The
Common Worship
Lectionary

New Revised Standard Version

ANGLICIZED EDITION

UNIVERSITY PRESS

OXFORD

UNIVERSITY PRESS

Great Clarendon Street, Oxford OX2 6DP

Oxford University Press is a department of the University of Oxford.
It furthers the University's objective of excellence in research, scholarship,
and education by publishing worldwide in

Oxford New York

Athens Auckland Bangkok Bogotá Buenos Aires Calcutta
Cape Town Chennai Dar es Salaam Delhi Florence Hong Kong Istanbul
Karachi Kuala Lumpur Madrid Melbourne Mexico City Mumbai
Nairobi Paris São Paulo Singapore Taipei Tokyo Toronto Warsaw

with associated companies in Berlin Ibadan

First published 1999

British Library Cataloging in Publication Data

Data available

ISBN 0-19-145610-1

1 3 5 7 9 10 8 6 4 2

Typeset in Swift and Meta
by Selwood Systems
Printed by Clays Ltd., St Ives PLC
Bungay, Suffolk

CONTENTS

PREFACE

FOR most people, how the Bible is read in Church is a practical question which they know to be important but which they are content to leave to others to decide. This is why—across the centuries—schemes for reading scripture at the principal Sunday services have varied from one place to another, and within different Christian traditions. And while some will certainly expect certain passages to be read at the great festivals—Holy Week would be incomplete without one of the passion narratives—it took a few centuries before detailed schemes were worked out in the churches of the East and West. The Reformation brought its own priorities to bear on the matter, opening out the scriptures to the people in their own tongue, even if—as in the case of the Book of Common Prayer—the Epistles and Gospels were taken largely from medieval practice, and remained largely unchanged.

In our own time, the single most significant achievement has been the production of the three-year Sunday Lectionary in 1969 after the Second Vatican Council in the Roman Catholic Church. It was the product of motivations comparable to the Reformation, which made available the riches of the Old and New Testaments at the Sunday Eucharist over a three-year period on a scale hitherto unknown. It was soon taken over—with adaptation—by other churches in North America as a 'Common Lectionary', and found its way increasingly into Anglican revisions in other parts of the world. *The Revised Common Lectionary* (1992) bore further testimony to this process of ecumenical reception at an international level, and it is this which, after minor alterations, was authorized for use in the Church of England in 1996.

Why a three-year scheme? The first reason stems from a desire to be as inclusive as possible for the Old Testament, Epistle, and Gospel Readings. The second reason reflects a growing interest in the narrative character of Holy Scripture, particularly when it comes to the Gospels, where each gospel writer has particular characteristics that come across in celebration as well as preaching when they are read 'in course'. The foundation of the three-year Lectionary, therefore, is to concentrate on Matthew in Year A, Mark in Year B, Luke in Year C, still using John's Gospel as well in all three, but inserting pragmatically into Year B other passages from the Fourth Gospel, since Mark is shorter than the other two. Worshippers are thus enabled to reflect on each gospel in turn at a profound level, aided by a similar approach to the Old Testament and the Epistle.

The version of the Bible used in this book is the *New Revised Standard Version Anglicized Edition*, which is gaining widespread acceptance in churches today. The layout of the lessons is intended to facilitate reading, and the collect and alternative post communion prayers authorized to accompany this Lectionary in the Church of England are printed as well, for use whether at lectern or altar.

No Lectionary is perfect, and every Lectionary necessarily has something of the provisional about it. As comprehensive a selection as this will inevitably require careful preparation, and—where appropriate—judicious simplification. But this particular scheme, with its rich accompanying psalmody and prayers will, it is hoped, nourish and sustain the people of God in their eucharistic worship for many years to come. The fruit of ecumenical collaboration, biblical as well as liturgical, it can claim to be a significant landmark in the Church catholic's attention to what the Spirit has to say to us as we gather around the Lord's Table.

✠ KENNETH STEVENSON
Bishop of Portsmouth

All Saints' Day 1998

A READER'S GUIDE TO
THE COMMON WORSHIP LECTIONARY

THE development of *The Common Worship Lectionary* has provided for the Church of England a resource that will ensure the scriptures are given due prominence in worship within a structure that enhances congregational understanding of the readings. The creation of this pattern, based largely on *The Revised Common Lectionary*, offers greater flexibility to individual churches, yet this flexibility also places demands on the structure and layout of the book. The editors and publishers of this volume have sought to make the material as easy to use as possible, but readers are strongly recommended to read these notes to assist in getting the greatest benefit from the material. It is also suggested that churches should obtain a copy of *The Christian Year: Calendar, Lectionary and Collects* (Church House Publishing 1997) which provides further guidance, together with a complete Calendar.

The New Revised Standard Version

The translation of the Bible chosen for this edition of the Lectionary is the *NRSV Anglicized Edition*, first published by Oxford University Press in 1995. It is widely recognized as an accurate and authoritative version of the scriptures, and is in use in numerous congregations. The translators of the NRSV had as one of their aims the intention of producing a Bible that was suitable for reading in public worship, and in this they have been successful, making the version a natural choice for *The Common Worship Lectionary*.

The verse numbers have been retained within the text to assist the congregation in locating readings when referred to in the sermon. The verse numbering system used is that adopted in the NRSV with the exception of readings taken from the Psalms. The use of a letter *a* or *b* after a verse number indicates the first or second half of the verse.

The NRSV text has been reproduced exactly in accordance with the original translation. Some readers may wish to substitute the appropriate noun where a passage begins with a personal pronoun.

The Psalms

The translation of the Psalms used in this edition of the Lectionary
is that produced by the Episcopal Church of the United States of
America in its Anglicized form, as used in *Celebrating Common Prayer*.
The verse numbers of that Psalter have been retained, and readers
preferring to use an alternative translation of the Psalms may need
to make appropriate adjustments. Where a Canticle is prescribed,
this uses the NRSV text and verse numbering.

Psalm responses have not been included in this Lectionary, nor
have possible insertion points been indicated, as this is a matter of
local usage that varies considerably.

Bracketed Material

Within Readings, Psalms, and Canticles, portions of text may be
found in square brackets. These are used to indicate optional
additional material that may be preferred by some congregations.
Where complete alternative readings are available, these are supplied
in full and noted accordingly.

Second and Third Service Lectionaries

The readings provided are for the principal service of the day. At the
end of each day may be found the references identifying material to
be used at other services. The Second Service Lectionary is intended
for a second main service, and a reading from the Gospels is always
included to enable this to be used for a celebration of Holy Communion. The Third Service Lectionary has shorter readings, and is
especially suitable for use at an office.

Ordinary Time

On the Sundays between the Presentation of Christ in the Temple
and the Second Sunday before Lent, and on the Sundays after Trinity,
the readings and collects are independent of each other. Tables have
been inserted in the relevant part of the book to assist the user in
identifying how to draw the two strands together. The collects and
post communions belong to the day, but the readings belong between
particular calendar dates. The use of the appropriate table should

make clear the starting point for this conjoining of the various items. Thereafter, both collects and readings advance one week at a time until the conclusion of Ordinary Time.

Continuous and Related Readings

Two sets of readings are included for Ordinary Time after Trinity, and on each day these are headed as 'Continuous' or 'Related'. The former allows the Old Testament reading and the Psalm to be independent of the other readings; the latter relates the theme of the Old Testament reading and the Psalm to the Gospel. It should be noted that one system only should be adopted throughout Ordinary Time within any one year.

Sundays and Principal Feasts and Holy Days

The first three sections of the book consist of the cycle of collects, readings, and post communions for use at services throughout the year, separated into the three–year cycle. In addition to the regular pattern of Sunday worship, this section also includes the readings for the Principal Feasts with the exception of the Annunciation of Our Lord (25 March). The structure of the Lectionary between the Presentation of Christ in the Temple and the Second Sunday before Lent makes it difficult to place this material in the main Lectionary, and it will therefore be found in The Holy Days.

The readings for Harvest Thanksgiving, Bible Sunday, and Dedication Festival, which may vary according to local usage, will be found at the end of each year.

The Holy Days

This section includes all the readings for the Festivals and certain of the Lesser Festivals in calendar order, together with the Principal Feast of the Annunciation of Our Lord. The readings for the Day of Thanksgiving for the Institution of Holy Communion (Corpus Christi) are also to be found here in recognition of the authority given in the new Calendar to observe the day as a festival.

Common of the Saints and Special Occasions

This section contains the collects and post communions only for other Commemorations. The structure of the book varies slightly here, in that the general collect and post communion appears first with a list of suggested readings, followed by the collects appointed for specific commemorations and appropriate readings. This structure, which is believed to be the most helpful, does require the placement of the various saints in specific groups (Bishops, Martyrs, etc.), and within these subsections the commemorations then appear in calendar order. A contents list at the beginning of the main section identifies the placement of the particular categories.

Index

A final feature which it is hoped will be of value is an index of all scripture readings found throughout the book where they are reproduced in full. Readings which appear only in the form of biblical references are not included. The locations of the readings are identified by reference to their place in the Calendar.

The introduction of *The Common Worship Lectionary* to the Church of England will bring numerous benefits in the reading and interpretation of the Bible within the liturgy. It is the hope of all involved with the production of this edition that this book may be an invaluable tool in the service of the Church, to the glory of God.

OXFORD

The Conversion of Paul 1999

SUNDAYS AND
PRINCIPAL FEASTS AND HOLY DAYS

YEAR A

ACKNOWLEDGEMENTS

THE Publishers wish to thank the following people for their invaluable contribution to the creation of this edition of *The Common Worship Lectionary*.

MANAGING EDITOR

Martin H. Manser

CONSULTANT EDITORS

The Reverend Canon Dr Martin Kitchen, Durham Cathedral
The Right Reverend Dr Kenneth Stevenson, Bishop of Portsmouth

Thanks are also expressed to the staff at Church House, London, for their helpful advice and guidance at all stages of this project.

ACKNOWLEDGEMENTS

The Liturgical Press for Collect 'God of Compassion' (Mothering Sunday); Post Communion 'Loving God ...' (Mothering Sunday); extract from the Liturgy of Malabar 'Strengthen for service, Lord ...'; all from *Enriching the Christian Year*, compiled by Michael Perham. Copyright © 1993 by The Order of St. Benedict, Inc. Published by The Liturgical Press, Collegeville, Minnesota. Used with permission.

Mowbray Publishers (an imprint of Cassell Plc) for prayers from *Prayers for use at the Alternative Services* by David Silk and from *After Communion* by C. L. MacDonnell.

Oxford University Press for prayers, some in adapted form, from *The Book of Common Worship of the Church of South India*.

The Society for Promoting Christian Knowledge for Collect 'God of Compassion' (Mothering Sunday); Post Communion, 'Loving God' (Mothering Sunday); extract from the Liturgy of Malabar 'Strengthen for Service Lord ...'; all from *Enriching the Christian Year*, compiled by Michael Perham (SPCK 1993).

THE DATE OF EASTER AND ACCOMPANYING FESTIVALS

YEAR	SUNDAYS BEFORE LENT BEGIN	ASH WEDNESDAY	EASTER DAY	ASCENSION DAY	PENTECOST (WHIT SUNDAY)	ADVENT SUNDAY
1999	7 Feb	17 Feb	4 Apr	13 May	23 May	28 Nov
2000	6 Feb	8 Mar	23 Apr	1 Jun	11 Jun	3 Dec
2001	4 Feb	28 Feb	15 Apr	24 May	3 Jun	2 Dec
2002	3 Feb	13 Feb	31 Mar	9 May	19 May	1 Dec
2003	9 Feb	5 Mar	20 Apr	29 May	8 Jun	30 Nov
2004	8 Feb	25 Feb	11 Apr	20 May	30 May	28 Nov
2005	6 Feb	9 Feb	27 Mar	5 May	15 May	27 Nov
2006	5 Feb	1 Mar	16 Apr	25 May	4 Jun	3 Dec
2007	4 Feb	21 Feb	8 Apr	17 May	27 May	2 Dec
2008	3 Feb	6 Feb	23 Mar	1 May	11 May	30 Nov
2009	8 Feb	25 Feb	12 Apr	21 May	31 May	29 Nov
2010	7 Feb	17 Feb	4 Apr	13 May	23 May	28 Nov
2011	6 Feb	9 Mar	24 Apr	2 Jun	12 Jun	27 Nov
2012	5 Feb	22 Feb	8 Apr	17 May	27 May	2 Dec
2013	3 Feb	13 Feb	31 Mar	9 May	19 May	1 Dec
2014	9 Feb	5 Mar	20 Apr	29 May	8 Jun	30 Nov
2015	8 Feb	18 Feb	5 Apr	14 May	24 May	29 Nov
2016	7 Feb	10 Feb	27 Mar	5 May	15 May	27 Nov
2017	5 Feb	1 Mar	16 Apr	25 May	4 Jun	3 Dec
2018	4 Feb	14 Feb	1 Apr	10 May	20 May	2 Dec
2019	3 Feb	6 Mar	21 Apr	30 May	9 Jun	1 Dec
2020	9 Feb	26 Feb	12 Apr	21 May	31 May	29 Nov

THE FIRST SUNDAY OF ADVENT

COLLECT

Almighty God,
give us grace to cast away the works of darkness
and to put on the armour of light,
now in the time of this mortal life,
in which your Son Jesus Christ
   came to us in great humility;
that on the last day,
when he shall come again in his glorious majesty
   to judge the living and the dead,
we may rise to the life immortal;
through him who is alive and reigns with you,
in the unity of the Holy Spirit,
one God, now and for ever.

This Collect may be used as the Post Communion on any day from the Second Sunday of Advent until Christmas Eve instead of the Post Communion provided

READING   Isaiah 2.1–5

¹ The word that Isaiah son of Amoz saw concerning Judah and Jerusalem.
² In days to come
     the mountain of the LORD's house
   shall be established as the highest of the mountains,
     and shall be raised above the hills;
   all the nations shall stream to it.
³   Many peoples shall come and say,
   'Come, let us go up to the mountain of the LORD,
     to the house of the God of Jacob;
   that he may teach us his ways
     and that we may walk in his paths.'
   For out of Zion shall go forth instruction,
     and the word of the LORD from Jerusalem.
⁴ He shall judge between the nations,
     and shall arbitrate for many peoples;
   they shall beat their swords into ploughshares,
     and their spears into pruning-hooks;
   nation shall not lift up sword against nation,
     neither shall they learn war any more.

⁵ O house of Jacob,
    come, let us walk
    in the light of the LORD!

PSALM   Psalm 122

¹ I was glad when they said to me,
    'Let us go to the house of the Lord.'
² Now our feet are standing
    within your gates, O Jerusalem.
³ Jerusalem is built as a city
    that is at unity with itself.
⁴ To which the tribes go up, the tribes of the Lord,
    the assembly of Israel, to praise the name of the Lord.
⁵ For there are the thrones of judgement,
    the thrones of the house of David.
⁶ Pray for the peace of Jerusalem:
    'May they prosper who love you.
⁷ Peace be within your walls
    and quietness within your towers.
⁸ For my family and companions' sake,
    I pray for your prosperity.
⁹ Because of the house of the Lord our God,
    I will seek to do you good.'

READING   Romans 13.11–14

¹¹ Besides this, you know what time it is, how it is now the moment for you to wake from sleep. For salvation is nearer to us now than when we became believers; ¹² the night is far gone, the day is near. Let us then lay aside the works of darkness and put on the armour of light; ¹³ let us live honourably as in the day, not in revelling and drunkenness, not in debauchery and licentiousness, not in quarrelling and jealousy. ¹⁴ Instead, put on the Lord Jesus Christ, and make no provision for the flesh, to gratify its desires.

GOSPEL   Matthew 24.36–44

³⁶ 'But about that day and hour no one knows, neither the angels of heaven, nor the Son, but only the Father. ³⁷ For as the days of Noah were, so will be the coming of the Son of Man. ³⁸ For as in those days before the flood they were eating and drinking, marrying and giving in marriage, until the day Noah entered the ark, ³⁹ and they knew nothing until the

flood came and swept them all away, so too will be the coming of the Son of Man. [40] Then two will be in the field; one will be taken and one will be left. [41] Two women will be grinding meal together; one will be taken and one will be left. [42] Keep awake therefore, for you do not know on what day your Lord is coming. [43] But understand this: if the owner of the house had known in what part of the night the thief was coming, he would have stayed awake and would not have let his house be broken into. [44] Therefore you also must be ready, for the Son of Man is coming at an unexpected hour.'

POST COMMUNION

O Lord our God,
make us watchful and keep us faithful
as we await the coming of your Son our Lord;
that, when he shall appear,
he may not find us sleeping in sin
but active in his service
and joyful in his praise;
through Jesus Christ our Lord.

SECOND SERVICE	THIRD SERVICE
Psalm 9.1–8, [9–20]	Psalm 44
Isaiah 52.1–12	Micah 4.1–7
Matthew 24.15–28	1 Thessalonians 5.1–11

THE SECOND SUNDAY OF ADVENT

COLLECT

O Lord, raise up, we pray, your power
and come among us,
and with great might succour us;
that whereas, through our sins and wickedness
we are grievously hindered
in running the race that is set before us,
your bountiful grace and mercy
may speedily help and deliver us;
through Jesus Christ your Son our Lord,

to whom with you and the Holy Spirit,
be honour and glory, now and for ever.

READING   Isaiah 11.1–10

¹ A shoot shall come out from the stock of Jesse,
    and a branch shall grow out of his roots.
² The spirit of the Lord shall rest on him,
    the spirit of wisdom and understanding,
    the spirit of counsel and might,
    the spirit of knowledge and the fear of the Lord.
³ His delight shall be in the fear of the Lord.
He shall not judge by what his eyes see,
    or decide by what his ears hear;
⁴ but with righteousness he shall judge the poor,
    and decide with equity for the meek of the earth;
he shall strike the earth with the rod of his mouth,
    and with the breath of his lips he shall kill the wicked.
⁵ Righteousness shall be the belt around his waist,
    and faithfulness the belt around his loins.
⁶ The wolf shall live with the lamb,
    the leopard shall lie down with the kid,
the calf and the lion and the fatling together,
    and a little child shall lead them.
⁷ The cow and the bear shall graze,
    their young shall lie down together;
    and the lion shall eat straw like the ox.
⁸ The nursing child shall play over the hole of the asp,
    and the weaned child shall put its hand on the adder's den.
⁹ They will not hurt or destroy
    on all my holy mountain;
for the earth will be full of the knowledge of the Lord
    as the waters cover the sea.

¹⁰ On that day the root of Jesse shall stand as a signal to the peoples; the nations shall inquire of him, and his dwelling shall be glorious.

PSALM   Psalm 72.1–7, [18–19]

¹ Give the king your justice, O God,
    and your righteousness to the king's son;
² .That he may rule your people righteously
    and the poor with justice;

3 That the mountains may bring prosperity to the people,
and the little hills bring righteousness.
4 He shall defend the needy among the people;
he shall rescue the poor and crush the oppressor.
5 He shall live as long as the sun and moon endure,
from one generation to another.
6 He shall come down like rain upon the mown field,
like showers that water the earth.
7 In his time shall the righteous flourish;
there shall be abundance of peace till the moon shall be no more.

[18 Blessèd be the Lord God, the God of Israel,
who alone does wondrous deeds!
19 And blessèd be his glorious name for ever!
and may all the earth be filled with his glory. Amen. Amen.]

READING   Romans 15.4–13

4 For whatever was written in former days was written for our instruction, so that by steadfastness and by the encouragement of the scriptures we might have hope. 5 May the God of steadfastness and encouragement grant you to live in harmony with one another, in accordance with Christ Jesus, 6 so that together you may with one voice glorify the God and Father of our Lord Jesus Christ.

7 Welcome one another, therefore, just as Christ has welcomed you, for the glory of God. 8 For I tell you that Christ has become a servant of the circumcised on behalf of the truth of God in order that he might confirm the promises given to the patriarchs, 9 and in order that the Gentiles might glorify God for his mercy. As it is written,
'Therefore I will confess you among the Gentiles,
and sing praises to your name';
10 and again he says,
'Rejoice, O Gentiles, with his people';
11 and again,
'Praise the Lord, all you Gentiles,
and let all the peoples praise him';
12 and again Isaiah says,
'The root of Jesse shall come,
the one who rises to rule the Gentiles;
in him the Gentiles shall hope.'
13 May the God of hope fill you with all joy and peace in believing, so that you may abound in hope by the power of the Holy Spirit.

GOSPEL   Matthew 3.1–12

[1] In those days John the Baptist appeared in the wilderness of Judea, proclaiming, [2] 'Repent, for the kingdom of heaven has come near.' [3] This is the one of whom the prophet Isaiah spoke when he said,

    'The voice of one crying out in the wilderness:

    "Prepare the way of the Lord,

      make his paths straight." '

[4] Now John wore clothing of camel's hair with a leather belt around his waist, and his food was locusts and wild honey. [5] Then the people of Jerusalem and all Judea were going out to him, and all the region along the Jordan, [6] and they were baptized by him in the river Jordan, confessing their sins.

[7] But when he saw many Pharisees and Sadducees coming for baptism, he said to them, 'You brood of vipers! Who warned you to flee from the wrath to come? [8] Bear fruit worthy of repentance. [9] Do not presume to say to yourselves, "We have Abraham as our ancestor"; for I tell you, God is able from these stones to raise up children to Abraham. [10] Even now the axe is lying at the root of the trees; every tree therefore that does not bear good fruit is cut down and thrown into the fire.

[11] 'I baptize you with water for repentance, but one who is more powerful than I is coming after me; I am not worthy to carry his sandals. He will baptize you with the Holy Spirit and fire. [12] His winnowing-fork is in his hand, and he will clear his threshing-floor and will gather his wheat into the granary; but the chaff he will burn with unquenchable fire.'

POST COMMUNION

Father in heaven,
who sent your Son to redeem the world
and will send him again to be our judge:
give us grace so to imitate him
   in the humility and purity of his first coming
that, when he comes again,
we may be ready to greet him
with joyful love and firm faith;
through Jesus Christ our Lord.

SECOND SERVICE	THIRD SERVICE
Psalms 11; [28]	Psalm 80
1 Kings 18.17–39	Amos 7
John 1.19–28	Luke 1.5–20

THE THIRD SUNDAY OF ADVENT

COLLECT

O Lord Jesus Christ,
who at your first coming sent your messenger
to prepare your way before you:
grant that the ministers and stewards of your mysteries
may likewise so prepare and make ready your way
by turning the hearts of the disobedient
   to the wisdom of the just,
that at your second coming to judge the world
we may be found an acceptable people in your sight;
for you are alive and reign with the Father
in the unity of the Holy Spirit,
one God, now and for ever.

READING   Isaiah 35.1–10

¹ The wilderness and the dry land shall be glad,
    the desert shall rejoice and blossom;
  like the crocus ² it shall blossom abundantly,
    and rejoice with joy and singing.
  The glory of Lebanon shall be given to it,
    the majesty of Carmel and Sharon.
  They shall see the glory of the LORD,
    the majesty of our God.
³ Strengthen the weak hands,
    and make firm the feeble knees.
⁴ Say to those who are of a fearful heart,
    'Be strong, do not fear!
  Here is your God.
    He will come with vengeance,
  with terrible recompense.
    He will come and save you.'

⁵ Then the eyes of the blind shall be opened,
  and the ears of the deaf unstopped;
⁶ then the lame shall leap like a deer,
  and the tongue of the speechless sing for joy.
  For waters shall break forth in the wilderness,
  and streams in the desert;
⁷ the burning sand shall become a pool,
  and the thirsty ground springs of water;
  the haunt of jackals shall become a swamp,
  the grass shall become reeds and rushes.
⁸ A highway shall be there,
  and it shall be called the Holy Way;
  the unclean shall not travel on it,
  but it shall be for God's people;
  no traveller, not even fools, shall go astray.
⁹ No lion shall be there,
  nor shall any ravenous beast come up on it;
  they shall not be found there,
  but the redeemed shall walk there.
¹⁰ And the ransomed of the LORD shall return,
  and come to Zion with singing;
  everlasting joy shall be upon their heads;
  they shall obtain joy and gladness,
  and sorrow and sighing shall flee away.

EITHER

PSALM   Psalm 146.4–9

⁴ Happy are they who have the God of Jacob for their help!
  whose hope is in the Lord their God;
⁵ Who made heaven and earth, the seas, and all that is in them;
  who keeps his promise for ever;
⁶ Who gives justice to those who are oppressed,
  and food to those who hunger.
⁷ The Lord sets the prisoners free; the Lord opens the eyes of the
    blind;
  the Lord lifts up those who are bowed down;
⁸ The Lord loves the righteous; the Lord cares for the stranger;
  he sustains the orphan and widow, but frustrates the way of the
    wicked.
⁹ The Lord shall reign for ever,
  your God, O Zion, throughout all generations. Alleluia!

OR

CANTICLE: Magnificat   Luke 1.46–55

46 My soul proclaims the greatness of the Lord,
47 my spirit rejoices in God my Saviour,
48 who has looked with favour on his lowly servant.
     From this day all generations will call me blessed:
49   the Almighty has done great things for me
     and holy is his name.
50   God has mercy on those who fear him,
     from generation to generation.
51 The Lord has shown strength with his arm
     and scattered the proud in their conceit,
52 casting down the mighty from their thrones
     and lifting up the lowly.
53 God has filled the hungry with good things
     and sent the rich away empty.
54 He has come to the aid of his servant Israel,
     to remember the promise of mercy,
55 the promise made to our forebears,
     to Abraham and his children for ever.

READING   James 5.7–10

7 Be patient, therefore, beloved, until the coming of the Lord. The farmer waits for the precious crop from the earth, being patient with it until it receives the early and the late rains. 8 You also must be patient. Strengthen your hearts, for the coming of the Lord is near. 9 Beloved, do not grumble against one another, so that you may not be judged. See, the Judge is standing at the doors! 10 As an example of suffering and patience, beloved, take the prophets who spoke in the name of the Lord.

GOSPEL   Matthew 11.2–11

2 When John heard in prison what the Messiah was doing, he sent word by his disciples 3 and said to him, 'Are you the one who is to come, or are we to wait for another?' 4 Jesus answered them, 'Go and tell John what you hear and see: 5 the blind receive their sight, the lame walk, the lepers are cleansed, the deaf hear, the dead are raised, and the poor have good news brought to them. 6 And blessed is anyone who takes no offence at me.'

⁷ As they went away, Jesus began to speak to the crowds about John: 'What did you go out into the wilderness to look at? A reed shaken by the wind? ⁸ What then did you go out to see? Someone dressed in soft robes? Look, those who wear soft robes are in royal palaces. ⁹ What then did you go out to see? A prophet? Yes, I tell you, and more than a prophet. ¹⁰ This is the one about whom it is written,

"See, I am sending my messenger ahead of you,
who will prepare your way before you."

¹¹ Truly I tell you, among those born of women no one has arisen greater than John the Baptist; yet the least in the kingdom of heaven is greater than he.'

POST COMMUNION

We give you thanks, O Lord, for these heavenly gifts;
kindle in us the fire of your Spirit
that when your Christ comes again
we may shine as lights before his face;
who is alive and reigns now and for ever.

SECOND SERVICE

Psalms 12; [14]
Isaiah 5.8–30
Acts 13.13–41

If the Second Service is a Eucharist, the following is read as a Gospel:

John 5.31–40

THIRD SERVICE

Psalm 68.1–20
Zephaniah 3.14–20
Philippians 4.4–7

THE FOURTH SUNDAY OF ADVENT

COLLECT

God our redeemer,
who prepared the Blessed Virgin Mary
to be the mother of your Son:
grant that, as she looked for his coming as our saviour,
so we may be ready to greet him
when he comes again as our judge;

who is alive and reigns with you,
in the unity of the Holy Spirit,
one God, now and for ever.

READING   Isaiah 7.10–16

¹⁰ Again the LORD spoke to Ahaz, saying, ¹¹ Ask a sign of the LORD your
God; let it be deep as Sheol or high as heaven. ¹² But Ahaz said, I will not
ask, and I will not put the LORD to the test. ¹³ Then Isaiah said: 'Hear then,
O house of David! Is it too little for you to weary mortals, that you weary
my God also? ¹⁴ Therefore the Lord himself will give you a sign. Look, the
young woman is with child and shall bear a son, and shall name him
Immanuel. ¹⁵ He shall eat curds and honey by the time he knows how to
refuse the evil and choose the good. ¹⁶ For before the child knows how to
refuse the evil and choose the good, the land before whose two kings you
are in dread will be deserted.

PSALM   Psalm 80.1–7, [16–18]

1   Hear, O Shepherd of Israel, leading Joseph like a flock;
       shine forth, you that are enthroned upon the cherubim.
2   In the presence of Ephraim, Benjamin and Manasseh,
       stir up your strength and come to help us.
3   Restore us, O God of hosts;
       show the light of your countenance and we shall be saved.
4   O Lord God of hosts,
       how long will you be angered despite the prayers of your people?
5   You have fed them with the bread of tears;
       you have given them bowls of tears to drink.
6   You have made us the derision of our neighbours,
       and our enemies laugh us to scorn.
7   Restore us, O God of hosts;
       show the light of your countenance and we shall be saved.

[16 Let your hand be upon the man of your right hand,
       the son of man you have made so strong for yourself.
17   And so will we never turn away from you;
       give us life, that we may call upon your name.
18   Restore us, O Lord God of hosts;
       show the light of your countenance and we shall be saved.]

READING   Romans 1.1–7

¹ Paul, a servant of Jesus Christ, called to be an apostle, set apart for the gospel of God, ² which he promised beforehand through his prophets in the holy scriptures, ³ the gospel concerning his Son, who was descended from David according to the flesh ⁴ and was declared to be Son of God with power according to the spirit of holiness by resurrection from the dead, Jesus Christ our Lord, ⁵ through whom we have received grace and apostleship to bring about the obedience of faith among all the Gentiles for the sake of his name, ⁶ including yourselves who are called to belong to Jesus Christ,

⁷ To all God's beloved in Rome, who are called to be saints:
Grace to you and peace from God our Father and the Lord Jesus Christ.

GOSPEL   Matthew 1.18–25

¹⁸ Now the birth of Jesus the Messiah took place in this way. When his mother Mary had been engaged to Joseph, but before they lived together, she was found to be with child from the Holy Spirit. ¹⁹ Her husband Joseph, being a righteous man and unwilling to expose her to public disgrace, planned to dismiss her quietly. ²⁰ But just when he had resolved to do this, an angel of the Lord appeared to him in a dream and said, 'Joseph, son of David, do not be afraid to take Mary as your wife, for the child conceived in her is from the Holy Spirit. ²¹ She will bear a son, and you are to name him Jesus, for he will save his people from their sins.' ²² All this took place to fulfil what had been spoken by the Lord through the prophet:
²³ 'Look, the virgin shall conceive and bear a son,
    and they shall name him Emmanuel',
which means, 'God is with us.'
²⁴ When Joseph awoke from sleep, he did as the angel of the Lord commanded him; he took her as his wife, ²⁵ but had no marital relations with her until she had borne a son; and he named him Jesus.

POST COMMUNION

Heavenly Father,
who chose the Blessed Virgin Mary
to be the mother of the promised saviour:
fill us your servants with your grace,
that in all things we may embrace your holy will
and with her rejoice in your salvation;
through Jesus Christ our Lord.

SECOND SERVICE

Psalms 113; [126]
1 Samuel 1.1–20
Revelation 22.6–21

*If the Second Service is a Eucharist, the
following is read as a Gospel:*

Luke 1.39–45

THIRD SERVICE

Psalm 144
Micah 5.2–5a
Luke 1.26–38

CHRISTMAS EVE

24 DECEMBER

COLLECT

Almighty God,
you make us glad with the yearly remembrance
    of the birth of your Son Jesus Christ:
grant that, as we joyfully receive him as our redeemer,
so we may with sure confidence behold him
when he shall come to be our judge;
who is alive and reigns with you,
in the unity of the Holy Spirit,
one God, now and for ever.

READING

2 Samuel 7.1–5, 8–11, 16

¹ Now when the king was settled in his house, and the Lord had given him rest from all his enemies around him, ² the king said to the prophet Nathan, 'See now, I am living in a house of cedar, but the ark of God stays in a tent.' ³ Nathan said to the king, 'Go, do all that you have in mind; for the Lord is with you.'

⁴ But that same night the word of the Lord came to Nathan: ⁵ Go and tell my servant David: Thus says the Lord: Are you the one to build me a house to live in?

⁸ Now therefore thus you shall say to my servant David: Thus says the Lord of hosts: I took you from the pasture, from following the sheep to be prince over my people Israel; ⁹ and I have been with you wherever you went, and have cut off all your enemies from before you; and I will make for you a great name, like the name of the great ones of the earth. ¹⁰ And I will appoint a place for my people Israel and will plant them, so that they may live in their own place, and be disturbed no more; and evildoers shall afflict

15

them no more, as formerly, [11] from the time that I appointed judges over my people Israel; and I will give you rest from all your enemies. Moreover, the LORD declares to you that the LORD will make you a house.

[16] Your house and your kingdom shall be made sure for ever before me; your throne shall be established for ever.

PSALM   Psalm 89.2, 21-27

[2] For I am persuaded that your love is established for ever;
    you have set your faithfulness firmly in the heavens.

[21] 'My hand will hold him fast
    and my arm will make him strong.
[22] No enemy shall deceive him,
    nor the wicked bring him down.
[23] I will crush his foes before him
    and strike down those who hate him.
[24] My faithfulness and love shall be with him,
    and he shall be victorious through my name.
[25] I shall make his dominion extend
    from the Great Sea to the River.
[26] He will say to me, "You are my Father,
    my God and the rock of my salvation."
[27] I will make him my first-born
    and higher than the kings of the earth.'

READING   Acts 13.16-26

[16] So Paul stood up and with a gesture began to speak:

'You Israelites, and others who fear God, listen. [17] The God of this people Israel chose our ancestors and made the people great during their stay in the land of Egypt, and with uplifted arm he led them out of it. [18] For about forty years he put up with them in the wilderness. [19] After he had destroyed seven nations in the land of Canaan, he gave them their land as an inheritance [20] for about four hundred and fifty years. After that he gave them judges until the time of the prophet Samuel. [21] Then they asked for a king; and God gave them Saul son of Kish, a man of the tribe of Benjamin, who reigned for forty years. [22] When he had removed him, he made David their king. In his testimony about him he said, "I have found David, son of Jesse, to be a man after my heart, who will carry out all my wishes." [23] Of this man's posterity God has brought to Israel a Saviour, Jesus, as he promised; [24] before his coming John had already proclaimed a baptism of repentance to all the people of Israel. [25] And as John was finishing his work, he said, "What do you suppose that I am? I am not he. No, but one is coming after me; I am not worthy to untie the thong of the sandals on his feet."

[26] 'My brothers, you descendants of Abraham's family, and others who fear God, to us the message of this salvation has been sent.'

GOSPEL   Luke 1.67–79

[67] Then his father Zechariah was filled with the Holy Spirit and spoke this prophecy:
[68] 'Blessed be the Lord God of Israel,
       for he has looked favourably on his people and redeemed them.
[69] He has raised up a mighty saviour for us
       in the house of his servant David,
[70] as he spoke through the mouth of his holy prophets from of old,
[71]   that we would be saved from our enemies and from the hand of all
          who hate us.
[72] Thus he has shown the mercy promised to our ancestors,
       and has remembered his holy covenant,
[73] the oath that he swore to our ancestor Abraham,
       to grant us [74] that we, being rescued from the hands of our enemies,
       might serve him without fear, [75] in holiness and righteousness
       before him all our days.
[76] And you, child, will be called the prophet of the Most High;
       for you will go before the Lord to prepare his ways,
[77] to give knowledge of salvation to his people
       by the forgiveness of their sins.
[78] By the tender mercy of our God,
       the dawn from on high will break upon us,
[79] to give light to those who sit in darkness and in the shadow of death,
       to guide our feet into the way of peace.'

POST COMMUNION

Eternal God, for whom we wait,
you have fed us with the bread of eternal life:
keep us ever watchful,
that we may be ready to stand before the Son of Man,
Jesus Christ our Lord.

CHRISTMAS DAY

Any of the following sets of readings may be used on the evening of Christmas Eve and on Christmas Day. Set III should be used at some service during the celebration.

SET I

COLLECT

CHRISTMAS NIGHT

Eternal God,
who made this most holy night
to shine with the brightness of your one true light:
bring us, who have known the revelation
    of that light on earth,
to see the radiance of your heavenly glory;
through Jesus Christ your Son our Lord,
who is alive and reigns with you,
in the unity of the Holy Spirit,
one God, now and for ever.

CHRISTMAS DAY

Almighty God,
you have given us your only-begotten Son
to take our nature upon him
and as at this time to be born of a pure virgin:
grant that we, who have been born again
and made your children by adoption and grace,
may daily be renewed by your Holy Spirit;
through Jesus Christ your Son our Lord,
who is alive and reigns with you,
in the unity of the Holy Spirit,
one God, now and for ever.

READING   Isaiah 9.2–7

2 The people who walked in darkness
    have seen a great light;
  those who lived in a land of deep darkness—
    on them light has shined.
3 You have multiplied the nation,
    you have increased its joy;
  they rejoice before you
    as with joy at the harvest,
    as people exult when dividing plunder.
4 For the yoke of their burden,
    and the bar across their shoulders,
    the rod of their oppressor,
    you have broken as on the day of Midian.
5 For all the boots of the tramping warriors
    and all the garments rolled in blood
    shall be burned as fuel for the fire.
6 For a child has been born for us,
    a son given to us;
  authority rests upon his shoulders;
    and he is named
  Wonderful Counsellor, Mighty God,
    Everlasting Father, Prince of Peace.
7 His authority shall grow continually,
    and there shall be endless peace
  for the throne of David and his kingdom.
    He will establish and uphold it
  with justice and with righteousness
    from this time onwards and for evermore.
  The zeal of the LORD of hosts will do this.

PSALM   Psalm 96

1 Sing to the Lord a new song;
  sing to the Lord, all the whole earth.
2 Sing to the Lord and bless his name;
  proclaim the good news of his salvation from day to day.
3 Declare his glory among the nations
  and his wonders among all peoples.
4 For great is the Lord and greatly to be praised;
  he is more to be feared than all gods.

5   As for all the gods of the nations, they are but idols;
    but it is the Lord who made the heavens.
6   O the majesty and magnificence of his presence!
    O the power and the splendour of his sanctuary!
7   Ascribe to the Lord, you families of the peoples;
    ascribe to the Lord honour and power.
8   Ascribe to the Lord the honour due to his name;
    bring offerings and come into his courts.
9   Worship the Lord in the beauty of holiness;
    let the whole earth tremble before him.
10 Tell it out among the nations: 'The Lord is king!
    he has made the world so firm that it cannot be moved; he will
        judge the peoples with equity.'
11 Let the heavens rejoice and let the earth be glad; let the sea
        thunder and all that is in it;
    let the field be joyful and all that is therein.
12 Then shall all the trees of the wood shout for joy before the Lord
        when he comes,
    when he comes to judge the earth.
13 He will judge the world with righteousness
    and the peoples with his truth.

READING   Titus 2.11–14

11 For the grace of God has appeared, bringing salvation to all, 12 training
us to renounce impiety and worldly passions, and in the present age to live
lives that are self-controlled, upright, and godly, 13 while we wait for the
blessed hope and the manifestation of the glory of our great God and
Saviour, Jesus Christ. 14 He it is who gave himself for us that he might
redeem us from all iniquity and purify for himself a people of his own who
are zealous for good deeds.

GOSPEL   Luke 2.1–14, [15–20]

1 In those days a decree went out from Emperor Augustus that all the
world should be registered. 2 This was the first registration and was taken
while Quirinius was governor of Syria. 3 All went to their own towns to be
registered. 4 Joseph also went from the town of Nazareth in Galilee to Judea,
to the city of David called Bethlehem, because he was descended from the
house and family of David. 5 He went to be registered with Mary, to whom
he was engaged and who was expecting a child. 6 While they were there,
the time came for her to deliver her child. 7 And she gave birth to her

firstborn son and wrapped him in bands of cloth, and laid him in a manger, because there was no place for them in the inn.

⁸ In that region there were shepherds living in the fields, keeping watch over their flock by night. ⁹ Then an angel of the Lord stood before them, and the glory of the Lord shone around them, and they were terrified. ¹⁰ But the angel said to them, 'Do not be afraid; for see—I am bringing you good news of great joy for all the people: ¹¹ to you is born this day in the city of David a Saviour, who is the Messiah, the Lord. ¹² This will be a sign for you: you will find a child wrapped in bands of cloth and lying in a manger.' ¹³ And suddenly there was with the angel a multitude of the heavenly host, praising God and saying,
¹⁴   'Glory to God in the highest heaven,
        and on earth peace among those whom he favours!'

[¹⁵ When the angels had left them and gone into heaven, the shepherds said to one another, 'Let us go now to Bethlehem and see this thing that has taken place, which the Lord has made known to us.' ¹⁶ So they went with haste and found Mary and Joseph, and the child lying in the manger. ¹⁷ When they saw this, they made known what had been told them about this child; ¹⁸ and all who heard it were amazed at what the shepherds told them. ¹⁹ But Mary treasured all these words and pondered them in her heart. ²⁰ The shepherds returned, glorifying and praising God for all they had heard and seen, as it had been told them.]

POST COMMUNION

CHRISTMAS NIGHT

God our Father,
in this night you have made known to us again
the coming of our Lord Jesus Christ:
confirm our faith and fix our eyes on him
until the day dawns
and Christ the Morning Star rises in our hearts.
To him be glory both now and for ever.

CHRISTMAS DAY

God our Father,
whose Word has come among us
in the Holy Child of Bethlehem:
may the light of faith illumine our hearts
and shine in our words and deeds;
through him who is Christ the Lord.

SET II

COLLECT

CHRISTMAS NIGHT

Eternal God,
who made this most holy night
to shine with the brightness of your one true light:
bring us, who have known the revelation
   of that light on earth,
to see the radiance of your heavenly glory;
through Jesus Christ your Son our Lord,
who is alive and reigns with you,
in the unity of the Holy Spirit,
one God, now and for ever.

CHRISTMAS DAY

Almighty God,
you have given us your only-begotten Son
to take our nature upon him
and as at this time to be born of a pure virgin:
grant that we, who have been born again
and made your children by adoption and grace,
may daily be renewed by your Holy Spirit;
through Jesus Christ your Son our Lord,
who is alive and reigns with you,
in the unity of the Holy Spirit,
one God, now and for ever.

READING   Isaiah 62.6–12

⁶ Upon your walls, O Jerusalem,
   I have posted sentinels;
all day and all night
   they shall never be silent.
You who remind the LORD,
   take no rest,
⁷ and give him no rest
   until he establishes Jerusalem
   and makes it renowned throughout the earth.

⁸ The LORD has sworn by his right hand
    and by his mighty arm:
  I will not again give your grain
    to be food for your enemies,
  and foreigners shall not drink the wine
    for which you have laboured;
⁹ but those who garner it shall eat it
    and praise the LORD,
  and those who gather it shall drink it
    in my holy courts.
¹⁰ Go through, go through the gates,
    prepare the way for the people;
  build up, build up the highway,
    clear it of stones,
    lift up an ensign over the peoples.
¹¹ The LORD has proclaimed
    to the end of the earth:
  Say to daughter Zion,
    'See, your salvation comes;
  his reward is with him,
    and his recompense before him.'
¹² They shall be called, 'The Holy People,
    The Redeemed of the LORD';
  and you shall be called, 'Sought Out,
    A City Not Forsaken.'

PSALM   Psalm 97

¹ The Lord is king; let the earth rejoice;
  let the multitude of the isles be glad.
² Clouds and darkness are round about him,
  righteousness and justice are the foundations of his throne.
³ A fire goes before him
  and burns up his enemies on every side.
⁴ His lightnings light up the world;
  the earth sees it and is afraid.
⁵ The mountains melt like wax at the presence of the Lord,
  at the presence of the Lord of the whole earth.
⁶ The heavens declare his righteousness,
  and all the peoples see his glory.
⁷ Confounded be all who worship carved images and delight in false
    gods!
  Bow down before him, all you gods.

8   Zion hears and is glad and the cities of Judah rejoice,
    because of your judgements, O Lord.
9   For you are the Lord: most high over all the earth;
    you are exalted far above all gods.
10 The Lord loves those who hate evil;
    he preserves the lives of his saints and delivers them from the
        hand of the wicked.
11 Light has sprung up for the righteous,
    and joyful gladness for those who are true-hearted.
12 Rejoice in the Lord, you righteous,
    and give thanks to his holy name.

READING   Titus 3.4–7

4 But when the goodness and loving-kindness of God our Saviour appeared,
5 he saved us, not because of any works of righteousness that we had done,
but according to his mercy, through the water of rebirth and renewal by
the Holy Spirit. 6 This Spirit he poured out on us richly through Jesus Christ
our Saviour, 7 so that, having been justified by his grace, we might become
heirs according to the hope of eternal life.

GOSPEL   Luke 2.[1–7,] 8–20

[1 In those days a decree went out from Emperor Augustus that all the
world should be registered. 2 This was the first registration and was taken
while Quirinius was governor of Syria. 3 All went to their own towns to be
registered. 4 Joseph also went from the town of Nazareth in Galilee to Judea,
to the city of David called Bethlehem, because he was descended from the
house and family of David. 5 He went to be registered with Mary, to whom
he was engaged and who was expecting a child. 6 While they were there,
the time came for her to deliver her child. 7 And she gave birth to her
firstborn son and wrapped him in bands of cloth, and laid him in a manger,
because there was no place for them in the inn.]

8 In that region there were shepherds living in the fields, keeping watch
over their flock by night. 9 Then an angel of the Lord stood before them,
and the glory of the Lord shone around them, and they were terrified.
10 But the angel said to them, 'Do not be afraid; for see—I am bringing you
good news of great joy for all the people: 11 to you is born this day in the
city of David a Saviour, who is the Messiah, the Lord. 12 This will be a sign
for you: you will find a child wrapped in bands of cloth and lying in a
manger.' 13 And suddenly there was with the angel a multitude of the
heavenly host, praising God and saying,

14 'Glory to God in the highest heaven,
and on earth peace among those whom he favours!'

15 When the angels had left them and gone into heaven, the shepherds said to one another, 'Let us go now to Bethlehem and see this thing that has taken place, which the Lord has made known to us.' 16 So they went with haste and found Mary and Joseph, and the child lying in the manger. 17 When they saw this, they made known what had been told them about this child; 18 and all who heard it were amazed at what the shepherds told them. 19 But Mary treasured all these words and pondered them in her heart. 20 The shepherds returned, glorifying and praising God for all they had heard and seen, as it had been told them.

POST COMMUNION

CHRISTMAS NIGHT

God our Father,
in this night you have made known to us again
the coming of our Lord Jesus Christ:
confirm our faith and fix our eyes on him
until the day dawns
and Christ the Morning Star rises in our hearts.
To him be glory both now and for ever.

CHRISTMAS DAY

God our Father,
whose Word has come among us
in the Holy Child of Bethlehem:
may the light of faith illumine our hearts
and shine in our words and deeds;
through him who is Christ the Lord.

SET III

COLLECT

CHRISTMAS NIGHT

Eternal God,
who made this most holy night
to shine with the brightness of your one true light:

25

bring us, who have known the revelation
   of that light on earth,
to see the radiance of your heavenly glory;
through Jesus Christ your Son our Lord,
who is alive and reigns with you,
in the unity of the Holy Spirit,
one God, now and for ever.

CHRISTMAS DAY

Almighty God,
you have given us your only-begotten Son
to take our nature upon him
and as at this time to be born of a pure virgin:
grant that we, who have been born again
and made your children by adoption and grace,
may daily be renewed by your Holy Spirit;
through Jesus Christ your Son our Lord,
who is alive and reigns with you,
in the unity of the Holy Spirit,
one God, now and for ever.

READING   Isaiah 52.7–10

7 How beautiful upon the mountains
      are the feet of the messenger who announces peace,
   who brings good news,
      who announces salvation,
      who says to Zion, 'Your God reigns.'
8 Listen! Your sentinels lift up their voices,
      together they sing for joy;
   for in plain sight they see
      the return of the LORD to Zion.
9 Break forth together into singing,
      you ruins of Jerusalem;
   for the LORD has comforted his people,
      he has redeemed Jerusalem.
10 The LORD has bared his holy arm
      before the eyes of all the nations;
   and all the ends of the earth shall see
      the salvation of our God.

PSALM   Psalm 98

1   Sing to the Lord a new song,
    for he has done marvellous things.
2   With his right hand and his holy arm
    has he won for himself the victory.
3   The Lord has made known his victory;
    his righteousness has he openly shown in the sight of the nations.
4   He remembers his mercy and faithfulness to the house of Israel,
    and all the ends of the earth have seen the victory of our God.
5   Shout with joy to the Lord, all you lands;
    lift up your voice, rejoice and sing.
6   Sing to the Lord with the harp,
    with the harp and the voice of song.
7   With trumpets and the sound of the horn
    shout with joy before the King, the Lord.
8   Let the sea make a noise and all that is in it,
    the lands and those who dwell therein.
9   Let the rivers clap their hands,
    and let the hills ring out with joy before the Lord, when he comes
      to judge the earth.
10 In righteousness shall he judge the world,
    and the peoples with equity.

READING   Hebrews 1.1–4, [5–12]

1 Long ago God spoke to our ancestors in many and various ways by the prophets, 2 but in these last days he has spoken to us by a Son, whom he appointed heir of all things, through whom he also created the worlds. 3 He is the reflection of God's glory and the exact imprint of God's very being, and he sustains all things by his powerful word. When he had made purification for sins, he sat down at the right hand of the Majesty on high, 4 having become as much superior to angels as the name he has inherited is more excellent than theirs.

[5 For to which of the angels did God ever say,
    'You are my Son;
      today I have begotten you'?
Or again,
    'I will be his Father,
      and he will be my Son'?
6 And again, when he brings the firstborn into the world, he says,
    'Let all God's angels worship him.'

⁷Of the angels he says,

    'He makes his angels winds,
      and his servants flames of fire.'

⁸But of the Son he says,

    'Your throne, O God, is for ever and ever,
      and the righteous sceptre is the sceptre of your kingdom.

⁹ You have loved righteousness and hated wickedness;
    therefore God, your God, has anointed you
      with the oil of gladness beyond your companions.'

¹⁰And,

    'In the beginning, Lord, you founded the earth,
      and the heavens are the work of your hands;

¹¹ they will perish, but you remain;
    they will all wear out like clothing;

¹² like a cloak you will roll them up,
    and like clothing they will be changed.
  But you are the same,
    and your years will never end.']

GOSPEL   John 1.1–14

¹In the beginning was the Word, and the Word was with God, and the Word was God. ²He was in the beginning with God. ³All things came into being through him, and without him not one thing came into being. What has come into being ⁴in him was life, and the life was the light of all people. ⁵The light shines in the darkness, and the darkness did not overcome it.

⁶There was a man sent from God, whose name was John. ⁷He came as a witness to testify to the light, so that all might believe through him. ⁸He himself was not the light, but he came to testify to the light. ⁹The true light, which enlightens everyone, was coming into the world.

¹⁰He was in the world, and the world came into being through him; yet the world did not know him. ¹¹He came to what was his own, and his own people did not accept him. ¹²But to all who received him, who believed in his name, he gave power to become children of God, ¹³who were born, not of blood or of the will of the flesh or of the will of man, but of God.

¹⁴And the Word became flesh and lived among us, and we have seen his glory, the glory as of a father's only son, full of grace and truth.

POST COMMUNION

CHRISTMAS NIGHT

God our Father,
in this night you have made known to us again
the coming of our Lord Jesus Christ:
confirm our faith and fix our eyes on him
until the day dawns
and Christ the Morning Star rises in our hearts.
To him be glory both now and for ever.

CHRISTMAS DAY

God our Father,
whose Word has come among us
in the Holy Child of Bethlehem:
may the light of faith illumine our hearts
    and shine in our words and deeds;
through him who is Christ the Lord.

SECOND SERVICE

Psalm 8
Isaiah 65.17–25
Philippians 2.5–11

or

Luke 2.1–20

*if it has not been used at the Principal Service
of the day*

THIRD SERVICE

Psalm 110
Isaiah 62.1–5
Matthew 1.18–25

THE FIRST SUNDAY OF CHRISTMAS

COLLECT

Almighty God,
who wonderfully created us in your own image
and yet more wonderfully restored us
through your Son Jesus Christ:
grant that, as he came to share in our humanity,
so we may share the life of his divinity;
who is alive and reigns with you,
in the unity of the Holy Spirit,
one God, now and for ever.

READING   Isaiah 63.7–9

7 I will recount the gracious deeds of the LORD,
       the praiseworthy acts of the LORD,
     because of all that the LORD has done for us,
        and the great favour to the house of Israel
     that he has shown them according to his mercy,
        according to the abundance of his steadfast love.
8 For he said, 'Surely they are my people,
        children who will not deal falsely';
     and he became their saviour
9   in all their distress.
     It was no messenger or angel
        but his presence that saved them;
     in his love and in his pity he redeemed them;
        he lifted them up and carried them all the days of old.

PSALM   Psalm 148.[1–6,] 7–14

[1 Alleluia! Praise the Lord from the heavens;
       praise him in the heights.
2 Praise him, all you angels of his;
       praise him, all his host.
3 Praise him, sun and moon;
       praise him, all you shining stars.
4 Praise him, heaven of heavens,
       and you waters above the heavens.

5   Let them praise the name of the Lord;
    for he commanded and they were created.
6   He made them stand fast for ever and ever;
    he gave them a law which shall not pass away.]
7   Praise the Lord from the earth,
    you sea-monsters and all deeps;
8   Fire and hail, snow and fog,
    tempestuous wind, doing his will;
9   Mountains and all hills,
    fruit trees and all cedars;
10 Wild beasts and all cattle,
    creeping things and winged birds;
11 Kings of the earth and all peoples,
    princes and all rulers of the world;
12 Young men and maidens,
    old and young together.
13 Let them praise the name of the Lord,
    for his name only is exalted, his splendour is over earth and heaven.
14 He has raised up strength for his people and praise for all his loyal
        servants,
    the children of Israel, a people who are near him. Alleluia!

READING   Hebrews 2.10–18

10 It was fitting that God, for whom and through whom all things exist, in bringing many children to glory, should make the pioneer of their salvation perfect through sufferings. 11 For the one who sanctifies and those who are sanctified all have one Father. For this reason Jesus is not ashamed to call them brothers and sisters, 12 saying,
    'I will proclaim your name to my brothers and sisters,
        in the midst of the congregation I will praise you.'
13 And again,
    'I will put my trust in him.'
And again,
    'Here am I and the children whom God has given me.'

14 Since, therefore, the children share flesh and blood, he himself likewise shared the same things, so that through death he might destroy the one who has the power of death, that is, the devil, 15 and free those who all their lives were held in slavery by the fear of death. 16 For it is clear that he did not come to help angels, but the descendants of Abraham. 17 Therefore he had to become like his brothers and sisters in every respect, so that he

might be a merciful and faithful high priest in the service of God, to make a sacrifice of atonement for the sins of the people. [18] Because he himself was tested by what he suffered, he is able to help those who are being tested.

GOSPEL   Matthew 2.13–23

[13] Now after they had left, an angel of the Lord appeared to Joseph in a dream and said, 'Get up, take the child and his mother, and flee to Egypt, and remain there until I tell you; for Herod is about to search for the child, to destroy him.' [14] Then Joseph got up, took the child and his mother by night, and went to Egypt, [15] and remained there until the death of Herod. This was to fulfil what had been spoken by the Lord through the prophet, 'Out of Egypt I have called my son.'

[16] When Herod saw that he had been tricked by the wise men, he was infuriated, and he sent and killed all the children in and around Bethlehem who were two years old or under, according to the time that he had learned from the wise men. [17] Then was fulfilled what had been spoken through the prophet Jeremiah:
[18] 'A voice was heard in Ramah,
        wailing and loud lamentation,
     Rachel weeping for her children;
        she refused to be consoled, because they are no more.'

[19] When Herod died, an angel of the Lord suddenly appeared in a dream to Joseph in Egypt and said, [20] 'Get up, take the child and his mother, and go to the land of Israel, for those who were seeking the child's life are dead.' [21] Then Joseph got up, took the child and his mother, and went to the land of Israel. [22] But when he heard that Archelaus was ruling over Judea in place of his father Herod, he was afraid to go there. And after being warned in a dream, he went away to the district of Galilee. [23] There he made his home in a town called Nazareth, so that what had been spoken through the prophets might be fulfilled, 'He will be called a Nazorean.'

POST COMMUNION

Heavenly Father,
whose blessed Son shared at Nazareth
   the life of an earthly home:
help your Church to live as one family,
united in love and obedience,
and bring us all at last to our home in heaven;
through Jesus Christ our Lord.

SECOND SERVICE

THIRD SERVICE

Psalm 132
Isaiah 49.7–13
Philippians 2.1–11

Psalm 105.1–9
Isaiah 35.1–6
Galatians 3.23–25

If the Second Service is a Eucharist, the following is read as a Gospel:

Luke 2.41–52

THE SECOND SUNDAY OF CHRISTMAS

COLLECT

Almighty God,
in the birth of your Son
you have poured on us the new light of your incarnate Word,
and shown us the fullness of your love:
help us to walk in his light and dwell in his love
that we may know the fullness of his joy;
who is alive and reigns with you,
in the unity of the Holy Spirit,
one God, now and for ever.

EITHER

READING   Jeremiah 31.7–14

7   For thus says the LORD:
    Sing aloud with gladness for Jacob,
        and raise shouts for the chief of the nations;
    proclaim, give praise, and say,
        'Save, O LORD, your people,
        the remnant of Israel.'
8   See, I am going to bring them from the land of the north,
        and gather them from the farthest parts of the earth,
    among them the blind and the lame,
        those with child and those in labour, together;
        a great company, they shall return here.

9   With weeping they shall come,
        and with consolations I will lead them back,
    I will let them walk by brooks of water,
        in a straight path in which they shall not stumble;
    for I have become a father to Israel,
        and Ephraim is my firstborn.
10 Hear the word of the LORD, O nations,
        and declare it in the coastlands far away;
    say, 'He who scattered Israel will gather him,
        and will keep him as a shepherd a flock.'
11 For the LORD has ransomed Jacob,
        and has redeemed him from hands too strong for him.
12 They shall come and sing aloud on the height of Zion,
        and they shall be radiant over the goodness of the LORD,
    over the grain, the wine, and the oil,
        and over the young of the flock and the herd;
    their life shall become like a watered garden,
        and they shall never languish again.
13 Then shall the young women rejoice in the dance,
        and the young men and the old shall be merry.
    I will turn their mourning into joy,
        I will comfort them, and give them gladness for sorrow.
14 I will give the priests their fill of fatness,
        and my people shall be satisfied with my bounty,

                                    says the LORD.

PSALM   Psalm 147.13–21

13 Worship the Lord, O Jerusalem;
        praise your God, O Zion;
14 For he has strengthened the bars of your gates;
        he has blessed your children within you.
15 He has established peace on your borders;
        he satisfies you with the finest wheat.
16 He sends out his command to the earth,
        and his word runs very swiftly.
17 He gives snow like wool;
        he scatters hoarfrost like ashes.
18 He scatters his hail like bread crumbs;
        who can stand against his cold?
19 He sends forth his word and melts them;
        he blows with his wind and the waters flow.

20 He declares his word to Jacob,
      his statutes and his judgements to Israel.
21 He has not done so to any other nation;
      to them he has not revealed his judgements. Alleluia!

READING   Ephesians 1.3–14

³ Blessed be the God and Father of our Lord Jesus Christ, who has blessed us in Christ with every spiritual blessing in the heavenly places, ⁴ just as he chose us in Christ before the foundation of the world to be holy and blameless before him in love. ⁵ He destined us for adoption as his children through Jesus Christ, according to the good pleasure of his will, ⁶ to the praise of his glorious grace that he freely bestowed on us in the Beloved. ⁷ In him we have redemption through his blood, the forgiveness of our trespasses, according to the riches of his grace ⁸ that he lavished on us. With all wisdom and insight ⁹ he has made known to us the mystery of his will, according to his good pleasure that he set forth in Christ, ¹⁰ as a plan for the fullness of time, to gather up all things in him, things in heaven and things on earth. ¹¹ In Christ we have also obtained an inheritance, having been destined according to the purpose of him who accomplishes all things according to his counsel and will, ¹² so that we, who were the first to set our hope on Christ, might live for the praise of his glory. ¹³ In him you also, when you had heard the word of truth, the gospel of your salvation, and had believed in him, were marked with the seal of the promised Holy Spirit; ¹⁴ this is the pledge of our inheritance towards redemption as God's own people, to the praise of his glory.

GOSPEL   John 1.[1–9,] 10–18

[¹ In the beginning was the Word, and the Word was with God, and the Word was God. ² He was in the beginning with God. ³ All things came into being through him, and without him not one thing came into being. What has come into being ⁴ in him was life, and the life was the light of all people. ⁵ The light shines in the darkness, and the darkness did not overcome it.

⁶ There was a man sent from God, whose name was John. ⁷ He came as a witness to testify to the light, so that all might believe through him. ⁸ He himself was not the light, but he came to testify to the light. ⁹ The true light, which enlightens everyone, was coming into the world.]

¹⁰ He was in the world, and the world came into being through him; yet the world did not know him. ¹¹ He came to what was his own, and his own people did not accept him. ¹² But to all who received him, who believed in

his name, he gave power to become children of God, [13] who were born, not of blood or of the will of the flesh or of the will of man, but of God.

[14] And the Word became flesh and lived among us, and we have seen his glory, the glory as of a father's only son, full of grace and truth. [15] (John testified to him and cried out, 'This was he of whom I said, "He who comes after me ranks ahead of me because he was before me." ') [16] From his fullness we have all received, grace upon grace. [17] The law indeed was given through Moses; grace and truth came through Jesus Christ. [18] No one has ever seen God. It is God the only Son, who is close to the Father's heart, who has made him known.

OR

READING   Ecclesiasticus 24.1–12

[1] Wisdom praises herself,
      and tells of her glory in the midst of her people.
[2] In the assembly of the Most High she opens her mouth,
      and in the presence of his hosts she tells of her glory:
[3] 'I came forth from the mouth of the Most High,
      and covered the earth like a mist.
[4] I dwelt in the highest heavens,
      and my throne was in a pillar of cloud.
[5] Alone I compassed the vault of heaven
      and traversed the depths of the abyss.
[6] Over waves of the sea, over all the earth,
      and over every people and nation I have held sway.
[7] Among all these I sought a resting-place;
      in whose territory should I abide?
[8] Then the Creator of all things gave me a command,
      and my Creator chose the place for my tent.
      He said, "Make your dwelling in Jacob,
      and in Israel receive your inheritance."
[9] Before the ages, in the beginning, he created me,
      and for all the ages I shall not cease to be.
[10] In the holy tent I ministered before him,
      and so I was established in Zion.
[11] Thus in the beloved city he gave me a resting-place,
      and in Jerusalem was my domain.
[12] I took root in an honoured people,
      in the portion of the Lord, his heritage.'

CANTICLE   **Wisdom 10.15–21**

15   A holy people and blameless race
     wisdom delivered from a nation of oppressors.
16   She entered the soul of a servant of the Lord,
     and withstood dread kings with wonders and signs.
17   She gave to holy people the reward of their labours;
     she guided them along a marvellous way,
     and became a shelter to them by day,
     and a starry flame through the night.
18   She brought them over the Red Sea,
     and led them through deep waters;
19   but she drowned their enemies,
     and cast them up from the depths of the sea.
20   Therefore the righteous plundered the ungodly;
     they sang hymns, O Lord, to your holy name,
     and praised with one accord your defending hand;
21   for wisdom opened the mouths of those who were mute,
     and made the tongues of infants speak clearly.

READING   **Ephesians 1.3–14**

3 Blessed be the God and Father of our Lord Jesus Christ, who has blessed us in Christ with every spiritual blessing in the heavenly places, 4 just as he chose us in Christ before the foundation of the world to be holy and blameless before him in love. 5 He destined us for adoption as his children through Jesus Christ, according to the good pleasure of his will, 6 to the praise of his glorious grace that he freely bestowed on us in the Beloved. 7 In him we have redemption through his blood, the forgiveness of our trespasses, according to the riches of his grace 8 that he lavished on us. With all wisdom and insight 9 he has made known to us the mystery of his will, according to his good pleasure that he set forth in Christ, 10 as a plan for the fullness of time, to gather up all things in him, things in heaven and things on earth. 11 In Christ we have also obtained an inheritance, having been destined according to the purpose of him who accomplishes all things according to his counsel and will, 12 so that we, who were the first to set our hope on Christ, might live for the praise of his glory. 13 In him you also, when you had heard the word of truth, the gospel of your salvation, and had believed in him, were marked with the seal of the promised Holy Spirit; 14 this is the pledge of our inheritance towards redemption as God's own people, to the praise of his glory.

GOSPEL   John 1.[1–9,] 10–18

[¹ In the beginning was the Word, and the Word was with God, and the Word was God. ² He was in the beginning with God. ³ All things came into being through him, and without him not one thing came into being. What has come into being ⁴ in him was life, and the life was the light of all people. ⁵ The light shines in the darkness, and the darkness did not overcome it.

⁶ There was a man sent from God, whose name was John. ⁷ He came as a witness to testify to the light, so that all might believe through him. ⁸ He himself was not the light, but he came to testify to the light. ⁹ The true light, which enlightens everyone, was coming into the world.]

¹⁰ He was in the world, and the world came into being through him; yet the world did not know him. ¹¹ He came to what was his own, and his own people did not accept him. ¹² But to all who received him, who believed in his name, he gave power to become children of God, ¹³ who were born, not of blood or of the will of the flesh or of the will of man, but of God.

¹⁴ And the Word became flesh and lived among us, and we have seen his glory, the glory as of a father's only son, full of grace and truth. ¹⁵ (John testified to him and cried out, 'This was he of whom I said, "He who comes after me ranks ahead of me because he was before me." ') ¹⁶ From his fullness we have all received, grace upon grace. ¹⁷ The law indeed was given through Moses; grace and truth came through Jesus Christ. ¹⁸ No one has ever seen God. It is God the only Son, who is close to the Father's heart, who has made him known.

POST COMMUNION

All praise to you,
almighty God and heavenly King,
who sent your Son into the world
to take our nature upon him
and to be born of a pure virgin:
grant that, as we are born again in him,
so he may continually dwell in us
and reign on earth as he reigns in heaven,
now and for ever.

SECOND SERVICE

Psalm 135.1–14, [15–21]
Isaiah 41.21–42.4
Colossians 1.1–14

*If the Second Service is a Eucharist, the
following is read as a Gospel:*

Matthew 2.13–23

THIRD SERVICE

Psalm 87
Jeremiah 31.15–17
2 Corinthians 1.3–12

THE EPIPHANY   6 JANUARY

COLLECT

O God,
who by the leading of a star
manifested your only Son to the peoples of the earth:
mercifully grant that we,
who know you now by faith,
may at last behold your glory face to face;
through Jesus Christ your Son our Lord,
who is alive and reigns with you,
in the unity of the Holy Spirit,
one God, now and for ever.

READING   Isaiah 60.1–6

1 Arise, shine; for your light has come,
      and the glory of the LORD has risen upon you.
2 For darkness shall cover the earth,
      and thick darkness the peoples;
   but the LORD will arise upon you,
      and his glory will appear over you.
3 Nations shall come to your light,
      and kings to the brightness of your dawn.
4 Lift up your eyes and look around;
      they all gather together, they come to you;
   your sons shall come from far away,
      and your daughters shall be carried on their nurses' arms.

5 Then you shall see and be radiant;
>   your heart shall thrill and rejoice,
> because the abundance of the sea shall be brought to you,
>   the wealth of the nations shall come to you.
6 A multitude of camels shall cover you,
>   the young camels of Midian and Ephah;
>   all those from Sheba shall come.
> They shall bring gold and frankincense,
>   and shall proclaim the praise of the LORD.

PSALM   Psalm 72.[1–9,] 10–15

[1 Give the king your justice, O God,
>   and your righteousness to the king's son;
2 That he may rule your people righteously
>   and the poor with justice;
3 That the mountains may bring prosperity to the people,
>   and the little hills bring righteousness.
4 He shall defend the needy among the people;
>   he shall rescue the poor and crush the oppressor.
5 He shall live as long as the sun and moon endure,
>   from one generation to another.
6 He shall come down like rain upon the mown field,
>   like showers that water the earth.
7 In his time shall the righteous flourish;
>   there shall be abundance of peace till the moon shall be no more.
8 He shall rule from sea to sea,
>   and from the River to the ends of the earth.
9 His foes shall bow down before him,
>   and his enemies lick the dust.]
10 The kings of Tarshish and of the isles shall pay tribute,
>   and the kings of Arabia and Saba offer gifts.
11 All kings shall bow down before him,
>   and all the nations do him service.
12 For he shall deliver the poor who cries out in distress,
>   and the oppressed who has no helper.
13 He shall have pity on the lowly and poor;
>   he shall preserve the lives of the needy.
14 He shall redeem their lives from oppression and violence,
>   and dear shall their blood be in his sight.
15 Long may he live, and may there be given to him gold from Arabia;
>   may prayer be made for him always, and may they bless him all
>   the day long.

READING   Ephesians 3.1-12

[1] This is the reason that I Paul am a prisoner for Christ Jesus for the sake of you Gentiles— [2] for surely you have already heard of the commission of God's grace that was given to me for you, [3] and how the mystery was made known to me by revelation, as I wrote above in a few words, [4] a reading of which will enable you to perceive my understanding of the mystery of Christ. [5] In former generations this mystery was not made known to human-kind, as it has now been revealed to his holy apostles and prophets by the Spirit: [6] that is, the Gentiles have become fellow-heirs, members of the same body, and sharers in the promise in Christ Jesus through the gospel.

[7] Of this gospel I have become a servant according to the gift of God's grace that was given to me by the working of his power. [8] Although I am the very least of all the saints, this grace was given to me to bring to the Gentiles the news of the boundless riches of Christ, [9] and to make everyone see what is the plan of the mystery hidden for ages in God who created all things; [10] so that through the church the wisdom of God in its rich variety might now be made known to the rulers and authorities in the heavenly places. [11] This was in accordance with the eternal purpose that he has carried out in Christ Jesus our Lord, [12] in whom we have access to God in boldness and confidence through faith in him.

GOSPEL   Matthew 2.1-12

[1] In the time of King Herod, after Jesus was born in Bethlehem of Judea, wise men from the East came to Jerusalem, [2] asking, 'Where is the child who has been born king of the Jews? For we observed his star at its rising, and have come to pay him homage.' [3] When King Herod heard this, he was frightened, and all Jerusalem with him; [4] and calling together all the chief priests and scribes of the people, he inquired of them where the Messiah was to be born. [5] They told him, 'In Bethlehem of Judea; for so it has been written by the prophet:
[6] "And you, Bethlehem, in the land of Judah,
        are by no means least among the rulers of Judah;
     for from you shall come a ruler
        who is to shepherd my people Israel." '

[7] Then Herod secretly called for the wise men and learned from them the exact time when the star had appeared. [8] Then he sent them to Bethlehem, saying, 'Go and search diligently for the child; and when you have found him, bring me word so that I may also go and pay him homage.' [9] When they had heard the king, they set out; and there, ahead of them, went the star that they had seen at its rising, until it stopped over the place where

the child was. [10] When they saw that the star had stopped, they were overwhelmed with joy. [11] On entering the house, they saw the child with Mary his mother; and they knelt down and paid him homage. Then, opening their treasure-chests, they offered him gifts of gold, frankincense, and myrrh. [12] And having been warned in a dream not to return to Herod, they left for their own country by another road.

POST COMMUNION

Lord God,
the bright splendour whom the nations seek:
may we who with the wise men
    have been drawn by your light
discern the glory of your presence in your Son,
the Word made flesh, Jesus Christ our Lord.

SECOND SERVICE

Psalms 98; 100
Baruch 4.36–5.9
or
Isaiah 60.1–9
John 2.1–11

THIRD SERVICE

Psalms 113; 132
Jeremiah 31.7–14
John 1.29–34

THE BAPTISM OF CHRIST
THE FIRST SUNDAY OF EPIPHANY

COLLECT

Eternal Father,
who at the baptism of Jesus
revealed him to be your Son,
anointing him with the Holy Spirit:
grant to us, who are born again by water and the Spirit,
that we may be faithful to our calling
    as your adopted children;
through Jesus Christ your Son our Lord,
who is alive and reigns with you,
in the unity of the Holy Spirit,
one God, now and for ever.

READING

1 Here is my servant, whom I uphold,
      my chosen, in whom my soul delights;
    I have put my spirit upon him;
      he will bring forth justice to the nations.
2 He will not cry or lift up his voice,
      or make it heard in the street;
3 a bruised reed he will not break,
      and a dimly burning wick he will not quench;
    he will faithfully bring forth justice.
4 He will not grow faint or be crushed
      until he has established justice in the earth;
      and the coastlands wait for his teaching.
5 Thus says God, the LORD,
      who created the heavens and stretched them out,
      who spread out the earth and what comes from it,
    who gives breath to the people upon it
      and spirit to those who walk in it:
6 I am the LORD, I have called you in righteousness,
      I have taken you by the hand and kept you;
    I have given you as a covenant to the people,
      a light to the nations,
7   to open the eyes that are blind,
    to bring out the prisoners from the dungeon,
      from the prison those who sit in darkness.
8 I am the LORD, that is my name;
      my glory I give to no other,
      nor my praise to idols.
9 See, the former things have come to pass,
      and new things I now declare;
    before they spring forth,
      I tell you of them.

PSALM

1 Ascribe to the Lord, you gods,
      ascribe to the Lord glory and strength.
2 Ascribe to the Lord the glory due to his name;
      worship the Lord in the beauty of holiness.
3 The voice of the Lord is upon the waters; the God of glory thunders;
      the Lord is upon the mighty waters.

⁴ The voice of the Lord is a powerful voice;
  the voice of the Lord is a voice of splendour.
⁵ The voice of the Lord breaks the cedar trees;
  the Lord breaks the cedars of Lebanon;
⁶ He makes Lebanon skip like a calf,
  and Mount Hermon like a young wild ox.
⁷ The voice of the Lord splits the flames of fire; the voice of the Lord
    shakes the wilderness;
  the Lord shakes the wilderness of Kadesh.
⁸ The voice of the Lord makes the oak trees writhe
  and strips the forests bare.
⁹ And in the temple of the Lord
  all are crying, 'Glory!'
¹⁰ The Lord sits enthroned above the flood;
   the Lord sits enthroned as king for evermore.
¹¹ The Lord shall give strength to his people;
   the Lord shall give his people the blessing of peace.

READING   Acts 10.34–43

³⁴ Then Peter began to speak to them: 'I truly understand that God shows
no partiality, ³⁵ but in every nation anyone who fears him and does what is
right is acceptable to him. ³⁶ You know the message he sent to the people
of Israel, preaching peace by Jesus Christ—he is Lord of all. ³⁷ That message
spread throughout Judea, beginning in Galilee after the baptism that John
announced: ³⁸ how God anointed Jesus of Nazareth with the Holy Spirit
and with power; how he went about doing good and healing all who were
oppressed by the devil, for God was with him. ³⁹ We are witnesses to all
that he did both in Judea and in Jerusalem. They put him to death by
hanging him on a tree; ⁴⁰ but God raised him on the third day and allowed
him to appear, ⁴¹ not to all the people but to us who were chosen by God as
witnesses, and who ate and drank with him after he rose from the dead.
⁴² He commanded us to preach to the people and to testify that he is the
one ordained by God as judge of the living and the dead. ⁴³ All the prophets
testify about him that everyone who believes in him receives forgiveness of
sins through his name.'

GOSPEL   Matthew 3.13–17

¹³ Then Jesus came from Galilee to John at the Jordan, to be baptized by
him. ¹⁴ John would have prevented him, saying, 'I need to be baptized by
you, and do you come to me?' ¹⁵ But Jesus answered him, 'Let it be so now;
for it is proper for us in this way to fulfil all righteousness.' Then he

consented. [16] And when Jesus had been baptized, just as he came up from the water, suddenly the heavens were opened to him and he saw the Spirit of God descending like a dove and alighting on him. [17] And a voice from heaven said, 'This is my Son, the Beloved, with whom I am well pleased.'

POST COMMUNION

Lord of all time and eternity,
you opened the heavens
    and revealed yourself as Father
in the baptism of Jesus your beloved Son:
by the power of your Spirit
complete the heavenly work of our rebirth
through the waters of the new creation;
through Jesus Christ our Lord.

SECOND SERVICE

Psalms 46; 47
Joshua 3.1–8, 14–17
Hebrews 1.1–12

If the Second Service is a Eucharist, the following is read as a Gospel:

Luke 3.15–22

THIRD SERVICE

Psalm 89.20–29
Exodus 14.15–22
1 John 5.6–9

THE SECOND SUNDAY OF EPIPHANY

COLLECT

Almighty God,
in Christ you make all things new:
transform the poverty of our nature
    by the riches of your grace,
and in the renewal of our lives
make known your heavenly glory;
through Jesus Christ your Son our Lord,
who is alive and reigns with you,
in the unity of the Holy Spirit,
one God, now and for ever.

READING   Isaiah 49.1–7

[1] Listen to me, O coastlands,
   pay attention, you peoples from far away!
The LORD called me before I was born,
   while I was in my mother's womb he named me.
[2] He made my mouth like a sharp sword,
   in the shadow of his hand he hid me;
he made me a polished arrow,
   in his quiver he hid me away.
[3] And he said to me, 'You are my servant,
   Israel, in whom I will be glorified.'
[4] But I said, 'I have laboured in vain,
   I have spent my strength for nothing and vanity;
yet surely my cause is with the LORD,
   and my reward with my God.'
[5] And now the LORD says,
   who formed me in the womb to be his servant,
to bring Jacob back to him,
   and that Israel might be gathered to him,
for I am honoured in the sight of the LORD,
   and my God has become my strength—
[6] he says,
'It is too light a thing that you should be my servant
   to raise up the tribes of Jacob
   and to restore the survivors of Israel;
I will give you as a light to the nations,
   that my salvation may reach to the end of the earth.'
[7] Thus says the LORD,
   the Redeemer of Israel and his Holy One,
to one deeply despised, abhorred by the nations,
   the slave of rulers,
'Kings shall see and stand up,
   princes, and they shall prostrate themselves,
because of the LORD, who is faithful,
   the Holy One of Israel, who has chosen you.'

PSALM   Psalm 40.1–12

[1] I waited patiently upon the Lord;
   he stooped to me and heard my cry.
[2] He lifted me out of the desolate pit, out of the mire and clay;
   he set my feet upon a high cliff and made my footing sure.

3　He put a new song in my mouth, a song of praise to our God;
　　many shall see and stand in awe and put their trust in the Lord.
4　Happy are they who trust in the Lord!
　　they do not resort to evil spirits or turn to false gods.
5　Great things are they that you have done, O Lord my God! how
　　　great your wonders and your plans for us!
　　there is none who can be compared with you.
6　O that I could make them known and tell them!
　　but they are more than I can count.
7　In sacrifice and offering you take no pleasure
　　you have given me ears to hear you;
8　Burnt-offering and sin-offering you have not required,
　　and so I said, 'Behold, I come.
9　In the roll of the book it is written concerning me:
　　"I love to do your will, O my God; your law is deep in my heart." '
10　I proclaimed righteousness in the great congregation;
　　behold, I did not restrain my lips; and that, O Lord, you know.
11　Your righteousness have I not hidden in my heart; I have spoken
　　　of your faithfulness and your deliverance;
　　I have not concealed your love and faithfulness from the great
　　　congregation.
12　You are the Lord; do not withhold your compassion from me;
　　let your love and your faithfulness keep me safe for ever.

READING   1 Corinthians 1.1–9

1 Paul, called to be an apostle of Christ Jesus by the will of God, and our brother Sosthenes,

2 To the church of God that is in Corinth, to those who are sanctified in Christ Jesus, called to be saints, together with all those who in every place call on the name of our Lord Jesus Christ, both their Lord and ours:

3 Grace to you and peace from God our Father and the Lord Jesus Christ.

4 I give thanks to my God always for you because of the grace of God that has been given you in Christ Jesus, 5 for in every way you have been enriched in him, in speech and knowledge of every kind— 6 just as the testimony of Christ has been strengthened among you— 7 so that you are not lacking in any spiritual gift as you wait for the revealing of our Lord Jesus Christ. 8 He will also strengthen you to the end, so that you may be blameless on the day of our Lord Jesus Christ. 9 God is faithful; by him you were called into the fellowship of his Son, Jesus Christ our Lord.

GOSPEL   John 1.29–42

[29] The next day he saw Jesus coming towards him and declared, 'Here is the Lamb of God who takes away the sin of the world! [30] This is he of whom I said, "After me comes a man who ranks ahead of me because he was before me." [31] I myself did not know him; but I came baptizing with water for this reason, that he might be revealed to Israel.' [32] And John testified, 'I saw the Spirit descending from heaven like a dove, and it remained on him. [33] I myself did not know him, but the one who sent me to baptize with water said to me, "He on whom you see the Spirit descend and remain is the one who baptizes with the Holy Spirit." [34] And I myself have seen and have testified that this is the Son of God.'

[35] The next day John again was standing with two of his disciples, [36] and as he watched Jesus walk by, he exclaimed, 'Look, here is the Lamb of God!' [37] The two disciples heard him say this, and they followed Jesus. [38] When Jesus turned and saw them following, he said to them, 'What are you looking for?' They said to him, 'Rabbi' (which translated means Teacher), 'where are you staying?' [39] He said to them, 'Come and see.' They came and saw where he was staying, and they remained with him that day. It was about four o'clock in the afternoon. [40] One of the two who heard John speak and followed him was Andrew, Simon Peter's brother. [41] He first found his brother Simon and said to him, 'We have found the Messiah' (which is translated Anointed). [42] He brought Simon to Jesus, who looked at him and said, 'You are Simon son of John. You are to be called Cephas' (which is translated Peter).

POST COMMUNION

God of glory,
you nourish us with your Word
who is the bread of life:
fill us with your Holy Spirit
that through us the light of your glory
may shine in all the world.
We ask this in the name of Jesus Christ our Lord.

SECOND SERVICE

Psalm 96
Ezekiel 2.1–3.4
Galatians 1.11–24

*If the Second Service is a Eucharist, the
following is read as a Gospel:*

John 1.43–51

THIRD SERVICE

Psalm 145.1–12
Jeremiah 1.4–10
Mark 1.14–20

THE THIRD SUNDAY OF EPIPHANY

COLLECT

Almighty God,
whose Son revealed in signs and miracles
the wonder of your saving presence:
renew your people with your heavenly grace,
and in all our weakness
sustain us by your mighty power;
through Jesus Christ your Son our Lord,
who is alive and reigns with you,
in the unity of the Holy Spirit,
one God, now and for ever.

READING   Isaiah 9.1–4

¹ But there will be no gloom for those who were in anguish. In the
former time he brought into contempt the land of Zebulun and the land
of Naphtali, but in the latter time he will make glorious the way of the sea,
the land beyond the Jordan, Galilee of the nations.
² The people who walked in darkness
    have seen a great light;
  those who lived in a land of deep darkness—
    on them light has shined.
³ You have multiplied the nation,
    you have increased its joy;
  they rejoice before you
    as with joy at the harvest,
    as people exult when dividing plunder.

⁴ For the yoke of their burden,
and the bar across their shoulders,
the rod of their oppressor,
you have broken as on the day of Midian.

PSALM   Psalm 27.1, [2–4,] 5–13

¹   The Lord is my light and my salvation; whom then shall I fear?
the Lord is the strength of my life; of whom then shall I be afraid?
[²   When evildoers came upon me to eat up my flesh,
it was they, my foes and my adversaries, who stumbled and fell.
³   Though an army should encamp against me,
yet my heart shall not be afraid;
⁴   And though war should rise up against me,
yet will I put my trust in him.]
⁵   One thing have I asked of the Lord; one thing I seek;
that I may dwell in the house of the Lord all the days of my life;
⁶   To behold the fair beauty of the Lord
and to seek him in his temple.
⁷   For in the day of trouble he shall keep me safe in his shelter;
he shall hide me in the secrecy of his dwelling and set me high
upon a rock.
⁸   Even now he lifts up my head
above my enemies round about me;
⁹   Therefore I will offer in his dwelling an oblation with sounds of
great gladness;
I will sing and make music to the Lord.
¹⁰   Hearken to my voice, O Lord, when I call;
have mercy on me and answer me.
¹¹   You speak in my heart and say, 'Seek my face.'
Your face, Lord, will I seek.
¹²   Hide not your face from me,
nor turn away your servant in displeasure.
¹³   You have been my helper; cast me not away;
do not forsake me, O God of my salvation.

READING   1 Corinthians 1.10–18

¹⁰ Now I appeal to you, brothers and sisters, by the name of our Lord Jesus Christ, that all of you should be in agreement and that there should be no divisions among you, but that you should be united in the same mind and the same purpose. ¹¹ For it has been reported to me by Chloe's people that there are quarrels among you, my brothers and sisters. ¹² What I mean is

that each of you says, 'I belong to Paul', or 'I belong to Apollos', or 'I belong to Cephas', or 'I belong to Christ.' ¹³ Has Christ been divided? Was Paul crucified for you? Or were you baptized in the name of Paul? ¹⁴ I thank God that I baptized none of you except Crispus and Gaius, ¹⁵ so that no one can say that you were baptized in my name. ¹⁶ (I did baptize also the household of Stephanas; beyond that, I do not know whether I baptized anyone else.) ¹⁷ For Christ did not send me to baptize but to proclaim the gospel, and not with eloquent wisdom, so that the cross of Christ might not be emptied of its power.

¹⁸ For the message about the cross is foolishness to those who are perishing, but to us who are being saved it is the power of God.

GOSPEL   Matthew 4.12–23

¹² Now when Jesus heard that John had been arrested, he withdrew to Galilee. ¹³ He left Nazareth and made his home in Capernaum by the lake, in the territory of Zebulun and Naphtali, ¹⁴ so that what had been spoken through the prophet Isaiah might be fulfilled:
¹⁵ 'Land of Zebulun, land of Naphtali,
      on the road by the sea, across the Jordan, Galilee of the Gentiles—
¹⁶ the people who sat in darkness
      have seen a great light,
   and for those who sat in the region and shadow of death
      light has dawned.'
¹⁷ From that time Jesus began to proclaim, 'Repent, for the kingdom of heaven has come near.'

¹⁸ As he walked by the Sea of Galilee, he saw two brothers, Simon, who is called Peter, and Andrew his brother, casting a net into the lake—for they were fishermen. ¹⁹ And he said to them, 'Follow me, and I will make you fish for people.' ²⁰ Immediately they left their nets and followed him. ²¹ As he went from there, he saw two other brothers, James son of Zebedee and his brother John, in the boat with their father Zebedee, mending their nets, and he called them. ²² Immediately they left the boat and their father, and followed him.

²³ Jesus went throughout Galilee, teaching in their synagogues and proclaiming the good news of the kingdom and curing every disease and every sickness among the people.

POST COMMUNION

Almighty Father,
whose Son our Saviour Jesus Christ
    is the light of the world:
may your people,
illumined by your word and sacraments,
shine with the radiance of his glory,
that he may be known, worshipped, and obeyed
    to the ends of the earth;
for he is alive and reigns, now and for ever.

SECOND SERVICE   THIRD SERVICE

Psalm 33.1–12, [13–22]   Psalm 113
Ecclesiastes 3.1–11   Amos 3.1–8
1 Peter 1.3–12   1 John 1.1–4

*If the Second Service is a Eucharist, the
following is read as a Gospel:*

Luke 4.14–21

THE FOURTH SUNDAY OF EPIPHANY

COLLECT

God our creator,
who in the beginning
commanded the light to shine out of darkness:
we pray that the light of the glorious gospel of Christ
may dispel the darkness of ignorance and unbelief,
shine into the hearts of all your people,
and reveal the knowledge of your glory
    in the face of Jesus Christ your Son our Lord,
who is alive and reigns with you,
in the unity of the Holy Spirit,
one God, now and for ever.

READING   1 Kings 17.8–16

⁸ Then the word of the LORD came to him, saying, ⁹ 'Go now to Zarephath, which belongs to Sidon, and live there; for I have commanded a widow there to feed you.' ¹⁰ So he set out and went to Zarephath. When he came to the gate of the town, a widow was there gathering sticks; he called to her and said, 'Bring me a little water in a vessel, so that I may drink.' ¹¹ As she was going to bring it, he called to her and said, 'Bring me a morsel of bread in your hand.' ¹² But she said, 'As the LORD your God lives, I have nothing baked, only a handful of meal in a jar, and a little oil in a jug; I am now gathering a couple of sticks, so that I may go home and prepare it for myself and my son, that we may eat it, and die.' ¹³ Elijah said to her, 'Do not be afraid; go and do as you have said; but first make me a little cake of it and bring it to me, and afterwards make something for yourself and your son. ¹⁴ For thus says the LORD the God of Israel: The jar of meal will not be emptied and the jug of oil will not fail until the day that the LORD sends rain on the earth.' ¹⁵ She went and did as Elijah said, so that she as well as he and her household ate for many days. ¹⁶ The jar of meal was not emptied, neither did the jug of oil fail, according to the word of the LORD that he spoke by Elijah.

PSALM   Psalm 36.5–10

5   Your love, O Lord, reaches to the heavens,
      and your faithfulness to the clouds.
6   Your righteousness is like the strong mountains, your justice like
          the great deep;
      you save both human and beast, O Lord.
7   How priceless is your love, O God!
      your people take refuge under the shadow of your wings.
8   They feast upon the abundance of your house;
      you give them drink from the river of your delights.
9   For with you is the well of life,
      and in your light we see light.
10 Continue your loving-kindness to those who know you,
      and your favour to those who are true of heart.

READING   1 Corinthians 1.18–31

¹⁸ For the message about the cross is foolishness to those who are perishing, but to us who are being saved it is the power of God. ¹⁹ For it is written,
      'I will destroy the wisdom of the wise,
          and the discernment of the discerning I will thwart.'

[20] Where is the one who is wise? Where is the scribe? Where is the debater of this age? Has not God made foolish the wisdom of the world? [21] For since, in the wisdom of God, the world did not know God through wisdom, God decided, through the foolishness of our proclamation, to save those who believe. [22] For Jews demand signs and Greeks desire wisdom, [23] but we proclaim Christ crucified, a stumbling-block to Jews and foolishness to Gentiles, [24] but to those who are the called, both Jews and Greeks, Christ the power of God and the wisdom of God. [25] For God's foolishness is wiser than human wisdom, and God's weakness is stronger than human strength.

[26] Consider your own call, brothers and sisters: not many of you were wise by human standards, not many were powerful, not many were of noble birth. [27] But God chose what is foolish in the world to shame the wise; God chose what is weak in the world to shame the strong; [28] God chose what is low and despised in the world, things that are not, to reduce to nothing things that are, [29] so that no one might boast in the presence of God. [30] He is the source of your life in Christ Jesus, who became for us wisdom from God, and righteousness and sanctification and redemption, [31] in order that, as it is written, 'Let the one who boasts, boast in the Lord.'

GOSPEL   John 2.1–11

[1] On the third day there was a wedding in Cana of Galilee, and the mother of Jesus was there. [2] Jesus and his disciples had also been invited to the wedding. [3] When the wine gave out, the mother of Jesus said to him, 'They have no wine.' [4] And Jesus said to her, 'Woman, what concern is that to you and to me? My hour has not yet come.' [5] His mother said to the servants, 'Do whatever he tells you.' [6] Now standing there were six stone water-jars for the Jewish rites of purification, each holding twenty or thirty gallons. [7] Jesus said to them, 'Fill the jars with water.' And they filled them up to the brim. [8] He said to them, 'Now draw some out, and take it to the chief steward.' So they took it. [9] When the steward tasted the water that had become wine, and did not know where it came from (though the servants who had drawn the water knew), the steward called the bridegroom [10] and said to him, 'Everyone serves the good wine first, and then the inferior wine after the guests have become drunk. But you have kept the good wine until now.' [11] Jesus did this, the first of his signs, in Cana of Galilee, and revealed his glory; and his disciples believed in him.

POST COMMUNION

Generous Lord,
in word and eucharist we have proclaimed
   the mystery of your love:
help us so to live out our days
that we may be signs of your wonders in the world;
through Jesus Christ our Saviour.

SECOND SERVICE

Psalm 34.1–10, [11–22]
Genesis 28.10–22
Philemon 1–16

*If the Second Service is a Eucharist, the
following is read as a Gospel:*

Mark 1.21–28

THIRD SERVICE

Psalm 71.1–6, 15–17
Haggai 2.1–9
1 Corinthians 3.10–17

THE PRESENTATION OF CHRIST IN THE TEMPLE
CANDLEMAS
2 FEBRUARY

COLLECT

Almighty and ever-living God,
clothed in majesty,
whose beloved Son
   was this day presented in the Temple,
in substance of our flesh:
grant that we may be presented to you
with pure and clean hearts,
by your Son Jesus Christ our Lord,
who is alive and reigns with you,
in the unity of the Holy Spirit,
one God, now and for ever.

READING   Malachi 3.1–5

¹ See, I am sending my messenger to prepare the way before me, and the Lord whom you seek will suddenly come to his temple. The messenger of the covenant in whom you delight—indeed, he is coming, says the LORD of hosts. ² But who can endure the day of his coming, and who can stand when he appears?

For he is like a refiner's fire and like fullers' soap; ³ he will sit as a refiner and purifier of silver, and he will purify the descendants of Levi and refine them like gold and silver, until they present offerings to the LORD in righteousness. ⁴ Then the offering of Judah and Jerusalem will be pleasing to the LORD as in the days of old and as in former years.

⁵ Then I will draw near to you for judgement; I will be swift to bear witness against the sorcerers, against the adulterers, against those who swear falsely, against those who oppress the hired workers in their wages, the widow, and the orphan, against those who thrust aside the alien, and do not fear me, says the LORD of hosts.

PSALM   Psalm 24.[1–6,] 7–10

[¹ The earth is the Lord's and all that is in it,
   the world and all who dwell therein.
² For it is he who founded it upon the seas
   and made it firm upon the rivers of the deep.
³ 'Who can ascend the hill of the Lord?
   and who can stand in his holy place?'
⁴ 'Those who have clean hands and a pure heart,
   who have not pledged themselves to falsehood, nor sworn by what
      is a fraud.
⁵ They shall receive a blessing from the Lord
   and a just reward from the God of their salvation.'
⁶ Such is the generation of those who seek him,
   of those who seek your face, O God of Jacob.]
⁷ Lift up your heads, O gates; lift them high, O everlasting doors;
   and the King of glory shall come in.
⁸ 'Who is this King of glory?'
   'The Lord, strong and mighty, the Lord, mighty in battle.'
⁹ Lift up your heads, O gates; lift them high, O everlasting doors;
   and the King of glory shall come in.
¹⁰ 'Who is he, this King of glory?'
   'The Lord of hosts, he is the King of glory.'

READING   Hebrews 2.14–18

[14] Since, therefore, the children share flesh and blood, he himself likewise shared the same things, so that through death he might destroy the one who has the power of death, that is, the devil, [15] and free those who all their lives were held in slavery by the fear of death. [16] For it is clear that he did not come to help angels, but the descendants of Abraham. [17] Therefore he had to become like his brothers and sisters in every respect, so that he might be a merciful and faithful high priest in the service of God, to make a sacrifice of atonement for the sins of the people. [18] Because he himself was tested by what he suffered, he is able to help those who are being tested.

GOSPEL   Luke 2.22–40

[22] When the time came for their purification according to the law of Moses, they brought him up to Jerusalem to present him to the Lord [23] (as it is written in the law of the Lord, 'Every firstborn male shall be designated as holy to the Lord'), [24] and they offered a sacrifice according to what is stated in the law of the Lord, 'a pair of turtle-doves or two young pigeons.'

[25] Now there was a man in Jerusalem whose name was Simeon; this man was righteous and devout, looking forward to the consolation of Israel, and the Holy Spirit rested on him. [26] It had been revealed to him by the Holy Spirit that he would not see death before he had seen the Lord's Messiah. [27] Guided by the Spirit, Simeon came into the temple; and when the parents brought in the child Jesus, to do for him what was customary under the law, [28] Simeon took him in his arms and praised God, saying,

[29]   'Master, now you are dismissing your servant in peace,
         according to your word;
[30]   for my eyes have seen your salvation,
[31]   which you have prepared in the presence of all peoples,
[32]   a light for revelation to the Gentiles
         and for glory to your people Israel.'

[33] And the child's father and mother were amazed at what was being said about him. [34] Then Simeon blessed them and said to his mother Mary, 'This child is destined for the falling and the rising of many in Israel, and to be a sign that will be opposed [35] so that the inner thoughts of many will be revealed—and a sword will pierce your own soul too.'

[36] There was also a prophet, Anna the daughter of Phanuel, of the tribe of Asher. She was of a great age, having lived with her husband for seven years after her marriage, [37] then as a widow to the age of eighty-four. She never

left the temple but worshipped there with fasting and prayer night and day. [38] At that moment she came, and began to praise God and to speak about the child to all who were looking for the redemption of Jerusalem.

[39] When they had finished everything required by the law of the Lord, they returned to Galilee, to their own town of Nazareth. [40] The child grew and became strong, filled with wisdom; and the favour of God was upon him.

POST COMMUNION

Lord, you fulfilled the hope of Simeon and Anna,
who lived to welcome the Messiah:
may we, who have received these gifts beyond words,
prepare to meet Christ Jesus when he comes
   to bring us to eternal life;
for he is alive and reigns, now and for ever.

SECOND SERVICE	THIRD SERVICE
Psalms 122; 132	**Psalms 42; 43; 48**
Haggai 2.1–9	**Exodus 13.1–16**
John 2.18–22	**Romans 12.1–5**

TABLE OF SUNDAYS BEFORE LENT DATES AND PROPERS

YEAR	LITURGICAL YEAR	FIFTH SUNDAY BEFORE LENT	FOURTH SUNDAY BEFORE LENT	THIRD SUNDAY BEFORE LENT	SECOND SUNDAY BEFORE LENT	FIRST SUNDAY BEFORE LENT
1999	A				7 Feb	14 Feb
2000	B	6 Feb (1)	13 Feb (2)	20 Feb (3)	27 Feb	5 Mar
2001	C		4 Feb (1)	11 Feb (2)	18 Feb	25 Feb
2002	A				3 Feb	10 Feb
2003	B		9 Feb (1)	16 Feb (2)	23 Feb	2 Mar
2004	C			8 Feb (1)	15 Feb	22 Feb
2005	A					6 Feb
2006	B		5 Feb (1)	12 Feb (2)	19 Feb	26 Feb
2007	C			4 Feb (1)	11 Feb	18 Feb
2008	A					3 Feb
2009	B			8 Feb (1)	15 Feb	22 Feb
2010	C				7 Feb	14 Feb
2011	A	6 Feb (1)	13 Feb (2)	20 Feb (3)	27 Feb	6 Mar
2012	B			5 Feb (1)	12 Feb	19 Feb
2013	C				3 Feb	10 Feb
2014	A		9 Feb (1)	16 Feb (2)	23 Feb	2 Mar
2015	B				8 Feb	15 Feb
2016	C					7 Feb
2017	A		5 Feb (1)	12 Feb (2)	19 Feb	26 Feb
2018	B				4 Feb	11 Feb
2019	C	3 Feb (1)	10 Feb (2)	17 Feb (3)	24 Feb	3 Mar
2020	A			9 Feb (1)	16 Feb	23 Feb

The figures in parentheses after dates indicate the appropriate Proper provisions for the day

THE FIFTH SUNDAY BEFORE LENT

COLLECT

Almighty God,
by whose grace alone we are accepted
    and called to your service:
strengthen us by your Holy Spirit
and make us worthy of our calling;
through Jesus Christ your Son our Lord,
who is alive and reigns with you,
in the unity of the Holy Spirit,
one God, now and for ever.

READINGS

See pages 62 to 65 and Table on page 59

POST COMMUNION

God of truth,
we have seen with our eyes
    and touched with our hands the bread of life:
strengthen our faith
that we may grow in love for you and for each other;
through Jesus Christ our Lord.

THE FOURTH SUNDAY BEFORE LENT

COLLECT

O God,
you know us to be set
in the midst of so many and great dangers,
that by reason of the frailty of our nature
we cannot always stand upright:
grant to us such strength and protection
as may support us in all dangers
and carry us through all temptations;
through Jesus Christ your Son our Lord,
who is alive and reigns with you,

in the unity of the Holy Spirit,
one God, now and for ever.

READINGS

See pages 62 to 66 and Table on page 59

POST COMMUNION

Go before us, Lord, in all we do
with your most gracious favour,
and guide us with your continual help,
that in all our works
begun, continued and ended in you,
we may glorify your holy name,
and finally by your mercy receive everlasting life;
through Jesus Christ our Lord.

THE THIRD SUNDAY BEFORE LENT

COLLECT

Almighty God,
who alone can bring order
to the unruly wills and passions of sinful humanity:
give your people grace
so to love what you command
and to desire what you promise,
that, among the many changes of this world,
our hearts may surely there be fixed
where true joys are to be found;
through Jesus Christ your Son our Lord,
who is alive and reigns with you,
in the unity of the Holy Spirit,
one God, now and for ever.

READINGS

See pages 62 to 69 and Table on page 59

POST COMMUNION

Merciful Father,
who gave Jesus Christ to be for us the bread of life,

that those who come to him should never hunger:
draw us to the Lord in faith and love,
that we may eat and drink with him
at his table in the kingdom,
where he is alive and reigns, now and for ever.

PROPER 1

Sunday between 3 and 9 February inclusive (if earlier than the Second Sunday before Lent)

COLLECT

See pages 60 to 61 and Table on page 59

READING   Isaiah 58.1–9a, [9b-12]

¹ Shout out, do not hold back!
    Lift up your voice like a trumpet!
Announce to my people their rebellion,
    to the house of Jacob their sins.
² Yet day after day they seek me
    and delight to know my ways,
as if they were a nation that practised righteousness
    and did not forsake the ordinance of their God;
they ask of me righteous judgements,
    they delight to draw near to God.
³ 'Why do we fast, but you do not see?
    Why humble ourselves, but you do not notice?'
Look, you serve your own interest on your fast-day,
    and oppress all your workers.
⁴ Look, you fast only to quarrel and to fight
    and to strike with a wicked fist.
Such fasting as you do today
    will not make your voice heard on high.
⁵ Is such the fast that I choose,
    a day to humble oneself?
Is it to bow down the head like a bulrush,
    and to lie in sackcloth and ashes?
Will you call this a fast,
    a day acceptable to the LORD?

⁶ Is not this the fast that I choose:
　　to loose the bonds of injustice,
　　to undo the thongs of the yoke,
　to let the oppressed go free,
　　and to break every yoke?
⁷ Is it not to share your bread with the hungry,
　　and bring the homeless poor into your house;
　when you see the naked, to cover them,
　　and not to hide yourself from your own kin?
⁸ Then your light shall break forth like the dawn,
　　and your healing shall spring up quickly;
　your vindicator shall go before you,
　　the glory of the LORD shall be your rearguard.
⁹ Then you shall call, and the LORD will answer;
　　you shall cry for help, and he will say, Here I am.
[　If you remove the yoke from among you,
　　the pointing of the finger, the speaking of evil,
¹⁰ if you offer your food to the hungry
　　and satisfy the needs of the afflicted,
　then your light shall rise in the darkness
　　and your gloom be like the noonday.
¹¹ The LORD will guide you continually,
　　and satisfy your needs in parched places,
　　and make your bones strong;
　and you shall be like a watered garden,
　　like a spring of water,
　　whose waters never fail.
¹² Your ancient ruins shall be rebuilt;
　　you shall raise up the foundations of many generations;
　you shall be called the repairer of the breach,
　　the restorer of streets to live in.]

PSALM　　　　　　　　　　　　　　**Psalm 112.1–9, [10]**

¹ Alleluia! Happy are they who fear the Lord
　and have great delight in his commandments!
² Their descendants will be mighty in the land;
　the generation of the upright will be blessed.
³ Wealth and riches will be in their house,
　and their righteousness will last for ever.
⁴ Light shines in the darkness for the upright;
　the righteous are merciful and full of compassion.

5   It is good for them to be generous in lending
    and to manage their affairs with justice.
6   For they will never be shaken;
    the righteous will be kept in everlasting remembrance.
7   They will not be afraid of any evil rumours;
    their heart is right; they put their trust in the Lord.
8   Their heart is established and will not shrink,
    until they see their desire upon their enemies.
9   They have given freely to the poor,
    and their righteousness stands fast for ever; they will hold up their
        head with honour.
[10 The wicked will see it and be angry; they will gnash their teeth
        and pine away;
    the desires of the wicked will perish.]

READING   1 Corinthians 2.1–12, [13–16]

1 When I came to you, brothers and sisters, I did not come proclaiming the mystery of God to you in lofty words or wisdom. 2 For I decided to know nothing among you except Jesus Christ, and him crucified. 3 And I came to you in weakness and in fear and in much trembling. 4 My speech and my proclamation were not with plausible words of wisdom, but with a demonstration of the Spirit and of power, 5 so that your faith might rest not on human wisdom but on the power of God.

6 Yet among the mature we do speak wisdom, though it is not a wisdom of this age or of the rulers of this age, who are doomed to perish. 7 But we speak God's wisdom, secret and hidden, which God decreed before the ages for our glory. 8 None of the rulers of this age understood this; for if they had, they would not have crucified the Lord of glory. 9 But, as it is written,
    'What no eye has seen, nor ear heard,
        nor the human heart conceived,
    what God has prepared for those who love him'—
10 these things God has revealed to us through the Spirit; for the Spirit searches everything, even the depths of God. 11 For what human being knows what is truly human except the human spirit that is within? So also no one comprehends what is truly God's except the Spirit of God. 12 Now we have received not the spirit of the world, but the Spirit that is from God, so that we may understand the gifts bestowed on us by God.
[13 And we speak of these things in words not taught by human wisdom but taught by the Spirit, interpreting spiritual things to those who are spiritual.

[14] Those who are unspiritual do not receive the gifts of God's Spirit, for they are foolishness to them, and they are unable to understand them because they are discerned spiritually. [15] Those who are spiritual discern all things, and they are themselves subject to no one else's scrutiny.
[16] 'For who has known the mind of the Lord
    so as to instruct him?'
But we have the mind of Christ.]

GOSPEL   Matthew 5.13–20

[13] 'You are the salt of the earth; but if salt has lost its taste, how can its saltiness be restored? It is no longer good for anything, but is thrown out and trampled under foot.

[14] 'You are the light of the world. A city built on a hill cannot be hidden. [15] No one after lighting a lamp puts it under the bushel basket, but on the lampstand, and it gives light to all in the house. [16] In the same way, let your light shine before others, so that they may see your good works and give glory to your Father in heaven.

[17] 'Do not think that I have come to abolish the law or the prophets; I have come not to abolish but to fulfil. [18] For truly I tell you, until heaven and earth pass away, not one letter, not one stroke of a letter, will pass from the law until all is accomplished. [19] Therefore, whoever breaks one of the least of these commandments, and teaches others to do the same, will be called least in the kingdom of heaven; but whoever does them and teaches them will be called great in the kingdom of heaven. [20] For I tell you, unless your righteousness exceeds that of the scribes and Pharisees, you will never enter the kingdom of heaven.'

POST COMMUNION

See pages 60 to 61 and Table on page 59

SECOND SERVICE   THIRD SERVICE

Psalms [1; 3;] 4   **Psalms 5; 6**
Amos 2.4–16   **Jeremiah 26.1–16**
Ephesians 4.17–32   **Acts 3.1–10**

If the Second Service is a Eucharist, the following is read as a Gospel:

Mark 1.29–39

PROPER 2

Sunday between 10 and 16 February inclusive (if earlier than the Second Sunday before Lent)

The provisions of Propers 2 and 3 are only used if there are more than four Sundays between 2 February and Ash Wednesday

COLLECT

See pages 60 to 61 and Table on page 59

READING

EITHER   **Deuteronomy 30.15–20**

¹⁵ See, I have set before you today life and prosperity, death and adversity. ¹⁶ If you obey the commandments of the LORD your God that I am commanding you today, by loving the LORD your God, walking in his ways, and observing his commandments, decrees, and ordinances, then you shall live and become numerous, and the LORD your God will bless you in the land that you are entering to possess. ¹⁷ But if your heart turns away and you do not hear, but are led astray to bow down to other gods and serve them, ¹⁸ I declare to you today that you shall perish; you shall not live long in the land that you are crossing the Jordan to enter and possess. ¹⁹ I call heaven and earth to witness against you today that I have set before you life and death, blessings and curses. Choose life so that you and your descendants may live, ²⁰ loving the LORD your God, obeying him, and holding fast to him; for that means life to you and length of days, so that you may live in the land that the LORD swore to give to your ancestors, to Abraham, to Isaac, and to Jacob.

OR   **Ecclesiasticus 15.15–20**

¹⁵ If you choose, you can keep the commandments,
      and to act faithfully is a matter of your own choice.
¹⁶ He has placed before you fire and water;
      stretch out your hand for whichever you choose.
¹⁷ Before each person are life and death,
      and whichever one chooses will be given.
¹⁸ For great is the wisdom of the Lord;
      he is mighty in power and sees everything;
¹⁹ ˙his eyes are on those who fear him,
      and he knows every human action.

²⁰ He has not commanded anyone to be wicked,
     and he has not given anyone permission to sin.

PSALM   Psalm 119.1–8

¹ Happy are they whose way is blameless,
    who walk in the law of the Lord!
² Happy are they who observe his decrees
    and seek him with all their hearts!
³ Who never do any wrong,
    but always walk in his ways.
⁴ You laid down your commandments,
    that we should fully keep them.
⁵ O that my ways were made so direct
    that I might keep your statutes!
⁶ Then I should not be put to shame,
    when I regard all your commandments.
⁷ I will thank you with an unfeigned heart,
    when I have learned your righteous judgements.
⁸ I will keep your statutes;
    do not utterly forsake me.

READING   1 Corinthians 3.1–9

¹ And so, brothers and sisters, I could not speak to you as spiritual people, but rather as people of the flesh, as infants in Christ. ² I fed you with milk, not solid food, for you were not ready for solid food. Even now you are still not ready, ³ for you are still of the flesh. For as long as there is jealousy and quarrelling among you, are you not of the flesh, and behaving according to human inclinations? ⁴ For when one says, 'I belong to Paul', and another, 'I belong to Apollos', are you not merely human?

⁵ What then is Apollos? What is Paul? Servants through whom you came to believe, as the Lord assigned to each. ⁶ I planted, Apollos watered, but God gave the growth. ⁷ So neither the one who plants nor the one who waters is anything, but only God who gives the growth. ⁸ The one who plants and the one who waters have a common purpose, and each will receive wages according to the labour of each. ⁹ For we are God's servants, working together; you are God's field, God's building.

GOSPEL   Matthew 5.21–37

^{21} 'You have heard that it was said to those of ancient times, "You shall not murder"; and "whoever murders shall be liable to judgement." ^{22} But I say to you that if you are angry with a brother or sister, you will be liable to judgement; and if you insult a brother or sister, you will be liable to the council; and if you say, "You fool", you will be liable to the hell of fire. ^{23} So when you are offering your gift at the altar, if you remember that your brother or sister has something against you, ^{24} leave your gift there before the altar and go; first be reconciled to your brother or sister, and then come and offer your gift. ^{25} Come to terms quickly with your accuser while you are on the way to court with him, or your accuser may hand you over to the judge, and the judge to the guard, and you will be thrown into prison. ^{26} Truly I tell you, you will never get out until you have paid the last penny.

^{27} 'You have heard that it was said, "You shall not commit adultery." ^{28} But I say to you that everyone who looks at a woman with lust has already committed adultery with her in his heart. ^{29} If your right eye causes you to sin, tear it out and throw it away; it is better for you to lose one of your members than for your whole body to be thrown into hell. ^{30} And if your right hand causes you to sin, cut it off and throw it away; it is better for you to lose one of your members than for your whole body to go into hell.

^{31} 'It was also said, "Whoever divorces his wife, let him give her a certificate of divorce." ^{32} But I say to you that anyone who divorces his wife, except on the ground of unchastity, causes her to commit adultery; and whoever marries a divorced woman commits adultery.

^{33} 'Again, you have heard that it was said to those of ancient times, "You shall not swear falsely, but carry out the vows you have made to the Lord." ^{34} But I say to you, Do not swear at all, either by heaven, for it is the throne of God, ^{35} or by the earth, for it is his footstool, or by Jerusalem, for it is the city of the great King. ^{36} And do not swear by your head, for you cannot make one hair white or black. ^{37} Let your word be "Yes, Yes" or "No, No"; anything more than this comes from the evil one.'

POST COMMUNION

See pages 60 to 61 and Table on page 59

SECOND SERVICE

Psalms [7;] 13
Amos 3.1–8
Ephesians 5.1–17

If the Second Service is a Eucharist, the following is read as a Gospel:

Mark 1.40–45

THIRD SERVICE

Psalm 10
Jeremiah 30.1–3, 10–22
Acts 6

PROPER 3

Sunday between 17 and 23 February inclusive (if earlier than the Second Sunday before Lent)

The provisions of Propers 2 and 3 are only used if there are more than four Sundays between 2 February and Ash Wednesday

COLLECT

See page 61 and Table on page 59

READING   Leviticus 19.1–2, 9–18

¹ The LORD spoke to Moses, saying:

² Speak to all the congregation of the people of Israel and say to them: You shall be holy, for I the LORD your God am holy.

⁹ When you reap the harvest of your land, you shall not reap to the very edges of your field, or gather the gleanings of your harvest. ¹⁰ You shall not strip your vineyard bare, or gather the fallen grapes of your vineyard; you shall leave them for the poor and the alien: I am the LORD your God.

¹¹ You shall not steal; you shall not deal falsely; and you shall not lie to one another. ¹² And you shall not swear falsely by my name, profaning the name of your God: I am the LORD.

¹³ You shall not defraud your neighbour; you shall not steal; and you shall not keep for yourself the wages of a labourer until morning. ¹⁴ You shall not revile the deaf or put a stumbling-block before the blind; you shall fear your God: I am the LORD.

¹⁵ You shall not render an unjust judgement; you shall not be partial to the poor or defer to the great: with justice you shall judge your neighbour. ¹⁶ You shall not go around as a slanderer among your people, and you shall not profit by the blood of your neighbour: I am the Lord.

¹⁷ You shall not hate in your heart anyone of your kin; you shall reprove your neighbour, or you will incur guilt yourself. ¹⁸ You shall not take vengeance or bear a grudge against any of your people, but you shall love your neighbour as yourself: I am the Lord.

PSALM   Psalm 119.33–40

33 Teach me, O Lord, the way of your statutes,
    and I shall keep it to the end.
34 Give me understanding and I shall keep your law;
    I shall keep it with all my heart.
35 Make me go in the path of your commandments,
    for that is my desire.
36 Incline my heart to your decrees
    and not to unjust gain.
37 Turn my eyes from watching what is worthless;
    give me life in your ways.
38 Fulfil your promise to your servant,
    which you make to those who fear you.
39 Turn away the reproach which I dread,
    because your judgements are good.
40 Behold, I long for your commandments;
    in your righteousness preserve my life.

READING   1 Corinthians 3.10–11, 16–23

¹⁰ According to the grace of God given to me, like a skilled master builder I laid a foundation, and someone else is building on it. Each builder must choose with care how to build on it. ¹¹ For no one can lay any foundation other than the one that has been laid; that foundation is Jesus Christ.

¹⁶ Do you not know that you are God's temple and that God's Spirit dwells in you? ¹⁷ If anyone destroys God's temple, God will destroy that person. For God's temple is holy, and you are that temple.

¹⁸ Do not deceive yourselves. If you think that you are wise in this age, you should become fools so that you may become wise. ¹⁹ For the wisdom of this world is foolishness with God. For it is written,
    'He catches the wise in their craftiness',

²⁰ and again,

'The Lord knows the thoughts of the wise,
   that they are futile.'

²¹ So let no one boast about human leaders. For all things are yours, ²² whether Paul or Apollos or Cephas or the world or life or death or the present or the future—all belong to you, ²³ and you belong to Christ, and Christ belongs to God.

GOSPEL   Matthew 5.38–48

³⁸ 'You have heard that it was said, "An eye for an eye and a tooth for a tooth." ³⁹ But I say to you, Do not resist an evildoer. But if anyone strikes you on the right cheek, turn the other also; ⁴⁰ and if anyone wants to sue you and take your coat, give your cloak as well; ⁴¹ and if anyone forces you to go one mile, go also the second mile. ⁴² Give to everyone who begs from you, and do not refuse anyone who wants to borrow from you.

⁴³ 'You have heard that it was said, "You shall love your neighbour and hate your enemy." ⁴⁴ But I say to you, Love your enemies and pray for those who persecute you, ⁴⁵ so that you may be children of your Father in heaven; for he makes his sun rise on the evil and on the good, and sends rain on the righteous and on the unrighteous. ⁴⁶ For if you love those who love you, what reward do you have? Do not even the tax-collectors do the same? ⁴⁷ And if you greet only your brothers and sisters, what more are you doing than others? Do not even the Gentiles do the same? ⁴⁸ Be perfect, therefore, as your heavenly Father is perfect.'

POST COMMUNION

See page 61 and Table on page 59

SECOND SERVICE	THIRD SERVICE
Psalm 18.1–20	Psalms 21; 23
or	Jeremiah 33.1–11
18.21–30	Acts 8.4–25
Amos 9.5–15	
Ephesians 6.1–20	

If the Second Service is a Eucharist, the
following is read as a Gospel:

Mark 2.1–12

THE SECOND SUNDAY BEFORE LENT

COLLECT

Almighty God,
you have created the heavens and the earth
and made us in your own image:
teach us to discern your hand in all your works
and your likeness in all your children;
through Jesus Christ your Son our Lord,
who with you and the Holy Spirit
  reigns supreme over all things,
now and for ever.

READING   Genesis 1.1–2.3

[1] In the beginning when God created the heavens and the earth, [2] the earth was a formless void and darkness covered the face of the deep, while a wind from God swept over the face of the waters. [3] Then God said, 'Let there be light'; and there was light. [4] And God saw that the light was good; and God separated the light from the darkness. [5] God called the light Day, and the darkness he called Night. And there was evening and there was morning, the first day.

[6] And God said, 'Let there be a dome in the midst of the waters, and let it separate the waters from the waters.' [7] So God made the dome and separated the waters that were under the dome from the waters that were above the dome. And it was so. [8] God called the dome Sky. And there was evening and there was morning, the second day.

[9] And God said, 'Let the waters under the sky be gathered together into one place, and let the dry land appear.' And it was so. [10] God called the dry land Earth, and the waters that were gathered together he called Seas. And God saw that it was good. [11] Then God said, 'Let the earth put forth vegetation: plants yielding seed, and fruit trees of every kind on earth that bear fruit with the seed in it.' And it was so. [12] The earth brought forth vegetation: plants yielding seed of every kind, and trees of every kind bearing fruit with the seed in it. And God saw that it was good. [13] And there was evening and there was morning, the third day.

[14] And God said, 'Let there be lights in the dome of the sky to separate the day from the night; and let them be for signs and for seasons and for days and years, [15] and let them be lights in the dome of the sky to give light upon the earth.' And it was so. [16] God made the two great lights—the greater light to rule the day and the lesser light to rule the night—and the stars. [17] God set them in the dome of the sky to give light upon the earth, [18] to rule over the day and over the night, and to separate the light from the darkness. And God saw that it was good. [19] And there was evening and there was morning, the fourth day.

[20] And God said, 'Let the waters bring forth swarms of living creatures, and let birds fly above the earth across the dome of the sky.' [21] So God created the great sea monsters and every living creature that moves, of every kind, with which the waters swarm, and every winged bird of every kind. And God saw that it was good. [22] God blessed them, saying, 'Be fruitful and multiply and fill the waters in the seas, and let birds multiply on the earth.' [23] And there was evening and there was morning, the fifth day.

[24] And God said, 'Let the earth bring forth living creatures of every kind: cattle and creeping things and wild animals of the earth of every kind.' And it was so. [25] God made the wild animals of the earth of every kind, and the cattle of every kind, and everything that creeps upon the ground of every kind. And God saw that it was good.

[26] Then God said, 'Let us make humankind in our image, according to our likeness; and let them have dominion over the fish of the sea, and over the birds of the air, and over the cattle, and over all the wild animals of the earth, and over every creeping thing that creeps upon the earth.'
[27] So God created humankind in his image,
     in the image of God he created them;
     male and female he created them.
[28] God blessed them, and God said to them, 'Be fruitful and multiply, and fill the earth and subdue it; and have dominion over the fish of the sea and over the birds of the air and over every living thing that moves upon the earth.' [29] God said, 'See, I have given you every plant yielding seed that is upon the face of all the earth, and every tree with seed in its fruit; you

shall have them for food. ³⁰ And to every beast of the earth, and to every bird of the air, and to everything that creeps on the earth, everything that has the breath of life, I have given every green plant for food.' And it was so. ³¹ God saw everything that he had made, and indeed, it was very good. And there was evening and there was morning, the sixth day. ¹ Thus the heavens and the earth were finished, and all their multitude. ² And on the seventh day God finished the work that he had done, and he rested on the seventh day from all the work that he had done. ³ So God blessed the seventh day and hallowed it, because on it God rested from all the work that he had done in creation.

PSALM   Psalm 136.1–9, [10–22,] 23–26

¹ Give thanks to the Lord, for he is good,
   for his mercy endures for ever.
² Give thanks to the God of gods,
   for his mercy endures for ever.
³ Give thanks to the Lord of lords,
   for his mercy endures for ever.
⁴ Who only does great wonders,
   for his mercy endures for ever;
⁵ Who by his wisdom made the heavens,
   for his mercy endures for ever;
⁶ Who spread out the earth upon the waters,
   for his mercy endures for ever;
⁷ Who created great lights,
   for his mercy endures for ever;
⁸ The sun to rule the day,
   for his mercy endures for ever;
⁹ The moon and the stars to govern the night,
   for his mercy endures for ever.
[¹⁰ Who struck down the first-born of Egypt,
   for his mercy endures for ever;
¹¹ And brought out Israel from among them,
   for his mercy endures for ever;
¹² With a mighty hand and a stretched-out arm,
   for his mercy endures for ever;
¹³ Who divided the Red Sea in two,
   for his mercy endures for ever;
¹⁴ And made Israel to pass through the midst of it,
   for his mercy endures for ever;
¹⁵ But swept Pharaoh and his army into the Red Sea,
   for his mercy endures for ever;

16   Who led his people through the wilderness,
     for his mercy endures for ever.
17   Who struck down great kings,
     for his mercy endures for ever;
18   And slew mighty kings,
     for his mercy endures for ever;
19   Sihon, king of the Amorites,
     for his mercy endures for ever;
20   And Og, the king of Bashan,
     for his mercy endures for ever;
21   And gave away their lands for an inheritance,
     for his mercy endures for ever;
22   An inheritance for Israel his servant,
     for his mercy endures for ever.]
23   Who remembered us in our low estate,
     for his mercy endures for ever;
24   And delivered us from our enemies,
     for his mercy endures for ever;
25   Who gives food to all creatures,
     for his mercy endures for ever;
26   Give thanks to the God of heaven,
     for his mercy endures for ever.

READING   Romans 8.18–25

18 I consider that the sufferings of this present time are not worth comparing with the glory about to be revealed to us. 19 For the creation waits with eager longing for the revealing of the children of God; 20 for the creation was subjected to futility, not of its own will but by the will of the one who subjected it, in hope 21 that the creation itself will be set free from its bondage to decay and will obtain the freedom of the glory of the children of God. 22 We know that the whole creation has been groaning in labour pains until now; 23 and not only the creation, but we ourselves, who have the first fruits of the Spirit, groan inwardly while we wait for adoption, the redemption of our bodies. 24 For in hope we were saved. Now hope that is seen is not hope. For who hopes for what is seen? 25 But if we hope for what we do not see, we wait for it with patience.

GOSPEL   Matthew 6.25–34

25 'Therefore I tell you, do not worry about your life, what you will eat or what you will drink, or about your body, what you will wear. Is not life more than food, and the body more than clothing? 26 Look at the birds of

the air; they neither sow nor reap nor gather into barns, and yet your heavenly Father feeds them. Are you not of more value than they? [27] And can any of you by worrying add a single hour to your span of life? [28] And why do you worry about clothing? Consider the lilies of the field, how they grow; they neither toil nor spin, [29] yet I tell you, even Solomon in all his glory was not clothed like one of these. [30] But if God so clothes the grass of the field, which is alive today and tomorrow is thrown into the oven, will he not much more clothe you—you of little faith? [31] Therefore do not worry, saying, "What will we eat?" or "What will we drink?" or "What will we wear?" [32] For it is the Gentiles who strive for all these things; and indeed your heavenly Father knows that you need all these things. [33] But strive first for the kingdom of God and his righteousness, and all these things will be given to you as well.

[34] 'So do not worry about tomorrow, for tomorrow will bring worries of its own. Today's trouble is enough for today.'

POST COMMUNION

God our creator, by your gift
the tree of life was set at the heart of the earthly paradise,
and the bread of life at the heart of your Church:
may we who have been nourished at your table on earth
be transformed by the glory of the Saviour's cross
and enjoy the delights of eternity;
through Jesus Christ our Lord.

SECOND SERVICE

Psalm 148
Proverbs 8.1, 22–31
Revelation 4

If the Second Service is a Eucharist, the following is read as a Gospel:

Luke 12.16–31

THIRD SERVICE

Psalms 100; 150
Job 38.1–21
Colossians 1.15–20

THE SUNDAY NEXT BEFORE LENT

COLLECT

Almighty Father,
whose Son was revealed in majesty
before he suffered death upon the cross:
give us grace to perceive his glory,
that we may be strengthened to suffer with him
and be changed into his likeness, from glory to glory;
who is alive and reigns with you,
in the unity of the Holy Spirit,
one God, now and for ever.

READING   Exodus 24.12–18

[12] The LORD said to Moses, 'Come up to me on the mountain, and wait there; and I will give you the tablets of stone, with the law and the commandment, which I have written for their instruction.' [13] So Moses set out with his assistant Joshua, and Moses went up into the mountain of God. [14] To the elders he had said, 'Wait here for us, until we come to you again; for Aaron and Hur are with you; whoever has a dispute may go to them.'

[15] Then Moses went up on the mountain, and the cloud covered the mountain. [16] The glory of the LORD settled on Mount Sinai, and the cloud covered it for six days; on the seventh day he called to Moses out of the cloud. [17] Now the appearance of the glory of the LORD was like a devouring fire on the top of the mountain in the sight of the people of Israel. [18] Moses entered the cloud, and went up on the mountain. Moses was on the mountain for forty days and forty nights.

PSALM

EITHER   Psalm 2

1   Why are the nations in an uproar?
    Why do the peoples mutter empty threats?
2   Why do the kings of the earth rise up in revolt, and the princes
        plot together,
    against the Lord and against his anointed?
3   'Let us break their yoke', they say; ·
    'let us cast off their bonds from us.'

4 He whose throne is in heaven is laughing;
  the Lord has them in derision.
5 Then he speaks to them in his wrath,
  and his rage fills them with terror.
6 'I myself have set my king
  upon my holy hill of Zion.'
7 Let me announce the decree of the Lord:
  he said to me, 'You are my Son; this day have I begotten you.
8 Ask of me and I will give you the nations for your inheritance
  and the ends of the earth for your possession.
9 You shall crush them with an iron rod
  and shatter them like a piece of pottery.'
10 And now, you kings, be wise;
  be warned, you rulers of the earth.
11 Submit to the Lord with fear,
  and with trembling bow before him;
12 Lest he be angry and you perish;
  for his wrath is quickly kindled.
13 Happy are they all
  who take refuge in him!

OR   **Psalm 99**

1 The Lord is king; let the people tremble;
  he is enthroned upon the cherubim; let the earth shake.
2 The Lord is great in Zion;
  he is high above all peoples.
3 Let them confess his name, which is great and awesome;
  he is the Holy One.
4 'O mighty King, lover of justice, you have established equity;
  you have executed justice and righteousness in Jacob.'
5 Proclaim the greatness of the Lord our God and fall down before
     his footstool;
  he is the Holy One.
6 Moses and Aaron among his priests, and Samuel among those who
     call upon his name,
  they called upon the Lord and he answered them.
7 He spoke to them out of the pillar of cloud;
  they kept his testimonies and the decree that he gave them.
8 'O Lord our God, you answered them indeed;
  you were a God who forgave them, yet punished them for their
     evil deeds.'

9 Proclaim the greatness of the Lord our God and worship him upon
   his holy hill;
  for the Lord our God is the Holy One.

READING   2 Peter 1.16–21

16 For we did not follow cleverly devised myths when we made known to
you the power and coming of our Lord Jesus Christ, but we had been
eyewitnesses of his majesty. 17 For he received honour and glory from God
the Father when that voice was conveyed to him by the Majestic Glory,
saying, 'This is my Son, my Beloved, with whom I am well pleased.' 18 We
ourselves heard this voice come from heaven, while we were with him on
the holy mountain.

19 So we have the prophetic message more fully confirmed. You will do
well to be attentive to this as to a lamp shining in a dark place, until the
day dawns and the morning star rises in your hearts. 20 First of all you must
understand this, that no prophecy of scripture is a matter of one's own
interpretation, 21 because no prophecy ever came by human will, but men
and women moved by the Holy Spirit spoke from God.

GOSPEL   Matthew 17.1–9

1 Six days later, Jesus took with him Peter and James and his brother John
and led them up a high mountain, by themselves. 2 And he was transfigured
before them, and his face shone like the sun, and his clothes became
dazzling white. 3 Suddenly there appeared to them Moses and Elijah,
talking with him. 4 Then Peter said to Jesus, 'Lord, it is good for us to be
here; if you wish, I will make three dwellings here, one for you, one for
Moses, and one for Elijah.' 5 While he was still speaking, suddenly a bright
cloud overshadowed them, and from the cloud a voice said, 'This is my Son,
the Beloved; with him I am well pleased; listen to him!' 6 When the disciples
heard this, they fell to the ground and were overcome by fear. 7 But Jesus
came and touched them, saying, 'Get up and do not be afraid.' 8 And when
they looked up, they saw no one except Jesus himself alone.

9 As they were coming down the mountain, Jesus ordered them, 'Tell no
one about the vision until after the Son of Man has been raised from the
dead.'

POST COMMUNION

Holy God,
we see your glory in the face of Jesus Christ:
may we who are partakers at his table
reflect his life in word and deed,
that all the world may know
    his power to change and save.
This we ask through Jesus Christ our Lord.

SECOND SERVICE

Psalm 84
Ecclesiasticus 48.1–10
or
2 Kings 2.1–12
Matthew 17.[1–8,] 9–23

THIRD SERVICE

Psalm 72
Exodus 34.29–35
2 Corinthians 4.3–6

THE ANNUNCIATION OF OUR LORD   25 MARCH

The readings for the Feast of the Annunciation will be found on page 1113

ASH WEDNESDAY

COLLECT

Almighty and everlasting God,
you hate nothing that you have made
and forgive the sins of all those who are penitent:
create and make in us new and contrite hearts
that we, worthily lamenting our sins
and acknowledging our wretchedness,
may receive from you, the God of all mercy,
perfect remission and forgiveness;
through Jesus Christ your Son our Lord,

who is alive and reigns with you,
in the unity of the Holy Spirit,
one God, now and for ever.

This Collect may be used as the Post Communion on any day from the First Sunday of Lent until the Saturday after the Fourth Sunday of Lent instead of the Post Communion provided

READING

EITHER   **Joel 2.1–2, 12–17**

¹ Blow the trumpet in Zion;
        sound the alarm on my holy mountain!
    Let all the inhabitants of the land tremble,
        for the day of the LORD is coming, it is near—
² a day of darkness and gloom,
        a day of clouds and thick darkness!
    Like blackness spread upon the mountains
        a great and powerful army comes;
    their like has never been from of old,
        nor will be again after them
        in ages to come.

¹² Yet even now, says the LORD,
        return to me with all your heart,
    with fasting, with weeping, and with mourning;
¹³   rend your hearts and not your clothing.
    Return to the LORD, your God,
        for he is gracious and merciful,
    slow to anger, and abounding in steadfast love,
        and relents from punishing.
¹⁴ Who knows whether he will not turn and relent,
        and leave a blessing behind him,
    a grain-offering and a drink-offering
        for the LORD, your God?
¹⁵ Blow the trumpet in Zion;
        sanctify a fast;
    call a solemn assembly;
¹⁶   gather the people.
    Sanctify the congregation;
        assemble the aged;
    gather the children,
        even infants at the breast.
    Let the bridegroom leave his room,
        and the bride her canopy.

¹⁷ Between the vestibule and the altar
    let the priests, the ministers of the L ORD, weep.
Let them say, 'Spare your people, O L ORD,
    and do not make your heritage a mockery,
    a byword among the nations.
Why should it be said among the peoples,
    "Where is their God?" '

OR   **Isaiah 58.1–12**

¹ Shout out, do not hold back!
    Lift up your voice like a trumpet!
Announce to my people their rebellion,
    to the house of Jacob their sins.
² Yet day after day they seek me
    and delight to know my ways,
as if they were a nation that practised righteousness
    and did not forsake the ordinance of their God;
they ask of me righteous judgements,
    they delight to draw near to God.
³ 'Why do we fast, but you do not see?
    Why humble ourselves, but you do not notice?'
Look, you serve your own interest on your fast-day,
    and oppress all your workers.
⁴ Look, you fast only to quarrel and to fight
    and to strike with a wicked fist.
Such fasting as you do today
    will not make your voice heard on high.
⁵ Is such the fast that I choose,
    a day to humble oneself?
Is it to bow down the head like a bulrush,
    and to lie in sackcloth and ashes?
Will you call this a fast,
    a day acceptable to the L ORD?
⁶ Is not this the fast that I choose:
    to loose the bonds of injustice,
    to undo the thongs of the yoke,
to let the oppressed go free,
    and to break every yoke?
⁷ Is it not to share your bread with the hungry,
    and bring the homeless poor into your house;
when you see the naked, to cover them,
    and not to hide yourself from your own kin?

8 Then your light shall break forth like the dawn,
   and your healing shall spring up quickly;
   your vindicator shall go before you,
   the glory of the LORD shall be your rearguard.
9 Then you shall call, and the LORD will answer;
   you shall cry for help, and he will say, Here I am.
   If you remove the yoke from among you,
   the pointing of the finger, the speaking of evil,
10 if you offer your food to the hungry
   and satisfy the needs of the afflicted,
   then your light shall rise in the darkness
   and your gloom be like the noonday.
11 The LORD will guide you continually,
   and satisfy your needs in parched places,
   and make your bones strong;
   and you shall be like a watered garden,
   like a spring of water,
   whose waters never fail.
12 Your ancient ruins shall be rebuilt;
   you shall raise up the foundations of many generations;
   you shall be called the repairer of the breach,
   the restorer of streets to live in.

PSALM   Psalm 51.1–18

1 Have mercy on me, O God, according to your loving-kindness;
   in your great compassion blot out my offences.
2 Wash me through and through from my wickedness
   and cleanse me from my sin.
3 For I know my transgressions,
   and my sin is ever before me.
4 Against you only have I sinned
   and done what is evil in your sight.
5 And so you are justified when you speak
   and upright in your judgement.
6 Indeed, I have been wicked from my birth,
   a sinner from my mother's womb.
7 For behold, you look for truth deep within me,
   and will make me understand wisdom secretly.
8 Purge me from my sin and I shall be pure;
   wash me and I shall be clean indeed.
9 Make me hear of joy and gladness,
   that the body you have broken may rejoice.

10 Hide your face from my sins
   and blot out all my iniquities.
11 Create in me a clean heart, O God,
   and renew a right spirit within me.
12 Cast me not away from your presence
   and take not your holy Spirit from me.
13 Give me the joy of your saving help again
   and sustain me with your bountiful Spirit.
14 I shall teach your ways to the wicked,
   and sinners shall return to you.
15 Deliver me from death, O God,
   and my tongue shall sing of your righteousness, O God of my
      salvation.
16 Open my lips, O Lord,
   and my mouth shall proclaim your praise.
17 Had you desired it, I would have offered sacrifice,
   but you take no delight in burnt-offerings.
18 The sacrifice of God is a troubled spirit;
   a broken and contrite heart, O God, you will not despise.

READING   2 Corinthians 5.20b–6.10

20 We entreat you on behalf of Christ, be reconciled to God. 21 For our sake
he made him to be sin who knew no sin, so that in him we might become
the righteousness of God.

   1 As we work together with him, we urge you also not to accept the grace
of God in vain. 2 For he says,
      'At an acceptable time I have listened to you,
         and on a day of salvation I have helped you.'
See, now is the acceptable time; see, now is the day of salvation! 3 We are
putting no obstacle in anyone's way, so that no fault may be found with
our ministry, 4 but as servants of God we have commended ourselves in
every way: through great endurance, in afflictions, hardships, calamities,
5 beatings, imprisonments, riots, labours, sleepless nights, hunger; 6 by
purity, knowledge, patience, kindness, holiness of spirit, genuine love,
7 truthful speech, and the power of God; with the weapons of righteousness
for the right hand and for the left; 8 in honour and dishonour, in ill
repute and good repute. We are treated as impostors, and yet are true; 9 as
unknown, and yet are well known; as dying, and see—we are alive; as
punished, and yet not killed; 10 as sorrowful, yet always rejoicing; as poor,
yet making many rich; as having nothing, and yet possessing everything.

GOSPEL

EITHER ## Matthew 6.1–6, 16–21

[1] 'Beware of practising your piety before others in order to be seen by them; for then you have no reward from your Father in heaven.

[2] 'So whenever you give alms, do not sound a trumpet before you, as the hypocrites do in the synagogues and in the streets, so that they may be praised by others. Truly I tell you, they have received their reward. [3] But when you give alms, do not let your left hand know what your right hand is doing, [4] so that your alms may be done in secret; and your Father who sees in secret will reward you.

[5] 'And whenever you pray, do not be like the hypocrites; for they love to stand and pray in the synagogues and at the street corners, so that they may be seen by others. Truly I tell you, they have received their reward. [6] But whenever you pray, go into your room and shut the door and pray to your Father who is in secret; and your Father who sees in secret will reward you.

[16] 'And whenever you fast, do not look dismal, like the hypocrites, for they disfigure their faces so as to show others that they are fasting. Truly I tell you, they have received their reward. [17] But when you fast, put oil on your head and wash your face, [18] so that your fasting may be seen not by others but by your Father who is in secret; and your Father who sees in secret will reward you.

[19] 'Do not store up for yourselves treasures on earth, where moth and rust consume and where thieves break in and steal; [20] but store up for yourselves treasures in heaven, where neither moth nor rust consumes and where thieves do not break in and steal. [21] For where your treasure is, there your heart will be also.'

OR ## John 8.2–11

[2] Early in the morning he came again to the temple. All the people came to him and he sat down and began to teach them. [3] The scribes and the Pharisees brought a woman who had been caught in adultery; and making her stand before all of them, [4] they said to him, 'Teacher, this woman was caught in the very act of committing adultery. [5] Now in the law Moses commanded us to stone such women. Now what do you say?' [6] They said this to test him, so that they might have some charge to bring against him. Jesus bent down and wrote with his finger on the ground. [7] When they kept on questioning him, he straightened up and said to them, 'Let anyone

among you who is without sin be the first to throw a stone at her.' [8] And once again he bent down and wrote on the ground. [9] When they heard it, they went away, one by one, beginning with the elders; and Jesus was left alone with the woman standing before him. [10] Jesus straightened up and said to her, 'Woman, where are they? Has no one condemned you?' [11] She said, 'No one, sir.' And Jesus said, 'Neither do I condemn you. Go your way, and from now on do not sin again.'

POST COMMUNION

Almighty God,
you have given your only Son to be for us
both a sacrifice for sin
and also an example of godly life:
give us grace
that we may always most thankfully receive
these his inestimable gifts,
and also daily endeavour to follow
   the blessed steps of his most holy life;
through Jesus Christ our Lord.

SECOND SERVICE

Psalm 102.1–17, [18–28]
Isaiah 1.10–18
Luke 15.11–32

THIRD SERVICE

Psalm 38
Daniel 9.3–6, 17–19
1 Timothy 6.6–19

THE FIRST SUNDAY OF LENT

COLLECT

Almighty God,
whose Son Jesus Christ fasted forty days in the wilderness,
and was tempted as we are, yet without sin:
give us grace to discipline ourselves
   in obedience to your Spirit;
and, as you know our weakness,
so may we know your power to save;

through Jesus Christ your Son our Lord,
who is alive and reigns with you,
in the unity of the Holy Spirit,
one God, now and for ever.

READING   Genesis 2.15–17; 3.1–7

¹⁵ The LORD God took the man and put him in the garden of Eden to till it
and keep it. ¹⁶ And the LORD God commanded the man, 'You may freely eat
of every tree of the garden; ¹⁷ but of the tree of the knowledge of good and
evil you shall not eat, for in the day that you eat of it you shall die.'

¹ Now the serpent was more crafty than any other wild animal that the
LORD God had made. He said to the woman, 'Did God say, "You shall not
eat from any tree in the garden"?' ² The woman said to the serpent, 'We
may eat of the fruit of the trees in the garden; ³ but God said, "You shall
not eat of the fruit of the tree that is in the middle of the garden, nor shall
you touch it, or you shall die." ' ⁴ But the serpent said to the woman, 'You
will not die; ⁵ for God knows that when you eat of it your eyes will be
opened, and you will be like God, knowing good and evil.' ⁶ So when the
woman saw that the tree was good for food, and that it was a delight to the
eyes, and that the tree was to be desired to make one wise, she took of its
fruit and ate; and she also gave some to her husband, who was with her,
and he ate. ⁷ Then the eyes of both were opened, and they knew that they
were naked; and they sewed fig leaves together and made loincloths for
themselves.

PSALM   Psalm 32

1 Happy are they whose transgressions are forgiven,
   and whose sin is put away!
2 Happy are they to whom the Lord imputes no guilt,
   and in whose spirit there is no guile!
3 While I held my tongue, my bones withered away,
   because of my groaning all day long.
4 For your hand was heavy upon me day and night;
   my moisture was dried up as in the heat of summer.
5 Then I acknowledged my sin to you,
   and did not conceal my guilt.
6 I said, 'I will confess my transgressions to the Lord':
   then you forgave me the guilt of my sin;

7   Therefore all the faithful will make their prayers to you in time of
      trouble;
  when the great waters overflow, they shall not reach them.
8   You are my hiding-place; you preserve me from trouble;
  you surround me with shouts of deliverance.
9   'I will instruct you and teach you in the way that you should go;
  I will guide you with my eye.
10   Do not be like horse or mule, which have no understanding;
  who must be fitted with bit and bridle, or else they will not stay
      near you.'
11   Great are the tribulations of the wicked;
  but mercy embraces those who trust in the Lord.
12   Be glad, you righteous, and rejoice in the Lord;
  shout for joy, all who are true of heart.

READING   Romans 5.12–19

12 Therefore, just as sin came into the world through one man, and death came through sin, and so death spread to all because all have sinned— 13 sin was indeed in the world before the law, but sin is not reckoned when there is no law. 14 Yet death exercised dominion from Adam to Moses, even over those whose sins were not like the transgression of Adam, who is a type of the one who was to come.

15 But the free gift is not like the trespass. For if the many died through the one man's trespass, much more surely have the grace of God and the free gift in the grace of the one man, Jesus Christ, abounded for the many. 16 And the free gift is not like the effect of the one man's sin. For the judgement following one trespass brought condemnation, but the free gift following many trespasses brings justification. 17 If, because of the one man's trespass, death exercised dominion through that one, much more surely will those who receive the abundance of grace and the free gift of righteousness exercise dominion in life through the one man, Jesus Christ.

18 Therefore just as one man's trespass led to condemnation for all, so one man's act of righteousness leads to justification and life for all. 19 For just as by the one man's disobedience the many were made sinners, so by the one man's obedience the many will be made righteous.

GOSPEL   Matthew 4.1–11

1 Then Jesus was led up by the Spirit into the wilderness to be tempted by the devil. 2 He fasted for forty days and forty nights, and afterwards he was famished. 3 The tempter came and said to him, 'If you are the Son of God,

command these stones to become loaves of bread.' ⁴ But he answered, 'It is written,

"One does not live by bread alone,
but by every word that comes from the mouth of God." '

⁵ Then the devil took him to the holy city and placed him on the pinnacle of the temple, ⁶ saying to him, 'If you are the Son of God, throw yourself down; for it is written,

"He will command his angels concerning you",
and "On their hands they will bear you up,
so that you will not dash your foot against a stone." '

⁷ Jesus said to him, 'Again it is written, "Do not put the Lord your God to the test." '

⁸ Again, the devil took him to a very high mountain and showed him all the kingdoms of the world and their splendour; ⁹ and he said to him, 'All these I will give you, if you will fall down and worship me.' ¹⁰ Jesus said to him, 'Away with you, Satan! for it is written,

"Worship the Lord your God,
and serve only him." '

¹¹ Then the devil left him, and suddenly angels came and waited on him.

POST COMMUNION

Lord God,
you have renewed us with the living bread from heaven;
by it you nourish our faith,
increase our hope,
and strengthen our love:
teach us always to hunger for him
   who is the true and living bread,
and enable us to live by every word
   that proceeds from out of your mouth;
through Jesus Christ our Lord.

SECOND SERVICE

Psalm 50.1–15
Deuteronomy 6.4–9, 16–25
Luke 15.1–10

THIRD SERVICE

Psalm 119.1–16
Jeremiah 18.1–11
Luke 18.9–14

THE SECOND SUNDAY OF LENT

COLLECT

Almighty God,
you show to those who are in error the light of your truth,
that they may return to the way of righteousness:
grant to all those who are admitted
    into the fellowship of Christ's religion,
that they may reject those things
    that are contrary to their profession,
and follow all such things as are agreeable to the same;
through our Lord Jesus Christ,
who is alive and reigns with you,
in the unity of the Holy Spirit,
one God, now and for ever.

READING   Genesis 12.1–4a

¹ Now the LORD said to Abram, 'Go from your country and your kindred and your father's house to the land that I will show you. ² I will make of you a great nation, and I will bless you, and make your name great, so that you will be a blessing. ³ I will bless those who bless you, and the one who curses you I will curse; and in you all the families of the earth shall be blessed.'

⁴ So Abram went, as the LORD had told him; and Lot went with him.

PSALM   Psalm 121

1   I lift up my eyes to the hills;
      from where is my help to come?
2   My help comes from the Lord,
      the maker of heaven and earth.
3   He will not let your foot be moved
      and he who watches over you will not fall asleep.
4   Behold, he who keeps watch over Israel
      shall neither slumber nor sleep;
5   The Lord himself watches over you;
      the Lord is your shade at your right hand,
6   ·So that the sun shall not strike you by day,
      nor the moon by night.

7 The Lord shall preserve you from all evil;
   it is he who shall keep you safe.
8 The Lord shall watch over your going out and your coming in,
   from this time forth for evermore.

READING   Romans 4.1–5, 13–17

1 What then are we to say was gained by Abraham, our ancestor according to the flesh? 2 For if Abraham was justified by works, he has something to boast about, but not before God. 3 For what does the scripture say? 'Abraham believed God, and it was reckoned to him as righteousness.' 4 Now to one who works, wages are not reckoned as a gift but as something due. 5 But to one who without works trusts him who justifies the ungodly, such faith is reckoned as righteousness.

13 For the promise that he would inherit the world did not come to Abraham or to his descendants through the law but through the righteousness of faith. 14 If it is the adherents of the law who are to be the heirs, faith is null and the promise is void. 15 For the law brings wrath; but where there is no law, neither is there violation.

16 For this reason it depends on faith, in order that the promise may rest on grace and be guaranteed to all his descendants, not only to the adherents of the law but also to those who share the faith of Abraham (for he is the father of all of us, 17 as it is written, 'I have made you the father of many nations')—in the presence of the God in whom he believed, who gives life to the dead and calls into existence the things that do not exist.

GOSPEL   John 3.1–17

1 Now there was a Pharisee named Nicodemus, a leader of the Jews. 2 He came to Jesus by night and said to him, 'Rabbi, we know that you are a teacher who has come from God; for no one can do these signs that you do apart from the presence of God.' 3 Jesus answered him, 'Very truly, I tell you, no one can see the kingdom of God without being born from above.' 4 Nicodemus said to him, 'How can anyone be born after having grown old? Can one enter a second time into the mother's womb and be born?' 5 Jesus answered, 'Very truly, I tell you, no one can enter the kingdom of God without being born of water and Spirit. 6 What is born of the flesh is flesh, and what is born of the Spirit is spirit. 7 Do not be astonished that I said to you, "You must be born from above." 8 The wind blows where it chooses, and you hear the sound of it, but you do not know where it comes from or where it goes. So it is with everyone who is born of the Spirit.' 9 Nicodemus

said to him, 'How can these things be?' [10] Jesus answered him, 'Are you a teacher of Israel, and yet you do not understand these things?

[11] 'Very truly, I tell you, we speak of what we know and testify to what we have seen; yet you do not receive our testimony. [12] If I have told you about earthly things and you do not believe, how can you believe if I tell you about heavenly things? [13] No one has ascended into heaven except the one who descended from heaven, the Son of Man. [14] And just as Moses lifted up the serpent in the wilderness, so must the Son of Man be lifted up, [15] that whoever believes in him may have eternal life.

[16] 'For God so loved the world that he gave his only Son, so that everyone who believes in him may not perish but may have eternal life.

[17] 'Indeed, God did not send the Son into the world to condemn the world, but in order that the world might be saved through him.'

POST COMMUNION

Almighty God,
you see that we have no power of ourselves to help ourselves:
keep us both outwardly in our bodies,
and inwardly in our souls;
that we may be defended from all adversities
    which may happen to the body,
and from all evil thoughts
    which may assault and hurt the soul;
through Jesus Christ our Lord.

SECOND SERVICE

Psalm 135.1–14, [15–21]
Numbers 21.4–9
Luke 14.27–33

THIRD SERVICE

Psalm 74
Jeremiah 22.1–9
Matthew 8.1–13

THE THIRD SUNDAY OF LENT

COLLECT

Almighty God,
whose most dear Son went not up to joy
    but first he suffered pain,
and entered not into glory before he was crucified:
mercifully grant that we, walking in the way of the cross,
may find it none other than the way of life and peace;
through Jesus Christ your Son our Lord,
who is alive and reigns with you,
in the unity of the Holy Spirit,
one God, now and for ever.

READING   Exodus 17.1–7

¹ From the wilderness of Sin the whole congregation of the Israelites journeyed by stages, as the LORD commanded. They camped at Rephidim, but there was no water for the people to drink. ² The people quarrelled with Moses, and said, 'Give us water to drink.' Moses said to them, 'Why do you quarrel with me? Why do you test the LORD?' ³ But the people thirsted there for water; and the people complained against Moses and said, 'Why did you bring us out of Egypt, to kill us and our children and livestock with thirst?' ⁴ So Moses cried out to the LORD, 'What shall I do with this people? They are almost ready to stone me.' ⁵ The LORD said to Moses, 'Go on ahead of the people, and take some of the elders of Israel with you; take in your hand the staff with which you struck the Nile, and go. ⁶ I will be standing there in front of you on the rock at Horeb. Strike the rock, and water will come out of it, so that the people may drink.' Moses did so, in the sight of the elders of Israel. ⁷ He called the place Massah and Meribah, because the Israelites quarrelled and tested the LORD, saying, 'Is the LORD among us or not?'

PSALM   Psalm 95

1   Come, let us sing to the Lord;
      let us shout for joy to the rock of our salvation.
2   Let us come before his presence with thanksgiving
      and raise a loud shout to him with psalms.
3   For the Lord is a great God,
      and a great king above all gods.

4   In his hand are the depths of the earth,
    and the heights of the hills are his also.
5   The sea is his, for he made it,
    and his hands have moulded the dry land.
6   Come, let us bow down and bend the knee,
    and kneel before the Lord our Maker.
7   For he is our God, and we are the people of his pasture and the
        sheep of his hand.
    O that today you would hearken to his voice!
8   'Harden not your hearts, as your forebears did in the wilderness,
    at Meribah, and on that day at Massah, when they tempted me.
9   They put me to the test,
    though they had seen my works.
10 Forty years long I detested that generation and said,
    "This people are wayward in their hearts; they do not know my
        ways."
11 So I swore in my wrath,
    "They shall not enter into my rest." '

READING   Romans 5.1–11

¹ Therefore, since we are justified by faith, we have peace with God
through our Lord Jesus Christ, ² through whom we have obtained access to
this grace in which we stand; and we boast in our hope of sharing the glory
of God. ³ And not only that, but we also boast in our sufferings, knowing
that suffering produces endurance, ⁴ and endurance produces character,
and character produces hope, ⁵ and hope does not disappoint us, because
God's love has been poured into our hearts through the Holy Spirit that
has been given to us.

⁶ For while we were still weak, at the right time Christ died for the
ungodly. ⁷ Indeed, rarely will anyone die for a righteous person—though
perhaps for a good person someone might actually dare to die. ⁸ But God
proves his love for us in that while we still were sinners Christ died for us.
⁹ Much more surely then, now that we have been justified by his blood, will
we be saved through him from the wrath of God. ¹⁰ For if while we were
enemies, we were reconciled to God through the death of his Son, much
more surely, having been reconciled, will we be saved by his life. ¹¹ But
more than that, we even boast in God through our Lord Jesus Christ,
through whom we have now received reconciliation.

GOSPEL

John 4.5–42

[5] So he came to a Samaritan city called Sychar, near the plot of ground that Jacob had given to his son Joseph. [6] Jacob's well was there, and Jesus, tired out by his journey, was sitting by the well. It was about noon.

[7] A Samaritan woman came to draw water, and Jesus said to her, 'Give me a drink'. [8] (His disciples had gone to the city to buy food.) [9] The Samaritan woman said to him, 'How is it that you, a Jew, ask a drink of me, a woman of Samaria?' (Jews do not share things in common with Samaritans.) [10] Jesus answered her, 'If you knew the gift of God, and who it is that is saying to you, "Give me a drink", you would have asked him, and he would have given you living water.' [11] The woman said to him, 'Sir, you have no bucket, and the well is deep. Where do you get that living water? [12] Are you greater than our ancestor Jacob, who gave us the well, and with his sons and his flocks drank from it?' [13] Jesus said to her, 'Everyone who drinks of this water will be thirsty again, [14] but those who drink of the water that I will give them will never be thirsty. The water that I will give will become in them a spring of water gushing up to eternal life.' [15] The woman said to him, 'Sir, give me this water, so that I may never be thirsty or have to keep coming here to draw water.'

[16] Jesus said to her, 'Go, call your husband, and come back.' [17] The woman answered him, 'I have no husband.' Jesus said to her, 'You are right in saying, "I have no husband"; [18] for you have had five husbands, and the one you have now is not your husband. What you have said is true!' [19] The woman said to him, 'Sir, I see that you are a prophet. [20] Our ancestors worshipped on this mountain, but you say that the place where people must worship is in Jerusalem.' [21] Jesus said to her, 'Woman, believe me, the hour is coming when you will worship the Father neither on this mountain nor in Jerusalem. [22] You worship what you do not know; we worship what we know, for salvation is from the Jews. [23] But the hour is coming, and is now here, when the true worshippers will worship the Father in spirit and truth, for the Father seeks such as these to worship him. [24] God is spirit, and those who worship him must worship in spirit and truth.' [25] The woman said to him, 'I know that Messiah is coming' (who is called Christ). 'When he comes, he will proclaim all things to us.' [26] Jesus said to her, 'I am he, the one who is speaking to you.'

[27] Just then his disciples came. They were astonished that he was speaking with a woman, but no one said, 'What do you want?' or, 'Why are you speaking with her?' [28] Then the woman left her water-jar and went back to the city. She said to the people, [29] 'Come and see a man who told me everything I have ever done! He cannot be the Messiah, can he?' [30] They left the city and were on their way to him.

³¹ Meanwhile the disciples were urging him, 'Rabbi, eat something.' ³² But he said to them, 'I have food to eat that you do not know about.' ³³ So the disciples said to one another, 'Surely no one has brought him something to eat?' ³⁴ Jesus said to them, 'My food is to do the will of him who sent me and to complete his work. ³⁵ Do you not say, "Four months more, then comes the harvest"? But I tell you, look around you, and see how the fields are ripe for harvesting. ³⁶ The reaper is already receiving wages and is gathering fruit for eternal life, so that sower and reaper may rejoice together. ³⁷ For here the saying holds true, "One sows and another reaps." ³⁸ I sent you to reap that for which you did not labour. Others have laboured, and you have entered into their labour.'

³⁹ Many Samaritans from that city believed in him because of the woman's testimony, 'He told me everything I have ever done.' ⁴⁰ So when the Samaritans came to him, they asked him to stay with them; and he stayed there for two days. ⁴¹ And many more believed because of his word. ⁴² They said to the woman, 'It is no longer because of what you said that we believe, for we have heard for ourselves, and we know that this is truly the Saviour of the world.'

POST COMMUNION

Merciful Lord,
grant your people grace to withstand the temptations
    of the world, the flesh and the devil,
and with pure hearts and minds to follow you,
    the only God;
through Jesus Christ our Lord.

SECOND SERVICE

Psalm 40
Joshua 1.1–9
Ephesians 6.10–20

If the Second Service is a Eucharist, the following is read as a Gospel:

John 2.13–22

THIRD SERVICE

Psalm 46
Amos 7.10–17
2 Corinthians 1.1–11

THE FOURTH SUNDAY OF LENT

Mothering Sunday may be celebrated in preference to the provision for the Fourth Sunday of Lent

COLLECT

Merciful Lord,
absolve your people from their offences,
that through your bountiful goodness
we may all be delivered from the chains of those sins
which by our frailty we have committed;
grant this, heavenly Father,
for Jesus Christ's sake, our blessed Lord and Saviour,
who is alive and reigns with you,
in the unity of the Holy Spirit,
one God, now and for ever.

READING   1 Samuel 16.1–13

[1] The LORD said to Samuel, 'How long will you grieve over Saul? I have rejected him from being king over Israel. Fill your horn with oil and set out; I will send you to Jesse the Bethlehemite, for I have provided for myself a king among his sons.' [2] Samuel said, 'How can I go? If Saul hears of it, he will kill me.' And the LORD said, 'Take a heifer with you, and say, "I have come to sacrifice to the LORD." [3] Invite Jesse to the sacrifice, and I will show you what you shall do; and you shall anoint for me the one whom I name to you.' [4] Samuel did what the LORD commanded, and came to Bethlehem. The elders of the city came to meet him trembling, and said, 'Do you come peaceably?' [5] He said, 'Peaceably; I have come to sacrifice to the LORD; sanctify yourselves and come with me to the sacrifice.' And he sanctified Jesse and his sons and invited them to the sacrifice.

[6] When they came, he looked on Eliab and thought, 'Surely the LORD's anointed is now before the LORD.' [7] But the LORD said to Samuel, 'Do not look on his appearance or on the height of his stature, because I have rejected him; for the LORD does not see as mortals see; they look on the outward appearance, but the LORD looks on the heart.' [8] Then Jesse called Abinadab, and made him pass before Samuel. He said, 'Neither has the LORD chosen this one.' [9] Then Jesse made Shammah pass by. And he said, 'Neither has the LORD chosen this one.' [10] Jesse made seven of his sons pass before Samuel, and Samuel said to Jesse, 'The LORD has not chosen any of these.' [11] Samuel said to Jesse, 'Are all your sons here?' And he said, 'There

remains yet the youngest, but he is keeping the sheep.' And Samuel said to Jesse, 'Send and bring him; for we will not sit down until he comes here.' [12] He sent and brought him in. Now he was ruddy, and had beautiful eyes, and was handsome. The LORD said, 'Rise and anoint him; for this is the one.' [13] Then Samuel took the horn of oil, and anointed him in the presence of his brothers; and the spirit of the LORD came mightily upon David from that day forward. Samuel then set out and went to Ramah.

PSALM   Psalm 23

1   The Lord is my shepherd;
     I shall not be in want.
2   He makes me lie down in green pastures
     and leads me beside still waters.
3   He revives my soul
     and guides me along right pathways for his name's sake.
4   Though I walk through the valley of the shadow of death, I shall
        fear no evil;
     for you are with me; your rod and your staff, they comfort me.
5   You spread a table before me in the presence of those who trouble
        me;
     you have anointed my head with oil, and my cup is running over.
6   Surely your goodness and mercy shall follow me all the days of my
        life,
     and I will dwell in the house of the Lord for ever.

READING   Ephesians 5.8–14

[8] For once you were darkness, but now in the Lord you are light. Live as children of light— [9] for the fruit of the light is found in all that is good and right and true. [10] Try to find out what is pleasing to the Lord. [11] Take no part in the unfruitful works of darkness, but instead expose them. [12] For it is shameful even to mention what such people do secretly; [13] but everything exposed by the light becomes visible, [14] for everything that becomes visible is light. Therefore it says,

    'Sleeper, awake!
       Rise from the dead,
    and Christ will shine on you.'

GOSPEL   John 9.1–41

¹ As he walked along, he saw a man blind from birth. ² His disciples asked him, 'Rabbi, who sinned, this man or his parents, that he was born blind?' ³ Jesus answered, 'Neither this man nor his parents sinned; he was born blind so that God's works might be revealed in him. ⁴ We must work the works of him who sent me while it is day; night is coming when no one can work. ⁵ As long as I am in the world, I am the light of the world.' ⁶ When he had said this, he spat on the ground and made mud with the saliva and spread the mud on the man's eyes, ⁷ saying to him, 'Go, wash in the pool of Siloam' (which means Sent). Then he went and washed and came back able to see. ⁸ The neighbours and those who had seen him before as a beggar began to ask, 'Is this not the man who used to sit and beg?' ⁹ Some were saying, 'It is he.' Others were saying, 'No, but it is someone like him.' He kept saying, 'I am the man.' ¹⁰ But they kept asking him, 'Then how were your eyes opened?' ¹¹ He answered, 'The man called Jesus made mud, spread it on my eyes, and said to me, "Go to Siloam and wash." Then I went and washed and received my sight.' ¹² They said to him, 'Where is he?' He said, 'I do not know.'

¹³ They brought to the Pharisees the man who had formerly been blind. ¹⁴ Now it was a sabbath day when Jesus made the mud and opened his eyes. ¹⁵ Then the Pharisees also began to ask him how he had received his sight. He said to them, 'He put mud on my eyes. Then I washed, and now I see.' ¹⁶ Some of the Pharisees said, 'This man is not from God, for he does not observe the sabbath.' But others said, 'How can a man who is a sinner perform such signs?' And they were divided. ¹⁷ So they said again to the blind man, 'What do you say about him? It was your eyes he opened.' He said, 'He is a prophet.'

¹⁸ The Jews did not believe that he had been blind and had received his sight until they called the parents of the man who had received his sight ¹⁹ and asked them, 'Is this your son, who you say was born blind? How then does he now see?' ²⁰ His parents answered, 'We know that this is our son, and that he was born blind; ²¹ but we do not know how it is that now he sees, nor do we know who opened his eyes. Ask him; he is of age. He will speak for himself.' ²² His parents said this because they were afraid of the Jews; for the Jews had already agreed that anyone who confessed Jesus to be the Messiah would be put out of the synagogue. ²³ Therefore his parents said, 'He is of age; ask him.'

²⁴ So for the second time they called the man who had been blind, and they said to him, 'Give glory to God! We know that this man is a sinner.' ²⁵ He answered, 'I do not know whether he is a sinner. One thing I do know, that though I was blind, now I see.' ²⁶ They said to him, 'What did he do to you? How did he open your eyes?' ²⁷ He answered them, 'I have told you already, and you would not listen. Why do you want to hear it again? Do you also want to become his disciples?' ²⁸ Then they reviled him, saying,

'You are his disciple, but we are disciples of Moses. [29] We know that God has spoken to Moses, but as for this man, we do not know where he comes from.' [30] The man answered, 'Here is an astonishing thing! You do not know where he comes from, and yet he opened my eyes. [31] We know that God does not listen to sinners, but he does listen to one who worships him and obeys his will. [32] Never since the world began has it been heard that anyone opened the eyes of a person born blind. [33] If this man were not from God, he could do nothing.' [34] They answered him, 'You were born entirely in sins, and are you trying to teach us?' And they drove him out.

[35] Jesus heard that they had driven him out, and when he found him, he said, 'Do you believe in the Son of Man?' [36] He answered, 'And who is he, sir? Tell me, so that I may believe in him.' [37] Jesus said to him, 'You have seen him, and the one speaking with you is he.' [38] He said, 'Lord, I believe.' And he worshipped him. [39] Jesus said, 'I came into this world for judgement so that those who do not see may see, and those who do see may become blind.' [40] Some of the Pharisees near him heard this and said to him, 'Surely we are not blind, are we?' [41] Jesus said to them, 'If you were blind, you would not have sin. But now that you say, "We see", your sin remains.'

If the Principal Service readings have been displaced by Mothering Sunday provisions, they may be used at the Second Service

POST COMMUNION

Lord God,
whose blessed Son our Saviour
gave his back to the smiters
and did not hide his face from shame:
give us grace to endure the sufferings of this present time
with sure confidence in the glory that shall be revealed;
through Jesus Christ our Lord.

SECOND SERVICE

Psalm 31.1–8, [9–16]
Micah 7

or

Prayer of Manasseh
James 5

If the Second Service is a Eucharist, the following is read as a Gospel:

John 3.14–21

THIRD SERVICE

Psalm 19
Isaiah 43.1–7
Ephesians 2.8–14

MOTHERING SUNDAY

Mothering Sunday may be celebrated in preference to any part of the provision for the Fourth Sunday of Lent. If it replaces a Second or Third Service, the Principal Service provision may still be used.

COLLECT

God of compassion,
whose Son Jesus Christ, the child of Mary,
shared the life of a home in Nazareth,
and on the cross drew the whole human family to himself:
strengthen us in our daily living
that in joy and in sorrow
we may know the power of your presence
   to bind together and to heal;
through Jesus Christ your Son our Lord,
who is alive and reigns with you,
in the unity of the Holy Spirit,
one God, now and for ever.

READING

EITHER   **Exodus 2.1–10**

[1] Now a man from the house of Levi went and married a Levite woman. [2] The woman conceived and bore a son; and when she saw that he was a fine baby, she hid him for three months. [3] When she could hide him no longer she got a papyrus basket for him, and plastered it with bitumen and pitch; she put the child in it and placed it among the reeds on the bank of the river. [4] His sister stood at a distance, to see what would happen to him.

[5] The daughter of Pharaoh came down to bathe at the river, while her attendants walked beside the river. She saw the basket among the reeds and sent her maid to bring it. [6] When she opened it, she saw the child. He was crying, and she took pity on him. 'This must be one of the Hebrews' children,' she said. [7] Then his sister said to Pharaoh's daughter, 'Shall I go and get you a nurse from the Hebrew women to nurse the child for you?' [8] Pharaoh's daughter said to her, 'Yes.' So the girl went and called the child's mother. [9] Pharaoh's daughter said to her, 'Take this child and nurse it for me, and I will give you your wages.' So the woman took the child and nursed it. [10] When the child grew up, she brought him to Pharaoh's daughter, and she took him as her son. She named him Moses, 'because', she said, 'I drew him out of the water.'

²⁰ In due time Hannah conceived and bore a son. She named him Samuel, for she said, 'I have asked him of the LORD.'

²¹ The man Elkanah and all his household went up to offer to the LORD the yearly sacrifice, and to pay his vow. ²² But Hannah did not go up, for she said to her husband, 'As soon as the child is weaned, I will bring him, that he may appear in the presence of the LORD, and remain there for ever; I will offer him as a nazirite for all time.' ²³ Her husband Elkanah said to her, 'Do what seems best to you, wait until you have weaned him; only— may the LORD establish his word.' So the woman remained and nursed her son, until she weaned him. ²⁴ When she had weaned him, she took him up with her, along with a three-year-old bull, an ephah of flour, and a skin of wine. She brought him to the house of the LORD at Shiloh; and the child was young. ²⁵ Then they slaughtered the bull, and they brought the child to Eli. ²⁶ And she said, 'Oh, my lord! As you live, my lord, I am the woman who was standing here in your presence, praying to the LORD. ²⁷ For this child I prayed; and the LORD has granted me the petition that I made to him. ²⁸ Therefore I have lent him to the LORD; as long as he lives, he is given to the LORD.'

She left him there for the LORD.

PSALM

¹¹   Come, children, and listen to me;
     I will teach you the fear of the Lord.
¹²   Who among you loves life
     and desires long life to enjoy prosperity?
¹³   Keep your tongue from evil-speaking
     and your lips from lying words.
¹⁴   Turn from evil and do good;
     seek peace and pursue it.
¹⁵   The eyes of the Lord are upon the righteous,
     and his ears are open to their cry.
¹⁶   The face of the Lord is against those who do evil,
     to root out the remembrance of them from the earth.
¹⁷   The righteous cry and the Lord hears them
     and delivers them from all their troubles.
¹⁸   The Lord is near to the brokenhearted
     and will save those whose spirits are crushed.

¹⁹ Many are the troubles of the righteous,
but the Lord will deliver him out of them all.
²⁰ He will keep safe all his bones;
not one of them shall be broken.

OR   Psalm 127.1–5

¹ Unless the Lord builds the house,
their labour is in vain who build it.
² Unless the Lord watches over the city,
in vain the guard keeps vigil.
³ It is in vain that you rise so early and go to bed so late;
vain, too, to eat the bread of toil, for he gives to his belovèd sleep.
⁴ Children are a heritage from the Lord,
and the fruit of the womb is a gift.
⁵ Like arrows in the hand of a warrior
are the children of one's youth.

READING

EITHER   2 Corinthians 1.3–7

³ Blessed be the God and Father of our Lord Jesus Christ, the Father of mercies and the God of all consolation, ⁴ who consoles us in all our affliction, so that we may be able to console those who are in any affliction with the consolation with which we ourselves are consoled by God. ⁵ For just as the sufferings of Christ are abundant for us, so also our consolation is abundant through Christ. ⁶ If we are being afflicted, it is for your consolation and salvation; if we are being consoled, it is for your consolation, which you experience when you patiently endure the same sufferings that we are also suffering. ⁷ Our hope for you is unshaken; for we know that as you share in our sufferings, so also you share in our consolation.

OR   Colossians 3.12–17

¹² As God's chosen ones, holy and beloved, clothe yourselves with compassion, kindness, humility, meekness, and patience. ¹³ Bear with one another and, if anyone has a complaint against another, forgive each other; just as the Lord has forgiven you, so you also must forgive. ¹⁴ Above all, clothe yourselves with love, which binds everything together in perfect harmony. ¹⁵ And let the peace of Christ rule in your hearts, to which indeed you were called in the one body. And be thankful. ¹⁶ Let the word of Christ dwell in you richly; teach and admonish one another in all wisdom; and

with gratitude in your hearts sing psalms, hymns, and spiritual songs to God. [17] And whatever you do, in word or deed, do everything in the name of the Lord Jesus, giving thanks to God the Father through him.

GOSPEL

EITHER   Luke 2.33–35

[33] And the child's father and mother were amazed at what was being said about him. [34] Then Simeon blessed them and said to his mother Mary, 'This child is destined for the falling and the rising of many in Israel, and to be a sign that will be opposed [35] so that the inner thoughts of many will be revealed—and a sword will pierce your own soul too.'

OR   John 19.25b-27

[25] Meanwhile, standing near the cross of Jesus were his mother, and his mother's sister, Mary the wife of Clopas, and Mary Magdalene. [26] When Jesus saw his mother and the disciple whom he loved standing beside her, he said to his mother, 'Woman, here is your son.' [27] Then he said to the disciple, 'Here is your mother.' And from that hour the disciple took her into his own home.

POST COMMUNION

Loving God,
as a mother feeds her children at the breast
you feed us in this sacrament
   with the food and drink of eternal life:
help us who have tasted your goodness
to grow in grace within the household of faith;
through Jesus Christ our Lord.

THE FIFTH SUNDAY OF LENT
PASSIONTIDE BEGINS

COLLECT

Most merciful God,
who by the death and resurrection of your Son Jesus Christ
delivered and saved the world:

grant that by faith in him who suffered on the cross
we may triumph in the power of his victory;
through Jesus Christ your Son our Lord,
who is alive and reigns with you,
in the unity of the Holy Spirit,
one God, now and for ever.

READING   Ezekiel 37.1–14

¹ The hand of the LORD came upon me, and he brought me out by the spirit of the LORD and set me down in the middle of a valley; it was full of bones. ² He led me all round them; there were very many lying in the valley, and they were very dry. ³ He said to me, 'Mortal, can these bones live?' I answered, 'O Lord GOD, you know.' ⁴ Then he said to me, 'Prophesy to these bones, and say to them: O dry bones, hear the word of the LORD. ⁵ Thus says the Lord GOD to these bones: I will cause breath to enter you, and you shall live. ⁶ I will lay sinews on you, and will cause flesh to come upon you, and cover you with skin, and put breath in you, and you shall live; and you shall know that I am the LORD.'

⁷ So I prophesied as I had been commanded; and as I prophesied, suddenly there was a noise, a rattling, and the bones came together, bone to its bone. ⁸ I looked, and there were sinews on them, and flesh had come upon them, and skin had covered them; but there was no breath in them. ⁹ Then he said to me, 'Prophesy to the breath, prophesy, mortal, and say to the breath: Thus says the Lord GOD: Come from the four winds, O breath, and breathe upon these slain, that they may live.' ¹⁰ I prophesied as he commanded me, and the breath came into them, and they lived, and stood on their feet, a vast multitude.

¹¹ Then he said to me, 'Mortal, these bones are the whole house of Israel. They say, "Our bones are dried up, and our hope is lost; we are cut off completely." ¹² Therefore prophesy, and say to them, Thus says the Lord GOD: I am going to open your graves, and bring you up from your graves, O my people; and I will bring you back to the land of Israel. ¹³ And you shall know that I am the LORD, when I open your graves, and bring you up from your graves, O my people. ¹⁴ I will put my spirit within you, and you shall live, and I will place you on your own soil; then you shall know that I, the LORD, have spoken and will act, says the LORD.'

PSALM

¹ Out of the depths have I called to you, O Lord; Lord, hear my voice;
   let your ears consider well the voice of my supplication.
² If you, Lord, were to note what is done amiss,
   O Lord, who could stand?
³ For there is forgiveness with you;
   therefore you shall be feared.
⁴ I wait for the Lord; my soul waits for him;
   in his word is my hope.
⁵ My soul waits for the Lord, more than the night-watch for the
      morning,
   more than the night-watch for the morning.
⁶ O Israel, wait for the Lord,
   for with the Lord there is mercy;
⁷ With him there is plenteous redemption,
   and he shall redeem Israel from all their sins.

READING

⁶ To set the mind on the flesh is death, but to set the mind on the Spirit is life and peace. ⁷ For this reason the mind that is set on the flesh is hostile to God; it does not submit to God's law—indeed it cannot, ⁸ and those who are in the flesh cannot please God.

⁹ But you are not in the flesh; you are in the Spirit, since the Spirit of God dwells in you. Anyone who does not have the Spirit of Christ does not belong to him. ¹⁰ But if Christ is in you, though the body is dead because of sin, the Spirit is life because of righteousness. ¹¹ If the Spirit of him who raised Jesus from the dead dwells in you, he who raised Christ from the dead will give life to your mortal bodies also through his Spirit that dwells in you.

GOSPEL

¹ Now a certain man was ill, Lazarus of Bethany, the village of Mary and her sister Martha. ² Mary was the one who anointed the Lord with perfume and wiped his feet with her hair; her brother Lazarus was ill. ³ So the sisters sent a message to Jesus, 'Lord, he whom you love is ill.' ⁴ But when Jesus heard it, he said, 'This illness does not lead to death; rather it is for God's glory, so that the Son of God may be glorified through it.' ⁵ Accordingly, though Jesus loved Martha and her sister and Lazarus, ⁶ after having heard that Lazarus was ill, he stayed two days longer in the place where he was.

[7] Then after this he said to the disciples, 'Let us go to Judea again.' [8] The disciples said to him, 'Rabbi, the Jews were just now trying to stone you, and are you going there again?' [9] Jesus answered, 'Are there not twelve hours of daylight? Those who walk during the day do not stumble, because they see the light of this world. [10] But those who walk at night stumble, because the light is not in them.' [11] After saying this, he told them, 'Our friend Lazarus has fallen asleep, but I am going there to awaken him.' [12] The disciples said to him, 'Lord, if he has fallen asleep, he will be all right.' [13] Jesus, however, had been speaking about his death, but they thought that he was referring merely to sleep. [14] Then Jesus told them plainly, 'Lazarus is dead. [15] For your sake I am glad I was not there, so that you may believe. But let us go to him.' [16] Thomas, who was called the Twin, said to his fellow-disciples, 'Let us also go, that we may die with him.'

[17] When Jesus arrived, he found that Lazarus had already been in the tomb for four days. [18] Now Bethany was near Jerusalem, some two miles away, [19] and many of the Jews had come to Martha and Mary to console them about their brother. [20] When Martha heard that Jesus was coming, she went and met him, while Mary stayed at home. [21] Martha said to Jesus, 'Lord, if you had been here, my brother would not have died. [22] But even now I know that God will give you whatever you ask of him.' [23] Jesus said to her, 'Your brother will rise again.' [24] Martha said to him, 'I know that he will rise again in the resurrection on the last day.' [25] Jesus said to her, 'I am the resurrection and the life. Those who believe in me, even though they die, will live, [26] and everyone who lives and believes in me will never die. Do you believe this?' [27] She said to him, 'Yes, Lord, I believe that you are the Messiah, the Son of God, the one coming into the world.'

[28] When she had said this, she went back and called her sister Mary, and told her privately, 'The Teacher is here and is calling for you.' [29] And when she heard it, she got up quickly and went to him. [30] Now Jesus had not yet come to the village, but was still at the place where Martha had met him. [31] The Jews who were with her in the house, consoling her, saw Mary get up quickly and go out. They followed her because they thought that she was going to the tomb to weep there. [32] When Mary came where Jesus was and saw him, she knelt at his feet and said to him, 'Lord, if you had been here, my brother would not have died.' [33] When Jesus saw her weeping, and the Jews who came with her also weeping, he was greatly disturbed in spirit and deeply moved. [34] He said, 'Where have you laid him?' They said to him, 'Lord, come and see.' [35] Jesus began to weep. [36] So the Jews said, 'See how he loved him!' [37] But some of them said, 'Could not he who opened the eyes of the blind man have kept this man from dying?'

[38] Then Jesus, again greatly disturbed, came to the tomb. It was a cave, and a stone was lying against it. [39] Jesus said, 'Take away the stone.' Martha, the

sister of the dead man, said to him, 'Lord, already there is a stench because he has been dead for four days.' [40] Jesus said to her, 'Did I not tell you that if you believed, you would see the glory of God?' [41] So they took away the stone. And Jesus looked upwards and said, 'Father, I thank you for having heard me. [42] I knew that you always hear me, but I have said this for the sake of the crowd standing here, so that they may believe that you sent me.' [43] When he had said this, he cried with a loud voice, 'Lazarus, come out!' [44] The dead man came out, his hands and feet bound with strips of cloth, and his face wrapped in a cloth. Jesus said to them, 'Unbind him, and let him go.'

[45] Many of the Jews therefore, who had come with Mary and had seen what Jesus did, believed in him.

POST COMMUNION

Lord Jesus Christ,
you have taught us
that what we do for the least of our brothers and sisters
we do also for you:
give us the will to be the servant of others
as you were the servant of all,
and gave up your life and died for us,
but are alive and reign, now and for ever.

SECOND SERVICE   THIRD SERVICE

Psalm 30   **Psalm 86**
Lamentations 3.19–33   **Jeremiah 31.27–37**
Matthew 20.17–34   **John 12.20–33**

PALM SUNDAY

LITURGY OF THE PALMS

GOSPEL   **Matthew 21.1–11**

[1] When they had come near Jerusalem and had reached Bethphage, at the Mount of Olives, Jesus sent two disciples, [2] saying to them, 'Go into the village ahead of you, and immediately you will find a donkey tied, and a colt with her; untie them and bring them to me. [3] If anyone says anything

to you, just say this, "The Lord needs them." And he will send them immediately.' [4] This took place to fulfil what had been spoken through the prophet, saying,

5   'Tell the daughter of Zion,
    Look, your king is coming to you,
        humble, and mounted on a donkey,
            and on a colt, the foal of a donkey.'

[6] The disciples went and did as Jesus had directed them; [7] they brought the donkey and the colt, and put their cloaks on them, and he sat on them. [8] A very large crowd spread their cloaks on the road, and others cut branches from the trees and spread them on the road. [9] The crowds that went ahead of him and that followed were shouting,

    'Hosanna to the Son of David!
    Blessed is the one who comes in the name of the Lord!
    Hosanna in the highest heaven!'

[10] When he entered Jerusalem, the whole city was in turmoil, asking, 'Who is this?' [11] The crowds were saying, 'This is the prophet Jesus from Nazareth in Galilee.'

PSALM   Psalm 118.[1–2,] 19–24, [25–29]

[¹   Give thanks to the Lord, for he is good;
        his mercy endures for ever.
 2   Let Israel now proclaim,
        'His mercy endures for ever.']

19   Open for me the gates of righteousness;
        I will enter them; I will offer thanks to the Lord.
20   'This is the gate of the Lord;
        he who is righteous may enter.'
21   I will give thanks to you, for you answered me
        and have become my salvation.
22   The same stone which the builders rejected
        has become the chief corner-stone.
23   This is the Lord's doing,
        and it is marvellous in our eyes.
24   On this day the Lord has acted;
        we will rejoice and be glad in it.
[25   Hosanna, Lord, hosanna!
        Lord, send us now success.
26   Blessèd is he who comes in the name of the Lord;
        we bless you from the house of the Lord.

27 God is the Lord; he has shined upon us;
   form a procession with branches up to the horns of the altar.
28 'You are my God and I will thank you;
   you are my God and I will exalt you.'
29 Give thanks to the Lord, for he is good;
   his mercy endures for ever.]

LITURGY OF THE PASSION

COLLECT

Almighty and everlasting God,
who in your tender love towards the human race
    sent your Son our Saviour Jesus Christ
to take upon him our flesh
and to suffer death upon the cross:
grant that we may follow the example
    of his patience and humility,
and also be made partakers of his resurrection;
through Jesus Christ your Son our Lord,
who is alive and reigns with you,
in the unity of the Holy Spirit,
one God, now and for ever.

READING   Isaiah 50.4–9a

4 The Lord GOD has given me
      the tongue of a teacher,
   that I may know how to sustain
      the weary with a word.
   Morning by morning he wakens—
      wakens my ear
      to listen as those who are taught.
5 The Lord GOD has opened my ear,
      and I was not rebellious,
      I did not turn backwards.
6 I gave my back to those who struck me,
      and my cheeks to those who pulled out the beard;
   I did not hide my face
      from insult and spitting.

7 The Lord GOD helps me;
   therefore I have not been disgraced;
   therefore I have set my face like flint,
      and I know that I shall not be put to shame;
8 he who vindicates me is near.
   Who will contend with me?
      Let us stand up together.
   Who are my adversaries?
      Let them confront me.
9 It is the Lord GOD who helps me;
   who will declare me guilty?

PSALM   Psalm 31.9–16, [17–18]

9 Have mercy on me, O Lord, for I am in trouble;
   my eye is consumed with sorrow, and also my throat and my belly.
10 For my life is wasted with grief, and my years with sighing;
   my strength fails me because of affliction, and my bones are
      consumed.
11 I have become a reproach to all my enemies and even to my
      neighbours, a dismay to those of my acquaintance;
   when they see me in the street they avoid me.
12 I am forgotten like the dead, out of mind;
   I am as useless as a broken pot.
13 For I have heard the whispering of the crowd; fear is all around;
   they put their heads together against me; they plot to take my life.
14 But as for me, I have trusted in you, O Lord.
   I have said, 'You are my God.
15 My times are in your hand;
   rescue me from the hand of my enemies, and from those who
      persecute me.
16 Make your face to shine upon your servant,
   and in your loving-kindness save me.'
[17 Lord, let me not be ashamed for having called upon you;
   rather, let the wicked be put to shame; let them be silent in the
      grave.
18 Let the lying lips be silenced which speak against the righteous,
   haughtily, disdainfully and with contempt.]

READING   Philippians 2.5–11

⁵ Let the same mind be in you that was in Christ Jesus,
  ⁶   who, though he was in the form of God,
        did not regard equality with God
        as something to be exploited,
  ⁷   but emptied himself,
        taking the form of a slave,
        being born in human likeness.
      And being found in human form,
  ⁸   he humbled himself
        and became obedient to the point of death—
        even death on a cross.
  ⁹   Therefore God also highly exalted him
        and gave him the name
        that is above every name,
 ¹⁰   so that at the name of Jesus
        every knee should bend,
        in heaven and on earth and under the earth,
 ¹¹   and every tongue should confess
        that Jesus Christ is Lord,
        to the glory of God the Father.

GOSPEL

EITHER   Matthew 26.14–27.66

¹⁴ Then one of the twelve, who was called Judas Iscariot, went to the chief priests ¹⁵ and said, 'What will you give me if I betray him to you?' They paid him thirty pieces of silver. ¹⁶ And from that moment he began to look for an opportunity to betray him.

¹⁷ On the first day of Unleavened Bread the disciples came to Jesus, saying, 'Where do you want us to make the preparations for you to eat the Passover?' ¹⁸ He said, 'Go into the city to a certain man, and say to him, "The Teacher says, My time is near; I will keep the Passover at your house with my disciples."' ¹⁹ So the disciples did as Jesus had directed them, and they prepared the Passover meal.

²⁰ When it was evening, he took his place with the twelve; ²¹ and while they were eating, he said, 'Truly I tell you, one of you will betray me.' ²² And they became greatly distressed and began to say to him one after another, 'Surely not I, Lord?' ²³ He answered, 'The one who has dipped his hand into the bowl with me will betray me. ²⁴ The Son of Man goes as it is written of

him, but woe to that one by whom the Son of Man is betrayed! It would have been better for that one not to have been born.' ²⁵ Judas, who betrayed him, said, 'Surely not I, Rabbi?' He replied, 'You have said so.'

²⁶ While they were eating, Jesus took a loaf of bread, and after blessing it he broke it, gave it to the disciples, and said, 'Take, eat; this is my body.' ²⁷ Then he took a cup, and after giving thanks he gave it to them, saying, 'Drink from it, all of you; ²⁸ for this is my blood of the covenant, which is poured out for many for the forgiveness of sins. ²⁹ I tell you, I will never again drink of this fruit of the vine until that day when I drink it new with you in my Father's kingdom.'

³⁰ When they had sung the hymn, they went out to the Mount of Olives.

³¹ Then Jesus said to them, 'You will all become deserters because of me this night; for it is written,

"I will strike the shepherd,

and the sheep of the flock will be scattered."

³² But after I am raised up, I will go ahead of you to Galilee.' ³³ Peter said to him, 'Though all become deserters because of you, I will never desert you.' ³⁴ Jesus said to him, 'Truly I tell you, this very night, before the cock crows, you will deny me three times.' ³⁵ Peter said to him, 'Even though I must die with you, I will not deny you.' And so said all the disciples.

³⁶ Then Jesus went with them to a place called Gethsemane; and he said to his disciples, 'Sit here while I go over there and pray.' ³⁷ He took with him Peter and the two sons of Zebedee, and began to be grieved and agitated. ³⁸ Then he said to them, 'I am deeply grieved, even to death; remain here, and stay awake with me.' ³⁹ And going a little farther, he threw himself on the ground and prayed, 'My Father, if it is possible, let this cup pass from me; yet not what I want but what you want.' ⁴⁰ Then he came to the disciples and found them sleeping; and he said to Peter, 'So, could you not stay awake with me one hour? ⁴¹ Stay awake and pray that you may not come into the time of trial; the spirit indeed is willing, but the flesh is weak.' ⁴² Again he went away for the second time and prayed, 'My Father, if this cannot pass unless I drink it, your will be done.' ⁴³ Again he came and found them sleeping, for their eyes were heavy. ⁴⁴ So leaving them again, he went away and prayed for the third time, saying the same words. ⁴⁵ Then he came to the disciples and said to them, 'Are you still sleeping and taking your rest? See, the hour is at hand, and the Son of Man is betrayed into the hands of sinners. ⁴⁶ Get up, let us be going. See, my betrayer is at hand.'

⁴⁷ While he was still speaking, Judas, one of the twelve, arrived; with him was a large crowd with swords and clubs, from the chief priests and the elders of the people. ⁴⁸ Now the betrayer had given them a sign, saying,

'The one I will kiss is the man; arrest him.' [49] At once he came up to Jesus and said, 'Greetings, Rabbi!' and kissed him. [50] Jesus said to him, 'Friend, do what you are here to do.' Then they came and laid hands on Jesus and arrested him. [51] Suddenly, one of those with Jesus put his hand on his sword, drew it, and struck the slave of the high priest, cutting off his ear. [52] Then Jesus said to him, 'Put your sword back into its place; for all who take the sword will perish by the sword. [53] Do you think that I cannot appeal to my Father, and he will at once send me more than twelve legions of angels? [54] But how then would the scriptures be fulfilled, which say it must happen in this way?' [55] At that hour Jesus said to the crowds, 'Have you come out with swords and clubs to arrest me as though I were a bandit? Day after day I sat in the temple teaching, and you did not arrest me. [56] But all this has taken place, so that the scriptures of the prophets may be fulfilled.' Then all the disciples deserted him and fled.

[57] Those who had arrested Jesus took him to Caiaphas the high priest, in whose house the scribes and the elders had gathered. [58] But Peter was following him at a distance, as far as the courtyard of the high priest; and going inside, he sat with the guards in order to see how this would end. [59] Now the chief priests and the whole council were looking for false testimony against Jesus so that they might put him to death, [60] but they found none, though many false witnesses came forward. At last two came forward [61] and said, 'This fellow said, "I am able to destroy the temple of God and to build it in three days."' [62] The high priest stood up and said, 'Have you no answer? What is it that they testify against you?' [63] But Jesus was silent. Then the high priest said to him, 'I put you under oath before the living God, tell us if you are the Messiah, the Son of God.' [64] Jesus said to him, 'You have said so. But I tell you,

From now on you will see the Son of Man

seated at the right hand of Power

and coming on the clouds of heaven.'

[65] Then the high priest tore his clothes and said, 'He has blasphemed! Why do we still need witnesses? You have now heard his blasphemy. [66] What is your verdict?' They answered, 'He deserves death.' [67] Then they spat in his face and struck him; and some slapped him, [68] saying, 'Prophesy to us, you Messiah! Who is it that struck you?'

[69] Now Peter was sitting outside in the courtyard. A servant-girl came to him and said, 'You also were with Jesus the Galilean.' [70] But he denied it before all of them, saying, 'I do not know what you are talking about.' [71] When he went out to the porch, another servant-girl saw him, and she said to the bystanders, 'This man was with Jesus of Nazareth.' [72] Again he denied it with an oath, 'I do not know the man.' [73] After a little while the bystanders came up and said to Peter, 'Certainly you are also one of them, for your accent betrays you.' [74] Then he began to curse, and he swore an

oath, 'I do not know the man!' At that moment the cock crowed. [75] Then Peter remembered what Jesus had said: 'Before the cock crows, you will deny me three times.' And he went out and wept bitterly.

[1] When morning came, all the chief priests and the elders of the people conferred together against Jesus in order to bring about his death. [2] They bound him, led him away, and handed him over to Pilate the governor.

[3] When Judas, his betrayer, saw that Jesus was condemned, he repented and brought back the thirty pieces of silver to the chief priests and the elders. [4] He said, 'I have sinned by betraying innocent blood.' But they said, 'What is that to us? See to it yourself.' [5] Throwing down the pieces of silver in the temple, he departed; and he went and hanged himself. [6] But the chief priests, taking the pieces of silver, said, 'It is not lawful to put them into the treasury, since they are blood money.' [7] After conferring together, they used them to buy the potter's field as a place to bury foreigners. [8] For this reason that field has been called the Field of Blood to this day. [9] Then was fulfilled what had been spoken through the prophet Jeremiah, 'And they took the thirty pieces of silver, the price of the one on whom a price had been set, on whom some of the people of Israel had set a price, [10] and they gave them for the potter's field, as the Lord commanded me.'

[11] Now Jesus stood before the governor; and the governor asked him, 'Are you the King of the Jews?' Jesus said, 'You say so.' [12] But when he was accused by the chief priests and elders, he did not answer. [13] Then Pilate said to him, 'Do you not hear how many accusations they make against you?' [14] But he gave him no answer, not even to a single charge, so that the governor was greatly amazed.

[15] Now at the festival the governor was accustomed to release a prisoner for the crowd, anyone whom they wanted. [16] At that time they had a notorious prisoner, called Jesus Barabbas. [17] So after they had gathered, Pilate said to them, 'Whom do you want me to release for you, Jesus Barabbas or Jesus who is called the Messiah?' [18] For he realized that it was out of jealousy that they had handed him over. [19] While he was sitting on the judgement seat, his wife sent word to him, 'Have nothing to do with that innocent man, for today I have suffered a great deal because of a dream about him.' [20] Now the chief priests and the elders persuaded the crowds to ask for Barabbas and to have Jesus killed. [21] The governor again said to them, 'Which of the two do you want me to release for you?' And they said, 'Barabbas.' [22] Pilate said to them, 'Then what should I do with Jesus who is called the Messiah?' All of them said, 'Let him be crucified!' [23] Then he asked, 'Why, what evil has he done?' But they shouted all the more, 'Let him be crucified!'

[24] So when Pilate saw that he could do nothing, but rather that a riot was beginning, he took some water and washed his hands before the crowd,

saying, 'I am innocent of this man's blood; see to it yourselves.' [25] Then the people as a whole answered, 'His blood be on us and on our children!' [26] So he released Barabbas for them; and after flogging Jesus, he handed him over to be crucified.

[27] Then the soldiers of the governor took Jesus into the governor's head-quarters, and they gathered the whole cohort around him. [28] They stripped him and put a scarlet robe on him, [29] and after twisting some thorns into a crown, they put it on his head. They put a reed in his right hand and knelt before him and mocked him, saying, 'Hail, King of the Jews!' [30] They spat on him, and took the reed and struck him on the head. [31] After mocking him, they stripped him of the robe and put his own clothes on him. Then they led him away to crucify him.

[32] As they went out, they came upon a man from Cyrene named Simon; they compelled this man to carry his cross. [33] And when they came to a place called Golgotha (which means Place of a Skull), [34] they offered him wine to drink, mixed with gall; but when he tasted it, he would not drink it. [35] And when they had crucified him, they divided his clothes among themselves by casting lots; [36] then they sat down there and kept watch over him. [37] Over his head they put the charge against him, which read, 'This is Jesus, the King of the Jews.'

[38] Then two bandits were crucified with him, one on his right and one on his left. [39] Those who passed by derided him, shaking their heads [40] and saying, 'You who would destroy the temple and build it in three days, save yourself! If you are the Son of God, come down from the cross.' [41] In the same way the chief priests also, along with the scribes and elders, were mocking him, saying, [42] 'He saved others; he cannot save himself. He is the King of Israel; let him come down from the cross now, and we will believe in him. [43] He trusts in God; let God deliver him now, if he wants to; for he said, "I am God's Son." ' [44] The bandits who were crucified with him also taunted him in the same way.

[45] From noon on, darkness came over the whole land until three in the afternoon. [46] And about three o'clock Jesus cried with a loud voice, 'Eli, Eli, lema sabachthani?' that is, 'My God, my God, why have you forsaken me?' [47] When some of the bystanders heard it, they said, 'This man is calling for Elijah.' [48] At once one of them ran and got a sponge, filled it with sour wine, put it on a stick, and gave it to him to drink. [49] But the others said, 'Wait, let us see whether Elijah will come to save him.' [50] Then Jesus cried again with a loud voice and breathed his last. [51] At that moment the curtain of the temple was torn in two, from top to bottom. The earth shook, and the rocks were split. [52] The tombs also were opened, and many bodies of the saints who had fallen asleep were raised. [53] After his resurrection they came out of the tombs and entered the holy city and appeared to

many. ⁵⁴ Now when the centurion and those with him, who were keeping watch over Jesus, saw the earthquake and what took place, they were terrified and said, 'Truly this man was God's Son!'

⁵⁵ Many women were also there, looking on from a distance; they had followed Jesus from Galilee and had provided for him. ⁵⁶ Among them were Mary Magdalene, and Mary the mother of James and Joseph, and the mother of the sons of Zebedee.

⁵⁷ When it was evening, there came a rich man from Arimathea, named Joseph, who was also a disciple of Jesus. ⁵⁸ He went to Pilate and asked for the body of Jesus; then Pilate ordered it to be given to him. ⁵⁹ So Joseph took the body and wrapped it in a clean linen cloth ⁶⁰ and laid it in his own new tomb, which he had hewn in the rock. He then rolled a great stone to the door of the tomb and went away. ⁶¹ Mary Magdalene and the other Mary were there, sitting opposite the tomb.

⁶² The next day, that is, after the day of Preparation, the chief priests and the Pharisees gathered before Pilate ⁶³ and said, 'Sir, we remember what that impostor said while he was still alive, "After three days I will rise again." ⁶⁴ Therefore command that the tomb be made secure until the third day; otherwise his disciples may go and steal him away, and tell the people, "He has been raised from the dead", and the last deception would be worse than the first.' ⁶⁵ Pilate said to them, 'You have a guard of soldiers; go, make it as secure as you can.' ⁶⁶ So they went with the guard and made the tomb secure by sealing the stone.

OR   **Matthew 27.11–54**

¹¹ Now Jesus stood before the governor; and the governor asked him, 'Are you the King of the Jews?' Jesus said, 'You say so.' ¹² But when he was accused by the chief priests and elders, he did not answer. ¹³ Then Pilate said to him, 'Do you not hear how many accusations they make against you?' ¹⁴ But he gave him no answer, not even to a single charge, so that the governor was greatly amazed.

¹⁵ Now at the festival the governor was accustomed to release a prisoner for the crowd, anyone whom they wanted. ¹⁶ At that time they had a notorious prisoner, called Jesus Barabbas. ¹⁷ So after they had gathered, Pilate said to them, 'Whom do you want me to release for you, Jesus Barabbas or Jesus who is called the Messiah?' ¹⁸ For he realized that it was out of jealousy that they had handed him over. ¹⁹ While he was sitting on the judgement seat, his wife sent word to him, 'Have nothing to do with that innocent man, for today I have suffered a great deal because of a dream about him.' ²⁰ Now the chief priests and the elders persuaded the crowds to ask for Barabbas and to have Jesus killed. ²¹ The governor again said to

them, 'Which of the two do you want me to release for you?' And they said, 'Barabbas.' 22 Pilate said to them, 'Then what should I do with Jesus who is called the Messiah?' All of them said, 'Let him be crucified!' 23 Then he asked, 'Why, what evil has he done?' But they shouted all the more, 'Let him be crucified!'

24 So when Pilate saw that he could do nothing, but rather that a riot was beginning, he took some water and washed his hands before the crowd, saying, 'I am innocent of this man's blood; see to it yourselves.' 25 Then the people as a whole answered, 'His blood be on us and on our children!' 26 So he released Barabbas for them; and after flogging Jesus, he handed him over to be crucified.

27 Then the soldiers of the governor took Jesus into the governor's head-quarters, and they gathered the whole cohort around him. 28 They stripped him and put a scarlet robe on him, 29 and after twisting some thorns into a crown, they put it on his head. They put a reed in his right hand and knelt before him and mocked him, saying, 'Hail, King of the Jews!' 30 They spat on him, and took the reed and struck him on the head. 31 After mocking him, they stripped him of the robe and put his own clothes on him. Then they led him away to crucify him.

32 As they went out, they came upon a man from Cyrene named Simon; they compelled this man to carry his cross. 33 And when they came to a place called Golgotha (which means Place of a Skull), 34 they offered him wine to drink, mixed with gall; but when he tasted it, he would not drink it. 35 And when they had crucified him, they divided his clothes among themselves by casting lots; 36 then they sat down there and kept watch over him. 37 Over his head they put the charge against him, which read, 'This is Jesus, the King of the Jews.'

38 Then two bandits were crucified with him, one on his right and one on his left. 39 Those who passed by derided him, shaking their heads 40 and saying, 'You who would destroy the temple and build it in three days, save yourself! If you are the Son of God, come down from the cross.' 41 In the same way the chief priests also, along with the scribes and elders, were mocking him, saying, 42 'He saved others; he cannot save himself. He is the King of Israel; let him come down from the cross now, and we will believe in him. 43 He trusts in God; let God deliver him now, if he wants to; for he said, "I am God's Son." ' 44 The bandits who were crucified with him also taunted him in the same way.

45 From noon on, darkness came over the whole land until three in the afternoon. 46 And about three o'clock Jesus cried with a loud voice, 'Eli, Eli, lema sabachthani?' that is, 'My God, my God, why have you forsaken me?' 47 When some of the bystanders heard it, they said, 'This man is calling for

Elijah.' ⁴⁸ At once one of them ran and got a sponge, filled it with sour wine, put it on a stick, and gave it to him to drink. ⁴⁹ But the others said, 'Wait, let us see whether Elijah will come to save him.' ⁵⁰ Then Jesus cried again with a loud voice and breathed his last. ⁵¹ At that moment the curtain of the temple was torn in two, from top to bottom. The earth shook, and the rocks were split. ⁵² The tombs also were opened, and many bodies of the saints who had fallen asleep were raised. ⁵³ After his resurrection they came out of the tombs and entered the holy city and appeared to many. ⁵⁴ Now when the centurion and those with him, who were keeping watch over Jesus, saw the earthquake and what took place, they were terrified and said, 'Truly this man was God's Son!'

POST COMMUNION

Lord Jesus Christ,
you humbled yourself in taking the form of a servant,
and in obedience died on the cross for our salvation:
give us the mind to follow you
and to proclaim you as Lord and King,
to the glory of God the Father.

SECOND SERVICE

Psalm 80
Isaiah 5.1–7
Matthew 21.33–46

THIRD SERVICE

Psalms 61; 62
Zechariah 9.9–12
Luke 16.19–31

MONDAY OF HOLY WEEK

COLLECT

Almighty and everlasting God,
who in your tender love towards the human race
    sent your Son our Saviour Jesus Christ
to take upon him our flesh
and to suffer death upon the cross:
grant that we may follow the example
    of his patience and humility,
and also be made partakers of his resurrection;

through Jesus Christ your Son our Lord,
who is alive and reigns with you,
in the unity of the Holy Spirit,
one God, now and for ever.

READING   Isaiah 42.1–9

¹ Here is my servant, whom I uphold,
    my chosen, in whom my soul delights;
  I have put my spirit upon him;
    he will bring forth justice to the nations.
² He will not cry or lift up his voice,
    or make it heard in the street;
³ a bruised reed he will not break,
    and a dimly burning wick he will not quench;
  he will faithfully bring forth justice.
⁴ He will not grow faint or be crushed
    until he has established justice in the earth;
  and the coastlands wait for his teaching.
⁵ Thus says God, the LORD,
    who created the heavens and stretched them out,
    who spread out the earth and what comes from it,
  who gives breath to the people upon it
  and spirit to those who walk in it:
⁶ I am the LORD, I have called you in righteousness,
    I have taken you by the hand and kept you;
  I have given you as a covenant to the people,
    a light to the nations,
⁷ to open the eyes that are blind,
  to bring out the prisoners from the dungeon,
    from the prison those who sit in darkness.
⁸ I am the LORD, that is my name;
    my glory I give to no other,
    nor my praise to idols.
⁹ See, the former things have come to pass,
    and new things I now declare;
  before they spring forth,
    I tell you of them.

PSALM   Psalm 36.5–11

5 Your love, O Lord, reaches to the heavens,
   and your faithfulness to the clouds.
6 Your righteousness is like the strong mountains, your justice like
      the great deep;
   you save both human and beast, O Lord.
7 How priceless is your love, O God!
   your people take refuge under the shadow of your wings.
8 They feast upon the abundance of your house;
   you give them drink from the river of your delights.
9 For with you is the well of life,
   and in your light we see light.
10 Continue your loving-kindness to those who know you,
   and your favour to those who are true of heart.
11 Let not the foot of the proud come near me,
   nor the hand of the wicked push me aside.

READING   Hebrews 9.11–15

11 But when Christ came as a high priest of the good things that have
come, then through the greater and perfect tent (not made with hands,
that is, not of this creation), 12 he entered once for all into the Holy Place,
not with the blood of goats and calves, but with his own blood, thus
obtaining eternal redemption. 13 For if the blood of goats and bulls, with
the sprinkling of the ashes of a heifer, sanctifies those who have been
defiled so that their flesh is purified, 14 how much more will the blood of
Christ, who through the eternal Spirit offered himself without blemish to
God, purify our conscience from dead works to worship the living God!

15 For this reason he is the mediator of a new covenant, so that those who
are called may receive the promised eternal inheritance, because a death
has occurred that redeems them from the transgressions under the first
covenant.

GOSPEL   John 12.1–11

1 Six days before the Passover Jesus came to Bethany, the home of Lazarus,
whom he had raised from the dead. 2 There they gave a dinner for him.
Martha served, and Lazarus was one of those at the table with him. 3 Mary
took a pound of costly perfume made of pure nard, anointed Jesus' feet,
and wiped them with her hair. The house was filled with the fragrance of
the perfume. 4 But Judas Iscariot, one of his disciples (the one who was
about to betray him), said, 5 'Why was this perfume not sold for three

hundred denarii and the money given to the poor?' ⁶ (He said this not because he cared about the poor, but because he was a thief; he kept the common purse and used to steal what was put into it.) ⁷ Jesus said, 'Leave her alone. She bought it so that she might keep it for the day of my burial. ⁸ You always have the poor with you, but you do not always have me.'

⁹ When the great crowd of the Jews learned that he was there, they came not only because of Jesus but also to see Lazarus, whom he had raised from the dead. ¹⁰ So the chief priests planned to put Lazarus to death as well, ¹¹ since it was on account of him that many of the Jews were deserting and were believing in Jesus.

POST COMMUNION

Lord Jesus Christ,
you humbled yourself in taking the form of a servant,
and in obedience died on the cross for our salvation:
give us the mind to follow you
and to proclaim you as Lord and King,
to the glory of God the Father.

SECOND SERVICE

Psalm 41
Lamentations 1.1–12a
Luke 22.1–23

THIRD SERVICE

Psalm 25
Lamentations 2.8–19
Colossians 1.18–23

TUESDAY OF HOLY WEEK

COLLECT

Almighty and everlasting God,
who in your tender love towards the human race
    sent your Son our Saviour Jesus Christ
to take upon him our flesh
and to suffer death upon the cross:
grant that we may follow the example
    of his patience and humility,
and also be made partakers of his resurrection;
through Jesus Christ your Son our Lord,
who is alive and reigns with you,
in the unity of the Holy Spirit,
one God, now and for ever.

READING   Isaiah 49.1–7

¹ Listen to me, O coastlands,
   pay attention, you peoples from far away!
 The LORD called me before I was born,
   while I was in my mother's womb he named me.
² He made my mouth like a sharp sword,
   in the shadow of his hand he hid me;
 he made me a polished arrow,
   in his quiver he hid me away.
³ And he said to me, 'You are my servant,
   Israel, in whom I will be glorified.'
⁴ But I said, 'I have laboured in vain,
   I have spent my strength for nothing and vanity;
 yet surely my cause is with the LORD,
   and my reward with my God.'
⁵ And now the LORD says,
   who formed me in the womb to be his servant,
 to bring Jacob back to him,
   and that Israel might be gathered to him,
 for I am honoured in the sight of the LORD,
   and my God has become my strength—
⁶ he says,
 'It is too light a thing that you should be my servant
   to raise up the tribes of Jacob
   and to restore the survivors of Israel;
 I will give you as a light to the nations,
   that my salvation may reach to the end of the earth.'
⁷ Thus says the LORD,
   the Redeemer of Israel and his Holy One,
 to one deeply despised, abhorred by the nations,
   the slave of rulers,
 'Kings shall see and stand up,
   princes, and they shall prostrate themselves,
 because of the LORD, who is faithful,
   the Holy One of Israel, who has chosen you.'

PSALM   Psalm 71.1–8, [9–14]

¹ In you, O Lord, have I taken refuge;
  let me never be ashamed.
² In your righteousness, deliver me and set me free;
  incline your ear to me and save me.

3   Be my strong rock, a castle to keep me safe;
     you are my crag and my stronghold.

4   Deliver me, my God, from the hand of the wicked,
     from the clutches of the evildoer and the oppressor.

5   For you are my hope, O Lord God,
     my confidence since I was young.

6   I have been sustained by you ever since I was born; from my
       mother's womb you have been my strength;
     my praise shall be always of you.

7   I have become a portent to many;
     but you are my refuge and my strength.

8   Let my mouth be full of your praise
     and your glory all the day long.

[9   Do not cast me off in my old age;
     forsake me not when my strength fails.

10   For my enemies are talking against me,
     and those who lie in wait for my life take counsel together.

11   They say, 'God has forsaken him; go after him and seize him;
     because there is none who will save.'

12   O God, be not far from me;
     come quickly to help me, O my God.

13   Let those who set themselves against me be put to shame and be
       disgraced;
     let those who seek to do me evil be covered with scorn and
       reproach.

14   But I shall always wait in patience,
     and shall praise you more and more.]

READING   1 Corinthians 1.18–31

18 For the message about the cross is foolishness to those who are per-ishing, but to us who are being saved it is the power of God. 19 For it is written,

    'I will destroy the wisdom of the wise,
      and the discernment of the discerning I will thwart.'

20 Where is the one who is wise? Where is the scribe? Where is the debater of this age? Has not God made foolish the wisdom of the world? 21 For since, in the wisdom of God, the world did not know God through wisdom, God decided, through the foolishness of our proclamation, to save those who believe. 22 For Jews demand signs and Greeks desire wisdom, 23 but we proclaim Christ crucified, a stumbling-block to Jews and foolishness to

Gentiles, [24] but to those who are the called, both Jews and Greeks, Christ the power of God and the wisdom of God. [25] For God's foolishness is wiser than human wisdom, and God's weakness is stronger than human strength.

[26] Consider your own call, brothers and sisters: not many of you were wise by human standards, not many were powerful, not many were of noble birth. [27] But God chose what is foolish in the world to shame the wise; God chose what is weak in the world to shame the strong; [28] God chose what is low and despised in the world, things that are not, to reduce to nothing things that are, [29] so that no one might boast in the presence of God. [30] He is the source of your life in Christ Jesus, who became for us wisdom from God, and righteousness and sanctification and redemption, [31] in order that, as it is written, 'Let the one who boasts, boast in the Lord.'

GOSPEL   John 12.20–36

[20] Now among those who went up to worship at the festival were some Greeks. [21] They came to Philip, who was from Bethsaida in Galilee, and said to him, 'Sir, we wish to see Jesus.' [22] Philip went and told Andrew; then Andrew and Philip went and told Jesus. [23] Jesus answered them, 'The hour has come for the Son of Man to be glorified. [24] Very truly, I tell you, unless a grain of wheat falls into the earth and dies, it remains just a single grain; but if it dies, it bears much fruit. [25] Those who love their life lose it, and those who hate their life in this world will keep it for eternal life. [26] Whoever serves me must follow me, and where I am, there will my servant be also. Whoever serves me, the Father will honour.

[27] 'Now my soul is troubled. And what should I say—"Father, save me from this hour"? No, it is for this reason that I have come to this hour. [28] Father, glorify your name.' Then a voice came from heaven, 'I have glorified it, and I will glorify it again.' [29] The crowd standing there heard it and said that it was thunder. Others said, 'An angel has spoken to him.' [30] Jesus answered, 'This voice has come for your sake, not for mine. [31] Now is the judgement of this world; now the ruler of this world will be driven out. [32] And I, when I am lifted up from the earth, will draw all people to myself.' [33] He said this to indicate the kind of death he was to die. [34] The crowd answered him, 'We have heard from the law that the Messiah remains for ever. How can you say that the Son of Man must be lifted up? Who is this Son of Man?' [35] Jesus said to them, 'The light is with you for a little longer. Walk while you have the light, so that the darkness may not overtake you. If you walk in the darkness, you do not know where you are going. [36] While you have the light, believe in the light, so that you may become children of light.'

After Jesus had said this, he departed and hid from them.

POST COMMUNION

Lord Jesus Christ,
you humbled yourself in taking the form of a servant,
and in obedience died on the cross for our salvation:
give us the mind to follow you
and to proclaim you as Lord and King,
to the glory of God the Father.

SECOND SERVICE	THIRD SERVICE
Psalm 27	Psalm 55.13–24
Lamentations 3.1–18	Lamentations 3.40–51
Luke 22.[24–38,] 39–53	Galatians 6.11–18

WEDNESDAY OF HOLY WEEK

COLLECT

Almighty and everlasting God,
who in your tender love towards the human race
    sent your Son our Saviour Jesus Christ
to take upon him our flesh
and to suffer death upon the cross:
grant that we may follow the example
    of his patience and humility,
and also be made partakers of his resurrection;
through Jesus Christ your Son our Lord,
who is alive and reigns with you,
in the unity of the Holy Spirit,
one God, now and for ever.

READING   Isaiah 50.4–9a

4   The Lord GOD has given me
        the tongue of a teacher,
    that I may know how to sustain
        the weary with a word.
    Morning by morning he wakens—
        wakens my ear
        to listen as those who are taught.

5 The Lord GOD has opened my ear,
    and I was not rebellious,
    I did not turn backwards.
6 I gave my back to those who struck me,
    and my cheeks to those who pulled out the beard;
    I did not hide my face
    from insult and spitting.
7 The Lord GOD helps me;
    therefore I have not been disgraced;
    therefore I have set my face like flint,
    and I know that I shall not be put to shame;
8   he who vindicates me is near.
    Who will contend with me?
    Let us stand up together.
    Who are my adversaries?
    Let them confront me.
9 It is the Lord GOD who helps me;
    who will declare me guilty?

PSALM   Psalm 70

1 Be pleased, O God, to deliver me;
    O Lord, make haste to help me.
2 Let those who seek my life be ashamed and altogether dismayed;
    let those who take pleasure in my misfortune draw back and be
        disgraced.
3 Let those who say to me 'Aha!' and gloat over me turn back,
    because they are ashamed.
4 Let all who seek you rejoice and be glad in you;
    let those who love your salvation say for ever, 'Great is the Lord!'
5 But as for me, I am poor and needy;
    come to me speedily, O God.
6 You are my helper and my deliverer;
    O Lord, do not tarry.

READING   Hebrews 12.1–3

1 Therefore, since we are surrounded by so great a cloud of witnesses, let us also lay aside every weight and the sin that clings so closely, and let us run with perseverance the race that is set before us, 2 looking to Jesus the pioneer and perfecter of our faith, who for the sake of the joy that was set

before him endured the cross, disregarding its shame, and has taken his seat at the right hand of the throne of God.

³ Consider him who endured such hostility against himself from sinners, so that you may not grow weary or lose heart.

GOSPEL   John 13.21–32

²¹ After saying this Jesus was troubled in spirit, and declared, 'Very truly, I tell you, one of you will betray me.' ²² The disciples looked at one another, uncertain of whom he was speaking. ²³ One of his disciples—the one whom Jesus loved—was reclining next to him; ²⁴ Simon Peter therefore motioned to him to ask Jesus of whom he was speaking. ²⁵ So while reclining next to Jesus, he asked him, 'Lord, who is it?' ²⁶ Jesus answered, 'It is the one to whom I give this piece of bread when I have dipped it in the dish.' So when he had dipped the piece of bread, he gave it to Judas son of Simon Iscariot. ²⁷ After he received the piece of bread, Satan entered into him. Jesus said to him, 'Do quickly what you are going to do.' ²⁸ Now no one at the table knew why he said this to him. ²⁹ Some thought that, because Judas had the common purse, Jesus was telling him, 'Buy what we need for the festival'; or, that he should give something to the poor. ³⁰ So, after receiving the piece of bread, he immediately went out. And it was night.

³¹ When he had gone out, Jesus said, 'Now the Son of Man has been glorified, and God has been glorified in him. ³² If God has been glorified in him, God will also glorify him in himself and will glorify him at once.'

POST COMMUNION

Lord Jesus Christ,
you humbled yourself in taking the form of a servant,
and in obedience died on the cross for our salvation:
give us the mind to follow you
and to proclaim you as Lord and King,
to the glory of God the Father.

SECOND SERVICE

Psalm 102.1–17, [18–28]
Wisdom 1.16–2.1; 2.12–22
or
Jeremiah 11.18–20
Luke 22.54–71

THIRD SERVICE

Psalm 88
Isaiah 63.1–9
Revelation 14.18–15.4

MAUNDY THURSDAY

COLLECT

God our Father,
you have invited us to share in the supper
which your Son gave to his Church
to proclaim his death until he comes:
may he nourish us by his presence,
and unite us in his love;
who is alive and reigns with you,
in the unity of the Holy Spirit,
one God, now and for ever.

At Morning and Evening Prayer the Collect of Palm Sunday is used

READING   Exodus 12.1–4, [5–10,] 11–14

¹ The LORD said to Moses and Aaron in the land of Egypt: ² This month shall mark for you the beginning of months; it shall be the first month of the year for you. ³ Tell the whole congregation of Israel that on the tenth of this month they are to take a lamb for each family, a lamb for each household. ⁴ If a household is too small for a whole lamb, it shall join its closest neighbour in obtaining one; the lamb shall be divided in proportion to the number of people who eat of it.
[⁵ Your lamb shall be without blemish, a year-old male; you may take it from the sheep or from the goats. ⁶ You shall keep it until the fourteenth day of this month; then the whole assembled congregation of Israel shall slaughter it at twilight. ⁷ They shall take some of the blood and put it on the two doorposts and the lintel of the houses in which they eat it. ⁸ They shall eat the lamb that same night; they shall eat it roasted over the fire with unleavened bread and bitter herbs. ⁹ Do not eat any of it raw or boiled in water, but roasted over the fire, with its head, legs, and inner organs. ¹⁰ You shall let none of it remain until the morning; anything that remains until the morning you shall burn.]
¹¹ This is how you shall eat it: your loins girded, your sandals on your feet, and your staff in your hand; and you shall eat it hurriedly. It is the passover of the LORD. ¹² For I will pass through the land of Egypt that night, and I will strike down every firstborn in the land of Egypt, both human beings and animals; on all the gods of Egypt I will execute judgements: I am the LORD. ¹³ The blood shall be a sign for you on the houses where you live: when I see the blood, I will pass over you, and no plague shall destroy you when I strike the land of Egypt.

¹⁴ This day shall be a day of remembrance for you. You shall celebrate it as a festival to the LORD; throughout your generations you shall observe it as a perpetual ordinance.

PSALM   Psalm 116.1, 10–17

¹   I love the Lord, because he has heard the voice of my supplication,
     because he has inclined his ear to me whenever I called upon him.

¹⁰ How shall I repay the Lord
     for all the good things he has done for me?
¹¹ I will lift up the cup of salvation
     and call upon the name of the Lord.
¹² I will fulfil my vows to the Lord
     in the presence of all his people.
¹³ Precious in the sight of the Lord
     is the death of his servants.
¹⁴ O Lord, I am your servant;
     I am your servant and the child of your handmaid; you have freed
         me from my bonds.
¹⁵ I will offer you the sacrifice of thanksgiving
     and call upon the name of the Lord.
¹⁶ I will fulfil my vows to the Lord
     in the presence of all his people.
¹⁷ In the courts of the Lord's house,
     in the midst of you, O Jerusalem. Praise the Lord.

OR, IF AN ALTERNATIVE TEXT IS PREFERRED   Psalm 116.9–17

⁹   I believed, even when I said, 'I have been brought very low.'
     In my distress I said, 'No one can be trusted.'
¹⁰ How shall I repay the Lord
     for all the good things he has done for me?
¹¹ I will lift up the cup of salvation
     and call upon the name of the Lord.
¹² I will fulfil my vows to the Lord
     in the presence of all his people.
¹³ Precious in the sight of the Lord
     is the death of his servants.
¹⁴ O Lord, I am your servant;
     I am your servant and the child of your handmaid; you have freed
         me from my bonds.
¹⁵ I will offer you the sacrifice of thanksgiving
     and call upon the name of the Lord.

16 I will fulfil my vows to the Lord
in the presence of all his people.
17 In the courts of the Lord's house,
in the midst of you, O Jerusalem. Praise the Lord.

READING   1 Corinthians 11.23–26

23 For I received from the Lord what I also handed on to you, that the Lord Jesus on the night when he was betrayed took a loaf of bread, 24 and when he had given thanks, he broke it and said, 'This is my body that is for you. Do this in remembrance of me.' 25 In the same way he took the cup also, after supper, saying, 'This cup is the new covenant in my blood. Do this, as often as you drink it, in remembrance of me.' 26 For as often as you eat this bread and drink the cup, you proclaim the Lord's death until he comes.

GOSPEL   John 13.1–17, 31b–35

1 Now before the festival of the Passover, Jesus knew that his hour had come to depart from this world and go to the Father. Having loved his own who were in the world, he loved them to the end. 2 The devil had already put it into the heart of Judas son of Simon Iscariot to betray him. And during supper 3 Jesus, knowing that the Father had given all things into his hands, and that he had come from God and was going to God, 4 got up from the table, took off his outer robe, and tied a towel around himself. 5 Then he poured water into a basin and began to wash the disciples' feet and to wipe them with the towel that was tied around him. 6 He came to Simon Peter, who said to him, 'Lord, are you going to wash my feet?' 7 Jesus answered, 'You do not know now what I am doing, but later you will understand.' 8 Peter said to him, 'You will never wash my feet.' Jesus answered, 'Unless I wash you, you have no share with me.' 9 Simon Peter said to him, 'Lord, not my feet only but also my hands and my head!' 10 Jesus said to him, 'One who has bathed does not need to wash, except for the feet, but is entirely clean. And you are clean, though not all of you.' 11 For he knew who was to betray him; for this reason he said, 'Not all of you are clean.'

12 After he had washed their feet, had put on his robe, and had returned to the table, he said to them, 'Do you know what I have done to you? 13 You call me Teacher and Lord—and you are right, for that is what I am. 14 So if I, your Lord and Teacher, have washed your feet, you also ought to wash one another's feet. 15 For I have set you an example, that you also should do as I have done to you. 16 Very truly, I tell you, servants are not greater

than their master, nor are messengers greater than the one who sent them. [17] If you know these things, you are blessed if you do them.'

[31] 'Now the Son of Man has been glorified, and God has been glorified in him. [32] If God has been glorified in him, God will also glorify him in himself and will glorify him at once. [33] Little children, I am with you only a little longer. You will look for me; and as I said to the Jews so now I say to you, "Where I am going, you cannot come." [34] I give you a new commandment, that you love one another. Just as I have loved you, you also should love one another. [35] By this everyone will know that you are my disciples, if you have love for one another.'

POST COMMUNION

Lord Jesus Christ,
we thank you that in this wonderful sacrament
you have given us the memorial of your passion:
grant us so to reverence the sacred mysteries
    of your body and blood
that we may know within ourselves
and show forth in our lives
the fruit of your redemption,
for you are alive and reign, now and for ever.

SECOND SERVICE   THIRD SERVICE

Psalm 39   Psalms 42; 43
Leviticus 16.2–24   Exodus 11
Luke 23.1–25   Ephesians 2.11–18

GOOD FRIDAY

COLLECT

Almighty Father,
look with mercy on this your family
for which our Lord Jesus Christ
    was content to be betrayed
    and given up into the hands of sinners
    and to suffer death upon the cross;

who is alive and glorified
      with you and the Holy Spirit,
one God, now and for ever.

READING   Isaiah 52.13–53.12

¹³ See, my servant shall prosper;
         he shall be exalted and lifted up,
         and shall be very high.
¹⁴ Just as there were many who were astonished at him
         —so marred was his appearance, beyond human semblance,
         and his form beyond that of mortals—
¹⁵ so he shall startle many nations;
         kings shall shut their mouths because of him;
      for that which had not been told them they shall see,
         and that which they had not heard they shall contemplate.
¹   Who has believed what we have heard?
         And to whom has the arm of the LORD been revealed?
²   For he grew up before him like a young plant,
         and like a root out of dry ground;
      he had no form or majesty that we should look at him,
         nothing in his appearance that we should desire him.
³   He was despised and rejected by others;
         a man of suffering and acquainted with infirmity;
      and as one from whom others hide their faces
         he was despised, and we held him of no account.
⁴   Surely he has borne our infirmities
         and carried our diseases;
      yet we accounted him stricken,
         struck down by God, and afflicted.
⁵   But he was wounded for our transgressions,
         crushed for our iniquities;
      upon him was the punishment that made us whole,
         and by his bruises we are healed.
⁶   All we like sheep have gone astray;
         we have all turned to our own way,
      and the LORD has laid on him
         the iniquity of us all.
⁷   He was oppressed, and he was afflicted,
         yet he did not open his mouth;
      like a lamb that is led to the slaughter,
         and like a sheep that before its shearers is silent,
         so he did not open his mouth.

8 By a perversion of justice he was taken away.
  Who could have imagined his future?
For he was cut off from the land of the living,
  stricken for the transgression of my people.
9 They made his grave with the wicked
  and his tomb with the rich,
although he had done no violence,
  and there was no deceit in his mouth.
10 Yet it was the will of the LORD to crush him with pain.
When you make his life an offering for sin,
  he shall see his offspring, and shall prolong his days;
through him the will of the LORD shall prosper.
11 Out of his anguish he shall see light;
he shall find satisfaction through his knowledge.
  The righteous one, my servant, shall make many righteous,
  and he shall bear their iniquities.
12 Therefore I will allot him a portion with the great,
  and he shall divide the spoil with the strong;
because he poured out himself to death,
  and was numbered with the transgressors;
yet he bore the sin of many,
  and made intercession for the transgressors.

PSALM   Psalm 22

IF A SHORTER TEXT IS PREFERRED, USE 1–11 OR 1–20

1 My God, my God, why have you forsaken me?
  and are so far from my cry and from the words of my distress?
2 O my God, I cry in the daytime, but you do not answer;
  by night as well, but I find no rest.
3 Yet you are the Holy One,
  enthroned upon the praises of Israel.
4 Our forebears put their trust in you;
  they trusted and you delivered them.
5 They cried out to you and were delivered;
  they trusted in you and were not put to shame.
6 But as for me, I am a worm and no man,
  scorned by all and despised by the people.
7 All who see me laugh me to scorn;
  they curl their lips and wag their heads, saying,
8 'He trusted in the Lord; let him deliver him;
  let him rescue him, if he delights in him.'

9   Yet you are he who took me out of the womb,
    and kept me safe upon my mother's breast.
10 I have been entrusted to you ever since I was born;
    you were my God when I was still in my mother's womb.
11 Be not far from me, for trouble is near,
    and there is none to help.
12 Many young bulls encircle me;
    strong bulls of Bashan surround me.
13 They open wide their jaws at me,
    like a ravening and a roaring lion.
14 I am poured out like water; all my bones are out of joint;
    my heart within my breast is melting wax.
15 My mouth is dried out like a pot-sherd; my tongue sticks to the
        roof of my mouth;
    and you have laid me in the dust of the grave.
16 Packs of dogs close me in, and gangs of evildoers circle around
        me;
    they pierce my hands and my feet; I can count all my bones.
17 They stare and gloat over me;
    they divide my garments among them; they cast lots for my
        clothing.
18 Be not far away, O Lord;
    you are my strength; hasten to help me.
19 Save me from the sword,
    my life from the power of the dog.
20 Save me from the lion's mouth,
    my wretched body from the horns of wild bulls.
21 I will declare your name to my people;
    in the midst of the congregation I will praise you.
22 Praise the Lord, you that fear him;
    stand in awe of him, O offspring of Israel; all you of Jacob's line,
        give glory.
23 For he does not despise nor abhor the poor in their poverty; neither
        does he hide his face from them;
    but when they cry to him he hears them.
24 My praise is of him in the great assembly;
    I will perform my vows in the presence of those who worship him.
25 The poor shall eat and be satisfied, and those who seek the Lord
        shall praise him:
    'May your heart live for ever!'
26 All the ends of the earth shall remember and turn to the Lord,
    and all the families of the nations shall bow before him.
27 For kingship belongs to the Lord;
    he rules over the nations.

28 To him alone all who sleep in the earth bow down in worship;
   all who go down to the dust fall before him.
29 My soul shall live for him; my descendants shall serve him;
   they shall be known as the Lord's for ever.
30 They shall come and make known to a people yet unborn
   the saving deeds that he has done.

READING

EITHER   **Hebrews 10.16–25**

16 'This is the covenant that I will make with them
       after those days, says the Lord:
   I will put my laws in their hearts,
       and I will write them on their minds',
17 he also adds,
   'I will remember their sins and their lawless deeds no more.'
18 Where there is forgiveness of these, there is no longer any offering for sin.

19 Therefore, my friends, since we have confidence to enter the sanctuary by the blood of Jesus, 20 by the new and living way that he opened for us through the curtain (that is, through his flesh), 21 and since we have a great priest over the house of God, 22 let us approach with a true heart in full assurance of faith, with our hearts sprinkled clean from an evil conscience and our bodies washed with pure water. 23 Let us hold fast to the confession of our hope without wavering, for he who has promised is faithful. 24 And let us consider how to provoke one another to love and good deeds, 25 not neglecting to meet together, as is the habit of some, but encouraging one another, and all the more as you see the Day approaching.

OR   **Hebrews 4.14–16; 5.7–9**

14 Since, then, we have a great high priest who has passed through the heavens, Jesus, the Son of God, let us hold fast to our confession. 15 For we do not have a high priest who is unable to sympathize with our weaknesses, but we have one who in every respect has been tested as we are, yet without sin. 16 Let us therefore approach the throne of grace with boldness, so that we may receive mercy and find grace to help in time of need.

7 In the days of his flesh, Jesus offered up prayers and supplications, with loud cries and tears, to the one who was able to save him from death, and

he was heard because of his reverent submission. [8] Although he was a Son, he learned obedience through what he suffered; [9] and having been made perfect, he became the source of eternal salvation for all who obey him.

GOSPEL   John 18.1–19.42

[1] After Jesus had spoken these words, he went out with his disciples across the Kidron valley to a place where there was a garden, which he and his disciples entered. [2] Now Judas, who betrayed him, also knew the place, because Jesus often met there with his disciples. [3] So Judas brought a detachment of soldiers together with police from the chief priests and the Pharisees, and they came there with lanterns and torches and weapons. [4] Then Jesus, knowing all that was to happen to him, came forward and asked them, 'For whom are you looking?' [5] They answered, 'Jesus of Nazareth.' Jesus replied, 'I am he.' Judas, who betrayed him, was standing with them. [6] When Jesus said to them, 'I am he', they stepped back and fell to the ground. [7] Again he asked them, 'For whom are you looking?' And they said, 'Jesus of Nazareth.' [8] Jesus answered, 'I told you that I am he. So if you are looking for me, let these men go.' [9] This was to fulfil the word that he had spoken, 'I did not lose a single one of those whom you gave me.' [10] Then Simon Peter, who had a sword, drew it, struck the high priest's slave, and cut off his right ear. The slave's name was Malchus. [11] Jesus said to Peter, 'Put your sword back into its sheath. Am I not to drink the cup that the Father has given me?'

[12] So the soldiers, their officer, and the Jewish police arrested Jesus and bound him. [13] First they took him to Annas, who was the father-in-law of Caiaphas, the high priest that year. [14] Caiaphas was the one who had advised the Jews that it was better to have one person die for the people.

[15] Simon Peter and another disciple followed Jesus. Since that disciple was known to the high priest, he went with Jesus into the courtyard of the high priest, [16] but Peter was standing outside at the gate. So the other disciple, who was known to the high priest, went out, spoke to the woman who guarded the gate, and brought Peter in. [17] The woman said to Peter, 'You are not also one of this man's disciples, are you?' He said, 'I am not.' [18] Now the slaves and the police had made a charcoal fire because it was cold, and they were standing round it and warming themselves. Peter also was standing with them and warming himself.

[19] Then the high priest questioned Jesus about his disciples and about his teaching. [20] Jesus answered, 'I have spoken openly to the world; I have always taught in synagogues and in the temple, where all the Jews come together. I have said nothing in secret. [21] Why do you ask me? Ask those who heard what I said to them; they know what I said.' [22] When he had

said this, one of the police standing nearby struck Jesus on the face, saying, 'Is that how you answer the high priest?' [23] Jesus answered, 'If I have spoken wrongly, testify to the wrong. But if I have spoken rightly, why do you strike me?' [24] Then Annas sent him bound to Caiaphas the high priest.

[25] Now Simon Peter was standing and warming himself. They asked him, 'You are not also one of his disciples, are you?' He denied it and said, 'I am not.' [26] One of the slaves of the high priest, a relative of the man whose ear Peter had cut off, asked, 'Did I not see you in the garden with him?' [27] Again Peter denied it, and at that moment the cock crowed.

[28] Then they took Jesus from Caiaphas to Pilate's headquarters. It was early in the morning. They themselves did not enter the headquarters, so as to avoid ritual defilement and to be able to eat the Passover. [29] So Pilate went out to them and said, 'What accusation do you bring against this man?' [30] They answered, 'If this man were not a criminal, we would not have handed him over to you.' [31] Pilate said to them, 'Take him yourselves and judge him according to your law.' The Jews replied, 'We are not permitted to put anyone to death.' [32] (This was to fulfil what Jesus had said when he indicated the kind of death he was to die.)

[33] Then Pilate entered the headquarters again, summoned Jesus, and asked him, 'Are you the King of the Jews?' [34] Jesus answered, 'Do you ask this on your own, or did others tell you about me?' [35] Pilate replied, 'I am not a Jew, am I? Your own nation and the chief priests have handed you over to me. What have you done?' [36] Jesus answered, 'My kingdom is not from this world. If my kingdom were from this world, my followers would be fighting to keep me from being handed over to the Jews. But as it is, my kingdom is not from here.' [37] Pilate asked him, 'So you are a king?' Jesus answered, 'You say that I am a king. For this I was born, and for this I came into the world, to testify to the truth. Everyone who belongs to the truth listens to my voice.' [38] Pilate asked him, 'What is truth?'

After he had said this, he went out to the Jews again and told them, 'I find no case against him. [39] But you have a custom that I release someone for you at the Passover. Do you want me to release for you the King of the Jews?' [40] They shouted in reply, 'Not this man, but Barabbas!' Now Barabbas was a bandit.

[1] Then Pilate took Jesus and had him flogged. [2] And the soldiers wove a crown of thorns and put it on his head, and they dressed him in a purple robe. [3] They kept coming up to him, saying, 'Hail, King of the Jews!' and striking him on the face. [4] Pilate went out again and said to them, 'Look, I am bringing him out to you to let you know that I find no case against him.' [5] So Jesus came out, wearing the crown of thorns and the purple robe. Pilate said to them, 'Here is the man!' [6] When the chief priests and the

police saw him, they shouted, 'Crucify him! Crucify him!' Pilate said to them, 'Take him yourselves and crucify him; I find no case against him.' [7] The Jews answered him, 'We have a law, and according to that law he ought to die because he has claimed to be the Son of God.'

[8] Now when Pilate heard this, he was more afraid than ever. [9] He entered his headquarters again and asked Jesus, 'Where are you from?' But Jesus gave him no answer. [10] Pilate therefore said to him, 'Do you refuse to speak to me? Do you not know that I have power to release you, and power to crucify you?' [11] Jesus answered him, 'You would have no power over me unless it had been given you from above; therefore the one who handed me over to you is guilty of a greater sin.' [12] From then on Pilate tried to release him, but the Jews cried out, 'If you release this man, you are no friend of the emperor. Everyone who claims to be a king sets himself against the emperor.'

[13] When Pilate heard these words, he brought Jesus outside and sat on the judge's bench at a place called The Stone Pavement, or in Hebrew Gabbatha. [14] Now it was the day of Preparation for the Passover; and it was about noon. He said to the Jews, 'Here is your King!' [15] They cried out, 'Away with him! Away with him! Crucify him!' Pilate asked them, 'Shall I crucify your King?' The chief priests answered, 'We have no king but the emperor.' [16] Then he handed him over to them to be crucified.

So they took Jesus; [17] and carrying the cross by himself, he went out to what is called The Place of the Skull, which in Hebrew is called Golgotha. [18] There they crucified him, and with him two others, one on either side, with Jesus between them. [19] Pilate also had an inscription written and put on the cross. It read, 'Jesus of Nazareth, the King of the Jews.' [20] Many of the Jews read this inscription, because the place where Jesus was crucified was near the city; and it was written in Hebrew, in Latin, and in Greek. [21] Then the chief priests of the Jews said to Pilate, 'Do not write, "The King of the Jews", but, "This man said, I am King of the Jews."' [22] Pilate answered, 'What I have written I have written.' [23] When the soldiers had crucified Jesus, they took his clothes and divided them into four parts, one for each soldier. They also took his tunic; now the tunic was seamless, woven in one piece from the top. [24] So they said to one another, 'Let us not tear it, but cast lots for it to see who will get it.' This was to fulfil what the scripture says,

'They divided my clothes among themselves,
and for my clothing they cast lots.'

[25] And that is what the soldiers did.

Meanwhile, standing near the cross of Jesus were his mother, and his mother's sister, Mary the wife of Clopas, and Mary Magdalene. [26] When Jesus saw his mother and the disciple whom he loved standing beside her, he said to his mother, 'Woman, here is your son.' ²⁷ Then he said to the disciple, 'Here is your mother.' And from that hour the disciple took her into his own home.

²⁸ After this, when Jesus knew that all was now finished, he said (in order to fulfil the scripture), 'I am thirsty.' ²⁹ A jar full of sour wine was standing there. So they put a sponge full of the wine on a branch of hyssop and held it to his mouth. ³⁰ When Jesus had received the wine, he said, 'It is finished.' Then he bowed his head and gave up his spirit.

³¹ Since it was the day of Preparation, the Jews did not want the bodies left on the cross during the sabbath, especially because that sabbath was a day of great solemnity. So they asked Pilate to have the legs of the crucified men broken and the bodies removed. ³² Then the soldiers came and broke the legs of the first and of the other who had been crucified with him. ³³ But when they came to Jesus and saw that he was already dead, they did not break his legs. ³⁴ Instead, one of the soldiers pierced his side with a spear, and at once blood and water came out. ³⁵ (He who saw this has testified so that you also may believe. His testimony is true, and he knows that he tells the truth.) ³⁶ These things occurred so that the scripture might be fulfilled, 'None of his bones shall be broken.' ³⁷ And again another passage of scripture says, 'They will look on the one whom they have pierced.'

³⁸ After these things, Joseph of Arimathea, who was a disciple of Jesus, though a secret one because of his fear of the Jews, asked Pilate to let him take away the body of Jesus. Pilate gave him permission; so he came and removed his body. ³⁹ Nicodemus, who had at first come to Jesus by night, also came, bringing a mixture of myrrh and aloes, weighing about a hundred pounds. ⁴⁰ They took the body of Jesus and wrapped it with the spices in linen cloths, according to the burial custom of the Jews. ⁴¹ Now there was a garden in the place where he was crucified, and in the garden there was a new tomb in which no one had ever been laid. ⁴² And so, because it was the Jewish day of Preparation, and the tomb was nearby, they laid Jesus there.

SECOND SERVICE	THIRD SERVICE
Psalms 130; 143	**Psalm 69**
Genesis 22.1–18	**Lamentations 5.15–22**
A part of	*A part of*
John 18–19	**John 18–19**
if not used at the Principal Service especially in the evening	*if not read at the Principal Service*
John 19.38–42	*or*
or	**Hebrews 10.1–10**
Colossians 1.18–23	

EASTER EVE

COLLECT

Grant, Lord,
that we who are baptized into the death
 of your Son our Saviour Jesus Christ
may continually put to death our evil desires
 and be buried with him;
and that through the grave and gate of death
we may pass to our joyful resurrection;
through his merits, who died and was buried
 and rose again for us,
your Son Jesus Christ our Lord.

These readings are for use at services other than the Easter Vigil

READING

EITHER   **Job 14.1–14**

¹ 'A mortal, born of woman, few of days and full of trouble,
²   comes up like a flower and withers,
      flees like a shadow and does not last.
³ Do you fix your eyes on such a one?
      Do you bring me into judgement with you?
⁴ Who can bring a clean thing out of an unclean?
      No one can.
⁵ Since their days are determined,
      and the number of their months is known to you,
      and you have appointed the bounds that they cannot pass,
⁶ look away from them, and desist,
      that they may enjoy, like labourers, their days.
⁷ For there is hope for a tree,
      if it is cut down, that it will sprout again,
      and that its shoots will not cease.
⁸ Though its root grows old in the earth,
      and its stump dies in the ground,
⁹ yet at the scent of water it will bud
      and put forth branches like a young plant.
¹⁰ But mortals die, and are laid low;
      humans expire, and where are they?

11 As waters fail from a lake,
    and a river wastes away and dries up,
12 so mortals lie down and do not rise again;
    until the heavens are no more, they will not awake
    or be roused out of their sleep.
13 O that you would hide me in Sheol,
    that you would conceal me until your wrath is past,
    that you would appoint me a set time, and remember me!
14 If mortals die, will they live again?
    All the days of my service I would wait
    until my release should come.'

OR   **Lamentations 3.1–9, 19–24**

1 I am one who has seen affliction
    under the rod of God's wrath;
2 he has driven and brought me
    into darkness without any light;
3 against me alone he turns his hand,
    again and again, all day long.
4 He has made my flesh and my skin waste away,
    and broken my bones;
5 he has besieged and enveloped me
    with bitterness and tribulation;
6 he has made me sit in darkness
    like the dead of long ago.
7 He has walled me about so that I cannot escape;
    he has put heavy chains on me;
8 though I call and cry for help,
    he shuts out my prayer;
9 he has blocked my ways with hewn stones,
    he has made my paths crooked.

19 The thought of my affliction and my homelessness
    is wormwood and gall!
20 My soul continually thinks of it
    and is bowed down within me.
21 But this I call to mind,
    and therefore I have hope:
22 The steadfast love of the LORD never ceases,
    his mercies never come to an end;

²³ they are new every morning;
     great is your faithfulness.
²⁴ 'The LORD is my portion,' says my soul,
     'therefore I will hope in him.'

PSALM   Psalm 31.1–4, 15–16

¹ In you, O Lord, have I taken refuge; let me never be put to shame;
    deliver me in your righteousness.
² Incline your ear to me;
    make haste to deliver me.
³ Be my strong rock, a castle to keep me safe, for you are my crag
       and my stronghold;
    for the sake of your name, lead me and guide me.
⁴ Take me out of the net that they have secretly set for me,
    for you are my tower of strength.

¹⁵ 'My times are in your hand;
     rescue me from the hand of my enemies, and from those who
        persecute me.
¹⁶ Make your face to shine upon your servant,
     and in your loving-kindness save me.'

OR, IF AN ALTERNATIVE TEXT IS PREFERRED   Psalm 31.1–5

¹ In you, O Lord, have I taken refuge; let me never be put to shame;
    deliver me in your righteousness.
² Incline your ear to me;
    make haste to deliver me.
³ Be my strong rock, a castle to keep me safe, for you are my crag
       and my stronghold;
    for the sake of your name, lead me and guide me.
⁴ Take me out of the net that they have secretly set for me,
    for you are my tower of strength.
⁵ Into your hands I commend my spirit,
    for you have redeemed me, O Lord, O God of truth.

READING   1 Peter 4.1–8

¹ Since therefore Christ suffered in the flesh, arm yourselves also with
the same intention (for whoever has suffered in the flesh has finished with
sin), ² so as to live for the rest of your earthly life no longer by human
desires but by the will of God. ³ You have already spent enough time
in doing what the Gentiles like to do, living in licentiousness, passions,
drunkenness, revels, carousing, and lawless idolatry. ⁴ They are surprised

that you no longer join them in the same excesses of dissipation, and so they blaspheme. [5] But they will have to give an account to him who stands ready to judge the living and the dead. [6] For this is the reason the gospel was proclaimed even to the dead, so that, though they had been judged in the flesh as everyone is judged, they might live in the spirit as God does.

[7] The end of all things is near; therefore be serious and discipline yourselves for the sake of your prayers. [8] Above all, maintain constant love for one another, for love covers a multitude of sins.

GOSPEL

EITHER   **Matthew 27.57–66**

[57] When it was evening, there came a rich man from Arimathea, named Joseph, who was also a disciple of Jesus. [58] He went to Pilate and asked for the body of Jesus; then Pilate ordered it to be given to him. [59] So Joseph took the body and wrapped it in a clean linen cloth [60] and laid it in his own new tomb, which he had hewn in the rock. He then rolled a great stone to the door of the tomb and went away. [61] Mary Magdalene and the other Mary were there, sitting opposite the tomb.

[62] The next day, that is, after the day of Preparation, the chief priests and the Pharisees gathered before Pilate [63] and said, 'Sir, we remember what that impostor said while he was still alive, "After three days I will rise again." [64] Therefore command that the tomb be made secure until the third day; otherwise his disciples may go and steal him away, and tell the people, "He has been raised from the dead", and the last deception would be worse than the first.' [65] Pilate said to them, 'You have a guard of soldiers; go, make it as secure as you can.' [66] So they went with the guard and made the tomb secure by sealing the stone.

OR   **John 19.38–42**

[38] After these things, Joseph of Arimathea, who was a disciple of Jesus, though a secret one because of his fear of the Jews, asked Pilate to let him take away the body of Jesus. Pilate gave him permission; so he came and removed his body. [39] Nicodemus, who had at first come to Jesus by night, also came, bringing a mixture of myrrh and aloes, weighing about a hundred pounds. [40] They took the body of Jesus and wrapped it with the spices in linen cloths, according to the burial custom of the Jews. [41] Now there was a garden in the place where he was crucified, and in the garden there was a new tomb in which no one had ever been laid. [42] And so, because it was the Jewish day of Preparation, and the tomb was nearby, they laid Jesus there.

SECOND SERVICE	THIRD SERVICE
Psalm 142	Psalm 116
Hosea 6.1–6	Job 19.21–27
John 2.18–22	1 John 5.5–12

EASTER VIGIL

COLLECT

Lord of all life and power,
who through the mighty resurrection of your Son
overcame the old order of sin and death
to make all things new in him:
grant that we, being dead to sin
and alive to you in Jesus Christ,
may reign with him in glory;
to whom with you and the Holy Spirit
be praise and honour, glory and might,
now and in all eternity.

A minimum of three Old Testament readings should be chosen. The reading from Exodus 14, along with its associated Canticle, the reading from Romans, Psalm 114, and the Gospel should always be used.

READING   Genesis 1.1–2.4a

[1] In the beginning when God created the heavens and the earth, [2] the earth was a formless void and darkness covered the face of the deep, while a wind from God swept over the face of the waters. [3] Then God said, 'Let there be light'; and there was light. [4] And God saw that the light was good; and God separated the light from the darkness. [5] God called the light Day, and the darkness he called Night. And there was evening and there was morning, the first day.

[6] And God said, 'Let there be a dome in the midst of the waters, and let it separate the waters from the waters.' [7] So God made the dome and separated the waters that were under the dome from the waters that were above the dome. And it was so. [8] God called the dome Sky. And there was evening and there was morning, the second day.

⁹ And God said, 'Let the waters under the sky be gathered together into one place, and let the dry land appear.' And it was so. ¹⁰ God called the dry land Earth, and the waters that were gathered together he called Seas. And God saw that it was good. ¹¹ Then God said, 'Let the earth put forth vegetation: plants yielding seed, and fruit trees of every kind on earth that bear fruit with the seed in it.' And it was so. ¹² The earth brought forth vegetation: plants yielding seed of every kind, and trees of every kind bearing fruit with the seed in it. And God saw that it was good. ¹³ And there was evening and there was morning, the third day.

¹⁴ And God said, 'Let there be lights in the dome of the sky to separate the day from the night; and let them be for signs and for seasons and for days and years, ¹⁵ and let them be lights in the dome of the sky to give light upon the earth.' And it was so. ¹⁶ God made the two great lights—the greater light to rule the day and the lesser light to rule the night—and the stars. ¹⁷ God set them in the dome of the sky to give light upon the earth, ¹⁸ to rule over the day and over the night, and to separate the light from the darkness. And God saw that it was good. ¹⁹ And there was evening and there was morning, the fourth day.

²⁰ And God said, 'Let the waters bring forth swarms of living creatures, and let birds fly above the earth across the dome of the sky.' ²¹ So God created the great sea monsters and every living creature that moves, of every kind, with which the waters swarm, and every winged bird of every kind. And God saw that it was good. ²² God blessed them, saying, 'Be fruitful and multiply and fill the waters in the seas, and let birds multiply on the earth.' ²³ And there was evening and there was morning, the fifth day.

²⁴ And God said, 'Let the earth bring forth living creatures of every kind: cattle and creeping things and wild animals of the earth of every kind.' And it was so. ²⁵ God made the wild animals of the earth of every kind, and the cattle of every kind, and everything that creeps upon the ground of every kind. And God saw that it was good.

²⁶ Then God said, 'Let us make humankind in our image, according to our likeness; and let them have dominion over the fish of the sea, and over the birds of the air, and over the cattle, and over all the wild animals of the earth, and over every creeping thing that creeps upon the earth.'
²⁷   So God created humankind in his image,
        in the image of God he created them;
        male and female he created them.
²⁸ God blessed them, and God said to them, 'Be fruitful and multiply, and fill the earth and subdue it; and have dominion over the fish of the sea and over the birds of the air and over every living thing that moves upon the earth.' ²⁹ God said, 'See, I have given you every plant yielding seed that is upon the face of all the earth, and every tree with seed in its fruit; you

shall have them for food. [30] And to every beast of the earth, and to every bird of the air, and to everything that creeps on the earth, everything that has the breath of life, I have given every green plant for food.' And it was so. [31] God saw everything that he had made, and indeed, it was very good. And there was evening and there was morning, the sixth day.

[1] Thus the heavens and the earth were finished, and all their multitude. [2] And on the seventh day God finished the work that he had done, and he rested on the seventh day from all the work that he had done. [3] So God blessed the seventh day and hallowed it, because on it God rested from all the work that he had done in creation.

[4] These are the generations of the heavens and the earth when they were created.

PSALM   Psalm 136.1–9, 23–26

[1]   Give thanks to the Lord, for he is good,
    for his mercy endures for ever.
[2]   Give thanks to the God of gods,
    for his mercy endures for ever.
[3]   Give thanks to the Lord of lords,
    for his mercy endures for ever.
[4]   Who only does great wonders,
    for his mercy endures for ever;
[5]   Who by his wisdom made the heavens,
    for his mercy endures for ever;
[6]   Who spread out the earth upon the waters,
    for his mercy endures for ever;
[7]   Who created great lights,
    for his mercy endures for ever;
[8]   The sun to rule the day,
    for his mercy endures for ever;
[9]   The moon and the stars to govern the night,
    for his mercy endures for ever.

[23]   Who remembered us in our low estate,
    for his mercy endures for ever;
[24]   And delivered us from our enemies,
    for his mercy endures for ever;
[25]   Who gives food to all creatures,
    for his mercy endures for ever;
[26]   Give thanks to the God of heaven,
    for his mercy endures for ever.

READING   **Genesis 7.1–5, 11–18; 8.6–18; 9.8–13**

¹ Then the LORD said to Noah, 'Go into the ark, you and all your household, for I have seen that you alone are righteous before me in this generation. ² Take with you seven pairs of all clean animals, the male and its mate; and a pair of the animals that are not clean, the male and its mate; ³ and seven pairs of the birds of the air also, male and female, to keep their kind alive on the face of all the earth. ⁴ For in seven days I will send rain on the earth for forty days and forty nights; and every living thing that I have made I will blot out from the face of the ground.' ⁵ And Noah did all that the LORD had commanded him.

¹¹ In the six-hundredth year of Noah's life, in the second month, on the seventeenth day of the month, on that day all the fountains of the great deep burst forth, and the windows of the heavens were opened. ¹² The rain fell on the earth for forty days and forty nights. ¹³ On the very same day Noah with his sons, Shem and Ham and Japheth, and Noah's wife and the three wives of his sons, entered the ark, ¹⁴ they and every wild animal of every kind, and all domestic animals of every kind, and every creeping thing that creeps on the earth, and every bird of every kind—every bird, every winged creature. ¹⁵ They went into the ark with Noah, two and two of all flesh in which there was the breath of life. ¹⁶ And those that entered, male and female of all flesh, went in as God had commanded him; and the LORD shut him in.

¹⁷ The flood continued for forty days on the earth; and the waters increased, and bore up the ark, and it rose high above the earth. ¹⁸ The waters swelled and increased greatly on the earth; and the ark floated on the face of the waters.

⁶ At the end of forty days Noah opened the window of the ark that he had made ⁷ and sent out the raven; and it went to and fro until the waters were dried up from the earth. ⁸ Then he sent out the dove from him, to see if the waters had subsided from the face of the ground; ⁹ but the dove found no place to set its foot, and it returned to him to the ark, for the waters were still on the face of the whole earth. So he put out his hand and took it and brought it into the ark with him. ¹⁰ He waited another seven days, and again he sent out the dove from the ark; ¹¹ and the dove came back to him in the evening, and there in its beak was a freshly plucked olive leaf; so Noah knew that the waters had subsided from the earth. ¹² Then he waited another seven days, and sent out the dove; and it did not return to him any more.

¹³ In the six hundred and first year, in the first month, on the first day of the month, the waters were dried up from the earth; and Noah removed

the covering of the ark, and looked, and saw that the face of the ground was drying. [14] In the second month, on the twenty-seventh day of the month, the earth was dry. [15] Then God said to Noah, [16] 'Go out of the ark, you and your wife, and your sons and your sons' wives with you. [17] Bring out with you every living thing that is with you of all flesh—birds and animals and every creeping thing that creeps on the earth—so that they may abound on the earth, and be fruitful and multiply on the earth.' [18] So Noah went out with his sons and his wife and his sons' wives.

[8] Then God said to Noah and to his sons with him, [9] 'As for me, I am establishing my covenant with you and your descendants after you, [10] and with every living creature that is with you, the birds, the domestic animals, and every animal of the earth with you, as many as came out of the ark. [11] I establish my covenant with you, that never again shall all flesh be cut off by the waters of a flood, and never again shall there be a flood to destroy the earth.' [12] God said, 'This is the sign of the covenant that I make between me and you and every living creature that is with you, for all future generations: [13] I have set my bow in the clouds, and it shall be a sign of the covenant between me and the earth.'

PSALM   Psalm 46

1 God is our refuge and strength,
   a very present help in trouble;
2 Therefore we will not fear, though the earth be moved,
   and though the mountains be toppled into the depths of the sea;
3 Though its waters rage and foam,
   and though the mountains tremble at its tumult.
4 The Lord of hosts is with us;
   the God of Jacob is our stronghold.
5 There is a river whose streams make glad the city of God,
   the holy habitation of the Most High.
6 God is in the midst of her; she shall not be overthrown;
   God shall help her at the break of day.
7 The nations make much ado and the kingdoms are shaken;
   God has spoken and the earth shall melt away.
8 The Lord of hosts is with us;
   the God of Jacob is our stronghold.
9 Come now and look upon the works of the Lord,
   what awesome things he has done on earth.
10 It is he who makes war to cease in all the world;
   he breaks the bow and shatters the spear and burns the shields
       with fire.

YEAR A

11 'Be still, then, and know that I am God;
   I will be exalted among the nations; I will be exalted in the earth.'
12 The Lord of hosts is with us;
   the God of Jacob is our stronghold.

READING   Genesis 22.1–18

¹ After these things God tested Abraham. He said to him, 'Abraham!' And
he said, 'Here I am.' ² He said, 'Take your son, your only son Isaac, whom
you love, and go to the land of Moriah, and offer him there as a burnt-
offering on one of the mountains that I shall show you.' ³ So Abraham rose
early in the morning, saddled his donkey, and took two of his young men
with him, and his son Isaac; he cut the wood for the burnt-offering, and
set out and went to the place in the distance that God had shown him. ⁴ On
the third day Abraham looked up and saw the place far away. ⁵ Then
Abraham said to his young men, 'Stay here with the donkey; the boy and I
will go over there; we will worship, and then we will come back to you.'
⁶ Abraham took the wood of the burnt-offering and laid it on his son Isaac,
and he himself carried the fire and the knife. So the two of them walked
on together. ⁷ Isaac said to his father Abraham, 'Father!' And he said, 'Here
I am, my son.' He said, 'The fire and the wood are here, but where is the
lamb for a burnt-offering?' ⁸ Abraham said, 'God himself will provide the
lamb for a burnt-offering, my son.' So the two of them walked on together.

⁹ When they came to the place that God had shown him, Abraham built
an altar there and laid the wood in order. He bound his son Isaac, and laid
him on the altar, on top of the wood. ¹⁰ Then Abraham reached out his
hand and took the knife to kill his son. ¹¹ But the angel of the LORD called
to him from heaven, and said, 'Abraham, Abraham!' And he said, 'Here I
am.' ¹² He said, 'Do not lay your hand on the boy or do anything to him; for
now I know that you fear God, since you have not withheld your son, your
only son, from me.' ¹³ And Abraham looked up and saw a ram, caught in a
thicket by its horns. Abraham went and took the ram and offered it up as
a burnt-offering instead of his son. ¹⁴ So Abraham called that place 'The
LORD will provide'; as it is said to this day, 'On the mount of the LORD it
shall be provided.'

¹⁵ The angel of the LORD called to Abraham a second time from heaven,
¹⁶ and said, 'By myself I have sworn, says the LORD: Because you have done
this, and have not withheld your son, your only son, ¹⁷ I will indeed bless
you, and I will make your offspring as numerous as the stars of heaven and
as the sand that is on the seashore. And your offspring shall possess the
gate of their enemies, ¹⁸ and by your offspring shall all the nations of the
earth gain blessing for themselves, because you have obeyed my voice.'

PSALM   Psalm 16

¹ Protect me, O God, for I take refuge in you;
   I have said to the Lord, 'You are my Lord, my good above all other.'
² All my delight is upon the godly that are in the land,
   upon those who are noble among the people.
³ But those who run after other gods
   shall have their troubles multiplied.
⁴ Their libations of blood I will not offer,
   nor take the names of their gods upon my lips.
⁵ O Lord, you are my portion and my cup;
   it is you who uphold my lot.
⁶ My boundaries enclose a pleasant land;
   indeed, I have a goodly heritage.
⁷ I will bless the Lord who gives me counsel;
   my heart teaches me, night after night.
⁸ I have set the Lord always before me;
   because he is at my right hand I shall not fall.
⁹ My heart, therefore, is glad and my spirit rejoices;
   my body also shall rest in hope.
¹⁰ For you will not abandon me to the grave,
   nor let your holy one see the Pit.
¹¹ You will show me the path of life;
   in your presence there is fullness of joy, and in your right hand
      are pleasures for evermore.

READING   Exodus 14.10–31; 15.20–21

¹⁰ As Pharaoh drew near, the Israelites looked back, and there were the Egyptians advancing on them. In great fear the Israelites cried out to the Lord. ¹¹ They said to Moses, 'Was it because there were no graves in Egypt that you have taken us away to die in the wilderness? What have you done to us, bringing us out of Egypt? ¹² Is this not the very thing we told you in Egypt, "Let us alone and let us serve the Egyptians"? For it would have been better for us to serve the Egyptians than to die in the wilderness.' ¹³ But Moses said to the people, 'Do not be afraid, stand firm, and see the deliverance that the Lord will accomplish for you today; for the Egyptians whom you see today you shall never see again. ¹⁴ The Lord will fight for you, and you have only to keep still.'

¹⁵ Then the Lord said to Moses, 'Why do you cry out to me? Tell the Israelites to go forward. ¹⁶ But you lift up your staff, and stretch out your hand over the sea and divide it, that the Israelites may go into the sea on dry ground. ¹⁷ Then I will harden the hearts of the Egyptians so that they

will go in after them; and so I will gain glory for myself over Pharaoh and all his army, his chariots, and his chariot drivers. [18] And the Egyptians shall know that I am the LORD, when I have gained glory for myself over Pharaoh, his chariots, and his chariot drivers.'

[19] The angel of God who was going before the Israelite army moved and went behind them; and the pillar of cloud moved from in front of them and took its place behind them. [20] It came between the army of Egypt and the army of Israel. And so the cloud was there with the darkness, and it lit up the night; one did not come near the other all night.

[21] Then Moses stretched out his hand over the sea. The LORD drove the sea back by a strong east wind all night, and turned the sea into dry land; and the waters were divided. [22] The Israelites went into the sea on dry ground, the waters forming a wall for them on their right and on their left. [23] The Egyptians pursued, and went into the sea after them, all of Pharaoh's horses, chariots, and chariot drivers. [24] At the morning watch the LORD in the pillar of fire and cloud looked down upon the Egyptian army, and threw the Egyptian army into panic. [25] He clogged their chariot wheels so that they turned with difficulty. The Egyptians said, 'Let us flee from the Israelites, for the LORD is fighting for them against Egypt.'

[26] Then the LORD said to Moses, 'Stretch out your hand over the sea, so that the water may come back upon the Egyptians, upon their chariots and chariot drivers.' [27] So Moses stretched out his hand over the sea, and at dawn the sea returned to its normal depth. As the Egyptians fled before it, the LORD tossed the Egyptians into the sea. [28] The waters returned and covered the chariots and the chariot drivers, the entire army of Pharaoh that had followed them into the sea; not one of them remained. [29] But the Israelites walked on dry ground through the sea, the waters forming a wall for them on their right and on their left.

[30] Thus the LORD saved Israel that day from the Egyptians; and Israel saw the Egyptians dead on the seashore. [31] Israel saw the great work that the LORD did against the Egyptians. So the people feared the LORD and believed in the LORD and in his servant Moses.

[20] Then the prophet Miriam, Aaron's sister, took a tambourine in her hand; and all the women went out after her with tambourines and with dancing. [21] And Miriam sang to them:

'Sing to the LORD, for he has triumphed gloriously;
horse and rider he has thrown into the sea.'

CANTICLE   Exodus 15.1b–13, 17–18

¹ 'I will sing to the LORD, for he has triumphed gloriously;
   horse and rider he has thrown into the sea.
² The LORD is my strength and my might,
   and he has become my salvation;
 this is my God, and I will praise him,
   my father's God, and I will exalt him.
³ The LORD is a warrior;
   the LORD is his name.
⁴ Pharaoh's chariots and his army he cast into the sea;
   his picked officers were sunk in the Red Sea.
⁵ The floods covered them;
   they went down into the depths like a stone.
⁶ Your right hand, O LORD, glorious in power—
   your right hand, O LORD, shattered the enemy.
⁷ In the greatness of your majesty you overthrew your adversaries;
   you sent out your fury, it consumed them like stubble.
⁸ At the blast of your nostrils the waters piled up,
   the floods stood up in a heap;
   the deeps congealed in the heart of the sea.
⁹ The enemy said, "I will pursue, I will overtake,
   I will divide the spoil, my desire shall have its fill of them.
   I will draw my sword, my hand shall destroy them."
¹⁰ You blew with your wind, the sea covered them;
   they sank like lead in the mighty waters.
¹¹ Who is like you, O LORD, among the gods?
   Who is like you, majestic in holiness,
   awesome in splendour, doing wonders?
¹² You stretched out your right hand,
   the earth swallowed them.
¹³ In your steadfast love you led the people whom you redeemed;
   you guided them by your strength to your holy abode.'

¹⁷ 'You brought them in and planted them on the mountain of your own possession,
   the place, O LORD, that you made your abode,
   the sanctuary, O LORD, that your hands have established.
¹⁸ The LORD will reign for ever and ever.'

READING   Isaiah 55.1–11

1 Ho, everyone who thirsts,
    come to the waters;
and you that have no money,
    come, buy and eat!
Come, buy wine and milk
    without money and without price.
2 Why do you spend your money for that which is not bread,
    and your labour for that which does not satisfy?
Listen carefully to me, and eat what is good,
    and delight yourselves in rich food.
3 Incline your ear, and come to me;
    listen, so that you may live.
I will make with you an everlasting covenant,
    my steadfast, sure love for David.
4 See, I made him a witness to the peoples,
    a leader and commander for the peoples.
5 See, you shall call nations that you do not know,
    and nations that do not know you shall run to you,
because of the LORD your God, the Holy One of Israel,
    for he has glorified you.
6 Seek the LORD while he may be found,
    call upon him while he is near;
7 let the wicked forsake their way,
    and the unrighteous their thoughts;
let them return to the LORD, that he may have mercy on them,
    and to our God, for he will abundantly pardon.
8 For my thoughts are not your thoughts,
    nor are your ways my ways, says the LORD.
9 For as the heavens are higher than the earth,
    so are my ways higher than your ways
    and my thoughts than your thoughts.
10 For as the rain and the snow come down from heaven,
    and do not return there until they have watered the earth,
making it bring forth and sprout,
    giving seed to the sower and bread to the eater,
11 so shall my word be that goes out from my mouth;
    it shall not return to me empty,
but it shall accomplish that which I purpose,
    and succeed in the thing for which I sent it.

CANTICLE

Isaiah 12.2–6

2 Surely God is my salvation;
    I will trust, and will not be afraid,
  for the LORD GOD is my strength and my might;
    he has become my salvation.

3 With joy you will draw water from the wells of salvation. 4 And you will
say on that day:
  Give thanks to the LORD,
    call on his name;
  make known his deeds among the nations;
    proclaim that his name is exalted.
5 Sing praises to the LORD, for he has done gloriously;
    let this be known in all the earth.
6 Shout aloud and sing for joy, O royal Zion,
    for great in your midst is the Holy One of Israel.

READING

EITHER

Baruch 3.9–15, 32–4.4

9   Hear the commandments of life, O Israel;
     give ear, and learn wisdom!
10 Why is it, O Israel, why is it that you are in the land of your enemies,
     that you are growing old in a foreign country,
    that you are defiled with the dead,
11   that you are counted among those in Hades?
12 You have forsaken the fountain of wisdom.
13 If you had walked in the way of God,
     you would be living in peace for ever.
14 Learn where there is wisdom,
     where there is strength,
     where there is understanding,
    so that you may at the same time discern
     where there is length of days, and life,
     where there is light for the eyes, and peace.
15 Who has found her place?
     And who has entered her storehouses?

³² But the one who knows all things knows her,
  he found her by his understanding.
The one who prepared the earth for all time
  filled it with four-footed creatures;
³³ the one who sends forth the light, and it goes;
  he called it, and it obeyed him, trembling;
³⁴ the stars shone in their watches, and were glad;
  he called them, and they said, 'Here we are!'
They shone with gladness for him who made them.
³⁵ This is our God;
  no other can be compared to him.
³⁶ He found the whole way to knowledge,
  and gave her to his servant Jacob
  and to Israel, whom he loved.
³⁷ Afterwards she appeared on earth
  and lived with humankind.
¹ She is the book of the commandments of God,
  the law that endures for ever.
All who hold her fast will live,
  and those who forsake her will die.
² Turn, O Jacob, and take her;
  walk towards the shining of her light.
³ Do not give your glory to another,
  or your advantages to an alien people.
⁴ Happy are we, O Israel,
  for we know what is pleasing to God.

OR   **Proverbs 8.1–8, 19–21; 9.4b–6**

¹ Does not wisdom call,
  and does not understanding raise her voice?
² On the heights, beside the way,
  at the crossroads she takes her stand;
³ beside the gates in front of the town,
  at the entrance of the portals she cries out:
⁴ 'To you, O people, I call,
  and my cry is to all that live.
⁵ O simple ones, learn prudence;
  acquire intelligence, you who lack it.
⁶ Hear, for I will speak noble things,
  and from my lips will come what is right;
⁷ for my mouth will utter truth;
  wickedness is an abomination to my lips.

⁸ All the words of my mouth are righteous;
  there is nothing twisted or crooked in them.

¹⁹ 'My fruit is better than gold, even fine gold,
  and my yield than choice silver.
²⁰ I walk in the way of righteousness,
  along the paths of justice,
²¹ endowing with wealth those who love me,
  and filling their treasuries.'

⁴ To those without sense she says,
⁵ 'Come, eat of my bread
  and drink of the wine I have mixed.
⁶ Lay aside immaturity, and live,
  and walk in the way of insight.'

PSALM   Psalm 19

¹ The heavens declare the glory of God,
  and the firmament shows his handiwork.
² One day tells its tale to another,
  and one night imparts knowledge to another.
³ Although they have no words or language,
  and their voices are not heard,
⁴ Their sound has gone out into all lands,
  and their message to the ends of the world.
⁵ In the deep has he set a pavilion for the sun;
  it comes forth like a bridegroom out of his chamber; it rejoices
    like a champion to run its course.
⁶ It goes forth from the uttermost edge of the heavens and runs
    about to the end of it again;
  nothing is hidden from its burning heat.
⁷ The law of the Lord is perfect and revives the soul;
  the testimony of the Lord is sure and gives wisdom to the innocent.
⁸ The statutes of the Lord are just and rejoice the heart;
  the commandment of the Lord is clear and gives light to the eyes.
⁹ The fear of the Lord is clean and endures for ever;
  the judgements of the Lord are true and righteous altogether.
¹⁰ More to be desired are they than gold, more than much fine gold,
  sweeter far than honey, than honey in the comb.
¹¹ By them also is your servant enlightened,
  and in keeping them there is great reward.
¹² Who can tell how often he offends?
  Cleanse me from my secret faults.

¹³ Above all, keep your servant from presumptuous sins; let them
    not get dominion over me;
then shall I be whole and sound, and innocent of a great offence.
¹⁴ Let the words of my mouth and the meditation of my heart be
    acceptable in your sight,
O Lord, my strength and my redeemer.

READING   Ezekiel 36.24–28

²⁴ I will take you from the nations, and gather you from all the countries, and bring you into your own land. ²⁵ I will sprinkle clean water upon you, and you shall be clean from all your uncleannesses, and from all your idols I will cleanse you. ²⁶ A new heart I will give you, and a new spirit I will put within you; and I will remove from your body the heart of stone and give you a heart of flesh. ²⁷ I will put my spirit within you, and make you follow my statutes and be careful to observe my ordinances. ²⁸ Then you shall live in the land that I gave to your ancestors; and you shall be my people, and I will be your God.

PSALMS   Psalm 42

¹ As the deer longs for the water-brooks,
    so longs my soul for you, O God.
² My soul is athirst for God, athirst for the living God;
    when shall I come to appear before the presence of God?
³ My tears have been my food day and night,
    while all day long they say to me, 'Where now is your God?'
⁴ I pour out my soul when I think on these things:
    how I went with the multitude and led them into the house of
        God,
⁵ With the voice of praise and thanksgiving,
    among those who keep holy-day.
⁶ Why are you so full of heaviness, O my soul?
    and why are you so disquieted within me?
⁷ Put your trust in God;
    for I will yet give thanks to him, who is the help of my countenance,
        and my God.
⁸ My soul is heavy within me;
    therefore I will remember you from the land of Jordan, and from
        the peak of Mizar among the heights of Hermon.
⁹ One deep calls to another in the noise of your cataracts;
    all your rapids and floods have gone over me.

¹⁰ The Lord grants his loving-kindness in the daytime;
    in the night season his song is with me, a prayer to the God of my
        life.
¹¹ I will say to the God of my strength, 'Why have you forgotten me?
    and why do I go so heavily while the enemy oppresses me?'
¹² While my bones are being broken,
    my enemies mock me to my face;
¹³ All day long they mock me
    say to me, 'Where now is your God?'
¹⁴ Why are you so full of heaviness, O my soul?
    and why are you so disquieted within me?
¹⁵ Put your trust in God;
    for I will yet give thanks to him, who is the help of my countenance,
        and my God.

Psalm 43

¹ Give judgement for me, O God, and defend my cause against an
    ungodly people;
    deliver me from the deceitful and the wicked.
² For you are the God of my strength; why have you put me from
    you?
    and why do I go so heavily while the enemy oppresses me?
³ Send out your light and your truth, that they may lead me,
    and bring me to your holy hill and to your dwelling;
⁴ That I may go to the altar of God, to the God of my joy and gladness;
    and on the harp I will give thanks to you, O God my God.
⁵ Why are you so full of heaviness, O my soul?
    and why are you so disquieted within me?
⁶ Put your trust in God;
    for I will yet give thanks to him, who is the help of my countenance,
        and my God.

READING   Ezekiel 37.1–14

¹ The hand of the LORD came upon me, and he brought me out by the
spirit of the LORD and set me down in the middle of a valley; it was full of
bones. ² He led me all round them; there were very many lying in the valley,
and they were very dry. ³ He said to me, 'Mortal, can these bones live?' I
answered, 'O Lord GOD, you know.' ⁴ Then he said to me, 'Prophesy to these
bones, and say to them: O dry bones, hear the word of the LORD. ⁵ Thus says
the Lord GOD to these bones: I will cause breath to enter you, and you shall
live. ⁶ I will lay sinews on you, and will cause flesh to come upon you, and

cover you with skin, and put breath in you, and you shall live; and you shall know that I am the LORD.'

⁷ So I prophesied as I had been commanded; and as I prophesied, suddenly there was a noise, a rattling, and the bones came together, bone to its bone. ⁸ I looked, and there were sinews on them, and flesh had come upon them, and skin had covered them; but there was no breath in them. ⁹ Then he said to me, 'Prophesy to the breath, prophesy, mortal, and say to the breath: Thus says the Lord GOD: Come from the four winds, O breath, and breathe upon these slain, that they may live.' ¹⁰ I prophesied as he commanded me, and the breath came into them, and they lived, and stood on their feet, a vast multitude.

¹¹ Then he said to me, 'Mortal, these bones are the whole house of Israel. They say, "Our bones are dried up, and our hope is lost; we are cut off completely." ¹² Therefore prophesy, and say to them, Thus says the Lord GOD: I am going to open your graves, and bring you up from your graves, O my people; and I will bring you back to the land of Israel. ¹³ And you shall know that I am the LORD, when I open your graves, and bring you up from your graves, O my people. ¹⁴ I will put my spirit within you, and you shall live, and I will place you on your own soil; then you shall know that I, the LORD, have spoken and will act, says the LORD.'

PSALM   Psalm 143

1   Lord, hear my prayer, and in your faithfulness heed my
       supplications;
     answer me in your righteousness.
2   Enter not into judgement with your servant,
     for in your sight shall no one living be justified.
3   For my enemy has sought my life and has crushed me to the
       ground;
     making me live in dark places like those who are long dead.
4   My spirit faints within me;
     my heart within me is desolate.
5   I remember the time past; I muse upon all your deeds;
     I consider the works of your hands.
6   I spread out my hands to you;
     my soul gasps to you like a thirsty land.
7   O Lord, make haste to answer me; my spirit fails me;
     do not hide your face from me or I shall be like those who go down
       to the Pit.

8 Let me hear of your loving-kindness in the morning, for I put my
    trust in you;
  show me the road that I must walk, for I lift up my soul to you.
9 Deliver me from my enemies, O Lord,
  for I flee to you for refuge.
10 Teach me to do what pleases you, for you are my God;
  let your good Spirit lead me on level ground.
11 Revive me, O Lord, for your name's sake;
  for your righteousness' sake, bring me out of trouble.
12 Of your goodness, destroy my enemies and bring all my foes to
    naught,
  for truly I am your servant.

READING   Zephaniah 3.14–20

14 Sing aloud, O daughter Zion;
  shout, O Israel!
  Rejoice and exult with all your heart,
    O daughter Jerusalem!
15 The LORD has taken away the judgements against you,
  he has turned away your enemies.
  The king of Israel, the LORD, is in your midst;
    you shall fear disaster no more.
16 On that day it shall be said to Jerusalem:
  Do not fear, O Zion;
    do not let your hands grow weak.
17 The LORD, your God, is in your midst,
    a warrior who gives victory;
  he will rejoice over you with gladness,
    he will renew you in his love;
  he will exult over you with loud singing
18   as on a day of festival.
  I will remove disaster from you,
    so that you will not bear reproach for it.
19 I will deal with all your oppressors
    at that time.
  And I will save the lame
    and gather the outcast,
  and I will change their shame into praise
    and renown in all the earth.

20 At that time I will bring you home,
 at the time when I gather you;
for I will make you renowned and praised
 among all the peoples of the earth,
when I restore your fortunes
 before your eyes, says the LORD.

PSALM   Psalm 98

1 Sing to the Lord a new song,
 for he has done marvellous things.
2 With his right hand and his holy arm
 has he won for himself the victory.
3 The Lord has made known his victory;
 his righteousness has he openly shown in the sight of the nations.
4 He remembers his mercy and faithfulness to the house of Israel,
 and all the ends of the earth have seen the victory of our God.
5 Shout with joy to the Lord, all you lands;
 lift up your voice, rejoice and sing.
6 Sing to the Lord with the harp,
 with the harp and the voice of song.
7 With trumpets and the sound of the horn
 shout with joy before the King, the Lord.
8 Let the sea make a noise and all that is in it,
 the lands and those who dwell therein.
9 Let the rivers clap their hands,
 and let the hills ring out with joy before the Lord, when he comes
  to judge the earth.
10 In righteousness shall he judge the world,
 and the peoples with equity.

READING   Romans 6.3–11

3 Do you not know that all of us who have been baptized into Christ Jesus were baptized into his death? 4 Therefore we have been buried with him by baptism into death, so that, just as Christ was raised from the dead by the glory of the Father, so we too might walk in newness of life.

5 For if we have been united with him in a death like his, we will certainly be united with him in a resurrection like his. 6 We know that our old self was crucified with him so that the body of sin might be destroyed, and we might no longer be enslaved to sin. 7 For whoever has died is freed from sin. 8 But if we have died with Christ, we believe that we will also live with

him. [9] We know that Christ, being raised from the dead, will never die again; death no longer has dominion over him. [10] The death he died, he died to sin, once for all; but the life he lives, he lives to God. [11] So you also must consider yourselves dead to sin and alive to God in Christ Jesus.

PSALM   Psalm 114

[1]   Alleluia! When Israel came out of Egypt,
      the house of Jacob from a people of strange speech,
[2]   Judah became God's sanctuary
      and Israel his dominion.
[3]   The sea beheld it and fled;
      Jordan turned and went back.
[4]   The mountains skipped like rams,
      and the little hills like young sheep.
[5]   What ailed you, O sea, that you fled?
      O Jordan, that you turned back?
[6]   You mountains, that you skipped like rams?
      you little hills like young sheep?
[7]   Tremble, O earth, at the presence of the Lord,
      at the presence of the God of Jacob,
[8]   Who turned the hard rock into a pool of water
      and flint-stone into a flowing spring.

GOSPEL   Matthew 28.1–10

[1] After the sabbath, as the first day of the week was dawning, Mary Magdalene and the other Mary went to see the tomb. [2] And suddenly there was a great earthquake; for an angel of the Lord, descending from heaven, came and rolled back the stone and sat on it. [3] His appearance was like lightning, and his clothing white as snow. [4] For fear of him the guards shook and became like dead men. [5] But the angel said to the women, 'Do not be afraid; I know that you are looking for Jesus who was crucified. [6] He is not here; for he has been raised, as he said. Come, see the place where he lay. [7] Then go quickly and tell his disciples, "He has been raised from the dead, and indeed he is going ahead of you to Galilee; there you will see him." This is my message for you.' [8] So they left the tomb quickly with fear and great joy, and ran to tell his disciples. [9] Suddenly Jesus met them and said, 'Greetings!' And they came to him, took hold of his feet, and worshipped him. [10] Then Jesus said to them, 'Do not be afraid; go and tell my brothers to go to Galilee; there they will see me.'

POST COMMUNION

God of Life,
who for our redemption gave your only-begotten Son
    to the death of the cross,
and by his glorious resurrection
have delivered us from the power of our enemy:
grant us so to die daily to sin,
that we may evermore live with him
    in the joy of his risen life;
through Jesus Christ our Lord.

EASTER DAY

COLLECT

Lord of all life and power,
who through the mighty resurrection of your Son
overcame the old order of sin and death
to make all things new in him:
grant that we, being dead to sin
and alive to you in Jesus Christ,
may reign with him in glory;
to whom with you and the Holy Spirit
be praise and honour, glory and might,
now and in all eternity.

READING

EITHER   Acts 10.34–43

34 Then Peter began to speak to them: 'I truly understand that God shows
no partiality, 35 but in every nation anyone who fears him and does what is
right is acceptable to him. 36 You know the message he sent to the people
of Israel, preaching peace by Jesus Christ—he is Lord of all. 37 That message
spread throughout Judea, beginning in Galilee after the baptism that John
announced: 38 how God anointed Jesus of Nazareth with the Holy Spirit
and with power; how he went about doing good and healing all who were
oppressed by the devil, for God was with him. 39 We are witnesses to all
that he did both in Judea and in Jerusalem. They put him to death by
hanging him on a tree; 40 but God raised him on the third day and allowed
him to appear, 41 not to all the people but to us who were chosen by God as

witnesses, and who ate and drank with him after he rose from the dead. [42] He commanded us to preach to the people and to testify that he is the one ordained by God as judge of the living and the dead. [43] All the prophets testify about him that everyone who believes in him receives forgiveness of sins through his name.'

OR   **Jeremiah 31.1–6**

[1]   At that time, says the LORD, I will be the God of all the families of Israel, and they shall be my people.
[2]   Thus says the LORD:
    The people who survived the sword
        found grace in the wilderness;
    when Israel sought for rest,
[3]   the LORD appeared to him from far away.
    I have loved you with an everlasting love;
        therefore I have continued my faithfulness to you.
[4]   Again I will build you, and you shall be built,
        O virgin Israel!
    Again you shall take your tambourines,
        and go forth in the dance of the merrymakers.
[5]   Again you shall plant vineyards
        on the mountains of Samaria;
    the planters shall plant,
        and shall enjoy the fruit.
[6]   For there shall be a day when sentinels will call
        in the hill country of Ephraim:
    'Come, let us go up to Zion,
        to the LORD our God.'

PSALM   **Psalm 118.[1–2,] 14–24**

[[1]   Give thanks to the Lord, for he is good;
    his mercy endures for ever.
[2]   Let Israel now proclaim,
    'His mercy endures for ever.']

[14]   The Lord is my strength and my song,
    and he has become my salvation.
[15]   There is a sound of exultation and victory
    in the tents of the righteous:
[16]   'The right hand of the Lord has triumphed!
    the right hand of the Lord is exalted! the right hand of the Lord
        has triumphed!'

17 I shall not die, but live,
     and declare the works of the Lord.
18 The Lord has punished me sorely,
     but he did not hand me over to death.
19 Open for me the gates of righteousness;
     I will enter them; I will offer thanks to the Lord.
20 'This is the gate of the Lord;
     he who is righteous may enter.'
21 I will give thanks to you, for you answered me
     and have become my salvation.
22 The same stone which the builders rejected
     has become the chief corner-stone.
23 This is the Lord's doing,
     and it is marvellous in our eyes.
24 On this day the Lord has acted;
     we will rejoice and be glad in it.

READING

EITHER   ### Colossians 3.1–4

¹ So if you have been raised with Christ, seek the things that are above, where Christ is, seated at the right hand of God. ² Set your minds on things that are above, not on things that are on earth, ³ for you have died, and your life is hidden with Christ in God. ⁴ When Christ who is your life is revealed, then you also will be revealed with him in glory.

OR   ### Acts 10.34–43

³⁴ Then Peter began to speak to them: 'I truly understand that God shows no partiality, ³⁵ but in every nation anyone who fears him and does what is right is acceptable to him. ³⁶ You know the message he sent to the people of Israel, preaching peace by Jesus Christ—he is Lord of all. ³⁷ That message spread throughout Judea, beginning in Galilee after the baptism that John announced: ³⁸ how God anointed Jesus of Nazareth with the Holy Spirit and with power; how he went about doing good and healing all who were oppressed by the devil, for God was with him. ³⁹ We are witnesses to all that he did both in Judea and in Jerusalem. They put him to death by hanging him on a tree; ⁴⁰ but God raised him on the third day and allowed him to appear, ⁴¹ not to all the people but to us who were chosen by God as witnesses, and who ate and drank with him after he rose from the dead.

⁴² He commanded us to preach to the people and to testify that he is the one ordained by God as judge of the living and the dead. ⁴³ All the prophets testify about him that everyone who believes in him receives forgiveness of sins through his name.'

GOSPEL

EITHER   John 20.1–18

¹ Early on the first day of the week, while it was still dark, Mary Magdalene came to the tomb and saw that the stone had been removed from the tomb. ² So she ran and went to Simon Peter and the other disciple, the one whom Jesus loved, and said to them, 'They have taken the Lord out of the tomb, and we do not know where they have laid him.' ³ Then Peter and the other disciple set out and went towards the tomb. ⁴ The two were running together, but the other disciple outran Peter and reached the tomb first. ⁵ He bent down to look in and saw the linen wrappings lying there, but he did not go in. ⁶ Then Simon Peter came, following him, and went into the tomb. He saw the linen wrappings lying there, ⁷ and the cloth that had been on Jesus' head, not lying with the linen wrappings but rolled up in a place by itself. ⁸ Then the other disciple, who reached the tomb first, also went in, and he saw and believed; ⁹ for as yet they did not understand the scripture, that he must rise from the dead. ¹⁰ Then the disciples returned to their homes.

¹¹ But Mary stood weeping outside the tomb. As she wept, she bent over to look into the tomb; ¹² and she saw two angels in white, sitting where the body of Jesus had been lying, one at the head and the other at the feet. ¹³ They said to her, 'Woman, why are you weeping?' She said to them, 'They have taken away my Lord, and I do not know where they have laid him.' ¹⁴ When she had said this, she turned round and saw Jesus standing there, but she did not know that it was Jesus. ¹⁵ Jesus said to her, 'Woman, why are you weeping? For whom are you looking?' Supposing him to be the gardener, she said to him, 'Sir, if you have carried him away, tell me where you have laid him, and I will take him away.' ¹⁶ Jesus said to her, 'Mary!' She turned and said to him in Hebrew, 'Rabbouni!' (which means Teacher). ¹⁷ Jesus said to her, 'Do not hold on to me, because I have not yet ascended to the Father. But go to my brothers and say to them, "I am ascending to my Father and your Father, to my God and your God." ' ¹⁸ Mary Magdalene went and announced to the disciples, 'I have seen the Lord'; and she told them that he had said these things to her.

OR
Matthew 28.1–10

[1] After the sabbath, as the first day of the week was dawning, Mary Magdalene and the other Mary went to see the tomb. [2] And suddenly there was a great earthquake; for an angel of the Lord, descending from heaven, came and rolled back the stone and sat on it. [3] His appearance was like lightning, and his clothing white as snow. [4] For fear of him the guards shook and became like dead men. [5] But the angel said to the women, 'Do not be afraid; I know that you are looking for Jesus who was crucified. [6] He is not here; for he has been raised, as he said. Come, see the place where he lay. [7] Then go quickly and tell his disciples, "He has been raised from the dead, and indeed he is going ahead of you to Galilee; there you will see him." This is my message for you.' [8] So they left the tomb quickly with fear and great joy, and ran to tell his disciples. [9] Suddenly Jesus met them and said, 'Greetings!' And they came to him, took hold of his feet, and worshipped him. [10] Then Jesus said to them, 'Do not be afraid; go and tell my brothers to go to Galilee; there they will see me.'

POST COMMUNION

God of Life,
who for our redemption gave your only-begotten Son
   to the death of the cross,
and by his glorious resurrection
have delivered us from the power of our enemy:
grant us so to die daily to sin,
that we may evermore live with him
   in the joy of his risen life;
through Jesus Christ our Lord.

SECOND SERVICE

Psalms 114; 117
Song of Solomon 3.2–5; 8.6–7
John 20.11–18
if not read at the Principal Service
or
Revelation 1.12–18

THIRD SERVICE

Psalms 105
or
66.1–11
Exodus 14.10–18, 26–15.2
Revelation 15.2–4

OLD TESTAMENT READINGS FOR SUNDAYS IN EASTERTIDE

For those who require an Old Testament reading on the Sundays in Eastertide, provision is made in this table. If used, the reading from Acts must be used as the second reading.

THE SECOND SUNDAY OF EASTER	Exodus 14.10–31; 15.20–21
THE THIRD SUNDAY OF EASTER	Zephaniah 3.14–20
THE FOURTH SUNDAY OF EASTER	Genesis 7
THE FIFTH SUNDAY OF EASTER	Genesis 8.1–19
THE SIXTH SUNDAY OF EASTER	Genesis 8.20–9.17
THE SEVENTH SUNDAY OF EASTER	Ezekiel 36.24–28

THE SECOND SUNDAY OF EASTER

The reading from Acts must be used. The second (New Testament) reading follows or, if the Old Testament reading is used, the Acts reading follows as the second reading.

COLLECT

Almighty Father,
you have given your only Son to die for our sins
and to rise again for our justification:
grant us so to put away the leaven of malice and wickedness
that we may always serve you
in pureness of living and truth;
through the merits of your Son Jesus Christ our Lord,
who is alive and reigns with you,
in the unity of the Holy Spirit,
one God, now and for ever.

READING   Acts 2.14a, 22–32

[14] But Peter, standing with the eleven, raised his voice and addressed them:

[22] 'You that are Israelites, listen to what I have to say: Jesus of Nazareth, a man attested to you by God with deeds of power, wonders, and signs that God did through him among you, as you yourselves know— [23] this man, handed over to you according to the definite plan and foreknowledge of God, you crucified and killed by the hands of those outside the law. [24] But

God raised him up, having freed him from death, because it was impossible for him to be held in its power. [25] For David says concerning him,

"I saw the Lord always before me,
for he is at my right hand so that I will not be shaken;
[26] therefore my heart was glad, and my tongue rejoiced;
moreover, my flesh will live in hope.
[27] For you will not abandon my soul to Hades,
or let your Holy One experience corruption.
[28] You have made known to me the ways of life;
you will make me full of gladness with your presence."

[29] 'Fellow Israelites, I may say to you confidently of our ancestor David that he both died and was buried, and his tomb is with us to this day. [30] Since he was a prophet, he knew that God had sworn with an oath to him that he would put one of his descendants on his throne. [31] Foreseeing this, David spoke of the resurrection of the Messiah, saying,

"He was not abandoned to Hades,
nor did his flesh experience corruption."
[32] This Jesus God raised up, and of that all of us are witnesses.'

PSALM   Psalm 16

1 Protect me, O God, for I take refuge in you;
   I have said to the Lord, 'You are my Lord, my good above all other.'
2 All my delight is upon the godly that are in the land,
   upon those who are noble among the people.
3 But those who run after other gods
   shall have their troubles multiplied.
4 Their libations of blood I will not offer,
   nor take the names of their gods upon my lips.
5 O Lord, you are my portion and my cup;
   it is you who uphold my lot.
6 My boundaries enclose a pleasant land;
   indeed, I have a goodly heritage.
7 I will bless the Lord who gives me counsel;
   my heart teaches me, night after night.
8 I have set the Lord always before me;
   because he is at my right hand I shall not fall.
9 My heart, therefore, is glad and my spirit rejoices;
   my body also shall rest in hope.
10 For you will not abandon me to the grave,
   nor let your holy one see the Pit.

[11] You will show me the path of life;
   in your presence there is fullness of joy, and in your right hand
      are pleasures for evermore.

READING   1 Peter 1.3–9

[3] Blessed be the God and Father of our Lord Jesus Christ! By his great mercy he has given us a new birth into a living hope through the resurrection of Jesus Christ from the dead, [4] and into an inheritance that is imperishable, undefiled, and unfading, kept in heaven for you, [5] who are being protected by the power of God through faith for a salvation ready to be revealed in the last time. [6] In this you rejoice, even if now for a little while you have had to suffer various trials, [7] so that the genuineness of your faith—being more precious than gold that, though perishable, is tested by fire—may be found to result in praise and glory and honour when Jesus Christ is revealed. [8] Although you have not seen him, you love him; and even though you do not see him now, you believe in him and rejoice with an indescribable and glorious joy, [9] for you are receiving the outcome of your faith, the salvation of your souls.

GOSPEL   John 20.19–31

[19] When it was evening on that day, the first day of the week, and the doors of the house where the disciples had met were locked for fear of the Jews, Jesus came and stood among them and said, 'Peace be with you.' [20] After he said this, he showed them his hands and his side. Then the disciples rejoiced when they saw the Lord. [21] Jesus said to them again, 'Peace be with you. As the Father has sent me, so I send you.' [22] When he had said this, he breathed on them and said to them, 'Receive the Holy Spirit. [23] If you forgive the sins of any, they are forgiven them; if you retain the sins of any, they are retained.'

[24] But Thomas (who was called the Twin), one of the twelve, was not with them when Jesus came. [25] So the other disciples told him, 'We have seen the Lord.' But he said to them, 'Unless I see the mark of the nails in his hands, and put my finger in the mark of the nails and my hand in his side, I will not believe.'

[26] A week later his disciples were again in the house, and Thomas was with them. Although the doors were shut, Jesus came and stood among them and said, 'Peace be with you.' [27] Then he said to Thomas, 'Put your finger here and see my hands. Reach out your hand and put it in my side. Do not doubt but believe.' [28] Thomas answered him, 'My Lord and my God!' [29] Jesus

said to him, 'Have you believed because you have seen me? Blessed are those who have not seen and yet have come to believe.'

[30] Now Jesus did many other signs in the presence of his disciples, which are not written in this book. [31] But these are written so that you may come to believe that Jesus is the Messiah, the Son of God, and that through believing you may have life in his name.

POST COMMUNION

Lord God our Father,
through our Saviour Jesus Christ
you have assured your children of eternal life
and in baptism have made us one with him:
deliver us from the death of sin
and raise us to new life in your love,
in the fellowship of the Holy Spirit,
by the grace of our Lord Jesus Christ.

SECOND SERVICE

Psalm 30.1–6
Daniel 6.1–23
or
6.6–23
Mark 15.46–16.8

THIRD SERVICE

Psalm 81.1–10
Exodus 12.1–17
1 Corinthians 5.6b-8

THE THIRD SUNDAY OF EASTER

The reading from Acts must be used. The second (New Testament) reading follows or, if the Old Testament reading is used, the Acts reading follows as the second reading.

COLLECT

Almighty Father,
who in your great mercy gladdened the disciples
    with the sight of the risen Lord:
give us such knowledge of his presence with us,
that we may be strengthened and sustained
    by his risen life
and serve you continually in righteousness and truth;

through Jesus Christ your Son our Lord,
who is alive and reigns with you,
in the unity of the Holy Spirit,
one God, now and for ever.

READING   Acts 2.14a, 36–41

[14] But Peter, standing with the eleven, raised his voice and addressed them:

[36] 'Therefore let the entire house of Israel know with certainty that God has made him both Lord and Messiah, this Jesus whom you crucified.'

[37] Now when they heard this, they were cut to the heart and said to Peter and to the other apostles, 'Brothers, what should we do?' [38] Peter said to them, 'Repent, and be baptized every one of you in the name of Jesus Christ so that your sins may be forgiven; and you will receive the gift of the Holy Spirit. [39] For the promise is for you, for your children, and for all who are far away, everyone whom the Lord our God calls to him.' [40] And he testified with many other arguments and exhorted them, saying, 'Save yourselves from this corrupt generation.' [41] So those who welcomed his message were baptized, and that day about three thousand persons were added.

PSALM   Psalm 116.1–3, 10–17

1   I love the Lord, because he has heard the voice of my supplication,
    because he has inclined his ear to me whenever I called upon him.
2   The cords of death entangled me; the grip of the grave took hold
        of me;
    I came to grief and sorrow.
3   Then I called upon the name of the Lord:
    'O Lord, I pray you, save my life.'

10 How shall I repay the Lord
    for all the good things he has done for me?
11 I will lift up the cup of salvation
    and call upon the name of the Lord.
12 I will fulfil my vows to the Lord
    in the presence of all his people.
13 Precious in the sight of the Lord
    is the death of his servants.
14 O Lord, I am your servant;
    I am your servant and the child of your handmaid; you have freed
        me from my bonds.
15 I will offer you the sacrifice of thanksgiving
    and call upon the name of the Lord.

16 I will fulfil my vows to the Lord
    in the presence of all his people.
17 In the courts of the Lord's house,
    in the midst of you, O Jerusalem. Alleluia!

OR, IF AN ALTERNATIVE TEXT IS PREFERRED   **Psalm 116.1–7**

1 I love the Lord, because he has heard the voice of my supplication,
   because he has inclined his ear to me whenever I called upon him.
2 The cords of death entangled me; the grip of the grave took hold
   of me;
   I came to grief and sorrow.
3 Then I called upon the name of the Lord:
   'O Lord, I pray you, save my life.'
4 Gracious is the Lord and righteous;
   our God is full of compassion.
5 The Lord watches over the innocent;
   I was brought very low and he helped me.
6 Turn again to your rest, O my soul,
   for the Lord has treated you well.
7 For you have rescued my life from death,
   my eyes from tears and my feet from stumbling.

READING   1 Peter 1.17–23

17 If you invoke as Father the one who judges all people impartially according to their deeds, live in reverent fear during the time of your exile. 18 You know that you were ransomed from the futile ways inherited from your ancestors, not with perishable things like silver or gold, 19 but with the precious blood of Christ, like that of a lamb without defect or blemish. 20 He was destined before the foundation of the world, but was revealed at the end of the ages for your sake. 21 Through him you have come to trust in God, who raised him from the dead and gave him glory, so that your faith and hope are set on God.

22 Now that you have purified your souls by your obedience to the truth so that you have genuine mutual love, love one another deeply from the heart. 23 You have been born anew, not of perishable but of imperishable seed, through the living and enduring word of God.

GOSPEL   Luke 24.13–35

13 Now on that same day two of them were going to a village called Emmaus, about seven miles from Jerusalem, 14 and talking with each other about all these things that had happened. 15 While they were talking and

discussing, Jesus himself came near and went with them, [16] but their eyes were kept from recognizing him. [17] And he said to them, 'What are you discussing with each other while you walk along?' They stood still, looking sad. [18] Then one of them, whose name was Cleopas, answered him, 'Are you the only stranger in Jerusalem who does not know the things that have taken place there in these days?' [19] He asked them, 'What things?' They replied, 'The things about Jesus of Nazareth, who was a prophet mighty in deed and word before God and all the people, [20] and how our chief priests and leaders handed him over to be condemned to death and crucified him. [21] But we had hoped that he was the one to redeem Israel. Yes, and besides all this, it is now the third day since these things took place. [22] Moreover, some women of our group astounded us. They were at the tomb early this morning, [23] and when they did not find his body there, they came back and told us that they had indeed seen a vision of angels who said that he was alive. [24] Some of those who were with us went to the tomb and found it just as the women had said; but they did not see him.' [25] Then he said to them, 'Oh, how foolish you are, and how slow of heart to believe all that the prophets have declared! [26] Was it not necessary that the Messiah should suffer these things and then enter into his glory?' [27] Then beginning with Moses and all the prophets, he interpreted to them the things about himself in all the scriptures.

[28] As they came near the village to which they were going, he walked ahead as if he were going on. [29] But they urged him strongly, saying, 'Stay with us, because it is almost evening and the day is now nearly over.' So he went in to stay with them. [30] When he was at the table with them, he took bread, blessed and broke it, and gave it to them. [31] Then their eyes were opened, and they recognized him; and he vanished from their sight. [32] They said to each other, 'Were not our hearts burning within us while he was talking to us on the road, while he was opening the scriptures to us?' [33] That same hour they got up and returned to Jerusalem; and they found the eleven and their companions gathered together. [34] They were saying, 'The Lord has risen indeed, and he has appeared to Simon!' [35] Then they told what had happened on the road, and how he had been made known to them in the breaking of the bread.

POST COMMUNION

Living God,
your Son made himself known to his disciples
in the breaking of bread:
open the eyes of our faith,
that we may see him in all his redeeming work;
who is alive and reigns, now and for ever.

SECOND SERVICE

Psalm 48
Haggai 1.13–2.9
1 Corinthians 3.10–17

If the Second Service is a Eucharist, the
following is read as a Gospel:

John 2.13–22

THIRD SERVICE

Psalm 23
Isaiah 40.1–11
1 Peter 5.1–11

THE FOURTH SUNDAY OF EASTER

The reading from Acts must be used. The second (New Testament) reading follows or,
if the Old Testament reading is used, the Acts reading follows as the second reading.

COLLECT

Almighty God,
whose Son Jesus Christ is the resurrection and the life:
raise us, who trust in him,
from the death of sin to the life of righteousness,
that we may seek those things which are above,
where he reigns with you
in the unity of the Holy Spirit,
one God, now and for ever.

READING   Acts 2.42–47

[42] They devoted themselves to the apostles' teaching and fellowship, to the breaking of bread and the prayers.

[43] Awe came upon everyone, because many wonders and signs were being done by the apostles. [44] All who believed were together and had all things in common; [45] they would sell their possessions and goods and distribute the proceeds to all, as any had need. [46] Day by day, as they spent much time together in the temple, they broke bread at home and ate their food with glad and generous hearts, [47] praising God and having the goodwill of all the people. And day by day the Lord added to their number those who were being saved.

PSALM   Psalm 23

[1] The Lord is my shepherd;
    I shall not be in want.

² He makes me lie down in green pastures
and leads me beside still waters.
³ He revives my soul
and guides me along right pathways for his name's sake.
⁴ Though I walk through the valley of the shadow of death, I shall fear no evil;
for you are with me; your rod and your staff, they comfort me.
⁵ You spread a table before me in the presence of those who trouble me;
you have anointed my head with oil, and my cup is running over.
⁶ Surely your goodness and mercy shall follow me all the days of my life,
and I will dwell in the house of the Lord for ever.

READING   1 Peter 2.19–25

¹⁹ For it is to your credit if, being aware of God, you endure pain while suffering unjustly. ²⁰ If you endure when you are beaten for doing wrong, where is the credit in that? But if you endure when you do right and suffer for it, you have God's approval. ²¹ For to this you have been called, because Christ also suffered for you, leaving you an example, so that you should follow in his steps.
²² 'He committed no sin,
and no deceit was found in his mouth.'
²³ When he was abused, he did not return abuse; when he suffered, he did not threaten; but he entrusted himself to the one who judges justly. ²⁴ He himself bore our sins in his body on the cross, so that, free from sins, we might live for righteousness; by his wounds you have been healed. ²⁵ For you were going astray like sheep, but now you have returned to the shepherd and guardian of your souls.

GOSPEL   John 10.1–10

¹ 'Very truly, I tell you, anyone who does not enter the sheepfold by the gate but climbs in by another way is a thief and a bandit. ² The one who enters by the gate is the shepherd of the sheep. ³ The gatekeeper opens the gate for him, and the sheep hear his voice. He calls his own sheep by name and leads them out. ⁴ When he has brought out all his own, he goes ahead of them, and the sheep follow him because they know his voice. ⁵ They will not follow a stranger, but they will run from him because they do not know the voice of strangers.' ⁶ Jesus used this figure of speech with them, but they did not understand what he was saying to them.

⁷ So again Jesus said to them, 'Very truly, I tell you, I am the gate for the sheep. ⁸ All who came before me are thieves and bandits; but the sheep did not listen to them. ⁹ I am the gate. Whoever enters by me will be saved, and will come in and go out and find pasture. ¹⁰ The thief comes only to steal and kill and destroy. I came that they may have life, and have it abundantly.'

POST COMMUNION

Merciful Father,
you gave your Son Jesus Christ to be the good shepherd,
and in his love for us to lay down his life and rise again:
keep us always under his protection,
and give us grace to follow in his steps;
through Jesus Christ our Lord.

SECOND SERVICE

Psalm 29.1–10
Ezra 3.1–13
Ephesians 2.11–22

If the Second Service is a Eucharist, the following is read as a Gospel:

Luke 19.37–48

THIRD SERVICE

Psalm 106.6–24
Nehemiah 9.6–15
1 Corinthians 10.1–13

THE FIFTH SUNDAY OF EASTER

The reading from Acts must be used. The second (New Testament) reading follows or, if the Old Testament reading is used, the Acts reading follows as the second reading.

COLLECT

Almighty God,
who through your only-begotten Son Jesus Christ
have overcome death and opened to us
    the gate of everlasting life:
grant that, as by your grace going before us
    you put into our minds good desires,
so by your continual help
we may bring them to good effect;
through Jesus Christ our risen Lord,
who is alive and reigns with you,
in the unity of the Holy Spirit,
one God, now and for ever.

READING   Acts 7.55–60

⁵⁵ But filled with the Holy Spirit, he gazed into heaven and saw the glory of God and Jesus standing at the right hand of God. ⁵⁶ 'Look,' he said, 'I see the heavens opened and the Son of Man standing at the right hand of God!' ⁵⁷ But they covered their ears, and with a loud shout all rushed together against him. ⁵⁸ Then they dragged him out of the city and began to stone him; and the witnesses laid their coats at the feet of a young man named Saul. ⁵⁹ While they were stoning Stephen, he prayed, 'Lord Jesus, receive my spirit.' ⁶⁰ Then he knelt down and cried out in a loud voice, 'Lord, do not hold this sin against them.' When he had said this, he died.

PSALM   Psalm 31.1–5, [15–16]

1   In you, O Lord, have I taken refuge; let me never be put to shame;
    deliver me in your righteousness.
2   Incline your ear to me;
    make haste to deliver me.
3   Be my strong rock, a castle to keep me safe, for you are my crag
        and my stronghold;
    for the sake of your name, lead me and guide me.
4   Take me out of the net that they have secretly set for me,
    for you are my tower of strength.
5   Into your hands I commend my spirit,
    for you have redeemed me, O Lord, O God of truth.

[15   'My times are in your hand;
    rescue me from the hand of my enemies, and from those who
        persecute me.
16   Make your face to shine upon your servant,
    and in your loving-kindness save me.']

READING   1 Peter 2.2–10

² Like newborn infants, long for the pure, spiritual milk, so that by it you may grow into salvation— ³ if indeed you have tasted that the Lord is good.

⁴ Come to him, a living stone, though rejected by mortals yet chosen and precious in God's sight, and ⁵ like living stones, let yourselves be built into a spiritual house, to be a holy priesthood, to offer spiritual sacrifices acceptable to God through Jesus Christ. ⁶ For it stands in scripture:
    'See, I am laying in Zion a stone,
        a cornerstone chosen and precious;
    and whoever believes in him will not be put to shame.'

[7] To you then who believe, he is precious; but for those who do not believe,

'The stone that the builders rejected
    has become the very head of the corner',

[8] and

'A stone that makes them stumble,
    and a rock that makes them fall.'

They stumble because they disobey the word, as they were destined to do.

[9] But you are a chosen race, a royal priesthood, a holy nation, God's own people, in order that you may proclaim the mighty acts of him who called you out of darkness into his marvellous light.

[10]   Once you were not a people,
    but now you are God's people;
once you had not received mercy,
    but now you have received mercy.

GOSPEL   John 14.1–14

[1] 'Do not let your hearts be troubled. Believe in God, believe also in me. [2] In my Father's house there are many dwelling-places. If it were not so, would I have told you that I go to prepare a place for you? [3] And if I go and prepare a place for you, I will come again and will take you to myself, so that where I am, there you may be also. [4] And you know the way to the place where I am going.' [5] Thomas said to him, 'Lord, we do not know where you are going. How can we know the way?' [6] Jesus said to him, 'I am the way, and the truth, and the life. No one comes to the Father except through me. [7] If you know me, you will know my Father also. From now on you do know him and have seen him.'

[8] Philip said to him, 'Lord, show us the Father, and we will be satisfied.' [9] Jesus said to him, 'Have I been with you all this time, Philip, and you still do not know me? Whoever has seen me has seen the Father. How can you say, "Show us the Father"? [10] Do you not believe that I am in the Father and the Father is in me? The words that I say to you I do not speak on my own; but the Father who dwells in me does his works. [11] Believe me that I am in the Father and the Father is in me; but if you do not, then believe me because of the works themselves. [12] Very truly, I tell you, the one who believes in me will also do the works that I do and, in fact, will do greater works than these, because I am going to the Father. [13] I will do whatever you ask in my name, so that the Father may be glorified in the Son. [14] If in my name you ask me for anything, I will do it.'

POST COMMUNION

Eternal God,
whose Son Jesus Christ is the way, the truth, and the life:
grant us to walk in his way,
to rejoice in his truth,
and to share his risen life;
who is alive and reigns, now and for ever.

SECOND SERVICE

Psalm 147.1–12
Zechariah 4.1–10
Revelation 21.1–14

*If the Second Service is a Eucharist, the
following is read as a Gospel:*

Luke 2.25–32, [33–38]

THIRD SERVICE

Psalm 30
Ezekiel 37.1–12
John 5.19–29

THE SIXTH SUNDAY OF EASTER

*The reading from Acts must be used. The second (New Testament) reading follows or,
if the Old Testament reading is used, the Acts reading follows as the second reading.*

COLLECT

God our redeemer,
you have delivered us from the power of darkness
and brought us into the kingdom of your Son:
grant, that as by his death he has recalled us to life,
so by his continual presence in us he may raise us
    to eternal joy;
through Jesus Christ your Son our Lord,
who is alive and reigns with you,
in the unity of the Holy Spirit,
one God, now and for ever.

READING   Acts 17.22–31

[22] Then Paul stood in front of the Areopagus and said, 'Athenians, I see how extremely religious you are in every way. [23] For as I went through the city and looked carefully at the objects of your worship, I found among them an altar with the inscription, "To an unknown god." What therefore you worship as unknown, this I proclaim to you. [24] The God who made the

world and everything in it, he who is Lord of heaven and earth, does not live in shrines made by human hands, 25 nor is he served by human hands, as though he needed anything, since he himself gives to all mortals life and breath and all things. 26 From one ancestor he made all nations to inhabit the whole earth, and he allotted the times of their existence and the boundaries of the places where they would live, 27 so that they would search for God and perhaps grope for him and find him—though indeed he is not far from each one of us. 28 For "In him we live and move and have our being"; as even some of your own poets have said,

"For we too are his offspring."

29 Since we are God's offspring, we ought not to think that the deity is like gold, or silver, or stone, an image formed by the art and imagination of mortals. 30 While God has overlooked the times of human ignorance, now he commands all people everywhere to repent, 31 because he has fixed a day on which he will have the world judged in righteousness by a man whom he has appointed, and of this he has given assurance to all by raising him from the dead.'

PSALM   Psalm 66.7–18

7 Bless our God, you peoples;
  make the voice of his praise to be heard;
8 Who holds our souls in life,
  and will not allow our feet to slip.
9 For you, O God, have proved us;
  you have tried us just as silver is tried.
10 You brought us into the snare;
  you laid heavy burdens upon our backs.
11 You let enemies ride over our heads; we went through fire and
    water;
  but you brought us out into a place of refreshment.
12 I will enter your house with burnt-offerings and will pay you my
    vows,
  which I promised with my lips and spoke with my mouth when I
    was in trouble.
13 I will offer you sacrifices of fat beasts with the smoke of rams;
  I will give you oxen and goats.
14 Come and listen, all you who fear God,
  and I will tell you what he has done for me.
15 I called out to him with my mouth,
  and his praise was on my tongue.
16 If I had found evil in my heart,
  the Lord would not have heard me;

17 But in truth God has heard me;
he has attended to the voice of my prayer.
18 Blessèd be God, who has not rejected my prayer,
nor withheld his love from me.

READING   1 Peter 3.13–22

13 Now who will harm you if you are eager to do what is good? 14 But even if you do suffer for doing what is right, you are blessed. Do not fear what they fear, and do not be intimidated, 15 but in your hearts sanctify Christ as Lord. Always be ready to make your defence to anyone who demands from you an account of the hope that is in you; 16 yet do it with gentleness and reverence. Keep your conscience clear, so that, when you are maligned, those who abuse you for your good conduct in Christ may be put to shame. 17 For it is better to suffer for doing good, if suffering should be God's will, than to suffer for doing evil. 18 For Christ also suffered for sins once for all, the righteous for the unrighteous, in order to bring you to God. He was put to death in the flesh, but made alive in the spirit, 19 in which also he went and made a proclamation to the spirits in prison, 20 who in former times did not obey, when God waited patiently in the days of Noah, during the building of the ark, in which a few, that is, eight people, were saved through water. 21 And baptism, which this prefigured, now saves you—not as a removal of dirt from the body, but as an appeal to God for a good conscience, through the resurrection of Jesus Christ, 22 who has gone into heaven and is at the right hand of God, with angels, authorities, and powers made subject to him.

GOSPEL   John 14.15–21

15 'If you love me, you will keep my commandments. 16 And I will ask the Father, and he will give you another Advocate, to be with you for ever. 17 This is the Spirit of truth, whom the world cannot receive, because it neither sees him nor knows him. You know him, because he abides with you, and he will be in you.

18 'I will not leave you orphaned; I am coming to you. 19 In a little while the world will no longer see me, but you will see me; because I live, you also will live. 20 On that day you will know that I am in my Father, and you in me, and I in you. 21 They who have my commandments and keep them are those who love me; and those who love me will be loved by my Father, and I will love them and reveal myself to them.'

POST COMMUNION

God our Father,
whose Son Jesus Christ gives the water of eternal life:
may we thirst for you,
the spring of life and source of goodness,
through him who is alive and reigns, now and for ever.

SECOND SERVICE   THIRD SERVICE

Psalms 87; 36.5–10   **Psalm 73.21–29**
Zechariah 8.1–13   **Job 14.1–2, 7–15; 19.23–27a**
Revelation 21.22–22.5   **1 Thessalonians 4.13–18**

*If the Second Service is a Eucharist, the
following is read as a Gospel:*

John 21.1–14

ASCENSION DAY

COLLECT

Grant, we pray, almighty God,
that as we believe your only-begotten Son
    our Lord Jesus Christ
to have ascended into the heavens,
so we in heart and mind may also ascend
and with him continually dwell;
who is alive and reigns with you,
in the unity of the Holy Spirit,
one God, now and for ever.

The reading from Acts must be used as either the first or second reading

READING

EITHER   **Acts 1.1–11**

[1] In the first book, Theophilus, I wrote about all that Jesus did and taught
from the beginning [2] until the day when he was taken up to heaven, after
giving instructions through the Holy Spirit to the apostles whom he had

chosen. [3] After his suffering he presented himself alive to them by many convincing proofs, appearing to them over the course of forty days and speaking about the kingdom of God. [4] While staying with them, he ordered them not to leave Jerusalem, but to wait there for the promise of the Father. 'This', he said, 'is what you have heard from me; [5] for John baptized with water, but you will be baptized with the Holy Spirit not many days from now.'

[6] So when they had come together, they asked him, 'Lord, is this the time when you will restore the kingdom to Israel?' [7] He replied, 'It is not for you to know the times or periods that the Father has set by his own authority. [8] But you will receive power when the Holy Spirit has come upon you; and you will be my witnesses in Jerusalem, in all Judea and Samaria, and to the ends of the earth.' [9] When he had said this, as they were watching, he was lifted up, and a cloud took him out of their sight. [10] While he was going and they were gazing up towards heaven, suddenly two men in white robes stood by them. [11] They said, 'Men of Galilee, why do you stand looking up towards heaven? This Jesus, who has been taken up from you into heaven, will come in the same way as you saw him go into heaven.'

OR   **Daniel 7.9–14**

[9] As I watched,
  thrones were set in place,
    and an Ancient One took his throne;
  his clothing was white as snow,
    and the hair of his head like pure wool;
  his throne was fiery flames,
    and its wheels were burning fire.
[10] A stream of fire issued
    and flowed out from his presence.
  A thousand thousand served him,
    and ten thousand times ten thousand stood attending him.
  The court sat in judgement,
    and the books were opened.
[11] I watched then because of the noise of the arrogant words that the horn was speaking. And as I watched, the beast was put to death, and its body destroyed and given over to be burned with fire. [12] As for the rest of the beasts, their dominion was taken away, but their lives were prolonged for a season and a time. [13] As I watched in the night visions,
  I saw one like a human being
    coming with the clouds of heaven.
  And he came to the Ancient One
    and was presented before him.

14 To him was given dominion
  and glory and kingship,
that all peoples, nations, and languages
  should serve him.
His dominion is an everlasting dominion
  that shall not pass away,
and his kingship is one
  that shall never be destroyed.

PSALM

EITHER   **Psalm 47**

1 Clap your hands, all you peoples;
  shout to God with a cry of joy.
2 For the Lord Most High is to be feared;
  he is the great king over all the earth.
3 He subdues the peoples under us,
  and the nations under our feet.
4 He chooses our inheritance for us,
  the pride of Jacob whom he loves.
5 God has gone up with a shout,
  the Lord with the sound of the ram's-horn.
6 Sing praises to God, sing praises;
  sing praises to our king, sing praises.
7 For God is king of all the earth;
  sing praises with all your skill.
8 God reigns over the nations;
  God sits upon his holy throne.
9 The nobles of the peoples have gathered together
  with the people of the God of Abraham.
10 The rulers of the earth belong to God,
  and he is highly exalted.

OR   **Psalm 93**

1 The Lord is king; he has put on splendid apparel;
  the Lord has put on his apparel and girded himself with strength.
2 He has made the whole world so sure
  that it cannot be moved;
3 Ever since the world began, your throne has been established;
  you are from everlasting.

4 The waters have lifted up, O Lord, the waters have lifted up their
   voice;
   the waters have lifted up their pounding waves.
5 Mightier than the sound of many waters, mightier than the
   breakers of the sea,
   mightier is the Lord who dwells on high.
6 Your testimonies are very sure,
   and holiness adorns your house, O Lord, for ever and for evermore.

READING

EITHER   Ephesians 1.15–23

15 I have heard of your faith in the Lord Jesus and your love towards all the
saints, and for this reason 16 I do not cease to give thanks for you as I
remember you in my prayers. 17 I pray that the God of our Lord Jesus Christ,
the Father of glory, may give you a spirit of wisdom and revelation as you
come to know him, 18 so that, with the eyes of your heart enlightened, you
may know what is the hope to which he has called you, what are the
riches of his glorious inheritance among the saints, 19 and what is the
immeasurable greatness of his power for us who believe, according to the
working of his great power. 20 God put this power to work in Christ when
he raised him from the dead and seated him at his right hand in the
heavenly places, 21 far above all rule and authority and power and
dominion, and above every name that is named, not only in this age but
also in the age to come. 22 And he has put all things under his feet and has
made him the head over all things for the church, 23 which is his body, the
fullness of him who fills all in all.

OR   Acts 1.1–11

1 In the first book, Theophilus, I wrote about all that Jesus did and taught
from the beginning 2 until the day when he was taken up to heaven, after
giving instructions through the Holy Spirit to the apostles whom he had
chosen. 3 After his suffering he presented himself alive to them by many
convincing proofs, appearing to them over the course of forty days and
speaking about the kingdom of God. 4 While staying with them, he ordered
them not to leave Jerusalem, but to wait there for the promise of the Father.
'This', he said, 'is what you have heard from me; 5 for John baptized with
water, but you will be baptized with the Holy Spirit not many days from
now.'

6 So when they had come together, they asked him, 'Lord, is this the time
when you will restore the kingdom to Israel?' 7 He replied, 'It is not for you

to know the times or periods that the Father has set by his own authority. [8] But you will receive power when the Holy Spirit has come upon you; and you will be my witnesses in Jerusalem, in all Judea and Samaria, and to the ends of the earth.' [9] When he had said this, as they were watching, he was lifted up, and a cloud took him out of their sight. [10] While he was going and they were gazing up towards heaven, suddenly two men in white robes stood by them. [11] They said, 'Men of Galilee, why do you stand looking up towards heaven? This Jesus, who has been taken up from you into heaven, will come in the same way as you saw him go into heaven.'

GOSPEL   Luke 24.44–53

[44] Then he said to them, 'These are my words that I spoke to you while I was still with you—that everything written about me in the law of Moses, the prophets, and the psalms must be fulfilled.' [45] Then he opened their minds to understand the scriptures, [46] and he said to them, 'Thus it is written, that the Messiah is to suffer and to rise from the dead on the third day, [47] and that repentance and forgiveness of sins is to be proclaimed in his name to all nations, beginning from Jerusalem. [48] You are witnesses of these things. [49] And see, I am sending upon you what my Father promised; so stay here in the city until you have been clothed with power from on high.'

[50] Then he led them out as far as Bethany, and, lifting up his hands, he blessed them. [51] While he was blessing them, he withdrew from them and was carried up into heaven. [52] And they worshipped him, and returned to Jerusalem with great joy; [53] and they were continually in the temple blessing God.

POST COMMUNION

God our Father,
you have raised our humanity in Christ
and have fed us with the bread of heaven:
mercifully grant that, nourished with such spiritual blessings,
we may set our hearts in the heavenly places;
through Jesus Christ our Lord.

SECOND SERVICE

Psalm 8
Prayer of Azariah 29–37

or

2 Kings 2.1–15
Revelation 5

*If the Second Service is a Eucharist, the
following is read as a Gospel:*

Mark 16.14–20

THIRD SERVICE

Psalm 110
Isaiah 52.7–15
Hebrews 7.[11–25,] 26–28

THE SEVENTH SUNDAY OF EASTER
SUNDAY AFTER ASCENSION DAY

*The reading from Acts must be used. The second (New Testament) reading follows or,
if the Old Testament reading is used, the Acts reading follows as the second reading.*

COLLECT

O God the king of glory,
you have exalted your only Son Jesus Christ
with great triumph to your kingdom in heaven:
we beseech you, leave us not comfortless,
but send your Holy Spirit to strengthen us
and exalt us to the place
   where our Saviour Christ is gone before,
who is alive and reigns with you,
in the unity of the Holy Spirit,
one God, now and for ever.

READING   Acts 1.6–14

⁶ So when they had come together, they asked him, 'Lord, is this the time when you will restore the kingdom to Israel?' ⁷ He replied, 'It is not for you to know the times or periods that the Father has set by his own authority. ⁸ But you will receive power when the Holy Spirit has come upon you; and you will be my witnesses in Jerusalem, in all Judea and Samaria, and to the ends of the earth.' ⁹ When he had said this, as they were watching, he was lifted up, and a cloud took him out of their sight. ¹⁰ While he was going and they were gazing up towards heaven, suddenly two men in white robes

stood by them. [11] They said, 'Men of Galilee, why do you stand looking up towards heaven? This Jesus, who has been taken up from you into heaven, will come in the same way as you saw him go into heaven.'

[12] Then they returned to Jerusalem from the mount called Olivet, which is near Jerusalem, a sabbath day's journey away. [13] When they had entered the city, they went to the room upstairs where they were staying, Peter, and John, and James, and Andrew, Philip and Thomas, Bartholomew and Matthew, James son of Alphaeus, and Simon the Zealot, and Judas son of James. [14] All these were constantly devoting themselves to prayer, together with certain women, including Mary the mother of Jesus, as well as his brothers.

PSALM   Psalm 68.1–10, [33–36]

1   Let God arise and let his enemies be scattered;
    let those who hate him flee before him.
2   Let them vanish like smoke when the wind drives it away;
    as the wax melts at the fire, so let the wicked perish at the presence
      of God.
3   But let the righteous be glad and rejoice before God;
    let them also be merry and joyful.
4   Sing to God, sing praises to his name; exalt him who rides upon
      the heavens;
    Yahweh is his name, rejoice before him!
5   Father of orphans, defender of widows,
    God in his holy habitation!
6   God gives the solitary a home and brings forth prisoners into
      freedom;
    but the rebels shall live in dry places.
7   O God, when you went forth before your people,
    when you marched through the wilderness,
8   The earth shook and the skies poured down rain, at the presence
      of God, the God of Sinai,
    at the presence of God, the God of Israel.
9   You sent a gracious rain, O God, upon your inheritance;
    you refreshed the land when it was weary.
10 Your people found their home in it;
    in your goodness, O God, you have made provision for the poor.

[33 Sing to God, O kingdoms of the earth;
    sing praises to the Lord.
34 He rides in the heavens, the ancient heavens;
    he sends forth his voice, his mighty voice.

³⁵ Ascribe power to God;
   his majesty is over Israel; his strength is in the skies.
³⁶ How wonderful is God in his holy places!
   the God of Israel giving strength and power to his people! Blessèd
      be God!]

READING   1 Peter 4.12‑14; 5.6‑11

¹² Beloved, do not be surprised at the fiery ordeal that is taking place among you to test you, as though something strange were happening to you. ¹³ But rejoice in so far as you are sharing Christ's sufferings, so that you may also be glad and shout for joy when his glory is revealed. ¹⁴ If you are reviled for the name of Christ, you are blessed, because the spirit of glory, which is the Spirit of God, is resting on you.

⁶ Humble yourselves therefore under the mighty hand of God, so that he may exalt you in due time. ⁷ Cast all your anxiety on him, because he cares for you. ⁸ Discipline yourselves; keep alert. Like a roaring lion your adversary the devil prowls around, looking for someone to devour. ⁹ Resist him, steadfast in your faith, for you know that your brothers and sisters throughout the world are undergoing the same kinds of suffering. ¹⁰ And after you have suffered for a little while, the God of all grace, who has called you to his eternal glory in Christ, will himself restore, support, strengthen, and establish you. ¹¹ To him be the power for ever and ever. Amen.

GOSPEL   John 17.1‑11

¹ After Jesus had spoken these words, he looked up to heaven and said, 'Father, the hour has come; glorify your Son so that the Son may glorify you, ² since you have given him authority over all people, to give eternal life to all whom you have given him. ³ And this is eternal life, that they may know you, the only true God, and Jesus Christ whom you have sent. ⁴ I glorified you on earth by finishing the work that you gave me to do. ⁵ So now, Father, glorify me in your own presence with the glory that I had in your presence before the world existed.

⁶ 'I have made your name known to those whom you gave me from the world. They were yours, and you gave them to me, and they have kept your word. ⁷ Now they know that everything you have given me is from you; ⁸ for the words that you gave to me I have given to them, and they have received them and know in truth that I came from you; and they have believed that you sent me. ⁹ I am asking on their behalf; I am not asking on behalf of the world, but on behalf of those whom you gave me, because they are yours.

¹⁰ All mine are yours, and yours are mine; and I have been glorified in them.
¹¹ And now I am no longer in the world, but they are in the world, and I am coming to you. Holy Father, protect them in your name that you have given me, so that they may be one, as we are one.'

POST COMMUNION

Eternal God, giver of love and power,
your Son Jesus Christ has sent us into all the world
to preach the gospel of his kingdom:
confirm us in this mission,
and help us to live the good news we proclaim;
through Jesus Christ our Lord.

SECOND SERVICE

Psalm 47
2 Samuel 23.1–5
Ephesians 1.15–23

If the Second Service is a Eucharist, the following is read as a Gospel:

Mark 16.14–20

THIRD SERVICE

Psalm 104.27–37
Isaiah 65.17–25
Revelation 21.1–8

DAY OF PENTECOST
WHIT SUNDAY

COLLECT

God, who as at this time
taught the hearts of your faithful people
by sending to them the light of your Holy Spirit:
grant us by the same Spirit
to have a right judgement in all things
and evermore to rejoice in his holy comfort;
through the merits of Christ Jesus our Saviour,
who is alive and reigns with you,
in the unity of the Holy Spirit,
one God, now and for ever.

The reading from Acts must be used as either the first or second reading

READING

Acts 2.1–21

[1] When the day of Pentecost had come, they were all together in one place. [2] And suddenly from heaven there came a sound like the rush of a violent wind, and it filled the entire house where they were sitting. [3] Divided tongues, as of fire, appeared among them, and a tongue rested on each of them. [4] All of them were filled with the Holy Spirit and began to speak in other languages, as the Spirit gave them ability.

[5] Now there were devout Jews from every nation under heaven living in Jerusalem. [6] And at this sound the crowd gathered and was bewildered, because each one heard them speaking in the native language of each. [7] Amazed and astonished, they asked, 'Are not all these who are speaking Galileans? [8] And how is it that we hear, each of us, in our own native language? [9] Parthians, Medes, Elamites, and residents of Mesopotamia, Judea and Cappadocia, Pontus and Asia, [10] Phrygia and Pamphylia, Egypt and the parts of Libya belonging to Cyrene, and visitors from Rome, both Jews and proselytes, [11] Cretans and Arabs—in our own languages we hear them speaking about God's deeds of power.' [12] All were amazed and perplexed, saying to one another, 'What does this mean?' [13] But others sneered and said, 'They are filled with new wine.'

[14] But Peter, standing with the eleven, raised his voice and addressed them: 'Men of Judea and all who live in Jerusalem, let this be known to you, and listen to what I say. [15] Indeed, these are not drunk, as you suppose, for it is only nine o'clock in the morning. [16] No, this is what was spoken through the prophet Joel:

[17]   "In the last days it will be, God declares,
        that I will pour out my Spirit upon all flesh,
            and your sons and your daughters shall prophesy,
        and your young men shall see visions,
            and your old men shall dream dreams.
[18]   Even upon my slaves, both men and women,
            in those days I will pour out my Spirit;
                and they shall prophesy.
[19]   And I will show portents in the heaven above
            and signs on the earth below,
                blood, and fire, and smoky mist.

20 The sun shall be turned to darkness
and the moon to blood,
before the coming of the Lord's great and glorious day.
21 Then everyone who calls on the name of the Lord shall be saved." '

OR   **Numbers 11.24–30**

24 So Moses went out and told the people the words of the LORD; and he gathered seventy elders of the people, and placed them all around the tent. 25 Then the LORD came down in the cloud and spoke to him, and took some of the spirit that was on him and put it on the seventy elders; and when the spirit rested upon them, they prophesied. But they did not do so again.

26 Two men remained in the camp, one named Eldad, and the other named Medad, and the spirit rested on them; they were among those registered, but they had not gone out to the tent, and so they prophesied in the camp. 27 And a young man ran and told Moses, 'Eldad and Medad are prophesying in the camp.' 28 And Joshua son of Nun, the assistant of Moses, one of his chosen men, said, 'My lord Moses, stop them!' 29 But Moses said to him, 'Are you jealous for my sake? Would that all the LORD's people were prophets, and that the LORD would put his spirit on them!' 30 And Moses and the elders of Israel returned to the camp.

PSALM   **Psalm 104.25–35, [36,] 37**

25 O Lord, how manifold are your works!
in wisdom you have made them all; the earth is full of your
creatures.
26 Yonder is the great and wide sea with its living things too many
to number,
creatures both small and great.
27 There move the ships, and there is that Leviathan,
which you have made for the sport of it.
28 All of them look to you
to give them their food in due season.
29 You give it to them, they gather it;
you open your hand and they are filled with good things.
30 You hide your face and they are terrified;
you take away their breath and they die and return to their dust.
31 You send forth your Spirit and they are created;
and so you renew the face of the earth.
32 May the glory of the Lord endure for ever;
may the Lord rejoice in all his works.

33 He looks at the earth and it trembles;
   he touches the mountains and they smoke.
34 I will sing to the Lord as long as I live;
   I will praise my God while I have my being.
35 May these words of mine please him;
   I will rejoice in the Lord.
[36 Let sinners be consumed out of the earth,
   and the wicked be no more.]
37 Bless the Lord, O my soul.
   Alleluia!

READING

EITHER   ### 1 Corinthians 12.3b–13

3 No one can say 'Jesus is Lord' except by the Holy Spirit.

4 Now there are varieties of gifts, but the same Spirit; 5 and there are varieties of services, but the same Lord; 6 and there are varieties of activities, but it is the same God who activates all of them in everyone. 7 To each is given the manifestation of the Spirit for the common good. 8 To one is given through the Spirit the utterance of wisdom, and to another the utterance of knowledge according to the same Spirit, 9 to another faith by the same Spirit, to another gifts of healing by the one Spirit, 10 to another the working of miracles, to another prophecy, to another the discernment of spirits, to another various kinds of tongues, to another the interpretation of tongues. 11 All these are activated by one and the same Spirit, who allots to each one individually just as the Spirit chooses.

12 For just as the body is one and has many members, and all the members of the body, though many, are one body, so it is with Christ. 13 For in the one Spirit we were all baptized into one body—Jews or Greeks, slaves or free—and we were all made to drink of one Spirit.

OR   ### Acts 2.1–21

1 When the day of Pentecost had come, they were all together in one place. 2 And suddenly from heaven there came a sound like the rush of a violent wind, and it filled the entire house where they were sitting. 3 Divided tongues, as of fire, appeared among them, and a tongue rested on each of them. 4 All of them were filled with the Holy Spirit and began to speak in other languages, as the Spirit gave them ability.

5 Now there were devout Jews from every nation under heaven living in Jerusalem. 6 And at this sound the crowd gathered and was bewildered,

because each one heard them speaking in the native language of each. [7] Amazed and astonished, they asked, 'Are not all these who are speaking Galileans? [8] And how is it that we hear, each of us, in our own native language? [9] Parthians, Medes, Elamites, and residents of Mesopotamia, Judea and Cappadocia, Pontus and Asia, [10] Phrygia and Pamphylia, Egypt and the parts of Libya belonging to Cyrene, and visitors from Rome, both Jews and proselytes, [11] Cretans and Arabs—in our own languages we hear them speaking about God's deeds of power.' [12] All were amazed and perplexed, saying to one another, 'What does this mean?' [13] But others sneered and said, 'They are filled with new wine.'

[14] But Peter, standing with the eleven, raised his voice and addressed them: 'Men of Judea and all who live in Jerusalem, let this be known to you, and listen to what I say. [15] Indeed, these are not drunk, as you suppose, for it is only nine o'clock in the morning. [16] No, this is what was spoken through the prophet Joel:

[17] "In the last days it will be, God declares,
     that I will pour out my Spirit upon all flesh,
         and your sons and your daughters shall prophesy,
     and your young men shall see visions,
         and your old men shall dream dreams.
[18] Even upon my slaves, both men and women,
         in those days I will pour out my Spirit;
             and they shall prophesy.
[19] And I will show portents in the heaven above
         and signs on the earth below,
             blood, and fire, and smoky mist.
[20] The sun shall be turned to darkness
         and the moon to blood,
             before the coming of the Lord's great and glorious day.
[21] Then everyone who calls on the name of the Lord shall be saved." '

GOSPEL

EITHER   John 20.19–23

[19] When it was evening on that day, the first day of the week, and the doors of the house where the disciples had met were locked for fear of the Jews, Jesus came and stood among them and said, 'Peace be with you.' [20] After he said this, he showed them his hands and his side. Then the disciples rejoiced when they saw the Lord. [21] Jesus said to them again, 'Peace be with you. As the Father has sent me, so I send you.' [22] When he

had said this, he breathed on them and said to them, 'Receive the Holy Spirit. [23] If you forgive the sins of any, they are forgiven them; if you retain the sins of any, they are retained.'

OR   ## John 7.37–39

[37] On the last day of the festival, the great day, while Jesus was standing there, he cried out, 'Let anyone who is thirsty come to me, [38] and let the one who believes in me drink. As the scripture has said, "Out of the believer's heart shall flow rivers of living water." ' [39] Now he said this about the Spirit, which believers in him were to receive; for as yet there was no Spirit, because Jesus was not yet glorified.

POST COMMUNION

Faithful God,
who fulfilled the promises of Easter
by sending us your Holy Spirit
and opening to every race and nation
the way of life eternal:
open our lips by your Spirit,
that every tongue may tell of your glory;
through Jesus Christ our Lord.

SECOND SERVICE

Psalms 67; 133
Joel 2.21–32
Acts 2.14–21, [22–38]

If the Second Service is a Eucharist, the following is read as a Gospel:

Luke 24.44–53

THIRD SERVICE

Psalm 87
Genesis 11.1–9
Acts 10.34–48

TRINITY SUNDAY

COLLECT

Almighty and everlasting God,
you have given us your servants grace,
by the confession of a true faith,
to acknowledge the glory of the eternal Trinity

and in the power of the divine majesty to worship the Unity:
keep us steadfast in this faith,
that we may evermore be defended from all adversities;
through Jesus Christ your Son our Lord,
who is alive and reigns with you,
in the unity of the Holy Spirit,
one God, now and for ever.

READING   Isaiah 40.12–17, 27–31

12 Who has measured the waters in the hollow of his hand
       and marked off the heavens with a span,
    enclosed the dust of the earth in a measure,
       and weighed the mountains in scales
       and the hills in a balance?
13 Who has directed the spirit of the LORD,
       or as his counsellor has instructed him?
14 Whom did he consult for his enlightenment,
       and who taught him the path of justice?
    Who taught him knowledge,
       and showed him the way of understanding?
15 Even the nations are like a drop from a bucket,
       and are accounted as dust on the scales;
       see, he takes up the isles like fine dust.
16 Lebanon would not provide fuel enough,
       nor are its animals enough for a burnt-offering.
17 All the nations are as nothing before him;
       they are accounted by him as less than nothing and emptiness.

27 Why do you say, O Jacob,
       and speak, O Israel,
    'My way is hidden from the LORD,
       and my right is disregarded by my God'?
28 Have you not known? Have you not heard?
    The LORD is the everlasting God,
       the Creator of the ends of the earth.
    He does not faint or grow weary;
       his understanding is unsearchable.
29 He gives power to the faint,
       and strengthens the powerless.
30 Even youths will faint and be weary,
       and the young will fall exhausted;

[31] but those who wait for the LORD shall renew their strength,
　　they shall mount up with wings like eagles,
　they shall run and not be weary,
　　they shall walk and not faint.

PSALM   Psalm 8

[1] O Lord our governor,
　　how exalted is your name in all the world!
[2] Out of the mouths of infants and children
　　your majesty is praised above the heavens.
[3] You have set up a stronghold against your adversaries,
　　to quell the enemy and the avenger.
[4] When I consider your heavens, the work of your fingers,
　　the moon and the stars you have set in their courses,
[5] What are mortals, that you should be mindful of them?
　　mere human beings, that you should seek them out?
[6] You have made them little lower than the angels;
　　you adorn them with glory and honour.
[7] You give them mastery over the works of your hands;
　　and put all things under their feet,
[8] All sheep and oxen,
　　even the wild beasts of the field,
[9] The birds of the air, the fish of the sea,
　　and whatsoever walks in the paths of the sea.
[10] O Lord our governor,
　　how exalted is your name in all the world!

READING   2 Corinthians 13.11–13

[11] Finally, brothers and sisters, farewell. Put things in order, listen to my appeal, agree with one another, live in peace; and the God of love and peace will be with you. [12] Greet one another with a holy kiss. All the saints greet you.

[13] The grace of the Lord Jesus Christ, the love of God, and the communion of the Holy Spirit be with all of you.

GOSPEL   Matthew 28.16–20

[16] Now the eleven disciples went to Galilee, to the mountain to which Jesus had directed them. [17] When they saw him, they worshipped him; but some doubted. [18] And Jesus came and said to them, 'All authority in heaven

and on earth has been given to me. [19] Go therefore and make disciples of all nations, baptizing them in the name of the Father and of the Son and of the Holy Spirit, [20] and teaching them to obey everything that I have commanded you. And remember, I am with you always, to the end of the age.'

POST COMMUNION

Almighty and eternal God,
you have revealed yourself as Father, Son and Holy Spirit,
and live and reign in the perfect unity of love:
hold us firm in this faith,
that we may know you in all your ways
and evermore rejoice in your eternal glory,
who are three Persons yet one God,
now and for ever.

SECOND SERVICE

Psalms 93; 150
Isaiah 6.1–8
John 16.5–15

THIRD SERVICE

Psalm 86.8–13
Exodus 3.1–6, 13–15
John 17.1–11

TABLE OF FIRST SUNDAY AFTER TRINITY DATES AND PROPERS

YEAR	LITURGICAL YEAR	FIRST SUNDAY AFTER TRINITY	PROPER
1999	A	6 Jun	5
2000	B	25 Jun	7
2001	C	17 Jun	6
2002	A	2 Jun	4
2003	B	23 Jun	7
2004	C	13 Jun	6
2005	A	29 May	4
2006	B	18 Jun	6
2007	C	10 Jun	5
2008	A	25 May	(3)*
2009	B	14 Jun	6
2010	C	6 Jun	5
2011	A	26 Jun	8
2012	B	10 Jun	5
2013	C	2 Jun	4
2014	A	22 Jun	7
2015	B	7 Jun	5
2016	C	29 May	4
2017	A	18 Jun	6
2018	B	3 Jun	4
2019	C	23 Jun	7
2020	A	14 Jun	6

* For Proper 3 use Second Sunday before Lent, Option B (8th Sunday after Epiphany)

THE FIRST SUNDAY AFTER TRINITY

COLLECT

O God,
the strength of all those who put their trust in you,
mercifully accept our prayers
and, because through the weakness of our mortal nature
we can do no good thing without you,
grant us the help of your grace,
that in the keeping of your commandments
we may please you both in will and deed;
through Jesus Christ your Son our Lord,
who is alive and reigns with you,
in the unity of the Holy Spirit,
one God, now and for ever.

READINGS

See page 69 and pages 219 to 242 and Table on page 201

POST COMMUNION

Eternal Father,
we thank you for nourishing us
with these heavenly gifts:
may our communion strengthen us in faith,
build us up in hope,
and make us grow in love;
for the sake of Jesus Christ our Lord.

THE SECOND SUNDAY AFTER TRINITY

COLLECT

Lord, you have taught us
that all our doings without love are nothing worth:
send your Holy Spirit
and pour into our hearts that most excellent gift of love,
the true bond of peace and of all virtues,

without which whoever lives is counted dead before you.
Grant this for your only Son Jesus Christ's sake,
who is alive and reigns with you,
in the unity of the Holy Spirit,
one God, now and for ever.

READINGS

See pages 219 to 247 and Table on page 201

POST COMMUNION

Loving Father,
we thank you for feeding us at the supper of your Son:
sustain us with your Spirit,
that we may serve you here on earth
until our joy is complete in heaven,
and we share in the eternal banquet
with Jesus Christ our Lord.

THE THIRD SUNDAY AFTER TRINITY

COLLECT

Almighty God,
you have broken the tyranny of sin
and have sent the Spirit of your Son into our hearts
    whereby we call you Father:
give us grace to dedicate our freedom to your service,
that we and all creation may be brought
    to the glorious liberty of the children of God;
through Jesus Christ your Son our Lord,
who is alive and reigns with you,
in the unity of the Holy Spirit,
one God, now and for ever.

READINGS

See pages 224 to 253 and Table on page 201

POST COMMUNION

O God, whose beauty is beyond our imagining
and whose power we cannot comprehend:
show us your glory as far as we can grasp it,
and shield us from knowing more than we can bear
until we may look upon you without fear;
through Jesus Christ our Saviour.

THE FOURTH SUNDAY AFTER TRINITY

COLLECT

O God, the protector of all who trust in you,
without whom nothing is strong, nothing is holy:
increase and multiply upon us your mercy;
that with you as our ruler and guide
we may so pass through things temporal
that we lose not our hold on things eternal;
grant this, heavenly Father,
for our Lord Jesus Christ's sake,
who is alive and reigns with you,
in the unity of the Holy Spirit,
one God, now and for ever.

READINGS

See pages 229 to 259 and Table on page 201

POST COMMUNION

Eternal God,
comfort of the afflicted and healer of the broken,
you have fed us at the table of life and hope:
teach us the ways of gentleness and peace,
that all the world may acknowledge
the kingdom of your Son Jesus Christ our Lord.

THE FIFTH SUNDAY AFTER TRINITY

COLLECT

Almighty and everlasting God,
by whose Spirit the whole body of the Church
   is governed and sanctified:
hear our prayer which we offer for all your faithful people,
that in their vocation and ministry
they may serve you in holiness and truth
to the glory of your name;
through our Lord and Saviour Jesus Christ,
who is alive and reigns with you,
in the unity of the Holy Spirit,
one God, now and for ever.

READINGS

See pages 236 to 264 and Table on page 201

POST COMMUNION

Grant, O Lord, we beseech you,
that the course of this world may be so peaceably ordered
   by your governance,
that your Church may joyfully serve you
   in all godly quietness;
through Jesus Christ our Lord.

THE SIXTH SUNDAY AFTER TRINITY

COLLECT

Merciful God,
you have prepared for those who love you
such good things as pass our understanding:
pour into our hearts such love toward you
that we, loving you in all things and above all things,
may obtain your promises,
which exceed all that we can desire;

through Jesus Christ your Son our Lord,
who is alive and reigns with you,
in the unity of the Holy Spirit,
one God, now and for ever.

READINGS

See pages 242 to 271 and Table on page 201

POST COMMUNION

God of our pilgrimage,
you have led us to the living water:
refresh and sustain us
as we go forward on our journey,
in the name of Jesus Christ our Lord.

THE SEVENTH SUNDAY AFTER TRINITY

COLLECT

Lord of all power and might,
the author and giver of all good things:
graft in our hearts the love of your name,
increase in us true religion,
nourish us with all goodness,
and of your great mercy keep us in the same;
through Jesus Christ your Son our Lord,
who is alive and reigns with you,
in the unity of the Holy Spirit,
one God, now and for ever.

READINGS

See pages 247 to 275 and Table on page 201

POST COMMUNION

Lord God, whose Son is the true vine and the source of life,
ever giving himself that the world may live:
may we so receive within ourselves
   the power of his death and passion
that, in his saving cup,
   we may share his glory and be made perfect in his love;
for he is alive and reigns, now and for ever.

THE EIGHTH SUNDAY AFTER TRINITY

COLLECT

Almighty Lord and everlasting God,
we beseech you to direct, sanctify and govern
   both our hearts and bodies
in the ways of your laws
   and the works of your commandments;
that through your most mighty protection, both here and ever,
we may be preserved in body and soul;
through our Lord and Saviour Jesus Christ,
who is alive and reigns with you,
in the unity of the Holy Spirit,
one God, now and for ever.

READINGS

See pages 253 to 281 and Table on page 201

POST COMMUNION

Strengthen for service, Lord,
the hands that have taken holy things;
may the ears which have heard your word
   be deaf to clamour and dispute;
may the tongues which have sung your praise
   be free from deceit;

may the eyes which have seen the tokens of your love
    shine with the light of hope;
and may the bodies which have been fed with your body
    be refreshed with the fullness of your life;
glory to you for ever.

THE NINTH SUNDAY AFTER TRINITY

COLLECT

Almighty God,
who sent your Holy Spirit
to be the life and light of your Church:
open our hearts to the riches of your grace,
that we may bring forth the fruit of the Spirit
in love and joy and peace;
through Jesus Christ your Son our Lord,
who is alive and reigns with you,
in the unity of the Holy Spirit,
one God, now and for ever.

READINGS

See pages 259 to 286 and Table on page 201

POST COMMUNION

Holy Father,
who gathered us here around the table of your Son
to share this meal with the whole household of God:
in that new world
    where you reveal the fullness of your peace,
gather people of every race and language
    to share in the eternal banquet
    of Jesus Christ our Lord.

THE TENTH SUNDAY AFTER TRINITY

COLLECT

Let your merciful ears, O Lord,
be open to the prayers of your humble servants;
and that they may obtain their petitions
make them to ask such things as shall please you;
through Jesus Christ your Son our Lord,
who is alive and reigns with you,
in the unity of the Holy Spirit,
one God, now and for ever.

READINGS

See pages 264 to 291 and Table on page 201

POST COMMUNION

God of our pilgrimage,
you have willed that the gate of mercy
should stand open for those who trust in you:
look upon us with your favour
that we who follow the path of your will
may never wander from the way of life;
through Jesus Christ our Lord.

THE ELEVENTH SUNDAY AFTER TRINITY

COLLECT

O God, you declare your almighty power
most chiefly in showing mercy and pity:
mercifully grant to us such a measure of your grace,
that we, running the way of your commandments,
may receive your gracious promises,
and be made partakers of your heavenly treasure;
through Jesus Christ your Son our Lord,

who is alive and reigns with you,
in the unity of the Holy Spirit,
one God, now and for ever.

READINGS

See pages 271 to 298 and Table on page 201

POST COMMUNION

Lord of all mercy,
we your faithful people have celebrated that one true sacrifice
    which takes away our sins and brings pardon and peace:
by our communion
keep us firm on the foundation of the gospel
and preserve us from all sin;
through Jesus Christ our Lord.

THE TWELFTH SUNDAY AFTER TRINITY

COLLECT

Almighty and everlasting God,
you are always more ready to hear than we to pray
and to give more than either we desire or deserve:
pour down upon us the abundance of your mercy,
forgiving us those things of which our conscience is afraid
and giving us those good things
    which we are not worthy to ask
but through the merits and mediation
of Jesus Christ your Son our Lord,
who is alive and reigns with you,
in the unity of the Holy Spirit,
one God, now and for ever.

READINGS

See pages 275 to 302 and Table on page 201

POST COMMUNION

God of all mercy,
in this eucharist you have set aside our sins
and given us your healing:
grant that we who are made whole in Christ
may bring that healing to this broken world,
in the name of Jesus Christ our Lord.

THE THIRTEENTH SUNDAY AFTER TRINITY

COLLECT

Almighty God,
who called your Church to bear witness
that you were in Christ reconciling the world to yourself:
help us to proclaim the good news of your love,
that all who hear it may be drawn to you;
through him who was lifted up on the cross,
and reigns with you in the unity of the Holy Spirit,
one God, now and for ever.

READINGS

See pages 281 to 308 and Table on page 201

POST COMMUNION

God our creator,
you feed your children with the true manna,
the living bread from heaven:
let this holy food sustain us through our earthly pilgrimage
until we come to that place
    where hunger and thirst are no more;
through Jesus Christ our Lord.

THE FOURTEENTH SUNDAY AFTER TRINITY

COLLECT

Almighty God,
whose only Son has opened for us
a new and living way into your presence:
give us pure hearts and steadfast wills
to worship you in spirit and in truth;
through Jesus Christ your Son our Lord,
who is alive and reigns with you,
in the unity of the Holy Spirit,
one God, now and for ever.

READINGS

See pages 286 to 314 and Table on page 201

POST COMMUNION

Lord God, the source of truth and love,
keep us faithful to the apostles' teaching and fellowship,
united in prayer and the breaking of bread,
and one in joy and simplicity of heart,
in Jesus Christ our Lord.

THE FIFTEENTH SUNDAY AFTER TRINITY

COLLECT

God, who in generous mercy sent the Holy Spirit
upon your Church in the burning fire of your love:
grant that your people may be fervent
in the fellowship of the gospel
that, always abiding in you,
they may be found steadfast in faith and active in service;
through Jesus Christ your Son our Lord,
who is alive and reigns with you,
in the unity of the Holy Spirit,
one God, now and for ever.

READINGS

See pages 291 to 320 and Table on page 201

POST COMMUNION

Keep, O Lord, your Church,
  with your perpetual mercy;
and, because without you our human frailty cannot but fall,
keep us ever by your help from all things hurtful,
and lead us to all things profitable to our salvation;
through Jesus Christ our Lord.

THE SIXTEENTH SUNDAY AFTER TRINITY

COLLECT

O Lord, we beseech you mercifully to hear the prayers
  of your people who call upon you;
and grant that they may both perceive and know
  what things they ought to do,
and also may have grace and power
  faithfully to fulfil them;
through Jesus Christ your Son our Lord,
who is alive and reigns with you,
in the unity of the Holy Spirit,
one God, now and for ever.

READINGS

See pages 298 to 327 and Table on page 201

POST COMMUNION

Almighty God,
you have taught us through your Son
that love is the fulfilling of the law:
grant that we may love you with our whole heart
and our neighbours as ourselves;
through Jesus Christ our Lord.

THE SEVENTEENTH SUNDAY AFTER TRINITY

COLLECT

Almighty God,
you have made us for yourself,
and our hearts are restless till they find their rest in you:
pour your love into our hearts and draw us to yourself,
and so bring us at last to your heavenly city
where we shall see you face to face;
through Jesus Christ your Son our Lord,
who is alive and reigns with you,
in the unity of the Holy Spirit,
one God, now and for ever.

READINGS

See pages 302 to 332 and Table on page 201

POST COMMUNION

Lord, we pray that your grace
    may always precede and follow us,
and make us continually to be given to all good works;
through Jesus Christ our Lord.

THE EIGHTEENTH SUNDAY AFTER TRINITY

COLLECT

Almighty and everlasting God,
increase in us your gift of faith
that, forsaking what lies behind
and reaching out to that which is before,
we may run the way of your commandments
and win the crown of everlasting joy;
through Jesus Christ your Son our Lord,

who is alive and reigns with you,
in the unity of the Holy Spirit,
one God, now and for ever.

READINGS

See pages 308 to 338 and Table on page 201

POST COMMUNION

We praise and thank you, O Christ, for this sacred feast:
for here we receive you,
here the memory of your passion is renewed,
here our minds are filled with grace,
and here a pledge of future glory is given,
when we shall feast at that table where you reign
with all your saints for ever.

THE NINETEENTH SUNDAY AFTER TRINITY

COLLECT

O God, forasmuch as without you
we are not able to please you;
mercifully grant that your Holy Spirit
may in all things direct and rule our hearts;
through Jesus Christ your Son our Lord,
who is alive and reigns with you,
in the unity of the Holy Spirit,
one God, now and for ever.

READINGS

See pages 314 to 338 and Table on page 201

POST COMMUNION

Holy and blessed God,
you have fed us with the body and blood of your Son
and filled us with your Holy Spirit:
may we honour you,

not only with our lips
but in lives dedicated to the service
  of Jesus Christ our Lord.

THE TWENTIETH SUNDAY AFTER TRINITY

COLLECT

God, the giver of life,
whose Holy Spirit wells up within your Church:
by the Spirit's gifts equip us to live the gospel of Christ
  and make us eager to do your will,
that we may share with the whole creation
  the joys of eternal life;
through Jesus Christ your Son our Lord,
who is alive and reigns with you,
in the unity of the Holy Spirit,
one God, now and for ever.

READINGS

See pages 320 to 338 and Table on page 201

POST COMMUNION

God our Father,
whose Son, the light unfailing,
has come from heaven to deliver the world
  from the darkness of ignorance:
let these holy mysteries open the eyes of our understanding
that we may know the way of life,
and walk in it without stumbling;
through Jesus Christ our Lord.

THE TWENTY-FIRST SUNDAY AFTER TRINITY

COLLECT

Grant, we beseech you, merciful Lord,
to your faithful people pardon and peace,
that they may be cleansed from all their sins
and serve you with a quiet mind;
through Jesus Christ your Son our Lord,
who is alive and reigns with you,
in the unity of the Holy Spirit,
one God, now and for ever.

READINGS

See pages 327 to 338 and Table on page 201

POST COMMUNION

Father of light,
in whom is no change or shadow of turning,
you give us every good and perfect gift
and have brought us to birth by your word of truth:
may we be a living sign of that kingdom
where your whole creation will be made perfect
    in Jesus Christ our Lord.

THE LAST SUNDAY AFTER TRINITY

COLLECT

Blessed Lord,
who caused all holy scriptures
    to be written for our learning:
help us so to hear them,
to read, mark, learn and inwardly digest them
that, through patience, and the comfort of your holy word,
we may embrace and for ever hold fast
    the hope of everlasting life,
which you have given us in our Saviour Jesus Christ,
who is alive and reigns with you,
in the unity of the Holy Spirit,
one God, now and for ever.

READINGS

See pages 332 to 338 and Table on page 201

POST COMMUNION

God of all grace,
your Son Jesus Christ fed the hungry
with the bread of his life
and the word of his kingdom:
renew your people with your heavenly grace,
and in all our weakness
sustain us by your true and living bread;
who is alive and reigns, now and for ever.

PROPER 4

Sunday between 29 May and 4 June inclusive (if after Trinity Sunday)

COLLECT

See page 202 and Table on page 201

CONTINUOUS

READING   Genesis 6.9–22; 7.24; 8.14–19

9 These are the descendants of Noah. Noah was a righteous man, blameless in his generation; Noah walked with God. 10 And Noah had three sons, Shem, Ham, and Japheth.

11 Now the earth was corrupt in God's sight, and the earth was filled with violence. 12 And God saw that the earth was corrupt; for all flesh had corrupted its ways upon the earth. 13 And God said to Noah, 'I have determined to make an end of all flesh, for the earth is filled with violence because of them; now I am going to destroy them along with the earth. 14 Make yourself an ark of cypress wood; make rooms in the ark, and cover it inside and out with pitch. 15 This is how you are to make it: the length of the ark three hundred cubits, its width fifty cubits, and its height thirty cubits. 16 Make a roof for the ark, and finish it to a cubit above; and put the door of the ark in its side; make it with lower, second, and third decks. 17 For my part, I am going to bring a flood of waters on the earth, to destroy from under heaven all flesh in which is the breath of life; everything that is on the earth shall die. 18 But I will establish my covenant with you; and you shall come into the ark, you, your sons, your wife, and your sons' wives with you. 19 And of every living thing, of all flesh, you shall bring two of every kind into the ark, to keep them alive with you; they shall be male and female. 20 Of the birds according to their kinds, and of the animals according to their kinds, of every creeping thing of the ground according to its kind, two of every kind shall come in to you, to keep them alive. 21 Also take with you every kind of food that is eaten, and store it up; and it shall serve as food for you and for them.' 22 Noah did this; he did all that God commanded him.

24 And the waters swelled on the earth for one hundred and fifty days.

14 In the second month, on the twenty-seventh day of the month, the earth was dry. 15 Then God said to Noah, 16 'Go out of the ark, you and your wife, and your sons and your sons' wives with you. 17 Bring out with you every

living thing that is with you of all flesh—birds and animals and every creeping thing that creeps on the earth—so that they may abound on the earth, and be fruitful and multiply on the earth.' ¹⁸ So Noah went out with his sons and his wife and his sons' wives. ¹⁹ And every animal, every creeping thing, and every bird, everything that moves on the earth, went out of the ark by families.

PSALM   Psalm 46

¹   God is our refuge and strength,
      a very present help in trouble;
²   Therefore we will not fear, though the earth be moved,
      and though the mountains be toppled into the depths of the sea;
³   Though its waters rage and foam,
      and though the mountains tremble at its tumult.
⁴   The Lord of hosts is with us;
      the God of Jacob is our stronghold.
⁵   There is a river whose streams make glad the city of God,
      the holy habitation of the Most High.
⁶   God is in the midst of her; she shall not be overthrown;
      God shall help her at the break of day.
⁷   The nations make much ado and the kingdoms are shaken;
      God has spoken and the earth shall melt away.
⁸   The Lord of hosts is with us;
      the God of Jacob is our stronghold.
⁹   Come now and look upon the works of the Lord,
      what awesome things he has done on earth.
¹⁰ It is he who makes war to cease in all the world;
      he breaks the bow and shatters the spear and burns the shields
        with fire.
¹¹ 'Be still, then, and know that I am God;
      I will be exalted among the nations; I will be exalted in the earth.'
¹² The Lord of hosts is with us;
      the God of Jacob is our stronghold.

READING   Romans 1.16–17; 3.22b–28, [29–31]

¹⁶ For I am not ashamed of the gospel; it is the power of God for salvation to everyone who has faith, to the Jew first and also to the Greek. ¹⁷ For in it the righteousness of God is revealed through faith for faith; as it is written, 'The one who is righteous will live by faith.'

²² For there is no distinction, ²³ since all have sinned and fall short of the glory of God; ²⁴ they are now justified by his grace as a gift, through the

redemption that is in Christ Jesus, [25] whom God put forward as a sacrifice of atonement by his blood, effective through faith. He did this to show his righteousness, because in his divine forbearance he had passed over the sins previously committed; [26] it was to prove at the present time that he himself is righteous and that he justifies the one who has faith in Jesus.

[27] Then what becomes of boasting? It is excluded. By what law? By that of works? No, but by the law of faith. [28] For we hold that a person is justified by faith apart from works prescribed by the law.
[[29] Or is God the God of Jews only? Is he not the God of Gentiles also? Yes, of Gentiles also, [30] since God is one; and he will justify the circumcised on the ground of faith and the uncircumcised through that same faith. [31] Do we then overthrow the law by this faith? By no means! On the contrary, we uphold the law.]

GOSPEL   Matthew 7.21–29

[21] 'Not everyone who says to me, "Lord, Lord", will enter the kingdom of heaven, but only one who does the will of my Father in heaven. [22] On that day many will say to me, "Lord, Lord, did we not prophesy in your name, and cast out demons in your name, and do many deeds of power in your name?" [23] Then I will declare to them, "I never knew you; go away from me, you evildoers."

[24] 'Everyone then who hears these words of mine and acts on them will be like a wise man who built his house on rock. [25] The rain fell, the floods came, and the winds blew and beat on that house, but it did not fall, because it had been founded on rock. [26] And everyone who hears these words of mine and does not act on them will be like a foolish man who built his house on sand. [27] The rain fell, and the floods came, and the winds blew and beat against that house, and it fell—and great was its fall!'

[28] Now when Jesus had finished saying these things, the crowds were astounded at his teaching, [29] for he taught them as one having authority, and not as their scribes.

RELATED

READING   Deuteronomy 11.18–21, 26–28

[18] You shall put these words of mine in your heart and soul, and you shall bind them as a sign on your hand, and fix them as an emblem on your forehead. [19] Teach them to your children, talking about them when you are at home and when you are away, when you lie down and when you rise.

²⁰ Write them on the doorposts of your house and on your gates, ²¹ so that your days and the days of your children may be multiplied in the land that the LORD swore to your ancestors to give them, as long as the heavens are above the earth.

²⁶ See, I am setting before you today a blessing and a curse: ²⁷ the blessing, if you obey the commandments of the LORD your God that I am commanding you today; ²⁸ and the curse, if you do not obey the commandments of the LORD your God, but turn from the way that I am commanding you today, to follow other gods that you have not known.

PSALM   Psalm 31.[1–5,] 19–24

[¹ In you, O Lord, have I taken refuge; let me never be put to shame;
    deliver me in your righteousness.
² Incline your ear to me;
    make haste to deliver me.
³ Be my strong rock, a castle to keep me safe, for you are my crag
        and my stronghold;
    for the sake of your name, lead me and guide me.
⁴ Take me out of the net that they have secretly set for me,
    for you are my tower of strength.
⁵ Into your hands I commend my spirit,
    for you have redeemed me, O Lord, O God of truth.]

¹⁹ How great is your goodness, O Lord, which you have laid up for
        those who fear you;
    which you have done in the sight of all for those who put their
        trust in you.
²⁰ You hide them in the covert of your presence from those who
        slander them;
    you keep them in your shelter from the strife of tongues.
²¹ Blessèd be the Lord!
    for he has shown me the wonders of his love in a besieged city.
²² Yet I said in my alarm, 'I have been cut off from the sight of your
        eyes.'
    Nevertheless, you heard the sound of my entreaty when I cried out
        to you.
²³ Love the Lord, all you who worship him;
    the Lord protects the faithful, but repays to the full those who act
        haughtily.
²⁴ Be strong and let your heart take courage,
    all you who wait for the Lord.

READING   Romans 1.16–17; 3.22b–28, [29–31]

¹⁶ For I am not ashamed of the gospel; it is the power of God for salvation to everyone who has faith, to the Jew first and also to the Greek. ¹⁷ For in it the righteousness of God is revealed through faith for faith; as it is written, 'The one who is righteous will live by faith.'

²² For there is no distinction, ²³ since all have sinned and fall short of the glory of God; ²⁴ they are now justified by his grace as a gift, through the redemption that is in Christ Jesus, ²⁵ whom God put forward as a sacrifice of atonement by his blood, effective through faith. He did this to show his righteousness, because in his divine forbearance he had passed over the sins previously committed; ²⁶ it was to prove at the present time that he himself is righteous and that he justifies the one who has faith in Jesus.

²⁷ Then what becomes of boasting? It is excluded. By what law? By that of works? No, but by the law of faith. ²⁸ For we hold that a person is justified by faith apart from works prescribed by the law.
[²⁹ Or is God the God of Jews only? Is he not the God of Gentiles also? Yes, of Gentiles also, ³⁰ since God is one; and he will justify the circumcised on the ground of faith and the uncircumcised through that same faith. ³¹ Do we then overthrow the law by this faith? By no means! On the contrary, we uphold the law.]

GOSPEL   Matthew 7.21–29

²¹ 'Not everyone who says to me, "Lord, Lord", will enter the kingdom of heaven, but only one who does the will of my Father in heaven. ²² On that day many will say to me, "Lord, Lord, did we not prophesy in your name, and cast out demons in your name, and do many deeds of power in your name?" ²³ Then I will declare to them, "I never knew you; go away from me, you evildoers."

²⁴ 'Everyone then who hears these words of mine and acts on them will be like a wise man who built his house on rock. ²⁵ The rain fell, the floods came, and the winds blew and beat on that house, but it did not fall, because it had been founded on rock. ²⁶ And everyone who hears these words of mine and does not act on them will be like a foolish man who built his house on sand. ²⁷ The rain fell, and the floods came, and the winds blew and beat against that house, and it fell—and great was its fall!'

²⁸ Now when Jesus had finished saying these things, the crowds were astounded at his teaching, ²⁹ for he taught them as one having authority, and not as their scribes.

223

POST COMMUNION

See pages 202 to 203 and Table on page 201

SECOND SERVICE

Psalm 33.[1–12,] 13–22
Ruth 2.1–20a
Luke 8.4–15

THIRD SERVICE

Psalm 37.1–18
Deuteronomy 5.1–21
Acts 21.17–39a

PROPER 5

Sunday between 5 and 11 June inclusive (if after Trinity Sunday)

COLLECT

See pages 202 to 203 and Table on page 201

CONTINUOUS

READING   Genesis 12.1–9

¹ Now the Lord said to Abram, 'Go from your country and your kindred
and your father's house to the land that I will show you. ² I will make of
you a great nation, and I will bless you, and make your name great, so that
you will be a blessing. ³ I will bless those who bless you, and the one who
curses you I will curse; and in you all the families of the earth shall be
blessed.'

⁴ So Abram went, as the Lord had told him; and Lot went with him.
Abram was seventy-five years old when he departed from Haran. ⁵ Abram
took his wife Sarai and his brother's son Lot, and all the possessions that
they had gathered, and the persons whom they had acquired in Haran; and
they set forth to go to the land of Canaan. When they had come to the land
of Canaan, ⁶ Abram passed through the land to the place at Shechem, to
the oak of Moreh. At that time the Canaanites were in the land. ⁷ Then the
Lord appeared to Abram, and said, 'To your offspring I will give this land.'
So he built there an altar to the Lord, who had appeared to him. ⁸ From
there he moved on to the hill country on the east of Bethel, and pitched
his tent, with Bethel on the west and Ai on the east; and there he built an
altar to the Lord and invoked the name of the Lord. ⁹ And Abram journeyed
on by stages towards the Negeb.

PSALM   Psalm 33.1–12

¹ Rejoice in the Lord, you righteous;
   it is good for the just to sing praises.
² Praise the Lord with the harp;
   play to him upon the psaltery and lyre.
³ Sing for him a new song;
   sound a fanfare with all your skill upon the trumpet.
⁴ For the word of the Lord is right,
   and all his works are sure.
⁵ He loves righteousness and justice;
   the loving-kindness of the Lord fills the whole earth.
⁶ By the word of the Lord were the heavens made,
   by the breath of his mouth all the heavenly hosts.
⁷ He gathers up the waters of the ocean as in a water-skin
   and stores up the depths of the sea.
⁸ Let all the earth fear the Lord;
   let all who dwell in the world stand in awe of him.
⁹ For he spoke and it came to pass;
   he commanded and it stood fast.
¹⁰ The Lord brings the will of the nations to naught;
   he thwarts the designs of the peoples.
¹¹ But the Lord's will stands fast for ever,
   and the designs of his heart from age to age.
¹² Happy is the nation whose God is the Lord!
   happy the people he has chosen to be his own!

READING   Romans 4.13–25

¹³ For the promise that he would inherit the world did not come to Abraham or to his descendants through the law but through the righteousness of faith. ¹⁴ If it is the adherents of the law who are to be the heirs, faith is null and the promise is void. ¹⁵ For the law brings wrath; but where there is no law, neither is there violation.

¹⁶ For this reason it depends on faith, in order that the promise may rest on grace and be guaranteed to all his descendants, not only to the adherents of the law but also to those who share the faith of Abraham (for he is the father of all of us, ¹⁷ as it is written, 'I have made you the father of many nations')—in the presence of the God in whom he believed, who gives life to the dead and calls into existence the things that do not exist. ¹⁸ Hoping against hope, he believed that he would become 'the father of many nations', according to what was said, 'So numerous shall your descendants be.' ¹⁹ He did not weaken in faith when he considered his own body, which

was already as good as dead (for he was about a hundred years old), or when he considered the barrenness of Sarah's womb. [20] No distrust made him waver concerning the promise of God, but he grew strong in his faith as he gave glory to God, [21] being fully convinced that God was able to do what he had promised. [22] Therefore his faith 'was reckoned to him as righteousness.' [23] Now the words, 'it was reckoned to him', were written not for his sake alone, [24] but for ours also. It will be reckoned to us who believe in him who raised Jesus our Lord from the dead, [25] who was handed over to death for our trespasses and was raised for our justification.

GOSPEL   Matthew 9.9–13, 18–26

[9] As Jesus was walking along, he saw a man called Matthew sitting at the tax booth; and he said to him, 'Follow me.' And he got up and followed him.

[10] And as he sat at dinner in the house, many tax-collectors and sinners came and were sitting with him and his disciples. [11] When the Pharisees saw this, they said to his disciples, 'Why does your teacher eat with tax-collectors and sinners?' [12] But when he heard this, he said, 'Those who are well have no need of a physician, but those who are sick. [13] Go and learn what this means, "I desire mercy, not sacrifice." For I have come to call not the righteous but sinners.'

[18] While he was saying these things to them, suddenly a leader of the synagogue came in and knelt before him, saying, 'My daughter has just died; but come and lay your hand on her, and she will live.' [19] And Jesus got up and followed him, with his disciples. [20] Then suddenly a woman who had been suffering from haemorrhages for twelve years came up behind him and touched the fringe of his cloak, [21] for she said to herself, 'If I only touch his cloak, I will be made well.' [22] Jesus turned, and seeing her he said, 'Take heart, daughter; your faith has made you well.' And instantly the woman was made well. [23] When Jesus came to the leader's house and saw the flute-players and the crowd making a commotion, [24] he said, 'Go away; for the girl is not dead but sleeping.' And they laughed at him. [25] But when the crowd had been put outside, he went in and took her by the hand, and the girl got up. [26] And the report of this spread throughout that district.

RELATED

READING   Hosea 5.15–6.6

¹⁵ I will return again to my place
    until they acknowledge their guilt and seek my face.
    In their distress they will beg my favour:
¹ 'Come, let us return to the LORD;
    for it is he who has torn, and he will heal us;
    he has struck down, and he will bind us up.
² After two days he will revive us;
    on the third day he will raise us up,
    that we may live before him.
³ Let us know, let us press on to know the LORD;
    his appearing is as sure as the dawn;
    he will come to us like the showers,
    like the spring rains that water the earth.'
⁴ What shall I do with you, O Ephraim?
    What shall I do with you, O Judah?
    Your love is like a morning cloud,
    like the dew that goes away early.
⁵ Therefore I have hewn them by the prophets,
    I have killed them by the words of my mouth,
    and my judgement goes forth as the light.
⁶ For I desire steadfast love and not sacrifice,
    the knowledge of God rather than burnt-offerings.

PSALM   Psalm 50.7–15

⁷ Hear, O my people, and I will speak: 'O Israel, I will bear witness
    against you;
    for I am God, your God.
⁸ I do not accuse you because of your sacrifices;
    your offerings are always before me.
⁹ I will take no bull-calf from your stalls,
    nor he-goats out of your pens;
¹⁰ For the beasts of the forest are mine,
    the herds in their thousands upon the hills.
¹¹ I know every bird in the sky,
    and the creatures of the fields are in my sight.
¹² If I were hungry, I would not tell you,
    for the whole world is mine and all that is in it.

¹³ Do you think I eat the flesh of bulls,
or drink the blood of goats?
¹⁴ Offer to God a sacrifice of thanksgiving
and make good your vows to the Most High.
¹⁵ Call upon me in the day of trouble;
I will deliver you and you shall honour me.'

READING   Romans 4.13–25

¹³ For the promise that he would inherit the world did not come to Abraham or to his descendants through the law but through the righteousness of faith. ¹⁴ If it is the adherents of the law who are to be the heirs, faith is null and the promise is void. ¹⁵ For the law brings wrath; but where there is no law, neither is there violation.

¹⁶ For this reason it depends on faith, in order that the promise may rest on grace and be guaranteed to all his descendants, not only to the adherents of the law but also to those who share the faith of Abraham (for he is the father of all of us, ¹⁷ as it is written, 'I have made you the father of many nations')—in the presence of the God in whom he believed, who gives life to the dead and calls into existence the things that do not exist. ¹⁸ Hoping against hope, he believed that he would become 'the father of many nations', according to what was said, 'So numerous shall your descendants be.' ¹⁹ He did not weaken in faith when he considered his own body, which was already as good as dead (for he was about a hundred years old), or when he considered the barrenness of Sarah's womb. ²⁰ No distrust made him waver concerning the promise of God, but he grew strong in his faith as he gave glory to God, ²¹ being fully convinced that God was able to do what he had promised. ²² Therefore his faith 'was reckoned to him as righteousness.' ²³ Now the words, 'it was reckoned to him', were written not for his sake alone, ²⁴ but for ours also. It will be reckoned to us who believe in him who raised Jesus our Lord from the dead, ²⁵ who was handed over to death for our trespasses and was raised for our justification.

GOSPEL   Matthew 9.9–13, 18–26

⁹ As Jesus was walking along, he saw a man called Matthew sitting at the tax booth; and he said to him, 'Follow me.' And he got up and followed him.

¹⁰ And as he sat at dinner in the house, many tax-collectors and sinners came and were sitting with him and his disciples. ¹¹ When the Pharisees saw this, they said to his disciples, 'Why does your teacher eat with tax-collectors and sinners?' ¹² But when he heard this, he said, 'Those who are

well have no need of a physician, but those who are sick. ¹³ Go and learn what this means, "I desire mercy, not sacrifice." For I have come to call not the righteous but sinners.'

¹⁸ While he was saying these things to them, suddenly a leader of the synagogue came in and knelt before him, saying, 'My daughter has just died; but come and lay your hand on her, and she will live.' ¹⁹ And Jesus got up and followed him, with his disciples. ²⁰ Then suddenly a woman who had been suffering from haemorrhages for twelve years came up behind him and touched the fringe of his cloak, ²¹ for she said to herself, 'If I only touch his cloak, I will be made well.' ²² Jesus turned, and seeing her he said, 'Take heart, daughter; your faith has made you well.' And instantly the woman was made well. ²³ When Jesus came to the leader's house and saw the flute-players and the crowd making a commotion, ²⁴ he said, 'Go away; for the girl is not dead but sleeping.' And they laughed at him. ²⁵ But when the crowd had been put outside, he went in and took her by the hand, and the girl got up. ²⁶ And the report of this spread throughout that district.

POST COMMUNION

See pages 202 to 204 and Table on page 201

SECOND SERVICE

Psalms [39;] 41
1 Samuel 18.1–16
Luke 8.41–56

THIRD SERVICE

Psalm 38
Deuteronomy 6.10–25
Acts 22.22–23.11

PROPER 6

Sunday between 12 and 18 June inclusive (if after Trinity Sunday)

COLLECT

See pages 202 to 204 and Table on page 201

CONTINUOUS

READING   **Genesis 18.1–15; [21.1–7]**

¹ The LORD appeared to Abraham by the oaks of Mamre, as he sat at the entrance of his tent in the heat of the day. ² He looked up and saw three men standing near him. When he saw them, he ran from the tent entrance

to meet them, and bowed down to the ground. ³ He said, 'My lord, if I find favour with you, do not pass by your servant. ⁴ Let a little water be brought, and wash your feet, and rest yourselves under the tree. ⁵ Let me bring a little bread, that you may refresh yourselves, and after that you may pass on—since you have come to your servant.' So they said, 'Do as you have said.' ⁶ And Abraham hastened into the tent to Sarah, and said, 'Make ready quickly three measures of choice flour, knead it, and make cakes.' ⁷ Abraham ran to the herd, and took a calf, tender and good, and gave it to the servant, who hastened to prepare it. ⁸ Then he took curds and milk and the calf that he had prepared, and set it before them; and he stood by them under the tree while they ate.

⁹ They said to him, 'Where is your wife Sarah?' And he said, 'There, in the tent.' ¹⁰ Then one said, 'I will surely return to you in due season, and your wife Sarah shall have a son.' And Sarah was listening at the tent entrance behind him. ¹¹ Now Abraham and Sarah were old, advanced in age; it had ceased to be with Sarah after the manner of women. ¹² So Sarah laughed to herself, saying, 'After I have grown old, and my husband is old, shall I have pleasure?' ¹³ The LORD said to Abraham, 'Why did Sarah laugh, and say, "Shall I indeed bear a child, now that I am old?" ¹⁴ Is anything too wonderful for the LORD? At the set time I will return to you, in due season, and Sarah shall have a son.' ¹⁵ But Sarah denied, saying, 'I did not laugh'; for she was afraid. He said, 'Oh yes, you did laugh.'

[¹ The LORD dealt with Sarah as he had said, and the LORD did for Sarah as he had promised. ² Sarah conceived and bore Abraham a son in his old age, at the time of which God had spoken to him. ³ Abraham gave the name Isaac to his son whom Sarah bore him. ⁴ And Abraham circumcised his son Isaac when he was eight days old, as God had commanded him. ⁵ Abraham was a hundred years old when his son Isaac was born to him. ⁶ Now Sarah said, 'God has brought laughter for me; everyone who hears will laugh with me.' ⁷ And she said, 'Who would ever have said to Abraham that Sarah would nurse children? Yet I have borne him a son in his old age.'

PSALM   Psalm 116.1, 10–17

1   I love the Lord, because he has heard the voice of my supplication,
    because he has inclined his ear to me whenever I called upon him.

10 How shall I repay the Lord
    for all the good things he has done for me?
11 I will lift up the cup of salvation
    and call upon the name of the Lord.

12   I will fulfil my vows to the Lord
     in the presence of all his people.
13   Precious in the sight of the Lord
     is the death of his servants.
14   O Lord, I am your servant;
     I am your servant and the child of your handmaid; you have freed
       me from my bonds.
15   I will offer you the sacrifice of thanksgiving
     and call upon the name of the Lord.
16   I will fulfil my vows to the Lord
     in the presence of all his people.
17   In the courts of the Lord's house,
     in the midst of you, O Jerusalem. Alleluia!

OR, IF AN ALTERNATIVE READING IS REQUIRED   **Psalm 116.9b–16**

9   In my distress I said, 'No one can be trusted.'
10   How shall I repay the Lord
     for all the good things he has done for me?
11   I will lift up the cup of salvation
     and call upon the name of the Lord.
12   I will fulfil my vows to the Lord
     in the presence of all his people.
13   Precious in the sight of the Lord
     is the death of his servants.
14   O Lord, I am your servant;
     I am your servant and the child of your handmaid; you have freed
      me from my bonds.
15   I will offer you the sacrifice of thanksgiving
     and call upon the name of the Lord.
16   I will fulfil my vows to the Lord
     in the presence of all his people.

READING   Romans 5.1–8

1 Therefore, since we are justified by faith, we have peace with God through our Lord Jesus Christ, 2 through whom we have obtained access to this grace in which we stand; and we boast in our hope of sharing the glory of God. 3 And not only that, but we also boast in our sufferings, knowing that suffering produces endurance, 4 and endurance produces character, and character produces hope, 5 and hope does not disappoint us, because God's love has been poured into our hearts through the Holy Spirit that has been given to us.

⁶ For while we were still weak, at the right time Christ died for the ungodly. ⁷ Indeed, rarely will anyone die for a righteous person—though perhaps for a good person someone might actually dare to die. ⁸ But God proves his love for us in that while we still were sinners Christ died for us.

GOSPEL   Matthew 9.35–10.8, [9–23]

³⁵ Then Jesus went about all the cities and villages, teaching in their synagogues, and proclaiming the good news of the kingdom, and curing every disease and every sickness. ³⁶ When he saw the crowds, he had compassion for them, because they were harassed and helpless, like sheep without a shepherd. ³⁷ Then he said to his disciples, 'The harvest is plentiful, but the labourers are few; ³⁸ therefore ask the Lord of the harvest to send out labourers into his harvest.'

¹ Then Jesus summoned his twelve disciples and gave them authority over unclean spirits, to cast them out, and to cure every disease and every sickness. ² These are the names of the twelve apostles: first, Simon, also known as Peter, and his brother Andrew; James son of Zebedee, and his brother John; ³ Philip and Bartholomew; Thomas and Matthew the tax-collector; James son of Alphaeus, and Thaddaeus; ⁴ Simon the Cananaean, and Judas Iscariot, the one who betrayed him.

⁵ These twelve Jesus sent out with the following instructions: 'Go nowhere among the Gentiles, and enter no town of the Samaritans, ⁶ but go rather to the lost sheep of the house of Israel. ⁷ As you go, proclaim the good news, "The kingdom of heaven has come near." ⁸ Cure the sick, raise the dead, cleanse the lepers, cast out demons. You received without payment; give without payment.'
[⁹ 'Take no gold, or silver, or copper in your belts, ¹⁰ no bag for your journey, or two tunics, or sandals, or a staff; for labourers deserve their food. ¹¹ Whatever town or village you enter, find out who in it is worthy, and stay there until you leave. ¹² As you enter the house, greet it. ¹³ If the house is worthy, let your peace come upon it; but if it is not worthy, let your peace return to you. ¹⁴ If anyone will not welcome you or listen to your words, shake off the dust from your feet as you leave that house or town. ¹⁵ Truly I tell you, it will be more tolerable for the land of Sodom and Gomorrah on the day of judgement than for that town.

¹⁶ 'See, I am sending you out like sheep into the midst of wolves; so be wise as serpents and innocent as doves. ¹⁷ Beware of them, for they will hand you over to councils and flog you in their synagogues; ¹⁸ and you will be dragged before governors and kings because of me, as a testimony to them and the Gentiles. ¹⁹ When they hand you over, do not worry about how you are to speak or what you are to say; for what you are to say will be

given to you at that time; [20] for it is not you who speak, but the Spirit of your Father speaking through you. [21] Brother will betray brother to death, and a father his child, and children will rise against parents and have them put to death; [22] and you will be hated by all because of my name. But the one who endures to the end will be saved. [23] When they persecute you in one town, flee to the next; for truly I tell you, you will not have gone through all the towns of Israel before the Son of Man comes.']

RELATED

READING   Exodus 19.2–8a

[2] They had journeyed from Rephidim, entered the wilderness of Sinai, and camped in the wilderness; Israel camped there in front of the mountain. [3] Then Moses went up to God; the LORD called to him from the mountain, saying, 'Thus you shall say to the house of Jacob, and tell the Israelites: [4] You have seen what I did to the Egyptians, and how I bore you on eagles' wings and brought you to myself. [5] Now therefore, if you obey my voice and keep my covenant, you shall be my treasured possession out of all the peoples. Indeed, the whole earth is mine, [6] but you shall be for me a priestly kingdom and a holy nation. These are the words that you shall speak to the Israelites.'

[7] So Moses came, summoned the elders of the people, and set before them all these words that the LORD had commanded him. [8] The people all answered as one: 'Everything that the LORD has spoken we will do.'

PSALM   Psalm 100

[1] Be joyful in the Lord, all you lands;
   serve the Lord with gladness and come before his presence with a song.
[2] Know this: The Lord himself is God;
   he himself has made us and we are his; we are his people and the sheep of his pasture.
[3] Enter his gates with thanksgiving; go into his courts with praise;
   give thanks to him and call upon his name.
[4] For the Lord is good; his mercy is everlasting;
   and his faithfulness endures from age to age.

READING   Romans 5.1–8

¹ Therefore, since we are justified by faith, we have peace with God through our Lord Jesus Christ, ² through whom we have obtained access to this grace in which we stand; and we boast in our hope of sharing the glory of God. ³ And not only that, but we also boast in our sufferings, knowing that suffering produces endurance, ⁴ and endurance produces character, and character produces hope, ⁵ and hope does not disappoint us, because God's love has been poured into our hearts through the Holy Spirit that has been given to us.

⁶ For while we were still weak, at the right time Christ died for the ungodly. ⁷ Indeed, rarely will anyone die for a righteous person—though perhaps for a good person someone might actually dare to die. ⁸ But God proves his love for us in that while we still were sinners Christ died for us.

GOSPEL   Matthew 9.35–10.8, [9–23]

³⁵ Then Jesus went about all the cities and villages, teaching in their synagogues, and proclaiming the good news of the kingdom, and curing every disease and every sickness. ³⁶ When he saw the crowds, he had compassion for them, because they were harassed and helpless, like sheep without a shepherd. ³⁷ Then he said to his disciples, 'The harvest is plentiful, but the labourers are few; ³⁸ therefore ask the Lord of the harvest to send out labourers into his harvest.'

¹ Then Jesus summoned his twelve disciples and gave them authority over unclean spirits, to cast them out, and to cure every disease and every sickness. ² These are the names of the twelve apostles: first, Simon, also known as Peter, and his brother Andrew; James son of Zebedee, and his brother John; ³ Philip and Bartholomew; Thomas and Matthew the tax-collector; James son of Alphaeus, and Thaddaeus; ⁴ Simon the Cananaean, and Judas Iscariot, the one who betrayed him.

⁵ These twelve Jesus sent out with the following instructions: 'Go nowhere among the Gentiles, and enter no town of the Samaritans, ⁶ but go rather to the lost sheep of the house of Israel. ⁷ As you go, proclaim the good news, "The kingdom of heaven has come near." ⁸ Cure the sick, raise the dead, cleanse the lepers, cast out demons. You received without payment; give without payment.'
[⁹ 'Take no gold, or silver, or copper in your belts, ¹⁰ no bag for your journey, or two tunics, or sandals, or a staff; for labourers deserve their food. ¹¹ Whatever town or village you enter, find out who in it is worthy, and stay there until you leave. ¹² As you enter the house, greet

it. ¹³ If the house is worthy, let your peace come upon it; but if it is not worthy, let your peace return to you. ¹⁴ If anyone will not welcome you or listen to your words, shake off the dust from your feet as you leave that house or town. ¹⁵ Truly I tell you, it will be more tolerable for the land of Sodom and Gomorrah on the day of judgement than for that town.

¹⁶ 'See, I am sending you out like sheep into the midst of wolves; so be wise as serpents and innocent as doves. ¹⁷ Beware of them, for they will hand you over to councils and flog you in their synagogues; ¹⁸ and you will be dragged before governors and kings because of me, as a testimony to them and the Gentiles. ¹⁹ When they hand you over, do not worry about how you are to speak or what you are to say; for what you are to say will be given to you at that time; ²⁰ for it is not you who speak, but the Spirit of your Father speaking through you. ²¹ Brother will betray brother to death, and a father his child, and children will rise against parents and have them put to death; ²² and you will be hated by all because of my name. But the one who endures to the end will be saved. ²³ When they persecute you in one town, flee to the next; for truly I tell you, you will not have gone through all the towns of Israel before the Son of Man comes.']

POST COMMUNION

See pages 202 to 204 and Table on page 201

SECOND SERVICE

Psalms [42;] 43
1 Samuel 21.1–15
Luke 11.14–28

THIRD SERVICE

Psalm 45
Deuteronomy 10.12–11.1
Acts 23.12–35

PROPER 7

Sunday between 19 and 25 June inclusive (if after Trinity Sunday)

COLLECT

See pages 202 to 205 and Table on page 201

CONTINUOUS

READING   Genesis 21.8–21

⁸ The child grew, and was weaned; and Abraham made a great feast on the day that Isaac was weaned. ⁹ But Sarah saw the son of Hagar the Egyptian, whom she had borne to Abraham, playing with her son Isaac. ¹⁰ So she said to Abraham, 'Cast out this slave woman with her son; for the son of this slave woman shall not inherit along with my son Isaac.' ¹¹ The matter was very distressing to Abraham on account of his son. ¹² But God said to Abraham, 'Do not be distressed because of the boy and because of your slave woman; whatever Sarah says to you, do as she tells you, for it is through Isaac that offspring shall be named after you. ¹³ As for the son of the slave woman, I will make a nation of him also, because he is your offspring.' ¹⁴ So Abraham rose early in the morning, and took bread and a skin of water, and gave it to Hagar, putting it on her shoulder, along with the child, and sent her away. And she departed, and wandered about in the wilderness of Beer-sheba.

¹⁵ When the water in the skin was gone, she cast the child under one of the bushes. ¹⁶ Then she went and sat down opposite him a good way off, about the distance of a bowshot; for she said, 'Do not let me look on the death of the child.' And as she sat opposite him, she lifted up her voice and wept. ¹⁷ And God heard the voice of the boy; and the angel of God called to Hagar from heaven, and said to her, 'What troubles you, Hagar? Do not be afraid; for God has heard the voice of the boy where he is. ¹⁸ Come, lift up the boy and hold him fast with your hand, for I will make a great nation of him.' ¹⁹ Then God opened her eyes, and she saw a well of water. She went, and filled the skin with water, and gave the boy a drink.

²⁰ God was with the boy, and he grew up; he lived in the wilderness, and became an expert with the bow. ²¹ He lived in the wilderness of Paran; and his mother got a wife for him from the land of Egypt.

PSALM Psalm 86.1–10, [16–17]

1   Bow down your ear, O Lord, and answer me,
    for I am poor and in misery.
2   Keep watch over my life, for I am faithful;
    save your servant who trusts in you.
3   Be merciful to me, O Lord, for you are my God;
    I call upon you all the day long.
4   Gladden the soul of your servant,
    for to you, O Lord, I lift up my soul.
5   For you, O Lord, are good and forgiving,
    and great is your love towards all who call upon you.
6   Give ear, O Lord, to my prayer,
    and attend to the voice of my supplications.
7   In the time of my trouble I will call upon you,
    for you will answer me.
8   Among the gods there is none like you, O Lord,
    nor anything like your works.
9   All nations you have made will come and worship you, O Lord,
    and glorify your name.
10 For you are great; you do wondrous things;
    and you alone are God.

[16 Turn to me and have mercy upon me;
    give your strength to your servant; and save the child of your
      handmaid.
17 Show me a sign of your favour, so that those who hate me may see
      it and be ashamed;
    because you, O Lord, have helped me and comforted me.]

READING Romans 6.1b–11

1 Should we continue in sin in order that grace may abound? 2 By no means! How can we who died to sin go on living in it? 3 Do you not know that all of us who have been baptized into Christ Jesus were baptized into his death? 4 Therefore we have been buried with him by baptism into death, so that, just as Christ was raised from the dead by the glory of the Father, so we too might walk in newness of life.

5 For if we have been united with him in a death like his, we will certainly be united with him in a resurrection like his. 6 We know that our old self was crucified with him so that the body of sin might be destroyed, and we might no longer be enslaved to sin. 7 For whoever has died is freed from sin. 8 But if we have died with Christ, we believe that we will also live with

him. [9] We know that Christ, being raised from the dead, will never die again; death no longer has dominion over him. [10] The death he died, he died to sin, once for all; but the life he lives, he lives to God. [11] So you also must consider yourselves dead to sin and alive to God in Christ Jesus.

GOSPEL   Matthew 10.24–39

[24] 'A disciple is not above the teacher, nor a slave above the master; [25] it is enough for the disciple to be like the teacher, and the slave like the master. If they have called the master of the house Beelzebul, how much more will they malign those of his household!

[26] 'So have no fear of them; for nothing is covered up that will not be uncovered, and nothing secret that will not become known. [27] What I say to you in the dark, tell in the light; and what you hear whispered, proclaim from the housetops. [28] Do not fear those who kill the body but cannot kill the soul; rather fear him who can destroy both soul and body in hell. [29] Are not two sparrows sold for a penny? Yet not one of them will fall to the ground unperceived by your Father. [30] And even the hairs of your head are all counted. [31] So do not be afraid; you are of more value than many sparrows.

[32] 'Everyone therefore who acknowledges me before others, I also will acknowledge before my Father in heaven; [33] but whoever denies me before others, I also will deny before my Father in heaven.

[34] 'Do not think that I have come to bring peace to the earth; I have not come to bring peace, but a sword.
[35]   For I have come to set a man against his father,
      and a daughter against her mother,
      and a daughter-in-law against her mother-in-law;
[36]   and one's foes will be members of one's own household.
[37] Whoever loves father or mother more than me is not worthy of me; and whoever loves son or daughter more than me is not worthy of me; [38] and whoever does not take up the cross and follow me is not worthy of me. [39] Those who find their life will lose it, and those who lose their life for my sake will find it.'

RELATED

READING   Jeremiah 20.7–13

⁷ O Lord, you have enticed me,
    and I was enticed;
  you have overpowered me,
    and you have prevailed.
  I have become a laughing-stock all day long;
    everyone mocks me.
⁸ For whenever I speak, I must cry out,
    I must shout, 'Violence and destruction!'
  For the word of the Lord has become for me
    a reproach and derision all day long.
⁹ If I say, 'I will not mention him,
    or speak any more in his name',
  then within me there is something like a burning fire
    shut up in my bones;
  I am weary with holding it in,
    and I cannot.
¹⁰ For I hear many whispering:
    'Terror is all around!
  Denounce him! Let us denounce him!'
    All my close friends
    are watching for me to stumble.
  'Perhaps he can be enticed,
    and we can prevail against him,
    and take our revenge on him.'
¹¹ But the Lord is with me like a dread warrior;
    therefore my persecutors will stumble,
    and they will not prevail.
  They will be greatly shamed,
    for they will not succeed.
  Their eternal dishonour
    will never be forgotten.
¹² O Lord of hosts, you test the righteous,
    you see the heart and the mind;
  let me see your retribution upon them,
    for to you I have committed my cause.
¹³ Sing to the Lord;
    praise the Lord!
  For he has delivered the life of the needy
    from the hands of evildoers.

PSALM   Psalm 69.8–11, [12–17,] 18–20

8 Surely, for your sake have I suffered reproach,
   and shame has covered my face.
9 I have become a stranger to my own kindred,
   an alien to my mother's children.
10 Zeal for your house has eaten me up;
   the scorn of those who scorn you has fallen upon me.
11 I humbled myself with fasting,
   but that was turned to my reproach.
[12 I put on sack-cloth also,
   and became a byword among them.
13 Those who sit at the gate murmur against me,
   and the drunkards make songs about me.
14 But as for me, this is my prayer to you,
   at the time you have set, O Lord:
15 'In your great mercy, O God,
   answer me with your unfailing help.
16 Save me from the mire; do not let me sink;
   let me be rescued from those who hate me and out of the deep
      waters.
17 Let not the torrent of waters wash over me, neither let the deep
      swallow me up;
   do not let the Pit shut its mouth upon me.']
18 'Answer me, O Lord, for your love is kind;
   in your great compassion, turn to me.
19 Hide not your face from your servant;
   be swift and answer me, for I am in distress.
20 Draw near to me and redeem me;
   because of my enemies deliver me.'

OR, IF AN ALTERNATIVE READING IS PREFERRED   Psalm 69.14–20

14 But as for me, this is my prayer to you,
   at the time you have set, O Lord:
15 'In your great mercy, O God,
   answer me with your unfailing help.
16 Save me from the mire; do not let me sink;
   let me be rescued from those who hate me and out of the deep
      waters.
17 Let not the torrent of waters wash over me, neither let the deep
      swallow me up;
   do not let the Pit shut its mouth upon me.

¹⁸ Answer me, O Lord, for your love is kind;
in your great compassion, turn to me.
¹⁹ Hide not your face from your servant;
be swift and answer me, for I am in distress.
²⁰ Draw near to me and redeem me;
because of my enemies deliver me.'

READING   Romans 6.1b–11

¹ Should we continue in sin in order that grace may abound? ² By no means! How can we who died to sin go on living in it? ³ Do you not know that all of us who have been baptized into Christ Jesus were baptized into his death? ⁴ Therefore we have been buried with him by baptism into death, so that, just as Christ was raised from the dead by the glory of the Father, so we too might walk in newness of life.

⁵ For if we have been united with him in a death like his, we will certainly be united with him in a resurrection like his. ⁶ We know that our old self was crucified with him so that the body of sin might be destroyed, and we might no longer be enslaved to sin. ⁷ For whoever has died is freed from sin. ⁸ But if we have died with Christ, we believe that we will also live with him. ⁹ We know that Christ, being raised from the dead, will never die again; death no longer has dominion over him. ¹⁰ The death he died, he died to sin, once for all; but the life he lives, he lives to God. ¹¹ So you also must consider yourselves dead to sin and alive to God in Christ Jesus.

GOSPEL   Matthew 10.24–39

²⁴ 'A disciple is not above the teacher, nor a slave above the master; ²⁵ it is enough for the disciple to be like the teacher, and the slave like the master. If they have called the master of the house Beelzebul, how much more will they malign those of his household!

²⁶ 'So have no fear of them; for nothing is covered up that will not be uncovered, and nothing secret that will not become known. ²⁷ What I say to you in the dark, tell in the light; and what you hear whispered, proclaim from the housetops. ²⁸ Do not fear those who kill the body but cannot kill the soul; rather fear him who can destroy both soul and body in hell. ²⁹ Are not two sparrows sold for a penny? Yet not one of them will fall to the ground unperceived by your Father. ³⁰ And even the hairs of your head are all counted. ³¹ So do not be afraid; you are of more value than many sparrows.

³² 'Everyone therefore who acknowledges me before others, I also will acknowledge before my Father in heaven; ³³ but whoever denies me before others, I also will deny before my Father in heaven.

³⁴ 'Do not think that I have come to bring peace to the earth; I have not come to bring peace, but a sword.
³⁵ For I have come to set a man against his father,
  and a daughter against her mother,
  and a daughter-in-law against her mother-in-law;
³⁶ and one's foes will be members of one's own household.
³⁷ Whoever loves father or mother more than me is not worthy of me; and whoever loves son or daughter more than me is not worthy of me; ³⁸ and whoever does not take up the cross and follow me is not worthy of me. ³⁹ Those who find their life will lose it, and those who lose their life for my sake will find it.'

POST COMMUNION

See pages 202 to 205 and Table on page 201

SECOND SERVICE

Psalms 46; [48]
1 Samuel 24.1–17
Luke 14.12–24

THIRD SERVICE

Psalm 49
Deuteronomy 11.1–15
Acts 27.1–12

PROPER 8

Sunday between 26 June and 2 July inclusive

COLLECT

See pages 202 to 205 and Table on page 201

CONTINUOUS

READING   Genesis 22.1–14

¹ After these things God tested Abraham. He said to him, 'Abraham!' And he said, 'Here I am.' ² He said, 'Take your son, your only son Isaac, whom you love, and go to the land of Moriah, and offer him there as a burnt-offering on one of the mountains that I shall show you.' ³ So Abraham rose

early in the morning, saddled his donkey, and took two of his young men with him, and his son Isaac; he cut the wood for the burnt-offering, and set out and went to the place in the distance that God had shown him. [4] On the third day Abraham looked up and saw the place far away. [5] Then Abraham said to his young men, 'Stay here with the donkey; the boy and I will go over there; we will worship, and then we will come back to you.' [6] Abraham took the wood of the burnt-offering and laid it on his son Isaac, and he himself carried the fire and the knife. So the two of them walked on together. [7] Isaac said to his father Abraham, 'Father!' And he said, 'Here I am, my son.' He said, 'The fire and the wood are here, but where is the lamb for a burnt-offering?' [8] Abraham said, 'God himself will provide the lamb for a burnt-offering, my son.' So the two of them walked on together.

[9] When they came to the place that God had shown him, Abraham built an altar there and laid the wood in order. He bound his son Isaac, and laid him on the altar, on top of the wood. [10] Then Abraham reached out his hand and took the knife to kill his son. [11] But the angel of the LORD called to him from heaven, and said, 'Abraham, Abraham!' And he said, 'Here I am.' [12] He said, 'Do not lay your hand on the boy or do anything to him; for now I know that you fear God, since you have not withheld your son, your only son, from me.' [13] And Abraham looked up and saw a ram, caught in a thicket by its horns. Abraham went and took the ram and offered it up as a burnt-offering instead of his son. [14] So Abraham called that place 'The LORD will provide'; as it is said to this day, 'On the mount of the LORD it shall be provided.'

PSALM   Psalm 13

1   How long, O Lord; will you forget me for ever?
    how long will you hide your face from me?
2   How long shall I have perplexity in my mind, and grief in my
        heart, day after day?
    how long shall my enemy triumph over me?
3   Look upon me and answer me, O Lord my God;
    give light to my eyes, lest I sleep in death;
4   Lest my enemy say, 'I have prevailed over him',
    and my foes rejoice that I have fallen.
5   But I put my trust in your mercy;
    my heart is joyful because of your saving help.
6   I will sing to the Lord, for he has dealt with me richly;
    I will praise the name of the Lord Most High.

READING   Romans 6.12–23

¹² Therefore, do not let sin exercise dominion in your mortal bodies, to make you obey their passions. ¹³ No longer present your members to sin as instruments of wickedness, but present yourselves to God as those who have been brought from death to life, and present your members to God as instruments of righteousness. ¹⁴ For sin will have no dominion over you, since you are not under law but under grace.

¹⁵ What then? Should we sin because we are not under law but under grace? By no means! ¹⁶ Do you not know that if you present yourselves to anyone as obedient slaves, you are slaves of the one whom you obey, either of sin, which leads to death, or of obedience, which leads to righteousness? ¹⁷ But thanks be to God that you, having once been slaves of sin, have become obedient from the heart to the form of teaching to which you were entrusted, ¹⁸ and that you, having been set free from sin, have become slaves of righteousness. ¹⁹ I am speaking in human terms because of your natural limitations. For just as you once presented your members as slaves to impurity and to greater and greater iniquity, so now present your members as slaves to righteousness for sanctification.

²⁰ When you were slaves of sin, you were free in regard to righteousness. ²¹ So what advantage did you then get from the things of which you now are ashamed? The end of those things is death. ²² But now that you have been freed from sin and enslaved to God, the advantage you get is sanctification. The end is eternal life. ²³ For the wages of sin is death, but the free gift of God is eternal life in Christ Jesus our Lord.

GOSPEL   Matthew 10.40–42

⁴⁰ 'Whoever welcomes you welcomes me, and whoever welcomes me welcomes the one who sent me. ⁴¹ Whoever welcomes a prophet in the name of a prophet will receive a prophet's reward; and whoever welcomes a righteous person in the name of a righteous person will receive the reward of the righteous; ⁴² and whoever gives even a cup of cold water to one of these little ones in the name of a disciple—truly I tell you, none of these will lose their reward.'

RELATED

READING   Jeremiah 28.5–9

⁵ Then the prophet Jeremiah spoke to the prophet Hananiah in the presence of the priests and all the people who were standing in the house of the Lord; ⁶ and the prophet Jeremiah said, 'Amen! May the Lord do so; may the Lord fulfil the words that you have prophesied, and bring back to this place from Babylon the vessels of the house of the Lord, and all the exiles. ⁷ But listen now to this word that I speak in your hearing and in the hearing of all the people. ⁸ The prophets who preceded you and me from ancient times prophesied war, famine, and pestilence against many countries and great kingdoms. ⁹ As for the prophet who prophesies peace, when the word of that prophet comes true, then it will be known that the Lord has truly sent the prophet.'

PSALM   Psalm 89.1–4, 15–18

1   Your love, O Lord, for ever will I sing;
     from age to age my mouth will proclaim your faithfulness.
2   For I am persuaded that your love is established for ever;
     you have set your faithfulness firmly in the heavens.
3   'I have made a covenant with my chosen one;
     I have sworn an oath to David my servant:
4   "I will establish your line for ever,
     and preserve your throne for all generations." '

15 Happy are the people who know the festal shout!
     they walk, O Lord, in the light of your presence.
16 They rejoice daily in your name;
     they are jubilant in your righteousness.
17 For you are the glory of their strength,
     and by your favour our might is exalted.
18 Truly, the Lord is our ruler;
     the Holy One of Israel is our king.

OR, IF AN ALTERNATIVE READING IS PREFERRED   **Psalm 89.8–18**

8   Who is like you, Lord God of hosts?
     O mighty Lord, your faithfulness is all around you.
9   You rule the raging of the sea
     and still the surging of its waves.
10 You have crushed Rahab of the deep with a deadly wound;
     you have scattered your enemies with your mighty arm.

11 Yours are the heavens; the earth also is yours;
   you laid the foundations of the world and all that is in it.
12 You have made the north and the south;
   Tabor and Hermon rejoice in your name.
13 You have a mighty arm;
   strong is your hand and high is your right hand.
14 Righteousness and justice are the foundations of your throne;
   love and truth go before your face.
15 Happy are the people who know the festal shout!
   they walk, O Lord, in the light of your presence.
16 They rejoice daily in your name;
   they are jubilant in your righteousness.
17 For you are the glory of their strength,
   and by your favour our might is exalted.
18 Truly, the Lord is our ruler;
   the Holy One of Israel is our king.

READING   Romans 6.12–23

12 Therefore, do not let sin exercise dominion in your mortal bodies, to make you obey their passions. 13 No longer present your members to sin as instruments of wickedness, but present yourselves to God as those who have been brought from death to life, and present your members to God as instruments of righteousness. 14 For sin will have no dominion over you, since you are not under law but under grace.

15 What then? Should we sin because we are not under law but under grace? By no means! 16 Do you not know that if you present yourselves to anyone as obedient slaves, you are slaves of the one whom you obey, either of sin, which leads to death, or of obedience, which leads to righteousness? 17 But thanks be to God that you, having once been slaves of sin, have become obedient from the heart to the form of teaching to which you were entrusted, 18 and that you, having been set free from sin, have become slaves of righteousness. 19 I am speaking in human terms because of your natural limitations. For just as you once presented your members as slaves to impurity and to greater and greater iniquity, so now present your members as slaves to righteousness for sanctification.

20 When you were slaves of sin, you were free in regard to righteousness. 21 So what advantage did you then get from the things of which you now are ashamed? The end of those things is death. 22 But now that you have been freed from sin and enslaved to God, the advantage you get is sanctification. The end is eternal life. 23 For the wages of sin is death, but the free gift of God is eternal life in Christ Jesus our Lord.

GOSPEL   Matthew 10.40–42

[40] 'Whoever welcomes you welcomes me, and whoever welcomes me welcomes the one who sent me. [41] Whoever welcomes a prophet in the name
of a prophet will receive a prophet's reward; and whoever welcomes a
righteous person in the name of a righteous person will receive the reward
of the righteous; [42] and whoever gives even a cup of cold water to one of
these little ones in the name of a disciple—truly I tell you, none of these
will lose their reward.'

POST COMMUNION

See pages 202 to 206 and Table on page 201

SECOND SERVICE   THIRD SERVICE

Psalm 50.1–15, [16–24]   Psalms 52; 53
1 Samuel 28.3–19   Deuteronomy 15.1–11
Luke 17.20–37   Acts 27.[13–32,] 33–44

PROPER 9

Sunday between 3 and 9 July inclusive

COLLECT

See pages 202 to 206 and Table on page 201

CONTINUOUS

READING   Genesis 24.34–38, 42–49, 58–67

[34] So he said, 'I am Abraham's servant. [35] The LORD has greatly blessed my
master, and he has become wealthy; he has given him flocks and herds,
silver and gold, male and female slaves, camels and donkeys. [36] And Sarah
my master's wife bore a son to my master when she was old; and he has
given him all that he has. [37] My master made me swear, saying, "You shall
not take a wife for my son from the daughters of the Canaanites, in whose
land I live; [38] but you shall go to my father's house, to my kindred, and get
a wife for my son." '

⁴² 'I came today to the spring, and said, "O LORD, the God of my master Abraham, if now you will only make successful the way I am going! ⁴³ I am standing here by the spring of water; let the young woman who comes out to draw, to whom I shall say, 'Please give me a little water from your jar to drink,' ⁴⁴ and who will say to me, 'Drink, and I will draw for your camels also'—let her be the woman whom the LORD has appointed for my master's son."

⁴⁵ 'Before I had finished speaking in my heart, there was Rebekah coming out with her water-jar on her shoulder; and she went down to the spring, and drew. I said to her, "Please let me drink." ⁴⁶ She quickly let down her jar from her shoulder, and said, "Drink, and I will also water your camels." So I drank, and she also watered the camels. ⁴⁷ Then I asked her, "Whose daughter are you?" She said, "The daughter of Bethuel, Nahor's son, whom Milcah bore to him." So I put the ring on her nose, and the bracelets on her arms. ⁴⁸ Then I bowed my head and worshipped the LORD, and blessed the LORD, the God of my master Abraham, who had led me by the right way to obtain the daughter of my master's kinsman for his son. ⁴⁹ Now then, if you will deal loyally and truly with my master, tell me; and if not, tell me, so that I may turn either to the right hand or to the left.'

⁵⁸ And they called Rebekah, and said to her, 'Will you go with this man?' She said, 'I will.' ⁵⁹ So they sent away their sister Rebekah and her nurse along with Abraham's servant and his men. ⁶⁰ And they blessed Rebekah and said to her,

'May you, our sister, become
   thousands of myriads;
may your offspring gain possession
   of the gates of their foes.'

⁶¹ Then Rebekah and her maids rose up, mounted the camels, and followed the man; thus the servant took Rebekah, and went his way.

⁶² Now Isaac had come from Beer-lahai-roi, and was settled in the Negeb. ⁶³ Isaac went out in the evening to walk in the field; and looking up, he saw camels coming. ⁶⁴ And Rebekah looked up, and when she saw Isaac, she slipped quickly from the camel, ⁶⁵ and said to the servant, 'Who is the man over there, walking in the field to meet us?' The servant said, 'It is my master.' So she took her veil and covered herself. ⁶⁶ And the servant told Isaac all the things that he had done. ⁶⁷ Then Isaac brought her into his mother Sarah's tent. He took Rebekah, and she became his wife; and he loved her. So Isaac was comforted after his mother's death.

EITHER

PSALM
Psalm 45.11–18

¹¹ 'Hear, O daughter; consider and listen closely;
    forget your people and your family's house.
¹² The king will have pleasure in your beauty;
    he is your master; therefore do him honour.
¹³ The people of Tyre are here with a gift;
    the rich among the people seek your favour.'
¹⁴ All glorious is the princess as she enters;
    her gown is cloth-of-gold.
¹⁵ In embroidered apparel she is brought to the king;
    after her the bridesmaids follow in procession.
¹⁶ With joy and gladness they are brought,
    and enter into the palace of the king.
¹⁷ 'In place of fathers, O king, you shall have sons;
    you shall make them princes over all the earth.
¹⁸ I will make your name to be remembered from one generation to
        another;
    therefore nations will praise you for ever and ever.'

OR

CANTICLE
Song of Solomon 2.8–13

⁸ The voice of my beloved!
        Look, he comes,
    leaping upon the mountains,
        bounding over the hills.
⁹ My beloved is like a gazelle
        or a young stag.
    Look, there he stands
        behind our wall,
    gazing in at the windows,
        looking through the lattice.
¹⁰ My beloved speaks and says to me:
    'Arise, my love, my fair one,
        and come away;
¹¹ for now the winter is past,
        the rain is over and gone.
¹² The flowers appear on the earth;
        the time of singing has come,
    and the voice of the turtle-dove
        is heard in our land.

13 The fig tree puts forth its figs,
    and the vines are in blossom;
    they give forth fragrance.
Arise, my love, my fair one,
    and come away.'

READING   Romans 7.15–25a

15 I do not understand my own actions. For I do not do what I want, but I do the very thing I hate. 16 Now if I do what I do not want, I agree that the law is good. 17 But in fact it is no longer I that do it, but sin that dwells within me. 18 For I know that nothing good dwells within me, that is, in my flesh. I can will what is right, but I cannot do it. 19 For I do not do the good I want, but the evil I do not want is what I do. 20 Now if I do what I do not want, it is no longer I that do it, but sin that dwells within me.

21 So I find it to be a law that when I want to do what is good, evil lies close at hand. 22 For I delight in the law of God in my inmost self, 23 but I see in my members another law at war with the law of my mind, making me captive to the law of sin that dwells in my members. 24 Wretched man that I am! Who will rescue me from this body of death? 25 Thanks be to God through Jesus Christ our Lord!

GOSPEL   Matthew 11.16–19, 25–30

16 'But to what will I compare this generation? It is like children sitting in the market-places and calling to one another,
17 "We played the flute for you, and you did not dance;
    we wailed, and you did not mourn."
18 For John came neither eating nor drinking, and they say, "He has a demon"; 19 the Son of Man came eating and drinking, and they say, "Look, a glutton and a drunkard, a friend of tax-collectors and sinners!" Yet wisdom is vindicated by her deeds.'

25 At that time Jesus said, 'I thank you, Father, Lord of heaven and earth, because you have hidden these things from the wise and the intelligent and have revealed them to infants; 26 yes, Father, for such was your gracious will. 27 All things have been handed over to me by my Father; and no one knows the Son except the Father, and no one knows the Father except the Son and anyone to whom the Son chooses to reveal him.

28 'Come to me, all you that are weary and are carrying heavy burdens, and I will give you rest. 29 Take my yoke upon you, and learn from me; for I

am gentle and humble in heart, and you will find rest for your souls. [30] For my yoke is easy, and my burden is light.'

RELATED

READING   Zechariah 9.9–12

[9] Rejoice greatly, O daughter Zion!
     Shout aloud, O daughter Jerusalem!
   Lo, your king comes to you;
     triumphant and victorious is he,
   humble and riding on a donkey,
     on a colt, the foal of a donkey.
[10] He will cut off the chariot from Ephraim
     and the warhorse from Jerusalem;
   and the battle-bow shall be cut off,
     and he shall command peace to the nations;
   his dominion shall be from sea to sea,
     and from the River to the ends of the earth.
[11] As for you also, because of the blood of my covenant with you,
     I will set your prisoners free from the waterless pit.
[12] Return to your stronghold, O prisoners of hope;
     today I declare that I will restore to you double.

PSALM   Psalm 145.8–15

[8] The Lord is gracious and full of compassion,
     slow to anger and of great kindness.
[9] The Lord is loving to everyone
     and his compassion is over all his works.
[10] All your works praise you, O Lord,
     and your faithful servants bless you.
[11] They make known the glory of your kingdom
     and speak of your power;
[12] That the peoples may know of your power
     and the glorious splendour of your kingdom.
[13] Your kingdom is an everlasting kingdom;
     your dominion endures throughout all ages.
[14] The Lord is faithful in all his words
     and merciful in all his deeds.
[15] The Lord upholds all those who fall;
     he lifts up those who are bowed down.

READING   Romans 7.15–25a

[15] I do not understand my own actions. For I do not do what I want, but I do the very thing I hate. [16] Now if I do what I do not want, I agree that the law is good. [17] But in fact it is no longer I that do it, but sin that dwells within me. [18] For I know that nothing good dwells within me, that is, in my flesh. I can will what is right, but I cannot do it. [19] For I do not do the good I want, but the evil I do not want is what I do. [20] Now if I do what I do not want, it is no longer I that do it, but sin that dwells within me.

[21] So I find it to be a law that when I want to do what is good, evil lies close at hand. [22] For I delight in the law of God in my inmost self, [23] but I see in my members another law at war with the law of my mind, making me captive to the law of sin that dwells in my members. [24] Wretched man that I am! Who will rescue me from this body of death? [25] Thanks be to God through Jesus Christ our Lord!

GOSPEL   Matthew 11.16–19, 25–30

[16] 'But to what will I compare this generation? It is like children sitting in the market-places and calling to one another,
[17]   "We played the flute for you, and you did not dance;
        we wailed, and you did not mourn."
[18] For John came neither eating nor drinking, and they say, "He has a demon"; [19] the Son of Man came eating and drinking, and they say, "Look, a glutton and a drunkard, a friend of tax-collectors and sinners!" Yet wisdom is vindicated by her deeds.'

[25] At that time Jesus said, 'I thank you, Father, Lord of heaven and earth, because you have hidden these things from the wise and the intelligent and have revealed them to infants; [26] yes, Father, for such was your gracious will. [27] All things have been handed over to me by my Father; and no one knows the Son except the Father, and no one knows the Father except the Son and anyone to whom the Son chooses to reveal him.

[28] 'Come to me, all you that are weary and are carrying heavy burdens, and I will give you rest. [29] Take my yoke upon you, and learn from me; for I am gentle and humble in heart, and you will find rest for your souls. [30] For my yoke is easy, and my burden is light.'

POST COMMUNION

See pages 203 to 207 and Table on page 201

SECOND SERVICE

Psalms 56; [57]
2 Samuel 2.1–11; 3.1
Luke 18.31–19.10

THIRD SERVICE

Psalm 55.1–16, 19–24
Deuteronomy 24.10–22
Acts 28.1–16

PROPER 10

Sunday between 10 and 16 July inclusive

COLLECT

See pages 203 to 207 and Table on page 201

CONTINUOUS

READING   Genesis 25.19–34

¹⁹ These are the descendants of Isaac, Abraham's son: Abraham was the father of Isaac, ²⁰ and Isaac was forty years old when he married Rebekah, daughter of Bethuel the Aramean of Paddan-aram, sister of Laban the Aramean. ²¹ Isaac prayed to the LORD for his wife, because she was barren; and the LORD granted his prayer, and his wife Rebekah conceived. ²² The children struggled together within her; and she said, 'If it is to be this way, why do I live?' So she went to inquire of the LORD. ²³ And the LORD said to her,

'Two nations are in your womb,
 and two peoples born of you shall be divided;
 one shall be stronger than the other,
  the elder shall serve the younger.'

²⁴ When her time to give birth was at hand, there were twins in her womb.
²⁵ The first came out red, all his body like a hairy mantle; so they named him Esau. ²⁶ Afterwards his brother came out, with his hand gripping Esau's heel; so he was named Jacob. Isaac was sixty years old when she bore them.

²⁷ When the boys grew up, Esau was a skilful hunter, a man of the field, while Jacob was a quiet man, living in tents. ²⁸ Isaac loved Esau, because he was fond of game; but Rebekah loved Jacob.

²⁹ Once when Jacob was cooking a stew, Esau came in from the field, and he was famished. ³⁰ Esau said to Jacob, 'Let me eat some of that red stuff, for I am famished!' (Therefore he was called Edom.) ³¹ Jacob said, 'First sell me your birthright.' ³² Esau said, 'I am about to die; of what use is a birthright to me?' ³³ Jacob said, 'Swear to me first.' So he swore to him, and sold his birthright to Jacob. ³⁴ Then Jacob gave Esau bread and lentil stew, and he ate and drank, and rose and went his way. Thus Esau despised his birthright.

PSALM   Psalm 119.105–112

105 Your word is a lantern to my feet
       and a light upon my path.
106 I have sworn and am determined
       to keep your righteous judgements.
107 I am deeply troubled;
       preserve my life, O Lord, according to your word.
108 Accept, O Lord, the willing tribute of my lips,
       and teach me your judgements.
109 My life is always in my hand,
       yet I do not forget your law.
110 The wicked have set a trap for me,
       but I have not strayed from your commandments.
111 Your decrees are my inheritance for ever;
       truly, they are the joy of my heart.
112 I have applied my heart to fulfil your statutes
       for ever and to the end.

READING   Romans 8.1–11

¹ There is therefore now no condemnation for those who are in Christ Jesus. ² For the law of the Spirit of life in Christ Jesus has set you free from the law of sin and of death. ³ For God has done what the law, weakened by the flesh, could not do: by sending his own Son in the likeness of sinful flesh, and to deal with sin, he condemned sin in the flesh, ⁴ so that the just requirement of the law might be fulfilled in us, who walk not according to the flesh but according to the Spirit. ⁵ For those who live according to the flesh set their minds on the things of the flesh, but those who live according to the Spirit set their minds on the things of the Spirit. ⁶ To set the mind

on the flesh is death, but to set the mind on the Spirit is life and peace. [7] For this reason the mind that is set on the flesh is hostile to God; it does not submit to God's law—indeed it cannot, [8] and those who are in the flesh cannot please God.

[9] But you are not in the flesh; you are in the Spirit, since the Spirit of God dwells in you. Anyone who does not have the Spirit of Christ does not belong to him. [10] But if Christ is in you, though the body is dead because of sin, the Spirit is life because of righteousness. [11] If the Spirit of him who raised Jesus from the dead dwells in you, he who raised Christ from the dead will give life to your mortal bodies also through his Spirit that dwells in you.

GOSPEL   Matthew 13.1–9, 18–23

[1] That same day Jesus went out of the house and sat beside the lake. [2] Such great crowds gathered around him that he got into a boat and sat there, while the whole crowd stood on the beach. [3] And he told them many things in parables, saying: 'Listen! A sower went out to sow. [4] And as he sowed, some seeds fell on the path, and the birds came and ate them up. [5] Other seeds fell on rocky ground, where they did not have much soil, and they sprang up quickly, since they had no depth of soil. [6] But when the sun rose, they were scorched; and since they had no root, they withered away. [7] Other seeds fell among thorns, and the thorns grew up and choked them. [8] Other seeds fell on good soil and brought forth grain, some a hundredfold, some sixty, some thirty. [9] Let anyone with ears listen!'

[18] 'Hear then the parable of the sower. [19] When anyone hears the word of the kingdom and does not understand it, the evil one comes and snatches away what is sown in the heart; this is what was sown on the path. [20] As for what was sown on rocky ground, this is the one who hears the word and immediately receives it with joy; [21] yet such a person has no root, but endures only for a while, and when trouble or persecution arises on account of the word, that person immediately falls away. [22] As for what was sown among thorns, this is the one who hears the word, but the cares of the world and the lure of wealth choke the word, and it yields nothing. [23] But as for what was sown on good soil, this is the one who hears the word and understands it, who indeed bears fruit and yields, in one case a hundredfold, in another sixty, and in another thirty.'

RELATED

READING   Isaiah 55.10–13

¹⁰ For as the rain and the snow come down from heaven,
    and do not return there until they have watered the earth,
  making it bring forth and sprout,
    giving seed to the sower and bread to the eater,
¹¹ so shall my word be that goes out from my mouth;
    it shall not return to me empty,
  but it shall accomplish that which I purpose,
    and succeed in the thing for which I sent it.
¹² For you shall go out in joy,
    and be led back in peace;
  the mountains and the hills before you
    shall burst into song,
    and all the trees of the field shall clap their hands.
¹³ Instead of the thorn shall come up the cypress;
    instead of the brier shall come up the myrtle;
  and it shall be to the LORD for a memorial,
    for an everlasting sign that shall not be cut off.

PSALM   Psalm 65.[1–8,] 9–14

[¹ You are to be praised, O God, in Zion;
  to you shall vows be performed in Jerusalem.
² To you that hear prayer shall all flesh come,
  because of their transgressions.
³ Our sins are stronger than we are,
  but you will blot them out.
⁴ Happy are they whom you choose and draw to your courts to dwell
    there!
  they will be satisfied by the beauty of your house, by the holiness
    of your temple.
⁵ Awesome things will you show us in your righteousness, O God of
    our salvation,
  O Hope of all the ends of the earth and of the seas that are far
    away.
⁶ You make fast the mountains by your power;
  they are girded about with might.
⁷ You still the roaring of the seas,
  the roaring of their waves, and the clamour of the peoples.

8 Those who dwell at the ends of the earth will tremble at your
    marvellous signs;
  you make the dawn and the dusk to sing for joy.]
9 You visit the earth and water it abundantly; you make it very
    plenteous;
  the river of God is full of water.
10 You prepare the grain,
  for so you provide for the earth.
11 You drench the furrows and smooth out the ridges;
  with heavy rain you soften the ground and bless its increase.
12 You crown the year with your goodness,
  and your paths overflow with plenty.
13 May the fields of the wilderness be rich for grazing,
  and the hills be clothed with joy.
14 May the meadows cover themselves with flocks, and the valleys
    cloak themselves with grain;
  let them shout for joy and sing.

READING   Romans 8.1–11

1 There is therefore now no condemnation for those who are in Christ Jesus. 2 For the law of the Spirit of life in Christ Jesus has set you free from the law of sin and of death. 3 For God has done what the law, weakened by the flesh, could not do: by sending his own Son in the likeness of sinful flesh, and to deal with sin, he condemned sin in the flesh, 4 so that the just requirement of the law might be fulfilled in us, who walk not according to the flesh but according to the Spirit. 5 For those who live according to the flesh set their minds on the things of the flesh, but those who live according to the Spirit set their minds on the things of the Spirit. 6 To set the mind on the flesh is death, but to set the mind on the Spirit is life and peace. 7 For this reason the mind that is set on the flesh is hostile to God; it does not submit to God's law—indeed it cannot, 8 and those who are in the flesh cannot please God.

9 But you are not in the flesh; you are in the Spirit, since the Spirit of God dwells in you. Anyone who does not have the Spirit of Christ does not belong to him. 10 But if Christ is in you, though the body is dead because of sin, the Spirit is life because of righteousness. 11 If the Spirit of him who raised Jesus from the dead dwells in you, he who raised Christ from the dead will give life to your mortal bodies also through his Spirit that dwells in you.

GOSPEL   Matthew 13.1–9, 18–23

[1] That same day Jesus went out of the house and sat beside the lake. [2] Such great crowds gathered around him that he got into a boat and sat there, while the whole crowd stood on the beach. [3] And he told them many things in parables, saying: 'Listen! A sower went out to sow. [4] And as he sowed, some seeds fell on the path, and the birds came and ate them up. [5] Other seeds fell on rocky ground, where they did not have much soil, and they sprang up quickly, since they had no depth of soil. [6] But when the sun rose, they were scorched; and since they had no root, they withered away. [7] Other seeds fell among thorns, and the thorns grew up and choked them. [8] Other seeds fell on good soil and brought forth grain, some a hundredfold, some sixty, some thirty. [9] Let anyone with ears listen!'

[18] 'Hear then the parable of the sower. [19] When anyone hears the word of the kingdom and does not understand it, the evil one comes and snatches away what is sown in the heart; this is what was sown on the path. [20] As for what was sown on rocky ground, this is the one who hears the word and immediately receives it with joy; [21] yet such a person has no root, but endures only for a while, and when trouble or persecution arises on account of the word, that person immediately falls away. [22] As for what was sown among thorns, this is the one who hears the word, but the cares of the world and the lure of wealth choke the word, and it yields nothing. [23] But as for what was sown on good soil, this is the one who hears the word and understands it, who indeed bears fruit and yields, in one case a hundredfold, in another sixty, and in another thirty.'

POST COMMUNION

See pages 203 to 207 and Table on page 201

SECOND SERVICE   THIRD SERVICE

Psalms 60; [63]   **Psalms 64; 65**
2 Samuel 7.18–29   **Deuteronomy 28.1–14**
Luke 19.41–20.8   **Acts 28.17–30**

PROPER 11

Sunday between 17 and 23 July inclusive

COLLECT

See pages 204 to 208 and Table on page 201

CONTINUOUS

READING   Genesis 28.10−19a

¹⁰ Jacob left Beer-sheba and went towards Haran. ¹¹ He came to a certain place and stayed there for the night, because the sun had set. Taking one of the stones of the place, he put it under his head and lay down in that place. ¹² And he dreamed that there was a ladder set up on the earth, the top of it reaching to heaven; and the angels of God were ascending and descending on it. ¹³ And the LORD stood beside him and said, 'I am the LORD, the God of Abraham your father and the God of Isaac; the land on which you lie I will give to you and to your offspring; ¹⁴ and your offspring shall be like the dust of the earth, and you shall spread abroad to the west and to the east and to the north and to the south; and all the families of the earth shall be blessed in you and in your offspring. ¹⁵ Know that I am with you and will keep you wherever you go, and will bring you back to this land; for I will not leave you until I have done what I have promised you.' ¹⁶ Then Jacob woke from his sleep and said, 'Surely the LORD is in this place—and I did not know it!' ¹⁷ And he was afraid, and said, 'How awesome is this place! This is none other than the house of God, and this is the gate of heaven.'

¹⁸ So Jacob rose early in the morning, and he took the stone that he had put under his head and set it up for a pillar and poured oil on the top of it. ¹⁹ He called that place Bethel.

PSALM   Psalm 139.1−11, [22−23]

¹   Lord, you have searched me out and known me;
       you know my sitting down and my rising up; you discern my
           thoughts from afar.
²   You trace my journeys and my resting-places
       and are acquainted with all my ways.
³   Indeed, there is not a word on my lips,
       but you, O Lord, know it altogether.

⁴ You press upon me behind and before
    and lay your hand upon me.
⁵ Such knowledge is too wonderful for me;
    it is so high that I cannot attain to it.
⁶ Where can I go then from your Spirit?
    where can I flee from your presence?
⁷ If I climb up to heaven, you are there;
    if I make the grave my bed, you are there also.
⁸ If I take the wings of the morning
    and dwell in the uttermost parts of the sea,
⁹ Even there your hand will lead me
    and your right hand hold me fast.
¹⁰ If I say, 'Surely the darkness will cover me,
    and the light around me turn to night',
¹¹ Darkness is not dark to you; the night is as bright as the day;
    darkness and light to you are both alike.

[²² Search me out, O God, and know my heart;
    try me and know my restless thoughts.
²³ Look well whether there be any wickedness in me
    and lead me in the way that is everlasting.]

READING   Romans 8.12–25

¹² So then, brothers and sisters, we are debtors, not to the flesh, to live according to the flesh— ¹³ for if you live according to the flesh, you will die; but if by the Spirit you put to death the deeds of the body, you will live. ¹⁴ For all who are led by the Spirit of God are children of God. ¹⁵ For you did not receive a spirit of slavery to fall back into fear, but you have received a spirit of adoption. When we cry, 'Abba! Father!' ¹⁶ it is that very Spirit bearing witness with our spirit that we are children of God, ¹⁷ and if children, then heirs, heirs of God and joint heirs with Christ—if, in fact, we suffer with him so that we may also be glorified with him.

¹⁸ I consider that the sufferings of this present time are not worth comparing with the glory about to be revealed to us. ¹⁹ For the creation waits with eager longing for the revealing of the children of God; ²⁰ for the creation was subjected to futility, not of its own will but by the will of the one who subjected it, in hope ²¹ that the creation itself will be set free from its bondage to decay and will obtain the freedom of the glory of the children of God. ²² We know that the whole creation has been groaning in labour pains until now; ²³ and not only the creation, but we ourselves, who have the first fruits of the Spirit, groan inwardly while we wait for adoption, the

redemption of our bodies. [24] For in hope we were saved. Now hope that is seen is not hope. For who hopes for what is seen? [25] But if we hope for what we do not see, we wait for it with patience.

GOSPEL   Matthew 13.24–30, 36–43

[24] He put before them another parable: 'The kingdom of heaven may be compared to someone who sowed good seed in his field; [25] but while everybody was asleep, an enemy came and sowed weeds among the wheat, and then went away. [26] So when the plants came up and bore grain, then the weeds appeared as well. [27] And the slaves of the householder came and said to him, "Master, did you not sow good seed in your field? Where, then, did these weeds come from?" [28] He answered, "An enemy has done this." The slaves said to him, "Then do you want us to go and gather them?" [29] But he replied, "No; for in gathering the weeds you would uproot the wheat along with them. [30] Let both of them grow together until the harvest; and at harvest time I will tell the reapers, Collect the weeds first and bind them in bundles to be burned, but gather the wheat into my barn." '

[36] Then he left the crowds and went into the house. And his disciples approached him, saying, 'Explain to us the parable of the weeds of the field.' [37] He answered, 'The one who sows the good seed is the Son of Man; [38] the field is the world, and the good seed are the children of the kingdom; the weeds are the children of the evil one, [39] and the enemy who sowed them is the devil; the harvest is the end of the age, and the reapers are angels. [40] Just as the weeds are collected and burned up with fire, so will it be at the end of the age. [41] The Son of Man will send his angels, and they will collect out of his kingdom all causes of sin and all evildoers, [42] and they will throw them into the furnace of fire, where there will be weeping and gnashing of teeth. [43] Then the righteous will shine like the sun in the kingdom of their Father. Let anyone with ears listen!'

RELATED

READING

EITHER   **Wisdom 12.13, 16–19**

[13] For neither is there any god besides you, whose care is for all people,
      to whom you should prove that you have not judged unjustly.

[16] For your strength is the source of righteousness,
      and your sovereignty over all causes you to spare all.

17 For you show your strength when people doubt the completeness of
    your power,
and you rebuke any insolence among those who know it.
18 Although you are sovereign in strength, you judge with mildness,
and with great forbearance you govern us;
for you have power to act whenever you choose.
19 Through such works you have taught your people
that the righteous must be kind,
and you have filled your children with good hope,
because you give repentance for sins.

OR   **Isaiah 44.6–8**

6 Thus says the Lord, the King of Israel
    and his Redeemer, the Lord of hosts:
I am the first and I am the last;
    besides me there is no god.
7 Who is like me? Let them proclaim it,
    let them declare and set it forth before me.
Who has announced from of old the things to come?
    Let them tell us what is yet to be.
8 Do not fear, or be afraid;
    have I not told you from of old and declared it?
    You are my witnesses!
Is there any god besides me?
    There is no other rock; I know not one.

PSALM   **Psalm 86.11–17**

11 Teach me your way, O Lord, and I will walk in your truth;
    knit my heart to you that I may fear your name.
12 I will thank you, O Lord my God, with all my heart,
    and glorify your name for evermore.
13 For great is your love towards me;
    you have delivered me from the nethermost Pit.
14 The arrogant rise up against me, O God, and a violent band seeks
    my life;
    they have not set you before their eyes.
15 But you, O Lord, are gracious and full of compassion,
    slow to anger and full of kindness and truth.
16 Turn to me and have mercy upon me;
    give your strength to your servant; and save the child of your
    handmaid.

[17] Show me a sign of your favour, so that those who hate me may see
it and be ashamed;
because you, O Lord, have helped me and comforted me.

READING   Romans 8.12–25

[12] So then, brothers and sisters, we are debtors, not to the flesh, to live according to the flesh— [13] for if you live according to the flesh, you will die; but if by the Spirit you put to death the deeds of the body, you will live. [14] For all who are led by the Spirit of God are children of God. [15] For you did not receive a spirit of slavery to fall back into fear, but you have received a spirit of adoption. When we cry, 'Abba! Father!' [16] it is that very Spirit bearing witness with our spirit that we are children of God, [17] and if children, then heirs, heirs of God and joint heirs with Christ—if, in fact, we suffer with him so that we may also be glorified with him.

[18] I consider that the sufferings of this present time are not worth comparing with the glory about to be revealed to us. [19] For the creation waits with eager longing for the revealing of the children of God; [20] for the creation was subjected to futility, not of its own will but by the will of the one who subjected it, in hope [21] that the creation itself will be set free from its bondage to decay and will obtain the freedom of the glory of the children of God. [22] We know that the whole creation has been groaning in labour pains until now; [23] and not only the creation, but we ourselves, who have the first fruits of the Spirit, groan inwardly while we wait for adoption, the redemption of our bodies. [24] For in hope we were saved. Now hope that is seen is not hope. For who hopes for what is seen? [25] But if we hope for what we do not see, we wait for it with patience.

GOSPEL   Matthew 13.24–30, 36–43

[24] He put before them another parable: 'The kingdom of heaven may be compared to someone who sowed good seed in his field; [25] but while everybody was asleep, an enemy came and sowed weeds among the wheat, and then went away. [26] So when the plants came up and bore grain, then the weeds appeared as well. [27] And the slaves of the householder came and said to him, "Master, did you not sow good seed in your field? Where, then, did these weeds come from?" [28] He answered, "An enemy has done this." The slaves said to him, "Then do you want us to go and gather them?" [29] But he replied, "No; for in gathering the weeds you would uproot the wheat along with them. [30] Let both of them grow together until the harvest; and at harvest time I will tell the reapers, Collect the weeds first and bind them in bundles to be burned, but gather the wheat into my barn." '

^{36} Then he left the crowds and went into the house. And his disciples approached him, saying, 'Explain to us the parable of the weeds of the field.' ^{37} He answered, 'The one who sows the good seed is the Son of Man; ^{38} the field is the world, and the good seed are the children of the kingdom; the weeds are the children of the evil one, ^{39} and the enemy who sowed them is the devil; the harvest is the end of the age, and the reapers are angels. ^{40} Just as the weeds are collected and burned up with fire, so will it be at the end of the age. ^{41} The Son of Man will send his angels, and they will collect out of his kingdom all causes of sin and all evildoers, ^{42} and they will throw them into the furnace of fire, where there will be weeping and gnashing of teeth. ^{43} Then the righteous will shine like the sun in the kingdom of their Father. Let anyone with ears listen!'

POST COMMUNION

See pages 204 to 208 and Table on page 201

SECOND SERVICE

Psalms 67; [70]
1 Kings 2.10–12; 3.16–28
Acts 4.1–22

If the Second Service is a Eucharist, the following is read as a Gospel:

Mark 6.30–34, 53–56

THIRD SERVICE

Psalm 71
Deuteronomy 30.1–10
1 Peter 3.8–18

PROPER 12

Sunday between 24 and 30 July inclusive

COLLECT

See pages 205 to 209 and Table on page 201

CONTINUOUS

READING   Genesis 29.15–28

^{15} Then Laban said to Jacob, 'Because you are my kinsman, should you therefore serve me for nothing? Tell me, what shall your wages be?' ^{16} Now Laban had two daughters; the name of the elder was Leah, and the name of the younger was Rachel. [17] Leah's eyes were lovely, and Rachel was grace-ful and beautiful. [18] Jacob loved Rachel; so he said, 'I will serve you seven years for your younger daughter Rachel.' [19] Laban said, 'It is better that I give her to you than that I should give her to any other man; stay with me.' [20] So Jacob served seven years for Rachel, and they seemed to him but a few days because of the love he had for her.

[21] Then Jacob said to Laban, 'Give me my wife that I may go in to her, for my time is completed.' [22] So Laban gathered together all the people of the place, and made a feast. [23] But in the evening he took his daughter Leah and brought her to Jacob; and he went in to her. [24] (Laban gave his maid Zilpah to his daughter Leah to be her maid.) [25] When morning came, it was Leah! And Jacob said to Laban, 'What is this you have done to me? Did I not serve with you for Rachel? Why then have you deceived me?' [26] Laban said, 'This is not done in our country—giving the younger before the firstborn. [27] Complete the week of this one, and we will give you the other also in return for serving me for another seven years.' [28] Jacob did so, and com-pleted her week; then Laban gave him his daughter Rachel as a wife.

PSALM

EITHER   **Psalm 105.1–11, [45b]**

1   Give thanks to the Lord and call upon his name;
     make known his deeds among the peoples.
2   Sing to him, sing praises to him,
     and speak of all his marvellous works.
3   Glory in his holy name;
     let the hearts of those who seek the Lord rejoice.
4   Search for the Lord and his strength;
     continually seek his face.
5   Remember the marvels he has done,
     his wonders and the judgements of his mouth,
6   O offspring of Abraham his servant,
     O children of Jacob his chosen.
7   He is the Lord our God;
     his judgements prevail in all the world.
8   He has always been mindful of his covenant,
     the promise he made for a thousand generations:
9   The covenant he made with Abraham,
     the oath that he swore to Isaac,

¹⁰ Which he established as a statute for Jacob,
   an everlasting covenant for Israel,
¹¹ Saying, 'To you will I give the land of Canaan
   to be your allotted inheritance.'

[⁴⁵ Alleluia!]

OR   Psalm 128

¹ Happy are they all who fear the Lord,
   and who follow in his ways!
² You shall eat the fruit of your labour;
   happiness and prosperity shall be yours.
³ Your wife shall be like a fruitful vine within your house,
   your children like olive shoots round about your table.
⁴ Whoever fears the Lord
   shall thus indeed be blessed.
⁵ The Lord bless you from Zion,
   and may you see the prosperity of Jerusalem all the days of your
      life.
⁶ May you live to see your children's children;
   may peace be upon Israel.

READING   Romans 8.26–39

²⁶ Likewise the Spirit helps us in our weakness; for we do not know how to pray as we ought, but that very Spirit intercedes with sighs too deep for words. ²⁷ And God, who searches the heart, knows what is the mind of the Spirit, because the Spirit intercedes for the saints according to the will of God.

²⁸ We know that all things work together for good for those who love God, who are called according to his purpose. ²⁹ For those whom he foreknew he also predestined to be conformed to the image of his Son, in order that he might be the firstborn within a large family. ³⁰ And those whom he predestined he also called; and those whom he called he also justified; and those whom he justified he also glorified.

³¹ What then are we to say about these things? If God is for us, who is against us? ³² He who did not withhold his own Son, but gave him up for all of us, will he not with him also give us everything else? ³³ Who will bring any charge against God's elect? It is God who justifies. ³⁴ Who is to condemn? It is Christ Jesus, who died, yes, who was raised, who is at the right hand of God, who indeed intercedes for us. ³⁵ Who will separate us

from the love of Christ? Will hardship, or distress, or persecution, or famine, or nakedness, or peril, or sword? [36] As it is written,

'For your sake we are being killed all day long;
we are accounted as sheep to be slaughtered.'

[37] No, in all these things we are more than conquerors through him who loved us. [38] For I am convinced that neither death, nor life, nor angels, nor rulers, nor things present, nor things to come, nor powers, [39] nor height, nor depth, nor anything else in all creation, will be able to separate us from the love of God in Christ Jesus our Lord.

GOSPEL   Matthew 13.31–33, 44–52

[31] He put before them another parable: 'The kingdom of heaven is like a mustard seed that someone took and sowed in his field; [32] it is the smallest of all the seeds, but when it has grown it is the greatest of shrubs and becomes a tree, so that the birds of the air come and make nests in its branches.'

[33] He told them another parable: 'The kingdom of heaven is like yeast that a woman took and mixed in with three measures of flour until all of it was leavened.'

[44] 'The kingdom of heaven is like treasure hidden in a field, which someone found and hid; then in his joy he goes and sells all that he has and buys that field.

[45] 'Again, the kingdom of heaven is like a merchant in search of fine pearls; [46] on finding one pearl of great value, he went and sold all that he had and bought it.

[47] 'Again, the kingdom of heaven is like a net that was thrown into the sea and caught fish of every kind; [48] when it was full, they drew it ashore, sat down, and put the good into baskets but threw out the bad. [49] So it will be at the end of the age. The angels will come out and separate the evil from the righteous [50] and throw them into the furnace of fire, where there will be weeping and gnashing of teeth.

[51] 'Have you understood all this?' They answered, 'Yes.' [52] And he said to them, 'Therefore every scribe who has been trained for the kingdom of heaven is like the master of a household who brings out of his treasure what is new and what is old.'

RELATED

READING   **1 Kings 3.5–12**

⁵ At Gibeon the LORD appeared to Solomon in a dream by night; and God said, 'Ask what I should give you.' ⁶ And Solomon said, 'You have shown great and steadfast love to your servant my father David, because he walked before you in faithfulness, in righteousness, and in uprightness of heart towards you; and you have kept for him this great and steadfast love, and have given him a son to sit on his throne today. ⁷ And now, O LORD my God, you have made your servant king in place of my father David, although I am only a little child; I do not know how to go out or come in. ⁸ And your servant is in the midst of the people whom you have chosen, a great people, so numerous they cannot be numbered or counted. ⁹ Give your servant therefore an understanding mind to govern your people, able to discern between good and evil; for who can govern this your great people?'

¹⁰ It pleased the Lord that Solomon had asked this. ¹¹ God said to him, 'Because you have asked this, and have not asked for yourself long life or riches, or for the life of your enemies, but have asked for yourself understanding to discern what is right, ¹² I now do according to your word. Indeed I give you a wise and discerning mind; no one like you has been before you and no one like you shall arise after you.'

PSALM   **Psalm 119.129–136**

129 Your decrees are wonderful;
     therefore I obey them with all my heart.
130 When your word goes forth it gives light;
     it gives understanding to the simple.
131 I open my mouth and pant;
     I long for your commandments.
132 Turn to me in mercy,
     as you always do to those who love your name.
133 Steady my footsteps in your word;
     let no iniquity have dominion over me.
134 Rescue me from those who oppress me,
     and I will keep your commandments.
135 Let your countenance shine upon your servant
     and teach me your statutes.
136 My eyes shed streams of tears,
     because people do not keep your law.

READING   Romans 8.26–39

[26] Likewise the Spirit helps us in our weakness; for we do not know how to pray as we ought, but that very Spirit intercedes with sighs too deep for words. [27] And God, who searches the heart, knows what is the mind of the Spirit, because the Spirit intercedes for the saints according to the will of God.

[28] We know that all things work together for good for those who love God, who are called according to his purpose. [29] For those whom he foreknew he also predestined to be conformed to the image of his Son, in order that he might be the firstborn within a large family. [30] And those whom he predestined he also called; and those whom he called he also justified; and those whom he justified he also glorified.

[31] What then are we to say about these things? If God is for us, who is against us? [32] He who did not withhold his own Son, but gave him up for all of us, will he not with him also give us everything else? [33] Who will bring any charge against God's elect? It is God who justifies. [34] Who is to condemn? It is Christ Jesus, who died, yes, who was raised, who is at the right hand of God, who indeed intercedes for us. [35] Who will separate us from the love of Christ? Will hardship, or distress, or persecution, or famine, or nakedness, or peril, or sword? [36] As it is written,
    'For your sake we are being killed all day long;
        we are accounted as sheep to be slaughtered.'
[37] No, in all these things we are more than conquerors through him who loved us. [38] For I am convinced that neither death, nor life, nor angels, nor rulers, nor things present, nor things to come, nor powers, [39] nor height, nor depth, nor anything else in all creation, will be able to separate us from the love of God in Christ Jesus our Lord.

GOSPEL   Matthew 13.31–33, 44–52

[31] He put before them another parable: 'The kingdom of heaven is like a mustard seed that someone took and sowed in his field; [32] it is the smallest of all the seeds, but when it has grown it is the greatest of shrubs and becomes a tree, so that the birds of the air come and make nests in its branches.'

[33] He told them another parable: 'The kingdom of heaven is like yeast that a woman took and mixed in with three measures of flour until all of it was leavened.'

⁴⁴ 'The kingdom of heaven is like treasure hidden in a field, which someone found and hid; then in his joy he goes and sells all that he has and buys that field.

⁴⁵ 'Again, the kingdom of heaven is like a merchant in search of fine pearls; ⁴⁶ on finding one pearl of great value, he went and sold all that he had and bought it.

⁴⁷ 'Again, the kingdom of heaven is like a net that was thrown into the sea and caught fish of every kind; ⁴⁸ when it was full, they drew it ashore, sat down, and put the good into baskets but threw out the bad. ⁴⁹ So it will be at the end of the age. The angels will come out and separate the evil from the righteous ⁵⁰ and throw them into the furnace of fire, where there will be weeping and gnashing of teeth.

⁵¹ 'Have you understood all this?' They answered, 'Yes.' ⁵² And he said to them, 'Therefore every scribe who has been trained for the kingdom of heaven is like the master of a household who brings out of his treasure what is new and what is old.'

POST COMMUNION

See pages 205 to 209 and Table on page 201

SECOND SERVICE

Psalms 75; [76]
1 Kings 6.11–14, 23–38
Acts 12.1–17

If the Second Service is a Eucharist, the following is read as a Gospel:

John 6.1–21

THIRD SERVICE

Psalm 77
Song of Solomon 2

or

1 Maccabees 2.[1–14,] 15–22
1 Peter 4.7–14

PROPER 13

Sunday between 31 July and 6 August inclusive

COLLECT

See pages 205 to 209 and Table on page 201

CONTINUOUS

READING   Genesis 32.22–31

²² The same night he got up and took his two wives, his two maids, and his eleven children, and crossed the ford of the Jabbok. ²³ He took them and sent them across the stream, and likewise everything that he had. ²⁴ Jacob was left alone; and a man wrestled with him until daybreak. ²⁵ When the man saw that he did not prevail against Jacob, he struck him on the hip socket; and Jacob's hip was put out of joint as he wrestled with him. ²⁶ Then he said, 'Let me go, for the day is breaking.' But Jacob said, 'I will not let you go, unless you bless me.' ²⁷ So he said to him, 'What is your name?' And he said, 'Jacob.' ²⁸ Then the man said, 'You shall no longer be called Jacob, but Israel, for you have striven with God and with humans, and have prevailed.' ²⁹ Then Jacob asked him, 'Please tell me your name.' But he said, 'Why is it that you ask my name?' And there he blessed him. ³⁰ So Jacob called the place Peniel, saying, 'For I have seen God face to face, and yet my life is preserved.' ³¹ The sun rose upon him as he passed Penuel, limping because of his hip.

PSALM   Psalm 17.1–7, [16]

1 Hear my plea of innocence, O Lord; give heed to my cry;
   listen to my prayer, which does not come from lying lips.
2 Let my vindication come forth from your presence;
   let your eyes be fixed on justice.
3 Weigh my heart, summon me by night,
   melt me down; you will find no impurity in me.
4 I give no offence with my mouth as others do;
   I have heeded the words of your lips.
5 My footsteps hold fast to the ways of your law;
   in your paths my feet shall not stumble.
6 I call upon you, O God, for you will answer me;
   incline your ear to me and hear my words.

7 Show me your marvellous loving-kindness,
   O Saviour of those who take refuge at your right hand from those
      who rise up against them.

[16 But at my vindication I shall see your face;
   when I awake, I shall be satisfied, beholding your likeness.]

READING   Romans 9.1–5

¹ I am speaking the truth in Christ—I am not lying; my conscience confirms it by the Holy Spirit— ² I have great sorrow and unceasing anguish in my heart. ³ For I could wish that I myself were accursed and cut off from Christ for the sake of my own people, my kindred according to the flesh. ⁴ They are Israelites, and to them belong the adoption, the glory, the covenants, the giving of the law, the worship, and the promises; ⁵ to them belong the patriarchs, and from them, according to the flesh, comes the Messiah, who is over all, God blessed for ever. Amen.

GOSPEL   Matthew 14.13–21

¹³ Now when Jesus heard this, he withdrew from there in a boat to a deserted place by himself. But when the crowds heard it, they followed him on foot from the towns. ¹⁴ When he went ashore, he saw a great crowd; and he had compassion for them and cured their sick. ¹⁵ When it was evening, the disciples came to him and said, 'This is a deserted place, and the hour is now late; send the crowds away so that they may go into the villages and buy food for themselves.' ¹⁶ Jesus said to them, 'They need not go away; you give them something to eat.' ¹⁷ They replied, 'We have nothing here but five loaves and two fish.' ¹⁸ And he said, 'Bring them here to me.' ¹⁹ Then he ordered the crowds to sit down on the grass. Taking the five loaves and the two fish, he looked up to heaven, and blessed and broke the loaves, and gave them to the disciples, and the disciples gave them to the crowds. ²⁰ And all ate and were filled; and they took up what was left over of the broken pieces, twelve baskets full. ²¹ And those who ate were about five thousand men, besides women and children.

RELATED

READING   Isaiah 55.1–5

1 Ho, everyone who thirsts,
        come to the waters;
    and you that have no money,
        come, buy and eat!
    Come, buy wine and milk
        without money and without price.
2 Why do you spend your money for that which is not bread,
        and your labour for that which does not satisfy?
    Listen carefully to me, and eat what is good,
        and delight yourselves in rich food.
3 Incline your ear, and come to me;
        listen, so that you may live.
    I will make with you an everlasting covenant,
        my steadfast, sure love for David.
4 See, I made him a witness to the peoples,
        a leader and commander for the peoples.
5 See, you shall call nations that you do not know,
        and nations that do not know you shall run to you,
    because of the LORD your God, the Holy One of Israel,
        for he has glorified you.

PSALM   Psalm 145.[8–9,] 15–22

[8 The Lord is gracious and full of compassion,
    slow to anger and of great kindness.
9 The Lord is loving to everyone
    and his compassion is over all his works.]

15 The Lord upholds all those who fall;
    he lifts up those who are bowed down.
16 The eyes of all wait upon you, O Lord,
    and you give them their food in due season.
17 You open wide your hand
    and satisfy the needs of every living creature.
18 The Lord is righteous in all his ways
    and loving in all his works.
19 The Lord is near to those who call upon him,
    to all who call upon him faithfully.

20 He fulfils the desire of those who fear him,
    he hears their cry and helps them.
21 The Lord preserves all those who love him,
    but he destroys all the wicked.
22 My mouth shall speak the praise of the Lord;
    let all flesh bless his holy name for ever and ever.

READING   Romans 9.1–5

¹ I am speaking the truth in Christ—I am not lying; my conscience confirms it by the Holy Spirit— ² I have great sorrow and unceasing anguish in my heart. ³ For I could wish that I myself were accursed and cut off from Christ for the sake of my own people, my kindred according to the flesh. ⁴ They are Israelites, and to them belong the adoption, the glory, the covenants, the giving of the law, the worship, and the promises; ⁵ to them belong the patriarchs, and from them, according to the flesh, comes the Messiah, who is over all, God blessed for ever. Amen.

GOSPEL   Matthew 14.13–21

¹³ Now when Jesus heard this, he withdrew from there in a boat to a deserted place by himself. But when the crowds heard it, they followed him on foot from the towns. ¹⁴ When he went ashore, he saw a great crowd; and he had compassion for them and cured their sick. ¹⁵ When it was evening, the disciples came to him and said, 'This is a deserted place, and the hour is now late; send the crowds away so that they may go into the villages and buy food for themselves.' ¹⁶ Jesus said to them, 'They need not go away; you give them something to eat.' ¹⁷ They replied, 'We have nothing here but five loaves and two fish.' ¹⁸ And he said, 'Bring them here to me.' ¹⁹ Then he ordered the crowds to sit down on the grass. Taking the five loaves and the two fish, he looked up to heaven, and blessed and broke the loaves, and gave them to the disciples, and the disciples gave them to the crowds. ²⁰ And all ate and were filled; and they took up what was left over of the broken pieces, twelve baskets full. ²¹ And those who ate were about five thousand men, besides women and children.

POST COMMUNION

See pages 206 to 210 and Table on page 201

SECOND SERVICE

Psalm 80.1–7, [8–18]
1 Kings 10.1–13
Acts 13.1–13

If the Second Service is a Eucharist, the following is read as a Gospel:

John 6.24–35

THIRD SERVICE

Psalm 85
Song of Solomon 5.2–16

or

1 Maccabees 3.1–12
2 Peter 1.1–15

PROPER 14

Sunday between 7 and 13 August inclusive

COLLECT

See pages 206 to 210 and Table on page 201

CONTINUOUS

READING   Genesis 37.1–4, 12–28

¹ Jacob settled in the land where his father had lived as an alien, the land of Canaan. ² This is the story of the family of Jacob.

Joseph, being seventeen years old, was shepherding the flock with his brothers; he was a helper to the sons of Bilhah and Zilpah, his father's wives; and Joseph brought a bad report of them to their father. ³ Now Israel loved Joseph more than any other of his children, because he was the son of his old age; and he had made him a long robe with sleeves. ⁴ But when his brothers saw that their father loved him more than all his brothers, they hated him, and could not speak peaceably to him.

¹² Now his brothers went to pasture their father's flock near Shechem. ¹³ And Israel said to Joseph, 'Are not your brothers pasturing the flock at Shechem? Come, I will send you to them.' He answered, 'Here I am.' ¹⁴ So he said to him, 'Go now, see if it is well with your brothers and with the flock; and bring word back to me.' So he sent him from the valley of Hebron.

He came to Shechem, ¹⁵ and a man found him wandering in the fields;

the man asked him, 'What are you seeking?' 16 'I am seeking my brothers,' he said; 'tell me, please, where they are pasturing the flock.' 17 The man said, 'They have gone away, for I heard them say, "Let us go to Dothan." ' So Joseph went after his brothers, and found them at Dothan. 18 They saw him from a distance, and before he came near to them, they conspired to kill him. 19 They said to one another, 'Here comes this dreamer. 20 Come now, let us kill him and throw him into one of the pits; then we shall say that a wild animal has devoured him, and we shall see what will become of his dreams.' 21 But when Reuben heard it, he delivered him out of their hands, saying, 'Let us not take his life.' 22 Reuben said to them, 'Shed no blood; throw him into this pit here in the wilderness, but lay no hand on him'— that he might rescue him out of their hand and restore him to his father. 23 So when Joseph came to his brothers, they stripped him of his robe, the long robe with sleeves that he wore; 24 and they took him and threw him into a pit. The pit was empty; there was no water in it.

25 Then they sat down to eat; and looking up they saw a caravan of Ishmaelites coming from Gilead, with their camels carrying gum, balm, and resin, on their way to carry it down to Egypt. 26 Then Judah said to his brothers, 'What profit is there if we kill our brother and conceal his blood? 27 Come, let us sell him to the Ishmaelites, and not lay our hands on him, for he is our brother, our own flesh.' And his brothers agreed. 28 When some Midianite traders passed by, they drew Joseph up, lifting him out of the pit, and sold him to the Ishmaelites for twenty pieces of silver. And they took Joseph to Egypt.

PSALM   Psalm 105.1–6, 16–22, 45b

1   Give thanks to the Lord and call upon his name;
    make known his deeds among the peoples.
2   Sing to him, sing praises to him,
    and speak of all his marvellous works.
3   Glory in his holy name;
    let the hearts of those who seek the Lord rejoice.
4   Search for the Lord and his strength;
    continually seek his face.
5   Remember the marvels he has done,
    his wonders and the judgements of his mouth,
6   O offspring of Abraham his servant,
    O children of Jacob his chosen.

16 Then he called for a famine in the land
    and destroyed the supply of bread.

17 He sent a man before them,
Joseph, who was sold as a slave.
18 They bruised his feet in fetters;
his neck they put in an iron collar.
19 Until his prediction came to pass,
the word of the Lord tested him.
20 The king sent and released him;
the ruler of the peoples set him free.
21 He set him as master over his household,
as a ruler over all his possessions,
22 To instruct his princes according to his will
and to teach his elders wisdom.

45 Alleluia!

OR, IF AN ALTERNATIVE READING IS PREFERRED   **Psalm 105.1–10**

1 Give thanks to the Lord and call upon his name;
make known his deeds among the peoples.
2 Sing to him, sing praises to him,
and speak of all his marvellous works.
3 Glory in his holy name;
let the hearts of those who seek the Lord rejoice.
4 Search for the Lord and his strength;
continually seek his face.
5 Remember the marvels he has done,
his wonders and the judgements of his mouth,
6 O offspring of Abraham his servant,
O children of Jacob his chosen.
7 He is the Lord our God;
his judgements prevail in all the world.
8 He has always been mindful of his covenant,
the promise he made for a thousand generations:
9 The covenant he made with Abraham,
the oath that he swore to Isaac,
10 Which he established as a statute for Jacob,
an everlasting covenant for Israel.

READING   Romans 10.5–15

5 Moses writes concerning the righteousness that comes from the law, that 'the person who does these things will live by them.' 6 But the righteousness that comes from faith says, 'Do not say in your heart, "Who will ascend into heaven?"' (that is, to bring Christ down) 7 'or "Who will

descend into the abyss?" ' (that is, to bring Christ up from the dead). [8] But what does it say?

'The word is near you,
on your lips and in your heart'

(that is, the word of faith that we proclaim); [9] because if you confess with your lips that Jesus is Lord and believe in your heart that God raised him from the dead, you will be saved. [10] For one believes with the heart and so is justified, and one confesses with the mouth and so is saved. [11] The scripture says, 'No one who believes in him will be put to shame.' [12] For there is no distinction between Jew and Greek; the same Lord is Lord of all and is generous to all who call on him. [13] For, 'Everyone who calls on the name of the Lord shall be saved.'

[14] But how are they to call on one in whom they have not believed? And how are they to believe in one of whom they have never heard? And how are they to hear without someone to proclaim him? [15] And how are they to proclaim him unless they are sent? As it is written, 'How beautiful are the feet of those who bring good news!'

GOSPEL   Matthew 14.22–33

[22] Immediately he made the disciples get into the boat and go on ahead to the other side, while he dismissed the crowds. [23] And after he had dismissed the crowds, he went up the mountain by himself to pray. When evening came, he was there alone, [24] but by this time the boat, battered by the waves, was far from the land, for the wind was against them. [25] And early in the morning he came walking towards them on the lake. [26] But when the disciples saw him walking on the lake, they were terrified, saying, 'It is a ghost!' And they cried out in fear. [27] But immediately Jesus spoke to them and said, 'Take heart, it is I; do not be afraid.'

[28] Peter answered him, 'Lord, if it is you, command me to come to you on the water.' [29] He said, 'Come.' So Peter got out of the boat, started walking on the water, and came towards Jesus. [30] But when he noticed the strong wind, he became frightened, and beginning to sink, he cried out, 'Lord, save me!' [31] Jesus immediately reached out his hand and caught him, saying to him, 'You of little faith, why did you doubt?' [32] When they got into the boat, the wind ceased. [33] And those in the boat worshipped him, saying, 'Truly you are the Son of God.'

RELATED

READING   1 Kings 19.9–18

⁹ At that place he came to a cave, and spent the night there.

Then the word of the LORD came to him, saying, 'What are you doing here, Elijah?' ¹⁰ He answered, 'I have been very zealous for the LORD, the God of hosts; for the Israelites have forsaken your covenant, thrown down your altars, and killed your prophets with the sword. I alone am left, and they are seeking my life, to take it away.'

¹¹ He said, 'Go out and stand on the mountain before the LORD, for the LORD is about to pass by.' Now there was a great wind, so strong that it was splitting mountains and breaking rocks in pieces before the LORD, but the LORD was not in the wind; and after the wind an earthquake, but the LORD was not in the earthquake; ¹² and after the earthquake a fire, but the LORD was not in the fire; and after the fire a sound of sheer silence. ¹³ When Elijah heard it, he wrapped his face in his mantle and went out and stood at the entrance of the cave. Then there came a voice to him that said, 'What are you doing here, Elijah?' ¹⁴ He answered, 'I have been very zealous for the LORD, the God of hosts; for the Israelites have forsaken your covenant, thrown down your altars, and killed your prophets with the sword. I alone am left, and they are seeking my life, to take it away.' ¹⁵ Then the LORD said to him, 'Go, return on your way to the wilderness of Damascus; when you arrive, you shall anoint Hazael as king over Aram. ¹⁶ Also you shall anoint Jehu son of Nimshi as king over Israel; and you shall anoint Elisha son of Shaphat of Abel-meholah as prophet in your place. ¹⁷ Whoever escapes from the sword of Hazael, Jehu shall kill; and whoever escapes from the sword of Jehu, Elisha shall kill. ¹⁸ Yet I will leave seven thousand in Israel, all the knees that have not bowed to Baal, and every mouth that has not kissed him.'

PSALM   Psalm 85.8–13

8 I will listen to what the Lord God is saying,
    for he is speaking peace to his faithful people and to those who
      turn their hearts to him.
9 Truly, his salvation is very near to those who fear him,
    that his glory may dwell in our land.
10 Mercy and truth have met together;
    righteousness and peace have kissed each other.
11 Truth shall spring up from the earth,
    and righteousness shall look down from heaven.

¹² The Lord will indeed grant prosperity,
   and our land will yield its increase.
¹³ Righteousness shall go before him,
   and peace shall be a pathway for his feet.

READING   Romans 10.5–15

⁵ Moses writes concerning the righteousness that comes from the law, that 'the person who does these things will live by them.' ⁶ But the righteousness that comes from faith says, 'Do not say in your heart, "Who will ascend into heaven?" ' (that is, to bring Christ down) ⁷ 'or "Who will descend into the abyss?" ' (that is, to bring Christ up from the dead). ⁸ But what does it say?

'The word is near you,
    on your lips and in your heart'

(that is, the word of faith that we proclaim); ⁹ because if you confess with your lips that Jesus is Lord and believe in your heart that God raised him from the dead, you will be saved. ¹⁰ For one believes with the heart and so is justified, and one confesses with the mouth and so is saved. ¹¹ The scripture says, 'No one who believes in him will be put to shame.' ¹² For there is no distinction between Jew and Greek; the same Lord is Lord of all and is generous to all who call on him. ¹³ For, 'Everyone who calls on the name of the Lord shall be saved.'

¹⁴ But how are they to call on one in whom they have not believed? And how are they to believe in one of whom they have never heard? And how are they to hear without someone to proclaim him? ¹⁵ And how are they to proclaim him unless they are sent? As it is written, 'How beautiful are the feet of those who bring good news!'

GOSPEL   Matthew 14.22–33

²² Immediately he made the disciples get into the boat and go on ahead to the other side, while he dismissed the crowds. ²³ And after he had dismissed the crowds, he went up the mountain by himself to pray. When evening came, he was there alone, ²⁴ but by this time the boat, battered by the waves, was far from the land, for the wind was against them. ²⁵ And early in the morning he came walking towards them on the lake. ²⁶ But when the disciples saw him walking on the lake, they were terrified, saying, 'It is a ghost!' And they cried out in fear. ²⁷ But immediately Jesus spoke to them and said, 'Take heart, it is I; do not be afraid.'

²⁸ Peter answered him, 'Lord, if it is you, command me to come to you on the water.' ²⁹ He said, 'Come.' So Peter got out of the boat, started walking

on the water, and came towards Jesus. ³⁰ But when he noticed the strong wind, he became frightened, and beginning to sink, he cried out, 'Lord, save me!' ³¹ Jesus immediately reached out his hand and caught him, saying to him, 'You of little faith, why did you doubt?' ³² When they got into the boat, the wind ceased. ³³ And those in the boat worshipped him, saying, 'Truly you are the Son of God.'

POST COMMUNION

See pages 207 to 211 and Table on page 201

SECOND SERVICE

Psalm 86
1 Kings 11.41–12.20
Acts 14.8–20

If the Second Service is a Eucharist, the following is read as a Gospel:

John 6.35, 41–51

THIRD SERVICE

Psalm 88
Song of Solomon 8.5–7

or

1 Maccabees 14.4–15
2 Peter 3.8–13

PROPER 15

Sunday between 14 and 20 August inclusive

COLLECT

See pages 207 to 211 and Table on page 201

CONTINUOUS

READING   Genesis 45.1–15

¹ Then Joseph could no longer control himself before all those who stood by him, and he cried out, 'Send everyone away from me.' So no one stayed with him when Joseph made himself known to his brothers. ² And he wept so loudly that the Egyptians heard it, and the household of Pharaoh heard it. ³ Joseph said to his brothers, 'I am Joseph. Is my father still alive?' But his brothers could not answer him, so dismayed were they at his presence.

⁴ Then Joseph said to his brothers, 'Come closer to me.' And they came closer. He said, 'I am your brother Joseph, whom you sold into Egypt. ⁵ And

now do not be distressed, or angry with yourselves, because you sold me here; for God sent me before you to preserve life. [6] For the famine has been in the land these two years; and there are five more years in which there will be neither ploughing nor harvest. [7] God sent me before you to preserve for you a remnant on earth, and to keep alive for you many survivors. [8] So it was not you who sent me here, but God; he has made me a father to Pharaoh, and lord of all his house and ruler over all the land of Egypt. [9] Hurry and go up to my father and say to him, "Thus says your son Joseph, God has made me lord of all Egypt; come down to me, do not delay. [10] You shall settle in the land of Goshen, and you shall be near me, you and your children and your children's children, as well as your flocks, your herds, and all that you have. [11] I will provide for you there—since there are five more years of famine to come—so that you and your household, and all that you have, will not come to poverty." [12] And now your eyes and the eyes of my brother Benjamin see that it is my own mouth that speaks to you. [13] You must tell my father how greatly I am honoured in Egypt, and all that you have seen. Hurry and bring my father down here.' [14] Then he fell upon his brother Benjamin's neck and wept, while Benjamin wept upon his neck. [15] And he kissed all his brothers and wept upon them; and after that his brothers talked with him.

PSALM   Psalm 133

1 O how good and pleasant it is,
   when a family lives together in unity!
2 It is like fine oil upon the head
   that runs down upon the beard,
3 Upon the beard of Aaron,
   and runs down upon the collar of his robe.
4 It is like the dew of Hermon
   that falls upon the hills of Zion.
5 For there the Lord has ordained the blessing:
   life for evermore.

READING   Romans 11.1–2a, 29–32

[1] I ask, then, has God rejected his people? By no means! I myself am an Israelite, a descendant of Abraham, a member of the tribe of Benjamin. [2] God has not rejected his people whom he foreknew.

[29] For the gifts and the calling of God are irrevocable. [30] Just as you were once disobedient to God but have now received mercy because of their

disobedience, [31] so they have now been disobedient in order that, by the mercy shown to you, they too may now receive mercy. [32] For God has imprisoned all in disobedience so that he may be merciful to all.

GOSPEL   Matthew 15.[10–20,] 21–28

[[10] Then he called the crowd to him and said to them, 'Listen and understand: [11] it is not what goes into the mouth that defiles a person, but it is what comes out of the mouth that defiles.' [12] Then the disciples approached and said to him, 'Do you know that the Pharisees took offence when they heard what you said?' [13] He answered, 'Every plant that my heavenly Father has not planted will be uprooted. [14] Let them alone; they are blind guides of the blind. And if one blind person guides another, both will fall into a pit.' [15] But Peter said to him, 'Explain this parable to us.' [16] Then he said, 'Are you also still without understanding? [17] Do you not see that whatever goes into the mouth enters the stomach, and goes out into the sewer? [18] But what comes out of the mouth proceeds from the heart, and this is what defiles. [19] For out of the heart come evil intentions, murder, adultery, fornication, theft, false witness, slander. [20] These are what defile a person, but to eat with unwashed hands does not defile.']

[21] Jesus left that place and went away to the district of Tyre and Sidon. [22] Just then a Canaanite woman from that region came out and started shouting, 'Have mercy on me, Lord, Son of David; my daughter is tormented by a demon.' [23] But he did not answer her at all. And his disciples came and urged him, saying, 'Send her away, for she keeps shouting after us.' [24] He answered, 'I was sent only to the lost sheep of the house of Israel.' [25] But she came and knelt before him, saying, 'Lord, help me.' [26] He answered, 'It is not fair to take the children's food and throw it to the dogs.' [27] She said, 'Yes, Lord, yet even the dogs eat the crumbs that fall from their masters' table.' [28] Then Jesus answered her, 'Woman, great is your faith! Let it be done for you as you wish.' And her daughter was healed instantly.

RELATED

READING   Isaiah 56.1, 6–8

[1]   Thus says the LORD:
        Maintain justice, and do what is right,
    for soon my salvation will come,
        and my deliverance be revealed.

6 And the foreigners who join themselves to the LORD,
    to minister to him, to love the name of the LORD,
      and to be his servants,
  all who keep the sabbath, and do not profane it,
      and hold fast my covenant—
7 these I will bring to my holy mountain,
    and make them joyful in my house of prayer;
  their burnt-offerings and their sacrifices
      will be accepted on my altar;
  for my house shall be called a house of prayer
      for all peoples.
8 Thus says the Lord GOD,
    who gathers the outcasts of Israel,
  I will gather others to them
      besides those already gathered.

PSALM   Psalm 67

1 May God be merciful to us and bless us,
    show us the light of his countenance and come to us.
2 Let your ways be known upon earth,
    your saving health among all nations.
3 Let the peoples praise you, O God;
    let all the peoples praise you.
4 Let the nations be glad and sing for joy,
    for you judge the peoples with equity and guide all the nations
      upon earth.
5 Let the peoples praise you, O God;
    let all the peoples praise you.
6 The earth has brought forth her increase;
    may God, our own God, give us his blessing.
7 May God give us his blessing,
    and may all the ends of the earth stand in awe of him.

READING   Romans 11.1–2a, 29–32

1 I ask, then, has God rejected his people? By no means! I myself am an Israelite, a descendant of Abraham, a member of the tribe of Benjamin. 2 God has not rejected his people whom he foreknew.

^{29} For the gifts and the calling of God are irrevocable. ^{30} Just as you were once disobedient to God but have now received mercy because of their disobedience, ^{31} so they have now been disobedient in order that, by the mercy shown to you, they too may now receive mercy. ^{32} For God has imprisoned all in disobedience so that he may be merciful to all.

GOSPEL   Matthew 15.[10–20,] 21–28

[^{10} Then he called the crowd to him and said to them, 'Listen and under-stand: ^{11} it is not what goes into the mouth that defiles a person, but it is what comes out of the mouth that defiles.' ^{12} Then the disciples approached and said to him, 'Do you know that the Pharisees took offence when they heard what you said?' ^{13} He answered, 'Every plant that my heavenly Father has not planted will be uprooted. ^{14} Let them alone; they are blind guides of the blind. And if one blind person guides another, both will fall into a pit.' ^{15} But Peter said to him, 'Explain this parable to us.' ^{16} Then he said, 'Are you also still without understanding? ^{17} Do you not see that whatever goes into the mouth enters the stomach, and goes out into the sewer? ^{18} But what comes out of the mouth proceeds from the heart, and this is what defiles. ^{19} For out of the heart come evil intentions, murder, adultery, fornication, theft, false witness, slander. ^{20} These are what defile a person, but to eat with unwashed hands does not defile.']

^{21} Jesus left that place and went away to the district of Tyre and Sidon. ^{22} Just then a Canaanite woman from that region came out and started shouting, 'Have mercy on me, Lord, Son of David; my daughter is tormented by a demon.' ^{23} But he did not answer her at all. And his disciples came and urged him, saying, 'Send her away, for she keeps shouting after us.' ^{24} He answered, 'I was sent only to the lost sheep of the house of Israel.' ^{25} But she came and knelt before him, saying, 'Lord, help me.' ^{26} He answered, 'It is not fair to take the children's food and throw it to the dogs.' ^{27} She said, 'Yes, Lord, yet even the dogs eat the crumbs that fall from their masters' table.' ^{28} Then Jesus answered her, 'Woman, great is your faith! Let it be done for you as you wish.' And her daughter was healed instantly.

POST COMMUNION

See pages 207 to 211 and Table on page 201

SECOND SERVICE	THIRD SERVICE
Psalm 90.1–12, [13–17]	Psalm 92
2 Kings 4.1–37	Jonah 1
Acts 16.1–15	*or*
If the Second Service is a Eucharist, the following is read as a Gospel:	Ecclesiasticus 3.1–15
	2 Peter 3.14–18
John 6.51–58	

PROPER 16

Sunday between 21 and 27 August inclusive

COLLECT

See pages 208 to 212 and Table on page 201

CONTINUOUS

READING   Exodus 1.8–2.10

⁸ Now a new king arose over Egypt, who did not know Joseph. ⁹ He said to his people, 'Look, the Israelite people are more numerous and more power-ful than we. ¹⁰ Come, let us deal shrewdly with them, or they will increase and, in the event of war, join our enemies and fight against us and escape from the land.' ¹¹ Therefore they set taskmasters over them to oppress them with forced labour. They built supply cities, Pithom and Rameses, for Pharaoh. ¹² But the more they were oppressed, the more they multiplied and spread, so that the Egyptians came to dread the Israelites. ¹³ The Egyp-tians became ruthless in imposing tasks on the Israelites, ¹⁴ and made their lives bitter with hard service in mortar and brick and in every kind of field labour. They were ruthless in all the tasks that they imposed on them.

¹⁵ The king of Egypt said to the Hebrew midwives, one of whom was named Shiphrah and the other Puah, ¹⁶ 'When you act as midwives to the Hebrew women, and see them on the birthstool, if it is a boy, kill him; but if it is a girl, she shall live.' ¹⁷ But the midwives feared God; they did not do as the king of Egypt commanded them, but they let the boys live. ¹⁸ So the king

of Egypt summoned the midwives and said to them, 'Why have you done this, and allowed the boys to live?' ¹⁹ The midwives said to Pharaoh, 'Because the Hebrew women are not like the Egyptian women; for they are vigorous and give birth before the midwife comes to them.' ²⁰ So God dealt well with the midwives; and the people multiplied and became very strong. ²¹ And because the midwives feared God, he gave them families. ²² Then Pharaoh commanded all his people, 'Every boy that is born to the Hebrews you shall throw into the Nile, but you shall let every girl live.'

¹ Now a man from the house of Levi went and married a Levite woman. ² The woman conceived and bore a son; and when she saw that he was a fine baby, she hid him for three months. ³ When she could hide him no longer she got a papyrus basket for him, and plastered it with bitumen and pitch; she put the child in it and placed it among the reeds on the bank of the river. ⁴ His sister stood at a distance, to see what would happen to him.

⁵ The daughter of Pharaoh came down to bathe at the river, while her attendants walked beside the river. She saw the basket among the reeds and sent her maid to bring it. ⁶ When she opened it, she saw the child. He was crying, and she took pity on him. 'This must be one of the Hebrews' children,' she said. ⁷ Then his sister said to Pharaoh's daughter, 'Shall I go and get you a nurse from the Hebrew women to nurse the child for you?' ⁸ Pharaoh's daughter said to her, 'Yes.' So the girl went and called the child's mother. ⁹ Pharaoh's daughter said to her, 'Take this child and nurse it for me, and I will give you your wages.' So the woman took the child and nursed it. ¹⁰ When the child grew up, she brought him to Pharaoh's daughter, and she took him as her son. She named him Moses, 'because', she said, 'I drew him out of the water.'

PSALM   Psalm 124

1   If the Lord had not been on our side,
     let Israel now say;
2   If the Lord had not been on our side,
     when enemies rose up against us;
3   Then would they have swallowed us up alive
     in their fierce anger towards us;
4   Then would the waters have overwhelmed us
     and the torrent gone over us;
5   Then would the raging waters
     have gone right over us.
6   Blessèd be the Lord!
     he has not given us over to be a prey for their teeth.

7   We have escaped like a bird from the snare of the fowler;
    the snare is broken and we have escaped.
8   Our help is in the name of the Lord,
    the maker of heaven and earth.

READING   Romans 12.1–8

¹ I appeal to you therefore, brothers and sisters, by the mercies of God, to present your bodies as a living sacrifice, holy and acceptable to God, which is your spiritual worship. ² Do not be conformed to this world, but be transformed by the renewing of your minds, so that you may discern what is the will of God—what is good and acceptable and perfect.

³ For by the grace given to me I say to everyone among you not to think of yourself more highly than you ought to think, but to think with sober judgement, each according to the measure of faith that God has assigned. ⁴ For as in one body we have many members, and not all the members have the same function, ⁵ so we, who are many, are one body in Christ, and individually we are members one of another. ⁶ We have gifts that differ according to the grace given to us: prophecy, in proportion to faith; ⁷ ministry, in ministering; the teacher, in teaching; ⁸ the exhorter, in exhortation; the giver, in generosity; the leader, in diligence; the compassionate, in cheerfulness.

GOSPEL   Matthew 16.13–20

¹³ Now when Jesus came into the district of Caesarea Philippi, he asked his disciples, 'Who do people say that the Son of Man is?' ¹⁴ And they said, 'Some say John the Baptist, but others Elijah, and still others Jeremiah or one of the prophets.' ¹⁵ He said to them, 'But who do you say that I am?' ¹⁶ Simon Peter answered, 'You are the Messiah, the Son of the living God.' ¹⁷ And Jesus answered him, 'Blessed are you, Simon son of Jonah! For flesh and blood has not revealed this to you, but my Father in heaven. ¹⁸ And I tell you, you are Peter, and on this rock I will build my church, and the gates of Hades will not prevail against it. ¹⁹ I will give you the keys of the kingdom of heaven, and whatever you bind on earth will be bound in heaven, and whatever you loose on earth will be loosed in heaven.' ²⁰ Then he sternly ordered the disciples not to tell anyone that he was the Messiah.

RELATED

READING   Isaiah 51.1–6

¹ Listen to me, you that pursue righteousness,
    you that seek the LORD.
 Look to the rock from which you were hewn,
    and to the quarry from which you were dug.
² Look to Abraham your father
    and to Sarah who bore you;
 for he was but one when I called him,
    but I blessed him and made him many.
³ For the LORD will comfort Zion;
    he will comfort all her waste places,
 and will make her wilderness like Eden,
    her desert like the garden of the LORD;
 joy and gladness will be found in her,
    thanksgiving and the voice of song.
⁴ Listen to me, my people,
    and give heed to me, my nation;
 for a teaching will go out from me,
    and my justice for a light to the peoples.
⁵ I will bring near my deliverance swiftly,
    my salvation has gone out
    and my arms will rule the peoples;
 the coastlands wait for me,
    and for my arm they hope.
⁶ Lift up your eyes to the heavens,
    and look at the earth beneath;
 for the heavens will vanish like smoke,
    the earth will wear out like a garment,
    and those who live on it will die like gnats;
 but my salvation will be for ever,
    and my deliverance will never be ended.

PSALM   Psalm 138

¹ I will give thanks to you, O Lord, with my whole heart;
 before the gods I will sing your praise.
² I will bow down towards your holy temple and praise your name,
 because of your love and faithfulness;
³ For you have glorified your name
 and your word above all things.

⁴ When I called, you answered me;
   you increased my strength within me.
⁵ All the kings of the earth will praise you, O Lord,
   when they have heard the words of your mouth.
⁶ They will sing of the ways of the Lord,
   that great is the glory of the Lord.
⁷ Though the Lord be high, he cares for the lowly;
   he perceives the haughty from afar.
⁸ Though I walk in the midst of trouble, you keep me safe;
   you stretch forth your hand against the fury of my enemies; your
     right hand shall save me.
⁹ The Lord will make good his purpose for me;
   O Lord, your love endures for ever; do not abandon the works of
     your hands.

READING   Romans 12.1–8

¹ I appeal to you therefore, brothers and sisters, by the mercies of God, to present your bodies as a living sacrifice, holy and acceptable to God, which is your spiritual worship. ² Do not be conformed to this world, but be transformed by the renewing of your minds, so that you may discern what is the will of God—what is good and acceptable and perfect.

³ For by the grace given to me I say to everyone among you not to think of yourself more highly than you ought to think, but to think with sober judgement, each according to the measure of faith that God has assigned. ⁴ For as in one body we have many members, and not all the members have the same function, ⁵ so we, who are many, are one body in Christ, and individually we are members one of another. ⁶ We have gifts that differ according to the grace given to us: prophecy, in proportion to faith; ⁷ ministry, in ministering; the teacher, in teaching; ⁸ the exhorter, in exhortation; the giver, in generosity; the leader, in diligence; the compassionate, in cheerfulness.

GOSPEL   Matthew 16.13–20

¹³ Now when Jesus came into the district of Caesarea Philippi, he asked his disciples, 'Who do people say that the Son of Man is?' ¹⁴ And they said, 'Some say John the Baptist, but others Elijah, and still others Jeremiah or one of the prophets.' ¹⁵ He said to them, 'But who do you say that I am?' ¹⁶ Simon Peter answered, 'You are the Messiah, the Son of the living God.' ¹⁷ And Jesus answered him, 'Blessed are you, Simon son of Jonah! For flesh and blood has not revealed this to you, but my Father in heaven. ¹⁸ And I

tell you, you are Peter, and on this rock I will build my church, and the gates of Hades will not prevail against it. [19] I will give you the keys of the kingdom of heaven, and whatever you bind on earth will be bound in heaven, and whatever you loose on earth will be loosed in heaven.' [20] Then he sternly ordered the disciples not to tell anyone that he was the Messiah.

POST COMMUNION

See pages 208 to 212 and Table on page 201

SECOND SERVICE	THIRD SERVICE
Psalm 95	Psalm 104.1–26
2 Kings 6.8–23	Jonah 2
Acts 17.15–34	*or*
If the Second Service is a Eucharist, the following is read as a Gospel:	Ecclesiasticus 3.17–29
	Revelation 1
John 6.56–69	

PROPER 17

Sunday between 28 August and 3 September inclusive

COLLECT

See pages 209 to 212 and Table on page 201

CONTINUOUS

READING   Exodus 3.1–15

[1] Moses was keeping the flock of his father-in-law Jethro, the priest of Midian; he led his flock beyond the wilderness, and came to Horeb, the mountain of God. [2] There the angel of the LORD appeared to him in a flame of fire out of a bush; he looked, and the bush was blazing, yet it was not consumed. [3] Then Moses said, 'I must turn aside and look at this great sight, and see why the bush is not burned up.' [4] When the LORD saw that he had turned aside to see, God called to him out of the bush, 'Moses, Moses!' And he said, 'Here I am.' [5] Then he said, 'Come no closer! Remove the sandals from your feet, for the place on which you are standing is holy ground.' [6] He said further, 'I am the God of your father, the God of Abraham,

the God of Isaac, and the God of Jacob.' And Moses hid his face, for he was afraid to look at God.

⁷ Then the LORD said, 'I have observed the misery of my people who are in Egypt; I have heard their cry on account of their taskmasters. Indeed, I know their sufferings, ⁸ and I have come down to deliver them from the Egyptians, and to bring them up out of that land to a good and broad land, a land flowing with milk and honey, to the country of the Canaanites, the Hittites, the Amorites, the Perizzites, the Hivites, and the Jebusites. ⁹ The cry of the Israelites has now come to me; I have also seen how the Egyptians oppress them. ¹⁰ So come, I will send you to Pharaoh to bring my people, the Israelites, out of Egypt.' ¹¹ But Moses said to God, 'Who am I that I should go to Pharaoh, and bring the Israelites out of Egypt?' ¹² He said, 'I will be with you; and this shall be the sign for you that it is I who sent you: when you have brought the people out of Egypt, you shall worship God on this mountain.'

¹³ But Moses said to God, 'If I come to the Israelites and say to them, "The God of your ancestors has sent me to you", and they ask me, "What is his name?" what shall I say to them?' ¹⁴ God said to Moses, 'I AM WHO I AM.' He said further, 'Thus you shall say to the Israelites, "I AM has sent me to you."' ¹⁵ God also said to Moses, 'Thus you shall say to the Israelites, "The LORD, the God of your ancestors, the God of Abraham, the God of Isaac, and the God of Jacob, has sent me to you":

This is my name for ever,
and this my title for all generations.'

PSALM   Psalm 105.1–6, 23–26, 45b

¹   Give thanks to the Lord and call upon his name;
    make known his deeds among the peoples.
²   Sing to him, sing praises to him,
    and speak of all his marvellous works.
³   Glory in his holy name;
    let the hearts of those who seek the Lord rejoice.
⁴   Search for the Lord and his strength;
    continually seek his face.
⁵   Remember the marvels he has done,
    his wonders and the judgements of his mouth,
⁶   O offspring of Abraham his servant,
    O children of Jacob his chosen.

²³ Israel came into Egypt,
    and Jacob became a sojourner in the land of Ham.

24 The Lord made his people exceedingly fruitful;
   he made them stronger than their enemies;
25 Whose heart he turned, so that they hated his people,
   and dealt unjustly with his servants.
26 He sent Moses his servant,
   and Aaron whom he had chosen.

45 Alleluia!

OR, IF AN ALTERNATIVE IS PREFERRED   **Psalm 115**

1 Not to us, O Lord, not to us, but to your name give glory;
   because of your love and because of your faithfulness.
2 Why should the heathen say,
   'Where then is their God?'
3 Our God is in heaven;
   whatever he wills to do he does.
4 Their idols are silver and gold,
   the work of human hands.
5 They have mouths, but they cannot speak;
   eyes have they, but they cannot see;
6 They have ears, but they cannot hear;
   noses, but they cannot smell;
7 They have hands, but they cannot feel; feet, but they cannot walk;
   they make no sound with their throat.
8 Those who make them are like them,
   and so are all who put their trust in them.
9 O Israel, trust in the Lord;
   he is their help and their shield.
10 O house of Aaron, trust in the Lord;
    he is their help and their shield.
11 You who fear the Lord, trust in the Lord;
    he is their help and their shield.
12 The Lord has been mindful of us and he will bless us;
    he will bless the house of Israel; he will bless the house of Aaron;
13 He will bless those who fear the Lord,
    both small and great together.
14 May the Lord increase you more and more,
    you and your children after you.
15 May you be blessed by the Lord,
    the maker of heaven and earth.
16 The heaven of heavens is the Lord's,
    but he entrusted the earth to its peoples.

17   The dead do not praise the Lord,
     nor all those who go down into silence;
18   But we will bless the Lord,
     from this time forth for evermore. Alleluia!

READING   Romans 12.9–21

⁹ Let love be genuine; hate what is evil, hold fast to what is good; ¹⁰ love one another with mutual affection; outdo one another in showing honour. ¹¹ Do not lag in zeal, be ardent in spirit, serve the Lord. ¹² Rejoice in hope, be patient in suffering, persevere in prayer. ¹³ Contribute to the needs of the saints; extend hospitality to strangers.

¹⁴ Bless those who persecute you; bless and do not curse them. ¹⁵ Rejoice with those who rejoice, weep with those who weep. ¹⁶ Live in harmony with one another; do not be haughty, but associate with the lowly; do not claim to be wiser than you are. ¹⁷ Do not repay anyone evil for evil, but take thought for what is noble in the sight of all. ¹⁸ If it is possible, so far as it depends on you, live peaceably with all. ¹⁹ Beloved, never avenge yourselves, but leave room for the wrath of God; for it is written, 'Vengeance is mine, I will repay, says the Lord.' ²⁰ No, 'if your enemies are hungry, feed them; if they are thirsty, give them something to drink; for by doing this you will heap burning coals on their heads.' ²¹ Do not be overcome by evil, but overcome evil with good.

GOSPEL   Matthew 16.21–28

²¹ From that time on, Jesus began to show his disciples that he must go to Jerusalem and undergo great suffering at the hands of the elders and chief priests and scribes, and be killed, and on the third day be raised. ²² And Peter took him aside and began to rebuke him, saying, 'God forbid it, Lord! This must never happen to you.' ²³ But he turned and said to Peter, 'Get behind me, Satan! You are a stumbling-block to me; for you are setting your mind not on divine things but on human things.'

²⁴ Then Jesus told his disciples, 'If any want to become my followers, let them deny themselves and take up their cross and follow me. ²⁵ For those who want to save their life will lose it, and those who lose their life for my sake will find it. ²⁶ For what will it profit them if they gain the whole world but forfeit their life? Or what will they give in return for their life?

²⁷ 'For the Son of Man is to come with his angels in the glory of his Father, and then he will repay everyone for what has been done. ²⁸ Truly I tell you, there are some standing here who will not taste death before they see the Son of Man coming in his kingdom.'

RELATED

READING   **Jeremiah 15.15–21**

¹⁵ O LORD, you know;
    remember me and visit me,
    and bring down retribution for me on my persecutors.
  In your forbearance do not take me away;
    know that on your account I suffer insult.
¹⁶ Your words were found, and I ate them,
    and your words became to me a joy
    and the delight of my heart;
  for I am called by your name,
    O LORD, God of hosts.
¹⁷ I did not sit in the company of merrymakers,
    nor did I rejoice;
  under the weight of your hand I sat alone,
    for you had filled me with indignation.
¹⁸ Why is my pain unceasing,
    my wound incurable,
    refusing to be healed?
  Truly, you are to me like a deceitful brook,
    like waters that fail.
¹⁹ Therefore, thus says the LORD:
  If you turn back, I will take you back,
    and you shall stand before me.
  If you utter what is precious, and not what is worthless,
    you shall serve as my mouth.
  It is they who will turn to you,
    not you who will turn to them.
²⁰ And I will make you to this people
    a fortified wall of bronze;
  they will fight against you,
    but they shall not prevail over you,
  for I am with you
    to save you and deliver you,

                  says the LORD.

²¹ I will deliver you out of the hand of the wicked,
    and redeem you from the grasp of the ruthless.

PSALM

Psalm 26.1–8

1 Give judgement for me, O Lord, for I have lived with integrity;
   I have trusted in the Lord and have not faltered.
2 Test me, O Lord, and try me;
   examine my heart and my mind.
3 For your love is before my eyes;
   I have walked faithfully with you.
4 I have not sat with the worthless,
   nor do I consort with the deceitful.
5 I have hated the company of evildoers;
   I will not sit down with the wicked.
6 I will wash my hands in innocence, O Lord,
   that I may go in procession round your altar,
7 Singing aloud a song of thanksgiving
   and recounting all your wonderful deeds.
8 Lord, I love the house in which you dwell
   and the place where your glory abides.

READING

Romans 12.9–21

9 Let love be genuine; hate what is evil, hold fast to what is good; 10 love one another with mutual affection; outdo one another in showing honour. 11 Do not lag in zeal, be ardent in spirit, serve the Lord. 12 Rejoice in hope, be patient in suffering, persevere in prayer. 13 Contribute to the needs of the saints; extend hospitality to strangers.

14 Bless those who persecute you; bless and do not curse them. 15 Rejoice with those who rejoice, weep with those who weep. 16 Live in harmony with one another; do not be haughty, but associate with the lowly; do not claim to be wiser than you are. 17 Do not repay anyone evil for evil, but take thought for what is noble in the sight of all. 18 If it is possible, so far as it depends on you, live peaceably with all. 19 Beloved, never avenge yourselves, but leave room for the wrath of God; for it is written, 'Vengeance is mine, I will repay, says the Lord.' 20 No, 'if your enemies are hungry, feed them; if they are thirsty, give them something to drink; for by doing this you will heap burning coals on their heads.' 21 Do not be overcome by evil, but overcome evil with good.

GOSPEL

Matthew 16.21–28

21 From that time on, Jesus began to show his disciples that he must go to Jerusalem and undergo great suffering at the hands of the elders and chief priests and scribes, and be killed, and on the third day be raised. 22 And

Peter took him aside and began to rebuke him, saying, 'God forbid it, Lord! This must never happen to you.' 23 But he turned and said to Peter, 'Get behind me, Satan! You are a stumbling-block to me; for you are setting your mind not on divine things but on human things.'

24 Then Jesus told his disciples, 'If any want to become my followers, let them deny themselves and take up their cross and follow me. 25 For those who want to save their life will lose it, and those who lose their life for my sake will find it. 26 For what will it profit them if they gain the whole world but forfeit their life? Or what will they give in return for their life?

27 'For the Son of Man is to come with his angels in the glory of his Father, and then he will repay everyone for what has been done. 28 Truly I tell you, there are some standing here who will not taste death before they see the Son of Man coming in his kingdom.'

POST COMMUNION

See pages 209 to 213 and Table on page 201

SECOND SERVICE

Psalm 105.1–15
2 Kings 6.24–25; 7.3–20
Acts 18.1–16

If the Second Service is a Eucharist, the following is read as a Gospel:

Mark 7.1–8, 14–15, 21–23

THIRD SERVICE

Psalm 107.1–32
Jonah 3.1–9

or

Ecclesiasticus 11.[7–18,] 19–28
Revelation 3.14–22

PROPER 18

Sunday between 4 and 10 September inclusive

COLLECT

See pages 209 to 213 and Table on page 201

CONTINUOUS

READING   Exodus 12.1–14

¹ The LORD said to Moses and Aaron in the land of Egypt: ² This month shall mark for you the beginning of months; it shall be the first month of the year for you. ³ Tell the whole congregation of Israel that on the tenth of this month they are to take a lamb for each family, a lamb for each household. ⁴ If a household is too small for a whole lamb, it shall join its closest neighbour in obtaining one; the lamb shall be divided in proportion to the number of people who eat of it. ⁵ Your lamb shall be without blemish, a year-old male; you may take it from the sheep or from the goats. ⁶ You shall keep it until the fourteenth day of this month; then the whole assembled congregation of Israel shall slaughter it at twilight. ⁷ They shall take some of the blood and put it on the two doorposts and the lintel of the houses in which they eat it. ⁸ They shall eat the lamb that same night; they shall eat it roasted over the fire with unleavened bread and bitter herbs. ⁹ Do not eat any of it raw or boiled in water, but roasted over the fire, with its head, legs, and inner organs. ¹⁰ You shall let none of it remain until the morning; anything that remains until the morning you shall burn. ¹¹ This is how you shall eat it: your loins girded, your sandals on your feet, and your staff in your hand; and you shall eat it hurriedly. It is the passover of the LORD. ¹² For I will pass through the land of Egypt that night, and I will strike down every firstborn in the land of Egypt, both human beings and animals; on all the gods of Egypt I will execute judgements: I am the LORD. ¹³ The blood shall be a sign for you on the houses where you live: when I see the blood, I will pass over you, and no plague shall destroy you when I strike the land of Egypt.

¹⁴ This day shall be a day of remembrance for you. You shall celebrate it as a festival to the LORD; throughout your generations you shall observe it as a perpetual ordinance.

PSALM   Psalm 149

[1] Alleluia! Sing to the Lord a new song;
   sing his praise in the congregation of the faithful.
[2] Let Israel rejoice in his maker;
   let the children of Zion be joyful in their king.
[3] Let them praise his name in the dance;
   let them sing praise to him with timbrel and harp.
[4] For the Lord takes pleasure in his people
   and adorns the poor with victory.
[5] Let the faithful rejoice in triumph;
   let them be joyful on their beds.
[6] Let the praises of God be in their throat
   and a two-edged sword in their hand;
[7] To wreak vengeance on the nations
   and punishment on the peoples;
[8] To bind their kings in chains
   and their nobles with links of iron;
[9] To inflict on them the judgement decreed;
   this is glory for all his faithful people. Alleluia!

READING   Romans 13.8–14

[8] Owe no one anything, except to love one another; for the one who loves another has fulfilled the law. [9] The commandments, 'You shall not commit adultery; You shall not murder; You shall not steal; You shall not covet'; and any other commandment, are summed up in this word, 'Love your neighbour as yourself.' [10] Love does no wrong to a neighbour; therefore, love is the fulfilling of the law.

[11] Besides this, you know what time it is, how it is now the moment for you to wake from sleep. For salvation is nearer to us now than when we became believers; [12] the night is far gone, the day is near. Let us then lay aside the works of darkness and put on the armour of light; [13] let us live honourably as in the day, not in revelling and drunkenness, not in debauchery and licentiousness, not in quarrelling and jealousy. [14] Instead, put on the Lord Jesus Christ, and make no provision for the flesh, to gratify its desires.

GOSPEL   Matthew 18.15–20

¹⁵ 'If another member of the church sins against you, go and point out the fault when the two of you are alone. If the member listens to you, you have regained that one. ¹⁶ But if you are not listened to, take one or two others along with you, so that every word may be confirmed by the evidence of two or three witnesses. ¹⁷ If the member refuses to listen to them, tell it to the church; and if the offender refuses to listen even to the church, let such a one be to you as a Gentile and a tax-collector. ¹⁸ Truly I tell you, whatever you bind on earth will be bound in heaven, and whatever you loose on earth will be loosed in heaven. ¹⁹ Again, truly I tell you, if two of you agree on earth about anything you ask, it will be done for you by my Father in heaven. ²⁰ For where two or three are gathered in my name, I am there among them.'

RELATED

READING   Ezekiel 33.7–11

⁷ So you, mortal, I have made a sentinel for the house of Israel; whenever you hear a word from my mouth, you shall give them warning from me. ⁸ If I say to the wicked, 'O wicked ones, you shall surely die', and you do not speak to warn the wicked to turn from their ways, the wicked shall die in their iniquity, but their blood I will require at your hand. ⁹ But if you warn the wicked to turn from their ways, and they do not turn from their ways, the wicked shall die in their iniquity, but you will have saved your life.

¹⁰ Now you, mortal, say to the house of Israel, Thus you have said: 'Our transgressions and our sins weigh upon us, and we waste away because of them; how then can we live?' ¹¹ Say to them, As I live, says the Lord GOD, I have no pleasure in the death of the wicked, but that the wicked turn from their ways and live; turn back, turn back from your evil ways; for why will you die, O house of Israel?

PSALM   Psalm 119.33–40

³³ Teach me, O Lord, the way of your statutes,
   and I shall keep it to the end.
³⁴ Give me understanding and I shall keep your law;
   I shall keep it with all my heart.
³⁵ Make me go in the path of your commandments,
   for that is my desire.

36 Incline my heart to your decrees
    and not to unjust gain.
37 Turn my eyes from watching what is worthless;
    give me life in your ways.
38 Fulfil your promise to your servant,
    which you make to those who fear you.
39 Turn away the reproach which I dread,
    because your judgements are good.
40 Behold, I long for your commandments;
    in your righteousness preserve my life.

READING   Romans 13.8-14

⁸ Owe no one anything, except to love one another; for the one who loves another has fulfilled the law. ⁹ The commandments, 'You shall not commit adultery; You shall not murder; You shall not steal; You shall not covet'; and any other commandment, are summed up in this word, 'Love your neighbour as yourself.' ¹⁰ Love does no wrong to a neighbour; therefore, love is the fulfilling of the law.

¹¹ Besides this, you know what time it is, how it is now the moment for you to wake from sleep. For salvation is nearer to us now than when we became believers; ¹² the night is far gone, the day is near. Let us then lay aside the works of darkness and put on the armour of light; ¹³ let us live honourably as in the day, not in revelling and drunkenness, not in debauchery and licentiousness, not in quarrelling and jealousy. ¹⁴ Instead, put on the Lord Jesus Christ, and make no provision for the flesh, to gratify its desires.

GOSPEL   Matthew 18.15-20

¹⁵ 'If another member of the church sins against you, go and point out the fault when the two of you are alone. If the member listens to you, you have regained that one. ¹⁶ But if you are not listened to, take one or two others along with you, so that every word may be confirmed by the evidence of two or three witnesses. ¹⁷ If the member refuses to listen to them, tell it to the church; and if the offender refuses to listen even to the church, let such a one be to you as a Gentile and a tax-collector. ¹⁸ Truly I tell you, whatever you bind on earth will be bound in heaven, and whatever you loose on earth will be loosed in heaven. ¹⁹ Again, truly I tell you, if two of you agree on earth about anything you ask, it will be done for you by my Father in heaven. ²⁰ For where two or three are gathered in my name, I am there among them.'

POST COMMUNION

See pages 210 to 213 and Table on page 201

SECOND SERVICE

Psalms 108; [115]
Ezekiel 12.21–13.16
Acts 19.1–20

If the Second Service is a Eucharist, the following is read as a Gospel:

Mark 7.24–37

THIRD SERVICE

Psalm 119.17–32
Jonah 3.10–4.11

or

Ecclesiasticus 27.30–28.9
Revelation 8.1–5

PROPER 19

Sunday between 11 and 17 September inclusive

COLLECT

See pages 210 to 214 and Table on page 201

CONTINUOUS

READING   Exodus 14.19–31

[19] The angel of God who was going before the Israelite army moved and went behind them; and the pillar of cloud moved from in front of them and took its place behind them. [20] It came between the army of Egypt and the army of Israel. And so the cloud was there with the darkness, and it lit up the night; one did not come near the other all night.

[21] Then Moses stretched out his hand over the sea. The LORD drove the sea back by a strong east wind all night, and turned the sea into dry land; and the waters were divided. [22] The Israelites went into the sea on dry ground, the waters forming a wall for them on their right and on their left. [23] The Egyptians pursued, and went into the sea after them, all of Pharaoh's horses, chariots, and chariot drivers. [24] At the morning watch the LORD in the pillar of fire and cloud looked down upon the Egyptian army, and threw the Egyptian army into panic. [25] He clogged their chariot wheels so that they turned with difficulty. The Egyptians said, 'Let us flee from the Israelites, for the LORD is fighting for them against Egypt.'

²⁶ Then the LORD said to Moses, 'Stretch out your hand over the sea, so that the water may come back upon the Egyptians, upon their chariots and chariot drivers.' ²⁷ So Moses stretched out his hand over the sea, and at dawn the sea returned to its normal depth. As the Egyptians fled before it, the LORD tossed the Egyptians into the sea. ²⁸ The waters returned and covered the chariots and the chariot drivers, the entire army of Pharaoh that had followed them into the sea; not one of them remained. ²⁹ But the Israelites walked on dry ground through the sea, the waters forming a wall for them on their right and on their left.

³⁰ Thus the LORD saved Israel that day from the Egyptians; and Israel saw the Egyptians dead on the seashore. ³¹ Israel saw the great work that the LORD did against the Egyptians. So the people feared the LORD and believed in the LORD and in his servant Moses.

EITHER

PSALM   Psalm 114

1   Alleluia! When Israel came out of Egypt,
    the house of Jacob from a people of strange speech,
2   Judah became God's sanctuary
    and Israel his dominion.
3   The sea beheld it and fled;
    Jordan turned and went back.
4   The mountains skipped like rams,
    and the little hills like young sheep.
5   What ailed you, O sea, that you fled?
    O Jordan, that you turned back?
6   You mountains, that you skipped like rams?
    you little hills like young sheep?
7   Tremble, O earth, at the presence of the Lord,
    at the presence of the God of Jacob,
8   Who turned the hard rock into a pool of water
    and flint-stone into a flowing spring.

OR

CANTICLE   Exodus 15.1b–11, 20–21

1   'I will sing to the LORD, for he has triumphed gloriously;
    horse and rider he has thrown into the sea.

2   The LORD is my strength and my might,
         and he has become my salvation;
      this is my God, and I will praise him,
         my father's God, and I will exalt him.
3   The LORD is a warrior;
         the LORD is his name.
4   Pharaoh's chariots and his army he cast into the sea;
         his picked officers were sunk in the Red Sea.
5   The floods covered them;
         they went down into the depths like a stone.
6   Your right hand, O LORD, glorious in power—
         your right hand, O LORD, shattered the enemy.
7   In the greatness of your majesty you overthrew your adversaries;
         you sent out your fury, it consumed them like stubble.
8   At the blast of your nostrils the waters piled up,
         the floods stood up in a heap;
         the deeps congealed in the heart of the sea.
9   The enemy said, "I will pursue, I will overtake,
         I will divide the spoil, my desire shall have its fill of them.
         I will draw my sword, my hand shall destroy them."
10   You blew with your wind, the sea covered them;
         they sank like lead in the mighty waters.
11   Who is like you, O LORD, among the gods?
         Who is like you, majestic in holiness,
         awesome in splendour, doing wonders?'

   20 Then the prophet Miriam, Aaron's sister, took a tambourine in her hand;
and all the women went out after her with tambourines and with dancing.
21 And Miriam sang to them:

      'Sing to the LORD, for he has triumphed gloriously;
      horse and rider he has thrown into the sea.'

READING   Romans 14.1–12

   1 Welcome those who are weak in faith, but not for the purpose of quarrelling over opinions. 2 Some believe in eating anything, while the weak
eat only vegetables. 3 Those who eat must not despise those who abstain,
and those who abstain must not pass judgement on those who eat; for God
has welcomed them. 4 Who are you to pass judgement on servants of
another? It is before their own lord that they stand or fall. And they will
be upheld, for the Lord is able to make them stand.

   5 Some judge one day to be better than another, while others judge all
days to be alike. Let all be fully convinced in their own minds. 6 Those who

observe the day, observe it in honour of the Lord. Also those who eat, eat in honour of the Lord, since they give thanks to God; while those who abstain, abstain in honour of the Lord and give thanks to God.

[7] We do not live to ourselves, and we do not die to ourselves. [8] If we live, we live to the Lord, and if we die, we die to the Lord; so then, whether we live or whether we die, we are the Lord's. [9] For to this end Christ died and lived again, so that he might be Lord of both the dead and the living.

[10] Why do you pass judgement on your brother or sister? Or you, why do you despise your brother or sister? For we will all stand before the judgement seat of God. [11] For it is written,

'As I live, says the Lord, every knee shall bow to me,
    and every tongue shall give praise to God.'
[12] So then, each of us will be accountable to God.

GOSPEL   Matthew 18.21–35

[21] Then Peter came and said to him, 'Lord, if another member of the church sins against me, how often should I forgive? As many as seven times?' [22] Jesus said to him, 'Not seven times, but, I tell you, seventy-seven times.

[23] 'For this reason the kingdom of heaven may be compared to a king who wished to settle accounts with his slaves. [24] When he began the reckoning, one who owed him ten thousand talents was brought to him; [25] and, as he could not pay, his lord ordered him to be sold, together with his wife and children and all his possessions, and payment to be made. [26] So the slave fell on his knees before him, saying, "Have patience with me, and I will pay you everything." [27] And out of pity for him, the lord of that slave released him and forgave him the debt. [28] But that same slave, as he went out, came upon one of his fellow-slaves who owed him a hundred denarii; and seizing him by the throat, he said, "Pay what you owe." [29] Then his fellow-slave fell down and pleaded with him, "Have patience with me, and I will pay you." [30] But he refused; then he went and threw him into prison until he should pay the debt. [31] When his fellow-slaves saw what had happened, they were greatly distressed, and they went and reported to their lord all that had taken place. [32] Then his lord summoned him and said to him, "You wicked slave! I forgave you all that debt because you pleaded with me. [33] Should you not have had mercy on your fellow-slave, as I had mercy on you?" [34] And in anger his lord handed him over to be tortured until he should pay his entire debt. [35] So my heavenly Father will also do to every one of you, if you do not forgive your brother or sister from your heart.'

RELATED

READING   Genesis 50.15–21

¹⁵ Realizing that their father was dead, Joseph's brothers said, 'What if Joseph still bears a grudge against us and pays us back in full for all the wrong that we did to him?' ¹⁶ So they approached Joseph, saying, 'Your father gave this instruction before he died, ¹⁷ "Say to Joseph: I beg you, forgive the crime of your brothers and the wrong they did in harming you." Now therefore please forgive the crime of the servants of the God of your father.' Joseph wept when they spoke to him. ¹⁸ Then his brothers also wept, fell down before him, and said, 'We are here as your slaves.' ¹⁹ But Joseph said to them, 'Do not be afraid! Am I in the place of God? ²⁰ Even though you intended to do harm to me, God intended it for good, in order to preserve a numerous people, as he is doing today. ²¹ So have no fear; I myself will provide for you and your little ones.' In this way he reassured them, speaking kindly to them.

PSALM   Psalm 103.[1–7,] 8–13

[¹ Bless the Lord, O my soul,
    and all that is within me, bless his holy name.
 ² Bless the Lord, O my soul,
    and forget not all his benefits.
 ³ He forgives all your sins
    and heals all your infirmities;
 ⁴ He redeems your life from the grave
    and crowns you with mercy and loving-kindness;
 ⁵ He satisfies you with good things,
    and your youth is renewed like an eagle's.
 ⁶ The Lord executes righteousness
    and judgement for all who are oppressed.
 ⁷ He made his ways known to Moses
    and his works to the children of Israel.]
 ⁸ The Lord is full of compassion and mercy,
    slow to anger and of great kindness.
 ⁹ He will not always accuse us,
    nor will he keep his anger for ever.
¹⁰ He has not dealt with us according to our sins,
    nor rewarded us according to our wickedness.
¹¹ For as the heavens are high above the earth,
    so is his mercy great upon those who fear him.

¹² As far as the east is from the west,
   so far has he removed our sins from us.
¹³ As a father cares for his children,
   so does the Lord care for those who fear him.

READING   Romans 14.1-12

¹ Welcome those who are weak in faith, but not for the purpose of quarrelling over opinions. ² Some believe in eating anything, while the weak eat only vegetables. ³ Those who eat must not despise those who abstain, and those who abstain must not pass judgement on those who eat; for God has welcomed them. ⁴ Who are you to pass judgement on servants of another? It is before their own lord that they stand or fall. And they will be upheld, for the Lord is able to make them stand.

⁵ Some judge one day to be better than another, while others judge all days to be alike. Let all be fully convinced in their own minds. ⁶ Those who observe the day, observe it in honour of the Lord. Also those who eat, eat in honour of the Lord, since they give thanks to God; while those who abstain, abstain in honour of the Lord and give thanks to God.

⁷ We do not live to ourselves, and we do not die to ourselves. ⁸ If we live, we live to the Lord, and if we die, we die to the Lord; so then, whether we live or whether we die, we are the Lord's. ⁹ For to this end Christ died and lived again, so that he might be Lord of both the dead and the living.

¹⁰ Why do you pass judgement on your brother or sister? Or you, why do you despise your brother or sister? For we will all stand before the judgement seat of God. ¹¹ For it is written,
   'As I live, says the Lord, every knee shall bow to me,
      and every tongue shall give praise to God.'
¹² So then, each of us will be accountable to God.

GOSPEL   Matthew 18.21-35

²¹ Then Peter came and said to him, 'Lord, if another member of the church sins against me, how often should I forgive? As many as seven times?' ²² Jesus said to him, 'Not seven times, but, I tell you, seventy-seven times.

²³ 'For this reason the kingdom of heaven may be compared to a king who wished to settle accounts with his slaves. ²⁴ When he began the reckoning, one who owed him ten thousand talents was brought to him; ²⁵ and, as he could not pay, his lord ordered him to be sold, together with his wife and children and all his possessions, and payment to be made. ²⁶ So the slave fell on his knees before him, saying, "Have patience with me, and I will pay you

everything." ²⁷ And out of pity for him, the lord of that slave released him and forgave him the debt. ²⁸ But that same slave, as he went out, came upon one of his fellow-slaves who owed him a hundred denarii; and seizing him by the throat, he said, "Pay what you owe." ²⁹ Then his fellow-slave fell down and pleaded with him, "Have patience with me, and I will pay you." ³⁰ But he refused; then he went and threw him into prison until he should pay the debt. ³¹ When his fellow-slaves saw what had happened, they were greatly distressed, and they went and reported to their lord all that had taken place. ³² Then his lord summoned him and said to him, "You wicked slave! I forgave you all that debt because you pleaded with me. ³³ Should you not have had mercy on your fellow-slave, as I had mercy on you?" ³⁴ And in anger his lord handed him over to be tortured until he should pay his entire debt. ³⁵ So my heavenly Father will also do to every one of you, if you do not forgive your brother or sister from your heart.'

POST COMMUNION

See pages 211 to 214 and Table on page 201

SECOND SERVICE

Psalm 119.41–48, [49–64]
Ezekiel 20.1–8, 33–44
Acts 20.17–38

If the Second Service is a Eucharist, the following is read as a Gospel:

Mark 8.27–38

THIRD SERVICE

Psalm 119.65–88
Isaiah 44.24–45.8
Revelation 12.1–12

PROPER 20

Sunday between 18 and 24 September inclusive

COLLECT

See pages 211 to 214 and Table on page 201

CONTINUOUS

READING   Exodus 16.2–15

² The whole congregation of the Israelites complained against Moses and Aaron in the wilderness. ³ The Israelites said to them, 'If only we had died

by the hand of the LORD in the land of Egypt, when we sat by the fleshpots and ate our fill of bread; for you have brought us out into this wilderness to kill this whole assembly with hunger.'

⁴ Then the LORD said to Moses, 'I am going to rain bread from heaven for you, and each day the people shall go out and gather enough for that day. In that way I will test them, whether they will follow my instruction or not. ⁵ On the sixth day, when they prepare what they bring in, it will be twice as much as they gather on other days.' ⁶ So Moses and Aaron said to all the Israelites, 'In the evening you shall know that it was the LORD who brought you out of the land of Egypt, ⁷ and in the morning you shall see the glory of the LORD, because he has heard your complaining against the LORD. For what are we, that you complain against us?' ⁸ And Moses said, 'When the LORD gives you meat to eat in the evening and your fill of bread in the morning, because the LORD has heard the complaining that you utter against him—what are we? Your complaining is not against us but against the LORD.'

⁹ Then Moses said to Aaron, 'Say to the whole congregation of the Israelites, "Draw near to the LORD, for he has heard your complaining." ' ¹⁰ And as Aaron spoke to the whole congregation of the Israelites, they looked towards the wilderness, and the glory of the LORD appeared in the cloud. ¹¹ The LORD spoke to Moses and said, ¹² 'I have heard the complaining of the Israelites; say to them, "At twilight you shall eat meat, and in the morning you shall have your fill of bread; then you shall know that I am the LORD your God." '

¹³ In the evening quails came up and covered the camp; and in the morning there was a layer of dew around the camp. ¹⁴ When the layer of dew lifted, there on the surface of the wilderness was a fine flaky substance, as fine as frost on the ground. ¹⁵ When the Israelites saw it, they said to one another, 'What is it?' For they did not know what it was. Moses said to them, 'It is the bread that the LORD has given you to eat.'

PSALM   Psalm 105.[1–6,] 37–45

[¹ Give thanks to the Lord and call upon his name;
    make known his deeds among the peoples.
² Sing to him, sing praises to him,
    and speak of all his marvellous works.
³ Glory in his holy name;
    let the hearts of those who seek the Lord rejoice.
⁴ Search for the Lord and his strength;
    continually seek his face.
⁵ Remember the marvels he has done,
    his wonders and the judgements of his mouth,

6 O offspring of Abraham his servant,
   O children of Jacob his chosen.]

37 He led out his people with silver and gold;
   in all their tribes there was not one that stumbled.

38 Egypt was glad of their going,
   because they were afraid of them.

39 He spread out a cloud for a covering
   and a fire to give light in the night season.

40 They asked and quails appeared,
   and he satisfied them with bread from heaven.

41 He opened the rock and water flowed,
   so the river ran in the dry places.

42 For God remembered his holy word
   and Abraham his servant.

43 So he led forth his people with gladness,
   his chosen with shouts of joy.

44 He gave his people the lands of the nations,
   and they took the fruit of others' toil,

45 That they might keep his statutes
   and observe his laws. Alleluia!

READING   Philippians 1.21–30

21 For to me, living is Christ and dying is gain. 22 If I am to live in the flesh, that means fruitful labour for me; and I do not know which I prefer. 23 I am hard pressed between the two: my desire is to depart and be with Christ, for that is far better; 24 but to remain in the flesh is more necessary for you. 25 Since I am convinced of this, I know that I will remain and continue with all of you for your progress and joy in faith, 26 so that I may share abundantly in your boasting in Christ Jesus when I come to you again.

27 Only, live your life in a manner worthy of the gospel of Christ, so that, whether I come and see you or am absent and hear about you, I will know that you are standing firm in one spirit, striving side by side with one mind for the faith of the gospel, 28 and are in no way intimidated by your opponents. For them this is evidence of their destruction, but of your salvation. And this is God's doing. 29 For he has graciously granted you the privilege not only of believing in Christ, but of suffering for him as well— 30 since you are having the same struggle that you saw I had and now hear that I still have.

GOSPEL   Matthew 20.1–16

¹ 'For the kingdom of heaven is like a landowner who went out early in the morning to hire labourers for his vineyard. ² After agreeing with the labourers for the usual daily wage, he sent them into his vineyard. ³ When he went out about nine o'clock, he saw others standing idle in the marketplace; ⁴ and he said to them, "You also go into the vineyard, and I will pay you whatever is right." So they went. ⁵ When he went out again about noon and about three o'clock, he did the same. ⁶ And about five o'clock he went out and found others standing around; and he said to them, "Why are you standing here idle all day?" ⁷ They said to him, "Because no one has hired us." He said to them, "You also go into the vineyard." ⁸ When evening came, the owner of the vineyard said to his manager, "Call the labourers and give them their pay, beginning with the last and then going to the first." ⁹ When those hired about five o'clock came, each of them received the usual daily wage. ¹⁰ Now when the first came, they thought they would receive more; but each of them also received the usual daily wage. ¹¹ And when they received it, they grumbled against the landowner, ¹² saying, "These last worked only one hour, and you have made them equal to us who have borne the burden of the day and the scorching heat." ¹³ But he replied to one of them, "Friend, I am doing you no wrong; did you not agree with me for the usual daily wage? ¹⁴ Take what belongs to you and go; I choose to give to this last the same as I give to you. ¹⁵ Am I not allowed to do what I choose with what belongs to me? Or are you envious because I am generous?" ¹⁶ So the last will be first, and the first will be last.'

RELATED

READING   Jonah 3.10–4.11

¹⁰ When God saw what they did, how they turned from their evil ways, God changed his mind about the calamity that he had said he would bring upon them; and he did not do it.

¹ But this was very displeasing to Jonah, and he became angry. ² He prayed to the LORD and said, 'O LORD! Is not this what I said while I was still in my own country? That is why I fled to Tarshish at the beginning; for I knew that you are a gracious God and merciful, slow to anger, and abounding in steadfast love, and ready to relent from punishing. ³ And now, O LORD, please take my life from me, for it is better for me to die than to live.' ⁴ And the LORD said, 'Is it right for you to be angry?' ⁵ Then Jonah went out of the city and sat down east of the city, and made a booth for himself there. He sat under it in the shade, waiting to see what would become of the city.

⁶ The LORD God appointed a bush, and made it come up over Jonah, to give shade over his head, to save him from his discomfort; so Jonah was very happy about the bush. ⁷ But when dawn came up the next day, God appointed a worm that attacked the bush, so that it withered. ⁸ When the sun rose, God prepared a sultry east wind, and the sun beat down on the head of Jonah so that he was faint and asked that he might die. He said, 'It is better for me to die than to live.'

⁹ But God said to Jonah, 'Is it right for you to be angry about the bush?' And he said, 'Yes, angry enough to die.' ¹⁰ Then the LORD said, 'You are concerned about the bush, for which you did not labour and which you did not grow; it came into being in a night and perished in a night. ¹¹ And should I not be concerned about Nineveh, that great city, in which there are more than a hundred and twenty thousand people who do not know their right hand from their left, and also many animals?'

PSALM   Psalm 145.1–8

¹   I will exalt you, O God my King,
    and bless your name for ever and ever.
²   Every day will I bless you
    and praise your name for ever and ever.
³   Great is the Lord and greatly to be praised;
    there is no end to his greatness.
⁴   One generation shall praise your works to another
    and shall declare your power.
⁵   I will ponder the glorious splendour of your majesty
    and all your marvellous works.
⁶   They shall speak of the might of your wondrous acts,
    and I will tell of your greatness.
⁷   They shall publish the remembrance of your great goodness;
    they shall sing of your righteous deeds.
⁸   The Lord is gracious and full of compassion,
    slow to anger and of great kindness.

READING   Philippians 1.21–30

²¹ For to me, living is Christ and dying is gain. ²² If I am to live in the flesh, that means fruitful labour for me; and I do not know which I prefer. ²³ I am hard pressed between the two: my desire is to depart and be with Christ, for that is far better; ²⁴ but to remain in the flesh is more necessary for you. ²⁵ Since I am convinced of this, I know that I will remain and continue with

all of you for your progress and joy in faith, [26] so that I may share abundantly in your boasting in Christ Jesus when I come to you again.

[27] Only, live your life in a manner worthy of the gospel of Christ, so that, whether I come and see you or am absent and hear about you, I will know that you are standing firm in one spirit, striving side by side with one mind for the faith of the gospel, [28] and are in no way intimidated by your opponents. For them this is evidence of their destruction, but of your salvation. And this is God's doing. [29] For he has graciously granted you the privilege not only of believing in Christ, but of suffering for him as well— [30] since you are having the same struggle that you saw I had and now hear that I still have.

GOSPEL   Matthew 20.1–16

[1] 'For the kingdom of heaven is like a landowner who went out early in the morning to hire labourers for his vineyard. [2] After agreeing with the labourers for the usual daily wage, he sent them into his vineyard. [3] When he went out about nine o'clock, he saw others standing idle in the market-place; [4] and he said to them, "You also go into the vineyard, and I will pay you whatever is right." So they went. [5] When he went out again about noon and about three o'clock, he did the same. [6] And about five o'clock he went out and found others standing around; and he said to them, "Why are you standing here idle all day?" [7] They said to him, "Because no one has hired us." He said to them, "You also go into the vineyard." [8] When evening came, the owner of the vineyard said to his manager, "Call the labourers and give them their pay, beginning with the last and then going to the first." [9] When those hired about five o'clock came, each of them received the usual daily wage. [10] Now when the first came, they thought they would receive more; but each of them also received the usual daily wage. [11] And when they received it, they grumbled against the landowner, [12] saying, "These last worked only one hour, and you have made them equal to us who have borne the burden of the day and the scorching heat." [13] But he replied to one of them, "Friend, I am doing you no wrong; did you not agree with me for the usual daily wage? [14] Take what belongs to you and go; I choose to give to this last the same as I give to you. [15] Am I not allowed to do what I choose with what belongs to me? Or are you envious because I am generous?" [16] So the last will be first, and the first will be last.'

POST COMMUNION

See pages 211 to 215 and Table on page 201

SECOND SERVICE

Psalm 119.[113–120,] 121–128, [129–136]
Ezekiel 33.23, 30–34.10
Acts 26.1, 9–25

If the Second Service is a Eucharist, the following is read as a Gospel:

Mark 9.30–37

THIRD SERVICE

Psalm 119.153–176
Isaiah 45.9–22
Revelation 14.1–5

PROPER 21

Sunday between 25 September and 1 October inclusive

COLLECT

See pages 212 to 215 and Table on page 201

CONTINUOUS

READING   Exodus 17.1–7

¹ From the wilderness of Sin the whole congregation of the Israelites journeyed by stages, as the LORD commanded. They camped at Rephidim, but there was no water for the people to drink. ² The people quarrelled with Moses, and said, 'Give us water to drink.' Moses said to them, 'Why do you quarrel with me? Why do you test the LORD?' ³ But the people thirsted there for water; and the people complained against Moses and said, 'Why did you bring us out of Egypt, to kill us and our children and livestock with thirst?' ⁴ So Moses cried out to the LORD, 'What shall I do with this people? They are almost ready to stone me.' ⁵ The LORD said to Moses, 'Go on ahead of the people, and take some of the elders of Israel with you; take in your hand the staff with which you struck the Nile, and go. ⁶ I will be standing there in front of you on the rock at Horeb. Strike the rock, and water will come out of it, so that the people may drink.' Moses did so, in the sight of the elders of Israel. ⁷ He called the place Massah and Meribah, because the Israelites quarrelled and tested the LORD, saying, 'Is the LORD among us or not?'

PSALM   Psalm 78.1–4, 12–16

1   Hear my teaching, O my people;
    incline your ears to the words of my mouth.
2   I will open my mouth in a parable;
    I will declare the mysteries of ancient times.
3   That which we have heard and known, and what our forebears
        have told us,
    we will not hide from their children.
4   We will recount to generations to come the praiseworthy deeds
        and the power of the Lord,
    and the wonderful works he has done.

12 He worked marvels in the sight of their forebears,
    in the land of Egypt, in the field of Zoan.
13 He split open the sea and let them pass through;
    he made the waters stand up like walls.
14 He led them with a cloud by day,
    and all the night through with a glow of fire.
15 He split the hard rocks in the wilderness
    and gave them drink as from the great deep.
16 He brought streams out of the cliff,
    and the waters gushed out like rivers.

OR, IF AN ALTERNATIVE READING IS PREFERRED   Psalm 78.1–7

1   Hear my teaching, O my people;
    incline your ears to the words of my mouth.
2   I will open my mouth in a parable;
    I will declare the mysteries of ancient times.
3   That which we have heard and known, and what our forebears
        have told us,
    we will not hide from their children.
4   We will recount to generations to come the praiseworthy deeds
        and the power of the Lord,
    and the wonderful works he has done.
5   He gave his decrees to Jacob and established a law for Israel,
    which he commanded them to teach their children;
6   That the generations to come might know, and the children yet
        unborn;
    that they in their turn might tell it to their children;
7   So that they might put their trust in God,
    and not forget the deeds of God, but keep his commandments.

READING   Philippians 2.1–13

¹ If then there is any encouragement in Christ, any consolation from love, any sharing in the Spirit, any compassion and sympathy, ² make my joy complete: be of the same mind, having the same love, being in full accord and of one mind. ³ Do nothing from selfish ambition or conceit, but in humility regard others as better than yourselves. ⁴ Let each of you look not to your own interests, but to the interests of others. ⁵ Let the same mind be in you that was in Christ Jesus,

⁶   who, though he was in the form of God,
     did not regard equality with God
     as something to be exploited,
⁷   but emptied himself,
     taking the form of a slave,
     being born in human likeness.
  And being found in human form,
⁸   he humbled himself
     and became obedient to the point of death—
     even death on a cross.
⁹   Therefore God also highly exalted him
     and gave him the name
     that is above every name,
¹⁰ so that at the name of Jesus
     every knee should bend,
     in heaven and on earth and under the earth,
¹¹ and every tongue should confess
     that Jesus Christ is Lord,
     to the glory of God the Father.

¹² Therefore, my beloved, just as you have always obeyed me, not only in my presence, but much more now in my absence, work out your own salvation with fear and trembling; ¹³ for it is God who is at work in you, enabling you both to will and to work for his good pleasure.

GOSPEL   Matthew 21.23–32

²³ When he entered the temple, the chief priests and the elders of the people came to him as he was teaching, and said, 'By what authority are you doing these things, and who gave you this authority?' ²⁴ Jesus said to them, 'I will also ask you one question; if you tell me the answer, then I will also tell you by what authority I do these things. ²⁵ Did the baptism of John come from heaven, or was it of human origin?' And they argued with one another, 'If we say, "From heaven", he will say to us, "Why then did you not believe him?" ²⁶ But if we say, "Of human origin", we are afraid of the

crowd; for all regard John as a prophet.' ²⁷ So they answered Jesus, 'We do not know.' And he said to them, 'Neither will I tell you by what authority I am doing these things.

²⁸ 'What do you think? A man had two sons; he went to the first and said, "Son, go and work in the vineyard today." ²⁹ He answered, "I will not"; but later he changed his mind and went. ³⁰ The father went to the second and said the same; and he answered, "I go, sir"; but he did not go. ³¹ Which of the two did the will of his father?' They said, 'The first.' Jesus said to them, 'Truly I tell you, the tax-collectors and the prostitutes are going into the kingdom of God ahead of you. ³² For John came to you in the way of righteousness and you did not believe him, but the tax-collectors and the prostitutes believed him; and even after you saw it, you did not change your minds and believe him.'

RELATED

READING   Ezekiel 18.1–4, 25–32

¹ The word of the LORD came to me: ² What do you mean by repeating this proverb concerning the land of Israel, 'The parents have eaten sour grapes, and the children's teeth are set on edge'? ³ As I live, says the Lord GOD, this proverb shall no more be used by you in Israel. ⁴ Know that all lives are mine; the life of the parent as well as the life of the child is mine: it is only the person who sins that shall die.

²⁵ Yet you say, 'The way of the Lord is unfair.' Hear now, O house of Israel: Is my way unfair? Is it not your ways that are unfair? ²⁶ When the righteous turn away from their righteousness and commit iniquity, they shall die for it; for the iniquity that they have committed they shall die. ²⁷ Again, when the wicked turn away from the wickedness they have committed and do what is lawful and right, they shall save their life. ²⁸ Because they considered and turned away from all the transgressions that they had committed, they shall surely live; they shall not die. ²⁹ Yet the house of Israel says, 'The way of the Lord is unfair.' O house of Israel, are my ways unfair? Is it not your ways that are unfair?

³⁰ Therefore I will judge you, O house of Israel, all of you according to your ways, says the Lord GOD. Repent and turn from all your transgressions; otherwise iniquity will be your ruin. ³¹ Cast away from you all the transgressions that you have committed against me, and get yourselves a new heart and a new spirit! Why will you die, O house of Israel? ³² For I have no pleasure in the death of anyone, says the Lord GOD. Turn, then, and live.

PSALM   Psalm 25.1–8

1 To you, O Lord, I lift up my soul; my God, I put my trust in you;
   let me not be humiliated, nor let my enemies triumph over me.
2 Let none who look to you be put to shame;
   let the treacherous be disappointed in their schemes.
3 Show me your ways, O Lord,
   and teach me your paths.
4 Lead me in your truth and teach me,
   for you are the God of my salvation; in you have I trusted all the
      day long.
5 Remember, O Lord, your compassion and love,
   for they are from everlasting.
6 Remember not the sins of my youth and my transgressions;
   remember me according to your love and for the sake of your
      goodness, O Lord.
7 Gracious and upright is the Lord;
   therefore he teaches sinners in his way.
8 He guides the humble in doing right
   and teaches his way to the lowly.

READING   Philippians 2.1–13

1 If then there is any encouragement in Christ, any consolation from love,
any sharing in the Spirit, any compassion and sympathy, 2 make my joy
complete: be of the same mind, having the same love, being in full accord
and of one mind. 3 Do nothing from selfish ambition or conceit, but in
humility regard others as better than yourselves. 4 Let each of you look not
to your own interests, but to the interests of others. 5 Let the same mind be
in you that was in Christ Jesus,
6 who, though he was in the form of God,
      did not regard equality with God
      as something to be exploited,
7 but emptied himself,
      taking the form of a slave,
      being born in human likeness.
   And being found in human form,
8   he humbled himself
      and became obedient to the point of death—
      even death on a cross.
9 Therefore God also highly exalted him
      and gave him the name
      that is above every name,

¹⁰ so that at the name of Jesus
    every knee should bend,
    in heaven and on earth and under the earth,
¹¹ and every tongue should confess
    that Jesus Christ is Lord,
    to the glory of God the Father.

¹² Therefore, my beloved, just as you have always obeyed me, not only in my presence, but much more now in my absence, work out your own salvation with fear and trembling; ¹³ for it is God who is at work in you, enabling you both to will and to work for his good pleasure.

GOSPEL   Matthew 21.23–32

²³ When he entered the temple, the chief priests and the elders of the people came to him as he was teaching, and said, 'By what authority are you doing these things, and who gave you this authority?' ²⁴ Jesus said to them, 'I will also ask you one question; if you tell me the answer, then I will also tell you by what authority I do these things. ²⁵ Did the baptism of John come from heaven, or was it of human origin?' And they argued with one another, 'If we say, "From heaven", he will say to us, "Why then did you not believe him?" ²⁶ But if we say, "Of human origin", we are afraid of the crowd; for all regard John as a prophet.' ²⁷ So they answered Jesus, 'We do not know.' And he said to them, 'Neither will I tell you by what authority I am doing these things.

²⁸ 'What do you think? A man had two sons; he went to the first and said, "Son, go and work in the vineyard today." ²⁹ He answered, "I will not"; but later he changed his mind and went. ³⁰ The father went to the second and said the same; and he answered, "I go, sir"; but he did not go. ³¹ Which of the two did the will of his father?' They said, 'The first.' Jesus said to them, 'Truly I tell you, the tax-collectors and the prostitutes are going into the kingdom of God ahead of you. ³² For John came to you in the way of righteousness and you did not believe him, but the tax-collectors and the prostitutes believed him; and even after you saw it, you did not change your minds and believe him.'

POST COMMUNION

See pages 212 to 216 and Table on page 201

SECOND SERVICE

Psalms [120; 123;] 124
Ezekiel 37.15–28
1 John 2.22–29

If the Second Service is a Eucharist, the following is read as a Gospel:

Mark 9.38–50

THIRD SERVICE

Psalms 125; 126; 127
Isaiah 48.12–21
Luke 11.37–54

PROPER 22

Sunday between 2 and 8 October inclusive

COLLECT

See pages 212 to 216 and Table on page 201

CONTINUOUS

READING   **Exodus 20.1–4, 7–9, 12–20**

¹ Then God spoke all these words:

² I am the Lᴏʀᴅ your God, who brought you out of the land of Egypt, out of the house of slavery; ³ you shall have no other gods before me.

⁴ You shall not make for yourself an idol, whether in the form of anything that is in heaven above, or that is on the earth beneath, or that is in the water under the earth.

⁷ You shall not make wrongful use of the name of the Lᴏʀᴅ your God, for the Lᴏʀᴅ will not acquit anyone who misuses his name.

⁸ Remember the sabbath day, and keep it holy. ⁹ For six days you shall labour and do all your work.

¹² Honour your father and your mother, so that your days may be long in the land that the Lᴏʀᴅ your God is giving you.

¹³ You shall not murder.

¹⁴ You shall not commit adultery.

¹⁵ You shall not steal.

¹⁶ You shall not bear false witness against your neighbour.

¹⁷ You shall not covet your neighbour's house; you shall not covet your neighbour's wife, or male or female slave, or ox, or donkey, or anything that belongs to your neighbour.

¹⁸ When all the people witnessed the thunder and lightning, the sound of the trumpet, and the mountain smoking, they were afraid and trembled and stood at a distance, ¹⁹ and said to Moses, 'You speak to us, and we will listen; but do not let God speak to us, or we will die.' ²⁰ Moses said to the people, 'Do not be afraid; for God has come only to test you and to put the fear of him upon you so that you do not sin.'

PSALM   **Psalm 19.[1–6,] 7–14**

[¹   The heavens declare the glory of God,
       and the firmament shows his handiwork.
 ²   One day tells its tale to another,
       and one night imparts knowledge to another.
 ³   Although they have no words or language,
       and their voices are not heard,
 ⁴   Their sound has gone out into all lands,
       and their message to the ends of the world.
 ⁵   In the deep has he set a pavilion for the sun;
       it comes forth like a bridegroom out of his chamber; it rejoices
         like a champion to run its course.
 ⁶   It goes forth from the uttermost edge of the heavens and runs
         about to the end of it again;
       nothing is hidden from its burning heat.]
 ⁷   The law of the Lord is perfect and revives the soul;
       the testimony of the Lord is sure and gives wisdom to the innocent.
 ⁸   The statutes of the Lord are just and rejoice the heart;
       the commandment of the Lord is clear and gives light to the eyes.
 ⁹   The fear of the Lord is clean and endures for ever;
       the judgements of the Lord are true and righteous altogether.
¹⁰   More to be desired are they than gold, more than much fine gold,
       sweeter far than honey, than honey in the comb.
¹¹   By them also is your servant enlightened,
       and in keeping them there is great reward.

¹² Who can tell how often he offends?
   Cleanse me from my secret faults.
¹³ Above all, keep your servant from presumptuous sins; let them
      not get dominion over me;
   then shall I be whole and sound, and innocent of a great offence.
¹⁴ Let the words of my mouth and the meditation of my heart be
      acceptable in your sight,
   O Lord, my strength and my redeemer.

READING   Philippians 3.4b–14

⁴ If anyone else has reason to be confident in the flesh, I have more: ⁵ circumcised on the eighth day, a member of the people of Israel, of the tribe of Benjamin, a Hebrew born of Hebrews; as to the law, a Pharisee; ⁶ as to zeal, a persecutor of the church; as to righteousness under the law, blameless.

⁷ Yet whatever gains I had, these I have come to regard as loss because of Christ. ⁸ More than that, I regard everything as loss because of the surpassing value of knowing Christ Jesus my Lord. For his sake I have suffered the loss of all things, and I regard them as rubbish, in order that I may gain Christ ⁹ and be found in him, not having a righteousness of my own that comes from the law, but one that comes through faith in Christ, the righteousness from God based on faith. ¹⁰ I want to know Christ and the power of his resurrection and the sharing of his sufferings by becoming like him in his death, ¹¹ if somehow I may attain the resurrection from the dead.

¹² Not that I have already obtained this or have already reached the goal; but I press on to make it my own, because Christ Jesus has made me his own. ¹³ Beloved, I do not consider that I have made it my own; but this one thing I do: forgetting what lies behind and straining forward to what lies ahead, ¹⁴ I press on towards the goal for the prize of the heavenly call of God in Christ Jesus.

GOSPEL   Matthew 21.33–46

³³ 'Listen to another parable. There was a landowner who planted a vineyard, put a fence around it, dug a wine press in it, and built a watch-tower. Then he leased it to tenants and went to another country. ³⁴ When the harvest time had come, he sent his slaves to the tenants to collect his produce. ³⁵ But the tenants seized his slaves and beat one, killed another, and stoned another. ³⁶ Again he sent other slaves, more than the first; and

they treated them in the same way. [37] Finally he sent his son to them, saying, "They will respect my son." [38] But when the tenants saw the son, they said to themselves, "This is the heir; come, let us kill him and get his inheritance." [39] So they seized him, threw him out of the vineyard, and killed him. [40] Now when the owner of the vineyard comes, what will he do to those tenants?' [41] They said to him, 'He will put those wretches to a miserable death, and lease the vineyard to other tenants who will give him the produce at the harvest time.'

[42] Jesus said to them, 'Have you never read in the scriptures:
"The stone that the builders rejected
   has become the cornerstone;
this was the Lord's doing,
   and it is amazing in our eyes"?
[43] Therefore I tell you, the kingdom of God will be taken away from you and given to a people that produces the fruits of the kingdom. [44] The one who falls on this stone will be broken to pieces; and it will crush anyone on whom it falls.'

[45] When the chief priests and the Pharisees heard his parables, they realized that he was speaking about them. [46] They wanted to arrest him, but they feared the crowds, because they regarded him as a prophet.

RELATED

READING   Isaiah 5.1–7

[1] Let me sing for my beloved
      my love-song concerning his vineyard:
   My beloved had a vineyard
      on a very fertile hill.
[2] He dug it and cleared it of stones,
      and planted it with choice vines;
   he built a watch-tower in the midst of it,
      and hewed out a wine vat in it;
   he expected it to yield grapes,
      but it yielded wild grapes.
[3] And now, inhabitants of Jerusalem
      and people of Judah,
   judge between me
      and my vineyard.

4 What more was there to do for my vineyard
      that I have not done in it?
   When I expected it to yield grapes,
      why did it yield wild grapes?
5 And now I will tell you
      what I will do to my vineyard.
   I will remove its hedge,
      and it shall be devoured;
   I will break down its wall,
      and it shall be trampled down.
6 I will make it a waste;
      it shall not be pruned or hoed,
      and it shall be overgrown with briers and thorns;
   I will also command the clouds
      that they rain no rain upon it.
7 For the vineyard of the LORD of hosts
      is the house of Israel,
   and the people of Judah
      are his pleasant planting;
   he expected justice,
      but saw bloodshed;
   righteousness,
      but heard a cry!

PSALM   Psalm 80.7–14

7 Restore us, O God of hosts;
   show the light of your countenance and we shall be saved.
8 You have brought a vine out of Egypt;
   you cast out the nations and planted it.
9 You prepared the ground for it;
   it took root and filled the land.
10 The mountains were covered by its shadow
   and the towering cedar trees by its boughs.
11 You stretched out its tendrils to the Sea
   and its branches to the River.
12 Why have you broken down its wall,
   so that all who pass by pluck off its grapes?
13 The wild boar of the forest has ravaged it,
   and the beasts of the field have grazed upon it.
14 Turn now, O God of hosts, look down from heaven; behold and
      tend this vine;
   preserve what your right hand has planted.

READING   Philippians 3.4b–14

[4] If anyone else has reason to be confident in the flesh, I have more: [5] circumcised on the eighth day, a member of the people of Israel, of the tribe of Benjamin, a Hebrew born of Hebrews; as to the law, a Pharisee; [6] as to zeal, a persecutor of the church; as to righteousness under the law, blameless.

[7] Yet whatever gains I had, these I have come to regard as loss because of Christ. [8] More than that, I regard everything as loss because of the surpassing value of knowing Christ Jesus my Lord. For his sake I have suffered the loss of all things, and I regard them as rubbish, in order that I may gain Christ [9] and be found in him, not having a righteousness of my own that comes from the law, but one that comes through faith in Christ, the righteousness from God based on faith. [10] I want to know Christ and the power of his resurrection and the sharing of his sufferings by becoming like him in his death, [11] if somehow I may attain the resurrection from the dead.

[12] Not that I have already obtained this or have already reached the goal; but I press on to make it my own, because Christ Jesus has made me his own. [13] Beloved, I do not consider that I have made it my own; but this one thing I do: forgetting what lies behind and straining forward to what lies ahead, [14] I press on towards the goal for the prize of the heavenly call of God in Christ Jesus.

GOSPEL   Matthew 21.33–46

[33] 'Listen to another parable. There was a landowner who planted a vineyard, put a fence around it, dug a wine press in it, and built a watch-tower. Then he leased it to tenants and went to another country. [34] When the harvest time had come, he sent his slaves to the tenants to collect his produce. [35] But the tenants seized his slaves and beat one, killed another, and stoned another. [36] Again he sent other slaves, more than the first; and they treated them in the same way. [37] Finally he sent his son to them, saying, "They will respect my son." [38] But when the tenants saw the son, they said to themselves, "This is the heir; come, let us kill him and get his inheritance." [39] So they seized him, threw him out of the vineyard, and killed him. [40] Now when the owner of the vineyard comes, what will he do to those tenants?' [41] They said to him, 'He will put those wretches to a miserable death, and lease the vineyard to other tenants who will give him the produce at the harvest time.'

⁴² Jesus said to them, 'Have you never read in the scriptures:
 "The stone that the builders rejected
  has become the cornerstone;
 this was the Lord's doing,
  and it is amazing in our eyes"?
⁴³ Therefore I tell you, the kingdom of God will be taken away from you and given to a people that produces the fruits of the kingdom. ⁴⁴ The one who falls on this stone will be broken to pieces; and it will crush anyone on whom it falls.'

⁴⁵ When the chief priests and the Pharisees heard his parables, they realized that he was speaking about them. ⁴⁶ They wanted to arrest him, but they feared the crowds, because they regarded him as a prophet.

POST COMMUNION

See pages 213 to 216 and Table on page 201

SECOND SERVICE

Psalm 136.1–9, [10–26]
Proverbs 2.1–11
1 John 2.1–17

If the Second Service is a Eucharist, the following is read as a Gospel:

Mark 10.2–16

THIRD SERVICE

Psalms 128; 129; 134
Isaiah 49.13–23
Luke 12.1–12

PROPER 23

Sunday between 9 and 15 October inclusive

COLLECT

See pages 213 to 217 and Table on page 201

CONTINUOUS

READING   Exodus 32.1–14

¹ When the people saw that Moses delayed to come down from the mountain, the people gathered around Aaron and said to him, 'Come, make gods for us, who shall go before us; as for this Moses, the man who brought us up out of the land of Egypt, we do not know what has become of him.' ² Aaron said to them, 'Take off the gold rings that are on the ears of your wives, your sons, and your daughters, and bring them to me.' ³ So all the people took off the gold rings from their ears, and brought them to Aaron. ⁴ He took the gold from them, formed it in a mould, and cast an image of a calf; and they said, 'These are your gods, O Israel, who brought you up out of the land of Egypt!' ⁵ When Aaron saw this, he built an altar before it; and Aaron made proclamation and said, 'Tomorrow shall be a festival to the LORD.' ⁶ They rose early the next day, and offered burnt-offerings and brought sacrifices of well-being; and the people sat down to eat and drink, and rose up to revel.

⁷ The LORD said to Moses, 'Go down at once! Your people, whom you brought up out of the land of Egypt, have acted perversely; ⁸ they have been quick to turn aside from the way that I commanded them; they have cast for themselves an image of a calf, and have worshipped it and sacrificed to it, and said, "These are your gods, O Israel, who brought you up out of the land of Egypt!" ' ⁹ The LORD said to Moses, 'I have seen this people, how stiffnecked they are. ¹⁰ Now let me alone, so that my wrath may burn hot against them and I may consume them; and of you I will make a great nation.'

¹¹ But Moses implored the LORD his God, and said, 'O LORD, why does your wrath burn hot against your people, whom you brought out of the land of Egypt with great power and with a mighty hand? ¹² Why should the Egyptians say, "It was with evil intent that he brought them out to kill them in the mountains, and to consume them from the face of the earth"? Turn from your fierce wrath; change your mind and do not bring disaster on your people. ¹³ Remember Abraham, Isaac, and Israel, your servants, how

327

you swore to them by your own self, saying to them, "I will multiply your descendants like the stars of heaven, and all this land that I have promised I will give to your descendants, and they shall inherit it for ever." ' ¹⁴ And the LORD changed his mind about the disaster that he planned to bring on his people.

PSALM   Psalm 106.1–6, [19–23]

¹ Alleluia! Give thanks to the Lord, for he is good,
   for his mercy endures for ever.
² Who can declare the mighty acts of the Lord
   or show forth all his praise?
³ Happy are those who act with justice
   and always do what is right!
⁴ Remember me, O Lord, with the favour you have for your people,
   and visit me with your saving help;
⁵ That I may see the prosperity of your elect and be glad with the
      gladness of your people,
   that I may glory with your inheritance.
⁶ We have sinned as our forebears did;
   we have done wrong and dealt wickedly.

[¹⁹ Israel made a bull-calf at Horeb
   and worshipped a molten image;
²⁰ And so they exchanged their Glory
   for the image of an ox that feeds on grass.
²¹ They forgot God their saviour,
   who had done great things in Egypt,
²² Wonderful deeds in the land of Ham,
   and fearful things at the Red Sea.
²³ So he would have destroyed them, had not Moses his chosen stood
      before him in the breach,
   to turn away his wrath from consuming them.]

READING   Philippians 4.1–9

¹ Therefore, my brothers and sisters, whom I love and long for, my joy and crown, stand firm in the Lord in this way, my beloved.

² I urge Euodia and I urge Syntyche to be of the same mind in the Lord. ³ Yes, and I ask you also, my loyal companion, help these women, for they have struggled beside me in the work of the gospel, together with Clement and the rest of my co-workers, whose names are in the book of life.

[4] Rejoice in the Lord always; again I will say, Rejoice. [5] Let your gentleness be known to everyone. The Lord is near. [6] Do not worry about anything, but in everything by prayer and supplication with thanksgiving let your requests be made known to God. [7] And the peace of God, which surpasses all understanding, will guard your hearts and your minds in Christ Jesus.

[8] Finally, beloved, whatever is true, whatever is honourable, whatever is just, whatever is pure, whatever is pleasing, whatever is commendable, if there is any excellence and if there is anything worthy of praise, think about these things. [9] Keep on doing the things that you have learned and received and heard and seen in me, and the God of peace will be with you.

GOSPEL   Matthew 22.1–14

[1] Once more Jesus spoke to them in parables, saying: [2] 'The kingdom of heaven may be compared to a king who gave a wedding banquet for his son. [3] He sent his slaves to call those who had been invited to the wedding banquet, but they would not come. [4] Again he sent other slaves, saying, "Tell those who have been invited: Look, I have prepared my dinner, my oxen and my fat calves have been slaughtered, and everything is ready; come to the wedding banquet." [5] But they made light of it and went away, one to his farm, another to his business, [6] while the rest seized his slaves, maltreated them, and killed them. [7] The king was enraged. He sent his troops, destroyed those murderers, and burned their city. [8] Then he said to his slaves, "The wedding is ready, but those invited were not worthy. [9] Go therefore into the main streets, and invite everyone you find to the wedding banquet." [10] Those slaves went out into the streets and gathered all whom they found, both good and bad; so the wedding hall was filled with guests.

[11] 'But when the king came in to see the guests, he noticed a man there who was not wearing a wedding robe, [12] and he said to him, "Friend, how did you get in here without a wedding robe?" And he was speechless. [13] Then the king said to the attendants, "Bind him hand and foot, and throw him into the outer darkness, where there will be weeping and gnashing of teeth." [14] For many are called, but few are chosen.'

RELATED

READING   Isaiah 25.1–9

¹ O LORD, you are my God;
    I will exalt you, I will praise your name;
   for you have done wonderful things,
        plans formed of old, faithful and sure.
² For you have made the city a heap,
        the fortified city a ruin;
   the palace of aliens is a city no more,
        it will never be rebuilt.
³ Therefore strong peoples will glorify you;
        cities of ruthless nations will fear you.
⁴ For you have been a refuge to the poor,
        a refuge to the needy in their distress,
        a shelter from the rainstorm and a shade from the heat.
   When the blast of the ruthless was like a winter rainstorm,
⁵   the noise of aliens like heat in a dry place,
   you subdued the heat with the shade of clouds;
        the song of the ruthless was stilled.
⁶ On this mountain the LORD of hosts will make for all peoples
        a feast of rich food, a feast of well-matured wines,
        of rich food filled with marrow, of well-matured wines strained clear.
⁷ And he will destroy on this mountain
        the shroud that is cast over all peoples,
        the sheet that is spread over all nations;
⁸ he will swallow up death for ever.
   Then the Lord GOD will wipe away the tears from all faces,
        and the disgrace of his people he will take away from all the earth,
        for the LORD has spoken.
⁹ It will be said on that day,
   Lo, this is our God; we have waited for him, so that he might save us.
   This is the LORD for whom we have waited;
        let us be glad and rejoice in his salvation.

PSALM   Psalm 23

¹ The Lord is my shepherd;
   I shall not be in want.
² He makes me lie down in green pastures
   and leads me beside still waters.

3 He revives my soul
   and guides me along right pathways for his name's sake.
4 Though I walk through the valley of the shadow of death, I shall
        fear no evil;
   for you are with me; your rod and your staff, they comfort me.
5 You spread a table before me in the presence of those who trouble
        me;
   you have anointed my head with oil, and my cup is running over.
6 Surely your goodness and mercy shall follow me all the days of my
        life,
   and I will dwell in the house of the Lord for ever.

READING   Philippians 4.1–9

¹ Therefore, my brothers and sisters, whom I love and long for, my joy and crown, stand firm in the Lord in this way, my beloved.

² I urge Euodia and I urge Syntyche to be of the same mind in the Lord. ³ Yes, and I ask you also, my loyal companion, help these women, for they have struggled beside me in the work of the gospel, together with Clement and the rest of my co-workers, whose names are in the book of life.

⁴ Rejoice in the Lord always; again I will say, Rejoice. ⁵ Let your gentleness be known to everyone. The Lord is near. ⁶ Do not worry about anything, but in everything by prayer and supplication with thanksgiving let your requests be made known to God. ⁷ And the peace of God, which surpasses all understanding, will guard your hearts and your minds in Christ Jesus.

⁸ Finally, beloved, whatever is true, whatever is honourable, whatever is just, whatever is pure, whatever is pleasing, whatever is commendable, if there is any excellence and if there is anything worthy of praise, think about these things. ⁹ Keep on doing the things that you have learned and received and heard and seen in me, and the God of peace will be with you.

GOSPEL   Matthew 22.1–14

¹ Once more Jesus spoke to them in parables, saying: ² 'The kingdom of heaven may be compared to a king who gave a wedding banquet for his son. ³ He sent his slaves to call those who had been invited to the wedding banquet, but they would not come. ⁴ Again he sent other slaves, saying, "Tell those who have been invited: Look, I have prepared my dinner, my oxen and my fat calves have been slaughtered, and everything is ready; come to the wedding banquet." ⁵ But they made light of it and went away, one to his farm, another to his business, ⁶ while the rest seized his slaves,

maltreated them, and killed them. ⁷ The king was enraged. He sent his troops, destroyed those murderers, and burned their city. ⁸ Then he said to his slaves, "The wedding is ready, but those invited were not worthy. ⁹ Go therefore into the main streets, and invite everyone you find to the wedding banquet." ¹⁰ Those slaves went out into the streets and gathered all whom they found, both good and bad; so the wedding hall was filled with guests.

¹¹ 'But when the king came in to see the guests, he noticed a man there who was not wearing a wedding robe, ¹² and he said to him, "Friend, how did you get in here without a wedding robe?" And he was speechless. ¹³ Then the king said to the attendants, "Bind him hand and foot, and throw him into the outer darkness, where there will be weeping and gnashing of teeth." ¹⁴ For many are called, but few are chosen.'

POST COMMUNION

See pages 213 to 217 and Table on page 201

SECOND SERVICE

Psalm 139.1–11, [12–17]
Proverbs 3.1–18
1 John 3.1–15

If the Second Service is a Eucharist, the following is read as a Gospel:

Mark 10.17–31

THIRD SERVICE

Psalms 138; 141
Isaiah 50.4–10
Luke 13.22–30

PROPER 24

Sunday between 16 and 22 October inclusive

COLLECT

See pages 214 to 218 and Table on page 201

CONTINUOUS

READING   Exodus 33.12–23

¹² Moses said to the LORD, 'See, you have said to me, "Bring up this people"; but you have not let me know whom you will send with me. Yet you have said, "I know you by name, and you have also found favour in my sight."

¹³ Now if I have found favour in your sight, show me your ways, so that I may know you and find favour in your sight. Consider too that this nation is your people.' ¹⁴ He said, 'My presence will go with you, and I will give you rest.' ¹⁵ And he said to him, 'If your presence will not go, do not carry us up from here. ¹⁶ For how shall it be known that I have found favour in your sight, I and your people, unless you go with us? In this way, we shall be distinct, I and your people, from every people on the face of the earth.'

¹⁷ The LORD said to Moses, 'I will do the very thing that you have asked; for you have found favour in my sight, and I know you by name.' ¹⁸ Moses said, 'Show me your glory, I pray.' ¹⁹ And he said, 'I will make all my goodness pass before you, and will proclaim before you the name, "The LORD"; and I will be gracious to whom I will be gracious, and will show mercy on whom I will show mercy. ²⁰ But', he said, 'you cannot see my face; for no one shall see me and live.' ²¹ And the LORD continued, 'See, there is a place by me where you shall stand on the rock; ²² and while my glory passes by I will put you in a cleft of the rock, and I will cover you with my hand until I have passed by; ²³ then I will take away my hand, and you shall see my back; but my face shall not be seen.'

PSALM   Psalm 99

¹ The Lord is king; let the people tremble;
    he is enthroned upon the cherubim; let the earth shake.
² The Lord is great in Zion;
    he is high above all peoples.
³ Let them confess his name, which is great and awesome;
    he is the Holy One.
⁴ 'O mighty King, lover of justice, you have established equity;
    you have executed justice and righteousness in Jacob.'
⁵ Proclaim the greatness of the Lord our God and fall down before
      his footstool;
    he is the Holy One.
⁶ Moses and Aaron among his priests, and Samuel among those who
      call upon his name,
    they called upon the Lord and he answered them.
⁷ He spoke to them out of the pillar of cloud;
    they kept his testimonies and the decree that he gave them.
⁸ 'O Lord our God, you answered them indeed;
    you were a God who forgave them, yet punished them for their
      evil deeds.'
⁹ Proclaim the greatness of the Lord our God and worship him upon
      his holy hill;
    for the Lord our God is the Holy One.

READING 1 Thessalonians 1.1–10

[1] Paul, Silvanus, and Timothy,

To the church of the Thessalonians in God the Father and the Lord Jesus Christ:

Grace to you and peace.

[2] We always give thanks to God for all of you and mention you in our prayers, constantly [3] remembering before our God and Father your work of faith and labour of love and steadfastness of hope in our Lord Jesus Christ. [4] For we know, brothers and sisters beloved by God, that he has chosen you, [5] because our message of the gospel came to you not in word only, but also in power and in the Holy Spirit and with full conviction; just as you know what kind of people we proved to be among you for your sake. [6] And you became imitators of us and of the Lord, for in spite of persecution you received the word with joy inspired by the Holy Spirit, [7] so that you became an example to all the believers in Macedonia and in Achaia. [8] For the word of the Lord has sounded forth from you not only in Macedonia and Achaia, but in every place where your faith in God has become known, so that we have no need to speak about it. [9] For the people of those regions report about us what kind of welcome we had among you, and how you turned to God from idols, to serve a living and true God, [10] and to wait for his Son from heaven, whom he raised from the dead—Jesus, who rescues us from the wrath that is coming.

GOSPEL Matthew 22.15–22

[15] Then the Pharisees went and plotted to entrap him in what he said. [16] So they sent their disciples to him, along with the Herodians, saying, 'Teacher, we know that you are sincere, and teach the way of God in accordance with truth, and show deference to no one; for you do not regard people with partiality. [17] Tell us, then, what you think. Is it lawful to pay taxes to the emperor, or not?' [18] But Jesus, aware of their malice, said, 'Why are you putting me to the test, you hypocrites? [19] Show me the coin used for the tax.' And they brought him a denarius. [20] Then he said to them, 'Whose head is this, and whose title?' [21] They answered, 'The emperor's.' Then he said to them, 'Give therefore to the emperor the things that are the emperor's, and to God the things that are God's.' [22] When they heard this, they were amazed; and they left him and went away.

RELATED

READING   Isaiah 45.1–7

1   Thus says the Lord to his anointed, to Cyrus,
        whose right hand I have grasped
     to subdue nations before him
        and strip kings of their robes,
     to open doors before him—
        and the gates shall not be closed:
2   I will go before you
        and level the mountains,
     I will break in pieces the doors of bronze
        and cut through the bars of iron,
3   I will give you the treasures of darkness
        and riches hidden in secret places,
     so that you may know that it is I, the Lord,
        the God of Israel, who call you by your name.
4   For the sake of my servant Jacob,
        and Israel my chosen,
     I call you by your name,
        I surname you, though you do not know me.
5   I am the Lord, and there is no other;
        besides me there is no god.
     I arm you, though you do not know me,
6   so that they may know, from the rising of the sun
        and from the west, that there is no one besides me;
     I am the Lord, and there is no other.
7   I form light and create darkness,
        I make weal and create woe;
        I the Lord do all these things.

PSALM   Psalm 96.1–9, [10–13]

1   Sing to the Lord a new song;
    sing to the Lord, all the whole earth.
2   Sing to the Lord and bless his name;
    proclaim the good news of his salvation from day to day.
3   Declare his glory among the nations
    and his wonders among all peoples.
4   For great is the Lord and greatly to be praised;
    he is more to be feared than all gods.

⁵ As for all the gods of the nations, they are but idols;
  but it is the Lord who made the heavens.
⁶ O the majesty and magnificence of his presence!
  O the power and the splendour of his sanctuary!
⁷ Ascribe to the Lord, you families of the peoples;
  ascribe to the Lord honour and power.
⁸ Ascribe to the Lord the honour due to his name;
  bring offerings and come into his courts.
⁹ Worship the Lord in the beauty of holiness;
  let the whole earth tremble before him.
[¹⁰ Tell it out among the nations: 'The Lord is king!
  he has made the world so firm that it cannot be moved; he will
    judge the peoples with equity.'
¹¹ Let the heavens rejoice and let the earth be glad; let the sea
    thunder and all that is in it;
  let the field be joyful and all that is therein.
¹² Then shall all the trees of the wood shout for joy before the Lord
    when he comes,
  when he comes to judge the earth.
¹³ He will judge the world with righteousness
  and the peoples with his truth.]

READING   1 Thessalonians 1.1–10

¹ Paul, Silvanus, and Timothy,

To the church of the Thessalonians in God the Father and the Lord Jesus Christ:

Grace to you and peace.

² We always give thanks to God for all of you and mention you in our prayers, constantly ³ remembering before our God and Father your work of faith and labour of love and steadfastness of hope in our Lord Jesus Christ. ⁴ For we know, brothers and sisters beloved by God, that he has chosen you, ⁵ because our message of the gospel came to you not in word only, but also in power and in the Holy Spirit and with full conviction; just as you know what kind of people we proved to be among you for your sake. ⁶ And you became imitators of us and of the Lord, for in spite of persecution you received the word with joy inspired by the Holy Spirit, ⁷ so that you became an example to all the believers in Macedonia and in Achaia. ⁸ For the word of the Lord has sounded forth from you not only in Macedonia and Achaia, but in every place where your faith in God has become known, so that we have no need to speak about it. ⁹ For the people of those regions report about us what kind of welcome we had among you, and how you turned to God from idols, to serve a living and true God, ¹⁰ and to wait for his Son

from heaven, whom he raised from the dead—Jesus, who rescues us from
the wrath that is coming.

GOSPEL   Matthew 22.15–22

[15] Then the Pharisees went and plotted to entrap him in what he said. [16] So
they sent their disciples to him, along with the Herodians, saying, 'Teacher,
we know that you are sincere, and teach the way of God in accordance with
truth, and show deference to no one; for you do not regard people with
partiality. [17] Tell us, then, what you think. Is it lawful to pay taxes to the
emperor, or not?' [18] But Jesus, aware of their malice, said, 'Why are you
putting me to the test, you hypocrites? [19] Show me the coin used for the
tax.' And they brought him a denarius. [20] Then he said to them, 'Whose
head is this, and whose title?' [21] They answered, 'The emperor's.' Then he
said to them, 'Give therefore to the emperor the things that are the
emperor's, and to God the things that are God's.' [22] When they heard this,
they were amazed; and they left him and went away.

POST COMMUNION

See pages 214 to 218 and Table on page 201

SECOND SERVICE

Psalms 142; [143.1–11]
Proverbs 4.1–18
1 John 3.16–4.6

*If the Second Service is a Eucharist, the
following is read as a Gospel:*

Mark 10.35–45

THIRD SERVICE

Psalms 145; 149
Isaiah 54.1–14
Luke 13.31–35

PROPER 25

Sunday between 23 and 29 October inclusive

COLLECT

See page 218 and Table on page 201

CONTINUOUS

READING   **Deuteronomy 34.1–12**

¹ Then Moses went up from the plains of Moab to Mount Nebo, to the top of Pisgah, which is opposite Jericho, and the LORD showed him the whole land: Gilead as far as Dan, ² all Naphtali, the land of Ephraim and Manasseh, all the land of Judah as far as the Western Sea, ³ the Negeb, and the Plain—that is, the valley of Jericho, the city of palm trees—as far as Zoar. ⁴ The LORD said to him, 'This is the land of which I swore to Abraham, to Isaac, and to Jacob, saying, "I will give it to your descendants"; I have let you see it with your eyes, but you shall not cross over there.' ⁵ Then Moses, the servant of the LORD, died there in the land of Moab, at the LORD's command. ⁶ He was buried in a valley in the land of Moab, opposite Beth-peor, but no one knows his burial place to this day. ⁷ Moses was one hundred and twenty years old when he died; his sight was unimpaired and his vigour had not abated. ⁸ The Israelites wept for Moses in the plains of Moab for thirty days; then the period of mourning for Moses was ended.

⁹ Joshua son of Nun was full of the spirit of wisdom, because Moses had laid his hands on him; and the Israelites obeyed him, doing as the LORD had commanded Moses.

¹⁰ Never since has there arisen a prophet in Israel like Moses, whom the LORD knew face to face. ¹¹ He was unequalled for all the signs and wonders that the LORD sent him to perform in the land of Egypt, against Pharaoh and all his servants and his entire land, ¹² and for all the mighty deeds and all the terrifying displays of power that Moses performed in the sight of all Israel.

PSALM   **Psalm 90.1–6, [13–17]**

¹   Lord, you have been our refuge
     from one generation to another.

² Before the mountains were brought forth, or the land and the
    earth were born,
  from age to age you are God.
³ You turn us back to the dust and say,
  'Go back, O child of earth.'
⁴ For a thousand years in your sight are like yesterday when it is
    past
  and like a watch in the night.
⁵ You sweep us away like a dream;
  we fade away suddenly like the grass.
⁶ In the morning it is green and flourishes;
  in the evening it is dried up and withered.

[¹³ Return, O Lord; how long will you tarry?
  be gracious to your servants.
¹⁴ Satisfy us by your loving-kindness in the morning;
  so shall we rejoice and be glad all the days of our life.
¹⁵ Make us glad by the measure of the days that you afflicted us
  and the years in which we suffered adversity.
¹⁶ Show your servants your works
  and your splendour to their children.
¹⁷ May the graciousness of the Lord our God be upon us;
  prosper the work of our hands; prosper our handiwork.]

READING   1 Thessalonians 2.1–8

¹ You yourselves know, brothers and sisters, that our coming to you was
not in vain, ² but though we had already suffered and been shamefully
maltreated at Philippi, as you know, we had courage in our God to declare
to you the gospel of God in spite of great opposition. ³ For our appeal does
not spring from deceit or impure motives or trickery, ⁴ but just as we have
been approved by God to be entrusted with the message of the gospel, even
so we speak, not to please mortals, but to please God who tests our hearts.
⁵ As you know and as God is our witness, we never came with words of
flattery or with a pretext for greed; ⁶ nor did we seek praise from mortals,
whether from you or from others, ⁷ though we might have made demands
as apostles of Christ. But we were gentle among you, like a nurse tenderly
caring for her own children. ⁸ So deeply do we care for you that we are
determined to share with you not only the gospel of God but also our own
selves, because you have become very dear to us.

GOSPEL   Matthew 22.34–46

³⁴ When the Pharisees heard that he had silenced the Sadducees, they gathered together, ³⁵ and one of them, a lawyer, asked him a question to test him. ³⁶ 'Teacher, which commandment in the law is the greatest?' ³⁷ He said to him, ' "You shall love the Lord your God with all your heart, and with all your soul, and with all your mind." ³⁸ This is the greatest and first commandment. ³⁹ And a second is like it: "You shall love your neighbour as yourself." ⁴⁰ On these two commandments hang all the law and the prophets.'

⁴¹ Now while the Pharisees were gathered together, Jesus asked them this question: ⁴² 'What do you think of the Messiah? Whose son is he?' They said to him, 'The son of David.' ⁴³ He said to them, 'How is it then that David by the Spirit calls him Lord, saying,

⁴⁴ "The Lord said to my Lord,
    'Sit at my right hand,
       until I put your enemies under your feet' "?

⁴⁵ If David thus calls him Lord, how can he be his son?' ⁴⁶ No one was able to give him an answer, nor from that day did anyone dare to ask him any more questions.

RELATED

READING   Leviticus 19.1–2, 15–18

¹ The Lord spoke to Moses, saying:

² Speak to all the congregation of the people of Israel and say to them: You shall be holy, for I the Lord your God am holy.

¹⁵ You shall not render an unjust judgement; you shall not be partial to the poor or defer to the great: with justice you shall judge your neighbour. ¹⁶ You shall not go around as a slanderer among your people, and you shall not profit by the blood of your neighbour: I am the Lord.

¹⁷ You shall not hate in your heart anyone of your kin; you shall reprove your neighbour, or you will incur guilt yourself. ¹⁸ You shall not take vengeance or bear a grudge against any of your people, but you shall love your neighbour as yourself: I am the Lord.

PSALM   Psalm 1

1   Happy are they who have not walked in the counsel of the wicked,
    nor lingered in the way of sinners, nor sat in the seats of the
        scornful!
2   Their delight is in the law of the Lord,
    and they meditate on his law day and night.
3   They are like trees planted by streams of water, bearing fruit in
        due season, with leaves that do not wither;
    everything they do shall prosper.
4   It is not so with the wicked:
    they are like chaff which the wind blows away;
5   Therefore the wicked shall not stand upright when judgement
        comes,
    nor the sinner in the council of the righteous.
6   For the Lord knows the way of the righteous,
    but the way of the wicked is doomed.

READING   1 Thessalonians 2.1–8

1 You yourselves know, brothers and sisters, that our coming to you was
not in vain, 2 but though we had already suffered and been shamefully
maltreated at Philippi, as you know, we had courage in our God to declare
to you the gospel of God in spite of great opposition. 3 For our appeal does
not spring from deceit or impure motives or trickery, 4 but just as we have
been approved by God to be entrusted with the message of the gospel, even
so we speak, not to please mortals, but to please God who tests our hearts.
5 As you know and as God is our witness, we never came with words of
flattery or with a pretext for greed; 6 nor did we seek praise from mortals,
whether from you or from others, 7 though we might have made demands
as apostles of Christ. But we were gentle among you, like a nurse tenderly
caring for her own children. 8 So deeply do we care for you that we are
determined to share with you not only the gospel of God but also our own
selves, because you have become very dear to us.

GOSPEL   Matthew 22.34–46

34 When the Pharisees heard that he had silenced the Sadducees, they
gathered together, 35 and one of them, a lawyer, asked him a question to
test him. 36 'Teacher, which commandment in the law is the greatest?' 37 He
said to him, ' "You shall love the Lord your God with all your heart, and
with all your soul, and with all your mind." 38 This is the greatest and first
commandment. 39 And a second is like it: "You shall love your neighbour
as yourself." 40 On these two commandments hang all the law and the
prophets.'

41 Now while the Pharisees were gathered together, Jesus asked them this question: 42 'What do you think of the Messiah? Whose son is he?' They said to him, 'The son of David.' 43 He said to them, 'How is it then that David by the Spirit calls him Lord, saying,

44 "The Lord said to my Lord,
'Sit at my right hand,
until I put your enemies under your feet' "?

45 If David thus calls him Lord, how can he be his son?' 46 No one was able to give him an answer, nor from that day did anyone dare to ask him any more questions.

POST COMMUNION

See page 218 and Table on page 201

SECOND SERVICE

Psalm 119.89–104
Ecclesiastes 11; 12
2 Timothy 2.1–7

If the Second Service is a Eucharist, the following is read as a Gospel:

Mark 12.28–34

THIRD SERVICE

Psalm 119.137–152
Isaiah 59.9–20
Luke 14.1–14

ALL SAINTS' DAY   1 NOVEMBER

Sunday between 30 October and 5 November or, if this is not kept as All Saints' Sunday, on 1 November itself

COLLECT

Almighty God,
you have knit together your elect
in one communion and fellowship
    in the mystical body of your Son Christ our Lord:
grant us grace so to follow your blessed saints
in all virtuous and godly living
that we may come to those inexpressible joys
that you have prepared for those who truly love you;
through Jesus Christ your Son our Lord,
who is alive and reigns with you,
in the unity of the Holy Spirit,
one God, now and for ever.

READING   Revelation 7.9–17

[9] After this I looked, and there was a great multitude that no one could count, from every nation, from all tribes and peoples and languages, standing before the throne and before the Lamb, robed in white, with palm branches in their hands. [10] They cried out in a loud voice, saying,

  'Salvation belongs to our God who is seated on the throne, and to the
    Lamb!'

[11] And all the angels stood around the throne and around the elders and the four living creatures, and they fell on their faces before the throne and worshipped God, [12] singing,

  'Amen! Blessing and glory and wisdom
  and thanksgiving and honour
  and power and might
  be to our God for ever and ever! Amen.'

[13] Then one of the elders addressed me, saying, 'Who are these, robed in white, and where have they come from?' [14] I said to him, 'Sir, you are the one that knows.' Then he said to me, 'These are they who have come out of the great ordeal; they have washed their robes and made them white in the blood of the Lamb.

[15]   For this reason they are before the throne of God,
      and worship him day and night within his temple,
      and the one who is seated on the throne will shelter them.
[16]   They will hunger no more, and thirst no more;
      the sun will not strike them,
      nor any scorching heat;
[17]   for the Lamb at the centre of the throne will be their shepherd,
      and he will guide them to springs of the water of life,
    and God will wipe away every tear from their eyes.'

PSALM   Psalm 34.1–10

[1]   I will bless the Lord at all times;
    his praise shall ever be in my mouth.
[2]   I will glory in the Lord;
    let the humble hear and rejoice.
[3]   Proclaim with me the greatness of the Lord;
    let us exalt his name together.
[4]   I sought the Lord and he answered me
    and delivered me out of all my terror.
[5]   Look upon him and be radiant,
    and let not your faces be ashamed.

⁶ I called in my affliction and the Lord heard me
   and saved me from all my troubles.
⁷ The angel of the Lord encompasses those who fear him,
   and he will deliver them.
⁸ Taste and see that the Lord is good;
   happy are they who trust in him!
⁹ Fear the Lord, you that are his saints,
   for those who fear him lack nothing.
¹⁰ The young lions lack and suffer hunger,
   but those who seek the Lord lack nothing that is good.

READING   1 John 3.1–3

¹ See what love the Father has given us, that we should be called children of God; and that is what we are. The reason the world does not know us is that it did not know him. ² Beloved, we are God's children now; what we will be has not yet been revealed. What we do know is this: when he is revealed, we will be like him, for we will see him as he is. ³ And all who have this hope in him purify themselves, just as he is pure.

GOSPEL   Matthew 5.1–12

¹ When Jesus saw the crowds, he went up the mountain; and after he sat down, his disciples came to him. ² Then he began to speak, and taught them, saying:

³ 'Blessed are the poor in spirit, for theirs is the kingdom of heaven.

⁴ 'Blessed are those who mourn, for they will be comforted.

⁵ 'Blessed are the meek, for they will inherit the earth.

⁶ 'Blessed are those who hunger and thirst for righteousness, for they will be filled.

⁷ 'Blessed are the merciful, for they will receive mercy.

⁸ 'Blessed are the pure in heart, for they will see God.

⁹ 'Blessed are the peacemakers, for they will be called children of God.

¹⁰ 'Blessed are those who are persecuted for righteousness' sake, for theirs is the kingdom of heaven.

¹¹ 'Blessed are you when people revile you and persecute you and utter all kinds of evil against you falsely on my account. ¹² Rejoice and be glad, for your reward is great in heaven, for in the same way they persecuted the prophets who were before you.'

POST COMMUNION

God, the source of all holiness
 and giver of all good things:
may we who have shared at this table
 as strangers and pilgrims here on earth
be welcomed with all your saints
 to the heavenly feast on the day of your kingdom;
through Jesus Christ our Lord.

On 1 November if the material above is used on the Sunday

COLLECT

Almighty God,
you have knit together your elect
in one communion and fellowship
 in the mystical body of your Son Christ our Lord:
grant us grace so to follow your blessed saints
in all virtuous and godly living
that we may come to those inexpressible joys
that you have prepared for those who truly love you;
through Jesus Christ your Son our Lord,
who is alive and reigns with you,
in the unity of the Holy Spirit,
one God, now and for ever.

READING

EITHER   Isaiah 56.3–8

³ Do not let the foreigner joined to the LORD say,
       'The LORD will surely separate me from his people';
    and do not let the eunuch say,
       'I am just a dry tree.'
⁴ For thus says the LORD:
    To the eunuchs who keep my sabbaths,
       who choose the things that please me
       and hold fast my covenant,
⁵ I will give, in my house and within my walls,
       a monument and a name
       better than sons and daughters;
    I will give them an everlasting name
       that shall not be cut off.

6 And the foreigners who join themselves to the LORD,
  to minister to him, to love the name of the LORD,
  and to be his servants,
all who keep the sabbath, and do not profane it,
  and hold fast my covenant—
7 these I will bring to my holy mountain,
  and make them joyful in my house of prayer;
their burnt-offerings and their sacrifices
  will be accepted on my altar;
for my house shall be called a house of prayer
  for all peoples.
8 Thus says the Lord GOD,
  who gathers the outcasts of Israel,
I will gather others to them
  besides those already gathered.

OR   2 Esdras 2.42–48

42 I, Ezra, saw on Mount Zion a great multitude that I could not number, and they all were praising the Lord with songs. 43 In their midst was a young man of great stature, taller than any of the others, and on the head of each of them he placed a crown, but he was more exalted than they. And I was held spellbound. 44 Then I asked an angel, 'Who are these, my lord?' 45 He answered and said to me, 'These are they who have put off mortal clothing and have put on the immortal, and have confessed the name of God. Now they are being crowned, and receive palms.' 46 Then I said to the angel, 'Who is that young man who is placing crowns on them and putting palms in their hands?' 47 He answered and said to me, 'He is the Son of God, whom they confessed in the world.' So I began to praise those who had stood valiantly for the name of the Lord. 48 Then the angel said to me, 'Go, tell my people how great and how many are the wonders of the Lord God that you have seen.'

PSALM   Psalm 33.1–5

1 Rejoice in the Lord, you righteous;
  it is good for the just to sing praises.
2 Praise the Lord with the harp;
  play to him upon the psaltery and lyre.
3 Sing for him a new song;
  sound a fanfare with all your skill upon the trumpet.

⁴ For the word of the Lord is right,
  and all his works are sure.
⁵ He loves righteousness and justice;
  the loving-kindness of the Lord fills the whole earth.

READING   Hebrews 12.18–24

¹⁸ You have not come to something that can be touched, a blazing fire, and darkness, and gloom, and a tempest, ¹⁹ and the sound of a trumpet, and a voice whose words made the hearers beg that not another word be spoken to them. ²⁰ (For they could not endure the order that was given, 'If even an animal touches the mountain, it shall be stoned to death.' ²¹ Indeed, so terrifying was the sight that Moses said, 'I tremble with fear.') ²² But you have come to Mount Zion and to the city of the living God, the heavenly Jerusalem, and to innumerable angels in festal gathering, ²³ and to the assembly of the firstborn who are enrolled in heaven, and to God the judge of all, and to the spirits of the righteous made perfect, ²⁴ and to Jesus, the mediator of a new covenant, and to the sprinkled blood that speaks a better word than the blood of Abel.

GOSPEL   Matthew 5.1–12

¹ When Jesus saw the crowds, he went up the mountain; and after he sat down, his disciples came to him. ² Then he began to speak, and taught them, saying:

³ 'Blessed are the poor in spirit, for theirs is the kingdom of heaven.

⁴ 'Blessed are those who mourn, for they will be comforted.

⁵ 'Blessed are the meek, for they will inherit the earth.

⁶ 'Blessed are those who hunger and thirst for righteousness, for they will be filled.

⁷ 'Blessed are the merciful, for they will receive mercy.

⁸ 'Blessed are the pure in heart, for they will see God.

⁹ 'Blessed are the peacemakers, for they will be called children of God.

¹⁰ 'Blessed are those who are persecuted for righteousness' sake, for theirs is the kingdom of heaven.

¹¹ 'Blessed are you when people revile you and persecute you and utter all kinds of evil against you falsely on my account. ¹² Rejoice and be glad, for your reward is great in heaven, for in the same way they persecuted the prophets who were before you.'

POST COMMUNION

God, the source of all holiness
   and giver of all good things:
may we who have shared at this table
   as strangers and pilgrims here on earth
be welcomed with all your saints
   to the heavenly feast on the day of your kingdom;
through Jesus Christ our Lord.

THE FOURTH SUNDAY BEFORE ADVENT

Sunday between 30 October and 5 November inclusive. For use if the Feast of All Saints was celebrated on 1 November and alternative propers are needed.

COLLECT

Almighty and eternal God,
you have kindled the flame of love
   in the hearts of the saints:
grant to us the same faith and power of love,
that, as we rejoice in their triumphs,
we may be sustained by their example and fellowship;
through Jesus Christ your Son our Lord,
who is alive and reigns with you,
in the unity of the Holy Spirit,
one God, now and for ever.

READING   Micah 3.5–12

5 Thus says the LORD concerning the prophets
   who lead my people astray,
who cry 'Peace'
   when they have something to eat,
but declare war against those
   who put nothing into their mouths.
6 Therefore it shall be night to you, without vision,
   and darkness to you, without revelation.
The sun shall go down upon the prophets,
   and the day shall be black over them;

7　the seers shall be disgraced,
　　　and the diviners put to shame;
　　they shall all cover their lips,
　　　for there is no answer from God.
8　But as for me, I am filled with power,
　　　with the spirit of the LORD,
　　　and with justice and might,
　　to declare to Jacob his transgression
　　　and to Israel his sin.
9　Hear this, you rulers of the house of Jacob
　　　and chiefs of the house of Israel,
　　who abhor justice
　　　and pervert all equity,
10　who build Zion with blood
　　　and Jerusalem with wrong!
11　Its rulers give judgement for a bribe,
　　　its priests teach for a price,
　　　its prophets give oracles for money;
　　yet they lean upon the LORD and say,
　　　'Surely the LORD is with us!
　　　No harm shall come upon us.'
12　Therefore because of you
　　　Zion shall be ploughed as a field;
　　Jerusalem shall become a heap of ruins,
　　　and the mountain of the house a wooded height.

PSALM   Psalm 43

1　Give judgement for me, O God, and defend my cause against an
　　　ungodly people;
　　deliver me from the deceitful and the wicked.
2　For you are the God of my strength; why have you put me from
　　　you?
　　and why do I go so heavily while the enemy oppresses me?
3　Send out your light and your truth, that they may lead me,
　　and bring me to your holy hill and to your dwelling;
4　That I may go to the altar of God, to the God of my joy and gladness;
　　and on the harp I will give thanks to you, O God my God.
5　Why are you so full of heaviness, O my soul?
　　and why are you so disquieted within me?
6　Put your trust in God;
　　for I will yet give thanks to him, who is the help of my countenance,
　　　and my God.

Psalm 107.1–8

¹ Give thanks to the Lord, for he is good,
   and his mercy endures for ever.
² Let all those whom the Lord has redeemed proclaim
   that he redeemed them from the hand of the foe.
³ He gathered them out of the lands;
   from the east and from the west, from the north and from the
      south.
⁴ Some wandered in desert wastes;
   they found no way to a city where they might dwell.
⁵ They were hungry and thirsty;
   their spirits languished within them.
⁶ Then they cried to the Lord in their trouble,
   and he delivered them from their distress.
⁷ He put their feet on a straight path
   to go to a city where they might dwell.
⁸ Let them give thanks to the Lord for his mercy
   and the wonders he does for his children.

READING   1 Thessalonians 2.9–13

⁹ You remember our labour and toil, brothers and sisters; we worked night and day, so that we might not burden any of you while we proclaimed to you the gospel of God. ¹⁰ You are witnesses, and God also, how pure, upright, and blameless our conduct was towards you believers. ¹¹ As you know, we dealt with each one of you like a father with his children, ¹² urging and encouraging you and pleading that you should lead a life worthy of God, who calls you into his own kingdom and glory.

¹³ We also constantly give thanks to God for this, that when you received the word of God that you heard from us, you accepted it not as a human word but as what it really is, God's word, which is also at work in you believers.

GOSPEL   Matthew 24.1–14

¹ As Jesus came out of the temple and was going away, his disciples came to point out to him the buildings of the temple. ² Then he asked them, 'You see all these, do you not? Truly I tell you, not one stone will be left here upon another; all will be thrown down.'

³ When he was sitting on the Mount of Olives, the disciples came to him privately, saying, 'Tell us, when will this be, and what will be the sign of

your coming and of the end of the age?' [4] Jesus answered them, 'Beware that no one leads you astray. [5] For many will come in my name, saying, "I am the Messiah!" and they will lead many astray. [6] And you will hear of wars and rumours of wars; see that you are not alarmed; for this must take place, but the end is not yet. [7] For nation will rise against nation, and kingdom against kingdom, and there will be famines and earthquakes in various places: [8] all this is but the beginning of the birth pangs.

[9] 'Then they will hand you over to be tortured and will put you to death, and you will be hated by all nations because of my name. [10] Then many will fall away, and they will betray one another and hate one another. [11] And many false prophets will arise and lead many astray. [12] And because of the increase of lawlessness, the love of many will grow cold. [13] But anyone who endures to the end will be saved. [14] And this good news of the kingdom will be proclaimed throughout the world, as a testimony to all the nations; and then the end will come.'

POST COMMUNION

Lord of heaven,
in this eucharist you have brought us near
   to an innumerable company of angels
   and to the spirits of the saints made perfect:
as in this food of our earthly pilgrimage
   we have shared their fellowship,
so may we come to share their joy in heaven;
through Jesus Christ our Lord.

SECOND SERVICE

Psalms 111; 117
Daniel 7.1–18
Luke 6.17–31

THIRD SERVICE

Psalm 33
Isaiah 66.20–23
Ephesians 1.11–23

THE THIRD SUNDAY BEFORE ADVENT

Sunday between 6 and 12 November inclusive

COLLECT

Almighty Father,
whose will is to restore all things
in your beloved Son, the king of all:
govern the hearts and minds of those in authority,
and bring the families of the nations,
divided and torn apart by the ravages of sin,
to be subject to his just and gentle rule;
who is alive and reigns with you,
in the unity of the Holy Spirit,
one God, now and for ever.

EITHER

READING   Wisdom 6.12–16

¹² Wisdom is radiant and unfading,
    and she is easily discerned by those who love her,
    and is found by those who seek her.
¹³ She hastens to make herself known to those who desire her.
¹⁴ One who rises early to seek her will have no difficulty,
    for she will be found sitting at the gate.
¹⁵ To fix one's thought on her is perfect understanding,
    and one who is vigilant on her account will soon be free from care,
¹⁶ because she goes about seeking those worthy of her,
    and she graciously appears to them in their paths,
    and meets them in every thought.

CANTICLE   Wisdom 6.17–20

¹⁷ The beginning of wisdom is the most sincere desire for instruction,
    and concern for instruction is love of her,
¹⁸ and love of her is the keeping of her laws,
    and giving heed to her laws is assurance of immortality,
¹⁹ and immortality brings one near to God;
²⁰ so the desire for wisdom leads to a kingdom.

READING   1 Thessalonians 4.13–18

[13] But we do not want you to be uninformed, brothers and sisters, about those who have died, so that you may not grieve as others do who have no hope. [14] For since we believe that Jesus died and rose again, even so, through Jesus, God will bring with him those who have died. [15] For this we declare to you by the word of the Lord, that we who are alive, who are left until the coming of the Lord, will by no means precede those who have died. [16] For the Lord himself, with a cry of command, with the archangel's call and with the sound of God's trumpet, will descend from heaven, and the dead in Christ will rise first. [17] Then we who are alive, who are left, will be caught up in the clouds together with them to meet the Lord in the air; and so we will be with the Lord for ever. [18] Therefore encourage one another with these words.

GOSPEL   Matthew 25.1–13

[1] 'Then the kingdom of heaven will be like this. Ten bridesmaids took their lamps and went to meet the bridegroom. [2] Five of them were foolish, and five were wise. [3] When the foolish took their lamps, they took no oil with them; [4] but the wise took flasks of oil with their lamps. [5] As the bridegroom was delayed, all of them became drowsy and slept. [6] But at midnight there was a shout, "Look! Here is the bridegroom! Come out to meet him." [7] Then all those bridesmaids got up and trimmed their lamps. [8] The foolish said to the wise, "Give us some of your oil, for our lamps are going out." [9] But the wise replied, "No! there will not be enough for you and for us; you had better go to the dealers and buy some for yourselves." [10] And while they went to buy it, the bridegroom came, and those who were ready went with him into the wedding banquet; and the door was shut. [11] Later the other bridesmaids came also, saying, "Lord, lord, open to us." [12] But he replied, "Truly I tell you, I do not know you." [13] Keep awake therefore, for you know neither the day nor the hour.'

OR

READING   Amos 5.18–24

[18]   Alas for you who desire the day of the LORD!
          Why do you want the day of the LORD?
       It is darkness, not light;
[19]   as if someone fled from a lion,
          and was met by a bear;
       or went into the house and rested a hand against the wall,
          and was bitten by a snake.

20   Is not the day of the LORD darkness, not light,
     and gloom with no brightness in it?
21   I hate, I despise your festivals,
     and I take no delight in your solemn assemblies.
22   Even though you offer me your burnt-offerings and grain-offerings,
     I will not accept them;
   and the offerings of well-being of your fatted animals
     I will not look upon.
23   Take away from me the noise of your songs;
     I will not listen to the melody of your harps.
24   But let justice roll down like waters,
     and righteousness like an ever-flowing stream.

PSALM   Psalm 70

1   Be pleased, O God, to deliver me;
   O Lord, make haste to help me.
2   Let those who seek my life be ashamed and altogether dismayed;
   let those who take pleasure in my misfortune draw back and be
    disgraced.
3   Let those who say to me 'Aha!' and gloat over me turn back,
   because they are ashamed.
4   Let all who seek you rejoice and be glad in you;
   let those who love your salvation say for ever, 'Great is the Lord!'
5   But as for me, I am poor and needy;
   come to me speedily, O God.
6   You are my helper and my deliverer;
   O Lord, do not tarry.

READING   1 Thessalonians 4.13–18

13 But we do not want you to be uninformed, brothers and sisters, about those who have died, so that you may not grieve as others do who have no hope. 14 For since we believe that Jesus died and rose again, even so, through Jesus, God will bring with him those who have died. 15 For this we declare to you by the word of the Lord, that we who are alive, who are left until the coming of the Lord, will by no means precede those who have died. 16 For the Lord himself, with a cry of command, with the archangel's call and with the sound of God's trumpet, will descend from heaven, and the dead in Christ will rise first. 17 Then we who are alive, who are left, will be caught up in the clouds together with them to meet the Lord in the air; and so we will be with the Lord for ever. 18 Therefore encourage one another with these words.

GOSPEL   Matthew 25.1–13

[1] 'Then the kingdom of heaven will be like this. Ten bridesmaids took their lamps and went to meet the bridegroom. [2] Five of them were foolish, and five were wise. [3] When the foolish took their lamps, they took no oil with them; [4] but the wise took flasks of oil with their lamps. [5] As the bridegroom was delayed, all of them became drowsy and slept. [6] But at midnight there was a shout, "Look! Here is the bridegroom! Come out to meet him." [7] Then all those bridesmaids got up and trimmed their lamps. [8] The foolish said to the wise, "Give us some of your oil, for our lamps are going out." [9] But the wise replied, "No! there will not be enough for you and for us; you had better go to the dealers and buy some for yourselves." [10] And while they went to buy it, the bridegroom came, and those who were ready went with him into the wedding banquet; and the door was shut. [11] Later the other bridesmaids came also, saying, "Lord, lord, open to us." [12] But he replied, "Truly I tell you, I do not know you." [13] Keep awake therefore, for you know neither the day nor the hour.'

POST COMMUNION

God of peace,
whose Son Jesus Christ proclaimed the kingdom
and restored the broken to wholeness of life:
look with compassion on the anguish of the world,
and by your healing power
make whole both people and nations;
through our Lord and Saviour Jesus Christ.

SECOND SERVICE   THIRD SERVICE

Psalms [20;] 82   Psalm 91
Judges 7.2–22   Deuteronomy 17.14–20
John 15.9–17   1 Timothy 2.1–7

THE SECOND SUNDAY BEFORE ADVENT

Sunday between 13 and 19 November inclusive

COLLECT

Heavenly Father,
whose blessed Son was revealed
    to destroy the works of the devil
and to make us the children of God and heirs of eternal life:
grant that we, having this hope,
may purify ourselves even as he is pure;
that when he shall appear in power and great glory
we may be made like him
    in his eternal and glorious kingdom;
where he is alive and reigns with you,
in the unity of the Holy Spirit,
one God, now and for ever.

READING   Zephaniah 1.7, 12–18

7 Be silent before the Lord God!
       For the day of the Lord is at hand;
   the Lord has prepared a sacrifice,
       he has consecrated his guests.

12 At that time I will search Jerusalem with lamps,
       and I will punish the people
   who rest complacently on their dregs,
       those who say in their hearts,
   'The Lord will not do good,
       nor will he do harm.'
13 Their wealth shall be plundered,
       and their houses laid waste.
   Though they build houses,
       they shall not inhabit them;
   though they plant vineyards,
       they shall not drink wine from them.
14 The great day of the Lord is near,
       near and hastening fast;
   the sound of the day of the Lord is bitter,
       the warrior cries aloud there.

¹⁵ That day will be a day of wrath,
     a day of distress and anguish,
   a day of ruin and devastation,
     a day of darkness and gloom,
   a day of clouds and thick darkness,
¹⁶   a day of trumpet blast and battle cry
   against the fortified cities
     and against the lofty battlements.
¹⁷ I will bring such distress upon people
     that they shall walk like the blind;
     because they have sinned against the LORD,
   their blood shall be poured out like dust,
     and their flesh like dung.
¹⁸ Neither their silver nor their gold
     will be able to save them
     on the day of the LORD's wrath;
   in the fire of his passion
     the whole earth shall be consumed;
   for a full, a terrible end
     he will make of all the inhabitants of the earth.

PSALM   Psalm 90.1–8, [9–11,] 12

¹ Lord, you have been our refuge
   from one generation to another.
² Before the mountains were brought forth, or the land and the
     earth were born,
   from age to age you are God.
³ You turn us back to the dust and say,
   'Go back, O child of earth.'
⁴ For a thousand years in your sight are like yesterday when it is
     past
   and like a watch in the night.
⁵ You sweep us away like a dream;
   we fade away suddenly like the grass.
⁶ In the morning it is green and flourishes;
   in the evening it is dried up and withered.
⁷ For we consume away in your displeasure;
   we are afraid because of your wrathful indignation.
⁸ Our iniquities you have set before you,
   and our secret sins in the light of your countenance.
[⁹ When you are angry, all our days are gone;
   we bring our years to an end like a sigh.

¹⁰ The span of our life is seventy years, perhaps in strength even
       eighty;
    yet the sum of them is but labour and sorrow, for they pass away
       quickly and we are gone.
¹¹ Who regards the power of your wrath?
    who rightly fears your indignation?]
¹² So teach us to number our days
    that we may apply our hearts to wisdom.

OR, IF AN ALTERNATIVE READING IS PREFERRED   **Psalm 90.1–8**

¹ Lord, you have been our refuge
   from one generation to another.
² Before the mountains were brought forth, or the land and the
      earth were born,
   from age to age you are God.
³ You turn us back to the dust and say,
   'Go back, O child of earth.'
⁴ For a thousand years in your sight are like yesterday when it is
      past
   and like a watch in the night.
⁵ You sweep us away like a dream;
   we fade away suddenly like the grass.
⁶ In the morning it is green and flourishes;
   in the evening it is dried up and withered.
⁷ For we consume away in your displeasure;
   we are afraid because of your wrathful indignation.
⁸ Our iniquities you have set before you,
   and our secret sins in the light of your countenance.

READING   1 Thessalonians 5.1–11

¹ Now concerning the times and the seasons, brothers and sisters, you do
not need to have anything written to you. ² For you yourselves know very
well that the day of the Lord will come like a thief in the night. ³ When
they say, 'There is peace and security', then sudden destruction will come
upon them, as labour pains come upon a pregnant woman, and there will
be no escape! ⁴ But you, beloved, are not in darkness, for that day to surprise
you like a thief; ⁵ for you are all children of light and children of the day;
we are not of the night or of darkness. ⁶ So then, let us not fall asleep as
others do, but let us keep awake and be sober; ⁷ for those who sleep sleep
at night, and those who are drunk get drunk at night. ⁸ But since we belong
to the day, let us be sober, and put on the breastplate of faith and love, and

for a helmet the hope of salvation. [9] For God has destined us not for wrath but for obtaining salvation through our Lord Jesus Christ, [10] who died for us, so that whether we are awake or asleep we may live with him. [11] Therefore encourage one another and build up each other, as indeed you are doing.

GOSPEL   Matthew 25.14–30

[14] 'For it is as if a man, going on a journey, summoned his slaves and entrusted his property to them; [15] to one he gave five talents, to another two, to another one, to each according to his ability. Then he went away. [16] The one who had received the five talents went off at once and traded with them, and made five more talents. [17] In the same way, the one who had the two talents made two more talents. [18] But the one who had received the one talent went off and dug a hole in the ground and hid his master's money. [19] After a long time the master of those slaves came and settled accounts with them. [20] Then the one who had received the five talents came forward, bringing five more talents, saying, "Master, you handed over to me five talents; see, I have made five more talents." [21] His master said to him, "Well done, good and trustworthy slave; you have been trustworthy in a few things, I will put you in charge of many things; enter into the joy of your master." [22] And the one with the two talents also came forward, saying, "Master, you handed over to me two talents; see, I have made two more talents." [23] His master said to him, "Well done, good and trustworthy slave; you have been trustworthy in a few things, I will put you in charge of many things; enter into the joy of your master." [24] Then the one who had received the one talent also came forward, saying, "Master, I knew that you were a harsh man, reaping where you did not sow, and gathering where you did not scatter seed; [25] so I was afraid, and I went and hid your talent in the ground. Here you have what is yours." [26] But his master replied, "You wicked and lazy slave! You knew, did you, that I reap where I did not sow, and gather where I did not scatter? [27] Then you ought to have invested my money with the bankers, and on my return I would have received what was my own with interest. [28] So take the talent from him, and give it to the one with the ten talents. [29] For to all those who have, more will be given, and they will have an abundance; but from those who have nothing, even what they have will be taken away. [30] As for this worthless slave, throw him into the outer darkness, where there will be weeping and gnashing of teeth." '

YEAR A

POST COMMUNION

Gracious Lord,
in this holy sacrament
you give substance to our hope:
bring us at the last
to that fullness of life for which we long;
through Jesus Christ our Saviour.

SECOND SERVICE   THIRD SERVICE

Psalm 89.19–29, [30–37]   **Psalm 98**
1 Kings 1.[1–14,] 15–40   **Daniel 10.19–21**
Revelation 1.4–18   **Revelation 4**

*If the Second Service is a Eucharist, the
following is read as a Gospel:*

Luke 9.1–6

CHRIST THE KING
THE SUNDAY NEXT BEFORE ADVENT

Sunday between 20 and 26 November inclusive

COLLECT

Eternal Father,
whose Son Jesus Christ ascended to the throne of heaven
    that he might rule over all things as Lord and King:
keep the Church in the unity of the Spirit
and in the bond of peace,
and bring the whole created order to worship at his feet;
who is alive and reigns with you,
in the unity of the Holy Spirit,
one God, now and for ever.

READING   Ezekiel 34.11–16, 20–24

[11] For thus says the Lord GOD: I myself will search for my sheep, and will
seek them out. [12] As shepherds seek out their flocks when they are among
their scattered sheep, so I will seek out my sheep. I will rescue them from
all the places to which they have been scattered on a day of clouds and

thick darkness. ¹³ I will bring them out from the peoples and gather them from the countries, and will bring them into their own land; and I will feed them on the mountains of Israel, by the watercourses, and in all the inhabited parts of the land. ¹⁴ I will feed them with good pasture, and the mountain heights of Israel shall be their pasture; there they shall lie down in good grazing land, and they shall feed on rich pasture on the mountains of Israel. ¹⁵ I myself will be the shepherd of my sheep, and I will make them lie down, says the Lord GOD. ¹⁶ I will seek the lost, and I will bring back the strayed, and I will bind up the injured, and I will strengthen the weak, but the fat and the strong I will destroy. I will feed them with justice.

²⁰ Therefore, thus says the Lord GOD to them: I myself will judge between the fat sheep and the lean sheep. ²¹ Because you pushed with flank and shoulder, and butted at all the weak animals with your horns until you scattered them far and wide, ²² I will save my flock, and they shall no longer be ravaged; and I will judge between sheep and sheep.

²³ I will set up over them one shepherd, my servant David, and he shall feed them: he shall feed them and be their shepherd. ²⁴ And I, the LORD, will be their God, and my servant David shall be prince among them; I, the LORD, have spoken.

PSALM   Psalm 95.1–7a, [7b]

¹ Come, let us sing to the Lord;
  let us shout for joy to the rock of our salvation.
² Let us come before his presence with thanksgiving
  and raise a loud shout to him with psalms.
³ For the Lord is a great God,
  and a great king above all gods.
⁴ In his hand are the depths of the earth,
  and the heights of the hills are his also.
⁵ The sea is his, for he made it,
  and his hands have moulded the dry land.
⁶ Come, let us bow down and bend the knee,
  and kneel before the Lord our Maker.
⁷ For he is our God, and we are the people of his pasture and the
    sheep of his hand.
[O that today you would hearken to his voice!]

READING   Ephesians 1.15–23

[15] I have heard of your faith in the Lord Jesus and your love towards all the saints, and for this reason [16] I do not cease to give thanks for you as I remember you in my prayers. [17] I pray that the God of our Lord Jesus Christ, the Father of glory, may give you a spirit of wisdom and revelation as you come to know him, [18] so that, with the eyes of your heart enlightened, you may know what is the hope to which he has called you, what are the riches of his glorious inheritance among the saints, [19] and what is the immeasurable greatness of his power for us who believe, according to the working of his great power. [20] God put this power to work in Christ when he raised him from the dead and seated him at his right hand in the heavenly places, [21] far above all rule and authority and power and dominion, and above every name that is named, not only in this age but also in the age to come. [22] And he has put all things under his feet and has made him the head over all things for the church, [23] which is his body, the fullness of him who fills all in all.

GOSPEL   Matthew 25.31–46

[31] 'When the Son of Man comes in his glory, and all the angels with him, then he will sit on the throne of his glory. [32] All the nations will be gathered before him, and he will separate people one from another as a shepherd separates the sheep from the goats, [33] and he will put the sheep at his right hand and the goats at the left. [34] Then the king will say to those at his right hand, "Come, you that are blessed by my Father, inherit the kingdom prepared for you from the foundation of the world; [35] for I was hungry and you gave me food, I was thirsty and you gave me something to drink, I was a stranger and you welcomed me, [36] I was naked and you gave me clothing, I was sick and you took care of me, I was in prison and you visited me." [37] Then the righteous will answer him, "Lord, when was it that we saw you hungry and gave you food, or thirsty and gave you something to drink? [38] And when was it that we saw you a stranger and welcomed you, or naked and gave you clothing? [39] And when was it that we saw you sick or in prison and visited you?" [40] And the king will answer them, "Truly I tell you, just as you did it to one of the least of these who are members of my family, you did it to me." [41] Then he will say to those at his left hand, "You that are accursed, depart from me into the eternal fire prepared for the devil and his angels; [42] for I was hungry and you gave me no food, I was thirsty and you gave me nothing to drink, [43] I was a stranger and you did not welcome me, naked and you did not give me clothing, sick and in prison and you did not visit me." [44] Then they also will answer, "Lord, when was it that we saw you hungry or thirsty or a stranger or naked or sick or in prison, and

did not take care of you?" [45] Then he will answer them, "Truly I tell you, just as you did not do it to one of the least of these, you did not do it to me." [46] And these will go away into eternal punishment, but the righteous into eternal life.'

POST COMMUNION

Stir up, O Lord, the wills of your faithful people;
that they, plenteously bringing forth the fruit of good works,
may by you be plenteously rewarded;
through Jesus Christ our Lord.

This Post Communion may be used as the Collect at Morning and Evening Prayer during this week

SECOND SERVICE

Psalms 93; [97]
2 Samuel 23.1–7
or
1 Maccabees 2.15–29
Matthew 28.16–20

THIRD SERVICE

Psalms 29; 110
Isaiah 4.2–5.7
Luke 19.29–38

HARVEST THANKSGIVING

COLLECT

Eternal God,
you crown the year with your goodness
and you give us the fruits of the earth in their season:
grant that we may use them to your glory,
    for the relief of those in need
    and for our own well-being;
through Jesus Christ your Son our Lord,
who is alive and reigns with you,
in the unity of the Holy Spirit,
one God, now and for ever.

READING

Deuteronomy 8.7–18

7 For the LORD your God is bringing you into a good land, a land with flowing streams, with springs and underground waters welling up in valleys and hills, 8 a land of wheat and barley, of vines and fig trees and pomegranates, a land of olive trees and honey, 9 a land where you may eat bread without scarcity, where you will lack nothing, a land whose stones are iron and from whose hills you may mine copper. 10 You shall eat your fill and bless the LORD your God for the good land that he has given you.

11 Take care that you do not forget the LORD your God, by failing to keep his commandments, his ordinances, and his statutes, which I am commanding you today. 12 When you have eaten your fill and have built fine houses and live in them, 13 and when your herds and flocks have multiplied, and your silver and gold is multiplied, and all that you have is multiplied, 14 then do not exalt yourself, forgetting the LORD your God, who brought you out of the land of Egypt, out of the house of slavery, 15 who led you through the great and terrible wilderness, an arid waste-land with poisonous snakes and scorpions. He made water flow for you from flint rock, 16 and fed you in the wilderness with manna that your ancestors did not know, to humble you and to test you, and in the end to do you good. 17 Do not say to yourself, 'My power and the might of my own hand have gained me this wealth.' 18 But remember the LORD your God, for it is he who gives you power to get wealth, so that he may confirm his covenant that he swore to your ancestors, as he is doing today.

OR ## Deuteronomy 28.1–14

1 If you will only obey the LORD your God, by diligently observing all his commandments that I am commanding you today, the LORD your God will set you high above all the nations of the earth; 2 all these blessings shall come upon you and overtake you, if you obey the LORD your God:

3 Blessed shall you be in the city, and blessed shall you be in the field.

4 Blessed shall be the fruit of your womb, the fruit of your ground, and the fruit of your livestock, both the increase of your cattle and the issue of your flock.

5 Blessed shall be your basket and your kneading-bowl.

6 Blessed shall you be when you come in, and blessed shall you be when you go out.

⁷ The Lᴏʀᴅ will cause your enemies who rise against you to be defeated before you; they shall come out against you one way, and flee before you seven ways. ⁸ The Lᴏʀᴅ will command the blessing upon you in your barns, and in all that you undertake; he will bless you in the land that the Lᴏʀᴅ your God is giving you. ⁹ The Lᴏʀᴅ will establish you as his holy people, as he has sworn to you, if you keep the commandments of the Lᴏʀᴅ your God and walk in his ways. ¹⁰ All the peoples of the earth shall see that you are called by the name of the Lᴏʀᴅ, and they shall be afraid of you. ¹¹ The Lᴏʀᴅ will make you abound in prosperity, in the fruit of your womb, in the fruit of your livestock, and in the fruit of your ground in the land that the Lᴏʀᴅ swore to your ancestors to give you. ¹² The Lᴏʀᴅ will open for you his rich storehouse, the heavens, to give the rain of your land in its season and to bless all your undertakings. You will lend to many nations, but you will not borrow. ¹³ The Lᴏʀᴅ will make you the head, and not the tail; you shall be only at the top, and not at the bottom—if you obey the commandments of the Lᴏʀᴅ your God, which I am commanding you today, by diligently observing them, ¹⁴ and if you do not turn aside from any of the words that I am commanding you today, either to the right or to the left, following other gods to serve them.

PSALM   Psalm 65

1   You are to be praised, O God, in Zion;
    to you shall vows be performed in Jerusalem.
2   To you that hear prayer shall all flesh come,
    because of their transgressions.
3   Our sins are stronger than we are,
    but you will blot them out.
4   Happy are they whom you choose and draw to your courts to dwell there!
    they will be satisfied by the beauty of your house, by the holiness of your temple.
5   Awesome things will you show us in your righteousness, O God of our salvation,
    O Hope of all the ends of the earth and of the seas that are far away.
6   You make fast the mountains by your power;
    they are girded about with might.
7   You still the roaring of the seas,
    the roaring of their waves, and the clamour of the peoples.
8   Those who dwell at the ends of the earth will tremble at your marvellous signs;
    you make the dawn and the dusk to sing for joy.

9 You visit the earth and water it abundantly; you make it very
   plenteous;
   the river of God is full of water.
10 You prepare the grain,
   for so you provide for the earth.
11 You drench the furrows and smooth out the ridges;
   with heavy rain you soften the ground and bless its increase.
12 You crown the year with your goodness,
   and your paths overflow with plenty.
13 May the fields of the wilderness be rich for grazing,
   and the hills be clothed with joy.
14 May the meadows cover themselves with flocks, and the valleys
   cloak themselves with grain;
   let them shout for joy and sing.

READING   2 Corinthians 9.6–15

6 The point is this: the one who sows sparingly will also reap sparingly,
and the one who sows bountifully will also reap bountifully. 7 Each of
you must give as you have made up your mind, not reluctantly or under
compulsion, for God loves a cheerful giver. 8 And God is able to provide you
with every blessing in abundance, so that by always having enough of
everything, you may share abundantly in every good work. 9 As it is written,
   'He scatters abroad, he gives to the poor;
      his righteousness endures for ever.'
10 He who supplies seed to the sower and bread for food will supply and
multiply your seed for sowing and increase the harvest of your righteousness. 11 You will be enriched in every way for your great generosity, which
will produce thanksgiving to God through us; 12 for the rendering of this
ministry not only supplies the needs of the saints but also overflows with
many thanksgivings to God. 13 Through the testing of this ministry you
glorify God by your obedience to the confession of the gospel of Christ and
by the generosity of your sharing with them and with all others, 14 while
they long for you and pray for you because of the surpassing grace of God
that he has given you. 15 Thanks be to God for his indescribable gift!

GOSPEL

EITHER   Luke 12.16–30

16 Then he told them a parable: 'The land of a rich man produced abundantly. 17 And he thought to himself, "What should I do, for I have no place
to store my crops?" 18 Then he said, "I will do this: I will pull down my barns
and build larger ones, and there I will store all my grain and my goods.
19 And I will say to my soul, Soul, you have ample goods laid up for many

years; relax, eat, drink, be merry." [20] But God said to him, "You fool! This very night your life is being demanded of you. And the things you have prepared, whose will they be?" [21] So it is with those who store up treasures for themselves but are not rich towards God.'

[22] He said to his disciples, 'Therefore I tell you, do not worry about your life, what you will eat, or about your body, what you will wear. [23] For life is more than food, and the body more than clothing. [24] Consider the ravens: they neither sow nor reap, they have neither storehouse nor barn, and yet God feeds them. Of how much more value are you than the birds! [25] And can any of you by worrying add a single hour to your span of life? [26] If then you are not able to do so small a thing as that, why do you worry about the rest? [27] Consider the lilies, how they grow: they neither toil nor spin; yet I tell you, even Solomon in all his glory was not clothed like one of these. [28] But if God so clothes the grass of the field, which is alive today and tomorrow is thrown into the oven, how much more will he clothe you— you of little faith! [29] And do not keep striving for what you are to eat and what you are to drink, and do not keep worrying. [30] For it is the nations of the world that strive after all these things, and your Father knows that you need them.'

OR   Luke 17.11–19

[11] On the way to Jerusalem Jesus was going through the region between Samaria and Galilee. [12] As he entered a village, ten lepers approached him. Keeping their distance, [13] they called out, saying, 'Jesus, Master, have mercy on us!' [14] When he saw them, he said to them, 'Go and show yourselves to the priests.' And as they went, they were made clean. [15] Then one of them, when he saw that he was healed, turned back, praising God with a loud voice. [16] He prostrated himself at Jesus' feet and thanked him. And he was a Samaritan. [17] Then Jesus asked, 'Were not ten made clean? But the other nine, where are they? [18] Was none of them found to return and give praise to God except this foreigner?' [19] Then he said to him, 'Get up and go on your way; your faith has made you well.'

POST COMMUNION

Lord of the harvest,
with joy we have offered thanksgiving
    for your love in creation
and have shared in the bread and the wine of the kingdom:
by your grace plant within us a reverence for all that you give us
and make us generous and wise stewards
of the good things we enjoy;
through Jesus Christ our Lord.

BIBLE SUNDAY

Bible Sunday may be celebrated in preference to the provision for the Last Sunday after Trinity

COLLECT

Blessed Lord,
who caused all holy scriptures
  to be written for our learning:
help us so to hear them,
to read, mark, learn, and inwardly digest them
that, through patience, and the comfort of your holy word,
we may embrace and for ever hold fast
  the hope of everlasting life,
which you have given us in our Saviour Jesus Christ,
who is alive and reigns with you,
in the unity of the Holy Spirit,
one God, now and for ever.

READING   Nehemiah 8.1–4a, [5–6,] 8–12

[1] All the people gathered together into the square before the Water Gate. They told the scribe Ezra to bring the book of the law of Moses, which the LORD had given to Israel. [2] Accordingly, the priest Ezra brought the law before the assembly, both men and women and all who could hear with understanding. This was on the first day of the seventh month. [3] He read from it facing the square before the Water Gate from early morning until midday, in the presence of the men and the women and those who could understand; and the ears of all the people were attentive to the book of the law. [4] The scribe Ezra stood on a wooden platform that had been made for the purpose.

[[5] And Ezra opened the book in the sight of all the people, for he was standing above all the people; and when he opened it, all the people stood up. [6] Then Ezra blessed the LORD, the great God, and all the people answered, 'Amen, Amen', lifting up their hands. Then they bowed their heads and worshipped the LORD with their faces to the ground.]

[8] So they read from the book, from the law of God, with interpretation. They gave the sense, so that the people understood the reading.

[9] And Nehemiah, who was the governor, and Ezra the priest and scribe, and the Levites who taught the people said to all the people, 'This day is

holy to the LORD your God; do not mourn or weep.' For all the people wept when they heard the words of the law. [10] Then he said to them, 'Go your way, eat the fat and drink sweet wine and send portions of them to those for whom nothing is prepared, for this day is holy to our LORD; and do not be grieved, for the joy of the LORD is your strength.' [11] So the Levites stilled all the people, saying, 'Be quiet, for this day is holy; do not be grieved.' [12] And all the people went their way to eat and drink and to send portions and to make great rejoicing, because they had understood the words that were declared to them.

PSALM   Psalm 119.9–16

[9] How shall the young cleanse their way?
     By keeping to your words.
[10] With my whole heart I seek you;
     let me not stray from your commandments.
[11] I treasure your promise in my heart,
     that I may not sin against you.
[12] Blessèd are you, O Lord;
     instruct me in your statutes.
[13] With my lips will I recite
     all the judgements of your mouth.
[14] I have taken greater delight in the way of your decrees
     than in all manner of riches.
[15] I will meditate on your commandments
     and give attention to your ways.
[16] My delight is in your statutes;
     I will not forget your word.

READING   Colossians 3.12–17

[12] As God's chosen ones, holy and beloved, clothe yourselves with compassion, kindness, humility, meekness, and patience. [13] Bear with one another and, if anyone has a complaint against another, forgive each other; just as the Lord has forgiven you, so you also must forgive. [14] Above all, clothe yourselves with love, which binds everything together in perfect harmony. [15] And let the peace of Christ rule in your hearts, to which indeed you were called in the one body. And be thankful. [16] Let the word of Christ dwell in you richly; teach and admonish one another in all wisdom; and with gratitude in your hearts sing psalms, hymns, and spiritual songs to God. [17] And whatever you do, in word or deed, do everything in the name of the Lord Jesus, giving thanks to God the Father through him.

GOSPEL   Matthew 24.30–35

[30] 'Then the sign of the Son of Man will appear in heaven, and then all the tribes of the earth will mourn, and they will see "the Son of Man coming on the clouds of heaven" with power and great glory. [31] And he will send out his angels with a loud trumpet call, and they will gather his elect from the four winds, from one end of heaven to the other.

[32] 'From the fig tree learn its lesson: as soon as its branch becomes tender and puts forth its leaves, you know that summer is near. [33] So also, when you see all these things, you know that he is near, at the very gates. [34] Truly I tell you, this generation will not pass away until all these things have taken place. [35] Heaven and earth will pass away, but my words will not pass away.'

POST COMMUNION

God of all grace,
your Son Jesus Christ fed the hungry
with the bread of his life
and the word of his kingdom:
renew your people with your heavenly grace,
and in all our weakness
sustain us by your true and living bread;
who is alive and reigns, now and for ever.

SECOND SERVICE   THIRD SERVICE

Psalm 119.89–104   Psalm 119.137–152
Isaiah 55.1–11   Deuteronomy 17.14–15, 18–20
Luke 4.14–30   John 5.36b-47

DEDICATION FESTIVAL

The First Sunday in October or Last Sunday after Trinity

COLLECT

Almighty God,
to whose glory we celebrate the dedication
   of this house of prayer:
we praise you for the many blessings

you have given to those who worship you here:
and we pray that all who seek you in this place
 may find you,
and, being filled with the Holy Spirit,
may become a living temple acceptable to you;
through Jesus Christ your Son our Lord,
who is alive and reigns with you,
in the unity of the Holy Spirit,
one God, now and for ever.

READING

EITHER   **1 Kings 8.22–30**

[22] Then Solomon stood before the altar of the LORD in the presence of all the assembly of Israel, and spread out his hands to heaven. [23] He said, 'O LORD, God of Israel, there is no God like you in heaven above or on earth beneath, keeping covenant and steadfast love for your servants who walk before you with all their heart, [24] the covenant that you kept for your servant my father David as you declared to him; you promised with your mouth and have this day fulfilled with your hand. [25] Therefore, O LORD, God of Israel, keep for your servant my father David that which you promised him, saying, "There shall never fail you a successor before me to sit on the throne of Israel, if only your children look to their way, to walk before me as you have walked before me." [26] Therefore, O God of Israel, let your word be confirmed, which you promised to your servant my father David.

[27] 'But will God indeed dwell on the earth? Even heaven and the highest heaven cannot contain you, much less this house that I have built! [28] Have regard to your servant's prayer and his plea, O LORD my God, heeding the cry and the prayer that your servant prays to you today; [29] that your eyes may be open night and day towards this house, the place of which you said, "My name shall be there", that you may heed the prayer that your servant prays towards this place. [30] Hear the plea of your servant and of your people Israel when they pray towards this place; O hear in heaven your dwelling-place; heed and forgive.'

OR   **Revelation 21.9–14**

[9] Then one of the seven angels who had the seven bowls full of the seven last plagues came and said to me, 'Come, I will show you the bride, the wife of the Lamb.' [10] And in the spirit he carried me away to a great, high mountain and showed me the holy city Jerusalem coming down out of heaven from God. [11] It has the glory of God and a radiance like a very rare

jewel, like jasper, clear as crystal. [12] It has a great, high wall with twelve gates, and at the gates twelve angels, and on the gates are inscribed the names of the twelve tribes of the Israelites; [13] on the east three gates, on the north three gates, on the south three gates, and on the west three gates. [14] And the wall of the city has twelve foundations, and on them are the twelve names of the twelve apostles of the Lamb.

PSALM   Psalm 122

1   I was glad when they said to me,
    'Let us go to the house of the Lord.'
2   Now our feet are standing
    within your gates, O Jerusalem.
3   Jerusalem is built as a city
    that is at unity with itself.
4   To which the tribes go up, the tribes of the Lord,
    the assembly of Israel, to praise the name of the Lord.
5   For there are the thrones of judgement,
    the thrones of the house of David.
6   Pray for the peace of Jerusalem:
    'May they prosper who love you.
7   Peace be within your walls
    and quietness within your towers.
8   For my family and companions' sake,
    I pray for your prosperity.
9   Because of the house of the Lord our God,
    I will seek to do you good.'

READING   Hebrews 12.18–24

[18] You have not come to something that can be touched, a blazing fire, and darkness, and gloom, and a tempest, [19] and the sound of a trumpet, and a voice whose words made the hearers beg that not another word be spoken to them. [20] (For they could not endure the order that was given, 'If even an animal touches the mountain, it shall be stoned to death.' [21] Indeed, so terrifying was the sight that Moses said, 'I tremble with fear.') [22] But you have come to Mount Zion and to the city of the living God, the heavenly Jerusalem, and to innumerable angels in festal gathering, [23] and to the assembly of the firstborn who are enrolled in heaven, and to God the judge of all, and to the spirits of the righteous made perfect, [24] and to Jesus, the mediator of a new covenant, and to the sprinkled blood that speaks a better word than the blood of Abel.

GOSPEL   Matthew 21.12–16

[12] Then Jesus entered the temple and drove out all who were selling and buying in the temple, and he overturned the tables of the money-changers and the seats of those who sold doves. [13] He said to them, 'It is written,
"My house shall be called a house of prayer";
but you are making it a den of robbers.'

[14] The blind and the lame came to him in the temple, and he cured them. [15] But when the chief priests and the scribes saw the amazing things that he did, and heard the children crying out in the temple, 'Hosanna to the Son of David', they became angry [16] and said to him, 'Do you hear what these are saying?' Jesus said to them, 'Yes; have you never read,
"Out of the mouths of infants and nursing babies
you have prepared praise for yourself"?'

POST COMMUNION

Father in heaven,
whose Church on earth is a sign of your heavenly peace,
an image of the new and eternal Jerusalem:
grant to us in the days of our pilgrimage
that, fed with the living bread of heaven,
and united in the body of your Son,
we may be the temple of your presence,
the place of your glory on earth,
and a sign of your peace in the world;
through Jesus Christ our Lord.

SECOND SERVICE   THIRD SERVICE

Psalm 132   Psalm 48
Jeremiah 7.1–11   Haggai 2.6–9
1 Corinthians 3.9–17   Hebrews 10.19–25

SUNDAYS AND
PRINCIPAL FEASTS AND HOLY DAYS

YEAR B

THE FIRST SUNDAY OF ADVENT

COLLECT

Almighty God,
give us grace to cast away the works of darkness
and to put on the armour of light,
now in the time of this mortal life,
in which your Son Jesus Christ
    came to us in great humility;
that on the last day,
when he shall come again in his glorious majesty
    to judge the living and the dead,
we may rise to the life immortal;
through him who is alive and reigns with you,
in the unity of the Holy Spirit,
one God, now and for ever.

*This Collect may be used as the Post Communion on any day from the Second Sunday
of Advent until Christmas Eve instead of the Post Communion provided*

READING   Isaiah 64.1–9

¹ O that you would tear open the heavens and come down,
    so that the mountains would quake at your presence—
² as when fire kindles brushwood
    and the fire causes water to boil—
    to make your name known to your adversaries,
    so that the nations might tremble at your presence!
³ When you did awesome deeds that we did not expect,
    you came down, the mountains quaked at your presence.
⁴ From ages past no one has heard,
    no ear has perceived,
    no eye has seen any God besides you,
    who works for those who wait for him.
⁵ You meet those who gladly do right,
    those who remember you in your ways.
    But you were angry, and we sinned;
    because you hid yourself we transgressed.
⁶ We have all become like one who is unclean,
    and all our righteous deeds are like a filthy cloth.
    We all fade like a leaf,
    and our iniquities, like the wind, take us away.

7   There is no one who calls on your name,
     or attempts to take hold of you;
  for you have hidden your face from us,
     and have delivered us into the hand of our iniquity.

8   Yet, O LORD, you are our Father;
     we are the clay, and you are our potter;
     we are all the work of your hand.

9   Do not be exceedingly angry, O LORD,
     and do not remember iniquity for ever.
     Now consider, we are all your people.

PSALM   Psalm 80.1–7, [16–18]

1   Hear, O Shepherd of Israel, leading Joseph like a flock;
     shine forth, you that are enthroned upon the cherubim.

2   In the presence of Ephraim, Benjamin and Manasseh,
     stir up your strength and come to help us.

3   Restore us, O God of hosts;
     show the light of your countenance and we shall be saved.

4   O Lord God of hosts,
     how long will you be angered despite the prayers of your people?

5   You have fed them with the bread of tears;
     you have given them bowls of tears to drink.

6   You have made us the derision of our neighbours,
     and our enemies laugh us to scorn.

7   Restore us, O God of hosts;
     show the light of your countenance and we shall be saved.

[16   Let your hand be upon the man of your right hand,
     the son of man you have made so strong for yourself.

17   And so will we never turn away from you;
     give us life, that we may call upon your name.

18   Restore us, O Lord God of hosts;
     show the light of your countenance and we shall be saved.]

READING   1 Corinthians 1.3–9

3 Grace to you and peace from God our Father and the Lord Jesus Christ.

4 I give thanks to my God always for you because of the grace of God that has been given you in Christ Jesus, 5 for in every way you have been enriched in him, in speech and knowledge of every kind— 6 just as the testimony of Christ has been strengthened among you— 7 so that you are not lacking in any spiritual gift as you wait for the revealing of our Lord Jesus Christ. 8 He

will also strengthen you to the end, so that you may be blameless on the day of our Lord Jesus Christ. [9] God is faithful; by him you were called into the fellowship of his Son, Jesus Christ our Lord.

GOSPEL   Mark 13.24–37

[24] 'But in those days, after that suffering,
   the sun will be darkened,
      and the moon will not give its light,
[25]   and the stars will be falling from heaven,
      and the powers in the heavens will be shaken.
[26] Then they will see "the Son of Man coming in clouds" with great power and glory. [27] Then he will send out the angels, and gather his elect from the four winds, from the ends of the earth to the ends of heaven.

[28] 'From the fig tree learn its lesson: as soon as its branch becomes tender and puts forth its leaves, you know that summer is near. [29] So also, when you see these things taking place, you know that he is near, at the very gates. [30] Truly I tell you, this generation will not pass away until all these things have taken place. [31] Heaven and earth will pass away, but my words will not pass away.

[32] 'But about that day or hour no one knows, neither the angels in heaven, nor the Son, but only the Father. [33] Beware, keep alert; for you do not know when the time will come. [34] It is like a man going on a journey, when he leaves home and puts his slaves in charge, each with his work, and commands the doorkeeper to be on the watch. [35] Therefore, keep awake—for you do not know when the master of the house will come, in the evening, or at midnight, or at cockcrow, or at dawn, [36] or else he may find you asleep when he comes suddenly. [37] And what I say to you I say to all: Keep awake.'

POST COMMUNION

O Lord our God,
make us watchful and keep us faithful
as we await the coming of your Son our Lord;
that, when he shall appear,
he may not find us sleeping in sin
but active in his service
and joyful in his praise;
through Jesus Christ our Lord.

SECOND SERVICE

Psalm 25.1–9, [10–21]
Isaiah 1.1–20
Matthew 21.1–13

THIRD SERVICE

Psalm 44
Isaiah 2.1–5
Luke 12.35–48

THE SECOND SUNDAY OF ADVENT

COLLECT

O Lord, raise up, we pray, your power
and come among us,
and with great might succour us;
that whereas, through our sins and wickedness
we are grievously hindered
in running the race that is set before us,
your bountiful grace and mercy
may speedily help and deliver us;
through Jesus Christ your Son our Lord,
to whom with you and the Holy Spirit,
be honour and glory, now and for ever.

READING   Isaiah 40.1–11

1 Comfort, O comfort my people,
    says your God.
2 Speak tenderly to Jerusalem,
    and cry to her
  that she has served her term,
    that her penalty is paid,
  that she has received from the LORD's hand
    double for all her sins.
3 A voice cries out:
  'In the wilderness prepare the way of the LORD,
    make straight in the desert a highway for our God.
4 Every valley shall be lifted up,
    and every mountain and hill be made low;
  the uneven ground shall become level,
    and the rough places a plain.

5 Then the glory of the LORD shall be revealed,
      and all people shall see it together,
      for the mouth of the LORD has spoken.'
6 A voice says, 'Cry out!'
      And I said, 'What shall I cry?'
   All people are grass,
      their constancy is like the flower of the field.
7 The grass withers, the flower fades,
      when the breath of the LORD blows upon it;
      surely the people are grass.
8 The grass withers, the flower fades;
      but the word of our God will stand for ever.
9 Get you up to a high mountain,
      O Zion, herald of good tidings;
   lift up your voice with strength,
      O Jerusalem, herald of good tidings,
      lift it up, do not fear;
   say to the cities of Judah,
      'Here is your God!'
10 See, the Lord GOD comes with might,
      and his arm rules for him;
   his reward is with him,
      and his recompense before him.
11 He will feed his flock like a shepherd;
      he will gather the lambs in his arms,
   and carry them in his bosom,
      and gently lead the mother sheep.

PSALM   Psalm 85.[1–2,] 8–13

[1 You have been gracious to your land, O Lord,
      you have restored the good fortune of Jacob.
 2 You have forgiven the iniquity of your people
      and blotted out all their sins.]

 8 I will listen to what the Lord God is saying,
      for he is speaking peace to his faithful people and to those who
         turn their hearts to him.
 9 Truly, his salvation is very near to those who fear him,
      that his glory may dwell in our land.
10 Mercy and truth have met together;
      righteousness and peace have kissed each other.
11 Truth shall spring up from the earth,
      and righteousness shall look down from heaven.

12 The Lord will indeed grant prosperity,
    and our land will yield its increase.
13 Righteousness shall go before him,
    and peace shall be a pathway for his feet.

READING   2 Peter 3.8–15a

8 But do not ignore this one fact, beloved, that with the Lord one day is like a thousand years, and a thousand years are like one day. 9 The Lord is not slow about his promise, as some think of slowness, but is patient with you, not wanting any to perish, but all to come to repentance. 10 But the day of the Lord will come like a thief, and then the heavens will pass away with a loud noise, and the elements will be dissolved with fire, and the earth and everything that is done on it will be disclosed.

11 Since all these things are to be dissolved in this way, what sort of people ought you to be in leading lives of holiness and godliness, 12 waiting for and hastening the coming of the day of God, because of which the heavens will be set ablaze and dissolved, and the elements will melt with fire? 13 But, in accordance with his promise, we wait for new heavens and a new earth, where righteousness is at home.

14 Therefore, beloved, while you are waiting for these things, strive to be found by him at peace, without spot or blemish; 15 and regard the patience of our Lord as salvation.

GOSPEL   Mark 1.1–8

1 The beginning of the good news of Jesus Christ, the Son of God.

2 As it is written in the prophet Isaiah,
  'See, I am sending my messenger ahead of you,
    who will prepare your way;
3   the voice of one crying out in the wilderness:
    "Prepare the way of the Lord,
    make his paths straight" ',
4 John the baptizer appeared in the wilderness, proclaiming a baptism of repentance for the forgiveness of sins. 5 And people from the whole Judean countryside and all the people of Jerusalem were going out to him, and were baptized by him in the river Jordan, confessing their sins. 6 Now John was clothed with camel's hair, with a leather belt around his waist, and he ate locusts and wild honey. 7 He proclaimed, 'The one who is more powerful

than I is coming after me; I am not worthy to stoop down and untie the thong of his sandals. [8] I have baptized you with water; but he will baptize you with the Holy Spirit.'

POST COMMUNION

Father in heaven,
who sent your Son to redeem the world
and will send him again to be our judge:
give us grace so to imitate him
    in the humility and purity of his first coming
that, when he comes again,
we may be ready to greet him
with joyful love and firm faith;
through Jesus Christ our Lord.

SECOND SERVICE

Psalm 40.[1–11,] 12–19
1 Kings 22.1–28
Romans 15.4–13

If the Second Service is a Eucharist, the following is read as a Gospel:

Matthew 11.2–11

THIRD SERVICE

Psalm 80
Baruch 5.1–9

or

Zephaniah 3.14–20
Luke 1.5–20

THE THIRD SUNDAY OF ADVENT

COLLECT

O Lord Jesus Christ,
who at your first coming sent your messenger
to prepare your way before you:
grant that the ministers and stewards of your mysteries
may likewise so prepare and make ready your way
by turning the hearts of the disobedient
    to the wisdom of the just,
that at your second coming to judge the world
we may be found an acceptable people in your sight;
for you are alive and reign with the Father
in the unity of the Holy Spirit,
one God, now and for ever.

READING   Isaiah 61.1–4, 8–11

¹ The spirit of the Lord GOD is upon me,
    because the LORD has anointed me;
  he has sent me to bring good news to the oppressed,
    to bind up the broken-hearted,
  to proclaim liberty to the captives,
    and release to the prisoners;
² to proclaim the year of the LORD's favour,
    and the day of vengeance of our God;
    to comfort all who mourn;
³ to provide for those who mourn in Zion—
    to give them a garland instead of ashes,
  the oil of gladness instead of mourning,
    the mantle of praise instead of a faint spirit.
  They will be called oaks of righteousness,
    the planting of the LORD, to display his glory.
⁴ They shall build up the ancient ruins,
    they shall raise up the former devastations;
  they shall repair the ruined cities,
    the devastations of many generations.

⁸ For I the LORD love justice,
    I hate robbery and wrongdoing;
  I will faithfully give them their recompense,
    and I will make an everlasting covenant with them.
⁹ Their descendants shall be known among the nations,
    and their offspring among the peoples;
  all who see them shall acknowledge
    that they are a people whom the LORD has blessed.
¹⁰ I will greatly rejoice in the LORD,
    my whole being shall exult in my God;
  for he has clothed me with the garments of salvation,
    he has covered me with the robe of righteousness,
  as a bridegroom decks himself with a garland,
    and as a bride adorns herself with her jewels.
¹¹ For as the earth brings forth its shoots,
    and as a garden causes what is sown in it to spring up,
  so the Lord GOD will cause righteousness and praise
    to spring up before all the nations.

EITHER

PSALM
Psalm 126

¹ When the Lord restored the fortunes of Zion,
   then were we like those who dream.
² Then was our mouth filled with laughter,
   and our tongue with shouts of joy.
³ Then they said among the nations,
   'The Lord has done great things for them.'
⁴ The Lord has done great things for us,
   and we are glad indeed.
⁵ Restore our fortunes, O Lord,
   like the watercourses of the Negev.
⁶ Those who sowed with tears
   will reap with songs of joy.
⁷ Those who go out weeping, carrying the seed,
   will come again with joy, shouldering their sheaves.

OR

CANTICLE: Magnificat
Luke 1.46–55

⁴⁶ My soul proclaims the greatness of the Lord,
⁴⁷ my spirit rejoices in God my Saviour,
⁴⁸ who has looked with favour on his lowly servant.
    From this day all generations will call me blessed:
⁴⁹   the Almighty has done great things for me
      and holy is his name.
⁵⁰   God has mercy on those who fear him,
      from generation to generation.
⁵¹ The Lord has shown strength with his arm
   and scattered the proud in their conceit,
⁵² casting down the mighty from their thrones
   and lifting up the lowly.
⁵³ God has filled the hungry with good things
   and sent the rich away empty.
⁵⁴ He has come to the aid of his servant Israel,
   to remember the promise of mercy,
⁵⁵ the promise made to our forebears,
   to Abraham and his children for ever.

READING   1 Thessalonians 5.16–24

[16] Rejoice always, [17] pray without ceasing, [18] give thanks in all circumstances; for this is the will of God in Christ Jesus for you. [19] Do not quench the Spirit. [20] Do not despise the words of prophets, [21] but test everything; hold fast to what is good; [22] abstain from every form of evil.

[23] May the God of peace himself sanctify you entirely; and may your spirit and soul and body be kept sound and blameless at the coming of our Lord Jesus Christ. [24] The one who calls you is faithful, and he will do this.

GOSPEL   John 1.6–8, 19–28

[6] There was a man sent from God, whose name was John. [7] He came as a witness to testify to the light, so that all might believe through him. [8] He himself was not the light, but he came to testify to the light.

[19] This is the testimony given by John when the Jews sent priests and Levites from Jerusalem to ask him, 'Who are you?' [20] He confessed and did not deny it, but confessed, 'I am not the Messiah.' [21] And they asked him, 'What then? Are you Elijah?' He said, 'I am not.' 'Are you the prophet?' He answered, 'No.' [22] Then they said to him, 'Who are you? Let us have an answer for those who sent us. What do you say about yourself?' [23] He said,

'I am the voice of one crying out in the wilderness,
     "Make straight the way of the Lord" ',
as the prophet Isaiah said.

[24] Now they had been sent from the Pharisees. [25] They asked him, 'Why then are you baptizing if you are neither the Messiah, nor Elijah, nor the prophet?' [26] John answered them, 'I baptize with water. Among you stands one whom you do not know, [27] the one who is coming after me; I am not worthy to untie the thong of his sandal.' [28] This took place in Bethany across the Jordan where John was baptizing.

POST COMMUNION

We give you thanks, O Lord, for these heavenly gifts;
kindle in us the fire of your Spirit
that when your Christ comes again
we may shine as lights before his face;
who is alive and reigns now and for ever.

SECOND SERVICE

Psalm 68.1–8, [9–20]
Malachi 3.1–4; 4
Philippians 4.4–7

*If the Second Service is a Eucharist, the
following is read as a Gospel:*

Matthew 14.1–12

THIRD SERVICE

Psalms 50.1–6; 62
Isaiah 12
Luke 1.57–66

THE FOURTH SUNDAY OF ADVENT

COLLECT

God our redeemer,
who prepared the Blessed Virgin Mary
to be the mother of your Son:
grant that, as she looked for his coming as our saviour,
so we may be ready to greet him
when he comes again as our judge;
who is alive and reigns with you,
in the unity of the Holy Spirit,
one God, now and for ever.

READING   2 Samuel 7.1–11, 16

¹ Now when the king was settled in his house, and the Lᴏʀᴅ had given him rest from all his enemies around him, ² the king said to the prophet Nathan, 'See now, I am living in a house of cedar, but the ark of God stays in a tent.' ³ Nathan said to the king, 'Go, do all that you have in mind; for the Lᴏʀᴅ is with you.'

⁴ But that same night the word of the Lᴏʀᴅ came to Nathan: ⁵ Go and tell my servant David: Thus says the Lᴏʀᴅ: Are you the one to build me a house to live in? ⁶ I have not lived in a house since the day I brought up the people of Israel from Egypt to this day, but I have been moving about in a tent and a tabernacle. ⁷ Wherever I have moved about among all the people of Israel, did I ever speak a word with any of the tribal leaders of Israel, whom I commanded to shepherd my people Israel, saying, 'Why have you not built me a house of cedar?' ⁸ Now therefore thus you shall say to my servant David: Thus says the Lᴏʀᴅ of hosts: I took you from the pasture, from following the sheep to be prince over my people Israel; ⁹ and I have been

with you wherever you went, and have cut off all your enemies from before you; and I will make for you a great name, like the name of the great ones of the earth. [10] And I will appoint a place for my people Israel and will plant them, so that they may live in their own place, and be disturbed no more; and evildoers shall afflict them no more, as formerly, [11] from the time that I appointed judges over my people Israel; and I will give you rest from all your enemies. Moreover, the LORD declares to you that the LORD will make you a house.

[16] Your house and your kingdom shall be made sure for ever before me; your throne shall be established for ever.

EITHER

CANTICLE: Magnificat   Luke 1.46–55

[46] My soul proclaims the greatness of the Lord,
[47] my spirit rejoices in God my Saviour,
[48] who has looked with favour on his lowly servant.
From this day all generations will call me blessed:
[49] the Almighty has done great things for me
and holy is his name.
[50] God has mercy on those who fear him,
from generation to generation.
[51] The Lord has shown strength with his arm
and scattered the proud in their conceit,
[52] casting down the mighty from their thrones
and lifting up the lowly.
[53] God has filled the hungry with good things
and sent the rich away empty.
[54] He has come to the aid of his servant Israel,
to remember the promise of mercy,
[55] the promise made to our forebears,
to Abraham and his children for ever.

OR

PSALM   Psalm 89.1–4, 19–26

[1] Your love, O Lord, for ever will I sing;
from age to age my mouth will proclaim your faithfulness.
[2] For I am persuaded that your love is established for ever;
you have set your faithfulness firmly in the heavens.

³ 'I have made a covenant with my chosen one;
I have sworn an oath to David my servant:

⁴ "I will establish your line for ever,
and preserve your throne for all generations." '

¹⁹ You spoke once in a vision and said to your faithful people:
'I have set the crown upon a warrior and have exalted one chosen
out of the people.

²⁰ I have found David my servant;
with my holy oil have I anointed him.

²¹ My hand will hold him fast
and my arm will make him strong.

²² No enemy shall deceive him,
nor the wicked bring him down.

²³ I will crush his foes before him
and strike down those who hate him.

²⁴ My faithfulness and love shall be with him,
and he shall be victorious through my name.

²⁵ I shall make his dominion extend
from the Great Sea to the River.

²⁶ He will say to me, "You are my Father,
my God and the rock of my salvation." '

OR, IF A SHORTER TEXT IS PREFERRED   **Psalm 89.1–8**

¹ Your love, O Lord, for ever will I sing;
from age to age my mouth will proclaim your faithfulness.

² For I am persuaded that your love is established for ever;
you have set your faithfulness firmly in the heavens.

³ 'I have made a covenant with my chosen one;
I have sworn an oath to David my servant:

⁴ "I will establish your line for ever,
and preserve your throne for all generations." '

⁵ The heavens bear witness to your wonders, O Lord,
and to your faithfulness in the assembly of the holy ones;

⁶ For who in the skies can be compared to the Lord?
who is like the Lord among the gods?

⁷ God is much to be feared in the council of the holy ones,
great and terrible to all those round about him.

⁸ Who is like you, Lord God of hosts?
O mighty Lord, your faithfulness is all around you.

READING   Romans 16.25–27

²⁵ Now to God who is able to strengthen you according to my gospel and the proclamation of Jesus Christ, according to the revelation of the mystery that was kept secret for long ages ²⁶ but is now disclosed, and through the prophetic writings is made known to all the Gentiles, according to the command of the eternal God, to bring about the obedience of faith— ²⁷ to the only wise God, through Jesus Christ, to whom be the glory for ever! Amen.

GOSPEL   Luke 1.26–38

²⁶ In the sixth month the angel Gabriel was sent by God to a town in Galilee called Nazareth, ²⁷ to a virgin engaged to a man whose name was Joseph, of the house of David. The virgin's name was Mary. ²⁸ And he came to her and said, 'Greetings, favoured one! The Lord is with you.' ²⁹ But she was much perplexed by his words and pondered what sort of greeting this might be. ³⁰ The angel said to her, 'Do not be afraid, Mary, for you have found favour with God. ³¹ And now, you will conceive in your womb and bear a son, and you will name him Jesus. ³² He will be great, and will be called the Son of the Most High, and the Lord God will give to him the throne of his ancestor David. ³³ He will reign over the house of Jacob for ever, and of his kingdom there will be no end.' ³⁴ Mary said to the angel, 'How can this be, since I am a virgin?' ³⁵ The angel said to her, 'The Holy Spirit will come upon you, and the power of the Most High will overshadow you; therefore the child to be born will be holy; he will be called Son of God. ³⁶ And now, your relative Elizabeth in her old age has also conceived a son; and this is the sixth month for her who was said to be barren. ³⁷ For nothing will be impossible with God.' ³⁸ Then Mary said, 'Here am I, the servant of the Lord; let it be with me according to your word.' Then the angel departed from her.

POST COMMUNION

Heavenly Father,
who chose the Blessed Virgin Mary
to be the mother of the promised saviour:
fill us your servants with your grace,
that in all things we may embrace your holy will
and with her rejoice in your salvation;
through Jesus Christ our Lord.

SECOND SERVICE

Psalms 113; [131]
Zechariah 2.10–13
Luke 1.39–55

THIRD SERVICE

Psalm 144
Isaiah 7.10–16
Romans 1.1–7

CHRISTMAS EVE

COLLECT

Almighty God,
you make us glad with the yearly remembrance
   of the birth of your Son Jesus Christ:
grant that, as we joyfully receive him as our redeemer,
so we may with sure confidence behold him
when he shall come to be our judge;
who is alive and reigns with you,
in the unity of the Holy Spirit,
one God, now and for ever.

READING   2 Samuel 7.1–5, 8–11, 16

[1] Now when the king was settled in his house, and the Lord had given him rest from all his enemies around him, [2] the king said to the prophet Nathan, 'See now, I am living in a house of cedar, but the ark of God stays in a tent.' [3] Nathan said to the king, 'Go, do all that you have in mind; for the Lord is with you.'

[4] But that same night the word of the Lord came to Nathan: [5] Go and tell my servant David: Thus says the Lord: Are you the one to build me a house to live in?

[8] Now therefore thus you shall say to my servant David: Thus says the Lord of hosts: I took you from the pasture, from following the sheep to be prince over my people Israel; [9] and I have been with you wherever you went, and have cut off all your enemies from before you; and I will make for you a great name, like the name of the great ones of the earth. [10] And I will appoint a place for my people Israel and will plant them, so that they may live in their own place, and be disturbed no more; and evildoers shall afflict

them no more, as formerly, [11] from the time that I appointed judges over my people Israel; and I will give you rest from all your enemies. Moreover, the LORD declares to you that the LORD will make you a house.

[16] Your house and your kingdom shall be made sure for ever before me; your throne shall be established for ever.

PSALM   Psalm 89.2, 21–27

[2]   For I am persuaded that your love is established for ever;
      you have set your faithfulness firmly in the heavens.

[21] 'My hand will hold him fast
      and my arm will make him strong.
[22] No enemy shall deceive him,
      nor the wicked bring him down.
[23] I will crush his foes before him
      and strike down those who hate him.
[24] My faithfulness and love shall be with him,
      and he shall be victorious through my name.
[25] I shall make his dominion extend
      from the Great Sea to the River.
[26] He will say to me, "You are my Father,
      my God and the rock of my salvation."
[27] I will make him my first-born
      and higher than the kings of the earth.'

READING   Acts 13.16–26

[16] So Paul stood up and with a gesture began to speak:

'You Israelites, and others who fear God, listen. [17] The God of this people Israel chose our ancestors and made the people great during their stay in the land of Egypt, and with uplifted arm he led them out of it. [18] For about forty years he put up with them in the wilderness. [19] After he had destroyed seven nations in the land of Canaan, he gave them their land as an inheritance [20] for about four hundred and fifty years. After that he gave them judges until the time of the prophet Samuel. [21] Then they asked for a king; and God gave them Saul son of Kish, a man of the tribe of Benjamin, who reigned for forty years. [22] When he had removed him, he made David their king. In his testimony about him he said, "I have found David, son of Jesse, to be a man after my heart, who will carry out all my wishes." [23] Of this man's posterity God has brought to Israel a Saviour, Jesus, as he promised; [24] before his coming John had already proclaimed a baptism of repentance to all the people of Israel. ²⁵ And as John was finishing his work, he said, "What do you suppose that I am? I am not he. No, but one is coming after me; I am not worthy to untie the thong of the sandals on his feet."

²⁶ 'My brothers, you descendants of Abraham's family, and others who fear God, to us the message of this salvation has been sent.'

GOSPEL   Luke 1.67–79

⁶⁷ Then his father Zechariah was filled with the Holy Spirit and spoke this prophecy:
⁶⁸ 'Blessed be the Lord God of Israel,
    for he has looked favourably on his people and redeemed them.
⁶⁹ He has raised up a mighty saviour for us
    in the house of his servant David,
⁷⁰ as he spoke through the mouth of his holy prophets from of old,
⁷¹   that we would be saved from our enemies and from the hand of all
    who hate us.
⁷² Thus he has shown the mercy promised to our ancestors,
    and has remembered his holy covenant,
⁷³ the oath that he swore to our ancestor Abraham,
    to grant us ⁷⁴ that we, being rescued from the hands of our enemies,
    might serve him without fear, ⁷⁵ in holiness and righteousness
    before him all our days.
⁷⁶ And you, child, will be called the prophet of the Most High;
    for you will go before the Lord to prepare his ways,
⁷⁷ to give knowledge of salvation to his people
    by the forgiveness of their sins.
⁷⁸ By the tender mercy of our God,
    the dawn from on high will break upon us,
⁷⁹ to give light to those who sit in darkness and in the shadow of death,
    to guide our feet into the way of peace.'

POST COMMUNION

Eternal God, for whom we wait,
you have fed us with the bread of eternal life:
keep us ever watchful,
that we may be ready to stand before the Son of Man,
Jesus Christ our Lord.

CHRISTMAS DAY

Any of the following sets of readings may be used on the evening of Christmas Eve and on Christmas Day. Set III should be used at some service during the celebration.

SET I

COLLECT

CHRISTMAS NIGHT

Eternal God,
who made this most holy night
to shine with the brightness of your one true light:
bring us, who have known the revelation
    of that light on earth,
to see the radiance of your heavenly glory;
through Jesus Christ your Son our Lord,
who is alive and reigns with you,
in the unity of the Holy Spirit,
one God, now and for ever.

CHRISTMAS DAY

Almighty God,
you have given us your only-begotten Son
to take our nature upon him
and as at this time to be born of a pure virgin:
grant that we, who have been born again
and made your children by adoption and grace,
may daily be renewed by your Holy Spirit;
through Jesus Christ your Son our Lord,
who is alive and reigns with you,
in the unity of the Holy Spirit,
one God, now and for ever.

READING   Isaiah 9.2–7

2 The people who walked in darkness
    have seen a great light;
 those who lived in a land of deep darkness—
    on them light has shined.
3 You have multiplied the nation,
    you have increased its joy;
 they rejoice before you
    as with joy at the harvest,
    as people exult when dividing plunder.
4 For the yoke of their burden,
    and the bar across their shoulders,
    the rod of their oppressor,
    you have broken as on the day of Midian.
5 For all the boots of the tramping warriors
    and all the garments rolled in blood
    shall be burned as fuel for the fire.
6 For a child has been born for us,
    a son given to us;
 authority rests upon his shoulders;
    and he is named
 Wonderful Counsellor, Mighty God,
    Everlasting Father, Prince of Peace.
7 His authority shall grow continually,
    and there shall be endless peace
 for the throne of David and his kingdom.
    He will establish and uphold it
 with justice and with righteousness
    from this time onwards and for evermore.
 The zeal of the Lord of hosts will do this.

PSALM   Psalm 96

1 Sing to the Lord a new song;
 sing to the Lord, all the whole earth.
2 Sing to the Lord and bless his name;
 proclaim the good news of his salvation from day to day.
3 Declare his glory among the nations
 and his wonders among all peoples.
4 For great is the Lord and greatly to be praised;
 he is more to be feared than all gods.

5 As for all the gods of the nations, they are but idols;
 but it is the Lord who made the heavens.
6 O the majesty and magnificence of his presence!
 O the power and the splendour of his sanctuary!
7 Ascribe to the Lord, you families of the peoples;
 ascribe to the Lord honour and power.
8 Ascribe to the Lord the honour due to his name;
 bring offerings and come into his courts.
9 Worship the Lord in the beauty of holiness;
 let the whole earth tremble before him.
10 Tell it out among the nations: 'The Lord is king!
 he has made the world so firm that it cannot be moved; he will
  judge the peoples with equity.'
11 Let the heavens rejoice and let the earth be glad; let the sea
  thunder and all that is in it;
 let the field be joyful and all that is therein.
12 Then shall all the trees of the wood shout for joy before the Lord
  when he comes,
 when he comes to judge the earth.
13 He will judge the world with righteousness
 and the peoples with his truth.

READING   Titus 2.11–14

11 For the grace of God has appeared, bringing salvation to all, 12 training us to renounce impiety and worldly passions, and in the present age to live lives that are self-controlled, upright, and godly, 13 while we wait for the blessed hope and the manifestation of the glory of our great God and Saviour, Jesus Christ. 14 He it is who gave himself for us that he might redeem us from all iniquity and purify for himself a people of his own who are zealous for good deeds.

GOSPEL   Luke 2.1–14, [15–20]

1 In those days a decree went out from Emperor Augustus that all the world should be registered. 2 This was the first registration and was taken while Quirinius was governor of Syria. 3 All went to their own towns to be registered. 4 Joseph also went from the town of Nazareth in Galilee to Judea, to the city of David called Bethlehem, because he was descended from the house and family of David. 5 He went to be registered with Mary, to whom he was engaged and who was expecting a child. 6 While they were there, the time came for her to deliver her child. 7 And she gave birth to her

firstborn son and wrapped him in bands of cloth, and laid him in a manger, because there was no place for them in the inn.

[8] In that region there were shepherds living in the fields, keeping watch over their flock by night. [9] Then an angel of the Lord stood before them, and the glory of the Lord shone around them, and they were terrified. [10] But the angel said to them, 'Do not be afraid; for see—I am bringing you good news of great joy for all the people: [11] to you is born this day in the city of David a Saviour, who is the Messiah, the Lord. [12] This will be a sign for you: you will find a child wrapped in bands of cloth and lying in a manger.' [13] And suddenly there was with the angel a multitude of the heavenly host, praising God and saying,

[14]   'Glory to God in the highest heaven,
       and on earth peace among those whom he favours!'

[[15] When the angels had left them and gone into heaven, the shepherds said to one another, 'Let us go now to Bethlehem and see this thing that has taken place, which the Lord has made known to us.' [16] So they went with haste and found Mary and Joseph, and the child lying in the manger. [17] When they saw this, they made known what had been told them about this child; [18] and all who heard it were amazed at what the shepherds told them. [19] But Mary treasured all these words and pondered them in her heart. [20] The shepherds returned, glorifying and praising God for all they had heard and seen, as it had been told them.]

POST COMMUNION

CHRISTMAS NIGHT

God our Father,
in this night you have made known to us again
the coming of our Lord Jesus Christ:
confirm our faith and fix our eyes on him
until the day dawns
and Christ the Morning Star rises in our hearts.
To him be glory both now and for ever.

CHRISTMAS DAY

God our Father,
whose Word has come among us
in the Holy Child of Bethlehem:
may the light of faith illumine our hearts
    and shine in our words and deeds;
through him who is Christ the Lord.

SET II

COLLECT

CHRISTMAS NIGHT

Eternal God,
who made this most holy night
to shine with the brightness of your one true light:
bring us, who have known the revelation
    of that light on earth,
to see the radiance of your heavenly glory;
through Jesus Christ your Son our Lord,
who is alive and reigns with you,
in the unity of the Holy Spirit,
one God, now and for ever.

CHRISTMAS DAY

Almighty God,
you have given us your only-begotten Son
to take our nature upon him
and as at this time to be born of a pure virgin:
grant that we, who have been born again
and made your children by adoption and grace,
may daily be renewed by your Holy Spirit;
through Jesus Christ your Son our Lord,
who is alive and reigns with you,
in the unity of the Holy Spirit,
one God, now and for ever.

READING   Isaiah 62.6–12

⁶ Upon your walls, O Jerusalem,
    I have posted sentinels;
  all day and all night
    they shall never be silent.
  You who remind the LORD,
    take no rest,
⁷ and give him no rest
    until he establishes Jerusalem
    and makes it renowned throughout the earth.

⁸ The Lᴏʀᴅ has sworn by his right hand
    and by his mighty arm:
I will not again give your grain
    to be food for your enemies,
and foreigners shall not drink the wine
    for which you have laboured;
⁹ but those who garner it shall eat it
    and praise the Lᴏʀᴅ,
and those who gather it shall drink it
    in my holy courts.
¹⁰ Go through, go through the gates,
    prepare the way for the people;
build up, build up the highway,
    clear it of stones,
    lift up an ensign over the peoples.
¹¹ The Lᴏʀᴅ has proclaimed
    to the end of the earth:
Say to daughter Zion,
    'See, your salvation comes;
his reward is with him,
    and his recompense before him.'
¹² They shall be called, 'The Holy People,
    The Redeemed of the Lᴏʀᴅ';
and you shall be called, 'Sought Out,
    A City Not Forsaken.'

PSALM   Psalm 97

¹ The Lord is king; let the earth rejoice;
    let the multitude of the isles be glad.
² Clouds and darkness are round about him,
    righteousness and justice are the foundations of his throne.
³ A fire goes before him
    and burns up his enemies on every side.
⁴ His lightnings light up the world;
    the earth sees it and is afraid.
⁵ The mountains melt like wax at the presence of the Lord,
    at the presence of the Lord of the whole earth.
⁶ The heavens declare his righteousness,
    and all the peoples see his glory.
⁷ Confounded be all who worship carved images and delight in false
    gods!
Bow down before him, all you gods.

8 Zion hears and is glad and the cities of Judah rejoice,
    because of your judgements, O Lord.
9 For you are the Lord: most high over all the earth;
    you are exalted far above all gods.
10 The Lord loves those who hate evil;
    he preserves the lives of his saints and delivers them from the
        hand of the wicked.
11 Light has sprung up for the righteous,
    and joyful gladness for those who are true-hearted.
12 Rejoice in the Lord, you righteous,
    and give thanks to his holy name.

READING   Titus 3.4–7

4 But when the goodness and loving-kindness of God our Saviour appeared,
5 he saved us, not because of any works of righteousness that we had done,
but according to his mercy, through the water of rebirth and renewal by
the Holy Spirit. 6 This Spirit he poured out on us richly through Jesus Christ
our Saviour, 7 so that, having been justified by his grace, we might become
heirs according to the hope of eternal life.

GOSPEL   Luke 2.[1–7,] 8–20

[1 In those days a decree went out from Emperor Augustus that all the
world should be registered. 2 This was the first registration and was taken
while Quirinius was governor of Syria. 3 All went to their own towns to be
registered. 4 Joseph also went from the town of Nazareth in Galilee to Judea,
to the city of David called Bethlehem, because he was descended from the
house and family of David. 5 He went to be registered with Mary, to whom
he was engaged and who was expecting a child. 6 While they were there,
the time came for her to deliver her child. 7 And she gave birth to her
firstborn son and wrapped him in bands of cloth, and laid him in a manger,
because there was no place for them in the inn.]

8 In that region there were shepherds living in the fields, keeping watch
over their flock by night. 9 Then an angel of the Lord stood before them,
and the glory of the Lord shone around them, and they were terrified.
10 But the angel said to them, 'Do not be afraid; for see—I am bringing you
good news of great joy for all the people: 11 to you is born this day in the
city of David a Saviour, who is the Messiah, the Lord. 12 This will be a sign
for you: you will find a child wrapped in bands of cloth and lying in a
manger.' 13 And suddenly there was with the angel a multitude of the
heavenly host, praising God and saying,

¹⁴ 'Glory to God in the highest heaven,
and on earth peace among those whom he favours!'

¹⁵ When the angels had left them and gone into heaven, the shepherds said to one another, 'Let us go now to Bethlehem and see this thing that has taken place, which the Lord has made known to us.' ¹⁶ So they went with haste and found Mary and Joseph, and the child lying in the manger. ¹⁷ When they saw this, they made known what had been told them about this child; ¹⁸ and all who heard it were amazed at what the shepherds told them. ¹⁹ But Mary treasured all these words and pondered them in her heart. ²⁰ The shepherds returned, glorifying and praising God for all they had heard and seen, as it had been told them.

POST COMMUNION

CHRISTMAS NIGHT

God our Father,
in this night you have made known to us again
the coming of our Lord Jesus Christ:
confirm our faith and fix our eyes on him
until the day dawns
and Christ the Morning Star rises in our hearts.
To him be glory both now and for ever.

CHRISTMAS DAY

God our Father,
whose Word has come among us
in the Holy Child of Bethlehem:
may the light of faith illumine our hearts
    and shine in our words and deeds;
through him who is Christ the Lord.

SET III

COLLECT

CHRISTMAS NIGHT

Eternal God,
who made this most holy night
to shine with the brightness of your one true light:

bring us, who have known the revelation
    of that light on earth,
to see the radiance of your heavenly glory;
through Jesus Christ your Son our Lord,
who is alive and reigns with you,
in the unity of the Holy Spirit,
one God, now and for ever.

CHRISTMAS DAY

Almighty God,
you have given us your only-begotten Son
to take our nature upon him
and as at this time to be born of a pure virgin:
grant that we, who have been born again
and made your children by adoption and grace,
may daily be renewed by your Holy Spirit;
through Jesus Christ your Son our Lord,
who is alive and reigns with you,
in the unity of the Holy Spirit,
one God, now and for ever.

READING   Isaiah 52.7–10

⁷ How beautiful upon the mountains
        are the feet of the messenger who announces peace,
    who brings good news,
        who announces salvation,
        who says to Zion, 'Your God reigns.'
⁸ Listen! Your sentinels lift up their voices,
        together they sing for joy;
    for in plain sight they see
        the return of the LORD to Zion.
⁹ Break forth together into singing,
        you ruins of Jerusalem;
    for the LORD has comforted his people,
        he has redeemed Jerusalem.
¹⁰ The LORD has bared his holy arm
        before the eyes of all the nations;
    and all the ends of the earth shall see
        the salvation of our God.

PSALM   Psalm 98

1   Sing to the Lord a new song,
    for he has done marvellous things.
2   With his right hand and his holy arm
    has he won for himself the victory.
3   The Lord has made known his victory;
    his righteousness has he openly shown in the sight of the nations.
4   He remembers his mercy and faithfulness to the house of Israel,
    and all the ends of the earth have seen the victory of our God.
5   Shout with joy to the Lord, all you lands;
    lift up your voice, rejoice and sing.
6   Sing to the Lord with the harp,
    with the harp and the voice of song.
7   With trumpets and the sound of the horn
    shout with joy before the King, the Lord.
8   Let the sea make a noise and all that is in it,
    the lands and those who dwell therein.
9   Let the rivers clap their hands,
    and let the hills ring out with joy before the Lord, when he comes
        to judge the earth.
10 In righteousness shall he judge the world,
    and the peoples with equity.

READING   Hebrews 1.1–4, [5–12]

1 Long ago God spoke to our ancestors in many and various ways by the
prophets, 2 but in these last days he has spoken to us by a Son, whom he
appointed heir of all things, through whom he also created the worlds.
3 He is the reflection of God's glory and the exact imprint of God's very
being, and he sustains all things by his powerful word. When he had made
purification for sins, he sat down at the right hand of the Majesty on high,
4 having become as much superior to angels as the name he has inherited
is more excellent than theirs.

[5 For to which of the angels did God ever say,
    'You are my Son;
        today I have begotten you'?
Or again,
    'I will be his Father,
        and he will be my Son'?
6 And again, when he brings the firstborn into the world, he says,
    'Let all God's angels worship him.'

⁷Of the angels he says,

'He makes his angels winds,
and his servants flames of fire.'

⁸But of the Son he says,

'Your throne, O God, is for ever and ever,
and the righteous sceptre is the sceptre of your kingdom.

⁹ You have loved righteousness and hated wickedness;
therefore God, your God, has anointed you
with the oil of gladness beyond your companions.'

¹⁰And,

'In the beginning, Lord, you founded the earth,
and the heavens are the work of your hands;

¹¹ they will perish, but you remain;
they will all wear out like clothing;

¹² like a cloak you will roll them up,
and like clothing they will be changed.

But you are the same,
and your years will never end.']

GOSPEL   John 1.1–14

¹ In the beginning was the Word, and the Word was with God, and the Word was God. ² He was in the beginning with God. ³ All things came into being through him, and without him not one thing came into being. What has come into being ⁴ in him was life, and the life was the light of all people. ⁵ The light shines in the darkness, and the darkness did not overcome it.

⁶ There was a man sent from God, whose name was John. ⁷ He came as a witness to testify to the light, so that all might believe through him. ⁸ He himself was not the light, but he came to testify to the light. ⁹ The true light, which enlightens everyone, was coming into the world.

¹⁰ He was in the world, and the world came into being through him; yet the world did not know him. ¹¹ He came to what was his own, and his own people did not accept him. ¹² But to all who received him, who believed in his name, he gave power to become children of God, ¹³ who were born, not of blood or of the will of the flesh or of the will of man, but of God.

¹⁴ And the Word became flesh and lived among us, and we have seen his glory, the glory as of a father's only son, full of grace and truth.

POST COMMUNION

CHRISTMAS NIGHT

God our Father,
in this night you have made known to us again
the coming of our Lord Jesus Christ:
confirm our faith and fix our eyes on him
until the day dawns
and Christ the Morning Star rises in our hearts.
To him be glory both now and for ever.

CHRISTMAS DAY

God our Father,
whose Word has come among us
in the Holy Child of Bethlehem:
may the light of faith illumine our hearts
    and shine in our words and deeds;
through him who is Christ the Lord.

SECOND SERVICE

Psalm 8
Isaiah 65.17–25
Philippians 2.5–11

or

Luke 2.1–20

*if it has not been used at the Principal Service
of the day*

THIRD SERVICE

Psalm 110
Isaiah 62.1–5
Matthew 1.18–25

THE FIRST SUNDAY OF CHRISTMAS

COLLECT

Almighty God,
who wonderfully created us in your own image
and yet more wonderfully restored us
through your Son Jesus Christ:
grant that, as he came to share in our humanity,
so we may share the life of his divinity;

who is alive and reigns with you,
in the unity of the Holy Spirit,
one God, now and for ever.

READING   Isaiah 61.10–62.3

10 I will greatly rejoice in the LORD,
       my whole being shall exult in my God;
    for he has clothed me with the garments of salvation,
       he has covered me with the robe of righteousness,
    as a bridegroom decks himself with a garland,
       and as a bride adorns herself with her jewels.
11 For as the earth brings forth its shoots,
       and as a garden causes what is sown in it to spring up,
    so the Lord GOD will cause righteousness and praise
       to spring up before all the nations.
1   For Zion's sake I will not keep silent,
       and for Jerusalem's sake I will not rest,
    until her vindication shines out like the dawn,
       and her salvation like a burning torch.
2   The nations shall see your vindication,
       and all the kings your glory;
    and you shall be called by a new name
       that the mouth of the LORD will give.
3   You shall be a crown of beauty in the hand of the LORD,
       and a royal diadem in the hand of your God.

PSALM   Psalm 148.[1–6,] 7–14

[1 Alleluia! Praise the Lord from the heavens;
       praise him in the heights.
2   Praise him, all you angels of his;
       praise him, all his host.
3   Praise him, sun and moon;
       praise him, all you shining stars.
4   Praise him, heaven of heavens,
       and you waters above the heavens.
5   Let them praise the name of the Lord;
       for he commanded and they were created.
6   He made them stand fast for ever and ever;
       he gave them a law which shall not pass away.]
7   Praise the Lord from the earth,
       you sea-monsters and all deeps;

8 Fire and hail, snow and fog,
   tempestuous wind, doing his will;
9 Mountains and all hills,
   fruit trees and all cedars;
10 Wild beasts and all cattle,
   creeping things and winged birds;
11 Kings of the earth and all peoples,
   princes and all rulers of the world;
12 Young men and maidens,
   old and young together.
13 Let them praise the name of the Lord,
   for his name only is exalted, his splendour is over earth and heaven.
14 He has raised up strength for his people and praise for all his loyal
      servants,
   the children of Israel, a people who are near him. Alleluia!

READING   Galatians 4.4–7

4 But when the fullness of time had come, God sent his Son, born of a
woman, born under the law, 5 in order to redeem those who were under
the law, so that we might receive adoption as children. 6 And because you
are children, God has sent the Spirit of his Son into our hearts, crying,
'Abba! Father!' 7 So you are no longer a slave but a child, and if a child then
also an heir, through God.

GOSPEL   Luke 2.15–21

15 When the angels had left them and gone into heaven, the shepherds
said to one another, 'Let us go now to Bethlehem and see this thing that
has taken place, which the Lord has made known to us.' 16 So they went
with haste and found Mary and Joseph, and the child lying in the manger.
17 When they saw this, they made known what had been told them about
this child; 18 and all who heard it were amazed at what the shepherds told
them. 19 But Mary treasured all these words and pondered them in her
heart. 20 The shepherds returned, glorifying and praising God for all they
had heard and seen, as it had been told them.

21 After eight days had passed, it was time to circumcise the child; and he
was called Jesus, the name given by the angel before he was conceived in
the womb.

POST COMMUNION

Heavenly Father,
whose blessed Son shared at Nazareth
   the life of an earthly home:
help your Church to live as one family,
united in love and obedience,
and bring us all at last to our home in heaven;
through Jesus Christ our Lord.

SECOND SERVICE

Psalm 132
Isaiah 35.1–10
Colossians 1.9–20

or

Luke 2.41–52

THIRD SERVICE

Psalm 105.1–9
Isaiah 63.7–9
Ephesians 3.5–12

THE SECOND SUNDAY OF CHRISTMAS

COLLECT

Almighty God,
in the birth of your Son
you have poured on us the new light of your incarnate Word,
and shown us the fullness of your love:
help us to walk in his light and dwell in his love
that we may know the fullness of his joy;
who is alive and reigns with you,
in the unity of the Holy Spirit,
one God, now and for ever.

EITHER

READING   Jeremiah 31.7–14

7 For thus says the Lord:
Sing aloud with gladness for Jacob,
   and raise shouts for the chief of the nations;
proclaim, give praise, and say,
   'Save, O Lord, your people,
   the remnant of Israel.'
8 See, I am going to bring them from the land of the north,
   and gather them from the farthest parts of the earth,
among them the blind and the lame,
   those with child and those in labour, together;
   a great company, they shall return here.
9 With weeping they shall come,
   and with consolations I will lead them back,
I will let them walk by brooks of water,
   in a straight path in which they shall not stumble;
for I have become a father to Israel,
   and Ephraim is my firstborn.
10 Hear the word of the Lord, O nations,
   and declare it in the coastlands far away;
say, 'He who scattered Israel will gather him,
   and will keep him as a shepherd a flock.'
11 For the Lord has ransomed Jacob,
   and has redeemed him from hands too strong for him.
12 They shall come and sing aloud on the height of Zion,
   and they shall be radiant over the goodness of the Lord,
over the grain, the wine, and the oil,
   and over the young of the flock and the herd;
their life shall become like a watered garden,
   and they shall never languish again.
13 Then shall the young women rejoice in the dance,
   and the young men and the old shall be merry.
I will turn their mourning into joy,
   I will comfort them, and give them gladness for sorrow.
14 I will give the priests their fill of fatness,
   and my people shall be satisfied with my bounty,

                                        says the Lord.

PSALM

Psalm 147.13–21

13 Worship the Lord, O Jerusalem;
   praise your God, O Zion;
14 For he has strengthened the bars of your gates;
   he has blessed your children within you.
15 He has established peace on your borders;
   he satisfies you with the finest wheat.
16 He sends out his command to the earth,
   and his word runs very swiftly.
17 He gives snow like wool;
   he scatters hoarfrost like ashes.
18 He scatters his hail like bread crumbs;
   who can stand against his cold?
19 He sends forth his word and melts them;
   he blows with his wind and the waters flow.
20 He declares his word to Jacob,
   his statutes and his judgements to Israel.
21 He has not done so to any other nation;
   to them he has not revealed his judgements. Alleluia!

READING

Ephesians 1.3–14

3 Blessed be the God and Father of our Lord Jesus Christ, who has blessed us in Christ with every spiritual blessing in the heavenly places, 4 just as he chose us in Christ before the foundation of the world to be holy and blameless before him in love. 5 He destined us for adoption as his children through Jesus Christ, according to the good pleasure of his will, 6 to the praise of his glorious grace that he freely bestowed on us in the Beloved. 7 In him we have redemption through his blood, the forgiveness of our trespasses, according to the riches of his grace 8 that he lavished on us. With all wisdom and insight 9 he has made known to us the mystery of his will, according to his good pleasure that he set forth in Christ, 10 as a plan for the fullness of time, to gather up all things in him, things in heaven and things on earth. 11 In Christ we have also obtained an inheritance, having been destined according to the purpose of him who accomplishes all things according to his counsel and will, 12 so that we, who were the first to set our hope on Christ, might live for the praise of his glory. 13 In him you also, when you had heard the word of truth, the gospel of your salvation, and had believed in him, were marked with the seal of the promised Holy Spirit; 14 this is the pledge of our inheritance towards redemption as God's own people, to the praise of his glory.

GOSPEL   John 1.[1–9,] 10–18

[[1] In the beginning was the Word, and the Word was with God, and the Word was God. [2] He was in the beginning with God. [3] All things came into being through him, and without him not one thing came into being. What has come into being [4] in him was life, and the life was the light of all people. [5] The light shines in the darkness, and the darkness did not overcome it.

[6] There was a man sent from God, whose name was John. [7] He came as a witness to testify to the light, so that all might believe through him. [8] He himself was not the light, but he came to testify to the light. [9] The true light, which enlightens everyone, was coming into the world.]

[10] He was in the world, and the world came into being through him; yet the world did not know him. [11] He came to what was his own, and his own people did not accept him. [12] But to all who received him, who believed in his name, he gave power to become children of God, [13] who were born, not of blood or of the will of the flesh or of the will of man, but of God.

[14] And the Word became flesh and lived among us, and we have seen his glory, the glory as of a father's only son, full of grace and truth. [15] (John testified to him and cried out, 'This was he of whom I said, "He who comes after me ranks ahead of me because he was before me." ') [16] From his fullness we have all received, grace upon grace. [17] The law indeed was given through Moses; grace and truth came through Jesus Christ. [18] No one has ever seen God. It is God the only Son, who is close to the Father's heart, who has made him known.

OR

READING   Ecclesiasticus 24.1–12

[1] Wisdom praises herself,
        and tells of her glory in the midst of her people.
[2] In the assembly of the Most High she opens her mouth,
        and in the presence of his hosts she tells of her glory:
[3] 'I came forth from the mouth of the Most High,
        and covered the earth like a mist.
[4] I dwelt in the highest heavens,
        and my throne was in a pillar of cloud.
[5] Alone I compassed the vault of heaven
        and traversed the depths of the abyss.
[6] Over waves of the sea, over all the earth,
        and over every people and nation I have held sway.

7 Among all these I sought a resting-place;
   in whose territory should I abide?
8 Then the Creator of all things gave me a command,
   and my Creator chose the place for my tent.
   He said, "Make your dwelling in Jacob,
   and in Israel receive your inheritance."
9 Before the ages, in the beginning, he created me,
   and for all the ages I shall not cease to be.
10 In the holy tent I ministered before him,
   and so I was established in Zion.
11 Thus in the beloved city he gave me a resting-place,
   and in Jerusalem was my domain.
12 I took root in an honoured people,
   in the portion of the Lord, his heritage.'

CANTICLE   Wisdom 10.15–21

15 A holy people and blameless race
   wisdom delivered from a nation of oppressors.
16 She entered the soul of a servant of the Lord,
   and withstood dread kings with wonders and signs.
17 She gave to holy people the reward of their labours;
   she guided them along a marvellous way,
   and became a shelter to them by day,
   and a starry flame through the night.
18 She brought them over the Red Sea,
   and led them through deep waters;
19 but she drowned their enemies,
   and cast them up from the depths of the sea.
20 Therefore the righteous plundered the ungodly;
   they sang hymns, O Lord, to your holy name,
   and praised with one accord your defending hand;
21 for wisdom opened the mouths of those who were mute,
   and made the tongues of infants speak clearly.

READING   Ephesians 1.3–14

3 Blessed be the God and Father of our Lord Jesus Christ, who has blessed us in Christ with every spiritual blessing in the heavenly places, 4 just as he chose us in Christ before the foundation of the world to be holy and blameless before him in love. 5 He destined us for adoption as his children through Jesus Christ, according to the good pleasure of his will, 6 to the praise of his glorious grace that he freely bestowed on us in the Beloved.

⁷ In him we have redemption through his blood, the forgiveness of our trespasses, according to the riches of his grace ⁸ that he lavished on us. With all wisdom and insight ⁹ he has made known to us the mystery of his will, according to his good pleasure that he set forth in Christ, ¹⁰ as a plan for the fullness of time, to gather up all things in him, things in heaven and things on earth. ¹¹ In Christ we have also obtained an inheritance, having been destined according to the purpose of him who accomplishes all things according to his counsel and will, ¹² so that we, who were the first to set our hope on Christ, might live for the praise of his glory. ¹³ In him you also, when you had heard the word of truth, the gospel of your salvation, and had believed in him, were marked with the seal of the promised Holy Spirit; ¹⁴ this is the pledge of our inheritance towards redemption as God's own people, to the praise of his glory.

GOSPEL   John 1.[1–9,] 10–18

[¹ In the beginning was the Word, and the Word was with God, and the Word was God. ² He was in the beginning with God. ³ All things came into being through him, and without him not one thing came into being. What has come into being ⁴ in him was life, and the life was the light of all people. ⁵ The light shines in the darkness, and the darkness did not overcome it.

⁶ There was a man sent from God, whose name was John. ⁷ He came as a witness to testify to the light, so that all might believe through him. ⁸ He himself was not the light, but he came to testify to the light. ⁹ The true light, which enlightens everyone, was coming into the world.]

¹⁰ He was in the world, and the world came into being through him; yet the world did not know him. ¹¹ He came to what was his own, and his own people did not accept him. ¹² But to all who received him, who believed in his name, he gave power to become children of God, ¹³ who were born, not of blood or of the will of the flesh or of the will of man, but of God.

¹⁴ And the Word became flesh and lived among us, and we have seen his glory, the glory as of a father's only son, full of grace and truth. ¹⁵ (John testified to him and cried out, 'This was he of whom I said, "He who comes after me ranks ahead of me because he was before me." ') ¹⁶ From his fullness we have all received, grace upon grace. ¹⁷ The law indeed was given through Moses; grace and truth came through Jesus Christ. ¹⁸ No one has ever seen God. It is God the only Son, who is close to the Father's heart, who has made him known.

POST COMMUNION

All praise to you,
almighty God and heavenly King,
who sent your Son into the world
to take our nature upon him
and to be born of a pure virgin:
grant that, as we are born again in him,
so he may continually dwell in us
and reign on earth as he reigns in heaven,
now and for ever.

SECOND SERVICE	THIRD SERVICE
Psalm 135.1–14, [15–21]	**Psalm 87**
Isaiah 46.3–13	**Zechariah 8.1–8**
Romans 12.1–8	**Luke 2.41–52**

If the Second Service is a Eucharist, the following is read as a Gospel:

Matthew 2.13–23

THE EPIPHANY   6 JANUARY

COLLECT

O God,
who by the leading of a star
manifested your only Son to the peoples of the earth:
mercifully grant that we,
who know you now by faith,
may at last behold your glory face to face;
through Jesus Christ your Son our Lord,
who is alive and reigns with you,
in the unity of the Holy Spirit,
one God, now and for ever.

READING   Isaiah 60.1–6

¹ Arise, shine; for your light has come,
    and the glory of the LORD has risen upon you.
² For darkness shall cover the earth,
    and thick darkness the peoples;
  but the LORD will arise upon you,
    and his glory will appear over you.
³ Nations shall come to your light,
    and kings to the brightness of your dawn.
⁴ Lift up your eyes and look around;
    they all gather together, they come to you;
  your sons shall come from far away,
    and your daughters shall be carried on their nurses' arms.
⁵ Then you shall see and be radiant;
    your heart shall thrill and rejoice,
  because the abundance of the sea shall be brought to you,
    the wealth of the nations shall come to you.
⁶ A multitude of camels shall cover you,
    the young camels of Midian and Ephah;
    all those from Sheba shall come.
  They shall bring gold and frankincense,
    and shall proclaim the praise of the LORD.

PSALM   Psalm 72.[1–9,] 10–15

[¹ Give the king your justice, O God,
    and your righteousness to the king's son;
² That he may rule your people righteously
    and the poor with justice;
³ That the mountains may bring prosperity to the people,
    and the little hills bring righteousness.
⁴ He shall defend the needy among the people;
  he shall rescue the poor and crush the oppressor.
⁵ He shall live as long as the sun and moon endure,
    from one generation to another.
⁶ He shall come down like rain upon the mown field,
    like showers that water the earth.
⁷ In his time shall the righteous flourish;
    there shall be abundance of peace till the moon shall be no more.
⁸ He shall rule from sea to sea,
    and from the River to the ends of the earth.

9   His foes shall bow down before him,
      and his enemies lick the dust.]
10 The kings of Tarshish and of the isles shall pay tribute,
      and the kings of Arabia and Saba offer gifts.
11 All kings shall bow down before him,
      and all the nations do him service.
12 For he shall deliver the poor who cries out in distress,
      and the oppressed who has no helper.
13 He shall have pity on the lowly and poor;
      he shall preserve the lives of the needy.
14 He shall redeem their lives from oppression and violence,
      and dear shall their blood be in his sight.
15 Long may he live, and may there be given to him gold from Arabia;
      may prayer be made for him always, and may they bless him all
          the day long.

READING   Ephesians 3.1–12

1 This is the reason that I Paul am a prisoner for Christ Jesus for the sake of you Gentiles— 2 for surely you have already heard of the commission of God's grace that was given to me for you, 3 and how the mystery was made known to me by revelation, as I wrote above in a few words, 4 a reading of which will enable you to perceive my understanding of the mystery of Christ. 5 In former generations this mystery was not made known to human-kind, as it has now been revealed to his holy apostles and prophets by the Spirit: 6 that is, the Gentiles have become fellow-heirs, members of the same body, and sharers in the promise in Christ Jesus through the gospel.

7 Of this gospel I have become a servant according to the gift of God's grace that was given to me by the working of his power. 8 Although I am the very least of all the saints, this grace was given to me to bring to the Gentiles the news of the boundless riches of Christ, 9 and to make everyone see what is the plan of the mystery hidden for ages in God who created all things; 10 so that through the church the wisdom of God in its rich variety might now be made known to the rulers and authorities in the heavenly places. 11 This was in accordance with the eternal purpose that he has carried out in Christ Jesus our Lord, 12 in whom we have access to God in boldness and confidence through faith in him.

GOSPEL   Matthew 2.1–12

¹ In the time of King Herod, after Jesus was born in Bethlehem of Judea, wise men from the East came to Jerusalem, ² asking, 'Where is the child who has been born king of the Jews? For we observed his star at its rising, and have come to pay him homage.' ³ When King Herod heard this, he was frightened, and all Jerusalem with him; ⁴ and calling together all the chief priests and scribes of the people, he inquired of them where the Messiah was to be born. ⁵ They told him, 'In Bethlehem of Judea; for so it has been written by the prophet:

⁶ "And you, Bethlehem, in the land of Judah,
     are by no means least among the rulers of Judah;
   for from you shall come a ruler
     who is to shepherd my people Israel." '

⁷ Then Herod secretly called for the wise men and learned from them the exact time when the star had appeared. ⁸ Then he sent them to Bethlehem, saying, 'Go and search diligently for the child; and when you have found him, bring me word so that I may also go and pay him homage.' ⁹ When they had heard the king, they set out; and there, ahead of them, went the star that they had seen at its rising, until it stopped over the place where the child was. ¹⁰ When they saw that the star had stopped, they were overwhelmed with joy. ¹¹ On entering the house, they saw the child with Mary his mother; and they knelt down and paid him homage. Then, opening their treasure-chests, they offered him gifts of gold, frankincense, and myrrh. ¹² And having been warned in a dream not to return to Herod, they left for their own country by another road.

POST COMMUNION

Lord God,
the bright splendour whom the nations seek:
may we who with the wise men
   have been drawn by your light
discern the glory of your presence in your Son,
the Word made flesh, Jesus Christ our Lord.

SECOND SERVICE	THIRD SERVICE
Psalms 98; 100	**Psalms 113; 132**
Baruch 4.36–5.9	**Jeremiah 31.7–14**
or	**John 1.29–34**
Isaiah 60.1–9	
John 2.1–11	

THE BAPTISM OF CHRIST
THE FIRST SUNDAY OF EPIPHANY

COLLECT

Eternal Father,
who at the baptism of Jesus
revealed him to be your Son,
anointing him with the Holy Spirit:
grant to us, who are born again by water and the Spirit,
that we may be faithful to our calling
   as your adopted children;
through Jesus Christ your Son our Lord,
who is alive and reigns with you,
in the unity of the Holy Spirit,
one God, now and for ever.

READING   Genesis 1.1–5

[1] In the beginning when God created the heavens and the earth, [2] the earth was a formless void and darkness covered the face of the deep, while a wind from God swept over the face of the waters. [3] Then God said, 'Let there be light'; and there was light. [4] And God saw that the light was good; and God separated the light from the darkness. [5] God called the light Day, and the darkness he called Night. And there was evening and there was morning, the first day.

PSALM   Psalm 29

1   Ascribe to the Lord, you gods,
    ascribe to the Lord glory and strength.
2   Ascribe to the Lord the glory due to his name;
    worship the Lord in the beauty of holiness.
3   The voice of the Lord is upon the waters; the God of glory thunders;
    the Lord is upon the mighty waters.
4   The voice of the Lord is a powerful voice;
    the voice of the Lord is a voice of splendour.
5   The voice of the Lord breaks the cedar trees;
    the Lord breaks the cedars of Lebanon;
6   He makes Lebanon skip like a calf,
    and Mount Hermon like a young wild ox.
7   The voice of the Lord splits the flames of fire; the voice of the Lord
        shakes the wilderness;
    the Lord shakes the wilderness of Kadesh.
8   The voice of the Lord makes the oak trees writhe
    and strips the forests bare.
9   And in the temple of the Lord
    all are crying, 'Glory!'
10 The Lord sits enthroned above the flood;
    the Lord sits enthroned as king for evermore.
11 The Lord shall give strength to his people;
    the Lord shall give his people the blessing of peace.

READING   Acts 19.1–7

1 While Apollos was in Corinth, Paul passed through the inland regions and came to Ephesus, where he found some disciples. 2 He said to them, 'Did you receive the Holy Spirit when you became believers?' They replied, 'No, we have not even heard that there is a Holy Spirit.' 3 Then he said, 'Into what then were you baptized?' They answered, 'Into John's baptism.' 4 Paul said, 'John baptized with the baptism of repentance, telling the people to believe in the one who was to come after him, that is, in Jesus.' 5 On hearing this, they were baptized in the name of the Lord Jesus. 6 When Paul had laid his hands on them, the Holy Spirit came upon them, and they spoke in tongues and prophesied— 7 altogether there were about twelve of them.

GOSPEL   Mark 1.4–11

⁴ John the baptizer appeared in the wilderness, proclaiming a baptism of repentance for the forgiveness of sins. ⁵ And people from the whole Judean countryside and all the people of Jerusalem were going out to him, and were baptized by him in the river Jordan, confessing their sins. ⁶ Now John was clothed with camel's hair, with a leather belt around his waist, and he ate locusts and wild honey. ⁷ He proclaimed, 'The one who is more powerful than I is coming after me; I am not worthy to stoop down and untie the thong of his sandals. ⁸ I have baptized you with water; but he will baptize you with the Holy Spirit.'

⁹ In those days Jesus came from Nazareth of Galilee and was baptized by John in the Jordan. ¹⁰ And just as he was coming up out of the water, he saw the heavens torn apart and the Spirit descending like a dove on him. ¹¹ And a voice came from heaven, 'You are my Son, the Beloved; with you I am well pleased.'

POST COMMUNION

Lord of all time and eternity,
you opened the heavens
     and revealed yourself as Father
in the baptism of Jesus your beloved Son:
by the power of your Spirit
complete the heavenly work of our rebirth
through the waters of the new creation;
through Jesus Christ our Lord.

SECOND SERVICE   THIRD SERVICE

Psalms 46; [47]   **Psalm 89.20–29**
Isaiah 42.1–9   **1 Samuel 16.1–3, 13**
Ephesians 2.1–10   **John 1.29–34**

If the Second Service is a Eucharist, the
following is read as a Gospel:

Matthew 3.13–17

THE SECOND SUNDAY OF EPIPHANY

COLLECT

Almighty God,
in Christ you make all things new:
transform the poverty of our nature
    by the riches of your grace,
and in the renewal of our lives
make known your heavenly glory;
through Jesus Christ your Son our Lord,
who is alive and reigns with you,
in the unity of the Holy Spirit,
one God, now and for ever.

READING   1 Samuel 3.1–10, [11–20]

[1] Now the boy Samuel was ministering to the LORD under Eli. The word of the LORD was rare in those days; visions were not widespread.

[2] At that time Eli, whose eyesight had begun to grow dim so that he could not see, was lying down in his room; [3] the lamp of God had not yet gone out, and Samuel was lying down in the temple of the LORD, where the ark of God was. [4] Then the LORD called, 'Samuel! Samuel!' and he said, 'Here I am!' [5] and ran to Eli, and said, 'Here I am, for you called me.' But he said, 'I did not call; lie down again.' So he went and lay down. [6] The LORD called again, 'Samuel!' Samuel got up and went to Eli, and said, 'Here I am, for you called me.' But he said, 'I did not call, my son; lie down again.' [7] Now Samuel did not yet know the LORD, and the word of the LORD had not yet been revealed to him. [8] The LORD called Samuel again, a third time. And he got up and went to Eli, and said, 'Here I am, for you called me.' Then Eli perceived that the LORD was calling the boy. [9] Therefore Eli said to Samuel, 'Go, lie down; and if he calls you, you shall say, "Speak, LORD, for your servant is listening." ' So Samuel went and lay down in his place.

[10] Now the LORD came and stood there, calling as before, 'Samuel! Samuel!' And Samuel said, 'Speak, for your servant is listening.'
[[11] Then the LORD said to Samuel, 'See, I am about to do something in Israel that will make both ears of anyone who hears of it tingle. [12] On that day I will fulfil against Eli all that I have spoken concerning his house, from beginning to end. [13] For I have told him that I am about to punish his house for ever, for the iniquity that he knew, because his sons were blaspheming God, and he did not restrain them. [14] Therefore I swear to the house of Eli

that the iniquity of Eli's house shall not be expiated by sacrifice or offering for ever.'

¹⁵ Samuel lay there until morning; then he opened the doors of the house of the LORD. Samuel was afraid to tell the vision to Eli. ¹⁶ But Eli called Samuel and said, 'Samuel, my son.' He said, 'Here I am.' ¹⁷ Eli said, 'What was it that he told you? Do not hide it from me. May God do so to you and more also, if you hide anything from me of all that he told you.' ¹⁸ So Samuel told him everything and hid nothing from him. Then he said, 'It is the LORD; let him do what seems good to him.'

¹⁹ As Samuel grew up, the LORD was with him and let none of his words fall to the ground. ²⁰ And all Israel from Dan to Beer-sheba knew that Samuel was a trustworthy prophet of the LORD.]

PSALM   Psalm 139.1–5, 12–17

¹ Lord, you have searched me out and known me;
   you know my sitting down and my rising up; you discern my
      thoughts from afar.
² You trace my journeys and my resting-places
   and are acquainted with all my ways.
³ Indeed, there is not a word on my lips,
   but you, O Lord, know it altogether.
⁴ You press upon me behind and before
   and lay your hand upon me.
⁵ Such knowledge is too wonderful for me;
   it is so high that I cannot attain to it.

¹² For you yourself created my inmost parts;
   you knit me together in my mother's womb.
¹³ I will thank you because I am marvellously made;
   your works are wonderful and I know it well.
¹⁴ My body was not hidden from you,
   while I was being made in secret and woven in the depths of the
      earth.
¹⁵ Your eyes beheld my limbs, yet unfinished in the womb; all of
      them were written in your book;
   they were fashioned day by day, when as yet there was none of
      them.
¹⁶ How deep I find your thoughts, O God!
   how great is the sum of them!
¹⁷ If I were to count them, they would be more in number than the
      sand;
   to count them all, my life span would need to be like yours.

OR, IF AN ALTERNATIVE READING IS PREFERRED **Psalm 139.1–9**

1 Lord, you have searched me out and known me;
    you know my sitting down and my rising up; you discern my
        thoughts from afar.
2 You trace my journeys and my resting-places
    and are acquainted with all my ways.
3 Indeed, there is not a word on my lips,
    but you, O Lord, know it altogether.
4 You press upon me behind and before
    and lay your hand upon me.
5 Such knowledge is too wonderful for me;
    it is so high that I cannot attain to it.
6 Where can I go then from your Spirit?
    where can I flee from your presence?
7 If I climb up to heaven, you are there;
    if I make the grave my bed, you are there also.
8 If I take the wings of the morning
    and dwell in the uttermost parts of the sea,
9 Even there your hand will lead me
    and your right hand hold me fast.

READING   Revelation 5.1–10

1 Then I saw in the right hand of the one seated on the throne a scroll written on the inside and on the back, sealed with seven seals; 2 and I saw a mighty angel proclaiming with a loud voice, 'Who is worthy to open the scroll and break its seals?' 3 And no one in heaven or on earth or under the earth was able to open the scroll or to look into it. 4 And I began to weep bitterly because no one was found worthy to open the scroll or to look into it. 5 Then one of the elders said to me, 'Do not weep. See, the Lion of the tribe of Judah, the Root of David, has conquered, so that he can open the scroll and its seven seals.'

6 Then I saw between the throne and the four living creatures and among the elders a Lamb standing as if it had been slaughtered, having seven horns and seven eyes, which are the seven spirits of God sent out into all the earth. 7 He went and took the scroll from the right hand of the one who was seated on the throne. 8 When he had taken the scroll, the four living creatures and the twenty-four elders fell before the Lamb, each

holding a harp and golden bowls full of incense, which are the prayers of the saints. [9] They sing a new song:

'You are worthy to take the scroll
and to open its seals,
for you were slaughtered and by your blood you ransomed for God
saints from every tribe and language and people and nation;
[10] you have made them to be a kingdom and priests serving our God,
and they will reign on earth.'

GOSPEL   John 1.43–51

[43] The next day Jesus decided to go to Galilee. He found Philip and said to him, 'Follow me.' [44] Now Philip was from Bethsaida, the city of Andrew and Peter. [45] Philip found Nathanael and said to him, 'We have found him about whom Moses in the law and also the prophets wrote, Jesus son of Joseph from Nazareth.' [46] Nathanael said to him, 'Can anything good come out of Nazareth?' Philip said to him, 'Come and see.' [47] When Jesus saw Nathanael coming towards him, he said of him, 'Here is truly an Israelite in whom there is no deceit!' [48] Nathanael asked him, 'Where did you come to know me?' Jesus answered, 'I saw you under the fig tree before Philip called you.' [49] Nathanael replied, 'Rabbi, you are the Son of God! You are the King of Israel!' [50] Jesus answered, 'Do you believe because I told you that I saw you under the fig tree? You will see greater things than these.' [51] And he said to him, 'Very truly, I tell you, you will see heaven opened and the angels of God ascending and descending upon the Son of Man.'

POST COMMUNION

God of glory,
you nourish us with your Word
who is the bread of life:
fill us with your Holy Spirit
that through us the light of your glory
may shine in all the world.
We ask this in the name of Jesus Christ our Lord.

SECOND SERVICE

Psalm 96
Isaiah 60.9–22
Hebrews 6.17–7.10

*If the Second Service is a Eucharist, the
following is read as a Gospel:*

Matthew 8.5–13

THIRD SERVICE

Psalm 145.1–12
Isaiah 62.1–5
1 Corinthians 6.11–20

THE THIRD SUNDAY OF EPIPHANY

COLLECT

Almighty God,
whose Son revealed in signs and miracles
the wonder of your saving presence:
renew your people with your heavenly grace,
and in all our weakness
sustain us by your mighty power;
through Jesus Christ your Son our Lord,
who is alive and reigns with you,
in the unity of the Holy Spirit,
one God, now and for ever.

READING   Genesis 14.17–20

[17] After his return from the defeat of Chedorlaomer and the kings who were with him, the king of Sodom went out to meet him at the Valley of Shaveh (that is, the King's Valley). [18] And King Melchizedek of Salem brought out bread and wine; he was priest of God Most High. [19] He blessed him and said,

'Blessed be Abram by God Most High,
　　maker of heaven and earth;
[20] and blessed be God Most High,
　　who has delivered your enemies into your hand!'
And Abram gave him one-tenth of everything.

PSALM   Psalm 128

1 Happy are they all who fear the Lord,
   and who follow in his ways!
2 You shall eat the fruit of your labour;
   happiness and prosperity shall be yours.
3 Your wife shall be like a fruitful vine within your house,
   your children like olive shoots round about your table.
4 Whoever fears the Lord
   shall thus indeed be blessed.
5 The Lord bless you from Zion,
   and may you see the prosperity of Jerusalem all the days of your
      life.
6 May you live to see your children's children;
   may peace be upon Israel.

READING   Revelation 19.6–10

6 Then I heard what seemed to be the voice of a great multitude, like the
sound of many waters and like the sound of mighty thunder-peals, crying
out,
   'Hallelujah!
   For the Lord our God
      the Almighty reigns.
7 Let us rejoice and exult
      and give him the glory,
   for the marriage of the Lamb has come,
      and his bride has made herself ready;
8 to her it has been granted to be clothed
      with fine linen, bright and pure'—
for the fine linen is the righteous deeds of the saints.

   9 And the angel said to me, 'Write this: Blessed are those who are invited
to the marriage supper of the Lamb.' And he said to me, 'These are true
words of God.' 10 Then I fell down at his feet to worship him, but he said to
me, 'You must not do that! I am a fellow-servant with you and your comrades
who hold the testimony of Jesus. Worship God! For the testimony of Jesus
is the spirit of prophecy.'

GOSPEL   John 2.1–11

   1 On the third day there was a wedding in Cana of Galilee, and the mother
of Jesus was there. 2 Jesus and his disciples had also been invited to the
wedding. 3 When the wine gave out, the mother of Jesus said to him, 'They

have no wine.' ⁴ And Jesus said to her, 'Woman, what concern is that to you and to me? My hour has not yet come.' ⁵ His mother said to the servants, 'Do whatever he tells you.' ⁶ Now standing there were six stone water-jars for the Jewish rites of purification, each holding twenty or thirty gallons. ⁷ Jesus said to them, 'Fill the jars with water.' And they filled them up to the brim. ⁸ He said to them, 'Now draw some out, and take it to the chief steward.' So they took it. ⁹ When the steward tasted the water that had become wine, and did not know where it came from (though the servants who had drawn the water knew), the steward called the bridegroom ¹⁰ and said to him, 'Everyone serves the good wine first, and then the inferior wine after the guests have become drunk. But you have kept the good wine until now.' ¹¹ Jesus did this, the first of his signs, in Cana of Galilee, and revealed his glory; and his disciples believed in him.

POST COMMUNION

Almighty Father,
whose Son our Saviour Jesus Christ
    is the light of the world:
may your people,
illumined by your word and sacraments,
shine with the radiance of his glory,
that he may be known, worshipped, and obeyed
    to the ends of the earth;
for he is alive and reigns, now and for ever.

SECOND SERVICE

Psalm 33.1–12, [13–22]
Jeremiah 3.21–4.2
Titus 2.1–8, 11–14

If the Second Service is a Eucharist, the following is read as a Gospel:

Matthew 4.12–23

THIRD SERVICE

Psalm 113
Jonah 3.1–5, 10
John 3.16–21

THE FOURTH SUNDAY OF EPIPHANY

COLLECT

God our creator,
who in the beginning
commanded the light to shine out of darkness:
we pray that the light of the glorious gospel of Christ
may dispel the darkness of ignorance and unbelief,
shine into the hearts of all your people,
and reveal the knowledge of your glory
    in the face of Jesus Christ your Son our Lord,
who is alive and reigns with you,
in the unity of the Holy Spirit,
one God, now and for ever.

READING   Deuteronomy 18.15–20

[15] The Lord your God will raise up for you a prophet like me from among
your own people; you shall heed such a prophet. [16] This is what you
requested of the Lord your God at Horeb on the day of the assembly when
you said: 'If I hear the voice of the Lord my God any more, or ever again
see this great fire, I will die.' [17] Then the Lord replied to me: 'They are right
in what they have said. [18] I will raise up for them a prophet like you from
among their own people; I will put my words in the mouth of the prophet,
who shall speak to them everything that I command. [19] Anyone who does
not heed the words that the prophet shall speak in my name, I myself will
hold accountable. [20] But any prophet who speaks in the name of other gods,
or who presumes to speak in my name a word that I have not commanded
the prophet to speak—that prophet shall die.'

PSALM   Psalm 111

[1]   Alleluia! I will give thanks to the Lord with my whole heart,
      in the assembly of the upright, in the congregation.
[2]   Great are the deeds of the Lord!
      they are studied by all who delight in them.
[3]   His work is full of majesty and splendour,
      and his righteousness endures for ever.
[4]   He makes his marvellous works to be remembered;
      the Lord is gracious and full of compassion.

5 He gives food to those who fear him;
 he is ever mindful of his covenant.
6 He has shown his people the power of his works
 in giving them the lands of the nations.
7 The works of his hands are faithfulness and justice;
 all his commandments are sure.
8 They stand fast for ever and ever,
 because they are done in truth and equity.
9 He sent redemption to his people; he commanded his covenant
  for ever;
 holy and awesome is his name.
10 The fear of the Lord is the beginning of wisdom;
 those who act accordingly have a good understanding; his praise
  endures for ever.

READING   Revelation 12.1–5a

1 A great portent appeared in heaven: a woman clothed with the sun,
with the moon under her feet, and on her head a crown of twelve stars.
2 She was pregnant and was crying out in birth pangs, in the agony of
giving birth. 3 Then another portent appeared in heaven: a great red dragon,
with seven heads and ten horns, and seven diadems on his heads. 4 His tail
swept down a third of the stars of heaven and threw them to the earth.
Then the dragon stood before the woman who was about to bear a child,
so that he might devour her child as soon as it was born. 5 And she gave
birth to a son, a male child, who is to rule all the nations with a rod of
iron.

GOSPEL   Mark 1.21–28

21 They went to Capernaum; and when the sabbath came, he entered the
synagogue and taught. 22 They were astounded at his teaching, for he taught
them as one having authority, and not as the scribes. 23 Just then there was
in their synagogue a man with an unclean spirit, 24 and he cried out, 'What
have you to do with us, Jesus of Nazareth? Have you come to destroy us? I
know who you are, the Holy One of God.' 25 But Jesus rebuked him, saying,
'Be silent, and come out of him!' 26 And the unclean spirit, throwing him
into convulsions and crying with a loud voice, came out of him. 27 They
were all amazed, and they kept on asking one another, 'What is this? A
new teaching—with authority! He commands even the unclean spirits,
and they obey him.' 28 At once his fame began to spread throughout the
surrounding region of Galilee.

POST COMMUNION

Generous Lord,
in word and eucharist we have proclaimed
    the mystery of your love:
help us so to live out our days
that we may be signs of your wonders in the world;
through Jesus Christ our Saviour.

SECOND SERVICE	THIRD SERVICE
Psalm 34.1–10, [11–22]	Psalm 71.1–6, 15–17
1 Samuel 3.1–20	Jeremiah 1.4–10
1 Corinthians 14.12–20	Mark 1.40–45

*If the Second Service is a Eucharist, the
following is read as a Gospel:*

Matthew 13.10–17

THE PRESENTATION OF CHRIST IN THE TEMPLE
CANDLEMAS   2 FEBRUARY

COLLECT

Almighty and ever-living God,
clothed in majesty,
whose beloved Son
    was this day presented in the Temple,
in substance of our flesh:
grant that we may be presented to you
with pure and clean hearts,
by your Son Jesus Christ our Lord,
who is alive and reigns with you,
in the unity of the Holy Spirit,
one God, now and for ever.

READING   Malachi 3.1–5

¹ See, I am sending my messenger to prepare the way before me, and the
Lord whom you seek will suddenly come to his temple. The messenger of
the covenant in whom you delight—indeed, he is coming, says the LORD of

hosts. [2] But who can endure the day of his coming, and who can stand when he appears?

For he is like a refiner's fire and like fullers' soap; [3] he will sit as a refiner and purifier of silver, and he will purify the descendants of Levi and refine them like gold and silver, until they present offerings to the LORD in righteousness. [4] Then the offering of Judah and Jerusalem will be pleasing to the LORD as in the days of old and as in former years.

[5] Then I will draw near to you for judgement; I will be swift to bear witness against the sorcerers, against the adulterers, against those who swear falsely, against those who oppress the hired workers in their wages, the widow, and the orphan, against those who thrust aside the alien, and do not fear me, says the LORD of hosts.

PSALM   Psalm 24.[1–6,] 7–10

[1   The earth is the Lord's and all that is in it,
      the world and all who dwell therein.
2   For it is he who founded it upon the seas
      and made it firm upon the rivers of the deep.
3   'Who can ascend the hill of the Lord?
      and who can stand in his holy place?'
4   'Those who have clean hands and a pure heart,
      who have not pledged themselves to falsehood, nor sworn by what
         is a fraud.
5   They shall receive a blessing from the Lord
      and a just reward from the God of their salvation.'
6   Such is the generation of those who seek him,
      of those who seek your face, O God of Jacob.]
7   Lift up your heads, O gates; lift them high, O everlasting doors;
      and the King of glory shall come in.
8   'Who is this King of glory?'
      'The Lord, strong and mighty, the Lord, mighty in battle.'
9   Lift up your heads, O gates; lift them high, O everlasting doors;
      and the King of glory shall come in.
10 'Who is he, this King of glory?'
      'The Lord of hosts, he is the King of glory.'

READING   Hebrews 2.14–18

[14] Since, therefore, the children share flesh and blood, he himself likewise shared the same things, so that through death he might destroy the one who has the power of death, that is, the devil, [15] and free those who all

their lives were held in slavery by the fear of death. [16] For it is clear that he did not come to help angels, but the descendants of Abraham. [17] Therefore he had to become like his brothers and sisters in every respect, so that he might be a merciful and faithful high priest in the service of God, to make a sacrifice of atonement for the sins of the people. [18] Because he himself was tested by what he suffered, he is able to help those who are being tested.

GOSPEL   Luke 2.22–40

[22] When the time came for their purification according to the law of Moses, they brought him up to Jerusalem to present him to the Lord [23] (as it is written in the law of the Lord, 'Every firstborn male shall be designated as holy to the Lord'), [24] and they offered a sacrifice according to what is stated in the law of the Lord, 'a pair of turtle-doves or two young pigeons.'

[25] Now there was a man in Jerusalem whose name was Simeon; this man was righteous and devout, looking forward to the consolation of Israel, and the Holy Spirit rested on him. [26] It had been revealed to him by the Holy Spirit that he would not see death before he had seen the Lord's Messiah. [27] Guided by the Spirit, Simeon came into the temple; and when the parents brought in the child Jesus, to do for him what was customary under the law, [28] Simeon took him in his arms and praised God, saying,

[29] 'Master, now you are dismissing your servant in peace,
        according to your word;
[30] for my eyes have seen your salvation,
[31]   which you have prepared in the presence of all peoples,
[32] a light for revelation to the Gentiles
        and for glory to your people Israel.'

[33] And the child's father and mother were amazed at what was being said about him. [34] Then Simeon blessed them and said to his mother Mary, 'This child is destined for the falling and the rising of many in Israel, and to be a sign that will be opposed [35] so that the inner thoughts of many will be revealed—and a sword will pierce your own soul too.'

[36] There was also a prophet, Anna the daughter of Phanuel, of the tribe of Asher. She was of a great age, having lived with her husband for seven years after her marriage, [37] then as a widow to the age of eighty-four. She never left the temple but worshipped there with fasting and prayer night and day. [38] At that moment she came, and began to praise God and to speak about the child to all who were looking for the redemption of Jerusalem.

[39] When they had finished everything required by the law of the Lord, they returned to Galilee, to their own town of Nazareth. [40] The child grew and became strong, filled with wisdom; and the favour of God was upon him.

POST COMMUNION

Lord, you fulfilled the hope of Simeon and Anna,
who lived to welcome the Messiah:
may we, who have received these gifts beyond words,
prepare to meet Christ Jesus when he comes
    to bring us to eternal life;
for he is alive and reigns, now and for ever.

SECOND SERVICE   THIRD SERVICE

Psalms 122; 132   Psalms 42; 43; 48
Haggai 2.1–9   Exodus 13.1–16
John 2.18–22   Romans 12.1–5

TABLE OF SUNDAYS BEFORE LENT
DATES AND PROPERS

YEAR	LITURGICAL YEAR	FIFTH SUNDAY BEFORE LENT	FOURTH SUNDAY BEFORE LENT	THIRD SUNDAY BEFORE LENT	SECOND SUNDAY BEFORE LENT	FIRST SUNDAY BEFORE LENT
1999	A				7 Feb	14 Feb
2000	B	6 Feb (1)	13 Feb (2)	20 Feb (3)	27 Feb	5 Mar
2001	C		4 Feb (1)	11 Feb (2)	18 Feb	25 Feb
2002	A				3 Feb	10 Feb
2003	B		9 Feb (1)	16 Feb (2)	23 Feb	2 Mar
2004	C			8 Feb (1)	15 Feb	22 Feb
2005	A					6 Feb
2006	B		5 Feb (1)	12 Feb (2)	19 Feb	26 Feb
2007	C			4 Feb (1)	11 Feb	18 Feb
2008	A					3 Feb
2009	B			8 Feb (1)	15 Feb	22 Feb
2010	C				7 Feb	14 Feb
2011	A	6 Feb (1)	13 Feb (2)	20 Feb (3)	27 Feb	6 Mar
2012	B			5 Feb (1)	12 Feb	19 Feb
2013	C				3 Feb	10 Feb
2014	A		9 Feb (1)	16 Feb (2)	23 Feb	2 Mar
2015	B				8 Feb	15 Feb
2016	C					7 Feb
2017	A		5 Feb (1)	12 Feb (2)	19 Feb	26 Feb
2018	B				4 Feb	11 Feb
2019	C	3 Feb (1)	10 Feb (2)	17 Feb (3)	24 Feb	3 Mar
2020	A			9 Feb (1)	16 Feb	23 Feb

The figures in parentheses after dates indicate the appropriate Proper provisions for the day

THE FIFTH SUNDAY BEFORE LENT

COLLECT

Almighty God,
by whose grace alone we are accepted
    and called to your service:
strengthen us by your Holy Spirit
and make us worthy of our calling;
through Jesus Christ your Son our Lord,
who is alive and reigns with you,
in the unity of the Holy Spirit,
one God, now and for ever.

READINGS

See pages 437 to 439 and table on page 434

POST COMMUNION

God of truth,
we have seen with our eyes
    and touched with our hands the bread of life:
strengthen our faith
that we may grow in love for you and for each other;
through Jesus Christ our Lord.

THE FOURTH SUNDAY BEFORE LENT

COLLECT

O God,
you know us to be set
in the midst of so many and great dangers,
that by reason of the frailty of our nature
we cannot always stand upright:
grant to us such strength and protection
as may support us in all dangers
and carry us through all temptations;
through Jesus Christ your Son our Lord,

who is alive and reigns with you,
in the unity of the Holy Spirit,
one God, now and for ever.

READINGS

See pages 437 to 442 and Table on page 434

POST COMMUNION

Go before us, Lord, in all we do
with your most gracious favour,
and guide us with your continual help,
that in all our works
begun, continued and ended in you,
we may glorify your holy name,
and finally by your mercy receive everlasting life;
through Jesus Christ our Lord.

THE THIRD SUNDAY BEFORE LENT

COLLECT

Almighty God,
who alone can bring order
to the unruly wills and passions of sinful humanity:
give your people grace
so to love what you command
and to desire what you promise,
that, among the many changes of this world,
our hearts may surely there be fixed
where true joys are to be found;
through Jesus Christ your Son our Lord,
who is alive and reigns with you,
in the unity of the Holy Spirit,
one God, now and for ever.

READINGS

See pages 437 to 445 and Table on page 434

POST COMMUNION

Merciful Father,
who gave Jesus Christ to be for us the bread of life,
that those who come to him should never hunger:
draw us to the Lord in faith and love,
that we may eat and drink with him
at his table in the kingdom,
where he is alive and reigns, now and for ever.

PROPER 1

Sunday between 3 and 9 February inclusive (if earlier than the Second Sunday before Lent)

COLLECT

See pages 435 to 436 and Table on page 434

READING   Isaiah 40.21–31

21 Have you not known? Have you not heard?
      Has it not been told you from the beginning?
      Have you not understood from the foundations of the earth?
22 It is he who sits above the circle of the earth,
      and its inhabitants are like grasshoppers;
    who stretches out the heavens like a curtain,
      and spreads them like a tent to live in;
23 who brings princes to naught,
      and makes the rulers of the earth as nothing.
24 Scarcely are they planted, scarcely sown,
      scarcely has their stem taken root in the earth,
    when he blows upon them, and they wither,
      and the tempest carries them off like stubble.
25 To whom then will you compare me,
      or who is my equal? says the Holy One.
26 Lift up your eyes on high and see:
      Who created these?
    He who brings out their host and numbers them,
      calling them all by name;
    because he is great in strength,
      mighty in power,
      not one is missing.

27 Why do you say, O Jacob,
   and speak, O Israel,
   'My way is hidden from the LORD,
   and my right is disregarded by my God'?
28 Have you not known? Have you not heard?
   The LORD is the everlasting God,
   the Creator of the ends of the earth.
   He does not faint or grow weary;
   his understanding is unsearchable.
29 He gives power to the faint,
   and strengthens the powerless.
30 Even youths will faint and be weary,
   and the young will fall exhausted;
31 but those who wait for the LORD shall renew their strength,
   they shall mount up with wings like eagles,
   they shall run and not be weary,
   they shall walk and not faint.

PSALM   Psalm 147.1–12, [21c]

1 Alleluia! How good it is to sing praises to our God!
   how pleasant it is to honour him with praise!
2 The Lord rebuilds Jerusalem;
   he gathers the exiles of Israel.
3 He heals the brokenhearted
   and binds up their wounds.
4 He counts the number of the stars
   and calls them all by their names.
5 Great is our Lord and mighty in power;
   there is no limit to his wisdom.
6 The Lord lifts up the lowly,
   but casts the wicked to the ground.
7 Sing to the Lord with thanksgiving;
   make music to our God upon the harp.
8 He covers the heavens with clouds
   and prepares rain for the earth;
9 He makes grass to grow upon the mountains
   and green plants to serve us all.
10 He provides food for flocks and herds
   and for the young ravens when they cry.
11 He is not impressed by the might of a horse,
   he has no pleasure in human strength;
12 But the Lord has pleasure in those who fear him,
   in those who await his gracious favour.

21 Alleluia!

READING   1 Corinthians 9.16–23

[16] If I proclaim the gospel, this gives me no ground for boasting, for an obligation is laid on me, and woe betide me if I do not proclaim the gospel! [17] For if I do this of my own will, I have a reward; but if not of my own will, I am entrusted with a commission. [18] What then is my reward? Just this: that in my proclamation I may make the gospel free of charge, so as not to make full use of my rights in the gospel.

[19] For though I am free with respect to all, I have made myself a slave to all, so that I might win more of them. [20] To the Jews I became as a Jew, in order to win Jews. To those under the law I became as one under the law (though I myself am not under the law) so that I might win those under the law. [21] To those outside the law I became as one outside the law (though I am not free from God's law but am under Christ's law) so that I might win those outside the law. [22] To the weak I became weak, so that I might win the weak. I have become all things to all people, so that I might by any means save some. [23] I do it all for the sake of the gospel, so that I may share in its blessings.

GOSPEL   Mark 1.29–39

[29] As soon as they left the synagogue, they entered the house of Simon and Andrew, with James and John. [30] Now Simon's mother-in-law was in bed with a fever, and they told him about her at once. [31] He came and took her by the hand and lifted her up. Then the fever left her, and she began to serve them.

[32] That evening, at sunset, they brought to him all who were sick or possessed with demons. [33] And the whole city was gathered around the door. [34] And he cured many who were sick with various diseases, and cast out many demons; and he would not permit the demons to speak, because they knew him.

[35] In the morning, while it was still very dark, he got up and went out to a deserted place, and there he prayed. [36] And Simon and his companions hunted for him. [37] When they found him, they said to him, 'Everyone is searching for you.' [38] He answered, 'Let us go on to the neighbouring towns, so that I may proclaim the message there also; for that is what I came out to do.' [39] And he went throughout Galilee, proclaiming the message in their synagogues and casting out demons.

POST COMMUNION

See pages 435 to 437 and Table on page 434

<table>
<tr><td>SECOND SERVICE</td><td>THIRD SERVICE</td></tr>
<tr><td>Psalm 5</td><td>Psalms 2; 3</td></tr>
<tr><td>Numbers 13.1–2, 27–33</td><td>Jeremiah 26.1–16</td></tr>
<tr><td>Philippians 2.12–28</td><td>Acts 3.1–10</td></tr>
</table>

If the Second Service is a Eucharist, the following is read as a Gospel:

Luke 5.1–11

PROPER 2

Sunday between 10 and 16 February inclusive (if earlier than the Second Sunday before Lent)

The provisions of Propers 2 and 3 are only used if there are more than four Sundays between 2 February and Ash Wednesday

COLLECT

See pages 435 to 436 and Table on page 434

READING   2 Kings 5.1–14

[1] Naaman, commander of the army of the king of Aram, was a great man and in high favour with his master, because by him the LORD had given victory to Aram. The man, though a mighty warrior, suffered from leprosy. [2] Now the Arameans on one of their raids had taken a young girl captive from the land of Israel, and she served Naaman's wife. [3] She said to her mistress, 'If only my lord were with the prophet who is in Samaria! He would cure him of his leprosy.' [4] So Naaman went in and told his lord just what the girl from the land of Israel had said. [5] And the king of Aram said, 'Go then, and I will send along a letter to the king of Israel.'

He went, taking with him ten talents of silver, six thousand shekels of gold, and ten sets of garments. [6] He brought the letter to the king of Israel, which read, 'When this letter reaches you, know that I have sent to you my servant Naaman, that you may cure him of his leprosy.' [7] When the king of Israel read the letter, he tore his clothes and said, 'Am I God, to give death or life, that this man sends word to me to cure a man of his leprosy? Just look and see how he is trying to pick a quarrel with me.'

⁸ But when Elisha the man of God heard that the king of Israel had torn his clothes, he sent a message to the king, 'Why have you torn your clothes? Let him come to me, that he may learn that there is a prophet in Israel.' ⁹ So Naaman came with his horses and chariots, and halted at the entrance of Elisha's house. ¹⁰ Elisha sent a messenger to him, saying, 'Go, wash in the Jordan seven times, and your flesh shall be restored and you shall be clean.' ¹¹ But Naaman became angry and went away, saying, 'I thought that for me he would surely come out, and stand and call on the name of the LORD his God, and would wave his hand over the spot, and cure the leprosy! ¹² Are not Abana and Pharpar, the rivers of Damascus, better than all the waters of Israel? Could I not wash in them, and be clean?' He turned and went away in a rage. ¹³ But his servants approached and said to him, 'Father, if the prophet had commanded you to do something difficult, would you not have done it? How much more, when all he said to you was, "Wash, and be clean"?' ¹⁴ So he went down and immersed himself seven times in the Jordan, according to the word of the man of God; his flesh was restored like the flesh of a young boy, and he was clean.

PSALM   Psalm 30

1 I will exalt you, O Lord, because you have lifted me up
   and have not let my enemies triumph over me.
2 O Lord my God, I cried out to you,
   and you restored me to health.
3 You brought me up, O Lord, from the dead;
   you restored my life as I was going down to the grave.
4 Sing to the Lord, you servants of his;
   give thanks for the remembrance of his holiness.
5 For his wrath endures but the twinkling of an eye,
   his favour for a lifetime.
6 Weeping may spend the night,
   but joy comes in the morning.
7 While I felt secure, I said, 'I shall never be disturbed.
   You, Lord, with your favour, made me as strong as the mountains.'
8 Then you hid your face,
   and I was filled with fear.
9 I cried to you, O Lord;
   I pleaded with the Lord, saying,
10 'What profit is there in my blood, if I go down to the Pit?
   will the dust praise you or declare your faithfulness?

11 Hear, O Lord, and have mercy upon me;
    O Lord, be my helper.'
12 You have turned my wailing into dancing;
    you have put off my sack-cloth and clothed me with joy;
13 Therefore my heart sings to you without ceasing;
    O Lord my God, I will give you thanks for ever.

READING   1 Corinthians 9.24–27

24 Do you not know that in a race the runners all compete, but only one receives the prize? Run in such a way that you may win it. 25 Athletes exercise self-control in all things; they do it to receive a perishable garland, but we an imperishable one. 26 So I do not run aimlessly, nor do I box as though beating the air; 27 but I punish my body and enslave it, so that after proclaiming to others I myself should not be disqualified.

GOSPEL   Mark 1.40–45

40 A leper came to him begging him, and kneeling he said to him, 'If you choose, you can make me clean.' 41 Moved with pity, Jesus stretched out his hand and touched him, and said to him, 'I do choose. Be made clean!' 42 Immediately the leprosy left him, and he was made clean. 43 After sternly warning him he sent him away at once, 44 saying to him, 'See that you say nothing to anyone; but go, show yourself to the priest, and offer for your cleansing what Moses commanded, as a testimony to them.' 45 But he went out and began to proclaim it freely, and to spread the word, so that Jesus could no longer go into a town openly, but stayed out in the country; and people came to him from every quarter.

POST COMMUNION

See pages 435 to 436 and Table on page 434

SECOND SERVICE   THIRD SERVICE

Psalm 6   **Psalm 7**
Numbers 20.2–13   **Jeremiah 30.1–3, 10–22**
Philippians 3.7–21   **Acts 6**

If the Second Service is a Eucharist, the
following is read as a Gospel:

Luke 6.17–26

PROPER 3

Sunday between 17 and 23 February inclusive (if earlier than the Second Sunday before Lent)
The provisions of Propers 2 and 3 are only used if there are more than four Sundays between 2 February and Ash Wednesday

COLLECT

See page 436 and Table on page 434

READING   Isaiah 43.18–25

¹⁸ Do not remember the former things,
   or consider the things of old.
¹⁹ I am about to do a new thing;
      now it springs forth, do you not perceive it?
   I will make a way in the wilderness
      and rivers in the desert.
²⁰ The wild animals will honour me,
      the jackals and the ostriches;
   for I give water in the wilderness,
      rivers in the desert,
   to give drink to my chosen people,
²¹   the people whom I formed for myself
   so that they might declare my praise.
²² Yet you did not call upon me, O Jacob;
      but you have been weary of me, O Israel!
²³ You have not brought me your sheep for burnt-offerings,
      or honoured me with your sacrifices.
   I have not burdened you with offerings,
      or wearied you with frankincense.
²⁴ You have not bought me sweet cane with money,
      or satisfied me with the fat of your sacrifices.
   But you have burdened me with your sins;
      you have wearied me with your iniquities.
²⁵ I, I am He
      who blots out your transgressions for my own sake,
      and I will not remember your sins.

PSALM   Psalm 41

1 Happy are they who consider the poor and needy!
   the Lord will deliver them in the time of trouble.
2 The Lord preserves them and keeps them alive, so that they may
     be happy in the land;
   he does not hand them over to the will of their enemies.
3 The Lord sustains them on their sick-bed
   and ministers to them in their illness.
4 I said, 'Lord, be merciful to me;
   heal me, for I have sinned against you.'
5 My enemies are saying wicked things about me:
   'When will he die and his name perish?'
6 Even if they come to see me, they speak empty words;
   their heart collects false rumours; they go outside and spread
     them.
7 All my enemies whisper together about me
   and devise evil against me.
8 'A deadly thing', they say, 'has fastened on him;
   he has taken to his bed and will never get up again.'
9 Even my best friend, whom I trusted, who broke bread with me,
   has lifted up his heel and turned against me.
10 But you, O Lord, be merciful to me and raise me up,
    and I shall repay them.
11 By this I know you are pleased with me,
    that my enemy does not triumph over me.
12 In my integrity you hold me fast,
    and shall set me before your face for ever.
13 Blessèd be the Lord God of Israel,
    from age to age. Amen. Amen.

READING   2 Corinthians 1.18–22

18 As surely as God is faithful, our word to you has not been 'Yes and No.'
19 For the Son of God, Jesus Christ, whom we proclaimed among you,
Silvanus and Timothy and I, was not 'Yes and No'; but in him it is always
'Yes.' 20 For in him every one of God's promises is a 'Yes.' For this reason it
is through him that we say the 'Amen', to the glory of God. 21 But it is God
who establishes us with you in Christ and has anointed us, 22 by putting
his seal on us and giving us his Spirit in our hearts as a first instalment.

GOSPEL   Mark 2.1–12

[1] When he returned to Capernaum after some days, it was reported that he was at home. [2] So many gathered around that there was no longer room for them, not even in front of the door; and he was speaking the word to them. [3] Then some people came, bringing to him a paralysed man, carried by four of them. [4] And when they could not bring him to Jesus because of the crowd, they removed the roof above him; and after having dug through it, they let down the mat on which the paralytic lay. [5] When Jesus saw their faith, he said to the paralytic, 'Son, your sins are forgiven.' [6] Now some of the scribes were sitting there, questioning in their hearts, [7] 'Why does this fellow speak in this way? It is blasphemy! Who can forgive sins but God alone?' [8] At once Jesus perceived in his spirit that they were discussing these questions among themselves; and he said to them, 'Why do you raise such questions in your hearts? [9] Which is easier, to say to the paralytic, "Your sins are forgiven", or to say, "Stand up and take your mat and walk"? [10] But so that you may know that the Son of Man has authority on earth to forgive sins'—he said to the paralytic— [11] 'I say to you, stand up, take your mat and go to your home.' [12] And he stood up, and immediately took the mat and went out before all of them; so that they were all amazed and glorified God, saying, 'We have never seen anything like this!'

POST COMMUNION

See page 436 and Table on page 434

SECOND SERVICE

Psalm 10
Numbers 22.21–23.12
Philippians 4.10–20

If the Second Service is a Eucharist, the following is read as a Gospel:

Luke 6.27–38

THIRD SERVICE

Psalm 9
Jeremiah 33.1–11
Acts 8.4–25

THE SECOND SUNDAY BEFORE LENT

COLLECT

Almighty God,
you have created the heavens and the earth
and made us in your own image:
teach us to discern your hand in all your works
and your likeness in all your children;
through Jesus Christ your Son our Lord,
who with you and the Holy Spirit
    reigns supreme over all things,
now and for ever.

READING   Proverbs 8.1, 22–31

1   Does not wisdom call,
        and does not understanding raise her voice?

22 The LORD created me at the beginning of his work,
        the first of his acts of long ago.
23 Ages ago I was set up,
        at the first, before the beginning of the earth.
24 When there were no depths I was brought forth,
        when there were no springs abounding with water.
25 Before the mountains had been shaped,
        before the hills, I was brought forth—
26 when he had not yet made earth and fields,
        or the world's first bits of soil.
27 When he established the heavens, I was there,
        when he drew a circle on the face of the deep,
28 when he made firm the skies above,
        when he established the fountains of the deep,
29 when he assigned to the sea its limit,
        so that the waters might not transgress his command,
        when he marked out the foundations of the earth,
30 then I was beside him, like a master worker;
    and I was daily his delight,
        rejoicing before him always,
31 rejoicing in his inhabited world
        and delighting in the human race.

PSALM   Psalm 104.25–37

25 O Lord, how manifold are your works!
      in wisdom you have made them all; the earth is full of your
            creatures.
26 Yonder is the great and wide sea with its living things too many
            to number,
      creatures both small and great.
27 There move the ships, and there is that Leviathan,
      which you have made for the sport of it.
28 All of them look to you
      to give them their food in due season.
29 You give it to them, they gather it;
      you open your hand and they are filled with good things.
30 You hide your face and they are terrified;
      you take away their breath and they die and return to their dust.
31 You send forth your Spirit and they are created;
      and so you renew the face of the earth.
32 May the glory of the Lord endure for ever;
      may the Lord rejoice in all his works.
33 He looks at the earth and it trembles;
      he touches the mountains and they smoke.
34 I will sing to the Lord as long as I live;
      I will praise my God while I have my being.
35 May these words of mine please him;
      I will rejoice in the Lord.
36 Let sinners be consumed out of the earth,
      and the wicked be no more.
37 Bless the Lord, O my soul.
      Alleluia!

READING   Colossians 1.15–20

15 He is the image of the invisible God, the firstborn of all creation; 16 for in him all things in heaven and on earth were created, things visible and invisible, whether thrones or dominions or rulers or powers—all things have been created through him and for him. 17 He himself is before all things, and in him all things hold together. 18 He is the head of the body, the church; he is the beginning, the firstborn from the dead, so that he might come to have first place in everything. 19 For in him all the fullness of God was pleased to dwell, 20 and through him God was pleased to reconcile to himself all things, whether on earth or in heaven, by making peace through the blood of his cross.

GOSPEL   John 1.1-14

[1] In the beginning was the Word, and the Word was with God, and the Word was God. [2] He was in the beginning with God. [3] All things came into being through him, and without him not one thing came into being. What has come into being [4] in him was life, and the life was the light of all people. [5] The light shines in the darkness, and the darkness did not overcome it.

[6] There was a man sent from God, whose name was John. [7] He came as a witness to testify to the light, so that all might believe through him. [8] He himself was not the light, but he came to testify to the light. [9] The true light, which enlightens everyone, was coming into the world.

[10] He was in the world, and the world came into being through him; yet the world did not know him. [11] He came to what was his own, and his own people did not accept him. [12] But to all who received him, who believed in his name, he gave power to become children of God, [13] who were born, not of blood or of the will of the flesh or of the will of man, but of God.

[14] And the Word became flesh and lived among us, and we have seen his glory, the glory as of a father's only son, full of grace and truth.

POST COMMUNION

God our creator, by your gift
the tree of life was set at the heart of the earthly paradise,
and the bread of life at the heart of your Church:
may we who have been nourished at your table on earth
be transformed by the glory of the Saviour's cross
and enjoy the delights of eternity;
through Jesus Christ our Lord.

SECOND SERVICE   THIRD SERVICE

Psalm 65   **Psalms 29; 67**
Genesis 2.4b-25   **Deuteronomy 8.1-10**
Luke 8.22-35   **Matthew 6.25-34**

THE SUNDAY NEXT BEFORE LENT

COLLECT

Almighty Father,
whose Son was revealed in majesty
before he suffered death upon the cross:
give us grace to perceive his glory,
that we may be strengthened to suffer with him
and be changed into his likeness, from glory to glory;
who is alive and reigns with you,
in the unity of the Holy Spirit,
one God, now and for ever.

READING   2 Kings 2.1–12

[1] Now when the LORD was about to take Elijah up to heaven by a whirl-wind, Elijah and Elisha were on their way from Gilgal. [2] Elijah said to Elisha, 'Stay here; for the LORD has sent me as far as Bethel.' But Elisha said, 'As the LORD lives, and as you yourself live, I will not leave you.' So they went down to Bethel. [3] The company of prophets who were in Bethel came out to Elisha, and said to him, 'Do you know that today the LORD will take your master away from you?' And he said, 'Yes, I know; keep silent.'

[4] Elijah said to him, 'Elisha, stay here; for the LORD has sent me to Jericho.' But he said, 'As the LORD lives, and as you yourself live, I will not leave you.' So they came to Jericho. [5] The company of prophets who were at Jericho drew near to Elisha, and said to him, 'Do you know that today the LORD will take your master away from you?' And he answered, 'Yes, I know; be silent.'

[6] Then Elijah said to him, 'Stay here; for the LORD has sent me to the Jordan.' But he said, 'As the LORD lives, and as you yourself live, I will not leave you.' So the two of them went on. [7] Fifty men of the company of prophets also went, and stood at some distance from them, as they both were standing by the Jordan. [8] Then Elijah took his mantle and rolled it up, and struck the water; the water was parted to the one side and to the other, until the two of them crossed on dry ground.

[9] When they had crossed, Elijah said to Elisha, 'Tell me what I may do for you, before I am taken from you.' Elisha said, 'Please let me inherit a double share of your spirit.' [10] He responded, 'You have asked a hard thing; yet, if you see me as I am being taken from you, it will be granted you; if not, it will not.' [11] As they continued walking and talking, a chariot of fire and

horses of fire separated the two of them, and Elijah ascended in a whirlwind into heaven. [12] Elisha kept watching and crying out, 'Father, father! The chariots of Israel and its horsemen!' But when he could no longer see him, he grasped his own clothes and tore them in two pieces.

PSALM   Psalm 50.1−6

[1] The Lord, the God of gods, has spoken;
      he has called the earth from the rising of the sun to its setting.
[2] Out of Zion, perfect in its beauty,
      God reveals himself in glory.
[3] Our God will come and will not keep silence;
      before him there is a consuming flame, and round about him a
         raging storm.
[4] He calls the heavens and the earth from above
      to witness the judgement of his people.
[5] 'Gather before me my loyal followers,
      those who have made a covenant with me and sealed it with
         sacrifice.'
[6] Let the heavens declare the rightness of his cause;
      for God himself is judge.

READING   2 Corinthians 4.3−6

[3] And even if our gospel is veiled, it is veiled to those who are perishing. [4] In their case the god of this world has blinded the minds of the unbelievers, to keep them from seeing the light of the gospel of the glory of Christ, who is the image of God. [5] For we do not proclaim ourselves; we proclaim Jesus Christ as Lord and ourselves as your slaves for Jesus' sake. [6] For it is the God who said, 'Let light shine out of darkness', who has shone in our hearts to give the light of the knowledge of the glory of God in the face of Jesus Christ.

GOSPEL   Mark 9.2−9

[2] Six days later, Jesus took with him Peter and James and John, and led them up a high mountain apart, by themselves. And he was transfigured before them, [3] and his clothes became dazzling white, such as no one on earth could bleach them. [4] And there appeared to them Elijah with Moses, who were talking with Jesus. [5] Then Peter said to Jesus, 'Rabbi, it is good for us to be here; let us make three dwellings, one for you, one for Moses, and one for Elijah.' [6] He did not know what to say, for they were terrified.

7 Then a cloud overshadowed them, and from the cloud there came a voice, 'This is my Son, the Beloved; listen to him!' 8 Suddenly when they looked around, they saw no one with them any more, but only Jesus.

9 As they were coming down the mountain, he ordered them to tell no one about what they had seen, until after the Son of Man had risen from the dead.

POST COMMUNION

Holy God,
we see your glory in the face of Jesus Christ:
may we who are partakers at his table
reflect his life in word and deed,
that all the world may know
    his power to change and save.
This we ask through Jesus Christ our Lord.

SECOND SERVICE

Psalms 2; [99]
1 Kings 19.1–16
2 Peter 1.16–21

If the Second Service is a Eucharist, the following is read as a Gospel:

Mark 9.[2–8,] 9–13

THIRD SERVICE

Psalms 27; 150
Exodus 24.12–18
2 Corinthians 3.12–18

THE ANNUNCIATION OF OUR LORD   25 MARCH

The readings for the Feast of the Annunciation will be found on page 1113

The readings for the Feast of the Annunciation will be found on page 1113

ASH WEDNESDAY

COLLECT

Almighty and everlasting God,
you hate nothing that you have made
and forgive the sins of all those who are penitent:
create and make in us new and contrite hearts

YEAR B

that we, worthily lamenting our sins
and acknowledging our wretchedness,
may receive from you, the God of all mercy,
perfect remission and forgiveness;
through Jesus Christ your Son our Lord,
who is alive and reigns with you,
in the unity of the Holy Spirit,
one God, now and for ever.

This Collect may be used as the Post Communion on any day from the First Sunday of Lent until the Saturday after the Fourth Sunday of Lent instead of the Post Communion provided

READING

EITHER   Joel 2.1–2, 12–17

¹ Blow the trumpet in Zion;
      sound the alarm on my holy mountain!
   Let all the inhabitants of the land tremble,
      for the day of the Lord is coming, it is near—
² a day of darkness and gloom,
      a day of clouds and thick darkness!
   Like blackness spread upon the mountains
      a great and powerful army comes;
   their like has never been from of old,
      nor will be again after them
      in ages to come.

¹² Yet even now, says the Lord,
      return to me with all your heart,
   with fasting, with weeping, and with mourning;
¹³   rend your hearts and not your clothing.
   Return to the Lord, your God,
      for he is gracious and merciful,
   slow to anger, and abounding in steadfast love,
      and relents from punishing.
¹⁴ Who knows whether he will not turn and relent,
      and leave a blessing behind him,
   a grain-offering and a drink-offering
      for the Lord, your God?
¹⁵ Blow the trumpet in Zion;
      sanctify a fast;
   call a solemn assembly;

16   gather the people.
    Sanctify the congregation;
      assemble the aged;
    gather the children,
      even infants at the breast.
    Let the bridegroom leave his room,
      and the bride her canopy.
17   Between the vestibule and the altar
      let the priests, the ministers of the LORD, weep.
    Let them say, 'Spare your people, O LORD,
      and do not make your heritage a mockery,
      a byword among the nations.
    Why should it be said among the peoples,
      "Where is their God?" '

OR   **Isaiah 58.1–12**

1   Shout out, do not hold back!
      Lift up your voice like a trumpet!
    Announce to my people their rebellion,
      to the house of Jacob their sins.
2   Yet day after day they seek me
      and delight to know my ways,
    as if they were a nation that practised righteousness
      and did not forsake the ordinance of their God;
    they ask of me righteous judgements,
      they delight to draw near to God.
3   'Why do we fast, but you do not see?
      Why humble ourselves, but you do not notice?'
    Look, you serve your own interest on your fast-day,
      and oppress all your workers.
4   Look, you fast only to quarrel and to fight
      and to strike with a wicked fist.
    Such fasting as you do today
      will not make your voice heard on high.
5   Is such the fast that I choose,
      a day to humble oneself?
    Is it to bow down the head like a bulrush,
      and to lie in sackcloth and ashes?
    Will you call this a fast,
      a day acceptable to the LORD?

6 Is not this the fast that I choose:
>> to loose the bonds of injustice,
>> to undo the thongs of the yoke,
> to let the oppressed go free,
>> and to break every yoke?

7 Is it not to share your bread with the hungry,
>> and bring the homeless poor into your house;
> when you see the naked, to cover them,
>> and not to hide yourself from your own kin?

8 Then your light shall break forth like the dawn,
>> and your healing shall spring up quickly;
> your vindicator shall go before you,
>> the glory of the LORD shall be your rearguard.

9 Then you shall call, and the LORD will answer;
>> you shall cry for help, and he will say, Here I am.
> If you remove the yoke from among you,
>> the pointing of the finger, the speaking of evil,

10 if you offer your food to the hungry
>> and satisfy the needs of the afflicted,
> then your light shall rise in the darkness
>> and your gloom be like the noonday.

11 The LORD will guide you continually,
>> and satisfy your needs in parched places,
>> and make your bones strong;
> and you shall be like a watered garden,
>> like a spring of water,
>> whose waters never fail.

12 Your ancient ruins shall be rebuilt;
>> you shall raise up the foundations of many generations;
> you shall be called the repairer of the breach,
>> the restorer of streets to live in.

PSALM   Psalm 51.1–18

1 Have mercy on me, O God, according to your loving-kindness;
> in your great compassion blot out my offences.

2 Wash me through and through from my wickedness
> and cleanse me from my sin.

3 For I know my transgressions,
> and my sin is ever before me.

4 Against you only have I sinned
> and done what is evil in your sight.

5 And so you are justified when you speak
   and upright in your judgement.
6 Indeed, I have been wicked from my birth,
   a sinner from my mother's womb.
7 For behold, you look for truth deep within me,
   and will make me understand wisdom secretly.
8 Purge me from my sin and I shall be pure;
   wash me and I shall be clean indeed.
9 Make me hear of joy and gladness,
   that the body you have broken may rejoice.
10 Hide your face from my sins
   and blot out all my iniquities.
11 Create in me a clean heart, O God,
   and renew a right spirit within me.
12 Cast me not away from your presence
   and take not your holy Spirit from me.
13 Give me the joy of your saving help again
   and sustain me with your bountiful Spirit.
14 I shall teach your ways to the wicked,
   and sinners shall return to you.
15 Deliver me from death, O God,
   and my tongue shall sing of your righteousness, O God of my
      salvation.
16 Open my lips, O Lord,
   and my mouth shall proclaim your praise.
17 Had you desired it, I would have offered sacrifice,
   but you take no delight in burnt-offerings.
18 The sacrifice of God is a troubled spirit;
   a broken and contrite heart, O God, you will not despise.

READING   2 Corinthians 5.20b–6.10

20 We entreat you on behalf of Christ, be reconciled to God. 21 For our sake
he made him to be sin who knew no sin, so that in him we might become
the righteousness of God.

   1 As we work together with him, we urge you also not to accept the grace
of God in vain. 2 For he says,
      'At an acceptable time I have listened to you,
         and on a day of salvation I have helped you.'
See, now is the acceptable time; see, now is the day of salvation!
3 We are putting no obstacle in anyone's way, so that no fault may be found
with our ministry, 4 but as servants of God we have commended ourselves
in every way: through great endurance, in afflictions, hardships, calamities,

⁵ beatings, imprisonments, riots, labours, sleepless nights, hunger; ⁶ by purity, knowledge, patience, kindness, holiness of spirit, genuine love, ⁷ truthful speech, and the power of God; with the weapons of righteousness for the right hand and for the left; ⁸ in honour and dishonour, in ill repute and good repute. We are treated as impostors, and yet are true; ⁹ as unknown, and yet are well known; as dying, and see—we are alive; as punished, and yet not killed; ¹⁰ as sorrowful, yet always rejoicing; as poor, yet making many rich; as having nothing, and yet possessing everything.

GOSPEL

EITHER   **Matthew 6.1–6, 16–21**

¹ 'Beware of practising your piety before others in order to be seen by them; for then you have no reward from your Father in heaven.

² 'So whenever you give alms, do not sound a trumpet before you, as the hypocrites do in the synagogues and in the streets, so that they may be praised by others. Truly I tell you, they have received their reward. ³ But when you give alms, do not let your left hand know what your right hand is doing, ⁴ so that your alms may be done in secret; and your Father who sees in secret will reward you.

⁵ 'And whenever you pray, do not be like the hypocrites; for they love to stand and pray in the synagogues and at the street corners, so that they may be seen by others. Truly I tell you, they have received their reward. ⁶ But whenever you pray, go into your room and shut the door and pray to your Father who is in secret; and your Father who sees in secret will reward you.'

¹⁶ 'And whenever you fast, do not look dismal, like the hypocrites, for they disfigure their faces so as to show others that they are fasting. Truly I tell you, they have received their reward. ¹⁷ But when you fast, put oil on your head and wash your face, ¹⁸ so that your fasting may be seen not by others but by your Father who is in secret; and your Father who sees in secret will reward you.

¹⁹ 'Do not store up for yourselves treasures on earth, where moth and rust consume and where thieves break in and steal; ²⁰ but store up for yourselves treasures in heaven, where neither moth nor rust consumes and where thieves do not break in and steal. ²¹ For where your treasure is, there your heart will be also.'

OR John 8.2–11

2 Early in the morning he came again to the temple. All the people came to him and he sat down and began to teach them. 3 The scribes and the Pharisees brought a woman who had been caught in adultery; and making her stand before all of them, 4 they said to him, 'Teacher, this woman was caught in the very act of committing adultery. 5 Now in the law Moses commanded us to stone such women. Now what do you say?' 6 They said this to test him, so that they might have some charge to bring against him. Jesus bent down and wrote with his finger on the ground. 7 When they kept on questioning him, he straightened up and said to them, 'Let anyone among you who is without sin be the first to throw a stone at her.' 8 And once again he bent down and wrote on the ground. 9 When they heard it, they went away, one by one, beginning with the elders; and Jesus was left alone with the woman standing before him. 10 Jesus straightened up and said to her, 'Woman, where are they? Has no one condemned you?' 11 She said, 'No one, sir.' And Jesus said, 'Neither do I condemn you. Go your way, and from now on do not sin again.'

POST COMMUNION

Almighty God,
you have given your only Son to be for us
both a sacrifice for sin
and also an example of godly life:
give us grace
that we may always most thankfully receive
these his inestimable gifts,
and also daily endeavour to follow
    the blessed steps of his most holy life;
through Jesus Christ our Lord.

SECOND SERVICE THIRD SERVICE

Psalm 102.1–17, [18–28] Psalm 38
Isaiah 1.10–18 Daniel 9.3–6, 17–19
Luke 15.11–32 1 Timothy 6.6–19

THE FIRST SUNDAY OF LENT

COLLECT

Almighty God,
whose Son Jesus Christ fasted forty days in the wilderness,
and was tempted as we are, yet without sin:
give us grace to discipline ourselves
   in obedience to your Spirit;
and, as you know our weakness,
so may we know your power to save;
through Jesus Christ your Son our Lord,
who is alive and reigns with you,
in the unity of the Holy Spirit,
one God, now and for ever.

READING   Genesis 9.8–17

[8] Then God said to Noah and to his sons with him, [9] 'As for me, I am establishing my covenant with you and your descendants after you, [10] and with every living creature that is with you, the birds, the domestic animals, and every animal of the earth with you, as many as came out of the ark. [11] I establish my covenant with you, that never again shall all flesh be cut off by the waters of a flood, and never again shall there be a flood to destroy the earth.' [12] God said, 'This is the sign of the covenant that I make between me and you and every living creature that is with you, for all future generations: [13] I have set my bow in the clouds, and it shall be a sign of the covenant between me and the earth. [14] When I bring clouds over the earth and the bow is seen in the clouds, [15] I will remember my covenant that is between me and you and every living creature of all flesh; and the waters shall never again become a flood to destroy all flesh. [16] When the bow is in the clouds, I will see it and remember the everlasting covenant between God and every living creature of all flesh that is on the earth.' [17] God said to Noah, 'This is the sign of the covenant that I have established between me and all flesh that is on the earth.'

PSALM   Psalm 25.1–9

[1] To you, O Lord, I lift up my soul; my God, I put my trust in you;
    let me not be humiliated, nor let my enemies triumph over me.
[2] Let none who look to you be put to shame;
    let the treacherous be disappointed in their schemes.

3 Show me your ways, O Lord,
and teach me your paths.

4 Lead me in your truth and teach me,
for you are the God of my salvation; in you have I trusted all the
day long.

5 Remember, O Lord, your compassion and love,
for they are from everlasting.

6 Remember not the sins of my youth and my transgressions;
remember me according to your love and for the sake of your
goodness, O Lord.

7 Gracious and upright is the Lord;
therefore he teaches sinners in his way.

8 He guides the humble in doing right
and teaches his way to the lowly.

9 All the paths of the Lord are love and faithfulness
to those who keep his covenant and his testimonies.

READING 1 Peter 3.18–22

18 For Christ also suffered for sins once for all, the righteous for the unright-eous, in order to bring you to God. He was put to death in the flesh, but made alive in the spirit, 19 in which also he went and made a proclamation to the spirits in prison, 20 who in former times did not obey, when God waited patiently in the days of Noah, during the building of the ark, in which a few, that is, eight people, were saved through water. 21 And baptism, which this prefigured, now saves you—not as a removal of dirt from the body, but as an appeal to God for a good conscience, through the res-urrection of Jesus Christ, 22 who has gone into heaven and is at the right hand of God, with angels, authorities, and powers made subject to him.

GOSPEL Mark 1.9–15

9 In those days Jesus came from Nazareth of Galilee and was baptized by John in the Jordan. 10 And just as he was coming up out of the water, he saw the heavens torn apart and the Spirit descending like a dove on him. 11 And a voice came from heaven, 'You are my Son, the Beloved; with you I am well pleased.'

12 And the Spirit immediately drove him out into the wilderness. 13 He was in the wilderness for forty days, tempted by Satan; and he was with the wild beasts; and the angels waited on him.

¹⁴ Now after John was arrested, Jesus came to Galilee, proclaiming the good news of God, ¹⁵ and saying, 'The time is fulfilled, and the kingdom of God has come near; repent, and believe in the good news.'

POST COMMUNION

Lord God,
you have renewed us with the living bread from heaven;
by it you nourish our faith,
increase our hope,
and strengthen our love:
teach us always to hunger for him
    who is the true and living bread,
and enable us to live by every word
    that proceeds from out of your mouth;
through Jesus Christ our Lord.

SECOND SERVICE	THIRD SERVICE
Psalm 119.17–32	**Psalm 77**
Genesis 2.15–17; 3.1–7	**Exodus 34.1–10**
Romans 5.12–19	**Romans 10.8b-13**

or

Luke 13.31–35

THE SECOND SUNDAY OF LENT

COLLECT

Almighty God,
you show to those who are in error the light of your truth,
that they may return to the way of righteousness:
grant to all those who are admitted
    into the fellowship of Christ's religion,
that they may reject those things
    that are contrary to their profession,
and follow all such things as are agreeable to the same;
through our Lord Jesus Christ,

who is alive and reigns with you,
in the unity of the Holy Spirit,
one God, now and for ever.

READING   Genesis 17.1–7, 15–16

¹ When Abram was ninety-nine years old, the Lᴏʀᴅ appeared to Abram, and said to him, 'I am God Almighty; walk before me, and be blameless. ² And I will make my covenant between me and you, and will make you exceedingly numerous.' ³ Then Abram fell on his face; and God said to him, ⁴ 'As for me, this is my covenant with you: You shall be the ancestor of a multitude of nations. ⁵ No longer shall your name be Abram, but your name shall be Abraham; for I have made you the ancestor of a multitude of nations. ⁶ I will make you exceedingly fruitful; and I will make nations of you, and kings shall come from you. ⁷ I will establish my covenant between me and you, and your offspring after you throughout their generations, for an everlasting covenant, to be God to you and to your offspring after you.'

¹⁵ God said to Abraham, 'As for Sarai your wife, you shall not call her Sarai, but Sarah shall be her name. ¹⁶ I will bless her, and moreover I will give you a son by her. I will bless her, and she shall give rise to nations; kings of peoples shall come from her.'

PSALM   Psalm 22.22–30

22 Praise the Lord, you that fear him;
    stand in awe of him, O offspring of Israel; all you of Jacob's line,
        give glory.
23 For he does not despise nor abhor the poor in their poverty; neither
        does he hide his face from them;
    but when they cry to him he hears them.
24 My praise is of him in the great assembly;
    I will perform my vows in the presence of those who worship him.
25 The poor shall eat and be satisfied, and those who seek the Lord
        shall praise him:
    'May your heart live for ever!'
26 All the ends of the earth shall remember and turn to the Lord,
    and all the families of the nations shall bow before him.
27 For kingship belongs to the Lord;
    he rules over the nations.
28 To him alone all who sleep in the earth bow down in worship;
    all who go down to the dust fall before him.

29 My soul shall live for him; my descendants shall serve him;
    they shall be known as the Lord's for ever.
30 They shall come and make known to a people yet unborn
    the saving deeds that he has done.

READING   Romans 4.13–25

13 For the promise that he would inherit the world did not come to
Abraham or to his descendants through the law but through the righteousness of faith. 14 If it is the adherents of the law who are to be the heirs, faith
is null and the promise is void. 15 For the law brings wrath; but where there
is no law, neither is there violation.

16 For this reason it depends on faith, in order that the promise may rest
on grace and be guaranteed to all his descendants, not only to the adherents
of the law but also to those who share the faith of Abraham (for he is the
father of all of us, 17 as it is written, 'I have made you the father of many
nations')—in the presence of the God in whom he believed, who gives life
to the dead and calls into existence the things that do not exist. 18 Hoping
against hope, he believed that he would become 'the father of many
nations', according to what was said, 'So numerous shall your descendants
be.' 19 He did not weaken in faith when he considered his own body, which
was already as good as dead (for he was about a hundred years old), or when
he considered the barrenness of Sarah's womb. 20 No distrust made him
waver concerning the promise of God, but he grew strong in his faith as he
gave glory to God, 21 being fully convinced that God was able to do what he
had promised. 22 Therefore his faith 'was reckoned to him as righteousness.'
23 Now the words, 'it was reckoned to him', were written not for his sake
alone, 24 but for ours also. It will be reckoned to us who believe in him who
raised Jesus our Lord from the dead, 25 who was handed over to death for
our trespasses and was raised for our justification.

GOSPEL   Mark 8.31–38

31 Then he began to teach them that the Son of Man must undergo great
suffering, and be rejected by the elders, the chief priests, and the scribes,
and be killed, and after three days rise again. 32 He said all this quite openly.
And Peter took him aside and began to rebuke him. 33 But turning and
looking at his disciples, he rebuked Peter and said, 'Get behind me, Satan!
For you are setting your mind not on divine things but on human things.'

34 He called the crowd with his disciples, and said to them, 'If any want to
become my followers, let them deny themselves and take up their cross and
follow me. 35 For those who want to save their life will lose it, and those

who lose their life for my sake, and for the sake of the gospel, will save it. [36] For what will it profit them to gain the whole world and forfeit their life? [37] Indeed, what can they give in return for their life? [38] Those who are ashamed of me and of my words in this adulterous and sinful generation, of them the Son of Man will also be ashamed when he comes in the glory of his Father with the holy angels.'

POST COMMUNION

Almighty God,
you see that we have no power of ourselves to help ourselves:
keep us both outwardly in our bodies,
and inwardly in our souls;
that we may be defended from all adversities
   which may happen to the body,
and from all evil thoughts
   which may assault and hurt the soul;
through Jesus Christ our Lord.

SECOND SERVICE

Psalm 135.1–14, [15–21]
Genesis 12.1–9
Hebrews 11.1–3, 8–16

THIRD SERVICE

Psalm 105.1–6, 37–45
Isaiah 51.1–11
Galatians 3.1–9, 23–29

THE THIRD SUNDAY OF LENT

COLLECT

Almighty God,
whose most dear Son went not up to joy
   but first he suffered pain,
and entered not into glory before he was crucified:
mercifully grant that we, walking in the way of the cross,
may find it none other than the way of life and peace;
through Jesus Christ your Son our Lord,
who is alive and reigns with you,
in the unity of the Holy Spirit,
one God, now and for ever.

READING   Exodus 20.1-17

¹ Then God spoke all these words:

² I am the LORD your God, who brought you out of the land of Egypt, out of the house of slavery; ³ you shall have no other gods before me.

⁴ You shall not make for yourself an idol, whether in the form of anything that is in heaven above, or that is on the earth beneath, or that is in the water under the earth. ⁵ You shall not bow down to them or worship them; for I the LORD your God am a jealous God, punishing children for the iniquity of parents, to the third and the fourth generation of those who reject me, ⁶ but showing steadfast love to the thousandth generation of those who love me and keep my commandments.

⁷ You shall not make wrongful use of the name of the LORD your God, for the LORD will not acquit anyone who misuses his name.

⁸ Remember the sabbath day, and keep it holy. ⁹ For six days you shall labour and do all your work. ¹⁰ But the seventh day is a sabbath to the LORD your God; you shall not do any work—you, your son or your daughter, your male or female slave, your livestock, or the alien resident in your towns. ¹¹ For in six days the LORD made heaven and earth, the sea, and all that is in them, but rested the seventh day; therefore the LORD blessed the sabbath day and consecrated it.

¹² Honour your father and your mother, so that your days may be long in the land that the LORD your God is giving you.

¹³ You shall not murder.

¹⁴ You shall not commit adultery.

¹⁵ You shall not steal.

¹⁶ You shall not bear false witness against your neighbour.

¹⁷ You shall not covet your neighbour's house; you shall not covet your neighbour's wife, or male or female slave, or ox, or donkey, or anything that belongs to your neighbour.

PSALM   Psalm 19.[1–6,] 7–14

[¹ The heavens declare the glory of God,
    and the firmament shows his handiwork.
 ² One day tells its tale to another,
    and one night imparts knowledge to another.

3 Although they have no words or language,
   and their voices are not heard,
4 Their sound has gone out into all lands,
   and their message to the ends of the world.
5 In the deep has he set a pavilion for the sun;
   it comes forth like a bridegroom out of his chamber; it rejoices
      like a champion to run its course.
6 It goes forth from the uttermost edge of the heavens and runs
      about to the end of it again;
   nothing is hidden from its burning heat.]
7 The law of the Lord is perfect and revives the soul;
   the testimony of the Lord is sure and gives wisdom to the innocent.
8 The statutes of the Lord are just and rejoice the heart;
   the commandment of the Lord is clear and gives light to the eyes.
9 The fear of the Lord is clean and endures for ever;
   the judgements of the Lord are true and righteous altogether.
10 More to be desired are they than gold, more than much fine gold,
   sweeter far than honey, than honey in the comb.
11 By them also is your servant enlightened,
   and in keeping them there is great reward.
12 Who can tell how often he offends?
   Cleanse me from my secret faults.
13 Above all, keep your servant from presumptuous sins; let them
      not get dominion over me;
   then shall I be whole and sound, and innocent of a great offence.
14 Let the words of my mouth and the meditation of my heart be
      acceptable in your sight,
   O Lord, my strength and my redeemer.

READING   1 Corinthians 1.18–25

18 For the message about the cross is foolishness to those who are perishing, but to us who are being saved it is the power of God. 19 For it is
written,
   'I will destroy the wisdom of the wise,
      and the discernment of the discerning I will thwart.'
20 Where is the one who is wise? Where is the scribe? Where is the debater
of this age? Has not God made foolish the wisdom of the world? 21 For since,
in the wisdom of God, the world did not know God through wisdom, God
decided, through the foolishness of our proclamation, to save those who
believe. 22 For Jews demand signs and Greeks desire wisdom, 23 but we
proclaim Christ crucified, a stumbling-block to Jews and foolishness to

Gentiles, ²⁴ but to those who are the called, both Jews and Greeks, Christ the power of God and the wisdom of God. ²⁵ For God's foolishness is wiser than human wisdom, and God's weakness is stronger than human strength.

GOSPEL   John 2.13–22

¹³ The Passover of the Jews was near, and Jesus went up to Jerusalem. ¹⁴ In the temple he found people selling cattle, sheep, and doves, and the money-changers seated at their tables. ¹⁵ Making a whip of cords, he drove all of them out of the temple, both the sheep and the cattle. He also poured out the coins of the money-changers and overturned their tables. ¹⁶ He told those who were selling the doves, 'Take these things out of here! Stop making my Father's house a market-place!' ¹⁷ His disciples remembered that it was written, 'Zeal for your house will consume me.' ¹⁸ The Jews then said to him, 'What sign can you show us for doing this?' ¹⁹ Jesus answered them, 'Destroy this temple, and in three days I will raise it up.' ²⁰ The Jews then said, 'This temple has been under construction for forty-six years, and will you raise it up in three days?' ²¹ But he was speaking of the temple of his body. ²² After he was raised from the dead, his disciples remembered that he had said this; and they believed the scripture and the word that Jesus had spoken.

POST COMMUNION

Merciful Lord,
grant your people grace to withstand the temptations
    of the world, the flesh and the devil,
and with pure hearts and minds to follow you,
    the only God;
through Jesus Christ our Lord.

SECOND SERVICE

THIRD SERVICE

Psalms 11; 12
Exodus 5.1–6.1
Philippians 3.4b-14

or

Matthew 10.16–22

Psalm 18.1–25
Jeremiah 38
Philippians 1.1–26

THE FOURTH SUNDAY OF LENT

Mothering Sunday may be celebrated in preference to the provision for the Fourth Sunday of Lent

COLLECT

Merciful Lord,
absolve your people from their offences,
that through your bountiful goodness
we may all be delivered from the chains of those sins
which by our frailty we have committed;
grant this, heavenly Father,
for Jesus Christ's sake, our blessed Lord and Saviour,
who is alive and reigns with you,
in the unity of the Holy Spirit,
one God, now and for ever.

READING   Numbers 21.4-9

⁴ From Mount Hor they set out by the way to the Red Sea, to go around the land of Edom; but the people became impatient on the way. ⁵ The people spoke against God and against Moses, 'Why have you brought us up out of Egypt to die in the wilderness? For there is no food and no water, and we detest this miserable food.' ⁶ Then the Lord sent poisonous serpents among the people, and they bit the people, so that many Israelites died. ⁷ The people came to Moses and said, 'We have sinned by speaking against the Lord and against you; pray to the Lord to take away the serpents from us.' So Moses prayed for the people. ⁸ And the Lord said to Moses, 'Make a poisonous serpent, and set it on a pole; and everyone who is bitten shall look at it and live.' ⁹ So Moses made a serpent of bronze, and put it upon a pole; and whenever a serpent bit someone, that person would look at the serpent of bronze and live.

PSALM   Psalm 107.1-3, 17-22

1   Give thanks to the Lord, for he is good,
     and his mercy endures for ever.
2   Let all those whom the Lord has redeemed proclaim
     that he redeemed them from the hand of the foe.
3   He gathered them out of the lands;
     from the east and from the west, from the north and from the
        south.

¹⁷ Some were fools and took to rebellious ways;
  they were afflicted because of their sins.
¹⁸ They abhorred all manner of food
  and drew near to death's door.
¹⁹ Then they cried to the Lord in their trouble,
  and he delivered them from their distress.
²⁰ He sent forth his word and healed them
  and saved them from the grave.
²¹ Let them give thanks to the Lord for his mercy
  and the wonders he does for his children.
²² Let them offer a sacrifice of thanksgiving
  and tell of his acts with shouts of joy.

OR, IF AN ALTERNATIVE TEXT IS PREFERRED   **Psalm 107.1–9**

¹ Give thanks to the Lord, for he is good,
  and his mercy endures for ever.
² Let all those whom the Lord has redeemed proclaim
  that he redeemed them from the hand of the foe.
³ He gathered them out of the lands;
  from the east and from the west, from the north and from the
    south.
⁴ Some wandered in desert wastes;
  they found no way to a city where they might dwell.
⁵ They were hungry and thirsty;
  their spirits languished within them.
⁶ Then they cried to the Lord in their trouble,
  and he delivered them from their distress.
⁷ He put their feet on a straight path
  to go to a city where they might dwell.
⁸ Let them give thanks to the Lord for his mercy
  and the wonders he does for his children.
⁹ For he satisfies the thirsty
  and fills the hungry with good things.

READING   **Ephesians 2.1–10**

¹ You were dead through the trespasses and sins ² in which you once lived, following the course of this world, following the ruler of the power of the air, the spirit that is now at work among those who are disobedient. ³ All of us once lived among them in the passions of our flesh, following the desires of flesh and senses, and we were by nature children of wrath, like everyone else. ⁴ But God, who is rich in mercy, out of the great love with

which he loved us [5] even when we were dead through our trespasses, made us alive together with Christ—by grace you have been saved— [6] and raised us up with him and seated us with him in the heavenly places in Christ Jesus, [7] so that in the ages to come he might show the immeasurable riches of his grace in kindness towards us in Christ Jesus. [8] For by grace you have been saved through faith, and this is not your own doing; it is the gift of God— [9] not the result of works, so that no one may boast. [10] For we are what he has made us, created in Christ Jesus for good works, which God prepared beforehand to be our way of life.

GOSPEL   John 3.14–21

[14] 'And just as Moses lifted up the serpent in the wilderness, so must the Son of Man be lifted up, [15] that whoever believes in him may have eternal life.

[16] 'For God so loved the world that he gave his only Son, so that everyone who believes in him may not perish but may have eternal life.

[17] 'Indeed, God did not send the Son into the world to condemn the world, but in order that the world might be saved through him. [18] Those who believe in him are not condemned; but those who do not believe are condemned already, because they have not believed in the name of the only Son of God. [19] And this is the judgement, that the light has come into the world, and people loved darkness rather than light because their deeds were evil. [20] For all who do evil hate the light and do not come to the light, so that their deeds may not be exposed. [21] But those who do what is true come to the light, so that it may be clearly seen that their deeds have been done in God.'

If the Principal Service readings have been displaced by Mothering Sunday provisions, they may be used at the Second Service

POST COMMUNION

Lord God,
whose blessed Son our Saviour
gave his back to the smiters
and did not hide his face from shame:
give us grace to endure the sufferings of this present time
with sure confidence in the glory that shall be revealed;
through Jesus Christ our Lord.

SECOND SERVICE	THIRD SERVICE
Psalms 13; 14	**Psalm 27**
Exodus 6.2–13	**1 Samuel 16.1–13**
Romans 5.1–11	**John 9.1–25**

If the Second Service is a Eucharist, the following is read as a Gospel:

John 12.1–8

MOTHERING SUNDAY

Mothering Sunday may be celebrated in preference to any part of the provision for the Fourth Sunday of Lent. If it replaces a Second or Third Service, the Principal Service provision may still be used.

COLLECT

God of compassion,
whose Son Jesus Christ, the child of Mary,
shared the life of a home in Nazareth,
and on the cross drew the whole human family to himself:
strengthen us in our daily living
that in joy and in sorrow
we may know the power of your presence
   to bind together and to heal;
through Jesus Christ your Son our Lord,
who is alive and reigns with you,
in the unity of the Holy Spirit,
one God, now and for ever.

READING

EITHER   **Exodus 2.1–10**

¹ Now a man from the house of Levi went and married a Levite woman. ² The woman conceived and bore a son; and when she saw that he was a fine baby, she hid him for three months. ³ When she could hide him no longer she got a papyrus basket for him, and plastered it with bitumen and pitch; she put the child in it and placed it among the reeds on the bank of the river. ⁴ His sister stood at a distance, to see what would happen to him.

⁵ The daughter of Pharaoh came down to bathe at the river, while her attendants walked beside the river. She saw the basket among the reeds and sent her maid to bring it. ⁶ When she opened it, she saw the child. He

was crying, and she took pity on him. 'This must be one of the Hebrews' children,' she said. ⁷ Then his sister said to Pharaoh's daughter, 'Shall I go and get you a nurse from the Hebrew women to nurse the child for you?' ⁸ Pharaoh's daughter said to her, 'Yes.' So the girl went and called the child's mother. ⁹ Pharaoh's daughter said to her, 'Take this child and nurse it for me, and I will give you your wages.' So the woman took the child and nursed it. ¹⁰ When the child grew up, she brought him to Pharaoh's daughter, and she took him as her son. She named him Moses, 'because', she said, 'I drew him out of the water.'

OR   1 Samuel 1.20–28

²⁰ In due time Hannah conceived and bore a son. She named him Samuel, for she said, 'I have asked him of the LORD.'

²¹ The man Elkanah and all his household went up to offer to the LORD the yearly sacrifice, and to pay his vow. ²² But Hannah did not go up, for she said to her husband, 'As soon as the child is weaned, I will bring him, that he may appear in the presence of the LORD, and remain there for ever; I will offer him as a nazirite for all time.' ²³ Her husband Elkanah said to her, 'Do what seems best to you, wait until you have weaned him; only— may the LORD establish his word.' So the woman remained and nursed her son, until she weaned him. ²⁴ When she had weaned him, she took him up with her, along with a three-year-old bull, an ephah of flour, and a skin of wine. She brought him to the house of the LORD at Shiloh; and the child was young. ²⁵ Then they slaughtered the bull, and they brought the child to Eli. ²⁶ And she said, 'Oh, my lord! As you live, my lord, I am the woman who was standing here in your presence, praying to the LORD. ²⁷ For this child I prayed; and the LORD has granted me the petition that I made to him. ²⁸ Therefore I have lent him to the LORD; as long as he lives, he is given to the LORD.'

She left him there for the LORD.

PSALM

EITHER   Psalm 34.11–20

11 Come, children, and listen to me;
      I will teach you the fear of the Lord.
12 Who among you loves life
      and desires long life to enjoy prosperity?
13 Keep your tongue from evil-speaking
      and your lips from lying words.
14 Turn from evil and do good;
      seek peace and pursue it.

15 The eyes of the Lord are upon the righteous,
    and his ears are open to their cry.
16 The face of the Lord is against those who do evil,
    to root out the remembrance of them from the earth.
17 The righteous cry and the Lord hears them
    and delivers them from all their troubles.
18 The Lord is near to the brokenhearted
    and will save those whose spirits are crushed.
19 Many are the troubles of the righteous,
    but the Lord will deliver him out of them all.
20 He will keep safe all his bones;
    not one of them shall be broken.

OR   Psalm 127.1–5

1 Unless the Lord builds the house,
    their labour is in vain who build it.
2 Unless the Lord watches over the city,
    in vain the guard keeps vigil.
3 It is in vain that you rise so early and go to bed so late;
    vain, too, to eat the bread of toil, for he gives to his belovèd sleep.
4 Children are a heritage from the Lord,
    and the fruit of the womb is a gift.
5 Like arrows in the hand of a warrior
    are the children of one's youth.

READING

EITHER   2 Corinthians 1.3–7

3 Blessed be the God and Father of our Lord Jesus Christ, the Father of mercies and the God of all consolation, 4 who consoles us in all our affliction, so that we may be able to console those who are in any affliction with the consolation with which we ourselves are consoled by God. 5 For just as the sufferings of Christ are abundant for us, so also our consolation is abundant through Christ. 6 If we are being afflicted, it is for your consolation and salvation; if we are being consoled, it is for your consolation, which you experience when you patiently endure the same sufferings that we are also suffering. 7 Our hope for you is unshaken; for we know that as you share in our sufferings, so also you share in our consolation.

OR   **Colossians 3.12–17**

[12] As God's chosen ones, holy and beloved, clothe yourselves with compassion, kindness, humility, meekness, and patience. [13] Bear with one another and, if anyone has a complaint against another, forgive each other; just as the Lord has forgiven you, so you also must forgive. [14] Above all, clothe yourselves with love, which binds everything together in perfect harmony. [15] And let the peace of Christ rule in your hearts, to which indeed you were called in the one body. And be thankful. [16] Let the word of Christ dwell in you richly; teach and admonish one another in all wisdom; and with gratitude in your hearts sing psalms, hymns, and spiritual songs to God. [17] And whatever you do, in word or deed, do everything in the name of the Lord Jesus, giving thanks to God the Father through him.

GOSPEL

EITHER   **Luke 2.33–35**

[33] And the child's father and mother were amazed at what was being said about him. [34] Then Simeon blessed them and said to his mother Mary, 'This child is destined for the falling and the rising of many in Israel, and to be a sign that will be opposed [35] so that the inner thoughts of many will be revealed—and a sword will pierce your own soul too.'

OR   **John 19.25b–27**

[25] Meanwhile, standing near the cross of Jesus were his mother, and his mother's sister, Mary the wife of Clopas, and Mary Magdalene. [26] When Jesus saw his mother and the disciple whom he loved standing beside her, he said to his mother, 'Woman, here is your son.' [27] Then he said to the disciple, 'Here is your mother.' And from that hour the disciple took her into his own home.

POST COMMUNION

Loving God,
as a mother feeds her children at the breast
you feed us in this sacrament
   with the food and drink of eternal life:
help us who have tasted your goodness
to grow in grace within the household of faith;
through Jesus Christ our Lord.

THE FIFTH SUNDAY OF LENT
PASSIONTIDE BEGINS

COLLECT

Most merciful God,
who by the death and resurrection of your Son Jesus Christ
delivered and saved the world:
grant that by faith in him who suffered on the cross
we may triumph in the power of his victory;
through Jesus Christ your Son our Lord,
who is alive and reigns with you,
in the unity of the Holy Spirit,
one God, now and for ever.

READING   Jeremiah 31.31–34

³¹ The days are surely coming, says the LORD, when I will make a new
covenant with the house of Israel and the house of Judah. ³² It will not be
like the covenant that I made with their ancestors when I took them by the
hand to bring them out of the land of Egypt—a covenant that they broke,
though I was their husband, says the LORD. ³³ But this is the covenant that
I will make with the house of Israel after those days, says the LORD: I will
put my law within them, and I will write it on their hearts; and I will be
their God, and they shall be my people. ³⁴ No longer shall they teach one
another, or say to each other, 'Know the LORD', for they shall all know me,
from the least of them to the greatest, says the LORD; for I will forgive their
iniquity, and remember their sin no more.

PSALM

EITHER   Psalm 51.1–13

1   Have mercy on me, O God, according to your loving-kindness;
    in your great compassion blot out my offences.
2   Wash me through and through from my wickedness
    and cleanse me from my sin.
3   For I know my transgressions,
    and my sin is ever before me.
4   Against you only have I sinned
    and done what is evil in your sight.

5   And so you are justified when you speak
    and upright in your judgement.
6   Indeed, I have been wicked from my birth,
    a sinner from my mother's womb.
7   For behold, you look for truth deep within me,
    and will make me understand wisdom secretly.
8   Purge me from my sin and I shall be pure;
    wash me and I shall be clean indeed.
9   Make me hear of joy and gladness,
    that the body you have broken may rejoice.
10 Hide your face from my sins
    and blot out all my iniquities.
11 Create in me a clean heart, O God,
    and renew a right spirit within me.
12 Cast me not away from your presence
    and take not your holy Spirit from me.
13 Give me the joy of your saving help again
    and sustain me with your bountiful Spirit.

OR   **Psalm 119.9–16**

9   How shall the young cleanse their way?
    By keeping to your words.
10 With my whole heart I seek you;
    let me not stray from your commandments.
11 I treasure your promise in my heart,
    that I may not sin against you.
12 Blessèd are you, O Lord;
    instruct me in your statutes.
13 With my lips will I recite
    all the judgements of your mouth.
14 I have taken greater delight in the way of your decrees
    than in all manner of riches.
15 I will meditate on your commandments
    and give attention to your ways.
16 My delight is in your statutes;
    I will not forget your word.

READING   Hebrews 5.5–10

⁵ So also Christ did not glorify himself in becoming a high priest, but was appointed by the one who said to him,
'You are my Son,
    today I have begotten you';
⁶ as he says also in another place,
'You are a priest for ever,
    according to the order of Melchizedek.'

⁷ In the days of his flesh, Jesus offered up prayers and supplications, with loud cries and tears, to the one who was able to save him from death, and he was heard because of his reverent submission. ⁸ Although he was a Son, he learned obedience through what he suffered; ⁹ and having been made perfect, he became the source of eternal salvation for all who obey him, ¹⁰ having been designated by God a high priest according to the order of Melchizedek.

GOSPEL   John 12.20–33

²⁰ Now among those who went up to worship at the festival were some Greeks. ²¹ They came to Philip, who was from Bethsaida in Galilee, and said to him, 'Sir, we wish to see Jesus.' ²² Philip went and told Andrew; then Andrew and Philip went and told Jesus. ²³ Jesus answered them, 'The hour has come for the Son of Man to be glorified. ²⁴ Very truly, I tell you, unless a grain of wheat falls into the earth and dies, it remains just a single grain; but if it dies, it bears much fruit. ²⁵ Those who love their life lose it, and those who hate their life in this world will keep it for eternal life. ²⁶ Whoever serves me must follow me, and where I am, there will my servant be also. Whoever serves me, the Father will honour.

²⁷ 'Now my soul is troubled. And what should I say—"Father, save me from this hour"? No, it is for this reason that I have come to this hour. ²⁸ Father, glorify your name.' Then a voice came from heaven, 'I have glorified it, and I will glorify it again.' ²⁹ The crowd standing there heard it and said that it was thunder. Others said, 'An angel has spoken to him.' ³⁰ Jesus answered, 'This voice has come for your sake, not for mine. ³¹ Now is the judgement of this world; now the ruler of this world will be driven out. ³² And I, when I am lifted up from the earth, will draw all people to myself.' ³³ He said this to indicate the kind of death he was to die.

POST COMMUNION

Lord Jesus Christ,
you have taught us
that what we do for the least of our brothers and sisters
we do also for you:
give us the will to be the servant of others
as you were the servant of all,
and gave up your life and died for us,
but are alive and reign, now and for ever.

SECOND SERVICE	THIRD SERVICE
Psalm 34.1–10, [11–22]	Psalm 107.1–22
Exodus 7.8–24	Exodus 24.3–8
Romans 5.12–21	Hebrews 12.18–29

If the Second Service is a Eucharist, the following is read as a Gospel:

Luke 22.1–13

PALM SUNDAY

LITURGY OF THE PALMS

GOSPEL

EITHER   **Mark 11.1–11**

¹ When they were approaching Jerusalem, at Bethphage and Bethany, near the Mount of Olives, he sent two of his disciples ² and said to them, 'Go into the village ahead of you, and immediately as you enter it, you will find tied there a colt that has never been ridden; untie it and bring it. ³ If anyone says to you, "Why are you doing this?" just say this, "The Lord needs it and will send it back here immediately." ' ⁴ They went away and found a colt tied near a door, outside in the street. As they were untying it, ⁵ some of the bystanders said to them, 'What are you doing, untying the colt?' ⁶ They told them what Jesus had said; and they allowed them to take it. ⁷ Then they brought the colt to Jesus and threw their cloaks on it; and he sat on it. ⁸ Many people spread their cloaks on the road, and others spread

leafy branches that they had cut in the fields. ⁹ Then those who went ahead and those who followed were shouting,

'Hosanna!
Blessed is the one who comes in the name of the Lord!
¹⁰   Blessed is the coming kingdom of our ancestor David!
Hosanna in the highest heaven!'

¹¹ Then he entered Jerusalem and went into the temple; and when he had looked around at everything, as it was already late, he went out to Bethany with the twelve.

OR   John 12.12–16

¹² The next day the great crowd that had come to the festival heard that Jesus was coming to Jerusalem. ¹³ So they took branches of palm trees and went out to meet him, shouting,

'Hosanna!
Blessed is the one who comes in the name of the Lord—
the King of Israel!'
¹⁴ Jesus found a young donkey and sat on it; as it is written:
¹⁵   'Do not be afraid, daughter of Zion.
Look, your king is coming,
sitting on a donkey's colt!'
¹⁶ His disciples did not understand these things at first; but when Jesus was glorified, then they remembered that these things had been written of him and had been done to him.

PSALM   Psalm 118.[1–2,] 19–24

[¹   Give thanks to the Lord, for he is good;
his mercy endures for ever.
²   Let Israel now proclaim,
'His mercy endures for ever.']

¹⁹   Open for me the gates of righteousness;
I will enter them; I will offer thanks to the Lord.
²⁰   'This is the gate of the Lord;
he who is righteous may enter.'
²¹   I will give thanks to you, for you answered me
and have become my salvation.
²²   The same stone which the builders rejected
has become the chief corner-stone.
²³   This is the Lord's doing,
and it is marvellous in our eyes.

24 On this day the Lord has acted;
    we will rejoice and be glad in it.

LITURGY OF THE PASSION

COLLECT

Almighty and everlasting God,
who in your tender love towards the human race
    sent your Son our Saviour Jesus Christ
to take upon him our flesh
and to suffer death upon the cross:
grant that we may follow the example
    of his patience and humility,
and also be made partakers of his resurrection;
through Jesus Christ your Son our Lord,
who is alive and reigns with you,
in the unity of the Holy Spirit,
one God, now and for ever.

READING   Isaiah 50.4–9a

4 The Lord GOD has given me
       the tongue of a teacher,
   that I may know how to sustain
       the weary with a word.
   Morning by morning he wakens—
       wakens my ear
       to listen as those who are taught.
5 The Lord GOD has opened my ear,
       and I was not rebellious,
       I did not turn backwards.
6 I gave my back to those who struck me,
       and my cheeks to those who pulled out the beard;
   I did not hide my face
       from insult and spitting.
7 The Lord GOD helps me;
       therefore I have not been disgraced;
   therefore I have set my face like flint,
       and I know that I shall not be put to shame;

8   he who vindicates me is near.
      Who will contend with me?
          Let us stand up together.
      Who are my adversaries?
          Let them confront me.
9   It is the Lord GOD who helps me;
      who will declare me guilty?

PSALM   Psalm 31.9-16, [17-18]

9   Have mercy on me, O Lord, for I am in trouble;
      my eye is consumed with sorrow, and also my throat and my belly.
10 For my life is wasted with grief, and my years with sighing;
      my strength fails me because of affliction, and my bones are
          consumed.
11 I have become a reproach to all my enemies and even to my
          neighbours, a dismay to those of my acquaintance;
      when they see me in the street they avoid me.
12 I am forgotten like the dead, out of mind;
      I am as useless as a broken pot.
13 For I have heard the whispering of the crowd; fear is all around;
      they put their heads together against me; they plot to take my life.
14 But as for me, I have trusted in you, O Lord.
      I have said, 'You are my God.
15 My times are in your hand;
      rescue me from the hand of my enemies, and from those who
          persecute me.
16 Make your face to shine upon your servant,
      and in your loving-kindness save me.'
[17 Lord, let me not be ashamed for having called upon you;
      rather, let the wicked be put to shame; let them be silent in the
          grave.
18 Let the lying lips be silenced which speak against the righteous,
      haughtily, disdainfully and with contempt.]

READING   Philippians 2.5-11

5 Let the same mind be in you that was in Christ Jesus,
  6   who, though he was in the form of God,
          did not regard equality with God
          as something to be exploited,

7   but emptied himself,
taking the form of a slave,
being born in human likeness.
And being found in human form,
8   he humbled himself
and became obedient to the point of death—
even death on a cross.
9   Therefore God also highly exalted him
and gave him the name
that is above every name,
10   so that at the name of Jesus
every knee should bend,
in heaven and on earth and under the earth,
11   and every tongue should confess
that Jesus Christ is Lord,
to the glory of God the Father.

GOSPEL

EITHER   **Mark 14.1–15.47**

¹ It was two days before the Passover and the festival of Unleavened Bread. The chief priests and the scribes were looking for a way to arrest Jesus by stealth and kill him; ² for they said, 'Not during the festival, or there may be a riot among the people.'

³ While he was at Bethany in the house of Simon the leper, as he sat at the table, a woman came with an alabaster jar of very costly ointment of nard, and she broke open the jar and poured the ointment on his head. ⁴ But some were there who said to one another in anger, 'Why was the ointment wasted in this way? ⁵ For this ointment could have been sold for more than three hundred denarii, and the money given to the poor.' And they scolded her. ⁶ But Jesus said, 'Let her alone; why do you trouble her? She has performed a good service for me. ⁷ For you always have the poor with you, and you can show kindness to them whenever you wish; but you will not always have me. ⁸ She has done what she could; she has anointed my body beforehand for its burial. ⁹ Truly I tell you, wherever the good news is proclaimed in the whole world, what she has done will be told in remembrance of her.'

¹⁰ Then Judas Iscariot, who was one of the twelve, went to the chief priests in order to betray him to them. ¹¹ When they heard it, they were greatly pleased, and promised to give him money. So he began to look for an opportunity to betray him.

¹² On the first day of Unleavened Bread, when the Passover lamb is sacrificed, his disciples said to him, 'Where do you want us to go and make the preparations for you to eat the Passover?' ¹³ So he sent two of his disciples, saying to them, 'Go into the city, and a man carrying a jar of water will meet you; follow him, ¹⁴ and wherever he enters, say to the owner of the house, "The Teacher asks, Where is my guest room where I may eat the Passover with my disciples?" ¹⁵ He will show you a large room upstairs, furnished and ready. Make preparations for us there.' ¹⁶ So the disciples set out and went to the city, and found everything as he had told them; and they prepared the Passover meal.

¹⁷ When it was evening, he came with the twelve. ¹⁸ And when they had taken their places and were eating, Jesus said, 'Truly I tell you, one of you will betray me, one who is eating with me.' ¹⁹ They began to be distressed and to say to him one after another, 'Surely, not I?' ²⁰ He said to them, 'It is one of the twelve, one who is dipping bread into the bowl with me. ²¹ For the Son of Man goes as it is written of him, but woe to that one by whom the Son of Man is betrayed! It would have been better for that one not to have been born.'

²² While they were eating, he took a loaf of bread, and after blessing it he broke it, gave it to them, and said, 'Take; this is my body.' ²³ Then he took a cup, and after giving thanks he gave it to them, and all of them drank from it. ²⁴ He said to them, 'This is my blood of the covenant, which is poured out for many. ²⁵ Truly I tell you, I will never again drink of the fruit of the vine until that day when I drink it new in the kingdom of God.'

²⁶ When they had sung the hymn, they went out to the Mount of Olives. ²⁷ And Jesus said to them, 'You will all become deserters; for it is written,

"I will strike the shepherd,
    and the sheep will be scattered."

²⁸ But after I am raised up, I will go before you to Galilee.' ²⁹ Peter said to him, 'Even though all become deserters, I will not.' ³⁰ Jesus said to him, 'Truly I tell you, this day, this very night, before the cock crows twice, you will deny me three times.' ³¹ But he said vehemently, 'Even though I must die with you, I will not deny you.' And all of them said the same.

³² They went to a place called Gethsemane; and he said to his disciples, 'Sit here while I pray.' ³³ He took with him Peter and James and John, and began to be distressed and agitated. ³⁴ And he said to them, 'I am deeply grieved, even to death; remain here, and keep awake.' ³⁵ And going a little farther, he threw himself on the ground and prayed that, if it were possible, the hour might pass from him. ³⁶ He said, 'Abba, Father, for you all things are possible; remove this cup from me; yet, not what I want, but what you want.' ³⁷ He came and found them sleeping; and he said to Peter, 'Simon, are you asleep? Could you not keep awake one hour? ³⁸ Keep awake and

pray that you may not come into the time of trial; the spirit indeed is willing, but the flesh is weak.' 39 And again he went away and prayed, saying the same words. 40 And once more he came and found them sleeping, for their eyes were very heavy; and they did not know what to say to him. 41 He came a third time and said to them, 'Are you still sleeping and taking your rest? Enough! The hour has come; the Son of Man is betrayed into the hands of sinners. 42 Get up, let us be going. See, my betrayer is at hand.'

43 Immediately, while he was still speaking, Judas, one of the twelve, arrived; and with him there was a crowd with swords and clubs, from the chief priests, the scribes, and the elders. 44 Now the betrayer had given them a sign, saying, 'The one I will kiss is the man; arrest him and lead him away under guard.' 45 So when he came, he went up to him at once and said, 'Rabbi!' and kissed him. 46 Then they laid hands on him and arrested him. 47 But one of those who stood near drew his sword and struck the slave of the high priest, cutting off his ear. 48 Then Jesus said to them, 'Have you come out with swords and clubs to arrest me as though I were a bandit? 49 Day after day I was with you in the temple teaching, and you did not arrest me. But let the scriptures be fulfilled.' 50 All of them deserted him and fled.

51 A certain young man was following him, wearing nothing but a linen cloth. They caught hold of him, 52 but he left the linen cloth and ran off naked.

53 They took Jesus to the high priest; and all the chief priests, the elders, and the scribes were assembled. 54 Peter had followed him at a distance, right into the courtyard of the high priest; and he was sitting with the guards, warming himself at the fire. 55 Now the chief priests and the whole council were looking for testimony against Jesus to put him to death; but they found none. 56 For many gave false testimony against him, and their testimony did not agree. 57 Some stood up and gave false testimony against him, saying, 58 'We heard him say, "I will destroy this temple that is made with hands, and in three days I will build another, not made with hands."' 59 But even on this point their testimony did not agree. 60 Then the high priest stood up before them and asked Jesus, 'Have you no answer? What is it that they testify against you?' 61 But he was silent and did not answer. Again the high priest asked him, 'Are you the Messiah, the Son of the Blessed One?' 62 Jesus said, 'I am; and

 "you will see the Son of Man

 seated at the right hand of the Power",

 and "coming with the clouds of heaven."'

63 Then the high priest tore his clothes and said, 'Why do we still need witnesses? 64 You have heard his blasphemy! What is your decision?' All of them condemned him as deserving death. 65 Some began to spit on him, to

blindfold him, and to strike him, saying to him, 'Prophesy!' The guards also took him over and beat him.

⁶⁶ While Peter was below in the courtyard, one of the servant-girls of the high priest came by. ⁶⁷ When she saw Peter warming himself, she stared at him and said, 'You also were with Jesus, the man from Nazareth.' ⁶⁸ But he denied it, saying, 'I do not know or understand what you are talking about.' And he went out into the forecourt. Then the cock crowed. ⁶⁹ And the servant-girl, on seeing him, began again to say to the bystanders, 'This man is one of them.' ⁷⁰ But again he denied it. Then after a little while the bystanders again said to Peter, 'Certainly you are one of them; for you are a Galilean.' ⁷¹ But he began to curse, and he swore an oath, 'I do not know this man you are talking about.' ⁷² At that moment the cock crowed for the second time. Then Peter remembered that Jesus had said to him, 'Before the cock crows twice, you will deny me three times.' And he broke down and wept.

¹ As soon as it was morning, the chief priests held a consultation with the elders and scribes and the whole council. They bound Jesus, led him away, and handed him over to Pilate. ² Pilate asked him, 'Are you the King of the Jews?' He answered him, 'You say so.' ³ Then the chief priests accused him of many things. ⁴ Pilate asked him again, 'Have you no answer? See how many charges they bring against you.' ⁵ But Jesus made no further reply, so that Pilate was amazed.

⁶ Now at the festival he used to release a prisoner for them, anyone for whom they asked. ⁷ Now a man called Barabbas was in prison with the rebels who had committed murder during the insurrection. ⁸ So the crowd came and began to ask Pilate to do for them according to his custom. ⁹ Then he answered them, 'Do you want me to release for you the King of the Jews?' ¹⁰ For he realized that it was out of jealousy that the chief priests had handed him over. ¹¹ But the chief priests stirred up the crowd to have him release Barabbas for them instead. ¹² Pilate spoke to them again, 'Then what do you wish me to do with the man you call the King of the Jews?' ¹³ They shouted back, 'Crucify him!' ¹⁴ Pilate asked them, 'Why, what evil has he done?' But they shouted all the more, 'Crucify him!' ¹⁵ So Pilate, wishing to satisfy the crowd, released Barabbas for them; and after flogging Jesus, he handed him over to be crucified.

¹⁶ Then the soldiers led him into the courtyard of the palace (that is, the governor's headquarters); and they called together the whole cohort. ¹⁷ And they clothed him in a purple cloak; and after twisting some thorns into a crown, they put it on him. ¹⁸ And they began saluting him, 'Hail, King of the Jews!' ¹⁹ They struck his head with a reed, spat upon him, and knelt down in homage to him. ²⁰ After mocking him, they stripped him of the

purple cloak and put his own clothes on him. Then they led him out to crucify him.

²¹ They compelled a passer-by, who was coming in from the country, to carry his cross; it was Simon of Cyrene, the father of Alexander and Rufus. ²² Then they brought Jesus to the place called Golgotha (which means the place of a skull). ²³ And they offered him wine mixed with myrrh; but he did not take it. ²⁴ And they crucified him, and divided his clothes among them, casting lots to decide what each should take.

²⁵ It was nine o'clock in the morning when they crucified him. ²⁶ The inscription of the charge against him read, 'The King of the Jews.' ²⁷ And with him they crucified two bandits, one on his right and one on his left. ²⁹ Those who passed by derided him, shaking their heads and saying, 'Aha! You who would destroy the temple and build it in three days, ³⁰ save yourself, and come down from the cross!' ³¹ In the same way the chief priests, along with the scribes, were also mocking him among themselves and saying, 'He saved others; he cannot save himself. ³² Let the Messiah, the King of Israel, come down from the cross now, so that we may see and believe.' Those who were crucified with him also taunted him.

³³ When it was noon, darkness came over the whole land until three in the afternoon. ³⁴ At three o'clock Jesus cried out with a loud voice, 'Eloi, Eloi, lema sabachthani?' which means, 'My God, my God, why have you forsaken me?' ³⁵ When some of the bystanders heard it, they said, 'Listen, he is calling for Elijah.' ³⁶ And someone ran, filled a sponge with sour wine, put it on a stick, and gave it to him to drink, saying, 'Wait, let us see whether Elijah will come to take him down.' ³⁷ Then Jesus gave a loud cry and breathed his last. ³⁸ And the curtain of the temple was torn in two, from top to bottom. ³⁹ Now when the centurion, who stood facing him, saw that in this way he breathed his last, he said, 'Truly this man was God's Son!'

⁴⁰ There were also women looking on from a distance; among them were Mary Magdalene, and Mary the mother of James the younger and of Joses, and Salome. ⁴¹ These used to follow him and provided for him when he was in Galilee; and there were many other women who had come up with him to Jerusalem.

⁴² When evening had come, and since it was the day of Preparation, that is, the day before the sabbath, ⁴³ Joseph of Arimathea, a respected member of the council, who was also himself waiting expectantly for the kingdom of God, went boldly to Pilate and asked for the body of Jesus. ⁴⁴ Then Pilate wondered if he were already dead; and summoning the centurion, he asked him whether he had been dead for some time. ⁴⁵ When he learned from the centurion that he was dead, he granted the body to Joseph. ⁴⁶ Then

Joseph bought a linen cloth, and taking down the body, wrapped it in the linen cloth, and laid it in a tomb that had been hewn out of the rock. He then rolled a stone against the door of the tomb. [47] Mary Magdalene and Mary the mother of Joses saw where the body was laid.

OR   **Mark 15.1–39, [40–47]**

[1] As soon as it was morning, the chief priests held a consultation with the elders and scribes and the whole council. They bound Jesus, led him away, and handed him over to Pilate. [2] Pilate asked him, 'Are you the King of the Jews?' He answered him, 'You say so.' [3] Then the chief priests accused him of many things. [4] Pilate asked him again, 'Have you no answer? See how many charges they bring against you.' [5] But Jesus made no further reply, so that Pilate was amazed.

[6] Now at the festival he used to release a prisoner for them, anyone for whom they asked. [7] Now a man called Barabbas was in prison with the rebels who had committed murder during the insurrection. [8] So the crowd came and began to ask Pilate to do for them according to his custom. [9] Then he answered them, 'Do you want me to release for you the King of the Jews?' [10] For he realized that it was out of jealousy that the chief priests had handed him over. [11] But the chief priests stirred up the crowd to have him release Barabbas for them instead. [12] Pilate spoke to them again, 'Then what do you wish me to do with the man you call the King of the Jews?' [13] They shouted back, 'Crucify him!' [14] Pilate asked them, 'Why, what evil has he done?' But they shouted all the more, 'Crucify him!' [15] So Pilate, wishing to satisfy the crowd, released Barabbas for them; and after flogging Jesus, he handed him over to be crucified.

[16] Then the soldiers led him into the courtyard of the palace (that is, the governor's headquarters); and they called together the whole cohort. [17] And they clothed him in a purple cloak; and after twisting some thorns into a crown, they put it on him. [18] And they began saluting him, 'Hail, King of the Jews!' [19] They struck his head with a reed, spat upon him, and knelt down in homage to him. [20] After mocking him, they stripped him of the purple cloak and put his own clothes on him. Then they led him out to crucify him.

[21] They compelled a passer-by, who was coming in from the country, to carry his cross; it was Simon of Cyrene, the father of Alexander and Rufus. [22] Then they brought Jesus to the place called Golgotha (which means the place of a skull). [23] And they offered him wine mixed with myrrh; but he did not take it. [24] And they crucified him, and divided his clothes among them, casting lots to decide what each should take.

²⁵ It was nine o'clock in the morning when they crucified him. ²⁶ The inscription of the charge against him read, 'The King of the Jews.' ²⁷ And with him they crucified two bandits, one on his right and one on his left. ²⁹ Those who passed by derided him, shaking their heads and saying, 'Aha! You who would destroy the temple and build it in three days, ³⁰ save yourself, and come down from the cross!' ³¹ In the same way the chief priests, along with the scribes, were also mocking him among themselves and saying, 'He saved others; he cannot save himself. ³² Let the Messiah, the King of Israel, come down from the cross now, so that we may see and believe.' Those who were crucified with him also taunted him.

³³ When it was noon, darkness came over the whole land until three in the afternoon. ³⁴ At three o'clock Jesus cried out with a loud voice, 'Eloi, Eloi, lema sabachthani?' which means, 'My God, my God, why have you forsaken me?' ³⁵ When some of the bystanders heard it, they said, 'Listen, he is calling for Elijah.' ³⁶ And someone ran, filled a sponge with sour wine, put it on a stick, and gave it to him to drink, saying, 'Wait, let us see whether Elijah will come to take him down.' ³⁷ Then Jesus gave a loud cry and breathed his last. ³⁸ And the curtain of the temple was torn in two, from top to bottom. ³⁹ Now when the centurion, who stood facing him, saw that in this way he breathed his last, he said, 'Truly this man was God's Son!'

[⁴⁰ There were also women looking on from a distance; among them were Mary Magdalene, and Mary the mother of James the younger and of Joses, and Salome. ⁴¹ These used to follow him and provided for him when he was in Galilee; and there were many other women who had come up with him to Jerusalem.

⁴² When evening had come, and since it was the day of Preparation, that is, the day before the sabbath, ⁴³ Joseph of Arimathea, a respected member of the council, who was also himself waiting expectantly for the kingdom of God, went boldly to Pilate and asked for the body of Jesus. ⁴⁴ Then Pilate wondered if he were already dead; and summoning the centurion, he asked him whether he had been dead for some time. ⁴⁵ When he learned from the centurion that he was dead, he granted the body to Joseph. ⁴⁶ Then Joseph bought a linen cloth, and taking down the body, wrapped it in the linen cloth, and laid it in a tomb that had been hewn out of the rock. He then rolled a stone against the door of the tomb. ⁴⁷ Mary Magdalene and Mary the mother of Joses saw where the body was laid.]

POST COMMUNION

Lord Jesus Christ,
you humbled yourself in taking the form of a servant,
and in obedience died on the cross for our salvation:
give us the mind to follow you
and to proclaim you as Lord and King,
to the glory of God the Father.

Psalm 69.1–20
Isaiah 5.1–7
Mark 12.1–12

THIRD SERVICE

Psalms 61; 62
Zechariah 9.9–12
1 Corinthians 2.1–12

MONDAY OF HOLY WEEK

COLLECT

Almighty and everlasting God,
who in your tender love towards the human race
    sent your Son our Saviour Jesus Christ
to take upon him our flesh
and to suffer death upon the cross:
grant that we may follow the example
    of his patience and humility,
and also be made partakers of his resurrection;
through Jesus Christ your Son our Lord,
who is alive and reigns with you,
in the unity of the Holy Spirit,
one God, now and for ever.

READING   Isaiah 42.1–9

1 Here is my servant, whom I uphold,
      my chosen, in whom my soul delights;
   I have put my spirit upon him;
      he will bring forth justice to the nations.
2 He will not cry or lift up his voice,
      or make it heard in the street;

3   a bruised reed he will not break,
     and a dimly burning wick he will not quench;
     he will faithfully bring forth justice.
4   He will not grow faint or be crushed
     until he has established justice in the earth;
     and the coastlands wait for his teaching.
5   Thus says God, the LORD,
     who created the heavens and stretched them out,
     who spread out the earth and what comes from it,
   who gives breath to the people upon it
     and spirit to those who walk in it:
6   I am the LORD, I have called you in righteousness,
     I have taken you by the hand and kept you;
   I have given you as a covenant to the people,
     a light to the nations,
7   to open the eyes that are blind,
   to bring out the prisoners from the dungeon,
     from the prison those who sit in darkness.
8   I am the LORD, that is my name;
     my glory I give to no other,
     nor my praise to idols.
9   See, the former things have come to pass,
     and new things I now declare;
   before they spring forth,
     I tell you of them.

PSALM   Psalm 36.5–11

5   Your love, O Lord, reaches to the heavens,
     and your faithfulness to the clouds.
6   Your righteousness is like the strong mountains, your justice like
     the great deep;
   you save both human and beast, O Lord.
7   How priceless is your love, O God!
   your people take refuge under the shadow of your wings.
8   They feast upon the abundance of your house;
   you give them drink from the river of your delights.
9   For with you is the well of life,
     and in your light we see light.
10   Continue your loving-kindness to those who know you,
     and your favour to those who are true of heart.
11   Let not the foot of the proud come near me,
     nor the hand of the wicked push me aside.

READING   Hebrews 9.11–15

[11] But when Christ came as a high priest of the good things that have come, then through the greater and perfect tent (not made with hands, that is, not of this creation), [12] he entered once for all into the Holy Place, not with the blood of goats and calves, but with his own blood, thus obtaining eternal redemption. [13] For if the blood of goats and bulls, with the sprinkling of the ashes of a heifer, sanctifies those who have been defiled so that their flesh is purified, [14] how much more will the blood of Christ, who through the eternal Spirit offered himself without blemish to God, purify our conscience from dead works to worship the living God!

[15] For this reason he is the mediator of a new covenant, so that those who are called may receive the promised eternal inheritance, because a death has occurred that redeems them from the transgressions under the first covenant.

GOSPEL   John 12.1–11

[1] Six days before the Passover Jesus came to Bethany, the home of Lazarus, whom he had raised from the dead. [2] There they gave a dinner for him. Martha served, and Lazarus was one of those at the table with him. [3] Mary took a pound of costly perfume made of pure nard, anointed Jesus' feet, and wiped them with her hair. The house was filled with the fragrance of the perfume. [4] But Judas Iscariot, one of his disciples (the one who was about to betray him), said, [5] 'Why was this perfume not sold for three hundred denarii and the money given to the poor?' [6] (He said this not because he cared about the poor, but because he was a thief; he kept the common purse and used to steal what was put into it.) [7] Jesus said, 'Leave her alone. She bought it so that she might keep it for the day of my burial. [8] You always have the poor with you, but you do not always have me.'

[9] When the great crowd of the Jews learned that he was there, they came not only because of Jesus but also to see Lazarus, whom he had raised from the dead. [10] So the chief priests planned to put Lazarus to death as well, [11] since it was on account of him that many of the Jews were deserting and were believing in Jesus.

POST COMMUNION

Lord Jesus Christ,
you humbled yourself in taking the form of a servant,
and in obedience died on the cross for our salvation:

give us the mind to follow you
and to proclaim you as Lord and King,
to the glory of God the Father.

SECOND SERVICE

Psalm 41
Lamentations 1.1–12a
Luke 22.1–23

THIRD SERVICE

Psalm 25
Lamentations 2.8–19
Colossians 1.18–23

TUESDAY OF HOLY WEEK

COLLECT

Almighty and everlasting God,
who in your tender love towards the human race
    sent your Son our Saviour Jesus Christ
to take upon him our flesh
and to suffer death upon the cross:
grant that we may follow the example
    of his patience and humility,
and also be made partakers of his resurrection;
through Jesus Christ your Son our Lord,
who is alive and reigns with you,
in the unity of the Holy Spirit,
one God, now and for ever.

READING   Isaiah 49.1–7

¹ Listen to me, O coastlands,
      pay attention, you peoples from far away!
   The LORD called me before I was born,
      while I was in my mother's womb he named me.
² He made my mouth like a sharp sword,
      in the shadow of his hand he hid me;
   he made me a polished arrow,
      in his quiver he hid me away.
³ And he said to me, 'You are my servant,
      Israel, in whom I will be glorified.'

4 But I said, 'I have laboured in vain,
     I have spent my strength for nothing and vanity;
    yet surely my cause is with the LORD,
     and my reward with my God.'

5 And now the LORD says,
     who formed me in the womb to be his servant,
    to bring Jacob back to him,
     and that Israel might be gathered to him,
    for I am honoured in the sight of the LORD,
     and my God has become my strength—

6 he says,
    'It is too light a thing that you should be my servant
     to raise up the tribes of Jacob
     and to restore the survivors of Israel;
    I will give you as a light to the nations,
     that my salvation may reach to the end of the earth.'

7 Thus says the LORD,
     the Redeemer of Israel and his Holy One,
    to one deeply despised, abhorred by the nations,
     the slave of rulers,
    'Kings shall see and stand up,
     princes, and they shall prostrate themselves,
    because of the LORD, who is faithful,
     the Holy One of Israel, who has chosen you.'

PSALM   Psalm 71.1–8, [9–14]

1 In you, O Lord, have I taken refuge;
    let me never be ashamed.

2 In your righteousness, deliver me and set me free;
    incline your ear to me and save me.

3 Be my strong rock, a castle to keep me safe;
    you are my crag and my stronghold.

4 Deliver me, my God, from the hand of the wicked,
    from the clutches of the evildoer and the oppressor.

5 For you are my hope, O Lord God,
    my confidence since I was young.

6 I have been sustained by you ever since I was born; from my
    mother's womb you have been my strength;
    my praise shall be always of you.

7 I have become a portent to many;
    but you are my refuge and my strength.

8   Let my mouth be full of your praise
    and your glory all the day long.
[9 Do not cast me off in my old age;
    forsake me not when my strength fails.
10 For my enemies are talking against me,
    and those who lie in wait for my life take counsel together.
11 They say, 'God has forsaken him; go after him and seize him;
    because there is none who will save.'
12 O God, be not far from me;
    come quickly to help me, O my God.
13 Let those who set themselves against me be put to shame and be
        disgraced;
    let those who seek to do me evil be covered with scorn and
        reproach.
14 But I shall always wait in patience,
    and shall praise you more and more.]

READING   1 Corinthians 1.18–31

18 For the message about the cross is foolishness to those who are perishing, but to us who are being saved it is the power of God. 19 For it is written,
    'I will destroy the wisdom of the wise,
        and the discernment of the discerning I will thwart.'
20 Where is the one who is wise? Where is the scribe? Where is the debater of this age? Has not God made foolish the wisdom of the world? 21 For since, in the wisdom of God, the world did not know God through wisdom, God decided, through the foolishness of our proclamation, to save those who believe. 22 For Jews demand signs and Greeks desire wisdom, 23 but we proclaim Christ crucified, a stumbling-block to Jews and foolishness to Gentiles, 24 but to those who are the called, both Jews and Greeks, Christ the power of God and the wisdom of God. 25 For God's foolishness is wiser than human wisdom, and God's weakness is stronger than human strength.

26 Consider your own call, brothers and sisters: not many of you were wise by human standards, not many were powerful, not many were of noble birth. 27 But God chose what is foolish in the world to shame the wise; God chose what is weak in the world to shame the strong; 28 God chose what is low and despised in the world, things that are not, to reduce to nothing things that are, 29 so that no one might boast in the presence of God. 30 He is the source of your life in Christ Jesus, who became for us wisdom from God, and righteousness and sanctification and redemption, 31 in order that, as it is written, 'Let the one who boasts, boast in the Lord.'

GOSPEL   John 12.20–36

²⁰ Now among those who went up to worship at the festival were some Greeks. ²¹ They came to Philip, who was from Bethsaida in Galilee, and said to him, 'Sir, we wish to see Jesus.' ²² Philip went and told Andrew; then Andrew and Philip went and told Jesus. ²³ Jesus answered them, 'The hour has come for the Son of Man to be glorified. ²⁴ Very truly, I tell you, unless a grain of wheat falls into the earth and dies, it remains just a single grain; but if it dies, it bears much fruit. ²⁵ Those who love their life lose it, and those who hate their life in this world will keep it for eternal life. ²⁶ Whoever serves me must follow me, and where I am, there will my servant be also. Whoever serves me, the Father will honour.

²⁷ 'Now my soul is troubled. And what should I say—"Father, save me from this hour"? No, it is for this reason that I have come to this hour. ²⁸ Father, glorify your name.' Then a voice came from heaven, 'I have glorified it, and I will glorify it again.' ²⁹ The crowd standing there heard it and said that it was thunder. Others said, 'An angel has spoken to him.' ³⁰ Jesus answered, 'This voice has come for your sake, not for mine. ³¹ Now is the judgement of this world; now the ruler of this world will be driven out. ³² And I, when I am lifted up from the earth, will draw all people to myself.' ³³ He said this to indicate the kind of death he was to die. ³⁴ The crowd answered him, 'We have heard from the law that the Messiah remains for ever. How can you say that the Son of Man must be lifted up? Who is this Son of Man?' ³⁵ Jesus said to them, 'The light is with you for a little longer. Walk while you have the light, so that the darkness may not overtake you. If you walk in the darkness, you do not know where you are going. ³⁶ While you have the light, believe in the light, so that you may become children of light.'

After Jesus had said this, he departed and hid from them.

POST COMMUNION

Lord Jesus Christ,
you humbled yourself in taking the form of a servant,
and in obedience died on the cross for our salvation:
give us the mind to follow you
and to proclaim you as Lord and King,
to the glory of God the Father.

SECOND SERVICE

Psalm 27
Lamentations 3.1–18
Luke 22.[24–38,] 39–53

THIRD SERVICE

Psalm 55.13–24
Lamentations 3.40–51
Galatians 6.11–18

WEDNESDAY OF HOLY WEEK

COLLECT

Almighty and everlasting God,
who in your tender love towards the human race
    sent your Son our Saviour Jesus Christ
to take upon him our flesh
and to suffer death upon the cross:
grant that we may follow the example
    of his patience and humility,
and also be made partakers of his resurrection;
through Jesus Christ your Son our Lord,
who is alive and reigns with you,
in the unity of the Holy Spirit,
one God, now and for ever.

READING   Isaiah 50.4–9a

⁴ The Lord GOD has given me
        the tongue of a teacher,
    that I may know how to sustain
        the weary with a word.
    Morning by morning he wakens—
        wakens my ear
        to listen as those who are taught.
⁵ The Lord GOD has opened my ear,
        and I was not rebellious,
        I did not turn backwards.
⁶ I gave my back to those who struck me,
        and my cheeks to those who pulled out the beard;
    I did not hide my face
        from insult and spitting.

7 The Lord GOD helps me;
 therefore I have not been disgraced;
 therefore I have set my face like flint,
  and I know that I shall not be put to shame;
8 he who vindicates me is near.
 Who will contend with me?
  Let us stand up together.
 Who are my adversaries?
  Let them confront me.
9 It is the Lord GOD who helps me;
 who will declare me guilty?

PSALM   Psalm 70

1 Be pleased, O God, to deliver me;
 O Lord, make haste to help me.
2 Let those who seek my life be ashamed and altogether dismayed;
 let those who take pleasure in my misfortune draw back and be
  disgraced.
3 Let those who say to me 'Aha!' and gloat over me turn back,
 because they are ashamed.
4 Let all who seek you rejoice and be glad in you;
 let those who love your salvation say for ever, 'Great is the Lord!'
5 But as for me, I am poor and needy;
 come to me speedily, O God.
6 You are my helper and my deliverer;
 O Lord, do not tarry.

READING   Hebrews 12.1–3

1 Therefore, since we are surrounded by so great a cloud of witnesses, let us also lay aside every weight and the sin that clings so closely, and let us run with perseverance the race that is set before us, 2 looking to Jesus the pioneer and perfecter of our faith, who for the sake of the joy that was set before him endured the cross, disregarding its shame, and has taken his seat at the right hand of the throne of God.

3 Consider him who endured such hostility against himself from sinners, so that you may not grow weary or lose heart.

GOSPEL   John 13.21–32

²¹ After saying this Jesus was troubled in spirit, and declared, 'Very truly, I tell you, one of you will betray me.' ²² The disciples looked at one another, uncertain of whom he was speaking. ²³ One of his disciples—the one whom Jesus loved—was reclining next to him; ²⁴ Simon Peter therefore motioned to him to ask Jesus of whom he was speaking. ²⁵ So while reclining next to Jesus, he asked him, 'Lord, who is it?' ²⁶ Jesus answered, 'It is the one to whom I give this piece of bread when I have dipped it in the dish.' So when he had dipped the piece of bread, he gave it to Judas son of Simon Iscariot. ²⁷ After he received the piece of bread, Satan entered into him. Jesus said to him, 'Do quickly what you are going to do.' ²⁸ Now no one at the table knew why he said this to him. ²⁹ Some thought that, because Judas had the common purse, Jesus was telling him, 'Buy what we need for the festival'; or, that he should give something to the poor. ³⁰ So, after receiving the piece of bread, he immediately went out. And it was night.

³¹ When he had gone out, Jesus said, 'Now the Son of Man has been glorified, and God has been glorified in him. ³² If God has been glorified in him, God will also glorify him in himself and will glorify him at once.'

POST COMMUNION

Lord Jesus Christ,
you humbled yourself in taking the form of a servant,
and in obedience died on the cross for our salvation:
give us the mind to follow you
and to proclaim you as Lord and King,
to the glory of God the Father.

SECOND SERVICE

Psalm 102.1–17, [18–28]
Wisdom 1.16–2.1; 2.12–22
or
Jeremiah 11.18–20
Luke 22.54–71

THIRD SERVICE

Psalm 88
Isaiah 63.1–9
Revelation 14.18–15.4

MAUNDY THURSDAY

COLLECT

God our Father,
you have invited us to share in the supper
which your Son gave to his Church
to proclaim his death until he comes:
may he nourish us by his presence,
and unite us in his love;
who is alive and reigns with you,
in the unity of the Holy Spirit,
one God, now and for ever.

At Morning and Evening Prayer the Collect of Palm Sunday is used

READING   Exodus 12.1–4, [5–10,] 11–14

¹ The LORD said to Moses and Aaron in the land of Egypt: ² This month shall mark for you the beginning of months; it shall be the first month of the year for you. ³ Tell the whole congregation of Israel that on the tenth of this month they are to take a lamb for each family, a lamb for each household. ⁴ If a household is too small for a whole lamb, it shall join its closest neighbour in obtaining one; the lamb shall be divided in proportion to the number of people who eat of it.

[⁵ Your lamb shall be without blemish, a year-old male; you may take it from the sheep or from the goats. ⁶ You shall keep it until the fourteenth day of this month; then the whole assembled congregation of Israel shall slaughter it at twilight. ⁷ They shall take some of the blood and put it on the two doorposts and the lintel of the houses in which they eat it. ⁸ They shall eat the lamb that same night; they shall eat it roasted over the fire with unleavened bread and bitter herbs. ⁹ Do not eat any of it raw or boiled in water, but roasted over the fire, with its head, legs, and inner organs. ¹⁰ You shall let none of it remain until the morning; anything that remains until the morning you shall burn.]

¹¹ This is how you shall eat it: your loins girded, your sandals on your feet, and your staff in your hand; and you shall eat it hurriedly. It is the passover of the LORD. ¹² For I will pass through the land of Egypt that night, and I will strike down every firstborn in the land of Egypt, both human beings and animals; on all the gods of Egypt I will execute judgements: I am the LORD. ¹³ The blood shall be a sign for you on the houses where you live: when I see the blood, I will pass over you, and no plague shall destroy you when I strike the land of Egypt.

[14] This day shall be a day of remembrance for you. You shall celebrate it as a festival to the LORD; throughout your generations you shall observe it as a perpetual ordinance.

PSALM   Psalm 116.1, 10–17

1   I love the Lord, because he has heard the voice of my supplication,
    because he has inclined his ear to me whenever I called upon him.

10 How shall I repay the Lord
    for all the good things he has done for me?
11 I will lift up the cup of salvation
    and call upon the name of the Lord.
12 I will fulfil my vows to the Lord
    in the presence of all his people.
13 Precious in the sight of the Lord
    is the death of his servants.
14 O Lord, I am your servant;
    I am your servant and the child of your handmaid; you have freed
      me from my bonds.
15 I will offer you the sacrifice of thanksgiving
    and call upon the name of the Lord.
16 I will fulfil my vows to the Lord
    in the presence of all his people.
17 In the courts of the Lord's house,
    in the midst of you, O Jerusalem. Praise the Lord.

OR, IF AN ALTERNATIVE TEXT IS PREFERRED   Psalm 116.9–17

9   I believed, even when I said, 'I have been brought very low.'
    In my distress I said, 'No one can be trusted.'
10 How shall I repay the Lord
    for all the good things he has done for me?
11 I will lift up the cup of salvation
    and call upon the name of the Lord.
12 I will fulfil my vows to the Lord
    in the presence of all his people.
13 Precious in the sight of the Lord
    is the death of his servants.
14 O Lord, I am your servant;
    I am your servant and the child of your handmaid; you have freed
      me from my bonds.
15 I will offer you the sacrifice of thanksgiving
    and call upon the name of the Lord.

16 I will fulfil my vows to the Lord
in the presence of all his people.
17 In the courts of the Lord's house,
in the midst of you, O Jerusalem. Praise the Lord.

READING   1 Corinthians 11.23–26

23 For I received from the Lord what I also handed on to you, that the Lord
Jesus on the night when he was betrayed took a loaf of bread, 24 and when
he had given thanks, he broke it and said, 'This is my body that is for you.
Do this in remembrance of me.' 25 In the same way he took the cup also,
after supper, saying, 'This cup is the new covenant in my blood. Do this, as
often as you drink it, in remembrance of me.' 26 For as often as you eat this
bread and drink the cup, you proclaim the Lord's death until he comes.

GOSPEL   John 13.1–17, 31b–35

1 Now before the festival of the Passover, Jesus knew that his hour had
come to depart from this world and go to the Father. Having loved his own
who were in the world, he loved them to the end. 2 The devil had already
put it into the heart of Judas son of Simon Iscariot to betray him. And
during supper 3 Jesus, knowing that the Father had given all things into
his hands, and that he had come from God and was going to God, 4 got up
from the table, took off his outer robe, and tied a towel around himself.
5 Then he poured water into a basin and began to wash the disciples' feet
and to wipe them with the towel that was tied around him. 6 He came to
Simon Peter, who said to him, 'Lord, are you going to wash my feet?' 7 Jesus
answered, 'You do not know now what I am doing, but later you will
understand.' 8 Peter said to him, 'You will never wash my feet.' Jesus answered, 'Unless I wash you, you have no share with me.' 9 Simon Peter said to
him, 'Lord, not my feet only but also my hands and my head!' 10 Jesus said
to him, 'One who has bathed does not need to wash, except for the feet,
but is entirely clean. And you are clean, though not all of you.' 11 For he
knew who was to betray him; for this reason he said, 'Not all of you are
clean.'

12 After he had washed their feet, had put on his robe, and had returned
to the table, he said to them, 'Do you know what I have done to you? 13 You
call me Teacher and Lord—and you are right, for that is what I am. 14 So if
I, your Lord and Teacher, have washed your feet, you also ought to wash
one another's feet. 15 For I have set you an example, that you also should
do as I have done to you. 16 Very truly, I tell you, servants are not greater

than their master, nor are messengers greater than the one who sent them. [17] If you know these things, you are blessed if you do them.'

[31] 'Now the Son of Man has been glorified, and God has been glorified in him. [32] If God has been glorified in him, God will also glorify him in himself and will glorify him at once. [33] Little children, I am with you only a little longer. You will look for me; and as I said to the Jews so now I say to you, "Where I am going, you cannot come." [34] I give you a new commandment, that you love one another. Just as I have loved you, you also should love one another. [35] By this everyone will know that you are my disciples, if you have love for one another.'

POST COMMUNION

Lord Jesus Christ,
we thank you that in this wonderful sacrament
you have given us the memorial of your passion:
grant us so to reverence the sacred mysteries
    of your body and blood
that we may know within ourselves
and show forth in our lives
the fruit of your redemption,
for you are alive and reign, now and for ever.

SECOND SERVICE

Psalm 39
Leviticus 16.2–24
Luke 23.1–25

THIRD SERVICE

Psalms 42; 43
Exodus 11
Ephesians 2.11–18

GOOD FRIDAY

COLLECT

Almighty Father,
look with mercy on this your family
for which our Lord Jesus Christ
    was content to be betrayed
    and given up into the hands of sinners
    and to suffer death upon the cross;

who is alive and glorified
   with you and the Holy Spirit,
one God, now and for ever.

READING   Isaiah 52.13–53.12

13 See, my servant shall prosper;
     he shall be exalted and lifted up,
     and shall be very high.
14 Just as there were many who were astonished at him
     —so marred was his appearance, beyond human semblance,
     and his form beyond that of mortals—
15 so he shall startle many nations;
     kings shall shut their mouths because of him;
    for that which had not been told them they shall see,
     and that which they had not heard they shall contemplate.
1 Who has believed what we have heard?
     And to whom has the arm of the Lord been revealed?
2 For he grew up before him like a young plant,
     and like a root out of dry ground;
    he had no form or majesty that we should look at him,
     nothing in his appearance that we should desire him.
3 He was despised and rejected by others;
     a man of suffering and acquainted with infirmity;
    and as one from whom others hide their faces
     he was despised, and we held him of no account.
4 Surely he has borne our infirmities
     and carried our diseases;
    yet we accounted him stricken,
     struck down by God, and afflicted.
5 But he was wounded for our transgressions,
     crushed for our iniquities;
    upon him was the punishment that made us whole,
     and by his bruises we are healed.
6 All we like sheep have gone astray;
     we have all turned to our own way,
    and the Lord has laid on him
     the iniquity of us all.
7 He was oppressed, and he was afflicted,
     yet he did not open his mouth;
    like a lamb that is led to the slaughter,
     and like a sheep that before its shearers is silent,
     so he did not open his mouth.

8 By a perversion of justice he was taken away.
   Who could have imagined his future?
   For he was cut off from the land of the living,
   stricken for the transgression of my people.
9 They made his grave with the wicked
   and his tomb with the rich,
   although he had done no violence,
   and there was no deceit in his mouth.
10 Yet it was the will of the LORD to crush him with pain.
   When you make his life an offering for sin,
   he shall see his offspring, and shall prolong his days;
   through him the will of the LORD shall prosper.
11   Out of his anguish he shall see light;
   he shall find satisfaction through his knowledge.
   The righteous one, my servant, shall make many righteous,
   and he shall bear their iniquities.
12 Therefore I will allot him a portion with the great,
   and he shall divide the spoil with the strong;
   because he poured out himself to death,
   and was numbered with the transgressors;
   yet he bore the sin of many,
   and made intercession for the transgressors.

PSALM   Psalm 22

IF A SHORTER TEXT IS PREFERRED, USE 1–11 OR 1–20

1 My God, my God, why have you forsaken me?
   and are so far from my cry and from the words of my distress?
2 O my God, I cry in the daytime, but you do not answer;
   by night as well, but I find no rest.
3 Yet you are the Holy One,
   enthroned upon the praises of Israel.
4 Our forebears put their trust in you;
   they trusted and you delivered them.
5 They cried out to you and were delivered;
   they trusted in you and were not put to shame.
6 But as for me, I am a worm and no man,
   scorned by all and despised by the people.
7 All who see me laugh me to scorn;
   they curl their lips and wag their heads, saying,
8 'He trusted in the Lord; let him deliver him;
   let him rescue him, if he delights in him.'

9 Yet you are he who took me out of the womb,
   and kept me safe upon my mother's breast.

10 I have been entrusted to you ever since I was born;
   you were my God when I was still in my mother's womb.

11 Be not far from me, for trouble is near,
   and there is none to help.

12 Many young bulls encircle me;
   strong bulls of Bashan surround me.

13 They open wide their jaws at me,
   like a ravening and a roaring lion.

14 I am poured out like water; all my bones are out of joint;
   my heart within my breast is melting wax.

15 My mouth is dried out like a pot-sherd; my tongue sticks to the
      roof of my mouth;
   and you have laid me in the dust of the grave.

16 Packs of dogs close me in, and gangs of evildoers circle around
      me;
   they pierce my hands and my feet; I can count all my bones.

17 They stare and gloat over me;
   they divide my garments among them; they cast lots for my
      clothing.

18 Be not far away, O Lord;
   you are my strength; hasten to help me.

19 Save me from the sword,
   my life from the power of the dog.

20 Save me from the lion's mouth,
   my wretched body from the horns of wild bulls.

21 I will declare your name to my people;
   in the midst of the congregation I will praise you.

22 Praise the Lord, you that fear him;
   stand in awe of him, O offspring of Israel; all you of Jacob's line,
      give glory.

23 For he does not despise nor abhor the poor in their poverty; neither
      does he hide his face from them;
   but when they cry to him he hears them.

24 My praise is of him in the great assembly;
   I will perform my vows in the presence of those who worship him.

25 The poor shall eat and be satisfied, and those who seek the Lord
      shall praise him:
   'May your heart live for ever!'

26 All the ends of the earth shall remember and turn to the Lord,
   and all the families of the nations shall bow before him.

27 For kingship belongs to the Lord;
   he rules over the nations.

²⁸ To him alone all who sleep in the earth bow down in worship;
 all who go down to the dust fall before him.
²⁹ My soul shall live for him; my descendants shall serve him;
 they shall be known as the Lord's for ever.
³⁰ They shall come and make known to a people yet unborn
 the saving deeds that he has done.

READING

EITHER   **Hebrews 10.16–25**

¹⁶ 'This is the covenant that I will make with them
   after those days, says the Lord:
 I will put my laws in their hearts,
   and I will write them on their minds',
¹⁷ he also adds,
   'I will remember their sins and their lawless deeds no more.'
¹⁸ Where there is forgiveness of these, there is no longer any offering for
sin.

¹⁹ Therefore, my friends, since we have confidence to enter the sanctuary
by the blood of Jesus, ²⁰ by the new and living way that he opened for us
through the curtain (that is, through his flesh), ²¹ and since we have a great
priest over the house of God, ²² let us approach with a true heart in full
assurance of faith, with our hearts sprinkled clean from an evil conscience
and our bodies washed with pure water. ²³ Let us hold fast to the confession
of our hope without wavering, for he who has promised is faithful. ²⁴ And
let us consider how to provoke one another to love and good deeds, ²⁵ not
neglecting to meet together, as is the habit of some, but encouraging one
another, and all the more as you see the Day approaching.

OR   **Hebrews 4.14–16; 5.7–9**

¹⁴ Since, then, we have a great high priest who has passed through the
heavens, Jesus, the Son of God, let us hold fast to our confession. ¹⁵ For we
do not have a high priest who is unable to sympathize with our weaknesses,
but we have one who in every respect has been tested as we are, yet without
sin. ¹⁶ Let us therefore approach the throne of grace with boldness, so that
we may receive mercy and find grace to help in time of need.

⁷ In the days of his flesh, Jesus offered up prayers and supplications, with
loud cries and tears, to the one who was able to save him from death, and

he was heard because of his reverent submission. [8] Although he was a Son, he learned obedience through what he suffered; [9] and having been made perfect, he became the source of eternal salvation for all who obey him.

GOSPEL   John 18.1–19.42

[1] After Jesus had spoken these words, he went out with his disciples across the Kidron valley to a place where there was a garden, which he and his disciples entered. [2] Now Judas, who betrayed him, also knew the place, because Jesus often met there with his disciples. [3] So Judas brought a detachment of soldiers together with police from the chief priests and the Pharisees, and they came there with lanterns and torches and weapons. [4] Then Jesus, knowing all that was to happen to him, came forward and asked them, 'For whom are you looking?' [5] They answered, 'Jesus of Nazareth.' Jesus replied, 'I am he.' Judas, who betrayed him, was standing with them. [6] When Jesus said to them, 'I am he', they stepped back and fell to the ground. [7] Again he asked them, 'For whom are you looking?' And they said, 'Jesus of Nazareth.' [8] Jesus answered, 'I told you that I am he. So if you are looking for me, let these men go.' [9] This was to fulfil the word that he had spoken, 'I did not lose a single one of those whom you gave me.' [10] Then Simon Peter, who had a sword, drew it, struck the high priest's slave, and cut off his right ear. The slave's name was Malchus. [11] Jesus said to Peter, 'Put your sword back into its sheath. Am I not to drink the cup that the Father has given me?'

[12] So the soldiers, their officer, and the Jewish police arrested Jesus and bound him. [13] First they took him to Annas, who was the father-in-law of Caiaphas, the high priest that year. [14] Caiaphas was the one who had advised the Jews that it was better to have one person die for the people.

[15] Simon Peter and another disciple followed Jesus. Since that disciple was known to the high priest, he went with Jesus into the courtyard of the high priest, [16] but Peter was standing outside at the gate. So the other disciple, who was known to the high priest, went out, spoke to the woman who guarded the gate, and brought Peter in. [17] The woman said to Peter, 'You are not also one of this man's disciples, are you?' He said, 'I am not.' [18] Now the slaves and the police had made a charcoal fire because it was cold, and they were standing round it and warming themselves. Peter also was standing with them and warming himself.

[19] Then the high priest questioned Jesus about his disciples and about his teaching. [20] Jesus answered, 'I have spoken openly to the world; I have always taught in synagogues and in the temple, where all the Jews come together. I have said nothing in secret. [21] Why do you ask me? Ask those who heard what I said to them; they know what I said.' [22] When he had

said this, one of the police standing nearby struck Jesus on the face, saying, 'Is that how you answer the high priest?' [23] Jesus answered, 'If I have spoken wrongly, testify to the wrong. But if I have spoken rightly, why do you strike me?' [24] Then Annas sent him bound to Caiaphas the high priest.

[25] Now Simon Peter was standing and warming himself. They asked him, 'You are not also one of his disciples, are you?' He denied it and said, 'I am not.' [26] One of the slaves of the high priest, a relative of the man whose ear Peter had cut off, asked, 'Did I not see you in the garden with him?' [27] Again Peter denied it, and at that moment the cock crowed.

[28] Then they took Jesus from Caiaphas to Pilate's headquarters. It was early in the morning. They themselves did not enter the headquarters, so as to avoid ritual defilement and to be able to eat the Passover. [29] So Pilate went out to them and said, 'What accusation do you bring against this man?' [30] They answered, 'If this man were not a criminal, we would not have handed him over to you.' [31] Pilate said to them, 'Take him yourselves and judge him according to your law.' The Jews replied, 'We are not permitted to put anyone to death.' [32] (This was to fulfil what Jesus had said when he indicated the kind of death he was to die.)

[33] Then Pilate entered the headquarters again, summoned Jesus, and asked him, 'Are you the King of the Jews?' [34] Jesus answered, 'Do you ask this on your own, or did others tell you about me?' [35] Pilate replied, 'I am not a Jew, am I? Your own nation and the chief priests have handed you over to me. What have you done?' [36] Jesus answered, 'My kingdom is not from this world. If my kingdom were from this world, my followers would be fighting to keep me from being handed over to the Jews. But as it is, my kingdom is not from here.' [37] Pilate asked him, 'So you are a king?' Jesus answered, 'You say that I am a king. For this I was born, and for this I came into the world, to testify to the truth. Everyone who belongs to the truth listens to my voice.' [38] Pilate asked him, 'What is truth?'

After he had said this, he went out to the Jews again and told them, 'I find no case against him. [39] But you have a custom that I release someone for you at the Passover. Do you want me to release for you the King of the Jews?' [40] They shouted in reply, 'Not this man, but Barabbas!' Now Barabbas was a bandit.

[1] Then Pilate took Jesus and had him flogged. [2] And the soldiers wove a crown of thorns and put it on his head, and they dressed him in a purple robe. [3] They kept coming up to him, saying, 'Hail, King of the Jews!' and striking him on the face. [4] Pilate went out again and said to them, 'Look, I am bringing him out to you to let you know that I find no case against him.' [5] So Jesus came out, wearing the crown of thorns and the purple robe. Pilate said to them, 'Here is the man!' [6] When the chief priests and the

police saw him, they shouted, 'Crucify him! Crucify him!' Pilate said to them, 'Take him yourselves and crucify him; I find no case against him.' [7] The Jews answered him, 'We have a law, and according to that law he ought to die because he has claimed to be the Son of God.'

[8] Now when Pilate heard this, he was more afraid than ever. [9] He entered his headquarters again and asked Jesus, 'Where are you from?' But Jesus gave him no answer. [10] Pilate therefore said to him, 'Do you refuse to speak to me? Do you not know that I have power to release you, and power to crucify you?' [11] Jesus answered him, 'You would have no power over me unless it had been given you from above; therefore the one who handed me over to you is guilty of a greater sin.' [12] From then on Pilate tried to release him, but the Jews cried out, 'If you release this man, you are no friend of the emperor. Everyone who claims to be a king sets himself against the emperor.'

[13] When Pilate heard these words, he brought Jesus outside and sat on the judge's bench at a place called The Stone Pavement, or in Hebrew Gabbatha. [14] Now it was the day of Preparation for the Passover; and it was about noon. He said to the Jews, 'Here is your King!' [15] They cried out, 'Away with him! Away with him! Crucify him!' Pilate asked them, 'Shall I crucify your King?' The chief priests answered, 'We have no king but the emperor.' [16] Then he handed him over to them to be crucified.

So they took Jesus; [17] and carrying the cross by himself, he went out to what is called The Place of the Skull, which in Hebrew is called Golgotha. [18] There they crucified him, and with him two others, one on either side, with Jesus between them. [19] Pilate also had an inscription written and put on the cross. It read, 'Jesus of Nazareth, the King of the Jews.' [20] Many of the Jews read this inscription, because the place where Jesus was crucified was near the city; and it was written in Hebrew, in Latin, and in Greek. [21] Then the chief priests of the Jews said to Pilate, 'Do not write, "The King of the Jews", but, "This man said, I am King of the Jews."' [22] Pilate answered, 'What I have written I have written.' [23] When the soldiers had crucified Jesus, they took his clothes and divided them into four parts, one for each soldier. They also took his tunic; now the tunic was seamless, woven in one piece from the top. [24] So they said to one another, 'Let us not tear it, but cast lots for it to see who will get it.' This was to fulfil what the scripture says,

'They divided my clothes among themselves,
   and for my clothing they cast lots.'

[25] And that is what the soldiers did.

Meanwhile, standing near the cross of Jesus were his mother, and his mother's sister, Mary the wife of Clopas, and Mary Magdalene. [26] When Jesus saw his mother and the disciple whom he loved standing beside her, he said to his mother, 'Woman, here is your son.' [27] Then he said to the disciple, 'Here is your mother.' And from that hour the disciple took her into his own home.

[28] After this, when Jesus knew that all was now finished, he said (in order to fulfil the scripture), 'I am thirsty.' [29] A jar full of sour wine was standing there. So they put a sponge full of the wine on a branch of hyssop and held it to his mouth. [30] When Jesus had received the wine, he said, 'It is finished.' Then he bowed his head and gave up his spirit.

[31] Since it was the day of Preparation, the Jews did not want the bodies left on the cross during the sabbath, especially because that sabbath was a day of great solemnity. So they asked Pilate to have the legs of the crucified men broken and the bodies removed. [32] Then the soldiers came and broke the legs of the first and of the other who had been crucified with him. [33] But when they came to Jesus and saw that he was already dead, they did not break his legs. [34] Instead, one of the soldiers pierced his side with a spear, and at once blood and water came out. [35] (He who saw this has testified so that you also may believe. His testimony is true, and he knows that he tells the truth.) [36] These things occurred so that the scripture might be fulfilled, 'None of his bones shall be broken.' [37] And again another passage of scripture says, 'They will look on the one whom they have pierced.'

[38] After these things, Joseph of Arimathea, who was a disciple of Jesus, though a secret one because of his fear of the Jews, asked Pilate to let him take away the body of Jesus. Pilate gave him permission; so he came and removed his body. [39] Nicodemus, who had at first come to Jesus by night, also came, bringing a mixture of myrrh and aloes, weighing about a hundred pounds. [40] They took the body of Jesus and wrapped it with the spices in linen cloths, according to the burial custom of the Jews. [41] Now there was a garden in the place where he was crucified, and in the garden there was a new tomb in which no one had ever been laid. [42] And so, because it was the Jewish day of Preparation, and the tomb was nearby, they laid Jesus there.

SECOND SERVICE

Psalms 130; 143
Genesis 22.1–18

A part of
John 18–19
if not used at the Principal Service especially in the evening

John 19.38–42
or
Colossians 1.18–23

THIRD SERVICE

Psalm 69
Lamentations 5.15–22

A part of
John 18–19
if not read at the Principal Service

or

Hebrews 10.1–10

EASTER EVE

COLLECT

Grant, Lord,
that we who are baptized into the death
   of your Son our Saviour Jesus Christ
may continually put to death our evil desires
   and be buried with him;
and that through the grave and gate of death
we may pass to our joyful resurrection;
through his merits, who died and was buried
   and rose again for us,
your Son Jesus Christ our Lord.

These readings are for use at services other than the Easter Vigil

READING

EITHER   **Job 14.1–14**

1 'A mortal, born of woman, few of days and full of trouble,
2   comes up like a flower and withers,
     flees like a shadow and does not last.
3 Do you fix your eyes on such a one?
     Do you bring me into judgement with you?
4 Who can bring a clean thing out of an unclean?
     No one can.
5 Since their days are determined,
     and the number of their months is known to you,
     and you have appointed the bounds that they cannot pass,
6 look away from them, and desist,
     that they may enjoy, like labourers, their days.
7 For there is hope for a tree,
     if it is cut down, that it will sprout again,
     and that its shoots will not cease.
8 Though its root grows old in the earth,
     and its stump dies in the ground,
9 yet at the scent of water it will bud
     and put forth branches like a young plant.
10 But mortals die, and are laid low;
     humans expire, and where are they?

11 As waters fail from a lake,
      and a river wastes away and dries up,
12 so mortals lie down and do not rise again;
      until the heavens are no more, they will not awake
      or be roused out of their sleep.
13 O that you would hide me in Sheol,
      that you would conceal me until your wrath is past,
      that you would appoint me a set time, and remember me!
14 If mortals die, will they live again?
      All the days of my service I would wait
      until my release should come.'

OR   **Lamentations 3.1–9, 19–24**

1 I am one who has seen affliction
      under the rod of God's wrath;
2 he has driven and brought me
      into darkness without any light;
3 against me alone he turns his hand,
      again and again, all day long.
4 He has made my flesh and my skin waste away,
      and broken my bones;
5 he has besieged and enveloped me
      with bitterness and tribulation;
6 he has made me sit in darkness
      like the dead of long ago.
7 He has walled me about so that I cannot escape;
      he has put heavy chains on me;
8 though I call and cry for help,
      he shuts out my prayer;
9 he has blocked my ways with hewn stones,
      he has made my paths crooked.

19 The thought of my affliction and my homelessness
      is wormwood and gall!
20 My soul continually thinks of it
      and is bowed down within me.
21 But this I call to mind,
      and therefore I have hope:
22 The steadfast love of the LORD never ceases,
      his mercies never come to an end;

²³ they are new every morning;
    great is your faithfulness.
²⁴ 'The LORD is my portion,' says my soul,
    'therefore I will hope in him.'

PSALM   Psalm 31.1-4, 15-16

¹ In you, O Lord, have I taken refuge; let me never be put to shame;
    deliver me in your righteousness.
² Incline your ear to me;
    make haste to deliver me.
³ Be my strong rock, a castle to keep me safe, for you are my crag
    and my stronghold;
    for the sake of your name, lead me and guide me.
⁴ Take me out of the net that they have secretly set for me,
    for you are my tower of strength.

¹⁵ 'My times are in your hand;
    rescue me from the hand of my enemies, and from those who
    persecute me.
¹⁶ Make your face to shine upon your servant,
    and in your loving-kindness save me.'

OR, IF AN ALTERNATIVE TEXT IS PREFERRED   Psalm 31.1-5

¹ In you, O Lord, have I taken refuge; let me never be put to shame;
    deliver me in your righteousness.
² Incline your ear to me;
    make haste to deliver me.
³ Be my strong rock, a castle to keep me safe, for you are my crag
    and my stronghold;
    for the sake of your name, lead me and guide me.
⁴ Take me out of the net that they have secretly set for me,
    for you are my tower of strength.
⁵ Into your hands I commend my spirit,
    for you have redeemed me, O Lord, O God of truth.

READING   1 Peter 4.1-8

¹ Since therefore Christ suffered in the flesh, arm yourselves also with the same intention (for whoever has suffered in the flesh has finished with sin), ² so as to live for the rest of your earthly life no longer by human desires but by the will of God. ³ You have already spent enough time in doing what the Gentiles like to do, living in licentiousness, passions, drunkenness, revels, carousing, and lawless idolatry. ⁴ They are surprised

that you no longer join them in the same excesses of dissipation, and so they blaspheme. ⁵ But they will have to give an account to him who stands ready to judge the living and the dead. ⁶ For this is the reason the gospel was proclaimed even to the dead, so that, though they had been judged in the flesh as everyone is judged, they might live in the spirit as God does.

⁷ The end of all things is near; therefore be serious and discipline yourselves for the sake of your prayers. ⁸ Above all, maintain constant love for one another, for love covers a multitude of sins.

GOSPEL

EITHER   Matthew 27.57–66

⁵⁷ When it was evening, there came a rich man from Arimathea, named Joseph, who was also a disciple of Jesus. ⁵⁸ He went to Pilate and asked for the body of Jesus; then Pilate ordered it to be given to him. ⁵⁹ So Joseph took the body and wrapped it in a clean linen cloth ⁶⁰ and laid it in his own new tomb, which he had hewn in the rock. He then rolled a great stone to the door of the tomb and went away. ⁶¹ Mary Magdalene and the other Mary were there, sitting opposite the tomb.

⁶² The next day, that is, after the day of Preparation, the chief priests and the Pharisees gathered before Pilate ⁶³ and said, 'Sir, we remember what that impostor said while he was still alive, "After three days I will rise again."' ⁶⁴ Therefore command that the tomb be made secure until the third day; otherwise his disciples may go and steal him away, and tell the people, "He has been raised from the dead", and the last deception would be worse than the first.' ⁶⁵ Pilate said to them, 'You have a guard of soldiers; go, make it as secure as you can.' ⁶⁶ So they went with the guard and made the tomb secure by sealing the stone.

OR   John 19.38–42

³⁸ After these things, Joseph of Arimathea, who was a disciple of Jesus, though a secret one because of his fear of the Jews, asked Pilate to let him take away the body of Jesus. Pilate gave him permission; so he came and removed his body. ³⁹ Nicodemus, who had at first come to Jesus by night, also came, bringing a mixture of myrrh and aloes, weighing about a hundred pounds. ⁴⁰ They took the body of Jesus and wrapped it with the spices in linen cloths, according to the burial custom of the Jews. ⁴¹ Now there was a garden in the place where he was crucified, and in the garden there was a new tomb in which no one had ever been laid. ⁴² And so, because it was the Jewish day of Preparation, and the tomb was nearby, they laid Jesus there.

SECOND SERVICE	THIRD SERVICE
Psalm 142	Psalm 116
Hosea 6.1–6	Job 19.21–27
John 2.18–22	1 John 5.5–12

EASTER VIGIL

COLLECT

Lord of all life and power,
who through the mighty resurrection of your Son
overcame the old order of sin and death
to make all things new in him:
grant that we, being dead to sin
and alive to you in Jesus Christ,
may reign with him in glory;
to whom with you and the Holy Spirit
be praise and honour, glory and might,
now and in all eternity.

A minimum of three Old Testament readings should be chosen. The reading from Exodus 14, along with its associated Canticle, the reading from Romans, Psalm 114, and the Gospel should always be used.

READING   Genesis 1.1–2.4a

¹ In the beginning when God created the heavens and the earth, ² the earth was a formless void and darkness covered the face of the deep, while a wind from God swept over the face of the waters. ³ Then God said, 'Let there be light'; and there was light. ⁴ And God saw that the light was good; and God separated the light from the darkness. ⁵ God called the light Day, and the darkness he called Night. And there was evening and there was morning, the first day.

⁶ And God said, 'Let there be a dome in the midst of the waters, and let it separate the waters from the waters.' ⁷ So God made the dome and separated the waters that were under the dome from the waters that were above the dome. And it was so. ⁸ God called the dome Sky. And there was evening and there was morning, the second day.

⁹ And God said, 'Let the waters under the sky be gathered together into one place, and let the dry land appear.' And it was so. ¹⁰ God called the dry land Earth, and the waters that were gathered together he called Seas. And God saw that it was good. ¹¹ Then God said, 'Let the earth put forth vegetation: plants yielding seed, and fruit trees of every kind on earth that bear fruit with the seed in it.' And it was so. ¹² The earth brought forth vegetation: plants yielding seed of every kind, and trees of every kind bearing fruit with the seed in it. And God saw that it was good. ¹³ And there was evening and there was morning, the third day.

¹⁴ And God said, 'Let there be lights in the dome of the sky to separate the day from the night; and let them be for signs and for seasons and for days and years, ¹⁵ and let them be lights in the dome of the sky to give light upon the earth.' And it was so. ¹⁶ God made the two great lights—the greater light to rule the day and the lesser light to rule the night—and the stars. ¹⁷ God set them in the dome of the sky to give light upon the earth, ¹⁸ to rule over the day and over the night, and to separate the light from the darkness. And God saw that it was good. ¹⁹ And there was evening and there was morning, the fourth day.

²⁰ And God said, 'Let the waters bring forth swarms of living creatures, and let birds fly above the earth across the dome of the sky.' ²¹ So God created the great sea monsters and every living creature that moves, of every kind, with which the waters swarm, and every winged bird of every kind. And God saw that it was good. ²² God blessed them, saying, 'Be fruitful and multiply and fill the waters in the seas, and let birds multiply on the earth.' ²³ And there was evening and there was morning, the fifth day.

²⁴ And God said, 'Let the earth bring forth living creatures of every kind: cattle and creeping things and wild animals of the earth of every kind.' And it was so. ²⁵ God made the wild animals of the earth of every kind, and the cattle of every kind, and everything that creeps upon the ground of every kind. And God saw that it was good.

²⁶ Then God said, 'Let us make humankind in our image, according to our likeness; and let them have dominion over the fish of the sea, and over the birds of the air, and over the cattle, and over all the wild animals of the earth, and over every creeping thing that creeps upon the earth.'
²⁷ So God created humankind in his image,
in the image of God he created them;
male and female he created them.
²⁸ God blessed them, and God said to them, 'Be fruitful and multiply, and fill the earth and subdue it; and have dominion over the fish of the sea and over the birds of the air and over every living thing that moves upon the earth.' ²⁹ God said, 'See, I have given you every plant yielding seed that is upon the face of all the earth, and every tree with seed in its fruit; you

shall have them for food. ³⁰ And to every beast of the earth, and to every bird of the air, and to everything that creeps on the earth, everything that has the breath of life, I have given every green plant for food.' And it was so. ³¹ God saw everything that he had made, and indeed, it was very good. And there was evening and there was morning, the sixth day.

¹ Thus the heavens and the earth were finished, and all their multitude. ² And on the seventh day God finished the work that he had done, and he rested on the seventh day from all the work that he had done. ³ So God blessed the seventh day and hallowed it, because on it God rested from all the work that he had done in creation.

⁴ These are the generations of the heavens and the earth when they were created.

PSALM   Psalm 136.1–9, 23–26

1 Give thanks to the Lord, for he is good,
   for his mercy endures for ever.
2 Give thanks to the God of gods,
   for his mercy endures for ever.
3 Give thanks to the Lord of lords,
   for his mercy endures for ever.
4 Who only does great wonders,
   for his mercy endures for ever;
5 Who by his wisdom made the heavens,
   for his mercy endures for ever;
6 Who spread out the earth upon the waters,
   for his mercy endures for ever;
7 Who created great lights,
   for his mercy endures for ever;
8 The sun to rule the day,
   for his mercy endures for ever;
9 The moon and the stars to govern the night,
   for his mercy endures for ever.

23 Who remembered us in our low estate,
    for his mercy endures for ever;
24 And delivered us from our enemies,
    for his mercy endures for ever;
25 Who gives food to all creatures,
    for his mercy endures for ever;
26 Give thanks to the God of heaven,
    for his mercy endures for ever.

READING   Genesis 7.1–5, 11–18; 8.6–18; 9.8–13

[1] Then the Lord said to Noah, 'Go into the ark, you and all your household, for I have seen that you alone are righteous before me in this generation. [2] Take with you seven pairs of all clean animals, the male and its mate; and a pair of the animals that are not clean, the male and its mate; [3] and seven pairs of the birds of the air also, male and female, to keep their kind alive on the face of all the earth. [4] For in seven days I will send rain on the earth for forty days and forty nights; and every living thing that I have made I will blot out from the face of the ground.' [5] And Noah did all that the Lord had commanded him.

[11] In the six-hundredth year of Noah's life, in the second month, on the seventeenth day of the month, on that day all the fountains of the great deep burst forth, and the windows of the heavens were opened. [12] The rain fell on the earth for forty days and forty nights. [13] On the very same day Noah with his sons, Shem and Ham and Japheth, and Noah's wife and the three wives of his sons, entered the ark, [14] they and every wild animal of every kind, and all domestic animals of every kind, and every creeping thing that creeps on the earth, and every bird of every kind—every bird, every winged creature. [15] They went into the ark with Noah, two and two of all flesh in which there was the breath of life. [16] And those that entered, male and female of all flesh, went in as God had commanded him; and the Lord shut him in.

[17] The flood continued for forty days on the earth; and the waters increased, and bore up the ark, and it rose high above the earth. [18] The waters swelled and increased greatly on the earth; and the ark floated on the face of the waters.

[6] At the end of forty days Noah opened the window of the ark that he had made [7] and sent out the raven; and it went to and fro until the waters were dried up from the earth. [8] Then he sent out the dove from him, to see if the waters had subsided from the face of the ground; [9] but the dove found no place to set its foot, and it returned to him to the ark, for the waters were still on the face of the whole earth. So he put out his hand and took it and brought it into the ark with him. [10] He waited another seven days, and again he sent out the dove from the ark; [11] and the dove came back to him in the evening, and there in its beak was a freshly plucked olive leaf; so Noah knew that the waters had subsided from the earth. [12] Then he waited another seven days, and sent out the dove; and it did not return to him any more.

[13] In the six hundred and first year, in the first month, on the first day of the month, the waters were dried up from the earth; and Noah removed

the covering of the ark, and looked, and saw that the face of the ground was drying. [14] In the second month, on the twenty-seventh day of the month, the earth was dry. [15] Then God said to Noah, [16] 'Go out of the ark, you and your wife, and your sons and your sons' wives with you. [17] Bring out with you every living thing that is with you of all flesh—birds and animals and every creeping thing that creeps on the earth—so that they may abound on the earth, and be fruitful and multiply on the earth.' [18] So Noah went out with his sons and his wife and his sons' wives.

[8] Then God said to Noah and to his sons with him, [9] 'As for me, I am establishing my covenant with you and your descendants after you, [10] and with every living creature that is with you, the birds, the domestic animals, and every animal of the earth with you, as many as came out of the ark. [11] I establish my covenant with you, that never again shall all flesh be cut off by the waters of a flood, and never again shall there be a flood to destroy the earth.' [12] God said, 'This is the sign of the covenant that I make between me and you and every living creature that is with you, for all future generations: [13] I have set my bow in the clouds, and it shall be a sign of the covenant between me and the earth.'

PSALM   Psalm 46

1   God is our refuge and strength,
     a very present help in trouble;
2   Therefore we will not fear, though the earth be moved,
     and though the mountains be toppled into the depths of the sea;
3   Though its waters rage and foam,
     and though the mountains tremble at its tumult.
4   The Lord of hosts is with us;
     the God of Jacob is our stronghold.
5   There is a river whose streams make glad the city of God,
     the holy habitation of the Most High.
6   God is in the midst of her; she shall not be overthrown;
     God shall help her at the break of day.
7   The nations make much ado and the kingdoms are shaken;
     God has spoken and the earth shall melt away.
8   The Lord of hosts is with us;
     the God of Jacob is our stronghold.
9   Come now and look upon the works of the Lord,
     what awesome things he has done on earth.
10 It is he who makes war to cease in all the world;
     he breaks the bow and shatters the spear and burns the shields
       with fire.

¹¹ 'Be still, then, and know that I am God;
   I will be exalted among the nations; I will be exalted in the earth.'
¹² The Lord of hosts is with us;
   the God of Jacob is our stronghold.

READING   Genesis 22.1–18

¹ After these things God tested Abraham. He said to him, 'Abraham!' And he said, 'Here I am.' ² He said, 'Take your son, your only son Isaac, whom you love, and go to the land of Moriah, and offer him there as a burnt-offering on one of the mountains that I shall show you.' ³ So Abraham rose early in the morning, saddled his donkey, and took two of his young men with him, and his son Isaac; he cut the wood for the burnt-offering, and set out and went to the place in the distance that God had shown him. ⁴ On the third day Abraham looked up and saw the place far away. ⁵ Then Abraham said to his young men, 'Stay here with the donkey; the boy and I will go over there; we will worship, and then we will come back to you.' ⁶ Abraham took the wood of the burnt-offering and laid it on his son Isaac, and he himself carried the fire and the knife. So the two of them walked on together. ⁷ Isaac said to his father Abraham, 'Father!' And he said, 'Here I am, my son.' He said, 'The fire and the wood are here, but where is the lamb for a burnt-offering?' ⁸ Abraham said, 'God himself will provide the lamb for a burnt-offering, my son.' So the two of them walked on together.

⁹ When they came to the place that God had shown him, Abraham built an altar there and laid the wood in order. He bound his son Isaac, and laid him on the altar, on top of the wood. ¹⁰ Then Abraham reached out his hand and took the knife to kill his son. ¹¹ But the angel of the LORD called to him from heaven, and said, 'Abraham, Abraham!' And he said, 'Here I am.' ¹² He said, 'Do not lay your hand on the boy or do anything to him; for now I know that you fear God, since you have not withheld your son, your only son, from me.' ¹³ And Abraham looked up and saw a ram, caught in a thicket by its horns. Abraham went and took the ram and offered it up as a burnt-offering instead of his son. ¹⁴ So Abraham called that place 'The LORD will provide'; as it is said to this day, 'On the mount of the LORD it shall be provided.'

¹⁵ The angel of the LORD called to Abraham a second time from heaven, ¹⁶ and said, 'By myself I have sworn, says the LORD: Because you have done this, and have not withheld your son, your only son, ¹⁷ I will indeed bless you, and I will make your offspring as numerous as the stars of heaven and as the sand that is on the seashore. And your offspring shall possess the gate of their enemies, ¹⁸ and by your offspring shall all the nations of the earth gain blessing for themselves, because you have obeyed my voice.'

PSALM   Psalm 16

1 Protect me, O God, for I take refuge in you;
   I have said to the Lord, 'You are my Lord, my good above all other.'
2 All my delight is upon the godly that are in the land,
   upon those who are noble among the people.
3 But those who run after other gods
   shall have their troubles multiplied.
4 Their libations of blood I will not offer,
   nor take the names of their gods upon my lips.
5 O Lord, you are my portion and my cup;
   it is you who uphold my lot.
6 My boundaries enclose a pleasant land;
   indeed, I have a goodly heritage.
7 I will bless the Lord who gives me counsel;
   my heart teaches me, night after night.
8 I have set the Lord always before me;
   because he is at my right hand I shall not fall.
9 My heart, therefore, is glad and my spirit rejoices;
   my body also shall rest in hope.
10 For you will not abandon me to the grave,
   nor let your holy one see the Pit.
11 You will show me the path of life;
   in your presence there is fullness of joy, and in your right hand
      are pleasures for evermore.

READING   Exodus 14.10–31; 15.20–21

10 As Pharaoh drew near, the Israelites looked back, and there were the Egyptians advancing on them. In great fear the Israelites cried out to the LORD. 11 They said to Moses, 'Was it because there were no graves in Egypt that you have taken us away to die in the wilderness? What have you done to us, bringing us out of Egypt? 12 Is this not the very thing we told you in Egypt, "Let us alone and let us serve the Egyptians"? For it would have been better for us to serve the Egyptians than to die in the wilderness.' 13 But Moses said to the people, 'Do not be afraid, stand firm, and see the deliverance that the LORD will accomplish for you today; for the Egyptians whom you see today you shall never see again. 14 The LORD will fight for you, and you have only to keep still.'

15 Then the LORD said to Moses, 'Why do you cry out to me? Tell the Israelites to go forward. 16 But you lift up your staff, and stretch out your hand over the sea and divide it, that the Israelites may go into the sea on dry ground. 17 Then I will harden the hearts of the Egyptians so that they

will go in after them; and so I will gain glory for myself over Pharaoh and all his army, his chariots, and his chariot drivers. [18] And the Egyptians shall know that I am the LORD, when I have gained glory for myself over Pharaoh, his chariots, and his chariot drivers.'

[19] The angel of God who was going before the Israelite army moved and went behind them; and the pillar of cloud moved from in front of them and took its place behind them. [20] It came between the army of Egypt and the army of Israel. And so the cloud was there with the darkness, and it lit up the night; one did not come near the other all night.

[21] Then Moses stretched out his hand over the sea. The LORD drove the sea back by a strong east wind all night, and turned the sea into dry land; and the waters were divided. [22] The Israelites went into the sea on dry ground, the waters forming a wall for them on their right and on their left. [23] The Egyptians pursued, and went into the sea after them, all of Pharaoh's horses, chariots, and chariot drivers. [24] At the morning watch the LORD in the pillar of fire and cloud looked down upon the Egyptian army, and threw the Egyptian army into panic. [25] He clogged their chariot wheels so that they turned with difficulty. The Egyptians said, 'Let us flee from the Israelites, for the LORD is fighting for them against Egypt.'

[26] Then the LORD said to Moses, 'Stretch out your hand over the sea, so that the water may come back upon the Egyptians, upon their chariots and chariot drivers.' [27] So Moses stretched out his hand over the sea, and at dawn the sea returned to its normal depth. As the Egyptians fled before it, the LORD tossed the Egyptians into the sea. [28] The waters returned and covered the chariots and the chariot drivers, the entire army of Pharaoh that had followed them into the sea; not one of them remained. [29] But the Israelites walked on dry ground through the sea, the waters forming a wall for them on their right and on their left.

[30] Thus the LORD saved Israel that day from the Egyptians; and Israel saw the Egyptians dead on the seashore. [31] Israel saw the great work that the LORD did against the Egyptians. So the people feared the LORD and believed in the LORD and in his servant Moses.

[20] Then the prophet Miriam, Aaron's sister, took a tambourine in her hand; and all the women went out after her with tambourines and with dancing. [21] And Miriam sang to them:
    'Sing to the LORD, for he has triumphed gloriously;
    horse and rider he has thrown into the sea.'

CANTICLE   Exodus 15.1b–13, 17–18

1 'I will sing to the Lord, for he has triumphed gloriously;
   horse and rider he has thrown into the sea.
2 The Lord is my strength and my might,
   and he has become my salvation;
   this is my God, and I will praise him,
   my father's God, and I will exalt him.
3 The Lord is a warrior;
   the Lord is his name.
4 Pharaoh's chariots and his army he cast into the sea;
   his picked officers were sunk in the Red Sea.
5 The floods covered them;
   they went down into the depths like a stone.
6 Your right hand, O Lord, glorious in power—
   your right hand, O Lord, shattered the enemy.
7 In the greatness of your majesty you overthrew your adversaries;
   you sent out your fury, it consumed them like stubble.
8 At the blast of your nostrils the waters piled up,
   the floods stood up in a heap;
   the deeps congealed in the heart of the sea.
9 The enemy said, "I will pursue, I will overtake,
   I will divide the spoil, my desire shall have its fill of them.
   I will draw my sword, my hand shall destroy them."
10 You blew with your wind, the sea covered them;
   they sank like lead in the mighty waters.
11 Who is like you, O Lord, among the gods?
   Who is like you, majestic in holiness,
   awesome in splendour, doing wonders?
12 You stretched out your right hand,
   the earth swallowed them.
13 In your steadfast love you led the people whom you redeemed;
   you guided them by your strength to your holy abode.'

17 'You brought them in and planted them on the mountain of your own
      possession,
   the place, O Lord, that you made your abode,
   the sanctuary, O Lord, that your hands have established.
18 The Lord will reign for ever and ever.'

READING   Isaiah 55.1–11

¹ Ho, everyone who thirsts,
 come to the waters;
and you that have no money,
 come, buy and eat!
Come, buy wine and milk
 without money and without price.
² Why do you spend your money for that which is not bread,
 and your labour for that which does not satisfy?
Listen carefully to me, and eat what is good,
 and delight yourselves in rich food.
³ Incline your ear, and come to me;
 listen, so that you may live.
I will make with you an everlasting covenant,
 my steadfast, sure love for David.
⁴ See, I made him a witness to the peoples,
 a leader and commander for the peoples.
⁵ See, you shall call nations that you do not know,
 and nations that do not know you shall run to you,
because of the LORD your God, the Holy One of Israel,
 for he has glorified you.
⁶ Seek the LORD while he may be found,
 call upon him while he is near;
⁷ let the wicked forsake their way,
 and the unrighteous their thoughts;
let them return to the LORD, that he may have mercy on them,
 and to our God, for he will abundantly pardon.
⁸ For my thoughts are not your thoughts,
 nor are your ways my ways, says the LORD.
⁹ For as the heavens are higher than the earth,
 so are my ways higher than your ways
 and my thoughts than your thoughts.
¹⁰ For as the rain and the snow come down from heaven,
 and do not return there until they have watered the earth,
making it bring forth and sprout,
 giving seed to the sower and bread to the eater,
¹¹ so shall my word be that goes out from my mouth;
 it shall not return to me empty,
but it shall accomplish that which I purpose,
 and succeed in the thing for which I sent it.

CANTICLE   Isaiah 12.2–6

2   Surely God is my salvation;
          I will trust, and will not be afraid,
       for the LORD GOD is my strength and my might;
          he has become my salvation.

3 With joy you will draw water from the wells of salvation. 4 And you will
say on that day:
       Give thanks to the LORD,
          call on his name;
       make known his deeds among the nations;
          proclaim that his name is exalted.
5   Sing praises to the LORD, for he has done gloriously;
          let this be known in all the earth.
6   Shout aloud and sing for joy, O royal Zion,
          for great in your midst is the Holy One of Israel.

READING

EITHER   Baruch 3.9–15, 32–4.4

9   Hear the commandments of life, O Israel;
          give ear, and learn wisdom!
10   Why is it, O Israel, why is it that you are in the land of your enemies,
          that you are growing old in a foreign country,
       that you are defiled with the dead,
11   that you are counted among those in Hades?
12   You have forsaken the fountain of wisdom.
13   If you had walked in the way of God,
          you would be living in peace for ever.
14   Learn where there is wisdom,
          where there is strength,
          where there is understanding,
       so that you may at the same time discern
          where there is length of days, and life,
          where there is light for the eyes, and peace.
15   Who has found her place?
          And who has entered her storehouses?

³² But the one who knows all things knows her,
    he found her by his understanding.
The one who prepared the earth for all time
    filled it with four-footed creatures;
³³ the one who sends forth the light, and it goes;
    he called it, and it obeyed him, trembling;
³⁴ the stars shone in their watches, and were glad;
    he called them, and they said, 'Here we are!'
    They shone with gladness for him who made them.
³⁵ This is our God;
    no other can be compared to him.
³⁶ He found the whole way to knowledge,
    and gave her to his servant Jacob
    and to Israel, whom he loved.
³⁷ Afterwards she appeared on earth
    and lived with humankind.
¹ She is the book of the commandments of God,
    the law that endures for ever.
All who hold her fast will live,
    and those who forsake her will die.
² Turn, O Jacob, and take her;
    walk towards the shining of her light.
³ Do not give your glory to another,
    or your advantages to an alien people.
⁴ Happy are we, O Israel,
    for we know what is pleasing to God.

OR   **Proverbs 8.1–8, 19–21; 9.4b–6**

¹ Does not wisdom call,
    and does not understanding raise her voice?
² On the heights, beside the way,
    at the crossroads she takes her stand;
³ beside the gates in front of the town,
    at the entrance of the portals she cries out:
⁴ 'To you, O people, I call,
    and my cry is to all that live.
⁵ O simple ones, learn prudence;
    acquire intelligence, you who lack it.
⁶ Hear, for I will speak noble things,
    and from my lips will come what is right;
⁷ for my mouth will utter truth;
    wickedness is an abomination to my lips.

8   All the words of my mouth are righteous;
      there is nothing twisted or crooked in them.

19 'My fruit is better than gold, even fine gold,
      and my yield than choice silver.
20 I walk in the way of righteousness,
      along the paths of justice,
21 endowing with wealth those who love me,
      and filling their treasuries.'

4   To those without sense she says,
5   'Come, eat of my bread
      and drink of the wine I have mixed.
6   Lay aside immaturity, and live,
      and walk in the way of insight.'

PSALM   Psalm 19

1   The heavens declare the glory of God,
      and the firmament shows his handiwork.
2   One day tells its tale to another,
      and one night imparts knowledge to another.
3   Although they have no words or language,
      and their voices are not heard,
4   Their sound has gone out into all lands,
      and their message to the ends of the world.
5   In the deep has he set a pavilion for the sun;
      it comes forth like a bridegroom out of his chamber; it rejoices
        like a champion to run its course.
6   It goes forth from the uttermost edge of the heavens and runs
        about to the end of it again;
      nothing is hidden from its burning heat.
7   The law of the Lord is perfect and revives the soul;
      the testimony of the Lord is sure and gives wisdom to the innocent.
8   The statutes of the Lord are just and rejoice the heart;
      the commandment of the Lord is clear and gives light to the eyes.
9   The fear of the Lord is clean and endures for ever;
      the judgements of the Lord are true and righteous altogether.
10 More to be desired are they than gold, more than much fine gold,
      sweeter far than honey, than honey in the comb.
11 By them also is your servant enlightened,
      and in keeping them there is great reward.
12 Who can tell how often he offends?
      Cleanse me from my secret faults.

¹³ Above all, keep your servant from presumptuous sins; let them
    not get dominion over me;
then shall I be whole and sound, and innocent of a great offence.
¹⁴ Let the words of my mouth and the meditation of my heart be
    acceptable in your sight,
O Lord, my strength and my redeemer.

READING   Ezekiel 36.24–28

²⁴ I will take you from the nations, and gather you from all the countries,
and bring you into your own land. ²⁵ I will sprinkle clean water upon you,
and you shall be clean from all your uncleannesses, and from all your idols
I will cleanse you. ²⁶ A new heart I will give you, and a new spirit I will put
within you; and I will remove from your body the heart of stone and give
you a heart of flesh. ²⁷ I will put my spirit within you, and make you follow
my statutes and be careful to observe my ordinances. ²⁸ Then you shall live
in the land that I gave to your ancestors; and you shall be my people, and I
will be your God.

PSALMS   Psalm 42

¹ As the deer longs for the water-brooks,
    so longs my soul for you, O God.
² My soul is athirst for God, athirst for the living God;
    when shall I come to appear before the presence of God?
³ My tears have been my food day and night,
    while all day long they say to me, 'Where now is your God?'
⁴ I pour out my soul when I think on these things:
    how I went with the multitude and led them into the house of
        God,
⁵ With the voice of praise and thanksgiving,
    among those who keep holy-day.
⁶ Why are you so full of heaviness, O my soul?
    and why are you so disquieted within me?
⁷ Put your trust in God;
    for I will yet give thanks to him, who is the help of my countenance,
        and my God.
⁸ My soul is heavy within me;
    therefore I will remember you from the land of Jordan, and from
        the peak of Mizar among the heights of Hermon.
⁹ One deep calls to another in the noise of your cataracts;
    all your rapids and floods have gone over me.

10   The Lord grants his loving-kindness in the daytime;
 in the night season his song is with me, a prayer to the God of my
  life.
11   I will say to the God of my strength, 'Why have you forgotten me?
 and why do I go so heavily while the enemy oppresses me?'
12   While my bones are being broken,
 my enemies mock me to my face;
13   All day long they mock me
 say to me, 'Where now is your God?'
14   Why are you so full of heaviness, O my soul?
 and why are you so disquieted within me?
15   Put your trust in God;
 for I will yet give thanks to him, who is the help of my countenance,
  and my God.

Psalm 43

1   Give judgement for me, O God, and defend my cause against an
  ungodly people;
 deliver me from the deceitful and the wicked.
2   For you are the God of my strength; why have you put me from
  you?
 and why do I go so heavily while the enemy oppresses me?
3   Send out your light and your truth, that they may lead me,
 and bring me to your holy hill and to your dwelling;
4   That I may go to the altar of God, to the God of my joy and gladness;
 and on the harp I will give thanks to you, O God my God.
5   Why are you so full of heaviness, O my soul?
 and why are you so disquieted within me?
6   Put your trust in God;
 for I will yet give thanks to him, who is the help of my countenance,
  and my God.

READING   Ezekiel 37.1–14

1 The hand of the LORD came upon me, and he brought me out by the
spirit of the LORD and set me down in the middle of a valley; it was full of
bones. 2 He led me all round them; there were very many lying in the valley,
and they were very dry. 3 He said to me, 'Mortal, can these bones live?' I
answered, 'O Lord GOD, you know.' 4 Then he said to me, 'Prophesy to these
bones, and say to them: O dry bones, hear the word of the LORD. 5 Thus says
the Lord GOD to these bones: I will cause breath to enter you, and you shall
live. 6 I will lay sinews on you, and will cause flesh to come upon you, and

cover you with skin, and put breath in you, and you shall live; and you shall know that I am the Lord.'

⁷ So I prophesied as I had been commanded; and as I prophesied, suddenly there was a noise, a rattling, and the bones came together, bone to its bone. ⁸ I looked, and there were sinews on them, and flesh had come upon them, and skin had covered them; but there was no breath in them. ⁹ Then he said to me, 'Prophesy to the breath, prophesy, mortal, and say to the breath: Thus says the Lord God: Come from the four winds, O breath, and breathe upon these slain, that they may live.' ¹⁰ I prophesied as he commanded me, and the breath came into them, and they lived, and stood on their feet, a vast multitude.

¹¹ Then he said to me, 'Mortal, these bones are the whole house of Israel. They say, "Our bones are dried up, and our hope is lost; we are cut off completely." ¹² Therefore prophesy, and say to them, Thus says the Lord God: I am going to open your graves, and bring you up from your graves, O my people; and I will bring you back to the land of Israel. ¹³ And you shall know that I am the Lord, when I open your graves, and bring you up from your graves, O my people. ¹⁴ I will put my spirit within you, and you shall live, and I will place you on your own soil; then you shall know that I, the Lord, have spoken and will act, says the Lord.'

PSALM   Psalm 143

1   Lord, hear my prayer, and in your faithfulness heed my
        supplications;
    answer me in your righteousness.
2   Enter not into judgement with your servant,
    for in your sight shall no one living be justified.
3   For my enemy has sought my life and has crushed me to the
        ground;
    making me live in dark places like those who are long dead.
4   My spirit faints within me;
    my heart within me is desolate.
5   I remember the time past; I muse upon all your deeds;
    I consider the works of your hands.
6   I spread out my hands to you;
    my soul gasps to you like a thirsty land.
7   O Lord, make haste to answer me; my spirit fails me;
    do not hide your face from me or I shall be like those who go down
        to the Pit.

8 Let me hear of your loving-kindness in the morning, for I put my
   trust in you;
   show me the road that I must walk, for I lift up my soul to you.
9 Deliver me from my enemies, O Lord,
   for I flee to you for refuge.
10 Teach me to do what pleases you, for you are my God;
   let your good Spirit lead me on level ground.
11 Revive me, O Lord, for your name's sake;
   for your righteousness' sake, bring me out of trouble.
12 Of your goodness, destroy my enemies and bring all my foes to
   naught,
   for truly I am your servant.

READING   Zephaniah 3.14–20

14 Sing aloud, O daughter Zion;
      shout, O Israel!
   Rejoice and exult with all your heart,
      O daughter Jerusalem!
15 The LORD has taken away the judgements against you,
      he has turned away your enemies.
   The king of Israel, the LORD, is in your midst;
      you shall fear disaster no more.
16 On that day it shall be said to Jerusalem:
   Do not fear, O Zion;
      do not let your hands grow weak.
17 The LORD, your God, is in your midst,
      a warrior who gives victory;
   he will rejoice over you with gladness,
      he will renew you in his love;
   he will exult over you with loud singing
18   as on a day of festival.
   I will remove disaster from you,
      so that you will not bear reproach for it.
19 I will deal with all your oppressors
      at that time.
   And I will save the lame
      and gather the outcast,
   and I will change their shame into praise
      and renown in all the earth.

²⁰ At that time I will bring you home,
    at the time when I gather you;
  for I will make you renowned and praised
    among all the peoples of the earth,
  when I restore your fortunes
    before your eyes, says the LORD.

PSALM   Psalm 98

¹ Sing to the Lord a new song,
  for he has done marvellous things.
² With his right hand and his holy arm
  has he won for himself the victory.
³ The Lord has made known his victory;
  his righteousness has he openly shown in the sight of the nations.
⁴ He remembers his mercy and faithfulness to the house of Israel,
  and all the ends of the earth have seen the victory of our God.
⁵ Shout with joy to the Lord, all you lands;
  lift up your voice, rejoice and sing.
⁶ Sing to the Lord with the harp,
  with the harp and the voice of song.
⁷ With trumpets and the sound of the horn
  shout with joy before the King, the Lord.
⁸ Let the sea make a noise and all that is in it,
  the lands and those who dwell therein.
⁹ Let the rivers clap their hands,
  and let the hills ring out with joy before the Lord, when he comes
    to judge the earth.
¹⁰ In righteousness shall he judge the world,
  and the peoples with equity.

READING   Romans 6.3–11

³ Do you not know that all of us who have been baptized into Christ Jesus
were baptized into his death? ⁴ Therefore we have been buried with him by
baptism into death, so that, just as Christ was raised from the dead by the
glory of the Father, so we too might walk in newness of life.

⁵ For if we have been united with him in a death like his, we will certainly
be united with him in a resurrection like his. ⁶ We know that our old self
was crucified with him so that the body of sin might be destroyed, and we
might no longer be enslaved to sin. ⁷ For whoever has died is freed from
sin. ⁸ But if we have died with Christ, we believe that we will also live with

him. [9] We know that Christ, being raised from the dead, will never die again; death no longer has dominion over him. [10] The death he died, he died to sin, once for all; but the life he lives, he lives to God. [11] So you also must consider yourselves dead to sin and alive to God in Christ Jesus.

PSALM   Psalm 114

1   Alleluia! When Israel came out of Egypt,
    the house of Jacob from a people of strange speech,
2   Judah became God's sanctuary
    and Israel his dominion.
3   The sea beheld it and fled;
    Jordan turned and went back.
4   The mountains skipped like rams,
    and the little hills like young sheep.
5   What ailed you, O sea, that you fled?
    O Jordan, that you turned back?
6   You mountains, that you skipped like rams?
    you little hills like young sheep?
7   Tremble, O earth, at the presence of the Lord,
    at the presence of the God of Jacob,
8   Who turned the hard rock into a pool of water
    and flint-stone into a flowing spring.

GOSPEL   Mark 16.1–8

[1] When the sabbath was over, Mary Magdalene, and Mary the mother of James, and Salome bought spices, so that they might go and anoint him. [2] And very early on the first day of the week, when the sun had risen, they went to the tomb. [3] They had been saying to one another, 'Who will roll away the stone for us from the entrance to the tomb?' [4] When they looked up, they saw that the stone, which was very large, had already been rolled back. [5] As they entered the tomb, they saw a young man, dressed in a white robe, sitting on the right side; and they were alarmed. [6] But he said to them, 'Do not be alarmed; you are looking for Jesus of Nazareth, who was crucified. He has been raised; he is not here. Look, there is the place they laid him. [7] But go, tell his disciples and Peter that he is going ahead of you to Galilee; there you will see him, just as he told you.' [8] So they went out and fled from the tomb, for terror and amazement had seized them; and they said nothing to anyone, for they were afraid.

POST COMMUNION

God of Life,
who for our redemption gave your only-begotten Son
    to the death of the cross,
and by his glorious resurrection
have delivered us from the power of our enemy:
grant us so to die daily to sin,
that we may evermore live with him
    in the joy of his risen life;
through Jesus Christ our Lord.

EASTER DAY

COLLECT

Lord of all life and power,
who through the mighty resurrection of your Son
overcame the old order of sin and death
to make all things new in him:
grant that we, being dead to sin
and alive to you in Jesus Christ,
may reign with him in glory;
to whom with you and the Holy Spirit
be praise and honour, glory and might,
now and in all eternity.

READING

EITHER   Acts 10.34–43

[34] Then Peter began to speak to them: 'I truly understand that God shows
no partiality, [35] but in every nation anyone who fears him and does what is
right is acceptable to him. [36] You know the message he sent to the people
of Israel, preaching peace by Jesus Christ—he is Lord of all. [37] That message
spread throughout Judea, beginning in Galilee after the baptism that John
announced: [38] how God anointed Jesus of Nazareth with the Holy Spirit
and with power; how he went about doing good and healing all who were
oppressed by the devil, for God was with him. [39] We are witnesses to all
that he did both in Judea and in Jerusalem. They put him to death by
hanging him on a tree; [40] but God raised him on the third day and allowed
him to appear, [41] not to all the people but to us who were chosen by God as

witnesses, and who ate and drank with him after he rose from the dead.
⁴² He commanded us to preach to the people and to testify that he is the
one ordained by God as judge of the living and the dead. ⁴³ All the prophets
testify about him that everyone who believes in him receives forgiveness of
sins through his name.'

OR   Isaiah 25.6–9

⁶ On this mountain the LORD of hosts will make for all peoples
       a feast of rich food, a feast of well-matured wines,
       of rich food filled with marrow, of well-matured wines strained clear.
⁷ And he will destroy on this mountain
       the shroud that is cast over all peoples,
       the sheet that is spread over all nations;
⁸ he will swallow up death for ever.
    Then the Lord GOD will wipe away the tears from all faces,
       and the disgrace of his people he will take away from all the earth,
       for the LORD has spoken.
⁹ It will be said on that day,
       Lo, this is our God; we have waited for him, so that he might save us.
    This is the LORD for whom we have waited;
       let us be glad and rejoice in his salvation.

PSALM   Psalm 118.[1–2,] 14–24

[¹ Give thanks to the Lord, for he is good;
      his mercy endures for ever.
 ² Let Israel now proclaim,
      'His mercy endures for ever.']

¹⁴ The Lord is my strength and my song,
      and he has become my salvation.
¹⁵ There is a sound of exultation and victory
      in the tents of the righteous:
¹⁶ 'The right hand of the Lord has triumphed!
      the right hand of the Lord is exalted! the right hand of the Lord
         has triumphed!'
¹⁷ I shall not die, but live,
      and declare the works of the Lord.
¹⁸ The Lord has punished me sorely,
      but he did not hand me over to death.
¹⁹ Open for me the gates of righteousness;
      I will enter them; I will offer thanks to the Lord.

20 'This is the gate of the Lord;
    he who is righteous may enter.'
21 I will give thanks to you, for you answered me
    and have become my salvation.
22 The same stone which the builders rejected
    has become the chief corner-stone.
23 This is the Lord's doing,
    and it is marvellous in our eyes.
24 On this day the Lord has acted;
    we will rejoice and be glad in it.

READING

EITHER   **1 Corinthians 15.1–11**

¹ Now I should remind you, brothers and sisters, of the good news that I proclaimed to you, which you in turn received, in which also you stand, ² through which also you are being saved, if you hold firmly to the message that I proclaimed to you—unless you have come to believe in vain.

³ For I handed on to you as of first importance what I in turn had received: that Christ died for our sins in accordance with the scriptures, ⁴ and that he was buried, and that he was raised on the third day in accordance with the scriptures, ⁵ and that he appeared to Cephas, then to the twelve. ⁶ Then he appeared to more than five hundred brothers and sisters at one time, most of whom are still alive, though some have died. ⁷ Then he appeared to James, then to all the apostles. ⁸ Last of all, as to someone untimely born, he appeared also to me. ⁹ For I am the least of the apostles, unfit to be called an apostle, because I persecuted the church of God. ¹⁰ But by the grace of God I am what I am, and his grace towards me has not been in vain. On the contrary, I worked harder than any of them—though it was not I, but the grace of God that is with me. ¹¹ Whether then it was I or they, so we proclaim and so you have come to believe.

OR   **Acts 10.34–43**

³⁴ Then Peter began to speak to them: 'I truly understand that God shows no partiality, ³⁵ but in every nation anyone who fears him and does what is right is acceptable to him. ³⁶ You know the message he sent to the people of Israel, preaching peace by Jesus Christ—he is Lord of all. ³⁷ That message spread throughout Judea, beginning in Galilee after the baptism that John announced: ³⁸ how God anointed Jesus of Nazareth with the Holy Spirit and with power; how he went about doing good and healing all who were oppressed by the devil, for God was with him. ³⁹ We are witnesses to all

that he did both in Judea and in Jerusalem. They put him to death by hanging him on a tree; [40] but God raised him on the third day and allowed him to appear, [41] not to all the people but to us who were chosen by God as witnesses, and who ate and drank with him after he rose from the dead. [42] He commanded us to preach to the people and to testify that he is the one ordained by God as judge of the living and the dead. [43] All the prophets testify about him that everyone who believes in him receives forgiveness of sins through his name.'

GOSPEL

EITHER   John 20.1–18

[1] Early on the first day of the week, while it was still dark, Mary Magdalene came to the tomb and saw that the stone had been removed from the tomb. [2] So she ran and went to Simon Peter and the other disciple, the one whom Jesus loved, and said to them, 'They have taken the Lord out of the tomb, and we do not know where they have laid him.' [3] Then Peter and the other disciple set out and went towards the tomb. [4] The two were running together, but the other disciple outran Peter and reached the tomb first. [5] He bent down to look in and saw the linen wrappings lying there, but he did not go in. [6] Then Simon Peter came, following him, and went into the tomb. He saw the linen wrappings lying there, [7] and the cloth that had been on Jesus' head, not lying with the linen wrappings but rolled up in a place by itself. [8] Then the other disciple, who reached the tomb first, also went in, and he saw and believed; [9] for as yet they did not understand the scripture, that he must rise from the dead. [10] Then the disciples returned to their homes.

[11] But Mary stood weeping outside the tomb. As she wept, she bent over to look into the tomb; [12] and she saw two angels in white, sitting where the body of Jesus had been lying, one at the head and the other at the feet. [13] They said to her, 'Woman, why are you weeping?' She said to them, 'They have taken away my Lord, and I do not know where they have laid him.' [14] When she had said this, she turned round and saw Jesus standing there, but she did not know that it was Jesus. [15] Jesus said to her, 'Woman, why are you weeping? For whom are you looking?' Supposing him to be the gardener, she said to him, 'Sir, if you have carried him away, tell me where you have laid him, and I will take him away.' [16] Jesus said to her, 'Mary!' She turned and said to him in Hebrew, 'Rabbouni!' (which means Teacher). [17] Jesus said to her, 'Do not hold on to me, because I have not yet ascended to the Father. But go to my brothers and say to them, "I am ascending to

my Father and your Father, to my God and your God." ' ¹⁸ Mary Magdalene went and announced to the disciples, 'I have seen the Lord'; and she told them that he had said these things to her.

OR   **Mark 16.1–8**

¹ When the sabbath was over, Mary Magdalene, and Mary the mother of James, and Salome bought spices, so that they might go and anoint him. ² And very early on the first day of the week, when the sun had risen, they went to the tomb. ³ They had been saying to one another, 'Who will roll away the stone for us from the entrance to the tomb?' ⁴ When they looked up, they saw that the stone, which was very large, had already been rolled back. ⁵ As they entered the tomb, they saw a young man, dressed in a white robe, sitting on the right side; and they were alarmed. ⁶ But he said to them, 'Do not be alarmed; you are looking for Jesus of Nazareth, who was crucified. He has been raised; he is not here. Look, there is the place they laid him. ⁷ But go, tell his disciples and Peter that he is going ahead of you to Galilee; there you will see him, just as he told you.' ⁸ So they went out and fled from the tomb, for terror and amazement had seized them; and they said nothing to anyone, for they were afraid.

POST COMMUNION

God of Life,
who for our redemption gave your only-begotten Son
    to the death of the cross,
and by his glorious resurrection
have delivered us from the power of our enemy:
grant us so to die daily to sin,
that we may evermore live with him
    in the joy of his risen life;
through Jesus Christ our Lord.

SECOND SERVICE   THIRD SERVICE

Psalms 114; 117   **Psalms 105**
Ezekiel 37.1–14   *or*
Luke 24.13–35   **66.1–11**
                                           Genesis 1.1–5, 26–31
                                           2 Corinthians 5.14–6.2

OLD TESTAMENT READINGS FOR SUNDAYS IN EASTERTIDE

For those who require an Old Testament reading on the Sundays in Eastertide, provision is made in this table. If used, the reading from Acts must be used as the second reading.

THE SECOND SUNDAY OF EASTER	Exodus 14.10–31; 15.20–21
THE THIRD SUNDAY OF EASTER	Zephaniah 3.14–20
THE FOURTH SUNDAY OF EASTER	Genesis 7.1–5, 11–18; 8.6–18; 9.8–13
THE FIFTH SUNDAY OF EASTER	Baruch 3.9–15, 32–4.4 *or* Genesis 22.1–18
THE SIXTH SUNDAY OF EASTER	Isaiah 55.1–11
THE SEVENTH SUNDAY OF EASTER	Ezekiel 36.24–28

THE SECOND SUNDAY OF EASTER

The reading from Acts must be used. The second (New Testament) reading follows or, if the Old Testament reading is used, the Acts reading follows as the second reading.

COLLECT

Almighty Father,
you have given your only Son to die for our sins
and to rise again for our justification:
grant us so to put away the leaven of malice and wickedness
that we may always serve you
in pureness of living and truth;
through the merits of your Son Jesus Christ our Lord,
who is alive and reigns with you,
in the unity of the Holy Spirit,
one God, now and for ever.

READING   Acts 4.32–35

[32] Now the whole group of those who believed were of one heart and soul, and no one claimed private ownership of any possessions, but everything they owned was held in common. [33] With great power the apostles gave their testimony to the resurrection of the Lord Jesus, and great grace was upon them all. [34] There was not a needy person among them, for as many as owned lands or houses sold them and brought the proceeds of what was sold. [35] They laid it at the apostles' feet, and it was distributed to each as any had need.

PSALM   Psalm 133

1 O how good and pleasant it is,
   when a family lives together in unity!
2 It is like fine oil upon the head
   that runs down upon the beard,
3 Upon the beard of Aarcn,
   and runs down upon the collar of his robe.
4 It is like the dew of Hermon
   that falls upon the hills of Zion.
5 For there the Lord has ordained the blessing:
   life for evermore.

READING   1 John 1.1–2.2

1 We declare to you what was from the beginning, what we have heard,
what we have seen with our eyes, what we have looked at and touched with
our hands, concerning the word of life— 2 this life was revealed, and we
have seen it and testify to it, and declare to you the eternal life that was
with the Father and was revealed to us— 3 we declare to you what we have
seen and heard so that you also may have fellowship with us; and truly our
fellowship is with the Father and with his Son Jesus Christ. 4 We are writing
these things so that our joy may be complete.

5 This is the message we have heard from him and proclaim to you, that
God is light and in him there is no darkness at all. 6 If we say that we have
fellowship with him while we are walking in darkness, we lie and do not
do what is true; 7 but if we walk in the light as he himself is in the light,
we have fellowship with one another, and the blood of Jesus his Son cleanses
us from all sin. 8 If we say that we have no sin, we deceive ourselves, and
the truth is not in us. 9 If we confess our sins, he who is faithful and just
will forgive us our sins and cleanse us from all unrighteousness. 10 If we say
that we have not sinned, we make him a liar, and his word is not in us.

1 My little children, I am writing these things to you so that you may not
sin. But if anyone does sin, we have an advocate with the Father, Jesus
Christ the righteous; 2 and he is the atoning sacrifice for our sins, and not
for ours only but also for the sins of the whole world.

GOSPEL   John 20.19–31

19 When it was evening on that day, the first day of the week, and the
doors of the house where the disciples had met were locked for fear of the
Jews, Jesus came and stood among them and said, 'Peace be with you.'
20 After he said this, he showed them his hands and his side. Then the

disciples rejoiced when they saw the Lord. [21] Jesus said to them again, 'Peace be with you. As the Father has sent me, so I send you.' [22] When he had said this, he breathed on them and said to them, 'Receive the Holy Spirit. [23] If you forgive the sins of any, they are forgiven them; if you retain the sins of any, they are retained.'

[24] But Thomas (who was called the Twin), one of the twelve, was not with them when Jesus came. [25] So the other disciples told him, 'We have seen the Lord.' But he said to them, 'Unless I see the mark of the nails in his hands, and put my finger in the mark of the nails and my hand in his side, I will not believe.'

[26] A week later his disciples were again in the house, and Thomas was with them. Although the doors were shut, Jesus came and stood among them and said, 'Peace be with you.' [27] Then he said to Thomas, 'Put your finger here and see my hands. Reach out your hand and put it in my side. Do not doubt but believe.' [28] Thomas answered him, 'My Lord and my God!' [29] Jesus said to him, 'Have you believed because you have seen me? Blessed are those who have not seen and yet have come to believe.'

[30] Now Jesus did many other signs in the presence of his disciples, which are not written in this book. [31] But these are written so that you may come to believe that Jesus is the Messiah, the Son of God, and that through believing you may have life in his name.

POST COMMUNION

Lord God our Father,
through our Saviour Jesus Christ
you have assured your children of eternal life
and in baptism have made us one with him:
deliver us from the death of sin
and raise us to new life in your love,
in the fellowship of the Holy Spirit,
by the grace of our Lord Jesus Christ.

SECOND SERVICE

Psalm 143.1–11
Isaiah 26.1–9, 19
Luke 24.1–12

THIRD SERVICE

Psalm 22.19–30
Isaiah 53.6–12
Romans 4.13–25

THE THIRD SUNDAY OF EASTER

The reading from Acts must be used. The second (New Testament) reading follows or, if the Old Testament reading is used, the Acts reading follows as the second reading.

COLLECT

Almighty Father,
who in your great mercy gladdened the disciples
   with the sight of the risen Lord:
give us such knowledge of his presence with us,
that we may be strengthened and sustained
   by his risen life
and serve you continually in righteousness and truth;
through Jesus Christ your Son our Lord,
who is alive and reigns with you,
in the unity of the Holy Spirit,
one God, now and for ever.

READING   Acts 3.12–19

[12] When Peter saw it, he addressed the people, 'You Israelites, why do you wonder at this, or why do you stare at us, as though by our own power or piety we had made him walk? [13] The God of Abraham, the God of Isaac, and the God of Jacob, the God of our ancestors has glorified his servant Jesus, whom you handed over and rejected in the presence of Pilate, though he had decided to release him. [14] But you rejected the Holy and Righteous One and asked to have a murderer given to you, [15] and you killed the Author of life, whom God raised from the dead. To this we are witnesses. [16] And by faith in his name, his name itself has made this man strong, whom you see and know; and the faith that is through Jesus has given him this perfect health in the presence of all of you.

[17] 'And now, friends, I know that you acted in ignorance, as did also your rulers. [18] In this way God fulfilled what he had foretold through all the prophets, that his Messiah would suffer. [19] Repent therefore, and turn to God so that your sins may be wiped out.'

PSALM   Psalm 4

[1] Answer me when I call, O God, defender of my cause;
    you set me free when I am hard-pressed; have mercy on me and
      hear my prayer.
[2] 'You mortals, how long will you dishonour my glory;
    how long will you worship dumb idols and run after false gods?'

3 Know that the Lord does wonders for the faithful;
   when I call upon the Lord, he will hear me.
4 Tremble, then, and do not sin;
   speak to your heart in silence upon your bed.
5 Offer the appointed sacrifices
   and put your trust in the Lord.
6 Many are saying, 'O that we might see better times!'
   Lift up the light of your countenance upon us, O Lord.
7 You have put gladness in my heart,
   more than when grain and wine and oil increase.
8 I lie down in peace; at once I fall asleep;
   for only you, Lord, make me dwell in safety.

READING   1 John 3.1–7

¹ See what love the Father has given us, that we should be called children of God; and that is what we are. The reason the world does not know us is that it did not know him. ² Beloved, we are God's children now; what we will be has not yet been revealed. What we do know is this: when he is revealed, we will be like him, for we will see him as he is. ³ And all who have this hope in him purify themselves, just as he is pure.

⁴ Everyone who commits sin is guilty of lawlessness; sin is lawlessness. ⁵ You know that he was revealed to take away sins, and in him there is no sin. ⁶ No one who abides in him sins; no one who sins has either seen him or known him. ⁷ Little children, let no one deceive you. Everyone who does what is right is righteous, just as he is righteous.

GOSPEL   Luke 24.36b–48

³⁶ Jesus himself stood among them and said to them, 'Peace be with you.' ³⁷ They were startled and terrified, and thought that they were seeing a ghost. ³⁸ He said to them, 'Why are you frightened, and why do doubts arise in your hearts? ³⁹ Look at my hands and my feet; see that it is I myself. Touch me and see; for a ghost does not have flesh and bones as you see that I have.' ⁴⁰ And when he had said this, he showed them his hands and his feet. ⁴¹ While in their joy they were disbelieving and still wondering, he said to them, 'Have you anything here to eat?' ⁴² They gave him a piece of broiled fish, ⁴³ and he took it and ate in their presence.

⁴⁴ Then he said to them, 'These are my words that I spoke to you while I was still with you—that everything written about me in the law of Moses, the prophets, and the psalms must be fulfilled.' ⁴⁵ Then he opened their minds to understand the scriptures, ⁴⁶ and he said to them, 'Thus it is

written, that the Messiah is to suffer and to rise from the dead on the third day, [47] and that repentance and forgiveness of sins is to be proclaimed in his name to all nations, beginning from Jerusalem. [48] You are witnesses of these things.'

POST COMMUNION

Living God,
your Son made himself known to his disciples
in the breaking of bread:
open the eyes of our faith,
that we may see him in all his redeeming work;
who is alive and reigns, now and for ever.

SECOND SERVICE

Psalm 142
Deuteronomy 7.7–13
Revelation 2.1–11

If the Second Service is a Eucharist, the following is read as a Gospel:

Luke 16.19–31

THIRD SERVICE

Psalm 77.11–20
Isaiah 63.7–15
1 Corinthians 10.1–13

THE FOURTH SUNDAY OF EASTER

The reading from Acts must be used. The second (New Testament) reading follows or, if the Old Testament reading is used, the Acts reading follows as the second reading.

COLLECT

Almighty God,
whose Son Jesus Christ is the resurrection and the life:
raise us, who trust in him,
from the death of sin to the life of righteousness,
that we may seek those things which are above,
where he reigns with you
in the unity of the Holy Spirit,
one God, now and for ever.

YEAR B

READING   Acts 4.5-12

⁵ The next day their rulers, elders, and scribes assembled in Jerusalem, ⁶ with Annas the high priest, Caiaphas, John, and Alexander, and all who were of the high-priestly family. ⁷ When they had made the prisoners stand in their midst, they inquired, 'By what power or by what name did you do this?' ⁸ Then Peter, filled with the Holy Spirit, said to them, 'Rulers of the people and elders, ⁹ if we are questioned today because of a good deed done to someone who was sick and are asked how this man has been healed, ¹⁰ let it be known to all of you, and to all the people of Israel, that this man is standing before you in good health by the name of Jesus Christ of Nazareth, whom you crucified, whom God raised from the dead. ¹¹ This Jesus is

"the stone that was rejected by you, the builders;
it has become the cornerstone."
¹² There is salvation in no one else, for there is no other name under heaven given among mortals by which we must be saved.'

PSALM   Psalm 23

¹ The Lord is my shepherd;
I shall not be in want.
² He makes me lie down in green pastures
and leads me beside still waters.
³ He revives my soul
and guides me along right pathways for his name's sake.
⁴ Though I walk through the valley of the shadow of death, I shall
fear no evil;
for you are with me; your rod and your staff, they comfort me.
⁵ You spread a table before me in the presence of those who trouble
me;
you have anointed my head with oil, and my cup is running over.
⁶ Surely your goodness and mercy shall follow me all the days of my
life,
and I will dwell in the house of the Lord for ever.

READING   1 John 3.16-24

¹⁶ We know love by this, that he laid down his life for us—and we ought to lay down our lives for one another. ¹⁷ How does God's love abide in anyone who has the world's goods and sees a brother or sister in need and yet refuses help?

544

[18] Little children, let us love, not in word or speech, but in truth and action. [19] And by this we will know that we are from the truth and will reassure our hearts before him [20] whenever our hearts condemn us; for God is greater than our hearts, and he knows everything. [21] Beloved, if our hearts do not condemn us, we have boldness before God; [22] and we receive from him whatever we ask, because we obey his commandments and do what pleases him.

[23] And this is his commandment, that we should believe in the name of his Son Jesus Christ and love one another, just as he has commanded us. [24] All who obey his commandments abide in him, and he abides in them. And by this we know that he abides in us, by the Spirit that he has given us.

GOSPEL   John 10.11–18

[11] 'I am the good shepherd. The good shepherd lays down his life for the sheep. [12] The hired hand, who is not the shepherd and does not own the sheep, sees the wolf coming and leaves the sheep and runs away—and the wolf snatches them and scatters them. [13] The hired hand runs away because a hired hand does not care for the sheep. [14] I am the good shepherd. I know my own and my own know me, [15] just as the Father knows me and I know the Father. And I lay down my life for the sheep. [16] I have other sheep that do not belong to this fold. I must bring them also, and they will listen to my voice. So there will be one flock, one shepherd. [17] For this reason the Father loves me, because I lay down my life in order to take it up again. [18] No one takes it from me, but I lay it down of my own accord. I have power to lay it down, and I have power to take it up again. I have received this command from my Father.'

POST COMMUNION

Merciful Father,
you gave your Son Jesus Christ to be the good shepherd,
and in his love for us to lay down his life and rise again:
keep us always under his protection,
and give us grace to follow in his steps;
through Jesus Christ our Lord.

SECOND SERVICE	THIRD SERVICE
Psalm 81.8–16	Psalm 119.89–96
Exodus 16.4–15	Nehemiah 8.1–12
Revelation 2.12–17	Luke 24.25–32

If the Second Service is a Eucharist, the following is read as a Gospel:

John 6.30–40

THE FIFTH SUNDAY OF EASTER

The reading from Acts must be used. The second (New Testament) reading follows or, if the Old Testament reading is used, the Acts reading follows as the second reading.

COLLECT

Almighty God,
who through your only-begotten Son Jesus Christ
have overcome death and opened to us
    the gate of everlasting life:
grant that, as by your grace going before us
    you put into our minds good desires,
so by your continual help
we may bring them to good effect;
through Jesus Christ our risen Lord,
who is alive and reigns with you,
in the unity of the Holy Spirit,
one God, now and for ever.

READING   Acts 8.26–40

²⁶ Then an angel of the Lord said to Philip, 'Get up and go towards the south to the road that goes down from Jerusalem to Gaza.' (This is a wilderness road.) ²⁷ So he got up and went. Now there was an Ethiopian eunuch, a court official of the Candace, queen of the Ethiopians, in charge of her entire treasury. He had come to Jerusalem to worship ²⁸ and was returning home; seated in his chariot, he was reading the prophet Isaiah. ²⁹ Then the Spirit said to Philip, 'Go over to this chariot and join it.' ³⁰ So Philip ran up to it and heard him reading the prophet Isaiah. He asked, 'Do you understand what you are reading?' ³¹ He replied, 'How can I, unless

someone guides me?' And he invited Philip to get in and sit beside him. ³² Now the passage of the scripture that he was reading was this:

'Like a sheep he was led to the slaughter,
and like a lamb silent before its shearer,
so he does not open his mouth.
³³ In his humiliation justice was denied him.
Who can describe his generation?
For his life is taken away from the earth.'

³⁴ The eunuch asked Philip, 'About whom, may I ask you, does the prophet say this, about himself or about someone else?' ³⁵ Then Philip began to speak, and starting with this scripture, he proclaimed to him the good news about Jesus. ³⁶ As they were going along the road, they came to some water; and the eunuch said, 'Look, here is water! What is to prevent me from being baptized?'

³⁸ He commanded the chariot to stop, and both of them, Philip and the eunuch, went down into the water, and Philip baptized him. ³⁹ When they came up out of the water, the Spirit of the Lord snatched Philip away; the eunuch saw him no more, and went on his way rejoicing. ⁴⁰ But Philip found himself at Azotus, and as he was passing through the region, he proclaimed the good news to all the towns until he came to Caesarea.

PSALM   Psalm 22.24–30

24 My praise is of him in the great assembly;
I will perform my vows in the presence of those who worship him.
25 The poor shall eat and be satisfied, and those who seek the Lord
shall praise him:
'May your heart live for ever!'
26 All the ends of the earth shall remember and turn to the Lord,
and all the families of the nations shall bow before him.
27 For kingship belongs to the Lord;
he rules over the nations.
28 To him alone all who sleep in the earth bow down in worship;
all who go down to the dust fall before him.
29 My soul shall live for him; my descendants shall serve him;
they shall be known as the Lord's for ever.
30 They shall come and make known to a people yet unborn
the saving deeds that he has done.

READING
1 John 4.7–21

⁷ Beloved, let us love one another, because love is from God; everyone who loves is born of God and knows God. ⁸ Whoever does not love does not know God, for God is love. ⁹ God's love was revealed among us in this way: God sent his only Son into the world so that we might live through him. ¹⁰ In this is love, not that we loved God but that he loved us and sent his Son to be the atoning sacrifice for our sins. ¹¹ Beloved, since God loved us so much, we also ought to love one another. ¹² No one has ever seen God; if we love one another, God lives in us, and his love is perfected in us.

¹³ By this we know that we abide in him and he in us, because he has given us of his Spirit. ¹⁴ And we have seen and do testify that the Father has sent his Son as the Saviour of the world. ¹⁵ God abides in those who confess that Jesus is the Son of God, and they abide in God. ¹⁶ So we have known and believe the love that God has for us.

God is love, and those who abide in love abide in God, and God abides in them. ¹⁷ Love has been perfected among us in this: that we may have boldness on the day of judgement, because as he is, so are we in this world. ¹⁸ There is no fear in love, but perfect love casts out fear; for fear has to do with punishment, and whoever fears has not reached perfection in love. ¹⁹ We love because he first loved us. ²⁰ Those who say, 'I love God', and hate their brothers or sisters, are liars; for those who do not love a brother or sister whom they have seen, cannot love God whom they have not seen. ²¹ The commandment we have from him is this: those who love God must love their brothers and sisters also.

GOSPEL
John 15.1–8

¹ 'I am the true vine, and my Father is the vine-grower. ² He removes every branch in me that bears no fruit. Every branch that bears fruit he prunes to make it bear more fruit. ³ You have already been cleansed by the word that I have spoken to you. ⁴ Abide in me as I abide in you. Just as the branch cannot bear fruit by itself unless it abides in the vine, neither can you unless you abide in me. ⁵ I am the vine, you are the branches. Those who abide in me and I in them bear much fruit, because apart from me you can do nothing. ⁶ Whoever does not abide in me is thrown away like a branch and withers; such branches are gathered, thrown into the fire, and burned. ⁷ If you abide in me, and my words abide in you, ask for whatever you wish, and it will be done for you. ⁸ My Father is glorified by this, that you bear much fruit and become my disciples.'

POST COMMUNION

Eternal God,
whose Son Jesus Christ is the way, the truth, and the life:
grant us to walk in his way,
to rejoice in his truth,
and to share his risen life;
who is alive and reigns, now and for ever.

SECOND SERVICE

THIRD SERVICE

Psalm 96
Isaiah 60.1–14
Revelation 3.1–13

*If the Second Service is a Eucharist, the
following is read as a Gospel:*

Mark 16.9–16

Psalm 44.15–26
2 Maccabees 7.7–14

or

Daniel 3.16–28
Hebrews 11.32–12.2

THE SIXTH SUNDAY OF EASTER

*The reading from Acts must be used. The second (New Testament) reading follows or,
if the Old Testament reading is used, the Acts reading follows as the second reading.*

COLLECT

God our redeemer,
you have delivered us from the power of darkness
and brought us into the kingdom of your Son:
grant, that as by his death he has recalled us to life,
so by his continual presence in us he may raise us
    to eternal joy;
through Jesus Christ your Son our Lord,
who is alive and reigns with you,
in the unity of the Holy Spirit,
one God, now and for ever.

READING
Acts 10.44–48

44 While Peter was still speaking, the Holy Spirit fell upon all who heard the word. 45 The circumcised believers who had come with Peter were astounded that the gift of the Holy Spirit had been poured out even on the

Gentiles, [46] for they heard them speaking in tongues and extolling God. Then Peter said, [47] 'Can anyone withhold the water for baptizing these people who have received the Holy Spirit just as we have?' [48] So he ordered them to be baptized in the name of Jesus Christ. Then they invited him to stay for several days.

PSALM   Psalm 98

1   Sing to the Lord a new song,
    for he has done marvellous things.
2   With his right hand and his holy arm
    has he won for himself the victory.
3   The Lord has made known his victory;
    his righteousness has he openly shown in the sight of the nations.
4   He remembers his mercy and faithfulness to the house of Israel,
    and all the ends of the earth have seen the victory of our God.
5   Shout with joy to the Lord, all you lands;
    lift up your voice, rejoice and sing.
6   Sing to the Lord with the harp,
    with the harp and the voice of song.
7   With trumpets and the sound of the horn
    shout with joy before the King, the Lord.
8   Let the sea make a noise and all that is in it,
    the lands and those who dwell therein.
9   Let the rivers clap their hands,
    and let the hills ring out with joy before the Lord, when he comes
        to judge the earth.
10 In righteousness shall he judge the world,
    and the peoples with equity.

READING   1 John 5.1–6

[1] Everyone who believes that Jesus is the Christ has been born of God, and everyone who loves the parent loves the child. [2] By this we know that we love the children of God, when we love God and obey his commandments. [3] For the love of God is this, that we obey his commandments. And his commandments are not burdensome, [4] for whatever is born of God conquers the world. And this is the victory that conquers the world, our faith. [5] Who is it that conquers the world but the one who believes that Jesus is the Son of God?

[6] This is the one who came by water and blood, Jesus Christ, not with the water only but with the water and the blood. And the Spirit is the one that testifies, for the Spirit is the truth.

GOSPEL   John 15.9–17

[9] 'As the Father has loved me, so I have loved you; abide in my love. [10] If you keep my commandments, you will abide in my love, just as I have kept my Father's commandments and abide in his love. [11] I have said these things to you so that my joy may be in you, and that your joy may be complete.

[12] 'This is my commandment, that you love one another as I have loved you. [13] No one has greater love than this, to lay down one's life for one's friends. [14] You are my friends if you do what I command you. [15] I do not call you servants any longer, because the servant does not know what the master is doing; but I have called you friends, because I have made known to you everything that I have heard from my Father. [16] You did not choose me but I chose you. And I appointed you to go and bear fruit, fruit that will last, so that the Father will give you whatever you ask him in my name. [17] I am giving you these commands so that you may love one another.'

POST COMMUNION

God our Father,
whose Son Jesus Christ gives the water of eternal life:
may we thirst for you,
the spring of life and source of goodness,
through him who is alive and reigns, now and for ever.

SECOND SERVICE   THIRD SERVICE

Psalm 45   **Psalm 104.27–33**
Song of Solomon 4.16–5.2; 8.6–7   **Ezekiel 47.1–12**
Revelation 3.14–22   **John 21.1–19**

If the Second Service is a Eucharist, the following is read as a Gospel:

Luke 22.24–30

ASCENSION DAY

COLLECT

Grant, we pray, almighty God,
that as we believe your only-begotten Son
   our Lord Jesus Christ
to have ascended into the heavens,
so we in heart and mind may also ascend
and with him continually dwell;
who is alive and reigns with you,
in the unity of the Holy Spirit,
one God, now and for ever.

The reading from Acts must be used as either the first or second reading

READING

EITHER   **Acts 1.1–11**

¹ In the first book, Theophilus, I wrote about all that Jesus did and taught from the beginning ² until the day when he was taken up to heaven, after giving instructions through the Holy Spirit to the apostles whom he had chosen. ³ After his suffering he presented himself alive to them by many convincing proofs, appearing to them over the course of forty days and speaking about the kingdom of God. ⁴ While staying with them, he ordered them not to leave Jerusalem, but to wait there for the promise of the Father. 'This', he said, 'is what you have heard from me; ⁵ for John baptized with water, but you will be baptized with the Holy Spirit not many days from now.'

⁶ So when they had come together, they asked him, 'Lord, is this the time when you will restore the kingdom to Israel?' ⁷ He replied, 'It is not for you to know the times or periods that the Father has set by his own authority. ⁸ But you will receive power when the Holy Spirit has come upon you; and you will be my witnesses in Jerusalem, in all Judea and Samaria, and to the ends of the earth.' ⁹ When he had said this, as they were watching, he was lifted up, and a cloud took him out of their sight. ¹⁰ While he was going and they were gazing up towards heaven, suddenly two men in white robes stood by them. ¹¹ They said, 'Men of Galilee, why do you stand looking up towards heaven? This Jesus, who has been taken up from you into heaven, will come in the same way as you saw him go into heaven.'

OR

Daniel 7.9–14

9 As I watched,
  thrones were set in place,
    and an Ancient One took his throne;
  his clothing was white as snow,
    and the hair of his head like pure wool;
  his throne was fiery flames,
    and its wheels were burning fire.
10 A stream of fire issued
    and flowed out from his presence.
  A thousand thousand served him,
    and ten thousand times ten thousand stood attending him.
  The court sat in judgement,
    and the books were opened.

11 I watched then because of the noise of the arrogant words that the horn was speaking. And as I watched, the beast was put to death, and its body destroyed and given over to be burned with fire. 12 As for the rest of the beasts, their dominion was taken away, but their lives were prolonged for a season and a time. 13 As I watched in the night visions,

  I saw one like a human being
    coming with the clouds of heaven.
  And he came to the Ancient One
    and was presented before him.
14 To him was given dominion
    and glory and kingship,
  that all peoples, nations, and languages
    should serve him.
  His dominion is an everlasting dominion
    that shall not pass away,
  and his kingship is one
    that shall never be destroyed.

PSALM

EITHER

Psalm 47

1 Clap your hands, all you peoples;
    shout to God with a cry of joy.
2 For the Lord Most High is to be feared;
    he is the great king over all the earth.
3 He subdues the peoples under us,
    and the nations under our feet.

4   He chooses our inheritance for us,
     the pride of Jacob whom he loves.
5   God has gone up with a shout,
     the Lord with the sound of the ram's-horn.
6   Sing praises to God, sing praises;
     sing praises to our king, sing praises.
7   For God is king of all the earth;
     sing praises with all your skill.
8   God reigns over the nations;
     God sits upon his holy throne.
9   The nobles of the peoples have gathered together
     with the people of the God of Abraham.
10 The rulers of the earth belong to God,
     and he is highly exalted.

OR   **Psalm 93**

1   The Lord is king; he has put on splendid apparel;
     the Lord has put on his apparel and girded himself with strength.
2   He has made the whole world so sure
     that it cannot be moved;
3   Ever since the world began, your throne has been established;
     you are from everlasting.
4   The waters have lifted up, O Lord, the waters have lifted up their
       voice;
     the waters have lifted up their pounding waves.
5   Mightier than the sound of many waters, mightier than the
       breakers of the sea,
     mightier is the Lord who dwells on high.
6   Your testimonies are very sure,
     and holiness adorns your house, O Lord, for ever and for evermore.

READING

EITHER   **Ephesians 1.15–23**

15 I have heard of your faith in the Lord Jesus and your love towards all the saints, and for this reason 16 I do not cease to give thanks for you as I remember you in my prayers. 17 I pray that the God of our Lord Jesus Christ, the Father of glory, may give you a spirit of wisdom and revelation as you come to know him, 18 so that, with the eyes of your heart enlightened, you may know what is the hope to which he has called you, what are the riches of his glorious inheritance among the saints, 19 and what is the

immeasurable greatness of his power for us who believe, according to the working of his great power. [20] God put this power to work in Christ when he raised him from the dead and seated him at his right hand in the heavenly places, [21] far above all rule and authority and power and dominion, and above every name that is named, not only in this age but also in the age to come. [22] And he has put all things under his feet and has made him the head over all things for the church, [23] which is his body, the fullness of him who fills all in all.

OR   **Acts 1.1–11**

[1] In the first book, Theophilus, I wrote about all that Jesus did and taught from the beginning [2] until the day when he was taken up to heaven, after giving instructions through the Holy Spirit to the apostles whom he had chosen. [3] After his suffering he presented himself alive to them by many convincing proofs, appearing to them over the course of forty days and speaking about the kingdom of God. [4] While staying with them, he ordered them not to leave Jerusalem, but to wait there for the promise of the Father. 'This', he said, 'is what you have heard from me; [5] for John baptized with water, but you will be baptized with the Holy Spirit not many days from now.'

[6] So when they had come together, they asked him, 'Lord, is this the time when you will restore the kingdom to Israel?' [7] He replied, 'It is not for you to know the times or periods that the Father has set by his own authority. [8] But you will receive power when the Holy Spirit has come upon you; and you will be my witnesses in Jerusalem, in all Judea and Samaria, and to the ends of the earth.' [9] When he had said this, as they were watching, he was lifted up, and a cloud took him out of their sight. [10] While he was going and they were gazing up towards heaven, suddenly two men in white robes stood by them. [11] They said, 'Men of Galilee, why do you stand looking up towards heaven? This Jesus, who has been taken up from you into heaven, will come in the same way as you saw him go into heaven.'

GOSPEL   **Luke 24.44–53**

[44] Then he said to them, 'These are my words that I spoke to you while I was still with you—that everything written about me in the law of Moses, the prophets, and the psalms must be fulfilled.' [45] Then he opened their minds to understand the scriptures, [46] and he said to them, 'Thus it is written, that the Messiah is to suffer and to rise from the dead on the third day, [47] and that repentance and forgiveness of sins is to be proclaimed in his name to all nations, beginning from Jerusalem. [48] You are witnesses of these things. [49] And see, I am sending upon you what my Father promised;

so stay here in the city until you have been clothed with power from on high.'

⁵⁰ Then he led them out as far as Bethany, and, lifting up his hands, he blessed them. ⁵¹ While he was blessing them, he withdrew from them and was carried up into heaven. ⁵² And they worshipped him, and returned to Jerusalem with great joy; ⁵³ and they were continually in the temple blessing God.

POST COMMUNION

God our Father,
you have raised our humanity in Christ
and have fed us with the bread of heaven:
mercifully grant that, nourished with such spiritual blessings,
we may set our hearts in the heavenly places;
through Jesus Christ our Lord.

SECOND SERVICE

Psalm 8
Prayer of Azariah 29–37
or
2 Kings 2.1–15
Revelation 5

If the Second Service is a Eucharist, the following is read as a Gospel:

Matthew 28.16–20

THIRD SERVICE

Psalm 110
Isaiah 52.7–15
Hebrews 7.[11–25,] 26–28

THE SEVENTH SUNDAY OF EASTER
SUNDAY AFTER ASCENSION DAY

The reading from Acts must be used. The second (New Testament) reading follows or,
if the Old Testament reading is used, the Acts reading follows as the second reading.

COLLECT

O God the king of glory,
you have exalted your only Son Jesus Christ
with great triumph to your kingdom in heaven:
we beseech you, leave us not comfortless,
but send your Holy Spirit to strengthen us
and exalt us to the place
    where our Saviour Christ is gone before,
who is alive and reigns with you,
in the unity of the Holy Spirit,
one God, now and for ever.

READING   Acts 1.15-17, 21-26

[15] In those days Peter stood up among the believers (together the crowd numbered about one hundred and twenty people) and said, [16] 'Friends, the scripture had to be fulfilled, which the Holy Spirit through David foretold concerning Judas, who became a guide for those who arrested Jesus— [17] for he was numbered among us and was allotted his share in this ministry.'

[21] 'So one of the men who have accompanied us throughout the time that the Lord Jesus went in and out among us, [22] beginning from the baptism of John until the day when he was taken up from us—one of these must become a witness with us to his resurrection.' [23] So they proposed two, Joseph called Barsabbas, who was also known as Justus, and Matthias. [24] Then they prayed and said, 'Lord, you know everyone's heart. Show us which one of these two you have chosen [25] to take the place in this ministry and apostleship from which Judas turned aside to go to his own place.' [26] And they cast lots for them, and the lot fell on Matthias; and he was added to the eleven apostles.

PSALM   Psalm 1

[1]   Happy are they who have not walked in the counsel of the wicked,
        nor lingered in the way of sinners, nor sat in the seats of the
        scornful!

2 Their delight is in the law of the Lord,
    and they meditate on his law day and night.
3 They are like trees planted by streams of water, bearing fruit in
      due season, with leaves that do not wither;
    everything they do shall prosper.
4 It is not so with the wicked:
    they are like chaff which the wind blows away;
5 Therefore the wicked shall not stand upright when judgement
    comes,
    nor the sinner in the council of the righteous.
6 For the Lord knows the way of the righteous,
    but the way of the wicked is doomed.

READING   1 John 5.9–13

9 If we receive human testimony, the testimony of God is greater; for this is the testimony of God that he has testified to his Son. 10 Those who believe in the Son of God have the testimony in their hearts. Those who do not believe in God have made him a liar by not believing in the testimony that God has given concerning his Son. 11 And this is the testimony: God gave us eternal life, and this life is in his Son. 12 Whoever has the Son has life; whoever does not have the Son of God does not have life.

13 I write these things to you who believe in the name of the Son of God, so that you may know that you have eternal life.

GOSPEL   John 17.6–19

6 'I have made your name known to those whom you gave me from the world. They were yours, and you gave them to me, and they have kept your word. 7 Now they know that everything you have given me is from you; 8 for the words that you gave to me I have given to them, and they have received them and know in truth that I came from you; and they have believed that you sent me. 9 I am asking on their behalf; I am not asking on behalf of the world, but on behalf of those whom you gave me, because they are yours. 10 All mine are yours, and yours are mine; and I have been glorified in them. 11 And now I am no longer in the world, but they are in the world, and I am coming to you. Holy Father, protect them in your name that you have given me, so that they may be one, as we are one. 12 While I was with them, I protected them in your name that you have given me. I guarded them, and not one of them was lost except the one destined to be lost, so that the scripture might be fulfilled. 13 But now I am coming to you, and I speak these things in the world so that they may have my joy made complete in

themselves. [14] I have given them your word, and the world has hated them because they do not belong to the world, just as I do not belong to the world. [15] I am not asking you to take them out of the world, but I ask you to protect them from the evil one. [16] They do not belong to the world, just as I do not belong to the world. [17] Sanctify them in the truth; your word is truth. [18] As you have sent me into the world, so I have sent them into the world. [19] And for their sakes I sanctify myself, so that they also may be sanctified in truth.'

POST COMMUNION

Eternal God, giver of love and power,
your Son Jesus Christ has sent us into all the world
to preach the gospel of his kingdom:
confirm us in this mission,
and help us to live the good news we proclaim;
through Jesus Christ our Lord.

SECOND SERVICE | THIRD SERVICE

Psalm 147.1–12 | **Psalm 76**
Isaiah 61.1–11 | **Isaiah 14.3–15**
Luke 4.14–21 | **Revelation 14.1–13**

DAY OF PENTECOST
WHIT SUNDAY

COLLECT

God, who as at this time
taught the hearts of your faithful people
by sending to them the light of your Holy Spirit:
grant us by the same Spirit
to have a right judgement in all things
and evermore to rejoice in his holy comfort;
through the merits of Christ Jesus our Saviour,
who is alive and reigns with you,
in the unity of the Holy Spirit,
one God, now and for ever.

The reading from Acts must be used as either the first or second reading

READING

EITHER   Acts 2.1–21

¹ When the day of Pentecost had come, they were all together in one place. ² And suddenly from heaven there came a sound like the rush of a violent wind, and it filled the entire house where they were sitting. ³ Divided tongues, as of fire, appeared among them, and a tongue rested on each of them. ⁴ All of them were filled with the Holy Spirit and began to speak in other languages, as the Spirit gave them ability.

⁵ Now there were devout Jews from every nation under heaven living in Jerusalem. ⁶ And at this sound the crowd gathered and was bewildered, because each one heard them speaking in the native language of each. ⁷ Amazed and astonished, they asked, 'Are not all these who are speaking Galileans? ⁸ And how is it that we hear, each of us, in our own native language? ⁹ Parthians, Medes, Elamites, and residents of Mesopotamia, Judea and Cappadocia, Pontus and Asia, ¹⁰ Phrygia and Pamphylia, Egypt and the parts of Libya belonging to Cyrene, and visitors from Rome, both Jews and proselytes, ¹¹ Cretans and Arabs—in our own languages we hear them speaking about God's deeds of power.' ¹² All were amazed and perplexed, saying to one another, 'What does this mean?' ¹³ But others sneered and said, 'They are filled with new wine.'

¹⁴ But Peter, standing with the eleven, raised his voice and addressed them: 'Men of Judea and all who live in Jerusalem, let this be known to you, and listen to what I say. ¹⁵ Indeed, these are not drunk, as you suppose, for it is only nine o'clock in the morning. ¹⁶ No, this is what was spoken through the prophet Joel:

¹⁷ "In the last days it will be, God declares,
     that I will pour out my Spirit upon all flesh,
         and your sons and your daughters shall prophesy,
     and your young men shall see visions,
         and your old men shall dream dreams.
¹⁸ Even upon my slaves, both men and women,
         in those days I will pour out my Spirit;
             and they shall prophesy.
¹⁹ And I will show portents in the heaven above
         and signs on the earth below,
             blood, and fire, and smoky mist.

²⁰ The sun shall be turned to darkness
    and the moon to blood,
        before the coming of the Lord's great and glorious day.
²¹ Then everyone who calls on the name of the Lord shall be saved." '

OR   ### Ezekiel 37.1–14

¹ The hand of the LORD came upon me, and he brought me out by the spirit of the LORD and set me down in the middle of a valley; it was full of bones. ² He led me all round them; there were very many lying in the valley, and they were very dry. ³ He said to me, 'Mortal, can these bones live?' I answered, 'O Lord GOD, you know.' ⁴ Then he said to me, 'Prophesy to these bones, and say to them: O dry bones, hear the word of the LORD. ⁵ Thus says the Lord GOD to these bones: I will cause breath to enter you, and you shall live. ⁶ I will lay sinews on you, and will cause flesh to come upon you, and cover you with skin, and put breath in you, and you shall live; and you shall know that I am the LORD.'

⁷ So I prophesied as I had been commanded; and as I prophesied, suddenly there was a noise, a rattling, and the bones came together, bone to its bone. ⁸ I looked, and there were sinews on them, and flesh had come upon them, and skin had covered them; but there was no breath in them. ⁹ Then he said to me, 'Prophesy to the breath, prophesy, mortal, and say to the breath: Thus says the Lord GOD: Come from the four winds, O breath, and breathe upon these slain, that they may live.' ¹⁰ I prophesied as he commanded me, and the breath came into them, and they lived, and stood on their feet, a vast multitude.

¹¹ Then he said to me, 'Mortal, these bones are the whole house of Israel. They say, "Our bones are dried up, and our hope is lost; we are cut off completely." ¹² Therefore prophesy, and say to them, Thus says the Lord GOD: I am going to open your graves, and bring you up from your graves, O my people; and I will bring you back to the land of Israel. ¹³ And you shall know that I am the LORD, when I open your graves, and bring you up from your graves, O my people. ¹⁴ I will put my spirit within you, and you shall live, and I will place you on your own soil; then you shall know that I, the LORD, have spoken and will act, says the LORD.'

PSALM   Psalm 104.25–35, [36,] 37

²⁵ O Lord, how manifold are your works!
    in wisdom you have made them all; the earth is full of your
        creatures.

26 Yonder is the great and wide sea with its living things too many
    to number,
  creatures both small and great.
27 There move the ships, and there is that Leviathan,
  which you have made for the sport of it.
28 All of them look to you
  to give them their food in due season.
29 You give it to them, they gather it;
  you open your hand and they are filled with good things.
30 You hide your face and they are terrified;
  you take away their breath and they die and return to their dust.
31 You send forth your Spirit and they are created;
  and so you renew the face of the earth.
32 May the glory of the Lord endure for ever;
  may the Lord rejoice in all his works.
33 He looks at the earth and it trembles;
  he touches the mountains and they smoke.
34 I will sing to the Lord as long as I live;
  I will praise my God while I have my being.
35 May these words of mine please him;
  I will rejoice in the Lord.
[36 Let sinners be consumed out of the earth,
  and the wicked be no more.]
37 Bless the Lord, O my soul.
  Alleluia!

READING

EITHER   **Romans 8.22–27**

22 We know that the whole creation has been groaning in labour pains until now; 23 and not only the creation, but we ourselves, who have the first fruits of the Spirit, groan inwardly while we wait for adoption, the redemption of our bodies. 24 For in hope we were saved. Now hope that is seen is not hope. For who hopes for what is seen? 25 But if we hope for what we do not see, we wait for it with patience.

26 Likewise the Spirit helps us in our weakness; for we do not know how to pray as we ought, but that very Spirit intercedes with sighs too deep for words. 27 And God, who searches the heart, knows what is the mind of the Spirit, because the Spirit intercedes for the saints according to the will of God.

OR   **Acts 2.1–21**

[1] When the day of Pentecost had come, they were all together in one place. [2] And suddenly from heaven there came a sound like the rush of a violent wind, and it filled the entire house where they were sitting. [3] Divided tongues, as of fire, appeared among them, and a tongue rested on each of them. [4] All of them were filled with the Holy Spirit and began to speak in other languages, as the Spirit gave them ability.

[5] Now there were devout Jews from every nation under heaven living in Jerusalem. [6] And at this sound the crowd gathered and was bewildered, because each one heard them speaking in the native language of each. [7] Amazed and astonished, they asked, 'Are not all these who are speaking Galileans? [8] And how is it that we hear, each of us, in our own native language? [9] Parthians, Medes, Elamites, and residents of Mesopotamia, Judea and Cappadocia, Pontus and Asia, [10] Phrygia and Pamphylia, Egypt and the parts of Libya belonging to Cyrene, and visitors from Rome, both Jews and proselytes, [11] Cretans and Arabs—in our own languages we hear them speaking about God's deeds of power.' [12] All were amazed and perplexed, saying to one another, 'What does this mean?' [13] But others sneered and said, 'They are filled with new wine.'

[14] But Peter, standing with the eleven, raised his voice and addressed them: 'Men of Judea and all who live in Jerusalem, let this be known to you, and listen to what I say. [15] Indeed, these are not drunk, as you suppose, for it is only nine o'clock in the morning. [16] No, this is what was spoken through the prophet Joel:
[17]   "In the last days it will be, God declares,
       that I will pour out my Spirit upon all flesh,
          and your sons and your daughters shall prophesy,
       and your young men shall see visions,
          and your old men shall dream dreams.
[18]   Even upon my slaves, both men and women,
          in those days I will pour out my Spirit;
             and they shall prophesy.
[19]   And I will show portents in the heaven above
          and signs on the earth below,
             blood, and fire, and smoky mist.
[20]   The sun shall be turned to darkness
          and the moon to blood,
             before the coming of the Lord's great and glorious day.
[21]   Then everyone who calls on the name of the Lord shall be saved." '

GOSPEL   John 15.26–27; 16.4b–15

²⁶ 'When the Advocate comes, whom I will send to you from the Father, the Spirit of truth who comes from the Father, he will testify on my behalf. ²⁷ You also are to testify because you have been with me from the beginning.'

⁴ 'I did not say these things to you from the beginning, because I was with you. ⁵ But now I am going to him who sent me; yet none of you asks me, "Where are you going?" ⁶ But because I have said these things to you, sorrow has filled your hearts. ⁷ Nevertheless, I tell you the truth: it is to your advantage that I go away, for if I do not go away, the Advocate will not come to you; but if I go, I will send him to you. ⁸ And when he comes, he will prove the world wrong about sin and righteousness and judgement: ⁹ about sin, because they do not believe in me; ¹⁰ about righteousness, because I am going to the Father and you will see me no longer; ¹¹ about judgement, because the ruler of this world has been condemned.

¹² 'I still have many things to say to you, but you cannot bear them now. ¹³ When the Spirit of truth comes, he will guide you into all the truth; for he will not speak on his own, but will speak whatever he hears, and he will declare to you the things that are to come. ¹⁴ He will glorify me, because he will take what is mine and declare it to you. ¹⁵ All that the Father has is mine. For this reason I said that he will take what is mine and declare it to you.'

POST COMMUNION

Faithful God,
who fulfilled the promises of Easter
by sending us your Holy Spirit
and opening to every race and nation
the way of life eternal:
open our lips by your Spirit,
that every tongue may tell of your glory;
through Jesus Christ our Lord.

SECOND SERVICE

Psalm 139.1–11, [12–17, 22–23]
Ezekiel 36.22–28
Acts 2.22–38

If the Second Service is a Eucharist, the following is read as a Gospel:

John 20.19–23

THIRD SERVICE

Psalm 145
Isaiah 11.1–9

or

Wisdom 7.15–23, [24–27]
1 Corinthians 12.4–13

TRINITY SUNDAY

COLLECT

Almighty and everlasting God,
you have given us your servants grace,
by the confession of a true faith,
to acknowledge the glory of the eternal Trinity
and in the power of the divine majesty to worship the Unity:
keep us steadfast in this faith,
that we may evermore be defended from all adversities;
through Jesus Christ your Son our Lord,
who is alive and reigns with you,
in the unity of the Holy Spirit,
one God, now and for ever.

READING   Isaiah 6.1–8

¹ In the year that King Uzziah died, I saw the Lord sitting on a throne, high and lofty; and the hem of his robe filled the temple. ² Seraphs were in attendance above him; each had six wings: with two they covered their faces, and with two they covered their feet, and with two they flew. ³ And one called to another and said:

'Holy, holy, holy is the LORD of hosts;
    the whole earth is full of his glory.'

⁴ The pivots on the thresholds shook at the voices of those who called, and the house filled with smoke. ⁵ And I said: 'Woe is me! I am lost, for I am a man of unclean lips, and I live among a people of unclean lips; yet my eyes have seen the King, the LORD of hosts!'

⁶ Then one of the seraphs flew to me, holding a live coal that had been taken from the altar with a pair of tongs. ⁷ The seraph touched my mouth with it and said: 'Now that this has touched your lips, your guilt has departed and your sin is blotted out.' ⁸ Then I heard the voice of the Lord saying, 'Whom shall I send, and who will go for us?' And I said, 'Here am I; send me!'

PSALM   Psalm 29

¹ Ascribe to the Lord, you gods,
      ascribe to the Lord glory and strength.
² Ascribe to the Lord the glory due to his name;
      worship the Lord in the beauty of holiness.

3 The voice of the Lord is upon the waters; the God of glory thunders;
the Lord is upon the mighty waters.
4 The voice of the Lord is a powerful voice;
the voice of the Lord is a voice of splendour.
5 The voice of the Lord breaks the cedar trees;
the Lord breaks the cedars of Lebanon;
6 He makes Lebanon skip like a calf,
and Mount Hermon like a young wild ox.
7 The voice of the Lord splits the flames of fire; the voice of the Lord
shakes the wilderness;
the Lord shakes the wilderness of Kadesh.
8 The voice of the Lord makes the oak trees writhe
and strips the forests bare.
9 And in the temple of the Lord
all are crying, 'Glory!'
10 The Lord sits enthroned above the flood;
the Lord sits enthroned as king for evermore.
11 The Lord shall give strength to his people;
the Lord shall give his people the blessing of peace.

READING   Romans 8.12–17

12 So then, brothers and sisters, we are debtors, not to the flesh, to live according to the flesh— 13 for if you live according to the flesh, you will die; but if by the Spirit you put to death the deeds of the body, you will live. 14 For all who are led by the Spirit of God are children of God. 15 For you did not receive a spirit of slavery to fall back into fear, but you have received a spirit of adoption. When we cry, 'Abba! Father!' 16 it is that very Spirit bearing witness with our spirit that we are children of God, 17 and if children, then heirs, heirs of God and joint heirs with Christ—if, in fact, we suffer with him so that we may also be glorified with him.

GOSPEL   John 3.1–17

1 Now there was a Pharisee named Nicodemus, a leader of the Jews. 2 He came to Jesus by night and said to him, 'Rabbi, we know that you are a teacher who has come from God; for no one can do these signs that you do apart from the presence of God.' 3 Jesus answered him, 'Very truly, I tell you, no one can see the kingdom of God without being born from above.' 4 Nicodemus said to him, 'How can anyone be born after having grown old? Can one enter a second time into the mother's womb and be born?' 5 Jesus answered, 'Very truly, I tell you, no one can enter the kingdom of God without being born of water and Spirit. 6 What is born of the flesh is flesh,

and what is born of the Spirit is spirit. ⁷ Do not be astonished that I said to you, "You must be born from above." ⁸ The wind blows where it chooses, and you hear the sound of it, but you do not know where it comes from or where it goes. So it is with everyone who is born of the Spirit.' ⁹ Nicodemus said to him, 'How can these things be?' ¹⁰ Jesus answered him, 'Are you a teacher of Israel, and yet you do not understand these things?

¹¹ 'Very truly, I tell you, we speak of what we know and testify to what we have seen; yet you do not receive our testimony. ¹² If I have told you about earthly things and you do not believe, how can you believe if I tell you about heavenly things? ¹³ No one has ascended into heaven except the one who descended from heaven, the Son of Man. ¹⁴ And just as Moses lifted up the serpent in the wilderness, so must the Son of Man be lifted up, ¹⁵ that whoever believes in him may have eternal life.

¹⁶ 'For God so loved the world that he gave his only Son, so that everyone who believes in him may not perish but may have eternal life.

¹⁷ 'Indeed, God did not send the Son into the world to condemn the world, but in order that the world might be saved through him.'

POST COMMUNION

Almighty and eternal God,
you have revealed yourself as Father, Son and Holy Spirit,
and live and reign in the perfect unity of love:
hold us firm in this faith,
that we may know you in all your ways
and evermore rejoice in your eternal glory,
who are three Persons yet one God,
now and for ever.

SECOND SERVICE

Psalm 104.1–9
Ezekiel 1.4–10, 22–28a
Revelation 4.1–11

If the Second Service is a Eucharist, the following is read as a Gospel:

Mark 1.1–13

THIRD SERVICE

Psalm 33.1–12
Proverbs 8.1–4, 22–31
2 Corinthians 13.[5–10,] 11–13

TABLE OF FIRST SUNDAY AFTER TRINITY DATES AND PROPERS

YEAR	LITURGICAL YEAR	FIRST SUNDAY AFTER TRINITY	PROPER
1999	A	6 Jun	5
2000	B	25 Jun	7
2001	C	17 Jun	6
2002	A	2 Jun	4
2003	B	22 Jun	7
2004	C	13 Jun	6
2005	A	29 May	4
2006	B	18 Jun	6
2007	C	10 Jun	5
2008	A	25 May	(3)*
2009	B	14 Jun	6
2010	C	6 Jun	5
2011	A	26 Jun	8
2012	B	10 Jun	5
2013	C	2 Jun	4
2014	A	22 Jun	7
2015	B	7 Jun	5
2016	C	29 May	4
2017	A	18 Jun	6
2018	B	3 Jun	4
2019	C	23 Jun	7
2020	A	14 Jun	6

* For Proper 3 use Second Sunday before Lent, Option B (8th Sunday after Epiphany)

THE FIRST SUNDAY AFTER TRINITY

COLLECT

O God,
the strength of all those who put their trust in you,
mercifully accept our prayers
and, because through the weakness of our mortal nature
we can do no good thing without you,
grant us the help of your grace,
that in the keeping of your commandments
we may please you both in will and deed;
through Jesus Christ your Son our Lord,
who is alive and reigns with you,
in the unity of the Holy Spirit,
one God, now and for ever.

READINGS

See page 443 and pages 585 to 608 and Table on page 568

POST COMMUNION

Eternal Father,
we thank you for nourishing us
with these heavenly gifts:
may our communion strengthen us in faith,
build us up in hope,
and make us grow in love;
for the sake of Jesus Christ our Lord.

THE SECOND SUNDAY AFTER TRINITY

COLLECT

Lord, you have taught us
that all our doings without love are nothing worth:
send your Holy Spirit
and pour into our hearts that most excellent gift of love,
the true bond of peace and of all virtues,

without which whoever lives is counted dead before you.
Grant this for your only Son Jesus Christ's sake,
who is alive and reigns with you,
in the unity of the Holy Spirit,
one God, now and for ever.

READINGS

See pages 585 to 615 and Table on page 568

POST COMMUNION

Loving Father,
we thank you for feeding us at the supper of your Son:
sustain us with your Spirit,
that we may serve you here on earth
until our joy is complete in heaven,
and we share in the eternal banquet
with Jesus Christ our Lord.

THE THIRD SUNDAY AFTER TRINITY

COLLECT

Almighty God,
you have broken the tyranny of sin
and have sent the Spirit of your Son into our hearts
    whereby we call you Father:
give us grace to dedicate our freedom to your service,
that we and all creation may be brought
    to the glorious liberty of the children of God;
through Jesus Christ your Son our Lord,
who is alive and reigns with you,
in the unity of the Holy Spirit,
one God, now and for ever.

READINGS

See pages 590 to 620 and Table on page 568

POST COMMUNION

O God, whose beauty is beyond our imagining
and whose power we cannot comprehend:
show us your glory as far as we can grasp it,
and shield us from knowing more than we can bear
until we may look upon you without fear;
through Jesus Christ our Saviour.

THE FOURTH SUNDAY AFTER TRINITY

COLLECT

O God, the protector of all who trust in you,
without whom nothing is strong, nothing is holy:
increase and multiply upon us your mercy;
that with you as our ruler and guide
we may so pass through things temporal
that we lose not our hold on things eternal;
grant this, heavenly Father,
for our Lord Jesus Christ's sake,
who is alive and reigns with you,
in the unity of the Holy Spirit,
one God, now and for ever.

READINGS

See pages 595 to 625 and Table on page 568

POST COMMUNION

Eternal God,
comfort of the afflicted and healer of the broken,
you have fed us at the table of life and hope:
teach us the ways of gentleness and peace,
that all the world may acknowledge
the kingdom of your Son Jesus Christ our Lord.

THE FIFTH SUNDAY AFTER TRINITY

COLLECT

Almighty and everlasting God,
by whose Spirit the whole body of the Church
    is governed and sanctified:
hear our prayer which we offer for all your faithful people,
that in their vocation and ministry
they may serve you in holiness and truth
to the glory of your name;
through our Lord and Saviour Jesus Christ,
who is alive and reigns with you,
in the unity of the Holy Spirit,
one God, now and for ever.

READINGS

See pages 601 to 631 and Table on page 568

POST COMMUNION

Grant, O Lord, we beseech you,
that the course of this world may be so peaceably ordered
    by your governance,
that your Church may joyfully serve you
    in all godly quietness;
through Jesus Christ our Lord.

THE SIXTH SUNDAY AFTER TRINITY

COLLECT

Merciful God,
you have prepared for those who love you
such good things as pass our understanding:
pour into our hearts such love toward you
that we, loving you in all things and above all things,
may obtain your promises,
which exceed all that we can desire;

through Jesus Christ your Son our Lord,
who is alive and reigns with you,
in the unity of the Holy Spirit,
one God, now and for ever.

READINGS

See pages 608 to 636 and Table on page 568

POST COMMUNION

God of our pilgrimage,
you have led us to the living water:
refresh and sustain us
as we go forward on our journey,
in the name of Jesus Christ our Lord.

THE SEVENTH SUNDAY AFTER TRINITY

COLLECT

Lord of all power and might,
the author and giver of all good things:
graft in our hearts the love of your name,
increase in us true religion,
nourish us with all goodness,
and of your great mercy keep us in the same;
through Jesus Christ your Son our Lord,
who is alive and reigns with you,
in the unity of the Holy Spirit,
one God, now and for ever.

READINGS

See pages 615 to 642 and Table on page 568

POST COMMUNION

Lord God, whose Son is the true vine and the source of life,
ever giving himself that the world may live:
may we so receive within ourselves
    the power of his death and passion
that, in his saving cup,
    we may share his glory and be made perfect in his love;
for he is alive and reigns, now and for ever.

THE EIGHTH SUNDAY AFTER TRINITY

COLLECT

Almighty Lord and everlasting God,
we beseech you to direct, sanctify and govern
    both our hearts and bodies
in the ways of your laws
    and the works of your commandments;
that through your most mighty protection, both here and ever,
we may be preserved in body and soul;
through our Lord and Saviour Jesus Christ,
who is alive and reigns with you,
in the unity of the Holy Spirit,
one God, now and for ever.

READINGS

See pages 620 to 647 and Table on page 568

POST COMMUNION

Strengthen for service, Lord,
the hands that have taken holy things;
may the ears which have heard your word
    be deaf to clamour and dispute;
may the tongues which have sung your praise
    be free from deceit;

may the eyes which have seen the tokens of your love
    shine with the light of hope;
and may the bodies which have been fed with your body
    be refreshed with the fullness of your life;
glory to you for ever.

THE NINTH SUNDAY AFTER TRINITY

COLLECT

Almighty God,
who sent your Holy Spirit
to be the life and light of your Church:
open our hearts to the riches of your grace,
that we may bring forth the fruit of the Spirit
in love and joy and peace;
through Jesus Christ your Son our Lord,
who is alive and reigns with you,
in the unity of the Holy Spirit,
one God, now and for ever.

READINGS

See pages 625 to 651 and Table on page 568

POST COMMUNION

Holy Father,
who gathered us here around the table of your Son
to share this meal with the whole household of God:
in that new world
    where you reveal the fullness of your peace,
gather people of every race and language
    to share in the eternal banquet
    of Jesus Christ our Lord.

THE TENTH SUNDAY AFTER TRINITY

COLLECT

Let your merciful ears, O Lord,
be open to the prayers of your humble servants;
and that they may obtain their petitions
make them to ask such things as shall please you;
through Jesus Christ your Son our Lord,
who is alive and reigns with you,
in the unity of the Holy Spirit,
one God, now and for ever.

READINGS

See pages 631 to 657 and Table on page 568

POST COMMUNION

God of our pilgrimage,
you have willed that the gate of mercy
should stand open for those who trust in you:
look upon us with your favour
that we who follow the path of your will
may never wander from the way of life;
through Jesus Christ our Lord.

THE ELEVENTH SUNDAY AFTER TRINITY

COLLECT

O God, you declare your almighty power
most chiefly in showing mercy and pity:
mercifully grant to us such a measure of your grace,
that we, running the way of your commandments,
may receive your gracious promises,
and be made partakers of your heavenly treasure;
through Jesus Christ your Son our Lord,

who is alive and reigns with you,
in the unity of the Holy Spirit,
one God, now and for ever.

READINGS

See pages 636 to 662 and Table on page 568

POST COMMUNION

Lord of all mercy,
we your faithful people have celebrated that one true sacrifice
    which takes away our sins and brings pardon and peace:
by our communion
keep us firm on the foundation of the gospel
and preserve us from all sin;
through Jesus Christ our Lord.

THE TWELFTH SUNDAY AFTER TRINITY

COLLECT

Almighty and everlasting God,
you are always more ready to hear than we to pray
and to give more than either we desire or deserve:
pour down upon us the abundance of your mercy,
forgiving us those things of which our conscience is afraid
and giving us those good things
    which we are not worthy to ask
but through the merits and mediation
of Jesus Christ your Son our Lord,
who is alive and reigns with you,
in the unity of the Holy Spirit,
one God, now and for ever.

READINGS

See pages 642 to 668 and Table on page 568

POST COMMUNION

God of all mercy,
in this eucharist you have set aside our sins
and given us your healing:
grant that we who are made whole in Christ
may bring that healing to this broken world,
in the name of Jesus Christ our Lord.

THE THIRTEENTH SUNDAY AFTER TRINITY

COLLECT

Almighty God,
who called your Church to bear witness
that you were in Christ reconciling the world to yourself:
help us to proclaim the good news of your love,
that all who hear it may be drawn to you;
through him who was lifted up on the cross,
and reigns with you in the unity of the Holy Spirit,
one God, now and for ever.

READINGS

See pages 647 to 674 and Table on page 568

POST COMMUNION

God our creator,
you feed your children with the true manna,
the living bread from heaven:
let this holy food sustain us through our earthly pilgrimage
until we come to that place
    where hunger and thirst are no more;
through Jesus Christ our Lord.

THE FOURTEENTH SUNDAY AFTER TRINITY

COLLECT

Almighty God,
whose only Son has opened for us
a new and living way into your presence:
give us pure hearts and steadfast wills
to worship you in spirit and in truth;
through Jesus Christ your Son our Lord,
who is alive and reigns with you,
in the unity of the Holy Spirit,
one God, now and for ever.

READINGS

See pages 651 to 680 and Table on page 568

POST COMMUNION

Lord God, the source of truth and love,
keep us faithful to the apostles' teaching and fellowship,
united in prayer and the breaking of bread,
and one in joy and simplicity of heart,
in Jesus Christ our Lord.

THE FIFTEENTH SUNDAY AFTER TRINITY

COLLECT

God, who in generous mercy sent the Holy Spirit
   upon your Church in the burning fire of your love:
grant that your people may be fervent
   in the fellowship of the gospel
that, always abiding in you,
they may be found steadfast in faith and active in service;
through Jesus Christ your Son our Lord,
who is alive and reigns with you,
in the unity of the Holy Spirit,
one God, now and for ever.

READINGS

See pages 657 to 685 and Table on page 568

POST COMMUNION

Keep, O Lord, your Church,
  with your perpetual mercy;
and, because without you our human frailty cannot but fall,
keep us ever by your help from all things hurtful,
and lead us to all things profitable to our salvation;
through Jesus Christ our Lord.

THE SIXTEENTH SUNDAY AFTER TRINITY

COLLECT

O Lord, we beseech you mercifully to hear the prayers
  of your people who call upon you;
and grant that they may both perceive and know
  what things they ought to do,
and also may have grace and power
  faithfully to fulfil them;
through Jesus Christ your Son our Lord,
who is alive and reigns with you,
in the unity of the Holy Spirit,
one God, now and for ever.

READINGS

See pages 662 to 690 and Table on page 568

POST COMMUNION

Almighty God,
you have taught us through your Son
that love is the fulfilling of the law:
grant that we may love you with our whole heart
and our neighbours as ourselves;
through Jesus Christ our Lord.

THE SEVENTEENTH SUNDAY AFTER TRINITY

COLLECT

Almighty God,
you have made us for yourself,
and our hearts are restless till they find their rest in you:
pour your love into our hearts and draw us to yourself,
and so bring us at last to your heavenly city
where we shall see you face to face;
through Jesus Christ your Son our Lord,
who is alive and reigns with you,
in the unity of the Holy Spirit,
one God, now and for ever.

READINGS

See pages 668 to 696 and Table on page 568

POST COMMUNION

Lord, we pray that your grace
    may always precede and follow us,
and make us continually to be given to all good works;
through Jesus Christ our Lord.

THE EIGHTEENTH SUNDAY AFTER TRINITY

COLLECT

Almighty and everlasting God,
increase in us your gift of faith
that, forsaking what lies behind
and reaching out to that which is before,
we may run the way of your commandments
and win the crown of everlasting joy;
through Jesus Christ your Son our Lord,

who is alive and reigns with you,
in the unity of the Holy Spirit,
one God, now and for ever.

READINGS

See pages 674 to 701 and Table on page 568

POST COMMUNION

We praise and thank you, O Christ, for this sacred feast:
for here we receive you,
here the memory of your passion is renewed,
here our minds are filled with grace,
and here a pledge of future glory is given,
when we shall feast at that table where you reign
with all your saints for ever.

THE NINETEENTH SUNDAY AFTER TRINITY

COLLECT

O God, forasmuch as without you
we are not able to please you;
mercifully grant that your Holy Spirit
may in all things direct and rule our hearts;
through Jesus Christ your Son our Lord,
who is alive and reigns with you,
in the unity of the Holy Spirit,
one God, now and for ever.

READINGS

See pages 680 to 701 and Table on page 568

POST COMMUNION

Holy and blessed God,
you have fed us with the body and blood of your Son
and filled us with your Holy Spirit:
may we honour you,

not only with our lips
but in lives dedicated to the service
    of Jesus Christ our Lord.

THE TWENTIETH SUNDAY AFTER TRINITY

COLLECT

God, the giver of life,
whose Holy Spirit wells up within your Church:
by the Spirit's gifts equip us to live the gospel of Christ
    and make us eager to do your will,
that we may share with the whole creation
    the joys of eternal life;
through Jesus Christ your Son our Lord,
who is alive and reigns with you,
in the unity of the Holy Spirit,
one God, now and for ever.

READINGS

See pages 685 to 701 and Table on page 568

POST COMMUNION

God our Father,
whose Son, the light unfailing,
has come from heaven to deliver the world
    from the darkness of ignorance:
let these holy mysteries open the eyes of our understanding
that we may know the way of life,
and walk in it without stumbling;
through Jesus Christ our Lord.

THE TWENTY-FIRST SUNDAY AFTER TRINITY

COLLECT

Grant, we beseech you, merciful Lord,
to your faithful people pardon and peace,
that they may be cleansed from all their sins
and serve you with a quiet mind;
through Jesus Christ your Son our Lord,
who is alive and reigns with you,
in the unity of the Holy Spirit,
one God, now and for ever.

READINGS

See pages 690 to 701 and Table on page 568

POST COMMUNION

Father of light,
in whom is no change or shadow of turning,
you give us every good and perfect gift
and have brought us to birth by your word of truth:
may we be a living sign of that kingdom
where your whole creation will be made perfect
    in Jesus Christ our Lord.

THE LAST SUNDAY AFTER TRINITY

COLLECT

Blessed Lord,
who caused all holy scriptures
    to be written for our learning:
help us so to hear them,
to read, mark, learn and inwardly digest them
that, through patience, and the comfort of your holy word,
we may embrace and for ever hold fast
    the hope of everlasting life,

which you have given us in our Saviour Jesus Christ,
who is alive and reigns with you,
in the unity of the Holy Spirit,
one God, now and for ever.

READINGS

See pages 696 to 701 and Table on page 568

POST COMMUNION

God of all grace,
your Son Jesus Christ fed the hungry
with the bread of his life
and the word of his kingdom:
renew your people with your heavenly grace,
and in all our weakness
sustain us by your true and living bread;
who is alive and reigns, now and for ever.

PROPER 4

Sunday between 29 May and 4 June inclusive (if after Trinity Sunday)

COLLECT

See page 569 and Table on page 568

CONTINUOUS

READING   1 Samuel 3.1–10, [11–20]

[1] Now the boy Samuel was ministering to the LORD under Eli. The word of the LORD was rare in those days; visions were not widespread.

[2] At that time Eli, whose eyesight had begun to grow dim so that he could not see, was lying down in his room; [3] the lamp of God had not yet gone out, and Samuel was lying down in the temple of the LORD, where the ark of God was. [4] Then the LORD called, 'Samuel! Samuel!' and he said, 'Here I am!' [5] and ran to Eli, and said, 'Here I am, for you called me.' But he said, 'I did not call; lie down again.' So he went and lay down. [6] The LORD called

again, 'Samuel!' Samuel got up and went to Eli, and said, 'Here I am, for you called me.' But he said, 'I did not call, my son; lie down again.' ⁷ Now Samuel did not yet know the LORD, and the word of the LORD had not yet been revealed to him. ⁸ The LORD called Samuel again, a third time. And he got up and went to Eli, and said, 'Here I am, for you called me.' Then Eli perceived that the LORD was calling the boy. ⁹ Therefore Eli said to Samuel, 'Go, lie down; and if he calls you, you shall say, "Speak, LORD, for your servant is listening." ' So Samuel went and lay down in his place.

¹⁰ Now the LORD came and stood there, calling as before, 'Samuel! Samuel!' And Samuel said, 'Speak, for your servant is listening.'
[¹¹ Then the LORD said to Samuel, 'See, I am about to do something in Israel that will make both ears of anyone who hears of it tingle. ¹² On that day I will fulfil against Eli all that I have spoken concerning his house, from beginning to end. ¹³ For I have told him that I am about to punish his house for ever, for the iniquity that he knew, because his sons were blaspheming God, and he did not restrain them. ¹⁴ Therefore I swear to the house of Eli that the iniquity of Eli's house shall not be expiated by sacrifice or offering for ever.'

¹⁵ Samuel lay there until morning; then he opened the doors of the house of the LORD. Samuel was afraid to tell the vision to Eli. ¹⁶ But Eli called Samuel and said, 'Samuel, my son.' He said, 'Here I am.' ¹⁷ Eli said, 'What was it that he told you? Do not hide it from me. May God do so to you and more also, if you hide anything from me of all that he told you.' ¹⁸ So Samuel told him everything and hid nothing from him. Then he said, 'It is the LORD; let him do what seems good to him.'

¹⁹ As Samuel grew up, the LORD was with him and let none of his words fall to the ground. ²⁰ And all Israel from Dan to Beer-sheba knew that Samuel was a trustworthy prophet of the LORD.]

PSALM   Psalm 139.1–5, 12–17

¹   Lord, you have searched me out and known me;
    you know my sitting down and my rising up; you discern my
        thoughts from afar.
²   You trace my journeys and my resting-places
    and are acquainted with all my ways.
³   Indeed, there is not a word on my lips,
    but you, O Lord, know it altogether.
⁴   You press upon me behind and before
    and lay your hand upon me.
⁵   Such knowledge is too wonderful for me;
    it is so high that I cannot attain to it.

12 For you yourself created my inmost parts;
   you knit me together in my mother's womb.
13 I will thank you because I am marvellously made;
   your works are wonderful and I know it well.
14 My body was not hidden from you,
   while I was being made in secret and woven in the depths of the
      earth.
15 Your eyes beheld my limbs, yet unfinished in the womb; all of
      them were written in your book;
   they were fashioned day by day, when as yet there was none of
      them.
16 How deep I find your thoughts, O God!
   how great is the sum of them!
17 If I were to count them, they would be more in number than the
      sand;
   to count them all, my life span would need to be like yours.

READING   2 Corinthians 4.5–12

5 For we do not proclaim ourselves; we proclaim Jesus Christ as Lord and
ourselves as your slaves for Jesus' sake. 6 For it is the God who said, 'Let
light shine out of darkness', who has shone in our hearts to give the light
of the knowledge of the glory of God in the face of Jesus Christ.

7 But we have this treasure in clay jars, so that it may be made clear that
this extraordinary power belongs to God and does not come from us. 8 We
are afflicted in every way, but not crushed; perplexed, but not driven to
despair; 9 persecuted, but not forsaken; struck down, but not destroyed;
10 always carrying in the body the death of Jesus, so that the life of Jesus
may also be made visible in our bodies. 11 For while we live, we are always
being given up to death for Jesus' sake, so that the life of Jesus may be made
visible in our mortal flesh. 12 So death is at work in us, but life in you.

GOSPEL   Mark 2.23–3.6

23 One sabbath he was going through the cornfields; and as they made
their way his disciples began to pluck heads of grain. 24 The Pharisees said
to him, 'Look, why are they doing what is not lawful on the sabbath?' 25 And
he said to them, 'Have you never read what David did when he and his
companions were hungry and in need of food? 26 He entered the house of
God, when Abiathar was high priest, and ate the bread of the Presence,
which it is not lawful for any but the priests to eat, and he gave some to
his companions.' 27 Then he said to them, 'The sabbath was made for

humankind, and not humankind for the sabbath; [28] so the Son of Man is lord even of the sabbath.'

[1] Again he entered the synagogue, and a man was there who had a withered hand. [2] They watched him to see whether he would cure him on the sabbath, so that they might accuse him. [3] And he said to the man who had the withered hand, 'Come forward.' [4] Then he said to them, 'Is it lawful to do good or to do harm on the sabbath, to save life or to kill?' But they were silent. [5] He looked around at them with anger; he was grieved at their hardness of heart and said to the man, 'Stretch out your hand.' He stretched it out, and his hand was restored. [6] The Pharisees went out and immediately conspired with the Herodians against him, how to destroy him.

RELATED

READING   Deuteronomy 5.12–15

[12] Observe the sabbath day and keep it holy, as the LORD your God commanded you. [13] For six days you shall labour and do all your work. [14] But the seventh day is a sabbath to the LORD your God; you shall not do any work—you, or your son or your daughter, or your male or female slave, or your ox or your donkey, or any of your livestock, or the resident alien in your towns, so that your male and female slave may rest as well as you. [15] Remember that you were a slave in the land of Egypt, and the LORD your God brought you out from there with a mighty hand and an outstretched arm; therefore the LORD your God commanded you to keep the sabbath day.

PSALM   Psalm 81.1–10

1   Sing with joy to God our strength
    and raise a loud shout to the God of Jacob.
2   Raise a song and sound the timbrel,
    the merry harp and the lyre.
3   Blow the ram's-horn at the new moon,
    and at the full moon, the day of our feast.
4   For this is a statute for Israel,
    a law of the God of Jacob.
5   He laid it as a solemn charge upon Joseph,
    when he came out of the land of Egypt.
6   I heard an unfamiliar voice saying,
    'I eased his shoulder from the burden; his hands were set free
        from bearing the load.'

7 You called on me in trouble and I saved you;
   I answered you from the secret place of thunder and tested you at
       the waters of Meribah.
8 Hear, O my people, and I will admonish you:
   O Israel, if you would but listen to me!
9 There shall be no strange god among you;
   you shall not worship a foreign god.
10 I am the Lord your God, who brought you out of the land of Egypt
       and said,
   'Open your mouth wide and I will fill it.'

READING   2 Corinthians 4.5–12

5 For we do not proclaim ourselves; we proclaim Jesus Christ as Lord and ourselves as your slaves for Jesus' sake. 6 For it is the God who said, 'Let light shine out of darkness', who has shone in our hearts to give the light of the knowledge of the glory of God in the face of Jesus Christ.

7 But we have this treasure in clay jars, so that it may be made clear that this extraordinary power belongs to God and does not come from us. 8 We are afflicted in every way, but not crushed; perplexed, but not driven to despair; 9 persecuted, but not forsaken; struck down, but not destroyed; 10 always carrying in the body the death of Jesus, so that the life of Jesus may also be made visible in our bodies. 11 For while we live, we are always being given up to death for Jesus' sake, so that the life of Jesus may be made visible in our mortal flesh. 12 So death is at work in us, but life in you.

GOSPEL   Mark 2.23–3.6

23 One sabbath he was going through the cornfields; and as they made their way his disciples began to pluck heads of grain. 24 The Pharisees said to him, 'Look, why are they doing what is not lawful on the sabbath?' 25 And he said to them, 'Have you never read what David did when he and his companions were hungry and in need of food? 26 He entered the house of God, when Abiathar was high priest, and ate the bread of the Presence, which it is not lawful for any but the priests to eat, and he gave some to his companions.' 27 Then he said to them, 'The sabbath was made for humankind, and not humankind for the sabbath; 28 so the Son of Man is lord even of the sabbath.'

1 Again he entered the synagogue, and a man was there who had a withered hand. 2 They watched him to see whether he would cure him on the sabbath, so that they might accuse him. 3 And he said to the man who had the withered hand, 'Come forward.' 4 Then he said to them, 'Is it lawful

to do good or to do harm on the sabbath, to save life or to kill?' But they were silent. ⁵ He looked around at them with anger; he was grieved at their hardness of heart and said to the man, 'Stretch out your hand.' He stretched it out, and his hand was restored. ⁶ The Pharisees went out and immediately conspired with the Herodians against him, how to destroy him.

POST COMMUNION

See pages 569 to 570 and Table on page 568

SECOND SERVICE

Psalm 35.1–10, [11–28]
Jeremiah 5.1–19
Romans 7.7–25

If the Second Service is a Eucharist, the following is read as a Gospel:

Luke 7.1–10

THIRD SERVICE

Psalms 28; 32
Deuteronomy 5.1–21
Acts 21.17–39a

PROPER 5

Sunday between 5 and 11 June inclusive (if after Trinity Sunday)

COLLECT

See pages 569 to 570 and Table on page 568

CONTINUOUS

READING   1 Samuel 8.4–11, [12–15,] 16–20; [11.14–15]

⁴ Then all the elders of Israel gathered together and came to Samuel at Ramah, ⁵ and said to him, 'You are old and your sons do not follow in your ways; appoint for us, then, a king to govern us, like other nations.' ⁶ But the thing displeased Samuel when they said, 'Give us a king to govern us.' Samuel prayed to the LORD, ⁷ and the LORD said to Samuel, 'Listen to the voice of the people in all that they say to you; for they have not rejected you, but they have rejected me from being king over them. ⁸ Just as they have done to me, from the day I brought them up out of Egypt to this day, forsaking me and serving other gods, so also they are doing to you. ⁹ Now

then, listen to their voice; only—you shall solemnly warn them, and show them the ways of the king who shall reign over them.'

10 So Samuel reported all the words of the LORD to the people who were asking him for a king. 11 He said, 'These will be the ways of the king who will reign over you: he will take your sons and appoint them to his chariots and to be his horsemen, and to run before his chariots;
[12 and he will appoint for himself commanders of thousands and commanders of fifties, and some to plough his ground and to reap his harvest, and to make his implements of war and the equipment of his chariots. 13 He will take your daughters to be perfumers and cooks and bakers. 14 He will take the best of your fields and vineyards and olive orchards and give them to his courtiers. 15 He will take one-tenth of your grain and of your vineyards and give it to his officers and his courtiers.]
16 He will take your male and female slaves, and the best of your cattle and donkeys, and put them to his work. 17 He will take one-tenth of your flocks, and you shall be his slaves. 18 And in that day you will cry out because of your king, whom you have chosen for yourselves; but the LORD will not answer you in that day.'

19 But the people refused to listen to the voice of Samuel; they said, 'No! but we are determined to have a king over us, 20 so that we also may be like other nations, and that our king may govern us and go out before us and fight our battles.'

[14 Samuel said to the people, 'Come, let us go to Gilgal and there renew the kingship.' 15 So all the people went to Gilgal, and there they made Saul king before the LORD in Gilgal. There they sacrificed offerings of well-being before the LORD, and there Saul and all the Israelites rejoiced greatly.]

PSALM   Psalm 138

1   I will give thanks to you, O Lord, with my whole heart;
    before the gods I will sing your praise.
2   I will bow down towards your holy temple and praise your name,
    because of your love and faithfulness;
3   For you have glorified your name
    and your word above all things.
4   When I called, you answered me;
    you increased my strength within me.
5   All the kings of the earth will praise you, O Lord,
    when they have heard the words of your mouth.
6   They will sing of the ways of the Lord,
    that great is the glory of the Lord.

7 Though the Lord be high, he cares for the lowly;
   he perceives the haughty from afar.
8 Though I walk in the midst of trouble, you keep me safe;
   you stretch forth your hand against the fury of my enemies; your
   right hand shall save me.
9 The Lord will make good his purpose for me;
   O Lord, your love endures for ever; do not abandon the works of
   your hands.

READING   2 Corinthians 4.13–5.1

^{13} But just as we have the same spirit of faith that is in accordance with
scripture—'I believed, and so I spoke'—we also believe, and so we speak,
^{14} because we know that the one who raised the Lord Jesus will raise us also
with Jesus, and will bring us with you into his presence. ^{15} Yes, everything
is for your sake, so that grace, as it extends to more and more people, may
increase thanksgiving, to the glory of God.

^{16} So we do not lose heart. Even though our outer nature is wasting away,
our inner nature is being renewed day by day. ^{17} For this slight momentary
affliction is preparing us for an eternal weight of glory beyond all measure,
^{18} because we look not at what can be seen but at what cannot be seen; for
what can be seen is temporary, but what cannot be seen is eternal.

^{1} For we know that if the earthly tent we live in is destroyed, we have a
building from God, a house not made with hands, eternal in the heavens.

GOSPEL   Mark 3.20–35

^{20} And the crowd came together again, so that they could not even eat.
^{21} When his family heard it, they went out to restrain him, for people were
saying, 'He has gone out of his mind.' ^{22} And the scribes who came down
from Jerusalem said, 'He has Beelzebul, and by the ruler of the demons he
casts out demons.' ^{23} And he called them to him, and spoke to them in
parables, 'How can Satan cast out Satan? ^{24} If a kingdom is divided against
itself, that kingdom cannot stand. ^{25} And if a house is divided against itself,
that house will not be able to stand. ^{26} And if Satan has risen up against
himself and is divided, he cannot stand, but his end has come. ^{27} But no
one can enter a strong man's house and plunder his property without first
tying up the strong man; then indeed the house can be plundered.

^{28} 'Truly I tell you, people will be forgiven for their sins and whatever
blasphemies they utter; ^{29} but whoever blasphemes against the Holy Spirit

can never have forgiveness, but is guilty of an eternal sin'— [30] for they had said, 'He has an unclean spirit.'

[31] Then his mother and his brothers came; and standing outside, they sent to him and called him. [32] A crowd was sitting around him; and they said to him, 'Your mother and your brothers and sisters are outside, asking for you.' [33] And he replied, 'Who are my mother and my brothers?' [34] And looking at those who sat around him, he said, 'Here are my mother and my brothers! [35] Whoever does the will of God is my brother and sister and mother.'

RELATED

READING   Genesis 3.8–15

[8] They heard the sound of the Lord God walking in the garden at the time of the evening breeze, and the man and his wife hid themselves from the presence of the Lord God among the trees of the garden. [9] But the Lord God called to the man, and said to him, 'Where are you?' [10] He said, 'I heard the sound of you in the garden, and I was afraid, because I was naked; and I hid myself.' [11] He said, 'Who told you that you were naked? Have you eaten from the tree of which I commanded you not to eat?' [12] The man said, 'The woman whom you gave to be with me, she gave me fruit from the tree, and I ate.' [13] Then the Lord God said to the woman, 'What is this that you have done?' The woman said, 'The serpent tricked me, and I ate.' [14] The Lord God said to the serpent,

'Because you have done this,
     cursed are you among all animals
     and among all wild creatures;
upon your belly you shall go,
     and dust you shall eat
     all the days of your life.
[15]   I will put enmity between you and the woman,
     and between your offspring and hers;
he will strike your head,
     and you will strike his heel.'

PSALM   Psalm 130

[1]   Out of the depths have I called to you, O Lord; Lord, hear my voice;
     let your ears consider well the voice of my supplication.
[2]   If you, Lord, were to note what is done amiss,
     O Lord, who could stand?

3   For there is forgiveness with you;
    therefore you shall be feared.
4   I wait for the Lord; my soul waits for him;
    in his word is my hope.
5   My soul waits for the Lord, more than the night-watch for the
        morning,
    more than the night-watch for the morning.
6   O Israel, wait for the Lord,
    for with the Lord there is mercy;
7   With him there is plenteous redemption,
    and he shall redeem Israel from all their sins.

READING   2 Corinthians 4.13–5.1

13 But just as we have the same spirit of faith that is in accordance with scripture—'I believed, and so I spoke'—we also believe, and so we speak, 14 because we know that the one who raised the Lord Jesus will raise us also with Jesus, and will bring us with you into his presence. 15 Yes, everything is for your sake, so that grace, as it extends to more and more people, may increase thanksgiving, to the glory of God.

16 So we do not lose heart. Even though our outer nature is wasting away, our inner nature is being renewed day by day. 17 For this slight momentary affliction is preparing us for an eternal weight of glory beyond all measure, 18 because we look not at what can be seen but at what cannot be seen; for what can be seen is temporary, but what cannot be seen is eternal.

1 For we know that if the earthly tent we live in is destroyed, we have a building from God, a house not made with hands, eternal in the heavens.

GOSPEL   Mark 3.20–35

20 And the crowd came together again, so that they could not even eat. 21 When his family heard it, they went out to restrain him, for people were saying, 'He has gone out of his mind.' 22 And the scribes who came down from Jerusalem said, 'He has Beelzebul, and by the ruler of the demons he casts out demons.' 23 And he called them to him, and spoke to them in parables, 'How can Satan cast out Satan? 24 If a kingdom is divided against itself, that kingdom cannot stand. 25 And if a house is divided against itself, that house will not be able to stand. 26 And if Satan has risen up against himself and is divided, he cannot stand, but his end has come. 27 But no one can enter a strong man's house and plunder his property without first tying up the strong man; then indeed the house can be plundered.

[28] 'Truly I tell you, people will be forgiven for their sins and whatever blasphemies they utter; [29] but whoever blasphemes against the Holy Spirit can never have forgiveness, but is guilty of an eternal sin'— [30] for they had said, 'He has an unclean spirit.'

[31] Then his mother and his brothers came; and standing outside, they sent to him and called him. [32] A crowd was sitting around him; and they said to him, 'Your mother and your brothers and sisters are outside, asking for you.' [33] And he replied, 'Who are my mother and my brothers?' [34] And looking at those who sat around him, he said, 'Here are my mother and my brothers! [35] Whoever does the will of God is my brother and sister and mother.'

POST COMMUNION

See pages 569 to 571 and Table on page 568

SECOND SERVICE

Psalm 37.1–12, [13–15]
Jeremiah 6.16–21
Romans 9.1–13

If the Second Service is a Eucharist, the following is read as a Gospel:

Luke 7.11–17

THIRD SERVICE

Psalm 36
Deuteronomy 6.10–25
Acts 22.22–23.11

PROPER 6

Sunday between 12 and 18 June inclusive (if after Trinity Sunday)

COLLECT

See pages 569 to 571 and Table on page 568

CONTINUOUS

READING   1 Samuel 15.34–16.13

[34] Then Samuel went to Ramah; and Saul went up to his house in Gibeah of Saul. [35] Samuel did not see Saul again until the day of his death, but Samuel grieved over Saul. And the Lord was sorry that he had made Saul king over Israel.

¹ The LORD said to Samuel, 'How long will you grieve over Saul? I have rejected him from being king over Israel. Fill your horn with oil and set out; I will send you to Jesse the Bethlehemite, for I have provided for myself a king among his sons.' ² Samuel said, 'How can I go? If Saul hears of it, he will kill me.' And the LORD said, 'Take a heifer with you, and say, "I have come to sacrifice to the LORD." ³ Invite Jesse to the sacrifice, and I will show you what you shall do; and you shall anoint for me the one whom I name to you.' ⁴ Samuel did what the LORD commanded, and came to Bethlehem. The elders of the city came to meet him trembling, and said, 'Do you come peaceably?' ⁵ He said, 'Peaceably; I have come to sacrifice to the LORD; sanctify yourselves and come with me to the sacrifice.' And he sanctified Jesse and his sons and invited them to the sacrifice.

⁶ When they came, he looked on Eliab and thought, 'Surely the LORD's anointed is now before the LORD.' ⁷ But the LORD said to Samuel, 'Do not look on his appearance or on the height of his stature, because I have rejected him; for the LORD does not see as mortals see; they look on the outward appearance, but the LORD looks on the heart.' ⁸ Then Jesse called Abinadab, and made him pass before Samuel. He said, 'Neither has the LORD chosen this one.' ⁹ Then Jesse made Shammah pass by. And he said, 'Neither has the LORD chosen this one.' ¹⁰ Jesse made seven of his sons pass before Samuel, and Samuel said to Jesse, 'The LORD has not chosen any of these.' ¹¹ Samuel said to Jesse, 'Are all your sons here?' And he said, 'There remains yet the youngest, but he is keeping the sheep.' And Samuel said to Jesse, 'Send and bring him; for we will not sit down until he comes here.' ¹² He sent and brought him in. Now he was ruddy, and had beautiful eyes, and was handsome. The LORD said, 'Rise and anoint him; for this is the one.' ¹³ Then Samuel took the horn of oil, and anointed him in the presence of his brothers; and the spirit of the LORD came mightily upon David from that day forward. Samuel then set out and went to Ramah.

PSALM   Psalm 20

¹   May the Lord answer you in the day of trouble,
     the name of the God of Jacob defend you;
²   Send you help from his holy place
     and strengthen you out of Zion;
³   Remember all your offerings
     and accept your burnt sacrifice;

4   Grant you your heart's desire
    and prosper all your plans.
5   We will shout for joy at your victory and triumph in the name of
      our God;
    may the Lord grant all your requests.
6   Now I know that the Lord gives victory to his anointed;
    he will answer him out of his holy heaven, with the victorious
      strength of his right hand.
7   Some put their trust in chariots and some in horses,
    but we will call upon the name of the Lord our God.
8   They collapse and fall down,
    but we will arise and stand upright.
9   O Lord, give victory to the king
    and answer us when we call.

READING   2 Corinthians 5.6–10, [11–13,] 14–17

6 So we are always confident; even though we know that while we are at home in the body we are away from the Lord— 7 for we walk by faith, not by sight. 8 Yes, we do have confidence, and we would rather be away from the body and at home with the Lord. 9 So whether we are at home or away, we make it our aim to please him. 10 For all of us must appear before the judgement seat of Christ, so that each may receive recompense for what has been done in the body, whether good or evil.

[11 Therefore, knowing the fear of the Lord, we try to persuade others; but we ourselves are well known to God, and I hope that we are also well known to your consciences. 12 We are not commending ourselves to you again, but giving you an opportunity to boast about us, so that you may be able to answer those who boast in outward appearance and not in the heart. 13 For if we are beside ourselves, it is for God; if we are in our right mind, it is for you.]
14 For the love of Christ urges us on, because we are convinced that one has died for all; therefore all have died. 15 And he died for all, so that those who live might live no longer for themselves, but for him who died and was raised for them.

16 From now on, therefore, we regard no one from a human point of view; even though we once knew Christ from a human point of view, we know him no longer in that way. 17 So if anyone is in Christ, there is a new creation: everything old has passed away; see, everything has become new!

GOSPEL   Mark 4.26–34

²⁶ He also said, 'The kingdom of God is as if someone would scatter seed on the ground, ²⁷ and would sleep and rise night and day, and the seed would sprout and grow, he does not know how. ²⁸ The earth produces of itself, first the stalk, then the head, then the full grain in the head. ²⁹ But when the grain is ripe, at once he goes in with his sickle, because the harvest has come.'

³⁰ He also said, 'With what can we compare the kingdom of God, or what parable will we use for it? ³¹ It is like a mustard seed, which, when sown upon the ground, is the smallest of all the seeds on earth; ³² yet when it is sown it grows up and becomes the greatest of all shrubs, and puts forth large branches, so that the birds of the air can make nests in its shade.'

³³ With many such parables he spoke the word to them, as they were able to hear it; ³⁴ he did not speak to them except in parables, but he explained everything in private to his disciples.

RELATED

READING   Ezekiel 17.22–24

²² Thus says the Lord GOD:
    I myself will take a sprig
        from the lofty top of a cedar;
        I will set it out.
    I will break off a tender one
        from the topmost of its young twigs;
    I myself will plant it
        on a high and lofty mountain.
²³   On the mountain height of Israel
        I will plant it,
    in order that it may produce boughs and bear fruit,
        and become a noble cedar.
    Under it every kind of bird will live;
        in the shade of its branches will nest
        winged creatures of every kind.

24 All the trees of the field shall know
    that I am the Lord.
I bring low the high tree,
    I make high the low tree;
I dry up the green tree
    and make the dry tree flourish.
I the Lord have spoken;
    I will accomplish it.

PSALM   Psalm 92.1–4, 11–14

1 It is a good thing to give thanks to the Lord,
    and to sing praises to your name, O Most High;
2 To tell of your loving-kindness early in the morning
    and of your faithfulness in the night season;
3 On the psaltery and on the lyre
    and to the melody of the harp.
4 For you have made me glad by your acts, O Lord;
    and I shout for joy because of the works of your hands.

11 The righteous shall flourish like a palm tree,
    and shall spread abroad like a cedar of Lebanon.
12 Those who are planted in the house of the Lord
    shall flourish in the courts of our God;
13 They shall still bear fruit in old age;
    they shall be green and succulent;
14 That they may show how upright the Lord is,
    my rock, in whom there is no fault.

OR, IF AN ALTERNATIVE READING IS PREFERRED   Psalm 92.1–7

1 It is a good thing to give thanks to the Lord,
    and to sing praises to your name, O Most High;
2 To tell of your loving-kindness early in the morning
    and of your faithfulness in the night season;
3 On the psaltery and on the lyre
    and to the melody of the harp.
4 For you have made me glad by your acts, O Lord;
    and I shout for joy because of the works of your hands.
5 Lord, how great are your works!
    your thoughts are very deep.

6 The dullard does not know, nor does the fool understand,
  that though the wicked grow like weeds, and all the workers of
    iniquity flourish,
7 They flourish only to be destroyed for ever;
  but you, O Lord, are exalted for evermore.

READING   2 Corinthians 5.6–10, [11–13,] 14–17

⁶ So we are always confident; even though we know that while we are at home in the body we are away from the Lord— ⁷ for we walk by faith, not by sight. ⁸ Yes, we do have confidence, and we would rather be away from the body and at home with the Lord. ⁹ So whether we are at home or away, we make it our aim to please him. ¹⁰ For all of us must appear before the judgement seat of Christ, so that each may receive recompense for what has been done in the body, whether good or evil.

[¹¹ Therefore, knowing the fear of the Lord, we try to persuade others; but we ourselves are well known to God, and I hope that we are also well known to your consciences. ¹² We are not commending ourselves to you again, but giving you an opportunity to boast about us, so that you may be able to answer those who boast in outward appearance and not in the heart. ¹³ For if we are beside ourselves, it is for God; if we are in our right mind, it is for you.]
¹⁴ For the love of Christ urges us on, because we are convinced that one has died for all; therefore all have died. ¹⁵ And he died for all, so that those who live might live no longer for themselves, but for him who died and was raised for them.

¹⁶ From now on, therefore, we regard no one from a human point of view; even though we once knew Christ from a human point of view, we know him no longer in that way. ¹⁷ So if anyone is in Christ, there is a new creation: everything old has passed away; see, everything has become new!

GOSPEL   Mark 4.26–34

²⁶ He also said, 'The kingdom of God is as if someone would scatter seed on the ground, ²⁷ and would sleep and rise night and day, and the seed would sprout and grow, he does not know how. ²⁸ The earth produces of itself, first the stalk, then the head, then the full grain in the head. ²⁹ But when the grain is ripe, at once he goes in with his sickle, because the harvest has come.'

³⁰ He also said, 'With what can we compare the kingdom of God, or what parable will we use for it? ³¹ It is like a mustard seed, which, when sown upon the ground, is the smallest of all the seeds on earth; ³² yet when it is

sown it grows up and becomes the greatest of all shrubs, and puts forth large branches, so that the birds of the air can make nests in its shade.'

[33] With many such parables he spoke the word to them, as they were able to hear it; [34] he did not speak to them except in parables, but he explained everything in private to his disciples.

POST COMMUNION

See pages 569 to 571 and Table on page 568

SECOND SERVICE

Psalm 39
Jeremiah 7.1–16
Romans 9.14–26

If the Second Service is a Eucharist, the following is read as a Gospel:

Luke 7.36–8.3

THIRD SERVICE

Psalms 42; 43
Deuteronomy 10.12–11.1
Acts 23.12–35

PROPER 7

Sunday between 19 and 25 June inclusive (if after Trinity Sunday)

COLLECT

See pages 569 to 572 and Table on page 568

CONTINUOUS

EITHER

READING   **1 Samuel 17.[1a, 4–11, 19–23,] 32–49**

[[1] Now the Philistines gathered their armies for battle.

[4] And there came out from the camp of the Philistines a champion named Goliath, of Gath, whose height was six cubits and a span. [5] He had a helmet of bronze on his head, and he was armoured with a coat of mail; the weight of the coat was five thousand shekels of bronze. [6] He had greaves of bronze on his legs and a javelin of bronze slung between his shoulders. [7] The shaft

of his spear was like a weaver's beam, and his spear's head weighed six hundred shekels of iron; and his shield-bearer went before him. ⁸ He stood and shouted to the ranks of Israel, 'Why have you come out to draw up for battle? Am I not a Philistine, and are you not servants of Saul? Choose a man for yourselves, and let him come down to me. ⁹ If he is able to fight with me and kill me, then we will be your servants; but if I prevail against him and kill him, then you shall be our servants and serve us.' ¹⁰ And the Philistine said, 'Today I defy the ranks of Israel! Give me a man, that we may fight together.' ¹¹ When Saul and all Israel heard these words of the Philistine, they were dismayed and greatly afraid.

¹⁹ Now Saul, and they, and all the men of Israel, were in the valley of Elah, fighting with the Philistines. ²⁰ David rose early in the morning, left someone in charge of the sheep, took the provisions, and went as Jesse had commanded him. He came to the encampment as the army was going forth to the battle line, shouting the war cry. ²¹ Israel and the Philistines drew up for battle, army against army. ²² David left the things in charge of the keeper of the baggage, ran to the ranks, and went and greeted his brothers. ²³ As he talked with them, the champion, the Philistine of Gath, Goliath by name, came up out of the ranks of the Philistines, and spoke the same words as before. And David heard him.]

³² David said to Saul, 'Let no one's heart fail because of him; your servant will go and fight with this Philistine.' ³³ Saul said to David, 'You are not able to go against this Philistine to fight with him; for you are just a boy, and he has been a warrior from his youth.' ³⁴ But David said to Saul, 'Your servant used to keep sheep for his father; and whenever a lion or a bear came, and took a lamb from the flock, ³⁵ I went after it and struck it down, rescuing the lamb from its mouth; and if it turned against me, I would catch it by the jaw, strike it down, and kill it. ³⁶ Your servant has killed both lions and bears; and this uncircumcised Philistine shall be like one of them, since he has defied the armies of the living God.' ³⁷ David said, 'The LORD, who saved me from the paw of the lion and from the paw of the bear, will save me from the hand of this Philistine.' So Saul said to David, 'Go, and may the LORD be with you!'

³⁸ Saul clothed David with his armour; he put a bronze helmet on his head and clothed him with a coat of mail. ³⁹ David strapped Saul's sword over the armour, and he tried in vain to walk, for he was not used to them. Then David said to Saul, 'I cannot walk with these; for I am not used to them.' So David removed them. ⁴⁰ Then he took his staff in his hand, and chose five smooth stones from the wadi, and put them in his shepherd's bag, in the pouch; his sling was in his hand, and he drew near to the Philistine.

⁴¹ The Philistine came on and drew near to David, with his shield-bearer in front of him. ⁴² When the Philistine looked and saw David, he disdained

him, for he was only a youth, ruddy and handsome in appearance. [43] The Philistine said to David, 'Am I a dog, that you come to me with sticks?' And the Philistine cursed David by his gods. [44] The Philistine said to David, 'Come to me, and I will give your flesh to the birds of the air and to the wild animals of the field.' [45] But David said to the Philistine, 'You come to me with sword and spear and javelin; but I come to you in the name of the LORD of hosts, the God of the armies of Israel, whom you have defied. [46] This very day the LORD will deliver you into my hand, and I will strike you down and cut off your head; and I will give the dead bodies of the Philistine army this very day to the birds of the air and to the wild animals of the earth, so that all the earth may know that there is a God in Israel, [47] and that all this assembly may know that the LORD does not save by sword and spear; for the battle is the LORD's and he will give you into our hand.'

[48] When the Philistine drew nearer to meet David, David ran quickly towards the battle line to meet the Philistine. [49] David put his hand in his bag, took out a stone, slung it, and struck the Philistine on his forehead; the stone sank into his forehead, and he fell face down on the ground.

PSALM   Psalm 9.9–20

9   The Lord will be a refuge for the oppressed,
     a refuge in time of trouble.
10 Those who know your name will put their trust in you,
     for you never forsake those who seek you, O Lord.
11 Sing praise to the Lord who dwells in Zion;
     proclaim to the peoples the things he has done.
12 The avenger of blood will remember them;
     he will not forget the cry of the afflicted.
13 Have pity on me, O Lord;
     see the misery I suffer from those who hate me, O you who lift me
        up from the gate of death;
14 So that I may tell of all your praises and rejoice in your salvation
     in the gates of the city of Zion.
15 The ungodly have fallen into the pit they dug,
     and in the snare they set is their own foot caught.
16 The Lord is known by his acts of justice;
     the wicked are trapped in the works of their own hands.
17 The wicked shall be given over to the grave,
     and also all the peoples that forget God.
18 For the needy shall not always be forgotten,
     and the hope of the poor shall not perish for ever.

¹⁹ Rise up, O Lord, let not the ungodly have the upper hand;
      let them be judged before you.
²⁰ Put fear upon them, O Lord;
      let the ungodly know they are but mortal.

OR

READING   1 Samuel 17.57–18.5, 10–16

⁵⁷ On David's return from killing the Philistine, Abner took him and brought him before Saul, with the head of the Philistine in his hand. ⁵⁸ Saul said to him, 'Whose son are you, young man?' And David answered, 'I am the son of your servant Jesse the Bethlehemite.'

¹ When David had finished speaking to Saul, the soul of Jonathan was bound to the soul of David, and Jonathan loved him as his own soul. ² Saul took him that day and would not let him return to his father's house. ³ Then Jonathan made a covenant with David, because he loved him as his own soul. ⁴ Jonathan stripped himself of the robe that he was wearing, and gave it to David, and his armour, and even his sword and his bow and his belt. ⁵ David went out and was successful wherever Saul sent him; as a result, Saul set him over the army. And all the people, even the servants of Saul, approved.

¹⁰ The next day an evil spirit from God rushed upon Saul, and he raved within his house, while David was playing the lyre, as he did day by day. Saul had his spear in his hand; ¹¹ and Saul threw the spear, for he thought, 'I will pin David to the wall.' But David eluded him twice.

¹² Saul was afraid of David, because the LORD was with him but had departed from Saul. ¹³ So Saul removed him from his presence, and made him a commander of a thousand; and David marched out and came in, leading the army. ¹⁴ David had success in all his undertakings; for the LORD was with him. ¹⁵ When Saul saw that he had great success, he stood in awe of him. ¹⁶ But all Israel and Judah loved David; for it was he who marched out and came in leading them.

PSALM   Psalm 133

¹ O how good and pleasant it is,
      when a family lives together in unity!
² It is like fine oil upon the head
      that runs down upon the beard,

³ Upon the beard of Aaron,
and runs down upon the collar of his robe.
⁴ It is like the dew of Hermon
that falls upon the hills of Zion.
⁵ For there the Lord has ordained the blessing:
life for evermore.

READING   2 Corinthians 6.1–13

¹ As we work together with him, we urge you also not to accept the grace of God in vain. ² For he says,
'At an acceptable time I have listened to you,
and on a day of salvation I have helped you.'
See, now is the acceptable time; see, now is the day of salvation! ³ We are putting no obstacle in anyone's way, so that no fault may be found with our ministry, ⁴ but as servants of God we have commended ourselves in every way: through great endurance, in afflictions, hardships, calamities, ⁵ beatings, imprisonments, riots, labours, sleepless nights, hunger; ⁶ by purity, knowledge, patience, kindness, holiness of spirit, genuine love, ⁷ truthful speech, and the power of God; with the weapons of righteousness for the right hand and for the left; ⁸ in honour and dishonour, in ill repute and good repute. We are treated as impostors, and yet are true; ⁹ as unknown, and yet are well known; as dying, and see—we are alive; as punished, and yet not killed; ¹⁰ as sorrowful, yet always rejoicing; as poor, yet making many rich; as having nothing, and yet possessing everything.

¹¹ We have spoken frankly to you Corinthians; our heart is wide open to you. ¹² There is no restriction in our affections, but only in yours. ¹³ In return—I speak as to children—open wide your hearts also.

GOSPEL   Mark 4.35–41

³⁵ On that day, when evening had come, he said to them, 'Let us go across to the other side.' ³⁶ And leaving the crowd behind, they took him with them in the boat, just as he was. Other boats were with him. ³⁷ A great gale arose, and the waves beat into the boat, so that the boat was already being swamped. ³⁸ But he was in the stern, asleep on the cushion; and they woke him up and said to him, 'Teacher, do you not care that we are perishing?' ³⁹ He woke up and rebuked the wind, and said to the sea, 'Peace! Be still!' Then the wind ceased, and there was a dead calm. ⁴⁰ He said to them, 'Why are you afraid? Have you still no faith?' ⁴¹ And they were filled with great awe and said to one another, 'Who then is this, that even the wind and the sea obey him?'

RELATED

READING   Job 38.1–11

¹ Then the LORD answered Job out of the whirlwind:
² 'Who is this that darkens counsel by words without knowledge?
³ Gird up your loins like a man,
    I will question you, and you shall declare to me.
⁴ Where were you when I laid the foundation of the earth?
    Tell me, if you have understanding.
⁵ Who determined its measurements—surely you know!
    Or who stretched the line upon it?
⁶ On what were its bases sunk,
    or who laid its cornerstone
⁷ when the morning stars sang together
    and all the heavenly beings shouted for joy?
⁸ Or who shut in the sea with doors
    when it burst out from the womb?—
⁹ when I made the clouds its garment,
    and thick darkness its swaddling band,
¹⁰ and prescribed bounds for it,
    and set bars and doors,
¹¹ and said, "Thus far shall you come, and no farther,
    and here shall your proud waves be stopped"?'

PSALM   Psalm 107.[1–3,] 23–32

[¹ Give thanks to the Lord, for he is good,
    and his mercy endures for ever.
² Let all those whom the Lord has redeemed proclaim
    that he redeemed them from the hand of the foe.
³ He gathered them out of the lands;
    from the east and from the west, from the north and from the
      south.]

²³ Some went down to the sea in ships
    and plied their trade in deep waters;
²⁴ They beheld the works of the Lord
    and his wonders in the deep.
²⁵ Then he spoke and a stormy wind arose,
    which tossed high the waves of the sea.
²⁶ They mounted up to the heavens and fell back to the depths;
    their hearts melted because of their peril.

27 They reeled and staggered like drunkards
and were at their wits' end.
28 Then they cried to the Lord in their trouble,
and he delivered them from their distress.
29 He stilled the storm to a whisper
and quieted the waves of the sea.
30 Then were they glad because of the calm,
and he brought them to the harbour they were bound for.
31 Let them give thanks to the Lord for his mercy
and the wonders he does for his children.
32 Let them exalt him in the congregation of the people
and praise him in the council of the elders.

READING   2 Corinthians 6.1-13

1 As we work together with him, we urge you also not to accept the grace of God in vain. 2 For he says,
'At an acceptable time I have listened to you,
and on a day of salvation I have helped you.'
See, now is the acceptable time; see, now is the day of salvation! 3 We are putting no obstacle in anyone's way, so that no fault may be found with our ministry, 4 but as servants of God we have commended ourselves in every way: through great endurance, in afflictions, hardships, calamities, 5 beatings, imprisonments, riots, labours, sleepless nights, hunger; 6 by purity, knowledge, patience, kindness, holiness of spirit, genuine love, 7 truthful speech, and the power of God; with the weapons of righteousness for the right hand and for the left; 8 in honour and dishonour, in ill repute and good repute. We are treated as impostors, and yet are true; 9 as unknown, and yet are well known; as dying, and see—we are alive; as punished, and yet not killed; 10 as sorrowful, yet always rejoicing; as poor, yet making many rich; as having nothing, and yet possessing everything.

11 We have spoken frankly to you Corinthians; our heart is wide open to you. 12 There is no restriction in our affections, but only in yours. 13 In return—I speak as to children—open wide your hearts also.

GOSPEL   Mark 4.35-41

35 On that day, when evening had come, he said to them, 'Let us go across to the other side.' 36 And leaving the crowd behind, they took him with them in the boat, just as he was. Other boats were with him. 37 A great gale arose, and the waves beat into the boat, so that the boat was already being swamped. 38 But he was in the stern, asleep on the cushion; and they woke

him up and said to him, 'Teacher, do you not care that we are perishing?' [39] He woke up and rebuked the wind, and said to the sea, 'Peace! Be still!' Then the wind ceased, and there was a dead calm. [40] He said to them, 'Why are you afraid? Have you still no faith?' [41] And they were filled with great awe and said to one another, 'Who then is this, that even the wind and the sea obey him?'

POST COMMUNION

See pages 569 to 572 and Table on page 568

SECOND SERVICE

Psalm 49
Jeremiah 10.1–16
Romans 11.25–36

If the Second Service is a Eucharist, the following is read as a Gospel:

Luke 8.26–39

THIRD SERVICE

Psalm 48
Deuteronomy 11.1–15
Acts 27.1–12

PROPER 8

Sunday between 26 June and 2 July inclusive

COLLECT

See pages 569 to 572 and Table on page 568

CONTINUOUS

READING   2 Samuel 1.1, 17–27

[1] After the death of Saul, when David had returned from defeating the Amalekites, David remained two days in Ziklag.

[17] David intoned this lamentation over Saul and his son Jonathan. [18] (He ordered that The Song of the Bow be taught to the people of Judah; it is written in the Book of Jashar.) He said:
[19]   Your glory, O Israel, lies slain upon your high places!
    How the mighty have fallen!

20 Tell it not in Gath,
    proclaim it not in the streets of Ashkelon;
or the daughters of the Philistines will rejoice,
    the daughters of the uncircumcised will exult.
21 You mountains of Gilboa,
    let there be no dew or rain upon you,
      nor bounteous fields!
For there the shield of the mighty was defiled,
    the shield of Saul, anointed with oil no more.
22 From the blood of the slain,
    from the fat of the mighty,
the bow of Jonathan did not turn back,
    nor the sword of Saul return empty.
23 Saul and Jonathan, beloved and lovely!
    In life and in death they were not divided;
they were swifter than eagles,
    they were stronger than lions.
24 O daughters of Israel, weep over Saul,
    who clothed you with crimson, in luxury,
    who put ornaments of gold on your apparel.
25 How the mighty have fallen
    in the midst of the battle!
Jonathan lies slain upon your high places.
26   I am distressed for you, my brother Jonathan;
greatly beloved were you to me;
    your love to me was wonderful,
    passing the love of women.
27 How the mighty have fallen,
    and the weapons of war perished!

PSALM   Psalm 130

1   Out of the depths have I called to you, O Lord; Lord, hear my voice;
    let your ears consider well the voice of my supplication.
2   If you, Lord, were to note what is done amiss,
    O Lord, who could stand?
3   For there is forgiveness with you;
    therefore you shall be feared.
4   I wait for the Lord; my soul waits for him;
    in his word is my hope.
5   My soul waits for the Lord, more than the night-watch for the
      morning,
    more than the night-watch for the morning.

6 O Israel, wait for the Lord,
   for with the Lord there is mercy;
7 With him there is plenteous redemption,
   and he shall redeem Israel from all their sins.

READING   2 Corinthians 8.7–15

⁷ Now as you excel in everything—in faith, in speech, in knowledge, in utmost eagerness, and in our love for you—so we want you to excel also in this generous undertaking.

⁸ I do not say this as a command, but I am testing the genuineness of your love against the earnestness of others. ⁹ For you know the generous act of our Lord Jesus Christ, that though he was rich, yet for your sakes he became poor, so that by his poverty you might become rich. ¹⁰ And in this matter I am giving my advice: it is appropriate for you who began last year not only to do something but even to desire to do something— ¹¹ now finish doing it, so that your eagerness may be matched by completing it according to your means. ¹² For if the eagerness is there, the gift is acceptable according to what one has—not according to what one does not have. ¹³ I do not mean that there should be relief for others and pressure on you, but it is a question of a fair balance between ¹⁴ your present abundance and their need, so that their abundance may be for your need, in order that there may be a fair balance. ¹⁵ As it is written,
    'The one who had much did not have too much,
       and the one who had little did not have too little.'

GOSPEL   Mark 5.21–43

²¹ When Jesus had crossed again in the boat to the other side, a great crowd gathered round him; and he was by the lake. ²² Then one of the leaders of the synagogue named Jairus came and, when he saw him, fell at his feet ²³ and begged him repeatedly, 'My little daughter is at the point of death. Come and lay your hands on her, so that she may be made well, and live.' ²⁴ So he went with him.

And a large crowd followed him and pressed in on him. ²⁵ Now there was a woman who had been suffering from haemorrhages for twelve years. ²⁶ She had endured much under many physicians, and had spent all that she had; and she was no better, but rather grew worse. ²⁷ She had heard about Jesus, and came up behind him in the crowd and touched his cloak, ²⁸ for she said, 'If I but touch his clothes, I will be made well.' ²⁹ Immediately her haemorrhage stopped; and she felt in her body that she was healed of her disease. ³⁰ Immediately aware that power had gone forth from him,

Jesus turned about in the crowd and said, 'Who touched my clothes?' ³¹ And his disciples said to him, 'You see the crowd pressing in on you; how can you say, "Who touched me?" ' ³² He looked all round to see who had done it. ³³ But the woman, knowing what had happened to her, came in fear and trembling, fell down before him, and told him the whole truth. ³⁴ He said to her, 'Daughter, your faith has made you well; go in peace, and be healed of your disease.'

³⁵ While he was still speaking, some people came from the leader's house to say, 'Your daughter is dead. Why trouble the teacher any further?' ³⁶ But overhearing what they said, Jesus said to the leader of the synagogue, 'Do not fear, only believe.' ³⁷ He allowed no one to follow him except Peter, James, and John, the brother of James. ³⁸ When they came to the house of the leader of the synagogue, he saw a commotion, people weeping and wailing loudly. ³⁹ When he had entered, he said to them, 'Why do you make a commotion and weep? The child is not dead but sleeping.' ⁴⁰ And they laughed at him. Then he put them all outside, and took the child's father and mother and those who were with him, and went in where the child was. ⁴¹ He took her by the hand and said to her, 'Talitha cum', which means, 'Little girl, get up!' ⁴² And immediately the girl got up and began to walk about (she was twelve years of age). At this they were overcome with amazement. ⁴³ He strictly ordered them that no one should know this, and told them to give her something to eat.

RELATED

READING

Lamentations 3.22–33 may be read as the first reading in place of Wisdom 1.13–15; 2.23–24

Wisdom 1.13–15; 2.23–24

¹³ God did not make death,
   and he does not delight in the death of the living.
¹⁴ For he created all things so that they might exist;
   the generative forces of the world are wholesome,
   and there is no destructive poison in them,
   and the dominion of Hades is not on earth.
¹⁵ For righteousness is immortal.

23 For God created us for incorruption,
   and made us in the image of his own eternity,
24 but through the devil's envy death entered the world,
   and those who belong to his company experience it.

EITHER

CANTICLE   Lamentations 3.22–33

22 The steadfast love of the LORD never ceases,
   his mercies never come to an end;
23 they are new every morning;
   great is your faithfulness.
24 'The LORD is my portion,' says my soul,
   'therefore I will hope in him.'
25 The LORD is good to those who wait for him,
   to the soul that seeks him.
26 It is good that one should wait quietly
   for the salvation of the LORD.
27 It is good for one to bear
   the yoke in youth,
28 to sit alone in silence
   when the Lord has imposed it,
29 to put one's mouth to the dust
   (there may yet be hope),
30 to give one's cheek to the smiter,
   and be filled with insults.
31 For the Lord will not
   reject for ever.
32 Although he causes grief, he will have compassion
   according to the abundance of his steadfast love;
33 for he does not willingly afflict
   or grieve anyone.

OR

PSALM   Psalm 30

1 I will exalt you, O Lord, because you have lifted me up
  and have not let my enemies triumph over me.
2 O Lord my God, I cried out to you,
  and you restored me to health.
3 You brought me up, O Lord, from the dead;
  you restored my life as I was going down to the grave.

4   Sing to the Lord, you servants of his;
     give thanks for the remembrance of his holiness.
5   For his wrath endures but the twinkling of an eye,
     his favour for a lifetime.
6   Weeping may spend the night,
     but joy comes in the morning.
7   While I felt secure, I said, 'I shall never be disturbed.
     You, Lord, with your favour, made me as strong as the mountains.'
8   Then you hid your face,
     and I was filled with fear.
9   I cried to you, O Lord;
     I pleaded with the Lord, saying,
10   'What profit is there in my blood, if I go down to the Pit?
     will the dust praise you or declare your faithfulness?
11   Hear, O Lord, and have mercy upon me;
     O Lord, be my helper.'
12   You have turned my wailing into dancing;
     you have put off my sack-cloth and clothed me with joy;
13   Therefore my heart sings to you without ceasing;
     O Lord my God, I will give you thanks for ever.

READING   2 Corinthians 8.7–15

7 Now as you excel in everything—in faith, in speech, in knowledge, in utmost eagerness, and in our love for you—so we want you to excel also in this generous undertaking.

8 I do not say this as a command, but I am testing the genuineness of your love against the earnestness of others. 9 For you know the generous act of our Lord Jesus Christ, that though he was rich, yet for your sakes he became poor, so that by his poverty you might become rich. 10 And in this matter I am giving my advice: it is appropriate for you who began last year not only to do something but even to desire to do something— 11 now finish doing it, so that your eagerness may be matched by completing it according to your means. 12 For if the eagerness is there, the gift is acceptable according to what one has—not according to what one does not have. 13 I do not mean that there should be relief for others and pressure on you, but it is a question of a fair balance between 14 your present abundance and their need, so that their abundance may be for your need, in order that there may be a fair balance. 15 As it is written,
     'The one who had much did not have too much,
        and the one who had little did not have too little.'

GOSPEL   Mark 5.21–43

[21] When Jesus had crossed again in the boat to the other side, a great crowd gathered round him; and he was by the lake. [22] Then one of the leaders of the synagogue named Jairus came and, when he saw him, fell at his feet [23] and begged him repeatedly, 'My little daughter is at the point of death. Come and lay your hands on her, so that she may be made well, and live.' [24] So he went with him.

And a large crowd followed him and pressed in on him. [25] Now there was a woman who had been suffering from haemorrhages for twelve years. [26] She had endured much under many physicians, and had spent all that she had; and she was no better, but rather grew worse. [27] She had heard about Jesus, and came up behind him in the crowd and touched his cloak, [28] for she said, 'If I but touch his clothes, I will be made well.' [29] Immediately her haemorrhage stopped; and she felt in her body that she was healed of her disease. [30] Immediately aware that power had gone forth from him, Jesus turned about in the crowd and said, 'Who touched my clothes?' [31] And his disciples said to him, 'You see the crowd pressing in on you; how can you say, "Who touched me?" ' [32] He looked all round to see who had done it. [33] But the woman, knowing what had happened to her, came in fear and trembling, fell down before him, and told him the whole truth. [34] He said to her, 'Daughter, your faith has made you well; go in peace, and be healed of your disease.'

[35] While he was still speaking, some people came from the leader's house to say, 'Your daughter is dead. Why trouble the teacher any further?' [36] But overhearing what they said, Jesus said to the leader of the synagogue, 'Do not fear, only believe.' [37] He allowed no one to follow him except Peter, James, and John, the brother of James. [38] When they came to the house of the leader of the synagogue, he saw a commotion, people weeping and wailing loudly. [39] When he had entered, he said to them, 'Why do you make a commotion and weep? The child is not dead but sleeping.' [40] And they laughed at him. Then he put them all outside, and took the child's father and mother and those who were with him, and went in where the child was. [41] He took her by the hand and said to her, 'Talitha cum', which means, 'Little girl, get up!' [42] And immediately the girl got up and began to walk about (she was twelve years of age). At this they were overcome with amazement. [43] He strictly ordered them that no one should know this, and told them to give her something to eat.

POST COMMUNION

See pages 569 to 573 and Table on page 568

SECOND SERVICE

Psalms [52;] 53
Jeremiah 11.1–14
Romans 13.1–10

If the Second Service is a Eucharist, the following is read as a Gospel:

Luke 9.51–62

THIRD SERVICE

Psalm 56
Deuteronomy 15.1–11
Acts 27.[13–32,] 33–44

PROPER 9

Sunday between 3 and 9 July inclusive

COLLECT

See pages 569 to 573 and Table on page 568

CONTINUOUS

READING   2 Samuel 5.1–5, 9–10

¹ Then all the tribes of Israel came to David at Hebron, and said, 'Look, we are your bone and flesh. ² For some time, while Saul was king over us, it was you who led out Israel and brought it in. The LORD said to you: It is you who shall be shepherd of my people Israel, you who shall be ruler over Israel.' ³ So all the elders of Israel came to the king at Hebron; and King David made a covenant with them at Hebron before the LORD, and they anointed David king over Israel. ⁴ David was thirty years old when he began to reign, and he reigned for forty years. ⁵ At Hebron he reigned over Judah for seven years and six months; and at Jerusalem he reigned over all Israel and Judah for thirty-three years.

⁹ David occupied the stronghold, and named it the city of David. David built the city all around from the Millo inwards. ¹⁰ And David became greater and greater, for the LORD, the God of hosts, was with him.

PSALM   Psalm 48

1 Great is the Lord and highly to be praised;
   in the city of our God is his holy hill.
2 Beautiful and lofty, the joy of all the earth, is the hill of Zion,
   the very centre of the world and the city of the great king.
3 God is in her citadels;
   he is known to be her sure refuge.
4 Behold, the kings of the earth assembled
   and marched forward together.
5 They looked and were astounded;
   they retreated and fled in terror.
6 Trembling seized them there;
   they writhed like a woman in childbirth, like ships of the sea when
      the east wind shatters them.
7 As we have heard, so have we seen, in the city of the Lord of hosts,
      in the city of our God;
   God has established her for ever.
8 We have waited in silence on your loving-kindness, O God,
   in the midst of your temple.
9 Your praise, like your name, O God, reaches to the world's end;
   your right hand is full of justice.
10 Let Mount Zion be glad and the cities of Judah rejoice,
   because of your judgements.
11 Make the circuit of Zion; walk round about her;
   count the number of her towers.
12 Consider well her bulwarks; examine her strongholds;
   that you may tell those who come after.
13 This God is our God for ever and ever;
   he shall be our guide for evermore.

READING   2 Corinthians 12.2–10

2 I know a person in Christ who fourteen years ago was caught up to the third heaven—whether in the body or out of the body I do not know; God knows. 3 And I know that such a person—whether in the body or out of the body I do not know; God knows— 4 was caught up into Paradise and heard things that are not to be told, that no mortal is permitted to repeat. 5 On behalf of such a one I will boast, but on my own behalf I will not boast, except of my weaknesses. 6 But if I wish to boast, I will not be a fool, for I will be speaking the truth. But I refrain from it, so that no one may think better of me than what is seen in me or heard from me, 7 even considering the exceptional character of the revelations. Therefore, to keep me from

being too elated, a thorn was given to me in the flesh, a messenger of Satan to torment me, to keep me from being too elated. ⁸ Three times I appealed to the Lord about this, that it would leave me, ⁹ but he said to me, 'My grace is sufficient for you, for power is made perfect in weakness.' So, I will boast all the more gladly of my weaknesses, so that the power of Christ may dwell in me. ¹⁰ Therefore I am content with weaknesses, insults, hardships, persecutions, and calamities for the sake of Christ; for whenever I am weak, then I am strong.

GOSPEL   Mark 6.1–13

¹ He left that place and came to his home town, and his disciples followed him. ² On the sabbath he began to teach in the synagogue, and many who heard him were astounded. They said, 'Where did this man get all this? What is this wisdom that has been given to him? What deeds of power are being done by his hands! ³ Is not this the carpenter, the son of Mary and brother of James and Joses and Judas and Simon, and are not his sisters here with us?' And they took offence at him. ⁴ Then Jesus said to them, 'Prophets are not without honour, except in their home town, and among their own kin, and in their own house.' ⁵ And he could do no deed of power there, except that he laid his hands on a few sick people and cured them. ⁶ And he was amazed at their unbelief.

Then he went about among the villages teaching. ⁷ He called the twelve and began to send them out two by two, and gave them authority over the unclean spirits. ⁸ He ordered them to take nothing for their journey except a staff; no bread, no bag, no money in their belts; ⁹ but to wear sandals and not to put on two tunics. ¹⁰ He said to them, 'Wherever you enter a house, stay there until you leave the place. ¹¹ If any place will not welcome you and they refuse to hear you, as you leave, shake off the dust that is on your feet as a testimony against them.' ¹² So they went out and proclaimed that all should repent. ¹³ They cast out many demons, and anointed with oil many who were sick and cured them.

RELATED

READING   Ezekiel 2.1–5

¹ He said to me: O mortal, stand up on your feet, and I will speak with you. ² And when he spoke to me, a spirit entered into me and set me on my feet; and I heard him speaking to me. ³ He said to me, Mortal, I am sending you to the people of Israel, to a nation of rebels who have rebelled against me; they and their ancestors have transgressed against me to this very day.

⁴ The descendants are impudent and stubborn. I am sending you to them, and you shall say to them, 'Thus says the Lord God.' ⁵ Whether they hear or refuse to hear (for they are a rebellious house), they shall know that there has been a prophet among them.

PSALM   Psalm 123

¹ To you I lift up my eyes,
    to you enthroned in the heavens.
² As the eyes of servants look to the hand of their masters,
    and the eyes of a maid to the hand of her mistress,
³ So our eyes look to the Lord our God,
    until he shows us his mercy.
⁴ Have mercy upon us, O Lord, have mercy,
    for we have had more than enough of contempt,
⁵ Too much of the scorn of the indolent rich,
    and of the derision of the proud.

READING   2 Corinthians 12.2–10

² I know a person in Christ who fourteen years ago was caught up to the third heaven—whether in the body or out of the body I do not know; God knows. ³ And I know that such a person—whether in the body or out of the body I do not know; God knows— ⁴ was caught up into Paradise and heard things that are not to be told, that no mortal is permitted to repeat. ⁵ On behalf of such a one I will boast, but on my own behalf I will not boast, except of my weaknesses. ⁶ But if I wish to boast, I will not be a fool, for I will be speaking the truth. But I refrain from it, so that no one may think better of me than what is seen in me or heard from me, ⁷ even considering the exceptional character of the revelations. Therefore, to keep me from being too elated, a thorn was given to me in the flesh, a messenger of Satan to torment me, to keep me from being too elated. ⁸ Three times I appealed to the Lord about this, that it would leave me, ⁹ but he said to me, 'My grace is sufficient for you, for power is made perfect in weakness.' So, I will boast all the more gladly of my weaknesses, so that the power of Christ may dwell in me. ¹⁰ Therefore I am content with weaknesses, insults, hardships, persecutions, and calamities for the sake of Christ; for whenever I am weak, then I am strong.

GOSPEL   Mark 6.1–13

¹ He left that place and came to his home town, and his disciples followed him. ² On the sabbath he began to teach in the synagogue, and many who heard him were astounded. They said, 'Where did this man get all this? What is this wisdom that has been given to him? What deeds of power are being done by his hands! ³ Is not this the carpenter, the son of Mary and brother of James and Joses and Judas and Simon, and are not his sisters here with us?' And they took offence at him. ⁴ Then Jesus said to them, 'Prophets are not without honour, except in their home town, and among their own kin, and in their own house.' ⁵ And he could do no deed of power there, except that he laid his hands on a few sick people and cured them. ⁶ And he was amazed at their unbelief.

Then he went about among the villages teaching. ⁷ He called the twelve and began to send them out two by two, and gave them authority over the unclean spirits. ⁸ He ordered them to take nothing for their journey except a staff; no bread, no bag, no money in their belts; ⁹ but to wear sandals and not to put on two tunics. ¹⁰ He said to them, 'Wherever you enter a house, stay there until you leave the place. ¹¹ If any place will not welcome you and they refuse to hear you, as you leave, shake off the dust that is on your feet as a testimony against them.' ¹² So they went out and proclaimed that all should repent. ¹³ They cast out many demons, and anointed with oil many who were sick and cured them.

POST COMMUNION

See pages 570 to 574 and Table on page 568

SECOND SERVICE

Psalms [63;] 64
Jeremiah 20.1–11a
Romans 14.1–17

If the Second Service is a Eucharist, the following is read as a Gospel:

Luke 10.1–11, 16–20

THIRD SERVICE

Psalm 57
Deuteronomy 24.10–22
Acts 28.1–16

PROPER 10

Sunday between 10 and 16 July inclusive

COLLECT

See pages 570 to 574 and Table on page 568

CONTINUOUS

READING   2 Samuel 6.1–5, 12b–19

¹ David again gathered all the chosen men of Israel, thirty thousand.
² David and all the people with him set out and went from Baale-judah, to
bring up from there the ark of God, which is called by the name of the
Lord of hosts who is enthroned on the cherubim. ³ They carried the ark of
God on a new cart, and brought it out of the house of Abinadab, which was
on the hill. Uzzah and Ahio, the sons of Abinadab, were driving the new
cart ⁴ with the ark of God; and Ahio went in front of the ark. ⁵ David and
all the house of Israel were dancing before the Lord with all their might,
with songs and lyres and harps and tambourines and castanets and
cymbals.

¹² So David went and brought up the ark of God from the house of Obed-
edom to the city of David with rejoicing; ¹³ and when those who bore the
ark of the Lord had gone six paces, he sacrificed an ox and a fatling. ¹⁴ David
danced before the Lord with all his might; David was girded with a linen
ephod. ¹⁵ So David and all the house of Israel brought up the ark of the
Lord with shouting, and with the sound of the trumpet.

¹⁶ As the ark of the Lord came into the city of David, Michal daughter of
Saul looked out of the window, and saw King David leaping and dancing
before the Lord; and she despised him in her heart.

¹⁷ They brought in the ark of the Lord, and set it in its place, inside the
tent that David had pitched for it; and David offered burnt-offerings and
offerings of well-being before the Lord. ¹⁸ When David had finished offering
the burnt-offerings and the offerings of well-being, he blessed the people
in the name of the Lord of hosts, ¹⁹ and distributed food among all the
people, the whole multitude of Israel, both men and women, to each a cake
of bread, a portion of meat, and a cake of raisins. Then all the people went
back to their homes.

PSALM   Psalm 24

1 The earth is the Lord's and all that is in it,
   the world and all who dwell therein.
2 For it is he who founded it upon the seas
   and made it firm upon the rivers of the deep.
3 'Who can ascend the hill of the Lord?
   and who can stand in his holy place?'
4 'Those who have clean hands and a pure heart,
   who have not pledged themselves to falsehood, nor sworn by what
      is a fraud.
5 They shall receive a blessing from the Lord
   and a just reward from the God of their salvation.'
6 Such is the generation of those who seek him,
   of those who seek your face, O God of Jacob.
7 Lift up your heads, O gates; lift them high, O everlasting doors;
   and the King of glory shall come in.
8 'Who is this King of glory?'
   'The Lord, strong and mighty, the Lord, mighty in battle.'
9 Lift up your heads, O gates; lift them high, O everlasting doors;
   and the King of glory shall come in.
10 'Who is he, this King of glory?'
   'The Lord of hosts, he is the King of glory.'

READING   Ephesians 1.3–14

3 Blessed be the God and Father of our Lord Jesus Christ, who has blessed us in Christ with every spiritual blessing in the heavenly places, 4 just as he chose us in Christ before the foundation of the world to be holy and blameless before him in love. 5 He destined us for adoption as his children through Jesus Christ, according to the good pleasure of his will, 6 to the praise of his glorious grace that he freely bestowed on us in the Beloved. 7 In him we have redemption through his blood, the forgiveness of our trespasses, according to the riches of his grace 8 that he lavished on us. With all wisdom and insight 9 he has made known to us the mystery of his will, according to his good pleasure that he set forth in Christ, 10 as a plan for the fullness of time, to gather up all things in him, things in heaven and things on earth. 11 In Christ we have also obtained an inheritance, having been destined according to the purpose of him who accomplishes all things according to his counsel and will, 12 so that we, who were the first to set our hope on Christ, might live for the praise of his glory. 13 In him you also, when you had heard the word of truth, the gospel of your salvation, and had believed in him, were marked with the seal of the

promised Holy Spirit; ¹⁴ this is the pledge of our inheritance towards redemption as God's own people, to the praise of his glory.

GOSPEL   Mark 6.14–29

¹⁴ King Herod heard of it, for Jesus' name had become known. Some were saying, 'John the baptizer has been raised from the dead; and for this reason these powers are at work in him.' ¹⁵ But others said, 'It is Elijah.' And others said, 'It is a prophet, like one of the prophets of old.' ¹⁶ But when Herod heard of it, he said, 'John, whom I beheaded, has been raised.'

¹⁷ For Herod himself had sent men who arrested John, bound him, and put him in prison on account of Herodias, his brother Philip's wife, because Herod had married her. ¹⁸ For John had been telling Herod, 'It is not lawful for you to have your brother's wife.' ¹⁹ And Herodias had a grudge against him, and wanted to kill him. But she could not, ²⁰ for Herod feared John, knowing that he was a righteous and holy man, and he protected him. When he heard him, he was greatly perplexed; and yet he liked to listen to him. ²¹ But an opportunity came when Herod on his birthday gave a banquet for his courtiers and officers and for the leaders of Galilee. ²² When his daughter Herodias came in and danced, she pleased Herod and his guests; and the king said to the girl, 'Ask me for whatever you wish, and I will give it.' ²³ And he solemnly swore to her, 'Whatever you ask me, I will give you, even half of my kingdom.' ²⁴ She went out and said to her mother, 'What should I ask for?' She replied, 'The head of John the baptizer.' ²⁵ Immediately she rushed back to the king and requested, 'I want you to give me at once the head of John the Baptist on a platter.' ²⁶ The king was deeply grieved; yet out of regard for his oaths and for the guests, he did not want to refuse her. ²⁷ Immediately the king sent a soldier of the guard with orders to bring John's head. He went and beheaded him in the prison, ²⁸ brought his head on a platter, and gave it to the girl. Then the girl gave it to her mother. ²⁹ When his disciples heard about it, they came and took his body, and laid it in a tomb.

RELATED

READING   Amos 7.7–15

⁷ This is what he showed me: the Lord was standing beside a wall built with a plumb-line, with a plumb-line in his hand. ⁸ And the LORD said to me, 'Amos, what do you see?' And I said, 'A plumb-line.' Then the Lord said,
'See, I am setting a plumb-line
    in the midst of my people Israel;
    I will never again pass them by;

⁹   the high places of Isaac shall be made desolate,
     and the sanctuaries of Israel shall be laid waste,
     and I will rise against the house of Jeroboam with the sword.'

¹⁰ Then Amaziah, the priest of Bethel, sent to King Jeroboam of Israel, saying, 'Amos has conspired against you in the very centre of the house of Israel; the land is not able to bear all his words. ¹¹ For thus Amos has said,
     "Jeroboam shall die by the sword,
       and Israel must go into exile
       away from his land."'
¹² And Amaziah said to Amos, 'O seer, go, flee away to the land of Judah, earn your bread there, and prophesy there; ¹³ but never again prophesy at Bethel, for it is the king's sanctuary, and it is a temple of the kingdom.'

¹⁴ Then Amos answered Amaziah, 'I am no prophet, nor a prophet's son; but I am a herdsman, and a dresser of sycomore trees, ¹⁵ and the LORD took me from following the flock, and the LORD said to me, "Go, prophesy to my people Israel."'

PSALM   Psalm 85.8–13

⁸   I will listen to what the Lord God is saying,
     for he is speaking peace to his faithful people and to those who
       turn their hearts to him.
⁹   Truly, his salvation is very near to those who fear him,
     that his glory may dwell in our land.
¹⁰   Mercy and truth have met together;
     righteousness and peace have kissed each other.
¹¹   Truth shall spring up from the earth,
     and righteousness shall look down from heaven.
¹²   The Lord will indeed grant prosperity,
     and our land will yield its increase.
¹³   Righteousness shall go before him,
     and peace shall be a pathway for his feet.

READING   Ephesians 1.3–14

³ Blessed be the God and Father of our Lord Jesus Christ, who has blessed us in Christ with every spiritual blessing in the heavenly places, ⁴ just as he chose us in Christ before the foundation of the world to be holy and blameless before him in love. ⁵ He destined us for adoption as his children

through Jesus Christ, according to the good pleasure of his will, [6] to the praise of his glorious grace that he freely bestowed on us in the Beloved. [7] In him we have redemption through his blood, the forgiveness of our trespasses, according to the riches of his grace [8] that he lavished on us. With all wisdom and insight [9] he has made known to us the mystery of his will, according to his good pleasure that he set forth in Christ, [10] as a plan for the fullness of time, to gather up all things in him, things in heaven and things on earth. [11] In Christ we have also obtained an inheritance, having been destined according to the purpose of him who accomplishes all things according to his counsel and will, [12] so that we, who were the first to set our hope on Christ, might live for the praise of his glory. [13] In him you also, when you had heard the word of truth, the gospel of your salvation, and had believed in him, were marked with the seal of the promised Holy Spirit; [14] this is the pledge of our inheritance towards redemption as God's own people, to the praise of his glory.

GOSPEL   Mark 6.14–29

[14] King Herod heard of it, for Jesus' name had become known. Some were saying, 'John the baptizer has been raised from the dead; and for this reason these powers are at work in him.' [15] But others said, 'It is Elijah.' And others said, 'It is a prophet, like one of the prophets of old.' [16] But when Herod heard of it, he said, 'John, whom I beheaded, has been raised.'

[17] For Herod himself had sent men who arrested John, bound him, and put him in prison on account of Herodias, his brother Philip's wife, because Herod had married her. [18] For John had been telling Herod, 'It is not lawful for you to have your brother's wife.' [19] And Herodias had a grudge against him, and wanted to kill him. But she could not, [20] for Herod feared John, knowing that he was a righteous and holy man, and he protected him. When he heard him, he was greatly perplexed; and yet he liked to listen to him. [21] But an opportunity came when Herod on his birthday gave a banquet for his courtiers and officers and for the leaders of Galilee. [22] When his daughter Herodias came in and danced, she pleased Herod and his guests; and the king said to the girl, 'Ask me for whatever you wish, and I will give it.' [23] And he solemnly swore to her, 'Whatever you ask me, I will give you, even half of my kingdom.' [24] She went out and said to her mother, 'What should I ask for?' She replied, 'The head of John the baptizer.' [25] Immediately she rushed back to the king and requested, 'I want you to give me at once the head of John the Baptist on a platter.' [26] The king was deeply grieved;

yet out of regard for his oaths and for the guests, he did not want to refuse her. [27] Immediately the king sent a soldier of the guard with orders to bring John's head. He went and beheaded him in the prison, [28] brought his head on a platter, and gave it to the girl. Then the girl gave it to her mother. [29] When his disciples heard about it, they came and took his body, and laid it in a tomb.

POST COMMUNION

See pages 571 to 574 and Table on page 568

SECOND SERVICE

Psalm 66.1-8, [9-18]
Job 4.1; 5.6-27
or
Ecclesiasticus 4.11-31
Romans 15.14-29

If the Second Service is a Eucharist, the following is read as a Gospel:

Luke 10.25-37

THIRD SERVICE

Psalm 65
Deuteronomy 28.1-14
Acts 28.17-30

PROPER 11

Sunday between 17 and 23 July inclusive

COLLECT

See pages 571 to 575 and Table on page 568

CONTINUOUS

READING   2 Samuel 7.1-14a

[1] Now when the king was settled in his house, and the LORD had given him rest from all his enemies around him, [2] the king said to the prophet Nathan, 'See now, I am living in a house of cedar, but the ark of God stays in a tent.' [3] Nathan said to the king, 'Go, do all that you have in mind; for the LORD is with you.'

⁴ But that same night the word of the LORD came to Nathan: ⁵ Go and tell my servant David: Thus says the LORD: Are you the one to build me a house to live in? ⁶ I have not lived in a house since the day I brought up the people of Israel from Egypt to this day, but I have been moving about in a tent and a tabernacle. ⁷ Wherever I have moved about among all the people of Israel, did I ever speak a word with any of the tribal leaders of Israel, whom I commanded to shepherd my people Israel, saying, 'Why have you not built me a house of cedar?' ⁸ Now therefore thus you shall say to my servant David: Thus says the LORD of hosts: I took you from the pasture, from following the sheep to be prince over my people Israel; ⁹ and I have been with you wherever you went, and have cut off all your enemies from before you; and I will make for you a great name, like the name of the great ones of the earth. ¹⁰ And I will appoint a place for my people Israel and will plant them, so that they may live in their own place, and be disturbed no more; and evildoers shall afflict them no more, as formerly, ¹¹ from the time that I appointed judges over my people Israel; and I will give you rest from all your enemies. Moreover, the LORD declares to you that the LORD will make you a house. ¹² When your days are fulfilled and you lie down with your ancestors, I will raise up your offspring after you, who shall come forth from your body, and I will establish his kingdom. ¹³ He shall build a house for my name, and I will establish the throne of his kingdom for ever. ¹⁴ I will be a father to him, and he shall be a son to me.

PSALM   Psalm 89.20–37

²⁰ 'I have found David my servant;
   with my holy oil have I anointed him.
²¹ My hand will hold him fast
   and my arm will make him strong.
²² No enemy shall deceive him,
   nor the wicked bring him down.
²³ I will crush his foes before him
   and strike down those who hate him.
²⁴ My faithfulness and love shall be with him,
   and he shall be victorious through my name.
²⁵ I shall make his dominion extend
   from the Great Sea to the River.
²⁶ He will say to me, "You are my Father,
   my God and the rock of my salvation."
²⁷ I will make him my first-born
   and higher than the kings of the earth.
²⁸ I will keep my love for him for ever,
   and my covenant will stand firm for him.

²⁹ I will establish his line for ever
and his throne as the days of heaven.
³⁰ If his children forsake my law
and do not walk according to my judgements;
³¹ If they break my statutes
and do not keep my commandments;
³² I will punish their transgressions with a rod
and their iniquities with the lash;
³³ But I will not take my love from him,
nor let my faithfulness prove false.
³⁴ I will not break my covenant,
nor change what has gone out of my lips.
³⁵ Once for all I have sworn by my holiness:
"I will not lie to David.
³⁶ His line shall endure for ever
and his throne as the sun before me;
³⁷ It shall stand fast for evermore like the moon,
the abiding witness in the sky." '

READING   Ephesians 2.11–22

¹¹ So then, remember that at one time you Gentiles by birth, called 'the uncircumcision' by those who are called 'the circumcision'—a physical circumcision made in the flesh by human hands— ¹² remember that you were at that time without Christ, being aliens from the commonwealth of Israel, and strangers to the covenants of promise, having no hope and without God in the world. ¹³ But now in Christ Jesus you who once were far off have been brought near by the blood of Christ. ¹⁴ For he is our peace; in his flesh he has made both groups into one and has broken down the dividing wall, that is, the hostility between us. ¹⁵ He has abolished the law with its commandments and ordinances, so that he might create in himself one new humanity in place of the two, thus making peace, ¹⁶ and might reconcile both groups to God in one body through the cross, thus putting to death that hostility through it. ¹⁷ So he came and proclaimed peace to you who were far off and peace to those who were near; ¹⁸ for through him both of us have access in one Spirit to the Father. ¹⁹ So then you are no longer strangers and aliens, but you are citizens with the saints and also members of the household of God, ²⁰ built upon the foundation of the apostles and prophets, with Christ Jesus himself as the cornerstone. ²¹ In him the whole structure is joined together and grows into a holy temple in the Lord; ²² in whom you also are built together spiritually into a dwelling-place for God.

YEAR B

GOSPEL   Mark 6.30–34, 53–56

³⁰ The apostles gathered around Jesus, and told him all that they had done and taught. ³¹ He said to them, 'Come away to a deserted place all by yourselves and rest a while.' For many were coming and going, and they had no leisure even to eat. ³² And they went away in the boat to a deserted place by themselves. ³³ Now many saw them going and recognized them, and they hurried there on foot from all the towns and arrived ahead of them. ³⁴ As he went ashore, he saw a great crowd; and he had compassion for them, because they were like sheep without a shepherd; and he began to teach them many things.

⁵³ When they had crossed over, they came to land at Gennesaret and moored the boat. ⁵⁴ When they got out of the boat, people at once recognized him, ⁵⁵ and rushed about that whole region and began to bring the sick on mats to wherever they heard he was. ⁵⁶ And wherever he went, into villages or cities or farms, they laid the sick in the market-places, and begged him that they might touch even the fringe of his cloak; and all who touched it were healed.

RELATED

READING   Jeremiah 23.1–6

¹ Woe to the shepherds who destroy and scatter the sheep of my pasture! says the LORD. ² Therefore, thus says the LORD, the God of Israel, concerning the shepherds who shepherd my people: It is you who have scattered my flock, and have driven them away, and you have not attended to them. So I will attend to you for your evil doings, says the LORD. ³ Then I myself will gather the remnant of my flock out of all the lands where I have driven them, and I will bring them back to their fold, and they shall be fruitful and multiply. ⁴ I will raise up shepherds over them who will shepherd them, and they shall not fear any longer, or be dismayed, nor shall any be missing, says the LORD.

⁵ The days are surely coming, says the LORD, when I will raise up for David a righteous Branch, and he shall reign as king and deal wisely, and shall execute justice and righteousness in the land. ⁶ In his days Judah will be saved and Israel will live in safety. And this is the name by which he will be called: 'The LORD is our righteousness.'

PSALM   Psalm 23

1 The Lord is my shepherd;
    I shall not be in want.
2 He makes me lie down in green pastures
    and leads me beside still waters.
3 He revives my soul
    and guides me along right pathways for his name's sake.
4 Though I walk through the valley of the shadow of death, I shall
       fear no evil;
    for you are with me; your rod and your staff, they comfort me.
5 You spread a table before me in the presence of those who trouble
       me;
    you have anointed my head with oil, and my cup is running over.
6 Surely your goodness and mercy shall follow me all the days of my
       life,
    and I will dwell in the house of the Lord for ever.

READING   Ephesians 2.11–22

[11] So then, remember that at one time you Gentiles by birth, called 'the uncircumcision' by those who are called 'the circumcision'—a physical circumcision made in the flesh by human hands— [12] remember that you were at that time without Christ, being aliens from the commonwealth of Israel, and strangers to the covenants of promise, having no hope and without God in the world. [13] But now in Christ Jesus you who once were far off have been brought near by the blood of Christ. [14] For he is our peace; in his flesh he has made both groups into one and has broken down the dividing wall, that is, the hostility between us. [15] He has abolished the law with its commandments and ordinances, so that he might create in himself one new humanity in place of the two, thus making peace, [16] and might reconcile both groups to God in one body through the cross, thus putting to death that hostility through it. [17] So he came and proclaimed peace to you who were far off and peace to those who were near; [18] for through him both of us have access in one Spirit to the Father. [19] So then you are no longer strangers and aliens, but you are citizens with the saints and also members of the household of God, [20] built upon the foundation of the apostles and prophets, with Christ Jesus himself as the cornerstone. [21] In him the whole structure is joined together and grows into a holy temple in the Lord; [22] in whom you also are built together spiritually into a dwelling-place for God.

GOSPEL   Mark 6.30–34, 53–56

³⁰ The apostles gathered around Jesus, and told him all that they had done and taught. ³¹ He said to them, 'Come away to a deserted place all by yourselves and rest a while.' For many were coming and going, and they had no leisure even to eat. ³² And they went away in the boat to a deserted place by themselves. ³³ Now many saw them going and recognized them, and they hurried there on foot from all the towns and arrived ahead of them. ³⁴ As he went ashore, he saw a great crowd; and he had compassion for them, because they were like sheep without a shepherd; and he began to teach them many things.

⁵³ When they had crossed over, they came to land at Gennesaret and moored the boat. ⁵⁴ When they got out of the boat, people at once recognized him, ⁵⁵ and rushed about that whole region and began to bring the sick on mats to wherever they heard he was. ⁵⁶ And wherever he went, into villages or cities or farms, they laid the sick in the market-places, and begged him that they might touch even the fringe of his cloak; and all who touched it were healed.

POST COMMUNION

See pages 571 to 575 and Table on page 568

SECOND SERVICE

Psalm 73.[1–20,] 21–29
Job 13.13–14.6

or

Ecclesiasticus 18.1–14
Hebrews 2.5–18

If the Second Service is a Eucharist, the following is read as a Gospel:

Luke 10.38–42

THIRD SERVICE

Psalms 67; 70
Deuteronomy 30.1–10
1 Peter 3.8–18

PROPER 12

Sunday between 24 and 30 July inclusive

COLLECT

See pages 572 to 576 and Table on page 568

CONTINUOUS

READING   2 Samuel 11.1–15

¹ In the spring of the year, the time when kings go out to battle, David sent Joab with his officers and all Israel with him; they ravaged the Ammonites, and besieged Rabbah. But David remained at Jerusalem.

² It happened, late one afternoon, when David rose from his couch and was walking about on the roof of the king's house, that he saw from the roof a woman bathing; the woman was very beautiful. ³ David sent someone to inquire about the woman. It was reported, 'This is Bathsheba daughter of Eliam, the wife of Uriah the Hittite.' ⁴ So David sent messengers to fetch her, and she came to him, and he lay with her. (Now she was purifying herself after her period.) Then she returned to her house. ⁵ The woman conceived; and she sent and told David, 'I am pregnant.'

⁶ So David sent word to Joab, 'Send me Uriah the Hittite.' And Joab sent Uriah to David. ⁷ When Uriah came to him, David asked how Joab and the people fared, and how the war was going. ⁸ Then David said to Uriah, 'Go down to your house, and wash your feet.' Uriah went out of the king's house, and there followed him a present from the king. ⁹ But Uriah slept at the entrance of the king's house with all the servants of his lord, and did not go down to his house. ¹⁰ When they told David, 'Uriah did not go down to his house', David said to Uriah, 'You have just come from a journey. Why did you not go down to your house?' ¹¹ Uriah said to David, 'The ark and Israel and Judah remain in booths; and my lord Joab and the servants of my lord are camping in the open field; shall I then go to my house, to eat and to drink, and to lie with my wife? As you live, and as your soul lives, I will not do such a thing.' ¹² Then David said to Uriah, 'Remain here today also, and tomorrow I will send you back.' So Uriah remained in Jerusalem that day. On the next day, ¹³ David invited him to eat and drink in his presence and made him drunk; and in the evening he went out to lie on his couch with the servants of his lord, but he did not go down to his house.

¹⁴ In the morning David wrote a letter to Joab, and sent it by the hand of Uriah. ¹⁵ In the letter he wrote, 'Set Uriah in the forefront of the hardest fighting, and then draw back from him, so that he may be struck down and die.'

PSALM   Psalm 14

1   The fool has said in his heart, 'There is no God.'
   All are corrupt and commit abominable acts; there is none who
     does any good.
2   The Lord looks down from heaven upon us all,
   to see if there is any who is wise, if there is one who seeks after
     God.
3   Everyone has proved faithless; all alike have turned bad;
   there is none who does good; no, not one.
4   Have they no knowledge, all those evildoers
   who eat up my people like bread and do not call upon the Lord?
5   See how they tremble with fear,
   because God is in the company of the righteous.
6   Their aim is to confound the plans of the afflicted,
   but the Lord is their refuge.
7   O that Israel's deliverance would come out of Zion!
   when the Lord restores the fortunes of his people, Jacob will rejoice
     and Israel be glad.

READING   Ephesians 3.14–21

¹⁴ For this reason I bow my knees before the Father, ¹⁵ from whom every family in heaven and on earth takes its name. ¹⁶ I pray that, according to the riches of his glory, he may grant that you may be strengthened in your inner being with power through his Spirit, ¹⁷ and that Christ may dwell in your hearts through faith, as you are being rooted and grounded in love. ¹⁸ I pray that you may have the power to comprehend, with all the saints, what is the breadth and length and height and depth, ¹⁹ and to know the love of Christ that surpasses knowledge, so that you may be filled with all the fullness of God.

²⁰ Now to him who by the power at work within us is able to accomplish abundantly far more than all we can ask or imagine, ²¹ to him be glory in the church and in Christ Jesus to all generations, for ever and ever. Amen.

GOSPEL   John 6.1–21

¹ After this Jesus went to the other side of the Sea of Galilee, also called the Sea of Tiberias. ² A large crowd kept following him, because they saw the signs that he was doing for the sick. ³ Jesus went up the mountain and sat down there with his disciples. ⁴ Now the Passover, the festival of the Jews, was near. ⁵ When he looked up and saw a large crowd coming towards him, Jesus said to Philip, 'Where are we to buy bread for these people to eat?' ⁶ He said this to test him, for he himself knew what he was going to do. ⁷ Philip answered him, 'Six months' wages would not buy enough bread for each of them to get a little.' ⁸ One of his disciples, Andrew, Simon Peter's brother, said to him, ⁹ 'There is a boy here who has five barley loaves and two fish. But what are they among so many people?' ¹⁰ Jesus said, 'Make the people sit down.' Now there was a great deal of grass in the place; so they sat down, about five thousand in all. ¹¹ Then Jesus took the loaves, and when he had given thanks, he distributed them to those who were seated; so also the fish, as much as they wanted. ¹² When they were satisfied, he told his disciples, 'Gather up the fragments left over, so that nothing may be lost.' ¹³ So they gathered them up, and from the fragments of the five barley loaves, left by those who had eaten, they filled twelve baskets. ¹⁴ When the people saw the sign that he had done, they began to say, 'This is indeed the prophet who is to come into the world.'

¹⁵ When Jesus realized that they were about to come and take him by force to make him king, he withdrew again to the mountain by himself.

¹⁶ When evening came, his disciples went down to the lake, ¹⁷ got into a boat, and started across the lake to Capernaum. It was now dark, and Jesus had not yet come to them. ¹⁸ The lake became rough because a strong wind was blowing. ¹⁹ When they had rowed about three or four miles, they saw Jesus walking on the lake and coming near the boat, and they were terrified. ²⁰ But he said to them, 'It is I; do not be afraid.' ²¹ Then they wanted to take him into the boat, and immediately the boat reached the land towards which they were going.

RELATED

READING   2 Kings 4.42–44

⁴² A man came from Baal-shalishah, bringing food from the first fruits to the man of God: twenty loaves of barley and fresh ears of grain in his sack. Elisha said, 'Give it to the people and let them eat.' ⁴³ But his servant said,

'How can I set this before a hundred people?' So he repeated, 'Give it to the people and let them eat, for thus says the LORD, "They shall eat and have some left." ' ⁴⁴ He set it before them, they ate, and had some left, according to the word of the LORD.

PSALM   Psalm 145.10–19

¹⁰ All your works praise you, O Lord,
    and your faithful servants bless you.
¹¹ They make known the glory of your kingdom
    and speak of your power;
¹² That the peoples may know of your power
    and the glorious splendour of your kingdom.
¹³ Your kingdom is an everlasting kingdom;
    your dominion endures throughout all ages.
¹⁴ The Lord is faithful in all his words
    and merciful in all his deeds.
¹⁵ The Lord upholds all those who fall;
    he lifts up those who are bowed down.
¹⁶ The eyes of all wait upon you, O Lord,
    and you give them their food in due season.
¹⁷ You open wide your hand
    and satisfy the needs of every living creature.
¹⁸ The Lord is righteous in all his ways
    and loving in all his works.
¹⁹ The Lord is near to those who call upon him,
    to all who call upon him faithfully.

READING   Ephesians 3.14–21

¹⁴ For this reason I bow my knees before the Father, ¹⁵ from whom every family in heaven and on earth takes its name. ¹⁶ I pray that, according to the riches of his glory, he may grant that you may be strengthened in your inner being with power through his Spirit, ¹⁷ and that Christ may dwell in your hearts through faith, as you are being rooted and grounded in love. ¹⁸ I pray that you may have the power to comprehend, with all the saints, what is the breadth and length and height and depth, ¹⁹ and to know the love of Christ that surpasses knowledge, so that you may be filled with all the fullness of God.

[20] Now to him who by the power at work within us is able to accomplish abundantly far more than all we can ask or imagine, [21] to him be glory in the church and in Christ Jesus to all generations, for ever and ever. Amen.

GOSPEL   John 6.1–21

[1] After this Jesus went to the other side of the Sea of Galilee, also called the Sea of Tiberias. [2] A large crowd kept following him, because they saw the signs that he was doing for the sick. [3] Jesus went up the mountain and sat down there with his disciples. [4] Now the Passover, the festival of the Jews, was near. [5] When he looked up and saw a large crowd coming towards him, Jesus said to Philip, 'Where are we to buy bread for these people to eat?' [6] He said this to test him, for he himself knew what he was going to do. [7] Philip answered him, 'Six months' wages would not buy enough bread for each of them to get a little.' [8] One of his disciples, Andrew, Simon Peter's brother, said to him, [9] 'There is a boy here who has five barley loaves and two fish. But what are they among so many people?' [10] Jesus said, 'Make the people sit down.' Now there was a great deal of grass in the place; so they sat down, about five thousand in all. [11] Then Jesus took the loaves, and when he had given thanks, he distributed them to those who were seated; so also the fish, as much as they wanted. [12] When they were satisfied, he told his disciples, 'Gather up the fragments left over, so that nothing may be lost.' [13] So they gathered them up, and from the fragments of the five barley loaves, left by those who had eaten, they filled twelve baskets. [14] When the people saw the sign that he had done, they began to say, 'This is indeed the prophet who is to come into the world.'

[15] When Jesus realized that they were about to come and take him by force to make him king, he withdrew again to the mountain by himself.

[16] When evening came, his disciples went down to the lake, [17] got into a boat, and started across the lake to Capernaum. It was now dark, and Jesus had not yet come to them. [18] The lake became rough because a strong wind was blowing. [19] When they had rowed about three or four miles, they saw Jesus walking on the lake and coming near the boat, and they were terrified. [20] But he said to them, 'It is I; do not be afraid.' [21] Then they wanted to take him into the boat, and immediately the boat reached the land towards which they were going.

YEAR B

POST COMMUNION

See pages 572 to 576 and Table on page 568

<table>
<tr><td>SECOND SERVICE</td><td>THIRD SERVICE</td></tr>
</table>

SECOND SERVICE

Psalm 74.[1–10,] 11–16, [17–22]
Job 19.1–27a

or

Ecclesiasticus 38.24–34
Hebrews 8

*If the Second Service is a Eucharist, the
following is read as a Gospel:*

Luke 11.1–13

THIRD SERVICE

Psalm 75
Song of Solomon 2

or

1 Maccabees 2.[1–14,] 15–22
1 Peter 4.7–14

PROPER 13

Sunday between 31 July and 6 August inclusive

COLLECT

See pages 572 to 576 and Table on page 568

CONTINUOUS

READING   2 Samuel 11.26–12.13a

26 When the wife of Uriah heard that her husband was dead, she made lamentation for him. 27 When the mourning was over, David sent and brought her to his house, and she became his wife, and bore him a son.

But the thing that David had done displeased the LORD, 1 and the LORD sent Nathan to David. He came to him, and said to him, 'There were two men in a certain city, one rich and the other poor. 2 The rich man had very many flocks and herds; 3 but the poor man had nothing but one little ewe lamb, which he had bought. He brought it up, and it grew up with him and with his children; it used to eat of his meagre fare, and drink from his cup, and lie in his bosom, and it was like a daughter to him. 4 Now there came a traveller to the rich man, and he was loath to take one of his own flock or herd to prepare for the wayfarer who had come to him, but he took the poor man's lamb, and prepared that for the guest who had come to him.' ⁵ Then David's anger was greatly kindled against the man. He said to Nathan, 'As the LORD lives, the man who has done this deserves to die; ⁶ he shall restore the lamb fourfold, because he did this thing, and because he had no pity.'

⁷ Nathan said to David, 'You are the man! Thus says the LORD, the God of Israel: I anointed you king over Israel, and I rescued you from the hand of Saul; ⁸ I gave you your master's house, and your master's wives into your bosom, and gave you the house of Israel and of Judah; and if that had been too little, I would have added as much more. ⁹ Why have you despised the word of the LORD, to do what is evil in his sight? You have struck down Uriah the Hittite with the sword, and have taken his wife to be your wife, and have killed him with the sword of the Ammonites. ¹⁰ Now therefore the sword shall never depart from your house, for you have despised me, and have taken the wife of Uriah the Hittite to be your wife. ¹¹ Thus says the LORD: I will raise up trouble against you from within your own house; and I will take your wives before your eyes, and give them to your neighbour, and he shall lie with your wives in the sight of this very sun. ¹² For you did it secretly; but I will do this thing before all Israel, and before the sun.' ¹³ David said to Nathan, 'I have sinned against the LORD.'

PSALM   Psalm 51.1–13

1   Have mercy on me, O God, according to your loving-kindness;
    in your great compassion blot out my offences.
2   Wash me through and through from my wickedness
    and cleanse me from my sin.
3   For I know my transgressions,
    and my sin is ever before me.
4   Against you only have I sinned
    and done what is evil in your sight.
5   And so you are justified when you speak
    and upright in your judgement.
6   Indeed, I have been wicked from my birth,
    a sinner from my mother's womb.
7   For behold, you look for truth deep within me,
    and will make me understand wisdom secretly.
8   Purge me from my sin and I shall be pure;
    wash me and I shall be clean indeed.
9   Make me hear of joy and gladness,
    that the body you have broken may rejoice.
10 Hide your face from my sins
    and blot out all my iniquities.

¹¹ Create in me a clean heart, O God,
   and renew a right spirit within me.
¹² Cast me not away from your presence
   and take not your holy Spirit from me.
¹³ Give me the joy of your saving help again
   and sustain me with your bountiful Spirit.

READING   Ephesians 4.1–16

¹ I therefore, the prisoner in the Lord, beg you to lead a life worthy of the calling to which you have been called, ² with all humility and gentleness, with patience, bearing with one another in love, ³ making every effort to maintain the unity of the Spirit in the bond of peace. ⁴ There is one body and one Spirit, just as you were called to the one hope of your calling, ⁵ one Lord, one faith, one baptism, ⁶ one God and Father of all, who is above all and through all and in all.

⁷ But each of us was given grace according to the measure of Christ's gift. ⁸ Therefore it is said,
   'When he ascended on high he made captivity itself a captive;
      he gave gifts to his people.'
⁹ (When it says, 'He ascended', what does it mean but that he had also descended into the lower parts of the earth? ¹⁰ He who descended is the same one who ascended far above all the heavens, so that he might fill all things.) ¹¹ The gifts he gave were that some would be apostles, some prophets, some evangelists, some pastors and teachers, ¹² to equip the saints for the work of ministry, for building up the body of Christ, ¹³ until all of us come to the unity of the faith and of the knowledge of the Son of God, to maturity, to the measure of the full stature of Christ. ¹⁴ We must no longer be children, tossed to and fro and blown about by every wind of doctrine, by people's trickery, by their craftiness in deceitful scheming. ¹⁵ But speaking the truth in love, we must grow up in every way into him who is the head, into Christ, ¹⁶ from whom the whole body, joined and knitted together by every ligament with which it is equipped, as each part is working properly, promotes the body's growth in building itself up in love.

GOSPEL   John 6.24–35

²⁴ So when the crowd saw that neither Jesus nor his disciples were there, they themselves got into the boats and went to Capernaum looking for Jesus.

25 When they found him on the other side of the lake, they said to him, 'Rabbi, when did you come here?' 26 Jesus answered them, 'Very truly, I tell you, you are looking for me, not because you saw signs, but because you ate your fill of the loaves. 27 Do not work for the food that perishes, but for the food that endures for eternal life, which the Son of Man will give you. For it is on him that God the Father has set his seal.' 28 Then they said to him, 'What must we do to perform the works of God?' 29 Jesus answered them, 'This is the work of God, that you believe in him whom he has sent.' 30 So they said to him, 'What sign are you going to give us then, so that we may see it and believe you? What work are you performing? 31 Our ancestors ate the manna in the wilderness; as it is written, "He gave them bread from heaven to eat." ' 32 Then Jesus said to them, 'Very truly, I tell you, it was not Moses who gave you the bread from heaven, but it is my Father who gives you the true bread from heaven. 33 For the bread of God is that which comes down from heaven and gives life to the world.' 34 They said to him, 'Sir, give us this bread always.'

35 Jesus said to them, 'I am the bread of life. Whoever comes to me will never be hungry, and whoever believes in me will never be thirsty.'

RELATED

READING   Exodus 16.2–4, 9–15

2 The whole congregation of the Israelites complained against Moses and Aaron in the wilderness. 3 The Israelites said to them, 'If only we had died by the hand of the LORD in the land of Egypt, when we sat by the fleshpots and ate our fill of bread; for you have brought us out into this wilderness to kill this whole assembly with hunger.'

4 Then the LORD said to Moses, 'I am going to rain bread from heaven for you, and each day the people shall go out and gather enough for that day. In that way I will test them, whether they will follow my instruction or not.'

9 Then Moses said to Aaron, 'Say to the whole congregation of the Israelites, "Draw near to the LORD, for he has heard your complaining." ' 10 And as Aaron spoke to the whole congregation of the Israelites, they looked towards the wilderness, and the glory of the LORD appeared in the cloud. 11 The LORD spoke to Moses and said, 12 'I have heard the complaining of the Israelites; say to them, "At twilight you shall eat meat, and in the morning you shall have your fill of bread; then you shall know that I am the LORD your God." '

¹³ In the evening quails came up and covered the camp; and in the morning there was a layer of dew around the camp. ¹⁴ When the layer of dew lifted, there on the surface of the wilderness was a fine flaky substance, as fine as frost on the ground. ¹⁵ When the Israelites saw it, they said to one another, 'What is it?' For they did not know what it was. Moses said to them, 'It is the bread that the LORD has given you to eat.'

PSALM

Psalm 78.23–29

23 So he commanded the clouds above
and opened the doors of heaven. .
24 He rained down manna upon them to eat
and gave them grain from heaven.
25 So mortals ate the bread of angels;
he provided for them food enough.
26 He caused the east wind to blow in the heavens
and led out the south wind by his might.
27 He rained down flesh upon them like dust
and winged birds like the sand of the sea.
28 He let it fall in the midst of their camp
and round about their dwellings.
29 So they ate and were well filled,
for he gave them what they craved.

READING

Ephesians 4.1–16

¹ I therefore, the prisoner in the Lord, beg you to lead a life worthy of the calling to which you have been called, ² with all humility and gentleness, with patience, bearing with one another in love, ³ making every effort to maintain the unity of the Spirit in the bond of peace. ⁴ There is one body and one Spirit, just as you were called to the one hope of your calling, ⁵ one Lord, one faith, one baptism, ⁶ one God and Father of all, who is above all and through all and in all.

⁷ But each of us was given grace according to the measure of Christ's gift. ⁸ Therefore it is said,

'When he ascended on high he made captivity itself a captive;
he gave gifts to his people.'
⁹ (When it says, 'He ascended', what does it mean but that he had also descended into the lower parts of the earth? ¹⁰ He who descended is the same one who ascended far above all the heavens, so that he might fill all things.) ¹¹ The gifts he gave were that some would be apostles, some prophets, some evangelists, some pastors and teachers, ¹² to equip the saints

for the work of ministry, for building up the body of Christ, ¹³ until all of us come to the unity of the faith and of the knowledge of the Son of God, to maturity, to the measure of the full stature of Christ. ¹⁴ We must no longer be children, tossed to and fro and blown about by every wind of doctrine, by people's trickery, by their craftiness in deceitful scheming. ¹⁵ But speaking the truth in love, we must grow up in every way into him who is the head, into Christ, ¹⁶ from whom the whole body, joined and knitted together by every ligament with which it is equipped, as each part is working properly, promotes the body's growth in building itself up in love.

GOSPEL   John 6.24–35

²⁴ So when the crowd saw that neither Jesus nor his disciples were there, they themselves got into the boats and went to Capernaum looking for Jesus.

²⁵ When they found him on the other side of the lake, they said to him, 'Rabbi, when did you come here?' ²⁶ Jesus answered them, 'Very truly, I tell you, you are looking for me, not because you saw signs, but because you ate your fill of the loaves. ²⁷ Do not work for the food that perishes, but for the food that endures for eternal life, which the Son of Man will give you. For it is on him that God the Father has set his seal.' ²⁸ Then they said to him, 'What must we do to perform the works of God?' ²⁹ Jesus answered them, 'This is the work of God, that you believe in him whom he has sent.' ³⁰ So they said to him, 'What sign are you going to give us then, so that we may see it and believe you? What work are you performing? ³¹ Our ancestors ate the manna in the wilderness; as it is written, "He gave them bread from heaven to eat." ' ³² Then Jesus said to them, 'Very truly, I tell you, it was not Moses who gave you the bread from heaven, but it is my Father who gives you the true bread from heaven. ³³ For the bread of God is that which comes down from heaven and gives life to the world.' ³⁴ They said to him, 'Sir, give us this bread always.'

³⁵ Jesus said to them, 'I am the bread of life. Whoever comes to me will never be hungry, and whoever believes in me will never be thirsty.'

POST COMMUNION

See pages 573 to 577 and Table on page 568

SECOND SERVICE	THIRD SERVICE
Psalm 88.1–10, [11–19]	Psalm 86
Job 28	Song of Solomon 5.2–16
or	*or*
Ecclesiasticus 42.15–25	1 Maccabees 3.1–12
Hebrews 11.17–31	2 Peter 1.1–15

If the Second Service is a Eucharist, the following is read as a Gospel:

Luke 12.13–21

PROPER 14

Sunday between 7 and 13 August inclusive

COLLECT

See pages 573 to 577 and Table on page 568

CONTINUOUS

READING   2 Samuel 18.5–9, 15, 31–33

⁵ The king gave orders to Joab and Abishai and Ittai, saying, 'Deal gently for my sake with the young man Absalom.' And all the people heard when the king gave orders to all the commanders concerning Absalom.

⁶ So the army went out into the field against Israel; and the battle was fought in the forest of Ephraim. ⁷ The men of Israel were defeated there by the servants of David, and the slaughter there was great on that day, twenty thousand men. ⁸ The battle spread over the face of all the country; and the forest claimed more victims that day than the sword.

⁹ Absalom happened to meet the servants of David. Absalom was riding on his mule, and the mule went under the thick branches of a great oak. His head caught fast in the oak, and he was left hanging between heaven and earth, while the mule that was under him went on.

¹⁵ And ten young men, Joab's armour-bearers, surrounded Absalom and struck him, and killed him.

³¹ Then the Cushite came; and the Cushite said, 'Good tidings for my lord the king! For the LORD has vindicated you this day, delivering you from the power of all who rose up against you.' ³² The king said to the Cushite, 'Is it well with the young man Absalom?' The Cushite answered, 'May the enemies of my lord the king, and all who rise up to do you harm, be like that young man.'

³³ The king was deeply moved, and went up to the chamber over the gate, and wept; and as he went, he said, 'O my son Absalom, my son, my son Absalom! Would that I had died instead of you, O Absalom, my son, my son!'

PSALM   Psalm 130

1 Out of the depths have I called to you, O Lord; Lord, hear my voice;
   let your ears consider well the voice of my supplication.
2 If you, Lord, were to note what is done amiss,
   O Lord, who could stand?
3 For there is forgiveness with you;
   therefore you shall be feared.
4 I wait for the Lord; my soul waits for him;
   in his word is my hope.
5 My soul waits for the Lord, more than the night-watch for the
   morning,
   more than the night-watch for the morning.
6 O Israel, wait for the Lord,
   for with the Lord there is mercy;
7 With him there is plenteous redemption,
   and he shall redeem Israel from all their sins.

READING   Ephesians 4.25–5.2

²⁵ So then, putting away falsehood, let all of us speak the truth to our neighbours, for we are members of one another. ²⁶ Be angry but do not sin; do not let the sun go down on your anger, ²⁷ and do not make room for the devil. ²⁸ Thieves must give up stealing; rather let them labour and work honestly with their own hands, so as to have something to share with the needy. ²⁹ Let no evil talk come out of your mouths, but only what is useful for building up, as there is need, so that your words may give grace to those who hear. ³⁰ And do not grieve the Holy Spirit of God, with which you were marked with a seal for the day of redemption. ³¹ Put away from you all bitterness and wrath and anger and wrangling and slander, together with

all malice, ³² and be kind to one another, tender-hearted, forgiving one another, as God in Christ has forgiven you. ¹ Therefore be imitators of God, as beloved children, ² and live in love, as Christ loved us and gave himself up for us, a fragrant offering and sacrifice to God.

GOSPEL   John 6.35, 41–51

³⁵ Jesus said to them, 'I am the bread of life. Whoever comes to me will never be hungry, and whoever believes in me will never be thirsty.'

⁴¹ Then the Jews began to complain about him because he said, 'I am the bread that came down from heaven.' ⁴² They were saying, 'Is not this Jesus, the son of Joseph, whose father and mother we know? How can he now say, "I have come down from heaven"?' ⁴³ Jesus answered them, 'Do not complain among yourselves. ⁴⁴ No one can come to me unless drawn by the Father who sent me; and I will raise that person up on the last day. ⁴⁵ It is written in the prophets, "And they shall all be taught by God." Everyone who has heard and learned from the Father comes to me. ⁴⁶ Not that anyone has seen the Father except the one who is from God; he has seen the Father. ⁴⁷ Very truly, I tell you, whoever believes has eternal life. ⁴⁸ I am the bread of life. ⁴⁹ Your ancestors ate the manna in the wilderness, and they died. ⁵⁰ This is the bread that comes down from heaven, so that one may eat of it and not die. ⁵¹ I am the living bread that came down from heaven. Whoever eats of this bread will live for ever; and the bread that I will give for the life of the world is my flesh.'

RELATED

READING   1 Kings 19.4–8

⁴ But he himself went a day's journey into the wilderness, and came and sat down under a solitary broom tree. He asked that he might die: 'It is enough; now, O LORD, take away my life, for I am no better than my ancestors.' ⁵ Then he lay down under the broom tree and fell asleep. Suddenly an angel touched him and said to him, 'Get up and eat.' ⁶ He looked, and there at his head was a cake baked on hot stones, and a jar of water. He ate and drank, and lay down again. ⁷ The angel of the LORD came a second time, touched him, and said, 'Get up and eat, otherwise the journey will be too much for you.' ⁸ He got up, and ate and drank; then he went in the strength of that food for forty days and forty nights to Horeb the mount of God.

PSALM

Psalm 34.1–8

1 I will bless the Lord at all times;
   his praise shall ever be in my mouth.
2 I will glory in the Lord;
   let the humble hear and rejoice.
3 Proclaim with me the greatness of the Lord;
   let us exalt his name together.
4 I sought the Lord and he answered me
   and delivered me out of all my terror.
5 Look upon him and be radiant,
   and let not your faces be ashamed.
6 I called in my affliction and the Lord heard me
   and saved me from all my troubles.
7 The angel of the Lord encompasses those who fear him,
   and he will deliver them.
8 Taste and see that the Lord is good;
   happy are they who trust in him!

READING

Ephesians 4.25–5.2

25 So then, putting away falsehood, let all of us speak the truth to our neighbours, for we are members of one another. 26 Be angry but do not sin; do not let the sun go down on your anger, 27 and do not make room for the devil. 28 Thieves must give up stealing; rather let them labour and work honestly with their own hands, so as to have something to share with the needy. 29 Let no evil talk come out of your mouths, but only what is useful for building up, as there is need, so that your words may give grace to those who hear. 30 And do not grieve the Holy Spirit of God, with which you were marked with a seal for the day of redemption. 31 Put away from you all bitterness and wrath and anger and wrangling and slander, together with all malice, 32 and be kind to one another, tender-hearted, forgiving one another, as God in Christ has forgiven you. 1 Therefore be imitators of God, as beloved children, 2 and live in love, as Christ loved us and gave himself up for us, a fragrant offering and sacrifice to God.

GOSPEL   John 6.35, 41–51

[35] Jesus said to them, 'I am the bread of life. Whoever comes to me will never be hungry, and whoever believes in me will never be thirsty.'

[41] Then the Jews began to complain about him because he said, 'I am the bread that came down from heaven.' [42] They were saying, 'Is not this Jesus, the son of Joseph, whose father and mother we know? How can he now say, "I have come down from heaven"?' [43] Jesus answered them, 'Do not complain among yourselves. [44] No one can come to me unless drawn by the Father who sent me; and I will raise that person up on the last day. [45] It is written in the prophets, "And they shall all be taught by God." Everyone who has heard and learned from the Father comes to me. [46] Not that anyone has seen the Father except the one who is from God; he has seen the Father. [47] Very truly, I tell you, whoever believes has eternal life. [48] I am the bread of life. [49] Your ancestors ate the manna in the wilderness, and they died. [50] This is the bread that comes down from heaven, so that one may eat of it and not die. [51] I am the living bread that came down from heaven. Whoever eats of this bread will live for ever; and the bread that I will give for the life of the world is my flesh.'

POST COMMUNION

See pages 574 to 578 and Table on page 568

SECOND SERVICE

Psalm 91.1–12, [13–16]
Job 39.1–40.4

or

Ecclesiasticus 43.13–33
Hebrews 12.1–17

If the Second Service is a Eucharist, the following is read as a Gospel:

Luke 12.32–40

THIRD SERVICE

Psalm 90
Song of Solomon 8.5–7

or

1 Maccabees 14.4–15
2 Peter 3.8–13

PROPER 15

Sunday between 14 and 20 August inclusive

COLLECT

See pages 574 to 578 and Table on page 568

CONTINUOUS

READING   1 Kings 2.10–12; 3.3–14

¹⁰ Then David slept with his ancestors, and was buried in the city of David. ¹¹ The time that David reigned over Israel was forty years; he reigned for seven years in Hebron, and thirty-three years in Jerusalem. ¹² So Solomon sat on the throne of his father David; and his kingdom was firmly established.

³ Solomon loved the LORD, walking in the statutes of his father David; only, he sacrificed and offered incense at the high places. ⁴ The king went to Gibeon to sacrifice there, for that was the principal high place; Solomon used to offer a thousand burnt-offerings on that altar. ⁵ At Gibeon the LORD appeared to Solomon in a dream by night; and God said, 'Ask what I should give you.' ⁶ And Solomon said, 'You have shown great and steadfast love to your servant my father David, because he walked before you in faithfulness, in righteousness, and in uprightness of heart towards you; and you have kept for him this great and steadfast love, and have given him a son to sit on his throne today. ⁷ And now, O LORD my God, you have made your servant king in place of my father David, although I am only a little child; I do not know how to go out or come in. ⁸ And your servant is in the midst of the people whom you have chosen, a great people, so numerous they cannot be numbered or counted. ⁹ Give your servant therefore an understanding mind to govern your people, able to discern between good and evil; for who can govern this your great people?'

¹⁰ It pleased the Lord that Solomon had asked this. ¹¹ God said to him, 'Because you have asked this, and have not asked for yourself long life or riches, or for the life of your enemies, but have asked for yourself understanding to discern what is right, ¹² I now do according to your word. Indeed I give you a wise and discerning mind; no one like you has been before you and no one like you shall arise after you. ¹³ I give you also what you have not asked, both riches and honour all your life; no other king

shall compare with you. ¹⁴ If you will walk in my ways, keeping my statutes and my commandments, as your father David walked, then I will lengthen your life.'

PSALM   Psalm 111

¹ Alleluia! I will give thanks to the Lord with my whole heart,
   in the assembly of the upright, in the congregation.
² Great are the deeds of the Lord!
   they are studied by all who delight in them.
³ His work is full of majesty and splendour,
   and his righteousness endures for ever.
⁴ He makes his marvellous works to be remembered;
   the Lord is gracious and full of compassion.
⁵ He gives food to those who fear him;
   he is ever mindful of his covenant.
⁶ He has shown his people the power of his works
   in giving them the lands of the nations.
⁷ The works of his hands are faithfulness and justice;
   all his commandments are sure.
⁸ They stand fast for ever and ever,
   because they are done in truth and equity.
⁹ He sent redemption to his people; he commanded his covenant
      for ever;
   holy and awesome is his name.
¹⁰ The fear of the Lord is the beginning of wisdom;
   those who act accordingly have a good understanding; his praise
      endures for ever.

READING   Ephesians 5.15–20

¹⁵ Be careful then how you live, not as unwise people but as wise, ¹⁶ making the most of the time, because the days are evil. ¹⁷ So do not be foolish, but understand what the will of the Lord is. ¹⁸ Do not get drunk with wine, for that is debauchery; but be filled with the Spirit, ¹⁹ as you sing psalms and hymns and spiritual songs among yourselves, singing and making melody to the Lord in your hearts, ²⁰ giving thanks to God the Father at all times and for everything in the name of our Lord Jesus Christ.

GOSPEL   John 6.51–58

[51] 'I am the living bread that came down from heaven. Whoever eats of this bread will live for ever; and the bread that I will give for the life of the world is my flesh.'

[52] The Jews then disputed among themselves, saying, 'How can this man give us his flesh to eat?' [53] So Jesus said to them, 'Very truly, I tell you, unless you eat the flesh of the Son of Man and drink his blood, you have no life in you. [54] Those who eat my flesh and drink my blood have eternal life, and I will raise them up on the last day; [55] for my flesh is true food and my blood is true drink. [56] Those who eat my flesh and drink my blood abide in me, and I in them. [57] Just as the living Father sent me, and I live because of the Father, so whoever eats me will live because of me. [58] This is the bread that came down from heaven, not like that which your ancestors ate, and they died. But the one who eats this bread will live for ever.'

RELATED

READING   Proverbs 9.1–6

[1] Wisdom has built her house,
        she has hewn her seven pillars.
[2] She has slaughtered her animals, she has mixed her wine,
        she has also set her table.
[3] She has sent out her servant-girls, she calls
        from the highest places in the town,
[4] 'You that are simple, turn in here!'
        To those without sense she says,
[5] 'Come, eat of my bread
        and drink of the wine I have mixed.
[6] Lay aside immaturity, and live,
        and walk in the way of insight.'

PSALM   Psalm 34.9–14

[9]   Fear the Lord, you that are his saints,
        for those who fear him lack nothing.
[10] The young lions lack and suffer hunger,
        but those who seek the Lord lack nothing that is good.
[11] Come, children, and listen to me;
        I will teach you the fear of the Lord.

12 Who among you loves life
and desires long life to enjoy prosperity?
13 Keep your tongue from evil-speaking
and your lips from lying words.
14 Turn from evil and do good;
seek peace and pursue it.

READING   Ephesians 5.15–20

15 Be careful then how you live, not as unwise people but as wise, 16 making the most of the time, because the days are evil. 17 So do not be foolish, but understand what the will of the Lord is. 18 Do not get drunk with wine, for that is debauchery; but be filled with the Spirit, 19 as you sing psalms and hymns and spiritual songs among yourselves, singing and making melody to the Lord in your hearts, 20 giving thanks to God the Father at all times and for everything in the name of our Lord Jesus Christ.

GOSPEL   John 6.51–58

51 'I am the living bread that came down from heaven. Whoever eats of this bread will live for ever; and the bread that I will give for the life of the world is my flesh.'

52 The Jews then disputed among themselves, saying, 'How can this man give us his flesh to eat?' 53 So Jesus said to them, 'Very truly, I tell you, unless you eat the flesh of the Son of Man and drink his blood, you have no life in you. 54 Those who eat my flesh and drink my blood have eternal life, and I will raise them up on the last day; 55 for my flesh is true food and my blood is true drink. 56 Those who eat my flesh and drink my blood abide in me, and I in them. 57 Just as the living Father sent me, and I live because of the Father, so whoever eats me will live because of me. 58 This is the bread that came down from heaven, not like that which your ancestors ate, and they died. But the one who eats this bread will live for ever.'

POST COMMUNION

See pages 574 to 578 and Table on page 568

PROPER 16

Sunday between 21 and 27 August inclusive

COLLECT

See pages 575 to 579 and Table on page 568

CONTINUOUS

READING   1 Kings 8.[1, 6, 10–11,] 22–30, 41–43

[¹ Then Solomon assembled the elders of Israel and all the heads of the tribes, the leaders of the ancestral houses of the Israelites, before King Solomon in Jerusalem, to bring up the ark of the covenant of the LORD out of the city of David, which is Zion.

⁶ Then the priests brought the ark of the covenant of the LORD to its place, in the inner sanctuary of the house, in the most holy place, underneath the wings of the cherubim.

¹⁰ And when the priests came out of the holy place, a cloud filled the house of the LORD, ¹¹ so that the priests could not stand to minister because of the cloud; for the glory of the LORD filled the house of the LORD.]

²² Then Solomon stood before the altar of the LORD in the presence of all the assembly of Israel, and spread out his hands to heaven. ²³ He said, 'O LORD, God of Israel, there is no God like you in heaven above or on earth beneath, keeping covenant and steadfast love for your servants who walk

before you with all their heart, ²⁴ the covenant that you kept for your servant my father David as you declared to him; you promised with your mouth and have this day fulfilled with your hand. ²⁵ Therefore, O LORD, God of Israel, keep for your servant my father David that which you promised him, saying, "There shall never fail you a successor before me to sit on the throne of Israel, if only your children look to their way, to walk before me as you have walked before me." ²⁶ Therefore, O God of Israel, let your word be confirmed, which you promised to your servant my father David.

²⁷ 'But will God indeed dwell on the earth? Even heaven and the highest heaven cannot contain you, much less this house that I have built! ²⁸ Have regard to your servant's prayer and his plea, O LORD my God, heeding the cry and the prayer that your servant prays to you today; ²⁹ that your eyes may be open night and day towards this house, the place of which you said, "My name shall be there", that you may heed the prayer that your servant prays towards this place. ³⁰ Hear the plea of your servant and of your people Israel when they pray towards this place; O hear in heaven your dwelling-place; heed and forgive.'

⁴¹ 'Likewise when a foreigner, who is not of your people Israel, comes from a distant land because of your name ⁴²—for they shall hear of your great name, your mighty hand, and your outstretched arm—when a foreigner comes and prays towards this house, ⁴³ then hear in heaven your dwelling-place, and do according to all that the foreigner calls to you, so that all the peoples of the earth may know your name and fear you, as do your people Israel, and so that they may know that your name has been invoked on this house that I have built.'

PSALM   Psalm 84

¹ How dear to me is your dwelling, O Lord of hosts!
   My soul has a desire and longing for the courts of the Lord; my
      heart and my flesh rejoice in the living God.
² The sparrow has found her a house and the swallow a nest where
      she may lay her young;
   by the side of your altars, O Lord of hosts, my King and my God.
³ Happy are they who dwell in your house!
   they will always be praising you.
⁴ Happy are the people whose strength is in you!
   whose hearts are set on the pilgrims' way.
⁵ Those who go through the desolate valley will find it a place of
      springs,
   for the early rains have covered it with pools of water.

6 They will climb from height to height,
   and the God of gods will reveal himself in Zion.
7 Lord God of hosts, hear my prayer;
   hearken, O God of Jacob.
8 Behold our defender, O God;
   and look upon the face of your anointed.
9 For one day in your courts is better than a thousand in my own
       room,
   and to stand at the threshold of the house of my God than to dwell
       in the tents of the wicked.
10 For the Lord God is both sun and shield;
    he will give grace and glory;
11 No good thing will the Lord withhold
    from those who walk with integrity.
12 O Lord of hosts,
    happy are they who put their trust in you!

READING   Ephesians 6.10–20

[10] Finally, be strong in the Lord and in the strength of his power. [11] Put on the whole armour of God, so that you may be able to stand against the wiles of the devil. [12] For our struggle is not against enemies of blood and flesh, but against the rulers, against the authorities, against the cosmic powers of this present darkness, against the spiritual forces of evil in the heavenly places. [13] Therefore take up the whole armour of God, so that you may be able to withstand on that evil day, and having done everything, to stand firm. [14] Stand therefore, and fasten the belt of truth around your waist, and put on the breastplate of righteousness. [15] As shoes for your feet put on whatever will make you ready to proclaim the gospel of peace. [16] With all of these, take the shield of faith, with which you will be able to quench all the flaming arrows of the evil one. [17] Take the helmet of salvation, and the sword of the Spirit, which is the word of God.

[18] Pray in the Spirit at all times in every prayer and supplication. To that end keep alert and always persevere in supplication for all the saints. [19] Pray also for me, so that when I speak, a message may be given to me to make known with boldness the mystery of the gospel, [20] for which I am an ambassador in chains. Pray that I may declare it boldly, as I must speak.

GOSPEL   John 6.56–69

⁵⁶ 'Those who eat my flesh and drink my blood abide in me, and I in them. ⁵⁷ Just as the living Father sent me, and I live because of the Father, so whoever eats me will live because of me. ⁵⁸ This is the bread that came down from heaven, not like that which your ancestors ate, and they died. But the one who eats this bread will live for ever.' ⁵⁹ He said these things while he was teaching in the synagogue at Capernaum.

⁶⁰ When many of his disciples heard it, they said, 'This teaching is difficult; who can accept it?' ⁶¹ But Jesus, being aware that his disciples were complaining about it, said to them, 'Does this offend you? ⁶² Then what if you were to see the Son of Man ascending to where he was before? ⁶³ It is the spirit that gives life; the flesh is useless. The words that I have spoken to you are spirit and life. ⁶⁴ But among you there are some who do not believe.' For Jesus knew from the first who were the ones that did not believe, and who was the one that would betray him. ⁶⁵ And he said, 'For this reason I have told you that no one can come to me unless it is granted by the Father.'

⁶⁶ Because of this many of his disciples turned back and no longer went about with him. ⁶⁷ So Jesus asked the twelve, 'Do you also wish to go away?' ⁶⁸ Simon Peter answered him, 'Lord, to whom can we go? You have the words of eternal life. ⁶⁹ We have come to believe and know that you are the Holy One of God.'

RELATED

READING   Joshua 24.1–2a, 14–18

¹ Then Joshua gathered all the tribes of Israel to Shechem, and summoned the elders, the heads, the judges, and the officers of Israel; and they presented themselves before God. ² And Joshua said to all the people,

¹⁴ 'Now therefore revere the LORD, and serve him in sincerity and in faithfulness; put away the gods that your ancestors served beyond the River and in Egypt, and serve the LORD. ¹⁵ Now if you are unwilling to serve the LORD, choose this day whom you will serve, whether the gods your ancestors served in the region beyond the River or the gods of the Amorites in whose land you are living; but as for me and my household, we will serve the LORD.'

¹⁶ Then the people answered, 'Far be it from us that we should forsake the LORD to serve other gods; ¹⁷ for it is the LORD our God who brought us and our ancestors up from the land of Egypt, out of the house of slavery, and

who did those great signs in our sight. He protected us along all the way that we went, and among all the peoples through whom we passed; [18] and the LORD drove out before us all the peoples, the Amorites who lived in the land. Therefore we also will serve the LORD, for he is our God.'

PSALM   Psalm 34.15–22

[15] The eyes of the Lord are upon the righteous,
    and his ears are open to their cry.
[16] The face of the Lord is against those who do evil,
    to root out the remembrance of them from the earth.
[17] The righteous cry and the Lord hears them
    and delivers them from all their troubles.
[18] The Lord is near to the brokenhearted
    and will save those whose spirits are crushed.
[19] Many are the troubles of the righteous,
    but the Lord will deliver him out of them all.
[20] He will keep safe all his bones;
    not one of them shall be broken.
[21] Evil shall slay the wicked,
    and those who hate the righteous will be punished.
[22] The Lord ransoms the life of his servants,
    and none will be punished who trust in him.

READING   Ephesians 6.10–20

[10] Finally, be strong in the Lord and in the strength of his power. [11] Put on the whole armour of God, so that you may be able to stand against the wiles of the devil. [12] For our struggle is not against enemies of blood and flesh, but against the rulers, against the authorities, against the cosmic powers of this present darkness, against the spiritual forces of evil in the heavenly places. [13] Therefore take up the whole armour of God, so that you may be able to withstand on that evil day, and having done everything, to stand firm. [14] Stand therefore, and fasten the belt of truth around your waist, and put on the breastplate of righteousness. [15] As shoes for your feet put on whatever will make you ready to proclaim the gospel of peace. [16] With all of these, take the shield of faith, with which you will be able to quench all the flaming arrows of the evil one. [17] Take the helmet of salvation, and the sword of the Spirit, which is the word of God.

[18] Pray in the Spirit at all times in every prayer and supplication. To that end keep alert and always persevere in supplication for all the saints. [19] Pray

also for me, so that when I speak, a message may be given to me to make known with boldness the mystery of the gospel, 20 for which I am an ambassador in chains. Pray that I may declare it boldly, as I must speak.

GOSPEL   John 6.56–69

56 'Those who eat my flesh and drink my blood abide in me, and I in them. 57 Just as the living Father sent me, and I live because of the Father, so whoever eats me will live because of me. 58 This is the bread that came down from heaven, not like that which your ancestors ate, and they died. But the one who eats this bread will live for ever.' 59 He said these things while he was teaching in the synagogue at Capernaum.

60 When many of his disciples heard it, they said, 'This teaching is difficult; who can accept it?' 61 But Jesus, being aware that his disciples were complaining about it, said to them, 'Does this offend you? 62 Then what if you were to see the Son of Man ascending to where he was before? 63 It is the spirit that gives life; the flesh is useless. The words that I have spoken to you are spirit and life. 64 But among you there are some who do not believe.' For Jesus knew from the first who were the ones that did not believe, and who was the one that would betray him. 65 And he said, 'For this reason I have told you that no one can come to me unless it is granted by the Father.'

66 Because of this many of his disciples turned back and no longer went about with him. 67 So Jesus asked the twelve, 'Do you also wish to go away?' 68 Simon Peter answered him, 'Lord, to whom can we go? You have the words of eternal life. 69 We have come to believe and know that you are the Holy One of God.'

POST COMMUNION

See pages 575 to 579 and Table on page 568

SECOND SERVICE

Psalm 116.[1–9,] 10–17
Exodus 4.27–5.1
Hebrews 13.16–21
If the Second Service is a Eucharist, the following is read as a Gospel:
Luke 13.10–17

THIRD SERVICE

Psalm 115
Jonah 2
or
Ecclesiasticus 3.17–29
Revelation 1

PROPER 17

Sunday between 28 August and 3 September inclusive

COLLECT

See pages 576 to 579 and Table on page 568

CONTINUOUS

READING   Song of Solomon 2.8–13

8 The voice of my beloved!
    Look, he comes,
leaping upon the mountains,
    bounding over the hills.
9 My beloved is like a gazelle
    or a young stag.
Look, there he stands
    behind our wall,
gazing in at the windows,
    looking through the lattice.
10 My beloved speaks and says to me:
'Arise, my love, my fair one,
    and come away;
11 for now the winter is past,
    the rain is over and gone.
12 The flowers appear on the earth;
    the time of singing has come,
and the voice of the turtle-dove
    is heard in our land.
13 The fig tree puts forth its figs,
    and the vines are in blossom;
    they give forth fragrance.
Arise, my love, my fair one,
    and come away.'

PSALM   Psalm 45.1–2, 7–10

1 My heart is stirring with a noble song; let me recite what I have
    fashioned for the king;
my tongue shall be the pen of a skilled writer.

2 You are the fairest of men;
   grace flows from your lips, because God has blessed you for ever.

7 Your throne, O God, endures for ever and ever,
   a sceptre of righteousness is the sceptre of your kingdom; you love
      righteousness and hate iniquity;

8 Therefore God, your God, has anointed you
   with the oil of gladness above your fellows.

9 All your garments are fragrant with myrrh, aloes and cassia,
   and the music of strings from ivory palaces makes you glad.

10 Kings' daughters stand among the ladies of the court;
   on your right hand is the queen, adorned with the gold of Ophir.

OR, IF AN ALTERNATIVE READING IS PREFERRED   **Psalm 45.1–8**

1 My heart is stirring with a noble song; let me recite what I have
      fashioned for the king;
   my tongue shall be the pen of a skilled writer.

2 You are the fairest of men;
   grace flows from your lips, because God has blessed you for ever.

3 Strap your sword upon your thigh, O mighty warrior,
   in your pride and in your majesty.

4 Ride out and conquer in the cause of truth
   and for the sake of justice.

5 Your right hand will show you marvellous things;
   your arrows are very sharp, O mighty warrior.

6 The peoples are falling at your feet,
   and the king's enemies are losing heart.

7 Your throne, O God, endures for ever and ever,
   a sceptre of righteousness is the sceptre of your kingdom; you love
      righteousness and hate iniquity;

8 Therefore God, your God, has anointed you
   with the oil of gladness above your fellows.

READING   James 1.17–27

17 Every generous act of giving, with every perfect gift, is from above,
coming down from the Father of lights, with whom there is no variation
or shadow due to change. 18 In fulfilment of his own purpose he gave us
birth by the word of truth, so that we would become a kind of first fruits
of his creatures.

¹⁹ You must understand this, my beloved: let everyone be quick to listen, slow to speak, slow to anger; ²⁰ for your anger does not produce God's righteousness. ²¹ Therefore rid yourselves of all sordidness and rank growth of wickedness, and welcome with meekness the implanted word that has the power to save your souls.

²² But be doers of the word, and not merely hearers who deceive themselves. ²³ For if any are hearers of the word and not doers, they are like those who look at themselves in a mirror; ²⁴ for they look at themselves and, on going away, immediately forget what they were like. ²⁵ But those who look into the perfect law, the law of liberty, and persevere, being not hearers who forget but doers who act—they will be blessed in their doing.

²⁶ If any think they are religious, and do not bridle their tongues but deceive their hearts, their religion is worthless. ²⁷ Religion that is pure and undefiled before God, the Father, is this: to care for orphans and widows in their distress, and to keep oneself unstained by the world.

GOSPEL   Mark 7.1–8, 14–15, 21–23

¹ Now when the Pharisees and some of the scribes who had come from Jerusalem gathered around him, ² they noticed that some of his disciples were eating with defiled hands, that is, without washing them. ³ (For the Pharisees, and all the Jews, do not eat unless they thoroughly wash their hands, thus observing the tradition of the elders; ⁴ and they do not eat anything from the market unless they wash it; and there are also many other traditions that they observe, the washing of cups, pots, and bronze kettles.) ⁵ So the Pharisees and the scribes asked him, 'Why do your disciples not live according to the tradition of the elders, but eat with defiled hands?' ⁶ He said to them, 'Isaiah prophesied rightly about you hypocrites, as it is written,

"This people honours me with their lips,
    but their hearts are far from me;
⁷   in vain do they worship me,
    teaching human precepts as doctrines."
⁸ You abandon the commandment of God and hold to human tradition.'

¹⁴ Then he called the crowd again and said to them, 'Listen to me, all of you, and understand: ¹⁵ there is nothing outside a person that by going in can defile, but the things that come out are what defile.'

²¹ 'For it is from within, from the human heart, that evil intentions come: fornication, theft, murder, ²² adultery, avarice, wickedness, deceit, licentiousness, envy, slander, pride, folly. ²³ All these evil things come from within, and they defile a person.'

RELATED

READING   Deuteronomy 4.1–2, 6–9

¹ So now, Israel, give heed to the statutes and ordinances that I am teaching you to observe, so that you may live to enter and occupy the land that the LORD, the God of your ancestors, is giving you. ² You must neither add anything to what I command you nor take away anything from it, but keep the commandments of the LORD your God with which I am charging you.

⁶ You must observe them diligently, for this will show your wisdom and discernment to the peoples, who, when they hear all these statutes, will say, 'Surely this great nation is a wise and discerning people!' ⁷ For what other great nation has a god so near to it as the LORD our God is whenever we call to him? ⁸ And what other great nation has statutes and ordinances as just as this entire law that I am setting before you today?

⁹ But take care and watch yourselves closely, so as neither to forget the things that your eyes have seen nor to let them slip from your mind all the days of your life; make them known to your children and your children's children.

PSALM   Psalm 15

¹ Lord, who may dwell in your tabernacle?
    who may abide upon your holy hill?
² Whoever leads a blameless life and does what is right,
    who speaks the truth from his heart.
³ There is no guile upon his tongue; he does no evil to his friend;
    he does not heap contempt upon his neighbour.
⁴ In his sight the wicked is rejected,
    but he honours those who fear the Lord.
⁵ He has sworn to do no wrong
    and does not take back his word.
⁶ He does not give his money in hope of gain,
    nor does he take a bribe against the innocent.
⁷ Whoever does these things
    shall never be overthrown.

READING   James 1.17–27

¹⁷ Every generous act of giving, with every perfect gift, is from above, coming down from the Father of lights, with whom there is no variation or shadow due to change. ¹⁸ In fulfilment of his own

purpose he gave us birth by the word of truth, so that we would become a kind of first fruits of his creatures.

¹⁹ You must understand this, my beloved: let everyone be quick to listen, slow to speak, slow to anger; ²⁰ for your anger does not produce God's righteousness. ²¹ Therefore rid yourselves of all sordidness and rank growth of wickedness, and welcome with meekness the implanted word that has the power to save your souls.

²² But be doers of the word, and not merely hearers who deceive themselves. ²³ For if any are hearers of the word and not doers, they are like those who look at themselves in a mirror; ²⁴ for they look at themselves and, on going away, immediately forget what they were like. ²⁵ But those who look into the perfect law, the law of liberty, and persevere, being not hearers who forget but doers who act—they will be blessed in their doing.

²⁶ If any think they are religious, and do not bridle their tongues but deceive their hearts, their religion is worthless. ²⁷ Religion that is pure and undefiled before God, the Father, is this: to care for orphans and widows in their distress, and to keep oneself unstained by the world.

GOSPEL   Mark 7.1–8, 14–15, 21–23

¹ Now when the Pharisees and some of the scribes who had come from Jerusalem gathered around him, ² they noticed that some of his disciples were eating with defiled hands, that is, without washing them. ³ (For the Pharisees, and all the Jews, do not eat unless they thoroughly wash their hands, thus observing the tradition of the elders; ⁴ and they do not eat anything from the market unless they wash it; and there are also many other traditions that they observe, the washing of cups, pots, and bronze kettles.) ⁵ So the Pharisees and the scribes asked him, 'Why do your disciples not live according to the tradition of the elders, but eat with defiled hands?' ⁶ He said to them, 'Isaiah prophesied rightly about you hypocrites, as it is written,

"This people honours me with their lips,
    but their hearts are far from me;
⁷   in vain do they worship me,
    teaching human precepts as doctrines."

⁸ You abandon the commandment of God and hold to human tradition.'

¹⁴ Then he called the crowd again and said to them, 'Listen to me, all of you, and understand: ¹⁵ there is nothing outside a person that by going in can defile, but the things that come out are what defile.'

²¹ 'For it is from within, from the human heart, that evil intentions come:

fornication, theft, murder, ²² adultery, avarice, wickedness, deceit, licentiousness, envy, slander, pride, folly. ²³ All these evil things come from within, and they defile a person.'

POST COMMUNION

See pages 576 to 580 and Table on page 568

SECOND SERVICE

Psalm 119.[1–8,] 9–16
Exodus 12.21–27
Matthew 4.23–5.20

THIRD SERVICE

Psalm 119.17–40
Jonah 3.1–9
or
Ecclesiasticus 11.[7–18,] 19–28
Revelation 3.14–22

PROPER 18

Sunday between 4 and 10 September inclusive

COLLECT

See pages 576 to 580 and Table on page 568

CONTINUOUS

READING   Proverbs 22.1–2, 8–9, 22–23

¹ A good name is to be chosen rather than great riches,
    and favour is better than silver or gold.
² The rich and the poor have this in common:
    the LORD is the maker of them all.

⁸ Whoever sows injustice will reap calamity,
    and the rod of anger will fail.
⁹ Those who are generous are blessed,
    for they share their bread with the poor.

22 Do not rob the poor because they are poor,
 or crush the afflicted at the gate;
23 for the LORD pleads their cause
 and despoils of life those who despoil them.

PSALM   Psalm 125

1 Those who trust in the Lord are like Mount Zion,
 which cannot be moved, but stands fast for ever.
2 The hills stand about Jerusalem;
 so does the Lord stand round about his people, from this time
 forth for evermore.
3 The sceptre of the wicked shall not hold sway over the land allotted
 to the just,
 so that the just shall not put their hands to evil.
4 Show your goodness, O Lord, to those who are good
 and to those who are true of heart.
5 As for those who turn aside to crooked ways, the Lord will lead
 them away with the evildoers;
 but peace be upon Israel.

READING   James 2.1–10, [11–13,] 14–17

1 My brothers and sisters, do you with your acts of favouritism really believe in our glorious Lord Jesus Christ? 2 For if a person with gold rings and in fine clothes comes into your assembly, and if a poor person in dirty clothes also comes in, 3 and if you take notice of the one wearing the fine clothes and say, 'Have a seat here, please', while to the one who is poor you say, 'Stand there', or, 'Sit at my feet', 4 have you not made distinctions among yourselves, and become judges with evil thoughts? 5 Listen, my beloved brothers and sisters. Has not God chosen the poor in the world to be rich in faith and to be heirs of the kingdom that he has promised to those who love him? 6 But you have dishonoured the poor. Is it not the rich who oppress you? Is it not they who drag you into court? 7 Is it not they who blaspheme the excellent name that was invoked over you?

8 You do well if you really fulfil the royal law according to the scripture, 'You shall love your neighbour as yourself.' 9 But if you show partiality, you commit sin and are convicted by the law as transgressors. 10 For whoever keeps the whole law but fails in one point has become accountable for all of it.
[11 For the one who said, 'You shall not commit adultery', also said, 'You shall not murder.' Now if you do not commit adultery but if you murder, you have become a transgressor of the law. 12 So speak and so act as those

who are to be judged by the law of liberty. [13] For judgement will be without mercy to anyone who has shown no mercy; mercy triumphs over judgement.]

[14] What good is it, my brothers and sisters, if you say you have faith but do not have works? Can faith save you? [15] If a brother or sister is naked and lacks daily food, [16] and one of you says to them, 'Go in peace; keep warm and eat your fill', and yet you do not supply their bodily needs, what is the good of that? [17] So faith by itself, if it has no works, is dead.

GOSPEL   Mark 7.24–37

[24] From there he set out and went away to the region of Tyre. He entered a house and did not want anyone to know he was there. Yet he could not escape notice, [25] but a woman whose little daughter had an unclean spirit immediately heard about him, and she came and bowed down at his feet. [26] Now the woman was a Gentile, of Syrophoenician origin. She begged him to cast the demon out of her daughter. [27] He said to her, 'Let the children be fed first, for it is not fair to take the children's food and throw it to the dogs.' [28] But she answered him, 'Sir, even the dogs under the table eat the children's crumbs.' [29] Then he said to her, 'For saying that, you may go— the demon has left your daughter.' [30] So she went home, found the child lying on the bed, and the demon gone.

[31] Then he returned from the region of Tyre, and went by way of Sidon towards the Sea of Galilee, in the region of the Decapolis. [32] They brought to him a deaf man who had an impediment in his speech; and they begged him to lay his hand on him. [33] He took him aside in private, away from the crowd, and put his fingers into his ears, and he spat and touched his tongue. [34] Then looking up to heaven, he sighed and said to him, 'Ephphatha', that is, 'Be opened.' [35] And immediately his ears were opened, his tongue was released, and he spoke plainly. [36] Then Jesus ordered them to tell no one; but the more he ordered them, the more zealously they proclaimed it. [37] They were astounded beyond measure, saying, 'He has done everything well; he even makes the deaf to hear and the mute to speak.'

RELATED

READING   Isaiah 35.4–7a

⁴ Say to those who are of a fearful heart,
    'Be strong, do not fear!
Here is your God.
    He will come with vengeance,
with terrible recompense.
    He will come and save you.'
⁵ Then the eyes of the blind shall be opened,
    and the ears of the deaf unstopped;
⁶ then the lame shall leap like a deer,
    and the tongue of the speechless sing for joy.
For waters shall break forth in the wilderness,
    and streams in the desert;
⁷ the burning sand shall become a pool,
    and the thirsty ground springs of water.

PSALM   Psalm 146

¹ Alleluia! Praise the Lord, O my soul!
I will praise the Lord as long as I live; I will sing praises to my God
    while I have my being.
² Put not your trust in rulers, nor in any child of earth,
for there is no help in them.
³ When they breathe their last, they return to earth,
and in that day their thoughts perish.
⁴ Happy are they who have the God of Jacob for their help!
whose hope is in the Lord their God;
⁵ Who made heaven and earth, the seas, and all that is in them;
who keeps his promise for ever;
⁶ Who gives justice to those who are oppressed,
and food to those who hunger.
⁷ The Lord sets the prisoners free; the Lord opens the eyes of the
    blind;
the Lord lifts up those who are bowed down;
⁸ The Lord loves the righteous; the Lord cares for the stranger;
he sustains the orphan and widow, but frustrates the way of the
    wicked.
⁹ The Lord shall reign for ever,
your God, O Zion, throughout all generations. Alleluia!

READING   James 2.1–10, [11–13,] 14–17

¹ My brothers and sisters, do you with your acts of favouritism really believe in our glorious Lord Jesus Christ? ² For if a person with gold rings and in fine clothes comes into your assembly, and if a poor person in dirty clothes also comes in, ³ and if you take notice of the one wearing the fine clothes and say, 'Have a seat here, please', while to the one who is poor you say, 'Stand there', or, 'Sit at my feet', ⁴ have you not made distinctions among yourselves, and become judges with evil thoughts? ⁵ Listen, my beloved brothers and sisters. Has not God chosen the poor in the world to be rich in faith and to be heirs of the kingdom that he has promised to those who love him? ⁶ But you have dishonoured the poor. Is it not the rich who oppress you? Is it not they who drag you into court? ⁷ Is it not they who blaspheme the excellent name that was invoked over you?

⁸ You do well if you really fulfil the royal law according to the scripture, 'You shall love your neighbour as yourself.' ⁹ But if you show partiality, you commit sin and are convicted by the law as transgressors. ¹⁰ For whoever keeps the whole law but fails in one point has become accountable for all of it.
[¹¹ For the one who said, 'You shall not commit adultery', also said, 'You shall not murder.' Now if you do not commit adultery but if you murder, you have become a transgressor of the law. ¹² So speak and so act as those who are to be judged by the law of liberty. ¹³ For judgement will be without mercy to anyone who has shown no mercy; mercy triumphs over judgement.]

¹⁴ What good is it, my brothers and sisters, if you say you have faith but do not have works? Can faith save you? ¹⁵ If a brother or sister is naked and lacks daily food, ¹⁶ and one of you says to them, 'Go in peace; keep warm and eat your fill', and yet you do not supply their bodily needs, what is the good of that? ¹⁷ So faith by itself, if it has no works, is dead.

GOSPEL   Mark 7.24–37

²⁴ From there he set out and went away to the region of Tyre. He entered a house and did not want anyone to know he was there. Yet he could not escape notice, ²⁵ but a woman whose little daughter had an unclean spirit immediately heard about him, and she came and bowed down at his feet. ²⁶ Now the woman was a Gentile, of Syrophoenician origin. She begged him to cast the demon out of her daughter. ²⁷ He said to her, 'Let the children be fed first, for it is not fair to take the children's food and throw it to the

dogs.' ²⁸ But she answered him, 'Sir, even the dogs under the table eat the children's crumbs.' ²⁹ Then he said to her, 'For saying that, you may go— the demon has left your daughter.' ³⁰ So she went home, found the child lying on the bed, and the demon gone.

³¹ Then he returned from the region of Tyre, and went by way of Sidon towards the Sea of Galilee, in the region of the Decapolis. ³² They brought to him a deaf man who had an impediment in his speech; and they begged him to lay his hand on him. ³³ He took him aside in private, away from the crowd, and put his fingers into his ears, and he spat and touched his tongue. ³⁴ Then looking up to heaven, he sighed and said to him, 'Ephphatha', that is, 'Be opened.' ³⁵ And immediately his ears were opened, his tongue was released, and he spoke plainly. ³⁶ Then Jesus ordered them to tell no one; but the more he ordered them, the more zealously they proclaimed it. ³⁷ They were astounded beyond measure, saying, 'He has done everything well; he even makes the deaf to hear and the mute to speak.'

POST COMMUNION

See pages 577 to 580 and Table on page 568

SECOND SERVICE

Psalm 119.41–48, [49–56]
Exodus 14.5–31
Matthew 6.1–18

THIRD SERVICE

Psalm 119.57–72
Jonah 3.10–4.11

or

Ecclesiasticus 27.30–28.9
Revelation 8.1–5

PROPER 19

Sunday between 11 and 17 September inclusive

COLLECT

See pages 577 to 581 and Table on page 568

CONTINUOUS

READING   Proverbs 1.20-33

20   Wisdom cries out in the street;
         in the squares she raises her voice.
21   At the busiest corner she cries out;
         at the entrance of the city gates she speaks:
22   'How long, O simple ones, will you love being simple?
     How long will scoffers delight in their scoffing
         and fools hate knowledge?
23   Give heed to my reproof;
     I will pour out my thoughts to you;
         I will make my words known to you.
24   Because I have called and you refused,
         have stretched out my hand and no one heeded,
25   and because you have ignored all my counsel
         and would have none of my reproof,
26   I also will laugh at your calamity;
         I will mock when panic strikes you,
27   when panic strikes you like a storm,
         and your calamity comes like a whirlwind,
         when distress and anguish come upon you.
28   Then they will call upon me, but I will not answer;
         they will seek me diligently, but will not find me.
29   Because they hated knowledge
         and did not choose the fear of the LORD,
30   would have none of my counsel,
         and despised all my reproof,
31   therefore they shall eat the fruit of their way
         and be sated with their own devices.
32   For waywardness kills the simple,
         and the complacency of fools destroys them;
33   but those who listen to me will be secure
         and will live at ease, without dread of disaster.'

EITHER

PSALM   Psalm 19.1–6, [7–14]

1 The heavens declare the glory of God,
  and the firmament shows his handiwork.
2 One day tells its tale to another,
  and one night imparts knowledge to another.
3 Although they have no words or language,
  and their voices are not heard,
4 Their sound has gone out into all lands,
  and their message to the ends of the world.
5 In the deep has he set a pavilion for the sun;
  it comes forth like a bridegroom out of his chamber; it rejoices
    like a champion to run its course.
6 It goes forth from the uttermost edge of the heavens and runs
    about to the end of it again;
  nothing is hidden from its burning heat.
[7 The law of the Lord is perfect and revives the soul;
  the testimony of the Lord is sure and gives wisdom to the innocent.
8 The statutes of the Lord are just and rejoice the heart;
  the commandment of the Lord is clear and gives light to the eyes.
9 The fear of the Lord is clean and endures for ever;
  the judgements of the Lord are true and righteous altogether.
10 More to be desired are they than gold, more than much fine gold,
  sweeter far than honey, than honey in the comb.
11 By them also is your servant enlightened,
  and in keeping them there is great reward.
12 Who can tell how often he offends?
  Cleanse me from my secret faults.
13 Above all, keep your servant from presumptuous sins; let them
    not get dominion over me;
  then shall I be whole and sound, and innocent of a great offence.
14 Let the words of my mouth and the meditation of my heart be
    acceptable in your sight,
  O Lord, my strength and my redeemer.]

OR

CANTICLE   Wisdom 7.26–8.1

26 For she is a reflection of eternal light,
  a spotless mirror of the working of God,
  and an image of his goodness.

²⁷ Although she is but one, she can do all things,
and while remaining in herself, she renews all things;
in every generation she passes into holy souls
and makes them friends of God, and prophets;
²⁸ for God loves nothing so much as the person who lives with wisdom.
²⁹ She is more beautiful than the sun,
and excels every constellation of the stars.
Compared with the light she is found to be superior,
³⁰ for it is succeeded by the night,
but against wisdom evil does not prevail.
¹ She reaches mightily from one end of the earth to the other,
and she orders all things well.

READING   James 3.1–12

¹ Not many of you should become teachers, my brothers and sisters, for you know that we who teach will be judged with greater strictness. ² For all of us make many mistakes. Anyone who makes no mistakes in speaking is perfect, able to keep the whole body in check with a bridle. ³ If we put bits into the mouths of horses to make them obey us, we guide their whole bodies. ⁴ Or look at ships: though they are so large that it takes strong winds to drive them, yet they are guided by a very small rudder wherever the will of the pilot directs. ⁵ So also the tongue is a small member, yet it boasts of great exploits.

How great a forest is set ablaze by a small fire! ⁶ And the tongue is a fire. The tongue is placed among our members as a world of iniquity; it stains the whole body, sets on fire the cycle of nature, and is itself set on fire by hell. ⁷ For every species of beast and bird, of reptile and sea creature, can be tamed and has been tamed by the human species, ⁸ but no one can tame the tongue—a restless evil, full of deadly poison. ⁹ With it we bless the Lord and Father, and with it we curse those who are made in the likeness of God. ¹⁰ From the same mouth come blessing and cursing. My brothers and sisters, this ought not to be so. ¹¹ Does a spring pour forth from the same opening both fresh and brackish water? ¹² Can a fig tree, my brothers and sisters, yield olives, or a grapevine figs? No more can salt water yield fresh.

GOSPEL   Mark 8.27–38

²⁷ Jesus went on with his disciples to the villages of Caesarea Philippi; and on the way he asked his disciples, 'Who do people say that I am?' ²⁸ And they answered him, 'John the Baptist; and others, Elijah; and still others, one of the prophets.' ²⁹ He asked them, 'But who do you say that I am?' Peter answered him, 'You are the Messiah.' ³⁰ And he sternly ordered them not to tell anyone about him.

³¹ Then he began to teach them that the Son of Man must undergo great suffering, and be rejected by the elders, the chief priests, and the scribes, and be killed, and after three days rise again. ³² He said all this quite openly. And Peter took him aside and began to rebuke him. ³³ But turning and looking at his disciples, he rebuked Peter and said, 'Get behind me, Satan! For you are setting your mind not on divine things but on human things.'

³⁴ He called the crowd with his disciples, and said to them, 'If any want to become my followers, let them deny themselves and take up their cross and follow me. ³⁵ For those who want to save their life will lose it, and those who lose their life for my sake, and for the sake of the gospel, will save it. ³⁶ For what will it profit them to gain the whole world and forfeit their life? ³⁷ Indeed, what can they give in return for their life? ³⁸ Those who are ashamed of me and of my words in this adulterous and sinful generation, of them the Son of Man will also be ashamed when he comes in the glory of his Father with the holy angels.'

RELATED

READING   Isaiah 50.4–9a

⁴ The Lord GOD has given me
        the tongue of a teacher,
    that I may know how to sustain
        the weary with a word.
    Morning by morning he wakens—
        wakens my ear
        to listen as those who are taught.
⁵ The Lord GOD has opened my ear,
        and I was not rebellious,
        I did not turn backwards.
⁶ I gave my back to those who struck me,
        and my cheeks to those who pulled out the beard;
    I did not hide my face
        from insult and spitting.
⁷ The Lord GOD helps me;
        therefore I have not been disgraced;
    therefore I have set my face like flint,
        and I know that I shall not be put to shame;

8   he who vindicates me is near.
    Who will contend with me?
        Let us stand up together.
    Who are my adversaries?
        Let them confront me.
9   It is the Lord GOD who helps me;
        who will declare me guilty?

PSALM   Psalm 116.1–8

1   I love the Lord, because he has heard the voice of my supplication,
        because he has inclined his ear to me whenever I called upon him.
2   The cords of death entangled me; the grip of the grave took hold
            of me;
        I came to grief and sorrow.
3   Then I called upon the name of the Lord:
        'O Lord, I pray you, save my life.'
4   Gracious is the Lord and righteous;
        our God is full of compassion.
5   The Lord watches over the innocent;
        I was brought very low and he helped me.
6   Turn again to your rest, O my soul,
        for the Lord has treated you well.
7   For you have rescued my life from death,
        my eyes from tears and my feet from stumbling.
8   I will walk in the presence of the Lord
        in the land of the living.

READING   James 3.1–12

1 Not many of you should become teachers, my brothers and sisters, for
you know that we who teach will be judged with greater strictness. 2 For
all of us make many mistakes. Anyone who makes no mistakes in speaking
is perfect, able to keep the whole body in check with a bridle. 3 If we put
bits into the mouths of horses to make them obey us, we guide their whole
bodies. 4 Or look at ships: though they are so large that it takes strong
winds to drive them, yet they are guided by a very small rudder wherever
the will of the pilot directs. 5 So also the tongue is a small member, yet it
boasts of great exploits.

How great a forest is set ablaze by a small fire! 6 And the tongue is a fire.
The tongue is placed among our members as a world of iniquity; it stains
the whole body, sets on fire the cycle of nature, and is itself set on fire by

hell. [7] For every species of beast and bird, of reptile and sea creature, can be tamed and has been tamed by the human species, [8] but no one can tame the tongue—a restless evil, full of deadly poison. [9] With it we bless the Lord and Father, and with it we curse those who are made in the likeness of God. [10] From the same mouth come blessing and cursing. My brothers and sisters, this ought not to be so. [11] Does a spring pour forth from the same opening both fresh and brackish water? [12] Can a fig tree, my brothers and sisters, yield olives, or a grapevine figs? No more can salt water yield fresh.

GOSPEL   Mark 8.27–38

[27] Jesus went on with his disciples to the villages of Caesarea Philippi; and on the way he asked his disciples, 'Who do people say that I am?' [28] And they answered him, 'John the Baptist; and others, Elijah; and still others, one of the prophets.' [29] He asked them, 'But who do you say that I am?' Peter answered him, 'You are the Messiah.' [30] And he sternly ordered them not to tell anyone about him.

[31] Then he began to teach them that the Son of Man must undergo great suffering, and be rejected by the elders, the chief priests, and the scribes, and be killed, and after three days rise again. [32] He said all this quite openly. And Peter took him aside and began to rebuke him. [33] But turning and looking at his disciples, he rebuked Peter and said, 'Get behind me, Satan! For you are setting your mind not on divine things but on human things.'

[34] He called the crowd with his disciples, and said to them, 'If any want to become my followers, let them deny themselves and take up their cross and follow me. [35] For those who want to save their life will lose it, and those who lose their life for my sake, and for the sake of the gospel, will save it. [36] For what will it profit them to gain the whole world and forfeit their life? [37] Indeed, what can they give in return for their life? [38] Those who are ashamed of me and of my words in this adulterous and sinful generation, of them the Son of Man will also be ashamed when he comes in the glory of his Father with the holy angels.'

POST COMMUNION

See pages 578 to 581 and Table on page 568

SECOND SERVICE   THIRD SERVICE

Psalm 119.73–80, [81–88]   Psalm 119.105–120
Exodus 18.13–26   Isaiah 44.24–45.8
Matthew 7.1–14   Revelation 12.1–12

PROPER 20

Sunday between 18 and 24 September inclusive

COLLECT

See pages 578 to 581 and Table on page 568

CONTINUOUS

READING   Proverbs 31.10–31

10   A capable wife who can find?
        She is far more precious than jewels.
11   The heart of her husband trusts in her,
        and he will have no lack of gain.
12   She does him good, and not harm,
        all the days of her life.
13   She seeks wool and flax,
        and works with willing hands.
14   She is like the ships of the merchant,
        she brings her food from far away.
15   She rises while it is still night
        and provides food for her household
        and tasks for her servant-girls.
16   She considers a field and buys it;
        with the fruit of her hands she plants a vineyard.
17   She girds herself with strength,
        and makes her arms strong.
18   She perceives that her merchandise is profitable.
        Her lamp does not go out at night.
19   She puts her hands to the distaff,
        and her hands hold the spindle.
20   She opens her hand to the poor,
        and reaches out her hands to the needy.
21   She is not afraid for her household when it snows,
        for all her household are clothed in crimson.
22   She makes herself coverings;
        her clothing is fine linen and purple.
23   Her husband is known in the city gates,
        taking his seat among the elders of the land.
24   She makes linen garments and sells them;
        she supplies the merchant with sashes.

25 Strength and dignity are her clothing,
  and she laughs at the time to come.
26 She opens her mouth with wisdom,
  and the teaching of kindness is on her tongue.
27 She looks well to the ways of her household,
  and does not eat the bread of idleness.
28 Her children rise up and call her happy;
  her husband too, and he praises her:
29 'Many women have done excellently,
  but you surpass them all.'
30 Charm is deceitful, and beauty is vain,
  but a woman who fears the LORD is to be praised.
31 Give her a share in the fruit of her hands,
  and let her works praise her in the city gates.

PSALM   Psalm 1

1 Happy are they who have not walked in the counsel of the wicked,
  nor lingered in the way of sinners, nor sat in the seats of the
    scornful!
2 Their delight is in the law of the Lord,
  and they meditate on his law day and night.
3 They are like trees planted by streams of water, bearing fruit in
    due season, with leaves that do not wither;
  everything they do shall prosper.
4 It is not so with the wicked:
  they are like chaff which the wind blows away;
5 Therefore the wicked shall not stand upright when judgement
    comes,
  nor the sinner in the council of the righteous.
6 For the Lord knows the way of the righteous,
  but the way of the wicked is doomed.

READING   James 3.13–4.3, 7–8a

13 Who is wise and understanding among you? Show by your good life that your works are done with gentleness born of wisdom. 14 But if you have bitter envy and selfish ambition in your hearts, do not be boastful and false to the truth. 15 Such wisdom does not come down from above, but is earthly, unspiritual, devilish. 16 For where there is envy and selfish ambition, there will also be disorder and wickedness of every kind. 17 But the wisdom from above is first pure, then peaceable, gentle, willing to yield, full of mercy

and good fruits, without a trace of partiality or hypocrisy. ¹⁸ And a harvest of righteousness is sown in peace for those who make peace.

¹ Those conflicts and disputes among you, where do they come from? Do they not come from your cravings that are at war within you? ² You want something and do not have it; so you commit murder. And you covet something and cannot obtain it; so you engage in disputes and conflicts. You do not have, because you do not ask. ³ You ask and do not receive, because you ask wrongly, in order to spend what you get on your pleasures.

⁷ Submit yourselves therefore to God. Resist the devil, and he will flee from you. ⁸ Draw near to God, and he will draw near to you.

GOSPEL   Mark 9.30–37

³⁰ They went on from there and passed through Galilee. He did not want anyone to know it; ³¹ for he was teaching his disciples, saying to them, 'The Son of Man is to be betrayed into human hands, and they will kill him, and three days after being killed, he will rise again.' ³² But they did not understand what he was saying and were afraid to ask him.

³³ Then they came to Capernaum; and when he was in the house he asked them, 'What were you arguing about on the way?' ³⁴ But they were silent, for on the way they had argued with one another about who was the greatest. ³⁵ He sat down, called the twelve, and said to them, 'Whoever wants to be first must be last of all and servant of all.' ³⁶ Then he took a little child and put it among them; and taking it in his arms, he said to them, ³⁷ 'Whoever welcomes one such child in my name welcomes me, and whoever welcomes me welcomes not me but the one who sent me.'

RELATED

READING

EITHER   **Wisdom 1.16–2.1, 12–22**

¹⁶   But the ungodly by their words and deeds summoned death;
      considering him a friend, they pined away
      and made a covenant with him,
      because they are fit to belong to his company.
¹   For they reasoned unsoundly, saying to themselves,
      'Short and sorrowful is our life,
      and there is no remedy when a life comes to its end,
      and no one has been known to return from Hades.'

12 'Let us lie in wait for the righteous man,
    because he is inconvenient to us and opposes our actions;
    he reproaches us for sins against the law,
    and accuses us of sins against our training.
13 He professes to have knowledge of God,
    and calls himself a child of the Lord.
14 He became to us a reproof of our thoughts;
15 the very sight of him is a burden to us,
    because his manner of life is unlike that of others,
    and his ways are strange.
16 We are considered by him as something base,
    and he avoids our ways as unclean;
    he calls the last end of the righteous happy,
    and boasts that God is his father.
17 Let us see if his words are true,
    and let us test what will happen at the end of his life;
18 for if the righteous man is God's child, he will help him,
    and will deliver him from the hand of his adversaries.
19 Let us test him with insult and torture,
    so that we may find out how gentle he is,
    and make trial of his forbearance.
20 Let us condemn him to a shameful death,
    for, according to what he says, he will be protected.'
21 Thus they reasoned, but they were led astray,
    for their wickedness blinded them,
22 and they did not know the secret purposes of God,
    nor hoped for the wages of holiness,
    nor discerned the prize for blameless souls.

OR   Jeremiah 11.18–20

18 It was the LORD who made it known to me, and I knew;
        then you showed me their evil deeds.
19 But I was like a gentle lamb
        led to the slaughter.
    And I did not know it was against me
        that they devised schemes, saying,
    'Let us destroy the tree with its fruit,
        let us cut him off from the land of the living,
        so that his name will no longer be remembered!'
20 But you, O LORD of hosts, who judge righteously,
        who try the heart and the mind,
    let me see your retribution upon them,
        for to you I have committed my cause.

PSALM   Psalm 54

¹ Save me, O God, by your name;
   in your might, defend my cause.
² Hear my prayer, O God;
   give ear to the words of my mouth.
³ For the arrogant have risen up against me, and the ruthless have
      sought my life,
   those who have no regard for God.
⁴ Behold, God is my helper;
   it is the Lord who sustains my life.
⁵ Render evil to those who spy on me;
   in your faithfulness, destroy them.
⁶ I will offer you a freewill sacrifice
   and praise your name, O Lord, for it is good.
⁷ For you have rescued me from every trouble,
   and my eye has seen the ruin of my foes.

READING   James 3.13–4.3, 7–8a

¹³ Who is wise and understanding among you? Show by your good life that your works are done with gentleness born of wisdom. ¹⁴ But if you have bitter envy and selfish ambition in your hearts, do not be boastful and false to the truth. ¹⁵ Such wisdom does not come down from above, but is earthly, unspiritual, devilish. ¹⁶ For where there is envy and selfish ambition, there will also be disorder and wickedness of every kind. ¹⁷ But the wisdom from above is first pure, then peaceable, gentle, willing to yield, full of mercy and good fruits, without a trace of partiality or hypocrisy. ¹⁸ And a harvest of righteousness is sown in peace for those who make peace.

¹ Those conflicts and disputes among you, where do they come from? Do they not come from your cravings that are at war within you? ² You want something and do not have it; so you commit murder. And you covet something and cannot obtain it; so you engage in disputes and conflicts. You do not have, because you do not ask. ³ You ask and do not receive, because you ask wrongly, in order to spend what you get on your pleasures.

⁷ Submit yourselves therefore to God. Resist the devil, and he will flee from you. ⁸ Draw near to God, and he will draw near to you.

GOSPEL   Mark 9.30–37

³⁰ They went on from there and passed through Galilee. He did not want anyone to know it; ³¹ for he was teaching his disciples, saying to them, 'The Son of Man is to be betrayed into human hands, and they will kill him, and three days after being killed, he will rise again.' ³² But they did not understand what he was saying and were afraid to ask him.

³³ Then they came to Capernaum; and when he was in the house he asked them, 'What were you arguing about on the way?' ³⁴ But they were silent, for on the way they had argued with one another about who was the greatest. ³⁵ He sat down, called the twelve, and said to them, 'Whoever wants to be first must be last of all and servant of all.' ³⁶ Then he took a little child and put it among them; and taking it in his arms, he said to them, ³⁷ 'Whoever welcomes one such child in my name welcomes me, and whoever welcomes me welcomes not me but the one who sent me.'

POST COMMUNION

See pages 578 to 582 and Table on page 568

SECOND SERVICE   THIRD SERVICE

Psalm 119.137–144, [145–152]   Psalm 119.153–176
Exodus 19.10–25   Isaiah 45.9–22
Matthew 8.23–34   Revelation 14.1–5

PROPER 21

Sunday between 25 September and 1 October inclusive

COLLECT

See pages 579 to 582 and Table on page 568

CONTINUOUS

READING   Esther 7.1–6, 9–10; 9.20–22

¹ So the king and Haman went in to feast with Queen Esther. ² On the second day, as they were drinking wine, the king again said to Esther, 'What is your petition, Queen Esther? It shall be granted you. And what is your request? Even to the half of my kingdom, it shall be fulfilled.' ³ Then Queen Esther answered, 'If I have won your favour, O king, and if it pleases the king, let my life be given me—that is my petition—and the lives of my people—that is my request. ⁴ For we have been sold, I and my people, to be destroyed, to be killed, and to be annihilated. If we had been sold merely as slaves, men and women, I would have held my peace; but no enemy can compensate for this damage to the king.' ⁵ Then King Ahasuerus said to Queen Esther, 'Who is he, and where is he, who has presumed to do this?' ⁶ Esther said, 'A foe and enemy, this wicked Haman!' Then Haman was terrified before the king and the queen.

⁹ Then Harbona, one of the eunuchs in attendance on the king, said, 'Look, the very gallows that Haman has prepared for Mordecai, whose word saved the king, stands at Haman's house, fifty cubits high.' And the king said, 'Hang him on that.' ¹⁰ So they hanged Haman on the gallows that he had prepared for Mordecai. Then the anger of the king abated.

²⁰ Mordecai recorded these things, and sent letters to all the Jews who were in all the provinces of King Ahasuerus, both near and far, ²¹ enjoining them that they should keep the fourteenth day of the month Adar and also the fifteenth day of the same month, year by year, ²² as the days on which the Jews gained relief from their enemies, and as the month that had been turned for them from sorrow into gladness and from mourning into a holiday; that they should make them days of feasting and gladness, days for sending gifts of food to one another and presents to the poor.

PSALM   Psalm 124

¹ If the Lord had not been on our side,
   let Israel now say;
² If the Lord had not been on our side,
   when enemies rose up against us;
³ Then would they have swallowed us up alive
   in their fierce anger towards us;
⁴ Then would the waters have overwhelmed us
   and the torrent gone over us;
⁵ Then would the raging waters
   have gone right over us.
⁶ Blessèd be the Lord!
   he has not given us over to be a prey for their teeth.
⁷ We have escaped like a bird from the snare of the fowler;
   the snare is broken and we have escaped.
⁸ Our help is in the name of the Lord,
   the maker of heaven and earth.

READING   James 5.13–20

¹³ Are any among you suffering? They should pray. Are any cheerful? They
should sing songs of praise. ¹⁴ Are any among you sick? They should call for
the elders of the church and have them pray over them, anointing them
with oil in the name of the Lord. ¹⁵ The prayer of faith will save the sick,
and the Lord will raise them up; and anyone who has committed sins will
be forgiven. ¹⁶ Therefore confess your sins to one another, and pray for one
another, so that you may be healed. The prayer of the righteous is powerful
and effective. ¹⁷ Elijah was a human being like us, and he prayed fervently
that it might not rain, and for three years and six months it did not rain
on the earth. ¹⁸ Then he prayed again, and the heaven gave rain and the
earth yielded its harvest.

¹⁹ My brothers and sisters, if anyone among you wanders from the truth
and is brought back by another, ²⁰ you should know that whoever brings
back a sinner from wandering will save the sinner's soul from death and
will cover a multitude of sins.

GOSPEL   Mark 9.38–50

³⁸ John said to him, 'Teacher, we saw someone casting out demons in your
name, and we tried to stop him, because he was not following us.' ³⁹ But
Jesus said, 'Do not stop him; for no one who does a deed of power in my
name will be able soon afterwards to speak evil of me. ⁴⁰ Whoever is not

against us is for us. [41] For truly I tell you, whoever gives you a cup of water to drink because you bear the name of Christ will by no means lose the reward.

[42] 'If any of you put a stumbling-block before one of these little ones who believe in me, it would be better for you if a great millstone were hung around your neck and you were thrown into the sea. [43] If your hand causes you to stumble, cut it off; it is better for you to enter life maimed than to have two hands and to go to hell, to the unquenchable fire. [45] And if your foot causes you to stumble, cut it off; it is better for you to enter life lame than to have two feet and to be thrown into hell. [47] And if your eye causes you to stumble, tear it out; it is better for you to enter the kingdom of God with one eye than to have two eyes and to be thrown into hell, [48] where their worm never dies, and the fire is never quenched.

[49] 'For everyone will be salted with fire. [50] Salt is good; but if salt has lost its saltiness, how can you season it? Have salt in yourselves, and be at peace with one another.'

RELATED

READING   **Numbers 11.4–6, 10–16, 24–29**

[4] The rabble among them had a strong craving; and the Israelites also wept again, and said, 'If only we had meat to eat! [5] We remember the fish we used to eat in Egypt for nothing, the cucumbers, the melons, the leeks, the onions, and the garlic; [6] but now our strength is dried up, and there is nothing at all but this manna to look at.'

[10] Moses heard the people weeping throughout their families, all at the entrances of their tents. Then the LORD became very angry, and Moses was displeased. [11] So Moses said to the LORD, 'Why have you treated your servant so badly? Why have I not found favour in your sight, that you lay the burden of all this people on me? [12] Did I conceive all this people? Did I give birth to them, that you should say to me, "Carry them in your bosom, as a nurse carries a sucking child", to the land that you promised on oath to their ancestors? [13] Where am I to get meat to give to all this people? For they come weeping to me and say, "Give us meat to eat!" [14] I am not able to carry all this people alone, for they are too heavy for me. [15] If this is the way you are going to treat me, put me to death at once—if I have found favour in your sight—and do not let me see my misery.'

¹⁶ So the LORD said to Moses, 'Gather for me seventy of the elders of Israel, whom you know to be the elders of the people and officers over them; bring them to the tent of meeting, and have them take their place there with you.'

²⁴ So Moses went out and told the people the words of the LORD; and he gathered seventy elders of the people, and placed them all around the tent. ²⁵ Then the LORD came down in the cloud and spoke to him, and took some of the spirit that was on him and put it on the seventy elders; and when the spirit rested upon them, they prophesied. But they did not do so again.

²⁶ Two men remained in the camp, one named Eldad, and the other named Medad, and the spirit rested on them; they were among those registered, but they had not gone out to the tent, and so they prophesied in the camp. ²⁷ And a young man ran and told Moses, 'Eldad and Medad are prophesying in the camp.' ²⁸ And Joshua son of Nun, the assistant of Moses, one of his chosen men, said, 'My lord Moses, stop them!' ²⁹ But Moses said to him, 'Are you jealous for my sake? Would that all the LORD's people were prophets, and that the LORD would put his spirit on them!'

PSALM   Psalm 19.7–14

⁷ The law of the Lord is perfect and revives the soul;
      the testimony of the Lord is sure and gives wisdom to the innocent.
⁸ The statutes of the Lord are just and rejoice the heart;
      the commandment of the Lord is clear and gives light to the eyes.
⁹ The fear of the Lord is clean and endures for ever;
      the judgements of the Lord are true and righteous altogether.
¹⁰ More to be desired are they than gold, more than much fine gold,
      sweeter far than honey, than honey in the comb.
¹¹ By them also is your servant enlightened,
      and in keeping them there is great reward.
¹² Who can tell how often he offends?
      Cleanse me from my secret faults.
¹³ Above all, keep your servant from presumptuous sins; let them
          not get dominion over me;
      then shall I be whole and sound, and innocent of a great offence.
¹⁴ Let the words of my mouth and the meditation of my heart be
          acceptable in your sight,
      O Lord, my strength and my redeemer.

READING   James 5.13–20

[13] Are any among you suffering? They should pray. Are any cheerful? They should sing songs of praise. [14] Are any among you sick? They should call for the elders of the church and have them pray over them, anointing them with oil in the name of the Lord. [15] The prayer of faith will save the sick, and the Lord will raise them up; and anyone who has committed sins will be forgiven. [16] Therefore confess your sins to one another, and pray for one another, so that you may be healed. The prayer of the righteous is powerful and effective. [17] Elijah was a human being like us, and he prayed fervently that it might not rain, and for three years and six months it did not rain on the earth. [18] Then he prayed again, and the heaven gave rain and the earth yielded its harvest.

[19] My brothers and sisters, if anyone among you wanders from the truth and is brought back by another, [20] you should know that whoever brings back a sinner from wandering will save the sinner's soul from death and will cover a multitude of sins.

GOSPEL   Mark 9.38–50

[38] John said to him, 'Teacher, we saw someone casting out demons in your name, and we tried to stop him, because he was not following us.' [39] But Jesus said, 'Do not stop him; for no one who does a deed of power in my name will be able soon afterwards to speak evil of me. [40] Whoever is not against us is for us. [41] For truly I tell you, whoever gives you a cup of water to drink because you bear the name of Christ will by no means lose the reward.

[42] 'If any of you put a stumbling-block before one of these little ones who believe in me, it would be better for you if a great millstone were hung around your neck and you were thrown into the sea. [43] If your hand causes you to stumble, cut it off; it is better for you to enter life maimed than to have two hands and to go to hell, to the unquenchable fire. [45] And if your foot causes you to stumble, cut it off; it is better for you to enter life lame than to have two feet and to be thrown into hell. [47] And if your eye causes you to stumble, tear it out; it is better for you to enter the kingdom of God with one eye than to have two eyes and to be thrown into hell, [48] where their worm never dies, and the fire is never quenched.

[49] 'For everyone will be salted with fire. [50] Salt is good; but if salt has lost its saltiness, how can you season it? Have salt in yourselves, and be at peace with one another.'

POST COMMUNION

See pages 579 to 582 and Table on page 568

SECOND SERVICE

Psalms 120; 121
Exodus 24
Matthew 9.1–8

THIRD SERVICE

Psalm 122
Isaiah 48.12–22
Luke 11.37–54

PROPER 22

Sunday between 2 and 8 October inclusive

COLLECT

See pages 579 to 583 and Table on page 568

CONTINUOUS

READING   Job 1.1; 2.1–10

¹ There was once a man in the land of Uz whose name was Job. That man was blameless and upright, one who feared God and turned away from evil.

¹ One day the heavenly beings came to present themselves before the Lord, and Satan also came among them to present himself before the Lord. ² The Lord said to Satan, 'Where have you come from?' Satan answered the Lord, 'From going to and fro on the earth, and from walking up and down on it.' ³ The Lord said to Satan, 'Have you considered my servant Job? There is no one like him on the earth, a blameless and upright man who fears God and turns away from evil. He still persists in his integrity, although you incited me against him, to destroy him for no reason.' ⁴ Then Satan answered the Lord, 'Skin for skin! All that people have they will give to save their lives. ⁵ But stretch out your hand now and touch his bone and his flesh, and he will curse you to your face.' ⁶ The Lord said to Satan, 'Very well, he is in your power; only spare his life.'

⁷ So Satan went out from the presence of the Lord, and inflicted loathsome sores on Job from the sole of his foot to the crown of his head. ⁸ Job took a potsherd with which to scrape himself, and sat among the ashes.

⁹ Then his wife said to him, 'Do you still persist in your integrity? Curse God, and die.' ¹⁰ But he said to her, 'You speak as any foolish woman would speak. Shall we receive the good at the hand of God, and not receive the bad?' In all this Job did not sin with his lips.

PSALM   Psalm 26

1 Give judgement for me, O Lord, for I have lived with integrity;
   I have trusted in the Lord and have not faltered.
2 Test me, O Lord, and try me;
   examine my heart and my mind.
3 For your love is before my eyes;
   I have walked faithfully with you.
4 I have not sat with the worthless,
   nor do I consort with the deceitful.
5 I have hated the company of evildoers;
   I will not sit down with the wicked.
6 I will wash my hands in innocence, O Lord,
   that I may go in procession round your altar,
7 Singing aloud a song of thanksgiving
   and recounting all your wonderful deeds.
8 Lord, I love the house in which you dwell
   and the place where your glory abides.
9 Do not sweep me away with sinners,
   nor my life with those who thirst for blood,
10 Whose hands are full of evil plots,
   and their right hand full of bribes.
11 As for me, I will live with integrity;
   redeem me, O Lord, and have pity on me.
12 My foot stands on level ground;
   in the full assembly I will bless the Lord.

READING   Hebrews 1.1–4; 2.5–12

¹ Long ago God spoke to our ancestors in many and various ways by the prophets, ² but in these last days he has spoken to us by a Son, whom he appointed heir of all things, through whom he also created the worlds. ³ He is the reflection of God's glory and the exact imprint of God's very being, and he sustains all things by his powerful word. When he had made purification for sins, he sat down at the right hand of the Majesty on high, ⁴ having become as much superior to angels as the name he has inherited is more excellent than theirs.

⁵ Now God did not subject the coming world, about which we are speaking, to angels. ⁶ But someone has testified somewhere,

'What are human beings that you are mindful of them,
or mortals, that you care for them?
⁷ You have made them for a little while lower than the angels;
you have crowned them with glory and honour,
⁸ subjecting all things under their feet.'

Now in subjecting all things to them, God left nothing outside their control. As it is, we do not yet see everything in subjection to them, ⁹ but we do see Jesus, who for a little while was made lower than the angels, now crowned with glory and honour because of the suffering of death, so that by the grace of God he might taste death for everyone.

¹⁰ It was fitting that God, for whom and through whom all things exist, in bringing many children to glory, should make the pioneer of their salvation perfect through sufferings. ¹¹ For the one who sanctifies and those who are sanctified all have one Father. For this reason Jesus is not ashamed to call them brothers and sisters, ¹² saying,

'I will proclaim your name to my brothers and sisters,
in the midst of the congregation I will praise you.'

GOSPEL   Mark 10.2–16

² Some Pharisees came, and to test him they asked, 'Is it lawful for a man to divorce his wife?' ³ He answered them, 'What did Moses command you?' ⁴ They said, 'Moses allowed a man to write a certificate of dismissal and to divorce her.' ⁵ But Jesus said to them, 'Because of your hardness of heart he wrote this commandment for you. ⁶ But from the beginning of creation, "God made them male and female." ⁷ "For this reason a man shall leave his father and mother and be joined to his wife, ⁸ and the two shall become one flesh." So they are no longer two, but one flesh. ⁹ Therefore what God has joined together, let no one separate.'

¹⁰ Then in the house the disciples asked him again about this matter. ¹¹ He said to them, 'Whoever divorces his wife and marries another commits adultery against her; ¹² and if she divorces her husband and marries another, she commits adultery.'

¹³ People were bringing little children to him in order that he might touch them; and the disciples spoke sternly to them. ¹⁴ But when Jesus saw this, he was indignant and said to them, 'Let the little children come to me; do not stop them; for it is to such as these that the kingdom of God belongs. ¹⁵ Truly I tell you, whoever does not receive the kingdom of God as a little child will never enter it.' ¹⁶ And he took them up in his arms, laid his hands on them, and blessed them.

RELATED

READING   Genesis 2.18–24

¹⁸ Then the LORD God said, 'It is not good that the man should be alone; I will make him a helper as his partner.' ¹⁹ So out of the ground the LORD God formed every animal of the field and every bird of the air, and brought them to the man to see what he would call them; and whatever the man called each living creature, that was its name. ²⁰ The man gave names to all cattle, and to the birds of the air, and to every animal of the field; but for the man there was not found a helper as his partner. ²¹ So the LORD God caused a deep sleep to fall upon the man, and he slept; then he took one of his ribs and closed up its place with flesh. ²² And the rib that the LORD God had taken from the man he made into a woman and brought her to the man. ²³ Then the man said,

'This at last is bone of my bones
and flesh of my flesh;
this one shall be called Woman,
for out of Man this one was taken.'
²⁴ Therefore a man leaves his father and his mother and clings to his wife, and they become one flesh.

PSALM   Psalm 8

1   O Lord our governor,
how exalted is your name in all the world!
2   Out of the mouths of infants and children
your majesty is praised above the heavens.
3   You have set up a stronghold against your adversaries,
to quell the enemy and the avenger.
4   When I consider your heavens, the work of your fingers,
the moon and the stars you have set in their courses,
5   What are mortals, that you should be mindful of them?
mere human beings, that you should seek them out?
6   You have made them little lower than the angels;
you adorn them with glory and honour.
7   You give them mastery over the works of your hands;
and put all things under their feet,
8   All sheep and oxen,
even the wild beasts of the field,

9   The birds of the air, the fish of the sea,
    and whatsoever walks in the paths of the sea.
10 O Lord our governor,
    how exalted is your name in all the world!

READING   Hebrews 1.1–4; 2.5–12

¹ Long ago God spoke to our ancestors in many and various ways by the prophets, ² but in these last days he has spoken to us by a Son, whom he appointed heir of all things, through whom he also created the worlds. ³ He is the reflection of God's glory and the exact imprint of God's very being, and he sustains all things by his powerful word. When he had made purification for sins, he sat down at the right hand of the Majesty on high, ⁴ having become as much superior to angels as the name he has inherited is more excellent than theirs.

⁵ Now God did not subject the coming world, about which we are speaking, to angels. ⁶ But someone has testified somewhere,
    'What are human beings that you are mindful of them,
        or mortals, that you care for them?
⁷   You have made them for a little while lower than the angels;
        you have crowned them with glory and honour,
⁸   subjecting all things under their feet.'
Now in subjecting all things to them, God left nothing outside their control. As it is, we do not yet see everything in subjection to them, ⁹ but we do see Jesus, who for a little while was made lower than the angels, now crowned with glory and honour because of the suffering of death, so that by the grace of God he might taste death for everyone.

¹⁰ It was fitting that God, for whom and through whom all things exist, in bringing many children to glory, should make the pioneer of their salvation perfect through sufferings. ¹¹ For the one who sanctifies and those who are sanctified all have one Father. For this reason Jesus is not ashamed to call them brothers and sisters, ¹² saying,
    'I will proclaim your name to my brothers and sisters,
        in the midst of the congregation I will praise you.'

GOSPEL   Mark 10.2–16

² Some Pharisees came, and to test him they asked, 'Is it lawful for a man to divorce his wife?' ³ He answered them, 'What did Moses command you?' ⁴ They said, 'Moses allowed a man to write a certificate of dismissal and to divorce her.' ⁵ But Jesus said to them, 'Because of your hardness of heart he wrote this commandment for you. ⁶ But from the beginning of creation,

"God made them male and female." ⁷ "For this reason a man shall leave his father and mother and be joined to his wife, ⁸ and the two shall become one flesh." So they are no longer two, but one flesh. ⁹ Therefore what God has joined together, let no one separate.'

¹⁰ Then in the house the disciples asked him again about this matter. ¹¹ He said to them, 'Whoever divorces his wife and marries another commits adultery against her; ¹² and if she divorces her husband and marries another, she commits adultery.'

¹³ People were bringing little children to him in order that he might touch them; and the disciples spoke sternly to them. ¹⁴ But when Jesus saw this, he was indignant and said to them, 'Let the little children come to me; do not stop them; for it is to such as these that the kingdom of God belongs. ¹⁵ Truly I tell you, whoever does not receive the kingdom of God as a little child will never enter it.' ¹⁶ And he took them up in his arms, laid his hands on them, and blessed them.

POST COMMUNION

See pages 580 to 583 and Table on page 568

SECOND SERVICE	THIRD SERVICE
Psalms 125; 126	Psalms 123; 124
Joshua 3.7–17	Isaiah 49.13–23
Matthew 10.1–22	Luke 12.1–12

PROPER 23

Sunday between 9 and 15 October inclusive

COLLECT

See pages 580 to 584 and Table on page 568

CONTINUOUS

READING   Job 23.1–9, 16–17

¹ Then Job answered:
² 'Today also my complaint is bitter;
    his hand is heavy despite my groaning.

3 O that I knew where I might find him,
   that I might come even to his dwelling!
4 I would lay my case before him,
   and fill my mouth with arguments.
5 I would learn what he would answer me,
   and understand what he would say to me.
6 Would he contend with me in the greatness of his power?
   No; but he would give heed to me.
7 There an upright person could reason with him,
   and I should be acquitted for ever by my judge.
8 If I go forward, he is not there;
   or backward, I cannot perceive him;
9 on the left he hides, and I cannot behold him;
   I turn to the right, but I cannot see him.

16 'God has made my heart faint;
   the Almighty has terrified me;
17 If only I could vanish in darkness,
   and thick darkness would cover my face!'

PSALM   Psalm 22.1–15

1 My God, my God, why have you forsaken me?
   and are so far from my cry and from the words of my distress?
2 O my God, I cry in the daytime, but you do not answer;
   by night as well, but I find no rest.
3 Yet you are the Holy One,
   enthroned upon the praises of Israel.
4 Our forebears put their trust in you;
   they trusted and you delivered them.
5 They cried out to you and were delivered;
   they trusted in you and were not put to shame.
6 But as for me, I am a worm and no man,
   scorned by all and despised by the people.
7 All who see me laugh me to scorn;
   they curl their lips and wag their heads, saying,
8 'He trusted in the Lord; let him deliver him;
   let him rescue him, if he delights in him.'
9 Yet you are he who took me out of the womb,
   and kept me safe upon my mother's breast.
10 I have been entrusted to you ever since I was born;
   you were my God when I was still in my mother's womb.
11 Be not far from me, for trouble is near,
   and there is none to help.

¹² Many young bulls encircle me;
  strong bulls of Bashan surround me.
¹³ They open wide their jaws at me,
  like a ravening and a roaring lion.
¹⁴ I am poured out like water; all my bones are out of joint;
  my heart within my breast is melting wax.
¹⁵ My mouth is dried out like a pot-sherd; my tongue sticks to the
    roof of my mouth;
  and you have laid me in the dust of the grave.

READING   Hebrews 4.12–16

¹² Indeed, the word of God is living and active, sharper than any two-edged sword, piercing until it divides soul from spirit, joints from marrow; it is able to judge the thoughts and intentions of the heart. ¹³ And before him no creature is hidden, but all are naked and laid bare to the eyes of the one to whom we must render an account.

¹⁴ Since, then, we have a great high priest who has passed through the heavens, Jesus, the Son of God, let us hold fast to our confession. ¹⁵ For we do not have a high priest who is unable to sympathize with our weaknesses, but we have one who in every respect has been tested as we are, yet without sin. ¹⁶ Let us therefore approach the throne of grace with boldness, so that we may receive mercy and find grace to help in time of need.

GOSPEL   Mark 10.17–31

¹⁷ As he was setting out on a journey, a man ran up and knelt before him, and asked him, 'Good Teacher, what must I do to inherit eternal life?' ¹⁸ Jesus said to him, 'Why do you call me good? No one is good but God alone. ¹⁹ You know the commandments: "You shall not murder; You shall not commit adultery; You shall not steal; You shall not bear false witness; You shall not defraud; Honour your father and mother." ' ²⁰ He said to him, 'Teacher, I have kept all these since my youth.' ²¹ Jesus, looking at him, loved him and said, 'You lack one thing; go, sell what you own, and give the money to the poor, and you will have treasure in heaven; then come, follow me.' ²² When he heard this, he was shocked and went away grieving, for he had many possessions.

²³ Then Jesus looked around and said to his disciples, 'How hard it will be for those who have wealth to enter the kingdom of God!' ²⁴ And the disciples were perplexed at these words. But Jesus said to them again, 'Children, how hard it is to enter the kingdom of God! ²⁵ It is easier for a camel to go through the eye of a needle than for someone who is rich to enter the

kingdom of God.' ²⁶ They were greatly astounded and said to one another, 'Then who can be saved?' ²⁷ Jesus looked at them and said, 'For mortals it is impossible, but not for God; for God all things are possible.'

²⁸ Peter began to say to him, 'Look, we have left everything and followed you.' ²⁹ Jesus said, 'Truly I tell you, there is no one who has left house or brothers or sisters or mother or father or children or fields, for my sake and for the sake of the good news, ³⁰ who will not receive a hundredfold now in this age—houses, brothers and sisters, mothers and children, and fields, with persecutions—and in the age to come eternal life. ³¹ But many who are first will be last, and the last will be first.'

RELATED

READING   Amos 5.6–7, 10–15

⁶   Seek the LORD and live,
        or he will break out against the house of Joseph like fire,
        and it will devour Bethel, with no one to quench it.
⁷   Ah, you that turn justice to wormwood,
        and bring righteousness to the ground!

¹⁰ They hate the one who reproves in the gate,
        and they abhor the one who speaks the truth.
¹¹ Therefore, because you trample on the poor
        and take from them levies of grain,
    you have built houses of hewn stone,
        but you shall not live in them;
    you have planted pleasant vineyards,
        but you shall not drink their wine.
¹² For I know how many are your transgressions,
        and how great are your sins—
    you who afflict the righteous, who take a bribe,
        and push aside the needy in the gate.
¹³ Therefore the prudent will keep silent in such a time;
        for it is an evil time.
¹⁴ Seek good and not evil,
        that you may live;
    and so the LORD, the God of hosts, will be with you,
        just as you have said.
¹⁵ Hate evil and love good,
        and establish justice in the gate;
    it may be that the LORD, the God of hosts,
        will be gracious to the remnant of Joseph.

PSALM   Psalm 90.12-17

¹² So teach us to number our days
　　that we may apply our hearts to wisdom.
¹³ Return, O Lord; how long will you tarry?
　　be gracious to your servants.
¹⁴ Satisfy us by your loving-kindness in the morning;
　　so shall we rejoice and be glad all the days of our life.
¹⁵ Make us glad by the measure of the days that you afflicted us
　　and the years in which we suffered adversity.
¹⁶ Show your servants your works
　　and your splendour to their children.
¹⁷ May the graciousness of the Lord our God be upon us;
　　prosper the work of our hands; prosper our handiwork.

READING   Hebrews 4.12-16

[12] Indeed, the word of God is living and active, sharper than any two-edged sword, piercing until it divides soul from spirit, joints from marrow; it is able to judge the thoughts and intentions of the heart. [13] And before him no creature is hidden, but all are naked and laid bare to the eyes of the one to whom we must render an account.

[14] Since, then, we have a great high priest who has passed through the heavens, Jesus, the Son of God, let us hold fast to our confession. [15] For we do not have a high priest who is unable to sympathize with our weaknesses, but we have one who in every respect has been tested as we are, yet without sin. [16] Let us therefore approach the throne of grace with boldness, so that we may receive mercy and find grace to help in time of need.

GOSPEL   Mark 10.17-31

[17] As he was setting out on a journey, a man ran up and knelt before him, and asked him, 'Good Teacher, what must I do to inherit eternal life?' [18] Jesus said to him, 'Why do you call me good? No one is good but God alone. [19] You know the commandments: "You shall not murder; You shall not commit adultery; You shall not steal; You shall not bear false witness; You shall not defraud; Honour your father and mother." ' [20] He said to him, 'Teacher, I have kept all these since my youth.' [21] Jesus, looking at him, loved him and said, 'You lack one thing; go, sell what you own, and give the money to the poor, and you will have treasure in heaven; then come, follow me.' [22] When he heard this, he was shocked and went away grieving, for he had many possessions.

23 Then Jesus looked around and said to his disciples, 'How hard it will be for those who have wealth to enter the kingdom of God!' 24 And the disciples were perplexed at these words. But Jesus said to them again, 'Children, how hard it is to enter the kingdom of God! 25 It is easier for a camel to go through the eye of a needle than for someone who is rich to enter the kingdom of God.' 26 They were greatly astounded and said to one another, 'Then who can be saved?' 27 Jesus looked at them and said, 'For mortals it is impossible, but not for God; for God all things are possible.'

28 Peter began to say to him, 'Look, we have left everything and followed you.' 29 Jesus said, 'Truly I tell you, there is no one who has left house or brothers or sisters or mother or father or children or fields, for my sake and for the sake of the good news, 30 who will not receive a hundredfold now in this age—houses, brothers and sisters, mothers and children, and fields, with persecutions—and in the age to come eternal life. 31 But many who are first will be last, and the last will be first.'

POST COMMUNION

See pages 580 to 584 and Table on page 568

SECOND SERVICE

Psalms 127; [128]
Joshua 5.13–6.20
Matthew 11.20–30

THIRD SERVICE

Psalms 129; 130
Isaiah 50.4–10
Luke 13.22–30

PROPER 24

Sunday between 16 and 22 October inclusive

COLLECT

See pages 581 to 584 and Table on page 568

CONTINUOUS

READING   Job 38.1–7, [34–41]

1   Then the LORD answered Job out of the whirlwind:
2   'Who is this that darkens counsel by words without knowledge?
3   Gird up your loins like a man,
     I will question you, and you shall declare to me.
4   Where were you when I laid the foundation of the earth?
     Tell me, if you have understanding.
5   Who determined its measurements—surely you know!
     Or who stretched the line upon it?
6   On what were its bases sunk,
     or who laid its cornerstone
7   when the morning stars sang together
     and all the heavenly beings shouted for joy?'

[34   'Can you lift up your voice to the clouds,
     so that a flood of waters may cover you?
35   Can you send forth lightnings, so that they may go
     and say to you, "Here we are"?
36   Who has put wisdom in the inward parts,
     or given understanding to the mind?
37   Who has the wisdom to number the clouds?
     Or who can tilt the waterskins of the heavens,
38   when the dust runs into a mass
     and the clods cling together?
39   Can you hunt the prey for the lion,
     or satisfy the appetite of the young lions,
40   when they crouch in their dens,
     or lie in wait in their covert?
41   Who provides for the raven its prey,
     when its young ones cry to God,
     and wander about for lack of food?']

PSALM   Psalm 104.1–9, [25, 37b]

1 Bless the Lord, O my soul;
> O Lord my God, how excellent is your greatness! you are clothed
> > with majesty and splendour.
2 You wrap yourself with light as with a cloak
> and spread out the heavens like a curtain.
3 You lay the beams of your chambers in the waters above;
> you make the clouds your chariot; you ride on the wings of the
> > wind.
4 You make the winds your messengers
> and flames of fire your servants.
5 You have set the earth upon its foundations,
> so that it never shall move at any time.
6 You covered it with the deep as with a mantle;
> the waters stood higher than the mountains.
7 At your rebuke they fled;
> at the voice of your thunder they hastened away.
8 They went up into the hills and down to the valleys beneath,
> to the places you had appointed for them.
9 You set the limits that they should not pass;
> they shall not again cover the earth.

[25 O Lord, how manifold are your works!
> in wisdom you have made them all; the earth is full of your
> > creatures.

37 Alleluia!]

READING   Hebrews 5.1–10

1 Every high priest chosen from among mortals is put in charge of things pertaining to God on their behalf, to offer gifts and sacrifices for sins. 2 He is able to deal gently with the ignorant and wayward, since he himself is subject to weakness; 3 and because of this he must offer sacrifice for his own sins as well as for those of the people. 4 And one does not presume to take this honour, but takes it only when called by God, just as Aaron was.

5 So also Christ did not glorify himself in becoming a high priest, but was appointed by the one who said to him,
> 'You are my Son,
> > today I have begotten you';
6 as he says also in another place,
> 'You are a priest for ever,
> > according to the order of Melchizedek.'

[7] In the days of his flesh, Jesus offered up prayers and supplications, with loud cries and tears, to the one who was able to save him from death, and he was heard because of his reverent submission. [8] Although he was a Son, he learned obedience through what he suffered; [9] and having been made perfect, he became the source of eternal salvation for all who obey him, [10] having been designated by God a high priest according to the order of Melchizedek.

GOSPEL   Mark 10.35–45

[35] James and John, the sons of Zebedee, came forward to him and said to him, 'Teacher, we want you to do for us whatever we ask of you.' [36] And he said to them, 'What is it you want me to do for you?' [37] And they said to him, 'Grant us to sit, one at your right hand and one at your left, in your glory.' [38] But Jesus said to them, 'You do not know what you are asking. Are you able to drink the cup that I drink, or be baptized with the baptism that I am baptized with?' [39] They replied, 'We are able.' Then Jesus said to them, 'The cup that I drink you will drink; and with the baptism with which I am baptized, you will be baptized; [40] but to sit at my right hand or at my left is not mine to grant, but it is for those for whom it has been prepared.'

[41] When the ten heard this, they began to be angry with James and John. [42] So Jesus called them and said to them, 'You know that among the Gentiles those whom they recognize as their rulers lord it over them, and their great ones are tyrants over them. [43] But it is not so among you; but whoever wishes to become great among you must be your servant, [44] and whoever wishes to be first among you must be slave of all. [45] For the Son of Man came not to be served but to serve, and to give his life a ransom for many.'

RELATED

READING   Isaiah 53.4–12

[4]   Surely he has borne our infirmities
          and carried our diseases;
       yet we accounted him stricken,
          struck down by God, and afflicted.
[5]   But he was wounded for our transgressions,
          crushed for our iniquities;
       upon him was the punishment that made us whole,
          and by his bruises we are healed.

6 All we like sheep have gone astray;
    we have all turned to our own way,
  and the LORD has laid on him
    the iniquity of us all.
7 He was oppressed, and he was afflicted,
    yet he did not open his mouth;
  like a lamb that is led to the slaughter,
    and like a sheep that before its shearers is silent,
    so he did not open his mouth.
8 By a perversion of justice he was taken away.
    Who could have imagined his future?
  For he was cut off from the land of the living,
    stricken for the transgression of my people.
9 They made his grave with the wicked
    and his tomb with the rich,
  although he had done no violence,
    and there was no deceit in his mouth.
10 Yet it was the will of the LORD to crush him with pain.
  When you make his life an offering for sin,
    he shall see his offspring, and shall prolong his days;
  through him the will of the LORD shall prosper.
11   Out of his anguish he shall see light;
  he shall find satisfaction through his knowledge.
    The righteous one, my servant, shall make many righteous,
    and he shall bear their iniquities.
12 Therefore I will allot him a portion with the great,
    and he shall divide the spoil with the strong;
  because he poured out himself to death,
    and was numbered with the transgressors;
  yet he bore the sin of many,
    and made intercession for the transgressors.

PSALM   Psalm 91.9–16

9 Because you have made the Lord your refuge,
    and the Most High your habitation.
10 There shall no evil happen to you,
    neither shall any plague come near your dwelling.
11 For he shall give his angels charge over you,
    to keep you in all your ways.
12 They shall bear you in their hands,
    lest you dash your foot against a stone.

13 You shall tread upon the lion and adder;
    you shall trample the young lion and the serpent under your feet.
14 Because he is bound to me in love, therefore will I deliver him;
    I will protect him, because he knows my name.
15 He shall call upon me and I will answer him;
    I am with him in trouble, I will rescue him and bring him to
        honour.
16 With long life will I satisfy him,
    and show him my salvation.

READING   Hebrews 5.1–10

¹ Every high priest chosen from among mortals is put in charge of things pertaining to God on their behalf, to offer gifts and sacrifices for sins. ² He is able to deal gently with the ignorant and wayward, since he himself is subject to weakness; ³ and because of this he must offer sacrifice for his own sins as well as for those of the people. ⁴ And one does not presume to take this honour, but takes it only when called by God, just as Aaron was.

⁵ So also Christ did not glorify himself in becoming a high priest, but was appointed by the one who said to him,
    'You are my Son,
        today I have begotten you';
⁶ as he says also in another place,
    'You are a priest for ever,
        according to the order of Melchizedek.'

⁷ In the days of his flesh, Jesus offered up prayers and supplications, with loud cries and tears, to the one who was able to save him from death, and he was heard because of his reverent submission. ⁸ Although he was a Son, he learned obedience through what he suffered; ⁹ and having been made perfect, he became the source of eternal salvation for all who obey him, ¹⁰ having been designated by God a high priest according to the order of Melchizedek.

GOSPEL   Mark 10.35–45

³⁵ James and John, the sons of Zebedee, came forward to him and said to him, 'Teacher, we want you to do for us whatever we ask of you.' ³⁶ And he said to them, 'What is it you want me to do for you?' ³⁷ And they said to him, 'Grant us to sit, one at your right hand and one at your left, in your glory.' ³⁸ But Jesus said to them, 'You do not know what you are asking. Are you able to drink the cup that I drink, or be baptized with the baptism that I am baptized with?' ³⁹ They replied, 'We are able.' Then Jesus said to them,

'The cup that I drink you will drink; and with the baptism with which I am baptized, you will be baptized; ⁴⁰ but to sit at my right hand or at my left is not mine to grant, but it is for those for whom it has been prepared.'

⁴¹ When the ten heard this, they began to be angry with James and John. ⁴² So Jesus called them and said to them, 'You know that among the Gentiles those whom they recognize as their rulers lord it over them, and their great ones are tyrants over them. ⁴³ But it is not so among you; but whoever wishes to become great among you must be your servant, ⁴⁴ and whoever wishes to be first among you must be slave of all. ⁴⁵ For the Son of Man came not to be served but to serve, and to give his life a ransom for many.'

POST COMMUNION

See pages 581 to 585 and Table on page 568

SECOND SERVICE

Psalm 141
Joshua 14.6–14
Matthew 12.1–21

THIRD SERVICE

Psalms 133; 134; 137.1–6
Isaiah 54.1–14
Luke 13.31–35

PROPER 25

Sunday between 23 and 29 October inclusive

COLLECT

See page 584 and Table on page 568

CONTINUOUS

READING   Job 42.1–6, 10–17

¹ Then Job answered the LORD:
² 'I know that you can do all things,
   and that no purpose of yours can be thwarted.
³ "Who is this that hides counsel without knowledge?"
   Therefore I have uttered what I did not understand,
   things too wonderful for me, which I did not know.
⁴ "Hear, and I will speak;
   I will question you, and you declare to me."

⁵   I had heard of you by the hearing of the ear,
    but now my eye sees you;
⁶   therefore I despise myself,
    and repent in dust and ashes.'

¹⁰ And the LORD restored the fortunes of Job when he had prayed for his friends; and the LORD gave Job twice as much as he had before. ¹¹ Then there came to him all his brothers and sisters and all who had known him before, and they ate bread with him in his house; they showed him sympathy and comforted him for all the evil that the LORD had brought upon him; and each of them gave him a piece of money and a gold ring. ¹² The LORD blessed the latter days of Job more than his beginning; and he had fourteen thousand sheep, six thousand camels, a thousand yoke of oxen, and a thousand donkeys. ¹³ He also had seven sons and three daughters. ¹⁴ He named the first Jemimah, the second Keziah, and the third Keren-happuch. ¹⁵ In all the land there were no women so beautiful as Job's daughters; and their father gave them an inheritance along with their brothers. ¹⁶ After this Job lived for one hundred and forty years, and saw his children, and his children's children, four generations. ¹⁷ And Job died, old and full of days.

PSALM   Psalm 34.1–8, [19–22]

¹   I will bless the Lord at all times;
    his praise shall ever be in my mouth.
²   I will glory in the Lord;
    let the humble hear and rejoice.
³   Proclaim with me the greatness of the Lord;
    let us exalt his name together.
⁴   I sought the Lord and he answered me
    and delivered me out of all my terror.
⁵   Look upon him and be radiant,
    and let not your faces be ashamed.
⁶   I called in my affliction and the Lord heard me
    and saved me from all my troubles.
⁷   The angel of the Lord encompasses those who fear him,
    and he will deliver them.
⁸   Taste and see that the Lord is good;
    happy are they who trust in him!

[¹⁹   Many are the troubles of the righteous,
    but the Lord will deliver him out of them all.
²⁰   He will keep safe all his bones;
    not one of them shall be broken.

21 Evil shall slay the wicked,
    and those who hate the righteous will be punished.
22 The Lord ransoms the life of his servants,
    and none will be punished who trust in him.]

READING   Hebrews 7.23–28

23 Furthermore, the former priests were many in number, because they were prevented by death from continuing in office; 24 but he holds his priesthood permanently, because he continues for ever. 25 Consequently he is able for all time to save those who approach God through him, since he always lives to make intercession for them.

26 For it was fitting that we should have such a high priest, holy, blameless, undefiled, separated from sinners, and exalted above the heavens. 27 Unlike the other high priests, he has no need to offer sacrifices day after day, first for his own sins, and then for those of the people; this he did once for all when he offered himself. 28 For the law appoints as high priests those who are subject to weakness, but the word of the oath, which came later than the law, appoints a Son who has been made perfect for ever.

GOSPEL   Mark 10.46–52

46 They came to Jericho. As he and his disciples and a large crowd were leaving Jericho, Bartimaeus son of Timaeus, a blind beggar, was sitting by the roadside. 47 When he heard that it was Jesus of Nazareth, he began to shout out and say, 'Jesus, Son of David, have mercy on me!' 48 Many sternly ordered him to be quiet, but he cried out even more loudly, 'Son of David, have mercy on me!' 49 Jesus stood still and said, 'Call him here.' And they called the blind man, saying to him, 'Take heart; get up, he is calling you.' 50 So throwing off his cloak, he sprang up and came to Jesus. 51 Then Jesus said to him, 'What do you want me to do for you?' The blind man said to him, 'My teacher, let me see again.' 52 Jesus said to him, 'Go; your faith has made you well.' Immediately he regained his sight and followed him on the way.

RELATED

READING   Jeremiah 31.7–9

⁷ For thus says the LORD:
  Sing aloud with gladness for Jacob,
    and raise shouts for the chief of the nations;
  proclaim, give praise, and say,
    'Save, O LORD, your people,
    the remnant of Israel.'
⁸ See, I am going to bring them from the land of the north,
    and gather them from the farthest parts of the earth,
  among them the blind and the lame,
    those with child and those in labour, together;
    a great company, they shall return here.
⁹ With weeping they shall come,
    and with consolations I will lead them back,
  I will let them walk by brooks of water,
    in a straight path in which they shall not stumble;
  for I have become a father to Israel,
    and Ephraim is my firstborn.

PSALM   Psalm 126

¹ When the Lord restored the fortunes of Zion,
  then were we like those who dream.
² Then was our mouth filled with laughter,
  and our tongue with shouts of joy.
³ Then they said among the nations,
  'The Lord has done great things for them.'
⁴ The Lord has done great things for us,
  and we are glad indeed.
⁵ Restore our fortunes, O Lord,
  like the watercourses of the Negev.
⁶ Those who sowed with tears
  will reap with songs of joy.
⁷ Those who go out weeping, carrying the seed,
  will come again with joy, shouldering their sheaves.

READING   Hebrews 7.23–28

²³ Furthermore, the former priests were many in number, because they were prevented by death from continuing in office; ²⁴ but he holds his

priesthood permanently, because he continues for ever. ²⁵ Consequently he is able for all time to save those who approach God through him, since he always lives to make intercession for them.

²⁶ For it was fitting that we should have such a high priest, holy, blameless, undefiled, separated from sinners, and exalted above the heavens. ²⁷ Unlike the other high priests, he has no need to offer sacrifices day after day, first for his own sins, and then for those of the people; this he did once for all when he offered himself. ²⁸ For the law appoints as high priests those who are subject to weakness, but the word of the oath, which came later than the law, appoints a Son who has been made perfect for ever.

GOSPEL   Mark 10.46–52

⁴⁶ They came to Jericho. As he and his disciples and a large crowd were leaving Jericho, Bartimaeus son of Timaeus, a blind beggar, was sitting by the roadside. ⁴⁷ When he heard that it was Jesus of Nazareth, he began to shout out and say, 'Jesus, Son of David, have mercy on me!' ⁴⁸ Many sternly ordered him to be quiet, but he cried out even more loudly, 'Son of David, have mercy on me!' ⁴⁹ Jesus stood still and said, 'Call him here.' And they called the blind man, saying to him, 'Take heart; get up, he is calling you.' ⁵⁰ So throwing off his cloak, he sprang up and came to Jesus. ⁵¹ Then Jesus said to him, 'What do you want me to do for you?' The blind man said to him, 'My teacher, let me see again.' ⁵² Jesus said to him, 'Go; your faith has made you well.' Immediately he regained his sight and followed him on the way.

POST COMMUNION

See page 585 and Table on page 568

SECOND SERVICE

Psalm 119.121–136
Ecclesiastes 11; 12
2 Timothy 2.1–7

If the Second Service is a Eucharist, the following is read as a Gospel:

Luke 18.9–14

THIRD SERVICE

Psalm 119.89–104
Isaiah 59.9–20
Luke 14.1–14

ALL SAINTS' DAY span style="float:right">1 NOVEMBER

Sunday between 30 October and 5 November or, if this is not kept as All Saints' Sunday, on 1 November itself

COLLECT

Almighty God,
you have knit together your elect
in one communion and fellowship
   in the mystical body of your Son Christ our Lord:
grant us grace so to follow your blessed saints
in all virtuous and godly living
that we may come to those inexpressible joys
that you have prepared for those who truly love you;
through Jesus Christ your Son our Lord,
who is alive and reigns with you,
in the unity of the Holy Spirit,
one God, now and for ever.

READING

EITHER span style="float:right">**Wisdom 3.1–9**

1 But the souls of the righteous are in the hand of God,
  and no torment will ever touch them.
2 In the eyes of the foolish they seemed to have died,
  and their departure was thought to be a disaster,
3 and their going from us to be their destruction;
  but they are at peace.
4 For though in the sight of others they were punished,
  their hope is full of immortality.
5 Having been disciplined a little, they will receive great good,
  because God tested them and found them worthy of himself;
6 like gold in the furnace he tried them,
  and like a sacrificial burnt-offering he accepted them.
7 In the time of their visitation they will shine forth,
  and will run like sparks through the stubble.
8 They will govern nations and rule over peoples,
  and the Lord will reign over them for ever.

⁹ Those who trust in him will understand truth,
   and the faithful will abide with him in love,
   because grace and mercy are upon his holy ones,
   and he watches over his elect.

OR   Isaiah 25.6–9

⁶ On this mountain the LORD of hosts will make for all peoples
     a feast of rich food, a feast of well-matured wines,
     of rich food filled with marrow, of well-matured wines strained clear.
⁷ And he will destroy on this mountain
     the shroud that is cast over all peoples,
     the sheet that is spread over all nations;
⁸ he will swallow up death for ever.
   Then the Lord GOD will wipe away the tears from all faces,
     and the disgrace of his people he will take away from all the earth,
     for the LORD has spoken.
⁹ It will be said on that day,
     Lo, this is our God; we have waited for him, so that he might save us.
     This is the LORD for whom we have waited;
     let us be glad and rejoice in his salvation.

PSALM   Psalm 24.1–6

¹ The earth is the Lord's and all that is in it,
   the world and all who dwell therein.
² For it is he who founded it upon the seas
   and made it firm upon the rivers of the deep.
³ 'Who can ascend the hill of the Lord?
   and who can stand in his holy place?'
⁴ 'Those who have clean hands and a pure heart,
   who have not pledged themselves to falsehood, nor sworn by what
     is a fraud.
⁵ They shall receive a blessing from the Lord
   and a just reward from the God of their salvation.'
⁶ Such is the generation of those who seek him,
   of those who seek your face, O God of Jacob.

READING   Revelation 21.1–6a

¹ Then I saw a new heaven and a new earth; for the first heaven and the
first earth had passed away, and the sea was no more. ² And I saw the holy
city, the new Jerusalem, coming down out of heaven from God, prepared

as a bride adorned for her husband. ³ And I heard a loud voice from the throne saying,

'See, the home of God is among mortals.
He will dwell with them;
they will be his peoples,
and God himself will be with them;
⁴ he will wipe every tear from their eyes.
Death will be no more;
mourning and crying and pain will be no more,
for the first things have passed away.'

⁵ And the one who was seated on the throne said, 'See, I am making all things new.' Also he said, 'Write this, for these words are trustworthy and true.' ⁶ Then he said to me, 'It is done! I am the Alpha and the Omega, the beginning and the end.'

GOSPEL   John 11.32–44

³² When Mary came where Jesus was and saw him, she knelt at his feet and said to him, 'Lord, if you had been here, my brother would not have died.' ³³ When Jesus saw her weeping, and the Jews who came with her also weeping, he was greatly disturbed in spirit and deeply moved. ³⁴ He said, 'Where have you laid him?' They said to him, 'Lord, come and see.' ³⁵ Jesus began to weep. ³⁶ So the Jews said, 'See how he loved him!' ³⁷ But some of them said, 'Could not he who opened the eyes of the blind man have kept this man from dying?'

³⁸ Then Jesus, again greatly disturbed, came to the tomb. It was a cave, and a stone was lying against it. ³⁹ Jesus said, 'Take away the stone.' Martha, the sister of the dead man, said to him, 'Lord, already there is a stench because he has been dead for four days.' ⁴⁰ Jesus said to her, 'Did I not tell you that if you believed, you would see the glory of God?' ⁴¹ So they took away the stone. And Jesus looked upwards and said, 'Father, I thank you for having heard me. ⁴² I knew that you always hear me, but I have said this for the sake of the crowd standing here, so that they may believe that you sent me.' ⁴³ When he had said this, he cried with a loud voice, 'Lazarus, come out!' ⁴⁴ The dead man came out, his hands and feet bound with strips of cloth, and his face wrapped in a cloth. Jesus said to them, 'Unbind him, and let him go.'

POST COMMUNION

God, the source of all holiness
   and giver of all good things:
may we who have shared at this table
   as strangers and pilgrims here on earth
be welcomed with all your saints
   to the heavenly feast on the day of your kingdom;
through Jesus Christ our Lord.

On 1 November if the material above is used on the Sunday

COLLECT

Almighty God,
you have knit together your elect
in one communion and fellowship
   in the mystical body of your Son Christ our Lord:
grant us grace so to follow your blessed saints
in all virtuous and godly living
that we may come to those inexpressible joys
that you have prepared for those who truly love you;
through Jesus Christ your Son our Lord,
who is alive and reigns with you,
in the unity of the Holy Spirit,
one God, now and for ever.

READING

EITHER   Isaiah 56.3–8

³ Do not let the foreigner joined to the Lord say,
   'The Lord will surely separate me from his people';
 and do not let the eunuch say,
   'I am just a dry tree.'
⁴ For thus says the Lord:
 To the eunuchs who keep my sabbaths,
   who choose the things that please me
   and hold fast my covenant,
⁵ I will give, in my house and within my walls,
   a monument and a name
   better than sons and daughters;
 I will give them an everlasting name
   that shall not be cut off.

6 And the foreigners who join themselves to the LORD,
    to minister to him, to love the name of the LORD,
    and to be his servants,
  all who keep the sabbath, and do not profane it,
    and hold fast my covenant—
7 these I will bring to my holy mountain,
    and make them joyful in my house of prayer;
  their burnt-offerings and their sacrifices
    will be accepted on my altar;
  for my house shall be called a house of prayer
    for all peoples.
8 Thus says the Lord GOD,
    who gathers the outcasts of Israel,
  I will gather others to them
    besides those already gathered.

OR   2 Esdras 2.42–48

42 I, Ezra, saw on Mount Zion a great multitude that I could not number, and they all were praising the Lord with songs. 43 In their midst was a young man of great stature, taller than any of the others, and on the head of each of them he placed a crown, but he was more exalted than they. And I was held spellbound. 44 Then I asked an angel, 'Who are these, my lord?' 45 He answered and said to me, 'These are they who have put off mortal clothing and have put on the immortal, and have confessed the name of God. Now they are being crowned, and receive palms.' 46 Then I said to the angel, 'Who is that young man who is placing crowns on them and putting palms in their hands?' 47 He answered and said to me, 'He is the Son of God, whom they confessed in the world.' So I began to praise those who had stood valiantly for the name of the Lord. 48 Then the angel said to me, 'Go, tell my people how great and how many are the wonders of the Lord God that you have seen.'

PSALM   Psalm 33.1–5

1 Rejoice in the Lord, you righteous;
    it is good for the just to sing praises.
2 Praise the Lord with the harp;
    play to him upon the psaltery and lyre.
3 Sing for him a new song;
    sound a fanfare with all your skill upon the trumpet.

4 For the word of the Lord is right,
   and all his works are sure.
5 He loves righteousness and justice;
   the loving-kindness of the Lord fills the whole earth.

READING   Hebrews 12.18–24

18 You have not come to something that can be touched, a blazing fire, and darkness, and gloom, and a tempest, 19 and the sound of a trumpet, and a voice whose words made the hearers beg that not another word be spoken to them. 20 (For they could not endure the order that was given, 'If even an animal touches the mountain, it shall be stoned to death.' 21 Indeed, so terrifying was the sight that Moses said, 'I tremble with fear.') 22 But you have come to Mount Zion and to the city of the living God, the heavenly Jerusalem, and to innumerable angels in festal gathering, 23 and to the assembly of the firstborn who are enrolled in heaven, and to God the judge of all, and to the spirits of the righteous made perfect, 24 and to Jesus, the mediator of a new covenant, and to the sprinkled blood that speaks a better word than the blood of Abel.

GOSPEL   Matthew 5.1–12

1 When Jesus saw the crowds, he went up the mountain; and after he sat down, his disciples came to him. 2 Then he began to speak, and taught them, saying:

3 'Blessed are the poor in spirit, for theirs is the kingdom of heaven.

4 'Blessed are those who mourn, for they will be comforted.

5 'Blessed are the meek, for they will inherit the earth.

6 'Blessed are those who hunger and thirst for righteousness, for they will be filled.

7 'Blessed are the merciful, for they will receive mercy.

8 'Blessed are the pure in heart, for they will see God.

9 'Blessed are the peacemakers, for they will be called children of God.

10 'Blessed are those who are persecuted for righteousness' sake, for theirs is the kingdom of heaven.

11 'Blessed are you when people revile you and persecute you and utter all kinds of evil against you falsely on my account. 12 Rejoice and be glad, for your reward is great in heaven, for in the same way they persecuted the prophets who were before you.'

POST COMMUNION

God, the source of all holiness
    and giver of all good things:
may we who have shared at this table
    as strangers and pilgrims here on earth
be welcomed with all your saints
    to the heavenly feast on the day of your kingdom;
through Jesus Christ our Lord.

THE FOURTH SUNDAY BEFORE ADVENT

Sunday between 30 October and 5 November inclusive. For use if the Feast of All Saints was celebrated on 1 November and alternative propers are needed.

COLLECT

Almighty and eternal God,
you have kindled the flame of love
    in the hearts of the saints:
grant to us the same faith and power of love,
that, as we rejoice in their triumphs,
we may be sustained by their example and fellowship;
through Jesus Christ your Son our Lord,
who is alive and reigns with you,
in the unity of the Holy Spirit,
one God, now and for ever.

READING   Deuteronomy 6.1–9

¹ Now this is the commandment—the statutes and the ordinances—that the LORD your God charged me to teach you to observe in the land that you are about to cross into and occupy, ² so that you and your children and your children's children may fear the LORD your God all the days of your life, and keep all his decrees and his commandments that I am commanding you, so that your days may be long. ³ Hear therefore, O Israel, and observe them diligently, so that it may go well with you, and so that you may multiply greatly in a land flowing with milk and honey, as the LORD, the God of your ancestors, has promised you.

⁴ Hear, O Israel: The LORD is our God, the LORD alone. ⁵ You shall love the LORD your God with all your heart, and with all your soul, and with all your might. ⁶ Keep these words that I am commanding you today in your

heart. [7] Recite them to your children and talk about them when you are at home and when you are away, when you lie down and when you rise. [8] Bind them as a sign on your hand, fix them as an emblem on your forehead, [9] and write them on the doorposts of your house and on your gates.

PSALM   Psalm 119.1–8

[1] Happy are they whose way is blameless,
     who walk in the law of the Lord!
[2] Happy are they who observe his decrees
     and seek him with all their hearts!
[3] Who never do any wrong,
     but always walk in his ways.
[4] You laid down your commandments,
     that we should fully keep them.
[5] O that my ways were made so direct
     that I might keep your statutes!
[6] Then I should not be put to shame,
     when I regard all your commandments.
[7] I will thank you with an unfeigned heart,
     when I have learned your righteous judgements.
[8] I will keep your statutes;
     do not utterly forsake me.

READING   Hebrews 9.11–14

[11] But when Christ came as a high priest of the good things that have come, then through the greater and perfect tent (not made with hands, that is, not of this creation), [12] he entered once for all into the Holy Place, not with the blood of goats and calves, but with his own blood, thus obtaining eternal redemption. [13] For if the blood of goats and bulls, with the sprinkling of the ashes of a heifer, sanctifies those who have been defiled so that their flesh is purified, [14] how much more will the blood of Christ, who through the eternal Spirit offered himself without blemish to God, purify our conscience from dead works to worship the living God!

GOSPEL   Mark 12.28–34

[28] One of the scribes came near and heard them disputing with one another, and seeing that he answered them well, he asked him, 'Which commandment is the first of all?' [29] Jesus answered, 'The first is, "Hear, O Israel: the Lord our God, the Lord is one; [30] you shall love the Lord your God with all your heart, and with all your soul, and with all your mind, and

with all your strength." [31] The second is this, "You shall love your neighbour as yourself." There is no other commandment greater than these.' [32] Then the scribe said to him, 'You are right, Teacher; you have truly said that "he is one, and besides him there is no other"; [33] and "to love him with all the heart, and with all the understanding, and with all the strength", and "to love one's neighbour as oneself",—this is much more important than all whole burnt-offerings and sacrifices.' [34] When Jesus saw that he answered wisely, he said to him, 'You are not far from the kingdom of God.' After that no one dared to ask him any question.

POST COMMUNION

Lord of heaven,
in this eucharist you have brought us near
   to an innumerable company of angels
   and to the spirits of the saints made perfect:
as in this food of our earthly pilgrimage
   we have shared their fellowship,
so may we come to share their joy in heaven;
through Jesus Christ our Lord.

SECOND SERVICE

THIRD SERVICE

Psalm 145.1–9, [10–22]
Daniel 2.1–11, [12–24,] 25–48
Revelation 7.9–17

Psalms 112; 149
Jeremiah 31.31–34
1 John 3.1–3

If the Second Service is a Eucharist, the following is read as a Gospel:

Matthew 5.1–12

THE THIRD SUNDAY BEFORE ADVENT

Sunday between 6 and 12 November inclusive

COLLECT

Almighty Father,
whose will is to restore all things
in your beloved Son, the king of all:
govern the hearts and minds of those in authority,
and bring the families of the nations,

divided and torn apart by the ravages of sin,
to be subject to his just and gentle rule;
who is alive and reigns with you,
in the unity of the Holy Spirit,
one God, now and for ever.

READING   Jonah 3.1–5, 10

¹ The word of the LORD came to Jonah a second time, saying, ² 'Get up, go
to Nineveh, that great city, and proclaim to it the message that I tell you.'
³ So Jonah set out and went to Nineveh, according to the word of the LORD.
Now Nineveh was an exceedingly large city, a three days' walk across.
⁴ Jonah began to go into the city, going a day's walk. And he cried out,
'Forty days more, and Nineveh shall be overthrown!' ⁵ And the people of
Nineveh believed God; they proclaimed a fast, and everyone, great and
small, put on sackcloth.

¹⁰ When God saw what they did, how they turned from their evil ways,
God changed his mind about the calamity that he had said he would bring
upon them; and he did not do it.

PSALM   Psalm 62.6–14

6   For God alone my soul in silence waits;
     truly, my hope is in him.
7   He alone is my rock and my salvation,
     my stronghold, so that I shall not be shaken.
8   In God is my safety and my honour;
     God is my strong rock and my refuge.
9   Put your trust in him always, O people,
     pour out your hearts before him, for God is our refuge.
10 Those of high degree are but a fleeting breath,
     even those of low estate cannot be trusted.
11 On the scales they are lighter than a breath,
     all of them together.
12 Put no trust in extortion; in robbery take no empty pride;
     though wealth increase, set not your heart upon it.
13 God has spoken once, twice have I heard it,
     that power belongs to God.
14 Steadfast love is yours, O Lord,
     for you repay everyone according to his deeds.

READING   Hebrews 9.24–28

[24] For Christ did not enter a sanctuary made by human hands, a mere copy of the true one, but he entered into heaven itself, now to appear in the presence of God on our behalf. [25] Nor was it to offer himself again and again, as the high priest enters the Holy Place year after year with blood that is not his own; [26] for then he would have had to suffer again and again since the foundation of the world. But as it is, he has appeared once for all at the end of the age to remove sin by the sacrifice of himself. [27] And just as it is appointed for mortals to die once, and after that the judgement, [28] so Christ, having been offered once to bear the sins of many, will appear a second time, not to deal with sin, but to save those who are eagerly waiting for him.

GOSPEL   Mark 1.14–20

[14] Now after John was arrested, Jesus came to Galilee, proclaiming the good news of God, [15] and saying, 'The time is fulfilled, and the kingdom of God has come near; repent, and believe in the good news.'

[16] As Jesus passed along the Sea of Galilee, he saw Simon and his brother Andrew casting a net into the lake—for they were fishermen. [17] And Jesus said to them, 'Follow me and I will make you fish for people.' [18] And immediately they left their nets and followed him. [19] As he went a little farther, he saw James son of Zebedee and his brother John, who were in their boat mending the nets. [20] Immediately he called them; and they left their father Zebedee in the boat with the hired men, and followed him.

POST COMMUNION

God of peace,
whose Son Jesus Christ proclaimed the kingdom
and restored the broken to wholeness of life:
look with compassion on the anguish of the world,
and by your healing power
make whole both people and nations;
through our Lord and Saviour Jesus Christ.

SECOND SERVICE

Psalms 46; [82]
Isaiah 10.33–11.9
John 14.[1–22,] 23–29

THIRD SERVICE

Psalm 136
Micah 4.1–5
Philippians 4.6–9

THE SECOND SUNDAY BEFORE ADVENT

Sunday between 13 and 19 November inclusive

COLLECT

Heavenly Father,
whose blessed Son was revealed
   to destroy the works of the devil
and to make us the children of God and heirs of eternal life:
grant that we, having this hope,
may purify ourselves even as he is pure;
that when he shall appear in power and great glory
we may be made like him
   in his eternal and glorious kingdom;
where he is alive and reigns with you,
in the unity of the Holy Spirit,
one God, now and for ever.

READING   Daniel 12.1–3

¹ 'At that time Michael, the great prince, the protector of your people, shall arise. There shall be a time of anguish, such as has never occurred since nations first came into existence. But at that time your people shall be delivered, everyone who is found written in the book. ² Many of those who sleep in the dust of the earth shall awake, some to everlasting life, and some to shame and everlasting contempt. ³ Those who are wise shall shine like the brightness of the sky, and those who lead many to righteousness, like the stars for ever and ever.'

PSALM   Psalm 16

¹   Protect me, O God, for I take refuge in you;
     I have said to the Lord, 'You are my Lord, my good above all other.'
²   All my delight is upon the godly that are in the land,
     upon those who are noble among the people.

3 But those who run after other gods
   shall have their troubles multiplied.
4 Their libations of blood I will not offer,
   nor take the names of their gods upon my lips.
5 O Lord, you are my portion and my cup;
   it is you who uphold my lot.
6 My boundaries enclose a pleasant land;
   indeed, I have a goodly heritage.
7 I will bless the Lord who gives me counsel;
   my heart teaches me, night after night.
8 I have set the Lord always before me;
   because he is at my right hand I shall not fall.
9 My heart, therefore, is glad and my spirit rejoices;
   my body also shall rest in hope.
10 For you will not abandon me to the grave,
   nor let your holy one see the Pit.
11 You will show me the path of life;
   in your presence there is fullness of joy, and in your right hand
      are pleasures for evermore.

READING   Hebrews 10.11–14, [15–18,] 19–25

11 And every priest stands day after day at his service, offering again and again the same sacrifices that can never take away sins. 12 But when Christ had offered for all time a single sacrifice for sins, 'he sat down at the right hand of God', 13 and since then has been waiting 'until his enemies would be made a footstool for his feet.' 14 For by a single offering he has perfected for all time those who are sanctified.

[15 And the Holy Spirit also testifies to us, for after saying,
16   'This is the covenant that I will make with them
         after those days, says the Lord:
      I will put my laws in their hearts,
         and I will write them on their minds',
17 he also adds,
      'I will remember their sins and their lawless deeds no more.'
18 Where there is forgiveness of these, there is no longer any offering for sin.]

19 Therefore, my friends, since we have confidence to enter the sanctuary by the blood of Jesus, 20 by the new and living way that he opened for us through the curtain (that is, through his flesh), 21 and since we have a great priest over the house of God, 22 let us approach with a true heart in full assurance of faith, with our hearts sprinkled clean from an evil conscience and our bodies washed with pure water. 23 Let us hold fast to the confession

of our hope without wavering, for he who has promised is faithful. [24] And let us consider how to provoke one another to love and good deeds, [25] not neglecting to meet together, as is the habit of some, but encouraging one another, and all the more as you see the Day approaching.

GOSPEL   Mark 13.1–8

[1] As he came out of the temple, one of his disciples said to him, 'Look, Teacher, what large stones and what large buildings!' [2] Then Jesus asked him, 'Do you see these great buildings? Not one stone will be left here upon another; all will be thrown down.'

[3] When he was sitting on the Mount of Olives opposite the temple, Peter, James, John, and Andrew asked him privately, [4] 'Tell us, when will this be, and what will be the sign that all these things are about to be accomplished?' [5] Then Jesus began to say to them, 'Beware that no one leads you astray. [6] Many will come in my name and say, "I am he!" and they will lead many astray. [7] When you hear of wars and rumours of wars, do not be alarmed; this must take place, but the end is still to come. [8] For nation will rise against nation, and kingdom against kingdom; there will be earthquakes in various places; there will be famines. This is but the beginning of the birth pangs.'

POST COMMUNION

Gracious Lord,
in this holy sacrament
you give substance to our hope:
bring us at the last
to that fullness of life for which we long;
through Jesus Christ our Saviour.

SECOND SERVICE   THIRD SERVICE

Psalm 95   **Psalm 96**
Daniel 3.[1–12,] 13–30   **1 Samuel 9.27–10.2a, 17–26**
Matthew 13.24–30, 36–43   **Matthew 13.31–35**

CHRIST THE KING
THE SUNDAY NEXT BEFORE ADVENT

Sunday between 20 and 26 November inclusive

COLLECT

Eternal Father,
whose Son Jesus Christ ascended to the throne of heaven
   that he might rule over all things as Lord and King:
keep the Church in the unity of the Spirit
and in the bond of peace,
and bring the whole created order to worship at his feet;
who is alive and reigns with you,
in the unity of the Holy Spirit,
one God, now and for ever.

READING   Daniel 7.9–10, 13–14

9 As I watched,
   thrones were set in place,
      and an Ancient One took his throne;
   his clothing was white as snow,
      and the hair of his head like pure wool;
   his throne was fiery flames,
      and its wheels were burning fire.
10 A stream of fire issued
   and flowed out from his presence.
A thousand thousand served him,
   and ten thousand times ten thousand stood attending him.
The court sat in judgement,
   and the books were opened.

13 As I watched in the night visions,
   I saw one like a human being
      coming with the clouds of heaven.
And he came to the Ancient One
   and was presented before him.

14 To him was given dominion
    and glory and kingship,
that all peoples, nations, and languages
    should serve him.
His dominion is an everlasting dominion
    that shall not pass away,
and his kingship is one
    that shall never be destroyed.

PSALM   Psalm 93

1 The Lord is king; he has put on splendid apparel;
    the Lord has put on his apparel and girded himself with strength.
2 He has made the whole world so sure
    that it cannot be moved;
3 Ever since the world began, your throne has been established;
    you are from everlasting.
4 The waters have lifted up, O Lord, the waters have lifted up their
    voice;
    the waters have lifted up their pounding waves.
5 Mightier than the sound of many waters, mightier than the
    breakers of the sea,
    mightier is the Lord who dwells on high.
6 Your testimonies are very sure,
    and holiness adorns your house, O Lord, for ever and for evermore.

READING   Revelation 1.4b–8

4 Grace to you and peace from him who is and who was and who is to come, and from the seven spirits who are before his throne, 5 and from Jesus Christ, the faithful witness, the firstborn of the dead, and the ruler of the kings of the earth.

To him who loves us and freed us from our sins by his blood, 6 and made us to be a kingdom, priests serving his God and Father, to him be glory and dominion for ever and ever. Amen.

7 Look! He is coming with the clouds;
    every eye will see him,
even those who pierced him;
    and on his account all the tribes of the earth will wail.
So it is to be. Amen.

8 'I am the Alpha and the Omega', says the Lord God, who is and who was and who is to come, the Almighty.

GOSPEL   John 18.33–37

[33] Then Pilate entered the headquarters again, summoned Jesus, and asked him, 'Are you the King of the Jews?' [34] Jesus answered, 'Do you ask this on your own, or did others tell you about me?' [35] Pilate replied, 'I am not a Jew, am I? Your own nation and the chief priests have handed you over to me. What have you done?' [36] Jesus answered, 'My kingdom is not from this world. If my kingdom were from this world, my followers would be fighting to keep me from being handed over to the Jews. But as it is, my kingdom is not from here.' [37] Pilate asked him, 'So you are a king?' Jesus answered, 'You say that I am a king. For this I was born, and for this I came into the world, to testify to the truth. Everyone who belongs to the truth listens to my voice.'

POST COMMUNION

Stir up, O Lord, the wills of your faithful people;
that they, plenteously bringing forth the fruit of good works,
may by you be plenteously rewarded;
through Jesus Christ our Lord.

This Post Communion may be used as the Collect at Morning and Evening Prayer during this week

SECOND SERVICE

Psalm 72.1–7, [8–19]
Daniel 5
John 6.1–15

THIRD SERVICE

Psalms 29; 110
Isaiah 32.1–8
Revelation 3.7–22

HARVEST THANKSGIVING

COLLECT

Eternal God,
you crown the year with your goodness
and you give us the fruits of the earth in their season:
grant that we may use them to your glory,
    for the relief of those in need
    and for our own well-being;
through Jesus Christ your Son our Lord,

who is alive and reigns with you,
in the unity of the Holy Spirit,
one God, now and for ever.

READING   Joel 2.21–27

21 Do not fear, O soil;
    be glad and rejoice,
      for the LORD has done great things!
22 Do not fear, you animals of the field,
    for the pastures of the wilderness are green;
    the tree bears its fruit,
      the fig tree and vine give their full yield.
23 O children of Zion, be glad
    and rejoice in the LORD your God;
    for he has given the early rain for your vindication,
    he has poured down for you abundant rain,
      the early and the later rain, as before.
24 The threshing-floors shall be full of grain,
    the vats shall overflow with wine and oil.
25 I will repay you for the years
    that the swarming locust has eaten,
    the hopper, the destroyer, and the cutter,
      my great army, which I sent against you.
26 You shall eat in plenty and be satisfied,
    and praise the name of the LORD your God,
    who has dealt wondrously with you.
And my people shall never again be put to shame.
27 You shall know that I am in the midst of Israel,
    and that I, the LORD, am your God and there is no other.
And my people shall never again
    be put to shame.

PSALM   Psalm 126

1 When the Lord restored the fortunes of Zion,
  then were we like those who dream.
2 Then was our mouth filled with laughter,
  and our tongue with shouts of joy.
3 Then they said among the nations,
  'The Lord has done great things for them.'
4 The Lord has done great things for us,
  and we are glad indeed.

⁵ Restore our fortunes, O Lord,
   like the watercourses of the Negev.
⁶ Those who sowed with tears
   will reap with songs of joy.
⁷ Those who go out weeping, carrying the seed,
   will come again with joy, shouldering their sheaves.

READING

EITHER   **1 Timothy 2.1–7**

¹ First of all, then, I urge that supplications, prayers, intercessions, and thanksgivings should be made for everyone, ² for kings and all who are in high positions, so that we may lead a quiet and peaceable life in all godliness and dignity. ³ This is right and is acceptable in the sight of God our Saviour, ⁴ who desires everyone to be saved and to come to the knowledge of the truth. ⁵ For
   there is one God;
      there is also one mediator between God and humankind,
   Christ Jesus, himself human,
⁶   who gave himself a ransom for all
—this was attested at the right time. ⁷ For this I was appointed a herald and an apostle (I am telling the truth, I am not lying), a teacher of the Gentiles in faith and truth.

OR   **1 Timothy 6.6–10**

⁶ Of course, there is great gain in godliness combined with contentment; ⁷ for we brought nothing into the world, so that we can take nothing out of it; ⁸ but if we have food and clothing, we will be content with these. ⁹ But those who want to be rich fall into temptation and are trapped by many senseless and harmful desires that plunge people into ruin and destruction. ¹⁰ For the love of money is a root of all kinds of evil, and in their eagerness to be rich some have wandered away from the faith and pierced themselves with many pains.

GOSPEL   **Matthew 6.25–33**

²⁵ 'Therefore I tell you, do not worry about your life, what you will eat or what you will drink, or about your body, what you will wear. Is not life more than food, and the body more than clothing? ²⁶ Look at the birds of the air; they neither sow nor reap nor gather into barns, and yet your heavenly Father feeds them. Are you not of more value than they? ²⁷ And

can any of you by worrying add a single hour to your span of life? [28] And why do you worry about clothing? Consider the lilies of the field, how they grow; they neither toil nor spin, [29] yet I tell you, even Solomon in all his glory was not clothed like one of these. [30] But if God so clothes the grass of the field, which is alive today and tomorrow is thrown into the oven, will he not much more clothe you—you of little faith? [31] Therefore do not worry, saying, "What will we eat?" or "What will we drink?" or "What will we wear?" [32] For it is the Gentiles who strive for all these things; and indeed your heavenly Father knows that you need all these things. [33] But strive first for the kingdom of God and his righteousness, and all these things will be given to you as well.'

POST COMMUNION

Lord of the harvest,
with joy we have offered thanksgiving
    for your love in creation
and have shared in the bread and the wine of the kingdom:
by your grace plant within us a reverence for all that you give us
and make us generous and wise stewards
of the good things we enjoy;
through Jesus Christ our Lord.

BIBLE SUNDAY

Bible Sunday may be celebrated in preference to the provision for the Last Sunday after Trinity

COLLECT

Blessed Lord,
who caused all holy scriptures
    to be written for our learning:
help us so to hear them,
to read, mark, learn, and inwardly digest them
that, through patience, and the comfort of your holy word,
we may embrace and for ever hold fast
    the hope of everlasting life,
which you have given us in our Saviour Jesus Christ,
who is alive and reigns with you,
in the unity of the Holy Spirit,
one God, now and for ever.

READING   Isaiah 55.1–11

¹ Ho, everyone who thirsts,
     come to the waters;
   and you that have no money,
     come, buy and eat!
   Come, buy wine and milk
     without money and without price.
² Why do you spend your money for that which is not bread,
     and your labour for that which does not satisfy?
   Listen carefully to me, and eat what is good,
     and delight yourselves in rich food.
³ Incline your ear, and come to me;
     listen, so that you may live.
   I will make with you an everlasting covenant,
     my steadfast, sure love for David.
⁴ See, I made him a witness to the peoples,
     a leader and commander for the peoples.
⁵ See, you shall call nations that you do not know,
     and nations that do not know you shall run to you,
   because of the LORD your God, the Holy One of Israel,
     for he has glorified you.
⁶ Seek the LORD while he may be found,
     call upon him while he is near;
⁷ let the wicked forsake their way,
     and the unrighteous their thoughts;
   let them return to the LORD, that he may have mercy on them,
     and to our God, for he will abundantly pardon.
⁸ For my thoughts are not your thoughts,
     nor are your ways my ways, says the LORD.
⁹ For as the heavens are higher than the earth,
     so are my ways higher than your ways
     and my thoughts than your thoughts.
¹⁰ For as the rain and the snow come down from heaven,
     and do not return there until they have watered the earth,
   making it bring forth and sprout,
     giving seed to the sower and bread to the eater,
¹¹ so shall my word be that goes out from my mouth;
     it shall not return to me empty,
   but it shall accomplish that which I purpose,
     and succeed in the thing for which I sent it.

PSALM   Psalm 19.7–14

7 The law of the Lord is perfect and revives the soul;
  the testimony of the Lord is sure and gives wisdom to the innocent.
8 The statutes of the Lord are just and rejoice the heart;
  the commandment of the Lord is clear and gives light to the eyes.
9 The fear of the Lord is clean and endures for ever;
  the judgements of the Lord are true and righteous altogether.
10 More to be desired are they than gold, more than much fine gold,
  sweeter far than honey, than honey in the comb.
11 By them also is your servant enlightened,
  and in keeping them there is great reward.
12 Who can tell how often he offends?
  Cleanse me from my secret faults.
13 Above all, keep your servant from presumptuous sins; let them
    not get dominion over me;
  then shall I be whole and sound, and innocent of a great offence.
14 Let the words of my mouth and the meditation of my heart be
    acceptable in your sight,
  O Lord, my strength and my redeemer.

READING   2 Timothy 3.14–4.5

14 But as for you, continue in what you have learned and firmly believed, knowing from whom you learned it, 15 and how from childhood you have known the sacred writings that are able to instruct you for salvation through faith in Christ Jesus. 16 All scripture is inspired by God and is useful for teaching, for reproof, for correction, and for training in righteousness, 17 so that everyone who belongs to God may be proficient, equipped for every good work.

1 In the presence of God and of Christ Jesus, who is to judge the living and the dead, and in view of his appearing and his kingdom, I solemnly urge you: 2 proclaim the message; be persistent whether the time is favourable or unfavourable; convince, rebuke, and encourage, with the utmost patience in teaching. 3 For the time is coming when people will not put up with sound doctrine, but having itching ears, they will accumulate for themselves teachers to suit their own desires, 4 and will turn away from listening to the truth and wander away to myths. 5 As for you, always be sober, endure suffering, do the work of an evangelist, carry out your ministry fully.

GOSPEL   John 5.36b–47

[36] 'The works that the Father has given me to complete, the very works that I am doing, testify on my behalf that the Father has sent me. [37] And the Father who sent me has himself testified on my behalf. You have never heard his voice or seen his form, [38] and you do not have his word abiding in you, because you do not believe him whom he has sent.

[39] 'You search the scriptures because you think that in them you have eternal life; and it is they that testify on my behalf. [40] Yet you refuse to come to me to have life. [41] I do not accept glory from human beings. [42] But I know that you do not have the love of God in you. [43] I have come in my Father's name, and you do not accept me; if another comes in his own name, you will accept him. [44] How can you believe when you accept glory from one another and do not seek the glory that comes from the one who alone is God? [45] Do not think that I will accuse you before the Father; your accuser is Moses, on whom you have set your hope. [46] If you believed Moses, you would believe me, for he wrote about me. [47] But if you do not believe what he wrote, how will you believe what I say?'

POST COMMUNION

God of all grace,
your Son Jesus Christ fed the hungry
with the bread of his life
and the word of his kingdom:
renew your people with your heavenly grace,
and in all our weakness
sustain us by your true and living bread;
who is alive and reigns, now and for ever.

SECOND SERVICE   THIRD SERVICE

Psalm 119.1–16   Psalm 119.89–104
2 Kings 22   Isaiah 45.22–45
Colossians 3.12–17   Matthew 24.30–35

                               or

                               Luke 14.1–14

DEDICATION FESTIVAL

The First Sunday in October or Last Sunday after Trinity

COLLECT

Almighty God,
to whose glory we celebrate the dedication
    of this house of prayer:
we praise you for the many blessings
you have given to those who worship you here:
and we pray that all who seek you in this place
    may find you,
and, being filled with the Holy Spirit,
may become a living temple acceptable to you;
through Jesus Christ your Son our Lord,
who is alive and reigns with you,
in the unity of the Holy Spirit,
one God, now and for ever.

READING

EITHER   **Genesis 28.11–18**

[11] He came to a certain place and stayed there for the night, because the sun had set. Taking one of the stones of the place, he put it under his head and lay down in that place. [12] And he dreamed that there was a ladder set up on the earth, the top of it reaching to heaven; and the angels of God were ascending and descending on it. [13] And the LORD stood beside him and said, 'I am the LORD, the God of Abraham your father and the God of Isaac; the land on which you lie I will give to you and to your offspring; [14] and your offspring shall be like the dust of the earth, and you shall spread abroad to the west and to the east and to the north and to the south; and all the families of the earth shall be blessed in you and in your offspring. [15] Know that I am with you and will keep you wherever you go, and will bring you back to this land; for I will not leave you until I have done what I have promised you.' [16] Then Jacob woke from his sleep and said, 'Surely the LORD is in this place—and I did not know it!' [17] And he was afraid, and said, 'How awesome is this place! This is none other than the house of God, and this is the gate of heaven.'

[18] So Jacob rose early in the morning, and he took the stone that he had put under his head and set it up for a pillar and poured oil on the top of it.

OR

Revelation 21.9–14

⁹ Then one of the seven angels who had the seven bowls full of the seven last plagues came and said to me, 'Come, I will show you the bride, the wife of the Lamb.' ¹⁰ And in the spirit he carried me away to a great, high mountain and showed me the holy city Jerusalem coming down out of heaven from God. ¹¹ It has the glory of God and a radiance like a very rare jewel, like jasper, clear as crystal. ¹² It has a great, high wall with twelve gates, and at the gates twelve angels, and on the gates are inscribed the names of the twelve tribes of the Israelites; ¹³ on the east three gates, on the north three gates, on the south three gates, and on the west three gates. ¹⁴ And the wall of the city has twelve foundations, and on them are the twelve names of the twelve apostles of the Lamb.

PSALM   Psalm 122

¹ I was glad when they said to me,
    'Let us go to the house of the Lord.'
² Now our feet are standing
    within your gates, O Jerusalem.
³ Jerusalem is built as a city
    that is at unity with itself.
⁴ To which the tribes go up, the tribes of the Lord,
    the assembly of Israel, to praise the name of the Lord.
⁵ For there are the thrones of judgement,
    the thrones of the house of David.
⁶ Pray for the peace of Jerusalem:
    'May they prosper who love you.
⁷ Peace be within your walls
    and quietness within your towers.
⁸ For my family and companions' sake,
    I pray for your prosperity.
⁹ Because of the house of the Lord our God,
    I will seek to do you good.'

READING   1 Peter 2.1–10

¹ Rid yourselves, therefore, of all malice, and all guile, insincerity, envy, and all slander. ² Like newborn infants, long for the pure, spiritual milk, so that by it you may grow into salvation— ³ if indeed you have tasted that the Lord is good.

⁴ Come to him, a living stone, though rejected by mortals yet chosen and precious in God's sight, and ⁵ like living stones, let yourselves be built

into a spiritual house, to be a holy priesthood, to offer spiritual sacrifices acceptable to God through Jesus Christ. [6] For it stands in scripture:

'See, I am laying in Zion a stone,
   a cornerstone chosen and precious;
and whoever believes in him will not be put to shame.'

[7] To you then who believe, he is precious; but for those who do not believe,

'The stone that the builders rejected
   has become the very head of the corner',

[8] and

'A stone that makes them stumble,
   and a rock that makes them fall.'

They stumble because they disobey the word, as they were destined to do.

[9] But you are a chosen race, a royal priesthood, a holy nation, God's own people, in order that you may proclaim the mighty acts of him who called you out of darkness into his marvellous light.

[10]   Once you were not a people,
   but now you are God's people;
once you had not received mercy,
   but now you have received mercy.

GOSPEL   John 10.22–29

[22] At that time the festival of the Dedication took place in Jerusalem. It was winter, [23] and Jesus was walking in the temple, in the portico of Solomon. [24] So the Jews gathered around him and said to him, 'How long will you keep us in suspense? If you are the Messiah, tell us plainly.' [25] Jesus answered, 'I have told you, and you do not believe. The works that I do in my Father's name testify to me; [26] but you do not believe, because you do not belong to my sheep. [27] My sheep hear my voice. I know them, and they follow me. [28] I give them eternal life, and they will never perish. No one will snatch them out of my hand. [29] What my Father has given me is greater than all else, and no one can snatch it out of the Father's hand.'

POST COMMUNION

Father in heaven,
whose Church on earth is a sign of your heavenly peace,
an image of the new and eternal Jerusalem:
grant to us in the days of our pilgrimage
that, fed with the living bread of heaven,
and united in the body of your Son,
we may be the temple of your presence,

the place of your glory on earth,
and a sign of your peace in the world;
through Jesus Christ our Lord.

SECOND SERVICE

Psalm 132
Jeremiah 7.1–11
Luke 19.1–10

THIRD SERVICE

Psalm 48
Haggai 2.6–9
Hebrews 10.19–25

SUNDAYS AND
PRINCIPAL FEASTS AND HOLY DAYS

YEAR C

THE FIRST SUNDAY OF ADVENT

COLLECT

Almighty God,
give us grace to cast away the works of darkness
and to put on the armour of light,
now in the time of this mortal life,
in which your Son Jesus Christ
    came to us in great humility;
that on the last day,
when he shall come again in his glorious majesty
    to judge the living and the dead,
we may rise to the life immortal;
through him who is alive and reigns with you,
in the unity of the Holy Spirit,
one God, now and for ever.

*This Collect may be used as the Post Communion on any day from the Second Sunday
of Advent until Christmas Eve instead of the Post Communion provided*

READING   Jeremiah 33.14–16

¹⁴ The days are surely coming, says the LORD, when I will fulfil the promise
I made to the house of Israel and the house of Judah. ¹⁵ In those days and
at that time I will cause a righteous Branch to spring up for David; and he
shall execute justice and righteousness in the land. ¹⁶ In those days Judah
will be saved and Jerusalem will live in safety. And this is the name by
which it will be called: 'The LORD is our righteousness.'

PSALM   Psalm 25.1–9

¹ To you, O Lord, I lift up my soul; my God, I put my trust in you;
      let me not be humiliated, nor let my enemies triumph over me.
² Let none who look to you be put to shame;
      let the treacherous be disappointed in their schemes.
³ Show me your ways, O Lord,
      and teach me your paths.
⁴ Lead me in your truth and teach me,
      for you are the God of my salvation; in you have I trusted all the
         day long.

⁵ Remember, O Lord, your compassion and love,
for they are from everlasting.
⁶ Remember not the sins of my youth and my transgressions;
remember me according to your love and for the sake of your
goodness, O Lord.
⁷ Gracious and upright is the Lord;
therefore he teaches sinners in his way.
⁸ He guides the humble in doing right
and teaches his way to the lowly.
⁹ All the paths of the Lord are love and faithfulness
to those who keep his covenant and his testimonies.

READING   1 Thessalonians 3.9-13

⁹ How can we thank God enough for you in return for all the joy that we feel before our God because of you? ¹⁰ Night and day we pray most earnestly that we may see you face to face and restore whatever is lacking in your faith.

¹¹ Now may our God and Father himself and our Lord Jesus direct our way to you. ¹² And may the Lord make you increase and abound in love for one another and for all, just as we abound in love for you. ¹³ And may he so strengthen your hearts in holiness that you may be blameless before our God and Father at the coming of our Lord Jesus with all his saints.

GOSPEL   Luke 21.25-36

²⁵ 'There will be signs in the sun, the moon, and the stars, and on the earth distress among nations confused by the roaring of the sea and the waves. ²⁶ People will faint from fear and foreboding of what is coming upon the world, for the powers of the heavens will be shaken. ²⁷ Then they will see "the Son of Man coming in a cloud" with power and great glory. ²⁸ Now when these things begin to take place, stand up and raise your heads, because your redemption is drawing near.'

²⁹ Then he told them a parable: 'Look at the fig tree and all the trees; ³⁰ as soon as they sprout leaves you can see for yourselves and know that summer is already near. ³¹ So also, when you see these things taking place, you know that the kingdom of God is near. ³² Truly I tell you, this generation will not pass away until all things have taken place. ³³ Heaven and earth will pass away, but my words will not pass away.

³⁴ 'Be on guard so that your hearts are not weighed down with dissipation and drunkenness and the worries of this life, and that day does not catch

you unexpectedly, [35] like a trap. For it will come upon all who live on the face of the whole earth. [36] Be alert at all times, praying that you may have the strength to escape all these things that will take place, and to stand before the Son of Man.'

POST COMMUNION

O Lord our God,
make us watchful and keep us faithful
as we await the coming of your Son our Lord;
that, when he shall appear,
he may not find us sleeping in sin
but active in his service
and joyful in his praise;
through Jesus Christ our Lord.

SECOND SERVICE

Psalm 9.1–8, [9–20]
Joel 3.9–21
Revelation 14.13–15.4

If the Second Service is a Eucharist, the following is read as a Gospel:

John 3.1–17

THIRD SERVICE

Psalm 44
Isaiah 51.4–11
Romans 13.11–14

THE SECOND SUNDAY OF ADVENT

COLLECT

O Lord, raise up, we pray, your power
and come among us,
and with great might succour us;
that whereas, through our sins and wickedness
we are grievously hindered
in running the race that is set before us,
your bountiful grace and mercy
may speedily help and deliver us;
through Jesus Christ your Son our Lord,
to whom with you and the Holy Spirit,
be honour and glory, now and for ever.

READING

Baruch 5.1–9

¹ Take off the garment of your sorrow and affliction, O Jerusalem,
  and put on for ever the beauty of the glory from God.
² Put on the robe of the righteousness that comes from God;
  put on your head the diadem of the glory of the Everlasting;
³ for God will show your splendour everywhere under heaven.
⁴ For God will give you evermore the name,
  'Righteous Peace, Godly Glory'.
⁵ Arise, O Jerusalem, stand upon the height;
  look towards the east,
and see your children gathered from west and east
  at the word of the Holy One,
  rejoicing that God has remembered them.
⁶ For they went out from you on foot,
  led away by their enemies;
but God will bring them back to you,
  carried in glory, as on a royal throne.
⁷ For God has ordered that every high mountain and the everlasting hills
    be made low
  and the valleys filled up, to make level ground,
  so that Israel may walk safely in the glory of God.
⁸ The woods and every fragrant tree
  have shaded Israel at God's command.
⁹ For God will lead Israel with joy,
  in the light of his glory,
  with the mercy and righteousness that come from him.

OR ## Malachi 3.1–4

¹ See, I am sending my messenger to prepare the way before me, and the Lord whom you seek will suddenly come to his temple. The messenger of the covenant in whom you delight—indeed, he is coming, says the LORD of hosts. ² But who can endure the day of his coming, and who can stand when he appears?

For he is like a refiner's fire and like fullers' soap; ³ he will sit as a refiner and purifier of silver, and he will purify the descendants of Levi and refine them like gold and silver, until they present offerings to the LORD in righteousness. ⁴ Then the offering of Judah and Jerusalem will be pleasing to the LORD as in the days of old and as in former years.

CANTICLE: Benedictus   Luke 1.68–79

68 Blessed be the Lord, the God of Israel,
   who has come to his people and set them free.
69 The Lord has raised up for us a mighty Saviour,
   born of the house of his servant David.
70 Through the holy prophets, God promised of old
71   to save us from our enemies,
     from the hands of all who hate us,
72   to show mercy to our forebears,
     and to remember his holy covenant.
73 This was the oath God swore to our father Abraham:
74   to set us free from the hands of our enemies,
     free to worship him without fear,
75   holy and righteous before him,
     all the days of our life.

76 And you, child, shall be called the prophet of the Most High,
   for you will go before the Lord to prepare his way,
77 to give his people knowledge of salvation
   by the forgiveness of their sins.
78 In the tender compassion of our God
   the dawn from on high shall break upon us,
79 to shine on those who dwell in darkness and the shadow of death,
   and to guide our feet into the way of peace.

READING   Philippians 1.3–11

3 I thank my God every time I remember you, 4 constantly praying with joy in every one of my prayers for all of you, 5 because of your sharing in the gospel from the first day until now. 6 I am confident of this, that the one who began a good work among you will bring it to completion by the day of Jesus Christ. 7 It is right for me to think this way about all of you, because you hold me in your heart, for all of you share in God's grace with me, both in my imprisonment and in the defence and confirmation of the gospel. 8 For God is my witness, how I long for all of you with the compassion of Christ Jesus. 9 And this is my prayer, that your love may overflow more and more with knowledge and full insight 10 to help you to determine what is best, so that on the day of Christ you may be pure and blameless, 11 having produced the harvest of righteousness that comes through Jesus Christ for the glory and praise of God.

GOSPEL   Luke 3.1–6

[1] In the fifteenth year of the reign of Emperor Tiberius, when Pontius Pilate was governor of Judea, and Herod was ruler of Galilee, and his brother Philip ruler of the region of Ituraea and Trachonitis, and Lysanias ruler of Abilene, [2] during the high-priesthood of Annas and Caiaphas, the word of God came to John son of Zechariah in the wilderness. [3] He went into all the region around the Jordan, proclaiming a baptism of repentance for the forgiveness of sins, [4] as it is written in the book of the words of the prophet Isaiah,

'The voice of one crying out in the wilderness:
"Prepare the way of the Lord,
   make his paths straight.
[5] Every valley shall be filled,
   and every mountain and hill shall be made low,
and the crooked shall be made straight,
   and the rough ways made smooth;
[6] and all flesh shall see the salvation of God." '

POST COMMUNION

Father in heaven,
who sent your Son to redeem the world
and will send him again to be our judge:
give us grace so to imitate him
   in the humility and purity of his first coming
that, when he comes again,
we may be ready to greet him
with joyful love and firm faith;
through Jesus Christ our Lord.

SECOND SERVICE   THIRD SERVICE

Psalms 75; [76]   Psalm 80
Isaiah 40.1–11   Isaiah 64.1–7
Luke 1.1–25   Matthew 11.2–11

THE THIRD SUNDAY OF ADVENT

COLLECT

O Lord Jesus Christ,
who at your first coming sent your messenger
to prepare your way before you:
grant that the ministers and stewards of your mysteries
may likewise so prepare and make ready your way
by turning the hearts of the disobedient
   to the wisdom of the just,
that at your second coming to judge the world
we may be found an acceptable people in your sight;
for you are alive and reign with the Father
in the unity of the Holy Spirit,
one God, now and for ever.

READING   Zephaniah 3.14–20

14   Sing aloud, O daughter Zion;
      shout, O Israel!
   Rejoice and exult with all your heart,
      O daughter Jerusalem!
15   The Lord has taken away the judgements against you,
      he has turned away your enemies.
   The king of Israel, the Lord, is in your midst;
      you shall fear disaster no more.
16   On that day it shall be said to Jerusalem:
   Do not fear, O Zion;
      do not let your hands grow weak.
17   The Lord, your God, is in your midst,
      a warrior who gives victory;
   he will rejoice over you with gladness,
      he will renew you in his love;
   he will exult over you with loud singing
18   as on a day of festival.
   I will remove disaster from you,
      so that you will not bear reproach for it.

19 I will deal with all your oppressors
    at that time.
And I will save the lame
    and gather the outcast,
and I will change their shame into praise
    and renown in all the earth.
20 At that time I will bring you home,
    at the time when I gather you;
for I will make you renowned and praised
    among all the peoples of the earth,
when I restore your fortunes
    before your eyes, says the LORD.

CANTICLE   Isaiah 12.2–6

2 Surely God is my salvation;
    I will trust, and will not be afraid,
for the LORD GOD is my strength and my might;
    he has become my salvation.

3 With joy you will draw water from the wells of salvation. 4 And you will
say on that day:
    Give thanks to the LORD,
        call on his name;
    make known his deeds among the nations;
        proclaim that his name is exalted.
5 Sing praises to the LORD, for he has done gloriously;
    let this be known in all the earth.
6 Shout aloud and sing for joy, O royal Zion,
    for great in your midst is the Holy One of Israel.

OR, IF AN ALTERNATIVE IS PREFERRED   Psalm 146.4–9

4 Happy are they who have the God of Jacob for their help!
    whose hope is in the Lord their God;
5 Who made heaven and earth, the seas, and all that is in them;
    who keeps his promise for ever;
6 Who gives justice to those who are oppressed,
    and food to those who hunger.
7 The Lord sets the prisoners free; the Lord opens the eyes of the
    blind;
    the Lord lifts up those who are bowed down;

⁸ The Lord loves the righteous; the Lord cares for the stranger;
he sustains the orphan and widow, but frustrates the way of the
wicked.
⁹ The Lord shall reign for ever,
your God, O Zion, throughout all generations. Alleluia!

READING   Philippians 4.4–7

⁴ Rejoice in the Lord always; again I will say, Rejoice. ⁵ Let your gentleness
be known to everyone. The Lord is near. ⁶ Do not worry about anything,
but in everything by prayer and supplication with thanksgiving let your
requests be made known to God. ⁷ And the peace of God, which surpasses
all understanding, will guard your hearts and your minds in Christ Jesus.

GOSPEL   Luke 3.7–18

⁷ John said to the crowds that came out to be baptized by him, 'You brood
of vipers! Who warned you to flee from the wrath to come? ⁸ Bear fruits
worthy of repentance. Do not begin to say to yourselves, "We have Abraham
as our ancestor"; for I tell you, God is able from these stones to raise up
children to Abraham. ⁹ Even now the axe is lying at the root of the trees;
every tree therefore that does not bear good fruit is cut down and thrown
into the fire.'

¹⁰ And the crowds asked him, 'What then should we do?' ¹¹ In reply he said
to them, 'Whoever has two coats must share with anyone who has none;
and whoever has food must do likewise.' ¹² Even tax-collectors came to be
baptized, and they asked him, 'Teacher, what should we do?' ¹³ He said to
them, 'Collect no more than the amount prescribed for you.' ¹⁴ Soldiers
also asked him, 'And we, what should we do?' He said to them, 'Do not
extort money from anyone by threats or false accusation, and be satisfied
with your wages.'

¹⁵ As the people were filled with expectation, and all were questioning in
their hearts concerning John, whether he might be the Messiah, ¹⁶ John
answered all of them by saying, 'I baptize you with water; but one who is
more powerful than I is coming; I am not worthy to untie the thong of his
sandals. He will baptize you with the Holy Spirit and fire. ¹⁷ His winnowing-
fork is in his hand, to clear his threshing-floor and to gather the wheat into
his granary; but the chaff he will burn with unquenchable fire.'

¹⁸ So, with many other exhortations, he proclaimed the good news to the
people.

POST COMMUNION

We give you thanks, O Lord, for these heavenly gifts;
kindle in us the fire of your Spirit
that when your Christ comes again
we may shine as lights before his face;
who is alive and reigns now and for ever.

SECOND SERVICE	THIRD SERVICE
Psalms 50.1–6; [62]	Psalms 12; 14
Isaiah 35	Isaiah 25.1–9
Luke 1.57–66, [67–80]	1 Corinthians 4.1–5

THE FOURTH SUNDAY OF ADVENT

COLLECT

God our redeemer,
who prepared the Blessed Virgin Mary
to be the mother of your Son:
grant that, as she looked for his coming as our saviour,
so we may be ready to greet him
when he comes again as our judge;
who is alive and reigns with you,
in the unity of the Holy Spirit,
one God, now and for ever.

READING   Micah 5.2–5a

² But you, O Bethlehem of Ephrathah,
    who are one of the little clans of Judah,
from you shall come forth for me
    one who is to rule in Israel,
whose origin is from of old,
    from ancient days.
³ Therefore he shall give them up until the time
    when she who is in labour has brought forth;
then the rest of his kindred shall return
    to the people of Israel.

4 And he shall stand and feed his flock in the strength of the LORD,
  in the majesty of the name of the LORD his God.
  And they shall live secure, for now he shall be great
    to the ends of the earth;
5 and he shall be the one of peace.

EITHER

CANTICLE: Magnificat   Luke 1.46–55

46 My soul proclaims the greatness of the Lord,
47 my spirit rejoices in God my Saviour,
48 who has looked with favour on his lowly servant.
   From this day all generations will call me blessed:
49   the Almighty has done great things for me
      and holy is his name.
50   God has mercy on those who fear him,
      from generation to generation.
51 The Lord has shown strength with his arm
   and scattered the proud in their conceit,
52 casting down the mighty from their thrones
   and lifting up the lowly.
53 God has filled the hungry with good things
   and sent the rich away empty.
54 He has come to the aid of his servant Israel,
   to remember the promise of mercy,
55 the promise made to our forebears,
   to Abraham and his children for ever.

OR

PSALM   Psalm 80.1–7

1 Hear, O Shepherd of Israel, leading Joseph like a flock;
  shine forth, you that are enthroned upon the cherubim.
2 In the presence of Ephraim, Benjamin and Manasseh,
  stir up your strength and come to help us.
3 Restore us, O God of hosts;
  show the light of your countenance and we shall be saved.
4 O Lord God of hosts,
  how long will you be angered despite the prayers of your people?
5 You have fed them with the bread of tears;
  you have given them bowls of tears to drink.

⁶ You have made us the derision of our neighbours,
       and our enemies laugh us to scorn.
⁷ Restore us, O God of hosts;
       show the light of your countenance and we shall be saved.

READING   Hebrews 10.5–10

⁵ Consequently, when Christ came into the world, he said,
       'Sacrifices and offerings you have not desired,
           but a body you have prepared for me;
⁶   in burnt-offerings and sin-offerings
           you have taken no pleasure.
⁷   Then I said, "See, God, I have come to do your will, O God"
           (in the scroll of the book it is written of me).'
⁸ When he said above, 'You have neither desired nor taken pleasure in
sacrifices and offerings and burnt-offerings and sin-offerings' (these are
offered according to the law), ⁹ then he added, 'See, I have come to do your
will.' He abolishes the first in order to establish the second. ¹⁰ And it is by
God's will that we have been sanctified through the offering of the body of
Jesus Christ once for all.

GOSPEL   Luke 1.39–45, [46–55]

³⁹ In those days Mary set out and went with haste to a Judean town in the
hill country, ⁴⁰ where she entered the house of Zechariah and greeted
Elizabeth. ⁴¹ When Elizabeth heard Mary's greeting, the child leapt in her
womb. And Elizabeth was filled with the Holy Spirit ⁴² and exclaimed with
a loud cry, 'Blessed are you among women, and blessed is the fruit of your
womb. ⁴³ And why has this happened to me, that the mother of my Lord
comes to me? ⁴⁴ For as soon as I heard the sound of your greeting, the child
in my womb leapt for joy. ⁴⁵ And blessed is she who believed that there
would be a fulfilment of what was spoken to her by the Lord.'

[⁴⁶ And Mary said,
       'My soul magnifies the Lord,
⁴⁷   and my spirit rejoices in God my Saviour,
⁴⁸   for he has looked with favour on the lowliness of his servant.
           Surely, from now on all generations will call me blessed;
⁴⁹   for the Mighty One has done great things for me,
           and holy is his name.
⁵⁰   His mercy is for those who fear him
           from generation to generation.

51 He has shown strength with his arm;
      he has scattered the proud in the thoughts of their hearts.
52 He has brought down the powerful from their thrones,
      and lifted up the lowly;
53 he has filled the hungry with good things,
      and sent the rich away empty.
54 He has helped his servant Israel,
      in remembrance of his mercy,
55 according to the promise he made to our ancestors,
      to Abraham and to his descendants for ever.']

POST COMMUNION

Heavenly Father,
who chose the Blessed Virgin Mary
to be the mother of the promised saviour:
fill us your servants with your grace,
that in all things we may embrace your holy will
and with her rejoice in your salvation;
through Jesus Christ our Lord.

SECOND SERVICE

Psalms 123; [131]
Isaiah 10.33–11.10
Matthew 1.18–25

THIRD SERVICE

Psalm 144
Isaiah 32.1–8
Revelation 22.6–21

CHRISTMAS EVE   24 DECEMBER

COLLECT

Almighty God,
you make us glad with the yearly remembrance
    of the birth of your Son Jesus Christ:
grant that, as we joyfully receive him as our redeemer,
so we may with sure confidence behold him
when he shall come to be our judge;
who is alive and reigns with you,
in the unity of the Holy Spirit,
one God, now and for ever.

READING   2 Samuel 7.1–5, 8–11, 16

¹ Now when the king was settled in his house, and the LORD had given him rest from all his enemies around him, ² the king said to the prophet Nathan, 'See now, I am living in a house of cedar, but the ark of God stays in a tent.' ³ Nathan said to the king, 'Go, do all that you have in mind; for the LORD is with you.'

⁴ But that same night the word of the LORD came to Nathan: ⁵ Go and tell my servant David: Thus says the LORD: Are you the one to build me a house to live in?

⁸ Now therefore thus you shall say to my servant David: Thus says the LORD of hosts: I took you from the pasture, from following the sheep to be prince over my people Israel; ⁹ and I have been with you wherever you went, and have cut off all your enemies from before you; and I will make for you a great name, like the name of the great ones of the earth. ¹⁰ And I will appoint a place for my people Israel and will plant them, so that they may live in their own place, and be disturbed no more; and evildoers shall afflict them no more, as formerly, ¹¹ from the time that I appointed judges over my people Israel; and I will give you rest from all your enemies. Moreover, the LORD declares to you that the LORD will make you a house.

¹⁶ Your house and your kingdom shall be made sure for ever before me; your throne shall be established for ever.

PSALM   Psalm 89.2, 21–27

²   For I am persuaded that your love is established for ever;
    you have set your faithfulness firmly in the heavens.

²¹ 'My hand will hold him fast
    and my arm will make him strong.
²² No enemy shall deceive him,
    nor the wicked bring him down.
²³ I will crush his foes before him
    and strike down those who hate him.
²⁴ My faithfulness and love shall be with him,
    and he shall be victorious through my name.
²⁵ I shall make his dominion extend
    from the Great Sea to the River.
²⁶ He will say to me, "You are my Father,
    my God and the rock of my salvation."
²⁷ I will make him my first-born
    and higher than the kings of the earth.'

CHRISTMAS EVE

READING   Acts 13.16-26

¹⁶ So Paul stood up and with a gesture began to speak:

'You Israelites, and others who fear God, listen. ¹⁷ The God of this people
Israel chose our ancestors and made the people great during their stay in
the land of Egypt, and with uplifted arm he led them out of it. ¹⁸ For about
forty years he put up with them in the wilderness. ¹⁹ After he had destroyed
seven nations in the land of Canaan, he gave them their land as an inheritance ²⁰ for about four hundred and fifty years. After that he gave them
judges until the time of the prophet Samuel. ²¹ Then they asked for a king;
and God gave them Saul son of Kish, a man of the tribe of Benjamin, who
reigned for forty years. ²² When he had removed him, he made David their
king. In his testimony about him he said, "I have found David, son of Jesse,
to be a man after my heart, who will carry out all my wishes." ²³ Of this
man's posterity God has brought to Israel a Saviour, Jesus, as he promised;
²⁴ before his coming John had already proclaimed a baptism of repentance
to all the people of Israel. ²⁵ And as John was finishing his work, he said,
"What do you suppose that I am? I am not he. No, but one is coming after
me; I am not worthy to untie the thong of the sandals on his feet."

²⁶ 'My brothers, you descendants of Abraham's family, and others who
fear God, to us the message of this salvation has been sent.'

GOSPEL   Luke 1.67-79

⁶⁷ Then his father Zechariah was filled with the Holy Spirit and spoke this
prophecy:
⁶⁸ 'Blessed be the Lord God of Israel,
        for he has looked favourably on his people and redeemed them.
⁶⁹ He has raised up a mighty saviour for us
        in the house of his servant David,
⁷⁰ as he spoke through the mouth of his holy prophets from of old,
⁷¹   that we would be saved from our enemies and from the hand of all
        who hate us.
⁷² Thus he has shown the mercy promised to our ancestors,
        and has remembered his holy covenant,
⁷³ the oath that he swore to our ancestor Abraham,
        to grant us ⁷⁴ that we, being rescued from the hands of our enemies,
    might serve him without fear, ⁷⁵ in holiness and righteousness
        before him all our days.
⁷⁶ And you, child, will be called the prophet of the Most High;
        for you will go before the Lord to prepare his ways,

77 to give knowledge of salvation to his people
   by the forgiveness of their sins.
78 By the tender mercy of our God,
   the dawn from on high will break upon us,
79 to give light to those who sit in darkness and in the shadow of death,
   to guide our feet into the way of peace.'

POST COMMUNION

Eternal God, for whom we wait,
you have fed us with the bread of eternal life:
keep us ever watchful,
that we may be ready to stand before the Son of Man,
Jesus Christ our Lord.

CHRISTMAS DAY   25 DECEMBER

Any of the following sets of readings may be used on the evening of Christmas Eve and on Christmas Day. Set III should be used at some service during the celebration.

SET I

COLLECT

CHRISTMAS NIGHT

Eternal God,
who made this most holy night
to shine with the brightness of your one true light:
bring us, who have known the revelation
   of that light on earth,
to see the radiance of your heavenly glory;
through Jesus Christ your Son our Lord,
who is alive and reigns with you,
in the unity of the Holy Spirit,
one God, now and for ever.

CHRISTMAS DAY

Almighty God,
you have given us your only-begotten Son
to take our nature upon him
and as at this time to be born of a pure virgin:
grant that we, who have been born again
and made your children by adoption and grace,
may daily be renewed by your Holy Spirit;
through Jesus Christ your Son our Lord,
who is alive and reigns with you,
in the unity of the Holy Spirit,
one God, now and for ever.

READING   Isaiah 9.2–7

2 The people who walked in darkness
       have seen a great light;
    those who lived in a land of deep darkness—
       on them light has shined.
3 You have multiplied the nation,
       you have increased its joy;
    they rejoice before you
       as with joy at the harvest,
       as people exult when dividing plunder.
4 For the yoke of their burden,
       and the bar across their shoulders,
       the rod of their oppressor,
       you have broken as on the day of Midian.
5 For all the boots of the tramping warriors
       and all the garments rolled in blood
       shall be burned as fuel for the fire.
6 For a child has been born for us,
       a son given to us;
    authority rests upon his shoulders;
       and he is named
    Wonderful Counsellor, Mighty God,
       Everlasting Father, Prince of Peace.

7 His authority shall grow continually,
    and there shall be endless peace
for the throne of David and his kingdom.
    He will establish and uphold it
with justice and with righteousness
    from this time onwards and for evermore.
The zeal of the LORD of hosts will do this.

PSALM   Psalm 96

1 Sing to the Lord a new song;
    sing to the Lord, all the whole earth.
2 Sing to the Lord and bless his name;
    proclaim the good news of his salvation from day to day.
3 Declare his glory among the nations
    and his wonders among all peoples.
4 For great is the Lord and greatly to be praised;
    he is more to be feared than all gods.
5 As for all the gods of the nations, they are but idols;
    but it is the Lord who made the heavens.
6 O the majesty and magnificence of his presence!
    O the power and the splendour of his sanctuary!
7 Ascribe to the Lord, you families of the peoples;
    ascribe to the Lord honour and power.
8 Ascribe to the Lord the honour due to his name;
    bring offerings and come into his courts.
9 Worship the Lord in the beauty of holiness;
    let the whole earth tremble before him.
10 Tell it out among the nations: 'The Lord is king!
    he has made the world so firm that it cannot be moved; he will
        judge the peoples with equity.'
11 Let the heavens rejoice and let the earth be glad; let the sea
        thunder and all that is in it;
    let the field be joyful and all that is therein.
12 Then shall all the trees of the wood shout for joy before the Lord
        when he comes,
    when he comes to judge the earth.
13 He will judge the world with righteousness
    and the peoples with his truth.

READING   **Titus 2.11–14**

[11] For the grace of God has appeared, bringing salvation to all, [12] training us to renounce impiety and worldly passions, and in the present age to live lives that are self-controlled, upright, and godly, [13] while we wait for the blessed hope and the manifestation of the glory of our great God and Saviour, Jesus Christ. [14] He it is who gave himself for us that he might redeem us from all iniquity and purify for himself a people of his own who are zealous for good deeds.

GOSPEL   **Luke 2.1–14, [15–20]**

[1] In those days a decree went out from Emperor Augustus that all the world should be registered. [2] This was the first registration and was taken while Quirinius was governor of Syria. [3] All went to their own towns to be registered. [4] Joseph also went from the town of Nazareth in Galilee to Judea, to the city of David called Bethlehem, because he was descended from the house and family of David. [5] He went to be registered with Mary, to whom he was engaged and who was expecting a child. [6] While they were there, the time came for her to deliver her child. [7] And she gave birth to her firstborn son and wrapped him in bands of cloth, and laid him in a manger, because there was no place for them in the inn.

[8] In that region there were shepherds living in the fields, keeping watch over their flock by night. [9] Then an angel of the Lord stood before them, and the glory of the Lord shone around them, and they were terrified. [10] But the angel said to them, 'Do not be afraid; for see—I am bringing you good news of great joy for all the people: [11] to you is born this day in the city of David a Saviour, who is the Messiah, the Lord. [12] This will be a sign for you: you will find a child wrapped in bands of cloth and lying in a manger.' [13] And suddenly there was with the angel a multitude of the heavenly host, praising God and saying,

[14] 'Glory to God in the highest heaven,
    and on earth peace among those whom he favours!'

[[15] When the angels had left them and gone into heaven, the shepherds said to one another, 'Let us go now to Bethlehem and see this thing that has taken place, which the Lord has made known to us.' [16] So they went with haste and found Mary and Joseph, and the child lying in the manger. [17] When they saw this, they made known what had been told them about this child; [18] and all who heard it were amazed at what the shepherds told them. [19] But Mary treasured all these words and pondered them in her heart. [20] The shepherds returned, glorifying and praising God for all they had heard and seen, as it had been told them.]

POST COMMUNION

CHRISTMAS NIGHT

God our Father,
in this night you have made known to us again
the coming of our Lord Jesus Christ:
confirm our faith and fix our eyes on him
until the day dawns
and Christ the Morning Star rises in our hearts.
To him be glory both now and for ever.

CHRISTMAS DAY

God our Father,
whose Word has come among us
in the Holy Child of Bethlehem:
may the light of faith illumine our hearts
    and shine in our words and deeds;
through him who is Christ the Lord.

SET II

COLLECT

CHRISTMAS NIGHT

Eternal God,
who made this most holy night
to shine with the brightness of your one true light:
bring us, who have known the revelation
    of that light on earth,
to see the radiance of your heavenly glory;
through Jesus Christ your Son our Lord,
who is alive and reigns with you,
in the unity of the Holy Spirit,
one God, now and for ever.

CHRISTMAS DAY

Almighty God,
you have given us your only-begotten Son
to take our nature upon him
and as at this time to be born of a pure virgin:
grant that we, who have been born again

and made your children by adoption and grace,
may daily be renewed by your Holy Spirit;
through Jesus Christ your Son our Lord,
who is alive and reigns with you,
in the unity of the Holy Spirit,
one God, now and for ever.

READING   Isaiah 62.6–12

6 Upon your walls, O Jerusalem,
       I have posted sentinels;
   all day and all night
       they shall never be silent.
   You who remind the LORD,
       take no rest,
7 and give him no rest
       until he establishes Jerusalem
       and makes it renowned throughout the earth.
8 The LORD has sworn by his right hand
       and by his mighty arm:
   I will not again give your grain
       to be food for your enemies,
   and foreigners shall not drink the wine
       for which you have laboured;
9 but those who garner it shall eat it
       and praise the LORD,
   and those who gather it shall drink it
       in my holy courts.
10 Go through, go through the gates,
       prepare the way for the people;
   build up, build up the highway,
       clear it of stones,
       lift up an ensign over the peoples.
11 The LORD has proclaimed
       to the end of the earth:
   Say to daughter Zion,
       'See, your salvation comes;
   his reward is with him,
       and his recompense before him.'
12 They shall be called, 'The Holy People,
       The Redeemed of the LORD';
   and you shall be called, 'Sought Out,
       A City Not Forsaken.'

PSALM   Psalm 97

¹ The Lord is king; let the earth rejoice;
   let the multitude of the isles be glad.
² Clouds and darkness are round about him,
   righteousness and justice are the foundations of his throne.
³ A fire goes before him
   and burns up his enemies on every side.
⁴ His lightnings light up the world;
   the earth sees it and is afraid.
⁵ The mountains melt like wax at the presence of the Lord,
   at the presence of the Lord of the whole earth.
⁶ The heavens declare his righteousness,
   and all the peoples see his glory.
⁷ Confounded be all who worship carved images and delight in false
   gods!
   Bow down before him, all you gods.
⁸ Zion hears and is glad and the cities of Judah rejoice,
   because of your judgements, O Lord.
⁹ For you are the Lord: most high over all the earth;
   you are exalted far above all gods.
¹⁰ The Lord loves those who hate evil;
   he preserves the lives of his saints and delivers them from the
      hand of the wicked.
¹¹ Light has sprung up for the righteous,
   and joyful gladness for those who are true-hearted.
¹² Rejoice in the Lord, you righteous,
   and give thanks to his holy name.

READING   Titus 3.4–7

⁴ But when the goodness and loving-kindness of God our Saviour appeared,
⁵ he saved us, not because of any works of righteousness that we had done,
but according to his mercy, through the water of rebirth and renewal by
the Holy Spirit. ⁶ This Spirit he poured out on us richly through Jesus Christ
our Saviour, ⁷ so that, having been justified by his grace, we might become
heirs according to the hope of eternal life.

GOSPEL   Luke 2.[1–7,] 8–20

[¹ In those days a decree went out from Emperor Augustus that all the
world should be registered. ² This was the first registration and was taken
while Quirinius was governor of Syria. ³ All went to their own towns to be

registered. [4] Joseph also went from the town of Nazareth in Galilee to Judea, to the city of David called Bethlehem, because he was descended from the house and family of David. [5] He went to be registered with Mary, to whom he was engaged and who was expecting a child. [6] While they were there, the time came for her to deliver her child. [7] And she gave birth to her firstborn son and wrapped him in bands of cloth, and laid him in a manger, because there was no place for them in the inn.]

[8] In that region there were shepherds living in the fields, keeping watch over their flock by night. [9] Then an angel of the Lord stood before them, and the glory of the Lord shone around them, and they were terrified. [10] But the angel said to them, 'Do not be afraid; for see—I am bringing you good news of great joy for all the people: [11] to you is born this day in the city of David a Saviour, who is the Messiah, the Lord. [12] This will be a sign for you: you will find a child wrapped in bands of cloth and lying in a manger.' [13] And suddenly there was with the angel a multitude of the heavenly host, praising God and saying,
[14] 'Glory to God in the highest heaven,
    and on earth peace among those whom he favours!'

[15] When the angels had left them and gone into heaven, the shepherds said to one another, 'Let us go now to Bethlehem and see this thing that has taken place, which the Lord has made known to us.' [16] So they went with haste and found Mary and Joseph, and the child lying in the manger. [17] When they saw this, they made known what had been told them about this child; [18] and all who heard it were amazed at what the shepherds told them. [19] But Mary treasured all these words and pondered them in her heart. [20] The shepherds returned, glorifying and praising God for all they had heard and seen, as it had been told them.

POST COMMUNION

CHRISTMAS NIGHT

God our Father,
in this night you have made known to us again
the coming of our Lord Jesus Christ:
confirm our faith and fix our eyes on him
until the day dawns
and Christ the Morning Star rises in our hearts.
To him be glory both now and for ever.

CHRISTMAS DAY

God our Father,
whose Word has come among us
in the Holy Child of Bethlehem:
may the light of faith illumine our hearts
   and shine in our words and deeds;
through him who is Christ the Lord.

SET III

COLLECT

CHRISTMAS NIGHT

Eternal God,
who made this most holy night
to shine with the brightness of your one true light:
bring us, who have known the revelation
   of that light on earth,
to see the radiance of your heavenly glory;
through Jesus Christ your Son our Lord,
who is alive and reigns with you,
in the unity of the Holy Spirit,
one God, now and for ever.

CHRISTMAS DAY

Almighty God,
you have given us your only-begotten Son
to take our nature upon him
and as at this time to be born of a pure virgin:
grant that we, who have been born again
and made your children by adoption and grace,
may daily be renewed by your Holy Spirit;
through Jesus Christ your Son our Lord,
who is alive and reigns with you,
in the unity of the Holy Spirit,
one God, now and for ever.

READING   Isaiah 52.7–10

⁷ How beautiful upon the mountains
   are the feet of the messenger who announces peace,
who brings good news,
   who announces salvation,
   who says to Zion, 'Your God reigns.'
⁸ Listen! Your sentinels lift up their voices,
   together they sing for joy;
for in plain sight they see
   the return of the LORD to Zion.
⁹ Break forth together into singing,
   you ruins of Jerusalem;
for the LORD has comforted his people,
   he has redeemed Jerusalem.
¹⁰ The LORD has bared his holy arm
   before the eyes of all the nations;
and all the ends of the earth shall see
   the salvation of our God.

PSALM   Psalm 98

¹ Sing to the Lord a new song,
   for he has done marvellous things.
² With his right hand and his holy arm
   has he won for himself the victory.
³ The Lord has made known his victory;
   his righteousness has he openly shown in the sight of the nations.
⁴ He remembers his mercy and faithfulness to the house of Israel,
   and all the ends of the earth have seen the victory of our God.
⁵ Shout with joy to the Lord, all you lands;
   lift up your voice, rejoice and sing.
⁶ Sing to the Lord with the harp,
   with the harp and the voice of song.
⁷ With trumpets and the sound of the horn
   shout with joy before the King, the Lord.
⁸ Let the sea make a noise and all that is in it,
   the lands and those who dwell therein.
⁹ Let the rivers clap their hands,
   and let the hills ring out with joy before the Lord, when he comes
      to judge the earth.
¹⁰ In righteousness shall he judge the world,
   and the peoples with equity.

READING   Hebrews 1.1–4, [5–12]

¹ Long ago God spoke to our ancestors in many and various ways by the prophets, ² but in these last days he has spoken to us by a Son, whom he appointed heir of all things, through whom he also created the worlds. ³ He is the reflection of God's glory and the exact imprint of God's very being, and he sustains all things by his powerful word. When he had made purification for sins, he sat down at the right hand of the Majesty on high, ⁴ having become as much superior to angels as the name he has inherited is more excellent than theirs.

[⁵ For to which of the angels did God ever say,
　　'You are my Son;
　　　today I have begotten you'?
Or again,
　　'I will be his Father,
　　　and he will be my Son'?
⁶ And again, when he brings the firstborn into the world, he says,
　　'Let all God's angels worship him.'
⁷ Of the angels he says,
　　'He makes his angels winds,
　　　and his servants flames of fire.'
⁸ But of the Son he says,
　　'Your throne, O God, is for ever and ever,
　　　and the righteous sceptre is the sceptre of your kingdom.
⁹　You have loved righteousness and hated wickedness;
　　therefore God, your God, has anointed you
　　　with the oil of gladness beyond your companions.'
¹⁰ And,
　　'In the beginning, Lord, you founded the earth,
　　　and the heavens are the work of your hands;
¹¹　they will perish, but you remain;
　　　they will all wear out like clothing;
¹²　like a cloak you will roll them up,
　　　and like clothing they will be changed.
　　But you are the same,
　　　and your years will never end.']

GOSPEL

John 1.1–14

[1] In the beginning was the Word, and the Word was with God, and the Word was God. [2] He was in the beginning with God. [3] All things came into being through him, and without him not one thing came into being. What has come into being [4] in him was life, and the life was the light of all people. [5] The light shines in the darkness, and the darkness did not overcome it.

[6] There was a man sent from God, whose name was John. [7] He came as a witness to testify to the light, so that all might believe through him. [8] He himself was not the light, but he came to testify to the light. [9] The true light, which enlightens everyone, was coming into the world.

[10] He was in the world, and the world came into being through him; yet the world did not know him. [11] He came to what was his own, and his own people did not accept him. [12] But to all who received him, who believed in his name, he gave power to become children of God, [13] who were born, not of blood or of the will of the flesh or of the will of man, but of God.

[14] And the Word became flesh and lived among us, and we have seen his glory, the glory as of a father's only son, full of grace and truth.

POST COMMUNION

CHRISTMAS NIGHT

God our Father,
in this night you have made known to us again
the coming of our Lord Jesus Christ:
confirm our faith and fix our eyes on him
until the day dawns
and Christ the Morning Star rises in our hearts.
To him be glory both now and for ever.

CHRISTMAS DAY

God our Father,
whose Word has come among us
in the Holy Child of Bethlehem:
may the light of faith illumine our hearts
    and shine in our words and deeds;
through him who is Christ the Lord.

YEAR C

SECOND SERVICE

Psalm 8
Isaiah 65.17–25
Philippians 2.5–11

or

Luke 2.1–20

if it has not been used at the Principal Service of the day

THIRD SERVICE

Psalm 110
Isaiah 62.1–5
Matthew 1.18–25

THE FIRST SUNDAY OF CHRISTMAS

COLLECT

Almighty God,
who wonderfully created us in your own image
and yet more wonderfully restored us
through your Son Jesus Christ:
grant that, as he came to share in our humanity,
so we may share the life of his divinity;
who is alive and reigns with you,
in the unity of the Holy Spirit,
one God, now and for ever.

READING   1 Samuel 2.18–20, 26

¹⁸ Samuel was ministering before the LORD, a boy wearing a linen ephod. ¹⁹ His mother used to make for him a little robe and take it to him each year, when she went up with her husband to offer the yearly sacrifice. ²⁰ Then Eli would bless Elkanah and his wife, and say, 'May the LORD repay you with children by this woman for the gift that she made to the LORD'; and then they would return to their home.

²⁶ Now the boy Samuel continued to grow both in stature and in favour with the LORD and with the people.

PSALM   Psalm 148.[1–6,] 7–14

[1 Alleluia! Praise the Lord from the heavens;
     praise him in the heights.
2 Praise him, all you angels of his;
    praise him, all his host.
3 Praise him, sun and moon;
    praise him, all you shining stars.
4 Praise him, heaven of heavens,
    and you waters above the heavens.
5 Let them praise the name of the Lord;
    for he commanded and they were created.
6 He made them stand fast for ever and ever;
    he gave them a law which shall not pass away.]
7 Praise the Lord from the earth,
    you sea-monsters and all deeps;
8 Fire and hail, snow and fog,
    tempestuous wind, doing his will;
9 Mountains and all hills,
    fruit trees and all cedars;
10 Wild beasts and all cattle,
     creeping things and winged birds;
11 Kings of the earth and all peoples,
     princes and all rulers of the world;
12 Young men and maidens,
     old and young together.
13 Let them praise the name of the Lord,
     for his name only is exalted, his splendour is over earth and heaven.
14 He has raised up strength for his people and praise for all his loyal
     servants,
     the children of Israel, a people who are near him. Alleluia!

READING   Colossians 3.12–17

12 As God's chosen ones, holy and beloved, clothe yourselves with compassion, kindness, humility, meekness, and patience. 13 Bear with one
another and, if anyone has a complaint against another, forgive each other;
just as the Lord has forgiven you, so you also must forgive. 14 Above all,
clothe yourselves with love, which binds everything together in perfect
harmony. 15 And let the peace of Christ rule in your hearts, to which indeed
you were called in the one body. And be thankful. 16 Let the word of Christ
dwell in you richly; teach and admonish one another in all wisdom; and

with gratitude in your hearts sing psalms, hymns, and spiritual songs to God. ¹⁷ And whatever you do, in word or deed, do everything in the name of the Lord Jesus, giving thanks to God the Father through him.

GOSPEL

Luke 2.41-52

⁴¹ Now every year his parents went to Jerusalem for the festival of the Passover. ⁴² And when he was twelve years old, they went up as usual for the festival. ⁴³ When the festival was ended and they started to return, the boy Jesus stayed behind in Jerusalem, but his parents did not know it. ⁴⁴ Assuming that he was in the group of travellers, they went a day's journey. Then they started to look for him among their relatives and friends. ⁴⁵ When they did not find him, they returned to Jerusalem to search for him. ⁴⁶ After three days they found him in the temple, sitting among the teachers, listening to them and asking them questions. ⁴⁷ And all who heard him were amazed at his understanding and his answers. ⁴⁸ When his parents saw him they were astonished; and his mother said to him, 'Child, why have you treated us like this? Look, your father and I have been searching for you in great anxiety.' ⁴⁹ He said to them, 'Why were you searching for me? Did you not know that I must be in my Father's house?' ⁵⁰ But they did not understand what he said to them. ⁵¹ Then he went down with them and came to Nazareth, and was obedient to them. His mother treasured all these things in her heart.

⁵² And Jesus increased in wisdom and in years, and in divine and human favour.

POST COMMUNION

Heavenly Father,
whose blessed Son shared at Nazareth
    the life of an earthly home:
help your Church to live as one family,
united in love and obedience,
and bring us all at last to our home in heaven;
through Jesus Christ our Lord.

SECOND SERVICE

Psalm 132
Isaiah 61
Galatians 3.27–4.7

If the Second Service is a Eucharist, the following is read as a Gospel:

Luke 2.15–21

THIRD SERVICE

Psalm 105.1–11
Isaiah 41.21–42.1
1 John 1.1–7

THE SECOND SUNDAY OF CHRISTMAS

COLLECT

Almighty God,
in the birth of your Son
you have poured on us the new light of your incarnate Word,
and shown us the fullness of your love:
help us to walk in his light and dwell in his love
that we may know the fullness of his joy;
who is alive and reigns with you,
in the unity of the Holy Spirit,
one God, now and for ever.

EITHER

READING   Jeremiah 31.7–14

7 For thus says the LORD:
  Sing aloud with gladness for Jacob,
    and raise shouts for the chief of the nations;
  proclaim, give praise, and say,
    'Save, O LORD, your people,
    the remnant of Israel.'
8 See, I am going to bring them from the land of the north,
    and gather them from the farthest parts of the earth,
  among them the blind and the lame,
    those with child and those in labour, together;
    a great company, they shall return here.

⁹ With weeping they shall come,
    and with consolations I will lead them back,
I will let them walk by brooks of water,
    in a straight path in which they shall not stumble;
for I have become a father to Israel,
    and Ephraim is my firstborn.

¹⁰ Hear the word of the LORD, O nations,
    and declare it in the coastlands far away;
say, 'He who scattered Israel will gather him,
    and will keep him as a shepherd a flock.'

¹¹ For the LORD has ransomed Jacob,
    and has redeemed him from hands too strong for him.

¹² They shall come and sing aloud on the height of Zion,
    and they shall be radiant over the goodness of the LORD,
over the grain, the wine, and the oil,
    and over the young of the flock and the herd;
their life shall become like a watered garden,
    and they shall never languish again.

¹³ Then shall the young women rejoice in the dance,
    and the young men and the old shall be merry.
I will turn their mourning into joy,
    I will comfort them, and give them gladness for sorrow.

¹⁴ I will give the priests their fill of fatness,
    and my people shall be satisfied with my bounty,

                  says the LORD.

PSALM   Psalm 147.13–21

¹³ Worship the Lord, O Jerusalem;
    praise your God, O Zion;

¹⁴ For he has strengthened the bars of your gates;
    he has blessed your children within you.

¹⁵ He has established peace on your borders;
    he satisfies you with the finest wheat.

¹⁶ He sends out his command to the earth,
    and his word runs very swiftly.

¹⁷ He gives snow like wool;
    he scatters hoarfrost like ashes.

¹⁸ He scatters his hail like bread crumbs;
    who can stand against his cold?

¹⁹ He sends forth his word and melts them;
    he blows with his wind and the waters flow.

8

20 He declares his word to Jacob,
  his statutes and his judgements to Israel.
21 He has not done so to any other nation;
  to them he has not revealed his judgements. Alleluia!

READING   Ephesians 1.3–14

3 Blessed be the God and Father of our Lord Jesus Christ, who has blessed us in Christ with every spiritual blessing in the heavenly places, 4 just as he chose us in Christ before the foundation of the world to be holy and blameless before him in love. 5 He destined us for adoption as his children through Jesus Christ, according to the good pleasure of his will, 6 to the praise of his glorious grace that he freely bestowed on us in the Beloved. 7 In him we have redemption through his blood, the forgiveness of our trespasses, according to the riches of his grace 8 that he lavished on us. With all wisdom and insight 9 he has made known to us the mystery of his will, according to his good pleasure that he set forth in Christ, 10 as a plan for the fullness of time, to gather up all things in him, things in heaven and things on earth. 11 In Christ we have also obtained an inheritance, having been destined according to the purpose of him who accomplishes all things according to his counsel and will, 12 so that we, who were the first to set our hope on Christ, might live for the praise of his glory. 13 In him you also, when you had heard the word of truth, the gospel of your salvation, and had believed in him, were marked with the seal of the promised Holy Spirit; 14 this is the pledge of our inheritance towards redemption as God's own people, to the praise of his glory.

GOSPEL   John 1.[1–9,] 10–18

[1 In the beginning was the Word, and the Word was with God, and the Word was God. 2 He was in the beginning with God. 3 All things came into being through him, and without him not one thing came into being. What has come into being 4 in him was life, and the life was the light of all people. 5 The light shines in the darkness, and the darkness did not overcome it.

6 There was a man sent from God, whose name was John. 7 He came as a witness to testify to the light, so that all might believe through him. 8 He himself was not the light, but he came to testify to the light. 9 The true light, which enlightens everyone, was coming into the world.]

10 He was in the world, and the world came into being through him; yet the world did not know him. 11 He came to what was his own, and his own people did not accept him. 12 But to all who received him, who believed in

his name, he gave power to become children of God, [13] who were born, not of blood or of the will of the flesh or of the will of man, but of God.

[14] And the Word became flesh and lived among us, and we have seen his glory, the glory as of a father's only son, full of grace and truth. [15] (John testified to him and cried out, 'This was he of whom I said, "He who comes after me ranks ahead of me because he was before me." ') [16] From his fullness we have all received, grace upon grace. [17] The law indeed was given through Moses; grace and truth came through Jesus Christ. [18] No one has ever seen God. It is God the only Son, who is close to the Father's heart, who has made him known.

OR

READING   Ecclesiasticus 24.1–12

[1] Wisdom praises herself,
   and tells of her glory in the midst of her people.
[2] In the assembly of the Most High she opens her mouth,
   and in the presence of his hosts she tells of her glory:
[3] 'I came forth from the mouth of the Most High,
   and covered the earth like a mist.
[4] I dwelt in the highest heavens,
   and my throne was in a pillar of cloud.
[5] Alone I compassed the vault of heaven
   and traversed the depths of the abyss.
[6] Over waves of the sea, over all the earth,
   and over every people and nation I have held sway.
[7] Among all these I sought a resting-place;
   in whose territory should I abide?
[8] Then the Creator of all things gave me a command,
   and my Creator chose the place for my tent.
   He said, "Make your dwelling in Jacob,
   and in Israel receive your inheritance."
[9] Before the ages, in the beginning, he created me,
   and for all the ages I shall not cease to be.
[10] In the holy tent I ministered before him,
   and so I was established in Zion.
[11] Thus in the beloved city he gave me a resting-place,
   and in Jerusalem was my domain.
[12] I took root in an honoured people,
   in the portion of the Lord, his heritage.'

CANTICLE   Wisdom 10.15–21

15 A holy people and blameless race
   wisdom delivered from a nation of oppressors.
16 She entered the soul of a servant of the Lord,
   and withstood dread kings with wonders and signs.
17 She gave to holy people the reward of their labours;
   she guided them along a marvellous way,
   and became a shelter to them by day,
   and a starry flame through the night.
18 She brought them over the Red Sea,
   and led them through deep waters;
19 but she drowned their enemies,
   and cast them up from the depths of the sea.
20 Therefore the righteous plundered the ungodly;
   they sang hymns, O Lord, to your holy name,
   and praised with one accord your defending hand;
21 for wisdom opened the mouths of those who were mute,
   and made the tongues of infants speak clearly.

READING   Ephesians 1.3–14

3 Blessed be the God and Father of our Lord Jesus Christ, who has blessed us in Christ with every spiritual blessing in the heavenly places, 4 just as he chose us in Christ before the foundation of the world to be holy and blameless before him in love. 5 He destined us for adoption as his children through Jesus Christ, according to the good pleasure of his will, 6 to the praise of his glorious grace that he freely bestowed on us in the Beloved. 7 In him we have redemption through his blood, the forgiveness of our trespasses, according to the riches of his grace 8 that he lavished on us. With all wisdom and insight 9 he has made known to us the mystery of his will, according to his good pleasure that he set forth in Christ, 10 as a plan for the fullness of time, to gather up all things in him, things in heaven and things on earth. 11 In Christ we have also obtained an inheritance, having been destined according to the purpose of him who accomplishes all things according to his counsel and will, 12 so that we, who were the first to set our hope on Christ, might live for the praise of his glory. 13 In him you also, when you had heard the word of truth, the gospel of your salvation, and had believed in him, were marked with the seal of the promised Holy Spirit; 14 this is the pledge of our inheritance towards redemption as God's own people, to the praise of his glory.

GOSPEL John 1.[1–9,] 10–18

[¹ In the beginning was the Word, and the Word was with God, and the Word was God. ² He was in the beginning with God. ³ All things came into being through him, and without him not one thing came into being. What has come into being ⁴ in him was life, and the life was the light of all people. ⁵ The light shines in the darkness, and the darkness did not overcome it.

⁶ There was a man sent from God, whose name was John. ⁷ He came as a witness to testify to the light, so that all might believe through him. ⁸ He himself was not the light, but he came to testify to the light. ⁹ The true light, which enlightens everyone, was coming into the world.]

¹⁰ He was in the world, and the world came into being through him; yet the world did not know him. ¹¹ He came to what was his own, and his own people did not accept him. ¹² But to all who received him, who believed in his name, he gave power to become children of God, ¹³ who were born, not of blood or of the will of the flesh or of the will of man, but of God.

¹⁴ And the Word became flesh and lived among us, and we have seen his glory, the glory as of a father's only son, full of grace and truth. ¹⁵ (John testified to him and cried out, 'This was he of whom I said, "He who comes after me ranks ahead of me because he was before me." ') ¹⁶ From his fullness we have all received, grace upon grace. ¹⁷ The law indeed was given through Moses; grace and truth came through Jesus Christ. ¹⁸ No one has ever seen God. It is God the only Son, who is close to the Father's heart, who has made him known.

POST COMMUNION

All praise to you,
almighty God and heavenly King,
who sent your Son into the world
to take our nature upon him
and to be born of a pure virgin:
grant that, as we are born again in him,
so he may continually dwell in us
and reign on earth as he reigns in heaven,
now and for ever.

SECOND SERVICE

Psalm 135
1 Samuel 1.20–28
1 John 4.7–16

If the Second Service is a Eucharist, the
following is read as a Gospel:

Matthew 2.13–23

THIRD SERVICE

Psalm 87
Isaiah 12
1 Thessalonians 2.1–8

THE EPIPHANY

6 JANUARY

COLLECT

O God,
who by the leading of a star
manifested your only Son to the peoples of the earth:
mercifully grant that we,
who know you now by faith,
may at last behold your glory face to face;
through Jesus Christ your Son our Lord,
who is alive and reigns with you,
in the unity of the Holy Spirit,
one God, now and for ever.

READING

Isaiah 60.1–6

1 Arise, shine; for your light has come,
    and the glory of the LORD has risen upon you.
2 For darkness shall cover the earth,
    and thick darkness the peoples;
   but the LORD will arise upon you,
    and his glory will appear over you.
3 Nations shall come to your light,
    and kings to the brightness of your dawn.
4 Lift up your eyes and look around;
    they all gather together, they come to you;
   your sons shall come from far away,
    and your daughters shall be carried on their nurses' arms.

5 Then you shall see and be radiant;
      your heart shall thrill and rejoice,
   because the abundance of the sea shall be brought to you,
      the wealth of the nations shall come to you.
6 A multitude of camels shall cover you,
      the young camels of Midian and Ephah;
   all those from Sheba shall come.
   They shall bring gold and frankincense,
      and shall proclaim the praise of the LORD.

PSALM   Psalm 72.[1–9,] 10–15

[1 Give the king your justice, O God,
      and your righteousness to the king's son;
2 That he may rule your people righteously
      and the poor with justice;
3 That the mountains may bring prosperity to the people,
      and the little hills bring righteousness.
4 He shall defend the needy among the people;
      he shall rescue the poor and crush the oppressor.
5 He shall live as long as the sun and moon endure,
      from one generation to another.
6 He shall come down like rain upon the mown field,
      like showers that water the earth.
7 In his time shall the righteous flourish;
      there shall be abundance of peace till the moon shall be no more.
8 He shall rule from sea to sea,
      and from the River to the ends of the earth.
9 His foes shall bow down before him,
      and his enemies lick the dust.]
10 The kings of Tarshish and of the isles shall pay tribute,
      and the kings of Arabia and Saba offer gifts.
11 All kings shall bow down before him,
      and all the nations do him service.
12 For he shall deliver the poor who cries out in distress,
      and the oppressed who has no helper.
13 He shall have pity on the lowly and poor;
      he shall preserve the lives of the needy.
14 He shall redeem their lives from oppression and violence,
      and dear shall their blood be in his sight.
15 Long may he live, and may there be given to him gold from Arabia;
      may prayer be made for him always, and may they bless him all
        the day long.

READING   Ephesians 3.1–12

[1] This is the reason that I Paul am a prisoner for Christ Jesus for the sake of you Gentiles— [2] for surely you have already heard of the commission of God's grace that was given to me for you, [3] and how the mystery was made known to me by revelation, as I wrote above in a few words, [4] a reading of which will enable you to perceive my understanding of the mystery of Christ. [5] In former generations this mystery was not made known to humankind, as it has now been revealed to his holy apostles and prophets by the Spirit: [6] that is, the Gentiles have become fellow-heirs, members of the same body, and sharers in the promise in Christ Jesus through the gospel.

[7] Of this gospel I have become a servant according to the gift of God's grace that was given to me by the working of his power. [8] Although I am the very least of all the saints, this grace was given to me to bring to the Gentiles the news of the boundless riches of Christ, [9] and to make everyone see what is the plan of the mystery hidden for ages in God who created all things; [10] so that through the church the wisdom of God in its rich variety might now be made known to the rulers and authorities in the heavenly places. [11] This was in accordance with the eternal purpose that he has carried out in Christ Jesus our Lord, [12] in whom we have access to God in boldness and confidence through faith in him.

GOSPEL   Matthew 2.1–12

[1] In the time of King Herod, after Jesus was born in Bethlehem of Judea, wise men from the East came to Jerusalem, [2] asking, 'Where is the child who has been born king of the Jews? For we observed his star at its rising, and have come to pay him homage.' [3] When King Herod heard this, he was frightened, and all Jerusalem with him; [4] and calling together all the chief priests and scribes of the people, he inquired of them where the Messiah was to be born. [5] They told him, 'In Bethlehem of Judea; for so it has been written by the prophet:
[6]   "And you, Bethlehem, in the land of Judah,
    are by no means least among the rulers of Judah;
  for from you shall come a ruler
    who is to shepherd my people Israel." '

[7] Then Herod secretly called for the wise men and learned from them the exact time when the star had appeared. [8] Then he sent them to Bethlehem, saying, 'Go and search diligently for the child; and when you have found him, bring me word so that I may also go and pay him homage.' [9] When they had heard the king, they set out; and there, ahead of them, went the star that they had seen at its rising, until it stopped over the place where

the child was. ¹⁰ When they saw that the star had stopped, they were overwhelmed with joy. ¹¹ On entering the house, they saw the child with Mary his mother; and they knelt down and paid him homage. Then, opening their treasure-chests, they offered him gifts of gold, frankincense, and myrrh. ¹² And having been warned in a dream not to return to Herod, they left for their own country by another road.

POST COMMUNION

Lord God,
the bright splendour whom the nations seek:
may we who with the wise men
   have been drawn by your light
discern the glory of your presence in your Son,
the Word made flesh, Jesus Christ our Lord.

SECOND SERVICE

Psalms 98; 100
Baruch 4.36–5.9

or

Isaiah 60.1–9
John 2.1–11

THIRD SERVICE

Psalms 113; 132
Jeremiah 31.7–14
John 1.29–34

THE BAPTISM OF CHRIST
THE FIRST SUNDAY OF EPIPHANY

COLLECT

Eternal Father,
who at the baptism of Jesus
revealed him to be your Son,
anointing him with the Holy Spirit:
grant to us, who are born again by water and the Spirit,
that we may be faithful to our calling
   as your adopted children;
through Jesus Christ your Son our Lord,
who is alive and reigns with you,
in the unity of the Holy Spirit,
one God, now and for ever.

READING   Isaiah 43.1-7

¹ But now thus says the LORD,
  he who created you, O Jacob,
  he who formed you, O Israel:
Do not fear, for I have redeemed you;
  I have called you by name, you are mine.
² When you pass through the waters, I will be with you;
  and through the rivers, they shall not overwhelm you;
when you walk through fire you shall not be burned,
  and the flame shall not consume you.
³ For I am the LORD your God,
  the Holy One of Israel, your Saviour.
I give Egypt as your ransom,
  Ethiopia and Seba in exchange for you.
⁴ Because you are precious in my sight,
  and honoured, and I love you,
I give people in return for you,
  nations in exchange for your life.
⁵ Do not fear, for I am with you;
  I will bring your offspring from the east,
  and from the west I will gather you;
⁶ I will say to the north, 'Give them up',
  and to the south, 'Do not withhold;
bring my sons from far away
  and my daughters from the end of the earth—
⁷ everyone who is called by my name,
  whom I created for my glory,
  whom I formed and made.'

PSALM   Psalm 29

¹ Ascribe to the Lord, you gods,
  ascribe to the Lord glory and strength.
² Ascribe to the Lord the glory due to his name;
  worship the Lord in the beauty of holiness.
³ The voice of the Lord is upon the waters; the God of glory thunders;
  the Lord is upon the mighty waters.
⁴ The voice of the Lord is a powerful voice;
  the voice of the Lord is a voice of splendour.
⁵ The voice of the Lord breaks the cedar trees;
  the Lord breaks the cedars of Lebanon;

6 He makes Lebanon skip like a calf,
    and Mount Hermon like a young wild ox.
7 The voice of the Lord splits the flames of fire; the voice of the Lord
    shakes the wilderness;
    the Lord shakes the wilderness of Kadesh.
8 The voice of the Lord makes the oak trees writhe
    and strips the forests bare.
9 And in the temple of the Lord
    all are crying, 'Glory!'
10 The Lord sits enthroned above the flood;
    the Lord sits enthroned as king for evermore.
11 The Lord shall give strength to his people;
    the Lord shall give his people the blessing of peace.

READING   Acts 8.14–17

14 Now when the apostles at Jerusalem heard that Samaria had accepted the word of God, they sent Peter and John to them. 15 The two went down and prayed for them that they might receive the Holy Spirit 16 (for as yet the Spirit had not come upon any of them; they had only been baptized in the name of the Lord Jesus). 17 Then Peter and John laid their hands on them, and they received the Holy Spirit.

GOSPEL   Luke 3.15–17, 21–22

15 As the people were filled with expectation, and all were questioning in their hearts concerning John, whether he might be the Messiah, 16 John answered all of them by saying, 'I baptize you with water; but one who is more powerful than I is coming; I am not worthy to untie the thong of his sandals. He will baptize you with the Holy Spirit and fire. 17 His winnowing-fork is in his hand, to clear his threshing-floor and to gather the wheat into his granary; but the chaff he will burn with unquenchable fire.'

21 Now when all the people were baptized, and when Jesus also had been baptized and was praying, the heaven was opened, 22 and the Holy Spirit descended upon him in bodily form like a dove. And a voice came from heaven, 'You are my Son, the Beloved; with you I am well pleased.'

POST COMMUNION

Lord of all time and eternity,
you opened the heavens
    and revealed yourself as Father
in the baptism of Jesus your beloved Son:
by the power of your Spirit
complete the heavenly work of our rebirth
through the waters of the new creation;
through Jesus Christ our Lord.

SECOND SERVICE

Psalms 46; 47
Isaiah 55.1–11
Romans 6.1–11

*If the Second Service is a Eucharist, the
following is read as a Gospel:*

Mark 1.4–11

THIRD SERVICE

Psalm 89.19–29
Isaiah 42.1–9
Acts 19.1–7

THE SECOND SUNDAY OF EPIPHANY

COLLECT

Almighty God,
in Christ you make all things new:
transform the poverty of our nature
    by the riches of your grace,
and in the renewal of our lives
make known your heavenly glory;
through Jesus Christ your Son our Lord,
who is alive and reigns with you,
in the unity of the Holy Spirit,
one God, now and for ever.

READING   Isaiah 62.1–5

¹ For Zion's sake I will not keep silent,
     and for Jerusalem's sake I will not rest,
   until her vindication shines out like the dawn,
     and her salvation like a burning torch.
² The nations shall see your vindication,
     and all the kings your glory;
   and you shall be called by a new name
     that the mouth of the LORD will give.
³ You shall be a crown of beauty in the hand of the LORD,
     and a royal diadem in the hand of your God.
⁴ You shall no more be termed Forsaken,
     and your land shall no more be termed Desolate;
   but you shall be called My Delight Is in Her,
     and your land Married;
   for the LORD delights in you,
     and your land shall be married.
⁵ For as a young man marries a young woman,
     so shall your builder marry you,
   and as the bridegroom rejoices over the bride,
     so shall your God rejoice over you.

PSALM   Psalm 36.5–10

⁵ Your love, O Lord, reaches to the heavens,
     and your faithfulness to the clouds.
⁶ Your righteousness is like the strong mountains, your justice like
     the great deep;
   you save both human and beast, O Lord.
⁷ How priceless is your love, O God!
     your people take refuge under the shadow of your wings.
⁸ They feast upon the abundance of your house;
     you give them drink from the river of your delights.
⁹ For with you is the well of life,
     and in your light we see light.
¹⁰ Continue your loving-kindness to those who know you,
     and your favour to those who are true of heart.

READING   **1 Corinthians 12.1–11**

¹ Now concerning spiritual gifts, brothers and sisters, I do not want you to be uninformed. ² You know that when you were pagans, you were enticed and led astray to idols that could not speak. ³ Therefore I want you to understand that no one speaking by the Spirit of God ever says 'Let Jesus be cursed!' and no one can say 'Jesus is Lord' except by the Holy Spirit.

⁴ Now there are varieties of gifts, but the same Spirit; ⁵ and there are varieties of services, but the same Lord; ⁶ and there are varieties of activities, but it is the same God who activates all of them in everyone. ⁷ To each is given the manifestation of the Spirit for the common good. ⁸ To one is given through the Spirit the utterance of wisdom, and to another the utterance of knowledge according to the same Spirit, ⁹ to another faith by the same Spirit, to another gifts of healing by the one Spirit, ¹⁰ to another the working of miracles, to another prophecy, to another the discernment of spirits, to another various kinds of tongues, to another the interpretation of tongues. ¹¹ All these are activated by one and the same Spirit, who allots to each one individually just as the Spirit chooses.

GOSPEL   **John 2.1–11**

¹ On the third day there was a wedding in Cana of Galilee, and the mother of Jesus was there. ² Jesus and his disciples had also been invited to the wedding. ³ When the wine gave out, the mother of Jesus said to him, 'They have no wine.' ⁴ And Jesus said to her, 'Woman, what concern is that to you and to me? My hour has not yet come.' ⁵ His mother said to the servants, 'Do whatever he tells you.' ⁶ Now standing there were six stone water-jars for the Jewish rites of purification, each holding twenty or thirty gallons. ⁷ Jesus said to them, 'Fill the jars with water.' And they filled them up to the brim. ⁸ He said to them, 'Now draw some out, and take it to the chief steward.' So they took it. ⁹ When the steward tasted the water that had become wine, and did not know where it came from (though the servants who had drawn the water knew), the steward called the bridegroom ¹⁰ and said to him, 'Everyone serves the good wine first, and then the inferior wine after the guests have become drunk. But you have kept the good wine until now.' ¹¹ Jesus did this, the first of his signs, in Cana of Galilee, and revealed his glory; and his disciples believed in him.

POST COMMUNION

God of glory,
you nourish us with your Word
who is the bread of life:
fill us with your Holy Spirit
that through us the light of your glory
may shine in all the world.
We ask this in the name of Jesus Christ our Lord.

SECOND SERVICE

Psalm 96
1 Samuel 3.1–20
Ephesians 4.1–16

*If the Second Service is a Eucharist, the
following is read as a Gospel:*

John 1.29–42

THIRD SERVICE

Psalm 145.1–14
Isaiah 49.1–7
Acts 16.11–15

THE THIRD SUNDAY OF EPIPHANY

COLLECT

Almighty God,
whose Son revealed in signs and miracles
the wonder of your saving presence:
renew your people with your heavenly grace,
and in all our weakness
sustain us by your mighty power;
through Jesus Christ your Son our Lord,
who is alive and reigns with you,
in the unity of the Holy Spirit,
one God, now and for ever.

READING   Nehemiah 8.1–3, 5–6, 8–10

[1] All the people gathered together into the square before the Water Gate.
They told the scribe Ezra to bring the book of the law of Moses, which the
LORD had given to Israel. [2] Accordingly, the priest Ezra brought the law
before the assembly, both men and women and all who could hear with

understanding. This was on the first day of the seventh month. ³ He read from it facing the square before the Water Gate from early morning until midday, in the presence of the men and the women and those who could understand; and the ears of all the people were attentive to the book of the law.

⁵ And Ezra opened the book in the sight of all the people, for he was standing above all the people; and when he opened it, all the people stood up. ⁶ Then Ezra blessed the Lord, the great God, and all the people answered, 'Amen, Amen', lifting up their hands. Then they bowed their heads and worshipped the Lord with their faces to the ground.

⁸ So they read from the book, from the law of God, with interpretation. They gave the sense, so that the people understood the reading.

⁹ And Nehemiah, who was the governor, and Ezra the priest and scribe, and the Levites who taught the people said to all the people, 'This day is holy to the Lord your God; do not mourn or weep.' For all the people wept when they heard the words of the law. ¹⁰ Then he said to them, 'Go your way, eat the fat and drink sweet wine and send portions of them to those for whom nothing is prepared, for this day is holy to our Lord; and do not be grieved, for the joy of the Lord is your strength.'

PSALM   Psalm 19.1–6, [7–14]

1   The heavens declare the glory of God,
    and the firmament shows his handiwork.
2   One day tells its tale to another,
    and one night imparts knowledge to another.
3   Although they have no words or language,
    and their voices are not heard,
4   Their sound has gone out into all lands,
    and their message to the ends of the world.
5   In the deep has he set a pavilion for the sun;
    it comes forth like a bridegroom out of his chamber; it rejoices
        like a champion to run its course.
6   It goes forth from the uttermost edge of the heavens and runs
        about to the end of it again;
    nothing is hidden from its burning heat.
[7 The law of the Lord is perfect and revives the soul;
    the testimony of the Lord is sure and gives wisdom to the innocent.
8   The statutes of the Lord are just and rejoice the heart;
    the commandment of the Lord is clear and gives light to the eyes.
9   The fear of the Lord is clean and endures for ever;
    the judgements of the Lord are true and righteous altogether.

¹⁰ More to be desired are they than gold, more than much fine gold,
    sweeter far than honey, than honey in the comb.
¹¹ By them also is your servant enlightened,
    and in keeping them there is great reward.
¹² Who can tell how often he offends?
    Cleanse me from my secret faults.
¹³ Above all, keep your servant from presumptuous sins; let them
      not get dominion over me;
    then shall I be whole and sound, and innocent of a great offence.
¹⁴ Let the words of my mouth and the meditation of my heart be
      acceptable in your sight,
    O Lord, my strength and my redeemer.]

READING   1 Corinthians 12.12–31a

¹² For just as the body is one and has many members, and all the members of the body, though many, are one body, so it is with Christ. ¹³ For in the one Spirit we were all baptized into one body—Jews or Greeks, slaves or free—and we were all made to drink of one Spirit.

¹⁴ Indeed, the body does not consist of one member but of many. ¹⁵ If the foot were to say, 'Because I am not a hand, I do not belong to the body', that would not make it any less a part of the body. ¹⁶ And if the ear were to say, 'Because I am not an eye, I do not belong to the body', that would not make it any less a part of the body. ¹⁷ If the whole body were an eye, where would the hearing be? If the whole body were hearing, where would the sense of smell be? ¹⁸ But as it is, God arranged the members in the body, each one of them, as he chose. ¹⁹ If all were a single member, where would the body be? ²⁰ As it is, there are many members, yet one body. ²¹ The eye cannot say to the hand, 'I have no need of you', nor again the head to the feet, 'I have no need of you.' ²² On the contrary, the members of the body that seem to be weaker are indispensable, ²³ and those members of the body that we think less honourable we clothe with greater honour, and our less respectable members are treated with greater respect; ²⁴ whereas our more respectable members do not need this. But God has so arranged the body, giving the greater honour to the inferior member, ²⁵ that there may be no dissension within the body, but the members may have the same care for one another. ²⁶ If one member suffers, all suffer together with it; if one member is honoured, all rejoice together with it.

²⁷ Now you are the body of Christ and individually members of it. ²⁸ And God has appointed in the church first apostles, second prophets, third teachers; then deeds of power, then gifts of healing, forms of assistance, forms of leadership, various kinds of tongues. ²⁹ Are all apostles? Are all

prophets? Are all teachers? Do all work miracles? [30] Do all possess gifts of healing? Do all speak in tongues? Do all interpret? [31] But strive for the greater gifts.

GOSPEL   Luke 4.14–21

[14] Then Jesus, filled with the power of the Spirit, returned to Galilee, and a report about him spread through all the surrounding country. [15] He began to teach in their synagogues and was praised by everyone.

[16] When he came to Nazareth, where he had been brought up, he went to the synagogue on the sabbath day, as was his custom. He stood up to read, [17] and the scroll of the prophet Isaiah was given to him. He unrolled the scroll and found the place where it was written:
[18] 'The Spirit of the Lord is upon me,
> because he has anointed me
>> to bring good news to the poor.
> He has sent me to proclaim release to the captives
>> and recovery of sight to the blind,
>>> to let the oppressed go free,
[19] to proclaim the year of the Lord's favour.'
[20] And he rolled up the scroll, gave it back to the attendant, and sat down. The eyes of all in the synagogue were fixed on him. [21] Then he began to say to them, 'Today this scripture has been fulfilled in your hearing.'

POST COMMUNION

Almighty Father,
whose Son our Saviour Jesus Christ
  is the light of the world:
may your people,
illumined by your word and sacraments,
shine with the radiance of his glory,
that he may be known, worshipped, and obeyed
  to the ends of the earth;
for he is alive and reigns, now and for ever.

SECOND SERVICE	THIRD SERVICE
Psalm 33	**Psalm 113**
Numbers 9.15–23	**Deuteronomy 30.11–15**
1 Corinthians 7.17–24	**3 John 1, 5–8**

If the Second Service is a Eucharist, the following is read as a Gospel:

Mark 1.21–28

THE FOURTH SUNDAY OF EPIPHANY

COLLECT

God our creator,
who in the beginning
commanded the light to shine out of darkness:
we pray that the light of the glorious gospel of Christ
may dispel the darkness of ignorance and unbelief,
shine into the hearts of all your people,
and reveal the knowledge of your glory
    in the face of Jesus Christ your Son our Lord,
who is alive and reigns with you,
in the unity of the Holy Spirit,
one God, now and for ever.

READING   Ezekiel 43.27–44.4

²⁷ When these days are over, then from the eighth day onwards the priests shall offer upon the altar your burnt-offerings and your offerings of well-being; and I will accept you, says the Lord GOD.

¹ Then he brought me back to the outer gate of the sanctuary, which faces east; and it was shut. ² The LORD said to me: This gate shall remain shut; it shall not be opened, and no one shall enter by it; for the LORD, the God of Israel, has entered by it; therefore it shall remain shut. ³ Only the prince, because he is a prince, may sit in it to eat food before the LORD; he shall enter by way of the vestibule of the gate, and shall go out by the same way.

⁴ Then he brought me by way of the north gate to the front of the temple; and I looked, and lo! the glory of the LORD filled the temple of the LORD; and I fell upon my face.

PSALM   Psalm 48

1 Great is the Lord and highly to be praised;
   in the city of our God is his holy hill.
2 Beautiful and lofty, the joy of all the earth, is the hill of Zion,
   the very centre of the world and the city of the great king.
3 God is in her citadels;
   he is known to be her sure refuge.
4 Behold, the kings of the earth assembled
   and marched forward together.
5 They looked and were astounded;
   they retreated and fled in terror.
6 Trembling seized them there;
   they writhed like a woman in childbirth, like ships of the sea when
      the east wind shatters them.
7 As we have heard, so have we seen, in the city of the Lord of hosts,
      in the city of our God;
   God has established her for ever.
8 We have waited in silence on your loving-kindness, O God,
   in the midst of your temple.
9 Your praise, like your name, O God, reaches to the world's end;
   your right hand is full of justice.
10 Let Mount Zion be glad and the cities of Judah rejoice,
   because of your judgements.
11 Make the circuit of Zion; walk round about her;
   count the number of her towers.
12 Consider well her bulwarks; examine her strongholds;
   that you may tell those who come after.
13 This God is our God for ever and ever;
   he shall be our guide for evermore.

READING   1 Corinthians 13.1–13

1 If I speak in the tongues of mortals and of angels, but do not have love,
I am a noisy gong or a clanging cymbal. 2 And if I have prophetic powers,
and understand all mysteries and all knowledge, and if I have all faith, so
as to remove mountains, but do not have love, I am nothing. 3 If I give away
all my possessions, and if I hand over my body so that I may boast, but do
not have love, I gain nothing.

4 Love is patient; love is kind; love is not envious or boastful or arrogant
5 or rude. It does not insist on its own way; it is not irritable or resentful;
6 it does not rejoice in wrongdoing, but rejoices in the truth. 7 It bears all
things, believes all things, hopes all things, endures all things.

⁸ Love never ends. But as for prophecies, they will come to an end; as for tongues, they will cease; as for knowledge, it will come to an end. ⁹ For we know only in part, and we prophesy only in part; ¹⁰ but when the complete comes, the partial will come to an end. ¹¹ When I was a child, I spoke like a child, I thought like a child, I reasoned like a child; when I became an adult, I put an end to childish ways. ¹² For now we see in a mirror, dimly, but then we will see face to face. Now I know only in part; then I will know fully, even as I have been fully known. ¹³ And now faith, hope, and love abide, these three; and the greatest of these is love.

GOSPEL   Luke 2.22–40

²² When the time came for their purification according to the law of Moses, they brought him up to Jerusalem to present him to the Lord ²³ (as it is written in the law of the Lord, 'Every firstborn male shall be designated as holy to the Lord'), ²⁴ and they offered a sacrifice according to what is stated in the law of the Lord, 'a pair of turtle-doves or two young pigeons.'

²⁵ Now there was a man in Jerusalem whose name was Simeon; this man was righteous and devout, looking forward to the consolation of Israel, and the Holy Spirit rested on him. ²⁶ It had been revealed to him by the Holy Spirit that he would not see death before he had seen the Lord's Messiah. ²⁷ Guided by the Spirit, Simeon came into the temple; and when the parents brought in the child Jesus, to do for him what was customary under the law, ²⁸ Simeon took him in his arms and praised God, saying,

²⁹ 'Master, now you are dismissing your servant in peace,
     according to your word;
³⁰ for my eyes have seen your salvation,
³¹   which you have prepared in the presence of all peoples,
³² a light for revelation to the Gentiles
     and for glory to your people Israel.'

³³ And the child's father and mother were amazed at what was being said about him. ³⁴ Then Simeon blessed them and said to his mother Mary, 'This child is destined for the falling and the rising of many in Israel, and to be a sign that will be opposed ³⁵ so that the inner thoughts of many will be revealed—and a sword will pierce your own soul too.'

³⁶ There was also a prophet, Anna the daughter of Phanuel, of the tribe of Asher. She was of a great age, having lived with her husband for seven years after her marriage, ³⁷ then as a widow to the age of eighty-four. She never left the temple but worshipped there with fasting and prayer night and day. ³⁸ At that moment she came, and began to praise God and to speak about the child to all who were looking for the redemption of Jerusalem.

[39] When they had finished everything required by the law of the Lord, they returned to Galilee, to their own town of Nazareth. [40] The child grew and became strong, filled with wisdom; and the favour of God was upon him.

POST COMMUNION

Generous Lord,
in word and eucharist we have proclaimed
   the mystery of your love:
help us so to live out our days
that we may be signs of your wonders in the world;
through Jesus Christ our Saviour.

SECOND SERVICE	THIRD SERVICE
Psalm 34	**Psalm 71.1–6, 15–17**
1 Chronicles 29.6–19	**Micah 6.1–8**
Acts 7.44–50	**1 Corinthians 6.12–20**

If the Second Service is a Eucharist, the following is read as a Gospel:

John 4.19–29a

THE PRESENTATION OF CHRIST IN THE TEMPLE
CANDLEMAS   2 FEBRUARY

COLLECT

Almighty and ever-living God,
clothed in majesty,
whose beloved Son
   was this day presented in the Temple,
in substance of our flesh:
grant that we may be presented to you
with pure and clean hearts,
by your Son Jesus Christ our Lord,
who is alive and reigns with you,
in the unity of the Holy Spirit,
one God, now and for ever.

READING   Malachi 3.1–5

¹ See, I am sending my messenger to prepare the way before me, and the Lord whom you seek will suddenly come to his temple. The messenger of the covenant in whom you delight—indeed, he is coming, says the LORD of hosts. ² But who can endure the day of his coming, and who can stand when he appears?

For he is like a refiner's fire and like fullers' soap; ³ he will sit as a refiner and purifier of silver, and he will purify the descendants of Levi and refine them like gold and silver, until they present offerings to the LORD in righteousness. ⁴ Then the offering of Judah and Jerusalem will be pleasing to the LORD as in the days of old and as in former years.

⁵ Then I will draw near to you for judgement; I will be swift to bear witness against the sorcerers, against the adulterers, against those who swear falsely, against those who oppress the hired workers in their wages, the widow, and the orphan, against those who thrust aside the alien, and do not fear me, says the LORD of hosts.

PSALM   Psalm 24.[1–6,] 7–10

[¹ The earth is the Lord's and all that is in it,
  the world and all who dwell therein.
² For it is he who founded it upon the seas
  and made it firm upon the rivers of the deep.
³ 'Who can ascend the hill of the Lord?
  and who can stand in his holy place?'
⁴ 'Those who have clean hands and a pure heart,
  who have not pledged themselves to falsehood, nor sworn by what
    is a fraud.
⁵ They shall receive a blessing from the Lord
  and a just reward from the God of their salvation.'
⁶ Such is the generation of those who seek him,
  of those who seek your face, O God of Jacob.]
⁷ Lift up your heads, O gates; lift them high, O everlasting doors;
  and the King of glory shall come in.
⁸ 'Who is this King of glory?'
  'The Lord, strong and mighty, the Lord, mighty in battle.'
⁹ Lift up your heads, O gates; lift them high, O everlasting doors;
  and the King of glory shall come in.
¹⁰ 'Who is he, this King of glory?'
  'The Lord of hosts, he is the King of glory.'

READING   Hebrews 2.14‒18

[14] Since, therefore, the children share flesh and blood, he himself likewise shared the same things, so that through death he might destroy the one who has the power of death, that is, the devil, [15] and free those who all their lives were held in slavery by the fear of death. [16] For it is clear that he did not come to help angels, but the descendants of Abraham. [17] Therefore he had to become like his brothers and sisters in every respect, so that he might be a merciful and faithful high priest in the service of God, to make a sacrifice of atonement for the sins of the people. [18] Because he himself was tested by what he suffered, he is able to help those who are being tested.

GOSPEL   Luke 2.22‒40

[22] When the time came for their purification according to the law of Moses, they brought him up to Jerusalem to present him to the Lord [23] (as it is written in the law of the Lord, 'Every firstborn male shall be designated as holy to the Lord'), [24] and they offered a sacrifice according to what is stated in the law of the Lord, 'a pair of turtle-doves or two young pigeons.'

[25] Now there was a man in Jerusalem whose name was Simeon; this man was righteous and devout, looking forward to the consolation of Israel, and the Holy Spirit rested on him. [26] It had been revealed to him by the Holy Spirit that he would not see death before he had seen the Lord's Messiah. [27] Guided by the Spirit, Simeon came into the temple; and when the parents brought in the child Jesus, to do for him what was customary under the law, [28] Simeon took him in his arms and praised God, saying,

[29]   'Master, now you are dismissing your servant in peace,
          according to your word;
[30]   for my eyes have seen your salvation,
[31]   which you have prepared in the presence of all peoples,
[32]   a light for revelation to the Gentiles
          and for glory to your people Israel.'

[33] And the child's father and mother were amazed at what was being said about him. [34] Then Simeon blessed them and said to his mother Mary, 'This child is destined for the falling and the rising of many in Israel, and to be a sign that will be opposed [35] so that the inner thoughts of many will be revealed—and a sword will pierce your own soul too.'

[36] There was also a prophet, Anna the daughter of Phanuel, of the tribe of Asher. She was of a great age, having lived with her husband for seven years after her marriage, [37] then as a widow to the age of eighty-four. She never left the temple but worshipped there with fasting and prayer night and

day. [38] At that moment she came, and began to praise God and to speak about the child to all who were looking for the redemption of Jerusalem.

[39] When they had finished everything required by the law of the Lord, they returned to Galilee, to their own town of Nazareth. [40] The child grew and became strong, filled with wisdom; and the favour of God was upon him.

POST COMMUNION

Lord, you fulfilled the hope of Simeon and Anna,
who lived to welcome the Messiah:
may we, who have received these gifts beyond words,
prepare to meet Christ Jesus when he comes
    to bring us to eternal life;
for he is alive and reigns, now and for ever.

SECOND SERVICE   THIRD SERVICE

Psalms 122; 132   Psalms 42; 43; 48
Haggai 2.1–9   Exodus 13.1–16
John 2.18–22   Romans 12.1–5

TABLE OF SUNDAYS BEFORE LENT
DATES AND PROPERS

YEAR	LITURGICAL YEAR	FIFTH SUNDAY BEFORE LENT	FOURTH SUNDAY BEFORE LENT	THIRD SUNDAY BEFORE LENT	SECOND SUNDAY BEFORE LENT	FIRST SUNDAY BEFORE LENT
1999	A				7 Feb	14 Feb
2000	B	6 Feb (1)	13 Feb (2)	20 Feb (3)	27 Feb	5 Mar
2001	C		4 Feb (1)	11 Feb (2)	18 Feb	25 Feb
2002	A				3 Feb	10 Feb
2003	B		9 Feb (1)	16 Feb (2)	23 Feb	2 Mar
2004	C			8 Feb (1)	15 Feb	22 Feb
2005	A					6 Feb
2006	B		5 Feb (1)	12 Feb (2)	19 Feb	26 Feb
2007	C			4 Feb (1)	11 Feb	18 Feb
2008	A					3 Feb
2009	B			8 Feb (1)	15 Feb	22 Feb
2010	C				7 Feb	14 Feb
2011	A	6 Feb (1)	13 Feb (2)	20 Feb (3)	27 Feb	6 Mar
2012	B			5 Feb (1)	12 Feb	19 Feb
2013	C				3 Feb	10 Feb
2014	A		9 Feb (1)	16 Feb (2)	23 Feb	2 Mar
2015	B				8 Feb	15 Feb
2016	C					7 Feb
2017	A		5 Feb (1)	12 Feb (2)	19 Feb	26 Feb
2018	B				4 Feb	11 Feb
2019	C	3 Feb (1)	10 Feb (2)	17 Feb (3)	24 Feb	3 Mar
2020	A			9 Feb (1)	16 Feb	23 Feb

The figures in parentheses after dates indicate the appropriate Proper provisions for the day

THE FIFTH SUNDAY BEFORE LENT

COLLECT

Almighty God,
by whose grace alone we are accepted
    and called to your service:
strengthen us by your Holy Spirit
and make us worthy of our calling;
through Jesus Christ your Son our Lord,
who is alive and reigns with you,
in the unity of the Holy Spirit,
one God, now and for ever.

READINGS

See pages 794 to 797 and Table on page 791

POST COMMUNION

God of truth,
we have seen with our eyes
    and touched with our hands the bread of life:
strengthen our faith
that we may grow in love for you and for each other;
through Jesus Christ our Lord.

THE FOURTH SUNDAY BEFORE LENT

COLLECT

O God,
you know us to be set
in the midst of so many and great dangers,
that by reason of the frailty of our nature
we cannot always stand upright:
grant to us such strength and protection
as may support us in all dangers
and carry us through all temptations;
through Jesus Christ your Son our Lord,

who is alive and reigns with you,
in the unity of the Holy Spirit,
one God, now and for ever.

READINGS

See pages 794 to 800 and Table on page 791

POST COMMUNION

Go before us, Lord, in all we do
with your most gracious favour,
and guide us with your continual help,
that in all our works
begun, continued and ended in you,
we may glorify your holy name,
and finally by your mercy receive everlasting life;
through Jesus Christ our Lord.

THE THIRD SUNDAY BEFORE LENT

COLLECT

Almighty God,
who alone can bring order
to the unruly wills and passions of sinful humanity:
give your people grace
so to love what you command
and to desire what you promise,
that, among the many changes of this world,
our hearts may surely there be fixed
where true joys are to be found;
through Jesus Christ your Son our Lord,
who is alive and reigns with you,
in the unity of the Holy Spirit,
one God, now and for ever.

READINGS

See pages 794 to 803 and Table on page 791

POST COMMUNION

Merciful Father,
who gave Jesus Christ to be for us the bread of life,
that those who come to him should never hunger:
draw us to the Lord in faith and love,
that we may eat and drink with him
at his table in the kingdom,
where he is alive and reigns, now and for ever.

PROPER 1

Sunday between 3 and 9 February inclusive (if earlier than the Second Sunday before Lent)

COLLECT

See pages 792 to 793 and Table on page 791

READING   Isaiah 6.1–8, [9–13]

¹ In the year that King Uzziah died, I saw the Lord sitting on a throne, high and lofty; and the hem of his robe filled the temple. ² Seraphs were in attendance above him; each had six wings: with two they covered their faces, and with two they covered their feet, and with two they flew. ³ And one called to another and said:

'Holy, holy, holy is the LORD of hosts;
    the whole earth is full of his glory.'
⁴ The pivots on the thresholds shook at the voices of those who called, and the house filled with smoke. ⁵ And I said: 'Woe is me! I am lost, for I am a man of unclean lips, and I live among a people of unclean lips; yet my eyes have seen the King, the LORD of hosts!'

⁶ Then one of the seraphs flew to me, holding a live coal that had been taken from the altar with a pair of tongs. ⁷ The seraph touched my mouth with it and said: 'Now that this has touched your lips, your guilt has departed and your sin is blotted out.' ⁸ Then I heard the voice of the Lord saying, 'Whom shall I send, and who will go for us?' And I said, 'Here am I; send me!'

[⁹ And he said, 'Go and say to this people:
    "Keep listening, but do not comprehend;
    keep looking, but do not understand."

10 Make the mind of this people dull,
        and stop their ears,
        and shut their eyes,
    so that they may not look with their eyes,
        and listen with their ears,
    and comprehend with their minds,
        and turn and be healed.'
11 Then I said, 'How long, O Lord?' And he said:
    'Until cities lie waste
        without inhabitant,
    and houses without people,
        and the land is utterly desolate;
12 until the LORD sends everyone far away,
        and vast is the emptiness in the midst of the land.
13 Even if a tenth part remains in it,
        it will be burned again,
    like a terebinth or an oak
        whose stump remains standing
        when it is felled.'
    The holy seed is its stump.]

PSALM   Psalm 138

1 I will give thanks to you, O Lord, with my whole heart;
    before the gods I will sing your praise.
2 I will bow down towards your holy temple and praise your name,
    because of your love and faithfulness;
3 For you have glorified your name
    and your word above all things.
4 When I called, you answered me;
    you increased my strength within me.
5 All the kings of the earth will praise you, O Lord,
    when they have heard the words of your mouth.
6 They will sing of the ways of the Lord,
    that great is the glory of the Lord.
7 Though the Lord be high, he cares for the lowly;
    he perceives the haughty from afar.
8 Though I walk in the midst of trouble, you keep me safe;
    you stretch forth your hand against the fury of my enemies; your
        right hand shall save me.
9 The Lord will make good his purpose for me;
    O Lord, your love endures for ever; do not abandon the works of
        your hands.

READING   1 Corinthians 15.1-11

¹ Now I should remind you, brothers and sisters, of the good news that I proclaimed to you, which you in turn received, in which also you stand, ² through which also you are being saved, if you hold firmly to the message that I proclaimed to you—unless you have come to believe in vain.

³ For I handed on to you as of first importance what I in turn had received: that Christ died for our sins in accordance with the scriptures, ⁴ and that he was buried, and that he was raised on the third day in accordance with the scriptures, ⁵ and that he appeared to Cephas, then to the twelve. ⁶ Then he appeared to more than five hundred brothers and sisters at one time, most of whom are still alive, though some have died. ⁷ Then he appeared to James, then to all the apostles. ⁸ Last of all, as to someone untimely born, he appeared also to me. ⁹ For I am the least of the apostles, unfit to be called an apostle, because I persecuted the church of God. ¹⁰ But by the grace of God I am what I am, and his grace towards me has not been in vain. On the contrary, I worked harder than any of them—though it was not I, but the grace of God that is with me. ¹¹ Whether then it was I or they, so we proclaim and so you have come to believe.

GOSPEL   Luke 5.1-11

¹ Once while Jesus was standing beside the lake of Gennesaret, and the crowd was pressing in on him to hear the word of God, ² he saw two boats there at the shore of the lake; the fishermen had gone out of them and were washing their nets. ³ He got into one of the boats, the one belonging to Simon, and asked him to put out a little way from the shore. Then he sat down and taught the crowds from the boat. ⁴ When he had finished speaking, he said to Simon, 'Put out into the deep water and let down your nets for a catch.' ⁵ Simon answered, 'Master, we have worked all night long but have caught nothing. Yet if you say so, I will let down the nets.' ⁶ When they had done this, they caught so many fish that their nets were beginning to break. ⁷ So they signalled to their partners in the other boat to come and help them. And they came and filled both boats, so that they began to sink. ⁸ But when Simon Peter saw it, he fell down at Jesus' knees, saying, 'Go away from me, Lord, for I am a sinful man!' ⁹ For he and all who were with him were amazed at the catch of fish that they had taken; ¹⁰ and so also were James and John, sons of Zebedee, who were partners with Simon. Then Jesus said to Simon, 'Do not be afraid; from now on you will be catching people.' ¹¹ When they had brought their boats to shore, they left everything and followed him.

POST COMMUNION

See pages 792 to 794 and Table on page 791

SECOND SERVICE   THIRD SERVICE

Psalms [1;] 2   **Psalms 3; 4**
Wisdom 6.1–21   **Jeremiah 26.1–16**
or   **Acts 3.1–10**

Hosea 1
Colossians 3.1–22

If the Second Service is a Eucharist, the
following is read as a Gospel:

Matthew 5.13–20

PROPER 2

Sunday between 10 and 16 February inclusive (if earlier than the Second Sunday before Lent)
The provisions of Propers 2 and 3 are only used if there are more than four Sundays between 2 February and Ash Wednesday

COLLECT

See pages 792 to 793 and Table on page 791

READING   **Jeremiah 17.5–10**

⁵ Thus says the LORD:
  Cursed are those who trust in mere mortals
    and make mere flesh their strength,
    whose hearts turn away from the LORD.
⁶ They shall be like a shrub in the desert,
    and shall not see when relief comes.
  They shall live in the parched places of the wilderness,
    in an uninhabited salt land.
⁷ Blessed are those who trust in the LORD,
    whose trust is the LORD.

8 They shall be like a tree planted by water,
   sending out its roots by the stream.
 It shall not fear when heat comes,
   and its leaves shall stay green;
 in the year of drought it is not anxious,
   and it does not cease to bear fruit.
9 The heart is devious above all else;
   it is perverse—
 who can understand it?
10 I the LORD test the mind
   and search the heart,
 to give to all according to their ways,
   according to the fruit of their doings.

PSALM   Psalm 1

1 Happy are they who have not walked in the counsel of the wicked,
   nor lingered in the way of sinners, nor sat in the seats of the
     scornful!
2 Their delight is in the law of the Lord,
   and they meditate on his law day and night.
3 They are like trees planted by streams of water, bearing fruit in
   due season, with leaves that do not wither;
 everything they do shall prosper.
4 It is not so with the wicked:
   they are like chaff which the wind blows away;
5 Therefore the wicked shall not stand upright when judgement
   comes,
 nor the sinner in the council of the righteous.
6 For the Lord knows the way of the righteous,
   but the way of the wicked is doomed.

READING   1 Corinthians 15.12–20

12 Now if Christ is proclaimed as raised from the dead, how can some of you say there is no resurrection of the dead? 13 If there is no resurrection of the dead, then Christ has not been raised; 14 and if Christ has not been raised, then our proclamation has been in vain and your faith has been in vain. 15 We are even found to be misrepresenting God, because we testified of God that he raised Christ—whom he did not raise if it is true that the dead are not raised. 16 For if the dead are not raised, then Christ has not been raised. 17 If Christ has not been raised, your faith is futile and you are still in your sins. 18 Then those also who have died in Christ have perished.

¹⁹ If for this life only we have hoped in Christ, we are of all people most to be pitied.

²⁰ But in fact Christ has been raised from the dead, the first fruits of those who have died.

GOSPEL   Luke 6.17–26

¹⁷ He came down with them and stood on a level place, with a great crowd of his disciples and a great multitude of people from all Judea, Jerusalem, and the coast of Tyre and Sidon. ¹⁸ They had come to hear him and to be healed of their diseases; and those who were troubled with unclean spirits were cured. ¹⁹ And all in the crowd were trying to touch him, for power came out from him and healed all of them.

²⁰ Then he looked up at his disciples and said:
  'Blessed are you who are poor,
    for yours is the kingdom of God.
²¹ Blessed are you who are hungry now,
      for you will be filled.
  Blessed are you who weep now,
      for you will laugh.

²² 'Blessed are you when people hate you, and when they exclude you, revile you, and defame you on account of the Son of Man. ²³ Rejoice on that day and leap for joy, for surely your reward is great in heaven; for that is what their ancestors did to the prophets.
²⁴ But woe to you who are rich,
      for you have received your consolation.
²⁵ Woe to you who are full now,
      for you will be hungry.
  Woe to you who are laughing now,
      for you will mourn and weep.

²⁶ 'Woe to you when all speak well of you, for that is what their ancestors did to the false prophets.'

POST COMMUNION

See pages 792 to 793 and Table on page 791

SECOND SERVICE	THIRD SERVICE
Psalms [5;] 6	Psalm 7
Wisdom 11.21–12.11	Jeremiah 30.1–3, 10–22
or	Acts 6
Hosea 10.1–8, 12	
Galatians 4.8–20	

If the Second Service is a Eucharist, the following is read as a Gospel:

Matthew 5.21–37

PROPER 3

Sunday between 17 and 23 February inclusive (if earlier than the Second Sunday before Lent)

The provisions of Propers 2 and 3 are only used if there are more than four Sundays between 2 February and Ash Wednesday

COLLECT

See page 793 and Table on page 791

READING   Genesis 45.3–11, 15

[3] Joseph said to his brothers, 'I am Joseph. Is my father still alive?' But his brothers could not answer him, so dismayed were they at his presence.

[4] Then Joseph said to his brothers, 'Come closer to me.' And they came closer. He said, 'I am your brother Joseph, whom you sold into Egypt. [5] And now do not be distressed, or angry with yourselves, because you sold me here; for God sent me before you to preserve life. [6] For the famine has been in the land these two years; and there are five more years in which there will be neither ploughing nor harvest. [7] God sent me before you to preserve for you a remnant on earth, and to keep alive for you many survivors. [8] So it was not you who sent me here, but God; he has made me a father to Pharaoh, and lord of all his house and ruler over all the land of Egypt. [9] Hurry and go up to my father and say to him, "Thus says your son Joseph,

God has made me lord of all Egypt; come down to me, do not delay. ¹⁰ You shall settle in the land of Goshen, and you shall be near me, you and your children and your children's children, as well as your flocks, your herds, and all that you have. ¹¹ I will provide for you there—since there are five more years of famine to come—so that you and your household, and all that you have, will not come to poverty." '

¹⁵ And he kissed all his brothers and wept upon them; and after that his brothers talked with him.

PSALM   Psalm 37.1–8, [9–12, 41–42]

¹ Do not fret yourself because of evildoers;
   do not be jealous of those who do wrong.
² For they shall soon wither like the grass,
   and like the green grass fade away.
³ Put your trust in the Lord and do good;
   dwell in the land and feed on its riches.
⁴ Take delight in the Lord,
   and he shall give you your heart's desire.
⁵ Commit your way to the Lord and put your trust in him,
   and he will bring it to pass.
⁶ He will make your righteousness as clear as the light
   and your just dealing as the noonday.
⁷ Be still before the Lord
   and wait patiently for him.
⁸ Do not fret yourself over the one who prospers,
   the one who succeeds in evil schemes.
[⁹ Refrain from anger, leave rage alone;
   do not fret yourself; it leads only to evil.
¹⁰ For evildoers shall be cut off,
   but those who wait upon the Lord shall possess the land.
¹¹ In a little while the wicked shall be no more;
   you shall search out their place, but they will not be there.
¹² But the lowly shall possess the land;
   they will delight in abundance of peace.

⁴¹ But the deliverance of the righteous comes from the Lord;
   he is their stronghold in time of trouble.
⁴² The Lord will help them and rescue them;
   he will rescue them from the wicked and deliver them, because
      they seek refuge in him.]

READING   1 Corinthians 15.35–38, 42–50

[35] But someone will ask, 'How are the dead raised? With what kind of body do they come?' [36] Fool! What you sow does not come to life unless it dies. [37] And as for what you sow, you do not sow the body that is to be, but a bare seed, perhaps of wheat or of some other grain. [38] But God gives it a body as he has chosen, and to each kind of seed its own body.

[42] So it is with the resurrection of the dead. What is sown is perishable, what is raised is imperishable. [43] It is sown in dishonour, it is raised in glory. It is sown in weakness, it is raised in power. [44] It is sown a physical body, it is raised a spiritual body. If there is a physical body, there is also a spiritual body. [45] Thus it is written, 'The first man, Adam, became a living being'; the last Adam became a life-giving spirit. [46] But it is not the spiritual that is first, but the physical, and then the spiritual. [47] The first man was from the earth, a man of dust; the second man is from heaven. [48] As was the man of dust, so are those who are of the dust; and as is the man of heaven, so are those who are of heaven. [49] Just as we have borne the image of the man of dust, we will also bear the image of the man of heaven.

[50] What I am saying, brothers and sisters, is this: flesh and blood cannot inherit the kingdom of God, nor does the perishable inherit the imperishable.

GOSPEL   Luke 6.27–38

[27] 'But I say to you that listen, Love your enemies, do good to those who hate you, [28] bless those who curse you, pray for those who abuse you. [29] If anyone strikes you on the cheek, offer the other also; and from anyone who takes away your coat do not withhold even your shirt. [30] Give to everyone who begs from you; and if anyone takes away your goods, do not ask for them again. [31] Do to others as you would have them do to you.

[32] 'If you love those who love you, what credit is that to you? For even sinners love those who love them. [33] If you do good to those who do good to you, what credit is that to you? For even sinners do the same. [34] If you lend to those from whom you hope to receive, what credit is that to you? Even sinners lend to sinners, to receive as much again. [35] But love your enemies, do good, and lend, expecting nothing in return. Your reward will be great, and you will be children of the Most High; for he is kind to the ungrateful and the wicked. [36] Be merciful, just as your Father is merciful.

[37] 'Do not judge, and you will not be judged; do not condemn, and you will not be condemned. Forgive, and you will be forgiven; [38] give, and it will be given to you. A good measure, pressed down, shaken together, running over, will be put into your lap; for the measure you give will be the measure you get back.'

POST COMMUNION

See page 793 and Table on page 791

SECOND SERVICE

Psalms [11;] 13
Hosea 14
Galatians 5.2–10

If the Second Service is a Eucharist, the following is read as a Gospel:

Matthew 6.1–8

THIRD SERVICE

Psalm 10
Jeremiah 33.1–11
Acts 8.4–25

THE SECOND SUNDAY BEFORE LENT

COLLECT

Almighty God,
you have created the heavens and the earth
and made us in your own image:
teach us to discern your hand in all your works
and your likeness in all your children;
through Jesus Christ your Son our Lord,
who with you and the Holy Spirit
    reigns supreme over all things,
now and for ever.

READING   Genesis 2.4b–9, 15–25

[4] In the day that the LORD God made the earth and the heavens, [5] when no plant of the field was yet in the earth and no herb of the field had yet sprung up—for the LORD God had not caused it to rain upon the earth, and there was no one to till the ground; [6] but a stream would rise from the earth, and water the whole face of the ground— [7] then the LORD God formed man from the dust of the ground, and breathed into his nostrils the breath of life; and the man became a living being. [8] And the LORD God planted a garden in Eden, in the east; and there he put the man whom he had formed. [9] Out of the ground the LORD God made to grow every tree

that is pleasant to the sight and good for food, the tree of life also in the midst of the garden, and the tree of the knowledge of good and evil.

¹⁵ The LORD God took the man and put him in the garden of Eden to till it and keep it. ¹⁶ And the LORD God commanded the man, 'You may freely eat of every tree of the garden; ¹⁷ but of the tree of the knowledge of good and evil you shall not eat, for in the day that you eat of it you shall die.'

¹⁸ Then the LORD God said, 'It is not good that the man should be alone; I will make him a helper as his partner.' ¹⁹ So out of the ground the LORD God formed every animal of the field and every bird of the air, and brought them to the man to see what he would call them; and whatever the man called each living creature, that was its name. ²⁰ The man gave names to all cattle, and to the birds of the air, and to every animal of the field; but for the man there was not found a helper as his partner. ²¹ So the LORD God caused a deep sleep to fall upon the man, and he slept; then he took one of his ribs and closed up its place with flesh. ²² And the rib that the LORD God had taken from the man he made into a woman and brought her to the man. ²³ Then the man said,

'This at last is bone of my bones
and flesh of my flesh;
this one shall be called Woman,
for out of Man this one was taken.'

²⁴ Therefore a man leaves his father and his mother and clings to his wife, and they become one flesh. ²⁵ And the man and his wife were both naked, and were not ashamed.

PSALM   Psalm 65

1   You are to be praised, O God, in Zion;
    to you shall vows be performed in Jerusalem.
2   To you that hear prayer shall all flesh come,
    because of their transgressions.
3   Our sins are stronger than we are,
    but you will blot them out.
4   Happy are they whom you choose and draw to your courts to dwell there!
    they will be satisfied by the beauty of your house, by the holiness of your temple.
5   Awesome things will you show us in your righteousness, O God of our salvation,
    O Hope of all the ends of the earth and of the seas that are far away.

6 You make fast the mountains by your power;
    they are girded about with might.
7 You still the roaring of the seas,
    the roaring of their waves, and the clamour of the peoples.
8 Those who dwell at the ends of the earth will tremble at your
        marvellous signs;
    you make the dawn and the dusk to sing for joy.
9 You visit the earth and water it abundantly; you make it very
        plenteous;
    the river of God is full of water.
10 You prepare the grain,
    for so you provide for the earth.
11 You drench the furrows and smooth out the ridges;
    with heavy rain you soften the ground and bless its increase.
12 You crown the year with your goodness,
    and your paths overflow with plenty.
13 May the fields of the wilderness be rich for grazing,
    and the hills be clothed with joy.
14 May the meadows cover themselves with flocks, and the valleys
        cloak themselves with grain;
    let them shout for joy and sing.

READING   Revelation 4

[1] After this I looked, and there in heaven a door stood open! And the first voice, which I had heard speaking to me like a trumpet, said, 'Come up here, and I will show you what must take place after this.' [2] At once I was in the spirit, and there in heaven stood a throne, with one seated on the throne! [3] And the one seated there looks like jasper and cornelian, and around the throne is a rainbow that looks like an emerald. [4] Around the throne are twenty-four thrones, and seated on the thrones are twenty-four elders, dressed in white robes, with golden crowns on their heads. [5] Coming from the throne are flashes of lightning, and rumblings and peals of thunder, and in front of the throne burn seven flaming torches, which are the seven spirits of God; [6] and in front of the throne there is something like a sea of glass, like crystal.

Around the throne, and on each side of the throne, are four living creatures, full of eyes in front and behind: [7] the first living creature like a lion, the second living creature like an ox, the third living creature with a face like a human face, and the fourth living creature like a flying eagle.

⁸ And the four living creatures, each of them with six wings, are full of eyes all around and inside. Day and night without ceasing they sing,

'Holy, holy, holy,
the Lord God the Almighty,
who was and is and is to come.'

⁹ And whenever the living creatures give glory and honour and thanks to the one who is seated on the throne, who lives for ever and ever, ¹⁰ the twenty-four elders fall before the one who is seated on the throne and worship the one who lives for ever and ever; they cast their crowns before the throne, singing,

¹¹ 'You are worthy, our Lord and God,
to receive glory and honour and power,
for you created all things,
and by your will they existed and were created.'

GOSPEL   Luke 8.22–25

²² One day he got into a boat with his disciples, and he said to them, 'Let us go across to the other side of the lake.' So they put out, ²³ and while they were sailing he fell asleep. A gale swept down on the lake, and the boat was filling with water, and they were in danger. ²⁴ They went to him and woke him up, shouting, 'Master, Master, we are perishing!' And he woke up and rebuked the wind and the raging waves; they ceased, and there was a calm. ²⁵ He said to them, 'Where is your faith?' They were afraid and amazed, and said to one another, 'Who then is this, that he commands even the winds and the water, and they obey him?'

POST COMMUNION

God our creator, by your gift
the tree of life was set at the heart of the earthly paradise,
and the bread of life at the heart of your Church:
may we who have been nourished at your table on earth
be transformed by the glory of the Saviour's cross
and enjoy the delights of eternity;
through Jesus Christ our Lord.

SECOND SERVICE

Psalm 147.[1–12,] 13–21
Genesis 1.1–2.3
Matthew 6.25–34

THIRD SERVICE

Psalm 104.1–26
Job 28.1–11
Acts 14.8–17

THE SUNDAY NEXT BEFORE LENT

COLLECT

Almighty Father,
whose Son was revealed in majesty
before he suffered death upon the cross:
give us grace to perceive his glory,
that we may be strengthened to suffer with him
and be changed into his likeness, from glory to glory;
who is alive and reigns with you,
in the unity of the Holy Spirit,
one God, now and for ever.

READING   Exodus 34.29–35

29 Moses came down from Mount Sinai. As he came down from the mountain with the two tablets of the covenant in his hand, Moses did not know
that the skin of his face shone because he had been talking with God.
30 When Aaron and all the Israelites saw Moses, the skin of his face was
shining, and they were afraid to come near him. 31 But Moses called to
them; and Aaron and all the leaders of the congregation returned to him,
and Moses spoke with them. 32 Afterwards all the Israelites came near, and
he gave them in commandment all that the Lord had spoken with him on
Mount Sinai. 33 When Moses had finished speaking with them, he put a veil
on his face; 34 but whenever Moses went in before the Lord to speak with
him, he would take the veil off, until he came out; and when he came out,
and told the Israelites what he had been commanded, 35 the Israelites would
see the face of Moses, that the skin of his face was shining; and Moses
would put the veil on his face again, until he went in to speak with him.

PSALM   Psalm 99

¹ The Lord is king; let the people tremble;
   he is enthroned upon the cherubim; let the earth shake.
² The Lord is great in Zion;
   he is high above all peoples.
³ Let them confess his name, which is great and awesome;
   he is the Holy One.
⁴ 'O mighty King, lover of justice, you have established equity;
   you have executed justice and righteousness in Jacob.'
⁵ Proclaim the greatness of the Lord our God and fall down before
      his footstool;
   he is the Holy One.
⁶ Moses and Aaron among his priests, and Samuel among those who
      call upon his name,
   they called upon the Lord and he answered them.
⁷ He spoke to them out of the pillar of cloud;
   they kept his testimonies and the decree that he gave them.
⁸ 'O Lord our God, you answered them indeed;
   you were a God who forgave them, yet punished them for their
      evil deeds.'
⁹ Proclaim the greatness of the Lord our God and worship him upon
      his holy hill;
   for the Lord our God is the Holy One.

READING   2 Corinthians 3.12–4.2

¹² Since, then, we have such a hope, we act with great boldness, ¹³ not like Moses, who put a veil over his face to keep the people of Israel from gazing at the end of the glory that was being set aside. ¹⁴ But their minds were hardened. Indeed, to this very day, when they hear the reading of the old covenant, that same veil is still there, since only in Christ is it set aside. ¹⁵ Indeed, to this very day whenever Moses is read, a veil lies over their minds; ¹⁶ but when one turns to the Lord, the veil is removed. ¹⁷ Now the Lord is the Spirit, and where the Spirit of the Lord is, there is freedom. ¹⁸ And all of us, with unveiled faces, seeing the glory of the Lord as though reflected in a mirror, are being transformed into the same image from one degree of glory to another; for this comes from the Lord, the Spirit.

¹ Therefore, since it is by God's mercy that we are engaged in this ministry, we do not lose heart. ² We have renounced the shameful things that one hides; we refuse to practise cunning or to falsify God's word; but by the open statement of the truth we commend ourselves to the conscience of everyone in the sight of God.

GOSPEL   Luke 9.28–36, [37–43]

[28] Now about eight days after these sayings Jesus took with him Peter and John and James, and went up on the mountain to pray. [29] And while he was praying, the appearance of his face changed, and his clothes became dazzling white. [30] Suddenly they saw two men, Moses and Elijah, talking to him. [31] They appeared in glory and were speaking of his departure, which he was about to accomplish at Jerusalem. [32] Now Peter and his companions were weighed down with sleep; but since they had stayed awake, they saw his glory and the two men who stood with him. [33] Just as they were leaving him, Peter said to Jesus, 'Master, it is good for us to be here; let us make three dwellings, one for you, one for Moses, and one for Elijah'—not knowing what he said. [34] While he was saying this, a cloud came and overshadowed them; and they were terrified as they entered the cloud. [35] Then from the cloud came a voice that said, 'This is my Son, my Chosen; listen to him!' [36] When the voice had spoken, Jesus was found alone. And they kept silent and in those days told no one any of the things they had seen.

[[37] On the next day, when they had come down from the mountain, a great crowd met him. [38] Just then a man from the crowd shouted, 'Teacher, I beg you to look at my son; he is my only child. [39] Suddenly a spirit seizes him, and all at once he shrieks. It throws him into convulsions until he foams at the mouth; it mauls him and will scarcely leave him. [40] I begged your disciples to cast it out, but they could not.' [41] Jesus answered, 'You faithless and perverse generation, how much longer must I be with you and bear with you? Bring your son here.' [42] While he was coming, the demon dashed him to the ground in convulsions. But Jesus rebuked the unclean spirit, healed the boy, and gave him back to his father. [43] And all were astounded at the greatness of God.]

POST COMMUNION

Holy God,
we see your glory in the face of Jesus Christ:
may we who are partakers at his table
reflect his life in word and deed,
that all the world may know
    his power to change and save.
This we ask through Jesus Christ our Lord.

809

YEAR C

SECOND SERVICE

Psalm 89.[1–4,] 5–12, [13–18]
Exodus 3.1–6
John 12.27–36a

THIRD SERVICE

Psalm 2
Exodus 33.17–23
1 John 3.1–3

THE ANNUNCIATION OF OUR LORD   25 MARCH

The readings for the Feast of the Annunciation will be found on page 1113

ASH WEDNESDAY

COLLECT

Almighty and everlasting God,
you hate nothing that you have made
and forgive the sins of all those who are penitent:
create and make in us new and contrite hearts
that we, worthily lamenting our sins
and acknowledging our wretchedness,
may receive from you, the God of all mercy,
perfect remission and forgiveness;
through Jesus Christ your Son our Lord,
who is alive and reigns with you,
in the unity of the Holy Spirit,
one God, now and for ever.

This Collect may be used as the Post Communion on any day from the First Sunday of Lent until the Saturday after the Fourth Sunday of Lent instead of the Post Communion provided

READING

EITHER   Joel 2.1–2, 12–17

¹ Blow the trumpet in Zion;
    sound the alarm on my holy mountain!
  Let all the inhabitants of the land tremble,
    for the day of the LORD is coming, it is near—

² a day of darkness and gloom,
    a day of clouds and thick darkness!
Like blackness spread upon the mountains
    a great and powerful army comes;
their like has never been from of old,
    nor will be again after them
    in ages to come.

¹² Yet even now, says the LORD,
    return to me with all your heart,
with fasting, with weeping, and with mourning;
¹³   rend your hearts and not your clothing.
Return to the LORD, your God,
    for he is gracious and merciful,
slow to anger, and abounding in steadfast love,
    and relents from punishing.
¹⁴ Who knows whether he will not turn and relent,
    and leave a blessing behind him,
a grain-offering and a drink-offering
    for the LORD, your God?
¹⁵ Blow the trumpet in Zion;
    sanctify a fast;
call a solemn assembly;
¹⁶   gather the people.
Sanctify the congregation;
    assemble the aged;
gather the children,
    even infants at the breast.
Let the bridegroom leave his room,
    and the bride her canopy.
¹⁷ Between the vestibule and the altar
    let the priests, the ministers of the LORD, weep.
Let them say, 'Spare your people, O LORD,
    and do not make your heritage a mockery,
    a byword among the nations.
Why should it be said among the peoples,
    "Where is their God?" '

OR   **Isaiah 58.1–12**

¹ Shout out, do not hold back!
    Lift up your voice like a trumpet!
Announce to my people their rebellion,
    to the house of Jacob their sins.

2 Yet day after day they seek me
    and delight to know my ways,
 as if they were a nation that practised righteousness
    and did not forsake the ordinance of their God;
 they ask of me righteous judgements,
    they delight to draw near to God.
3 'Why do we fast, but you do not see?
    Why humble ourselves, but you do not notice?'
 Look, you serve your own interest on your fast-day,
    and oppress all your workers.
4 Look, you fast only to quarrel and to fight
    and to strike with a wicked fist.
 Such fasting as you do today
    will not make your voice heard on high.
5 Is such the fast that I choose,
    a day to humble oneself?
 Is it to bow down the head like a bulrush,
    and to lie in sackcloth and ashes?
 Will you call this a fast,
    a day acceptable to the LORD?
6 Is not this the fast that I choose:
    to loose the bonds of injustice,
    to undo the thongs of the yoke,
 to let the oppressed go free,
    and to break every yoke?
7 Is it not to share your bread with the hungry,
    and bring the homeless poor into your house;
 when you see the naked, to cover them,
    and not to hide yourself from your own kin?
8 Then your light shall break forth like the dawn,
    and your healing shall spring up quickly;
 your vindicator shall go before you,
    the glory of the LORD shall be your rearguard.
9 Then you shall call, and the LORD will answer;
    you shall cry for help, and he will say, Here I am.
 If you remove the yoke from among you,
    the pointing of the finger, the speaking of evil,
10 if you offer your food to the hungry
    and satisfy the needs of the afflicted,
 then your light shall rise in the darkness
    and your gloom be like the noonday.

¹¹ The LORD will guide you continually,
>   and satisfy your needs in parched places,
>   and make your bones strong;
> and you shall be like a watered garden,
>   like a spring of water,
>   whose waters never fail.

¹² Your ancient ruins shall be rebuilt;
>   you shall raise up the foundations of many generations;
> you shall be called the repairer of the breach,
>   the restorer of streets to live in.

PSALM   Psalm 51.1–18

¹ Have mercy on me, O God, according to your loving-kindness;
>   in your great compassion blot out my offences.

² Wash me through and through from my wickedness
>   and cleanse me from my sin.

³ For I know my transgressions,
>   and my sin is ever before me.

⁴ Against you only have I sinned
>   and done what is evil in your sight.

⁵ And so you are justified when you speak
>   and upright in your judgement.

⁶ Indeed, I have been wicked from my birth,
>   a sinner from my mother's womb.

⁷ For behold, you look for truth deep within me,
>   and will make me understand wisdom secretly.

⁸ Purge me from my sin and I shall be pure;
>   wash me and I shall be clean indeed.

⁹ Make me hear of joy and gladness,
>   that the body you have broken may rejoice.

¹⁰ Hide your face from my sins
>   and blot out all my iniquities.

¹¹ Create in me a clean heart, O God,
>   and renew a right spirit within me.

¹² Cast me not away from your presence
>   and take not your holy Spirit from me.

¹³ Give me the joy of your saving help again
>   and sustain me with your bountiful Spirit.

¹⁴ I shall teach your ways to the wicked,
>   and sinners shall return to you.

15 Deliver me from death, O God,
    and my tongue shall sing of your righteousness, O God of my
       salvation.
16 Open my lips, O Lord,
    and my mouth shall proclaim your praise.
17 Had you desired it, I would have offered sacrifice,
    but you take no delight in burnt-offerings.
18 The sacrifice of God is a troubled spirit;
    a broken and contrite heart, O God, you will not despise.

READING   2 Corinthians 5.20b–6.10

20 We entreat you on behalf of Christ, be reconciled to God. 21 For our sake
he made him to be sin who knew no sin, so that in him we might become
the righteousness of God.

   1 As we work together with him, we urge you also not to accept the grace
of God in vain. 2 For he says,
      'At an acceptable time I have listened to you,
         and on a day of salvation I have helped you.'
See, now is the acceptable time; see, now is the day of salvation! 3 We are
putting no obstacle in anyone's way, so that no fault may be found with
our ministry, 4 but as servants of God we have commended ourselves in
every way: through great endurance, in afflictions, hardships, calamities,
5 beatings, imprisonments, riots, labours, sleepless nights, hunger; 6 by
purity, knowledge, patience, kindness, holiness of spirit, genuine love,
7 truthful speech, and the power of God; with the weapons of righteousness
for the right hand and for the left; 8 in honour and dishonour, in ill
repute and good repute. We are treated as impostors, and yet are true; 9 as
unknown, and yet are well known; as dying, and see—we are alive; as
punished, and yet not killed; 10 as sorrowful, yet always rejoicing; as poor,
yet making many rich; as having nothing, and yet possessing everything.

GOSPEL

EITHER   Matthew 6.1–6, 16–21

   1 'Beware of practising your piety before others in order to be seen by
them; for then you have no reward from your Father in heaven.

   2 'So whenever you give alms, do not sound a trumpet before you, as the
hypocrites do in the synagogues and in the streets, so that they may be
praised by others. Truly I tell you, they have received their reward. 3 But
when you give alms, do not let your left hand know what your right hand

is doing, [4] so that your alms may be done in secret; and your Father who sees in secret will reward you.

[5] 'And whenever you pray, do not be like the hypocrites; for they love to stand and pray in the synagogues and at the street corners, so that they may be seen by others. Truly I tell you, they have received their reward. [6] But whenever you pray, go into your room and shut the door and pray to your Father who is in secret; and your Father who sees in secret will reward you.'

[16] 'And whenever you fast, do not look dismal, like the hypocrites, for they disfigure their faces so as to show others that they are fasting. Truly I tell you, they have received their reward. [17] But when you fast, put oil on your head and wash your face, [18] so that your fasting may be seen not by others but by your Father who is in secret; and your Father who sees in secret will reward you.

[19] 'Do not store up for yourselves treasures on earth, where moth and rust consume and where thieves break in and steal; [20] but store up for yourselves treasures in heaven, where neither moth nor rust consumes and where thieves do not break in and steal. [21] For where your treasure is, there your heart will be also.'

OR   John 8.2–11

[2] Early in the morning he came again to the temple. All the people came to him and he sat down and began to teach them. [3] The scribes and the Pharisees brought a woman who had been caught in adultery; and making her stand before all of them, [4] they said to him, 'Teacher, this woman was caught in the very act of committing adultery. [5] Now in the law Moses commanded us to stone such women. Now what do you say?' [6] They said this to test him, so that they might have some charge to bring against him. Jesus bent down and wrote with his finger on the ground. [7] When they kept on questioning him, he straightened up and said to them, 'Let anyone among you who is without sin be the first to throw a stone at her.' [8] And once again he bent down and wrote on the ground. [9] When they heard it, they went away, one by one, beginning with the elders; and Jesus was left alone with the woman standing before him. [10] Jesus straightened up and said to her, 'Woman, where are they? Has no one condemned you?' [11] She said, 'No one, sir.' And Jesus said, 'Neither do I condemn you. Go your way, and from now on do not sin again.'

POST COMMUNION

Almighty God,
you have given your only Son to be for us
both a sacrifice for sin
and also an example of godly life:
give us grace
that we may always most thankfully receive
these his inestimable gifts,
and also daily endeavour to follow
   the blessed steps of his most holy life;
through Jesus Christ our Lord.

SECOND SERVICE

Psalm 102.1–17, [18–28]
Isaiah 1.10–18
Luke 15.11–32

THIRD SERVICE

Psalm 38
Daniel 9.3–6, 17–19
1 Timothy 6.6–19

THE FIRST SUNDAY OF LENT

COLLECT

Almighty God,
whose Son Jesus Christ fasted forty days in the wilderness,
and was tempted as we are, yet without sin:
give us grace to discipline ourselves
   in obedience to your Spirit;
and, as you know our weakness,
so may we know your power to save;
through Jesus Christ your Son our Lord,
who is alive and reigns with you,
in the unity of the Holy Spirit,
one God, now and for ever.

READING   Deuteronomy 26.1–11

¹ When you have come into the land that the LORD your God is giving you as an inheritance to possess, and you possess it, and settle in it, ² you shall take some of the first of all the fruit of the ground, which you harvest from the land that the LORD your God is giving you, and you shall put it in a

basket and go to the place that the LORD your God will choose as a dwelling for his name. ³ You shall go to the priest who is in office at that time, and say to him, 'Today I declare to the LORD your God that I have come into the land that the LORD swore to our ancestors to give us.' ⁴ When the priest takes the basket from your hand and sets it down before the altar of the LORD your God, ⁵ you shall make this response before the LORD your God: 'A wandering Aramean was my ancestor; he went down into Egypt and lived there as an alien, few in number, and there he became a great nation, mighty and populous. ⁶ When the Egyptians treated us harshly and afflicted us, by imposing hard labour on us, ⁷ we cried to the LORD, the God of our ancestors; the LORD heard our voice and saw our affliction, our toil, and our oppression. ⁸ The LORD brought us out of Egypt with a mighty hand and an outstretched arm, with a terrifying display of power, and with signs and wonders; ⁹ and he brought us into this place and gave us this land, a land flowing with milk and honey. ¹⁰ So now I bring the first of the fruit of the ground that you, O LORD, have given me.' You shall set it down before the LORD your God and bow down before the LORD your God. ¹¹ Then you, together with the Levites and the aliens who reside among you, shall celebrate with all the bounty that the LORD your God has given to you and to your house.

PSALM   Psalm 91.1-2, 9-16

¹ He who dwells in the shelter of the Most High,
      abides under the shadow of the Almighty.
² He shall say to the Lord, 'You are my refuge and my stronghold,
      my God in whom I put my trust.'

⁹ Because you have made the Lord your refuge,
      and the Most High your habitation.
¹⁰ There shall no evil happen to you,
      neither shall any plague come near your dwelling.
¹¹ For he shall give his angels charge over you,
      to keep you in all your ways.
¹² They shall bear you in their hands,
      lest you dash your foot against a stone.
¹³ You shall tread upon the lion and adder;
      you shall trample the young lion and the serpent under your feet.
¹⁴ Because he is bound to me in love, therefore will I deliver him;
      I will protect him, because he knows my name.
¹⁵ He shall call upon me and I will answer him;
      I am with him in trouble, I will rescue him and bring him to
         honour.

16 With long life will I satisfy him,
and show him my salvation.

OR, IF AN ALTERNATIVE READING IS PREFERRED   **Psalm 91.1–11**

1 He who dwells in the shelter of the Most High,
abides under the shadow of the Almighty.
2 He shall say to the Lord, 'You are my refuge and my stronghold,
my God in whom I put my trust.'
3 He shall deliver you from the snare of the hunter
and from the deadly pestilence.
4 He shall cover you with his pinions, and you shall find refuge
under his wings;
his faithfulness shall be a shield and buckler.
5 You shall not be afraid of any terror by night,
nor of the arrow that flies by day;
6 Of the plague that stalks in the darkness,
nor of the sickness that lays waste at midday.
7 A thousand shall fall at your side and ten thousand at your right
hand,
but it shall not come near you.
8 Your eyes have only to behold
to see the reward of the wicked.
9 Because you have made the Lord your refuge,
and the Most High your habitation.
10 There shall no evil happen to you,
neither shall any plague come near your dwelling.
11 For he shall give his angels charge over you,
to keep you in all your ways.

READING   Romans 10.8b–13

8 'The word is near you,
on your lips and in your heart'
(that is, the word of faith that we proclaim); 9 because if you confess with
your lips that Jesus is Lord and believe in your heart that God raised him
from the dead, you will be saved. 10 For one believes with the heart and so
is justified, and one confesses with the mouth and so is saved. 11 The
scripture says, 'No one who believes in him will be put to shame.' 12 For
there is no distinction between Jew and Greek; the same Lord is Lord of all
and is generous to all who call on him. 13 For, 'Everyone who calls on the
name of the Lord shall be saved.'

GOSPEL   Luke 4.1–13

¹ Jesus, full of the Holy Spirit, returned from the Jordan and was led by the Spirit in the wilderness, ² where for forty days he was tempted by the devil. He ate nothing at all during those days, and when they were over, he was famished. ³ The devil said to him, 'If you are the Son of God, command this stone to become a loaf of bread.' ⁴ Jesus answered him, 'It is written, "One does not live by bread alone." '

⁵ Then the devil led him up and showed him in an instant all the kingdoms of the world. ⁶ And the devil said to him, 'To you I will give their glory and all this authority; for it has been given over to me, and I give it to anyone I please. ⁷ If you, then, will worship me, it will all be yours.' ⁸ Jesus answered him, 'It is written,

"Worship the Lord your God,

and serve only him." '

⁹ Then the devil took him to Jerusalem, and placed him on the pinnacle of the temple, saying to him, 'If you are the Son of God, throw yourself down from here, ¹⁰ for it is written,

"He will command his angels concerning you,

to protect you",

¹¹ and

"On their hands they will bear you up,

so that you will not dash your foot against a stone." '

¹² Jesus answered him, 'It is said, "Do not put the Lord your God to the test." ' ¹³ When the devil had finished every test, he departed from him until an opportune time.

POST COMMUNION

Lord God,
you have renewed us with the living bread from heaven;
by it you nourish our faith,
increase our hope,
and strengthen our love:
teach us always to hunger for him
   who is the true and living bread,
and enable us to live by every word
   that proceeds from out of your mouth;
through Jesus Christ our Lord.

YEAR C

SECOND SERVICE	THIRD SERVICE
Psalm 119.73–88	**Psalm 50.1–15**
Jonah 3	**Micah 6.1–8**
Luke 18.9–14	**Luke 5.27–39**

THE SECOND SUNDAY OF LENT

COLLECT

Almighty God,
you show to those who are in error the light of your truth,
that they may return to the way of righteousness:
grant to all those who are admitted
   into the fellowship of Christ's religion,
that they may reject those things
   that are contrary to their profession,
and follow all such things as are agreeable to the same;
through our Lord Jesus Christ,
who is alive and reigns with you,
in the unity of the Holy Spirit,
one God, now and for ever.

READING   Genesis 15.1–12, 17–18

¹ After these things the word of the Lord came to Abram in a vision, 'Do not be afraid, Abram, I am your shield; your reward shall be very great.' ² But Abram said, 'O Lord God, what will you give me, for I continue childless, and the heir of my house is Eliezer of Damascus?' ³ And Abram said, 'You have given me no offspring, and so a slave born in my house is to be my heir.' ⁴ But the word of the Lord came to him, 'This man shall not be your heir; no one but your very own issue shall be your heir.' ⁵ He brought him outside and said, 'Look towards heaven and count the stars, if you are able to count them.' Then he said to him, 'So shall your descendants be.' ⁶ And he believed the Lord; and the Lord reckoned it to him as righteousness.

⁷ Then he said to him, 'I am the Lord who brought you from Ur of the Chaldeans, to give you this land to possess.' ⁸ But he said, 'O Lord God, how am I to know that I shall possess it?' ⁹ He said to him, 'Bring me a heifer three years old, a female goat three years old, a ram three years old, a turtle-dove, and a young pigeon.' ¹⁰ He brought him all these and cut them

in two, laying each half over against the other; but he did not cut the birds in two. [11] And when birds of prey came down on the carcasses, Abram drove them away.

[12] As the sun was going down, a deep sleep fell upon Abram, and a deep and terrifying darkness descended upon him.

[17] When the sun had gone down and it was dark, a smoking fire-pot and a flaming torch passed between these pieces. [18] On that day the LORD made a covenant with Abram, saying, 'To your descendants I give this land, from the river of Egypt to the great river, the river Euphrates.'

PSALM
Psalm 27

1 The Lord is my light and my salvation; whom then shall I fear?
   the Lord is the strength of my life; of whom then shall I be afraid?
2 When evildoers came upon me to eat up my flesh,
   it was they, my foes and my adversaries, who stumbled and fell.
3 Though an army should encamp against me,
   yet my heart shall not be afraid;
4 And though war should rise up against me,
   yet will I put my trust in him.
5 One thing have I asked of the Lord; one thing I seek;
   that I may dwell in the house of the Lord all the days of my life;
6 To behold the fair beauty of the Lord
   and to seek him in his temple.
7 For in the day of trouble he shall keep me safe in his shelter;
   he shall hide me in the secrecy of his dwelling and set me high
      upon a rock.
8 Even now he lifts up my head
   above my enemies round about me;
9 Therefore I will offer in his dwelling an oblation with sounds of
      great gladness;
   I will sing and make music to the Lord.
10 Hearken to my voice, O Lord, when I call;
   have mercy on me and answer me.
11 You speak in my heart and say, 'Seek my face.'
   Your face, Lord, will I seek.
12 Hide not your face from me,
   nor turn away your servant in displeasure.
13 You have been my helper; cast me not away;
   do not forsake me, O God of my salvation.
14 Though my father and my mother forsake me,
   the Lord will sustain me.

15 Show me your way, O Lord;
   lead me on a level path, because of my enemies.
16 Deliver me not into the hand of my adversaries,
   for false witnesses have risen up against me, and also those who
   speak malice.
17 What if I had not believed that I should see the goodness of the
   Lord
   in the land of the living!
18 O tarry and await the Lord's pleasure; be strong and he shall
   comfort your heart;
   wait patiently for the Lord.

READING   Philippians 3.17–4.1

17 Brothers and sisters, join in imitating me, and observe those who live
according to the example you have in us. 18 For many live as enemies of the
cross of Christ; I have often told you of them, and now I tell you even with
tears. 19 Their end is destruction; their god is the belly; and their glory is
in their shame; their minds are set on earthly things. 20 But our citizenship
is in heaven, and it is from there that we are expecting a Saviour, the Lord
Jesus Christ. 21 He will transform the body of our humiliation so that it
may be conformed to the body of his glory, by the power that also enables
him to make all things subject to himself. 1 Therefore, my brothers and
sisters, whom I love and long for, my joy and crown, stand firm in the Lord
in this way, my beloved.

GOSPEL   Luke 13.31–35

31 At that very hour some Pharisees came and said to him, 'Get away from
here, for Herod wants to kill you.' 32 He said to them, 'Go and tell that fox
for me, "Listen, I am casting out demons and performing cures today and
tomorrow, and on the third day I finish my work. 33 Yet today, tomorrow,
and the next day I must be on my way, because it is impossible for a prophet
to be killed away from Jerusalem." 34 Jerusalem, Jerusalem, the city that
kills the prophets and stones those who are sent to it! How often have I
desired to gather your children together as a hen gathers her brood under
her wings, and you were not willing! 35 See, your house is left to you. And I
tell you, you will not see me until the time comes when you say, "Blessed
is the one who comes in the name of the Lord." '

POST COMMUNION

Almighty God,
you see that we have no power of ourselves to help ourselves:
keep us both outwardly in our bodies,
and inwardly in our souls;
that we may be defended from all adversities
  which may happen to the body,
and from all evil thoughts
  which may assault and hurt the soul;
through Jesus Christ our Lord.

SECOND SERVICE

Psalm 135
Jeremiah 22.1–9, 13–17
Luke 14.27–33

THIRD SERVICE

Psalm 119.161–176
Genesis 17.1–7, 15–16
Romans 11.13–24

THE THIRD SUNDAY OF LENT

COLLECT

Almighty God,
whose most dear Son went not up to joy
  but first he suffered pain,
and entered not into glory before he was crucified:
mercifully grant that we, walking in the way of the cross,
may find it none other than the way of life and peace;
through Jesus Christ your Son our Lord,
who is alive and reigns with you,
in the unity of the Holy Spirit,
one God, now and for ever.

READING   Isaiah 55.1–9

[1] Ho, everyone who thirsts,
        come to the waters;
      and you that have no money,
        come, buy and eat!

Come, buy wine and milk
    without money and without price.
2 Why do you spend your money for that which is not bread,
    and your labour for that which does not satisfy?
Listen carefully to me, and eat what is good,
    and delight yourselves in rich food.
3 Incline your ear, and come to me;
    listen, so that you may live.
I will make with you an everlasting covenant,
    my steadfast, sure love for David.
4 See, I made him a witness to the peoples,
    a leader and commander for the peoples.
5 See, you shall call nations that you do not know,
    and nations that do not know you shall run to you,
because of the LORD your God, the Holy One of Israel,
    for he has glorified you.
6 Seek the LORD while he may be found,
    call upon him while he is near;
7 let the wicked forsake their way,
    and the unrighteous their thoughts;
let them return to the LORD, that he may have mercy on them,
    and to our God, for he will abundantly pardon.
8 For my thoughts are not your thoughts,
    nor are your ways my ways, says the LORD.
9 For as the heavens are higher than the earth,
    so are my ways higher than your ways
    and my thoughts than your thoughts.

PSALM   Psalm 63.1–8

1 O God, you are my God; eagerly I seek you;
    my soul thirsts for you, my flesh faints for you, as in a barren and
        dry land where there is no water;
2 Therefore I have gazed upon you in your holy place,
    that I might behold your power and your glory.
3 For your loving-kindness is better than life itself;
    my lips shall give you praise.
4 So will I bless you as long as I live
    and lift up my hands in your name.
5 My soul is content, as with marrow and fatness,
    and my mouth praises you with joyful lips,

6   When I remember you upon my bed,
    and meditate on you in the night watches.
7   For you have been my helper,
    and under the shadow of your wings I will rejoice.
8   My soul clings to you;
    your right hand holds me fast.

READING   1 Corinthians 10.1–13

1 I do not want you to be unaware, brothers and sisters, that our ancestors were all under the cloud, and all passed through the sea, 2 and all were baptized into Moses in the cloud and in the sea, 3 and all ate the same spiritual food, 4 and all drank the same spiritual drink. For they drank from the spiritual rock that followed them, and the rock was Christ. 5 Nevertheless, God was not pleased with most of them, and they were struck down in the wilderness.

6 Now these things occurred as examples for us, so that we might not desire evil as they did. 7 Do not become idolaters as some of them did; as it is written, 'The people sat down to eat and drink, and they rose up to play.' 8 We must not indulge in sexual immorality as some of them did, and twenty-three thousand fell in a single day. 9 We must not put Christ to the test, as some of them did, and were destroyed by serpents. 10 And do not complain as some of them did, and were destroyed by the destroyer. 11 These things happened to them to serve as an example, and they were written down to instruct us, on whom the ends of the ages have come. 12 So if you think you are standing, watch out that you do not fall. 13 No testing has overtaken you that is not common to everyone. God is faithful, and he will not let you be tested beyond your strength, but with the testing he will also provide the way out so that you may be able to endure it.

GOSPEL   Luke 13.1–9

1 At that very time there were some present who told him about the Galileans whose blood Pilate had mingled with their sacrifices. 2 He asked them, 'Do you think that because these Galileans suffered in this way they were worse sinners than all other Galileans? 3 No, I tell you; but unless you repent, you will all perish as they did. 4 Or those eighteen who were killed when the tower of Siloam fell on them—do you think that they were worse offenders than all the others living in Jerusalem? 5 No, I tell you; but unless you repent, you will all perish just as they did.'

825

⁶ Then he told this parable: 'A man had a fig tree planted in his vineyard; and he came looking for fruit on it and found none. ⁷ So he said to the gardener, "See here! For three years I have come looking for fruit on this fig tree, and still I find none. Cut it down! Why should it be wasting the soil?" ⁸ He replied, "Sir, let it alone for one more year, until I dig round it and put manure on it. ⁹ If it bears fruit next year, well and good; but if not, you can cut it down." '

POST COMMUNION

Merciful Lord,
grant your people grace to withstand the temptations
    of the world, the flesh and the devil,
and with pure hearts and minds to follow you,
    the only God;
through Jesus Christ our Lord.

SECOND SERVICE

THIRD SERVICE

Psalms 12; 13
Genesis 28.10–19a
John 1.35–51

Psalms 26; 28
Deuteronomy 6.4–9
John 17.1a, 11b-19

THE FOURTH SUNDAY OF LENT

Mothering Sunday may be celebrated in preference to the provision for the Fourth Sunday of Lent

COLLECT

Merciful Lord,
absolve your people from their offences,
that through your bountiful goodness
we may all be delivered from the chains of those sins
which by our frailty we have committed;
grant this, heavenly Father,
for Jesus Christ's sake, our blessed Lord and Saviour,
who is alive and reigns with you,
in the unity of the Holy Spirit,
one God, now and for ever.

READING   Joshua 5.9–12

[9] The Lord said to Joshua, 'Today I have rolled away from you the disgrace of Egypt.' And so that place is called Gilgal to this day.

[10] While the Israelites were encamped in Gilgal they kept the passover in the evening on the fourteenth day of the month in the plains of Jericho. [11] On the day after the passover, on that very day, they ate the produce of the land, unleavened cakes and parched grain. [12] The manna ceased on the day they ate the produce of the land, and the Israelites no longer had manna; they ate the crops of the land of Canaan that year.

PSALM   Psalm 32

1   Happy are they whose transgressions are forgiven,
    and whose sin is put away!
2   Happy are they to whom the Lord imputes no guilt,
    and in whose spirit there is no guile!
3   While I held my tongue, my bones withered away,
    because of my groaning all day long.
4   For your hand was heavy upon me day and night;
    my moisture was dried up as in the heat of summer.
5   Then I acknowledged my sin to you,
    and did not conceal my guilt.
6   I said, 'I will confess my transgressions to the Lord':
    then you forgave me the guilt of my sin;
7   Therefore all the faithful will make their prayers to you in time of
        trouble;
    when the great waters overflow, they shall not reach them.
8   You are my hiding-place; you preserve me from trouble;
    you surround me with shouts of deliverance.
9   'I will instruct you and teach you in the way that you should go;
    I will guide you with my eye.
10 Do not be like horse or mule, which have no understanding;
    who must be fitted with bit and bridle, or else they will not stay
        near you.'
11 Great are the tribulations of the wicked;
    but mercy embraces those who trust in the Lord.
12 Be glad, you righteous, and rejoice in the Lord;
    shout for joy, all who are true of heart.

READING   2 Corinthians 5.16–21

¹⁶ From now on, therefore, we regard no one from a human point of view; even though we once knew Christ from a human point of view, we know him no longer in that way. ¹⁷ So if anyone is in Christ, there is a new creation: everything old has passed away; see, everything has become new! ¹⁸ All this is from God, who reconciled us to himself through Christ, and has given us the ministry of reconciliation; ¹⁹ that is, in Christ God was reconciling the world to himself, not counting their trespasses against them, and entrusting the message of reconciliation to us. ²⁰ So we are ambassadors for Christ, since God is making his appeal through us; we entreat you on behalf of Christ, be reconciled to God. ²¹ For our sake he made him to be sin who knew no sin, so that in him we might become the righteousness of God.

GOSPEL   Luke 15.1–3, 11b–32

¹ Now all the tax-collectors and sinners were coming near to listen to him. ² And the Pharisees and the scribes were grumbling and saying, 'This fellow welcomes sinners and eats with them.'

³ So he told them this parable:

¹¹ 'There was a man who had two sons. ¹² The younger of them said to his father, "Father, give me the share of the property that will belong to me." So he divided his property between them. ¹³ A few days later the younger son gathered all he had and travelled to a distant country, and there he squandered his property in dissolute living. ¹⁴ When he had spent everything, a severe famine took place throughout that country, and he began to be in need. ¹⁵ So he went and hired himself out to one of the citizens of that country, who sent him to his fields to feed the pigs. ¹⁶ He would gladly have filled himself with the pods that the pigs were eating; and no one gave him anything. ¹⁷ But when he came to himself he said, "How many of my father's hired hands have bread enough and to spare, but here I am dying of hunger! ¹⁸ I will get up and go to my father, and I will say to him, 'Father, I have sinned against heaven and before you; ¹⁹ I am no longer worthy to be called your son; treat me like one of your hired hands.' " ²⁰ So he set off and went to his father. But while he was still far off, his father saw him and was filled with compassion; he ran and put his arms around him and kissed him. ²¹ Then the son said to him, "Father, I have sinned against heaven and before you; I am no longer worthy to be called your son." ²² But the father said to his slaves, "Quickly, bring out a robe—the best one—and put it on him; put a ring on his finger and sandals on his feet. ²³ And get the fatted calf and kill it, and let us eat and celebrate; ²⁴ for

this son of mine was dead and is alive again; he was lost and is found!" And they began to celebrate.

[25] 'Now his elder son was in the field; and when he came and approached the house, he heard music and dancing. [26] He called one of the slaves and asked what was going on. [27] He replied, "Your brother has come, and your father has killed the fatted calf, because he has got him back safe and sound." [28] Then he became angry and refused to go in. His father came out and began to plead with him. [29] But he answered his father, "Listen! For all these years I have been working like a slave for you, and I have never disobeyed your command; yet you have never given me even a young goat so that I might celebrate with my friends. [30] But when this son of yours came back, who has devoured your property with prostitutes, you killed the fatted calf for him!" [31] Then the father said to him, "Son, you are always with me, and all that is mine is yours. [32] But we had to celebrate and rejoice, because this brother of yours was dead and has come to life; he was lost and has been found." '

If the Principal Service readings have been displaced by Mothering Sunday provisions, they may be used at the Second Service

POST COMMUNION

Lord God,
whose blessed Son our Saviour
gave his back to the smiters
and did not hide his face from shame:
give us grace to endure the sufferings of this present time
with sure confidence in the glory that shall be revealed;
through Jesus Christ our Lord.

SECOND SERVICE

THIRD SERVICE

Psalm 30
Prayer of Manasseh

or

Isaiah 40.27–41.13
2 Timothy 4.1–18

If the Second Service is a Eucharist, the following is read as a Gospel:

John 11.17–44

Psalms 84; 85
Genesis 37.3–4, 12–36
1 Peter 2.16–25

MOTHERING SUNDAY

Mothering Sunday may be celebrated in preference to any part of the provision for the Fourth Sunday of Lent. If it replaces a Second or Third Service, the Principal Service provision may still be used.

COLLECT

God of compassion,
whose Son Jesus Christ, the child of Mary,
shared the life of a home in Nazareth,
and on the cross drew the whole human family to himself:
strengthen us in our daily living
that in joy and in sorrow
we may know the power of your presence
   to bind together and to heal;
through Jesus Christ your Son our Lord,
who is alive and reigns with you,
in the unity of the Holy Spirit,
one God, now and for ever.

READING

EITHER   **Exodus 2.1–10**

[1] Now a man from the house of Levi went and married a Levite woman. [2] The woman conceived and bore a son; and when she saw that he was a fine baby, she hid him for three months. [3] When she could hide him no longer she got a papyrus basket for him, and plastered it with bitumen and pitch; she put the child in it and placed it among the reeds on the bank of the river. [4] His sister stood at a distance, to see what would happen to him.

[5] The daughter of Pharaoh came down to bathe at the river, while her attendants walked beside the river. She saw the basket among the reeds and sent her maid to bring it. [6] When she opened it, she saw the child. He was crying, and she took pity on him. 'This must be one of the Hebrews' children,' she said. [7] Then his sister said to Pharaoh's daughter, 'Shall I go and get you a nurse from the Hebrew women to nurse the child for you?' [8] Pharaoh's daughter said to her, 'Yes.' So the girl went and called the child's mother. [9] Pharaoh's daughter said to her, 'Take this child and nurse it for me, and I will give you your wages.' So the woman took the child and nursed it. [10] When the child grew up, she brought him to Pharaoh's daughter, and

she took him as her son. She named him Moses, 'because', she said, 'I drew him out of the water.'

OR   **1 Samuel 1.20–28**

[20] In due time Hannah conceived and bore a son. She named him Samuel, for she said, 'I have asked him of the LORD.'

[21] The man Elkanah and all his household went up to offer to the LORD the yearly sacrifice, and to pay his vow. [22] But Hannah did not go up, for she said to her husband, 'As soon as the child is weaned, I will bring him, that he may appear in the presence of the LORD, and remain there for ever; I will offer him as a nazirite for all time.' [23] Her husband Elkanah said to her, 'Do what seems best to you, wait until you have weaned him; only— may the LORD establish his word.' So the woman remained and nursed her son, until she weaned him. [24] When she had weaned him, she took him up with her, along with a three-year-old bull, an ephah of flour, and a skin of wine. She brought him to the house of the LORD at Shiloh; and the child was young. [25] Then they slaughtered the bull, and they brought the child to Eli. [26] And she said, 'Oh, my lord! As you live, my lord, I am the woman who was standing here in your presence, praying to the LORD. [27] For this child I prayed; and the LORD has granted me the petition that I made to him. [28] Therefore I have lent him to the LORD; as long as he lives, he is given to the LORD.'

She left him there for the LORD.

PSALM

EITHER   **Psalm 34.11–20**

[11]   Come, children, and listen to me;
       I will teach you the fear of the Lord.
[12]   Who among you loves life
       and desires long life to enjoy prosperity?
[13]   Keep your tongue from evil-speaking
       and your lips from lying words.
[14]   Turn from evil and do good;
       seek peace and pursue it.
[15]   The eyes of the Lord are upon the righteous,
       and his ears are open to their cry.
[16]   The face of the Lord is against those who do evil,
       to root out the remembrance of them from the earth.

¹⁷ The righteous cry and the Lord hears them
and delivers them from all their troubles.
¹⁸ The Lord is near to the brokenhearted
and will save those whose spirits are crushed.
¹⁹ Many are the troubles of the righteous,
but the Lord will deliver him out of them all.
²⁰ He will keep safe all his bones;
not one of them shall be broken.

OR   Psalm 127.1–5

¹ Unless the Lord builds the house,
their labour is in vain who build it.
² Unless the Lord watches over the city,
in vain the guard keeps vigil.
³ It is in vain that you rise so early and go to bed so late;
vain, too, to eat the bread of toil, for he gives to his belovèd sleep.
⁴ Children are a heritage from the Lord,
and the fruit of the womb is a gift.
⁵ Like arrows in the hand of a warrior
are the children of one's youth.

READING

EITHER   2 Corinthians 1.3–7

³ Blessed be the God and Father of our Lord Jesus Christ, the Father of
mercies and the God of all consolation, ⁴ who consoles us in all our affliction, so that we may be able to console those who are in any affliction with
the consolation with which we ourselves are consoled by God. ⁵ For just as
the sufferings of Christ are abundant for us, so also our consolation is
abundant through Christ. ⁶ If we are being afflicted, it is for your consolation and salvation; if we are being consoled, it is for your consolation,
which you experience when you patiently endure the same sufferings that
we are also suffering. ⁷ Our hope for you is unshaken; for we know that as
you share in our sufferings, so also you share in our consolation.

OR   Colossians 3.12–17

¹² As God's chosen ones, holy and beloved, clothe yourselves with com-
passion, kindness, humility, meekness, and patience. ¹³ Bear with one
another and, if anyone has a complaint against another, forgive each other;
just as the Lord has forgiven you, so you also must forgive. ¹⁴ Above all,
clothe yourselves with love, which binds everything together in perfect

harmony. [15] And let the peace of Christ rule in your hearts, to which indeed you were called in the one body. And be thankful. [16] Let the word of Christ dwell in you richly; teach and admonish one another in all wisdom; and with gratitude in your hearts sing psalms, hymns, and spiritual songs to God. [17] And whatever you do, in word or deed, do everything in the name of the Lord Jesus, giving thanks to God the Father through him.

GOSPEL

EITHER   Luke 2.33–35

[33] And the child's father and mother were amazed at what was being said about him. [34] Then Simeon blessed them and said to his mother Mary, 'This child is destined for the falling and the rising of many in Israel, and to be a sign that will be opposed [35] so that the inner thoughts of many will be revealed—and a sword will pierce your own soul too.'

OR   John 19.25b–27

[25] Meanwhile, standing near the cross of Jesus were his mother, and his mother's sister, Mary the wife of Clopas, and Mary Magdalene. [26] When Jesus saw his mother and the disciple whom he loved standing beside her, he said to his mother, 'Woman, here is your son.' [27] Then he said to the disciple, 'Here is your mother.' And from that hour the disciple took her into his own home.

POST COMMUNION

Loving God,
as a mother feeds her children at the breast
you feed us in this sacrament
    with the food and drink of eternal life:
help us who have tasted your goodness
to grow in grace within the household of faith;
through Jesus Christ our Lord.

THE FIFTH SUNDAY OF LENT
PASSIONTIDE BEGINS

COLLECT

Most merciful God,
who by the death and resurrection of your Son Jesus Christ
delivered and saved the world:
grant that by faith in him who suffered on the cross
we may triumph in the power of his victory;
through Jesus Christ your Son our Lord,
who is alive and reigns with you,
in the unity of the Holy Spirit,
one God, now and for ever.

READING   Isaiah 43.16–21

16 Thus says the LORD,
    who makes a way in the sea,
    a path in the mighty waters,
17 who brings out chariot and horse,
    army and warrior;
  they lie down, they cannot rise,
    they are extinguished, quenched like a wick:
18 Do not remember the former things,
    or consider the things of old.
19 I am about to do a new thing;
    now it springs forth, do you not perceive it?
  I will make a way in the wilderness
    and rivers in the desert.
20 The wild animals will honour me,
    the jackals and the ostriches;
  for I give water in the wilderness,
    rivers in the desert,
  to give drink to my chosen people,
21   the people whom I formed for myself
  so that they might declare my praise.

PSALM   Psalm 126

1 When the Lord restored the fortunes of Zion,
    then were we like those who dream.

² Then was our mouth filled with laughter,
  and our tongue with shouts of joy.
³ Then they said among the nations,
  'The Lord has done great things for them.'
⁴ The Lord has done great things for us,
  and we are glad indeed.
⁵ Restore our fortunes, O Lord,
  like the watercourses of the Negev.
⁶ Those who sowed with tears
  will reap with songs of joy.
⁷ Those who go out weeping, carrying the seed,
  will come again with joy, shouldering their sheaves.

READING   Philippians 3.4b–14

⁴ If anyone else has reason to be confident in the flesh, I have more:
⁵ circumcised on the eighth day, a member of the people of Israel, of the tribe of Benjamin, a Hebrew born of Hebrews; as to the law, a Pharisee; ⁶ as to zeal, a persecutor of the church; as to righteousness under the law, blameless.

⁷ Yet whatever gains I had, these I have come to regard as loss because of Christ. ⁸ More than that, I regard everything as loss because of the surpassing value of knowing Christ Jesus my Lord. For his sake I have suffered the loss of all things, and I regard them as rubbish, in order that I may gain Christ ⁹ and be found in him, not having a righteousness of my own that comes from the law, but one that comes through faith in Christ, the righteousness from God based on faith. ¹⁰ I want to know Christ and the power of his resurrection and the sharing of his sufferings by becoming like him in his death, ¹¹ if somehow I may attain the resurrection from the dead.

¹² Not that I have already obtained this or have already reached the goal; but I press on to make it my own, because Christ Jesus has made me his own. ¹³ Beloved, I do not consider that I have made it my own; but this one thing I do: forgetting what lies behind and straining forward to what lies ahead, ¹⁴ I press on towards the goal for the prize of the heavenly call of God in Christ Jesus.

GOSPEL   John 12.1–8

¹ Six days before the Passover Jesus came to Bethany, the home of Lazarus, whom he had raised from the dead. ² There they gave a dinner for him. Martha served, and Lazarus was one of those at the table with him. ³ Mary

took a pound of costly perfume made of pure nard, anointed Jesus' feet, and wiped them with her hair. The house was filled with the fragrance of the perfume. ⁴ But Judas Iscariot, one of his disciples (the one who was about to betray him), said, ⁵ 'Why was this perfume not sold for three hundred denarii and the money given to the poor?' ⁶ (He said this not because he cared about the poor, but because he was a thief; he kept the common purse and used to steal what was put into it.) ⁷ Jesus said, 'Leave her alone. She bought it so that she might keep it for the day of my burial. ⁸ You always have the poor with you, but you do not always have me.'

POST COMMUNION

Lord Jesus Christ,
you have taught us
that what we do for the least of our brothers and sisters
we do also for you:
give us the will to be the servant of others
as you were the servant of all,
and gave up your life and died for us,
but are alive and reign, now and for ever.

SECOND SERVICE   THIRD SERVICE

Psalm 35.1–9, [10–28]   **Psalms 111; 112**
2 Chronicles 35.1–6, 10–16   **Isaiah 35.1–10**
Luke 22.1–13   **Romans 7.21–8.4**

PALM SUNDAY

LITURGY OF THE PALMS

GOSPEL   Luke 19.28–40

²⁸ After he had said this, he went on ahead, going up to Jerusalem.

²⁹ When he had come near Bethphage and Bethany, at the place called the Mount of Olives, he sent two of the disciples, ³⁰ saying, 'Go into the village ahead of you, and as you enter it you will find tied there a colt that has never been ridden. Untie it and bring it here. ³¹ If anyone asks you, "Why

are you untying it?" just say this: "The Lord needs it." ' ³² So those who were sent departed and found it as he had told them. ³³ As they were untying the colt, its owners asked them, 'Why are you untying the colt?' ³⁴ They said, 'The Lord needs it.' ³⁵ Then they brought it to Jesus; and after throwing their cloaks on the colt, they set Jesus on it. ³⁶ As he rode along, people kept spreading their cloaks on the road. ³⁷ As he was now approaching the path down from the Mount of Olives, the whole multitude of the disciples began to praise God joyfully with a loud voice for all the deeds of power that they had seen, ³⁸ saying,

'Blessed is the king
who comes in the name of the Lord!
Peace in heaven,
and glory in the highest heaven!'

³⁹ Some of the Pharisees in the crowd said to him, 'Teacher, order your disciples to stop.' ⁴⁰ He answered, 'I tell you, if these were silent, the stones would shout out.'

PSALM   Psalm 118.[1–2,] 19–24, [25–29]

[¹ Give thanks to the Lord, for he is good;
   his mercy endures for ever.
² Let Israel now proclaim,
   'His mercy endures for ever.']

¹⁹ Open for me the gates of righteousness;
   I will enter them; I will offer thanks to the Lord.
²⁰ 'This is the gate of the Lord;
   he who is righteous may enter.'
²¹ I will give thanks to you, for you answered me
   and have become my salvation.
²² The same stone which the builders rejected
   has become the chief corner-stone.
²³ This is the Lord's doing,
   and it is marvellous in our eyes.
²⁴ On this day the Lord has acted;
   we will rejoice and be glad in it.
[²⁵ Hosanna, Lord, hosanna!
   Lord, send us now success.
²⁶ Blessèd is he who comes in the name of the Lord;
   we bless you from the house of the Lord.
²⁷ God is the Lord; he has shined upon us;
   form a procession with branches up to the horns of the altar.

²⁸ 'You are my God and I will thank you;
    you are my God and I will exalt you.'
²⁹ Give thanks to the Lord, for he is good;
    his mercy endures for ever.]

LITURGY OF THE PASSION

COLLECT

Almighty and everlasting God,
who in your tender love towards the human race
    sent your Son our Saviour Jesus Christ
to take upon him our flesh
and to suffer death upon the cross:
grant that we may follow the example
    of his patience and humility,
and also be made partakers of his resurrection;
through Jesus Christ your Son our Lord,
who is alive and reigns with you,
in the unity of the Holy Spirit,
one God, now and for ever.

READING   Isaiah 50.4–9a

⁴ The Lord GOD has given me
        the tongue of a teacher,
    that I may know how to sustain
        the weary with a word.
    Morning by morning he wakens—
        wakens my ear
    to listen as those who are taught.
⁵ The Lord GOD has opened my ear,
        and I was not rebellious,
        I did not turn backwards.
⁶ I gave my back to those who struck me,
        and my cheeks to those who pulled out the beard;
    I did not hide my face
        from insult and spitting.
⁷ The Lord GOD helps me;
        therefore I have not been disgraced;
    therefore I have set my face like flint,
        and I know that I shall not be put to shame;

8   he who vindicates me is near.
    Who will contend with me?
      Let us stand up together.
    Who are my adversaries?
      Let them confront me.
9   It is the Lord God who helps me;
      who will declare me guilty?

PSALM   Psalm 31.9–16, [17–18]

9   Have mercy on me, O Lord, for I am in trouble;
    my eye is consumed with sorrow, and also my throat and my belly.
10   For my life is wasted with grief, and my years with sighing;
    my strength fails me because of affliction, and my bones are
      consumed.
11   I have become a reproach to all my enemies and even to my
      neighbours, a dismay to those of my acquaintance;
    when they see me in the street they avoid me.
12   I am forgotten like the dead, out of mind;
    I am as useless as a broken pot.
13   For I have heard the whispering of the crowd; fear is all around;
    they put their heads together against me; they plot to take my life.
14   But as for me, I have trusted in you, O Lord.
    I have said, 'You are my God.
15   My times are in your hand;
    rescue me from the hand of my enemies, and from those who
      persecute me.
16   Make your face to shine upon your servant,
    and in your loving-kindness save me.'
[17   Lord, let me not be ashamed for having called upon you;
    rather, let the wicked be put to shame; let them be silent in the
      grave.
18   Let the lying lips be silenced which speak against the righteous,
    haughtily, disdainfully and with contempt.]

READING   Philippians 2.5–11

5 Let the same mind be in you that was in Christ Jesus,
  6   who, though he was in the form of God,
      did not regard equality with God
      as something to be exploited,

7 but emptied himself,
    taking the form of a slave,
    being born in human likeness.
  And being found in human form,
8   he humbled himself
    and became obedient to the point of death—
    even death on a cross.
9 Therefore God also highly exalted him
    and gave him the name
    that is above every name,
10 so that at the name of Jesus
    every knee should bend,
    in heaven and on earth and under the earth,
11 and every tongue should confess
    that Jesus Christ is Lord,
    to the glory of God the Father.

GOSPEL

EITHER   Luke 22.14–23.56

14 When the hour came, he took his place at the table, and the apostles with him. 15 He said to them, 'I have eagerly desired to eat this Passover with you before I suffer; 16 for I tell you, I will not eat it until it is fulfilled in the kingdom of God.' 17 Then he took a cup, and after giving thanks he said, 'Take this and divide it among yourselves; 18 for I tell you that from now on I will not drink of the fruit of the vine until the kingdom of God comes.' 19 Then he took a loaf of bread, and when he had given thanks, he broke it and gave it to them, saying, 'This is my body, which is given for you. Do this in remembrance of me.' 20 And he did the same with the cup after supper, saying, 'This cup that is poured out for you is the new covenant in my blood. 21 But see, the one who betrays me is with me, and his hand is on the table. 22 For the Son of Man is going as it has been determined, but woe to that one by whom he is betrayed!' 23 Then they began to ask one another which one of them it could be who would do this.

24 A dispute also arose among them as to which one of them was to be regarded as the greatest. 25 But he said to them, 'The kings of the Gentiles lord it over them; and those in authority over them are called benefactors. 26 But not so with you; rather the greatest among you must become like the youngest, and the leader like one who serves. 27 For who is greater, the one who is at the table or the one who serves? Is it not the one at the table? But I am among you as one who serves.

[28] 'You are those who have stood by me in my trials; [29] and I confer on you, just as my Father has conferred on me, a kingdom, [30] so that you may eat and drink at my table in my kingdom, and you will sit on thrones judging the twelve tribes of Israel.

[31] 'Simon, Simon, listen! Satan has demanded to sift all of you like wheat, [32] but I have prayed for you that your own faith may not fail; and you, when once you have turned back, strengthen your brothers.' [33] And he said to him, 'Lord, I am ready to go with you to prison and to death!' [34] Jesus said, 'I tell you, Peter, the cock will not crow this day, until you have denied three times that you know me.'

[35] He said to them, 'When I sent you out without a purse, bag, or sandals, did you lack anything?' They said, 'No, not a thing.' [36] He said to them, 'But now, the one who has a purse must take it, and likewise a bag. And the one who has no sword must sell his cloak and buy one. [37] For I tell you, this scripture must be fulfilled in me, "And he was counted among the lawless"; and indeed what is written about me is being fulfilled.' [38] They said, 'Lord, look, here are two swords.' He replied, 'It is enough.'

[39] He came out and went, as was his custom, to the Mount of Olives; and the disciples followed him. [40] When he reached the place, he said to them, 'Pray that you may not come into the time of trial.' [41] Then he withdrew from them about a stone's throw, knelt down, and prayed, [42] 'Father, if you are willing, remove this cup from me; yet, not my will but yours be done.' [43] Then an angel from heaven appeared to him and gave him strength. [44] In his anguish he prayed more earnestly, and his sweat became like great drops of blood falling down on the ground. [45] When he got up from prayer, he came to the disciples and found them sleeping because of grief, [46] and he said to them, 'Why are you sleeping? Get up and pray that you may not come into the time of trial.'

[47] While he was still speaking, suddenly a crowd came, and the one called Judas, one of the twelve, was leading them. He approached Jesus to kiss him; [48] but Jesus said to him, 'Judas, is it with a kiss that you are betraying the Son of Man?' [49] When those who were around him saw what was coming, they asked, 'Lord, should we strike with the sword?' [50] Then one of them struck the slave of the high priest and cut off his right ear. [51] But Jesus said, 'No more of this!' And he touched his ear and healed him. [52] Then Jesus said to the chief priests, the officers of the temple police, and the elders who had come for him, 'Have you come out with swords and clubs as if I were a bandit? [53] When I was with you day after day in the temple, you did not lay hands on me. But this is your hour, and the power of darkness!'

54 Then they seized him and led him away, bringing him into the high priest's house. But Peter was following at a distance. 55 When they had kindled a fire in the middle of the courtyard and sat down together, Peter sat among them. 56 Then a servant-girl, seeing him in the firelight, stared at him and said, 'This man also was with him.' 57 But he denied it, saying, 'Woman, I do not know him.' 58 A little later someone else, on seeing him, said, 'You also are one of them.' But Peter said, 'Man, I am not!' 59 Then about an hour later yet another kept insisting, 'Surely this man also was with him; for he is a Galilean.' 60 But Peter said, 'Man, I do not know what you are talking about!' At that moment, while he was still speaking, the cock crowed. 61 The Lord turned and looked at Peter. Then Peter remembered the word of the Lord, how he had said to him, 'Before the cock crows today, you will deny me three times.' 62 And he went out and wept bitterly.

63 Now the men who were holding Jesus began to mock him and beat him; 64 they also blindfolded him and kept asking him, 'Prophesy! Who is it that struck you?' 65 They kept heaping many other insults on him.

66 When day came, the assembly of the elders of the people, both chief priests and scribes, gathered together, and they brought him to their council. 67 They said, 'If you are the Messiah, tell us.' He replied, 'If I tell you, you will not believe; 68 and if I question you, you will not answer. 69 But from now on the Son of Man will be seated at the right hand of the power of God.' 70 All of them asked, 'Are you, then, the Son of God?' He said to them, 'You say that I am.' 71 Then they said, 'What further testimony do we need? We have heard it ourselves from his own lips!'

1 Then the assembly rose as a body and brought Jesus before Pilate. 2 They began to accuse him, saying, 'We found this man perverting our nation, forbidding us to pay taxes to the emperor, and saying that he himself is the Messiah, a king.' 3 Then Pilate asked him, 'Are you the king of the Jews?' He answered, 'You say so.' 4 Then Pilate said to the chief priests and the crowds, 'I find no basis for an accusation against this man.' 5 But they were insistent and said, 'He stirs up the people by teaching throughout all Judea, from Galilee where he began even to this place.'

6 When Pilate heard this, he asked whether the man was a Galilean. 7 And when he learned that he was under Herod's jurisdiction, he sent him off to Herod, who was himself in Jerusalem at that time. 8 When Herod saw Jesus, he was very glad, for he had been wanting to see him for a long time, because he had heard about him and was hoping to see him perform some sign. 9 He questioned him at some length, but Jesus gave him no answer. 10 The chief priests and the scribes stood by, vehemently accusing him. 11 Even Herod with his soldiers treated him with contempt and mocked him; then he put an elegant robe on him, and sent him back to Pilate.

¹² That same day Herod and Pilate became friends with each other; before this they had been enemies.

¹³ Pilate then called together the chief priests, the leaders, and the people, ¹⁴ and said to them, 'You brought me this man as one who was perverting the people; and here I have examined him in your presence and have not found this man guilty of any of your charges against him. ¹⁵ Neither has Herod, for he sent him back to us. Indeed, he has done nothing to deserve death. ¹⁶ I will therefore have him flogged and release him.'

¹⁸ Then they all shouted out together, 'Away with this fellow! Release Barabbas for us!' ¹⁹ (This was a man who had been put in prison for an insurrection that had taken place in the city, and for murder.) ²⁰ Pilate, wanting to release Jesus, addressed them again; ²¹ but they kept shouting, 'Crucify, crucify him!' ²² A third time he said to them, 'Why, what evil has he done? I have found in him no ground for the sentence of death; I will therefore have him flogged and then release him.' ²³ But they kept urgently demanding with loud shouts that he should be crucified; and their voices prevailed. ²⁴ So Pilate gave his verdict that their demand should be granted. ²⁵ He released the man they asked for, the one who had been put in prison for insurrection and murder, and he handed Jesus over as they wished.

²⁶ As they led him away, they seized a man, Simon of Cyrene, who was coming from the country, and they laid the cross on him, and made him carry it behind Jesus. ²⁷ A great number of the people followed him, and among them were women who were beating their breasts and wailing for him. ²⁸ But Jesus turned to them and said, 'Daughters of Jerusalem, do not weep for me, but weep for yourselves and for your children. ²⁹ For the days are surely coming when they will say, "Blessed are the barren, and the wombs that never bore, and the breasts that never nursed." ³⁰ Then they will begin to say to the mountains, "Fall on us"; and to the hills, "Cover us." ³¹ For if they do this when the wood is green, what will happen when it is dry?'

³² Two others also, who were criminals, were led away to be put to death with him. ³³ When they came to the place that is called The Skull, they crucified Jesus there with the criminals, one on his right and one on his left. ³⁴ Then Jesus said, 'Father, forgive them; for they do not know what they are doing.' And they cast lots to divide his clothing. ³⁵ And the people stood by, watching; but the leaders scoffed at him, saying, 'He saved others; let him save himself if he is the Messiah of God, his chosen one!' ³⁶ The soldiers also mocked him, coming up and offering him sour wine, ³⁷ and saying, 'If you are the King of the Jews, save yourself!' ³⁸ There was also an inscription over him, 'This is the King of the Jews.'

[39] One of the criminals who were hanged there kept deriding him and saying, 'Are you not the Messiah? Save yourself and us!' [40] But the other rebuked him, saying, 'Do you not fear God, since you are under the same sentence of condemnation? [41] And we indeed have been condemned justly, for we are getting what we deserve for our deeds, but this man has done nothing wrong.' [42] Then he said, 'Jesus, remember me when you come into your kingdom.' [43] He replied, 'Truly I tell you, today you will be with me in Paradise.'

[44] It was now about noon, and darkness came over the whole land until three in the afternoon, [45] while the sun's light failed; and the curtain of the temple was torn in two. [46] Then Jesus, crying with a loud voice, said, 'Father, into your hands I commend my spirit.' Having said this, he breathed his last. [47] When the centurion saw what had taken place, he praised God and said, 'Certainly this man was innocent.' [48] And when all the crowds who had gathered there for this spectacle saw what had taken place, they returned home, beating their breasts. [49] But all his acquaintances, including the women who had followed him from Galilee, stood at a distance, watching these things.

[50] Now there was a good and righteous man named Joseph, who, though a member of the council, [51] had not agreed to their plan and action. He came from the Jewish town of Arimathea, and he was waiting expectantly for the kingdom of God. [52] This man went to Pilate and asked for the body of Jesus. [53] Then he took it down, wrapped it in a linen cloth, and laid it in a rock-hewn tomb where no one had ever been laid. [54] It was the day of Preparation, and the sabbath was beginning. [55] The women who had come with him from Galilee followed, and they saw the tomb and how his body was laid. [56] Then they returned, and prepared spices and ointments.

On the sabbath they rested according to the commandment.

OR   Luke 23.1–49

[1] Then the assembly rose as a body and brought Jesus before Pilate. [2] They began to accuse him, saying, 'We found this man perverting our nation, forbidding us to pay taxes to the emperor, and saying that he himself is the Messiah, a king.' [3] Then Pilate asked him, 'Are you the king of the Jews?' He answered, 'You say so.' [4] Then Pilate said to the chief priests and the crowds, 'I find no basis for an accusation against this man.' [5] But they were insistent and said, 'He stirs up the people by teaching throughout all Judea, from Galilee where he began even to this place.'

[6] When Pilate heard this, he asked whether the man was a Galilean. [7] And when he learned that he was under Herod's jurisdiction, he sent him off to Herod, who was himself in Jerusalem at that time. [8] When Herod saw

Jesus, he was very glad, for he had been wanting to see him for a long time, because he had heard about him and was hoping to see him perform some sign. 9 He questioned him at some length, but Jesus gave him no answer. 10 The chief priests and the scribes stood by, vehemently accusing him. 11 Even Herod with his soldiers treated him with contempt and mocked him; then he put an elegant robe on him, and sent him back to Pilate. 12 That same day Herod and Pilate became friends with each other; before this they had been enemies.

13 Pilate then called together the chief priests, the leaders, and the people, 14 and said to them, 'You brought me this man as one who was perverting the people; and here I have examined him in your presence and have not found this man guilty of any of your charges against him. 15 Neither has Herod, for he sent him back to us. Indeed, he has done nothing to deserve death. 16 I will therefore have him flogged and release him.'

18 Then they all shouted out together, 'Away with this fellow! Release Barabbas for us!' 19 (This was a man who had been put in prison for an insurrection that had taken place in the city, and for murder.) 20 Pilate, wanting to release Jesus, addressed them again; 21 but they kept shouting, 'Crucify, crucify him!' 22 A third time he said to them, 'Why, what evil has he done? I have found in him no ground for the sentence of death; I will therefore have him flogged and then release him.' 23 But they kept urgently demanding with loud shouts that he should be crucified; and their voices prevailed. 24 So Pilate gave his verdict that their demand should be granted. 25 He released the man they asked for, the one who had been put in prison for insurrection and murder, and he handed Jesus over as they wished.

26 As they led him away, they seized a man, Simon of Cyrene, who was coming from the country, and they laid the cross on him, and made him carry it behind Jesus. 27 A great number of the people followed him, and among them were women who were beating their breasts and wailing for him. 28 But Jesus turned to them and said, 'Daughters of Jerusalem, do not weep for me, but weep for yourselves and for your children. 29 For the days are surely coming when they will say, "Blessed are the barren, and the wombs that never bore, and the breasts that never nursed." 30 Then they will begin to say to the mountains, "Fall on us"; and to the hills, "Cover us." 31 For if they do this when the wood is green, what will happen when it is dry?'

32 Two others also, who were criminals, were led away to be put to death with him. 33 When they came to the place that is called The Skull, they crucified Jesus there with the criminals, one on his right and one on his left. 34 Then Jesus said, 'Father, forgive them; for they do not know what they are doing.' And they cast lots to divide his clothing. 35 And the people stood by, watching; but the leaders scoffed at him, saying, 'He saved others;

let him save himself if he is the Messiah of God, his chosen one!' [36] The soldiers also mocked him, coming up and offering him sour wine, [37] and saying, 'If you are the King of the Jews, save yourself!' [38] There was also an inscription over him, 'This is the King of the Jews.'

[39] One of the criminals who were hanged there kept deriding him and saying, 'Are you not the Messiah? Save yourself and us!' [40] But the other rebuked him, saying, 'Do you not fear God, since you are under the same sentence of condemnation? [41] And we indeed have been condemned justly, for we are getting what we deserve for our deeds, but this man has done nothing wrong.' [42] Then he said, 'Jesus, remember me when you come into your kingdom.' [43] He replied, 'Truly I tell you, today you will be with me in Paradise.'

[44] It was now about noon, and darkness came over the whole land until three in the afternoon, [45] while the sun's light failed; and the curtain of the temple was torn in two. [46] Then Jesus, crying with a loud voice, said, 'Father, into your hands I commend my spirit.' Having said this, he breathed his last. [47] When the centurion saw what had taken place, he praised God and said, 'Certainly this man was innocent.' [48] And when all the crowds who had gathered there for this spectacle saw what had taken place, they returned home, beating their breasts. [49] But all his acquaintances, including the women who had followed him from Galilee, stood at a distance, watching these things.

POST COMMUNION

Lord Jesus Christ,
you humbled yourself in taking the form of a servant,
and in obedience died on the cross for our salvation:
give us the mind to follow you
and to proclaim you as Lord and King,
to the glory of God the Father.

SECOND SERVICE

Psalm 69.1–20
Isaiah 5.1–7
Luke 20.9–19

THIRD SERVICE

Psalms 61; 62
Zechariah 9.9–12
1 Corinthians 2.1–12

MONDAY OF HOLY WEEK

COLLECT

Almighty and everlasting God,
who in your tender love towards the human race
    sent your Son our Saviour Jesus Christ
to take upon him our flesh
and to suffer death upon the cross:
grant that we may follow the example
    of his patience and humility,
and also be made partakers of his resurrection;
through Jesus Christ your Son our Lord,
who is alive and reigns with you,
in the unity of the Holy Spirit,
one God, now and for ever.

READING   Isaiah 42.1–9

1   Here is my servant, whom I uphold,
        my chosen, in whom my soul delights;
    I have put my spirit upon him;
        he will bring forth justice to the nations.
2   He will not cry or lift up his voice,
        or make it heard in the street;
3   a bruised reed he will not break,
        and a dimly burning wick he will not quench;
        he will faithfully bring forth justice.
4   He will not grow faint or be crushed
        until he has established justice in the earth;
        and the coastlands wait for his teaching.
5   Thus says God, the LORD,
        who created the heavens and stretched them out,
        who spread out the earth and what comes from it,
    who gives breath to the people upon it
        and spirit to those who walk in it:
6   I am the LORD, I have called you in righteousness,
        I have taken you by the hand and kept you;
    I have given you as a covenant to the people,
        a light to the nations,

7   to open the eyes that are blind,
    to bring out the prisoners from the dungeon,
        from the prison those who sit in darkness.
8   I am the LORD, that is my name;
        my glory I give to no other,
        nor my praise to idols.
9   See, the former things have come to pass,
        and new things I now declare;
    before they spring forth,
        I tell you of them.

PSALM   Psalm 36.5–11

5   Your love, O Lord, reaches to the heavens,
        and your faithfulness to the clouds.
6   Your righteousness is like the strong mountains, your justice like
        the great deep;
    you save both human and beast, O Lord.
7   How priceless is your love, O God!
    your people take refuge under the shadow of your wings.
8   They feast upon the abundance of your house;
    you give them drink from the river of your delights.
9   For with you is the well of life,
        and in your light we see light.
10 Continue your loving-kindness to those who know you,
        and your favour to those who are true of heart.
11 Let not the foot of the proud come near me,
        nor the hand of the wicked push me aside.

READING   Hebrews 9.11–15

11 But when Christ came as a high priest of the good things that have
come, then through the greater and perfect tent (not made with hands,
that is, not of this creation), 12 he entered once for all into the Holy Place,
not with the blood of goats and calves, but with his own blood, thus
obtaining eternal redemption. 13 For if the blood of goats and bulls, with
the sprinkling of the ashes of a heifer, sanctifies those who have been
defiled so that their flesh is purified, 14 how much more will the blood of
Christ, who through the eternal Spirit offered himself without blemish to
God, purify our conscience from dead works to worship the living God!

15 For this reason he is the mediator of a new covenant, so that those who
are called may receive the promised eternal inheritance, because a death

has occurred that redeems them from the transgressions under the first covenant.

GOSPEL John 12.1–11

¹ Six days before the Passover Jesus came to Bethany, the home of Lazarus, whom he had raised from the dead. ² There they gave a dinner for him. Martha served, and Lazarus was one of those at the table with him. ³ Mary took a pound of costly perfume made of pure nard, anointed Jesus' feet, and wiped them with her hair. The house was filled with the fragrance of the perfume. ⁴ But Judas Iscariot, one of his disciples (the one who was about to betray him), said, ⁵ 'Why was this perfume not sold for three hundred denarii and the money given to the poor?' ⁶ (He said this not because he cared about the poor, but because he was a thief; he kept the common purse and used to steal what was put into it.) ⁷ Jesus said, 'Leave her alone. She bought it so that she might keep it for the day of my burial. ⁸ You always have the poor with you, but you do not always have me.'

⁹ When the great crowd of the Jews learned that he was there, they came not only because of Jesus but also to see Lazarus, whom he had raised from the dead. ¹⁰ So the chief priests planned to put Lazarus to death as well, ¹¹ since it was on account of him that many of the Jews were deserting and were believing in Jesus.

POST COMMUNION

Lord Jesus Christ,
you humbled yourself in taking the form of a servant,
and in obedience died on the cross for our salvation:
give us the mind to follow you
and to proclaim you as Lord and King,
to the glory of God the Father.

SECOND SERVICE

Psalm 41
Lamentations 1.1–12a
Luke 22.1–23

THIRD SERVICE

Psalm 25
Lamentations 2.8–19
Colossians 1.18–23

TUESDAY OF HOLY WEEK

COLLECT

Almighty and everlasting God,
who in your tender love towards the human race
   sent your Son our Saviour Jesus Christ
to take upon him our flesh
and to suffer death upon the cross:
grant that we may follow the example
   of his patience and humility,
and also be made partakers of his resurrection;
through Jesus Christ your Son our Lord,
who is alive and reigns with you,
in the unity of the Holy Spirit,
one God, now and for ever.

READING   Isaiah 49.1–7

¹ Listen to me, O coastlands,
    pay attention, you peoples from far away!
The Lord called me before I was born,
    while I was in my mother's womb he named me.
² He made my mouth like a sharp sword,
    in the shadow of his hand he hid me;
he made me a polished arrow,
    in his quiver he hid me away.
³ And he said to me, 'You are my servant,
    Israel, in whom I will be glorified.'
⁴ But I said, 'I have laboured in vain,
    I have spent my strength for nothing and vanity;
yet surely my cause is with the Lord,
    and my reward with my God.'
⁵ And now the Lord says,
    who formed me in the womb to be his servant,
to bring Jacob back to him,
    and that Israel might be gathered to him,
for I am honoured in the sight of the Lord,
    and my God has become my strength—

⁶ he says,
  'It is too light a thing that you should be my servant
    to raise up the tribes of Jacob
    and to restore the survivors of Israel;
  I will give you as a light to the nations,
    that my salvation may reach to the end of the earth.'
⁷ Thus says the LORD,
    the Redeemer of Israel and his Holy One,
  to one deeply despised, abhorred by the nations,
    the slave of rulers,
  'Kings shall see and stand up,
    princes, and they shall prostrate themselves,
  because of the LORD, who is faithful,
    the Holy One of Israel, who has chosen you.'

PSALM   Psalm 71.1–8, [9–14]

¹ In you, O Lord, have I taken refuge;
    let me never be ashamed.
² In your righteousness, deliver me and set me free;
    incline your ear to me and save me.
³ Be my strong rock, a castle to keep me safe;
    you are my crag and my stronghold.
⁴ Deliver me, my God, from the hand of the wicked,
    from the clutches of the evildoer and the oppressor.
⁵ For you are my hope, O Lord God,
    my confidence since I was young.
⁶ I have been sustained by you ever since I was born; from my
      mother's womb you have been my strength;
    my praise shall be always of you.
⁷ I have become a portent to many;
    but you are my refuge and my strength.
⁸ Let my mouth be full of your praise
    and your glory all the day long.
[⁹ Do not cast me off in my old age;
    forsake me not when my strength fails.
¹⁰ For my enemies are talking against me,
    and those who lie in wait for my life take counsel together.
¹¹ They say, 'God has forsaken him; go after him and seize him;
    because there is none who will save.'
¹² O God, be not far from me;
    come quickly to help me, O my God.

¹³ Let those who set themselves against me be put to shame and be
   disgraced;
   let those who seek to do me evil be covered with scorn and
   reproach.
¹⁴ But I shall always wait in patience,
   and shall praise you more and more.]

READING   1 Corinthians 1.18–31

¹⁸ For the message about the cross is foolishness to those who are per-
ishing, but to us who are being saved it is the power of God. ¹⁹ For it is
written,
   'I will destroy the wisdom of the wise,
      and the discernment of the discerning I will thwart.'
²⁰ Where is the one who is wise? Where is the scribe? Where is the debater
of this age? Has not God made foolish the wisdom of the world? ²¹ For since,
in the wisdom of God, the world did not know God through wisdom, God
decided, through the foolishness of our proclamation, to save those who
believe. ²² For Jews demand signs and Greeks desire wisdom, ²³ but we
proclaim Christ crucified, a stumbling-block to Jews and foolishness to
Gentiles, ²⁴ but to those who are the called, both Jews and Greeks, Christ
the power of God and the wisdom of God. ²⁵ For God's foolishness is wiser
than human wisdom, and God's weakness is stronger than human strength.

²⁶ Consider your own call, brothers and sisters: not many of you were wise
by human standards, not many were powerful, not many were of noble
birth. ²⁷ But God chose what is foolish in the world to shame the wise; God
chose what is weak in the world to shame the strong; ²⁸ God chose what is
low and despised in the world, things that are not, to reduce to nothing
things that are, ²⁹ so that no one might boast in the presence of God. ³⁰ He
is the source of your life in Christ Jesus, who became for us wisdom from
God, and righteousness and sanctification and redemption, ³¹ in order that,
as it is written, 'Let the one who boasts, boast in the Lord.'

GOSPEL   John 12.20–36

²⁰ Now among those who went up to worship at the festival were some
Greeks. ²¹ They came to Philip, who was from Bethsaida in Galilee, and said
to him, 'Sir, we wish to see Jesus.' ²² Philip went and told Andrew; then
Andrew and Philip went and told Jesus. ²³ Jesus answered them, 'The hour
has come for the Son of Man to be glorified. ²⁴ Very truly, I tell you, unless
a grain of wheat falls into the earth and dies, it remains just a single grain;
but if it dies, it bears much fruit. ²⁵ Those who love their life lose it, and

those who hate their life in this world will keep it for eternal life. [26] Whoever serves me must follow me, and where I am, there will my servant be also. Whoever serves me, the Father will honour.

[27] 'Now my soul is troubled. And what should I say—"Father, save me from this hour"? No, it is for this reason that I have come to this hour. [28] Father, glorify your name.' Then a voice came from heaven, 'I have glorified it, and I will glorify it again.' [29] The crowd standing there heard it and said that it was thunder. Others said, 'An angel has spoken to him.' [30] Jesus answered, 'This voice has come for your sake, not for mine. [31] Now is the judgement of this world; now the ruler of this world will be driven out. [32] And I, when I am lifted up from the earth, will draw all people to myself.' [33] He said this to indicate the kind of death he was to die. [34] The crowd answered him, 'We have heard from the law that the Messiah remains for ever. How can you say that the Son of Man must be lifted up? Who is this Son of Man?' [35] Jesus said to them, 'The light is with you for a little longer. Walk while you have the light, so that the darkness may not overtake you. If you walk in the darkness, you do not know where you are going. [36] While you have the light, believe in the light, so that you may become children of light.'

After Jesus had said this, he departed and hid from them.

POST COMMUNION

Lord Jesus Christ,
you humbled yourself in taking the form of a servant,
and in obedience died on the cross for our salvation:
give us the mind to follow you
and to proclaim you as Lord and King,
to the glory of God the Father.

SECOND SERVICE

Psalm 27
Lamentations 3.1–18
Luke 22.[24–38,] 39–53

THIRD SERVICE

Psalm 55.13–24
Lamentations 3.40–51
Galatians 6.11–18

WEDNESDAY OF HOLY WEEK

COLLECT

Almighty and everlasting God,
who in your tender love towards the human race
    sent your Son our Saviour Jesus Christ
to take upon him our flesh
and to suffer death upon the cross:
grant that we may follow the example
    of his patience and humility,
and also be made partakers of his resurrection;
through Jesus Christ your Son our Lord,
who is alive and reigns with you,
in the unity of the Holy Spirit,
one God, now and for ever.

READING   Isaiah 50.4–9a

⁴ The Lord GOD has given me
        the tongue of a teacher,
    that I may know how to sustain
        the weary with a word.
    Morning by morning he wakens—
        wakens my ear
        to listen as those who are taught.
⁵ The Lord GOD has opened my ear,
        and I was not rebellious,
        I did not turn backwards.
⁶ I gave my back to those who struck me,
        and my cheeks to those who pulled out the beard;
    I did not hide my face
        from insult and spitting.
⁷ The Lord GOD helps me;
        therefore I have not been disgraced;
    therefore I have set my face like flint,
        and I know that I shall not be put to shame;
⁸   he who vindicates me is near.
    Who will contend with me?
        Let us stand up together.
    Who are my adversaries?
        Let them confront me.

⁹ It is the Lord GOD who helps me;
    who will declare me guilty?

PSALM   Psalm 70

¹ Be pleased, O God, to deliver me;
    O Lord, make haste to help me.
² Let those who seek my life be ashamed and altogether dismayed;
    let those who take pleasure in my misfortune draw back and be
      disgraced.
³ Let those who say to me 'Aha!' and gloat over me turn back,
    because they are ashamed.
⁴ Let all who seek you rejoice and be glad in you;
    let those who love your salvation say for ever, 'Great is the Lord!'
⁵ But as for me, I am poor and needy;
    come to me speedily, O God.
⁶ You are my helper and my deliverer;
    O Lord, do not tarry.

READING   Hebrews 12.1–3

¹ Therefore, since we are surrounded by so great a cloud of witnesses, let
us also lay aside every weight and the sin that clings so closely, and let us
run with perseverance the race that is set before us, ² looking to Jesus the
pioneer and perfecter of our faith, who for the sake of the joy that was set
before him endured the cross, disregarding its shame, and has taken his
seat at the right hand of the throne of God.

³ Consider him who endured such hostility against himself from sinners,
so that you may not grow weary or lose heart.

GOSPEL   John 13.21–32

²¹ After saying this Jesus was troubled in spirit, and declared, 'Very truly,
I tell you, one of you will betray me.' ²² The disciples looked at one another,
uncertain of whom he was speaking. ²³ One of his disciples—the one whom
Jesus loved—was reclining next to him; ²⁴ Simon Peter therefore motioned
to him to ask Jesus of whom he was speaking. ²⁵ So while reclining next to
Jesus, he asked him, 'Lord, who is it?' ²⁶ Jesus answered, 'It is the one to
whom I give this piece of bread when I have dipped it in the dish.' So when
he had dipped the piece of bread, he gave it to Judas son of Simon Iscariot.
²⁷ After he received the piece of bread, Satan entered into him. Jesus said
to him, 'Do quickly what you are going to do.' ²⁸ Now no one at the table

knew why he said this to him. [29] Some thought that, because Judas had the common purse, Jesus was telling him, 'Buy what we need for the festival'; or, that he should give something to the poor. [30] So, after receiving the piece of bread, he immediately went out. And it was night.

[31] When he had gone out, Jesus said, 'Now the Son of Man has been glorified, and God has been glorified in him. [32] If God has been glorified in him, God will also glorify him in himself and will glorify him at once.'

POST COMMUNION

Lord Jesus Christ,
you humbled yourself in taking the form of a servant,
and in obedience died on the cross for our salvation:
give us the mind to follow you
and to proclaim you as Lord and King,
to the glory of God the Father.

SECOND SERVICE

THIRD SERVICE

Psalm 102.1–17, [18–28]
Wisdom 1.16–2.1; 2.12–22
or
Jeremiah 11.18–20
Luke 22.54–71

Psalm 88
Isaiah 63.1–9
Revelation 14.18–15.4

MAUNDY THURSDAY

COLLECT

God our Father,
you have invited us to share in the supper
which your Son gave to his Church
to proclaim his death until he comes:
may he nourish us by his presence,
and unite us in his love;
who is alive and reigns with you,
in the unity of the Holy Spirit,
one God, now and for ever.

At Morning and Evening Prayer the Collect of Palm Sunday is used

READING   Exodus 12.1–4, [5–10,] 11–14

¹ The LORD said to Moses and Aaron in the land of Egypt: ² This month shall mark for you the beginning of months; it shall be the first month of the year for you. ³ Tell the whole congregation of Israel that on the tenth of this month they are to take a lamb for each family, a lamb for each household. ⁴ If a household is too small for a whole lamb, it shall join its closest neighbour in obtaining one; the lamb shall be divided in proportion to the number of people who eat of it.

[⁵ Your lamb shall be without blemish, a year-old male; you may take it from the sheep or from the goats. ⁶ You shall keep it until the fourteenth day of this month; then the whole assembled congregation of Israel shall slaughter it at twilight. ⁷ They shall take some of the blood and put it on the two doorposts and the lintel of the houses in which they eat it. ⁸ They shall eat the lamb that same night; they shall eat it roasted over the fire with unleavened bread and bitter herbs. ⁹ Do not eat any of it raw or boiled in water, but roasted over the fire, with its head, legs, and inner organs. ¹⁰ You shall let none of it remain until the morning; anything that remains until the morning you shall burn.]

¹¹ This is how you shall eat it: your loins girded, your sandals on your feet, and your staff in your hand; and you shall eat it hurriedly. It is the passover of the LORD. ¹² For I will pass through the land of Egypt that night, and I will strike down every firstborn in the land of Egypt, both human beings and animals; on all the gods of Egypt I will execute judgements: I am the LORD. ¹³ The blood shall be a sign for you on the houses where you live: when I see the blood, I will pass over you, and no plague shall destroy you when I strike the land of Egypt.

¹⁴ This day shall be a day of remembrance for you. You shall celebrate it as a festival to the LORD; throughout your generations you shall observe it as a perpetual ordinance.

PSALM   Psalm 116.1, 10–17

¹   I love the Lord, because he has heard the voice of my supplication,
    because he has inclined his ear to me whenever I called upon him.

¹⁰   How shall I repay the Lord
     for all the good things he has done for me?
¹¹   I will lift up the cup of salvation
     and call upon the name of the Lord.
¹²   I will fulfil my vows to the Lord
     in the presence of all his people.

13 Precious in the sight of the Lord
   is the death of his servants.
14 O Lord, I am your servant;
   I am your servant and the child of your handmaid; you have freed
      me from my bonds.
15 I will offer you the sacrifice of thanksgiving
   and call upon the name of the Lord.
16 I will fulfil my vows to the Lord
   in the presence of all his people.
17 In the courts of the Lord's house,
   in the midst of you, O Jerusalem. Praise the Lord.

OR, IF AN ALTERNATIVE TEXT IS PREFERRED   Psalm 116.9–17

9 I believed, even when I said, 'I have been brought very low.'
   In my distress I said, 'No one can be trusted.'
10 How shall I repay the Lord
   for all the good things he has done for me?
11 I will lift up the cup of salvation
   and call upon the name of the Lord.
12 I will fulfil my vows to the Lord
   in the presence of all his people.
13 Precious in the sight of the Lord
   is the death of his servants.
14 O Lord, I am your servant;
   I am your servant and the child of your handmaid; you have freed
      me from my bonds.
15 I will offer you the sacrifice of thanksgiving
   and call upon the name of the Lord.
16 I will fulfil my vows to the Lord
   in the presence of all his people.
17 In the courts of the Lord's house,
   in the midst of you, O Jerusalem. Praise the Lord.

READING   1 Corinthians 11.23–26

23 For I received from the Lord what I also handed on to you, that the Lord
Jesus on the night when he was betrayed took a loaf of bread, 24 and when
he had given thanks, he broke it and said, 'This is my body that is for you.
Do this in remembrance of me.' 25 In the same way he took the cup also,
after supper, saying, 'This cup is the new covenant in my blood. Do this, as
often as you drink it, in remembrance of me.' 26 For as often as you eat this
bread and drink the cup, you proclaim the Lord's death until he comes.

GOSPEL   John 13.1–17, 31b–35

[1] Now before the festival of the Passover, Jesus knew that his hour had come to depart from this world and go to the Father. Having loved his own who were in the world, he loved them to the end. [2] The devil had already put it into the heart of Judas son of Simon Iscariot to betray him. And during supper [3] Jesus, knowing that the Father had given all things into his hands, and that he had come from God and was going to God, [4] got up from the table, took off his outer robe, and tied a towel around himself. [5] Then he poured water into a basin and began to wash the disciples' feet and to wipe them with the towel that was tied around him. [6] He came to Simon Peter, who said to him, 'Lord, are you going to wash my feet?' [7] Jesus answered, 'You do not know now what I am doing, but later you will understand.' [8] Peter said to him, 'You will never wash my feet.' Jesus answered, 'Unless I wash you, you have no share with me.' [9] Simon Peter said to him, 'Lord, not my feet only but also my hands and my head!' [10] Jesus said to him, 'One who has bathed does not need to wash, except for the feet, but is entirely clean. And you are clean, though not all of you.' [11] For he knew who was to betray him; for this reason he said, 'Not all of you are clean.'

[12] After he had washed their feet, had put on his robe, and had returned to the table, he said to them, 'Do you know what I have done to you? [13] You call me Teacher and Lord—and you are right, for that is what I am. [14] So if I, your Lord and Teacher, have washed your feet, you also ought to wash one another's feet. [15] For I have set you an example, that you also should do as I have done to you. [16] Very truly, I tell you, servants are not greater than their master, nor are messengers greater than the one who sent them. [17] If you know these things, you are blessed if you do them.'

[31] 'Now the Son of Man has been glorified, and God has been glorified in him. [32] If God has been glorified in him, God will also glorify him in himself and will glorify him at once. [33] Little children, I am with you only a little longer. You will look for me; and as I said to the Jews so now I say to you, "Where I am going, you cannot come." [34] I give you a new commandment, that you love one another. Just as I have loved you, you also should love one another. [35] By this everyone will know that you are my disciples, if you have love for one another.'

POST COMMUNION

Lord Jesus Christ,
we thank you that in this wonderful sacrament
you have given us the memorial of your passion:
grant us so to reverence the sacred mysteries

of your body and blood
that we may know within ourselves
and show forth in our lives
the fruit of your redemption,
for you are alive and reign, now and for ever.

SECOND SERVICE | THIRD SERVICE

Psalm 39 | Psalms 42; 43
Leviticus 16.2–24 | Exodus 11
Luke 23.1–25 | Ephesians 2.11–18

GOOD FRIDAY

COLLECT

Almighty Father,
look with mercy on this your family
for which our Lord Jesus Christ
  was content to be betrayed
  and given up into the hands of sinners
  and to suffer death upon the cross;
who is alive and glorified
  with you and the Holy Spirit,
one God, now and for ever.

READING   Isaiah 52.13–53.12

13 See, my servant shall prosper;
      he shall be exalted and lifted up,
      and shall be very high.
14 Just as there were many who were astonished at him
      —so marred was his appearance, beyond human semblance,
      and his form beyond that of mortals—
15 so he shall startle many nations;
      kings shall shut their mouths because of him;
    for that which had not been told them they shall see,
      and that which they had not heard they shall contemplate.
1 Who has believed what we have heard?
      And to whom has the arm of the LORD been revealed?

² For he grew up before him like a young plant,
  and like a root out of dry ground;
he had no form or majesty that we should look at him,
  nothing in his appearance that we should desire him.
³ He was despised and rejected by others;
  a man of suffering and acquainted with infirmity;
and as one from whom others hide their faces
  he was despised, and we held him of no account.
⁴ Surely he has borne our infirmities
  and carried our diseases;
yet we accounted him stricken,
  struck down by God, and afflicted.
⁵ But he was wounded for our transgressions,
  crushed for our iniquities;
upon him was the punishment that made us whole,
  and by his bruises we are healed.
⁶ All we like sheep have gone astray;
  we have all turned to our own way,
and the Lord has laid on him
  the iniquity of us all.
⁷ He was oppressed, and he was afflicted,
  yet he did not open his mouth;
like a lamb that is led to the slaughter,
  and like a sheep that before its shearers is silent,
  so he did not open his mouth.
⁸ By a perversion of justice he was taken away.
  Who could have imagined his future?
For he was cut off from the land of the living,
  stricken for the transgression of my people.
⁹ They made his grave with the wicked
  and his tomb with the rich,
although he had done no violence,
  and there was no deceit in his mouth.
¹⁰ Yet it was the will of the Lord to crush him with pain.
  When you make his life an offering for sin,
  he shall see his offspring, and shall prolong his days;
through him the will of the Lord shall prosper.
¹¹   Out of his anguish he shall see light;
he shall find satisfaction through his knowledge.
    The righteous one, my servant, shall make many righteous,
    and he shall bear their iniquities.

¹² Therefore I will allot him a portion with the great,
    and he shall divide the spoil with the strong;
because he poured out himself to death,
    and was numbered with the transgressors;
yet he bore the sin of many,
    and made intercession for the transgressors.

PSALM   Psalm 22

IF A SHORTER TEXT IS PREFERRED, USE 1–11 OR 1–20

¹ My God, my God, why have you forsaken me?
    and are so far from my cry and from the words of my distress?
² O my God, I cry in the daytime, but you do not answer;
    by night as well, but I find no rest.
³ Yet you are the Holy One,
    enthroned upon the praises of Israel.
⁴ Our forebears put their trust in you;
    they trusted and you delivered them.
⁵ They cried out to you and were delivered;
    they trusted in you and were not put to shame.
⁶ But as for me, I am a worm and no man,
    scorned by all and despised by the people.
⁷ All who see me laugh me to scorn;
    they curl their lips and wag their heads, saying,
⁸ 'He trusted in the Lord; let him deliver him;
    let him rescue him, if he delights in him.'
⁹ Yet you are he who took me out of the womb,
    and kept me safe upon my mother's breast.
¹⁰ I have been entrusted to you ever since I was born;
    you were my God when I was still in my mother's womb.
¹¹ Be not far from me, for trouble is near,
    and there is none to help.
¹² Many young bulls encircle me;
    strong bulls of Bashan surround me.
¹³ They open wide their jaws at me,
    like a ravening and a roaring lion.
¹⁴ I am poured out like water; all my bones are out of joint;
    my heart within my breast is melting wax.
¹⁵ My mouth is dried out like a pot-sherd; my tongue sticks to the
    roof of my mouth;
and you have laid me in the dust of the grave.

16 Packs of dogs close me in, and gangs of evildoers circle around me;
they pierce my hands and my feet; I can count all my bones.

17 They stare and gloat over me;
they divide my garments among them; they cast lots for my clothing.

18 Be not far away, O Lord;
you are my strength; hasten to help me.

19 Save me from the sword,
my life from the power of the dog.

20 Save me from the lion's mouth,
my wretched body from the horns of wild bulls.

21 I will declare your name to my people;
in the midst of the congregation I will praise you.

22 Praise the Lord, you that fear him;
stand in awe of him, O offspring of Israel; all you of Jacob's line, give glory.

23 For he does not despise nor abhor the poor in their poverty; neither does he hide his face from them;
but when they cry to him he hears them.

24 My praise is of him in the great assembly;
I will perform my vows in the presence of those who worship him.

25 The poor shall eat and be satisfied, and those who seek the Lord shall praise him:
'May your heart live for ever!'

26 All the ends of the earth shall remember and turn to the Lord,
and all the families of the nations shall bow before him.

27 For kingship belongs to the Lord;
he rules over the nations.

28 To him alone all who sleep in the earth bow down in worship;
all who go down to the dust fall before him.

29 My soul shall live for him; my descendants shall serve him;
they shall be known as the Lord's for ever.

30 They shall come and make known to a people yet unborn
the saving deeds that he has done.

READING

EITHER ### Hebrews 10.16–25

¹⁶ 'This is the covenant that I will make with them
    after those days, says the Lord:
 I will put my laws in their hearts,
    and I will write them on their minds',
¹⁷ he also adds,
 'I will remember their sins and their lawless deeds no more.'
¹⁸ Where there is forgiveness of these, there is no longer any offering for sin.

¹⁹ Therefore, my friends, since we have confidence to enter the sanctuary by the blood of Jesus, ²⁰ by the new and living way that he opened for us through the curtain (that is, through his flesh), ²¹ and since we have a great priest over the house of God, ²² let us approach with a true heart in full assurance of faith, with our hearts sprinkled clean from an evil conscience and our bodies washed with pure water. ²³ Let us hold fast to the confession of our hope without wavering, for he who has promised is faithful. ²⁴ And let us consider how to provoke one another to love and good deeds, ²⁵ not neglecting to meet together, as is the habit of some, but encouraging one another, and all the more as you see the Day approaching.

OR ### Hebrews 4.14–16; 5.7–9

¹⁴ Since, then, we have a great high priest who has passed through the heavens, Jesus, the Son of God, let us hold fast to our confession. ¹⁵ For we do not have a high priest who is unable to sympathize with our weaknesses, but we have one who in every respect has been tested as we are, yet without sin. ¹⁶ Let us therefore approach the throne of grace with boldness, so that we may receive mercy and find grace to help in time of need.

⁷ In the days of his flesh, Jesus offered up prayers and supplications, with loud cries and tears, to the one who was able to save him from death, and he was heard because of his reverent submission. ⁸ Although he was a Son, he learned obedience through what he suffered; ⁹ and having been made perfect, he became the source of eternal salvation for all who obey him.

GOSPEL ### John 18.1–19.42

¹ After Jesus had spoken these words, he went out with his disciples across the Kidron valley to a place where there was a garden, which he and his disciples entered. ² Now Judas, who betrayed him, also knew the place,

because Jesus often met there with his disciples. ³ So Judas brought a detachment of soldiers together with police from the chief priests and the Pharisees, and they came there with lanterns and torches and weapons. ⁴ Then Jesus, knowing all that was to happen to him, came forward and asked them, 'For whom are you looking?' ⁵ They answered, 'Jesus of Nazareth.' Jesus replied, 'I am he.' Judas, who betrayed him, was standing with them. ⁶ When Jesus said to them, 'I am he', they stepped back and fell to the ground. ⁷ Again he asked them, 'For whom are you looking?' And they said, 'Jesus of Nazareth.' ⁸ Jesus answered, 'I told you that I am he. So if you are looking for me, let these men go.' ⁹ This was to fulfil the word that he had spoken, 'I did not lose a single one of those whom you gave me.' ¹⁰ Then Simon Peter, who had a sword, drew it, struck the high priest's slave, and cut off his right ear. The slave's name was Malchus. ¹¹ Jesus said to Peter, 'Put your sword back into its sheath. Am I not to drink the cup that the Father has given me?'

¹² So the soldiers, their officer, and the Jewish police arrested Jesus and bound him. ¹³ First they took him to Annas, who was the father-in-law of Caiaphas, the high priest that year. ¹⁴ Caiaphas was the one who had advised the Jews that it was better to have one person die for the people.

¹⁵ Simon Peter and another disciple followed Jesus. Since that disciple was known to the high priest, he went with Jesus into the courtyard of the high priest, ¹⁶ but Peter was standing outside at the gate. So the other disciple, who was known to the high priest, went out, spoke to the woman who guarded the gate, and brought Peter in. ¹⁷ The woman said to Peter, 'You are not also one of this man's disciples, are you?' He said, 'I am not.' ¹⁸ Now the slaves and the police had made a charcoal fire because it was cold, and they were standing round it and warming themselves. Peter also was standing with them and warming himself.

¹⁹ Then the high priest questioned Jesus about his disciples and about his teaching. ²⁰ Jesus answered, 'I have spoken openly to the world; I have always taught in synagogues and in the temple, where all the Jews come together. I have said nothing in secret. ²¹ Why do you ask me? Ask those who heard what I said to them; they know what I said.' ²² When he had said this, one of the police standing nearby struck Jesus on the face, saying, 'Is that how you answer the high priest?' ²³ Jesus answered, 'If I have spoken wrongly, testify to the wrong. But if I have spoken rightly, why do you strike me?' ²⁴ Then Annas sent him bound to Caiaphas the high priest.

²⁵ Now Simon Peter was standing and warming himself. They asked him, 'You are not also one of his disciples, are you?' He denied it and said, 'I am not.' ²⁶ One of the slaves of the high priest, a relative of the man whose ear Peter had cut off, asked, 'Did I not see you in the garden with him?' ²⁷ Again Peter denied it, and at that moment the cock crowed.

²⁸ Then they took Jesus from Caiaphas to Pilate's headquarters. It was early in the morning. They themselves did not enter the headquarters, so as to avoid ritual defilement and to be able to eat the Passover. ²⁹ So Pilate went out to them and said, 'What accusation do you bring against this man?' ³⁰ They answered, 'If this man were not a criminal, we would not have handed him over to you.' ³¹ Pilate said to them, 'Take him yourselves and judge him according to your law.' The Jews replied, 'We are not permitted to put anyone to death.' ³² (This was to fulfil what Jesus had said when he indicated the kind of death he was to die.)

³³ Then Pilate entered the headquarters again, summoned Jesus, and asked him, 'Are you the King of the Jews?' ³⁴ Jesus answered, 'Do you ask this on your own, or did others tell you about me?' ³⁵ Pilate replied, 'I am not a Jew, am I? Your own nation and the chief priests have handed you over to me. What have you done?' ³⁶ Jesus answered, 'My kingdom is not from this world. If my kingdom were from this world, my followers would be fighting to keep me from being handed over to the Jews. But as it is, my kingdom is not from here.' ³⁷ Pilate asked him, 'So you are a king?' Jesus answered, 'You say that I am a king. For this I was born, and for this I came into the world, to testify to the truth. Everyone who belongs to the truth listens to my voice.' ³⁸ Pilate asked him, 'What is truth?'

After he had said this, he went out to the Jews again and told them, 'I find no case against him. ³⁹ But you have a custom that I release someone for you at the Passover. Do you want me to release for you the King of the Jews?' ⁴⁰ They shouted in reply, 'Not this man, but Barabbas!' Now Barabbas was a bandit.

¹ Then Pilate took Jesus and had him flogged. ² And the soldiers wove a crown of thorns and put it on his head, and they dressed him in a purple robe. ³ They kept coming up to him, saying, 'Hail, King of the Jews!' and striking him on the face. ⁴ Pilate went out again and said to them, 'Look, I am bringing him out to you to let you know that I find no case against him.' ⁵ So Jesus came out, wearing the crown of thorns and the purple robe. Pilate said to them, 'Here is the man!' ⁶ When the chief priests and the police saw him, they shouted, 'Crucify him! Crucify him!' Pilate said to them, 'Take him yourselves and crucify him; I find no case against him.' ⁷ The Jews answered him, 'We have a law, and according to that law he ought to die because he has claimed to be the Son of God.'

⁸ Now when Pilate heard this, he was more afraid than ever. ⁹ He entered his headquarters again and asked Jesus, 'Where are you from?' But Jesus gave him no answer. ¹⁰ Pilate therefore said to him, 'Do you refuse to speak to me? Do you not know that I have power to release you, and power to crucify you?' ¹¹ Jesus answered him, 'You would have no power over me unless it had been given you from above; therefore the one who handed

me over to you is guilty of a greater sin.' [12] From then on Pilate tried to release him, but the Jews cried out, 'If you release this man, you are no friend of the emperor. Everyone who claims to be a king sets himself against the emperor.'

[13] When Pilate heard these words, he brought Jesus outside and sat on the judge's bench at a place called The Stone Pavement, or in Hebrew Gabbatha. [14] Now it was the day of Preparation for the Passover; and it was about noon. He said to the Jews, 'Here is your King!' [15] They cried out, 'Away with him! Away with him! Crucify him!' Pilate asked them, 'Shall I crucify your King?' The chief priests answered, 'We have no king but the emperor.' [16] Then he handed him over to them to be crucified.

So they took Jesus; [17] and carrying the cross by himself, he went out to what is called The Place of the Skull, which in Hebrew is called Golgotha. [18] There they crucified him, and with him two others, one on either side, with Jesus between them. [19] Pilate also had an inscription written and put on the cross. It read, 'Jesus of Nazareth, the King of the Jews.' [20] Many of the Jews read this inscription, because the place where Jesus was crucified was near the city; and it was written in Hebrew, in Latin, and in Greek. [21] Then the chief priests of the Jews said to Pilate, 'Do not write, "The King of the Jews", but, "This man said, I am King of the Jews." ' [22] Pilate answered, 'What I have written I have written.' [23] When the soldiers had crucified Jesus, they took his clothes and divided them into four parts, one for each soldier. They also took his tunic; now the tunic was seamless, woven in one piece from the top. [24] So they said to one another, 'Let us not tear it, but cast lots for it to see who will get it.' This was to fulfil what the scripture says,

'They divided my clothes among themselves,
    and for my clothing they cast lots.'
[25] And that is what the soldiers did.

Meanwhile, standing near the cross of Jesus were his mother, and his mother's sister, Mary the wife of Clopas, and Mary Magdalene. [26] When Jesus saw his mother and the disciple whom he loved standing beside her, he said to his mother, 'Woman, here is your son.' [27] Then he said to the disciple, 'Here is your mother.' And from that hour the disciple took her into his own home.

[28] After this, when Jesus knew that all was now finished, he said (in order to fulfil the scripture), 'I am thirsty.' [29] A jar full of sour wine was standing there. So they put a sponge full of the wine on a branch of hyssop and held it to his mouth. [30] When Jesus had received the wine, he said, 'It is finished.' Then he bowed his head and gave up his spirit.

³¹ Since it was the day of Preparation, the Jews did not want the bodies left on the cross during the sabbath, especially because that sabbath was a day of great solemnity. So they asked Pilate to have the legs of the crucified men broken and the bodies removed. ³² Then the soldiers came and broke the legs of the first and of the other who had been crucified with him. ³³ But when they came to Jesus and saw that he was already dead, they did not break his legs. ³⁴ Instead, one of the soldiers pierced his side with a spear, and at once blood and water came out. ³⁵ (He who saw this has testified so that you also may believe. His testimony is true, and he knows that he tells the truth.) ³⁶ These things occurred so that the scripture might be fulfilled, 'None of his bones shall be broken.' ³⁷ And again another passage of scripture says, 'They will look on the one whom they have pierced.'

³⁸ After these things, Joseph of Arimathea, who was a disciple of Jesus, though a secret one because of his fear of the Jews, asked Pilate to let him take away the body of Jesus. Pilate gave him permission; so he came and removed his body. ³⁹ Nicodemus, who had at first come to Jesus by night, also came, bringing a mixture of myrrh and aloes, weighing about a hundred pounds. ⁴⁰ They took the body of Jesus and wrapped it with the spices in linen cloths, according to the burial custom of the Jews. ⁴¹ Now there was a garden in the place where he was crucified, and in the garden there was a new tomb in which no one had ever been laid. ⁴² And so, because it was the Jewish day of Preparation, and the tomb was nearby, they laid Jesus there.

SECOND SERVICE

Psalms 130; 143
Genesis 22.1–18

A part of

John 18–19
if not used at the Principal Service especially in the evening

John 19.38–42

or

Colossians 1.18–23

THIRD SERVICE

Psalm 69
Lamentations 5.15–22

A part of

John 18–19
if not read at the Principal Service

or

Hebrews 10.1–10

EASTER EVE

COLLECT

Grant, Lord,
that we who are baptized into the death
   of your Son our Saviour Jesus Christ
may continually put to death our evil desires
   and be buried with him;
and that through the grave and gate of death
we may pass to our joyful resurrection;
through his merits, who died and was buried
   and rose again for us,
your Son Jesus Christ our Lord.

These readings are for use at services other than the Easter Vigil

READING

EITHER   **Job 14.1–14**

1   'A mortal, born of woman, few of days and full of trouble,
2   comes up like a flower and withers,
        flees like a shadow and does not last.
3   Do you fix your eyes on such a one?
        Do you bring me into judgement with you?
4   Who can bring a clean thing out of an unclean?
        No one can.
5   Since their days are determined,
        and the number of their months is known to you,
        and you have appointed the bounds that they cannot pass,
6   look away from them, and desist,
        that they may enjoy, like labourers, their days.
7   For there is hope for a tree,
        if it is cut down, that it will sprout again,
        and that its shoots will not cease.
8   Though its root grows old in the earth,
        and its stump dies in the ground,
9   yet at the scent of water it will bud
        and put forth branches like a young plant.
10   But mortals die, and are laid low;
        humans expire, and where are they?

11 As waters fail from a lake,
    and a river wastes away and dries up,
12 so mortals lie down and do not rise again;
    until the heavens are no more, they will not awake
    or be roused out of their sleep.
13 O that you would hide me in Sheol,
    that you would conceal me until your wrath is past,
    that you would appoint me a set time, and remember me!
14 If mortals die, will they live again?
    All the days of my service I would wait
    until my release should come.'

OR   **Lamentations 3.1–9, 19–24**

1 I am one who has seen affliction
    under the rod of God's wrath;
2 he has driven and brought me
    into darkness without any light;
3 against me alone he turns his hand,
    again and again, all day long.
4 He has made my flesh and my skin waste away,
    and broken my bones;
5 he has besieged and enveloped me
    with bitterness and tribulation;
6 he has made me sit in darkness
    like the dead of long ago.
7 He has walled me about so that I cannot escape;
    he has put heavy chains on me;
8 though I call and cry for help,
    he shuts out my prayer;
9 he has blocked my ways with hewn stones,
    he has made my paths crooked.

19 The thought of my affliction and my homelessness
    is wormwood and gall!
20 My soul continually thinks of it
    and is bowed down within me.
21 But this I call to mind,
    and therefore I have hope:
22 The steadfast love of the LORD never ceases,
    his mercies never come to an end;

²³ they are new every morning;
   great is your faithfulness.
²⁴ 'The LORD is my portion,' says my soul,
   'therefore I will hope in him.'

PSALM   Psalm 31.1–4, 15–16

¹ In you, O Lord, have I taken refuge; let me never be put to shame;
   deliver me in your righteousness.
² Incline your ear to me;
   make haste to deliver me.
³ Be my strong rock, a castle to keep me safe, for you are my crag
     and my stronghold;
   for the sake of your name, lead me and guide me.
⁴ Take me out of the net that they have secretly set for me,
   for you are my tower of strength.

¹⁵ 'My times are in your hand;
   rescue me from the hand of my enemies, and from those who
     persecute me.
¹⁶ Make your face to shine upon your servant,
   and in your loving-kindness save me.'

OR, IF AN ALTERNATIVE TEXT IS PREFERRED   **Psalm 31.1–5**

¹ In you, O Lord, have I taken refuge; let me never be put to shame;
   deliver me in your righteousness.
² Incline your ear to me;
   make haste to deliver me.
³ Be my strong rock, a castle to keep me safe, for you are my crag
     and my stronghold;
   for the sake of your name, lead me and guide me.
⁴ Take me out of the net that they have secretly set for me,
   for you are my tower of strength.
⁵ Into your hands I commend my spirit,
   for you have redeemed me, O Lord, O God of truth.

READING   1 Peter 4.1–8

¹ Since therefore Christ suffered in the flesh, arm yourselves also with the same intention (for whoever has suffered in the flesh has finished with sin), ² so as to live for the rest of your earthly life no longer by human desires but by the will of God. ³ You have already spent enough time in doing what the Gentiles like to do, living in licentiousness, passions,

drunkenness, revels, carousing, and lawless idolatry. ⁴ They are surprised that you no longer join them in the same excesses of dissipation, and so they blaspheme. ⁵ But they will have to give an account to him who stands ready to judge the living and the dead. ⁶ For this is the reason the gospel was proclaimed even to the dead, so that, though they had been judged in the flesh as everyone is judged, they might live in the spirit as God does.

⁷ The end of all things is near; therefore be serious and discipline yourselves for the sake of your prayers. ⁸ Above all, maintain constant love for one another, for love covers a multitude of sins.

GOSPEL

EITHER   **Matthew 27.57–66**

⁵⁷ When it was evening, there came a rich man from Arimathea, named Joseph, who was also a disciple of Jesus. ⁵⁸ He went to Pilate and asked for the body of Jesus; then Pilate ordered it to be given to him. ⁵⁹ So Joseph took the body and wrapped it in a clean linen cloth ⁶⁰ and laid it in his own new tomb, which he had hewn in the rock. He then rolled a great stone to the door of the tomb and went away. ⁶¹ Mary Magdalene and the other Mary were there, sitting opposite the tomb.

⁶² The next day, that is, after the day of Preparation, the chief priests and the Pharisees gathered before Pilate ⁶³ and said, 'Sir, we remember what that impostor said while he was still alive, "After three days I will rise again." ⁶⁴ Therefore command that the tomb be made secure until the third day; otherwise his disciples may go and steal him away, and tell the people, "He has been raised from the dead", and the last deception would be worse than the first.' ⁶⁵ Pilate said to them, 'You have a guard of soldiers; go, make it as secure as you can.' ⁶⁶ So they went with the guard and made the tomb secure by sealing the stone.

OR   **John 19.38–42**

³⁸ After these things, Joseph of Arimathea, who was a disciple of Jesus, though a secret one because of his fear of the Jews, asked Pilate to let him take away the body of Jesus. Pilate gave him permission; so he came and removed his body. ³⁹ Nicodemus, who had at first come to Jesus by night, also came, bringing a mixture of myrrh and aloes, weighing about a hundred pounds. ⁴⁰ They took the body of Jesus and wrapped it with the spices in linen cloths, according to the burial custom of the Jews. ⁴¹ Now there was a garden in the place where he was crucified, and in the garden

there was a new tomb in which no one had ever been laid. [42] And so, because it was the Jewish day of Preparation, and the tomb was nearby, they laid Jesus there.

SECOND SERVICE	THIRD SERVICE
Psalm 142	**Psalm 116**
Hosea 6.1–6	**Job 19.21–27**
John 2.18–22	**1 John 5.5–12**

EASTER VIGIL

COLLECT

Lord of all life and power,
who through the mighty resurrection of your Son
overcame the old order of sin and death
to make all things new in him:
grant that we, being dead to sin
and alive to you in Jesus Christ,
may reign with him in glory;
to whom with you and the Holy Spirit
be praise and honour, glory and might,
now and in all eternity.

A minimum of three Old Testament readings should be chosen. The reading from Exodus 14, along with its associated Canticle, the reading from Romans, Psalm 114 and the Gospel should always be used.

READING   Genesis 1.1–2.4a

[1] In the beginning when God created the heavens and the earth, [2] the earth was a formless void and darkness covered the face of the deep, while a wind from God swept over the face of the waters. [3] Then God said, 'Let there be light'; and there was light. [4] And God saw that the light was good; and God separated the light from the darkness. [5] God called the light Day, and the darkness he called Night. And there was evening and there was morning, the first day.

[6] And God said, 'Let there be a dome in the midst of the waters, and let it separate the waters from the waters.' [7] So God made the dome and separated

the waters that were under the dome from the waters that were above the dome. And it was so. [8] God called the dome Sky. And there was evening and there was morning, the second day.

[9] And God said, 'Let the waters under the sky be gathered together into one place, and let the dry land appear.' And it was so. [10] God called the dry land Earth, and the waters that were gathered together he called Seas. And God saw that it was good. [11] Then God said, 'Let the earth put forth vegetation: plants yielding seed, and fruit trees of every kind on earth that bear fruit with the seed in it.' And it was so. [12] The earth brought forth vegetation: plants yielding seed of every kind, and trees of every kind bearing fruit with the seed in it. And God saw that it was good. [13] And there was evening and there was morning, the third day.

[14] And God said, 'Let there be lights in the dome of the sky to separate the day from the night; and let them be for signs and for seasons and for days and years, [15] and let them be lights in the dome of the sky to give light upon the earth.' And it was so. [16] God made the two great lights—the greater light to rule the day and the lesser light to rule the night—and the stars. [17] God set them in the dome of the sky to give light upon the earth, [18] to rule over the day and over the night, and to separate the light from the darkness. And God saw that it was good. [19] And there was evening and there was morning, the fourth day.

[20] And God said, 'Let the waters bring forth swarms of living creatures, and let birds fly above the earth across the dome of the sky.' [21] So God created the great sea monsters and every living creature that moves, of every kind, with which the waters swarm, and every winged bird of every kind. And God saw that it was good. [22] God blessed them, saying, 'Be fruitful and multiply and fill the waters in the seas, and let birds multiply on the earth.' [23] And there was evening and there was morning, the fifth day.

[24] And God said, 'Let the earth bring forth living creatures of every kind: cattle and creeping things and wild animals of the earth of every kind.' And it was so. [25] God made the wild animals of the earth of every kind, and the cattle of every kind, and everything that creeps upon the ground of every kind. And God saw that it was good.

[26] Then God said, 'Let us make humankind in our image, according to our likeness; and let them have dominion over the fish of the sea, and over the birds of the air, and over the cattle, and over all the wild animals of the earth, and over every creeping thing that creeps upon the earth.'
[27] So God created humankind in his image,
    in the image of God he created them;
    male and female he created them.

²⁸ God blessed them, and God said to them, 'Be fruitful and multiply, and fill the earth and subdue it; and have dominion over the fish of the sea and over the birds of the air and over every living thing that moves upon the earth.' ²⁹ God said, 'See, I have given you every plant yielding seed that is upon the face of all the earth, and every tree with seed in its fruit; you shall have them for food. ³⁰ And to every beast of the earth, and to every bird of the air, and to everything that creeps on the earth, everything that has the breath of life, I have given every green plant for food.' And it was so. ³¹ God saw everything that he had made, and indeed, it was very good. And there was evening and there was morning, the sixth day.

¹ Thus the heavens and the earth were finished, and all their multitude. ² And on the seventh day God finished the work that he had done, and he rested on the seventh day from all the work that he had done. ³ So God blessed the seventh day and hallowed it, because on it God rested from all the work that he had done in creation.

⁴ These are the generations of the heavens and the earth when they were created.

PSALM   Psalm 136.1–9, 23–26

1 Give thanks to the Lord, for he is good,
   for his mercy endures for ever.
2 Give thanks to the God of gods,
   for his mercy endures for ever.
3 Give thanks to the Lord of lords,
   for his mercy endures for ever.
4 Who only does great wonders,
   for his mercy endures for ever;
5 Who by his wisdom made the heavens,
   for his mercy endures for ever;
6 Who spread out the earth upon the waters,
   for his mercy endures for ever;
7 Who created great lights,
   for his mercy endures for ever;
8 The sun to rule the day,
   for his mercy endures for ever;
9 The moon and the stars to govern the night,
   for his mercy endures for ever.

23 Who remembered us in our low estate,
    for his mercy endures for ever;
24 And delivered us from our enemies,
    for his mercy endures for ever;

25 Who gives food to all creatures,
    for his mercy endures for ever;
26 Give thanks to the God of heaven,
    for his mercy endures for ever.

READING   Genesis 7.1–5, 11–18; 8.6–18; 9.8–13

¹ Then the Lord said to Noah, 'Go into the ark, you and all your household, for I have seen that you alone are righteous before me in this generation. ² Take with you seven pairs of all clean animals, the male and its mate; and a pair of the animals that are not clean, the male and its mate; ³ and seven pairs of the birds of the air also, male and female, to keep their kind alive on the face of all the earth. ⁴ For in seven days I will send rain on the earth for forty days and forty nights; and every living thing that I have made I will blot out from the face of the ground.' ⁵ And Noah did all that the Lord had commanded him.

¹¹ In the six-hundredth year of Noah's life, in the second month, on the seventeenth day of the month, on that day all the fountains of the great deep burst forth, and the windows of the heavens were opened. ¹² The rain fell on the earth for forty days and forty nights. ¹³ On the very same day Noah with his sons, Shem and Ham and Japheth, and Noah's wife and the three wives of his sons, entered the ark, ¹⁴ they and every wild animal of every kind, and all domestic animals of every kind, and every creeping thing that creeps on the earth, and every bird of every kind—every bird, every winged creature. ¹⁵ They went into the ark with Noah, two and two of all flesh in which there was the breath of life. ¹⁶ And those that entered, male and female of all flesh, went in as God had commanded him; and the Lord shut him in.

¹⁷ The flood continued for forty days on the earth; and the waters increased, and bore up the ark, and it rose high above the earth. ¹⁸ The waters swelled and increased greatly on the earth; and the ark floated on the face of the waters.

⁶ At the end of forty days Noah opened the window of the ark that he had made ⁷ and sent out the raven; and it went to and fro until the waters were dried up from the earth. ⁸ Then he sent out the dove from him, to see if the waters had subsided from the face of the ground; ⁹ but the dove found no place to set its foot, and it returned to him to the ark, for the waters were still on the face of the whole earth. So he put out his hand and took it and brought it into the ark with him. ¹⁰ He waited another seven days, and again he sent out the dove from the ark; ¹¹ and the dove came back to him in the evening, and there in its beak was a freshly plucked olive leaf; so

Noah knew that the waters had subsided from the earth. [12] Then he waited another seven days, and sent out the dove; and it did not return to him any more.

[13] In the six hundred and first year, in the first month, on the first day of the month, the waters were dried up from the earth; and Noah removed the covering of the ark, and looked, and saw that the face of the ground was drying. [14] In the second month, on the twenty-seventh day of the month, the earth was dry. [15] Then God said to Noah, [16] 'Go out of the ark, you and your wife, and your sons and your sons' wives with you. [17] Bring out with you every living thing that is with you of all flesh—birds and animals and every creeping thing that creeps on the earth—so that they may abound on the earth, and be fruitful and multiply on the earth.' [18] So Noah went out with his sons and his wife and his sons' wives.

[8] Then God said to Noah and to his sons with him, [9] 'As for me, I am establishing my covenant with you and your descendants after you, [10] and with every living creature that is with you, the birds, the domestic animals, and every animal of the earth with you, as many as came out of the ark. [11] I establish my covenant with you, that never again shall all flesh be cut off by the waters of a flood, and never again shall there be a flood to destroy the earth.' [12] God said, 'This is the sign of the covenant that I make between me and you and every living creature that is with you, for all future generations: [13] I have set my bow in the clouds, and it shall be a sign of the covenant between me and the earth.'

PSALM   Psalm 46

1   God is our refuge and strength,
    a very present help in trouble;
2   Therefore we will not fear, though the earth be moved,
    and though the mountains be toppled into the depths of the sea;
3   Though its waters rage and foam,
    and though the mountains tremble at its tumult.
4   The Lord of hosts is with us;
    the God of Jacob is our stronghold.
5   There is a river whose streams make glad the city of God,
    the holy habitation of the Most High.
6   God is in the midst of her; she shall not be overthrown;
    God shall help her at the break of day.
7   The nations make much ado and the kingdoms are shaken;
    God has spoken and the earth shall melt away.
8   The Lord of hosts is with us;
    the God of Jacob is our stronghold.

9   Come now and look upon the works of the Lord,
    what awesome things he has done on earth.
10 It is he who makes war to cease in all the world;
    he breaks the bow and shatters the spear and burns the shields
        with fire.
11 'Be still, then, and know that I am God;
    I will be exalted among the nations; I will be exalted in the earth.'
12 The Lord of hosts is with us;
    the God of Jacob is our stronghold.

READING   Genesis 22.1–18

¹ After these things God tested Abraham. He said to him, 'Abraham!' And
he said, 'Here I am.' ² He said, 'Take your son, your only son Isaac, whom
you love, and go to the land of Moriah, and offer him there as a burnt-
offering on one of the mountains that I shall show you.' ³ So Abraham rose
early in the morning, saddled his donkey, and took two of his young men
with him, and his son Isaac; he cut the wood for the burnt-offering, and
set out and went to the place in the distance that God had shown him. ⁴ On
the third day Abraham looked up and saw the place far away. ⁵ Then
Abraham said to his young men, 'Stay here with the donkey; the boy and I
will go over there; we will worship, and then we will come back to you.'
⁶ Abraham took the wood of the burnt-offering and laid it on his son Isaac,
and he himself carried the fire and the knife. So the two of them walked
on together. ⁷ Isaac said to his father Abraham, 'Father!' And he said, 'Here
I am, my son.' He said, 'The fire and the wood are here, but where is the
lamb for a burnt-offering?' ⁸ Abraham said, 'God himself will provide the
lamb for a burnt-offering, my son.' So the two of them walked on together.

⁹ When they came to the place that God had shown him, Abraham built
an altar there and laid the wood in order. He bound his son Isaac, and laid
him on the altar, on top of the wood. ¹⁰ Then Abraham reached out his
hand and took the knife to kill his son. ¹¹ But the angel of the LORD called
to him from heaven, and said, 'Abraham, Abraham!' And he said, 'Here I
am.' ¹² He said, 'Do not lay your hand on the boy or do anything to him; for
now I know that you fear God, since you have not withheld your son, your
only son, from me.' ¹³ And Abraham looked up and saw a ram, caught in a
thicket by its horns. Abraham went and took the ram and offered it up as
a burnt-offering instead of his son. ¹⁴ So Abraham called that place 'The
LORD will provide'; as it is said to this day, 'On the mount of the LORD it
shall be provided.'

¹⁵ The angel of the LORD called to Abraham a second time from heaven,
¹⁶ and said, 'By myself I have sworn, says the LORD: Because you have done

this, and have not withheld your son, your only son, ¹⁷ I will indeed bless you, and I will make your offspring as numerous as the stars of heaven and as the sand that is on the seashore. And your offspring shall possess the gate of their enemies, ¹⁸ and by your offspring shall all the nations of the earth gain blessing for themselves, because you have obeyed my voice.'

PSALM   Psalm 16

¹ Protect me, O God, for I take refuge in you;
     I have said to the Lord, 'You are my Lord, my good above all other.'
² All my delight is upon the godly that are in the land,
     upon those who are noble among the people.
³ But those who run after other gods
     shall have their troubles multiplied.
⁴ Their libations of blood I will not offer,
     nor take the names of their gods upon my lips.
⁵ O Lord, you are my portion and my cup;
     it is you who uphold my lot.
⁶ My boundaries enclose a pleasant land;
     indeed, I have a goodly heritage.
⁷ I will bless the Lord who gives me counsel;
     my heart teaches me, night after night.
⁸ I have set the Lord always before me;
     because he is at my right hand I shall not fall.
⁹ My heart, therefore, is glad and my spirit rejoices;
     my body also shall rest in hope.
¹⁰ For you will not abandon me to the grave,
     nor let your holy one see the Pit.
¹¹ You will show me the path of life;
     in your presence there is fullness of joy, and in your right hand
        are pleasures for evermore.

READING   Exodus 14.10–31; 15.20–21

¹⁰ As Pharaoh drew near, the Israelites looked back, and there were the Egyptians advancing on them. In great fear the Israelites cried out to the LORD. ¹¹ They said to Moses, 'Was it because there were no graves in Egypt that you have taken us away to die in the wilderness? What have you done to us, bringing us out of Egypt? ¹² Is this not the very thing we told you in Egypt, "Let us alone and let us serve the Egyptians"? For it would have been better for us to serve the Egyptians than to die in the wilderness.' ¹³ But Moses said to the people, 'Do not be afraid, stand firm, and see the deliverance that the LORD will accomplish for you today; for the Egyptians whom

you see today you shall never see again. ¹⁴ The LORD will fight for you, and you have only to keep still.'

¹⁵ Then the LORD said to Moses, 'Why do you cry out to me? Tell the Israelites to go forward. ¹⁶ But you lift up your staff, and stretch out your hand over the sea and divide it, that the Israelites may go into the sea on dry ground. ¹⁷ Then I will harden the hearts of the Egyptians so that they will go in after them; and so I will gain glory for myself over Pharaoh and all his army, his chariots, and his chariot drivers. ¹⁸ And the Egyptians shall know that I am the LORD, when I have gained glory for myself over Pharaoh, his chariots, and his chariot drivers.'

¹⁹ The angel of God who was going before the Israelite army moved and went behind them; and the pillar of cloud moved from in front of them and took its place behind them. ²⁰ It came between the army of Egypt and the army of Israel. And so the cloud was there with the darkness, and it lit up the night; one did not come near the other all night.

²¹ Then Moses stretched out his hand over the sea. The LORD drove the sea back by a strong east wind all night, and turned the sea into dry land; and the waters were divided. ²² The Israelites went into the sea on dry ground, the waters forming a wall for them on their right and on their left. ²³ The Egyptians pursued, and went into the sea after them, all of Pharaoh's horses, chariots, and chariot drivers. ²⁴ At the morning watch the LORD in the pillar of fire and cloud looked down upon the Egyptian army, and threw the Egyptian army into panic. ²⁵ He clogged their chariot wheels so that they turned with difficulty. The Egyptians said, 'Let us flee from the Israelites, for the LORD is fighting for them against Egypt.'

²⁶ Then the LORD said to Moses, 'Stretch out your hand over the sea, so that the water may come back upon the Egyptians, upon their chariots and chariot drivers.' ²⁷ So Moses stretched out his hand over the sea, and at dawn the sea returned to its normal depth. As the Egyptians fled before it, the LORD tossed the Egyptians into the sea. ²⁸ The waters returned and covered the chariots and the chariot drivers, the entire army of Pharaoh that had followed them into the sea; not one of them remained. ²⁹ But the Israelites walked on dry ground through the sea, the waters forming a wall for them on their right and on their left.

³⁰ Thus the LORD saved Israel that day from the Egyptians; and Israel saw the Egyptians dead on the seashore. ³¹ Israel saw the great work that the LORD did against the Egyptians. So the people feared the LORD and believed in the LORD and in his servant Moses.

²⁰ Then the prophet Miriam, Aaron's sister, took a tambourine in her hand; and all the women went out after her with tambourines and with dancing. ²¹ And Miriam sang to them:

'Sing to the Lord, for he has triumphed gloriously;
horse and rider he has thrown into the sea.'

CANTICLE   Exodus 15.1b–13, 17–18

¹ 'I will sing to the Lord, for he has triumphed gloriously;
   horse and rider he has thrown into the sea.
² The Lord is my strength and my might,
   and he has become my salvation;
   this is my God, and I will praise him,
   my father's God, and I will exalt him.
³ The Lord is a warrior;
   the Lord is his name.
⁴ Pharaoh's chariots and his army he cast into the sea;
   his picked officers were sunk in the Red Sea.
⁵ The floods covered them;
   they went down into the depths like a stone.
⁶ Your right hand, O Lord, glorious in power—
   your right hand, O Lord, shattered the enemy.
⁷ In the greatness of your majesty you overthrew your adversaries;
   you sent out your fury, it consumed them like stubble.
⁸ At the blast of your nostrils the waters piled up,
   the floods stood up in a heap;
   the deeps congealed in the heart of the sea.
⁹ The enemy said, "I will pursue, I will overtake,
   I will divide the spoil, my desire shall have its fill of them.
   I will draw my sword, my hand shall destroy them."
¹⁰ You blew with your wind, the sea covered them;
   they sank like lead in the mighty waters.
¹¹ Who is like you, O Lord, among the gods?
   Who is like you, majestic in holiness,
   awesome in splendour, doing wonders?
¹² You stretched out your right hand,
   the earth swallowed them.
¹³ In your steadfast love you led the people whom you redeemed;
   you guided them by your strength to your holy abode.'

¹⁷ 'You brought them in and planted them on the mountain of your own possession,

    the place, O LORD, that you made your abode,

    the sanctuary, O LORD, that your hands have established.

¹⁸ The LORD will reign for ever and ever.'

READING   Isaiah 55.1–11

¹ Ho, everyone who thirsts,

    come to the waters;

and you that have no money,

    come, buy and eat!

Come, buy wine and milk

    without money and without price.

² Why do you spend your money for that which is not bread,

    and your labour for that which does not satisfy?

Listen carefully to me, and eat what is good,

    and delight yourselves in rich food.

³ Incline your ear, and come to me;

    listen, so that you may live.

I will make with you an everlasting covenant,

    my steadfast, sure love for David.

⁴ See, I made him a witness to the peoples,

    a leader and commander for the peoples.

⁵ See, you shall call nations that you do not know,

    and nations that do not know you shall run to you,

because of the LORD your God, the Holy One of Israel,

    for he has glorified you.

⁶ Seek the LORD while he may be found,

    call upon him while he is near;

⁷ let the wicked forsake their way,

    and the unrighteous their thoughts;

let them return to the LORD, that he may have mercy on them,

    and to our God, for he will abundantly pardon.

⁸ For my thoughts are not your thoughts,

    nor are your ways my ways, says the LORD.

⁹ For as the heavens are higher than the earth,

    so are my ways higher than your ways

    and my thoughts than your thoughts.

¹⁰ For as the rain and the snow come down from heaven,

    and do not return there until they have watered the earth,

making it bring forth and sprout,

    giving seed to the sower and bread to the eater,

¹¹ so shall my word be that goes out from my mouth;
    it shall not return to me empty,
but it shall accomplish that which I purpose,
    and succeed in the thing for which I sent it.

CANTICLE   Isaiah 12.2-6

² Surely God is my salvation;
    I will trust, and will not be afraid,
for the LORD GOD is my strength and my might;
    he has become my salvation.

³ With joy you will draw water from the wells of salvation. ⁴ And you will say on that day:
    Give thanks to the LORD,
        call on his name;
    make known his deeds among the nations;
        proclaim that his name is exalted.
⁵ Sing praises to the LORD, for he has done gloriously;
    let this be known in all the earth.
⁶ Shout aloud and sing for joy, O royal Zion,
    for great in your midst is the Holy One of Israel.

READING

EITHER   Baruch 3.9-15, 32-4.4

⁹ Hear the commandments of life, O Israel;
    give ear, and learn wisdom!
¹⁰ Why is it, O Israel, why is it that you are in the land of your enemies,
    that you are growing old in a foreign country,
that you are defiled with the dead,
¹¹   that you are counted among those in Hades?
¹² You have forsaken the fountain of wisdom.
¹³ If you had walked in the way of God,
    you would be living in peace for ever.
¹⁴ Learn where there is wisdom,
    where there is strength,
    where there is understanding,
so that you may at the same time discern
    where there is length of days, and life,
    where there is light for the eyes, and peace.

15 Who has found her place?
    And who has entered her storehouses?

32 But the one who knows all things knows her,
    he found her by his understanding.
  The one who prepared the earth for all time
    filled it with four-footed creatures;
33 the one who sends forth the light, and it goes;
    he called it, and it obeyed him, trembling;
34 the stars shone in their watches, and were glad;
    he called them, and they said, 'Here we are!'
  They shone with gladness for him who made them.
35 This is our God;
    no other can be compared to him.
36 He found the whole way to knowledge,
    and gave her to his servant Jacob
    and to Israel, whom he loved.
37 Afterwards she appeared on earth
    and lived with humankind.
1 She is the book of the commandments of God,
    the law that endures for ever.
  All who hold her fast will live,
    and those who forsake her will die.
2 Turn, O Jacob, and take her;
    walk towards the shining of her light.
3 Do not give your glory to another,
    or your advantages to an alien people.
4 Happy are we, O Israel,
    for we know what is pleasing to God.

OR   **Proverbs 8.1–8, 19–21; 9.4b–6**

1 Does not wisdom call,
    and does not understanding raise her voice?
2 On the heights, beside the way,
    at the crossroads she takes her stand;
3 beside the gates in front of the town,
    at the entrance of the portals she cries out:
4 'To you, O people, I call,
    and my cry is to all that live.
5 O simple ones, learn prudence;
    acquire intelligence, you who lack it.
6 Hear, for I will speak noble things,
    and from my lips will come what is right;

⁷ for my mouth will utter truth;
  wickedness is an abomination to my lips.
⁸ All the words of my mouth are righteous;
  there is nothing twisted or crooked in them.

¹⁹ 'My fruit is better than gold, even fine gold,
  and my yield than choice silver.
²⁰ I walk in the way of righteousness,
  along the paths of justice,
²¹ endowing with wealth those who love me,
  and filling their treasuries.'

⁴ To those without sense she says,
⁵ 'Come, eat of my bread
  and drink of the wine I have mixed.
⁶ Lay aside immaturity, and live,
  and walk in the way of insight.'

PSALM   Psalm 19

¹ The heavens declare the glory of God,
  and the firmament shows his handiwork.
² One day tells its tale to another,
  and one night imparts knowledge to another.
³ Although they have no words or language,
  and their voices are not heard,
⁴ Their sound has gone out into all lands,
  and their message to the ends of the world.
⁵ In the deep has he set a pavilion for the sun;
  it comes forth like a bridegroom out of his chamber; it rejoices
    like a champion to run its course.
⁶ It goes forth from the uttermost edge of the heavens and runs
    about to the end of it again;
  nothing is hidden from its burning heat.
⁷ The law of the Lord is perfect and revives the soul;
  the testimony of the Lord is sure and gives wisdom to the innocent.
⁸ The statutes of the Lord are just and rejoice the heart;
  the commandment of the Lord is clear and gives light to the eyes.
⁹ The fear of the Lord is clean and endures for ever;
  the judgements of the Lord are true and righteous altogether.
¹⁰ More to be desired are they than gold, more than much fine gold,
  sweeter far than honey, than honey in the comb.
¹¹ By them also is your servant enlightened,
  and in keeping them there is great reward.

¹² Who can tell how often he offends?
Cleanse me from my secret faults.
¹³ Above all, keep your servant from presumptuous sins; let them
not get dominion over me;
then shall I be whole and sound, and innocent of a great offence.
¹⁴ Let the words of my mouth and the meditation of my heart be
acceptable in your sight,
O Lord, my strength and my redeemer.

READING   Ezekiel 36.24–28

²⁴ I will take you from the nations, and gather you from all the countries,
and bring you into your own land. ²⁵ I will sprinkle clean water upon you,
and you shall be clean from all your uncleannesses, and from all your idols
I will cleanse you. ²⁶ A new heart I will give you, and a new spirit I will put
within you; and I will remove from your body the heart of stone and give
you a heart of flesh. ²⁷ I will put my spirit within you, and make you follow
my statutes and be careful to observe my ordinances. ²⁸ Then you shall live
in the land that I gave to your ancestors; and you shall be my people, and I
will be your God.

PSALMS   Psalm 42

¹ As the deer longs for the water-brooks,
so longs my soul for you, O God.
² My soul is athirst for God, athirst for the living God;
when shall I come to appear before the presence of God?
³ My tears have been my food day and night,
while all day long they say to me, 'Where now is your God?'
⁴ I pour out my soul when I think on these things:
how I went with the multitude and led them into the house of
God,
⁵ With the voice of praise and thanksgiving,
among those who keep holy-day.
⁶ Why are you so full of heaviness, O my soul?
and why are you so disquieted within me?
⁷ Put your trust in God;
for I will yet give thanks to him, who is the help of my countenance,
and my God.
⁸ My soul is heavy within me;
therefore I will remember you from the land of Jordan, and from
the peak of Mizar among the heights of Hermon.

9 One deep calls to another in the noise of your cataracts;
   all your rapids and floods have gone over me.
10 The Lord grants his loving-kindness in the daytime;
   in the night season his song is with me, a prayer to the God of my
      life.
11 I will say to the God of my strength, 'Why have you forgotten me?
   and why do I go so heavily while the enemy oppresses me?'
12 While my bones are being broken,
   my enemies mock me to my face;
13 All day long they mock me
   say to me, 'Where now is your God?'
14 Why are you so full of heaviness, O my soul?
   and why are you so disquieted within me?
15 Put your trust in God;
   for I will yet give thanks to him, who is the help of my countenance,
      and my God.

Psalm 43

1 Give judgement for me, O God, and defend my cause against an
      ungodly people;
   deliver me from the deceitful and the wicked.
2 For you are the God of my strength; why have you put me from
      you?
   and why do I go so heavily while the enemy oppresses me?
3 Send out your light and your truth, that they may lead me,
   and bring me to your holy hill and to your dwelling;
4 That I may go to the altar of God, to the God of my joy and gladness;
   and on the harp I will give thanks to you, O God my God.
5 Why are you so full of heaviness, O my soul?
   and why are you so disquieted within me?
6 Put your trust in God;
   for I will yet give thanks to him, who is the help of my countenance,
      and my God.

READING   Ezekiel 37.1–14

1 The hand of the LORD came upon me, and he brought me out by the
spirit of the LORD and set me down in the middle of a valley; it was full of
bones. 2 He led me all round them; there were very many lying in the valley,
and they were very dry. 3 He said to me, 'Mortal, can these bones live?' I
answered, 'O Lord GOD, you know.' 4 Then he said to me, 'Prophesy to these
bones, and say to them: O dry bones, hear the word of the LORD. 5 Thus says

the Lord GOD to these bones: I will cause breath to enter you, and you shall live. ⁶ I will lay sinews on you, and will cause flesh to come upon you, and cover you with skin, and put breath in you, and you shall live; and you shall know that I am the LORD.'

⁷ So I prophesied as I had been commanded; and as I prophesied, suddenly there was a noise, a rattling, and the bones came together, bone to its bone. ⁸ I looked, and there were sinews on them, and flesh had come upon them, and skin had covered them; but there was no breath in them. ⁹ Then he said to me, 'Prophesy to the breath, prophesy, mortal, and say to the breath: Thus says the Lord GOD: Come from the four winds, O breath, and breathe upon these slain, that they may live.' ¹⁰ I prophesied as he commanded me, and the breath came into them, and they lived, and stood on their feet, a vast multitude.

¹¹ Then he said to me, 'Mortal, these bones are the whole house of Israel. They say, "Our bones are dried up, and our hope is lost; we are cut off completely." ¹² Therefore prophesy, and say to them, Thus says the Lord GOD: I am going to open your graves, and bring you up from your graves, O my people; and I will bring you back to the land of Israel. ¹³ And you shall know that I am the LORD, when I open your graves, and bring you up from your graves, O my people. ¹⁴ I will put my spirit within you, and you shall live, and I will place you on your own soil; then you shall know that I, the LORD, have spoken and will act, says the LORD.'

PSALM   Psalm 143

1 Lord, hear my prayer, and in your faithfulness heed my
     supplications;
   answer me in your righteousness.
2 Enter not into judgement with your servant,
   for in your sight shall no one living be justified.
3 For my enemy has sought my life and has crushed me to the
     ground;
   making me live in dark places like those who are long dead.
4 My spirit faints within me;
   my heart within me is desolate.
5 I remember the time past; I muse upon all your deeds;
   I consider the works of your hands.
6 I spread out my hands to you;
   my soul gasps to you like a thirsty land.
7 O Lord, make haste to answer me; my spirit fails me;
   do not hide your face from me or I shall be like those who go down
     to the Pit.

⁸ Let me hear of your loving-kindness in the morning, for I put my
  trust in you;
  show me the road that I must walk, for I lift up my soul to you.
⁹ Deliver me from my enemies, O Lord,
  for I flee to you for refuge.
¹⁰ Teach me to do what pleases you, for you are my God;
  let your good Spirit lead me on level ground.
¹¹ Revive me, O Lord, for your name's sake;
  for your righteousness' sake, bring me out of trouble.
¹² Of your goodness, destroy my enemies and bring all my foes to
  naught,
  for truly I am your servant.

READING   Zephaniah 3.14–20

¹⁴ Sing aloud, O daughter Zion;
     shout, O Israel!
   Rejoice and exult with all your heart,
     O daughter Jerusalem!
¹⁵ The LORD has taken away the judgements against you,
     he has turned away your enemies.
   The king of Israel, the LORD, is in your midst;
     you shall fear disaster no more.
¹⁶ On that day it shall be said to Jerusalem:
   Do not fear, O Zion;
     do not let your hands grow weak.
¹⁷ The LORD, your God, is in your midst,
     a warrior who gives victory;
   he will rejoice over you with gladness,
     he will renew you in his love;
   he will exult over you with loud singing
¹⁸   as on a day of festival.
   I will remove disaster from you,
     so that you will not bear reproach for it.
¹⁹ I will deal with all your oppressors
     at that time.
   And I will save the lame
     and gather the outcast,
   and I will change their shame into praise
     and renown in all the earth.

²⁰ At that time I will bring you home,
  at the time when I gather you;
 for I will make you renowned and praised
  among all the peoples of the earth,
 when I restore your fortunes
  before your eyes, says the Lord.

PSALM   Psalm 98

¹ Sing to the Lord a new song,
 for he has done marvellous things.
² With his right hand and his holy arm
 has he won for himself the victory.
³ The Lord has made known his victory;
 his righteousness has he openly shown in the sight of the nations.
⁴ He remembers his mercy and faithfulness to the house of Israel,
 and all the ends of the earth have seen the victory of our God.
⁵ Shout with joy to the Lord, all you lands;
 lift up your voice, rejoice and sing.
⁶ Sing to the Lord with the harp,
 with the harp and the voice of song.
⁷ With trumpets and the sound of the horn
 shout with joy before the King, the Lord.
⁸ Let the sea make a noise and all that is in it,
 the lands and those who dwell therein.
⁹ Let the rivers clap their hands,
 and let the hills ring out with joy before the Lord, when he comes
  to judge the earth.
¹⁰ In righteousness shall he judge the world,
 and the peoples with equity.

READING   Romans 6.3–11

³ Do you not know that all of us who have been baptized into Christ Jesus were baptized into his death? ⁴ Therefore we have been buried with him by baptism into death, so that, just as Christ was raised from the dead by the glory of the Father, so we too might walk in newness of life.

 ⁵ For if we have been united with him in a death like his, we will certainly be united with him in a resurrection like his. ⁶ We know that our old self was crucified with him so that the body of sin might be destroyed, and we might no longer be enslaved to sin. ⁷ For whoever has died is freed from sin. ⁸ But if we have died with Christ, we believe that we will also live with

him. [9] We know that Christ, being raised from the dead, will never die again; death no longer has dominion over him. [10] The death he died, he died to sin, once for all; but the life he lives, he lives to God. [11] So you also must consider yourselves dead to sin and alive to God in Christ Jesus.

PSALM   Psalm 114

[1] Alleluia! When Israel came out of Egypt,
     the house of Jacob from a people of strange speech,
[2] Judah became God's sanctuary
     and Israel his dominion.
[3] The sea beheld it and fled;
     Jordan turned and went back.
[4] The mountains skipped like rams,
     and the little hills like young sheep.
[5] What ailed you, O sea, that you fled?
     O Jordan, that you turned back?
[6] You mountains, that you skipped like rams?
     you little hills like young sheep?
[7] Tremble, O earth, at the presence of the Lord,
     at the presence of the God of Jacob,
[8] Who turned the hard rock into a pool of water
     and flint-stone into a flowing spring.

GOSPEL   Luke 24.1–12

[1] But on the first day of the week, at early dawn, they came to the tomb, taking the spices that they had prepared. [2] They found the stone rolled away from the tomb, [3] but when they went in, they did not find the body. [4] While they were perplexed about this, suddenly two men in dazzling clothes stood beside them. [5] The women were terrified and bowed their faces to the ground, but the men said to them, 'Why do you look for the living among the dead? He is not here, but has risen. [6] Remember how he told you, while he was still in Galilee, [7] that the Son of Man must be handed over to sinners, and be crucified, and on the third day rise again.' [8] Then they remembered his words, [9] and returning from the tomb, they told all this to the eleven and to all the rest. [10] Now it was Mary Magdalene, Joanna, Mary the mother of James, and the other women with them who told this to the apostles. [11] But these words seemed to them an idle tale, and they did not believe them. [12] But Peter got up and ran to the tomb; stooping and looking in, he saw the linen cloths by themselves; then he went home, amazed at what had happened.

POST COMMUNION

God of Life,
who for our redemption gave your only-begotten Son
    to the death of the cross,
and by his glorious resurrection
have delivered us from the power of our enemy:
grant us so to die daily to sin,
that we may evermore live with him
    in the joy of his risen life;
through Jesus Christ our Lord.

EASTER DAY

COLLECT

Lord of all life and power,
who through the mighty resurrection of your Son
overcame the old order of sin and death
to make all things new in him:
grant that we, being dead to sin
and alive to you in Jesus Christ,
may reign with him in glory;
to whom with you and the Holy Spirit
be praise and honour, glory and might,
now and in all eternity.

READING

EITHER   Acts 10.34–43

³⁴ Then Peter began to speak to them: 'I truly understand that God shows
no partiality, ³⁵ but in every nation anyone who fears him and does what is
right is acceptable to him. ³⁶ You know the message he sent to the people
of Israel, preaching peace by Jesus Christ—he is Lord of all. ³⁷ That message
spread throughout Judea, beginning in Galilee after the baptism that John
announced: ³⁸ how God anointed Jesus of Nazareth with the Holy Spirit
and with power; how he went about doing good and healing all who were
oppressed by the devil, for God was with him. ³⁹ We are witnesses to all
that he did both in Judea and in Jerusalem. They put him to death by
hanging him on a tree; ⁴⁰ but God raised him on the third day and allowed
him to appear, ⁴¹ not to all the people but to us who were chosen by God as

witnesses, and who ate and drank with him after he rose from the dead. [42] He commanded us to preach to the people and to testify that he is the one ordained by God as judge of the living and the dead. [43] All the prophets testify about him that everyone who believes in him receives forgiveness of sins through his name.'

OR   # Isaiah 65.17–25

[17] For I am about to create new heavens
  and a new earth;
 the former things shall not be remembered
  or come to mind.
[18] But be glad and rejoice for ever
  in what I am creating;
 for I am about to create Jerusalem as a joy,
  and its people as a delight.
[19] I will rejoice in Jerusalem,
  and delight in my people;
 no more shall the sound of weeping be heard in it,
  or the cry of distress.
[20] No more shall there be in it
  an infant that lives but a few days,
  or an old person who does not live out a lifetime;
 for one who dies at a hundred years will be considered a youth,
  and one who falls short of a hundred will be considered accursed.
[21] They shall build houses and inhabit them;
  they shall plant vineyards and eat their fruit.
[22] They shall not build and another inhabit;
  they shall not plant and another eat;
 for like the days of a tree shall the days of my people be,
  and my chosen shall long enjoy the work of their hands.
[23] They shall not labour in vain,
  or bear children for calamity;
 for they shall be offspring blessed by the LORD—
  and their descendants as well.
[24] Before they call I will answer,
  while they are yet speaking I will hear.
[25] The wolf and the lamb shall feed together,
  the lion shall eat straw like the ox;
  but the serpent—its food shall be dust!
 They shall not hurt or destroy
  on all my holy mountain,
   says the LORD.

PSALM   Psalm 118.[1–2,] 14–24

[¹ Give thanks to the Lord, for he is good;
    his mercy endures for ever.
² Let Israel now proclaim,
    'His mercy endures for ever.']

¹⁴ The Lord is my strength and my song,
     and he has become my salvation.
¹⁵ There is a sound of exultation and victory
     in the tents of the righteous:
¹⁶ 'The right hand of the Lord has triumphed!
     the right hand of the Lord is exalted! the right hand of the Lord
       has triumphed!'
¹⁷ I shall not die, but live,
     and declare the works of the Lord.
¹⁸ The Lord has punished me sorely,
     but he did not hand me over to death.
¹⁹ Open for me the gates of righteousness;
     I will enter them; I will offer thanks to the Lord.
²⁰ 'This is the gate of the Lord;
     he who is righteous may enter.'
²¹ I will give thanks to you, for you answered me
     and have become my salvation.
²² The same stone which the builders rejected
     has become the chief corner-stone.
²³ This is the Lord's doing,
     and it is marvellous in our eyes.
²⁴ On this day the Lord has acted;
     we will rejoice and be glad in it.

READING

EITHER   1 Corinthians 15.19–26

¹⁹ If for this life only we have hoped in Christ, we are of all people most to
be pitied.

²⁰ But in fact Christ has been raised from the dead, the first fruits of
those who have died. ²¹ For since death came through a human being, the
resurrection of the dead has also come through a human being; ²² for as
all die in Adam, so all will be made alive in Christ. ²³ But each in his own
order: Christ the first fruits, then at his coming those who belong to Christ.
²⁴ Then comes the end, when he hands over the kingdom to God the Father,

after he has destroyed every ruler and every authority and power. [25] For he must reign until he has put all his enemies under his feet. [26] The last enemy to be destroyed is death.

OR   Acts 10.34–43

[34] Then Peter began to speak to them: 'I truly understand that God shows no partiality, [35] but in every nation anyone who fears him and does what is right is acceptable to him. [36] You know the message he sent to the people of Israel, preaching peace by Jesus Christ—he is Lord of all. [37] That message spread throughout Judea, beginning in Galilee after the baptism that John announced: [38] how God anointed Jesus of Nazareth with the Holy Spirit and with power; how he went about doing good and healing all who were oppressed by the devil, for God was with him. [39] We are witnesses to all that he did both in Judea and in Jerusalem. They put him to death by hanging him on a tree; [40] but God raised him on the third day and allowed him to appear, [41] not to all the people but to us who were chosen by God as witnesses, and who ate and drank with him after he rose from the dead. [42] He commanded us to preach to the people and to testify that he is the one ordained by God as judge of the living and the dead. [43] All the prophets testify about him that everyone who believes in him receives forgiveness of sins through his name.'

GOSPEL

EITHER   John 20.1–18

[1] Early on the first day of the week, while it was still dark, Mary Magdalene came to the tomb and saw that the stone had been removed from the tomb. [2] So she ran and went to Simon Peter and the other disciple, the one whom Jesus loved, and said to them, 'They have taken the Lord out of the tomb, and we do not know where they have laid him.' [3] Then Peter and the other disciple set out and went towards the tomb. [4] The two were running together, but the other disciple outran Peter and reached the tomb first. [5] He bent down to look in and saw the linen wrappings lying there, but he did not go in. [6] Then Simon Peter came, following him, and went into the tomb. He saw the linen wrappings lying there, [7] and the cloth that had been on Jesus' head, not lying with the linen wrappings but rolled up in a place by itself. [8] Then the other disciple, who reached the tomb first, also went in, and he saw and believed; [9] for as yet they did not understand the scripture, that he must rise from the dead. [10] Then the disciples returned to their homes.

¹¹ But Mary stood weeping outside the tomb. As she wept, she bent over to look into the tomb; ¹² and she saw two angels in white, sitting where the body of Jesus had been lying, one at the head and the other at the feet. ¹³ They said to her, 'Woman, why are you weeping?' She said to them, 'They have taken away my Lord, and I do not know where they have laid him.' ¹⁴ When she had said this, she turned round and saw Jesus standing there, but she did not know that it was Jesus. ¹⁵ Jesus said to her, 'Woman, why are you weeping? For whom are you looking?' Supposing him to be the gardener, she said to him, 'Sir, if you have carried him away, tell me where you have laid him, and I will take him away.' ¹⁶ Jesus said to her, 'Mary!' She turned and said to him in Hebrew, 'Rabbouni!' (which means Teacher). ¹⁷ Jesus said to her, 'Do not hold on to me, because I have not yet ascended to the Father. But go to my brothers and say to them, "I am ascending to my Father and your Father, to my God and your God." ' ¹⁸ Mary Magdalene went and announced to the disciples, 'I have seen the Lord'; and she told them that he had said these things to her.

OR   Luke 24.1–12

¹ But on the first day of the week, at early dawn, they came to the tomb, taking the spices that they had prepared. ² They found the stone rolled away from the tomb, ³ but when they went in, they did not find the body. ⁴ While they were perplexed about this, suddenly two men in dazzling clothes stood beside them. ⁵ The women were terrified and bowed their faces to the ground, but the men said to them, 'Why do you look for the living among the dead? He is not here, but has risen. ⁶ Remember how he told you, while he was still in Galilee, ⁷ that the Son of Man must be handed over to sinners, and be crucified, and on the third day rise again.' ⁸ Then they remembered his words, ⁹ and returning from the tomb, they told all this to the eleven and to all the rest. ¹⁰ Now it was Mary Magdalene, Joanna, Mary the mother of James, and the other women with them who told this to the apostles. ¹¹ But these words seemed to them an idle tale, and they did not believe them. ¹² But Peter got up and ran to the tomb; stooping and looking in, he saw the linen cloths by themselves; then he went home, amazed at what had happened.

POST COMMUNION

God of Life,
who for our redemption gave your only-begotten Son
    to the death of the cross,
and by his glorious resurrection
have delivered us from the power of our enemy:

grant us so to die daily to sin,
that we may evermore live with him
   in the joy of his risen life;
through Jesus Christ our Lord.

SECOND SERVICE

Psalms 66; 114; 117
Isaiah 43.1–21
1 Corinthians 15.1–11

or

John 20.19–23

THIRD SERVICE

Psalms 114; 117
Ezekiel 47.1–12
John 2.13–22

OLD TESTAMENT READINGS FOR SUNDAYS IN EASTERTIDE

For those who require an Old Testament reading on the Sundays in Eastertide, provision is made in this table. If used, the reading from Acts must be used as the second reading.

THE SECOND SUNDAY OF EASTER	Exodus 14.10–31; 15.20–21
THE THIRD SUNDAY OF EASTER	Zephaniah 3.14–20
THE FOURTH SUNDAY OF EASTER	Genesis 7.1–5, 11–18; 8.6–18; 9.8–13
THE FIFTH SUNDAY OF EASTER	Baruch 3.9–15, 32–4.4 *or* Genesis 22.1–18
THE SIXTH SUNDAY OF EASTER	Ezekiel 37.1–14
THE SEVENTH SUNDAY OF EASTER	Ezekiel 36.24–28

THE SECOND SUNDAY OF EASTER

The reading from Acts must be used. The second (New Testament) reading follows or, if the Old Testament reading is used, the Acts reading follows as the second reading.

COLLECT

Almighty Father,
you have given your only Son to die for our sins
and to rise again for our justification:
grant us so to put away the leaven of malice and wickedness
that we may always serve you
in pureness of living and truth;

through the merits of your Son Jesus Christ our Lord,
who is alive and reigns with you,
in the unity of the Holy Spirit,
one God, now and for ever.

READING   Acts 5.27–32

[27] When they had brought them, they had them stand before the council. The high priest questioned them, [28] saying, 'We gave you strict orders not to teach in this name, yet here you have filled Jerusalem with your teaching and you are determined to bring this man's blood on us.' [29] But Peter and the apostles answered, 'We must obey God rather than any human authority. [30] The God of our ancestors raised up Jesus, whom you had killed by hanging him on a tree. [31] God exalted him at his right hand as Leader and Saviour, so that he might give repentance to Israel and forgiveness of sins. [32] And we are witnesses to these things, and so is the Holy Spirit whom God has given to those who obey him.'

PSALM

EITHER   Psalm 118.14–29

[14] The Lord is my strength and my song,
      and he has become my salvation.
[15] There is a sound of exultation and victory
      in the tents of the righteous:
[16] 'The right hand of the Lord has triumphed!
      the right hand of the Lord is exalted! the right hand of the Lord
         has triumphed!'
[17] I shall not die, but live,
      and declare the works of the Lord.
[18] The Lord has punished me sorely,
      but he did not hand me over to death.
[19] Open for me the gates of righteousness;
      I will enter them; I will offer thanks to the Lord.
[20] 'This is the gate of the Lord;
      he who is righteous may enter.'
[21] I will give thanks to you, for you answered me
      and have become my salvation.
[22] The same stone which the builders rejected
      has become the chief corner-stone.
[23] This is the Lord's doing,
      and it is marvellous in our eyes.

24 On this day the Lord has acted;
    we will rejoice and be glad in it.
25 Hosanna, Lord, hosanna!
    Lord, send us now success.
26 Blessèd is he who comes in the name of the Lord;
    we bless you from the house of the Lord.
27 God is the Lord; he has shined upon us;
    form a procession with branches up to the horns of the altar.
28 'You are my God and I will thank you;
    you are my God and I will exalt you.'
29 Give thanks to the Lord, for he is good;
    his mercy endures for ever.

OR   **Psalm 150**

1 Alleluia! Praise God in his holy temple;
   praise him in the firmament of his power.
2 Praise him for his mighty acts;
   praise him for his excellent greatness.
3 Praise him with the blast of the ram's-horn;
   praise him with lyre and harp.
4 Praise him with timbrel and dance;
   praise him with strings and pipe.
5 Praise him with resounding cymbals;
   praise him with loud-clanging cymbals.
6 Let everything that has breath
   praise the Lord. Alleluia!

READING   Revelation 1.4–8

⁴ John to the seven churches that are in Asia:

Grace to you and peace from him who is and who was and who is to
come, and from the seven spirits who are before his throne, ⁵ and from
Jesus Christ, the faithful witness, the firstborn of the dead, and the ruler
of the kings of the earth.

To him who loves us and freed us from our sins by his blood, ⁶ and made
us to be a kingdom, priests serving his God and Father, to him be glory and
dominion for ever and ever. Amen.

7   Look! He is coming with the clouds;
        every eye will see him,
     even those who pierced him;
        and on his account all the tribes of the earth will wail.
So it is to be. Amen.

8 'I am the Alpha and the Omega', says the Lord God, who is and who was
and who is to come, the Almighty.

GOSPEL   John 20.19–31

19 When it was evening on that day, the first day of the week, and the
doors of the house where the disciples had met were locked for fear of the
Jews, Jesus came and stood among them and said, 'Peace be with you.'
20 After he said this, he showed them his hands and his side. Then the
disciples rejoiced when they saw the Lord. 21 Jesus said to them again,
'Peace be with you. As the Father has sent me, so I send you.' 22 When he
had said this, he breathed on them and said to them, 'Receive the Holy
Spirit. 23 If you forgive the sins of any, they are forgiven them; if you retain
the sins of any, they are retained.'

24 But Thomas (who was called the Twin), one of the twelve, was not with
them when Jesus came. 25 So the other disciples told him, 'We have seen
the Lord.' But he said to them, 'Unless I see the mark of the nails in his
hands, and put my finger in the mark of the nails and my hand in his side,
I will not believe.'

26 A week later his disciples were again in the house, and Thomas was with
them. Although the doors were shut, Jesus came and stood among them
and said, 'Peace be with you.' 27 Then he said to Thomas, 'Put your finger
here and see my hands. Reach out your hand and put it in my side. Do not
doubt but believe.' 28 Thomas answered him, 'My Lord and my God!' 29 Jesus
said to him, 'Have you believed because you have seen me? Blessed are those
who have not seen and yet have come to believe.'

30 Now Jesus did many other signs in the presence of his disciples, which
are not written in this book. 31 But these are written so that you may come
to believe that Jesus is the Messiah, the Son of God, and that through
believing you may have life in his name.

POST COMMUNION

Lord God our Father,
through our Saviour Jesus Christ
you have assured your children of eternal life
and in baptism have made us one with him:
deliver us from the death of sin
and raise us to new life in your love,
in the fellowship of the Holy Spirit,
by the grace of our Lord Jesus Christ.

SECOND SERVICE   THIRD SERVICE

Psalm 16   **Psalm 136.1–16**
Isaiah 52.13–53.12   **Exodus 12.1–13**
or   **1 Peter 1.3–12**

53.1–6, 9–12
Luke 24.13–35

THE THIRD SUNDAY OF EASTER

*The reading from Acts must be used. The second (New Testament) reading follows or,
if the Old Testament reading is used, the Acts reading follows as the second reading.*

COLLECT

Almighty Father,
who in your great mercy gladdened the disciples
    with the sight of the risen Lord:
give us such knowledge of his presence with us,
that we may be strengthened and sustained
    by his risen life
and serve you continually in righteousness and truth;
through Jesus Christ your Son our Lord,
who is alive and reigns with you,
in the unity of the Holy Spirit,
one God, now and for ever.

READING   Acts 9.1–6, [7–20]

[1] Meanwhile Saul, still breathing threats and murder against the disciples of the Lord, went to the high priest [2] and asked him for letters to the synagogues at Damascus, so that if he found any who belonged to the Way, men or women, he might bring them bound to Jerusalem. [3] Now as he was going along and approaching Damascus, suddenly a light from heaven flashed around him. [4] He fell to the ground and heard a voice saying to him, 'Saul, Saul, why do you persecute me?' [5] He asked, 'Who are you, Lord?' The reply came, 'I am Jesus, whom you are persecuting. [6] But get up and enter the city, and you will be told what you are to do.'

[[7] The men who were travelling with him stood speechless because they heard the voice but saw no one. [8] Saul got up from the ground, and though his eyes were open, he could see nothing; so they led him by the hand and brought him into Damascus. [9] For three days he was without sight, and neither ate nor drank.

[10] Now there was a disciple in Damascus named Ananias. The Lord said to him in a vision, 'Ananias.' He answered, 'Here I am, Lord.' [11] The Lord said to him, 'Get up and go to the street called Straight, and at the house of Judas look for a man of Tarsus named Saul. At this moment he is praying, [12] and he has seen in a vision a man named Ananias come in and lay his hands on him so that he might regain his sight.' [13] But Ananias answered, 'Lord, I have heard from many about this man, how much evil he has done to your saints in Jerusalem; [14] and here he has authority from the chief priests to bind all who invoke your name.' [15] But the Lord said to him, 'Go, for he is an instrument whom I have chosen to bring my name before Gentiles and kings and before the people of Israel; [16] I myself will show him how much he must suffer for the sake of my name.' [17] So Ananias went and entered the house. He laid his hands on Saul and said, 'Brother Saul, the Lord Jesus, who appeared to you on your way here, has sent me so that you may regain your sight and be filled with the Holy Spirit.' [18] And immediately something like scales fell from his eyes, and his sight was restored. Then he got up and was baptized, [19] and after taking some food, he regained his strength.

For several days he was with the disciples in Damascus, [20] and immediately he began to proclaim Jesus in the synagogues, saying, 'He is the Son of God.']

PSALM   Psalm 30

[1] I will exalt you, O Lord, because you have lifted me up
     and have not let my enemies triumph over me.

2 O Lord my God, I cried out to you,
   and you restored me to health.
3 You brought me up, O Lord, from the dead;
   you restored my life as I was going down to the grave.
4 Sing to the Lord, you servants of his;
   give thanks for the remembrance of his holiness.
5 For his wrath endures but the twinkling of an eye,
   his favour for a lifetime.
6 Weeping may spend the night,
   but joy comes in the morning.
7 While I felt secure, I said, 'I shall never be disturbed.
   You, Lord, with your favour, made me as strong as the mountains.'
8 Then you hid your face,
   and I was filled with fear.
9 I cried to you, O Lord;
   I pleaded with the Lord, saying,
10 'What profit is there in my blood, if I go down to the Pit?
   will the dust praise you or declare your faithfulness?
11 Hear, O Lord, and have mercy upon me;
   O Lord, be my helper.'
12 You have turned my wailing into dancing;
   you have put off my sack-cloth and clothed me with joy;
13 Therefore my heart sings to you without ceasing;
   O Lord my God, I will give you thanks for ever.

READING   Revelation 5.11–14

[11] Then I looked, and I heard the voice of many angels surrounding the throne and the living creatures and the elders; they numbered myriads of myriads and thousands of thousands, [12] singing with full voice,

   'Worthy is the Lamb that was slaughtered
   to receive power and wealth and wisdom and might
   and honour and glory and blessing!'

[13] Then I heard every creature in heaven and on earth and under the earth and in the sea, and all that is in them, singing,

   'To the one seated on the throne and to the Lamb
   be blessing and honour and glory and might
   for ever and ever!'

[14] And the four living creatures said, 'Amen!' And the elders fell down and worshipped.

GOSPEL   John 21.1–19

¹ After these things Jesus showed himself again to the disciples by the Sea of Tiberias; and he showed himself in this way. ² Gathered there together were Simon Peter, Thomas called the Twin, Nathanael of Cana in Galilee, the sons of Zebedee, and two others of his disciples. ³ Simon Peter said to them, 'I am going fishing.' They said to him, 'We will go with you.' They went out and got into the boat, but that night they caught nothing.

⁴ Just after daybreak, Jesus stood on the beach; but the disciples did not know that it was Jesus. ⁵ Jesus said to them, 'Children, you have no fish, have you?' They answered him, 'No.' ⁶ He said to them, 'Cast the net to the right side of the boat, and you will find some.' So they cast it, and now they were not able to haul it in because there were so many fish. ⁷ That disciple whom Jesus loved said to Peter, 'It is the Lord!' When Simon Peter heard that it was the Lord, he put on some clothes, for he was naked, and jumped into the lake. ⁸ But the other disciples came in the boat, dragging the net full of fish, for they were not far from the land, only about a hundred yards off.

⁹ When they had gone ashore, they saw a charcoal fire there, with fish on it, and bread. ¹⁰ Jesus said to them, 'Bring some of the fish that you have just caught.' ¹¹ So Simon Peter went aboard and hauled the net ashore, full of large fish, a hundred and fifty-three of them; and though there were so many, the net was not torn. ¹² Jesus said to them, 'Come and have breakfast.' Now none of the disciples dared to ask him, 'Who are you?' because they knew it was the Lord. ¹³ Jesus came and took the bread and gave it to them, and did the same with the fish. ¹⁴ This was now the third time that Jesus appeared to the disciples after he was raised from the dead.

¹⁵ When they had finished breakfast, Jesus said to Simon Peter, 'Simon son of John, do you love me more than these?' He said to him, 'Yes, Lord; you know that I love you.' Jesus said to him, 'Feed my lambs.' ¹⁶ A second time he said to him, 'Simon son of John, do you love me?' He said to him, 'Yes, Lord; you know that I love you.' Jesus said to him, 'Tend my sheep.' ¹⁷ He said to him the third time, 'Simon son of John, do you love me?' Peter felt hurt because he said to him the third time, 'Do you love me?' And he said to him, 'Lord, you know everything; you know that I love you.' Jesus said to him, 'Feed my sheep. ¹⁸ Very truly, I tell you, when you were younger, you used to fasten your own belt and to go wherever you wished. But when you grow old, you will stretch out your hands, and someone else will fasten a belt around you and take you where you do not wish to go.' ¹⁹ (He said this to indicate the kind of death by which he would glorify God.) After this he said to him, 'Follow me.'

POST COMMUNION

Living God,
your Son made himself known to his disciples
in the breaking of bread:
open the eyes of our faith,
that we may see him in all his redeeming work;
who is alive and reigns, now and for ever.

SECOND SERVICE   THIRD SERVICE

Psalm 86   **Psalm 80.1–7**
Isaiah 38.9–20   **Exodus 15.1–2, 9–18**
John 11.[17–26,] 27–44   **John 10.1–19**

THE FOURTH SUNDAY OF EASTER

The reading from Acts must be used. The second (New Testament) reading follows or, if the Old Testament reading is used, the Acts reading follows as the second reading.

COLLECT

Almighty God,
whose Son Jesus Christ is the resurrection and the life:
raise us, who trust in him,
from the death of sin to the life of righteousness,
that we may seek those things which are above,
where he reigns with you
in the unity of the Holy Spirit,
one God, now and for ever.

READING   Acts 9.36–43

36 Now in Joppa there was a disciple whose name was Tabitha, which in Greek is Dorcas. She was devoted to good works and acts of charity. 37 At that time she became ill and died. When they had washed her, they laid her in a room upstairs. 38 Since Lydda was near Joppa, the disciples, who heard that Peter was there, sent two men to him with the request, 'Please come to us without delay.' 39 So Peter got up and went with them; and when he arrived, they took him to the room upstairs. All the widows stood beside him, weeping and showing tunics and other clothing that Dorcas had made while she was with them. 40 Peter put all of them outside, and

then he knelt down and prayed. He turned to the body and said, 'Tabitha, get up.' Then she opened her eyes, and seeing Peter, she sat up. [41] He gave her his hand and helped her up. Then calling the saints and widows, he showed her to be alive. [42] This became known throughout Joppa, and many believed in the Lord. [43] Meanwhile he stayed in Joppa for some time with a certain Simon, a tanner.

PSALM   Psalm 23

[1] The Lord is my shepherd;
   I shall not be in want.
[2] He makes me lie down in green pastures
   and leads me beside still waters.
[3] He revives my soul
   and guides me along right pathways for his name's sake.
[4] Though I walk through the valley of the shadow of death, I shall
      fear no evil;
   for you are with me; your rod and your staff, they comfort me.
[5] You spread a table before me in the presence of those who trouble
      me;
   you have anointed my head with oil, and my cup is running over.
[6] Surely your goodness and mercy shall follow me all the days of my
      life,
   and I will dwell in the house of the Lord for ever.

READING   Revelation 7.9–17

[9] After this I looked, and there was a great multitude that no one could count, from every nation, from all tribes and peoples and languages, standing before the throne and before the Lamb, robed in white, with palm branches in their hands. [10] They cried out in a loud voice, saying,

'Salvation belongs to our God who is seated on the throne, and to the
   Lamb!'

[11] And all the angels stood around the throne and around the elders and the four living creatures, and they fell on their faces before the throne and worshipped God, [12] singing,

'Amen! Blessing and glory and wisdom
   and thanksgiving and honour
   and power and might
   be to our God for ever and ever! Amen.'

[13] Then one of the elders addressed me, saying, 'Who are these, robed in white, and where have they come from?' [14] I said to him, 'Sir, you are the

one that knows.' Then he said to me, 'These are they who have come out of the great ordeal; they have washed their robes and made them white in the blood of the Lamb.

¹⁵ For this reason they are before the throne of God,
    and worship him day and night within his temple,
    and the one who is seated on the throne will shelter them.
¹⁶ They will hunger no more, and thirst no more;
    the sun will not strike them,
    nor any scorching heat;
¹⁷ for the Lamb at the centre of the throne will be their shepherd,
    and he will guide them to springs of the water of life,
    and God will wipe away every tear from their eyes.'

GOSPEL   John 10.22–30

²² At that time the festival of the Dedication took place in Jerusalem. It was winter, ²³ and Jesus was walking in the temple, in the portico of Solomon. ²⁴ So the Jews gathered around him and said to him, 'How long will you keep us in suspense? If you are the Messiah, tell us plainly.' ²⁵ Jesus answered, 'I have told you, and you do not believe. The works that I do in my Father's name testify to me; ²⁶ but you do not believe, because you do not belong to my sheep. ²⁷ My sheep hear my voice. I know them, and they follow me. ²⁸ I give them eternal life, and they will never perish. No one will snatch them out of my hand. ²⁹ What my Father has given me is greater than all else, and no one can snatch it out of the Father's hand. ³⁰ The Father and I are one.'

POST COMMUNION

Merciful Father,
you gave your Son Jesus Christ to be the good shepherd,
and in his love for us to lay down his life and rise again:
keep us always under his protection,
and give us grace to follow in his steps;
through Jesus Christ our Lord.

SECOND SERVICE	THIRD SERVICE
Psalms 113; 114	Psalm 146
Isaiah 63.7–14	1 Kings 17.17–24
Luke 24.36–49	Luke 7.11–23

THE FIFTH SUNDAY OF EASTER

The reading from Acts must be used. The second (New Testament) reading follows or, if the Old Testament reading is used, the Acts reading follows as the second reading.

COLLECT

Almighty God,
who through your only-begotten Son Jesus Christ
have overcome death and opened to us
  the gate of everlasting life:
grant that, as by your grace going before us
  you put into our minds good desires,
so by your continual help
we may bring them to good effect;
through Jesus Christ our risen Lord,
who is alive and reigns with you,
in the unity of the Holy Spirit,
one God, now and for ever.

READING   Acts 11.1–18

¹ Now the apostles and the believers who were in Judea heard that the Gentiles had also accepted the word of God. ² So when Peter went up to Jerusalem, the circumcised believers criticized him, ³ saying, 'Why did you go to uncircumcised men and eat with them?' ⁴ Then Peter began to explain it to them, step by step, saying, ⁵ 'I was in the city of Joppa praying, and in a trance I saw a vision. There was something like a large sheet coming down from heaven, being lowered by its four corners; and it came close to me. ⁶ As I looked at it closely I saw four-footed animals, beasts of prey, reptiles, and birds of the air. ⁷ I also heard a voice saying to me, "Get up, Peter; kill and eat." ⁸ But I replied, "By no means, Lord; for nothing profane or unclean has ever entered my mouth." ⁹ But a second time the voice answered from heaven, "What God has made clean, you must not call profane." ¹⁰ This happened three times; then everything was pulled up again to heaven. ¹¹ At that very moment three men, sent to me from Caesarea, arrived at the house where we were. ¹² The Spirit told me to go with them and not to make a distinction between them and us. These six brothers also accompanied me, and we entered the man's house. ¹³ He told us how he had seen the angel standing in his house and saying, "Send to Joppa and bring Simon, who is called Peter; ¹⁴ he will give you a message by which you and your entire household will be saved." ¹⁵ And as I began to speak, the Holy Spirit fell upon them just as it had upon us at the

beginning. [16] And I remembered the word of the Lord, how he had said, "John baptized with water, but you will be baptized with the Holy Spirit." [17] If then God gave them the same gift that he gave us when we believed in the Lord Jesus Christ, who was I that I could hinder God?' [18] When they heard this, they were silenced. And they praised God, saying, 'Then God has given even to the Gentiles the repentance that leads to life.'

PSALM   Psalm 148.1–6, [7–14]

1   Alleluia! Praise the Lord from the heavens;
    praise him in the heights.
2   Praise him, all you angels of his;
    praise him, all his host.
3   Praise him, sun and moon;
    praise him, all you shining stars.
4   Praise him, heaven of heavens,
    and you waters above the heavens.
5   Let them praise the name of the Lord;
    for he commanded and they were created.
6   He made them stand fast for ever and ever;
    he gave them a law which shall not pass away.
[7   Praise the Lord from the earth,
    you sea-monsters and all deeps;
8   Fire and hail, snow and fog,
    tempestuous wind, doing his will;
9   Mountains and all hills,
    fruit trees and all cedars;
10 Wild beasts and all cattle,
    creeping things and winged birds;
11 Kings of the earth and all peoples,
    princes and all rulers of the world;
12 Young men and maidens,
    old and young together.
13 Let them praise the name of the Lord,
    for his name only is exalted, his splendour is over earth and heaven.
14 He has raised up strength for his people and praise for all his loyal
        servants,
    the children of Israel, a people who are near him. Alleluia!]

READING   Revelation 21.1–6

[1] Then I saw a new heaven and a new earth; for the first heaven and the first earth had passed away, and the sea was no more. [2] And I saw the holy

city, the new Jerusalem, coming down out of heaven from God, prepared as a bride adorned for her husband. ³ And I heard a loud voice from the throne saying,

'See, the home of God is among mortals.
He will dwell with them;
they will be his peoples,
and God himself will be with them;
⁴ he will wipe every tear from their eyes.
Death will be no more;
mourning and crying and pain will be no more,
for the first things have passed away.'

⁵ And the one who was seated on the throne said, 'See, I am making all things new.' Also he said, 'Write this, for these words are trustworthy and true.' ⁶ Then he said to me, 'It is done! I am the Alpha and the Omega, the beginning and the end. To the thirsty I will give water as a gift from the spring of the water of life.'

GOSPEL   John 13.31–35

³¹ When he had gone out, Jesus said, 'Now the Son of Man has been glorified, and God has been glorified in him. ³² If God has been glorified in him, God will also glorify him in himself and will glorify him at once. ³³ Little children, I am with you only a little longer. You will look for me; and as I said to the Jews so now I say to you, "Where I am going, you cannot come." ³⁴ I give you a new commandment, that you love one another. Just as I have loved you, you also should love one another. ³⁵ By this everyone will know that you are my disciples, if you have love for one another.'

POST COMMUNION

Eternal God,
whose Son Jesus Christ is the way, the truth, and the life:
grant us to walk in his way,
to rejoice in his truth,
and to share his risen life;
who is alive and reigns, now and for ever.

SECOND SERVICE	THIRD SERVICE
Psalm 98	Psalm 16
Daniel 6.[1–5,] 6–23	2 Samuel 7.4–13
Mark 15.46–16.8	Acts 2.14a, 22–32, [33–36]

THE SIXTH SUNDAY OF EASTER

The reading from Acts must be used. The second (New Testament) reading follows or, if the Old Testament reading is used, the Acts reading follows as the second reading.

COLLECT

God our redeemer,
you have delivered us from the power of darkness
and brought us into the kingdom of your Son:
grant, that as by his death he has recalled us to life,
so by his continual presence in us he may raise us
    to eternal joy;
through Jesus Christ your Son our Lord,
who is alive and reigns with you,
in the unity of the Holy Spirit,
one God, now and for ever.

READING   Acts 16.9–15

[9] During the night Paul had a vision: there stood a man of Macedonia pleading with him and saying, 'Come over to Macedonia and help us.' [10] When he had seen the vision, we immediately tried to cross over to Macedonia, being convinced that God had called us to proclaim the good news to them.

[11] We set sail from Troas and took a straight course to Samothrace, the following day to Neapolis, [12] and from there to Philippi, which is a leading city of the district of Macedonia and a Roman colony. We remained in this city for some days. [13] On the sabbath day we went outside the gate by the river, where we supposed there was a place of prayer; and we sat down and spoke to the women who had gathered there. [14] A certain woman named Lydia, a worshipper of God, was listening to us; she was from the city of Thyatira and a dealer in purple cloth. The Lord opened her heart to listen eagerly to what was said by Paul. [15] When she and her household were baptized, she urged us, saying, 'If you have judged me to be faithful to the Lord, come and stay at my home.' And she prevailed upon us.

PSALM   Psalm 67

¹ May God be merciful to us and bless us,
   show us the light of his countenance and come to us.
² Let your ways be known upon earth,
   your saving health among all nations.
³ Let the peoples praise you, O God;
   let all the peoples praise you.
⁴ Let the nations be glad and sing for joy,
   for you judge the peoples with equity and guide all the nations
      upon earth.
⁵ Let the peoples praise you, O God;
   let all the peoples praise you.
⁶ The earth has brought forth her increase;
   may God, our own God, give us his blessing.
⁷ May God give us his blessing,
   and may all the ends of the earth stand in awe of him.

READING   Revelation 21.10, 22–22.5

¹⁰ And in the spirit he carried me away to a great, high mountain and showed me the holy city Jerusalem coming down out of heaven from God.

²² I saw no temple in the city, for its temple is the Lord God the Almighty and the Lamb. ²³ And the city has no need of sun or moon to shine on it, for the glory of God is its light, and its lamp is the Lamb. ²⁴ The nations will walk by its light, and the kings of the earth will bring their glory into it. ²⁵ Its gates will never be shut by day—and there will be no night there. ²⁶ People will bring into it the glory and the honour of the nations. ²⁷ But nothing unclean will enter it, nor anyone who practises abomination or falsehood, but only those who are written in the Lamb's book of life.

¹ Then the angel showed me the river of the water of life, bright as crystal, flowing from the throne of God and of the Lamb ² through the middle of the street of the city. On either side of the river is the tree of life with its twelve kinds of fruit, producing its fruit each month; and the leaves of the tree are for the healing of the nations. ³ Nothing accursed will be found there any more. But the throne of God and of the Lamb will be in it, and his servants will worship him; ⁴ they will see his face, and his name will be on their foreheads. ⁵ And there will be no more night; they need no light of lamp or sun, for the Lord God will be their light, and they will reign for ever and ever.

GOSPEL

EITHER   **John 14.23–29**

²³ Jesus answered him, 'Those who love me will keep my word, and my Father will love them, and we will come to them and make our home with them. ²⁴ Whoever does not love me does not keep my words; and the word that you hear is not mine, but is from the Father who sent me.

²⁵ 'I have said these things to you while I am still with you. ²⁶ But the Advocate, the Holy Spirit, whom the Father will send in my name, will teach you everything, and remind you of all that I have said to you. ²⁷ Peace I leave with you; my peace I give to you. I do not give to you as the world gives. Do not let your hearts be troubled, and do not let them be afraid. ²⁸ You heard me say to you, "I am going away, and I am coming to you." If you loved me, you would rejoice that I am going to the Father, because the Father is greater than I. ²⁹ And now I have told you this before it occurs, so that when it does occur, you may believe.'

OR   **John 5.1–9**

¹ After this there was a festival of the Jews, and Jesus went up to Jerusalem.

² Now in Jerusalem by the Sheep Gate there is a pool, called in Hebrew Beth-zatha, which has five porticoes. ³ In these lay many invalids—blind, lame, and paralysed. ⁵ One man was there who had been ill for thirty-eight years. ⁶ When Jesus saw him lying there and knew that he had been there a long time, he said to him, 'Do you want to be made well?' ⁷ The sick man answered him, 'Sir, I have no one to put me into the pool when the water is stirred up; and while I am making my way, someone else steps down ahead of me.' ⁸ Jesus said to him, 'Stand up, take your mat and walk.' ⁹ At once the man was made well, and he took up his mat and began to walk.

Now that day was a sabbath.

POST COMMUNION

God our Father,
whose Son Jesus Christ gives the water of eternal life:
may we thirst for you,
the spring of life and source of goodness,
through him who is alive and reigns, now and for ever.

SECOND SERVICE

Psalms 126; 127
Zephaniah 3.14–20
Matthew 28.1–10, 16–20

THIRD SERVICE

Psalm 40.1–9
Genesis 1.26–28, [29–31]
Colossians 3.1–11

ASCENSION DAY

COLLECT

Grant, we pray, almighty God,
that as we believe your only-begotten Son
   our Lord Jesus Christ
to have ascended into the heavens,
so we in heart and mind may also ascend
and with him continually dwell;
who is alive and reigns with you,
in the unity of the Holy Spirit,
one God, now and for ever.

The reading from Acts must be used as either the first or second reading

READING

EITHER   Acts 1.1–11

[1] In the first book, Theophilus, I wrote about all that Jesus did and taught from the beginning [2] until the day when he was taken up to heaven, after giving instructions through the Holy Spirit to the apostles whom he had chosen. [3] After his suffering he presented himself alive to them by many convincing proofs, appearing to them over the course of forty days and speaking about the kingdom of God. [4] While staying with them, he ordered them not to leave Jerusalem, but to wait there for the promise of the Father. 'This', he said, 'is what you have heard from me; [5] for John baptized with water, but you will be baptized with the Holy Spirit not many days from now.'

[6] So when they had come together, they asked him, 'Lord, is this the time when you will restore the kingdom to Israel?' [7] He replied, 'It is not for you to know the times or periods that the Father has set by his own authority. [8] But you will receive power when the Holy Spirit has come upon you; and

you will be my witnesses in Jerusalem, in all Judea and Samaria, and to the ends of the earth.' ⁹ When he had said this, as they were watching, he was lifted up, and a cloud took him out of their sight. ¹⁰ While he was going and they were gazing up towards heaven, suddenly two men in white robes stood by them. ¹¹ They said, 'Men of Galilee, why do you stand looking up towards heaven? This Jesus, who has been taken up from you into heaven, will come in the same way as you saw him go into heaven.'

OR   **Daniel 7.9–14**

⁹   As I watched,
     thrones were set in place,
         and an Ancient One took his throne;
     his clothing was white as snow,
         and the hair of his head like pure wool;
     his throne was fiery flames,
         and its wheels were burning fire.
¹⁰ A stream of fire issued
         and flowed out from his presence.
     A thousand thousand served him,
         and ten thousand times ten thousand stood attending him.
     The court sat in judgement,
         and the books were opened.
¹¹ I watched then because of the noise of the arrogant words that the horn was speaking. And as I watched, the beast was put to death, and its body destroyed and given over to be burned with fire. ¹² As for the rest of the beasts, their dominion was taken away, but their lives were prolonged for a season and a time. ¹³ As I watched in the night visions,
     I saw one like a human being
         coming with the clouds of heaven.
     And he came to the Ancient One
         and was presented before him.
¹⁴ To him was given dominion
         and glory and kingship,
     that all peoples, nations, and languages
         should serve him.
     His dominion is an everlasting dominion
         that shall not pass away,
     and his kingship is one
         that shall never be destroyed.

PSALM

EITHER **Psalm 47**

1 Clap your hands, all you peoples;
   shout to God with a cry of joy.
2 For the Lord Most High is to be feared;
   he is the great king over all the earth.
3 He subdues the peoples under us,
   and the nations under our feet.
4 He chooses our inheritance for us,
   the pride of Jacob whom he loves.
5 God has gone up with a shout,
   the Lord with the sound of the ram's-horn.
6 Sing praises to God, sing praises;
   sing praises to our king, sing praises.
7 For God is king of all the earth;
   sing praises with all your skill.
8 God reigns over the nations;
   God sits upon his holy throne.
9 The nobles of the peoples have gathered together
   with the people of the God of Abraham.
10 The rulers of the earth belong to God,
   and he is highly exalted.

OR **Psalm 93**

1 The Lord is king; he has put on splendid apparel;
   the Lord has put on his apparel and girded himself with strength.
2 He has made the whole world so sure
   that it cannot be moved;
3 Ever since the world began, your throne has been established;
   you are from everlasting.
4 The waters have lifted up, O Lord, the waters have lifted up their
      voice;
   the waters have lifted up their pounding waves.
5 Mightier than the sound of many waters, mightier than the
      breakers of the sea,
   mightier is the Lord who dwells on high.
6 Your testimonies are very sure,
   and holiness adorns your house, O Lord, for ever and for evermore.

READING

EITHER   Ephesians 1.15–23

¹⁵ I have heard of your faith in the Lord Jesus and your love towards all the saints, and for this reason ¹⁶ I do not cease to give thanks for you as I remember you in my prayers. ¹⁷ I pray that the God of our Lord Jesus Christ, the Father of glory, may give you a spirit of wisdom and revelation as you come to know him, ¹⁸ so that, with the eyes of your heart enlightened, you may know what is the hope to which he has called you, what are the riches of his glorious inheritance among the saints, ¹⁹ and what is the immeasurable greatness of his power for us who believe, according to the working of his great power. ²⁰ God put this power to work in Christ when he raised him from the dead and seated him at his right hand in the heavenly places, ²¹ far above all rule and authority and power and dominion, and above every name that is named, not only in this age but also in the age to come. ²² And he has put all things under his feet and has made him the head over all things for the church, ²³ which is his body, the fullness of him who fills all in all.

OR   Acts 1.1–11

¹ In the first book, Theophilus, I wrote about all that Jesus did and taught from the beginning ² until the day when he was taken up to heaven, after giving instructions through the Holy Spirit to the apostles whom he had chosen. ³ After his suffering he presented himself alive to them by many convincing proofs, appearing to them over the course of forty days and speaking about the kingdom of God. ⁴ While staying with them, he ordered them not to leave Jerusalem, but to wait there for the promise of the Father. 'This', he said, 'is what you have heard from me; ⁵ for John baptized with water, but you will be baptized with the Holy Spirit not many days from now.'

⁶ So when they had come together, they asked him, 'Lord, is this the time when you will restore the kingdom to Israel?' ⁷ He replied, 'It is not for you to know the times or periods that the Father has set by his own authority. ⁸ But you will receive power when the Holy Spirit has come upon you; and you will be my witnesses in Jerusalem, in all Judea and Samaria, and to the ends of the earth.' ⁹ When he had said this, as they were watching, he was lifted up, and a cloud took him out of their sight. ¹⁰ While he was going and they were gazing up towards heaven, suddenly two men in white robes stood by them. ¹¹ They said, 'Men of Galilee, why do you stand looking up towards heaven? This Jesus, who has been taken up from you into heaven, will come in the same way as you saw him go into heaven.'

GOSPEL   Luke 24.44–53

⁴⁴ Then he said to them, 'These are my words that I spoke to you while I was still with you—that everything written about me in the law of Moses, the prophets, and the psalms must be fulfilled.' ⁴⁵ Then he opened their minds to understand the scriptures, ⁴⁶ and he said to them, 'Thus it is written, that the Messiah is to suffer and to rise from the dead on the third day, ⁴⁷ and that repentance and forgiveness of sins is to be proclaimed in his name to all nations, beginning from Jerusalem. ⁴⁸ You are witnesses of these things. ⁴⁹ And see, I am sending upon you what my Father promised; so stay here in the city until you have been clothed with power from on high.'

⁵⁰ Then he led them out as far as Bethany, and, lifting up his hands, he blessed them. ⁵¹ While he was blessing them, he withdrew from them and was carried up into heaven. ⁵² And they worshipped him, and returned to Jerusalem with great joy; ⁵³ and they were continually in the temple blessing God.

POST COMMUNION

God our Father,
you have raised our humanity in Christ
and have fed us with the bread of heaven:
mercifully grant that, nourished with such spiritual blessings,
we may set our hearts in the heavenly places;
through Jesus Christ our Lord.

SECOND SERVICE   THIRD SERVICE

Psalm 8   **Psalm 110**
Prayer of Azariah 29–37   **Isaiah 52.7–15**
or   **Hebrews 7.[11–25,] 26–28**

2 Kings 2.1–15
Revelation 5

If the Second Service is a Eucharist, the following is read as a Gospel:

Matthew 28.16–20

THE SEVENTH SUNDAY OF EASTER
SUNDAY AFTER ASCENSION DAY

The reading from Acts must be used. The second (New Testament) reading follows or, if the Old Testament reading is used, the Acts reading follows as the second reading.

COLLECT

O God the king of glory,
you have exalted your only Son Jesus Christ
with great triumph to your kingdom in heaven:
we beseech you, leave us not comfortless,
but send your Holy Spirit to strengthen us
and exalt us to the place
   where our Saviour Christ is gone before,
who is alive and reigns with you,
in the unity of the Holy Spirit,
one God, now and for ever.

READING   Acts 16.16–34

[16] One day, as we were going to the place of prayer, we met a slave-girl who had a spirit of divination and brought her owners a great deal of money by fortune-telling. [17] While she followed Paul and us, she would cry out, 'These men are slaves of the Most High God, who proclaim to you a way of salvation.' [18] She kept doing this for many days. But Paul, very much annoyed, turned and said to the spirit, 'I order you in the name of Jesus Christ to come out of her.' And it came out that very hour.

[19] But when her owners saw that their hope of making money was gone, they seized Paul and Silas and dragged them into the market-place before the authorities. [20] When they had brought them before the magistrates, they said, 'These men are disturbing our city; they are Jews [21] and are advocating customs that are not lawful for us as Romans to adopt or observe.' [22] The crowd joined in attacking them, and the magistrates had them stripped of their clothing and ordered them to be beaten with rods. [23] After they had given them a severe flogging, they threw them into prison and ordered the jailer to keep them securely. [24] Following these instructions, he put them in the innermost cell and fastened their feet in the stocks.

[25] About midnight Paul and Silas were praying and singing hymns to God, and the prisoners were listening to them. [26] Suddenly there was an earthquake, so violent that the foundations of the prison were shaken;

and immediately all the doors were opened and everyone's chains were unfastened. [27] When the jailer woke up and saw the prison doors wide open, he drew his sword and was about to kill himself, since he supposed that the prisoners had escaped. [28] But Paul shouted in a loud voice, 'Do not harm yourself, for we are all here.' [29] The jailer called for lights, and rushing in, he fell down trembling before Paul and Silas. [30] Then he brought them outside and said, 'Sirs, what must I do to be saved?' [31] They answered, 'Believe on the Lord Jesus, and you will be saved, you and your household.' [32] They spoke the word of the Lord to him and to all who were in his house. [33] At the same hour of the night he took them and washed their wounds; then he and his entire family were baptized without delay. [34] He brought them up into the house and set food before them; and he and his entire household rejoiced that he had become a believer in God.

PSALM   Psalm 97

1   The Lord is king; let the earth rejoice;
     let the multitude of the isles be glad.
2   Clouds and darkness are round about him,
     righteousness and justice are the foundations of his throne.
3   A fire goes before him
     and burns up his enemies on every side.
4   His lightnings light up the world;
     the earth sees it and is afraid.
5   The mountains melt like wax at the presence of the Lord,
     at the presence of the Lord of the whole earth.
6   The heavens declare his righteousness,
     and all the peoples see his glory.
7   Confounded be all who worship carved images and delight in false
          gods!
     Bow down before him, all you gods.
8   Zion hears and is glad and the cities of Judah rejoice,
     because of your judgements, O Lord.
9   For you are the Lord: most high over all the earth;
     you are exalted far above all gods.
10   The Lord loves those who hate evil;
     he preserves the lives of his saints and delivers them from the
          hand of the wicked.
11   Light has sprung up for the righteous,
     and joyful gladness for those who are true-hearted.
12   Rejoice in the Lord, you righteous,
     and give thanks to his holy name.

READING   Revelation 22.12-14, 16-17, 20-21

¹² 'See, I am coming soon; my reward is with me, to repay according to everyone's work. ¹³ I am the Alpha and the Omega, the first and the last, the beginning and the end.'

¹⁴ Blessed are those who wash their robes, so that they will have the right to the tree of life and may enter the city by the gates.

¹⁶ 'It is I, Jesus, who sent my angel to you with this testimony for the churches. I am the root and the descendant of David, the bright morning star.'
¹⁷ The Spirit and the bride say, 'Come.'
    And let everyone who hears say, 'Come.'
    And let everyone who is thirsty come.
    Let anyone who wishes take the water of life as a gift.

²⁰ The one who testifies to these things says, 'Surely I am coming soon.'
   Amen. Come, Lord Jesus!

²¹ The grace of the Lord Jesus be with all the saints. Amen.

GOSPEL   John 17.20-26

²⁰ 'I ask not only on behalf of these, but also on behalf of those who will believe in me through their word, ²¹ that they may all be one. As you, Father, are in me and I am in you, may they also be in us, so that the world may believe that you have sent me. ²² The glory that you have given me I have given them, so that they may be one, as we are one, ²³ I in them and you in me, that they may become completely one, so that the world may know that you have sent me and have loved them even as you have loved me. ²⁴ Father, I desire that those also, whom you have given me, may be with me where I am, to see my glory, which you have given me because you loved me before the foundation of the world.

²⁵ 'Righteous Father, the world does not know you, but I know you; and these know that you have sent me. ²⁶ I made your name known to them, and I will make it known, so that the love with which you have loved me may be in them, and I in them.'

POST COMMUNION

Eternal God, giver of love and power,
your Son Jesus Christ has sent us into all the world
to preach the gospel of his kingdom:
confirm us in this mission,
and help us to live the good news we proclaim;
through Jesus Christ our Lord.

SECOND SERVICE

THIRD SERVICE

**Psalm 68.1–14, [15–18,] 19–20,
[21–36]
Isaiah 44.1–8
Ephesians 4.7–16**

*If the Second Service is a Eucharist, the
following is read as a Gospel:*

Luke 24.44–53

**Psalm 99
Deuteronomy 34
Luke 24.44–53**

or

Acts 1.1–8

DAY OF PENTECOST
WHIT SUNDAY

COLLECT

God, who as at this time
taught the hearts of your faithful people
by sending to them the light of your Holy Spirit:
grant us by the same Spirit
to have a right judgement in all things
and evermore to rejoice in his holy comfort;
through the merits of Christ Jesus our Saviour,
who is alive and reigns with you,
in the unity of the Holy Spirit,
one God, now and for ever.

The reading from Acts must be used as either the first or second reading

READING

EITHER   Acts 2.1–21

¹ When the day of Pentecost had come, they were all together in one place. ² And suddenly from heaven there came a sound like the rush of a violent wind, and it filled the entire house where they were sitting. ³ Divided tongues, as of fire, appeared among them, and a tongue rested on each of them. ⁴ All of them were filled with the Holy Spirit and began to speak in other languages, as the Spirit gave them ability.

⁵ Now there were devout Jews from every nation under heaven living in Jerusalem. ⁶ And at this sound the crowd gathered and was bewildered, because each one heard them speaking in the native language of each. ⁷ Amazed and astonished, they asked, 'Are not all these who are speaking Galileans? ⁸ And how is it that we hear, each of us, in our own native language? ⁹ Parthians, Medes, Elamites, and residents of Mesopotamia, Judea and Cappadocia, Pontus and Asia, ¹⁰ Phrygia and Pamphylia, Egypt and the parts of Libya belonging to Cyrene, and visitors from Rome, both Jews and proselytes, ¹¹ Cretans and Arabs—in our own languages we hear them speaking about God's deeds of power.' ¹² All were amazed and perplexed, saying to one another, 'What does this mean?' ¹³ But others sneered and said, 'They are filled with new wine.'

¹⁴ But Peter, standing with the eleven, raised his voice and addressed them: 'Men of Judea and all who live in Jerusalem, let this be known to you, and listen to what I say. ¹⁵ Indeed, these are not drunk, as you suppose, for it is only nine o'clock in the morning. ¹⁶ No, this is what was spoken through the prophet Joel:
¹⁷   "In the last days it will be, God declares,
      that I will pour out my Spirit upon all flesh,
         and your sons and your daughters shall prophesy,
      and your young men shall see visions,
         and your old men shall dream dreams.
¹⁸   Even upon my slaves, both men and women,
         in those days I will pour out my Spirit;
            and they shall prophesy.
¹⁹   And I will show portents in the heaven above
         and signs on the earth below,
            blood, and fire, and smoky mist.

²⁰ The sun shall be turned to darkness
 and the moon to blood,
   before the coming of the Lord's great and glorious day.
²¹ Then everyone who calls on the name of the Lord shall be saved." '

OR   **Genesis 11.1–9**

¹ Now the whole earth had one language and the same words. ² And as
they migrated from the east, they came upon a plain in the land of Shinar
and settled there. ³ And they said to one another, 'Come, let us make bricks,
and burn them thoroughly.' And they had brick for stone, and bitumen for
mortar. ⁴ Then they said, 'Come, let us build ourselves a city, and a tower
with its top in the heavens, and let us make a name for ourselves; otherwise
we shall be scattered abroad upon the face of the whole earth.' ⁵ The Lord
came down to see the city and the tower, which mortals had built. ⁶ And
the Lord said, 'Look, they are one people, and they have all one language;
and this is only the beginning of what they will do; nothing that they
propose to do will now be impossible for them. ⁷ Come, let us go down,
and confuse their language there, so that they will not understand one
another's speech.' ⁸ So the Lord scattered them abroad from there over the
face of all the earth, and they left off building the city. ⁹ Therefore it was
called Babel, because there the Lord confused the language of all the earth;
and from there the Lord scattered them abroad over the face of all the
earth.

PSALM   **Psalm 104.25–35, [36,] 37**

²⁵ O Lord, how manifold are your works!
   in wisdom you have made them all; the earth is full of your
     creatures.
²⁶ Yonder is the great and wide sea with its living things too many
     to number,
   creatures both small and great.
²⁷ There move the ships, and there is that Leviathan,
   which you have made for the sport of it.
²⁸ All of them look to you
   to give them their food in due season.
²⁹ You give it to them, they gather it;
   you open your hand and they are filled with good things.
³⁰ You hide your face and they are terrified;
   you take away their breath and they die and return to their dust.
³¹ You send forth your Spirit and they are created;
   and so you renew the face of the earth.

³² May the glory of the Lord endure for ever;
    may the Lord rejoice in all his works.
³³ He looks at the earth and it trembles;
    he touches the mountains and they smoke.
³⁴ I will sing to the Lord as long as I live;
    I will praise my God while I have my being.
³⁵ May these words of mine please him;
    I will rejoice in the Lord.
[³⁶ Let sinners be consumed out of the earth,
    and the wicked be no more.]
³⁷ Bless the Lord, O my soul.
    Alleluia!

READING

EITHER   **Romans 8.14–17**

¹⁴ For all who are led by the Spirit of God are children of God. ¹⁵ For you did not receive a spirit of slavery to fall back into fear, but you have received a spirit of adoption. When we cry, 'Abba! Father!' ¹⁶ it is that very Spirit bearing witness with our spirit that we are children of God, ¹⁷ and if children, then heirs, heirs of God and joint heirs with Christ—if, in fact, we suffer with him so that we may also be glorified with him.

OR   **Acts 2.1–21**

¹ When the day of Pentecost had come, they were all together in one place. ² And suddenly from heaven there came a sound like the rush of a violent wind, and it filled the entire house where they were sitting. ³ Divided tongues, as of fire, appeared among them, and a tongue rested on each of them. ⁴ All of them were filled with the Holy Spirit and began to speak in other languages, as the Spirit gave them ability.

⁵ Now there were devout Jews from every nation under heaven living in Jerusalem. ⁶ And at this sound the crowd gathered and was bewildered, because each one heard them speaking in the native language of each. ⁷ Amazed and astonished, they asked, 'Are not all these who are speaking Galileans? ⁸ And how is it that we hear, each of us, in our own native language? ⁹ Parthians, Medes, Elamites, and residents of Mesopotamia, Judea and Cappadocia, Pontus and Asia, ¹⁰ Phrygia and Pamphylia, Egypt and the parts of Libya belonging to Cyrene, and visitors from Rome, both Jews and proselytes, ¹¹ Cretans and Arabs—in our own languages we hear them speaking about God's deeds of power.' ¹² All were amazed and perplexed, saying to one another, 'What does this mean?' ¹³ But others sneered and said, 'They are filled with new wine.'

¹⁴ But Peter, standing with the eleven, raised his voice and addressed them: 'Men of Judea and all who live in Jerusalem, let this be known to you, and listen to what I say. ¹⁵ Indeed, these are not drunk, as you suppose, for it is only nine o'clock in the morning. ¹⁶ No, this is what was spoken through the prophet Joel:

¹⁷ "In the last days it will be, God declares,
  that I will pour out my Spirit upon all flesh,
    and your sons and your daughters shall prophesy,
  and your young men shall see visions,
    and your old men shall dream dreams.
¹⁸ Even upon my slaves, both men and women,
  in those days I will pour out my Spirit;
    and they shall prophesy.
¹⁹ And I will show portents in the heaven above
  and signs on the earth below,
    blood, and fire, and smoky mist.
²⁰ The sun shall be turned to darkness
  and the moon to blood,
    before the coming of the Lord's great and glorious day.
²¹ Then everyone who calls on the name of the Lord shall be saved." '

GOSPEL   John 14.8–17, [25–27]

⁸ Philip said to him, 'Lord, show us the Father, and we will be satisfied.' ⁹ Jesus said to him, 'Have I been with you all this time, Philip, and you still do not know me? Whoever has seen me has seen the Father. How can you say, "Show us the Father"? ¹⁰ Do you not believe that I am in the Father and the Father is in me? The words that I say to you I do not speak on my own; but the Father who dwells in me does his works. ¹¹ Believe me that I am in the Father and the Father is in me; but if you do not, then believe me because of the works themselves. ¹² Very truly, I tell you, the one who believes in me will also do the works that I do and, in fact, will do greater works than these, because I am going to the Father. ¹³ I will do whatever you ask in my name, so that the Father may be glorified in the Son. ¹⁴ If in my name you ask me for anything, I will do it.

¹⁵ 'If you love me, you will keep my commandments. ¹⁶ And I will ask the Father, and he will give you another Advocate, to be with you for ever. ¹⁷ This is the Spirit of truth, whom the world cannot receive, because it neither sees him nor knows him. You know him, because he abides with you, and he will be in you.'

[[25] 'I have said these things to you while I am still with you. [26] But the Advocate, the Holy Spirit, whom the Father will send in my name, will teach you everything, and remind you of all that I have said to you. [27] Peace I leave with you; my peace I give to you. I do not give to you as the world gives. Do not let your hearts be troubled, and do not let them be afraid.']

POST COMMUNION

Faithful God,
who fulfilled the promises of Easter
by sending us your Holy Spirit
and opening to every race and nation
the way of life eternal:
open our lips by your Spirit,
that every tongue may tell of your glory;
through Jesus Christ our Lord.

SECOND SERVICE

Psalms 36.5–10; 150
Exodus 33.7–20
2 Corinthians 3.4–18

If the Second Service is a Eucharist, the following is read as a Gospel:

John 16.4b–15

THIRD SERVICE

Psalm 33.1–12
Isaiah 40.12–23

or

Wisdom 9.9–17
1 Corinthians 2.6–16

TRINITY SUNDAY

COLLECT

Almighty and everlasting God,
you have given us your servants grace,
by the confession of a true faith,
to acknowledge the glory of the eternal Trinity
and in the power of the divine majesty to worship the Unity:
keep us steadfast in this faith,
that we may evermore be defended from all adversities;
through Jesus Christ your Son our Lord,

who is alive and reigns with you,
in the unity of the Holy Spirit,
one God, now and for ever.

READING   Proverbs 8.1–4, 22–31

¹ Does not wisdom call,
   and does not understanding raise her voice?
² On the heights, beside the way,
   at the crossroads she takes her stand;
³ beside the gates in front of the town,
   at the entrance of the portals she cries out:
⁴ 'To you, O people, I call,
   and my cry is to all that live.'

²² 'The LORD created me at the beginning of his work,
   the first of his acts of long ago.
²³ Ages ago I was set up,
   at the first, before the beginning of the earth.
²⁴ When there were no depths I was brought forth,
   when there were no springs abounding with water.
²⁵ Before the mountains had been shaped,
   before the hills, I was brought forth—
²⁶ when he had not yet made earth and fields,
   or the world's first bits of soil.
²⁷ When he established the heavens, I was there,
   when he drew a circle on the face of the deep,
²⁸ when he made firm the skies above,
   when he established the fountains of the deep,
²⁹ when he assigned to the sea its limit,
   so that the waters might not transgress his command,
when he marked out the foundations of the earth,
³⁰ then I was beside him, like a master worker;
and I was daily his delight,
   rejoicing before him always,
³¹ rejoicing in his inhabited world
   and delighting in the human race.'

PSALM   Psalm 8

¹ O Lord our governor,
   how exalted is your name in all the world!

2 Out of the mouths of infants and children
     your majesty is praised above the heavens.
3 You have set up a stronghold against your adversaries,
     to quell the enemy and the avenger.
4 When I consider your heavens, the work of your fingers,
     the moon and the stars you have set in their courses,
5 What are mortals, that you should be mindful of them?
     mere human beings, that you should seek them out?
6 You have made them little lower than the angels;
     you adorn them with glory and honour.
7 You give them mastery over the works of your hands;
     and put all things under their feet,
8 All sheep and oxen,
     even the wild beasts of the field,
9 The birds of the air, the fish of the sea,
     and whatsoever walks in the paths of the sea.
10 O Lord our governor,
     how exalted is your name in all the world!

READING   Romans 5.1–5

[1] Therefore, since we are justified by faith, we have peace with God through our Lord Jesus Christ, [2] through whom we have obtained access to this grace in which we stand; and we boast in our hope of sharing the glory of God. [3] And not only that, but we also boast in our sufferings, knowing that suffering produces endurance, [4] and endurance produces character, and character produces hope, [5] and hope does not disappoint us, because God's love has been poured into our hearts through the Holy Spirit that has been given to us.

GOSPEL   John 16.12–15

[12] 'I still have many things to say to you, but you cannot bear them now. [13] When the Spirit of truth comes, he will guide you into all the truth; for he will not speak on his own, but will speak whatever he hears, and he will declare to you the things that are to come. [14] He will glorify me, because he will take what is mine and declare it to you. [15] All that the Father has is mine. For this reason I said that he will take what is mine and declare it to you.'

YEAR C

POST COMMUNION

Almighty and eternal God,
you have revealed yourself as Father, Son and Holy Spirit,
and live and reign in the perfect unity of love:
hold us firm in this faith,
that we may know you in all your ways
and evermore rejoice in your eternal glory,
who are three Persons yet one God,
now and for ever.

SECOND SERVICE

Psalm 73.1–3, 16–29
Exodus 3.1–15
John 3.1–17

THIRD SERVICE

Psalm 29
Isaiah 6.1–8
Revelation 4

TABLE OF FIRST SUNDAY AFTER TRINITY DATES AND PROPERS

YEAR	LITURGICAL YEAR	FIRST SUNDAY AFTER TRINITY	PROPER
1999	A	6 Jun	5
2000	B	25 Jun	7
2001	C	17 Jun	6
2002	A	2 Jun	4
2003	B	22 Jun	7
2004	C	13 Jun	6
2005	A	29 May	4
2006	B	18 Jun	6
2007	C	10 Jun	5
2008	A	25 May	(3)*
2009	B	14 Jun	6
2010	C	6 Jun	5
2011	A	26 Jun	8
2012	B	10 Jun	5
2013	C	2 Jun	4
2014	A	22 Jun	7
2015	B	7 Jun	5
2016	C	29 May	4
2017	A	18 Jun	6
2018	B	3 Jun	4
2019	C	23 Jun	7
2020	A	14 Jun	6

*For Proper 3 use Second Sunday before Lent, Option B (8th Sunday after Epiphany)

THE FIRST SUNDAY AFTER TRINITY

COLLECT

O God,
the strength of all those who put their trust in you,
mercifully accept our prayers
and, because through the weakness of our mortal nature
we can do no good thing without you,
grant us the help of your grace,
that in the keeping of your commandments
we may please you both in will and deed;
through Jesus Christ your Son our Lord,
who is alive and reigns with you,
in the unity of the Holy Spirit,
one God, now and for ever.

READINGS

See page 800 and pages 949 to 972 and Table on page 931

POST COMMUNION

Eternal Father,
we thank you for nourishing us
with these heavenly gifts:
may our communion strengthen us in faith,
build us up in hope,
and make us grow in love;
for the sake of Jesus Christ our Lord.

THE SECOND SUNDAY AFTER TRINITY

COLLECT

Lord, you have taught us
that all our doings without love are nothing worth:
send your Holy Spirit
and pour into our hearts that most excellent gift of love,
the true bond of peace and of all virtues,

without which whoever lives is counted dead before you.
Grant this for your only Son Jesus Christ's sake,
who is alive and reigns with you,
in the unity of the Holy Spirit,
one God, now and for ever.

READINGS

See pages 949 to 978 and Table on page 931

POST COMMUNION

Loving Father,
we thank you for feeding us at the supper of your Son:
sustain us with your Spirit,
that we may serve you here on earth
until our joy is complete in heaven,
and we share in the eternal banquet
with Jesus Christ our Lord.

THE THIRD SUNDAY AFTER TRINITY

COLLECT

Almighty God,
you have broken the tyranny of sin
and have sent the Spirit of your Son into our hearts
    whereby we call you Father:
give us grace to dedicate our freedom to your service,
that we and all creation may be brought
    to the glorious liberty of the children of God;
through Jesus Christ your Son our Lord,
who is alive and reigns with you,
in the unity of the Holy Spirit,
one God, now and for ever.

READINGS

See pages 954 to 984 and Table on page 931

POST COMMUNION

O God, whose beauty is beyond our imagining
and whose power we cannot comprehend:
show us your glory as far as we can grasp it,
and shield us from knowing more than we can bear
until we may look upon you without fear;
through Jesus Christ our Saviour.

THE FOURTH SUNDAY AFTER TRINITY

COLLECT

O God, the protector of all who trust in you,
without whom nothing is strong, nothing is holy:
increase and multiply upon us your mercy;
that with you as our ruler and guide
we may so pass through things temporal
that we lose not our hold on things eternal;
grant this, heavenly Father,
for our Lord Jesus Christ's sake,
who is alive and reigns with you,
in the unity of the Holy Spirit,
one God, now and for ever.

READINGS

See pages 959 to 989 and Table on page 931

POST COMMUNION

Eternal God,
comfort of the afflicted and healer of the broken,
you have fed us at the table of life and hope:
teach us the ways of gentleness and peace,
that all the world may acknowledge
the kingdom of your Son Jesus Christ our Lord.

THE FIFTH SUNDAY AFTER TRINITY

COLLECT

Almighty and everlasting God,
by whose Spirit the whole body of the Church
   is governed and sanctified:
hear our prayer which we offer for all your faithful people,
that in their vocation and ministry
they may serve you in holiness and truth
to the glory of your name;
through our Lord and Saviour Jesus Christ,
who is alive and reigns with you,
in the unity of the Holy Spirit,
one God, now and for ever.

READINGS

See pages 966 to 995 and Table on page 931

POST COMMUNION

Grant, O Lord, we beseech you,
that the course of this world may be so peaceably ordered
   by your governance,
that your Church may joyfully serve you
   in all godly quietness;
through Jesus Christ our Lord.

THE SIXTH SUNDAY AFTER TRINITY

COLLECT

Merciful God,
you have prepared for those who love you
such good things as pass our understanding:
pour into our hearts such love toward you
that we, loving you in all things and above all things,
may obtain your promises,
which exceed all that we can desire;

through Jesus Christ your Son our Lord,
who is alive and reigns with you,
in the unity of the Holy Spirit,
one God, now and for ever.

READINGS

See pages 972 to 1001 and Table on page 931

POST COMMUNION

God of our pilgrimage,
you have led us to the living water:
refresh and sustain us
as we go forward on our journey,
in the name of Jesus Christ our Lord.

THE SEVENTH SUNDAY AFTER TRINITY

COLLECT

Lord of all power and might,
the author and giver of all good things:
graft in our hearts the love of your name,
increase in us true religion,
nourish us with all goodness,
and of your great mercy keep us in the same;
through Jesus Christ your Son our Lord,
who is alive and reigns with you,
in the unity of the Holy Spirit,
one God, now and for ever.

READINGS

See pages 978 to 1006 and Table on page 931

POST COMMUNION

Lord God, whose Son is the true vine and the source of life,
ever giving himself that the world may live:
may we so receive within ourselves
 the power of his death and passion
that, in his saving cup,
 we may share his glory and be made perfect in his love;
for he is alive and reigns, now and for ever.

THE EIGHTH SUNDAY AFTER TRINITY

COLLECT

Almighty Lord and everlasting God,
we beseech you to direct, sanctify and govern
 both our hearts and bodies
in the ways of your laws
 and the works of your commandments;
that through your most mighty protection, both here and ever,
we may be preserved in body and soul;
through our Lord and Saviour Jesus Christ,
who is alive and reigns with you,
in the unity of the Holy Spirit,
one God, now and for ever.

READINGS

See pages 984 to 1012 and Table on page 931

POST COMMUNION

Strengthen for service, Lord,
the hands that have taken holy things;
may the ears which have heard your word
 be deaf to clamour and dispute;
may the tongues which have sung your praise
 be free from deceit;

may the eyes which have seen the tokens of your love
   shine with the light of hope;
and may the bodies which have been fed with your body
   be refreshed with the fullness of your life;
glory to you for ever.

THE NINTH SUNDAY AFTER TRINITY

COLLECT

Almighty God,
who sent your Holy Spirit
to be the life and light of your Church:
open our hearts to the riches of your grace,
that we may bring forth the fruit of the Spirit
in love and joy and peace;
through Jesus Christ your Son our Lord,
who is alive and reigns with you,
in the unity of the Holy Spirit,
one God, now and for ever.

READINGS

See pages 989 to 1018 and Table on page 931

POST COMMUNION

Holy Father,
who gathered us here around the table of your Son
to share this meal with the whole household of God:
in that new world
   where you reveal the fullness of your peace,
gather people of every race and language
   to share in the eternal banquet
   of Jesus Christ our Lord.

THE TENTH SUNDAY AFTER TRINITY

COLLECT

Let your merciful ears, O Lord,
be open to the prayers of your humble servants;
and that they may obtain their petitions
make them to ask such things as shall please you;
through Jesus Christ your Son our Lord,
who is alive and reigns with you,
in the unity of the Holy Spirit,
one God, now and for ever.

READINGS

See pages 995 to 1023 and Table on page 931

POST COMMUNION

God of our pilgrimage,
you have willed that the gate of mercy
should stand open for those who trust in you:
look upon us with your favour
that we who follow the path of your will
may never wander from the way of life;
through Jesus Christ our Lord.

THE ELEVENTH SUNDAY AFTER TRINITY

COLLECT

O God, you declare your almighty power
most chiefly in showing mercy and pity:
mercifully grant to us such a measure of your grace,
that we, running the way of your commandments,
may receive your gracious promises,
and be made partakers of your heavenly treasure;
through Jesus Christ your Son our Lord,

who is alive and reigns with you,
in the unity of the Holy Spirit,
one God, now and for ever.

READINGS

See pages 1001 to 1029 and Table on page 931

POST COMMUNION

Lord of all mercy,
we your faithful people have celebrated that one true sacrifice
    which takes away our sins and brings pardon and peace:
by our communion
keep us firm on the foundation of the gospel
and preserve us from all sin;
through Jesus Christ our Lord.

THE TWELFTH SUNDAY AFTER TRINITY

COLLECT

Almighty and everlasting God,
you are always more ready to hear than we to pray
and to give more than either we desire or deserve:
pour down upon us the abundance of your mercy,
forgiving us those things of which our conscience is afraid
and giving us those good things
    which we are not worthy to ask
but through the merits and mediation
of Jesus Christ your Son our Lord,
who is alive and reigns with you,
in the unity of the Holy Spirit,
one God, now and for ever.

READINGS

See pages 1006 to 1035 and Table on page 931

POST COMMUNION

God of all mercy,
in this eucharist you have set aside our sins
and given us your healing:
grant that we who are made whole in Christ
may bring that healing to this broken world,
in the name of Jesus Christ our Lord.

THE THIRTEENTH SUNDAY AFTER TRINITY

COLLECT

Almighty God,
who called your Church to bear witness
that you were in Christ reconciling the world to yourself:
help us to proclaim the good news of your love,
that all who hear it may be drawn to you;
through him who was lifted up on the cross,
and reigns with you in the unity of the Holy Spirit,
one God, now and for ever.

READINGS

See pages 1012 to 1040 and Table on page 931

POST COMMUNION

God our creator,
you feed your children with the true manna,
the living bread from heaven:
let this holy food sustain us through our earthly pilgrimage
until we come to that place
    where hunger and thirst are no more;
through Jesus Christ our Lord.

THE FOURTEENTH SUNDAY AFTER TRINITY

COLLECT

Almighty God,
whose only Son has opened for us
a new and living way into your presence:
give us pure hearts and steadfast wills
to worship you in spirit and in truth;
through Jesus Christ your Son our Lord,
who is alive and reigns with you,
in the unity of the Holy Spirit,
one God, now and for ever.

READINGS

See pages 1018 to 1044 and Table on page 931

POST COMMUNION

Lord God, the source of truth and love,
keep us faithful to the apostles' teaching and fellowship,
united in prayer and the breaking of bread,
and one in joy and simplicity of heart,
in Jesus Christ our Lord.

THE FIFTEENTH SUNDAY AFTER TRINITY

COLLECT

God, who in generous mercy sent the Holy Spirit
    upon your Church in the burning fire of your love:
grant that your people may be fervent
    in the fellowship of the gospel
that, always abiding in you,
they may be found steadfast in faith and active in service;
through Jesus Christ your Son our Lord,
who is alive and reigns with you,
in the unity of the Holy Spirit,
one God, now and for ever.

READINGS

See pages 1023 to 1050 and Table on page 931

POST COMMUNION

Keep, O Lord, your Church,
    with your perpetual mercy;
and, because without you our human frailty cannot but fall,
keep us ever by your help from all things hurtful,
and lead us to all things profitable to our salvation;
through Jesus Christ our Lord.

THE SIXTEENTH SUNDAY AFTER TRINITY

COLLECT

O Lord, we beseech you mercifully to hear the prayers
    of your people who call upon you;
and grant that they may both perceive and know
    what things they ought to do,
and also may have grace and power
    faithfully to fulfil them;
through Jesus Christ your Son our Lord,
who is alive and reigns with you,
in the unity of the Holy Spirit,
one God, now and for ever.

READINGS

See pages 1029 to 1056 and Table on page 931

POST COMMUNION

Almighty God,
you have taught us through your Son
that love is the fulfilling of the law:
grant that we may love you with our whole heart
and our neighbours as ourselves;
through Jesus Christ our Lord.

THE SEVENTEENTH SUNDAY AFTER TRINITY

COLLECT

Almighty God,
you have made us for yourself,
and our hearts are restless till they find their rest in you:
pour your love into our hearts and draw us to yourself,
and so bring us at last to your heavenly city
where we shall see you face to face;
through Jesus Christ your Son our Lord,
who is alive and reigns with you,
in the unity of the Holy Spirit,
one God, now and for ever.

READINGS

See pages 1035 to 1061 and Table on page 931

POST COMMUNION

Lord, we pray that your grace
    may always precede and follow us,
and make us continually to be given to all good works;
through Jesus Christ our Lord.

THE EIGHTEENTH SUNDAY AFTER TRINITY

COLLECT

Almighty and everlasting God,
increase in us your gift of faith
that, forsaking what lies behind
and reaching out to that which is before,
we may run the way of your commandments
and win the crown of everlasting joy;
through Jesus Christ your Son our Lord,

who is alive and reigns with you,
in the unity of the Holy Spirit,
one God, now and for ever.

READINGS

See pages 1040 to 1065 and Table on page 931

POST COMMUNION

We praise and thank you, O Christ, for this sacred feast:
for here we receive you,
here the memory of your passion is renewed,
here our minds are filled with grace,
and here a pledge of future glory is given,
when we shall feast at that table where you reign
with all your saints for ever.

THE NINETEENTH SUNDAY AFTER TRINITY

COLLECT

O God, forasmuch as without you
we are not able to please you;
mercifully grant that your Holy Spirit
may in all things direct and rule our hearts;
through Jesus Christ your Son our Lord,
who is alive and reigns with you,
in the unity of the Holy Spirit,
one God, now and for ever.

READINGS

See pages 1044 to 1065 and Table on page 931

POST COMMUNION

Holy and blessed God,
you have fed us with the body and blood of your Son
and filled us with your Holy Spirit:
may we honour you,

not only with our lips
but in lives dedicated to the service
   of Jesus Christ our Lord.

THE TWENTIETH SUNDAY AFTER TRINITY

COLLECT

God, the giver of life,
whose Holy Spirit wells up within your Church:
by the Spirit's gifts equip us to live the gospel of Christ
   and make us eager to do your will,
that we may share with the whole creation
   the joys of eternal life;
through Jesus Christ your Son our Lord,
who is alive and reigns with you,
in the unity of the Holy Spirit,
one God, now and for ever.

READINGS

See pages 1050 to 1065 and Table on page 931

POST COMMUNION

God our Father,
whose Son, the light unfailing,
has come from heaven to deliver the world
   from the darkness of ignorance:
let these holy mysteries open the eyes of our understanding
that we may know the way of life,
and walk in it without stumbling;
through Jesus Christ our Lord.

THE TWENTY-FIRST SUNDAY AFTER TRINITY

COLLECT

Grant, we beseech you, merciful Lord,
to your faithful people pardon and peace,
that they may be cleansed from all their sins
and serve you with a quiet mind;
through Jesus Christ your Son our Lord,
who is alive and reigns with you,
in the unity of the Holy Spirit,
one God, now and for ever.

READINGS

See pages 1056 to 1065 and Table on page 931

POST COMMUNION

Father of light,
in whom is no change or shadow of turning,
you give us every good and perfect gift
and have brought us to birth by your word of truth:
may we be a living sign of that kingdom
where your whole creation will be made perfect
    in Jesus Christ our Lord.

THE LAST SUNDAY AFTER TRINITY

COLLECT

Blessed Lord,
who caused all holy scriptures
    to be written for our learning:
help us so to hear them,
to read, mark, learn and inwardly digest them
that, through patience, and the comfort of your holy word,
we may embrace and for ever hold fast
    the hope of everlasting life,
which you have given us in our Saviour Jesus Christ,
who is alive and reigns with you,
in the unity of the Holy Spirit,
one God, now and for ever.

READINGS

See pages 1061 to 1065 and Table on page 931

POST COMMUNION

God of all grace,
your Son Jesus Christ fed the hungry
with the bread of his life
and the word of his kingdom:
renew your people with your heavenly grace,
and in all our weakness
sustain us by your true and living bread;
who is alive and reigns, now and for ever.

PROPER 4

Sunday between 29 May and 4 June inclusive (if after Trinity Sunday)

COLLECT

See page 932 and Table on page 931

CONTINUOUS

READING   **1 Kings 18.20–21, [22–29,] 30–39**

²⁰ So Ahab sent to all the Israelites, and assembled the prophets at Mount Carmel. ²¹ Elijah then came near to all the people, and said, 'How long will you go limping with two different opinions? If the LORD is God, follow him; but if Baal, then follow him.' The people did not answer him a word.

[²² Then Elijah said to the people, 'I, even I only, am left a prophet of the LORD; but Baal's prophets number four hundred and fifty. ²³ Let two bulls be given to us; let them choose one bull for themselves, cut it in pieces, and lay it on the wood, but put no fire to it; I will prepare the other bull and lay it on the wood, but put no fire to it. ²⁴ Then you call on the name of your god and I will call on the name of the LORD; the god who answers by fire is indeed God.' All the people answered, 'Well spoken!' ²⁵ Then Elijah said to the prophets of Baal, 'Choose for yourselves one bull and prepare it first, for you are many; then call on the name of your god, but put no fire to it.' ²⁶ So they took the bull that was given them, prepared it, and called on the name of Baal from morning until noon, crying, 'O Baal, answer us!' But there was no voice, and no answer. They limped about the altar that they had made. ²⁷ At noon Elijah mocked them, saying, 'Cry aloud! Surely he is a god; either he is meditating, or he has wandered away, or he is on a journey, or perhaps he is asleep and must be awakened.' ²⁸ Then they cried aloud and, as was their custom, they cut themselves with swords and lances until the blood gushed out over them. ²⁹ As midday passed, they raved on until the time of the offering of the oblation, but there was no voice, no answer, and no response.]

³⁰ Then Elijah said to all the people, 'Come closer to me'; and all the people came closer to him. First he repaired the altar of the LORD that had been thrown down; ³¹ Elijah took twelve stones, according to the number of the tribes of the sons of Jacob, to whom the word of the LORD came, saying, 'Israel shall be your name'; ³² with the stones he built an altar in the name of the LORD. Then he made a trench around the altar, large enough to contain two measures of seed. ³³ Next he put the wood in order, cut the

bull in pieces, and laid it on the wood. He said, 'Fill four jars with water and pour it on the burnt-offering and on the wood.' ³⁴ Then he said, 'Do it a second time'; and they did it a second time. Again he said, 'Do it a third time'; and they did it a third time, ³⁵ so that the water ran all round the altar, and filled the trench also with water.

³⁶ At the time of the offering of the oblation, the prophet Elijah came near and said, 'O LORD, God of Abraham, Isaac, and Israel, let it be known this day that you are God in Israel, that I am your servant, and that I have done all these things at your bidding. ³⁷ Answer me, O LORD, answer me, so that this people may know that you, O LORD, are God, and that you have turned their hearts back.' ³⁸ Then the fire of the LORD fell and consumed the burnt-offering, the wood, the stones, and the dust, and even licked up the water that was in the trench. ³⁹ When all the people saw it, they fell on their faces and said, 'The LORD indeed is God; the LORD indeed is God.'

PSALM   Psalm 96

1 Sing to the Lord a new song;
   sing to the Lord, all the whole earth.
2 Sing to the Lord and bless his name;
   proclaim the good news of his salvation from day to day.
3 Declare his glory among the nations
   and his wonders among all peoples.
4 For great is the Lord and greatly to be praised;
   he is more to be feared than all gods.
5 As for all the gods of the nations, they are but idols;
   but it is the Lord who made the heavens.
6 O the majesty and magnificence of his presence!
   O the power and the splendour of his sanctuary!
7 Ascribe to the Lord, you families of the peoples;
   ascribe to the Lord honour and power.
8 Ascribe to the Lord the honour due to his name;
   bring offerings and come into his courts.
9 Worship the Lord in the beauty of holiness;
   let the whole earth tremble before him.
10 Tell it out among the nations: 'The Lord is king!
   he has made the world so firm that it cannot be moved; he will
      judge the peoples with equity.'
11 Let the heavens rejoice and let the earth be glad; let the sea
      thunder and all that is in it;
   let the field be joyful and all that is therein.

12 Then shall all the trees of the wood shout for joy before the Lord
  when he comes,
  when he comes to judge the earth.
13 He will judge the world with righteousness
  and the peoples with his truth.

READING   Galatians 1.1–12

¹ Paul an apostle—sent neither by human commission nor from human authorities, but through Jesus Christ and God the Father, who raised him from the dead— ² and all the members of God's family who are with me,

To the churches of Galatia:

³ Grace to you and peace from God our Father and the Lord Jesus Christ, ⁴ who gave himself for our sins to set us free from the present evil age, according to the will of our God and Father, ⁵ to whom be the glory for ever and ever. Amen.

⁶ I am astonished that you are so quickly deserting the one who called you in the grace of Christ and are turning to a different gospel— ⁷ not that there is another gospel, but there are some who are confusing you and want to pervert the gospel of Christ. ⁸ But even if we or an angel from heaven should proclaim to you a gospel contrary to what we proclaimed to you, let that one be accursed! ⁹ As we have said before, so now I repeat, if anyone proclaims to you a gospel contrary to what you received, let that one be accursed!

¹⁰ Am I now seeking human approval, or God's approval? Or am I trying to please people? If I were still pleasing people, I would not be a servant of Christ.

¹¹ For I want you to know, brothers and sisters, that the gospel that was proclaimed by me is not of human origin; ¹² for I did not receive it from a human source, nor was I taught it, but I received it through a revelation of Jesus Christ.

GOSPEL   Luke 7.1–10

¹ After Jesus had finished all his sayings in the hearing of the people, he entered Capernaum. ² A centurion there had a slave whom he valued highly, and who was ill and close to death. ³ When he heard about Jesus, he sent some Jewish elders to him, asking him to come and heal his slave. ⁴ When they came to Jesus, they appealed to him earnestly, saying, 'He is worthy of having you do this for him, ⁵ for he loves our people, and it is he who built

our synagogue for us.' [6] And Jesus went with them, but when he was not far from the house, the centurion sent friends to say to him, 'Lord, do not trouble yourself, for I am not worthy to have you come under my roof; [7] therefore I did not presume to come to you. But only speak the word, and let my servant be healed. [8] For I also am a man set under authority, with soldiers under me; and I say to one, "Go", and he goes, and to another, "Come", and he comes, and to my slave, "Do this", and the slave does it.' [9] When Jesus heard this he was amazed at him, and turning to the crowd that followed him, he said, 'I tell you, not even in Israel have I found such faith.' [10] When those who had been sent returned to the house, they found the slave in good health.

RELATED

READING   1 Kings 8.22–23, 41–43

[22] Then Solomon stood before the altar of the LORD in the presence of all the assembly of Israel, and spread out his hands to heaven. [23] He said, 'O LORD, God of Israel, there is no God like you in heaven above or on earth beneath, keeping covenant and steadfast love for your servants who walk before you with all their heart.'

[41] 'Likewise when a foreigner, who is not of your people Israel, comes from a distant land because of your name [42] —for they shall hear of your great name, your mighty hand, and your outstretched arm—when a foreigner comes and prays towards this house, [43] then hear in heaven your dwelling-place, and do according to all that the foreigner calls to you, so that all the peoples of the earth may know your name and fear you, as do your people Israel, and so that they may know that your name has been invoked on this house that I have built.'

PSALM   Psalm 96.1–9

1   Sing to the Lord a new song;
      sing to the Lord, all the whole earth.
2   Sing to the Lord and bless his name;
      proclaim the good news of his salvation from day to day.
3   Declare his glory among the nations
      and his wonders among all peoples.
4   For great is the Lord and greatly to be praised;
      he is more to be feared than all gods.

5 As for all the gods of the nations, they are but idols;
  but it is the Lord who made the heavens.
6 O the majesty and magnificence of his presence!
  O the power and the splendour of his sanctuary!
7 Ascribe to the Lord, you families of the peoples;
  ascribe to the Lord honour and power.
8 Ascribe to the Lord the honour due to his name;
  bring offerings and come into his courts.
9 Worship the Lord in the beauty of holiness;
  let the whole earth tremble before him.

READING   Galatians 1.1–12

1 Paul an apostle—sent neither by human commission nor from human authorities, but through Jesus Christ and God the Father, who raised him from the dead— 2 and all the members of God's family who are with me,

To the churches of Galatia:

3 Grace to you and peace from God our Father and the Lord Jesus Christ, 4 who gave himself for our sins to set us free from the present evil age, according to the will of our God and Father, 5 to whom be the glory for ever and ever. Amen.

6 I am astonished that you are so quickly deserting the one who called you in the grace of Christ and are turning to a different gospel— 7 not that there is another gospel, but there are some who are confusing you and want to pervert the gospel of Christ. 8 But even if we or an angel from heaven should proclaim to you a gospel contrary to what we proclaimed to you, let that one be accursed! 9 As we have said before, so now I repeat, if anyone proclaims to you a gospel contrary to what you received, let that one be accursed!

10 Am I now seeking human approval, or God's approval? Or am I trying to please people? If I were still pleasing people, I would not be a servant of Christ.

11 For I want you to know, brothers and sisters, that the gospel that was proclaimed by me is not of human origin; 12 for I did not receive it from a human source, nor was I taught it, but I received it through a revelation of Jesus Christ.

GOSPEL   Luke 7.1–10

¹ After Jesus had finished all his sayings in the hearing of the people, he entered Capernaum. ² A centurion there had a slave whom he valued highly, and who was ill and close to death. ³ When he heard about Jesus, he sent some Jewish elders to him, asking him to come and heal his slave. ⁴ When they came to Jesus, they appealed to him earnestly, saying, 'He is worthy of having you do this for him, ⁵ for he loves our people, and it is he who built our synagogue for us.' ⁶ And Jesus went with them, but when he was not far from the house, the centurion sent friends to say to him, 'Lord, do not trouble yourself, for I am not worthy to have you come under my roof; ⁷ therefore I did not presume to come to you. But only speak the word, and let my servant be healed. ⁸ For I also am a man set under authority, with soldiers under me; and I say to one, "Go", and he goes, and to another, "Come", and he comes, and to my slave, "Do this", and the slave does it.' ⁹ When Jesus heard this he was amazed at him, and turning to the crowd that followed him, he said, 'I tell you, not even in Israel have I found such faith.' ¹⁰ When those who had been sent returned to the house, they found the slave in good health.

POST COMMUNION

See pages 932 to 933 and Table on page 931

SECOND SERVICE	THIRD SERVICE
Psalm 39	Psalm 41
Genesis 4.1–16	Deuteronomy 5.1–21
Mark 3.7–19	Acts 21.17–39a

PROPER 5

Sunday between 5 and 11 June inclusive (if after Trinity Sunday)

COLLECT

See pages 932 to 933 and Table on page 931

CONTINUOUS

READING   1 Kings 17.8–16, [17–24]

⁸ Then the word of the LORD came to him, saying, ⁹ 'Go now to Zarephath, which belongs to Sidon, and live there; for I have commanded a widow

there to feed you.' ¹⁰ So he set out and went to Zarephath. When he came to the gate of the town, a widow was there gathering sticks; he called to her and said, 'Bring me a little water in a vessel, so that I may drink.' ¹¹ As she was going to bring it, he called to her and said, 'Bring me a morsel of bread in your hand.' ¹² But she said, 'As the LORD your God lives, I have nothing baked, only a handful of meal in a jar, and a little oil in a jug; I am now gathering a couple of sticks, so that I may go home and prepare it for myself and my son, that we may eat it, and die.' ¹³ Elijah said to her, 'Do not be afraid; go and do as you have said; but first make me a little cake of it and bring it to me, and afterwards make something for yourself and your son. ¹⁴ For thus says the LORD the God of Israel: The jar of meal will not be emptied and the jug of oil will not fail until the day that the LORD sends rain on the earth.' ¹⁵ She went and did as Elijah said, so that she as well as he and her household ate for many days. ¹⁶ The jar of meal was not emptied, neither did the jug of oil fail, according to the word of the LORD that he spoke by Elijah.

[¹⁷ After this the son of the woman, the mistress of the house, became ill; his illness was so severe that there was no breath left in him. ¹⁸ She then said to Elijah, 'What have you against me, O man of God? You have come to me to bring my sin to remembrance, and to cause the death of my son!' ¹⁹ But he said to her, 'Give me your son.' He took him from her bosom, carried him up into the upper chamber where he was lodging, and laid him on his own bed. ²⁰ He cried out to the LORD, 'O LORD my God, have you brought calamity even upon the widow with whom I am staying, by killing her son?' ²¹ Then he stretched himself upon the child three times, and cried out to the LORD, 'O LORD my God, let this child's life come into him again.' ²² The LORD listened to the voice of Elijah; the life of the child came into him again, and he revived. ²³ Elijah took the child, brought him down from the upper chamber into the house, and gave him to his mother; then Elijah said, 'See, your son is alive.' ²⁴ So the woman said to Elijah, 'Now I know that you are a man of God, and that the word of the LORD in your mouth is truth.']

PSALM   Psalm 146

¹   Alleluia! Praise the Lord, O my soul!
    I will praise the Lord as long as I live; I will sing praises to my God
        while I have my being.
²   Put not your trust in rulers, nor in any child of earth,
    for there is no help in them.
³   When they breathe their last, they return to earth,
    and in that day their thoughts perish.

4 Happy are they who have the God of Jacob for their help!
  whose hope is in the Lord their God;
5 Who made heaven and earth, the seas, and all that is in them;
  who keeps his promise for ever;
6 Who gives justice to those who are oppressed,
  and food to those who hunger.
7 The Lord sets the prisoners free; the Lord opens the eyes of the
    blind;
  the Lord lifts up those who are bowed down;
8 The Lord loves the righteous; the Lord cares for the stranger;
  he sustains the orphan and widow, but frustrates the way of the
    wicked.
9 The Lord shall reign for ever,
  your God, O Zion, throughout all generations. Alleluia!

READING   Galatians 1.11–24

11 For I want you to know, brothers and sisters, that the gospel that was proclaimed by me is not of human origin; 12 for I did not receive it from a human source, nor was I taught it, but I received it through a revelation of Jesus Christ.

13 You have heard, no doubt, of my earlier life in Judaism. I was violently persecuting the church of God and was trying to destroy it. 14 I advanced in Judaism beyond many among my people of the same age, for I was far more zealous for the traditions of my ancestors. 15 But when God, who had set me apart before I was born and called me through his grace, was pleased 16 to reveal his Son to me, so that I might proclaim him among the Gentiles, I did not confer with any human being, 17 nor did I go up to Jerusalem to those who were already apostles before me, but I went away at once into Arabia, and afterwards I returned to Damascus.

18 Then after three years I did go up to Jerusalem to visit Cephas and stayed with him for fifteen days; 19 but I did not see any other apostle except James the Lord's brother. 20 In what I am writing to you, before God, I do not lie! 21 Then I went into the regions of Syria and Cilicia, 22 and I was still unknown by sight to the churches of Judea that are in Christ; 23 they only heard it said, 'The one who formerly was persecuting us is now proclaiming the faith he once tried to destroy.' 24 And they glorified God because of me.

GOSPEL   Luke 7.11–17

11 Soon afterwards he went to a town called Nain, and his disciples and a large crowd went with him. 12 As he approached the gate of the town, a

man who had died was being carried out. He was his mother's only son, and she was a widow; and with her was a large crowd from the town. [13] When the Lord saw her, he had compassion for her and said to her, 'Do not weep.' [14] Then he came forward and touched the bier, and the bearers stood still. And he said, 'Young man, I say to you, rise!' [15] The dead man sat up and began to speak, and Jesus gave him to his mother. [16] Fear seized all of them; and they glorified God, saying, 'A great prophet has risen among us!' and 'God has looked favourably on his people!' [17] This word about him spread throughout Judea and all the surrounding country.

RELATED

READING   1 Kings 17.17–24

[17] After this the son of the woman, the mistress of the house, became ill; his illness was so severe that there was no breath left in him. [18] She then said to Elijah, 'What have you against me, O man of God? You have come to me to bring my sin to remembrance, and to cause the death of my son!' [19] But he said to her, 'Give me your son.' He took him from her bosom, carried him up into the upper chamber where he was lodging, and laid him on his own bed. [20] He cried out to the LORD, 'O LORD my God, have you brought calamity even upon the widow with whom I am staying, by killing her son?' [21] Then he stretched himself upon the child three times, and cried out to the LORD, 'O LORD my God, let this child's life come into him again.' [22] The LORD listened to the voice of Elijah; the life of the child came into him again, and he revived. [23] Elijah took the child, brought him down from the upper chamber into the house, and gave him to his mother; then Elijah said, 'See, your son is alive.' [24] So the woman said to Elijah, 'Now I know that you are a man of God, and that the word of the LORD in your mouth is truth.'

PSALM   Psalm 30

1 I will exalt you, O Lord, because you have lifted me up
    and have not let my enemies triumph over me.
2 O Lord my God, I cried out to you,
    and you restored me to health.
3 You brought me up, O Lord, from the dead;
    you restored my life as I was going down to the grave.
4 Sing to the Lord, you servants of his;
    give thanks for the remembrance of his holiness.

⁵ For his wrath endures but the twinkling of an eye,
  his favour for a lifetime.
⁶ Weeping may spend the night,
  but joy comes in the morning.
⁷ While I felt secure, I said, 'I shall never be disturbed.
  You, Lord, with your favour, made me as strong as the mountains.'
⁸ Then you hid your face,
  and I was filled with fear.
⁹ I cried to you, O Lord;
  I pleaded with the Lord, saying,
¹⁰ 'What profit is there in my blood, if I go down to the Pit?
  will the dust praise you or declare your faithfulness?
¹¹ Hear, O Lord, and have mercy upon me;
  O Lord, be my helper.'
¹² You have turned my wailing into dancing;
  you have put off my sack-cloth and clothed me with joy;
¹³ Therefore my heart sings to you without ceasing;
  O Lord my God, I will give you thanks for ever.

READING   Galatians 1.11–24

¹¹ For I want you to know, brothers and sisters, that the gospel that was proclaimed by me is not of human origin; ¹² for I did not receive it from a human source, nor was I taught it, but I received it through a revelation of Jesus Christ.

¹³ You have heard, no doubt, of my earlier life in Judaism. I was violently persecuting the church of God and was trying to destroy it. ¹⁴ I advanced in Judaism beyond many among my people of the same age, for I was far more zealous for the traditions of my ancestors. ¹⁵ But when God, who had set me apart before I was born and called me through his grace, was pleased ¹⁶ to reveal his Son to me, so that I might proclaim him among the Gentiles, I did not confer with any human being, ¹⁷ nor did I go up to Jerusalem to those who were already apostles before me, but I went away at once into Arabia, and afterwards I returned to Damascus.

¹⁸ Then after three years I did go up to Jerusalem to visit Cephas and stayed with him for fifteen days; ¹⁹ but I did not see any other apostle except James the Lord's brother. ²⁰ In what I am writing to you, before God, I do not lie! ²¹ Then I went into the regions of Syria and Cilicia, ²² and I was still unknown by sight to the churches of Judea that are in Christ; ²³ they only heard it said, 'The one who formerly was persecuting us is now proclaiming the faith he once tried to destroy.' ²⁴ And they glorified God because of me.

GOSPEL   Luke 7.11–17

¹¹ Soon afterwards he went to a town called Nain, and his disciples and a large crowd went with him. ¹² As he approached the gate of the town, a man who had died was being carried out. He was his mother's only son, and she was a widow; and with her was a large crowd from the town. ¹³ When the Lord saw her, he had compassion for her and said to her, 'Do not weep.' ¹⁴ Then he came forward and touched the bier, and the bearers stood still. And he said, 'Young man, I say to you, rise!' ¹⁵ The dead man sat up and began to speak, and Jesus gave him to his mother. ¹⁶ Fear seized all of them; and they glorified God, saying, 'A great prophet has risen among us!' and 'God has looked favourably on his people!' ¹⁷ This word about him spread throughout Judea and all the surrounding country.

POST COMMUNION

See pages 932 to 934 and Table on page 931

SECOND SERVICE   THIRD SERVICE

Psalm 44.1–8, [9–26]   Psalm 45
Genesis 8.15–9.17   Deuteronomy 6.10–25
Mark 4.1–20   Acts 22.22–23.11

PROPER 6

Sunday between 12 and 18 June inclusive (if after Trinity Sunday)

COLLECT

See pages 932 to 934 and Table on page 931

CONTINUOUS

READING   1 Kings 21.1–10, [11–14,] 15–21a

¹ Later the following events took place: Naboth the Jezreelite had a vineyard in Jezreel, beside the palace of King Ahab of Samaria. ² And Ahab said to Naboth, 'Give me your vineyard, so that I may have it for a vegetable garden, because it is near my house; I will give you a better vineyard for it; or, if it seems good to you, I will give you its value in money.' ³ But Naboth

said to Ahab, 'The Lord forbid that I should give you my ancestral inheritance.' ⁴ Ahab went home resentful and sullen because of what Naboth the Jezreelite had said to him; for he had said, 'I will not give you my ancestral inheritance.' He lay down on his bed, turned away his face, and would not eat.

⁵ His wife Jezebel came to him and said, 'Why are you so depressed that you will not eat?' ⁶ He said to her, 'Because I spoke to Naboth the Jezreelite and said to him, "Give me your vineyard for money; or else, if you prefer, I will give you another vineyard for it"; but he answered, "I will not give you my vineyard."' ⁷ His wife Jezebel said to him, 'Do you now govern Israel? Get up, eat some food, and be cheerful; I will give you the vineyard of Naboth the Jezreelite.'

⁸ So she wrote letters in Ahab's name and sealed them with his seal; she sent the letters to the elders and the nobles who lived with Naboth in his city. ⁹ She wrote in the letters, 'Proclaim a fast, and seat Naboth at the head of the assembly; ¹⁰ seat two scoundrels opposite him, and have them bring a charge against him, saying, "You have cursed God and the king." Then take him out, and stone him to death.'
[¹¹ The men of his city, the elders and the nobles who lived in his city, did as Jezebel had sent word to them. Just as it was written in the letters that she had sent to them, ¹² they proclaimed a fast and seated Naboth at the head of the assembly. ¹³ The two scoundrels came in and sat opposite him; and the scoundrels brought a charge against Naboth, in the presence of the people, saying, 'Naboth cursed God and the king.' So they took him outside the city, and stoned him to death. ¹⁴ Then they sent to Jezebel, saying, 'Naboth has been stoned; he is dead.']

¹⁵ As soon as Jezebel heard that Naboth had been stoned and was dead, Jezebel said to Ahab, 'Go, take possession of the vineyard of Naboth the Jezreelite, which he refused to give you for money; for Naboth is not alive, but dead.' ¹⁶ As soon as Ahab heard that Naboth was dead, Ahab set out to go down to the vineyard of Naboth the Jezreelite, to take possession of it.

¹⁷ Then the word of the Lord came to Elijah the Tishbite, saying: ¹⁸ Go down to meet King Ahab of Israel, who rules in Samaria; he is now in the vineyard of Naboth, where he has gone to take possession. ¹⁹ You shall say to him, 'Thus says the Lord: Have you killed, and also taken possession?' You shall say to him, 'Thus says the Lord: In the place where dogs licked up the blood of Naboth, dogs will also lick up your blood.'

²⁰ Ahab said to Elijah, 'Have you found me, O my enemy?' He answered, 'I have found you. Because you have sold yourself to do what is evil in the sight of the Lord, ²¹ I will bring disaster on you.'

PSALM   Psalm 5.1–8

1 Give ear to my words, O Lord;
  consider my meditation.
2 Hearken to my cry for help, my King and my God,
  for I make my prayer to you.
3 In the morning, Lord, you hear my voice;
  early in the morning I make my appeal and watch for you.
4 For you are not a God who takes pleasure in wickedness
  and evil cannot dwell with you.
5 Braggarts cannot stand in your sight;
  you hate all those who work wickedness.
6 You destroy those who speak lies;
  the bloodthirsty and deceitful, O Lord, you abhor.
7 But as for me, through the greatness of your mercy, I will go into
    your house;
  I will bow down towards your holy temple in awe of you.
8 Lead me, O Lord, in your righteousness, because of those who lie
    in wait for me;
   make your way straight before me.

READING   Galatians 2.15–21

15 We ourselves are Jews by birth and not Gentile sinners; 16 yet we know that a person is justified not by the works of the law but through faith in Jesus Christ. And we have come to believe in Christ Jesus, so that we might be justified by faith in Christ, and not by doing the works of the law, because no one will be justified by the works of the law. 17 But if, in our effort to be justified in Christ, we ourselves have been found to be sinners, is Christ then a servant of sin? Certainly not! 18 But if I build up again the very things that I once tore down, then I demonstrate that I am a transgressor. 19 For through the law I died to the law, so that I might live to God. I have been crucified with Christ; 20 and it is no longer I who live, but it is Christ who lives in me. And the life I now live in the flesh I live by faith in the Son of God, who loved me and gave himself for me. 21 I do not nullify the grace of God; for if justification comes through the law, then Christ died for nothing.

GOSPEL   Luke 7.36–8.3

36 One of the Pharisees asked Jesus to eat with him, and he went into the Pharisee's house and took his place at the table. 37 And a woman in the city, who was a sinner, having learned that he was eating in the Pharisee's

house, brought an alabaster jar of ointment. [38] She stood behind him at his feet, weeping, and began to bathe his feet with her tears and to dry them with her hair. Then she continued kissing his feet and anointing them with the ointment. [39] Now when the Pharisee who had invited him saw it, he said to himself, 'If this man were a prophet, he would have known who and what kind of woman this is who is touching him—that she is a sinner.' [40] Jesus spoke up and said to him, 'Simon, I have something to say to you.' 'Teacher,' he replied, 'speak.' [41] 'A certain creditor had two debtors; one owed five hundred denarii, and the other fifty. [42] When they could not pay, he cancelled the debts for both of them. Now which of them will love him more?' [43] Simon answered, 'I suppose the one for whom he cancelled the greater debt.' And Jesus said to him, 'You have judged rightly.' [44] Then turning towards the woman, he said to Simon, 'Do you see this woman? I entered your house; you gave me no water for my feet, but she has bathed my feet with her tears and dried them with her hair. [45] You gave me no kiss, but from the time I came in she has not stopped kissing my feet. [46] You did not anoint my head with oil, but she has anointed my feet with ointment. [47] Therefore, I tell you, her sins, which were many, have been forgiven; hence she has shown great love. But the one to whom little is forgiven, loves little.' [48] Then he said to her, 'Your sins are forgiven.' [49] But those who were at the table with him began to say among themselves, 'Who is this who even forgives sins?' [50] And he said to the woman, 'Your faith has saved you; go in peace.'

[1] Soon afterwards he went on through cities and villages, proclaiming and bringing the good news of the kingdom of God. The twelve were with him, [2] as well as some women who had been cured of evil spirits and infirmities: Mary, called Magdalene, from whom seven demons had gone out, [3] and Joanna, the wife of Herod's steward Chuza, and Susanna, and many others, who provided for them out of their resources.

RELATED

READING   **2 Samuel 11.26–12.10, 13–15**

[26] When the wife of Uriah heard that her husband was dead, she made lamentation for him. [27] When the mourning was over, David sent and brought her to his house, and she became his wife, and bore him a son.

But the thing that David had done displeased the LORD, [1] and the LORD sent Nathan to David. He came to him, and said to him, 'There were two men in a certain city, one rich and the other poor. [2] The rich man had very many flocks and herds; [3] but the poor man had nothing but one little ewe lamb, which he had bought. He brought it up, and it grew up with him and with his children; it used to eat of his meagre fare, and drink from his cup, and lie in his bosom, and it was like a daughter to him. ⁴ Now there came a traveller to the rich man, and he was loath to take one of his own flock or herd to prepare for the wayfarer who had come to him, but he took the poor man's lamb, and prepared that for the guest who had come to him.' ⁵ Then David's anger was greatly kindled against the man. He said to Nathan, 'As the LORD lives, the man who has done this deserves to die; ⁶ he shall restore the lamb fourfold, because he did this thing, and because he had no pity.'

⁷ Nathan said to David, 'You are the man! Thus says the LORD, the God of Israel: I anointed you king over Israel, and I rescued you from the hand of Saul; ⁸ I gave you your master's house, and your master's wives into your bosom, and gave you the house of Israel and of Judah; and if that had been too little, I would have added as much more. ⁹ Why have you despised the word of the LORD, to do what is evil in his sight? You have struck down Uriah the Hittite with the sword, and have taken his wife to be your wife, and have killed him with the sword of the Ammonites. ¹⁰ Now therefore the sword shall never depart from your house, for you have despised me, and have taken the wife of Uriah the Hittite to be your wife.'

¹³ David said to Nathan, 'I have sinned against the LORD.' Nathan said to David, 'Now the LORD has put away your sin; you shall not die. ¹⁴ Nevertheless, because by this deed you have utterly scorned the LORD, the child that is born to you shall die.' ¹⁵ Then Nathan went to his house.

PSALM   Psalm 32

1   Happy are they whose transgressions are forgiven,
      and whose sin is put away!
2   Happy are they to whom the Lord imputes no guilt,
      and in whose spirit there is no guile!
3   While I held my tongue, my bones withered away,
      because of my groaning all day long.
4   For your hand was heavy upon me day and night;
      my moisture was dried up as in the heat of summer.
5   Then I acknowledged my sin to you,
      and did not conceal my guilt.
6   I said, 'I will confess my transgressions to the Lord':
      then you forgave me the guilt of my sin;
7   Therefore all the faithful will make their prayers to you in time of
          trouble;
      when the great waters overflow, they shall not reach them.

⁸ You are my hiding-place; you preserve me from trouble;
 you surround me with shouts of deliverance.
⁹ 'I will instruct you and teach you in the way that you should go;
 I will guide you with my eye.
¹⁰ Do not be like horse or mule, which have no understanding;
 who must be fitted with bit and bridle, or else they will not stay
 near you.'
¹¹ Great are the tribulations of the wicked;
 but mercy embraces those who trust in the Lord.
¹² Be glad, you righteous, and rejoice in the Lord;
 shout for joy, all who are true of heart.

READING   Galatians 2.15–21

¹⁵ We ourselves are Jews by birth and not Gentile sinners; ¹⁶ yet we know that a person is justified not by the works of the law but through faith in Jesus Christ. And we have come to believe in Christ Jesus, so that we might be justified by faith in Christ, and not by doing the works of the law, because no one will be justified by the works of the law. ¹⁷ But if, in our effort to be justified in Christ, we ourselves have been found to be sinners, is Christ then a servant of sin? Certainly not! ¹⁸ But if I build up again the very things that I once tore down, then I demonstrate that I am a transgressor. ¹⁹ For through the law I died to the law, so that I might live to God. I have been crucified with Christ; ²⁰ and it is no longer I who live, but it is Christ who lives in me. And the life I now live in the flesh I live by faith in the Son of God, who loved me and gave himself for me. ²¹ I do not nullify the grace of God; for if justification comes through the law, then Christ died for nothing.

GOSPEL   Luke 7.36–8.3

³⁶ One of the Pharisees asked Jesus to eat with him, and he went into the Pharisee's house and took his place at the table. ³⁷ And a woman in the city, who was a sinner, having learned that he was eating in the Pharisee's house, brought an alabaster jar of ointment. ³⁸ She stood behind him at his feet, weeping, and began to bathe his feet with her tears and to dry them with her hair. Then she continued kissing his feet and anointing them with the ointment. ³⁹ Now when the Pharisee who had invited him saw it, he said to himself, 'If this man were a prophet, he would have known who and what kind of woman this is who is touching him—that she is a sinner.' ⁴⁰ Jesus spoke up and said to him, 'Simon, I have something to say to you.' 'Teacher,' he replied, 'speak.' ⁴¹ 'A certain creditor had two debtors; one owed five hundred denarii, and the other fifty. ⁴² When they could not pay,

he cancelled the debts for both of them. Now which of them will love him more?' ⁴³ Simon answered, 'I suppose the one for whom he cancelled the greater debt.' And Jesus said to him, 'You have judged rightly.' ⁴⁴ Then turning towards the woman, he said to Simon, 'Do you see this woman? I entered your house; you gave me no water for my feet, but she has bathed my feet with her tears and dried them with her hair. ⁴⁵ You gave me no kiss, but from the time I came in she has not stopped kissing my feet. ⁴⁶ You did not anoint my head with oil, but she has anointed my feet with ointment. ⁴⁷ Therefore, I tell you, her sins, which were many, have been forgiven; hence she has shown great love. But the one to whom little is forgiven, loves little.' ⁴⁸ Then he said to her, 'Your sins are forgiven.' ⁴⁹ But those who were at the table with him began to say among themselves, 'Who is this who even forgives sins?' ⁵⁰ And he said to the woman, 'Your faith has saved you; go in peace.'

¹ Soon afterwards he went on through cities and villages, proclaiming and bringing the good news of the kingdom of God. The twelve were with him, ² as well as some women who had been cured of evil spirits and infirmities: Mary, called Magdalene, from whom seven demons had gone out, ³ and Joanna, the wife of Herod's steward Chuza, and Susanna, and many others, who provided for them out of their resources.

POST COMMUNION

See pages 932 to 934 and Table on page 931

SECOND SERVICE

Psalms 52; [53]
Genesis 13
Mark 4.21–41

THIRD SERVICE

Psalm 49
Deuteronomy 10.12–11.1
Acts 23.12–35

PROPER 7

Sunday between 19 and 25 June inclusive (if after Trinity Sunday)

COLLECT

See pages 932 to 935 and Table on page 931

CONTINUOUS

READING   1 Kings 19.1–4, [5–7,] 8–15a

¹ Ahab told Jezebel all that Elijah had done, and how he had killed all the prophets with the sword. ² Then Jezebel sent a messenger to Elijah, saying, 'So may the gods do to me, and more also, if I do not make your life like the life of one of them by this time tomorrow.' ³ Then he was afraid; he got up and fled for his life, and came to Beer-sheba, which belongs to Judah; he left his servant there.

⁴ But he himself went a day's journey into the wilderness, and came and sat down under a solitary broom tree. He asked that he might die: 'It is enough; now, O Lord, take away my life, for I am no better than my ancestors.'
[⁵ Then he lay down under the broom tree and fell asleep. Suddenly an angel touched him and said to him, 'Get up and eat.' ⁶ He looked, and there at his head was a cake baked on hot stones, and a jar of water. He ate and drank, and lay down again. ⁷ The angel of the Lord came a second time, touched him, and said, 'Get up and eat, otherwise the journey will be too much for you.']
⁸ He got up, and ate and drank; then he went in the strength of that food for forty days and forty nights to Horeb the mount of God. ⁹ At that place he came to a cave, and spent the night there.

Then the word of the Lord came to him, saying, 'What are you doing here, Elijah?' ¹⁰ He answered, 'I have been very zealous for the Lord, the God of hosts; for the Israelites have forsaken your covenant, thrown down your altars, and killed your prophets with the sword. I alone am left, and they are seeking my life, to take it away.'

¹¹ He said, 'Go out and stand on the mountain before the Lord, for the Lord is about to pass by.' Now there was a great wind, so strong that it was splitting mountains and breaking rocks in pieces before the Lord, but the Lord was not in the wind; and after the wind an earthquake, but the Lord was not in the earthquake; ¹² and after the earthquake a fire, but the Lord

was not in the fire; and after the fire a sound of sheer silence. ¹³ When Elijah heard it, he wrapped his face in his mantle and went out and stood at the entrance of the cave. Then there came a voice to him that said, 'What are you doing here, Elijah?' ¹⁴ He answered, 'I have been very zealous for the LORD, the God of hosts; for the Israelites have forsaken your covenant, thrown down your altars, and killed your prophets with the sword. I alone am left, and they are seeking my life, to take it away.' ¹⁵ Then the LORD said to him, 'Go, return on your way to the wilderness of Damascus.'

PSALMS   Psalm 42

1   As the deer longs for the water-brooks,
      so longs my soul for you, O God.
2   My soul is athirst for God, athirst for the living God;
      when shall I come to appear before the presence of God?
3   My tears have been my food day and night,
      while all day long they say to me, 'Where now is your God?'
4   I pour out my soul when I think on these things:
      how I went with the multitude and led them into the house of
        God,
5   With the voice of praise and thanksgiving,
      among those who keep holy-day.
6   Why are you so full of heaviness, O my soul?
      and why are you so disquieted within me?
7   Put your trust in God;
      for I will yet give thanks to him, who is the help of my countenance,
        and my God.
8   My soul is heavy within me;
      therefore I will remember you from the land of Jordan, and from
        the peak of Mizar among the heights of Hermon.
9   One deep calls to another in the noise of your cataracts;
      all your rapids and floods have gone over me.
10 The Lord grants his loving-kindness in the daytime;
      in the night season his song is with me, a prayer to the God of my
        life.
11 I will say to the God of my strength, 'Why have you forgotten me?
      and why do I go so heavily while the enemy oppresses me?'
12 While my bones are being broken,
      my enemies mock me to my face;
13 All day long they mock me
      say to me, 'Where now is your God?'
14 Why are you so full of heaviness, O my soul?
      and why are you so disquieted within me?

¹⁵ Put your trust in God;
  for I will yet give thanks to him, who is the help of my countenance,
    and my God.

Psalm 43

¹ Give judgement for me, O God, and defend my cause against an
    ungodly people;
  deliver me from the deceitful and the wicked.
² For you are the God of my strength; why have you put me from
    you?
  and why do I go so heavily while the enemy oppresses me?
³ Send out your light and your truth, that they may lead me,
  and bring me to your holy hill and to your dwelling;
⁴ That I may go to the altar of God, to the God of my joy and gladness;
  and on the harp I will give thanks to you, O God my God.
⁵ Why are you so full of heaviness, O my soul?
  and why are you so disquieted within me?
⁶ Put your trust in God;
  for I will yet give thanks to him, who is the help of my countenance,
    and my God.

OR, IF AN ALTERNATIVE READING IS PREFERRED, USE EITHER
PSALM 42 OR PSALM 43

READING

Galatians 3.23–29

²³ Now before faith came, we were imprisoned and guarded under the law until faith would be revealed. ²⁴ Therefore the law was our disciplinarian until Christ came, so that we might be justified by faith. ²⁵ But now that faith has come, we are no longer subject to a disciplinarian, ²⁶ for in Christ Jesus you are all children of God through faith. ²⁷ As many of you as were baptized into Christ have clothed yourselves with Christ. ²⁸ There is no longer Jew or Greek, there is no longer slave or free, there is no longer male and female; for all of you are one in Christ Jesus. ²⁹ And if you belong to Christ, then you are Abraham's offspring, heirs according to the promise.

GOSPEL

Luke 8.26–39

²⁶ Then they arrived at the country of the Gerasenes, which is opposite Galilee. ²⁷ As he stepped out on land, a man of the city who had demons met him. For a long time he had worn no clothes, and he did not live in a house but in the tombs. ²⁸ When he saw Jesus, he fell down before him and

shouted at the top of his voice, 'What have you to do with me, Jesus, Son of the Most High God? I beg you, do not torment me'— ²⁹ for Jesus had commanded the unclean spirit to come out of the man. (For many times it had seized him; he was kept under guard and bound with chains and shackles, but he would break the bonds and be driven by the demon into the wilds.) ³⁰ Jesus then asked him, 'What is your name?' He said, 'Legion'; for many demons had entered him. ³¹ They begged him not to order them to go back into the abyss.

³² Now there on the hillside a large herd of swine was feeding; and the demons begged Jesus to let them enter these. So he gave them permission. ³³ Then the demons came out of the man and entered the swine, and the herd rushed down the steep bank into the lake and was drowned.

³⁴ When the swineherds saw what had happened, they ran off and told it in the city and in the country. ³⁵ Then people came out to see what had happened, and when they came to Jesus, they found the man from whom the demons had gone sitting at the feet of Jesus, clothed and in his right mind. And they were afraid. ³⁶ Those who had seen it told them how the one who had been possessed by demons had been healed. ³⁷ Then all the people of the surrounding country of the Gerasenes asked Jesus to leave them; for they were seized with great fear. So he got into the boat and returned. ³⁸ The man from whom the demons had gone begged that he might be with him; but Jesus sent him away, saying, ³⁹ 'Return to your home, and declare how much God has done for you.' So he went away, proclaiming throughout the city how much Jesus had done for him.

RELATED

READING   Isaiah 65.1–9

¹ I was ready to be sought out by those who did not ask,
      to be found by those who did not seek me.
   I said, 'Here I am, here I am',
      to a nation that did not call on my name.
² I held out my hands all day long
      to a rebellious people,
   who walk in a way that is not good,
      following their own devices;
³ a people who provoke me
      to my face continually,
   sacrificing in gardens
      and offering incense on bricks;

4 who sit inside tombs,
  and spend the night in secret places;
who eat swine's flesh,
  with broth of abominable things in their vessels;
5 who say, 'Keep to yourself,
  do not come near me, for I am too holy for you.'
These are a smoke in my nostrils,
  a fire that burns all day long.
6 See, it is written before me:
  I will not keep silent, but I will repay;
I will indeed repay into their laps
7   their iniquities and their ancestors' iniquities together,
    says the LORD;
because they offered incense on the mountains
  and reviled me on the hills,
I will measure into their laps
  full payment for their actions.
8 Thus says the LORD:
As the wine is found in the cluster,
  and they say, 'Do not destroy it,
  for there is a blessing in it',
so I will do for my servants' sake,
  and not destroy them all.
9 I will bring forth descendants from Jacob,
  and from Judah inheritors of my mountains;
my chosen shall inherit it,
  and my servants shall settle there.

PSALM   Psalm 22.18–27

18 Be not far away, O Lord;
  you are my strength; hasten to help me.
19 Save me from the sword,
  my life from the power of the dog.
20 Save me from the lion's mouth,
  my wretched body from the horns of wild bulls.
21 I will declare your name to my people;
  in the midst of the congregation I will praise you.
22 Praise the Lord, you that fear him;
  stand in awe of him, O offspring of Israel; all you of Jacob's line,
    give glory.

23 For he does not despise nor abhor the poor in their poverty; neither
     does he hide his face from them;
    but when they cry to him he hears them.
24 My praise is of him in the great assembly;
    I will perform my vows in the presence of those who worship him.
25 The poor shall eat and be satisfied, and those who seek the Lord
     shall praise him:
    'May your heart live for ever!'
26 All the ends of the earth shall remember and turn to the Lord,
    and all the families of the nations shall bow before him.
27 For kingship belongs to the Lord;
    he rules over the nations.

READING   Galatians 3.23–29

23 Now before faith came, we were imprisoned and guarded under the law
until faith would be revealed. 24 Therefore the law was our disciplinarian
until Christ came, so that we might be justified by faith. 25 But now that
faith has come, we are no longer subject to a disciplinarian, 26 for in Christ
Jesus you are all children of God through faith. 27 As many of you as were
baptized into Christ have clothed yourselves with Christ. 28 There is no
longer Jew or Greek, there is no longer slave or free, there is no longer male
and female; for all of you are one in Christ Jesus. 29 And if you belong to
Christ, then you are Abraham's offspring, heirs according to the promise.

GOSPEL   Luke 8.26–39

26 Then they arrived at the country of the Gerasenes, which is opposite
Galilee. 27 As he stepped out on land, a man of the city who had demons
met him. For a long time he had worn no clothes, and he did not live in a
house but in the tombs. 28 When he saw Jesus, he fell down before him and
shouted at the top of his voice, 'What have you to do with me, Jesus, Son
of the Most High God? I beg you, do not torment me'— 29 for Jesus had
commanded the unclean spirit to come out of the man. (For many times it
had seized him; he was kept under guard and bound with chains and
shackles, but he would break the bonds and be driven by the demon into
the wilds.) 30 Jesus then asked him, 'What is your name?' He said, 'Legion';
for many demons had entered him. 31 They begged him not to order them
to go back into the abyss.

32 Now there on the hillside a large herd of swine was feeding; and the
demons begged Jesus to let them enter these. So he gave them permission.

[33] Then the demons came out of the man and entered the swine, and the herd rushed down the steep bank into the lake and was drowned.

[34] When the swineherds saw what had happened, they ran off and told it in the city and in the country. [35] Then people came out to see what had happened, and when they came to Jesus, they found the man from whom the demons had gone sitting at the feet of Jesus, clothed and in his right mind. And they were afraid. [36] Those who had seen it told them how the one who had been possessed by demons had been healed. [37] Then all the people of the surrounding country of the Gerasenes asked Jesus to leave them; for they were seized with great fear. So he got into the boat and returned. [38] The man from whom the demons had gone begged that he might be with him; but Jesus sent him away, saying, [39] 'Return to your home, and declare how much God has done for you.' So he went away, proclaiming throughout the city how much Jesus had done for him.

POST COMMUNION

See pages 932 to 935 and Table on page 931

SECOND SERVICE

Psalms [50;] 57
Genesis 24.1–27
Mark 5.21–43

THIRD SERVICE

Psalm 55.1–15, 17–20
Deuteronomy 11.1–15
Acts 27.1–12

PROPER 8

Sunday between 26 June and 2 July inclusive

COLLECT

See pages 932 to 935 and Table on page 931

CONTINUOUS

READING   2 Kings 2.1–2, 6–14

[1] Now when the LORD was about to take Elijah up to heaven by a whirlwind, Elijah and Elisha were on their way from Gilgal. [2] Elijah said to Elisha, 'Stay here; for the LORD has sent me as far as Bethel.' But Elisha said, 'As

the LORD lives, and as you yourself live, I will not leave you.' So they went down to Bethel.

⁶ Then Elijah said to him, 'Stay here; for the LORD has sent me to the Jordan.' But he said, 'As the LORD lives, and as you yourself live, I will not leave you.' So the two of them went on. ⁷ Fifty men of the company of prophets also went, and stood at some distance from them, as they both were standing by the Jordan. ⁸ Then Elijah took his mantle and rolled it up, and struck the water; the water was parted to the one side and to the other, until the two of them crossed on dry ground.

⁹ When they had crossed, Elijah said to Elisha, 'Tell me what I may do for you, before I am taken from you.' Elisha said, 'Please let me inherit a double share of your spirit.' ¹⁰ He responded, 'You have asked a hard thing; yet, if you see me as I am being taken from you, it will be granted you; if not, it will not.' ¹¹ As they continued walking and talking, a chariot of fire and horses of fire separated the two of them, and Elijah ascended in a whirlwind into heaven. ¹² Elisha kept watching and crying out, 'Father, father! The chariots of Israel and its horsemen!' But when he could no longer see him, he grasped his own clothes and tore them in two pieces.

¹³ He picked up the mantle of Elijah that had fallen from him, and went back and stood on the bank of the Jordan. ¹⁴ He took the mantle of Elijah that had fallen from him, and struck the water, saying, 'Where is the LORD, the God of Elijah?' When he had struck the water, the water was parted to the one side and to the other, and Elisha went over.

PSALM   Psalm 77.[1–2,] 11–20

[¹ I will cry aloud to God;
    I will cry aloud and he will hear me.
 ² In the day of my trouble I sought the Lord;
    my hands were stretched out by night and did not tire; I refused
        to be comforted.]

¹¹ I will remember the works of the Lord,
    and call to mind your wonders of old time.
¹² I will meditate on all your acts
    and ponder your mighty deeds.
¹³ Your way, O God, is holy;
    who is so great a god as our God?
¹⁴ You are the God who works wonders
    and have declared your power among the peoples.
¹⁵ By your strength you have redeemed your people,
    the children of Jacob and Joseph.

16   The waters saw you, O God; the waters saw you and trembled;
      the very depths were shaken.
17   The clouds poured out water; the skies thundered;
      your arrows flashed to and fro;
18   The sound of your thunder was in the whirlwind; your lightnings
        lit up the world;
      the earth trembled and shook.
19   Your way was in the sea, and your paths in the great waters,
      yet your footsteps were not seen.
20   You led your people like a flock
      by the hand of Moses and Aaron.

READING   Galatians 5.1, 13–25

1 For freedom Christ has set us free. Stand firm, therefore, and do not
submit again to a yoke of slavery.

13 For you were called to freedom, brothers and sisters; only do not use
your freedom as an opportunity for self-indulgence, but through love
become slaves to one another. 14 For the whole law is summed up in a single
commandment, 'You shall love your neighbour as yourself.' 15 If, however,
you bite and devour one another, take care that you are not consumed by
one another.

16 Live by the Spirit, I say, and do not gratify the desires of the flesh. 17 For
what the flesh desires is opposed to the Spirit, and what the Spirit desires
is opposed to the flesh; for these are opposed to each other, to prevent you
from doing what you want. 18 But if you are led by the Spirit, you are not
subject to the law. 19 Now the works of the flesh are obvious: fornication,
impurity, licentiousness, 20 idolatry, sorcery, enmities, strife, jealousy,
anger, quarrels, dissensions, factions, 21 envy, drunkenness, carousing, and
things like these. I am warning you, as I warned you before: those who do
such things will not inherit the kingdom of God.

22 By contrast, the fruit of the Spirit is love, joy, peace, patience, kindness,
generosity, faithfulness, 23 gentleness, and self-control. There is no law
against such things. 24 And those who belong to Christ Jesus have crucified
the flesh with its passions and desires. 25 If we live by the Spirit, let us also
be guided by the Spirit.

GOSPEL   Luke 9.51–62

[51] When the days drew near for him to be taken up, he set his face to go to Jerusalem. [52] And he sent messengers ahead of him. On their way they entered a village of the Samaritans to make ready for him; [53] but they did not receive him, because his face was set towards Jerusalem. [54] When his disciples James and John saw it, they said, 'Lord, do you want us to command fire to come down from heaven and consume them?' [55] But he turned and rebuked them. [56] Then they went on to another village.

[57] As they were going along the road, someone said to him, 'I will follow you wherever you go.' [58] And Jesus said to him, 'Foxes have holes, and birds of the air have nests; but the Son of Man has nowhere to lay his head.' [59] To another he said, 'Follow me.' But he said, 'Lord, first let me go and bury my father.' [60] But Jesus said to him, 'Let the dead bury their own dead; but as for you, go and proclaim the kingdom of God.' [61] Another said, 'I will follow you, Lord; but let me first say farewell to those at my home.' [62] Jesus said to him, 'No one who puts a hand to the plough and looks back is fit for the kingdom of God.'

RELATED

READING   1 Kings 19.15–16, 19–21

[15] Then the LORD said to him, 'Go, return on your way to the wilderness of Damascus; when you arrive, you shall anoint Hazael as king over Aram. [16] Also you shall anoint Jehu son of Nimshi as king over Israel; and you shall anoint Elisha son of Shaphat of Abel-meholah as prophet in your place.'

[19] So he set out from there, and found Elisha son of Shaphat, who was ploughing. There were twelve yoke of oxen ahead of him, and he was with the twelfth. Elijah passed by him and threw his mantle over him. [20] He left the oxen, ran after Elijah, and said, 'Let me kiss my father and my mother, and then I will follow you.' Then Elijah said to him, 'Go back again; for what have I done to you?' [21] He returned from following him, took the yoke of oxen, and slaughtered them; using the equipment from the oxen, he boiled their flesh, and gave it to the people, and they ate. Then he set out and followed Elijah, and became his servant.

PSALM   Psalm 16

¹ Protect me, O God, for I take refuge in you;
   I have said to the Lord, 'You are my Lord, my good above all other.'
² All my delight is upon the godly that are in the land,
   upon those who are noble among the people.
³ But those who run after other gods
   shall have their troubles multiplied.
⁴ Their libations of blood I will not offer,
   nor take the names of their gods upon my lips.
⁵ O Lord, you are my portion and my cup;
   it is you who uphold my lot.
⁶ My boundaries enclose a pleasant land;
   indeed, I have a goodly heritage.
⁷ I will bless the Lord who gives me counsel;
   my heart teaches me, night after night.
⁸ I have set the Lord always before me;
   because he is at my right hand I shall not fall.
⁹ My heart, therefore, is glad and my spirit rejoices;
   my body also shall rest in hope.
¹⁰ For you will not abandon me to the grave,
   nor let your holy one see the Pit.
¹¹ You will show me the path of life;
   in your presence there is fullness of joy, and in your right hand
       are pleasures for evermore.

READING   Galatians 5.1, 13–25

¹ For freedom Christ has set us free. Stand firm, therefore, and do not submit again to a yoke of slavery.

¹³ For you were called to freedom, brothers and sisters; only do not use your freedom as an opportunity for self-indulgence, but through love become slaves to one another. ¹⁴ For the whole law is summed up in a single commandment, 'You shall love your neighbour as yourself.' ¹⁵ If, however, you bite and devour one another, take care that you are not consumed by one another.

¹⁶ Live by the Spirit, I say, and do not gratify the desires of the flesh. ¹⁷ For what the flesh desires is opposed to the Spirit, and what the Spirit desires is opposed to the flesh; for these are opposed to each other, to prevent you from doing what you want. ¹⁸ But if you are led by the Spirit, you are not subject to the law. ¹⁹ Now the works of the flesh are obvious: fornication, impurity, licentiousness, ²⁰ idolatry, sorcery, enmities, strife, jealousy,

anger, quarrels, dissensions, factions, 21 envy, drunkenness, carousing, and things like these. I am warning you, as I warned you before: those who do such things will not inherit the kingdom of God.

22 By contrast, the fruit of the Spirit is love, joy, peace, patience, kindness, generosity, faithfulness, 23 gentleness, and self-control. There is no law against such things. 24 And those who belong to Christ Jesus have crucified the flesh with its passions and desires. 25 If we live by the Spirit, let us also be guided by the Spirit.

GOSPEL   Luke 9.51–62

51 When the days drew near for him to be taken up, he set his face to go to Jerusalem. 52 And he sent messengers ahead of him. On their way they entered a village of the Samaritans to make ready for him; 53 but they did not receive him, because his face was set towards Jerusalem. 54 When his disciples James and John saw it, they said, 'Lord, do you want us to command fire to come down from heaven and consume them?' 55 But he turned and rebuked them. 56 Then they went on to another village.

57 As they were going along the road, someone said to him, 'I will follow you wherever you go.' 58 And Jesus said to him, 'Foxes have holes, and birds of the air have nests; but the Son of Man has nowhere to lay his head.' 59 To another he said, 'Follow me.' But he said, 'Lord, first let me go and bury my father.' 60 But Jesus said to him, 'Let the dead bury their own dead; but as for you, go and proclaim the kingdom of God.' 61 Another said, 'I will follow you, Lord; but let me first say farewell to those at my home.' 62 Jesus said to him, 'No one who puts a hand to the plough and looks back is fit for the kingdom of God.'

POST COMMUNION

See pages 932 to 936 and Table on page 931

SECOND SERVICE

Psalms [59.1–6, 18–20;] 60
Genesis 27.1–40
Mark 6.1–6

THIRD SERVICE

Psalm 64
Deuteronomy 15.1–11
Acts 27.[13–32,] 33–44

PROPER 9

Sunday between 3 and 9 July inclusive

COLLECT

See pages 932 to 936 and Table on page 931

CONTINUOUS

READING   2 Kings 5.1–14

¹ Naaman, commander of the army of the king of Aram, was a great man and in high favour with his master, because by him the Lord had given victory to Aram. The man, though a mighty warrior, suffered from leprosy. ² Now the Arameans on one of their raids had taken a young girl captive from the land of Israel, and she served Naaman's wife. ³ She said to her mistress, 'If only my lord were with the prophet who is in Samaria! He would cure him of his leprosy.' ⁴ So Naaman went in and told his lord just what the girl from the land of Israel had said. ⁵ And the king of Aram said, 'Go then, and I will send along a letter to the king of Israel.'

He went, taking with him ten talents of silver, six thousand shekels of gold, and ten sets of garments. ⁶ He brought the letter to the king of Israel, which read, 'When this letter reaches you, know that I have sent to you my servant Naaman, that you may cure him of his leprosy.' ⁷ When the king of Israel read the letter, he tore his clothes and said, 'Am I God, to give death or life, that this man sends word to me to cure a man of his leprosy? Just look and see how he is trying to pick a quarrel with me.'

⁸ But when Elisha the man of God heard that the king of Israel had torn his clothes, he sent a message to the king, 'Why have you torn your clothes? Let him come to me, that he may learn that there is a prophet in Israel.' ⁹ So Naaman came with his horses and chariots, and halted at the entrance of Elisha's house. ¹⁰ Elisha sent a messenger to him, saying, 'Go, wash in the Jordan seven times, and your flesh shall be restored and you shall be clean.' ¹¹ But Naaman became angry and went away, saying, 'I thought that for me he would surely come out, and stand and call on the name of the Lord his God, and would wave his hand over the spot, and cure the leprosy! ¹² Are not Abana and Pharpar, the rivers of Damascus, better than all the waters of Israel? Could I not wash in them, and be clean?' He turned and went away in a rage. ¹³ But his servants approached and said to him, 'Father, if the prophet had commanded you to do something difficult, would you not have done it? How much more, when all he said to you was, "Wash,

and be clean"?' ¹⁴ So he went down and immersed himself seven times in the Jordan, according to the word of the man of God; his flesh was restored like the flesh of a young boy, and he was clean.

PSALM   Psalm 30

¹ I will exalt you, O Lord, because you have lifted me up
    and have not let my enemies triumph over me.
² O Lord my God, I cried out to you,
    and you restored me to health.
³ You brought me up, O Lord, from the dead;
    you restored my life as I was going down to the grave.
⁴ Sing to the Lord, you servants of his;
    give thanks for the remembrance of his holiness.
⁵ For his wrath endures but the twinkling of an eye,
    his favour for a lifetime.
⁶ Weeping may spend the night,
    but joy comes in the morning.
⁷ While I felt secure, I said, 'I shall never be disturbed.
    You, Lord, with your favour, made me as strong as the mountains.'
⁸ Then you hid your face,
    and I was filled with fear.
⁹ I cried to you, O Lord;
    I pleaded with the Lord, saying,
¹⁰ 'What profit is there in my blood, if I go down to the Pit?
    will the dust praise you or declare your faithfulness?
¹¹ Hear, O Lord, and have mercy upon me;
    O Lord, be my helper.'
¹² You have turned my wailing into dancing;
    you have put off my sack-cloth and clothed me with joy;
¹³ Therefore my heart sings to you without ceasing;
    O Lord my God, I will give you thanks for ever.

READING   Galatians 6.[1–6,] 7–16

[¹ My friends, if anyone is detected in a transgression, you who have received the Spirit should restore such a one in a spirit of gentleness. Take care that you yourselves are not tempted. ² Bear one another's burdens, and in this way you will fulfil the law of Christ. ³ For if those who are nothing think they are something, they deceive themselves. ⁴ All must test their own work; then that work, rather than their neighbour's work, will become a cause for pride. ⁵ For all must carry their own loads.

⁶ Those who are taught the word must share in all good things with their teacher.]

⁷ Do not be deceived; God is not mocked, for you reap whatever you sow. ⁸ If you sow to your own flesh, you will reap corruption from the flesh; but if you sow to the Spirit, you will reap eternal life from the Spirit. ⁹ So let us not grow weary in doing what is right, for we will reap at harvest time, if we do not give up. ¹⁰ So then, whenever we have an opportunity, let us work for the good of all, and especially for those of the family of faith.

¹¹ See what large letters I make when I am writing in my own hand! ¹² It is those who want to make a good showing in the flesh that try to compel you to be circumcised—only that they may not be persecuted for the cross of Christ. ¹³ Even the circumcised do not themselves obey the law, but they want you to be circumcised so that they may boast about your flesh. ¹⁴ May I never boast of anything except the cross of our Lord Jesus Christ, by which the world has been crucified to me, and I to the world. ¹⁵ For neither circumcision nor uncircumcision is anything; but a new creation is everything! ¹⁶ As for those who will follow this rule—peace be upon them, and mercy, and upon the Israel of God.

GOSPEL   Luke 10.1–11, 16–20

¹ After this the Lord appointed seventy others and sent them on ahead of him in pairs to every town and place where he himself intended to go. ² He said to them, 'The harvest is plentiful, but the labourers are few; therefore ask the Lord of the harvest to send out labourers into his harvest. ³ Go on your way. See, I am sending you out like lambs into the midst of wolves. ⁴ Carry no purse, no bag, no sandals; and greet no one on the road. ⁵ Whatever house you enter, first say, "Peace to this house!" ⁶ And if anyone is there who shares in peace, your peace will rest on that person; but if not, it will return to you. ⁷ Remain in the same house, eating and drinking whatever they provide, for the labourer deserves to be paid. Do not move about from house to house. ⁸ Whenever you enter a town and its people welcome you, eat what is set before you; ⁹ cure the sick who are there, and say to them, "The kingdom of God has come near to you." ¹⁰ But whenever you enter a town and they do not welcome you, go out into its streets and say, ¹¹ "Even the dust of your town that clings to our feet, we wipe off in protest against you. Yet know this: the kingdom of God has come near." '

¹⁶ 'Whoever listens to you listens to me, and whoever rejects you rejects me, and whoever rejects me rejects the one who sent me.'

¹⁷ The seventy returned with joy, saying, 'Lord, in your name even the demons submit to us!' ¹⁸ He said to them, 'I watched Satan fall from heaven

like a flash of lightning. ¹⁹ See, I have given you authority to tread on snakes and scorpions, and over all the power of the enemy; and nothing will hurt you. ²⁰ Nevertheless, do not rejoice at this, that the spirits submit to you, but rejoice that your names are written in heaven.'

RELATED

READING   Isaiah 66.10–14

¹⁰ Rejoice with Jerusalem, and be glad for her,
      all you who love her;
   rejoice with her in joy,
      all you who mourn over her—
¹¹ that you may nurse and be satisfied
      from her consoling breast;
   that you may drink deeply with delight
      from her glorious bosom.
¹² For thus says the LORD:
   I will extend prosperity to her like a river,
      and the wealth of the nations like an overflowing stream;
   and you shall nurse and be carried on her arm,
      and dandled on her knees.
¹³ As a mother comforts her child,
      so I will comfort you;
   you shall be comforted in Jerusalem.
¹⁴ You shall see, and your heart shall rejoice;
      your bodies shall flourish like the grass;
   and it shall be known that the hand of the LORD is with his servants,
      and his indignation is against his enemies.

PSALM   Psalm 66.1–8

¹ Be joyful in God, all you lands;
   sing the glory of his name; sing the glory of his praise.
² Say to God, 'How awesome are your deeds!
   because of your great strength your enemies cringe before you.
³ All the earth bows down before you,
   sings to you, sings out your name.'
⁴ Come now and see the works of God,
   how wonderful he is in his doing towards all people.

5   He turned the sea into dry land, so that they went through the
      water on foot,
      and there we rejoiced in him.
6   In his might he rules for ever; his eyes keep watch over the nations;
      let no rebel rise up against him.
7   Bless our God, you peoples;
      make the voice of his praise to be heard;
8   Who holds our souls in life,
      and will not allow our feet to slip.

READING   Galatians 6.[1-6,] 7-16

[¹ My friends, if anyone is detected in a transgression, you who have
received the Spirit should restore such a one in a spirit of gentleness. Take
care that you yourselves are not tempted. ² Bear one another's burdens, and
in this way you will fulfil the law of Christ. ³ For if those who are nothing
think they are something, they deceive themselves. ⁴ All must test their
own work; then that work, rather than their neighbour's work, will become
a cause for pride. ⁵ For all must carry their own loads.

⁶ Those who are taught the word must share in all good things with their
teacher.]

⁷ Do not be deceived; God is not mocked, for you reap whatever you sow.
⁸ If you sow to your own flesh, you will reap corruption from the flesh; but
if you sow to the Spirit, you will reap eternal life from the Spirit. ⁹ So let us
not grow weary in doing what is right, for we will reap at harvest time, if
we do not give up. ¹⁰ So then, whenever we have an opportunity, let us work
for the good of all, and especially for those of the family of faith.

¹¹ See what large letters I make when I am writing in my own hand! ¹² It
is those who want to make a good showing in the flesh that try to compel
you to be circumcised—only that they may not be persecuted for the cross
of Christ. ¹³ Even the circumcised do not themselves obey the law, but they
want you to be circumcised so that they may boast about your flesh. ¹⁴ May
I never boast of anything except the cross of our Lord Jesus Christ, by which
the world has been crucified to me, and I to the world. ¹⁵ For neither
circumcision nor uncircumcision is anything; but a new creation is everything! ¹⁶ As for those who will follow this rule—peace be upon them, and
mercy, and upon the Israel of God.

GOSPEL   Luke 10.1–11, 16–20

¹ After this the Lord appointed seventy others and sent them on ahead of him in pairs to every town and place where he himself intended to go. ² He said to them, 'The harvest is plentiful, but the labourers are few; therefore ask the Lord of the harvest to send out labourers into his harvest. ³ Go on your way. See, I am sending you out like lambs into the midst of wolves. ⁴ Carry no purse, no bag, no sandals; and greet no one on the road. ⁵ Whatever house you enter, first say, "Peace to this house!" ⁶ And if anyone is there who shares in peace, your peace will rest on that person; but if not, it will return to you. ⁷ Remain in the same house, eating and drinking whatever they provide, for the labourer deserves to be paid. Do not move about from house to house. ⁸ Whenever you enter a town and its people welcome you, eat what is set before you; ⁹ cure the sick who are there, and say to them, "The kingdom of God has come near to you." ¹⁰ But whenever you enter a town and they do not welcome you, go out into its streets and say, ¹¹ "Even the dust of your town that clings to our feet, we wipe off in protest against you. Yet know this: the kingdom of God has come near." '

¹⁶ 'Whoever listens to you listens to me, and whoever rejects you rejects me, and whoever rejects me rejects the one who sent me.'

¹⁷ The seventy returned with joy, saying, 'Lord, in your name even the demons submit to us!' ¹⁸ He said to them, 'I watched Satan fall from heaven like a flash of lightning. ¹⁹ See, I have given you authority to tread on snakes and scorpions, and over all the power of the enemy; and nothing will hurt you. ²⁰ Nevertheless, do not rejoice at this, that the spirits submit to you, but rejoice that your names are written in heaven.'

POST COMMUNION

See pages 933 to 937 and Table on page 931

SECOND SERVICE	THIRD SERVICE
Psalms 65; [70]	**Psalm 74**
Genesis 29.1–20	**Deuteronomy 24.10–22**
Mark 6.7–29	**Acts 28.1–16**

PROPER 10

Sunday between 10 and 16 July inclusive

COLLECT

See pages 933 to 937 and Table on page 931

CONTINUOUS

READING   Amos 7.7–17

⁷ This is what he showed me: the Lord was standing beside a wall built with a plumb-line, with a plumb-line in his hand. ⁸ And the LORD said to me, 'Amos, what do you see?' And I said, 'A plumb-line.' Then the Lord said,

   'See, I am setting a plumb-line
     in the midst of my people Israel;
     I will never again pass them by;
⁹   the high places of Isaac shall be made desolate,
     and the sanctuaries of Israel shall be laid waste,
     and I will rise against the house of Jeroboam with the sword.'

¹⁰ Then Amaziah, the priest of Bethel, sent to King Jeroboam of Israel, saying, 'Amos has conspired against you in the very centre of the house of Israel; the land is not able to bear all his words. ¹¹ For thus Amos has said,

   "Jeroboam shall die by the sword,
     and Israel must go into exile
     away from his land." '

¹² And Amaziah said to Amos, 'O seer, go, flee away to the land of Judah, earn your bread there, and prophesy there; ¹³ but never again prophesy at Bethel, for it is the king's sanctuary, and it is a temple of the kingdom.'

¹⁴ Then Amos answered Amaziah, 'I am no prophet, nor a prophet's son; but I am a herdsman, and a dresser of sycomore trees, ¹⁵ and the LORD took me from following the flock, and the LORD said to me, "Go, prophesy to my people Israel."
¹⁶ 'Now therefore hear the word of the LORD.

   You say, "Do not prophesy against Israel,
     and do not preach against the house of Isaac."

[17] Therefore, thus says the LORD:
"Your wife shall become a prostitute in the city,
and your sons and your daughters shall fall by the sword,
and your land shall be parcelled out by line;
you yourself shall die in an unclean land,
and Israel shall surely go into exile away from its land."'

PSALM   Psalm 82

[1] God takes his stand in the council of heaven;
he gives judgement in the midst of the gods:
[2] 'How long will you judge unjustly,
and show favour to the wicked?
[3] Save the weak and the orphan;
defend the humble and needy;
[4] Rescue the weak and the poor;
deliver them from the power of the wicked.
[5] They do not know, neither do they understand; they go about in
darkness;
all the foundations of the earth are shaken.
[6] Now I say to you, "You are gods,
and all of you children of the Most High;
[7] Nevertheless, you shall die like mortals,
and fall like any prince."'
[8] Arise, O God, and rule the earth,
for you shall take all nations for your own.

READING   Colossians 1.1–14

[1] Paul, an apostle of Christ Jesus by the will of God, and Timothy our brother,

[2] To the saints and faithful brothers and sisters in Christ in Colossae:
Grace to you and peace from God our Father.

[3] In our prayers for you we always thank God, the Father of our Lord Jesus Christ, [4] for we have heard of your faith in Christ Jesus and of the love that you have for all the saints, [5] because of the hope laid up for you in heaven. You have heard of this hope before in the word of the truth, the gospel [6] that has come to you. Just as it is bearing fruit and growing in the whole world, so it has been bearing fruit among yourselves from the day you heard it and truly comprehended the grace of God. [7] This you learned from Epaphras, our beloved fellow-servant. He is a faithful minister of Christ on your behalf, [8] and he has made known to us your love in the Spirit.

⁹ For this reason, since the day we heard it, we have not ceased praying for you and asking that you may be filled with the knowledge of God's will in all spiritual wisdom and understanding, ¹⁰ so that you may lead lives worthy of the Lord, fully pleasing to him, as you bear fruit in every good work and as you grow in the knowledge of God. ¹¹ May you be made strong with all the strength that comes from his glorious power, and may you be prepared to endure everything with patience, while joyfully ¹² giving thanks to the Father, who has enabled you to share in the inheritance of the saints in the light. ¹³ He has rescued us from the power of darkness and transferred us into the kingdom of his beloved Son, ¹⁴ in whom we have redemption, the forgiveness of sins.

GOSPEL   Luke 10.25-37

²⁵ Just then a lawyer stood up to test Jesus. 'Teacher,' he said, 'what must I do to inherit eternal life?' ²⁶ He said to him, 'What is written in the law? What do you read there?' ²⁷ He answered, 'You shall love the Lord your God with all your heart, and with all your soul, and with all your strength, and with all your mind; and your neighbour as yourself.' ²⁸ And he said to him, 'You have given the right answer; do this, and you will live.'

²⁹ But wanting to justify himself, he asked Jesus, 'And who is my neighbour?' ³⁰ Jesus replied, 'A man was going down from Jerusalem to Jericho, and fell into the hands of robbers, who stripped him, beat him, and went away, leaving him half dead. ³¹ Now by chance a priest was going down that road; and when he saw him, he passed by on the other side. ³² So likewise a Levite, when he came to the place and saw him, passed by on the other side. ³³ But a Samaritan while travelling came near him; and when he saw him, he was moved with pity. ³⁴ He went to him and bandaged his wounds, having poured oil and wine on them. Then he put him on his own animal, brought him to an inn, and took care of him. ³⁵ The next day he took out two denarii, gave them to the innkeeper, and said, "Take care of him; and when I come back, I will repay you whatever more you spend." ³⁶ Which of these three, do you think, was a neighbour to the man who fell into the hands of the robbers?' ³⁷ He said, 'The one who showed him mercy.' Jesus said to him, 'Go and do likewise.'

RELATED

READING   Deuteronomy 30.9–14

⁹ And the Lᴏʀᴅ your God will make you abundantly prosperous in all your undertakings, in the fruit of your body, in the fruit of your livestock, and in the fruit of your soil. For the Lᴏʀᴅ will again take delight in prospering you, just as he delighted in prospering your ancestors, ¹⁰ when you obey the Lᴏʀᴅ your God by observing his commandments and decrees that are written in this book of the law, because you turn to the Lᴏʀᴅ your God with all your heart and with all your soul.

¹¹ Surely, this commandment that I am commanding you today is not too hard for you, nor is it too far away. ¹² It is not in heaven, that you should say, 'Who will go up to heaven for us, and get it for us so that we may hear it and observe it?' ¹³ Neither is it beyond the sea, that you should say, 'Who will cross to the other side of the sea for us, and get it for us so that we may hear it and observe it?' ¹⁴ No, the word is very near to you; it is in your mouth and in your heart for you to observe.

PSALM   Psalm 25.1–9

1 To you, O Lord, I lift up my soul; my God, I put my trust in you;
   let me not be humiliated, nor let my enemies triumph over me.
2 Let none who look to you be put to shame;
   let the treacherous be disappointed in their schemes.
3 Show me your ways, O Lord,
   and teach me your paths.
4 Lead me in your truth and teach me,
   for you are the God of my salvation; in you have I trusted all the
      day long.
5 Remember, O Lord, your compassion and love,
   for they are from everlasting.
6 Remember not the sins of my youth and my transgressions;
   remember me according to your love and for the sake of your
      goodness, O Lord.
7 Gracious and upright is the Lord;
   therefore he teaches sinners in his way.
8 He guides the humble in doing right
   and teaches his way to the lowly.
9 All the paths of the Lord are love and faithfulness
   to those who keep his covenant and his testimonies.

READING   Colossians 1.1–14

¹ Paul, an apostle of Christ Jesus by the will of God, and Timothy our brother,

² To the saints and faithful brothers and sisters in Christ in Colossae: Grace to you and peace from God our Father.

³ In our prayers for you we always thank God, the Father of our Lord Jesus Christ, ⁴ for we have heard of your faith in Christ Jesus and of the love that you have for all the saints, ⁵ because of the hope laid up for you in heaven. You have heard of this hope before in the word of the truth, the gospel ⁶ that has come to you. Just as it is bearing fruit and growing in the whole world, so it has been bearing fruit among yourselves from the day you heard it and truly comprehended the grace of God. ⁷ This you learned from Epaphras, our beloved fellow-servant. He is a faithful minister of Christ on your behalf, ⁸ and he has made known to us your love in the Spirit.

⁹ For this reason, since the day we heard it, we have not ceased praying for you and asking that you may be filled with the knowledge of God's will in all spiritual wisdom and understanding, ¹⁰ so that you may lead lives worthy of the Lord, fully pleasing to him, as you bear fruit in every good work and as you grow in the knowledge of God. ¹¹ May you be made strong with all the strength that comes from his glorious power, and may you be prepared to endure everything with patience, while joyfully ¹² giving thanks to the Father, who has enabled you to share in the inheritance of the saints in the light. ¹³ He has rescued us from the power of darkness and transferred us into the kingdom of his beloved Son, ¹⁴ in whom we have redemption, the forgiveness of sins.

GOSPEL   Luke 10.25–37

²⁵ Just then a lawyer stood up to test Jesus. 'Teacher,' he said, 'what must I do to inherit eternal life?' ²⁶ He said to him, 'What is written in the law? What do you read there?' ²⁷ He answered, 'You shall love the Lord your God with all your heart, and with all your soul, and with all your strength, and with all your mind; and your neighbour as yourself.' ²⁸ And he said to him, 'You have given the right answer; do this, and you will live.'

²⁹ But wanting to justify himself, he asked Jesus, 'And who is my neighbour?' ³⁰ Jesus replied, 'A man was going down from Jerusalem to Jericho, and fell into the hands of robbers, who stripped him, beat him, and went away, leaving him half dead. ³¹ Now by chance a priest was going down that road; and when he saw him, he passed by on the other side. ³² So likewise a Levite, when he came to the place and saw him, passed by on the other

side. [33] But a Samaritan while travelling came near him; and when he saw him, he was moved with pity. [34] He went to him and bandaged his wounds, having poured oil and wine on them. Then he put him on his own animal, brought him to an inn, and took care of him. [35] The next day he took out two denarii, gave them to the innkeeper, and said, "Take care of him; and when I come back, I will repay you whatever more you spend." [36] Which of these three, do you think, was a neighbour to the man who fell into the hands of the robbers?' [37] He said, 'The one who showed him mercy.' Jesus said to him, 'Go and do likewise.'

POST COMMUNION

See pages 934 to 937 and Table on page 931

SECOND SERVICE

Psalm 77.1–12, [13–20]
Genesis 32.9–30
Mark 7.1–23

THIRD SERVICE

Psalm 76
Deuteronomy 28.1–14
Acts 28.17–31

PROPER 11

Sunday between 17 and 23 July inclusive

COLLECT

See pages 934 to 938 and Table on page 931

CONTINUOUS

READING   Amos 8.1–12

[1] This is what the Lord God showed me—a basket of summer fruit. [2] He said, 'Amos, what do you see?' And I said, 'A basket of summer fruit.' Then the Lord said to me,

'The end has come upon my people Israel;
    I will never again pass them by.
[3]   The songs of the temple shall become wailings on that day,'

says the Lord God;

'the dead bodies shall be many,
    cast out in every place. Be silent!'

⁴ Hear this, you that trample on the needy,
    and bring to ruin the poor of the land,
⁵ saying, 'When will the new moon be over
    so that we may sell grain;
and the sabbath,
    so that we may offer wheat for sale?
We will make the ephah small and the shekel great,
    and practise deceit with false balances,
⁶ buying the poor for silver
    and the needy for a pair of sandals,
    and selling the sweepings of the wheat.'
⁷ The LORD has sworn by the pride of Jacob:
Surely I will never forget any of their deeds.
⁸ Shall not the land tremble on this account,
    and everyone mourn who lives in it,
and all of it rise like the Nile,
    and be tossed about and sink again, like the Nile of Egypt?
⁹ On that day, says the Lord GOD,
    I will make the sun go down at noon,
    and darken the earth in broad daylight.
¹⁰ I will turn your feasts into mourning,
    and all your songs into lamentation;
I will bring sackcloth on all loins,
    and baldness on every head;
I will make it like the mourning for an only son,
    and the end of it like a bitter day.
¹¹ The time is surely coming, says the Lord GOD,
    when I will send a famine on the land;
not a famine of bread, or a thirst for water,
    but of hearing the words of the LORD.
¹² They shall wander from sea to sea,
    and from north to east;
they shall run to and fro, seeking the word of the LORD,
    but they shall not find it.

PSALM   Psalm 52

¹ You tyrant, why do you boast of wickedness
    against the godly all day long?
² You plot ruin; your tongue is like a sharpened razor,
    O worker of deception.
³ You love evil more than good
    and lying more than speaking the truth.

4   You love all words that hurt,
    O you deceitful tongue.
5   O that God would demolish you utterly,
    topple you and snatch you from your dwelling and root you out of
      the land of the living!
6   The righteous shall see and tremble,
    and they shall laugh, saying,
7   'This is the one who did not take God for a refuge,
    but trusted in great wealth and relied upon wickedness.'
8   But I am like a green olive tree in the house of God;
    I trust in the mercy of God for ever and ever.
9   I will give you thanks for what you have done
    and declare the goodness of your name in the presence of the
      godly.

READING   Colossians 1.15–28

¹⁵ He is the image of the invisible God, the firstborn of all creation; ¹⁶ for
in him all things in heaven and on earth were created, things visible and
invisible, whether thrones or dominions or rulers or powers—all things
have been created through him and for him. ¹⁷ He himself is before all
things, and in him all things hold together. ¹⁸ He is the head of the body,
the church; he is the beginning, the firstborn from the dead, so that he
might come to have first place in everything. ¹⁹ For in him all the fullness
of God was pleased to dwell, ²⁰ and through him God was pleased to reconcile to himself all things, whether on earth or in heaven, by making
peace through the blood of his cross.

²¹ And you who were once estranged and hostile in mind, doing evil deeds,
²² he has now reconciled in his fleshly body through death, so as to present
you holy and blameless and irreproachable before him— ²³ provided that
you continue securely established and steadfast in the faith, without shifting from the hope promised by the gospel that you heard, which has been
proclaimed to every creature under heaven. I, Paul, became a servant of
this gospel.

²⁴ I am now rejoicing in my sufferings for your sake, and in my flesh I am
completing what is lacking in Christ's afflictions for the sake of his body,
that is, the church. ²⁵ I became its servant according to God's commission
that was given to me for you, to make the word of God fully known, ²⁶ the
mystery that has been hidden throughout the ages and generations but
has now been revealed to his saints. ²⁷ To them God chose to make known
how great among the Gentiles are the riches of the glory of this mystery,

which is Christ in you, the hope of glory. [28] It is he whom we proclaim, warning everyone and teaching everyone in all wisdom, so that we may present everyone mature in Christ.

GOSPEL   Luke 10.38–42

[38] Now as they went on their way, he entered a certain village, where a woman named Martha welcomed him into her home. [39] She had a sister named Mary, who sat at the Lord's feet and listened to what he was saying. [40] But Martha was distracted by her many tasks; so she came to him and asked, 'Lord, do you not care that my sister has left me to do all the work by myself? Tell her then to help me.' [41] But the Lord answered her, 'Martha, Martha, you are worried and distracted by many things; [42] there is need of only one thing. Mary has chosen the better part, which will not be taken away from her.'

RELATED

READING   Genesis 18.1–10a

[1] The LORD appeared to Abraham by the oaks of Mamre, as he sat at the entrance of his tent in the heat of the day. [2] He looked up and saw three men standing near him. When he saw them, he ran from the tent entrance to meet them, and bowed down to the ground. [3] He said, 'My lord, if I find favour with you, do not pass by your servant. [4] Let a little water be brought, and wash your feet, and rest yourselves under the tree. [5] Let me bring a little bread, that you may refresh yourselves, and after that you may pass on—since you have come to your servant.' So they said, 'Do as you have said.' [6] And Abraham hastened into the tent to Sarah, and said, 'Make ready quickly three measures of choice flour, knead it, and make cakes.' [7] Abraham ran to the herd, and took a calf, tender and good, and gave it to the servant, who hastened to prepare it. [8] Then he took curds and milk and the calf that he had prepared, and set it before them; and he stood by them under the tree while they ate.

[9] They said to him, 'Where is your wife Sarah?' And he said, 'There, in the tent.' [10] Then one said, 'I will surely return to you in due season, and your wife Sarah shall have a son.'

PSALM   Psalm 15

¹ Lord, who may dwell in your tabernacle?
who may abide upon your holy hill?
² Whoever leads a blameless life and does what is right,
who speaks the truth from his heart.
³ There is no guile upon his tongue; he does no evil to his friend;
he does not heap contempt upon his neighbour.
⁴ In his sight the wicked is rejected,
but he honours those who fear the Lord.
⁵ He has sworn to do no wrong
and does not take back his word.
⁶ He does not give his money in hope of gain,
nor does he take a bribe against the innocent.
⁷ Whoever does these things
shall never be overthrown.

READING   Colossians 1.15–28

¹⁵ He is the image of the invisible God, the firstborn of all creation; ¹⁶ for in him all things in heaven and on earth were created, things visible and invisible, whether thrones or dominions or rulers or powers—all things have been created through him and for him. ¹⁷ He himself is before all things, and in him all things hold together. ¹⁸ He is the head of the body, the church; he is the beginning, the firstborn from the dead, so that he might come to have first place in everything. ¹⁹ For in him all the fullness of God was pleased to dwell, ²⁰ and through him God was pleased to reconcile to himself all things, whether on earth or in heaven, by making peace through the blood of his cross.

²¹ And you who were once estranged and hostile in mind, doing evil deeds, ²² he has now reconciled in his fleshly body through death, so as to present you holy and blameless and irreproachable before him— ²³ provided that you continue securely established and steadfast in the faith, without shifting from the hope promised by the gospel that you heard, which has been proclaimed to every creature under heaven. I, Paul, became a servant of this gospel.

²⁴ I am now rejoicing in my sufferings for your sake, and in my flesh I am completing what is lacking in Christ's afflictions for the sake of his body, that is, the church. ²⁵ I became its servant according to God's commission that was given to me for you, to make the word of God fully known, ²⁶ the mystery that has been hidden throughout the ages and generations but has now been revealed to his saints. ²⁷ To them God chose to make known

how great among the Gentiles are the riches of the glory of this mystery, which is Christ in you, the hope of glory. [28] It is he whom we proclaim, warning everyone and teaching everyone in all wisdom, so that we may present everyone mature in Christ.

GOSPEL   Luke 10.38–42

[38] Now as they went on their way, he entered a certain village, where a woman named Martha welcomed him into her home. [39] She had a sister named Mary, who sat at the Lord's feet and listened to what he was saying. [40] But Martha was distracted by her many tasks; so she came to him and asked, 'Lord, do you not care that my sister has left me to do all the work by myself? Tell her then to help me.' [41] But the Lord answered her, 'Martha, Martha, you are worried and distracted by many things; [42] there is need of only one thing. Mary has chosen the better part, which will not be taken away from her.'

POST COMMUNION

See pages 934 to 938 and Table on page 931

SECOND SERVICE   THIRD SERVICE

Psalm 81   **Psalms 82; 100**
Genesis 41.1–16, 25–37   **Deuteronomy 30.1–10**
1 Corinthians 4.8–13   **1 Peter 3.8–18**

*If the Second Service is a Eucharist, the
following is read as a Gospel:*

John 4.31–35

PROPER 12

Sunday between 24 and 30 July inclusive

COLLECT

See pages 935 to 939 and Table on page 931

CONTINUOUS

READING   Hosea 1.2–10

² When the LORD first spoke through Hosea, the LORD said to Hosea, 'Go, take for yourself a wife of whoredom and have children of whoredom, for the land commits great whoredom by forsaking the LORD.' ³ So he went and took Gomer daughter of Diblaim, and she conceived and bore him a son.

⁴ And the LORD said to him, 'Name him Jezreel; for in a little while I will punish the house of Jehu for the blood of Jezreel, and I will put an end to the kingdom of the house of Israel. ⁵ On that day I will break the bow of Israel in the valley of Jezreel.'

⁶ She conceived again and bore a daughter. Then the LORD said to him, 'Name her Lo-ruhamah, for I will no longer have pity on the house of Israel or forgive them. ⁷ But I will have pity on the house of Judah, and I will save them by the LORD their God; I will not save them by bow, or by sword, or by war, or by horses, or by horsemen.'

⁸ When she had weaned Lo-ruhamah, she conceived and bore a son. ⁹ Then the LORD said, 'Name him Lo-ammi, for you are not my people and I am not your God.'

¹⁰ Yet the number of the people of Israel shall be like the sand of the sea, which can be neither measured nor numbered; and in the place where it was said to them, 'You are not my people', it shall be said to them, 'Children of the living God.'

PSALM   Psalm 85.1–7, [8–13]

1   You have been gracious to your land, O Lord,
     you have restored the good fortune of Jacob.
2   You have forgiven the iniquity of your people
     and blotted out all their sins.

³ You have withdrawn all your fury
   and turned yourself from your wrathful indignation.
⁴ Restore us then, O God our Saviour;
   let your anger depart from us.
⁵ Will you be displeased with us for ever?
   will you prolong your anger from age to age?
⁶ Will you not give us life again,
   that your people may rejoice in you?
⁷ Show us your mercy, O Lord,
   and grant us your salvation.
[⁸ I will listen to what the Lord God is saying,
   for he is speaking peace to his faithful people and to those who
      turn their hearts to him.
⁹ Truly, his salvation is very near to those who fear him,
   that his glory may dwell in our land.
¹⁰ Mercy and truth have met together;
   righteousness and peace have kissed each other.
¹¹ Truth shall spring up from the earth,
   and righteousness shall look down from heaven.
¹² The Lord will indeed grant prosperity,
   and our land will yield its increase.
¹³ Righteousness shall go before him,
   and peace shall be a pathway for his feet.]

READING   Colossians 2.6–15, [16–19]

⁶ As you therefore have received Christ Jesus the Lord, continue to live your lives in him, ⁷ rooted and built up in him and established in the faith, just as you were taught, abounding in thanksgiving.

⁸ See to it that no one takes you captive through philosophy and empty deceit, according to human tradition, according to the elemental spirits of the universe, and not according to Christ. ⁹ For in him the whole fullness of deity dwells bodily, ¹⁰ and you have come to fullness in him, who is the head of every ruler and authority. ¹¹ In him also you were circumcised with a spiritual circumcision, by putting off the body of the flesh in the circumcision of Christ; ¹² when you were buried with him in baptism, you were also raised with him through faith in the power of God, who raised him from the dead. ¹³ And when you were dead in trespasses and the uncircumcision of your flesh, God made you alive together with him, when he forgave us all our trespasses, ¹⁴ erasing the record that stood against us with its legal demands. He set this aside, nailing it to the cross. ¹⁵ He disarmed the rulers and authorities and made a public example of them, triumphing over them in it.

[¹⁶ Therefore do not let anyone condemn you in matters of food and drink or of observing festivals, new moons, or sabbaths. ¹⁷ These are only a shadow of what is to come, but the substance belongs to Christ. ¹⁸ Do not let anyone disqualify you, insisting on self-abasement and worship of angels, dwelling on visions, puffed up without cause by a human way of thinking, ¹⁹ and not holding fast to the head, from whom the whole body, nourished and held together by its ligaments and sinews, grows with a growth that is from God.]

GOSPEL   Luke 11.1–13

¹ He was praying in a certain place, and after he had finished, one of his disciples said to him, 'Lord, teach us to pray, as John taught his disciples.' ² He said to them, 'When you pray, say:
Father, hallowed be your name.
Your kingdom come.
³   Give us each day our daily bread.
⁴   And forgive us our sins,
      for we ourselves forgive everyone indebted to us.
      And do not bring us to the time of trial.'

⁵ And he said to them, 'Suppose one of you has a friend, and you go to him at midnight and say to him, "Friend, lend me three loaves of bread; ⁶ for a friend of mine has arrived, and I have nothing to set before him." ⁷ And he answers from within, "Do not bother me; the door has already been locked, and my children are with me in bed; I cannot get up and give you anything." ⁸ I tell you, even though he will not get up and give him anything because he is his friend, at least because of his persistence he will get up and give him whatever he needs.

⁹ 'So I say to you, Ask, and it will be given to you; search, and you will find; knock, and the door will be opened for you. ¹⁰ For everyone who asks receives, and everyone who searches finds, and for everyone who knocks, the door will be opened. ¹¹ Is there anyone among you who, if your child asks for a fish, will give a snake instead of a fish? ¹² Or if the child asks for an egg, will give a scorpion? ¹³ If you then, who are evil, know how to give good gifts to your children, how much more will the heavenly Father give the Holy Spirit to those who ask him!'

RELATED

READING   Genesis 18.20–32

²⁰ Then the LORD said, 'How great is the outcry against Sodom and Gomorrah and how very grave their sin! ²¹ I must go down and see whether they have done altogether according to the outcry that has come to me; and if not, I will know.'

²² So the men turned from there, and went towards Sodom, while Abraham remained standing before the LORD. ²³ Then Abraham came near and said, 'Will you indeed sweep away the righteous with the wicked? ²⁴ Suppose there are fifty righteous within the city; will you then sweep away the place and not forgive it for the fifty righteous who are in it? ²⁵ Far be it from you to do such a thing, to slay the righteous with the wicked, so that the righteous fare as the wicked! Far be that from you! Shall not the Judge of all the earth do what is just?' ²⁶ And the LORD said, 'If I find at Sodom fifty righteous in the city, I will forgive the whole place for their sake.' ²⁷ Abraham answered, 'Let me take it upon myself to speak to the Lord, I who am but dust and ashes. ²⁸ Suppose five of the fifty righteous are lacking? Will you destroy the whole city for lack of five?' And he said, 'I will not destroy it if I find forty-five there.' ²⁹ Again he spoke to him, 'Suppose forty are found there.' He answered, 'For the sake of forty I will not do it.' ³⁰ Then he said, 'Oh do not let the Lord be angry if I speak. Suppose thirty are found there.' He answered, 'I will not do it, if I find thirty there.' ³¹ He said, 'Let me take it upon myself to speak to the Lord. Suppose twenty are found there.' He answered, 'For the sake of twenty I will not destroy it.' ³² Then he said, 'Oh do not let the Lord be angry if I speak just once more. Suppose ten are found there.' He answered, 'For the sake of ten I will not destroy it.'

PSALM   Psalm 138

¹ I will give thanks to you, O Lord, with my whole heart;
    before the gods I will sing your praise.
² I will bow down towards your holy temple and praise your name,
    because of your love and faithfulness;
³ For you have glorified your name
    and your word above all things.
⁴ When I called, you answered me;
    you increased my strength within me.
⁵ All the kings of the earth will praise you, O Lord,
    when they have heard the words of your mouth.

6   They will sing of the ways of the Lord,
      that great is the glory of the Lord.
7   Though the Lord be high, he cares for the lowly;
      he perceives the haughty from afar.
8   Though I walk in the midst of trouble, you keep me safe;
      you stretch forth your hand against the fury of my enemies; your
        right hand shall save me.
9   The Lord will make good his purpose for me;
      O Lord, your love endures for ever; do not abandon the works of
        your hands.

READING   Colossians 2.6–15, [16–19]

⁶ As you therefore have received Christ Jesus the Lord, continue to live
your lives in him, ⁷ rooted and built up in him and established in the faith,
just as you were taught, abounding in thanksgiving.

⁸ See to it that no one takes you captive through philosophy and empty
deceit, according to human tradition, according to the elemental spirits of
the universe, and not according to Christ. ⁹ For in him the whole fullness
of deity dwells bodily, ¹⁰ and you have come to fullness in him, who is the
head of every ruler and authority. ¹¹ In him also you were circumcised
with a spiritual circumcision, by putting off the body of the flesh in the
circumcision of Christ; ¹² when you were buried with him in baptism, you
were also raised with him through faith in the power of God, who raised
him from the dead. ¹³ And when you were dead in trespasses and the
uncircumcision of your flesh, God made you alive together with him, when
he forgave us all our trespasses, ¹⁴ erasing the record that stood against us
with its legal demands. He set this aside, nailing it to the cross. ¹⁵ He
disarmed the rulers and authorities and made a public example of them,
triumphing over them in it.

[¹⁶ Therefore do not let anyone condemn you in matters of food and drink
or of observing festivals, new moons, or sabbaths. ¹⁷ These are only a shadow
of what is to come, but the substance belongs to Christ. ¹⁸ Do not let anyone
disqualify you, insisting on self-abasement and worship of angels, dwelling
on visions, puffed up without cause by a human way of thinking, ¹⁹ and
not holding fast to the head, from whom the whole body, nourished and
held together by its ligaments and sinews, grows with a growth that is
from God.]

GOSPEL   Luke 11.1–13

¹ He was praying in a certain place, and after he had finished, one of his disciples said to him, 'Lord, teach us to pray, as John taught his disciples.' ² He said to them, 'When you pray, say:

Father, hallowed be your name.
   Your kingdom come.
³   Give us each day our daily bread.
⁴   And forgive us our sins,
      for we ourselves forgive everyone indebted to us.
   And do not bring us to the time of trial.'

⁵ And he said to them, 'Suppose one of you has a friend, and you go to him at midnight and say to him, "Friend, lend me three loaves of bread; ⁶ for a friend of mine has arrived, and I have nothing to set before him." ⁷ And he answers from within, "Do not bother me; the door has already been locked, and my children are with me in bed; I cannot get up and give you anything." ⁸ I tell you, even though he will not get up and give him anything because he is his friend, at least because of his persistence he will get up and give him whatever he needs.

⁹ 'So I say to you, Ask, and it will be given to you; search, and you will find; knock, and the door will be opened for you. ¹⁰ For everyone who asks receives, and everyone who searches finds, and for everyone who knocks, the door will be opened. ¹¹ Is there anyone among you who, if your child asks for a fish, will give a snake instead of a fish? ¹² Or if the child asks for an egg, will give a scorpion? ¹³ If you then, who are evil, know how to give good gifts to your children, how much more will the heavenly Father give the Holy Spirit to those who ask him!'

POST COMMUNION

See pages 935 to 939 and Table on page 931

SECOND SERVICE

Psalm 88.1–10, [11–19]
Genesis 42.1–25
1 Corinthians 10.1–24

If the Second Service is a Eucharist, the following is read as a Gospel:

Matthew 13.24–30, [31–43]

THIRD SERVICE

Psalm 95
Song of Solomon 2

or

1 Maccabees 2.[1–14,] 15–22
1 Peter 4.7–14

PROPER 13

Sunday between 31 July and 6 August inclusive

COLLECT

See pages 935 to 939 and Table on page 931

CONTINUOUS

READING   Hosea 11.1-11

¹ When Israel was a child, I loved him,
    and out of Egypt I called my son.
² The more I called them,
    the more they went from me;
  they kept sacrificing to the Baals,
    and offering incense to idols.
³ Yet it was I who taught Ephraim to walk,
    I took them up in my arms;
    but they did not know that I healed them.
⁴ I led them with cords of human kindness,
    with bands of love.
  I was to them like those
    who lift infants to their cheeks.
    I bent down to them and fed them.
⁵ They shall return to the land of Egypt,
    and Assyria shall be their king,
    because they have refused to return to me.
⁶ The sword rages in their cities,
    it consumes their oracle-priests,
    and devours because of their schemes.
⁷ My people are bent on turning away from me.
    To the Most High they call,
    but he does not raise them up at all.
⁸ How can I give you up, Ephraim?
    How can I hand you over, O Israel?
  How can I make you like Admah?
    How can I treat you like Zeboiim?
  My heart recoils within me;
    my compassion grows warm and tender.

9 I will not execute my fierce anger;
     I will not again destroy Ephraim;
  for I am God and no mortal,
     the Holy One in your midst,
     and I will not come in wrath.
10 They shall go after the LORD,
     who roars like a lion;
  when he roars,
     his children shall come trembling from the west.
11 They shall come trembling like birds from Egypt,
     and like doves from the land of Assyria;
     and I will return them to their homes, says the LORD.

PSALM   Psalm 107.1–9, [43]

1 Give thanks to the Lord, for he is good,
    and his mercy endures for ever.
2 Let all those whom the Lord has redeemed proclaim
    that he redeemed them from the hand of the foe.
3 He gathered them out of the lands;
    from the east and from the west, from the north and from the
      south.
4 Some wandered in desert wastes;
    they found no way to a city where they might dwell.
5 They were hungry and thirsty;
    their spirits languished within them.
6 Then they cried to the Lord in their trouble,
    and he delivered them from their distress.
7 He put their feet on a straight path
    to go to a city where they might dwell.
8 Let them give thanks to the Lord for his mercy
    and the wonders he does for his children.
9 For he satisfies the thirsty
    and fills the hungry with good things.

[43 Whoever is wise will ponder these things,
    and consider well the mercies of the Lord.]

READING   Colossians 3.1–11

1 So if you have been raised with Christ, seek the things that are above, where Christ is, seated at the right hand of God. 2 Set your minds on things that are above, not on things that are on earth, 3 for you have died, and

your life is hidden with Christ in God. ⁴ When Christ who is your life is revealed, then you also will be revealed with him in glory.

⁵ Put to death, therefore, whatever in you is earthly: fornication, impurity, passion, evil desire, and greed (which is idolatry). ⁶ On account of these the wrath of God is coming on those who are disobedient. ⁷ These are the ways you also once followed, when you were living that life. ⁸ But now you must get rid of all such things—anger, wrath, malice, slander, and abusive language from your mouth. ⁹ Do not lie to one another, seeing that you have stripped off the old self with its practices ¹⁰ and have clothed yourselves with the new self, which is being renewed in knowledge according to the image of its creator. ¹¹ In that renewal there is no longer Greek and Jew, circumcised and uncircumcised, barbarian, Scythian, slave and free; but Christ is all and in all!

GOSPEL   Luke 12.13–21

¹³ Someone in the crowd said to him, 'Teacher, tell my brother to divide the family inheritance with me.' ¹⁴ But he said to him, 'Friend, who set me to be a judge or arbitrator over you?' ¹⁵ And he said to them, 'Take care! Be on your guard against all kinds of greed; for one's life does not consist in the abundance of possessions.' ¹⁶ Then he told them a parable: 'The land of a rich man produced abundantly. ¹⁷ And he thought to himself, "What should I do, for I have no place to store my crops?" ¹⁸ Then he said, "I will do this: I will pull down my barns and build larger ones, and there I will store all my grain and my goods. ¹⁹ And I will say to my soul, Soul, you have ample goods laid up for many years; relax, eat, drink, be merry." ²⁰ But God said to him, "You fool! This very night your life is being demanded of you. And the things you have prepared, whose will they be?" ²¹ So it is with those who store up treasures for themselves but are not rich towards God.'

RELATED

READING   Ecclesiastes 1.2, 12–14; 2.18–23

² Vanity of vanities, says the Teacher,
   vanity of vanities! All is vanity.

¹² I, the Teacher, when king over Israel in Jerusalem, ¹³ applied my mind to seek and to search out by wisdom all that is done under heaven; it is an unhappy business that God has given to human beings to be busy with. ¹⁴ I saw all the deeds that are done under the sun; and see, all is vanity and a chasing after wind.

18 I hated all my toil in which I had toiled under the sun, seeing that I must leave it to those who come after me 19 —and who knows whether they will be wise or foolish? Yet they will be master of all for which I toiled and used my wisdom under the sun. This also is vanity. 20 So I turned and gave my heart up to despair concerning all the toil of my labours under the sun, 21 because sometimes one who has toiled with wisdom and knowledge and skill must leave all to be enjoyed by another who did not toil for it. This also is vanity and a great evil. 22 What do mortals get from all the toil and strain with which they toil under the sun? 23 For all their days are full of pain, and their work is a vexation; even at night their minds do not rest. This also is vanity.

PSALM   Psalm 49.1–8, [9–11]

1   Hear this, all you peoples; hearken, all you who dwell in the world,
    you of high degree and low, rich and poor together.
2   My mouth shall speak of wisdom,
    and my heart shall meditate on understanding.
3   I will incline my ear to a proverb
    and set forth my riddle upon the harp.
4   Why should I be afraid in evil days,
    when the wickedness of those at my heels surrounds me,
5   The wickedness of those who put their trust in their goods,
    and boast of their great riches?
6   We can never ransom ourselves,
    or deliver to God the price of our life;
7   For the ransom of our life is so great,
    that we should never have enough to pay it,
8   In order to live for ever and ever,
    and never see the grave.
[9 For we see that the wise die also; like the dull and stupid they
       perish
    and leave their wealth to those who come after them.
10 Their graves shall be their homes for ever, their dwelling places
       from generation to generation,
    though they call the lands after their own names.
11 Even though honoured, they cannot live for ever;
    they are like the beasts that perish.]

READING   Colossians 3.1–11

¹ So if you have been raised with Christ, seek the things that are above, where Christ is, seated at the right hand of God. ² Set your minds on things that are above, not on things that are on earth, ³ for you have died, and your life is hidden with Christ in God. ⁴ When Christ who is your life is revealed, then you also will be revealed with him in glory.

⁵ Put to death, therefore, whatever in you is earthly: fornication, impurity, passion, evil desire, and greed (which is idolatry). ⁶ On account of these the wrath of God is coming on those who are disobedient. ⁷ These are the ways you also once followed, when you were living that life. ⁸ But now you must get rid of all such things—anger, wrath, malice, slander, and abusive language from your mouth. ⁹ Do not lie to one another, seeing that you have stripped off the old self with its practices ¹⁰ and have clothed yourselves with the new self, which is being renewed in knowledge according to the image of its creator. ¹¹ In that renewal there is no longer Greek and Jew, circumcised and uncircumcised, barbarian, Scythian, slave and free; but Christ is all and in all!

GOSPEL   Luke 12.13–21

¹³ Someone in the crowd said to him, 'Teacher, tell my brother to divide the family inheritance with me.' ¹⁴ But he said to him, 'Friend, who set me to be a judge or arbitrator over you?' ¹⁵ And he said to them, 'Take care! Be on your guard against all kinds of greed; for one's life does not consist in the abundance of possessions.' ¹⁶ Then he told them a parable: 'The land of a rich man produced abundantly. ¹⁷ And he thought to himself, "What should I do, for I have no place to store my crops?" ¹⁸ Then he said, "I will do this: I will pull down my barns and build larger ones, and there I will store all my grain and my goods. ¹⁹ And I will say to my soul, Soul, you have ample goods laid up for many years; relax, eat, drink, be merry." ²⁰ But God said to him, "You fool! This very night your life is being demanded of you. And the things you have prepared, whose will they be?" ²¹ So it is with those who store up treasures for themselves but are not rich towards God.'

POST COMMUNION

See pages 936 to 940 and Table on page 931

YEAR C

SECOND SERVICE

Psalm 107.1–12, [13–32]
Genesis 50.4–26
1 Corinthians 14.1–19

*If the Second Service is a Eucharist, the
following is read as a Gospel:*

Mark 6.45–52

THIRD SERVICE

Psalm 106.1–10
Song of Solomon 5.2–16

or

1 Maccabees 3.1–12
2 Peter 1.1–15

PROPER 14

Sunday between 7 and 13 August inclusive

COLLECT

See pages 936 to 940 and Table on page 931

CONTINUOUS

READING   Isaiah 1.1, 10–20

¹ The vision of Isaiah son of Amoz, which he saw concerning Judah and
Jerusalem in the days of Uzziah, Jotham, Ahaz, and Hezekiah, kings of
Judah.

¹⁰   Hear the word of the LORD,
         you rulers of Sodom!
      Listen to the teaching of our God,
         you people of Gomorrah!
¹¹   What to me is the multitude of your sacrifices?
         says the LORD;
      I have had enough of burnt-offerings of rams
         and the fat of fed beasts;
      I do not delight in the blood of bulls,
         or of lambs, or of goats.
¹²   When you come to appear before me,
         who asked this from your hand?
      Trample my courts no more;
¹³   bringing offerings is futile;
         incense is an abomination to me.
      New moon and sabbath and calling of convocation—
         I cannot endure solemn assemblies with iniquity.

14 Your new moons and your appointed festivals
    my soul hates;
  they have become a burden to me,
    I am weary of bearing them.
15 When you stretch out your hands,
    I will hide my eyes from you;
  even though you make many prayers,
    I will not listen;
      your hands are full of blood.
16 Wash yourselves; make yourselves clean;
    remove the evil of your doings
    from before my eyes;
  cease to do evil,
17   learn to do good;
  seek justice,
    rescue the oppressed,
  defend the orphan,
    plead for the widow.
18 Come now, let us argue it out,
    says the LORD:
  though your sins are like scarlet,
    they shall be like snow;
  though they are red like crimson,
    they shall become like wool.
19 If you are willing and obedient,
    you shall eat the good of the land;
20 but if you refuse and rebel,
    you shall be devoured by the sword;
    for the mouth of the LORD has spoken.

PSALM   Psalm 50.1–7, [8, 23–24]

1 The Lord, the God of gods, has spoken;
   he has called the earth from the rising of the sun to its setting.
2 Out of Zion, perfect in its beauty,
   God reveals himself in glory.
3 Our God will come and will not keep silence;
   before him there is a consuming flame, and round about him a
     raging storm.
4 He calls the heavens and the earth from above
   to witness the judgement of his people.

5 'Gather before me my loyal followers,
  those who have made a covenant with me and sealed it with
      sacrifice.'
6 Let the heavens declare the rightness of his cause;
  for God himself is judge.
7 Hear, O my people, and I will speak: 'O Israel, I will bear witness
      against you;
  for I am God, your God.
[8 I do not accuse you because of your sacrifices;
  your offerings are always before me.'

23 'Consider this well, you who forget God,
  lest I rend you and there be none to deliver you.
24 Whoever offers me the sacrifice of thanksgiving honours me;
  but to those who keep in my way will I show the salvation of God.']

READING   Hebrews 11.1–3, 8–16

¹ Now faith is the assurance of things hoped for, the conviction of things
not seen. ² Indeed, by faith our ancestors received approval. ³ By faith we
understand that the worlds were prepared by the word of God, so that what
is seen was made from things that are not visible.

⁸ By faith Abraham obeyed when he was called to set out for a place that
he was to receive as an inheritance; and he set out, not knowing where he
was going. ⁹ By faith he stayed for a time in the land he had been promised,
as in a foreign land, living in tents, as did Isaac and Jacob, who were heirs
with him of the same promise. ¹⁰ For he looked forward to the city that has
foundations, whose architect and builder is God. ¹¹ By faith he received
power of procreation, even though he was too old—and Sarah herself was
barren—because he considered him faithful who had promised. ¹² Therefore from one person, and this one as good as dead, descendants were born,
'as many as the stars of heaven and as the innumerable grains of sand by
the seashore.'

¹³ All of these died in faith without having received the promises, but
from a distance they saw and greeted them. They confessed that they were
strangers and foreigners on the earth, ¹⁴ for people who speak in this way
make it clear that they are seeking a homeland. ¹⁵ If they had been thinking
of the land that they had left behind, they would have had opportunity to
return. ¹⁶ But as it is, they desire a better country, that is, a heavenly
one. Therefore God is not ashamed to be called their God; indeed, he has
prepared a city for them.

GOSPEL   Luke 12.32–40

³² 'Do not be afraid, little flock, for it is your Father's good pleasure to give you the kingdom. ³³ Sell your possessions, and give alms. Make purses for yourselves that do not wear out, an unfailing treasure in heaven, where no thief comes near and no moth destroys. ³⁴ For where your treasure is, there your heart will be also.

³⁵ 'Be dressed for action and have your lamps lit; ³⁶ be like those who are waiting for their master to return from the wedding banquet, so that they may open the door for him as soon as he comes and knocks. ³⁷ Blessed are those slaves whom the master finds alert when he comes; truly I tell you, he will fasten his belt and have them sit down to eat, and he will come and serve them. ³⁸ If he comes during the middle of the night, or near dawn, and finds them so, blessed are those slaves.

³⁹ 'But know this: if the owner of the house had known at what hour the thief was coming, he would not have let his house be broken into. ⁴⁰ You also must be ready, for the Son of Man is coming at an unexpected hour.'

RELATED

READING   Genesis 15.1–6

¹ After these things the word of the LORD came to Abram in a vision, 'Do not be afraid, Abram, I am your shield; your reward shall be very great.' ² But Abram said, 'O Lord GOD, what will you give me, for I continue childless, and the heir of my house is Eliezer of Damascus?' ³ And Abram said, 'You have given me no offspring, and so a slave born in my house is to be my heir.' ⁴ But the word of the LORD came to him, 'This man shall not be your heir; no one but your very own issue shall be your heir.' ⁵ He brought him outside and said, 'Look towards heaven and count the stars, if you are able to count them.' Then he said to him, 'So shall your descendants be.' ⁶ And he believed the LORD; and the LORD reckoned it to him as righteousness.

PSALM   Psalm 33.12–21, [22]

12 Happy is the nation whose God is the Lord!
   happy the people he has chosen to be his own!
13 The Lord looks down from heaven,
   and beholds all the people in the world.
14 From where he sits enthroned he turns his gaze
   on all who dwell on the earth.
15 He fashions all the hearts of them
   and understands all their works.
16 There is no king that can be saved by a mighty army;
   the strong are not delivered by great strength.
17 The horse is a vain hope for deliverance;
   for all its strength it cannot save.
18 Behold, the eye of the Lord is upon those who fear him,
   on those who wait upon his love,
19 To pluck their lives from death,
   and to feed them in time of famine.
20 Our soul waits for the Lord;
   he is our help and our shield.
21 Indeed, our heart rejoices in him,
   for in his holy name we put our trust.
[22 Let your loving-kindness, O Lord, be upon us,
   as we have put our trust in you.]

READING   Hebrews 11.1–3, 8–16

¹ Now faith is the assurance of things hoped for, the conviction of things not seen. ² Indeed, by faith our ancestors received approval. ³ By faith we understand that the worlds were prepared by the word of God, so that what is seen was made from things that are not visible.

⁸ By faith Abraham obeyed when he was called to set out for a place that he was to receive as an inheritance; and he set out, not knowing where he was going. ⁹ By faith he stayed for a time in the land he had been promised, as in a foreign land, living in tents, as did Isaac and Jacob, who were heirs with him of the same promise. ¹⁰ For he looked forward to the city that has foundations, whose architect and builder is God. ¹¹ By faith he received power of procreation, even though he was too old—and Sarah herself was barren—because he considered him faithful who had promised. ¹² Therefore from one person, and this one as good as dead, descendants were born, 'as many as the stars of heaven and as the innumerable grains of sand by the seashore.'

¹³ All of these died in faith without having received the promises, but from a distance they saw and greeted them. They confessed that they were strangers and foreigners on the earth, ¹⁴ for people who speak in this way make it clear that they are seeking a homeland. ¹⁵ If they had been thinking of the land that they had left behind, they would have had opportunity to return. ¹⁶ But as it is, they desire a better country, that is, a heavenly one. Therefore God is not ashamed to be called their God; indeed, he has prepared a city for them.

GOSPEL   Luke 12.32–40

³² 'Do not be afraid, little flock, for it is your Father's good pleasure to give you the kingdom. ³³ Sell your possessions, and give alms. Make purses for yourselves that do not wear out, an unfailing treasure in heaven, where no thief comes near and no moth destroys. ³⁴ For where your treasure is, there your heart will be also.

³⁵ 'Be dressed for action and have your lamps lit; ³⁶ be like those who are waiting for their master to return from the wedding banquet, so that they may open the door for him as soon as he comes and knocks. ³⁷ Blessed are those slaves whom the master finds alert when he comes; truly I tell you, he will fasten his belt and have them sit down to eat, and he will come and serve them. ³⁸ If he comes during the middle of the night, or near dawn, and finds them so, blessed are those slaves.

³⁹ 'But know this: if the owner of the house had known at what hour the thief was coming, he would not have let his house be broken into. ⁴⁰ You also must be ready, for the Son of Man is coming at an unexpected hour.'

POST COMMUNION

See pages 937 to 941 and Table on page 931

SECOND SERVICE

Psalms 108; [116]
Isaiah 11.10–12.6
2 Corinthians 1.1–22

If the Second Service is a Eucharist, the following is read as a Gospel:
Mark 7.24–30

THIRD SERVICE

Psalm 115
Song of Solomon 8.5–7

or

1 Maccabees 14.4–15
2 Peter 3.8–13

PROPER 15

Sunday between 14 and 20 August inclusive

COLLECT

See pages 937 to 941 and Table on page 931

CONTINUOUS

READING   Isaiah 5.1–7

¹ Let me sing for my beloved
    my love-song concerning his vineyard:
My beloved had a vineyard
    on a very fertile hill.
² He dug it and cleared it of stones,
    and planted it with choice vines;
he built a watch-tower in the midst of it,
    and hewed out a wine vat in it;
he expected it to yield grapes,
    but it yielded wild grapes.
³ And now, inhabitants of Jerusalem
    and people of Judah,
judge between me
    and my vineyard.
⁴ What more was there to do for my vineyard
    that I have not done in it?
When I expected it to yield grapes,
    why did it yield wild grapes?
⁵ And now I will tell you
    what I will do to my vineyard.
I will remove its hedge,
    and it shall be devoured;
I will break down its wall,
    and it shall be trampled down.
⁶ I will make it a waste;
    it shall not be pruned or hoed,
    and it shall be overgrown with briers and thorns;
I will also command the clouds
    that they rain no rain upon it.

7 For the vineyard of the LORD of hosts
       is the house of Israel,
   and the people of Judah
       are his pleasant planting;
   he expected justice,
       but saw bloodshed;
   righteousness,
       but heard a cry!

PSALM   Psalm 80.[1-2,] 8-18

[1 Hear, O Shepherd of Israel, leading Joseph like a flock;
       shine forth, you that are enthroned upon the cherubim.
 2 In the presence of Ephraim, Benjamin and Manasseh,
       stir up your strength and come to help us.]

 8 You have brought a vine out of Egypt;
       you cast out the nations and planted it.
 9 You prepared the ground for it;
       it took root and filled the land.
10 The mountains were covered by its shadow
       and the towering cedar trees by its boughs.
11 You stretched out its tendrils to the Sea
       and its branches to the River.
12 Why have you broken down its wall,
       so that all who pass by pluck off its grapes?
13 The wild boar of the forest has ravaged it,
       and the beasts of the field have grazed upon it.
14 Turn now, O God of hosts, look down from heaven; behold and
       tend this vine;
       preserve what your right hand has planted.
15 They burn it with fire like rubbish;
       at the rebuke of your countenance let them perish.
16 Let your hand be upon the man of your right hand,
       the son of man you have made so strong for yourself.
17 And so will we never turn away from you;
       give us life, that we may call upon your name.
18 Restore us, O Lord God of hosts;
       show the light of your countenance and we shall be saved.

READING — Hebrews 11.29–12.2

[29] By faith the people passed through the Red Sea as if it were dry land, but when the Egyptians attempted to do so they were drowned. [30] By faith the walls of Jericho fell after they had been encircled for seven days. [31] By faith Rahab the prostitute did not perish with those who were disobedient, because she had received the spies in peace.

[32] And what more should I say? For time would fail me to tell of Gideon, Barak, Samson, Jephthah, of David and Samuel and the prophets— [33] who through faith conquered kingdoms, administered justice, obtained promises, shut the mouths of lions, [34] quenched raging fire, escaped the edge of the sword, won strength out of weakness, became mighty in war, put foreign armies to flight. [35] Women received their dead by resurrection. Others were tortured, refusing to accept release, in order to obtain a better resurrection. [36] Others suffered mocking and flogging, and even chains and imprisonment. [37] They were stoned to death, they were sawn in two, they were killed by the sword; they went about in skins of sheep and goats, destitute, persecuted, tormented— [38] of whom the world was not worthy. They wandered in deserts and mountains, and in caves and holes in the ground.

[39] Yet all these, though they were commended for their faith, did not receive what was promised, [40] since God had provided something better so that they would not, without us, be made perfect.

[1] Therefore, since we are surrounded by so great a cloud of witnesses, let us also lay aside every weight and the sin that clings so closely, and let us run with perseverance the race that is set before us, [2] looking to Jesus the pioneer and perfecter of our faith, who for the sake of the joy that was set before him endured the cross, disregarding its shame, and has taken his seat at the right hand of the throne of God.

GOSPEL — Luke 12.49–56

[49] 'I came to bring fire to the earth, and how I wish it were already kindled! [50] I have a baptism with which to be baptized, and what stress I am under until it is completed! [51] Do you think that I have come to bring peace to the earth? No, I tell you, but rather division! [52] From now on, five in one

1014

household will be divided, three against two and two against three; [53] they will be divided:

> father against son
>> and son against father,
> mother against daughter
>> and daughter against mother,
> mother-in-law against her daughter-in-law
>> and daughter-in-law against mother-in-law.'

[54] He also said to the crowds, 'When you see a cloud rising in the west, you immediately say, "It is going to rain"; and so it happens. [55] And when you see the south wind blowing, you say, "There will be scorching heat"; and it happens. [56] You hypocrites! You know how to interpret the appearance of earth and sky, but why do you not know how to interpret the present time?'

RELATED

READING   Jeremiah 23.23–29

[23] Am I a God near by, says the LORD, and not a God far off? [24] Who can hide in secret places so that I cannot see them? says the LORD. Do I not fill heaven and earth? says the LORD. [25] I have heard what the prophets have said who prophesy lies in my name, saying, 'I have dreamed, I have dreamed!' [26] How long? Will the hearts of the prophets ever turn back—those who prophesy lies, and who prophesy the deceit of their own heart? [27] They plan to make my people forget my name by their dreams that they tell one another, just as their ancestors forgot my name for Baal. [28] Let the prophet who has a dream tell the dream, but let the one who has my word speak my word faithfully. What has straw in common with wheat? says the LORD. [29] Is not my word like fire, says the LORD, and like a hammer that breaks a rock in pieces?

PSALM   Psalm 82

[1] God takes his stand in the council of heaven;
     he gives judgement in the midst of the gods:
[2] 'How long will you judge unjustly,
     and show favour to the wicked?
[3] Save the weak and the orphan;
     defend the humble and needy;
[4] Rescue the weak and the poor;
     deliver them from the power of the wicked.

⁵ They do not know, neither do they understand; they go about in
   darkness;
all the foundations of the earth are shaken.
⁶ Now I say to you, "You are gods,
and all of you children of the Most High;
⁷ Nevertheless, you shall die like mortals,
and fall like any prince." '
⁸ Arise, O God, and rule the earth,
for you shall take all nations for your own.

READING   Hebrews 11.29–12.2

²⁹ By faith the people passed through the Red Sea as if it were dry land,
but when the Egyptians attempted to do so they were drowned. ³⁰ By faith
the walls of Jericho fell after they had been encircled for seven days. ³¹ By
faith Rahab the prostitute did not perish with those who were disobedient,
because she had received the spies in peace.

³² And what more should I say? For time would fail me to tell of Gideon,
Barak, Samson, Jephthah, of David and Samuel and the prophets— ³³ who
through faith conquered kingdoms, administered justice, obtained promises, shut the mouths of lions, ³⁴ quenched raging fire, escaped the edge of
the sword, won strength out of weakness, became mighty in war, put
foreign armies to flight. ³⁵ Women received their dead by resurrection.
Others were tortured, refusing to accept release, in order to obtain a better
resurrection. ³⁶ Others suffered mocking and flogging, and even chains and
imprisonment. ³⁷ They were stoned to death, they were sawn in two, they
were killed by the sword; they went about in skins of sheep and goats,
destitute, persecuted, tormented— ³⁸ of whom the world was not worthy.
They wandered in deserts and mountains, and in caves and holes in the
ground.

³⁹ Yet all these, though they were commended for their faith, did not
receive what was promised, ⁴⁰ since God had provided something better so
that they would not, without us, be made perfect.

¹ Therefore, since we are surrounded by so great a cloud of witnesses, let
us also lay aside every weight and the sin that clings so closely, and let us
run with perseverance the race that is set before us, ² looking to Jesus the
pioneer and perfecter of our faith, who for the sake of the joy that was set
before him endured the cross, disregarding its shame, and has taken his
seat at the right hand of the throne of God.

GOSPEL   Luke 12.49–56

[49] 'I came to bring fire to the earth, and how I wish it were already kindled! [50] I have a baptism with which to be baptized, and what stress I am under until it is completed! [51] Do you think that I have come to bring peace to the earth? No, I tell you, but rather division! [52] From now on, five in one household will be divided, three against two and two against three; [53] they will be divided:

father against son
    and son against father,
mother against daughter
    and daughter against mother,
mother-in-law against her daughter-in-law
    and daughter-in-law against mother-in-law.'

[54] He also said to the crowds, 'When you see a cloud rising in the west, you immediately say, "It is going to rain"; and so it happens. [55] And when you see the south wind blowing, you say, "There will be scorching heat"; and it happens. [56] You hypocrites! You know how to interpret the appearance of earth and sky, but why do you not know how to interpret the present time?'

POST COMMUNION

See pages 937 to 941 and Table on page 931

SECOND SERVICE

Psalm 119.17–24, [25–32]
Isaiah 28.9–22
2 Corinthians 8.1–9

If the Second Service is a Eucharist, the following is read as a Gospel:

Matthew 20.1–16

THIRD SERVICE

Psalm 119.33–48
Jonah 1

or

Ecclesiasticus 3.1–15
2 Peter 3.14–18

PROPER 16

Sunday between 21 and 27 August inclusive

COLLECT

See pages 938 to 942 and Table on page 931

CONTINUOUS

READING   Jeremiah 1.4–10

⁴ Now the word of the LORD came to me saying,
⁵ 'Before I formed you in the womb I knew you,
   and before you were born I consecrated you;
   I appointed you a prophet to the nations.'
⁶ Then I said, 'Ah, Lord GOD! Truly I do not know how to speak, for I am only
a boy.' ⁷ But the LORD said to me,
   'Do not say, "I am only a boy";
   for you shall go to all to whom I send you,
   and you shall speak whatever I command you.
⁸ Do not be afraid of them,
   for I am with you to deliver you,
        says the LORD.'
⁹ Then the LORD put out his hand and touched my mouth; and the LORD
said to me,
   'Now I have put my words in your mouth.
¹⁰ See, today I appoint you over nations and over kingdoms,
   to pluck up and to pull down,
   to destroy and to overthrow,
   to build and to plant.'

PSALM   Psalm 71.1–6

1 In you, O Lord, have I taken refuge;
   let me never be ashamed.
2 In your righteousness, deliver me and set me free;
   incline your ear to me and save me.
3 Be my strong rock, a castle to keep me safe;
   you are my crag and my stronghold.
4 Deliver me, my God, from the hand of the wicked,
   from the clutches of the evildoer and the oppressor.

5 For you are my hope, O Lord God,
   my confidence since I was young.
6 I have been sustained by you ever since I was born; from my
      mother's womb you have been my strength;
   my praise shall be always of you.

READING   Hebrews 12.18–29

18 You have not come to something that can be touched, a blazing fire, and darkness, and gloom, and a tempest, 19 and the sound of a trumpet, and a voice whose words made the hearers beg that not another word be spoken to them. 20 (For they could not endure the order that was given, 'If even an animal touches the mountain, it shall be stoned to death.' 21 Indeed, so terrifying was the sight that Moses said, 'I tremble with fear.') 22 But you have come to Mount Zion and to the city of the living God, the heavenly Jerusalem, and to innumerable angels in festal gathering, 23 and to the assembly of the firstborn who are enrolled in heaven, and to God the judge of all, and to the spirits of the righteous made perfect, 24 and to Jesus, the mediator of a new covenant, and to the sprinkled blood that speaks a better word than the blood of Abel.

25 See that you do not refuse the one who is speaking; for if they did not escape when they refused the one who warned them on earth, how much less will we escape if we reject the one who warns from heaven! 26 At that time his voice shook the earth; but now he has promised, 'Yet once more I will shake not only the earth but also the heaven.' 27 This phrase 'Yet once more' indicates the removal of what is shaken—that is, created things—so that what cannot be shaken may remain. 28 Therefore, since we are receiving a kingdom that cannot be shaken, let us give thanks, by which we offer to God an acceptable worship with reverence and awe; 29 for indeed our God is a consuming fire.

GOSPEL   Luke 13.10–17

10 Now he was teaching in one of the synagogues on the sabbath. 11 And just then there appeared a woman with a spirit that had crippled her for eighteen years. She was bent over and was quite unable to stand up straight. 12 When Jesus saw her, he called her over and said, 'Woman, you are set free from your ailment.' 13 When he laid his hands on her, immediately she stood up straight and began praising God. 14 But the leader of the synagogue, indignant because Jesus had cured on the sabbath, kept saying to the crowd, 'There are six days on which work ought to be done; come on those days and be cured, and not on the sabbath day.' 15 But the Lord

answered him and said, 'You hypocrites! Does not each of you on the sabbath untie his ox or his donkey from the manger, and lead it away to give it water? ¹⁶ And ought not this woman, a daughter of Abraham whom Satan bound for eighteen long years, be set free from this bondage on the sabbath day?' ¹⁷ When he said this, all his opponents were put to shame; and the entire crowd was rejoicing at all the wonderful things that he was doing.

RELATED

READING   Isaiah 58.9b–14

⁹ If you remove the yoke from among you,
    the pointing of the finger, the speaking of evil,
¹⁰ if you offer your food to the hungry
    and satisfy the needs of the afflicted,
  then your light shall rise in the darkness
    and your gloom be like the noonday.
¹¹ The Lord will guide you continually,
    and satisfy your needs in parched places,
    and make your bones strong;
  and you shall be like a watered garden,
    like a spring of water,
    whose waters never fail.
¹² Your ancient ruins shall be rebuilt;
    you shall raise up the foundations of many generations;
  you shall be called the repairer of the breach,
    the restorer of streets to live in.
¹³ If you refrain from trampling the sabbath,
    from pursuing your own interests on my holy day;
  if you call the sabbath a delight
    and the holy day of the Lord honourable;
  if you honour it, not going your own ways,
    serving your own interests, or pursuing your own affairs;
¹⁴ then you shall take delight in the Lord,
    and I will make you ride upon the heights of the earth;
  I will feed you with the heritage of your ancestor Jacob,
    for the mouth of the Lord has spoken.

PSALM
Psalm 103.1–8

1 Bless the Lord, O my soul,
   and all that is within me, bless his holy name.
2 Bless the Lord, O my soul,
   and forget not all his benefits.
3 He forgives all your sins
   and heals all your infirmities;
4 He redeems your life from the grave
   and crowns you with mercy and loving-kindness;
5 He satisfies you with good things,
   and your youth is renewed like an eagle's.
6 The Lord executes righteousness
   and judgement for all who are oppressed.
7 He made his ways known to Moses
   and his works to the children of Israel.
8 The Lord is full of compassion and mercy,
   slow to anger and of great kindness.

READING
Hebrews 12.18–29

18 You have not come to something that can be touched, a blazing fire, and darkness, and gloom, and a tempest, 19 and the sound of a trumpet, and a voice whose words made the hearers beg that not another word be spoken to them. 20 (For they could not endure the order that was given, 'If even an animal touches the mountain, it shall be stoned to death.' 21 Indeed, so terrifying was the sight that Moses said, 'I tremble with fear.') 22 But you have come to Mount Zion and to the city of the living God, the heavenly Jerusalem, and to innumerable angels in festal gathering, 23 and to the assembly of the firstborn who are enrolled in heaven, and to God the judge of all, and to the spirits of the righteous made perfect, 24 and to Jesus, the mediator of a new covenant, and to the sprinkled blood that speaks a better word than the blood of Abel.

25 See that you do not refuse the one who is speaking; for if they did not escape when they refused the one who warned them on earth, how much less will we escape if we reject the one who warns from heaven! 26 At that time his voice shook the earth; but now he has promised, 'Yet once more I will shake not only the earth but also the heaven.' 27 This phrase 'Yet once more' indicates the removal of what is shaken—that is, created things—so that what cannot be shaken may remain. 28 Therefore, since we are receiving a kingdom that cannot be shaken, let us give thanks, by which we offer to God an acceptable worship with reverence and awe; 29 for indeed our God is a consuming fire.

GOSPEL   Luke 13.10–17

¹⁰ Now he was teaching in one of the synagogues on the sabbath. ¹¹ And just then there appeared a woman with a spirit that had crippled her for eighteen years. She was bent over and was quite unable to stand up straight. ¹² When Jesus saw her, he called her over and said, 'Woman, you are set free from your ailment.' ¹³ When he laid his hands on her, immediately she stood up straight and began praising God. ¹⁴ But the leader of the synagogue, indignant because Jesus had cured on the sabbath, kept saying to the crowd, 'There are six days on which work ought to be done; come on those days and be cured, and not on the sabbath day.' ¹⁵ But the Lord answered him and said, 'You hypocrites! Does not each of you on the sabbath untie his ox or his donkey from the manger, and lead it away to give it water? ¹⁶ And ought not this woman, a daughter of Abraham whom Satan bound for eighteen long years, be set free from this bondage on the sabbath day?' ¹⁷ When he said this, all his opponents were put to shame; and the entire crowd was rejoicing at all the wonderful things that he was doing.

POST COMMUNION

See pages 938 to 942 and Table on page 931

SECOND SERVICE

Psalm 119.49–56, [57–72]
Isaiah 30.8–21
2 Corinthians 9

If the Second Service is a Eucharist, the following is read as a Gospel:

Matthew 21.28–32

THIRD SERVICE

Psalm 119.73–88
Jonah 2

or

Ecclesiasticus 3.17–29
Revelation 1

PROPER 17

Sunday between 28 August and 3 September inclusive

COLLECT

See pages 939 to 942 and Table on page 931

CONTINUOUS

READING   Jeremiah 2.4–13

⁴ Hear the word of the LORD, O house of Jacob, and all the families of the house of Israel. ⁵ Thus says the LORD:
> What wrong did your ancestors find in me
>> that they went far from me,
> and went after worthless things, and became worthless themselves?
⁶ They did not say, 'Where is the LORD
>> who brought us up from the land of Egypt,
> who led us in the wilderness,
>> in a land of deserts and pits,
> in a land of drought and deep darkness,
>> in a land that no one passes through,
>> where no one lives?'
⁷ I brought you into a plentiful land
>> to eat its fruits and its good things.
> But when you entered you defiled my land,
>> and made my heritage an abomination.
⁸ The priests did not say, 'Where is the LORD?'
>> Those who handle the law did not know me;
> the rulers transgressed against me;
>> the prophets prophesied by Baal,
>> and went after things that do not profit.
⁹ Therefore once more I accuse you,
>> says the LORD,
> and I accuse your children's children.
¹⁰ Cross to the coasts of Cyprus and look,
>> send to Kedar and examine with care;
>> see if there has ever been such a thing.
¹¹ Has a nation changed its gods,
>> even though they are no gods?
> But my people have changed their glory
>> for something that does not profit.

¹² Be appalled, O heavens, at this,
>> be shocked, be utterly desolate,
>>> says the LORD,
¹³ for my people have committed two evils:
>> they have forsaken me,
> the fountain of living water,
>> and dug out cisterns for themselves,
> cracked cisterns
>> that can hold no water.

PSALM   Psalm 81.1, 10–16

¹ Sing with joy to God our strength
> and raise a loud shout to the God of Jacob.

¹⁰ I am the Lord your God, who brought you out of the land of Egypt
>> and said,
> 'Open your mouth wide and I will fill it.'
¹¹ And yet my people did not hear my voice,
> and Israel would not obey me.
¹² So I gave them over to the stubbornness of their hearts,
> to follow their own devices.
¹³ O that my people would listen to me!
> that Israel would walk in my ways!
¹⁴ I should soon subdue their enemies
> and turn my hand against their foes.
¹⁵ Those who hate the Lord would cringe before him,
> and their punishment would last for ever.
¹⁶ But Israel would I feed with the finest wheat
> and satisfy him with honey from the rock.

OR, IF AN ALTERNATIVE READING IS PREFERRED   Psalm 81.1–11

¹ Sing with joy to God our strength
> and raise a loud shout to the God of Jacob.
² Raise a song and sound the timbrel,
> the merry harp and the lyre.
³ Blow the ram's-horn at the new moon,
> and at the full moon, the day of our feast.
⁴ For this is a statute for Israel,
> a law of the God of Jacob.
⁵ He laid it as a solemn charge upon Joseph,
> when he came out of the land of Egypt.

⁶ I heard an unfamiliar voice saying,
  'I eased his shoulder from the burden; his hands were set free
    from bearing the load.'
⁷ You called on me in trouble and I saved you;
  I answered you from the secret place of thunder and tested you at
    the waters of Meribah.
⁸ Hear, O my people, and I will admonish you:
  O Israel, if you would but listen to me!
⁹ There shall be no strange god among you;
  you shall not worship a foreign god.
¹⁰ I am the Lord your God, who brought you out of the land of Egypt
    and said,
  'Open your mouth wide and I will fill it.'
¹¹ And yet my people did not hear my voice,
  and Israel would not obey me.

READING   Hebrews 13.1–8, 15–16

¹ Let mutual love continue. ² Do not neglect to show hospitality to strangers, for by doing that some have entertained angels without knowing it. ³ Remember those who are in prison, as though you were in prison with them; those who are being tortured, as though you yourselves were being tortured. ⁴ Let marriage be held in honour by all, and let the marriage bed be kept undefiled; for God will judge fornicators and adulterers. ⁵ Keep your lives free from the love of money, and be content with what you have; for he has said, 'I will never leave you or forsake you.' ⁶ So we can say with confidence,
  'The Lord is my helper;
    I will not be afraid.
  What can anyone do to me?'

⁷ Remember your leaders, those who spoke the word of God to you; consider the outcome of their way of life, and imitate their faith. ⁸ Jesus Christ is the same yesterday and today and for ever.

¹⁵ Through him, then, let us continually offer a sacrifice of praise to God, that is, the fruit of lips that confess his name. ¹⁶ Do not neglect to do good and to share what you have, for such sacrifices are pleasing to God.

GOSPEL   Luke 14.1, 7–14

¹ On one occasion when Jesus was going to the house of a leader of the Pharisees to eat a meal on the sabbath, they were watching him closely.

⁷ When he noticed how the guests chose the places of honour, he told them a parable. ⁸ 'When you are invited by someone to a wedding banquet, do not sit down at the place of honour, in case someone more distinguished than you has been invited by your host; ⁹ and the host who invited both of you may come and say to you, "Give this person your place", and then in disgrace you would start to take the lowest place. ¹⁰ But when you are invited, go and sit down at the lowest place, so that when your host comes, he may say to you, "Friend, move up higher"; then you will be honoured in the presence of all who sit at the table with you. ¹¹ For all who exalt themselves will be humbled, and those who humble themselves will be exalted.'

¹² He said also to the one who had invited him, 'When you give a luncheon or a dinner, do not invite your friends or your brothers or your relatives or rich neighbours, in case they may invite you in return, and you would be repaid. ¹³ But when you give a banquet, invite the poor, the crippled, the lame, and the blind. ¹⁴ And you will be blessed, because they cannot repay you, for you will be repaid at the resurrection of the righteous.'

RELATED

READING

EITHER   Ecclesiasticus 10.12–18

¹² The beginning of human pride is to forsake the Lord;
    the heart has withdrawn from its Maker.
¹³ For the beginning of pride is sin,
    and the one who clings to it pours out abominations.
  Therefore the Lord brings upon them unheard-of calamities,
    and destroys them completely.
¹⁴ The Lord overthrows the thrones of rulers,
    and enthrones the lowly in their place.
¹⁵ The Lord plucks up the roots of the nations,
    and plants the humble in their place.
¹⁶ The Lord lays waste the lands of the nations,
    and destroys them to the foundations of the earth.

¹⁷ He removes some of them and destroys them,
    and erases the memory of them from the earth.
¹⁸ Pride was not created for human beings,
    or violent anger for those born of women.

OR   **Proverbs 25.6–7**

⁶ Do not put yourself forward in the king's presence
    or stand in the place of the great;
⁷ for it is better to be told, 'Come up here',
    than to be put lower in the presence of a noble.

PSALM   Psalm 112

¹ Alleluia! Happy are they who fear the Lord
    and have great delight in his commandments!
² Their descendants will be mighty in the land;
    the generation of the upright will be blessed.
³ Wealth and riches will be in their house,
    and their righteousness will last for ever.
⁴ Light shines in the darkness for the upright;
    the righteous are merciful and full of compassion.
⁵ It is good for them to be generous in lending
    and to manage their affairs with justice.
⁶ For they will never be shaken;
    the righteous will be kept in everlasting remembrance.
⁷ They will not be afraid of any evil rumours;
    their heart is right; they put their trust in the Lord.
⁸ Their heart is established and will not shrink,
    until they see their desire upon their enemies.
⁹ They have given freely to the poor,
    and their righteousness stands fast for ever; they will hold up their
      head with honour.
¹⁰ The wicked will see it and be angry; they will gnash their teeth
    and pine away;
    the desires of the wicked will perish.

READING   Hebrews 13.1–8, 15–16

¹ Let mutual love continue. ² Do not neglect to show hospitality to strangers, for by doing that some have entertained angels without knowing it. ³ Remember those who are in prison, as though you were in prison with them; those who are being tortured, as though you yourselves were being

tortured. ⁴ Let marriage be held in honour by all, and let the marriage bed be kept undefiled; for God will judge fornicators and adulterers. ⁵ Keep your lives free from the love of money, and be content with what you have; for he has said, 'I will never leave you or forsake you.' ⁶ So we can say with confidence,

'The Lord is my helper;
I will not be afraid.
What can anyone do to me?'

⁷ Remember your leaders, those who spoke the word of God to you; consider the outcome of their way of life, and imitate their faith. ⁸ Jesus Christ is the same yesterday and today and for ever.

¹⁵ Through him, then, let us continually offer a sacrifice of praise to God, that is, the fruit of lips that confess his name. ¹⁶ Do not neglect to do good and to share what you have, for such sacrifices are pleasing to God.

GOSPEL   Luke 14.1, 7–14

¹ On one occasion when Jesus was going to the house of a leader of the Pharisees to eat a meal on the sabbath, they were watching him closely.

⁷ When he noticed how the guests chose the places of honour, he told them a parable. ⁸ 'When you are invited by someone to a wedding banquet, do not sit down at the place of honour, in case someone more distinguished than you has been invited by your host; ⁹ and the host who invited both of you may come and say to you, "Give this person your place", and then in disgrace you would start to take the lowest place. ¹⁰ But when you are invited, go and sit down at the lowest place, so that when your host comes, he may say to you, "Friend, move up higher"; then you will be honoured in the presence of all who sit at the table with you. ¹¹ For all who exalt themselves will be humbled, and those who humble themselves will be exalted.'

¹² He said also to the one who had invited him, 'When you give a luncheon or a dinner, do not invite your friends or your brothers or your relatives or rich neighbours, in case they may invite you in return, and you would be repaid. ¹³ But when you give a banquet, invite the poor, the crippled, the lame, and the blind. ¹⁴ And you will be blessed, because they cannot repay you, for you will be repaid at the resurrection of the righteous.'

POST COMMUNION

See pages 939 to 943 and Table on page 931

SECOND SERVICE

Psalm 119.81–88, [89–96]
Isaiah 33.13–22
John 3.22–36

THIRD SERVICE

Psalm 119.161–176
Jonah 3.1–9

or

Ecclesiasticus 11.[7–17,] 18–28
Revelation 3.14–22

PROPER 18

Sunday between 4 and 10 September inclusive

COLLECT

See pages 939 to 943 and Table on page 931

CONTINUOUS

READING   Jeremiah 18.1–11

¹ The word that came to Jeremiah from the LORD: ² 'Come, go down to the potter's house, and there I will let you hear my words.' ³ So I went down to the potter's house, and there he was working at his wheel. ⁴ The vessel he was making of clay was spoiled in the potter's hand, and he reworked it into another vessel, as seemed good to him.

⁵ Then the word of the LORD came to me: ⁶ Can I not do with you, O house of Israel, just as this potter has done? says the LORD. Just like the clay in the potter's hand, so are you in my hand, O house of Israel. ⁷ At one moment I may declare concerning a nation or a kingdom, that I will pluck up and break down and destroy it, ⁸ but if that nation, concerning which I have spoken, turns from its evil, I will change my mind about the disaster that I intended to bring on it. ⁹ And at another moment I may declare concerning a nation or a kingdom that I will build and plant it, ¹⁰ but if it does evil in my sight, not listening to my voice, then I will change my mind about the good that I had intended to do to it. ¹¹ Now, therefore, say to the people of

Judah and the inhabitants of Jerusalem: Thus says the LORD: Look, I am a potter shaping evil against you and devising a plan against you. Turn now, all of you from your evil way, and amend your ways and your doings.

PSALM   Psalm 139.1–5, 12–17

1   Lord, you have searched me out and known me;
     you know my sitting down and my rising up; you discern my
       thoughts from afar.
2   You trace my journeys and my resting-places
     and are acquainted with all my ways.
3   Indeed, there is not a word on my lips,
     but you, O Lord, know it altogether.
4   You press upon me behind and before
     and lay your hand upon me.
5   Such knowledge is too wonderful for me;
     it is so high that I cannot attain to it.

12 For you yourself created my inmost parts;
     you knit me together in my mother's womb.
13 I will thank you because I am marvellously made;
     your works are wonderful and I know it well.
14 My body was not hidden from you,
     while I was being made in secret and woven in the depths of the
       earth.
15 Your eyes beheld my limbs, yet unfinished in the womb; all of
       them were written in your book;
     they were fashioned day by day, when as yet there was none of
       them.
16 How deep I find your thoughts, O God!
     how great is the sum of them!
17 If I were to count them, they would be more in number than the
       sand;
     to count them all, my life span would need to be like yours.

OR, IF AN ALTERNATIVE READING IS PREFERRED   **Psalm 139.1–7**

1   Lord, you have searched me out and known me;
     you know my sitting down and my rising up; you discern my
       thoughts from afar.
2   You trace my journeys and my resting-places
     and are acquainted with all my ways.
3   Indeed, there is not a word on my lips,
     but you, O Lord, know it altogether.

4 You press upon me behind and before
and lay your hand upon me.
5 Such knowledge is too wonderful for me;
it is so high that I cannot attain to it.
6 Where can I go then from your Spirit?
where can I flee from your presence?
7 If I climb up to heaven, you are there;
if I make the grave my bed, you are there also.

READING   Philemon 1–21

¹ Paul, a prisoner of Christ Jesus, and Timothy our brother,

To Philemon our dear friend and co-worker, ² to Apphia our sister, to Archippus our fellow-soldier, and to the church in your house:

³ Grace to you and peace from God our Father and the Lord Jesus Christ.

⁴ When I remember you in my prayers, I always thank my God ⁵ because I hear of your love for all the saints and your faith towards the Lord Jesus. ⁶ I pray that the sharing of your faith may become effective when you perceive all the good that we may do for Christ. ⁷ I have indeed received much joy and encouragement from your love, because the hearts of the saints have been refreshed through you, my brother.

⁸ For this reason, though I am bold enough in Christ to command you to do your duty, ⁹ yet I would rather appeal to you on the basis of love—and I, Paul, do this as an old man, and now also as a prisoner of Christ Jesus. ¹⁰ I am appealing to you for my child, Onesimus, whose father I have become during my imprisonment. ¹¹ Formerly he was useless to you, but now he is indeed useful both to you and to me. ¹² I am sending him, that is, my own heart, back to you. ¹³ I wanted to keep him with me, so that he might be of service to me in your place during my imprisonment for the gospel; ¹⁴ but I preferred to do nothing without your consent, in order that your good deed might be voluntary and not something forced. ¹⁵ Perhaps this is the reason he was separated from you for a while, so that you might have him back for ever, ¹⁶ no longer as a slave but as more than a slave, a beloved brother—especially to me but how much more to you, both in the flesh and in the Lord.

¹⁷ So if you consider me your partner, welcome him as you would welcome me. ¹⁸ If he has wronged you in any way, or owes you anything, charge that to my account. ¹⁹ I, Paul, am writing this with my own hand: I will repay it. I say nothing about your owing me even your own self. ²⁰ Yes, brother, let

me have this benefit from you in the Lord! Refresh my heart in Christ.
[21] Confident of your obedience, I am writing to you, knowing that you will do even more than I say.

GOSPEL   Luke 14.25–33

[25] Now large crowds were travelling with him; and he turned and said to them, [26] 'Whoever comes to me and does not hate father and mother, wife and children, brothers and sisters, yes, and even life itself, cannot be my disciple. [27] Whoever does not carry the cross and follow me cannot be my disciple. [28] For which of you, intending to build a tower, does not first sit down and estimate the cost, to see whether he has enough to complete it? [29] Otherwise, when he has laid a foundation and is not able to finish, all who see it will begin to ridicule him, [30] saying, "This fellow began to build and was not able to finish." [31] Or what king, going out to wage war against another king, will not sit down first and consider whether he is able with ten thousand to oppose the one who comes against him with twenty thousand? [32] If he cannot, then, while the other is still far away, he sends a delegation and asks for the terms of peace. [33] So therefore, none of you can become my disciple if you do not give up all your possessions.'

RELATED

READING   Deuteronomy 30.15–20

[15] See, I have set before you today life and prosperity, death and adversity. [16] If you obey the commandments of the LORD your God that I am commanding you today, by loving the LORD your God, walking in his ways, and observing his commandments, decrees, and ordinances, then you shall live and become numerous, and the LORD your God will bless you in the land that you are entering to possess. [17] But if your heart turns away and you do not hear, but are led astray to bow down to other gods and serve them, [18] I declare to you today that you shall perish; you shall not live long in the land that you are crossing the Jordan to enter and possess. [19] I call heaven and earth to witness against you today that I have set before you life and death, blessings and curses. Choose life so that you and your descendants may live, [20] loving the LORD your God, obeying him, and holding fast to him; for that means life to you and length of days, so that you may live in the land that the LORD swore to give to your ancestors, to Abraham, to Isaac, and to Jacob.

PSALM   Psalm 1

1 Happy are they who have not walked in the counsel of the wicked,
   nor lingered in the way of sinners, nor sat in the seats of the
   scornful!
2 Their delight is in the law of the Lord,
   and they meditate on his law day and night.
3 They are like trees planted by streams of water, bearing fruit in
   due season, with leaves that do not wither;
   everything they do shall prosper.
4 It is not so with the wicked:
   they are like chaff which the wind blows away;
5 Therefore the wicked shall not stand upright when judgement
   comes,
   nor the sinner in the council of the righteous.
6 For the Lord knows the way of the righteous,
   but the way of the wicked is doomed.

READING   Philemon 1–21

¹ Paul, a prisoner of Christ Jesus, and Timothy our brother,

To Philemon our dear friend and co-worker, ² to Apphia our sister, to Archippus our fellow-soldier, and to the church in your house:

³ Grace to you and peace from God our Father and the Lord Jesus Christ.

⁴ When I remember you in my prayers, I always thank my God ⁵ because I hear of your love for all the saints and your faith towards the Lord Jesus. ⁶ I pray that the sharing of your faith may become effective when you perceive all the good that we may do for Christ. ⁷ I have indeed received much joy and encouragement from your love, because the hearts of the saints have been refreshed through you, my brother.

⁸ For this reason, though I am bold enough in Christ to command you to do your duty, ⁹ yet I would rather appeal to you on the basis of love—and I, Paul, do this as an old man, and now also as a prisoner of Christ Jesus. ¹⁰ I am appealing to you for my child, Onesimus, whose father I have become during my imprisonment. ¹¹ Formerly he was useless to you, but now he is indeed useful both to you and to me. ¹² I am sending him, that is, my own heart, back to you. ¹³ I wanted to keep him with me, so that he might be of service to me in your place during my imprisonment for the gospel; ¹⁴ but I preferred to do nothing without your consent, in order that your good deed might be voluntary and not something forced. ¹⁵ Perhaps this is the reason he was separated from you for a while, so that you might have him

back for ever, [16] no longer as a slave but as more than a slave, a beloved brother—especially to me but how much more to you, both in the flesh and in the Lord.

[17] So if you consider me your partner, welcome him as you would welcome me. [18] If he has wronged you in any way, or owes you anything, charge that to my account. [19] I, Paul, am writing this with my own hand: I will repay it. I say nothing about your owing me even your own self. [20] Yes, brother, let me have this benefit from you in the Lord! Refresh my heart in Christ. [21] Confident of your obedience, I am writing to you, knowing that you will do even more than I say.

GOSPEL   Luke 14.25–33

[25] Now large crowds were travelling with him; and he turned and said to them, [26] 'Whoever comes to me and does not hate father and mother, wife and children, brothers and sisters, yes, and even life itself, cannot be my disciple. [27] Whoever does not carry the cross and follow me cannot be my disciple. [28] For which of you, intending to build a tower, does not first sit down and estimate the cost, to see whether he has enough to complete it? [29] Otherwise, when he has laid a foundation and is not able to finish, all who see it will begin to ridicule him, [30] saying, "This fellow began to build and was not able to finish." [31] Or what king, going out to wage war against another king, will not sit down first and consider whether he is able with ten thousand to oppose the one who comes against him with twenty thousand? [32] If he cannot, then, while the other is still far away, he sends a delegation and asks for the terms of peace. [33] So therefore, none of you can become my disciple if you do not give up all your possessions.'

POST COMMUNION

See pages 940 to 943 and Table on page 931

SECOND SERVICE

Psalms [120;] 121
Isaiah 43.14–44.5
John 5.30–47

THIRD SERVICE

Psalms 122; 123
Jonah 3.10–4.11
or
Ecclesiasticus 27.30–28.9
Revelation 8.1–5

PROPER 19

Sunday between 11 and 17 September inclusive

COLLECT

See pages 940 to 944 and Table on page 931

CONTINUOUS

READING   Jeremiah 4.11–12, 22–28

¹¹ At that time it will be said to this people and to Jerusalem: A hot wind comes from me out of the bare heights in the desert towards my poor people, not to winnow or cleanse— ¹² a wind too strong for that. Now it is I who speak in judgement against them.

²² 'For my people are foolish,
   they do not know me;
they are stupid children,
   they have no understanding.
They are skilled in doing evil,
   but do not know how to do good.'
²³ I looked on the earth, and lo, it was waste and void;
   and to the heavens, and they had no light.
²⁴ I looked on the mountains, and lo, they were quaking,
   and all the hills moved to and fro.
²⁵ I looked, and lo, there was no one at all,
   and all the birds of the air had fled.
²⁶ I looked, and lo, the fruitful land was a desert,
   and all its cities were laid in ruins
   before the LORD, before his fierce anger.

²⁷ For thus says the LORD: The whole land shall be a desolation; yet I will not make a full end.
²⁸ Because of this the earth shall mourn,
   and the heavens above grow black;
for I have spoken, I have purposed;
   I have not relented nor will I turn back.

PSALM   Psalm 14

1   The fool has said in his heart, 'There is no God.'
    All are corrupt and commit abominable acts; there is none who
        does any good.
2   The Lord looks down from heaven upon us all,
    to see if there is any who is wise, if there is one who seeks after
        God.
3   Everyone has proved faithless; all alike have turned bad;
    there is none who does good; no, not one.
4   Have they no knowledge, all those evildoers
    who eat up my people like bread and do not call upon the Lord?
5   See how they tremble with fear,
    because God is in the company of the righteous.
6   Their aim is to confound the plans of the afflicted,
    but the Lord is their refuge.
7   O that Israel's deliverance would come out of Zion!
    when the Lord restores the fortunes of his people, Jacob will rejoice
        and Israel be glad.

READING   1 Timothy 1.12–17

[12] I am grateful to Christ Jesus our Lord, who has strengthened me, because
he judged me faithful and appointed me to his service, [13] even though I
was formerly a blasphemer, a persecutor, and a man of violence. But I
received mercy because I had acted ignorantly in unbelief, [14] and the grace
of our Lord overflowed for me with the faith and love that are in Christ
Jesus. [15] The saying is sure and worthy of full acceptance, that Christ Jesus
came into the world to save sinners—of whom I am the foremost. [16] But for
that very reason I received mercy, so that in me, as the foremost, Jesus
Christ might display the utmost patience, making me an example to those
who would come to believe in him for eternal life. [17] To the King of the
ages, immortal, invisible, the only God, be honour and glory for ever and
ever. Amen.

GOSPEL   Luke 15.1–10

[1] Now all the tax-collectors and sinners were coming near to listen to
him. [2] And the Pharisees and the scribes were grumbling and saying, 'This
fellow welcomes sinners and eats with them.'

[3] So he told them this parable: [4] 'Which one of you, having a hundred
sheep and losing one of them, does not leave the ninety-nine in the wilderness and go after the one that is lost until he finds it? [5] When he has

found it, he lays it on his shoulders and rejoices. ⁶ And when he comes home, he calls together his friends and neighbours, saying to them, "Rejoice with me, for I have found my sheep that was lost." ⁷ Just so, I tell you, there will be more joy in heaven over one sinner who repents than over ninety-nine righteous people who need no repentance.

⁸ 'Or what woman having ten silver coins, if she loses one of them, does not light a lamp, sweep the house, and search carefully until she finds it? ⁹ When she has found it, she calls together her friends and neighbours, saying, "Rejoice with me, for I have found the coin that I had lost." ¹⁰ Just so, I tell you, there is joy in the presence of the angels of God over one sinner who repents.'

RELATED

READING   Exodus 32.7–14

⁷ The LORD said to Moses, 'Go down at once! Your people, whom you brought up out of the land of Egypt, have acted perversely; ⁸ they have been quick to turn aside from the way that I commanded them; they have cast for themselves an image of a calf, and have worshipped it and sacrificed to it, and said, "These are your gods, O Israel, who brought you up out of the land of Egypt!" ' ⁹ The LORD said to Moses, 'I have seen this people, how stiff-necked they are. ¹⁰ Now let me alone, so that my wrath may burn hot against them and I may consume them; and of you I will make a great nation.'

¹¹ But Moses implored the LORD his God, and said, 'O LORD, why does your wrath burn hot against your people, whom you brought out of the land of Egypt with great power and with a mighty hand? ¹² Why should the Egyptians say, "It was with evil intent that he brought them out to kill them in the mountains, and to consume them from the face of the earth"? Turn from your fierce wrath; change your mind and do not bring disaster on your people. ¹³ Remember Abraham, Isaac, and Israel, your servants, how you swore to them by your own self, saying to them, "I will multiply your descendants like the stars of heaven, and all this land that I have promised I will give to your descendants, and they shall inherit it for ever." ' ¹⁴ And the LORD changed his mind about the disaster that he planned to bring on his people.

PSALM   Psalm 51.1–11

1 Have mercy on me, O God, according to your loving-kindness;
   in your great compassion blot out my offences.
2 Wash me through and through from my wickedness
   and cleanse me from my sin.
3 For I know my transgressions,
   and my sin is ever before me.
4 Against you only have I sinned
   and done what is evil in your sight.
5 And so you are justified when you speak
   and upright in your judgement.
6 Indeed, I have been wicked from my birth,
   a sinner from my mother's womb.
7 For behold, you look for truth deep within me,
   and will make me understand wisdom secretly.
8 Purge me from my sin and I shall be pure;
   wash me and I shall be clean indeed.
9 Make me hear of joy and gladness,
   that the body you have broken may rejoice.
10 Hide your face from my sins
   and blot out all my iniquities.
11 Create in me a clean heart, O God,
   and renew a right spirit within me.

READING   1 Timothy 1.12–17

12 I am grateful to Christ Jesus our Lord, who has strengthened me, because he judged me faithful and appointed me to his service, 13 even though I was formerly a blasphemer, a persecutor, and a man of violence. But I received mercy because I had acted ignorantly in unbelief, 14 and the grace of our Lord overflowed for me with the faith and love that are in Christ Jesus. 15 The saying is sure and worthy of full acceptance, that Christ Jesus came into the world to save sinners—of whom I am the foremost. 16 But for that very reason I received mercy, so that in me, as the foremost, Jesus Christ might display the utmost patience, making me an example to those who would come to believe in him for eternal life. 17 To the King of the ages, immortal, invisible, the only God, be honour and glory for ever and ever. Amen.

GOSPEL   Luke 15.1–10

[1] Now all the tax-collectors and sinners were coming near to listen to him. [2] And the Pharisees and the scribes were grumbling and saying, 'This fellow welcomes sinners and eats with them.'

[3] So he told them this parable: [4] 'Which one of you, having a hundred sheep and losing one of them, does not leave the ninety-nine in the wilderness and go after the one that is lost until he finds it? [5] When he has found it, he lays it on his shoulders and rejoices. [6] And when he comes home, he calls together his friends and neighbours, saying to them, "Rejoice with me, for I have found my sheep that was lost." [7] Just so, I tell you, there will be more joy in heaven over one sinner who repents than over ninety-nine righteous people who need no repentance.

[8] 'Or what woman having ten silver coins, if she loses one of them, does not light a lamp, sweep the house, and search carefully until she finds it? [9] When she has found it, she calls together her friends and neighbours, saying, "Rejoice with me, for I have found the coin that I had lost." [10] Just so, I tell you, there is joy in the presence of the angels of God over one sinner who repents.'

POST COMMUNION

See pages 941 to 944 and Table on page 931

SECOND SERVICE   THIRD SERVICE

Psalms 124; 125   **Psalms 126; 127**
Isaiah 60   **Isaiah 44.24–45.8**
John 6.51–69   **Revelation 12.1–12**

PROPER 20

Sunday between 18 and 24 September inclusive

COLLECT

See pages 941 to 944 and Table on page 931

CONTINUOUS

READING   Jeremiah 8.18–9.1

¹⁸ My joy is gone, grief is upon me,
    my heart is sick.
¹⁹ Hark, the cry of my poor people
    from far and wide in the land:
  'Is the Lord not in Zion?
    Is her King not in her?'
  ('Why have they provoked me to anger with their images,
    with their foreign idols?')
²⁰ 'The harvest is past, the summer is ended,
    and we are not saved.'
²¹ For the hurt of my poor people I am hurt,
    I mourn, and dismay has taken hold of me.
²² Is there no balm in Gilead?
    Is there no physician there?
  Why then has the health of my poor people
    not been restored?

 ¹ O that my head were a spring of water,
    and my eyes a fountain of tears,
  so that I might weep day and night
    for the slain of my poor people!

PSALM   Psalm 79.1–9

¹ O God, the heathen have come into your inheritance; they have
    profaned your holy temple;
  they have made Jerusalem a heap of rubble.
² They have given the bodies of your servants as food for the birds
    of the air,
  and the flesh of your faithful ones to the beasts of the field.

3 They have shed their blood like water on every side of Jerusalem,
   and there was no one to bury them.
4 We have become a reproach to our neighbours,
   an object of scorn and derision to those around us.
5 How long will you be angry, O Lord?
   will your fury blaze like fire for ever?
6 Pour out your wrath upon the heathen who have not known you
   and upon the kingdoms that have not called upon your name.
7 For they have devoured Jacob
   and made his dwelling a ruin.
8 Remember not our past sins; let your compassion be swift to meet
   us;
   for we have been brought very low.
9 Help us, O God our Saviour, for the glory of your name;
   deliver us and forgive us our sins, for your name's sake.

READING   1 Timothy 2.1–7

1 First of all, then, I urge that supplications, prayers, intercessions, and thanksgivings should be made for everyone, 2 for kings and all who are in high positions, so that we may lead a quiet and peaceable life in all godliness and dignity. 3 This is right and is acceptable in the sight of God our Saviour, 4 who desires everyone to be saved and to come to the knowledge of the truth. 5 For
   there is one God;
      there is also one mediator between God and humankind,
   Christ Jesus, himself human,
6   who gave himself a ransom for all
—this was attested at the right time. 7 For this I was appointed a herald and an apostle (I am telling the truth, I am not lying), a teacher of the Gentiles in faith and truth.

GOSPEL   Luke 16.1–13

1 Then Jesus said to the disciples, 'There was a rich man who had a manager, and charges were brought to him that this man was squandering his property. 2 So he summoned him and said to him, "What is this that I hear about you? Give me an account of your management, because you cannot be my manager any longer." 3 Then the manager said to himself, "What will I do, now that my master is taking the position away from me? I am not strong enough to dig, and I am ashamed to beg. 4 I have decided what to do so that, when I am dismissed as manager, people may welcome me into their homes." 5 So, summoning his master's debtors one by one,

he asked the first, "How much do you owe my master?" [6] He answered, "A hundred jugs of olive oil." He said to him, "Take your bill, sit down quickly, and make it fifty." [7] Then he asked another, "And how much do you owe?" He replied, "A hundred containers of wheat." He said to him, "Take your bill and make it eighty." [8] And his master commended the dishonest manager because he had acted shrewdly; for the children of this age are more shrewd in dealing with their own generation than are the children of light. [9] And I tell you, make friends for yourselves by means of dishonest wealth so that when it is gone, they may welcome you into the eternal homes.

[10] 'Whoever is faithful in a very little is faithful also in much; and whoever is dishonest in a very little is dishonest also in much. [11] If then you have not been faithful with the dishonest wealth, who will entrust to you the true riches? [12] And if you have not been faithful with what belongs to another, who will give you what is your own? [13] No slave can serve two masters; for a slave will either hate the one and love the other, or be devoted to the one and despise the other. You cannot serve God and wealth.'

RELATED

READING   Amos 8.4–7

[4]   Hear this, you that trample on the needy,
          and bring to ruin the poor of the land,
[5]   saying, 'When will the new moon be over
          so that we may sell grain;
      and the sabbath,
          so that we may offer wheat for sale?
      We will make the ephah small and the shekel great,
          and practise deceit with false balances,
[6]   buying the poor for silver
          and the needy for a pair of sandals,
          and selling the sweepings of the wheat.'
[7]   The LORD has sworn by the pride of Jacob:
      Surely I will never forget any of their deeds.

PSALM   Psalm 113

[1]   Alleluia! Give praise, you servants of the Lord;
      praise the name of the Lord.
[2]   Let the name of the Lord be blessed,
      from this time forth for evermore.

3   From the rising of the sun to its going down
    let the name of the Lord be praised.
4   The Lord is high above all nations,
    and his glory above the heavens.
5   Who is like the Lord our God, who sits enthroned on high,
    but stoops to behold the heavens and the earth?
6   He takes up the weak out of the dust
    and lifts up the poor from the ashes.
7   He sets them with the princes,
    with the princes of his people.
8   He makes the woman of a childless house
    to be a joyful mother of children.

READING   1 Timothy 2.1-7

¹ First of all, then, I urge that supplications, prayers, intercessions, and thanksgivings should be made for everyone, ² for kings and all who are in high positions, so that we may lead a quiet and peaceable life in all godliness and dignity. ³ This is right and is acceptable in the sight of God our Saviour, ⁴ who desires everyone to be saved and to come to the knowledge of the truth. ⁵ For
    there is one God;
        there is also one mediator between God and humankind,
    Christ Jesus, himself human,
6   who gave himself a ransom for all
—this was attested at the right time. ⁷ For this I was appointed a herald and an apostle (I am telling the truth, I am not lying), a teacher of the Gentiles in faith and truth.

GOSPEL   Luke 16.1-13

¹ Then Jesus said to the disciples, 'There was a rich man who had a manager, and charges were brought to him that this man was squandering his property. ² So he summoned him and said to him, "What is this that I hear about you? Give me an account of your management, because you cannot be my manager any longer." ³ Then the manager said to himself, "What will I do, now that my master is taking the position away from me? I am not strong enough to dig, and I am ashamed to beg. ⁴ I have decided what to do so that, when I am dismissed as manager, people may welcome me into their homes." ⁵ So, summoning his master's debtors one by one, he asked the first, "How much do you owe my master?" ⁶ He answered, "A hundred jugs of olive oil." He said to him, "Take your bill, sit down quickly, and make it fifty." ⁷ Then he asked another, "And how much do you owe?"

He replied, "A hundred containers of wheat." He said to him, "Take your bill and make it eighty." [8] And his master commended the dishonest manager because he had acted shrewdly; for the children of this age are more shrewd in dealing with their own generation than are the children of light. [9] And I tell you, make friends for yourselves by means of dishonest wealth so that when it is gone, they may welcome you into the eternal homes.

[10] 'Whoever is faithful in a very little is faithful also in much; and whoever is dishonest in a very little is dishonest also in much. [11] If then you have not been faithful with the dishonest wealth, who will entrust to you the true riches? [12] And if you have not been faithful with what belongs to another, who will give you what is your own? [13] No slave can serve two masters; for a slave will either hate the one and love the other, or be devoted to the one and despise the other. You cannot serve God and wealth.'

POST COMMUNION

See pages 941 to 945 and Table on page 931

SECOND SERVICE	THIRD SERVICE
Psalms [128;] 129	Psalms 130; 131
Ezra 1	Isaiah 45.9–22
John 7.14–36	Revelation 14.1–5

PROPER 21

Sunday between 25 September and 1 October inclusive

COLLECT

See pages 942 to 945 and Table on page 931

CONTINUOUS

READING   Jeremiah 32.1–3a, 6–15

[1] The word that came to Jeremiah from the LORD in the tenth year of King Zedekiah of Judah, which was the eighteenth year of Nebuchadrezzar. [2] At that time the army of the king of Babylon was besieging Jerusalem, and the prophet Jeremiah was confined in the court of the guard that was in

the palace of the king of Judah, ³ where King Zedekiah of Judah had confined him.

⁶ Jeremiah said, The word of the LORD came to me: ⁷ Hanamel son of your uncle Shallum is going to come to you and say, 'Buy my field that is at Anathoth, for the right of redemption by purchase is yours.' ⁸ Then my cousin Hanamel came to me in the court of the guard, in accordance with the word of the LORD, and said to me, 'Buy my field that is at Anathoth in the land of Benjamin, for the right of possession and redemption is yours; buy it for yourself.' Then I knew that this was the word of the LORD.

⁹ And I bought the field at Anathoth from my cousin Hanamel, and weighed out the money to him, seventeen shekels of silver. ¹⁰ I signed the deed, sealed it, got witnesses, and weighed the money on scales. ¹¹ Then I took the sealed deed of purchase, containing the terms and conditions, and the open copy; ¹² and I gave the deed of purchase to Baruch son of Neriah son of Mahseiah, in the presence of my cousin Hanamel, in the presence of the witnesses who signed the deed of purchase, and in the presence of all the Judeans who were sitting in the court of the guard. ¹³ In their presence I charged Baruch, saying, ¹⁴ Thus says the LORD of hosts, the God of Israel: Take these deeds, both this sealed deed of purchase and this open deed, and put them in an earthenware jar, in order that they may last for a long time. ¹⁵ For thus says the LORD of hosts, the God of Israel: Houses and fields and vineyards shall again be bought in this land.

PSALM   Psalm 91.1–6, 14–16

1   He who dwells in the shelter of the Most High,
    abides under the shadow of the Almighty.
2   He shall say to the Lord, 'You are my refuge and my stronghold,
    my God in whom I put my trust.'
3   He shall deliver you from the snare of the hunter
    and from the deadly pestilence.
4   He shall cover you with his pinions, and you shall find refuge
        under his wings;
    his faithfulness shall be a shield and buckler.
5   You shall not be afraid of any terror by night,
    nor of the arrow that flies by day;
6   Of the plague that stalks in the darkness,
    nor of the sickness that lays waste at midday.

14 Because he is bound to me in love, therefore will I deliver him;
    I will protect him, because he knows my name.

¹⁵ He shall call upon me and I will answer him;
  I am with him in trouble, I will rescue him and bring him to
    honour.
¹⁶ With long life will I satisfy him,
  and show him my salvation.

OR, IF AN ALTERNATIVE READING IS PREFERRED **Psalm 91.11–16**

¹¹ For he shall give his angels charge over you,
  to keep you in all your ways.
¹² They shall bear you in their hands,
  lest you dash your foot against a stone.
¹³ You shall tread upon the lion and adder;
  you shall trample the young lion and the serpent under your feet.
¹⁴ Because he is bound to me in love, therefore will I deliver him;
  I will protect him, because he knows my name.
¹⁵ He shall call upon me and I will answer him;
  I am with him in trouble, I will rescue him and bring him to
    honour.
¹⁶ With long life will I satisfy him,
  and show him my salvation.

READING   1 Timothy 6.6–19

⁶ Of course, there is great gain in godliness combined with contentment; ⁷ for we brought nothing into the world, so that we can take nothing out of it; ⁸ but if we have food and clothing, we will be content with these. ⁹ But those who want to be rich fall into temptation and are trapped by many senseless and harmful desires that plunge people into ruin and destruction. ¹⁰ For the love of money is a root of all kinds of evil, and in their eagerness to be rich some have wandered away from the faith and pierced themselves with many pains.

¹¹ But as for you, man of God, shun all this; pursue righteousness, godliness, faith, love, endurance, gentleness. ¹² Fight the good fight of the faith; take hold of the eternal life, to which you were called and for which you made the good confession in the presence of many witnesses. ¹³ In the presence of God, who gives life to all things, and of Christ Jesus, who in his testimony before Pontius Pilate made the good confession, I charge you ¹⁴ to keep the commandment without spot or blame until the manifestation of our Lord Jesus Christ, ¹⁵ which he will bring about at the right time—he who is the blessed and only Sovereign, the King of kings and Lord of lords. ¹⁶ It is he alone who has immortality and dwells in unapproachable light,

whom no one has ever seen or can see; to him be honour and eternal dominion. Amen.

¹⁷ As for those who in the present age are rich, command them not to be haughty, or to set their hopes on the uncertainty of riches, but rather on God who richly provides us with everything for our enjoyment. ¹⁸ They are to do good, to be rich in good works, generous, and ready to share, ¹⁹ thus storing up for themselves the treasure of a good foundation for the future, so that they may take hold of the life that really is life.

GOSPEL   Luke 16.19–31

¹⁹ 'There was a rich man who was dressed in purple and fine linen and who feasted sumptuously every day. ²⁰ And at his gate lay a poor man named Lazarus, covered with sores, ²¹ who longed to satisfy his hunger with what fell from the rich man's table; even the dogs would come and lick his sores. ²² The poor man died and was carried away by the angels to be with Abraham. The rich man also died and was buried. ²³ In Hades, where he was being tormented, he looked up and saw Abraham far away with Lazarus by his side. ²⁴ He called out, "Father Abraham, have mercy on me, and send Lazarus to dip the tip of his finger in water and cool my tongue; for I am in agony in these flames." ²⁵ But Abraham said, "Child, remember that during your lifetime you received your good things, and Lazarus in like manner evil things; but now he is comforted here, and you are in agony. ²⁶ Besides all this, between you and us a great chasm has been fixed, so that those who might want to pass from here to you cannot do so, and no one can cross from there to us." ²⁷ He said, "Then, father, I beg you to send him to my father's house— ²⁸ for I have five brothers—that he may warn them, so that they will not also come into this place of torment." ²⁹ Abraham replied, "They have Moses and the prophets; they should listen to them." ³⁰ He said, "No, father Abraham; but if someone goes to them from the dead, they will repent." ³¹ He said to him, "If they do not listen to Moses and the prophets, neither will they be convinced even if someone rises from the dead." '

RELATED

READING   Amos 6.1a, 4–7

¹ Alas for those who are at ease in Zion,
      and for those who feel secure on Mount Samaria.

⁴ Alas for those who lie on beds of ivory,
      and lounge on their couches,
   and eat lambs from the flock,
      and calves from the stall;
⁵ who sing idle songs to the sound of the harp,
      and like David improvise on instruments of music;
⁶ who drink wine from bowls,
      and anoint themselves with the finest oils,
      but are not grieved over the ruin of Joseph!
⁷ Therefore they shall now be the first to go into exile,
      and the revelry of the loungers shall pass away.

PSALM   Psalm 146

¹ Alleluia! Praise the Lord, O my soul!
   I will praise the Lord as long as I live; I will sing praises to my God
      while I have my being.
² Put not your trust in rulers, nor in any child of earth,
   for there is no help in them.
³ When they breathe their last, they return to earth,
   and in that day their thoughts perish.
⁴ Happy are they who have the God of Jacob for their help!
   whose hope is in the Lord their God;
⁵ Who made heaven and earth, the seas, and all that is in them;
   who keeps his promise for ever;
⁶ Who gives justice to those who are oppressed,
   and food to those who hunger.
⁷ The Lord sets the prisoners free; the Lord opens the eyes of the
      blind;
   the Lord lifts up those who are bowed down;
⁸ The Lord loves the righteous; the Lord cares for the stranger;
   he sustains the orphan and widow, but frustrates the way of the
      wicked.
⁹ The Lord shall reign for ever,
   your God, O Zion, throughout all generations. Alleluia!

READING   1 Timothy 6.6–19

⁶ Of course, there is great gain in godliness combined with contentment;
⁷ for we brought nothing into the world, so that we can take nothing out
of it; ⁸ but if we have food and clothing, we will be content with these. ⁹ But
those who want to be rich fall into temptation and are trapped by many
senseless and harmful desires that plunge people into ruin and destruction.
¹⁰ For the love of money is a root of all kinds of evil, and in their eagerness
to be rich some have wandered away from the faith and pierced themselves
with many pains.

¹¹ But as for you, man of God, shun all this; pursue righteousness, godliness, faith, love, endurance, gentleness. ¹² Fight the good fight of the faith;
take hold of the eternal life, to which you were called and for which you
made the good confession in the presence of many witnesses. ¹³ In the
presence of God, who gives life to all things, and of Christ Jesus, who in his
testimony before Pontius Pilate made the good confession, I charge you
¹⁴ to keep the commandment without spot or blame until the manifestation
of our Lord Jesus Christ, ¹⁵ which he will bring about at the right time—he
who is the blessed and only Sovereign, the King of kings and Lord of lords.
¹⁶ It is he alone who has immortality and dwells in unapproachable light,
whom no one has ever seen or can see; to him be honour and eternal
dominion. Amen.

¹⁷ As for those who in the present age are rich, command them not to be
haughty, or to set their hopes on the uncertainty of riches, but rather on
God who richly provides us with everything for our enjoyment. ¹⁸ They are
to do good, to be rich in good works, generous, and ready to share, ¹⁹ thus
storing up for themselves the treasure of a good foundation for the future,
so that they may take hold of the life that really is life.

GOSPEL   Luke 16.19–31

¹⁹ 'There was a rich man who was dressed in purple and fine linen and
who feasted sumptuously every day. ²⁰ And at his gate lay a poor man named
Lazarus, covered with sores, ²¹ who longed to satisfy his hunger with what
fell from the rich man's table; even the dogs would come and lick his sores.
²² The poor man died and was carried away by the angels to be with
Abraham. The rich man also died and was buried. ²³ In Hades, where he
was being tormented, he looked up and saw Abraham far away with Lazarus
by his side. ²⁴ He called out, "Father Abraham, have mercy on me, and send
Lazarus to dip the tip of his finger in water and cool my tongue; for I am
in agony in these flames." ²⁵ But Abraham said, "Child, remember that
during your lifetime you received your good things, and Lazarus in like

manner evil things; but now he is comforted here, and you are in agony. [26] Besides all this, between you and us a great chasm has been fixed, so that those who might want to pass from here to you cannot do so, and no one can cross from there to us." [27] He said, "Then, father, I beg you to send him to my father's house— [28] for I have five brothers—that he may warn them, so that they will not also come into this place of torment." [29] Abraham replied, "They have Moses and the prophets; they should listen to them." [30] He said, "No, father Abraham; but if someone goes to them from the dead, they will repent." [31] He said to him, "If they do not listen to Moses and the prophets, neither will they be convinced even if someone rises from the dead." '

POST COMMUNION

See pages 942 to 946 and Table on page 931

SECOND SERVICE

Psalms 134; 135.1–14, [15–21]
Nehemiah 2
John 8.31–38, 48–59

THIRD SERVICE

Psalm 132
Isaiah 48.12–22
Luke 11.37–54

PROPER 22

Sunday between 2 and 8 October inclusive

COLLECT

See pages 942 to 946 and Table on page 931

CONTINUOUS

READING   Lamentations 1.1–6

[1] How lonely sits the city
   that once was full of people!
How like a widow she has become,
   she that was great among the nations!
She that was a princess among the provinces
   has become a vassal.

2 She weeps bitterly in the night,
       with tears on her cheeks;
   among all her lovers
       she has no one to comfort her;
   all her friends have dealt treacherously with her,
       they have become her enemies.
3 Judah has gone into exile with suffering
       and hard servitude;
   she lives now among the nations,
       and finds no resting-place;
   her pursuers have all overtaken her
       in the midst of her distress.
4 The roads to Zion mourn,
       for no one comes to the festivals;
   all her gates are desolate,
       her priests groan;
   her young girls grieve,
       and her lot is bitter.
5 Her foes have become the masters,
       her enemies prosper,
   because the LORD has made her suffer
       for the multitude of her transgressions;
   her children have gone away,
       captives before the foe.
6 From daughter Zion has departed
       all her majesty.
   Her princes have become like stags
       that find no pasture;
   they fled without strength
       before the pursuer.

EITHER

CANTICLE   Lamentations 3.19–26

19 The thought of my affliction and my homelessness
        is wormwood and gall!
20 My soul continually thinks of it
        and is bowed down within me.
21 But this I call to mind,
        and therefore I have hope:
22 The steadfast love of the LORD never ceases,
        his mercies never come to an end;

²³ they are new every morning;
    great is your faithfulness.
²⁴ 'The LORD is my portion,' says my soul,
    'therefore I will hope in him.'
²⁵ The LORD is good to those who wait for him,
    to the soul that seeks him.
²⁶ It is good that one should wait quietly
    for the salvation of the LORD.

OR

PSALM   Psalm 137.1–6, [7–9]

¹ By the waters of Babylon we sat down and wept,
    when we remembered you, O Zion.
² As for our harps, we hung them up
    on the trees in the midst of that land.
³ For those who led us away captive asked us for a song, and our
    oppressors called for mirth:
    'Sing us one of the songs of Zion.'
⁴ How shall we sing the Lord's song
    upon an alien soil?
⁵ If I forget you, O Jerusalem,
    let my right hand forget its skill.
⁶ Let my tongue cleave to the roof of my mouth if I do not remember
    you,
    if I do not set Jerusalem above my highest joy.
[⁷ Remember the day of Jerusalem, O Lord, against the people of
    Edom,
    who said, 'Down with it! down with it! even to the ground!'
⁸ O Daughter of Babylon, doomed to destruction,
    happy the one who pays you back for what you have done to us!
⁹ Happy shall he be who takes your little ones,
    and dashes them against the rock!]

READING   2 Timothy 1.1–14

¹ Paul, an apostle of Christ Jesus by the will of God, for the sake of the promise of life that is in Christ Jesus,

² To Timothy, my beloved child:

Grace, mercy, and peace from God the Father and Christ Jesus our Lord.

3 I am grateful to God—whom I worship with a clear conscience, as my ancestors did—when I remember you constantly in my prayers night and day. 4 Recalling your tears, I long to see you so that I may be filled with joy. 5 I am reminded of your sincere faith, a faith that lived first in your grandmother Lois and your mother Eunice and now, I am sure, lives in you. 6 For this reason I remind you to rekindle the gift of God that is within you through the laying on of my hands; 7 for God did not give us a spirit of cowardice, but rather a spirit of power and of love and of self-discipline.

8 Do not be ashamed, then, of the testimony about our Lord or of me his prisoner, but join with me in suffering for the gospel, relying on the power of God, 9 who saved us and called us with a holy calling, not according to our works but according to his own purpose and grace. This grace was given to us in Christ Jesus before the ages began, 10 but it has now been revealed through the appearing of our Saviour Christ Jesus, who abolished death and brought life and immortality to light through the gospel. 11 For this gospel I was appointed a herald and an apostle and a teacher, 12 and for this reason I suffer as I do. But I am not ashamed, for I know the one in whom I have put my trust, and I am sure that he is able to guard until that day what I have entrusted to him. 13 Hold to the standard of sound teaching that you have heard from me, in the faith and love that are in Christ Jesus. 14 Guard the good treasure entrusted to you, with the help of the Holy Spirit living in us.

GOSPEL   Luke 17.5–10

5 The apostles said to the Lord, 'Increase our faith!' 6 The Lord replied, 'If you had faith the size of a mustard seed, you could say to this mulberry tree, "Be uprooted and planted in the sea", and it would obey you.

7 'Who among you would say to your slave who has just come in from ploughing or tending sheep in the field, "Come here at once and take your place at the table"? 8 Would you not rather say to him, "Prepare supper for me, put on your apron and serve me while I eat and drink; later you may eat and drink"? 9 Do you thank the slave for doing what was commanded? 10 So you also, when you have done all that you were ordered to do, say, "We are worthless slaves; we have done only what we ought to have done!" '

RELATED

READING Habakkuk 1.1-4; 2.1-4

¹ The oracle that the prophet Habakkuk saw.
² O Lord, how long shall I cry for help,
and you will not listen?
Or cry to you 'Violence!'
and you will not save?
³ Why do you make me see wrongdoing
and look at trouble?
Destruction and violence are before me;
strife and contention arise.
⁴ So the law becomes slack
and justice never prevails.
The wicked surround the righteous—
therefore judgement comes forth perverted.

¹ I will stand at my watch-post,
and station myself on the rampart;
I will keep watch to see what he will say to me,
and what he will answer concerning my complaint.
² Then the Lord answered me and said:
Write the vision;
make it plain on tablets,
so that a runner may read it.
³ For there is still a vision for the appointed time;
it speaks of the end, and does not lie.
If it seems to tarry, wait for it;
it will surely come, it will not delay.
⁴ Look at the proud!
Their spirit is not right in them,
but the righteous live by their faith.

PSALM Psalm 37.1-10

¹ Do not fret yourself because of evildoers;
do not be jealous of those who do wrong.
² For they shall soon wither like the grass,
and like the green grass fade away.
³ Put your trust in the Lord and do good;
dwell in the land and feed on its riches.

4   Take delight in the Lord,
     and he shall give you your heart's desire.
5   Commit your way to the Lord and put your trust in him,
     and he will bring it to pass.
6   He will make your righteousness as clear as the light
     and your just dealing as the noonday.
7   Be still before the Lord
     and wait patiently for him.
8   Do not fret yourself over the one who prospers,
     the one who succeeds in evil schemes.
9   Refrain from anger, leave rage alone;
     do not fret yourself; it leads only to evil.
10 For evildoers shall be cut off,
     but those who wait upon the Lord shall possess the land.

READING   2 Timothy 1.1–14

1 Paul, an apostle of Christ Jesus by the will of God, for the sake of the promise of life that is in Christ Jesus,

2 To Timothy, my beloved child:

Grace, mercy, and peace from God the Father and Christ Jesus our Lord.

3 I am grateful to God—whom I worship with a clear conscience, as my ancestors did—when I remember you constantly in my prayers night and day. 4 Recalling your tears, I long to see you so that I may be filled with joy. 5 I am reminded of your sincere faith, a faith that lived first in your grandmother Lois and your mother Eunice and now, I am sure, lives in you. 6 For this reason I remind you to rekindle the gift of God that is within you through the laying on of my hands; 7 for God did not give us a spirit of cowardice, but rather a spirit of power and of love and of self-discipline.

8 Do not be ashamed, then, of the testimony about our Lord or of me his prisoner, but join with me in suffering for the gospel, relying on the power of God, 9 who saved us and called us with a holy calling, not according to our works but according to his own purpose and grace. This grace was given to us in Christ Jesus before the ages began, 10 but it has now been revealed through the appearing of our Saviour Christ Jesus, who abolished death and brought life and immortality to light through the gospel. 11 For this gospel I was appointed a herald and an apostle and a teacher, 12 and for this reason I suffer as I do. But I am not ashamed, for I know the one in whom I have put my trust, and I am sure that he is able to guard until that day what I have entrusted to him. 13 Hold to the standard of sound teaching that you have heard from me, in the faith and love that are in Christ Jesus. 14 Guard the good treasure entrusted to you, with the help of the Holy Spirit living in us.

GOSPEL   Luke 17.5-10

⁵ The apostles said to the Lord, 'Increase our faith!' ⁶ The Lord replied, 'If you had faith the size of a mustard seed, you could say to this mulberry tree, "Be uprooted and planted in the sea", and it would obey you.

⁷ 'Who among you would say to your slave who has just come in from ploughing or tending sheep in the field, "Come here at once and take your place at the table"? ⁸ Would you not rather say to him, "Prepare supper for me, put on your apron and serve me while I eat and drink; later you may eat and drink"? ⁹ Do you thank the slave for doing what was commanded? ¹⁰ So you also, when you have done all that you were ordered to do, say, "We are worthless slaves; we have done only what we ought to have done!" '

POST COMMUNION

See pages 943 to 946 and Table on page 931

SECOND SERVICE   THIRD SERVICE

Psalm 142   Psalm 141
Nehemiah 5.1–13   Isaiah 49.13–23
John 9   Luke 12.1–12

PROPER 23

Sunday between 9 and 15 October inclusive

COLLECT

See pages 943 to 947 and Table on page 931

CONTINUOUS

READING   Jeremiah 29.1, 4–7

¹ These are the words of the letter that the prophet Jeremiah sent from Jerusalem to the remaining elders among the exiles, and to the priests, the prophets, and all the people, whom Nebuchadnezzar had taken into exile from Jerusalem to Babylon.

4 Thus says the LORD of hosts, the God of Israel, to all the exiles whom I have sent into exile from Jerusalem to Babylon: 5 Build houses and live in them; plant gardens and eat what they produce. 6 Take wives and have sons and daughters; take wives for your sons, and give your daughters in marriage, that they may bear sons and daughters; multiply there, and do not decrease. 7 But seek the welfare of the city where I have sent you into exile, and pray to the LORD on its behalf, for in its welfare you will find your welfare.

PSALM   Psalm 66.1–11

1   Be joyful in God, all you lands;
    sing the glory of his name; sing the glory of his praise.
2   Say to God, 'How awesome are your deeds!
    because of your great strength your enemies cringe before you.
3   All the earth bows down before you,
    sings to you, sings out your name.'
4   Come now and see the works of God,
    how wonderful he is in his doing towards all people.
5   He turned the sea into dry land, so that they went through the
        water on foot,
    and there we rejoiced in him.
6   In his might he rules for ever; his eyes keep watch over the nations;
    let no rebel rise up against him.
7   Bless our God, you peoples;
    make the voice of his praise to be heard;
8   Who holds our souls in life,
    and will not allow our feet to slip.
9   For you, O God, have proved us;
    you have tried us just as silver is tried.
10 You brought us into the snare;
    you laid heavy burdens upon our backs.
11 You let enemies ride over our heads; we went through fire and
        water;
    but you brought us out into a place of refreshment.

READING   2 Timothy 2.8–15

8 Remember Jesus Christ, raised from the dead, a descendant of David—that is my gospel, 9 for which I suffer hardship, even to the point of being chained like a criminal. But the word of God is not chained. 10 Therefore I

endure everything for the sake of the elect, so that they may also obtain the salvation that is in Christ Jesus, with eternal glory. ¹¹ The saying is sure:
If we have died with him, we will also live with him;
¹² if we endure, we will also reign with him;
if we deny him, he will also deny us;
¹³ if we are faithless, he remains faithful—
for he cannot deny himself.

¹⁴ Remind them of this, and warn them before God that they are to avoid wrangling over words, which does no good but only ruins those who are listening. ¹⁵ Do your best to present yourself to God as one approved by him, a worker who has no need to be ashamed, rightly explaining the word of truth.

GOSPEL   Luke 17.11–19

¹¹ On the way to Jerusalem Jesus was going through the region between Samaria and Galilee. ¹² As he entered a village, ten lepers approached him. Keeping their distance, ¹³ they called out, saying, 'Jesus, Master, have mercy on us!' ¹⁴ When he saw them, he said to them, 'Go and show yourselves to the priests.' And as they went, they were made clean. ¹⁵ Then one of them, when he saw that he was healed, turned back, praising God with a loud voice. ¹⁶ He prostrated himself at Jesus' feet and thanked him. And he was a Samaritan. ¹⁷ Then Jesus asked, 'Were not ten made clean? But the other nine, where are they? ¹⁸ Was none of them found to return and give praise to God except this foreigner?' ¹⁹ Then he said to him, 'Get up and go on your way; your faith has made you well.'

RELATED

READING   2 Kings 5.1–3, 7–15c

¹ Naaman, commander of the army of the king of Aram, was a great man and in high favour with his master, because by him the LORD had given victory to Aram. The man, though a mighty warrior, suffered from leprosy. ² Now the Arameans on one of their raids had taken a young girl captive from the land of Israel, and she served Naaman's wife. ³ She said to her mistress, 'If only my lord were with the prophet who is in Samaria! He would cure him of his leprosy.'

7 When the king of Israel read the letter, he tore his clothes and said, 'Am I God, to give death or life, that this man sends word to me to cure a man of his leprosy? Just look and see how he is trying to pick a quarrel with me.'

8 But when Elisha the man of God heard that the king of Israel had torn his clothes, he sent a message to the king, 'Why have you torn your clothes? Let him come to me, that he may learn that there is a prophet in Israel.' 9 So Naaman came with his horses and chariots, and halted at the entrance of Elisha's house. 10 Elisha sent a messenger to him, saying, 'Go, wash in the Jordan seven times, and your flesh shall be restored and you shall be clean.' 11 But Naaman became angry and went away, saying, 'I thought that for me he would surely come out, and stand and call on the name of the LORD his God, and would wave his hand over the spot, and cure the leprosy! 12 Are not Abana and Pharpar, the rivers of Damascus, better than all the waters of Israel? Could I not wash in them, and be clean?' He turned and went away in a rage. 13 But his servants approached and said to him, 'Father, if the prophet had commanded you to do something difficult, would you not have done it? How much more, when all he said to you was, "Wash, and be clean"?' 14 So he went down and immersed himself seven times in the Jordan, according to the word of the man of God; his flesh was restored like the flesh of a young boy, and he was clean.

15 Then he returned to the man of God, he and all his company; he came and stood before him and said, 'Now I know that there is no God in all the earth except in Israel.'

PSALM   Psalm 111

1   Alleluia! I will give thanks to the Lord with my whole heart,
     in the assembly of the upright, in the congregation.
2   Great are the deeds of the Lord!
     they are studied by all who delight in them.
3   His work is full of majesty and splendour,
     and his righteousness endures for ever.
4   He makes his marvellous works to be remembered;
     the Lord is gracious and full of compassion.
5   He gives food to those who fear him;
     he is ever mindful of his covenant.
6   He has shown his people the power of his works
     in giving them the lands of the nations.
7   The works of his hands are faithfulness and justice;
     all his commandments are sure.
8   They stand fast for ever and ever,
     because they are done in truth and equity.

⁹ He sent redemption to his people; he commanded his covenant
    for ever;
  holy and awesome is his name.
¹⁰ The fear of the Lord is the beginning of wisdom;
    those who act accordingly have a good understanding; his praise
    endures for ever.

READING   2 Timothy 2.8–15

⁸ Remember Jesus Christ, raised from the dead, a descendant of David—
that is my gospel, ⁹ for which I suffer hardship, even to the point of being
chained like a criminal. But the word of God is not chained. ¹⁰ Therefore I
endure everything for the sake of the elect, so that they may also obtain
the salvation that is in Christ Jesus, with eternal glory. ¹¹ The saying is sure:
  If we have died with him, we will also live with him;
¹² if we endure, we will also reign with him;
  if we deny him, he will also deny us;
¹³ if we are faithless, he remains faithful—
  for he cannot deny himself.

¹⁴ Remind them of this, and warn them before God that they are to avoid
wrangling over words, which does no good but only ruins those who are
listening. ¹⁵ Do your best to present yourself to God as one approved by him,
a worker who has no need to be ashamed, rightly explaining the word of
truth.

GOSPEL   Luke 17.11–19

¹¹ On the way to Jerusalem Jesus was going through the region between
Samaria and Galilee. ¹² As he entered a village, ten lepers approached him.
Keeping their distance, ¹³ they called out, saying, 'Jesus, Master, have mercy
on us!' ¹⁴ When he saw them, he said to them, 'Go and show yourselves to
the priests.' And as they went, they were made clean. ¹⁵ Then one of them,
when he saw that he was healed, turned back, praising God with a loud
voice. ¹⁶ He prostrated himself at Jesus' feet and thanked him. And he was
a Samaritan. ¹⁷ Then Jesus asked, 'Were not ten made clean? But the other
nine, where are they? ¹⁸ Was none of them found to return and give praise
to God except this foreigner?' ¹⁹ Then he said to him, 'Get up and go on
your way; your faith has made you well.'

POST COMMUNION

See pages 943 to 947 and Table on page 931

SECOND SERVICE

Psalm 144
Nehemiah 6.1–16
John 15.12–27

THIRD SERVICE

Psalm 143
Isaiah 50.4–10
Luke 13.22–30

PROPER 24

Sunday between 16 and 22 October inclusive

COLLECT

See pages 944 to 948 and Table on page 931

CONTINUOUS

READING   Jeremiah 31.27–34

²⁷ The days are surely coming, says the LORD, when I will sow the house of Israel and the house of Judah with the seed of humans and the seed of animals. ²⁸ And just as I have watched over them to pluck up and break down, to overthrow, destroy, and bring evil, so I will watch over them to build and to plant, says the LORD. ²⁹ In those days they shall no longer say:

'The parents have eaten sour grapes,
    and the children's teeth are set on edge.'

³⁰ But all shall die for their own sins; the teeth of everyone who eats sour grapes shall be set on edge.

³¹ The days are surely coming, says the LORD, when I will make a new covenant with the house of Israel and the house of Judah. ³² It will not be like the covenant that I made with their ancestors when I took them by the hand to bring them out of the land of Egypt—a covenant that they broke, though I was their husband, says the LORD. ³³ But this is the covenant that I will make with the house of Israel after those days, says the LORD: I will put my law within them, and I will write it on their hearts; and I will be their God, and they shall be my people. ³⁴ No longer shall they teach one

another, or say to each other, 'Know the LORD', for they shall all know me, from the least of them to the greatest, says the LORD; for I will forgive their iniquity, and remember their sin no more.

PSALM   Psalm 119.97–104

⁹⁷ O how I love your law!
   all the day long it is in my mind.
⁹⁸ Your commandment has made me wiser than my enemies,
   and it is always with me.
⁹⁹ I have more understanding than all my teachers,
   for your decrees are my study.
¹⁰⁰ I am wiser than the elders,
   because I observe your commandments.
¹⁰¹ I restrain my feet from every evil way,
   that I may keep your word.
¹⁰² I do not shrink from your judgements,
   because you yourself have taught me.
¹⁰³ How sweet are your words to my taste!
   they are sweeter than honey to my mouth.
¹⁰⁴ Through your commandments I gain understanding;
   therefore I hate every lying way.

READING   2 Timothy 3.14–4.5

¹⁴ But as for you, continue in what you have learned and firmly believed, knowing from whom you learned it, ¹⁵ and how from childhood you have known the sacred writings that are able to instruct you for salvation through faith in Christ Jesus. ¹⁶ All scripture is inspired by God and is useful for teaching, for reproof, for correction, and for training in righteousness, ¹⁷ so that everyone who belongs to God may be proficient, equipped for every good work.

¹ In the presence of God and of Christ Jesus, who is to judge the living and the dead, and in view of his appearing and his kingdom, I solemnly urge you: ² proclaim the message; be persistent whether the time is favourable or unfavourable; convince, rebuke, and encourage, with the utmost patience in teaching. ³ For the time is coming when people will not put up with sound doctrine, but having itching ears, they will accumulate for themselves teachers to suit their own desires, ⁴ and will turn away from listening to the truth and wander away to myths. ⁵ As for you, always be sober, endure suffering, do the work of an evangelist, carry out your ministry fully.

GOSPEL   Luke 18.1–8

¹ Then Jesus told them a parable about their need to pray always and not to lose heart. ² He said, 'In a certain city there was a judge who neither feared God nor had respect for people. ³ In that city there was a widow who kept coming to him and saying, "Grant me justice against my opponent." ⁴ For a while he refused; but later he said to himself, "Though I have no fear of God and no respect for anyone, ⁵ yet because this widow keeps bothering me, I will grant her justice, so that she may not wear me out by continually coming." ' ⁶ And the Lord said, 'Listen to what the unjust judge says. ⁷ And will not God grant justice to his chosen ones who cry to him day and night? Will he delay long in helping them? ⁸ I tell you, he will quickly grant justice to them. And yet, when the Son of Man comes, will he find faith on earth?'

RELATED

READING   Genesis 32.22–31

²² The same night he got up and took his two wives, his two maids, and his eleven children, and crossed the ford of the Jabbok. ²³ He took them and sent them across the stream, and likewise everything that he had. ²⁴ Jacob was left alone; and a man wrestled with him until daybreak. ²⁵ When the man saw that he did not prevail against Jacob, he struck him on the hip socket; and Jacob's hip was put out of joint as he wrestled with him. ²⁶ Then he said, 'Let me go, for the day is breaking.' But Jacob said, 'I will not let you go, unless you bless me.' ²⁷ So he said to him, 'What is your name?' And he said, 'Jacob.' ²⁸ Then the man said, 'You shall no longer be called Jacob, but Israel, for you have striven with God and with humans, and have prevailed.' ²⁹ Then Jacob asked him, 'Please tell me your name.' But he said, 'Why is it that you ask my name?' And there he blessed him. ³⁰ So Jacob called the place Peniel, saying, 'For I have seen God face to face, and yet my life is preserved.' ³¹ The sun rose upon him as he passed Penuel, limping because of his hip.

PSALM   Psalm 121

1   I lift up my eyes to the hills;
      from where is my help to come?
2   My help comes from the Lord,
      the maker of heaven and earth.

3 He will not let your foot be moved
and he who watches over you will not fall asleep.
4 Behold, he who keeps watch over Israel
shall neither slumber nor sleep;
5 The Lord himself watches over you;
the Lord is your shade at your right hand,
6 So that the sun shall not strike you by day,
nor the moon by night.
7 The Lord shall preserve you from all evil;
it is he who shall keep you safe.
8 The Lord shall watch over your going out and your coming in,
from this time forth for evermore.

READING   2 Timothy 3.14–4.5

14 But as for you, continue in what you have learned and firmly believed, knowing from whom you learned it, 15 and how from childhood you have known the sacred writings that are able to instruct you for salvation through faith in Christ Jesus. 16 All scripture is inspired by God and is useful for teaching, for reproof, for correction, and for training in righteousness, 17 so that everyone who belongs to God may be proficient, equipped for every good work.

1 In the presence of God and of Christ Jesus, who is to judge the living and the dead, and in view of his appearing and his kingdom, I solemnly urge you: 2 proclaim the message; be persistent whether the time is favourable or unfavourable; convince, rebuke, and encourage, with the utmost patience in teaching. 3 For the time is coming when people will not put up with sound doctrine, but having itching ears, they will accumulate for themselves teachers to suit their own desires, 4 and will turn away from listening to the truth and wander away to myths. 5 As for you, always be sober, endure suffering, do the work of an evangelist, carry out your ministry fully.

GOSPEL   Luke 18.1–8

1 Then Jesus told them a parable about their need to pray always and not to lose heart. 2 He said, 'In a certain city there was a judge who neither feared God nor had respect for people. 3 In that city there was a widow who kept coming to him and saying, "Grant me justice against my opponent." 4 For a while he refused; but later he said to himself, "Though I have no fear of God and no respect for anyone, 5 yet because this widow keeps bothering me, I will grant her justice, so that she may not wear me out by continually coming." ' 6 And the Lord said, 'Listen to what the unjust judge

says. ⁷ And will not God grant justice to his chosen ones who cry to him day and night? Will he delay long in helping them? ⁸ I tell you, he will quickly grant justice to them. And yet, when the Son of Man comes, will he find faith on earth?'

POST COMMUNION

See pages 944 to 948 and Table on page 931

SECOND SERVICE   THIRD SERVICE

Psalms [146;] 149   **Psalm 147**
Nehemiah 8.9–18   **Isaiah 54.1–14**
John 16.1–11   **Luke 13.31–35**

PROPER 25

Sunday between 23 and 29 October inclusive

COLLECT

See page 948 and Table on page 931

CONTINUOUS

READING   Joel 2.23–32

²³ O children of Zion, be glad
        and rejoice in the LORD your God;
    for he has given the early rain for your vindication,
        he has poured down for you abundant rain,
        the early and the later rain, as before.
²⁴ The threshing-floors shall be full of grain,
        the vats shall overflow with wine and oil.
²⁵ I will repay you for the years
        that the swarming locust has eaten,
    the hopper, the destroyer, and the cutter,
        my great army, which I sent against you.

²⁶ You shall eat in plenty and be satisfied,
    and praise the name of the LORD your God,
    who has dealt wondrously with you.
And my people shall never again be put to shame.
²⁷ You shall know that I am in the midst of Israel,
    and that I, the LORD, am your God and there is no other.
And my people shall never again
    be put to shame.
²⁸ Then afterwards
    I will pour out my spirit on all flesh;
your sons and your daughters shall prophesy,
    your old men shall dream dreams,
    and your young men shall see visions.
²⁹ Even on the male and female slaves,
    in those days, I will pour out my spirit.

³⁰ I will show portents in the heavens and on the earth, blood and fire and columns of smoke. ³¹ The sun shall be turned to darkness, and the moon to blood, before the great and terrible day of the LORD comes. ³² Then everyone who calls on the name of the LORD shall be saved; for in Mount Zion and in Jerusalem there shall be those who escape, as the LORD has said, and among the survivors shall be those whom the LORD calls.

PSALM   Psalm 65.1–8, [9–14]

¹ You are to be praised, O God, in Zion;
    to you shall vows be performed in Jerusalem.
² To you that hear prayer shall all flesh come,
    because of their transgressions.
³ Our sins are stronger than we are,
    but you will blot them out.
⁴ Happy are they whom you choose and draw to your courts to dwell there!
    they will be satisfied by the beauty of your house, by the holiness of your temple.
⁵ Awesome things will you show us in your righteousness, O God of our salvation,
    O Hope of all the ends of the earth and of the seas that are far away.
⁶ You make fast the mountains by your power;
    they are girded about with might.
⁷ You still the roaring of the seas,
    the roaring of their waves, and the clamour of the peoples.

⁸ Those who dwell at the ends of the earth will tremble at your
    marvellous signs;
  you make the dawn and the dusk to sing for joy.
[⁹ You visit the earth and water it abundantly; you make it very
    plenteous;
  the river of God is full of water.
¹⁰ You prepare the grain,
  for so you provide for the earth.
¹¹ You drench the furrows and smooth out the ridges;
  with heavy rain you soften the ground and bless its increase.
¹² You crown the year with your goodness,
  and your paths overflow with plenty.
¹³ May the fields of the wilderness be rich for grazing,
  and the hills be clothed with joy.
¹⁴ May the meadows cover themselves with flocks, and the valleys
    cloak themselves with grain;
  let them shout for joy and sing.]

READING   2 Timothy 4.6–8, 16–18

⁶ As for me, I am already being poured out as a libation, and the time of
my departure has come. ⁷ I have fought the good fight, I have finished the
race, I have kept the faith. ⁸ From now on there is reserved for me the crown
of righteousness, which the Lord, the righteous judge, will give to me on
that day, and not only to me but also to all who have longed for his
appearing.

¹⁶ At my first defence no one came to my support, but all deserted me. May
it not be counted against them! ¹⁷ But the Lord stood by me and gave me
strength, so that through me the message might be fully proclaimed and
all the Gentiles might hear it. So I was rescued from the lion's mouth.
¹⁸ The Lord will rescue me from every evil attack and save me for his
heavenly kingdom. To him be the glory for ever and ever. Amen.

GOSPEL   Luke 18.9–14

⁹ He also told this parable to some who trusted in themselves that they
were righteous and regarded others with contempt: ¹⁰ 'Two men went up
to the temple to pray, one a Pharisee and the other a tax-collector. ¹¹ The
Pharisee, standing by himself, was praying thus, "God, I thank you that I
am not like other people: thieves, rogues, adulterers, or even like this tax-
collector. ¹² I fast twice a week; I give a tenth of all my income." ¹³ But the
tax-collector, standing far off, would not even look up to heaven, but was

beating his breast and saying, "God, be merciful to me, a sinner!" ¹⁴ I tell you, this man went down to his home justified rather than the other; for all who exalt themselves will be humbled, but all who humble themselves will be exalted.'

RELATED

READING

EITHER   Ecclesiasticus 35.12-17

¹² Give to the Most High as he has given to you,
       and as generously as you can afford.
¹³ For the Lord is the one who repays,
       and he will repay you sevenfold.
¹⁴ Do not offer him a bribe, for he will not accept it;
¹⁵   and do not rely on a dishonest sacrifice;
     for the Lord is the judge,
       and with him there is no partiality.
¹⁶ He will not show partiality to the poor;
       but he will listen to the prayer of one who is wronged.
¹⁷ He will not ignore the supplication of the orphan,
       or the widow when she pours out her complaint.

OR   Jeremiah 14.7-10, 19-22

⁷ Although our iniquities testify against us,
       act, O Lord, for your name's sake;
     our apostasies indeed are many,
       and we have sinned against you.
⁸ O hope of Israel,
       its saviour in time of trouble,
     why should you be like a stranger in the land,
       like a traveller turning aside for the night?
⁹ Why should you be like someone confused,
       like a mighty warrior who cannot give help?
     Yet you, O Lord, are in the midst of us,
       and we are called by your name;
       do not forsake us!

10 Thus says the LORD concerning this people:
Truly they have loved to wander,
   they have not restrained their feet;
therefore the LORD does not accept them,
   now he will remember their iniquity
   and punish their sins.

19 Have you completely rejected Judah?
   Does your heart loathe Zion?
Why have you struck us down
   so that there is no healing for us?
We look for peace, but find no good;
   for a time of healing, but there is terror instead.
20 We acknowledge our wickedness, O LORD,
   the iniquity of our ancestors,
   for we have sinned against you.
21 Do not spurn us, for your name's sake;
   do not dishonour your glorious throne;
   remember and do not break your covenant with us.
22 Can any idols of the nations bring rain?
   Or can the heavens give showers?
Is it not you, O LORD our God?
   We set our hope on you,
   for it is you who do all this.

PSALM   Psalm 84.1–6

1 How dear to me is your dwelling, O Lord of hosts!
My soul has a desire and longing for the courts of the Lord; my
   heart and my flesh rejoice in the living God.
2 The sparrow has found her a house and the swallow a nest where
   she may lay her young;
by the side of your altars, O Lord of hosts, my King and my God.
3 Happy are they who dwell in your house!
they will always be praising you.
4 Happy are the people whose strength is in you!
whose hearts are set on the pilgrims' way.
5 Those who go through the desolate valley will find it a place of
   springs,
for the early rains have covered it with pools of water.
6 They will climb from height to height,
and the God of gods will reveal himself in Zion.

YEAR C

READING   2 Timothy 4.6–8, 16–18

⁶ As for me, I am already being poured out as a libation, and the time of my departure has come. ⁷ I have fought the good fight, I have finished the race, I have kept the faith. ⁸ From now on there is reserved for me the crown of righteousness, which the Lord, the righteous judge, will give to me on that day, and not only to me but also to all who have longed for his appearing.

¹⁶ At my first defence no one came to my support, but all deserted me. May it not be counted against them! ¹⁷ But the Lord stood by me and gave me strength, so that through me the message might be fully proclaimed and all the Gentiles might hear it. So I was rescued from the lion's mouth. ¹⁸ The Lord will rescue me from every evil attack and save me for his heavenly kingdom. To him be the glory for ever and ever. Amen.

GOSPEL   Luke 18.9–14

⁹ He also told this parable to some who trusted in themselves that they were righteous and regarded others with contempt: ¹⁰ 'Two men went up to the temple to pray, one a Pharisee and the other a tax-collector. ¹¹ The Pharisee, standing by himself, was praying thus, "God, I thank you that I am not like other people: thieves, rogues, adulterers, or even like this tax-collector. ¹² I fast twice a week; I give a tenth of all my income." ¹³ But the tax-collector, standing far off, would not even look up to heaven, but was beating his breast and saying, "God, be merciful to me, a sinner!" ¹⁴ I tell you, this man went down to his home justified rather than the other; for all who exalt themselves will be humbled, but all who humble themselves will be exalted.'

POST COMMUNION

See page 948 and Table on page 931

SECOND SERVICE

Psalm 119.1–16
Ecclesiastes 11; 12
2 Timothy 2.1–7

If the Second Service is a Eucharist, the following is read as a Gospel:

Matthew 22.34–46

THIRD SERVICE

Psalm 119.105–128
Isaiah 59.9–20
Luke 14.1–14

ALL SAINTS' DAY   1 NOVEMBER

Sunday between 30 October and 5 November or, if this is not kept as All Saints' Sunday, on 1 November itself

COLLECT

Almighty God,
you have knit together your elect
in one communion and fellowship
    in the mystical body of your Son Christ our Lord:
grant us grace so to follow your blessed saints
in all virtuous and godly living
that we may come to those inexpressible joys
that you have prepared for those who truly love you;
through Jesus Christ your Son our Lord,
who is alive and reigns with you,
in the unity of the Holy Spirit,
one God, now and for ever.

READING   Daniel 7.1–3, 15–18

¹ In the first year of King Balshazzar of Babylon, Daniel had a dream and visions of his head as he lay in bed. Then he wrote down the dream: ² I, Daniel, saw in my vision by night the four winds of heaven stirring up the great seas, ³ and four great beasts came up out of the sea, different from one another.

¹⁵ As for me, Daniel, my spirit was troubled within me, and the visions of my head terrified me. ¹⁶ I approached one of the attendants to ask him the truth concerning all this. So he said that he would disclose to me the interpretation of the matter: ¹⁷ 'As for these four great beasts, four kings shall arise out of the earth. ¹⁸ But the holy ones of the Most High shall receive the kingdom and possess the kingdom for ever—for ever and ever.'

PSALM   Psalm 149

1   Alleluia! Sing to the Lord a new song;
        sing his praise in the congregation of the faithful.
2   Let Israel rejoice in his maker;
        let the children of Zion be joyful in their king.
3   Let them praise his name in the dance;
        let them sing praise to him with timbrel and harp.

⁴ For the Lord takes pleasure in his people
and adorns the poor with victory.
⁵ Let the faithful rejoice in triumph;
let them be joyful on their beds.
⁶ Let the praises of God be in their throat
and a two-edged sword in their hand;
⁷ To wreak vengeance on the nations
and punishment on the peoples;
⁸ To bind their kings in chains
and their nobles with links of iron;
⁹ To inflict on them the judgement decreed;
this is glory for all his faithful people. Alleluia!

READING   Ephesians 1.11–23

¹¹ In Christ we have also obtained an inheritance, having been destined according to the purpose of him who accomplishes all things according to his counsel and will, ¹² so that we, who were the first to set our hope on Christ, might live for the praise of his glory. ¹³ In him you also, when you had heard the word of truth, the gospel of your salvation, and had believed in him, were marked with the seal of the promised Holy Spirit; ¹⁴ this is the pledge of our inheritance towards redemption as God's own people, to the praise of his glory.

¹⁵ I have heard of your faith in the Lord Jesus and your love towards all the saints, and for this reason ¹⁶ I do not cease to give thanks for you as I remember you in my prayers. ¹⁷ I pray that the God of our Lord Jesus Christ, the Father of glory, may give you a spirit of wisdom and revelation as you come to know him, ¹⁸ so that, with the eyes of your heart enlightened, you may know what is the hope to which he has called you, what are the riches of his glorious inheritance among the saints, ¹⁹ and what is the immeasurable greatness of his power for us who believe, according to the working of his great power. ²⁰ God put this power to work in Christ when he raised him from the dead and seated him at his right hand in the heavenly places, ²¹ far above all rule and authority and power and dominion, and above every name that is named, not only in this age but also in the age to come. ²² And he has put all things under his feet and has made him the head over all things for the church, ²³ which is his body, the fullness of him who fills all in all.

GOSPEL   Luke 6.20–31

²⁰ Then he looked up at his disciples and said:
'Blessed are you who are poor,
    for yours is the kingdom of God.
²¹   Blessed are you who are hungry now,
        for you will be filled.
    Blessed are you who weep now,
        for you will laugh.

²² 'Blessed are you when people hate you, and when they exclude you, revile you, and defame you on account of the Son of Man. ²³ Rejoice on that day and leap for joy, for surely your reward is great in heaven; for that is what their ancestors did to the prophets.
²⁴   But woe to you who are rich,
        for you have received your consolation.
²⁵   Woe to you who are full now,
        for you will be hungry.
    Woe to you who are laughing now,
        for you will mourn and weep.

²⁶ 'Woe to you when all speak well of you, for that is what their ancestors did to the false prophets.

²⁷ 'But I say to you that listen, Love your enemies, do good to those who hate you, ²⁸ bless those who curse you, pray for those who abuse you. ²⁹ If anyone strikes you on the cheek, offer the other also; and from anyone who takes away your coat do not withhold even your shirt. ³⁰ Give to everyone who begs from you; and if anyone takes away your goods, do not ask for them again. ³¹ Do to others as you would have them do to you.'

POST COMMUNION

God, the source of all holiness
    and giver of all good things:
may we who have shared at this table
    as strangers and pilgrims here on earth
be welcomed with all your saints
    to the heavenly feast on the day of your kingdom;
through Jesus Christ our Lord.

On 1 November if the material above is used on the Sunday

COLLECT

Almighty God,
you have knit together your elect
in one communion and fellowship
   in the mystical body of your Son Christ our Lord:
grant us grace so to follow your blessed saints
in all virtuous and godly living
that we may come to those inexpressible joys
that you have prepared for those who truly love you;
through Jesus Christ your Son our Lord,
who is alive and reigns with you,
in the unity of the Holy Spirit,
one God, now and for ever.

READING

EITHER   **Isaiah 56.3–8**

3 Do not let the foreigner joined to the Lord say,
    'The Lord will surely separate me from his people';
  and do not let the eunuch say,
    'I am just a dry tree.'
4 For thus says the Lord:
  To the eunuchs who keep my sabbaths,
    who choose the things that please me
    and hold fast my covenant,
5 I will give, in my house and within my walls,
    a monument and a name
    better than sons and daughters;
  I will give them an everlasting name
    that shall not be cut off.
6 And the foreigners who join themselves to the Lord,
    to minister to him, to love the name of the Lord,
    and to be his servants,
  all who keep the sabbath, and do not profane it,
    and hold fast my covenant—
7 these I will bring to my holy mountain,
    and make them joyful in my house of prayer;
  their burnt-offerings and their sacrifices
    will be accepted on my altar;
  for my house shall be called a house of prayer
    for all peoples.

⁸ Thus says the Lord G<small>OD</small>,
   who gathers the outcasts of Israel,
 I will gather others to them
   besides those already gathered.

OR   **2 Esdras 2.42–48**

⁴² I, Ezra, saw on Mount Zion a great multitude that I could not number, and they all were praising the Lord with songs. ⁴³ In their midst was a young man of great stature, taller than any of the others, and on the head of each of them he placed a crown, but he was more exalted than they. And I was held spellbound. ⁴⁴ Then I asked an angel, 'Who are these, my lord?' ⁴⁵ He answered and said to me, 'These are they who have put off mortal clothing and have put on the immortal, and have confessed the name of God. Now they are being crowned, and receive palms.' ⁴⁶ Then I said to the angel, 'Who is that young man who is placing crowns on them and putting palms in their hands?' ⁴⁷ He answered and said to me, 'He is the Son of God, whom they confessed in the world.' So I began to praise those who had stood valiantly for the name of the Lord. ⁴⁸ Then the angel said to me, 'Go, tell my people how great and how many are the wonders of the Lord God that you have seen.'

PSALM   **Psalm 33.1–5**

¹ Rejoice in the Lord, you righteous;
  it is good for the just to sing praises.
² Praise the Lord with the harp;
  play to him upon the psaltery and lyre.
³ Sing for him a new song;
  sound a fanfare with all your skill upon the trumpet.
⁴ For the word of the Lord is right,
  and all his works are sure.
⁵ He loves righteousness and justice;
  the loving-kindness of the Lord fills the whole earth.

READING   **Hebrews 12.18–24**

¹⁸ You have not come to something that can be touched, a blazing fire, and darkness, and gloom, and a tempest, ¹⁹ and the sound of a trumpet, and a voice whose words made the hearers beg that not another word be spoken to them. ²⁰ (For they could not endure the order that was given, 'If even an animal touches the mountain, it shall be stoned to death.' ²¹ Indeed, so terrifying was the sight that Moses said, 'I tremble with fear.') ²² But you

have come to Mount Zion and to the city of the living God, the heavenly Jerusalem, and to innumerable angels in festal gathering, 23 and to the assembly of the firstborn who are enrolled in heaven, and to God the judge of all, and to the spirits of the righteous made perfect, 24 and to Jesus, the mediator of a new covenant, and to the sprinkled blood that speaks a better word than the blood of Abel.

GOSPEL   Matthew 5.1–12

1 When Jesus saw the crowds, he went up the mountain; and after he sat down, his disciples came to him. 2 Then he began to speak, and taught them, saying:

3 'Blessed are the poor in spirit, for theirs is the kingdom of heaven.

4 'Blessed are those who mourn, for they will be comforted.

5 'Blessed are the meek, for they will inherit the earth.

6 'Blessed are those who hunger and thirst for righteousness, for they will be filled.

7 'Blessed are the merciful, for they will receive mercy.

8 'Blessed are the pure in heart, for they will see God.

9 'Blessed are the peacemakers, for they will be called children of God.

10 'Blessed are those who are persecuted for righteousness' sake, for theirs is the kingdom of heaven.

11 'Blessed are you when people revile you and persecute you and utter all kinds of evil against you falsely on my account. 12 Rejoice and be glad, for your reward is great in heaven, for in the same way they persecuted the prophets who were before you.'

POST COMMUNION

God, the source of all holiness
    and giver of all good things:
may we who have shared at this table
    as strangers and pilgrims here on earth
be welcomed with all your saints
    to the heavenly feast on the day of your kingdom;
through Jesus Christ our Lord.

THE FOURTH SUNDAY BEFORE ADVENT

Sunday between 30 October and 5 November inclusive. For use if the Feast of All Saints was celebrated on 1 November and alternative propers are needed.

COLLECT

Almighty and eternal God,
you have kindled the flame of love
   in the hearts of the saints:
grant to us the same faith and power of love,
that, as we rejoice in their triumphs,
we may be sustained by their example and fellowship;
through Jesus Christ your Son our Lord,
who is alive and reigns with you,
in the unity of the Holy Spirit,
one God, now and for ever.

READING   Isaiah 1.10–18

¹⁰ Hear the word of the LORD,
   you rulers of Sodom!
Listen to the teaching of our God,
   you people of Gomorrah!
¹¹ What to me is the multitude of your sacrifices?
   says the LORD;
I have had enough of burnt-offerings of rams
   and the fat of fed beasts;
I do not delight in the blood of bulls,
   or of lambs, or of goats.
¹² When you come to appear before me,
   who asked this from your hand?
Trample my courts no more;
¹³ bringing offerings is futile;
   incense is an abomination to me.
New moon and sabbath and calling of convocation—
   I cannot endure solemn assemblies with iniquity.
¹⁴ Your new moons and your appointed festivals
   my soul hates;
they have become a burden to me,
   I am weary of bearing them.

15 When you stretch out your hands,
    I will hide my eyes from you;
   even though you make many prayers,
    I will not listen;
   your hands are full of blood.
16 Wash yourselves; make yourselves clean;
    remove the evil of your doings
    from before my eyes;
   cease to do evil,
17   learn to do good;
   seek justice,
    rescue the oppressed,
   defend the orphan,
    plead for the widow.
18 Come now, let us argue it out,
    says the LORD:
   though your sins are like scarlet,
    they shall be like snow;
   though they are red like crimson,
    they shall become like wool.

PSALM   Psalm 32.1–8

1 Happy are they whose transgressions are forgiven,
   and whose sin is put away!
2 Happy are they to whom the Lord imputes no guilt,
   and in whose spirit there is no guile!
3 While I held my tongue, my bones withered away,
   because of my groaning all day long.
4 For your hand was heavy upon me day and night;
   my moisture was dried up as in the heat of summer.
5 Then I acknowledged my sin to you,
   and did not conceal my guilt.
6 I said, 'I will confess my transgressions to the Lord':
   then you forgave me the guilt of my sin;
7 Therefore all the faithful will make their prayers to you in time of
     trouble;
   when the great waters overflow, they shall not reach them.
8 You are my hiding-place; you preserve me from trouble;
   you surround me with shouts of deliverance.

READING   **2 Thessalonians 1.1–12**

¹ Paul, Silvanus, and Timothy,
To the church of the Thessalonians in God our Father and the Lord Jesus
Christ:

² Grace to you and peace from God our Father and the Lord Jesus Christ.

³ We must always give thanks to God for you, brothers and sisters, as is
right, because your faith is growing abundantly, and the love of every one
of you for one another is increasing. ⁴ Therefore we ourselves boast of you
among the churches of God for your steadfastness and faith during all your
persecutions and the afflictions that you are enduring.

⁵ This is evidence of the righteous judgement of God, and is intended to
make you worthy of the kingdom of God, for which you are also suffering.
⁶ For it is indeed just of God to repay with affliction those who afflict you,
⁷ and to give relief to the afflicted as well as to us, when the Lord Jesus is
revealed from heaven with his mighty angels ⁸ in flaming fire, inflicting
vengeance on those who do not know God and on those who do not obey
the gospel of our Lord Jesus. ⁹ These will suffer the punishment of eternal
destruction, separated from the presence of the Lord and from the glory of
his might, ¹⁰ when he comes to be glorified by his saints and to be marvelled
at on that day among all who have believed, because our testimony to you
was believed. ¹¹ To this end we always pray for you, asking that our God will
make you worthy of his call and will fulfil by his power every good resolve
and work of faith, ¹² so that the name of our Lord Jesus may be glorified in
you, and you in him, according to the grace of our God and the Lord Jesus
Christ.

GOSPEL   **Luke 19.1–10**

¹ He entered Jericho and was passing through it. ² A man was there named
Zacchaeus; he was a chief tax-collector and was rich. ³ He was trying to see
who Jesus was, but on account of the crowd he could not, because he was
short in stature. ⁴ So he ran ahead and climbed a sycamore tree to see him,
because he was going to pass that way. ⁵ When Jesus came to the place, he
looked up and said to him, 'Zacchaeus, hurry and come down; for I must
stay at your house today.' ⁶ So he hurried down and was happy to welcome
him. ⁷ All who saw it began to grumble and said, 'He has gone to be the
guest of one who is a sinner.' ⁸ Zacchaeus stood there and said to the Lord,
'Look, half of my possessions, Lord, I will give to the poor; and if I have
defrauded anyone of anything, I will pay back four times as much.' ⁹ Then

Jesus said to him, 'Today salvation has come to this house, because he too is a son of Abraham. [10] For the Son of Man came to seek out and to save the lost.'

POST COMMUNION

Lord of heaven,
in this eucharist you have brought us near
to an innumerable company of angels
and to the spirits of the saints made perfect:
as in this food of our earthly pilgrimage
we have shared their fellowship,
so may we come to share their joy in heaven;
through Jesus Christ our Lord.

SECOND SERVICE	THIRD SERVICE
Psalm 145.1–9, [10–22]	Psalm 87
Lamentations 3.22–33	Job 19.21–27a
John 11.[1–31,] 32–44	Colossians 1.9–14

THE THIRD SUNDAY BEFORE ADVENT

Sunday between 6 and 12 November inclusive

COLLECT

Almighty Father,
whose will is to restore all things
in your beloved Son, the king of all:
govern the hearts and minds of those in authority,
and bring the families of the nations,
divided and torn apart by the ravages of sin,
to be subject to his just and gentle rule;
who is alive and reigns with you,
in the unity of the Holy Spirit,
one God, now and for ever.

READING   Job 19.23–27a

23 'O that my words were written down!
      O that they were inscribed in a book!
24 O that with an iron pen and with lead
      they were engraved on a rock for ever!
25 For I know that my Redeemer lives,
      and that at the last he will stand upon the earth;
26 and after my skin has been thus destroyed,
      then in my flesh I shall see God,
27 whom I shall see on my side,
      and my eyes shall behold, and not another.'

PSALM   Psalm 17.1–8, [9]

1 Hear my plea of innocence, O Lord; give heed to my cry;
      listen to my prayer, which does not come from lying lips.
2 Let my vindication come forth from your presence;
      let your eyes be fixed on justice.
3 Weigh my heart, summon me by night,
      melt me down; you will find no impurity in me.
4 I give no offence with my mouth as others do;
      I have heeded the words of your lips.
5 My footsteps hold fast to the ways of your law;
      in your paths my feet shall not stumble.
6 I call upon you, O God, for you will answer me;
      incline your ear to me and hear my words.
7 Show me your marvellous loving-kindness,
      O Saviour of those who take refuge at your right hand from those
            who rise up against them.
8 Keep me as the apple of your eye;
      hide me under the shadow of your wings,
[9 From the wicked who assault me,
      from my deadly enemies who surround me.]

READING   2 Thessalonians 2.1–5, 13–17

¹ As to the coming of our Lord Jesus Christ and our being gathered
together to him, we beg you, brothers and sisters, ² not to be quickly shaken
in mind or alarmed, either by spirit or by word or by letter, as though from
us, to the effect that the day of the Lord is already here. ³ Let no one deceive
you in any way; for that day will not come unless the rebellion comes first
and the lawless one is revealed, the one destined for destruction. ⁴ He

opposes and exalts himself above every so-called god or object of worship, so that he takes his seat in the temple of God, declaring himself to be God. [5] Do you not remember that I told you these things when I was still with you?

[13] But we must always give thanks to God for you, brothers and sisters beloved by the Lord, because God chose you as the first fruits for salvation through sanctification by the Spirit and through belief in the truth. [14] For this purpose he called you through our proclamation of the good news, so that you may obtain the glory of our Lord Jesus Christ. [15] So then, brothers and sisters, stand firm and hold fast to the traditions that you were taught by us, either by word of mouth or by our letter.

[16] Now may our Lord Jesus Christ himself and God our Father, who loved us and through grace gave us eternal comfort and good hope, [17] comfort your hearts and strengthen them in every good work and word.

GOSPEL   Luke 20.27–38

[27] Some Sadducees, those who say there is no resurrection, came to him [28] and asked him a question, 'Teacher, Moses wrote for us that if a man's brother dies, leaving a wife but no children, the man shall marry the widow and raise up children for his brother. [29] Now there were seven brothers; the first married, and died childless; [30] then the second [31] and the third married her, and so in the same way all seven died childless. [32] Finally the woman also died. [33] In the resurrection, therefore, whose wife will the woman be? For the seven had married her.'

[34] Jesus said to them, 'Those who belong to this age marry and are given in marriage; [35] but those who are considered worthy of a place in that age and in the resurrection from the dead neither marry nor are given in marriage. [36] Indeed they cannot die any more, because they are like angels and are children of God, being children of the resurrection. [37] And the fact that the dead are raised Moses himself showed, in the story about the bush, where he speaks of the Lord as the God of Abraham, the God of Isaac, and the God of Jacob. [38] Now he is God not of the dead, but of the living; for to him all of them are alive.'

POST COMMUNION

God of peace,
whose Son Jesus Christ proclaimed the kingdom
and restored the broken to wholeness of life:
look with compassion on the anguish of the world,

and by your healing power
make whole both people and nations;
through our Lord and Saviour Jesus Christ.

SECOND SERVICE

Psalm 40
1 Kings 3.1–15
Romans 8.31–39

*If the Second Service is a Eucharist, the
following is read as a Gospel:*

Matthew 22.15–22

THIRD SERVICE

Psalms 20; 90
Isaiah 2.1–5
James 3.13–18

THE SECOND SUNDAY BEFORE ADVENT

Sunday between 13 and 19 November inclusive

COLLECT

Heavenly Father,
whose blessed Son was revealed
   to destroy the works of the devil
and to make us the children of God and heirs of eternal life:
grant that we, having this hope,
may purify ourselves even as he is pure;
that when he shall appear in power and great glory
we may be made like him
   in his eternal and glorious kingdom;
where he is alive and reigns with you,
in the unity of the Holy Spirit,
one God, now and for ever.

READING   Malachi 4.1–2a

[1] See, the day is coming, burning like an oven, when all the arrogant and
all evildoers will be stubble; the day that comes shall burn them up, says
the LORD of hosts, so that it will leave them neither root nor branch. [2] But
for you who revere my name the sun of righteousness shall rise, with
healing in its wings.

PSALM   Psalm 98

1 Sing to the Lord a new song,
   for he has done marvellous things.
2 With his right hand and his holy arm
   has he won for himself the victory.
3 The Lord has made known his victory;
   his righteousness has he openly shown in the sight of the nations.
4 He remembers his mercy and faithfulness to the house of Israel,
   and all the ends of the earth have seen the victory of our God.
5 Shout with joy to the Lord, all you lands;
   lift up your voice, rejoice and sing.
6 Sing to the Lord with the harp,
   with the harp and the voice of song.
7 With trumpets and the sound of the horn
   shout with joy before the King, the Lord.
8 Let the sea make a noise and all that is in it,
   the lands and those who dwell therein.
9 Let the rivers clap their hands,
   and let the hills ring out with joy before the Lord, when he comes
        to judge the earth.
10 In righteousness shall he judge the world,
   and the peoples with equity.

READING   2 Thessalonians 3.6–13

6 Now we command you, beloved, in the name of our Lord Jesus Christ, to keep away from believers who are living in idleness and not according to the tradition that they received from us. 7 For you yourselves know how you ought to imitate us; we were not idle when we were with you, 8 and we did not eat anyone's bread without paying for it; but with toil and labour we worked night and day, so that we might not burden any of you. 9 This was not because we do not have that right, but in order to give you an example to imitate. 10 For even when we were with you, we gave you this command: Anyone unwilling to work should not eat. 11 For we hear that some of you are living in idleness, mere busybodies, not doing any work. 12 Now such persons we command and exhort in the Lord Jesus Christ to do their work quietly and to earn their own living. 13 Brothers and sisters, do not be weary in doing what is right.

GOSPEL   Luke 21.5–19

⁵ When some were speaking about the temple, how it was adorned with beautiful stones and gifts dedicated to God, he said, ⁶ 'As for these things that you see, the days will come when not one stone will be left upon another; all will be thrown down.'

⁷ They asked him, 'Teacher, when will this be, and what will be the sign that this is about to take place?' ⁸ And he said, 'Beware that you are not led astray; for many will come in my name and say, "I am he!" and, "The time is near!" Do not go after them.

⁹ 'When you hear of wars and insurrections, do not be terrified; for these things must take place first, but the end will not follow immediately.' ¹⁰ Then he said to them, 'Nation will rise against nation, and kingdom against kingdom; ¹¹ there will be great earthquakes, and in various places famines and plagues; and there will be dreadful portents and great signs from heaven.

¹² 'But before all this occurs, they will arrest you and persecute you; they will hand you over to synagogues and prisons, and you will be brought before kings and governors because of my name. ¹³ This will give you an opportunity to testify. ¹⁴ So make up your minds not to prepare your defence in advance; ¹⁵ for I will give you words and a wisdom that none of your opponents will be able to withstand or contradict. ¹⁶ You will be betrayed even by parents and brothers, by relatives and friends; and they will put some of you to death. ¹⁷ You will be hated by all because of my name. ¹⁸ But not a hair of your head will perish. ¹⁹ By your endurance you will gain your souls.'

POST COMMUNION

Gracious Lord,
in this holy sacrament
you give substance to our hope:
bring us at the last
to that fullness of life for which we long;
through Jesus Christ our Saviour.

CHRIST THE KING
THE SUNDAY NEXT BEFORE ADVENT

Sunday between 20 and 26 November inclusive

COLLECT

Eternal Father,
whose Son Jesus Christ ascended to the throne of heaven
   that he might rule over all things as Lord and King:
keep the Church in the unity of the Spirit
and in the bond of peace,
and bring the whole created order to worship at his feet;
who is alive and reigns with you,
in the unity of the Holy Spirit,
one God, now and for ever.

READING   Jeremiah 23.1–6

[1] Woe to the shepherds who destroy and scatter the sheep of my pasture! says the LORD. [2] Therefore, thus says the LORD, the God of Israel, concerning the shepherds who shepherd my people: It is you who have scattered my flock, and have driven them away, and you have not attended to them. So I will attend to you for your evil doings, says the LORD. [3] Then I myself will gather the remnant of my flock out of all the lands where I have driven them, and I will bring them back to their fold, and they shall be fruitful and multiply. [4] I will raise up shepherds over them who will shepherd them, and they shall not fear any longer, or be dismayed, nor shall any be missing, says the LORD.

[5] The days are surely coming, says the LORD, when I will raise up for David a righteous Branch, and he shall reign as king and deal wisely, and shall execute justice and righteousness in the land. [6] In his days Judah will be saved and Israel will live in safety. And this is the name by which he will be called: 'The LORD is our righteousness.'

PSALM   Psalm 46

1 God is our refuge and strength,
   a very present help in trouble;
2 Therefore we will not fear, though the earth be moved,
   and though the mountains be toppled into the depths of the sea;
3 Though its waters rage and foam,
   and though the mountains tremble at its tumult.
4 The Lord of hosts is with us;
   the God of Jacob is our stronghold.
5 There is a river whose streams make glad the city of God,
   the holy habitation of the Most High.
6 God is in the midst of her; she shall not be overthrown;
   God shall help her at the break of day.
7 The nations make much ado and the kingdoms are shaken;
   God has spoken and the earth shall melt away.
8 The Lord of hosts is with us;
   the God of Jacob is our stronghold.
9 Come now and look upon the works of the Lord,
   what awesome things he has done on earth.
10 It is he who makes war to cease in all the world;
   he breaks the bow and shatters the spear and burns the shields
   with fire.
11 'Be still, then, and know that I am God;
   I will be exalted among the nations; I will be exalted in the earth.'
12 The Lord of hosts is with us;
   the God of Jacob is our stronghold.

READING   Colossians 1.11–20

11 May you be made strong with all the strength that comes from his glorious power, and may you be prepared to endure everything with patience, while joyfully 12 giving thanks to the Father, who has enabled you to share in the inheritance of the saints in the light. 13 He has rescued us from the power of darkness and transferred us into the kingdom of his beloved Son, 14 in whom we have redemption, the forgiveness of sins.

15 He is the image of the invisible God, the firstborn of all creation; 16 for in him all things in heaven and on earth were created, things visible and invisible, whether thrones or dominions or rulers or powers—all things have been created through him and for him. 17 He himself is before all things, and in him all things hold together. 18 He is the head of the body, the church; he is the beginning, the firstborn from the dead, so that he might come to have first place in everything. 19 For in him all the fullness

of God was pleased to dwell, ²⁰ and through him God was pleased to reconcile to himself all things, whether on earth or in heaven, by making peace through the blood of his cross.

GOSPEL   Luke 23.33–43

³³ When they came to the place that is called The Skull, they crucified Jesus there with the criminals, one on his right and one on his left. ³⁴ Then Jesus said, 'Father, forgive them; for they do not know what they are doing.' And they cast lots to divide his clothing. ³⁵ And the people stood by, watching; but the leaders scoffed at him, saying, 'He saved others; let him save himself if he is the Messiah of God, his chosen one!' ³⁶ The soldiers also mocked him, coming up and offering him sour wine, ³⁷ and saying, 'If you are the King of the Jews, save yourself!' ³⁸ There was also an inscription over him, 'This is the King of the Jews.'

³⁹ One of the criminals who were hanged there kept deriding him and saying, 'Are you not the Messiah? Save yourself and us!' ⁴⁰ But the other rebuked him, saying, 'Do you not fear God, since you are under the same sentence of condemnation? ⁴¹ And we indeed have been condemned justly, for we are getting what we deserve for our deeds, but this man has done nothing wrong.' ⁴² Then he said, 'Jesus, remember me when you come into your kingdom.' ⁴³ He replied, 'Truly I tell you, today you will be with me in Paradise.'

POST COMMUNION

Stir up, O Lord, the wills of your faithful people;
that they, plenteously bringing forth the fruit of good works,
may by you be plenteously rewarded;
through Jesus Christ our Lord.

This Post Communion may be used as the Collect at Morning and Evening Prayer during this week

SECOND SERVICE   THIRD SERVICE

Psalm 72.1–7, [8–19]   Psalms 29; 110
1 Samuel 8.4–20   Zechariah 6.9–15
John 18.33–37   Revelation 11.15–18

HARVEST THANKSGIVING

COLLECT

Eternal God,
you crown the year with your goodness
and you give us the fruits of the earth in their season:
grant that we may use them to your glory,
for the relief of those in need
and for our own well-being;
through Jesus Christ your Son our Lord,
who is alive and reigns with you,
in the unity of the Holy Spirit,
one God, now and for ever.

READING   Deuteronomy 26.1–11

[1] When you have come into the land that the LORD your God is giving you as an inheritance to possess, and you possess it, and settle in it, [2] you shall take some of the first of all the fruit of the ground, which you harvest from the land that the LORD your God is giving you, and you shall put it in a basket and go to the place that the LORD your God will choose as a dwelling for his name. [3] You shall go to the priest who is in office at that time, and say to him, 'Today I declare to the LORD your God that I have come into the land that the LORD swore to our ancestors to give us.' [4] When the priest takes the basket from your hand and sets it down before the altar of the LORD your God, [5] you shall make this response before the LORD your God: 'A wandering Aramean was my ancestor; he went down into Egypt and lived there as an alien, few in number, and there he became a great nation, mighty and populous. [6] When the Egyptians treated us harshly and afflicted us, by imposing hard labour on us, [7] we cried to the LORD, the God of our ancestors; the LORD heard our voice and saw our affliction, our toil, and our oppression. [8] The LORD brought us out of Egypt with a mighty hand and an outstretched arm, with a terrifying display of power, and with signs and wonders; [9] and he brought us into this place and gave us this land, a land flowing with milk and honey. [10] So now I bring the first of the fruit of the ground that you, O LORD, have given me.' You shall set it down before the LORD your God and bow down before the LORD your God. [11] Then you, together with the Levites and the aliens who reside among you, shall celebrate with all the bounty that the LORD your God has given to you and to your house.

PSALM   Psalm 100

¹ Be joyful in the Lord, all you lands;
  serve the Lord with gladness and come before his presence with a
      song.
² Know this: The Lord himself is God;
  he himself has made us and we are his; we are his people and the
      sheep of his pasture.
³ Enter his gates with thanksgiving; go into his courts with praise;
  give thanks to him and call upon his name.
⁴ For the Lord is good; his mercy is everlasting;
  and his faithfulness endures from age to age.

READING

EITHER   Philippians 4.4–9

⁴ Rejoice in the Lord always; again I will say, Rejoice. ⁵ Let your gentleness be known to everyone. The Lord is near. ⁶ Do not worry about anything, but in everything by prayer and supplication with thanksgiving let your requests be made known to God. ⁷ And the peace of God, which surpasses all understanding, will guard your hearts and your minds in Christ Jesus.

⁸ Finally, beloved, whatever is true, whatever is honourable, whatever is just, whatever is pure, whatever is pleasing, whatever is commendable, if there is any excellence and if there is anything worthy of praise, think about these things. ⁹ Keep on doing the things that you have learned and received and heard and seen in me, and the God of peace will be with you.

OR   Revelation 14.14–18

¹⁴ Then I looked, and there was a white cloud, and seated on the cloud was one like the Son of Man, with a golden crown on his head, and a sharp sickle in his hand! ¹⁵ Another angel came out of the temple, calling with a loud voice to the one who sat on the cloud, 'Use your sickle and reap, for the hour to reap has come, because the harvest of the earth is fully ripe.' ¹⁶ So the one who sat on the cloud swung his sickle over the earth, and the earth was reaped.

¹⁷ Then another angel came out of the temple in heaven, and he too had a sharp sickle. ¹⁸ Then another angel came out from the altar, the angel who has authority over fire, and he called with a loud voice to him who had the sharp sickle, 'Use your sharp sickle and gather the clusters of the vine of the earth, for its grapes are ripe.'

GOSPEL   John 6.25–35

²⁵ When they found him on the other side of the lake, they said to him, 'Rabbi, when did you come here?' ²⁶ Jesus answered them, 'Very truly, I tell you, you are looking for me, not because you saw signs, but because you ate your fill of the loaves. ²⁷ Do not work for the food that perishes, but for the food that endures for eternal life, which the Son of Man will give you. For it is on him that God the Father has set his seal.' ²⁸ Then they said to him, 'What must we do to perform the works of God?' ²⁹ Jesus answered them, 'This is the work of God, that you believe in him whom he has sent.' ³⁰ So they said to him, 'What sign are you going to give us then, so that we may see it and believe you? What work are you performing? ³¹ Our ancestors ate the manna in the wilderness; as it is written, "He gave them bread from heaven to eat." ' ³² Then Jesus said to them, 'Very truly, I tell you, it was not Moses who gave you the bread from heaven, but it is my Father who gives you the true bread from heaven. ³³ For the bread of God is that which comes down from heaven and gives life to the world.' ³⁴ They said to him, 'Sir, give us this bread always.'

³⁵ Jesus said to them, 'I am the bread of life. Whoever comes to me will never be hungry, and whoever believes in me will never be thirsty.'

POST COMMUNION

Lord of the harvest,
with joy we have offered thanksgiving
    for your love in creation
and have shared in the bread and the wine of the kingdom:
by your grace plant within us a reverence for all that you give us
and make us generous and wise stewards
of the good things we enjoy;
through Jesus Christ our Lord.

BIBLE SUNDAY

Bible Sunday may be celebrated in preference to the provision for the Last Sunday after Trinity

COLLECT

Blessed Lord,
who caused all holy scriptures
    to be written for our learning:
help us so to hear them,
to read, mark, learn, and inwardly digest them
that, through patience, and the comfort of your holy word,
we may embrace and for ever hold fast
    the hope of everlasting life,
which you have given us in our Saviour Jesus Christ,
who is alive and reigns with you,
in the unity of the Holy Spirit,
one God, now and for ever.

READING   Isaiah 45.22–25

²² Turn to me and be saved,
        all the ends of the earth!
        For I am God, and there is no other.
²³ By myself I have sworn,
        from my mouth has gone forth in righteousness
        a word that shall not return:
    'To me every knee shall bow,
        every tongue shall swear.'
²⁴ Only in the LORD, it shall be said of me,
        are righteousness and strength;
    all who were incensed against him
        shall come to him and be ashamed.
²⁵ In the LORD all the offspring of Israel
        shall triumph and glory.

PSALM   Psalm 119.129–136

¹²⁹ Your decrees are wonderful;
        therefore I obey them with all my heart.
¹³⁰ When your word goes forth it gives light;
        it gives understanding to the simple.

131 I open my mouth and pant;
  I long for your commandments.
132 Turn to me in mercy,
  as you always do to those who love your name.
133 Steady my footsteps in your word;
  let no iniquity have dominion over me.
134 Rescue me from those who oppress me,
  and I will keep your commandments.
135 Let your countenance shine upon your servant
  and teach me your statutes.
136 My eyes shed streams of tears,
  because people do not keep your law.

READING   Romans 15.1–6

1 We who are strong ought to put up with the failings of the weak, and not to please ourselves. 2 Each of us must please our neighbour for the good purpose of building up the neighbour. 3 For Christ did not please himself; but, as it is written, 'The insults of those who insult you have fallen on me.' 4 For whatever was written in former days was written for our instruction, so that by steadfastness and by the encouragement of the scriptures we might have hope. 5 May the God of steadfastness and encouragement grant you to live in harmony with one another, in accordance with Christ Jesus, 6 so that together you may with one voice glorify the God and Father of our Lord Jesus Christ.

GOSPEL   Luke 4.16–24

16 When he came to Nazareth, where he had been brought up, he went to the synagogue on the sabbath day, as was his custom. He stood up to read, 17 and the scroll of the prophet Isaiah was given to him. He unrolled the scroll and found the place where it was written:
18 'The Spirit of the Lord is upon me,
    because he has anointed me
      to bring good news to the poor.
  He has sent me to proclaim release to the captives
    and recovery of sight to the blind,
      to let the oppressed go free,
19   to proclaim the year of the Lord's favour.'
20 And he rolled up the scroll, gave it back to the attendant, and sat down. The eyes of all in the synagogue were fixed on him. 21 Then he began to say to them, 'Today this scripture has been fulfilled in your hearing.' 22 All spoke well of him and were amazed at the gracious words that came

from his mouth. They said, 'Is not this Joseph's son?' [23] He said to them, 'Doubtless you will quote to me this proverb, "Doctor, cure yourself!" And you will say, "Do here also in your home town the things that we have heard you did at Capernaum." ' [24] And he said, 'Truly I tell you, no prophet is accepted in the prophet's home town.'

POST COMMUNION

God of all grace,
your Son Jesus Christ fed the hungry
with the bread of his life
and the word of his kingdom:
renew your people with your heavenly grace,
and in all our weakness
sustain us by your true and living bread;
who is alive and reigns, now and for ever.

SECOND SERVICE	THIRD SERVICE
Psalm 119.1–16	**Psalm 119.105–128**
Jeremiah 36.9–32	**1 Kings 22.1–17**
Romans 10.5–17	**Romans 15.4–13**
If the Second Service is a Eucharist, the following is read as a Gospel:	*or*
	Luke 14.1–14
Matthew 22.34–40	

DEDICATION FESTIVAL

The First Sunday in October or Last Sunday after Trinity

COLLECT

Almighty God,
to whose glory we celebrate the dedication
  of this house of prayer:
we praise you for the many blessings
you have given to those who worship you here:
and we pray that all who seek you in this place
  may find you,

and, being filled with the Holy Spirit,
may become a living temple acceptable to you;
through Jesus Christ your Son our Lord,
who is alive and reigns with you,
in the unity of the Holy Spirit,
one God, now and for ever.

READING   1 Chronicles 29.6–19

⁶ Then the leaders of ancestral houses made their freewill-offerings, as did also the leaders of the tribes, the commanders of the thousands and of the hundreds, and the officers over the king's work. ⁷ They gave for the service of the house of God five thousand talents and ten thousand darics of gold, ten thousand talents of silver, eighteen thousand talents of bronze, and one hundred thousand talents of iron. ⁸ Whoever had precious stones gave them to the treasury of the house of the LORD, into the care of Jehiel the Gershonite. ⁹ Then the people rejoiced because these had given willingly, for with single mind they had offered freely to the LORD; King David also rejoiced greatly.

¹⁰ Then David blessed the LORD in the presence of all the assembly; David said: 'Blessed are you, O LORD, the God of our ancestor Israel, for ever and ever. ¹¹ Yours, O LORD, are the greatness, the power, the glory, the victory, and the majesty; for all that is in the heavens and on the earth is yours; yours is the kingdom, O LORD, and you are exalted as head above all. ¹² Riches and honour come from you, and you rule over all. In your hand are power and might; and it is in your hand to make great and to give strength to all. ¹³ And now, our God, we give thanks to you and praise your glorious name.

¹⁴ 'But who am I, and what is my people, that we should be able to make this freewill-offering? For all things come from you, and of your own have we given you. ¹⁵ For we are aliens and transients before you, as were all our ancestors; our days on the earth are like a shadow, and there is no hope. ¹⁶ O LORD our God, all this abundance that we have provided for building you a house for your holy name comes from your hand and is all your own. ¹⁷ I know, my God, that you search the heart, and take pleasure in uprightness; in the uprightness of my heart I have freely offered all these things, and now I have seen your people, who are present here, offering freely and joyously to you. ¹⁸ O LORD, the God of Abraham, Isaac, and Israel, our ancestors, keep for ever such purposes and thoughts in the hearts of your people, and direct their hearts towards you. ¹⁹ Grant to my son

Solomon that with single mind he may keep your commandments, your decrees, and your statutes, performing all of them, and that he may build the temple for which I have made provision.'

PSALM   Psalm 122

[1] I was glad when they said to me,
   'Let us go to the house of the Lord.'
[2] Now our feet are standing
   within your gates, O Jerusalem.
[3] Jerusalem is built as a city
   that is at unity with itself.
[4] To which the tribes go up, the tribes of the Lord,
   the assembly of Israel, to praise the name of the Lord.
[5] For there are the thrones of judgement,
   the thrones of the house of David.
[6] Pray for the peace of Jerusalem:
   'May they prosper who love you.
[7] Peace be within your walls
   and quietness within your towers.
[8] For my family and companions' sake,
   I pray for your prosperity.
[9] Because of the house of the Lord our God,
   I will seek to do you good.'

READING   Ephesians 2.19–22

[19] So then you are no longer strangers and aliens, but you are citizens with the saints and also members of the household of God, [20] built upon the foundation of the apostles and prophets, with Christ Jesus himself as the cornerstone. [21] In him the whole structure is joined together and grows into a holy temple in the Lord; [22] in whom you also are built together spiritually into a dwelling-place for God.

GOSPEL   John 2.13–22

[13] The Passover of the Jews was near, and Jesus went up to Jerusalem. [14] In the temple he found people selling cattle, sheep, and doves, and the money-changers seated at their tables. [15] Making a whip of cords, he drove all of them out of the temple, both the sheep and the cattle. He also poured out the coins of the money-changers and overturned their tables. [16] He told those who were selling the doves, 'Take these things out of here! Stop making my Father's house a market-place!' [17] His disciples remembered

that it was written, 'Zeal for your house will consume me.' [18] The Jews then said to him, 'What sign can you show us for doing this?' [19] Jesus answered them, 'Destroy this temple, and in three days I will raise it up.' [20] The Jews then said, 'This temple has been under construction for forty-six years, and will you raise it up in three days?' [21] But he was speaking of the temple of his body. [22] After he was raised from the dead, his disciples remembered that he had said this; and they believed the scripture and the word that Jesus had spoken.

POST COMMUNION

Father in heaven,
whose Church on earth is a sign of your heavenly peace,
an image of the new and eternal Jerusalem:
grant to us in the days of our pilgrimage
that, fed with the living bread of heaven,
and united in the body of your Son,
we may be the temple of your presence,
the place of your glory on earth,
and a sign of your peace in the world;
through Jesus Christ our Lord.

SECOND SERVICE

Psalm 132
Jeremiah 7.1–11
Luke 19.1–10

THIRD SERVICE

Psalm 48
Haggai 2.6–9
Hebrews 10.19–25

HOLY DAYS

HOLY DAYS

COLLECT

Almighty God,
whose blessed Son was circumcised
in obedience to the law for our sake
and given the Name that is above every name:
give us grace faithfully to bear his Name,
to worship him in the freedom of the Spirit,
and to proclaim him as the Saviour of the world;
who is alive and reigns with you,
in the unity of the Holy Spirit,
one God, now and for ever.

READING   Numbers 6.22–27

²² The LORD spoke to Moses, saying: ²³ Speak to Aaron and his sons, saying,
Thus you shall bless the Israelites: You shall say to them,
²⁴ The LORD bless you and keep you;
²⁵ the LORD make his face to shine upon you, and be gracious to you;
²⁶ the LORD lift up his countenance upon you, and give you peace.

²⁷ So they shall put my name on the Israelites, and I will bless them.

PSALM   Psalm 8

¹ O Lord our governor,
   how exalted is your name in all the world!
² Out of the mouths of infants and children
   your majesty is praised above the heavens.
³ You have set up a stronghold against your adversaries,
   to quell the enemy and the avenger.
⁴ When I consider your heavens, the work of your fingers,
   the moon and the stars you have set in their courses,
⁵ What are mortals, that you should be mindful of them?
   mere human beings, that you should seek them out?
⁶ You have made them little lower than the angels;
   you adorn them with glory and honour.
⁷ You give them mastery over the works of your hands;
   and put all things under their feet,

⁸ All sheep and oxen,
   even the wild beasts of the field,
⁹ The birds of the air, the fish of the sea,
   and whatsoever walks in the paths of the sea.
¹⁰ O Lord our governor,
   how exalted is your name in all the world!

READING   Galatians 4.4–7

⁴ But when the fullness of time had come, God sent his Son, born of a
woman, born under the law, ⁵ in order to redeem those who were under
the law, so that we might receive adoption as children. ⁶ And because you
are children, God has sent the Spirit of his Son into our hearts, crying,
'Abba! Father!' ⁷ So you are no longer a slave but a child, and if a child then
also an heir, through God.

GOSPEL   Luke 2.15–21

¹⁵ When the angels had left them and gone into heaven, the shepherds
said to one another, 'Let us go now to Bethlehem and see this thing that
has taken place, which the Lord has made known to us.' ¹⁶ So they went
with haste and found Mary and Joseph, and the child lying in the manger.
¹⁷ When they saw this, they made known what had been told them about
this child; ¹⁸ and all who heard it were amazed at what the shepherds told
them. ¹⁹ But Mary treasured all these words and pondered them in her
heart. ²⁰ The shepherds returned, glorifying and praising God for all they
had heard and seen, as it had been told them.

²¹ After eight days had passed, it was time to circumcise the child; and he
was called Jesus, the name given by the angel before he was conceived in
the womb.

POST COMMUNION

Eternal God,
whose incarnate Son was given the Name of Saviour:
grant that we who have shared
   in this sacrament of our salvation
may live out our years in the power
   of the Name above all other names,
Jesus Christ our Lord.

THE CONVERSION OF PAUL 25 JANUARY

FESTIVAL

COLLECT

Almighty God,
who caused the light of the gospel
to shine throughout the world
through the preaching of your servant Saint Paul:
grant that we who celebrate his wonderful conversion
may follow him in bearing witness to your truth;
through Jesus Christ your Son our Lord,
who is alive and reigns with you,
in the unity of the Holy Spirit,
one God, now and for ever.

EITHER

READING Jeremiah 1.4–10

4 Now the word of the LORD came to me saying,
5   'Before I formed you in the womb I knew you,
    and before you were born I consecrated you;
    I appointed you a prophet to the nations.'
6 Then I said, 'Ah, Lord GOD! Truly I do not know how to speak, for I am only
a boy.' 7 But the LORD said to me,
    'Do not say, "I am only a boy";
    for you shall go to all to whom I send you,
    and you shall speak whatever I command you.
8   Do not be afraid of them,
    for I am with you to deliver you,
        says the LORD.'
9 Then the LORD put out his hand and touched my mouth; and the LORD
said to me,
    'Now I have put my words in your mouth.
10 See, today I appoint you over nations and over kingdoms,
    to pluck up and to pull down,
    to destroy and to overthrow,
    to build and to plant.'

PSALM

Psalm 67

¹ May God be merciful to us and bless us,
   show us the light of his countenance and come to us.
² Let your ways be known upon earth,
   your saving health among all nations.
³ Let the peoples praise you, O God;
   let all the peoples praise you.
⁴ Let the nations be glad and sing for joy,
   for you judge the peoples with equity and guide all the nations
      upon earth.
⁵ Let the peoples praise you, O God;
   let all the peoples praise you.
⁶ The earth has brought forth her increase;
   may God, our own God, give us his blessing.
⁷ May God give us his blessing,
   and may all the ends of the earth stand in awe of him.

READING

Acts 9.1–22

¹ Meanwhile Saul, still breathing threats and murder against the disciples of the Lord, went to the high priest ² and asked him for letters to the synagogues at Damascus, so that if he found any who belonged to the Way, men or women, he might bring them bound to Jerusalem. ³ Now as he was going along and approaching Damascus, suddenly a light from heaven flashed around him. ⁴ He fell to the ground and heard a voice saying to him, 'Saul, Saul, why do you persecute me?' ⁵ He asked, 'Who are you, Lord?' The reply came, 'I am Jesus, whom you are persecuting. ⁶ But get up and enter the city, and you will be told what you are to do.' ⁷ The men who were travelling with him stood speechless because they heard the voice but saw no one. ⁸ Saul got up from the ground, and though his eyes were open, he could see nothing; so they led him by the hand and brought him into Damascus. ⁹ For three days he was without sight, and neither ate nor drank.

¹⁰ Now there was a disciple in Damascus named Ananias. The Lord said to him in a vision, 'Ananias.' He answered, 'Here I am, Lord.' ¹¹ The Lord said to him, 'Get up and go to the street called Straight, and at the house of Judas look for a man of Tarsus named Saul. At this moment he is praying, ¹² and he has seen in a vision a man named Ananias come in and lay his hands on him so that he might regain his sight.' ¹³ But Ananias answered, 'Lord, I have heard from many about this man, how much evil he has done to your saints in Jerusalem; ¹⁴ and here he has authority from the chief priests to bind all who invoke your name.' ¹⁵ But the Lord said to him, 'Go, for he is an instrument whom I have chosen to bring my name before

Gentiles and kings and before the people of Israel; [16] I myself will show him how much he must suffer for the sake of my name.' [17] So Ananias went and entered the house. He laid his hands on Saul and said, 'Brother Saul, the Lord Jesus, who appeared to you on your way here, has sent me so that you may regain your sight and be filled with the Holy Spirit.' [18] And immediately something like scales fell from his eyes, and his sight was restored. Then he got up and was baptized, [19] and after taking some food, he regained his strength.

For several days he was with the disciples in Damascus, [20] and immediately he began to proclaim Jesus in the synagogues, saying, 'He is the Son of God.' [21] All who heard him were amazed and said, 'Is not this the man who made havoc in Jerusalem among those who invoked this name? And has he not come here for the purpose of bringing them bound before the chief priests?' [22] Saul became increasingly more powerful and confounded the Jews who lived in Damascus by proving that Jesus was the Messiah.

GOSPEL   Matthew 19.27–30

[27] Then Peter said in reply, 'Look, we have left everything and followed you. What then will we have?' [28] Jesus said to them, 'Truly I tell you, at the renewal of all things, when the Son of Man is seated on the throne of his glory, you who have followed me will also sit on twelve thrones, judging the twelve tribes of Israel. [29] And everyone who has left houses or brothers or sisters or father or mother or children or fields, for my name's sake, will receive a hundredfold, and will inherit eternal life. [30] But many who are first will be last, and the last will be first.'

OR

READING   Acts 9.1–22

[1] Meanwhile Saul, still breathing threats and murder against the disciples of the Lord, went to the high priest [2] and asked him for letters to the synagogues at Damascus, so that if he found any who belonged to the Way, men or women, he might bring them bound to Jerusalem. [3] Now as he was going along and approaching Damascus, suddenly a light from heaven flashed around him. [4] He fell to the ground and heard a voice saying to him, 'Saul, Saul, why do you persecute me?' [5] He asked, 'Who are you, Lord?' The reply came, 'I am Jesus, whom you are persecuting. [6] But get up and enter the city, and you will be told what you are to do.' [7] The men who were travelling with him stood speechless because they heard the voice but saw no one. [8] Saul got up from the ground, and though his eyes were open, he could see nothing; so they led him by the hand and brought him into

Damascus. [9] For three days he was without sight, and neither ate nor drank.

[10] Now there was a disciple in Damascus named Ananias. The Lord said to him in a vision, 'Ananias.' He answered, 'Here I am, Lord.' [11] The Lord said to him, 'Get up and go to the street called Straight, and at the house of Judas look for a man of Tarsus named Saul. At this moment he is praying, [12] and he has seen in a vision a man named Ananias come in and lay his hands on him so that he might regain his sight.' [13] But Ananias answered, 'Lord, I have heard from many about this man, how much evil he has done to your saints in Jerusalem; [14] and here he has authority from the chief priests to bind all who invoke your name.' [15] But the Lord said to him, 'Go, for he is an instrument whom I have chosen to bring my name before Gentiles and kings and before the people of Israel; [16] I myself will show him how much he must suffer for the sake of my name.' [17] So Ananias went and entered the house. He laid his hands on Saul and said, 'Brother Saul, the Lord Jesus, who appeared to you on your way here, has sent me so that you may regain your sight and be filled with the Holy Spirit.' [18] And immediately something like scales fell from his eyes, and his sight was restored. Then he got up and was baptized, [19] and after taking some food, he regained his strength.

For several days he was with the disciples in Damascus, [20] and immediately he began to proclaim Jesus in the synagogues, saying, 'He is the Son of God.' [21] All who heard him were amazed and said, 'Is not this the man who made havoc in Jerusalem among those who invoked this name? And has he not come here for the purpose of bringing them bound before the chief priests?' [22] Saul became increasingly more powerful and confounded the Jews who lived in Damascus by proving that Jesus was the Messiah.

PSALM   Psalm 67

1   May God be merciful to us and bless us,
    show us the light of his countenance and come to us.
2   Let your ways be known upon earth,
    your saving health among all nations.
3   Let the peoples praise you, O God;
    let all the peoples praise you.
4   Let the nations be glad and sing for joy,
    for you judge the peoples with equity and guide all the nations
       upon earth.
5   Let the peoples praise you, O God;
    let all the peoples praise you.

6 The earth has brought forth her increase;
may God, our own God, give us his blessing.
7 May God give us his blessing,
and may all the ends of the earth stand in awe of him.

READING   Galatians 1.11–16

11 For I want you to know, brothers and sisters, that the gospel that was proclaimed by me is not of human origin; 12 for I did not receive it from a human source, nor was I taught it, but I received it through a revelation of Jesus Christ.

13 You have heard, no doubt, of my earlier life in Judaism. I was violently persecuting the church of God and was trying to destroy it. 14 I advanced in Judaism beyond many among my people of the same age, for I was far more zealous for the traditions of my ancestors. 15 But when God, who had set me apart before I was born and called me through his grace, was pleased 16 to reveal his Son to me, so that I might proclaim him among the Gentiles, I did not confer with any human being.

GOSPEL   Matthew 19.27–30

27 Then Peter said in reply, 'Look, we have left everything and followed you. What then will we have?' 28 Jesus said to them, 'Truly I tell you, at the renewal of all things, when the Son of Man is seated on the throne of his glory, you who have followed me will also sit on twelve thrones, judging the twelve tribes of Israel. 29 And everyone who has left houses or brothers or sisters or father or mother or children or fields, for my name's sake, will receive a hundredfold, and will inherit eternal life. 30 But many who are first will be last, and the last will be first.'

POST COMMUNION

EITHER

Almighty God,
who on the day of Pentecost
sent your Holy Spirit to the apostles
with the wind from heaven and in tongues of flame,
filling them with joy and boldness to preach the gospel:
by the power of the same Spirit
strengthen us to witness to your truth
and to draw everyone to the fire of your love;
through Jesus Christ our Lord.

OR

Lord God, the source of truth and love,
keep us faithful to the apostles' teaching and fellowship,
united in prayer and the breaking of bread,
and one in joy and simplicity of heart,
in Jesus Christ our Lord.

TIMOTHY AND TITUS
COMPANIONS OF PAUL

COLLECT

Heavenly Father,
who sent your apostle Paul to preach the gospel,
and gave him Timothy and Titus
    to be his companions in the faith:
grant that our fellowship in the Holy Spirit
may bear witness to the name of Jesus,
who is alive and reigns with you,
in the unity of the Holy Spirit,
one God, now and for ever.

READING   Isaiah 61.1–3a

¹ The spirit of the Lord God is upon me,
    because the Lord has anointed me;
  he has sent me to bring good news to the oppressed,
    to bind up the broken-hearted,
  to proclaim liberty to the captives,
    and release to the prisoners;
² to proclaim the year of the Lord's favour,
    and the day of vengeance of our God;
  to comfort all who mourn;
³ to provide for those who mourn in Zion—
    to give them a garland instead of ashes,
  the oil of gladness instead of mourning,
    the mantle of praise instead of a faint spirit.

PSALM   Psalm 100

1 Be joyful in the Lord, all you lands;
   serve the Lord with gladness and come before his presence with a
      song.
2 Know this: The Lord himself is God;
   he himself has made us and we are his; we are his people and the
      sheep of his pasture.
3 Enter his gates with thanksgiving; go into his courts with praise;
   give thanks to him and call upon his name.
4 For the Lord is good; his mercy is everlasting;
   and his faithfulness endures from age to age.

READING

EITHER   2 Timothy 2.1–8

¹ You then, my child, be strong in the grace that is in Christ Jesus; ² and what you have heard from me through many witnesses entrust to faithful people who will be able to teach others as well. ³ Share in suffering like a good soldier of Christ Jesus. ⁴ No one serving in the army gets entangled in everyday affairs; the soldier's aim is to please the enlisting officer. ⁵ And in the case of an athlete, no one is crowned without competing according to the rules. ⁶ It is the farmer who does the work who ought to have the first share of the crops. ⁷ Think over what I say, for the Lord will give you understanding in all things.

⁸ Remember Jesus Christ, raised from the dead, a descendant of David—that is my gospel.

OR   Titus 1.1–5

¹ Paul, a servant of God and an apostle of Jesus Christ, for the sake of the faith of God's elect and the knowledge of the truth that is in accordance with godliness, ² in the hope of eternal life that God, who never lies, promised before the ages began— ³ in due time he revealed his word through the proclamation with which I have been entrusted by the command of God our Saviour,

⁴ To Titus, my loyal child in the faith we share:

Grace and peace from God the Father and Christ Jesus our Saviour.

⁵ I left you behind in Crete for this reason, that you should put in order what remained to be done, and should appoint elders in every town, as I directed you.

GOSPEL   Luke 10.1–9

¹ After this the Lord appointed seventy others and sent them on ahead of him in pairs to every town and place where he himself intended to go. ² He said to them, 'The harvest is plentiful, but the labourers are few; therefore ask the Lord of the harvest to send out labourers into his harvest. ³ Go on your way. See, I am sending you out like lambs into the midst of wolves. ⁴ Carry no purse, no bag, no sandals; and greet no one on the road. ⁵ Whatever house you enter, first say, "Peace to this house!" ⁶ And if anyone is there who shares in peace, your peace will rest on that person; but if not, it will return to you. ⁷ Remain in the same house, eating and drinking whatever they provide, for the labourer deserves to be paid. Do not move about from house to house. ⁸ Whenever you enter a town and its people welcome you, eat what is set before you; ⁹ cure the sick who are there, and say to them, "The kingdom of God has come near to you." '

POST COMMUNION

Holy Father,
who gathered us here around the table of your Son
to share this meal with the whole household of God:
in that new world where you reveal
    the fullness of your peace,
gather people of every race and language
to share with Timothy and Titus and all your saints
in the eternal banquet of Jesus Christ our Lord.

JOSEPH OF NAZARETH   19 MARCH

FESTIVAL

COLLECT

God our Father,
who from the family of your servant David
raised up Joseph the carpenter
to be the guardian of your incarnate Son
and husband of the Blessed Virgin Mary:
give us grace to follow him
in faithful obedience to your commands;
through Jesus Christ your Son our Lord,
who is alive and reigns with you,
in the unity of the Holy Spirit,
one God, now and for ever.

READING   2 Samuel 7.4-16

⁴ But that same night the word of the LORD came to Nathan: ⁵ Go and tell my servant David: Thus says the LORD: Are you the one to build me a house to live in? ⁶ I have not lived in a house since the day I brought up the people of Israel from Egypt to this day, but I have been moving about in a tent and a tabernacle. ⁷ Wherever I have moved about among all the people of Israel, did I ever speak a word with any of the tribal leaders of Israel, whom I commanded to shepherd my people Israel, saying, 'Why have you not built me a house of cedar?' ⁸ Now therefore thus you shall say to my servant David: Thus says the LORD of hosts: I took you from the pasture, from following the sheep to be prince over my people Israel; ⁹ and I have been with you wherever you went, and have cut off all your enemies from before you; and I will make for you a great name, like the name of the great ones of the earth. ¹⁰ And I will appoint a place for my people Israel and will plant them, so that they may live in their own place, and be disturbed no more; and evildoers shall afflict them no more, as formerly, ¹¹ from the time that I appointed judges over my people Israel; and I will give you rest from all your enemies. Moreover, the LORD declares to you that the LORD will make you a house. ¹² When your days are fulfilled and you lie down with your ancestors, I will raise up your offspring after you, who shall come forth from your body, and I will establish his kingdom. ¹³ He shall build a house for my name, and I will establish the throne of his kingdom for ever. ¹⁴ I will be a father to him, and he shall be a son to me. When he commits iniquity, I will punish him with a rod such as mortals use, with blows inflicted by human beings. ¹⁵ But I will not take my steadfast love from him, as I took it from Saul, whom I put away from before you. ¹⁶ Your house and your kingdom shall be made sure for ever before me; your throne shall be established for ever.

PSALM   Psalm 89.27-36

27 'I will make him my first-born
    and higher than the kings of the earth.
28 I will keep my love for him for ever,
    and my covenant will stand firm for him.
29 I will establish his line for ever
    and his throne as the days of heaven.
30 If his children forsake my law
    and do not walk according to my judgements;
31 If they break my statutes
    and do not keep my commandments;

32 I will punish their transgressions with a rod
    and their iniquities with the lash;
33 But I will not take my love from him,
    nor let my faithfulness prove false.
34 I will not break my covenant,
    nor change what has gone out of my lips.
35 Once for all I have sworn by my holiness:
    "I will not lie to David.
36 His line shall endure for ever
    and his throne as the sun before me." '

READING   Romans 4.13–18

13 For the promise that he would inherit the world did not come to Abraham or to his descendants through the law but through the righteousness of faith. 14 If it is the adherents of the law who are to be the heirs, faith is null and the promise is void. 15 For the law brings wrath; but where there is no law, neither is there violation.

16 For this reason it depends on faith, in order that the promise may rest on grace and be guaranteed to all his descendants, not only to the adherents of the law but also to those who share the faith of Abraham (for he is the father of all of us, 17 as it is written, 'I have made you the father of many nations')—in the presence of the God in whom he believed, who gives life to the dead and calls into existence the things that do not exist. 18 Hoping against hope, he believed that he would become 'the father of many nations', according to what was said, 'So numerous shall your descendants be.'

GOSPEL   Matthew 1.18–25

18 Now the birth of Jesus the Messiah took place in this way. When his mother Mary had been engaged to Joseph, but before they lived together, she was found to be with child from the Holy Spirit. 19 Her husband Joseph, being a righteous man and unwilling to expose her to public disgrace, planned to dismiss her quietly. 20 But just when he had resolved to do this, an angel of the Lord appeared to him in a dream and said, 'Joseph, son of David, do not be afraid to take Mary as your wife, for the child conceived in her is from the Holy Spirit. 21 She will bear a son, and you are to name him Jesus, for he will save his people from their sins.' 22 All this took place to fulfil what had been spoken by the Lord through the prophet:
23   'Look, the virgin shall conceive and bear a son,
        and they shall name him Emmanuel',

which means, 'God is with us.' [24] When Joseph awoke from sleep, he did as the angel of the Lord commanded him; he took her as his wife, [25] but had no marital relations with her until she had borne a son; and he named him Jesus.

POST COMMUNION

Heavenly Father,
whose Son grew in wisdom and stature
in the home of Joseph the carpenter of Nazareth
and on the wood of the cross perfected the work
    of the world's salvation:
help us, strengthened by this sacrament of his passion,
to count the wisdom of the world as foolishness,
and to walk with him in simplicity and trust;
through Jesus Christ our Lord.

THE ANNUNCIATION OF OUR LORD   25 MARCH

PRINCIPAL FEAST

COLLECT

We beseech you, O Lord,
pour your grace into our hearts,
that as we have known the incarnation
    of your Son Jesus Christ
by the message of an angel,
so by his cross and passion
we may be brought to the glory of his resurrection;
through Jesus Christ your Son our Lord,
who is alive and reigns with you,
in the unity of the Holy Spirit,
one God, now and for ever.

READING   Isaiah 7.10–14

¹⁰ Again the LORD spoke to Ahaz, saying, ¹¹ Ask a sign of the LORD your God; let it be deep as Sheol or high as heaven. ¹² But Ahaz said, I will not ask, and I will not put the LORD to the test. ¹³ Then Isaiah said: 'Hear then, O house of David! Is it too little for you to weary mortals, that you weary my God also? ¹⁴ Therefore the Lord himself will give you a sign. Look, the young woman is with child and shall bear a son, and shall name him Immanuel.'

PSALM   Psalm 40.5–11

⁵ Great things are they that you have done, O Lord my God! how
       great your wonders and your plans for us!
    there is none who can be compared with you.
⁶ O that I could make them known and tell them!
    but they are more than I can count.
⁷ In sacrifice and offering you take no pleasure
    you have given me ears to hear you;
⁸ Burnt-offering and sin-offering you have not required,
    and so I said, 'Behold, I come.
⁹ In the roll of the book it is written concerning me:
    "I love to do your will, O my God; your law is deep in my heart." '
¹⁰ I proclaimed righteousness in the great congregation;
    behold, I did not restrain my lips; and that, O Lord, you know.
¹¹ Your righteousness have I not hidden in my heart; I have spoken
       of your faithfulness and your deliverance;
    I have not concealed your love and faithfulness from the great
       congregation.

READING   Hebrews 10.4–10

⁴ For it is impossible for the blood of bulls and goats to take away sins.
⁵ Consequently, when Christ came into the world, he said,
    'Sacrifices and offerings you have not desired,
       but a body you have prepared for me;
⁶ in burnt-offerings and sin-offerings
       you have taken no pleasure.
⁷ Then I said, "See, God, I have come to do your will, O God"
       (in the scroll of the book it is written of me).'
⁸ When he said above, 'You have neither desired nor taken pleasure in sacrifices and offerings and burnt-offerings and sin-offerings' (these are offered according to the law), ⁹ then he added, 'See, I have come to do your

will.' He abolishes the first in order to establish the second. [10] And it is by God's will that we have been sanctified through the offering of the body of Jesus Christ once for all.

GOSPEL   Luke 1.26–38

[26] In the sixth month the angel Gabriel was sent by God to a town in Galilee called Nazareth, [27] to a virgin engaged to a man whose name was Joseph, of the house of David. The virgin's name was Mary. [28] And he came to her and said, 'Greetings, favoured one! The Lord is with you.' [29] But she was much perplexed by his words and pondered what sort of greeting this might be. [30] The angel said to her, 'Do not be afraid, Mary, for you have found favour with God. [31] And now, you will conceive in your womb and bear a son, and you will name him Jesus. [32] He will be great, and will be called the Son of the Most High, and the Lord God will give to him the throne of his ancestor David. [33] He will reign over the house of Jacob for ever, and of his kingdom there will be no end.' [34] Mary said to the angel, 'How can this be, since I am a virgin?' [35] The angel said to her, 'The Holy Spirit will come upon you, and the power of the Most High will overshadow you; therefore the child to be born will be holy; he will be called Son of God. [36] And now, your relative Elizabeth in her old age has also conceived a son; and this is the sixth month for her who was said to be barren. [37] For nothing will be impossible with God.' [38] Then Mary said, 'Here am I, the servant of the Lord; let it be with me according to your word.' Then the angel departed from her.

POST COMMUNION

God most high,
whose handmaid bore the Word made flesh:
we thank you that in this sacrament of our redemption
you visit us with your Holy Spirit
and overshadow us by your power;
strengthen us to walk with Mary the joyful path of obedience
and so to bring forth the fruits of holiness;
through Jesus Christ our Lord.

GEORGE
MARTYR, PATRON OF ENGLAND, c.304

23 APRIL

FESTIVAL

COLLECT

God of hosts,
who so kindled the flame of love
in the heart of your servant George
that he bore witness to the risen Lord
by his life and by his death:
give us the same faith and power of love
that we who rejoice in his triumphs
may come to share with him the fullness of the resurrection;
through Jesus Christ your Son our Lord,
who is alive and reigns with you,
in the unity of the Holy Spirit,
one God, now and for ever.

READING

EITHER   1 Maccabees 2.59–64

[59] 'Hananiah, Azariah, and Mishael believed and were saved from the flame.
[60] Daniel, because of his innocence, was delivered from the mouth of the lions.

[61] 'And so observe, from generation to generation, that none of those who put their trust in him will lack strength. [62] Do not fear the words of sinners, for their splendour will turn into dung and worms. [63] Today they will be exalted, but tomorrow they will not be found, because they will have returned to the dust, and their plans will have perished. [64] My children, be courageous and grow strong in the law, for by it you will gain honour.'

OR   Revelation 12.7–12

[7] And war broke out in heaven; Michael and his angels fought against the dragon. The dragon and his angels fought back, [8] but they were defeated, and there was no longer any place for them in heaven. [9] The great dragon was thrown down, that ancient serpent, who is called the Devil and Satan, the deceiver of the whole world—he was thrown down to the earth, and his angels were thrown down with him.

¹⁰ Then I heard a loud voice in heaven, proclaiming,
   'Now have come the salvation and the power
     and the kingdom of our God
     and the authority of his Messiah,
   for the accuser of our comrades has been thrown down,
     who accuses them day and night before our God.
¹¹ But they have conquered him by the blood of the Lamb
     and by the word of their testimony,
   for they did not cling to life even in the face of death.
¹² Rejoice then, you heavens
     and those who dwell in them!
   But woe to the earth and the sea,
     for the devil has come down to you
   with great wrath,
     because he knows that his time is short!'

PSALM   Psalm 126

¹ When the Lord restored the fortunes of Zion,
   then were we like those who dream.
² Then was our mouth filled with laughter,
   and our tongue with shouts of joy.
³ Then they said among the nations,
   'The Lord has done great things for them.'
⁴ The Lord has done great things for us,
   and we are glad indeed.
⁵ Restore our fortunes, O Lord,
   like the watercourses of the Negev.
⁶ Those who sowed with tears
   will reap with songs of joy.
⁷ Those who go out weeping, carrying the seed,
   will come again with joy, shouldering their sheaves.

READING   2 Timothy 2.3–13

³ Share in suffering like a good soldier of Christ Jesus. ⁴ No one serving in the army gets entangled in everyday affairs; the soldier's aim is to please the enlisting officer. ⁵ And in the case of an athlete, no one is crowned without competing according to the rules. ⁶ It is the farmer who does the work who ought to have the first share of the crops. ⁷ Think over what I say, for the Lord will give you understanding in all things.

⁸ Remember Jesus Christ, raised from the dead, a descendant of David—that is my gospel, ⁹ for which I suffer hardship, even to the point of being chained like a criminal. But the word of God is not chained. ¹⁰ Therefore I endure everything for the sake of the elect, so that they may also obtain the salvation that is in Christ Jesus, with eternal glory. ¹¹ The saying is sure:

If we have died with him, we will also live with him;
¹² if we endure, we will also reign with him;
if we deny him, he will also deny us;
¹³ if we are faithless, he remains faithful—
for he cannot deny himself.

GOSPEL   John 15.18–21

¹⁸ 'If the world hates you, be aware that it hated me before it hated you. ¹⁹ If you belonged to the world, the world would love you as its own. Because you do not belong to the world, but I have chosen you out of the world—therefore the world hates you. ²⁰ Remember the word that I said to you, "Servants are not greater than their master." If they persecuted me, they will persecute you; if they kept my word, they will keep yours also. ²¹ But they will do all these things to you on account of my name, because they do not know him who sent me.'

POST COMMUNION

EITHER

Eternal God,
who gave us this holy meal
in which we have celebrated the glory of the cross
and the victory of your martyr George:
by our communion with Christ
in his saving death and resurrection,
give us with all your saints the courage to conquer evil
and so to share the fruit of the tree of life;
through Jesus Christ our Lord.

OR

God our redeemer,
whose Church was strengthened by the blood of your martyr George:
so bind us, in life and death, to Christ's sacrifice
that our lives, broken and offered with his,
may carry his death and proclaim his resurrection in the world;
through Jesus Christ our Lord.

MARK
EVANGELIST

COLLECT

Almighty God,
who enlightened your holy Church
through the inspired witness
   of your evangelist Saint Mark:
grant that we, being firmly grounded
   in the truth of the gospel,
may be faithful to its teaching both in word and deed;
through Jesus Christ your Son our Lord,
who is alive and reigns with you,
in the unity of the Holy Spirit,
one God, now and for ever.

READING

EITHER   **Proverbs 15.28–33**

28 The mind of the righteous ponders how to answer,
    but the mouth of the wicked pours out evil.
29 The LORD is far from the wicked,
    but he hears the prayer of the righteous.
30 The light of the eyes rejoices the heart,
    and good news refreshes the body.
31 The ear that heeds wholesome admonition
    will lodge among the wise.
32 Those who ignore instruction despise themselves,
    but those who heed admonition gain understanding.
33 The fear of the LORD is instruction in wisdom,
    and humility goes before honour.

OR   **Acts 15.35–41**

35 But Paul and Barnabas remained in Antioch, and there, with many others, they taught and proclaimed the word of the Lord.

36 After some days Paul said to Barnabas, 'Come, let us return and visit the believers in every city where we proclaimed the word of the Lord and see how they are doing.' 37 Barnabas wanted to take with them John called

Mark. ³⁸ But Paul decided not to take with them one who had deserted them in Pamphylia and had not accompanied them in the work. ³⁹ The disagreement became so sharp that they parted company; Barnabas took Mark with him and sailed away to Cyprus. ⁴⁰ But Paul chose Silas and set out, the believers commending him to the grace of the Lord. ⁴¹ He went through Syria and Cilicia, strengthening the churches.

PSALM   Psalm 119.9–16

9   How shall the young cleanse their way?
    By keeping to your words.
10   With my whole heart I seek you;
    let me not stray from your commandments.
11   I treasure your promise in my heart,
    that I may not sin against you.
12   Blessèd are you, O Lord;
    instruct me in your statutes.
13   With my lips will I recite
    all the judgements of your mouth.
14   I have taken greater delight in the way of your decrees
    than in all manner of riches.
15   I will meditate on your commandments
    and give attention to your ways.
16   My delight is in your statutes;
    I will not forget your word.

READING   Ephesians 4.7–16

⁷ But each of us was given grace according to the measure of Christ's gift. ⁸ Therefore it is said,
    'When he ascended on high he made captivity itself a captive;
      he gave gifts to his people.'
⁹ (When it says, 'He ascended', what does it mean but that he had also descended into the lower parts of the earth? ¹⁰ He who descended is the same one who ascended far above all the heavens, so that he might fill all things.) ¹¹ The gifts he gave were that some would be apostles, some prophets, some evangelists, some pastors and teachers, ¹² to equip the saints for the work of ministry, for building up the body of Christ, ¹³ until all of us come to the unity of the faith and of the knowledge of the Son of God, to maturity, to the measure of the full stature of Christ. ¹⁴ We must no longer be children, tossed to and fro and blown about by every wind of doctrine, by people's trickery, by their craftiness in deceitful scheming. ¹⁵ But speaking the truth in love, we must grow up in every way into him

who is the head, into Christ, [16] from whom the whole body, joined and knitted together by every ligament with which it is equipped, as each part is working properly, promotes the body's growth in building itself up in love.

GOSPEL   Mark 13.5-13

[5] Then Jesus began to say to them, 'Beware that no one leads you astray. [6] Many will come in my name and say, "I am he!" and they will lead many astray. [7] When you hear of wars and rumours of wars, do not be alarmed; this must take place, but the end is still to come. [8] For nation will rise against nation, and kingdom against kingdom; there will be earthquakes in various places; there will be famines. This is but the beginning of the birth pangs.

[9] 'As for yourselves, beware; for they will hand you over to councils; and you will be beaten in synagogues; and you will stand before governors and kings because of me, as a testimony to them. [10] And the good news must first be proclaimed to all nations. [11] When they bring you to trial and hand you over, do not worry beforehand about what you are to say; but say whatever is given you at that time, for it is not you who speak, but the Holy Spirit. [12] Brother will betray brother to death, and a father his child, and children will rise against parents and have them put to death; [13] and you will be hated by all because of my name. But the one who endures to the end will be saved.'

POST COMMUNION

EITHER

Almighty God,
who on the day of Pentecost
sent your Holy Spirit to the apostles
with the wind from heaven and in tongues of flame,
filling them with joy and boldness to preach the gospel:
by the power of the same Spirit
strengthen us to witness to your truth
and to draw everyone to the fire of your love;
through Jesus Christ our Lord.

OR

Lord God, the source of truth and love,
keep us faithful to the apostles' teaching and fellowship,
united in prayer and the breaking of bread,
and one in joy and simplicity of heart,
in Jesus Christ our Lord.

PHILIP AND JAMES
APOSTLES

1 MAY

FESTIVAL

COLLECT

Almighty Father,
whom truly to know is eternal life:
teach us to know your Son Jesus Christ
as the way, the truth, and the life;
that we may follow the steps
   of your holy apostles Philip and James,
and walk steadfastly in the way that leads to your glory;
through Jesus Christ your Son our Lord,
who is alive and reigns with you,
in the unity of the Holy Spirit,
one God, now and for ever.

READING

Isaiah 30.15–21

¹⁵ For thus said the Lord GOD, the Holy One of Israel:
   In returning and rest you shall be saved;
     in quietness and in trust shall be your strength.
   But you refused ¹⁶ and said,
   'No! We will flee upon horses'—
     therefore you shall flee!
   and, 'We will ride upon swift steeds'—
     therefore your pursuers shall be swift!
¹⁷ A thousand shall flee at the threat of one,
     at the threat of five you shall flee,
   until you are left
     like a flagstaff on the top of a mountain,
     like a signal on a hill.

¹⁸ Therefore the LORD waits to be gracious to you;
 therefore he will rise up to show mercy to you.
For the LORD is a God of justice;
 blessed are all those who wait for him.

¹⁹ Truly, O people in Zion, inhabitants of Jerusalem, you shall weep no more. He will surely be gracious to you at the sound of your cry; when he hears it, he will answer you. ²⁰ Though the Lord may give you the bread of adversity and the water of affliction, yet your Teacher will not hide himself any more, but your eyes shall see your Teacher. ²¹ And when you turn to the right or when you turn to the left, your ears shall hear a word behind you, saying, 'This is the way; walk in it.'

PSALM   Psalm 119.1–8

¹ Happy are they whose way is blameless,
 who walk in the law of the Lord!
² Happy are they who observe his decrees
 and seek him with all their hearts!
³ Who never do any wrong,
 but always walk in his ways.
⁴ You laid down your commandments,
 that we should fully keep them.
⁵ O that my ways were made so direct
 that I might keep your statutes!
⁶ Then I should not be put to shame,
 when I regard all your commandments.
⁷ I will thank you with an unfeigned heart,
 when I have learned your righteous judgements.
⁸ I will keep your statutes;
 do not utterly forsake me.

READING   Ephesians 1.3–10

³ Blessed be the God and Father of our Lord Jesus Christ, who has blessed us in Christ with every spiritual blessing in the heavenly places, ⁴ just as he chose us in Christ before the foundation of the world to be holy and blameless before him in love. ⁵ He destined us for adoption as his children through Jesus Christ, according to the good pleasure of his will, ⁶ to the praise of his glorious grace that he freely bestowed on us in the Beloved. ⁷ In him we have redemption through his blood, the forgiveness of our trespasses, according to the riches of his grace ⁸ that he lavished on us. With all wisdom and insight ⁹ he has made known to us the mystery of his

will, according to his good pleasure that he set forth in Christ, [10] as a plan for the fullness of time, to gather up all things in him, things in heaven and things on earth.

GOSPEL   John 14.1–14

[1] 'Do not let your hearts be troubled. Believe in God, believe also in me. [2] In my Father's house there are many dwelling-places. If it were not so, would I have told you that I go to prepare a place for you? [3] And if I go and prepare a place for you, I will come again and will take you to myself, so that where I am, there you may be also. [4] And you know the way to the place where I am going.' [5] Thomas said to him, 'Lord, we do not know where you are going. How can we know the way?' [6] Jesus said to him, 'I am the way, and the truth, and the life. No one comes to the Father except through me. [7] If you know me, you will know my Father also. From now on you do know him and have seen him.'

[8] Philip said to him, 'Lord, show us the Father, and we will be satisfied.' [9] Jesus said to him, 'Have I been with you all this time, Philip, and you still do not know me? Whoever has seen me has seen the Father. How can you say, "Show us the Father"? [10] Do you not believe that I am in the Father and the Father is in me? The words that I say to you I do not speak on my own; but the Father who dwells in me does his works. [11] Believe me that I am in the Father and the Father is in me; but if you do not, then believe me because of the works themselves. [12] Very truly, I tell you, the one who believes in me will also do the works that I do and, in fact, will do greater works than these, because I am going to the Father. [13] I will do whatever you ask in my name, so that the Father may be glorified in the Son. [14] If in my name you ask me for anything, I will do it.'

POST COMMUNION

EITHER

Almighty God,
who on the day of Pentecost
sent your Holy Spirit to the apostles
with the wind from heaven and in tongues of flame,
filling them with joy and boldness to preach the gospel:
by the power of the same Spirit
strengthen us to witness to your truth
and to draw everyone to the fire of your love;
through Jesus Christ our Lord.

OR

Lord God, the source of truth and love,
keep us faithful to the apostles' teaching and fellowship,
united in prayer and the breaking of bread,
and one in joy and simplicity of heart,
in Jesus Christ our Lord.

ENGLISH SAINTS AND MARTYRS OF THE REFORMATION ERA

4 MAY

LESSER FESTIVAL

COLLECT

Merciful God,
who, when your Church on earth was torn apart
   by the ravages of sin,
raised up men and women in this land
who witnessed to their faith with courage and constancy:
give to your Church that peace which is your will,
and grant that those who have been divided on earth
   may be reconciled in heaven,
and share together in the vision of your glory;
through Jesus Christ your Son our Lord,
who is alive and reigns with you,
in the unity of the Holy Spirit,
one God, now and for ever.

READING

EITHER   Isaiah 43.1–7

¹ But now thus says the LORD,
      he who created you, O Jacob,
      he who formed you, O Israel:
   Do not fear, for I have redeemed you;
      I have called you by name, you are mine.
² When you pass through the waters, I will be with you;
      and through the rivers, they shall not overwhelm you;
   when you walk through fire you shall not be burned,
      and the flame shall not consume you.

³ For I am the LORD your God,
    the Holy One of Israel, your Saviour.
  I give Egypt as your ransom,
    Ethiopia and Seba in exchange for you.
⁴ Because you are precious in my sight,
    and honoured, and I love you,
  I give people in return for you,
    nations in exchange for your life.
⁵ Do not fear, for I am with you;
    I will bring your offspring from the east,
    and from the west I will gather you;
⁶ I will say to the north, 'Give them up',
    and to the south, 'Do not withhold;
  bring my sons from far away
    and my daughters from the end of the earth—
⁷ everyone who is called by my name,
    whom I created for my glory,
    whom I formed and made.'

OR   **Ecclesiasticus 2.10–17**

¹⁰ Consider the generations of old and see:
    has anyone trusted in the Lord and been disappointed?
  Or has anyone persevered in the fear of the Lord and been forsaken?
    Or has anyone called upon him and been neglected?
¹¹ For the Lord is compassionate and merciful;
    he forgives sins and saves in time of distress.
¹² Woe to timid hearts and to slack hands,
    and to the sinner who walks a double path!
¹³ Woe to the faint-hearted who have no trust!
    Therefore they will have no shelter.
¹⁴ Woe to you who have lost your nerve!
    What will you do when the Lord's reckoning comes?
¹⁵ Those who fear the Lord do not disobey his words,
    and those who love him keep his ways.
¹⁶ Those who fear the Lord seek to please him,
    and those who love him are filled with his law.
¹⁷ Those who fear the Lord prepare their hearts,
    and humble themselves before him.

PSALM
Psalm 87

1 On the holy mountain stands the city he has founded;
   the Lord loves the gates of Zion more than all the dwellings of
   Jacob.
2 Glorious things are spoken of you,
   O city of our God.
3 I count Egypt and Babylon among those who know me;
   behold Philistia, Tyre and Ethiopia: in Zion were they born.
4 Of Zion it shall be said, 'Everyone was born in her,
   and the Most High himself shall sustain her.'
5 The Lord will record as he enrols the peoples,
   'These also were born there.'
6 The singers and the dancers will say,
   'All my fresh springs are in you.'

READING
2 Corinthians 4.5–12

5 For we do not proclaim ourselves; we proclaim Jesus Christ as Lord and ourselves as your slaves for Jesus' sake. 6 For it is the God who said, 'Let light shine out of darkness', who has shone in our hearts to give the light of the knowledge of the glory of God in the face of Jesus Christ.

7 But we have this treasure in clay jars, so that it may be made clear that this extraordinary power belongs to God and does not come from us. 8 We are afflicted in every way, but not crushed; perplexed, but not driven to despair; 9 persecuted, but not forsaken; struck down, but not destroyed; 10 always carrying in the body the death of Jesus, so that the life of Jesus may also be made visible in our bodies. 11 For while we live, we are always being given up to death for Jesus' sake, so that the life of Jesus may be made visible in our mortal flesh. 12 So death is at work in us, but life in you.

GOSPEL
John 12.20–26

20 Now among those who went up to worship at the festival were some Greeks. 21 They came to Philip, who was from Bethsaida in Galilee, and said to him, 'Sir, we wish to see Jesus.' 22 Philip went and told Andrew; then Andrew and Philip went and told Jesus. 23 Jesus answered them, 'The hour has come for the Son of Man to be glorified. 24 Very truly, I tell you, unless a grain of wheat falls into the earth and dies, it remains just a single grain; but if it dies, it bears much fruit. 25 Those who love their life lose it, and those who hate their life in this world will keep it for eternal life. 26 Whoever serves me must follow me, and where I am, there will my servant be also. Whoever serves me, the Father will honour.'

POST COMMUNION

God, the source of all holiness
  and giver of all good things:
may we who have shared at this table
  as strangers and pilgrims here on earth
be welcomed with all your saints
  to the heavenly feast on the day of your kingdom;
through Jesus Christ our Lord.

MATTHIAS
APOSTLE   14 MAY

FESTIVAL

COLLECT

Almighty God,
who in the place of the traitor Judas
chose your faithful servant Matthias
to be of the number of the Twelve:
preserve your Church from false apostles
and, by the ministry of faithful pastors and teachers,
keep us steadfast in your truth;
through Jesus Christ your Son our Lord,
who is alive and reigns with you,
in the unity of the Holy Spirit,
one God, now and for ever.

EITHER

READING   Isaiah 22.15–25

¹⁵ Thus says the Lord GOD of hosts: Come, go to this steward, to Shebna, who is master of the household, and say to him: ¹⁶ What right do you have here? Who are your relatives here, that you have cut out a tomb here for yourself, cutting a tomb on the height, and carving a habitation for yourself in the rock? ¹⁷ The LORD is about to hurl you away violently, my man. He will seize firm hold of you, ¹⁸ whirl you round and round, and throw you like a ball into a wide land; there you shall die, and there your splendid chariots shall lie, O you disgrace to your master's house! ¹⁹ I will thrust you from your office, and you will be pulled down from your post.

²⁰ On that day I will call my servant Eliakim son of Hilkiah, ²¹ and will clothe him with your robe and bind your sash on him. I will commit your authority to his hand, and he shall be a father to the inhabitants of Jerusalem and to the house of Judah. ²² I will place on his shoulder the key of the house of David; he shall open, and no one shall shut; he shall shut, and no one shall open. ²³ I will fasten him like a peg in a secure place, and he will become a throne of honour to his ancestral house. ²⁴ And they will hang on him the whole weight of his ancestral house, the offspring and issue, every small vessel, from the cups to all the flagons. ²⁵ On that day, says the LORD of hosts, the peg that was fastened in a secure place will give way; it will be cut down and fall, and the load that was on it will perish, for the LORD has spoken.

PSALM   Psalm 15

¹   Lord, who may dwell in your tabernacle?
    who may abide upon your holy hill?
²   Whoever leads a blameless life and does what is right,
    who speaks the truth from his heart.
³   There is no guile upon his tongue; he does no evil to his friend;
    he does not heap contempt upon his neighbour.
⁴   In his sight the wicked is rejected,
    but he honours those who fear the Lord.
⁵   He has sworn to do no wrong
    and does not take back his word.
⁶   He does not give his money in hope of gain,
    nor does he take a bribe against the innocent.
⁷   Whoever does these things
    shall never be overthrown.

READING   Acts 1.15–26

¹⁵ In those days Peter stood up among the believers (together the crowd numbered about one hundred and twenty people) and said, ¹⁶ 'Friends, the scripture had to be fulfilled, which the Holy Spirit through David foretold concerning Judas, who became a guide for those who arrested Jesus— ¹⁷ for he was numbered among us and was allotted his share in this ministry.' ¹⁸ (Now this man acquired a field with the reward of his wickedness; and falling headlong, he burst open in the middle and all his bowels gushed out. ¹⁹ This became known to all the residents of Jerusalem, so that the field was called in their language Hakeldama, that is, Field of Blood.) ²⁰ 'For it is written in the book of Psalms,

"Let his homestead become desolate,
　　and let there be no one to live in it";
and
　　"Let another take his position of overseer."
[21] So one of the men who have accompanied us throughout the time that the Lord Jesus went in and out among us, [22] beginning from the baptism of John until the day when he was taken up from us—one of these must become a witness with us to his resurrection.' [23] So they proposed two, Joseph called Barsabbas, who was also known as Justus, and Matthias. [24] Then they prayed and said, 'Lord, you know everyone's heart. Show us which one of these two you have chosen [25] to take the place in this ministry and apostleship from which Judas turned aside to go to his own place.' [26] And they cast lots for them, and the lot fell on Matthias; and he was added to the eleven apostles.

GOSPEL   John 15.9–17

[9] 'As the Father has loved me, so I have loved you; abide in my love. [10] If you keep my commandments, you will abide in my love, just as I have kept my Father's commandments and abide in his love. [11] I have said these things to you so that my joy may be in you, and that your joy may be complete.

[12] 'This is my commandment, that you love one another as I have loved you. [13] No one has greater love than this, to lay down one's life for one's friends. [14] You are my friends if you do what I command you. [15] I do not call you servants any longer, because the servant does not know what the master is doing; but I have called you friends, because I have made known to you everything that I have heard from my Father. [16] You did not choose me but I chose you. And I appointed you to go and bear fruit, fruit that will last, so that the Father will give you whatever you ask him in my name. [17] I am giving you these commands so that you may love one another.'

OR

READING   Acts 1.15–26

[15] In those days Peter stood up among the believers (together the crowd numbered about one hundred and twenty people) and said, [16] 'Friends, the scripture had to be fulfilled, which the Holy Spirit through David foretold concerning Judas, who became a guide for those who arrested Jesus— [17] for he was numbered among us and was allotted his share in this ministry.' [18] (Now this man acquired a field with the reward of his wickedness; and falling headlong, he burst open in the middle and all his bowels gushed out. [19] This became known to all the residents of Jerusalem, so that the

field was called in their language Hakeldama, that is, Field of Blood.) [20] 'For it is written in the book of Psalms,

"Let his homestead become desolate,
and let there be no one to live in it";

and

"Let another take his position of overseer."

[21] So one of the men who have accompanied us throughout the time that the Lord Jesus went in and out among us, [22] beginning from the baptism of John until the day when he was taken up from us—one of these must become a witness with us to his resurrection.' [23] So they proposed two, Joseph called Barsabbas, who was also known as Justus, and Matthias. [24] Then they prayed and said, 'Lord, you know everyone's heart. Show us which one of these two you have chosen [25] to take the place in this ministry and apostleship from which Judas turned aside to go to his own place.' [26] And they cast lots for them, and the lot fell on Matthias; and he was added to the eleven apostles.

PSALM   Psalm 15

[1] Lord, who may dwell in your tabernacle?
    who may abide upon your holy hill?
[2] Whoever leads a blameless life and does what is right,
    who speaks the truth from his heart.
[3] There is no guile upon his tongue; he does no evil to his friend;
    he does not heap contempt upon his neighbour.
[4] In his sight the wicked is rejected,
    but he honours those who fear the Lord.
[5] He has sworn to do no wrong
    and does not take back his word.
[6] He does not give his money in hope of gain,
    nor does he take a bribe against the innocent.
[7] Whoever does these things
    shall never be overthrown.

READING   1 Corinthians 4.1–7

[1] Think of us in this way, as servants of Christ and stewards of God's mysteries. [2] Moreover, it is required of stewards that they should be found trustworthy. [3] But with me it is a very small thing that I should be judged by you or by any human court. I do not even judge myself. [4] I am not aware of anything against myself, but I am not thereby acquitted. It is the Lord who judges me. [5] Therefore do not pronounce judgement before the time, before the Lord comes, who will bring to light the things now hidden in

darkness and will disclose the purposes of the heart. Then each one will receive commendation from God.

⁶ I have applied all this to Apollos and myself for your benefit, brothers and sisters, so that you may learn through us the meaning of the saying, 'Nothing beyond what is written', so that none of you will be puffed up in favour of one against another. ⁷ For who sees anything different in you? What do you have that you did not receive? And if you received it, why do you boast as if it were not a gift?

GOSPEL   John 15.9–17

⁹ 'As the Father has loved me, so I have loved you; abide in my love. ¹⁰ If you keep my commandments, you will abide in my love, just as I have kept my Father's commandments and abide in his love. ¹¹ I have said these things to you so that my joy may be in you, and that your joy may be complete.

¹² 'This is my commandment, that you love one another as I have loved you. ¹³ No one has greater love than this, to lay down one's life for one's friends. ¹⁴ You are my friends if you do what I command you. ¹⁵ I do not call you servants any longer, because the servant does not know what the master is doing; but I have called you friends, because I have made known to you everything that I have heard from my Father. ¹⁶ You did not choose me but I chose you. And I appointed you to go and bear fruit, fruit that will last, so that the Father will give you whatever you ask him in my name. ¹⁷ I am giving you these commands so that you may love one another.'

POST COMMUNION

EITHER

Almighty God,
who on the day of Pentecost
sent your Holy Spirit to the apostles
with the wind from heaven and in tongues of flame,
filling them with joy and boldness to preach the gospel:
by the power of the same Spirit
strengthen us to witness to your truth
and to draw everyone to the fire of your love;
through Jesus Christ our Lord.

OR

Lord God, the source of truth and love,
keep us faithful to the apostles' teaching and fellowship,
united in prayer and the breaking of bread,
and one in joy and simplicity of heart,
in Jesus Christ our Lord.

THE VISIT OF THE BLESSED VIRGIN MARY TO ELIZABETH

31 MAY

FESTIVAL

COLLECT

Mighty God,
by whose grace Elizabeth rejoiced with Mary
and greeted her as the mother of the Lord:
look with favour on your lowly servants
that, with Mary, we may magnify your holy name
and rejoice to acclaim her Son our Saviour,
who is alive and reigns with you,
in the unity of the Holy Spirit,
one God, now and for ever.

READING   Zephaniah 3.14–18

¹⁴ Sing aloud, O daughter Zion;
        shout, O Israel!
    Rejoice and exult with all your heart,
        O daughter Jerusalem!
¹⁵ The LORD has taken away the judgements against you,
        he has turned away your enemies.
    The king of Israel, the LORD, is in your midst;
        you shall fear disaster no more.
¹⁶ On that day it shall be said to Jerusalem:
    Do not fear, O Zion;
        do not let your hands grow weak.
¹⁷ The LORD, your God, is in your midst,
        a warrior who gives victory;
    he will rejoice over you with gladness,
        he will renew you in his love;
    he will exult over you with loud singing

¹⁸ as on a day of festival.
   I will remove disaster from you,
      so that you will not bear reproach for it.

PSALM   Psalm 113

¹ Alleluia! Give praise, you servants of the Lord;
   praise the name of the Lord.
² Let the name of the Lord be blessed,
   from this time forth for evermore.
³ From the rising of the sun to its going down
   let the name of the Lord be praised.
⁴ The Lord is high above all nations,
   and his glory above the heavens.
⁵ Who is like the Lord our God, who sits enthroned on high,
   but stoops to behold the heavens and the earth?
⁶ He takes up the weak out of the dust
   and lifts up the poor from the ashes.
⁷ He sets them with the princes,
   with the princes of his people.
⁸ He makes the woman of a childless house
   to be a joyful mother of children.

READING   Romans 12.9–16

⁹ Let love be genuine; hate what is evil, hold fast to what is good; ¹⁰ love one another with mutual affection; outdo one another in showing honour. ¹¹ Do not lag in zeal, be ardent in spirit, serve the Lord. ¹² Rejoice in hope, be patient in suffering, persevere in prayer. ¹³ Contribute to the needs of the saints; extend hospitality to strangers.

¹⁴ Bless those who persecute you; bless and do not curse them. ¹⁵ Rejoice with those who rejoice, weep with those who weep. ¹⁶ Live in harmony with one another; do not be haughty, but associate with the lowly; do not claim to be wiser than you are.

GOSPEL   Luke 1.39–49, [50–56]

³⁹ In those days Mary set out and went with haste to a Judean town in the hill country, ⁴⁰ where she entered the house of Zechariah and greeted Elizabeth. ⁴¹ When Elizabeth heard Mary's greeting, the child leapt in her womb. And Elizabeth was filled with the Holy Spirit ⁴² and exclaimed with a loud cry, 'Blessed are you among women, and blessed is the fruit of your

womb. ⁴³ And why has this happened to me, that the mother of my Lord comes to me? ⁴⁴ For as soon as I heard the sound of your greeting, the child in my womb leapt for joy. ⁴⁵ And blessed is she who believed that there would be a fulfilment of what was spoken to her by the Lord.'

⁴⁶ And Mary said,
'My soul magnifies the Lord,
⁴⁷   and my spirit rejoices in God my Saviour,
⁴⁸ for he has looked with favour on the lowliness of his servant.
       Surely, from now on all generations will call me blessed;
⁴⁹ for the Mighty One has done great things for me,
       and holy is his name.'
[⁵⁰ 'His mercy is for those who fear him
       from generation to generation.
⁵¹ He has shown strength with his arm;
       he has scattered the proud in the thoughts of their hearts.
⁵² He has brought down the powerful from their thrones,
       and lifted up the lowly;
⁵³ he has filled the hungry with good things,
       and sent the rich away empty.
⁵⁴ He has helped his servant Israel,
       in remembrance of his mercy,
⁵⁵ according to the promise he made to our ancestors,
       to Abraham and to his descendants for ever.'

⁵⁶ And Mary remained with her for about three months and then returned to her home.]

POST COMMUNION

Gracious God,
who gave joy to Elizabeth and Mary
as they recognized the signs of redemption
    at work within them:
help us, who have shared in the joy of this eucharist,
to know the Lord deep within us
and his love shining out in our lives,
that the world may rejoice in your salvation;
through Jesus Christ our Lord.

YEARS A, B, AND C

DAY OF THANKSGIVING FOR THE INSTITUTION OF HOLY COMMUNION
THURSDAY AFTER TRINITY SUNDAY (CORPUS CHRISTI)

OPTIONAL FESTIVAL

COLLECT

Lord Jesus Christ,
we thank you that in this wonderful sacrament
you have given us the memorial of your passion:
grant us so to reverence the sacred mysteries
    of your body and blood
that we may know within ourselves
and show forth in our lives
the fruits of your redemption;
for you are alive and reign with the Father
in the unity of the Holy Spirit, one God, now and forever.

READING   Genesis 14.18–20

[18] And King Melchizedek of Salam brought out bread and wine; he was priest of God Most High. [19] He blessed him and said,
    'Blessed be Abram by God Most High,
        maker of heaven and earth;
[20] and blessed be God Most High,
        who has delivered your enemies into your hand!'
And Abram gave him one-tenth of everything.

PSALM   Psalm 116.10–17

[10] How shall I repay the Lord
        for all the good things he has done for me?
[11] I will lift up the cup of salvation
        and call upon the name of the Lord.
[12] I will fulfil my vows to the Lord
        in the presence of all his people.
[13] Precious in the sight of the Lord
        is the death of his servants.
[14] O Lord, I am your servant;
        I am your servant and the child of your handmaid; you have freed
        me from my bonds.

15 I will offer you the sacrifice of thanksgiving
    and call upon the name of the Lord.
16 I will fulfil my vows to the Lord
    in the presence of all his people.
17 IIn the courts of the Lord's house,
    in the midst of you, O Jerusalem. Alleluia!

READING   1 Corinthians 11.23–26

23 For I received from the Lord what I also handed on to you, that the Lord
Jesus on the night when he was betrayed took a loaf of bread, 24 and when
he had given thanks, he broke it and said, 'This is my body that is for you.
Do this in remembrance of me.' 25 In the same way he took the cup also,
after supper, saying, 'This cup is the new covenant in my blood. Do this, as
often as you drink it, in remembrance of me.' 26 For as often as you eat this
bread and drink the cup, you proclaim the Lord's death until he comes.

GOSPEL   John 6.51–58

51 'I am the living bread that came down from heaven. Whoever eats of this
bread will live for ever; and the bread that I will give for the life of the
world is my flesh.'

52 The Jews then disputed among themselves, saying, 'How can this man
give us his flesh to eat?' 53 So Jesus said to them, 'Very truly, I tell you, unless
you eat the flesh of the Son of Man and drink his blood, you have no life in
you. 54 Those who eat my flesh and drink my blood have eternal life, and I
will raise them up on the last day; 55 for my flesh is true food and my blood
is true drink. 56 Those who eat my flesh and drink my blood abide in me,
and I in them. 57 Just as the living Father sent me, and I live because of the
Father, so whoever eats me will live because of me. 58 This is the bread that
came down from heaven, not like that which your ancestors ate, and they
died. But the one who eats this bread will live for ever.'

POST COMMUNION

All praise to you, our God and Father,
for you have fed us with the bread of heaven
and quenched our thirst from the true vine:
hear our prayer that, being grafted into Christ,
we may grow together in unity
and feast with him in his kingdom;
through Jesus Christ our Lord.

BARNABAS

COLLECT

Bountiful God, giver of all gifts,
who poured your Spirit upon your servant Barnabas
and gave him grace to encourage others:
help us, by his example,
to be generous in our judgements
and unselfish in our service;
through Jesus Christ your Son our Lord,
who is alive and reigns with you,
in the unity of the Holy Spirit,
one God, now and for ever.

EITHER

READING   Job 29.11–16

11 'When the ear heard, it commended me,
   and when the eye saw, it approved;
12 because I delivered the poor who cried,
   and the orphan who had no helper.
13 The blessing of the wretched came upon me,
   and I caused the widow's heart to sing for joy.
14 I put on righteousness, and it clothed me;
   my justice was like a robe and a turban.
15 I was eyes to the blind,
   and feet to the lame.
16 I was a father to the needy,
   and I championed the cause of the stranger.'

PSALM   Psalm 112

1 Alleluia! Happy are they who fear the Lord
  and have great delight in his commandments!
2 Their descendants will be mighty in the land;
  the generation of the upright will be blessed.
3 Wealth and riches will be in their house,
  and their righteousness will last for ever.

4 Light shines in the darkness for the upright;
the righteous are merciful and full of compassion.

5 It is good for them to be generous in lending
and to manage their affairs with justice.

6 For they will never be shaken;
the righteous will be kept in everlasting remembrance.

7 They will not be afraid of any evil rumours;
their heart is right; they put their trust in the Lord.

8 Their heart is established and will not shrink,
until they see their desire upon their enemies.

9 They have given freely to the poor,
and their righteousness stands fast for ever; they will hold up their
head with honour.

10 The wicked will see it and be angry; they will gnash their teeth
and pine away;
the desires of the wicked will perish.

READING   Acts 11.19–30

19 Now those who were scattered because of the persecution that took place over Stephen travelled as far as Phoenicia, Cyprus, and Antioch, and they spoke the word to no one except Jews. 20 But among them were some men of Cyprus and Cyrene who, on coming to Antioch, spoke to the Hellenists also, proclaiming the Lord Jesus. 21 The hand of the Lord was with them, and a great number became believers and turned to the Lord. 22 News of this came to the ears of the church in Jerusalem, and they sent Barnabas to Antioch. 23 When he came and saw the grace of God, he rejoiced, and he exhorted them all to remain faithful to the Lord with steadfast devotion; 24 for he was a good man, full of the Holy Spirit and of faith. And a great many people were brought to the Lord. 25 Then Barnabas went to Tarsus to look for Saul, 26 and when he had found him, he brought him to Antioch. So it was that for an entire year they associated with the church and taught a great many people, and it was in Antioch that the disciples were first called 'Christians'.

27 At that time prophets came down from Jerusalem to Antioch. 28 One of them named Agabus stood up and predicted by the Spirit that there would be a severe famine over all the world; and this took place during the reign of Claudius. 29 The disciples determined that according to their ability, each would send relief to the believers living in Judea; 30 this they did, sending it to the elders by Barnabas and Saul.

GOSPEL   John 15.12-17

[12] 'This is my commandment, that you love one another as I have loved you. [13] No one has greater love than this, to lay down one's life for one's friends. [14] You are my friends if you do what I command you. [15] I do not call you servants any longer, because the servant does not know what the master is doing; but I have called you friends, because I have made known to you everything that I have heard from my Father. [16] You did not choose me but I chose you. And I appointed you to go and bear fruit, fruit that will last, so that the Father will give you whatever you ask him in my name. [17] I am giving you these commands so that you may love one another.'

OR

READING   Acts 11.19-30

[19] Now those who were scattered because of the persecution that took place over Stephen travelled as far as Phoenicia, Cyprus, and Antioch, and they spoke the word to no one except Jews. [20] But among them were some men of Cyprus and Cyrene who, on coming to Antioch, spoke to the Hellenists also, proclaiming the Lord Jesus. [21] The hand of the Lord was with them, and a great number became believers and turned to the Lord. [22] News of this came to the ears of the church in Jerusalem, and they sent Barnabas to Antioch. [23] When he came and saw the grace of God, he rejoiced, and he exhorted them all to remain faithful to the Lord with steadfast devotion; [24] for he was a good man, full of the Holy Spirit and of faith. And a great many people were brought to the Lord. [25] Then Barnabas went to Tarsus to look for Saul, [26] and when he had found him, he brought him to Antioch. So it was that for an entire year they associated with the church and taught a great many people, and it was in Antioch that the disciples were first called 'Christians'.

[27] At that time prophets came down from Jerusalem to Antioch. [28] One of them named Agabus stood up and predicted by the Spirit that there would be a severe famine over all the world; and this took place during the reign of Claudius. [29] The disciples determined that according to their ability, each would send relief to the believers living in Judea; [30] this they did, sending it to the elders by Barnabas and Saul.

PSALM   Psalm 112

1 Alleluia! Happy are they who fear the Lord
   and have great delight in his commandments!
2 Their descendants will be mighty in the land;
   the generation of the upright will be blessed.
3 Wealth and riches will be in their house,
   and their righteousness will last for ever.
4 Light shines in the darkness for the upright;
   the righteous are merciful and full of compassion.
5 It is good for them to be generous in lending
   and to manage their affairs with justice.
6 For they will never be shaken;
   the righteous will be kept in everlasting remembrance.
7 They will not be afraid of any evil rumours;
   their heart is right; they put their trust in the Lord.
8 Their heart is established and will not shrink,
   until they see their desire upon their enemies.
9 They have given freely to the poor,
   and their righteousness stands fast for ever; they will hold up their
      head with honour.
10 The wicked will see it and be angry; they will gnash their teeth
      and pine away;
   the desires of the wicked will perish.

READING   Galatians 2.1–10

   1 Then after fourteen years I went up again to Jerusalem with Barnabas,
taking Titus along with me. 2 I went up in response to a revelation. Then I
laid before them (though only in a private meeting with the acknowledged
leaders) the gospel that I proclaim among the Gentiles, in order to make
sure that I was not running, or had not run, in vain. 3 But even Titus, who
was with me, was not compelled to be circumcised, though he was a Greek.
4 But because of false believers secretly brought in, who slipped in to spy
on the freedom we have in Christ Jesus, so that they might enslave us—
5 we did not submit to them even for a moment, so that the truth of the
gospel might always remain with you. 6 And from those who were supposed
to be acknowledged leaders (what they actually were makes no difference
to me; God shows no partiality)—those leaders contributed nothing to me.
7 On the contrary, when they saw that I had been entrusted with the gospel
for the uncircumcised, just as Peter had been entrusted with the gospel for
the circumcised 8 (for he who worked through Peter making him an apostle
to the circumcised also worked through me in sending me to the Gentiles),

[9] and when James and Cephas and John, who were acknowledged pillars, recognized the grace that had been given to me, they gave to Barnabas and me the right hand of fellowship, agreeing that we should go to the Gentiles and they to the circumcised. [10] They asked only one thing, that we remember the poor, which was actually what I was eager to do.

GOSPEL   John 15.12–17

[12] 'This is my commandment, that you love one another as I have loved you. [13] No one has greater love than this, to lay down one's life for one's friends. [14] You are my friends if you do what I command you. [15] I do not call you servants any longer, because the servant does not know what the master is doing; but I have called you friends, because I have made known to you everything that I have heard from my Father. [16] You did not choose me but I chose you. And I appointed you to go and bear fruit, fruit that will last, so that the Father will give you whatever you ask him in my name. [17] I am giving you these commands so that you may love one another.'

POST COMMUNION

EITHER

Almighty God,
who on the day of Pentecost
sent your Holy Spirit to the apostles
with the wind from heaven and in tongues of flame,
filling them with joy and boldness to preach the gospel:
by the power of the same Spirit
strengthen us to witness to your truth
and to draw everyone to the fire of your love;
through Jesus Christ our Lord.

OR

Lord God, the source of truth and love,
keep us faithful to the apostles' teaching and fellowship,
united in prayer and the breaking of bread,
and one in joy and simplicity of heart,
in Jesus Christ our Lord.

THE BIRTH OF JOHN THE BAPTIST   24 JUNE

COLLECT

Almighty God,
by whose providence your servant John the Baptist
was wonderfully born,
and sent to prepare the way of your Son our Saviour
by the preaching of repentance:
lead us to repent according to his preaching
and, after his example,
constantly to speak the truth, boldly to rebuke vice,
and patiently to suffer for the truth's sake;
through Jesus Christ your Son our Lord,
who is alive and reigns with you,
in the unity of the Holy Spirit,
one God, now and for ever.

READING   Isaiah 40.1–11

1   Comfort, O comfort my people,
        says your God.
2   Speak tenderly to Jerusalem,
        and cry to her
    that she has served her term,
        that her penalty is paid,
    that she has received from the LORD's hand
        double for all her sins.
3   A voice cries out:
    'In the wilderness prepare the way of the LORD,
        make straight in the desert a highway for our God.
4   Every valley shall be lifted up,
        and every mountain and hill be made low;
    the uneven ground shall become level,
        and the rough places a plain.
5   Then the glory of the LORD shall be revealed,
        and all people shall see it together,
        for the mouth of the LORD has spoken.'
6   A voice says, 'Cry out!'
        And I said, 'What shall I cry?'
    All people are grass,
        their constancy is like the flower of the field.

7 The grass withers, the flower fades,
  when the breath of the LORD blows upon it;
  surely the people are grass.
8 The grass withers, the flower fades;
  but the word of our God will stand for ever.
9 Get you up to a high mountain,
  O Zion, herald of good tidings;
lift up your voice with strength,
  O Jerusalem, herald of good tidings,
  lift it up, do not fear;
say to the cities of Judah,
  'Here is your God!'
10 See, the Lord GOD comes with might,
  and his arm rules for him;
his reward is with him,
  and his recompense before him.
11 He will feed his flock like a shepherd;
  he will gather the lambs in his arms,
and carry them in his bosom,
  and gently lead the mother sheep.

PSALM   Psalm 85.7–13

7 Show us your mercy, O Lord,
  and grant us your salvation.
8 I will listen to what the Lord God is saying,
  for he is speaking peace to his faithful people and to those who
    turn their hearts to him.
9 Truly, his salvation is very near to those who fear him,
  that his glory may dwell in our land.
10 Mercy and truth have met together;
  righteousness and peace have kissed each other.
11 Truth shall spring up from the earth,
  and righteousness shall look down from heaven.
12 The Lord will indeed grant prosperity,
  and our land will yield its increase.
13 Righteousness shall go before him,
  and peace shall be a pathway for his feet.

READING

EITHER   ## Acts 13.14b–26

¹⁴ And on the sabbath day they went into the synagogue and sat down. ¹⁵ After the reading of the law and the prophets, the officials of the synagogue sent them a message, saying, 'Brothers, if you have any word of exhortation for the people, give it.' ¹⁶ So Paul stood up and with a gesture began to speak:

'You Israelites, and others who fear God, listen. ¹⁷ The God of this people Israel chose our ancestors and made the people great during their stay in the land of Egypt, and with uplifted arm he led them out of it. ¹⁸ For about forty years he put up with them in the wilderness. ¹⁹ After he had destroyed seven nations in the land of Canaan, he gave them their land as an inheritance ²⁰ for about four hundred and fifty years. After that he gave them judges until the time of the prophet Samuel. ²¹ Then they asked for a king; and God gave them Saul son of Kish, a man of the tribe of Benjamin, who reigned for forty years. ²² When he had removed him, he made David their king. In his testimony about him he said, "I have found David, son of Jesse, to be a man after my heart, who will carry out all my wishes." ²³ Of this man's posterity God has brought to Israel a Saviour, Jesus, as he promised; ²⁴ before his coming John had already proclaimed a baptism of repentance to all the people of Israel. ²⁵ And as John was finishing his work, he said, "What do you suppose that I am? I am not he. No, but one is coming after me; I am not worthy to untie the thong of the sandals on his feet."

²⁶ 'My brothers, you descendants of Abraham's family, and others who fear God, to us the message of this salvation has been sent.'

OR   ## Galatians 3.23–29

²³ Now before faith came, we were imprisoned and guarded under the law until faith would be revealed. ²⁴ Therefore the law was our disciplinarian until Christ came, so that we might be justified by faith. ²⁵ But now that faith has come, we are no longer subject to a disciplinarian, ²⁶ for in Christ Jesus you are all children of God through faith. ²⁷ As many of you as were baptized into Christ have clothed yourselves with Christ. ²⁸ There is no longer Jew or Greek, there is no longer slave or free, there is no longer male and female; for all of you are one in Christ Jesus. ²⁹ And if you belong to Christ, then you are Abraham's offspring, heirs according to the promise.

GOSPEL   Luke 1.57–66, 80

[57] Now the time came for Elizabeth to give birth, and she bore a son. [58] Her neighbours and relatives heard that the Lord had shown his great mercy to her, and they rejoiced with her.

[59] On the eighth day they came to circumcise the child, and they were going to name him Zechariah after his father. [60] But his mother said, 'No; he is to be called John.' [61] They said to her, 'None of your relatives has this name.' [62] Then they began motioning to his father to find out what name he wanted to give him. [63] He asked for a writing-tablet and wrote, 'His name is John.' And all of them were amazed. [64] Immediately his mouth was opened and his tongue freed, and he began to speak, praising God. [65] Fear came over all their neighbours, and all these things were talked about throughout the entire hill country of Judea. [66] All who heard them pondered them and said, 'What then will this child become?' For, indeed, the hand of the Lord was with him.

[80] The child grew and became strong in spirit, and he was in the wilderness until the day he appeared publicly to Israel.

POST COMMUNION

Merciful Lord,
whose prophet John the Baptist
proclaimed your Son as the Lamb of God
   who takes away the sin of the world:
grant that we who in this sacrament have known
   your forgiveness and your life-giving love
may ever tell of your mercy and your peace;
through Jesus Christ our Lord.

PETER AND PAUL
APOSTLES   29 JUNE

For Peter only, see page 1151

COLLECT

Almighty God,
whose blessed apostles Peter and Paul
glorified you in their death as in their life:
grant that your Church,
inspired by their teaching and example,
and made one by your Spirit,
may ever stand firm on the one foundation,
Jesus Christ your Son our Lord,
who is alive and reigns with you,
in the unity of the Holy Spirit,
one God, now and for ever.

EITHER

READING   Zechariah 4.1–6a, 10b–14

¹ The angel who talked with me came again, and wakened me, as one is wakened from sleep. ² He said to me, 'What do you see?' And I said, 'I see a lampstand all of gold, with a bowl on the top of it; there are seven lamps on it, with seven lips on each of the lamps that are on the top of it. ³ And by it there are two olive trees, one on the right of the bowl and the other on its left.' ⁴ I said to the angel who talked with me, 'What are these, my lord?' ⁵ Then the angel who talked with me answered me, 'Do you not know what these are?' I said, 'No, my lord.' ⁶ He said to me,

¹⁰ 'These seven are the eyes of the LORD, which range through the whole earth.' ¹¹ Then I said to him, 'What are these two olive trees on the right and the left of the lampstand?' ¹² And a second time I said to him, 'What are these two branches of the olive trees, which pour out the oil through the two golden pipes?' ¹³ He said to me, 'Do you not know what these are?' I said, 'No, my lord.' ¹⁴ Then he said, 'These are the two anointed ones who stand by the Lord of the whole earth.'

PSALM   Psalm 125

1 Those who trust in the Lord are like Mount Zion,
    which cannot be moved, but stands fast for ever.
2 The hills stand about Jerusalem;
    so does the Lord stand round about his people, from this time
       forth for evermore.
3 The sceptre of the wicked shall not hold sway over the land allotted
       to the just,
    so that the just shall not put their hands to evil.
4 Show your goodness, O Lord, to those who are good
    and to those who are true of heart.
5 As for those who turn aside to crooked ways, the Lord will lead
       them away with the evildoers;
    but peace be upon Israel.

READING   Acts 12.1–11

1 About that time King Herod laid violent hands upon some who belonged
to the church. 2 He had James, the brother of John, killed with the sword.
3 After he saw that it pleased the Jews, he proceeded to arrest Peter also.
(This was during the festival of Unleavened Bread.) 4 When he had seized
him, he put him in prison and handed him over to four squads of soldiers
to guard him, intending to bring him out to the people after the Passover.
5 While Peter was kept in prison, the church prayed fervently to God for
him.

6 The very night before Herod was going to bring him out, Peter, bound
with two chains, was sleeping between two soldiers, while guards in front
of the door were keeping watch over the prison. 7 Suddenly an angel of the
Lord appeared and a light shone in the cell. He tapped Peter on the side
and woke him, saying, 'Get up quickly.' And the chains fell off his wrists.
8 The angel said to him, 'Fasten your belt and put on your sandals.' He did
so. Then he said to him, 'Wrap your cloak around you and follow me.'
9 Peter went out and followed him; he did not realize that what was happening with the angel's help was real; he thought he was seeing a vision.
10 After they had passed the first and the second guard, they came before
the iron gate leading into the city. It opened for them of its own accord,
and they went outside and walked along a lane, when suddenly the angel
left him. 11 Then Peter came to himself and said, 'Now I am sure that the
Lord has sent his angel and rescued me from the hands of Herod and from
all that the Jewish people were expecting.'

GOSPEL

Matthew 16.13–19

¹³ Now when Jesus came into the district of Caesarea Philippi, he asked his disciples, 'Who do people say that the Son of Man is?' ¹⁴ And they said, 'Some say John the Baptist, but others Elijah, and still others Jeremiah or one of the prophets.' ¹⁵ He said to them, 'But who do you say that I am?' ¹⁶ Simon Peter answered, 'You are the Messiah, the Son of the living God.' ¹⁷ And Jesus answered him, 'Blessed are you, Simon son of Jonah! For flesh and blood has not revealed this to you, but my Father in heaven. ¹⁸ And I tell you, you are Peter, and on this rock I will build my church, and the gates of Hades will not prevail against it. ¹⁹ I will give you the keys of the kingdom of heaven, and whatever you bind on earth will be bound in heaven, and whatever you loose on earth will be loosed in heaven.'

OR

READING

Acts 12.1–11

¹ About that time King Herod laid violent hands upon some who belonged to the church. ² He had James, the brother of John, killed with the sword. ³ After he saw that it pleased the Jews, he proceeded to arrest Peter also. (This was during the festival of Unleavened Bread.) ⁴ When he had seized him, he put him in prison and handed him over to four squads of soldiers to guard him, intending to bring him out to the people after the Passover. ⁵ While Peter was kept in prison, the church prayed fervently to God for him.

⁶ The very night before Herod was going to bring him out, Peter, bound with two chains, was sleeping between two soldiers, while guards in front of the door were keeping watch over the prison. ⁷ Suddenly an angel of the Lord appeared and a light shone in the cell. He tapped Peter on the side and woke him, saying, 'Get up quickly.' And the chains fell off his wrists. ⁸ The angel said to him, 'Fasten your belt and put on your sandals.' He did so. Then he said to him, 'Wrap your cloak around you and follow me.' ⁹ Peter went out and followed him; he did not realize that what was happening with the angel's help was real; he thought he was seeing a vision. ¹⁰ After they had passed the first and the second guard, they came before the iron gate leading into the city. It opened for them of its own accord, and they went outside and walked along a lane, when suddenly the angel left him. ¹¹ Then Peter came to himself and said, 'Now I am sure that the Lord has sent his angel and rescued me from the hands of Herod and from all that the Jewish people were expecting.'

PSALM   Psalm 125

¹ Those who trust in the Lord are like Mount Zion,
   which cannot be moved, but stands fast for ever.
² The hills stand about Jerusalem;
   so does the Lord stand round about his people, from this time
      forth for evermore.
³ The sceptre of the wicked shall not hold sway over the land allotted
      to the just,
   so that the just shall not put their hands to evil.
⁴ Show your goodness, O Lord, to those who are good
   and to those who are true of heart.
⁵ As for those who turn aside to crooked ways, the Lord will lead
      them away with the evildoers;
   but peace be upon Israel.

READING   2 Timothy 4.6–8, 17–18

⁶ As for me, I am already being poured out as a libation, and the time of my departure has come. ⁷ I have fought the good fight, I have finished the race, I have kept the faith. ⁸ From now on there is reserved for me the crown of righteousness, which the Lord, the righteous judge, will give to me on that day, and not only to me but also to all who have longed for his appearing.

¹⁷ But the Lord stood by me and gave me strength, so that through me the message might be fully proclaimed and all the Gentiles might hear it. So I was rescued from the lion's mouth. ¹⁸ The Lord will rescue me from every evil attack and save me for his heavenly kingdom. To him be the glory for ever and ever. Amen.

GOSPEL   Matthew 16.13–19

¹³ Now when Jesus came into the district of Caesarea Philippi, he asked his disciples, 'Who do people say that the Son of Man is?' ¹⁴ And they said, 'Some say John the Baptist, but others Elijah, and still others Jeremiah or one of the prophets.' ¹⁵ He said to them, 'But who do you say that I am?' ¹⁶ Simon Peter answered, 'You are the Messiah, the Son of the living God.' ¹⁷ And Jesus answered him, 'Blessed are you, Simon son of Jonah! For flesh and blood has not revealed this to you, but my Father in heaven. ¹⁸ And I tell you, you are Peter, and on this rock I will build my church, and the gates of Hades will not prevail against it. ¹⁹ I will give you the keys of the kingdom of heaven, and whatever you bind on earth will be bound in heaven, and whatever you loose on earth will be loosed in heaven.'

POST COMMUNION

EITHER

Almighty God,
who on the day of Pentecost
sent your Holy Spirit to the apostles
with the wind from heaven and in tongues of flame,
filling them with joy and boldness to preach the gospel:
by the power of the same Spirit
strengthen us to witness to your truth
and to draw everyone to the fire of your love;
through Jesus Christ our Lord.

OR

Lord God, the source of truth and love,
keep us faithful to the apostles' teaching and fellowship,
united in prayer and the breaking of bread,
and one in joy and simplicity of heart,
in Jesus Christ our Lord.

PETER only

APOSTLE   29 JUNE

FESTIVAL

COLLECT

Almighty God,
who inspired your apostle Saint Peter
to confess Jesus as Christ and Son of the living God:
build up your Church upon this rock,
that in unity and peace it may proclaim one truth
and follow one Lord, your Son our Saviour Christ,
who is alive and reigns with you,
in the unity of the Holy Spirit,
one God, now and for ever.

EITHER

READING   Ezekiel 3.22–27

²² Then the hand of the Lᴏʀᴅ was upon me there; and he said to me, Rise up, go out into the valley, and there I will speak with you. ²³ So I rose up and went out into the valley; and the glory of the Lᴏʀᴅ stood there, like the glory that I had seen by the river Chebar; and I fell on my face. ²⁴ The spirit entered into me, and set me on my feet; and he spoke with me and said to me: Go, shut yourself inside your house. ²⁵ As for you, mortal, cords shall be placed on you, and you shall be bound with them, so that you cannot go out among the people; ²⁶ and I will make your tongue cling to the roof of your mouth, so that you shall be speechless and unable to reprove them; for they are a rebellious house. ²⁷ But when I speak with you, I will open your mouth, and you shall say to them, 'Thus says the Lord Gᴏᴅ'; let those who will hear, hear; and let those who refuse to hear, refuse; for they are a rebellious house.

PSALM   Psalm 125

¹ Those who trust in the Lord are like Mount Zion,
    which cannot be moved, but stands fast for ever.
² The hills stand about Jerusalem;
    so does the Lord stand round about his people, from this time
        forth for evermore.
³ The sceptre of the wicked shall not hold sway over the land allotted
        to the just,
    so that the just shall not put their hands to evil.
⁴ Show your goodness, O Lord, to those who are good
    and to those who are true of heart.
⁵ As for those who turn aside to crooked ways, the Lord will lead
        them away with the evildoers;
    but peace be upon Israel.

READING   Acts 12.1–11

¹ About that time King Herod laid violent hands upon some who belonged to the church. ² He had James, the brother of John, killed with the sword. ³ After he saw that it pleased the Jews, he proceeded to arrest Peter also. (This was during the festival of Unleavened Bread.) ⁴ When he had seized him, he put him in prison and handed him over to four squads of soldiers to guard him, intending to bring him out to the people after the Passover.

[5] While Peter was kept in prison, the church prayed fervently to God for him.

[6] The very night before Herod was going to bring him out, Peter, bound with two chains, was sleeping between two soldiers, while guards in front of the door were keeping watch over the prison. [7] Suddenly an angel of the Lord appeared and a light shone in the cell. He tapped Peter on the side and woke him, saying, 'Get up quickly.' And the chains fell off his wrists. [8] The angel said to him, 'Fasten your belt and put on your sandals.' He did so. Then he said to him, 'Wrap your cloak around you and follow me.' [9] Peter went out and followed him; he did not realize that what was happening with the angel's help was real; he thought he was seeing a vision. [10] After they had passed the first and the second guard, they came before the iron gate leading into the city. It opened for them of its own accord, and they went outside and walked along a lane, when suddenly the angel left him. [11] Then Peter came to himself and said, 'Now I am sure that the Lord has sent his angel and rescued me from the hands of Herod and from all that the Jewish people were expecting.'

GOSPEL   Matthew 16.13–19

[13] Now when Jesus came into the district of Caesarea Philippi, he asked his disciples, 'Who do people say that the Son of Man is?' [14] And they said, 'Some say John the Baptist, but others Elijah, and still others Jeremiah or one of the prophets.' [15] He said to them, 'But who do you say that I am?' [16] Simon Peter answered, 'You are the Messiah, the Son of the living God.' [17] And Jesus answered him, 'Blessed are you, Simon son of Jonah! For flesh and blood has not revealed this to you, but my Father in heaven. [18] And I tell you, you are Peter, and on this rock I will build my church, and the gates of Hades will not prevail against it. [19] I will give you the keys of the kingdom of heaven, and whatever you bind on earth will be bound in heaven, and whatever you loose on earth will be loosed in heaven.'

OR

READING   Acts 12.1–11

[1] About that time King Herod laid violent hands upon some who belonged to the church. [2] He had James, the brother of John, killed with the sword. [3] After he saw that it pleased the Jews, he proceeded to arrest Peter also. (This was during the festival of Unleavened Bread.) [4] When he had seized him, he put him in prison and handed him over to four squads of soldiers to guard him, intending to bring him out to the people after the Passover.

[5] While Peter was kept in prison, the church prayed fervently to God for him.

[6] The very night before Herod was going to bring him out, Peter, bound with two chains, was sleeping between two soldiers, while guards in front of the door were keeping watch over the prison. [7] Suddenly an angel of the Lord appeared and a light shone in the cell. He tapped Peter on the side and woke him, saying, 'Get up quickly.' And the chains fell off his wrists. [8] The angel said to him, 'Fasten your belt and put on your sandals.' He did so. Then he said to him, 'Wrap your cloak around you and follow me.' [9] Peter went out and followed him; he did not realize that what was happening with the angel's help was real; he thought he was seeing a vision. [10] After they had passed the first and the second guard, they came before the iron gate leading into the city. It opened for them of its own accord, and they went outside and walked along a lane, when suddenly the angel left him. [11] Then Peter came to himself and said, 'Now I am sure that the Lord has sent his angel and rescued me from the hands of Herod and from all that the Jewish people were expecting.'

PSALM   Psalm 125

1   Those who trust in the Lord are like Mount Zion,
     which cannot be moved, but stands fast for ever.
2   The hills stand about Jerusalem;
     so does the Lord stand round about his people, from this time
          forth for evermore.
3   The sceptre of the wicked shall not hold sway over the land allotted
          to the just,
     so that the just shall not put their hands to evil.
4   Show your goodness, O Lord, to those who are good
     and to those who are true of heart.
5   As for those who turn aside to crooked ways, the Lord will lead
          them away with the evildoers;
     but peace be upon Israel.

READING   1 Peter 2.19–25

[19] For it is to your credit if, being aware of God, you endure pain while suffering unjustly. [20] If you endure when you are beaten for doing wrong, where is the credit in that? But if you endure when you do right and suffer for it, you have God's approval. [21] For to this you have been called, because Christ also suffered for you, leaving you an example, so that you should follow in his steps.

²² 'He committed no sin,
and no deceit was found in his mouth.'
²³ When he was abused, he did not return abuse; when he suffered, he did not threaten; but he entrusted himself to the one who judges justly. ²⁴ He himself bore our sins in his body on the cross, so that, free from sins, we might live for righteousness; by his wounds you have been healed. ²⁵ For you were going astray like sheep, but now you have returned to the shepherd and guardian of your souls.

GOSPEL   Matthew 16.13–19

¹³ Now when Jesus came into the district of Caesarea Philippi, he asked his disciples, 'Who do people say that the Son of Man is?' ¹⁴ And they said, 'Some say John the Baptist, but others Elijah, and still others Jeremiah or one of the prophets.' ¹⁵ He said to them, 'But who do you say that I am?' ¹⁶ Simon Peter answered, 'You are the Messiah, the Son of the living God.' ¹⁷ And Jesus answered him, 'Blessed are you, Simon son of Jonah! For flesh and blood has not revealed this to you, but my Father in heaven. ¹⁸ And I tell you, you are Peter, and on this rock I will build my church, and the gates of Hades will not prevail against it. ¹⁹ I will give you the keys of the kingdom of heaven, and whatever you bind on earth will be bound in heaven, and whatever you loose on earth will be loosed in heaven.'

POST COMMUNION

EITHER

Almighty God,
who on the day of Pentecost
sent your Holy Spirit to the apostles
with the wind from heaven and in tongues of flame,
filling them with joy and boldness to preach the gospel:
by the power of the same Spirit
strengthen us to witness to your truth
and to draw everyone to the fire of your love;
through Jesus Christ our Lord.

OR

Lord God, the source of truth and love,
keep us faithful to the apostles' teaching and fellowship,
united in prayer and the breaking of bread,
and one in joy and simplicity of heart,
in Jesus Christ our Lord.

THOMAS
APOSTLE 3 JULY

FESTIVAL

COLLECT

Almighty and eternal God,
who, for the firmer foundation of our faith,
allowed your holy apostle Thomas
   to doubt the resurrection of your Son
till word and sight convinced him:
grant to us, who have not seen, that we also may believe
and so confess Christ as our Lord and our God;
who is alive and reigns with you,
in the unity of the Holy Spirit,
one God, now and for ever.

READING   Habakkuk 2.1-4

1   I will stand at my watch-post,
        and station myself on the rampart;
    I will keep watch to see what he will say to me,
        and what he will answer concerning my complaint.
2   Then the LORD answered me and said:
    Write the vision;
        make it plain on tablets,
        so that a runner may read it.
3   For there is still a vision for the appointed time;
        it speaks of the end, and does not lie.
    If it seems to tarry, wait for it;
        it will surely come, it will not delay.
4   Look at the proud!
        Their spirit is not right in them,
        but the righteous live by their faith.

PSALM   Psalm 31.1-6

1   In you, O Lord, have I taken refuge; let me never be put to shame;
    deliver me in your righteousness.
2   Incline your ear to me;
    make haste to deliver me.

3 Be my strong rock, a castle to keep me safe, for you are my crag
      and my stronghold;
   for the sake of your name, lead me and guide me.
4 Take me out of the net that they have secretly set for me,
   for you are my tower of strength.
5 Into your hands I commend my spirit,
   for you have redeemed me, O Lord, O God of truth.
6 I hate those who cling to worthless idols,
   and I put my trust in the Lord.

READING   Ephesians 2.19–22

19 So then you are no longer strangers and aliens, but you are citizens with
the saints and also members of the household of God, 20 built upon the
foundation of the apostles and prophets, with Christ Jesus himself as the
cornerstone. 21 In him the whole structure is joined together and grows
into a holy temple in the Lord; 22 in whom you also are built together
spiritually into a dwelling-place for God.

GOSPEL   John 20.24–29

24 But Thomas (who was called the Twin), one of the twelve, was not with
them when Jesus came. 25 So the other disciples told him, 'We have seen
the Lord.' But he said to them, 'Unless I see the mark of the nails in his
hands, and put my finger in the mark of the nails and my hand in his side,
I will not believe.'

26 A week later his disciples were again in the house, and Thomas was with
them. Although the doors were shut, Jesus came and stood among them
and said, 'Peace be with you.' 27 Then he said to Thomas, 'Put your finger
here and see my hands. Reach out your hand and put it in my side. Do not
doubt but believe.' 28 Thomas answered him, 'My Lord and my God!' 29 Jesus
said to him, 'Have you believed because you have seen me? Blessed are those
who have not seen and yet have come to believe.'

POST COMMUNION

EITHER

Almighty God,
who on the day of Pentecost
sent your Holy Spirit to the apostles
with the wind from heaven and in tongues of flame,
filling them with joy and boldness to preach the gospel:

by the power of the same Spirit
strengthen us to witness to your truth
and to draw everyone to the fire of your love;
through Jesus Christ our Lord.

OR

Lord God, the source of truth and love,
keep us faithful to the apostles' teaching and fellowship,
united in prayer and the breaking of bread,
and one in joy and simplicity of heart,
in Jesus Christ our Lord.

MARY MAGDALENE

22 JULY

FESTIVAL

COLLECT

Almighty God,
whose Son restored Mary Magdalene
   to health of mind and body
and called her to be a witness to his resurrection:
forgive our sins and heal us by your grace,
that we may serve you in the power of his risen life;
who is alive and reigns with you,
in the unity of the Holy Spirit,
one God, now and for ever.

READING   Song of Solomon 3.1–4

¹ Upon my bed at night
   I sought him whom my soul loves;
I sought him, but found him not;
   I called him, but he gave no answer.
² 'I will rise now and go about the city,
   in the streets and in the squares;
I will seek him whom my soul loves.'
   I sought him, but found him not.
³ The sentinels found me,
   as they went about in the city.
'Have you seen him whom my soul loves?'

4 Scarcely had I passed them,
   when I found him whom my soul loves.
  I held him, and would not let him go
   until I brought him into my mother's house,
   and into the chamber of her that conceived me.

PSALM   Psalm 42.1–9

1 As the deer longs for the water-brooks,
   so longs my soul for you, O God.
2 My soul is athirst for God, athirst for the living God;
   when shall I come to appear before the presence of God?
3 My tears have been my food day and night,
   while all day long they say to me, 'Where now is your God?'
4 I pour out my soul when I think on these things:
   how I went with the multitude and led them into the house of
      God,
5 With the voice of praise and thanksgiving,
   among those who keep holy-day.
6 Why are you so full of heaviness, O my soul?
   and why are you so disquieted within me?
7 Put your trust in God;
   for I will yet give thanks to him, who is the help of my countenance,
      and my God.
8 My soul is heavy within me;
   therefore I will remember you from the land of Jordan, and from
      the peak of Mizar among the heights of Hermon.
9 One deep calls to another in the noise of your cataracts;
   all your rapids and floods have gone over me.

READING   2 Corinthians 5.14–17

14 For the love of Christ urges us on, because we are convinced that one has died for all; therefore all have died. 15 And he died for all, so that those who live might live no longer for themselves, but for him who died and was raised for them.

16 From now on, therefore, we regard no one from a human point of view; even though we once knew Christ from a human point of view, we know him no longer in that way. 17 So if anyone is in Christ, there is a new creation: everything old has passed away; see, everything has become new!

GOSPEL

John 20.1–2, 11–18

[1] Early on the first day of the week, while it was still dark, Mary Magdalene came to the tomb and saw that the stone had been removed from the tomb. [2] So she ran and went to Simon Peter and the other disciple, the one whom Jesus loved, and said to them, 'They have taken the Lord out of the tomb, and we do not know where they have laid him.'

[11] But Mary stood weeping outside the tomb. As she wept, she bent over to look into the tomb; [12] and she saw two angels in white, sitting where the body of Jesus had been lying, one at the head and the other at the feet. [13] They said to her, 'Woman, why are you weeping?' She said to them, 'They have taken away my Lord, and I do not know where they have laid him.' [14] When she had said this, she turned round and saw Jesus standing there, but she did not know that it was Jesus. [15] Jesus said to her, 'Woman, why are you weeping? For whom are you looking?' Supposing him to be the gardener, she said to him, 'Sir, if you have carried him away, tell me where you have laid him, and I will take him away.' [16] Jesus said to her, 'Mary!' She turned and said to him in Hebrew, 'Rabbouni!' (which means Teacher). [17] Jesus said to her, 'Do not hold on to me, because I have not yet ascended to the Father. But go to my brothers and say to them, "I am ascending to my Father and your Father, to my God and your God." ' [18] Mary Magdalene went and announced to the disciples, 'I have seen the Lord'; and she told them that he had said these things to her.

POST COMMUNION

God of life and love,
whose risen Son called Mary Magdalene by name
and sent her to tell of his resurrection to his apostles:
in your mercy, help us,
who have been united with him in this eucharist,
to proclaim the good news
    that he is alive and reigns, now and for ever.

JAMES
APOSTLE

COLLECT

Merciful God,
whose holy apostle Saint James,
leaving his father and all that he had,
was obedient to the calling of your Son Jesus Christ
and followed him even to death:
help us, forsaking the false attractions of the world,
to be ready at all times to answer your call without delay;
through Jesus Christ your Son our Lord,
who is alive and reigns with you,
in the unity of the Holy Spirit,
one God, now and for ever.

EITHER

READING   Jeremiah 45.1–5

[1] The word that the prophet Jeremiah spoke to Baruch son of Neriah, when he wrote these words in a scroll at the dictation of Jeremiah, in the fourth year of King Jehoiakim son of Josiah of Judah: [2] Thus says the LORD, the God of Israel, to you, O Baruch: [3] You said, 'Woe is me! The LORD has added sorrow to my pain; I am weary with my groaning, and I find no rest.' [4] Thus you shall say to him, 'Thus says the LORD: I am going to break down what I have built, and pluck up what I have planted—that is, the whole land. [5] And you, do you seek great things for yourself? Do not seek them; for I am going to bring disaster upon all flesh, says the LORD; but I will give you your life as a prize of war in every place to which you may go.'

PSALM   Psalm 126

1   When the Lord restored the fortunes of Zion,
    then were we like those who dream.
2   Then was our mouth filled with laughter,
    and our tongue with shouts of joy.
3   Then they said among the nations,
    'The Lord has done great things for them.'
4   The Lord has done great things for us,
    and we are glad indeed.

5 Restore our fortunes, O Lord,
   like the watercourses of the Negev.
6 Those who sowed with tears
   will reap with songs of joy.
7 Those who go out weeping, carrying the seed,
   will come again with joy, shouldering their sheaves.

READING   Acts 11.27–12.2

²⁷ At that time prophets came down from Jerusalem to Antioch. ²⁸ One of them named Agabus stood up and predicted by the Spirit that there would be a severe famine over all the world; and this took place during the reign of Claudius. ²⁹ The disciples determined that according to their ability, each would send relief to the believers living in Judea; ³⁰ this they did, sending it to the elders by Barnabas and Saul.

¹ About that time King Herod laid violent hands upon some who belonged to the church. ² He had James, the brother of John, killed with the sword.

GOSPEL   Matthew 20.20–28

²⁰ Then the mother of the sons of Zebedee came to him with her sons, and kneeling before him, she asked a favour of him. ²¹ And he said to her, 'What do you want?' She said to him, 'Declare that these two sons of mine will sit, one at your right hand and one at your left, in your kingdom.' ²² But Jesus answered, 'You do not know what you are asking. Are you able to drink the cup that I am about to drink?' They said to him, 'We are able.' ²³ He said to them, 'You will indeed drink my cup, but to sit at my right hand and at my left, this is not mine to grant, but it is for those for whom it has been prepared by my Father.'

²⁴ When the ten heard it, they were angry with the two brothers. ²⁵ But Jesus called them to him and said, 'You know that the rulers of the Gentiles lord it over them, and their great ones are tyrants over them. ²⁶ It will not be so among you; but whoever wishes to be great among you must be your servant, ²⁷ and whoever wishes to be first among you must be your slave; ²⁸ just as the Son of Man came not to be served but to serve, and to give his life a ransom for many.'

OR

READING Acts 11.27-12.2

[27] At that time prophets came down from Jerusalem to Antioch. [28] One of them named Agabus stood up and predicted by the Spirit that there would be a severe famine over all the world; and this took place during the reign of Claudius. [29] The disciples determined that according to their ability, each would send relief to the believers living in Judea; [30] this they did, sending it to the elders by Barnabas and Saul.

[1] About that time King Herod laid violent hands upon some who belonged to the church. [2] He had James, the brother of John, killed with the sword.

PSALM Psalm 126

[1] When the Lord restored the fortunes of Zion,
     then were we like those who dream.
[2] Then was our mouth filled with laughter,
     and our tongue with shouts of joy.
[3] Then they said among the nations,
     'The Lord has done great things for them.'
[4] The Lord has done great things for us,
     and we are glad indeed.
[5] Restore our fortunes, O Lord,
     like the watercourses of the Negev.
[6] Those who sowed with tears
     will reap with songs of joy.
[7] Those who go out weeping, carrying the seed,
     will come again with joy, shouldering their sheaves.

READING 2 Corinthians 4.7-15

[7] But we have this treasure in clay jars, so that it may be made clear that this extraordinary power belongs to God and does not come from us. [8] We are afflicted in every way, but not crushed; perplexed, but not driven to despair; [9] persecuted, but not forsaken; struck down, but not destroyed; [10] always carrying in the body the death of Jesus, so that the life of Jesus may also be made visible in our bodies. [11] For while we live, we are always being given up to death for Jesus' sake, so that the life of Jesus may be made visible in our mortal flesh. [12] So death is at work in us, but life in you.

[13] But just as we have the same spirit of faith that is in accordance with scripture—'I believed, and so I spoke'—we also believe, and so we speak, [14] because we know that the one who raised the Lord Jesus will raise us also

with Jesus, and will bring us with you into his presence. [15] Yes, everything is for your sake, so that grace, as it extends to more and more people, may increase thanksgiving, to the glory of God.

GOSPEL   Matthew 20.20–28

[20] Then the mother of the sons of Zebedee came to him with her sons, and kneeling before him, she asked a favour of him. [21] And he said to her, 'What do you want?' She said to him, 'Declare that these two sons of mine will sit, one at your right hand and one at your left, in your kingdom.' [22] But Jesus answered, 'You do not know what you are asking. Are you able to drink the cup that I am about to drink?' They said to him, 'We are able.' [23] He said to them, 'You will indeed drink my cup, but to sit at my right hand and at my left, this is not mine to grant, but it is for those for whom it has been prepared by my Father.'

[24] When the ten heard it, they were angry with the two brothers. [25] But Jesus called them to him and said, 'You know that the rulers of the Gentiles lord it over them, and their great ones are tyrants over them. [26] It will not be so among you; but whoever wishes to be great among you must be your servant, [27] and whoever wishes to be first among you must be your slave; [28] just as the Son of Man came not to be served but to serve, and to give his life a ransom for many.'

POST COMMUNION

EITHER

Almighty God,
who on the day of Pentecost
sent your Holy Spirit to the apostles
with the wind from heaven and in tongues of flame,
filling them with joy and boldness to preach the gospel:
by the power of the same Spirit
strengthen us to witness to your truth
and to draw everyone to the fire of your love;
through Jesus Christ our Lord.

OR

Lord God, the source of truth and love,
keep us faithful to the apostles' teaching and fellowship,
united in prayer and the breaking of bread,
and one in joy and simplicity of heart,
in Jesus Christ our Lord.

ANNE AND JOACHIM
PARENTS OF THE BLESSED VIRGIN MARY   26 JULY

LESSER FESTIVAL

COLLECT

Lord God of Israel,
who bestowed such grace on Anne and Joachim
that their daughter Mary grew up obedient to your word
and made ready to be the mother of your Son:
help us to commit ourselves in all things to your keeping
and grant us the salvation you promised to your people;
through Jesus Christ your Son our Lord,
who is alive and reigns with you,
in the unity of the Holy Spirit,
one God, now and for ever.

READING   Zechariah 2.10–13

[10] Sing and rejoice, O daughter Zion! For lo, I will come and dwell in your
midst, says the LORD. [11] Many nations shall join themselves to the LORD on
that day, and shall be my people; and I will dwell in your midst. And you
shall know that the LORD of hosts has sent me to you. [12] The LORD will inherit
Judah as his portion in the holy land, and will again choose Jerusalem.

[13] Be silent, all people, before the LORD; for he has roused himself from
his holy dwelling.

PSALM   Psalm 127

1   Unless the Lord builds the house,
    their labour is in vain who build it.
2   Unless the Lord watches over the city,
    in vain the guard keeps vigil.
3   It is in vain that you rise so early and go to bed so late;
    vain, too, to eat the bread of toil, for he gives to his belovèd sleep.
4   Children are a heritage from the Lord,
    and the fruit of the womb is a gift.
5   Like arrows in the hand of a warrior
    are the children of one's youth.
6   Happy are they who have their quiver full of them!
    they shall not be put to shame when they contend with their
        enemies in the gate.

READING   Romans 8.28–30

^{28} We know that all things work together for good for those who love God, who are called according to his purpose. ^{29} For those whom he foreknew he also predestined to be conformed to the image of his Son, in order that he might be the firstborn within a large family. ^{30} And those whom he predestined he also called; and those whom he called he also justified; and those whom he justified he also glorified.

GOSPEL   Matthew 13.16–17

^{16} 'But blessed are your eyes, for they see, and your ears, for they hear. ^{17} Truly I tell you, many prophets and righteous people longed to see what you see, but did not see it, and to hear what you hear, but did not hear it.'

POST COMMUNION

Father,
from whom every family in heaven and on earth takes its name,
your servants Anne and Joachim revealed your goodness
    in a life of tranquillity and service:
grant that we who have gathered in faith around this table
may like them know the love of Christ
    that surpasses knowledge
and be filled with all your fullness;
through Jesus Christ our Lord.

or another Post Communion for 'Any Saint' (page 1267)

MARY, MARTHA, AND LAZARUS
COMPANIONS OF OUR LORD   29 JULY

LESSER FESTIVAL

COLLECT

God our Father,
whose Son enjoyed the love of his friends,
    Mary, Martha and Lazarus,
in learning, argument and hospitality:
may we so rejoice in your love

that the world may come to know
the depths of your wisdom, the wonder of your compassion,
and your power to bring life out of death;
through the merits of Jesus Christ,
our friend and brother,
who is alive and reigns with you,
in the unity of the Holy Spirit,
one God, now and for ever.

READING   Isaiah 25.6–9

6   On this mountain the LORD of hosts will make for all peoples
        a feast of rich food, a feast of well-matured wines,
            of rich food filled with marrow, of well-matured wines strained clear.
7   And he will destroy on this mountain
        the shroud that is cast over all peoples,
        the sheet that is spread over all nations;
8   he will swallow up death for ever.
    Then the Lord GOD will wipe away the tears from all faces,
        and the disgrace of his people he will take away from all the earth,
        for the LORD has spoken.
9   It will be said on that day,
        Lo, this is our God; we have waited for him, so that he might save us.
        This is the LORD for whom we have waited;
            let us be glad and rejoice in his salvation.

PSALM   Psalm 49.4–9, 16

4   Why should I be afraid in evil days,
        when the wickedness of those at my heels surrounds me,
5   The wickedness of those who put their trust in their goods,
        and boast of their great riches?
6   We can never ransom ourselves,
        or deliver to God the price of our life;
7   For the ransom of our life is so great,
        that we should never have enough to pay it,
8   In order to live for ever and ever,
        and never see the grave.
9   For we see that the wise die also; like the dull and stupid they
        perish
        and leave their wealth to those who come after them.

16 Do not be envious when some become rich,
        or when the grandeur of their house increases.

READING   Hebrews 2.10‑15

[10] It was fitting that God, for whom and through whom all things exist, in bringing many children to glory, should make the pioneer of their salvation perfect through sufferings. [11] For the one who sanctifies and those who are sanctified all have one Father. For this reason Jesus is not ashamed to call them brothers and sisters, [12] saying,
   'I will proclaim your name to my brothers and sisters,
      in the midst of the congregation I will praise you.'
[13] And again,
   'I will put my trust in him.'
And again,
   'Here am I and the children whom God has given me.'

[14] Since, therefore, the children share flesh and blood, he himself likewise shared the same things, so that through death he might destroy the one who has the power of death, that is, the devil, [15] and free those who all their lives were held in slavery by the fear of death.

GOSPEL   John 12.1‑8

[1] Six days before the Passover Jesus came to Bethany, the home of Lazarus, whom he had raised from the dead. [2] There they gave a dinner for him. Martha served, and Lazarus was one of those at the table with him. [3] Mary took a pound of costly perfume made of pure nard, anointed Jesus' feet, and wiped them with her hair. The house was filled with the fragrance of the perfume. [4] But Judas Iscariot, one of his disciples (the one who was about to betray him), said, [5] 'Why was this perfume not sold for three hundred denarii and the money given to the poor?' [6] (He said this not because he cared about the poor, but because he was a thief; he kept the common purse and used to steal what was put into it.) [7] Jesus said, 'Leave her alone. She bought it so that she might keep it for the day of my burial. [8] You always have the poor with you, but you do not always have me.'

POST COMMUNION

Father,
from whom every family in heaven and on earth takes its name,
your servants Mary, Martha and Lazarus revealed your goodness
   in a life of tranquillity and service:

grant that we who have gathered in faith around this table
may like them know the love of Christ
   that surpasses knowledge
and be filled with all your fullness;
through Jesus Christ our Lord.

or another Post Communion for 'Any Saint' (page 1267)

THE TRANSFIGURATION OF OUR LORD   6 AUGUST

FESTIVAL

COLLECT

Father in heaven,
whose Son Jesus Christ was wonderfully transfigured
before chosen witnesses upon the holy mountain,
and spoke of the exodus he would accomplish at Jerusalem:
give us strength so to hear his voice and bear our cross
that in the world to come we may see him as he is;
who is alive and reigns with you,
in the unity of the Holy Spirit,
one God, now and for ever.

READING   Daniel 7.9–10, 13–14

9   As I watched,
     thrones were set in place,
       and an Ancient One took his throne;
     his clothing was white as snow,
       and the hair of his head like pure wool;
     his throne was fiery flames,
       and its wheels were burning fire.
10 A stream of fire issued
     and flowed out from his presence.
     A thousand thousand served him,
       and ten thousand times ten thousand stood attending him.
     The court sat in judgement,
       and the books were opened.

¹³ As I watched in the night visions,
  I saw one like a human being
    coming with the clouds of heaven.
  And he came to the Ancient One
    and was presented before him.
¹⁴ To him was given dominion
    and glory and kingship,
  that all peoples, nations, and languages
    should serve him.
  His dominion is an everlasting dominion
    that shall not pass away,
  and his kingship is one
    that shall never be destroyed.

PSALM   Psalm 97

¹ The Lord is king; let the earth rejoice;
   let the multitude of the isles be glad.
² Clouds and darkness are round about him,
   righteousness and justice are the foundations of his throne.
³ A fire goes before him
   and burns up his enemies on every side.
⁴ His lightnings light up the world;
   the earth sees it and is afraid.
⁵ The mountains melt like wax at the presence of the Lord,
   at the presence of the Lord of the whole earth.
⁶ The heavens declare his righteousness,
   and all the peoples see his glory.
⁷ Confounded be all who worship carved images and delight in false
     gods!
   Bow down before him, all you gods.
⁸ Zion hears and is glad and the cities of Judah rejoice,
   because of your judgements, O Lord.
⁹ For you are the Lord: most high over all the earth;
   you are exalted far above all gods.
¹⁰ The Lord loves those who hate evil;
   he preserves the lives of his saints and delivers them from the
     hand of the wicked.
¹¹ Light has sprung up for the righteous,
   and joyful gladness for those who are true-hearted.
¹² Rejoice in the Lord, you righteous,
   and give thanks to his holy name.

READING   2 Peter 1.16–19

¹⁶ For we did not follow cleverly devised myths when we made known to you the power and coming of our Lord Jesus Christ, but we had been eyewitnesses of his majesty. ¹⁷ For he received honour and glory from God the Father when that voice was conveyed to him by the Majestic Glory, saying, 'This is my Son, my Beloved, with whom I am well pleased.' ¹⁸ We ourselves heard this voice come from heaven, while we were with him on the holy mountain.

¹⁹ So we have the prophetic message more fully confirmed. You will do well to be attentive to this as to a lamp shining in a dark place, until the day dawns and the morning star rises in your hearts.

GOSPEL   Luke 9.28–36

²⁸ Now about eight days after these sayings Jesus took with him Peter and John and James, and went up on the mountain to pray. ²⁹ And while he was praying, the appearance of his face changed, and his clothes became dazzling white. ³⁰ Suddenly they saw two men, Moses and Elijah, talking to him. ³¹ They appeared in glory and were speaking of his departure, which he was about to accomplish at Jerusalem. ³² Now Peter and his companions were weighed down with sleep; but since they had stayed awake, they saw his glory and the two men who stood with him. ³³ Just as they were leaving him, Peter said to Jesus, 'Master, it is good for us to be here; let us make three dwellings, one for you, one for Moses, and one for Elijah'—not knowing what he said. ³⁴ While he was saying this, a cloud came and overshadowed them; and they were terrified as they entered the cloud. ³⁵ Then from the cloud came a voice that said, 'This is my Son, my Chosen; listen to him!' ³⁶ When the voice had spoken, Jesus was found alone. And they kept silent and in those days told no one any of the things they had seen.

POST COMMUNION

Holy God,
we see your glory in the face of Jesus Christ:
may we who are partakers at his table
reflect his life in word and deed,
that all the world may know
    his power to change and save.
This we ask through Jesus Christ our Lord.

1171

THE BLESSED VIRGIN MARY   15 AUGUST

COLLECT

Almighty God,
who looked upon the lowliness of the Blessed Virgin Mary
and chose her to be the mother of your only Son:
grant that we who are redeemed by his blood
may share with her in the glory of your eternal kingdom;
through Jesus Christ your Son our Lord,
who is alive and reigns with you,
in the unity of the Holy Spirit,
one God, now and for ever.

READING

EITHER   Isaiah 61.10–11

10   I will greatly rejoice in the LORD,
         my whole being shall exult in my God;
      for he has clothed me with the garments of salvation,
         he has covered me with the robe of righteousness,
      as a bridegroom decks himself with a garland,
         and as a bride adorns herself with her jewels.
11   For as the earth brings forth its shoots,
         and as a garden causes what is sown in it to spring up,
      so the Lord GOD will cause righteousness and praise
         to spring up before all the nations.

OR   Revelation 11.19–12.6, 10

19 Then God's temple in heaven was opened, and the ark of his covenant
was seen within his temple; and there were flashes of lightning, rumblings,
peals of thunder, an earthquake, and heavy hail.

  1 A great portent appeared in heaven: a woman clothed with the sun,
with the moon under her feet, and on her head a crown of twelve stars.
2 She was pregnant and was crying out in birth pangs, in the agony of
giving birth. 3 Then another portent appeared in heaven: a great red dragon,
with seven heads and ten horns, and seven diadems on his heads. 4 His tail
swept down a third of the stars of heaven and threw them to the earth.
Then the dragon stood before the woman who was about to bear a child,
so that he might devour her child as soon as it was born. 5 And she gave

birth to a son, a male child, who is to rule all the nations with a rod of iron. But her child was snatched away and taken to God and to his throne; 6 and the woman fled into the wilderness, where she has a place prepared by God, so that there she can be nourished for one thousand two hundred and sixty days.

10 Then I heard a loud voice in heaven, proclaiming,
  'Now have come the salvation and the power
    and the kingdom of our God
    and the authority of his Messiah,
  for the accuser of our comrades has been thrown down,
    who accuses them day and night before our God.'

PSALM   Psalm 45.11–18

11 'Hear, O daughter; consider and listen closely;
    forget your people and your family's house.
12 The king will have pleasure in your beauty;
    he is your master; therefore do him honour.
13 The people of Tyre are here with a gift;
    the rich among the people seek your favour.'
14 All glorious is the princess as she enters;
    her gown is cloth-of-gold.
15 In embroidered apparel she is brought to the king;
    after her the bridesmaids follow in procession.
16 With joy and gladness they are brought,
    and enter into the palace of the king.
17 'In place of fathers, O king, you shall have sons;
    you shall make them princes over all the earth.
18 I will make your name to be remembered from one generation to
      another;
    therefore nations will praise you for ever and ever.'

READING   Galatians 4.4–7

4 But when the fullness of time had come, God sent his Son, born of a woman, born under the law, 5 in order to redeem those who were under the law, so that we might receive adoption as children. 6 And because you are children, God has sent the Spirit of his Son into our hearts, crying, 'Abba! Father!' 7 So you are no longer a slave but a child, and if a child then also an heir, through God.

GOSPEL

Luke 1.46–55

46 And Mary said,
   'My soul magnifies the Lord,
47   and my spirit rejoices in God my Saviour,
48 for he has looked with favour on the lowliness of his servant.
   Surely, from now on all generations will call me blessed;
49 for the Mighty One has done great things for me,
   and holy is his name.
50 His mercy is for those who fear him
   from generation to generation.
51 He has shown strength with his arm;
   he has scattered the proud in the thoughts of their hearts.
52 He has brought down the powerful from their thrones,
   and lifted up the lowly;
53 he has filled the hungry with good things,
   and sent the rich away empty.
54 He has helped his servant Israel,
   in remembrance of his mercy,
55 according to the promise he made to our ancestors,
   to Abraham and to his descendants for ever.'

POST COMMUNION

God most high,
whose handmaid bore the Word made flesh:
we thank you that in this sacrament of our redemption
you visit us with your Holy Spirit
and overshadow us by your power;
strengthen us to walk with Mary the joyful path of obedience
and so to bring forth the fruits of holiness;
through Jesus Christ our Lord.

BARTHOLOMEW
APOSTLE

24 AUGUST

COLLECT

Almighty and everlasting God,
who gave to your apostle Bartholomew grace
   truly to believe and to preach your word:
grant that your Church
may love that word which he believed
and may faithfully preach and receive the same;
through Jesus Christ your Son our Lord,
who is alive and reigns with you,
in the unity of the Holy Spirit,
one God, now and for ever.

EITHER

READING

Isaiah 43.8–13

8   Bring forth the people who are blind, yet have eyes,
     who are deaf, yet have ears!
9   Let all the nations gather together,
     and let the peoples assemble.
   Who among them declared this,
     and foretold to us the former things?
   Let them bring their witnesses to justify them,
     and let them hear and say, 'It is true.'
10 You are my witnesses, says the LORD,
     and my servant whom I have chosen,
   so that you may know and believe me
     and understand that I am he.
   Before me no god was formed,
     nor shall there be any after me.
11 I, I am the LORD,
     and besides me there is no saviour.
12 I declared and saved and proclaimed,
     when there was no strange god among you;
     and you are my witnesses, says the LORD.
13 I am God, and also henceforth I am He;
     there is no one who can deliver from my hand;
     I work and who can hinder it?

PSALM   Psalm 145.1-7

¹ I will exalt you, O God my King,
   and bless your name for ever and ever.
² Every day will I bless you
   and praise your name for ever and ever.
³ Great is the Lord and greatly to be praised;
   there is no end to his greatness.
⁴ One generation shall praise your works to another
   and shall declare your power.
⁵ I will ponder the glorious splendour of your majesty
   and all your marvellous works.
⁶ They shall speak of the might of your wondrous acts,
   and I will tell of your greatness.
⁷ They shall publish the remembrance of your great goodness;
   they shall sing of your righteous deeds.

READING   Acts 5.12-16

¹² Now many signs and wonders were done among the people through the apostles. And they were all together in Solomon's Portico. ¹³ None of the rest dared to join them, but the people held them in high esteem. ¹⁴ Yet more than ever believers were added to the Lord, great numbers of both men and women, ¹⁵ so that they even carried out the sick into the streets, and laid them on cots and mats, in order that Peter's shadow might fall on some of them as he came by. ¹⁶ A great number of people would also gather from the towns around Jerusalem, bringing the sick and those tormented by unclean spirits, and they were all cured.

GOSPEL   Luke 22.24-30

²⁴ A dispute also arose among them as to which one of them was to be regarded as the greatest. ²⁵ But he said to them, 'The kings of the Gentiles lord it over them; and those in authority over them are called benefactors. ²⁶ But not so with you; rather the greatest among you must become like the youngest, and the leader like one who serves. ²⁷ For who is greater, the one who is at the table or the one who serves? Is it not the one at the table? But I am among you as one who serves.

²⁸ 'You are those who have stood by me in my trials; ²⁹ and I confer on you, just as my Father has conferred on me, a kingdom, ³⁰ so that you may eat and drink at my table in my kingdom, and you will sit on thrones judging the twelve tribes of Israel.'

OR

READING   Acts 5.12–16

¹² Now many signs and wonders were done among the people through the apostles. And they were all together in Solomon's Portico. ¹³ None of the rest dared to join them, but the people held them in high esteem. ¹⁴ Yet more than ever believers were added to the Lord, great numbers of both men and women, ¹⁵ so that they even carried out the sick into the streets, and laid them on cots and mats, in order that Peter's shadow might fall on some of them as he came by. ¹⁶ A great number of people would also gather from the towns around Jerusalem, bringing the sick and those tormented by unclean spirits, and they were all cured.

PSALM   Psalm 145.1–7

¹ I will exalt you, O God my King,
    and bless your name for ever and ever.
² Every day will I bless you
    and praise your name for ever and ever.
³ Great is the Lord and greatly to be praised;
    there is no end to his greatness.
⁴ One generation shall praise your works to another
    and shall declare your power.
⁵ I will ponder the glorious splendour of your majesty
    and all your marvellous works.
⁶ They shall speak of the might of your wondrous acts,
    and I will tell of your greatness.
⁷ They shall publish the remembrance of your great goodness;
    they shall sing of your righteous deeds.

READING   1 Corinthians 4.9–15

⁹ For I think that God has exhibited us apostles as last of all, as though sentenced to death, because we have become a spectacle to the world, to angels and to mortals. ¹⁰ We are fools for the sake of Christ, but you are wise in Christ. We are weak, but you are strong. You are held in honour, but we in disrepute. ¹¹ To the present hour we are hungry and thirsty, we are poorly clothed and beaten and homeless, ¹² and we grow weary from the work of our own hands. When reviled, we bless; when persecuted, we endure; ¹³ when slandered, we speak kindly. We have become like the rubbish of the world, the dregs of all things, to this very day.

¹⁴ I am not writing this to make you ashamed, but to admonish you as my beloved children. ¹⁵ For though you might have ten thousand guardians in Christ, you do not have many fathers. Indeed, in Christ Jesus I became your father through the gospel.

GOSPEL   Luke 22.24–30

²⁴ A dispute also arose among them as to which one of them was to be regarded as the greatest. ²⁵ But he said to them, 'The kings of the Gentiles lord it over them; and those in authority over them are called benefactors. ²⁶ But not so with you; rather the greatest among you must become like the youngest, and the leader like one who serves. ²⁷ For who is greater, the one who is at the table or the one who serves? Is it not the one at the table? But I am among you as one who serves.

²⁸ 'You are those who have stood by me in my trials; ²⁹ and I confer on you, just as my Father has conferred on me, a kingdom, ³⁰ so that you may eat and drink at my table in my kingdom, and you will sit on thrones judging the twelve tribes of Israel.'

POST COMMUNION

EITHER

Almighty God,
who on the day of Pentecost
sent your Holy Spirit to the apostles
with the wind from heaven and in tongues of flame,
filling them with joy and boldness to preach the gospel:
by the power of the same Spirit
strengthen us to witness to your truth
and to draw everyone to the fire of your love;
through Jesus Christ our Lord.

OR

Lord God, the source of truth and love,
keep us faithful to the apostles' teaching and fellowship,
united in prayer and the breaking of bread,
and one in joy and simplicity of heart,
in Jesus Christ our Lord.

THE BEHEADING OF JOHN THE BAPTIST   29 AUGUST

LESSER FESTIVAL

COLLECT

Almighty God,
who called your servant John the Baptist
to be the forerunner of your Son in birth and death:
strengthen us by your grace
that, as he suffered for the truth,
so we may boldly resist corruption and vice
and receive with him the unfading crown of glory;
through Jesus Christ your Son our Lord,
who is alive and reigns with you,
in the unity of the Holy Spirit,
one God, now and for ever.

READING   Jeremiah 1.4–10

⁴ Now the word of the LORD came to me saying,

⁵ 'Before I formed you in the womb I knew you,
   and before you were born I consecrated you;
   I appointed you a prophet to the nations.'

⁶ Then I said, 'Ah, Lord GOD! Truly I do not know how to speak, for I am only a boy.' ⁷ But the LORD said to me,

   'Do not say, "I am only a boy";
   for you shall go to all to whom I send you,
   and you shall speak whatever I command you.

⁸ Do not be afraid of them,
   for I am with you to deliver you,
            says the LORD.'

⁹ Then the LORD put out his hand and touched my mouth; and the LORD said to me,

   'Now I have put my words in your mouth.

¹⁰ See, today I appoint you over nations and over kingdoms,
   to pluck up and to pull down,
   to destroy and to overthrow,
   to build and to plant.'

PSALM   Psalm 11

1   In the Lord have I taken refuge;
    how then can you say to me, 'Fly away like a bird to the hilltop;
2   For see how the wicked bend the bow and fit their arrows to the
        string,
    to shoot from ambush at the true of heart.
3   When the foundations are being destroyed,
    what can the righteous do?'
4   The Lord is in his holy temple;
    the Lord's throne is in heaven.
5   His eyes behold the inhabited world;
    his piercing eye weighs our worth.
6   The Lord weighs the righteous as well as the wicked,
    but those who delight in violence he abhors.
7   Upon the wicked he shall rain coals of fire and burning sulphur;
    a scorching wind shall be their lot.
8   For the Lord is righteous; he delights in righteous deeds;
    and the just shall see his face.

READING   Hebrews 11.32–12.2

32 And what more should I say? For time would fail me to tell of Gideon, Barak, Samson, Jephthah, of David and Samuel and the prophets— 33 who through faith conquered kingdoms, administered justice, obtained promises, shut the mouths of lions, 34 quenched raging fire, escaped the edge of the sword, won strength out of weakness, became mighty in war, put foreign armies to flight. 35 Women received their dead by resurrection. Others were tortured, refusing to accept release, in order to obtain a better resurrection. 36 Others suffered mocking and flogging, and even chains and imprisonment. 37 They were stoned to death, they were sawn in two, they were killed by the sword; they went about in skins of sheep and goats, destitute, persecuted, tormented— 38 of whom the world was not worthy. They wandered in deserts and mountains, and in caves and holes in the ground.

39 Yet all these, though they were commended for their faith, did not receive what was promised, 40 since God had provided something better so that they would not, without us, be made perfect.

1 Therefore, since we are surrounded by so great a cloud of witnesses, let us also lay aside every weight and the sin that clings so closely, and let us run with perseverance the race that is set before us, 2 looking to Jesus the

pioneer and perfecter of our faith, who for the sake of the joy that was set before him endured the cross, disregarding its shame, and has taken his seat at the right hand of the throne of God.

GOSPEL   Matthew 14.1-12

[1] At that time Herod the ruler heard reports about Jesus; [2] and he said to his servants, 'This is John the Baptist; he has been raised from the dead, and for this reason these powers are at work in him.' [3] For Herod had arrested John, bound him, and put him in prison on account of Herodias, his brother Philip's wife, [4] because John had been telling him, 'It is not lawful for you to have her.' [5] Though Herod wanted to put him to death, he feared the crowd, because they regarded him as a prophet. [6] But when Herod's birthday came, the daughter of Herodias danced before the company, and she pleased Herod [7] so much that he promised on oath to grant her whatever she might ask. [8] Prompted by her mother, she said, 'Give me the head of John the Baptist here on a platter.' [9] The king was grieved, yet out of regard for his oaths and for the guests, he commanded it to be given; [10] he sent and had John beheaded in the prison. [11] The head was brought on a platter and given to the girl, who brought it to her mother. [12] His disciples came and took the body and buried it; then they went and told Jesus.

POST COMMUNION

Merciful Lord,
whose prophet John the Baptist
proclaimed your Son as the Lamb of God
   who takes away the sin of the world:
grant that we who in this sacrament have known
   your forgiveness and your life-giving love
may ever tell of your mercy and your peace;
through Jesus Christ our Lord.

HOLY CROSS DAY 14 SEPTEMBER

COLLECT

Almighty God,
who in the passion of your blessed Son
made an instrument of painful death
to be for us the means of life and peace:
grant us so to glory in the cross of Christ
that we may gladly suffer for his sake;
who is alive and reigns with you,
in the unity of the Holy Spirit,
one God, now and for ever.

READING Numbers 21.4–9

⁴ From Mount Hor they set out by the way to the Red Sea, to go around the land of Edom; but the people became impatient on the way. ⁵ The people spoke against God and against Moses, 'Why have you brought us up out of Egypt to die in the wilderness? For there is no food and no water, and we detest this miserable food.' ⁶ Then the Lord sent poisonous serpents among the people, and they bit the people, so that many Israelites died. ⁷ The people came to Moses and said, 'We have sinned by speaking against the Lord and against you; pray to the Lord to take away the serpents from us.' So Moses prayed for the people. ⁸ And the Lord said to Moses, 'Make a poisonous serpent, and set it on a pole; and everyone who is bitten shall look at it and live.' ⁹ So Moses made a serpent of bronze, and put it upon a pole; and whenever a serpent bit someone, that person would look at the serpent of bronze and live.

PSALM Psalm 22.22–27

22 Praise the Lord, you that fear him;
    stand in awe of him, O offspring of Israel; all you of Jacob's line,
      give glory.
23 For he does not despise nor abhor the poor in their poverty; neither
    does he hide his face from them;
    but when they cry to him he hears them.
24 My praise is of him in the great assembly;
    I will perform my vows in the presence of those who worship him.

25 The poor shall eat and be satisfied, and those who seek the Lord
   shall praise him:
   'May your heart live for ever!'
26 All the ends of the earth shall remember and turn to the Lord,
   and all the families of the nations shall bow before him.
27 For kingship belongs to the Lord;
   he rules over the nations.

READING   Philippians 2.6–11

6 Christ Jesus, who, though he was in the form of God,
     did not regard equality with God
     as something to be exploited,
7 but emptied himself,
     taking the form of a slave,
     being born in human likeness.
   And being found in human form,
8   he humbled himself
     and became obedient to the point of death—
     even death on a cross.
9 Therefore God also highly exalted him
     and gave him the name
     that is above every name,
10   so that at the name of Jesus
     every knee should bend,
     in heaven and on earth and under the earth,
11   and every tongue should confess
     that Jesus Christ is Lord,
     to the glory of God the Father.

GOSPEL   John 3.13–17

13 'No one has ascended into heaven except the one who descended from
heaven, the Son of Man. 14 And just as Moses lifted up the serpent in the
wilderness, so must the Son of Man be lifted up, 15 that whoever believes
in him may have eternal life.

16 'For God so loved the world that he gave his only Son, so that everyone
who believes in him may not perish but may have eternal life.

17 'Indeed, God did not send the Son into the world to condemn the world,
but in order that the world might be saved through him.'

POST COMMUNION

Faithful God,
whose Son bore our sins in his body on the tree
and gave us this sacrament to show forth his death
   until he comes:
give us grace to glory in the cross of our Lord Jesus Christ,
for he is our salvation, our life and our hope,
who reigns as Lord, now and for ever.

MATTHEW
APOSTLE AND EVANGELIST   21 SEPTEMBER

FESTIVAL

COLLECT

O Almighty God,
whose blessed Son called Matthew the tax-collector
to be an apostle and evangelist:
give us grace to forsake the selfish pursuit of gain
   and the possessive love of riches
that we may follow in the way of your Son Jesus Christ,
who is alive and reigns with you,
in the unity of the Holy Spirit,
one God, now and for ever.

READING   Proverbs 3.13–18

13 Happy are those who find wisdom,
     and those who get understanding,
14 for her income is better than silver,
     and her revenue better than gold.
15 She is more precious than jewels,
     and nothing you desire can compare with her.
16 Long life is in her right hand;
     in her left hand are riches and honour.
17 Her ways are ways of pleasantness,
     and all her paths are peace.
18 She is a tree of life to those who lay hold of her;
     those who hold her fast are called happy.

PSALM   Psalm 119.65–72

⁶⁵ O Lord, you have dealt graciously with your servant,
   according to your word.
⁶⁶ Teach me discernment and knowledge,
   for I have believed in your commandments.
⁶⁷ Before I was afflicted I went astray,
   but now I keep your word.
⁶⁸ You are good and you bring forth good;
   instruct me in your statutes.
⁶⁹ The proud have smeared me with lies,
   but I will keep your commandments with my whole heart.
⁷⁰ Their heart is gross and fat,
   but my delight is in your law.
⁷¹ It is good for me that I have been afflicted,
   that I might learn your statutes.
⁷² The law of your mouth is dearer to me
   than thousands in gold and silver.

READING   2 Corinthians 4.1–6

¹ Therefore, since it is by God's mercy that we are engaged in this ministry, we do not lose heart. ² We have renounced the shameful things that one hides; we refuse to practise cunning or to falsify God's word; but by the open statement of the truth we commend ourselves to the conscience of everyone in the sight of God. ³ And even if our gospel is veiled, it is veiled to those who are perishing. ⁴ In their case the god of this world has blinded the minds of the unbelievers, to keep them from seeing the light of the gospel of the glory of Christ, who is the image of God. ⁵ For we do not proclaim ourselves; we proclaim Jesus Christ as Lord and ourselves as your slaves for Jesus' sake. ⁶ For it is the God who said, 'Let light shine out of darkness', who has shone in our hearts to give the light of the knowledge of the glory of God in the face of Jesus Christ.

GOSPEL   Matthew 9.9–13

⁹ As Jesus was walking along, he saw a man called Matthew sitting at the tax booth; and he said to him, 'Follow me.' And he got up and followed him.

¹⁰ And as he sat at dinner in the house, many tax-collectors and sinners came and were sitting with him and his disciples. ¹¹ When the Pharisees saw this, they said to his disciples, 'Why does your teacher eat with tax-collectors and sinners?' ¹² But when he heard this, he said, 'Those who are

well have no need of a physician, but those who are sick. [13] Go and learn
what this means, "I desire mercy, not sacrifice." For I have come to call not
the righteous but sinners.'

POST COMMUNION

EITHER

Almighty God,
who on the day of Pentecost
sent your Holy Spirit to the apostles
with the wind from heaven and in tongues of flame,
filling them with joy and boldness to preach the gospel:
by the power of the same Spirit
strengthen us to witness to your truth
and to draw everyone to the fire of your love;
through Jesus Christ our Lord.

OR

Lord God, the source of truth and love,
keep us faithful to the apostles' teaching and fellowship,
united in prayer and the breaking of bread,
and one in joy and simplicity of heart,
in Jesus Christ our Lord.

MICHAEL AND ALL ANGELS   29 SEPTEMBER

FESTIVAL

COLLECT

Everlasting God,
you have ordained and constituted the ministries
    of angels and mortals in a wonderful order:
grant that as your holy angels
    always serve you in heaven,
so, at your command,
they may help and defend us on earth;
through Jesus Christ your Son our Lord,
who is alive and reigns with you,
in the unity of the Holy Spirit,
one God, now and for ever.

READING

Genesis 28.10–17

[10] Jacob left Beer-sheba and went towards Haran. [11] He came to a certain place and stayed there for the night, because the sun had set. Taking one of the stones of the place, he put it under his head and lay down in that place. [12] And he dreamed that there was a ladder set up on the earth, the top of it reaching to heaven; and the angels of God were ascending and descending on it. [13] And the LORD stood beside him and said, 'I am the LORD, the God of Abraham your father and the God of Isaac; the land on which you lie I will give to you and to your offspring; [14] and your offspring shall be like the dust of the earth, and you shall spread abroad to the west and to the east and to the north and to the south; and all the families of the earth shall be blessed in you and in your offspring. [15] Know that I am with you and will keep you wherever you go, and will bring you back to this land; for I will not leave you until I have done what I have promised you.' [16] Then Jacob woke from his sleep and said, 'Surely the LORD is in this place—and I did not know it!' [17] And he was afraid, and said, 'How awesome is this place! This is none other than the house of God, and this is the gate of heaven.'

PSALM   **Psalm 103.19–22**

19 The Lord has set his throne in heaven,
      and his kingship has dominion over all.
20 Bless the Lord, you angels of his, you mighty ones who do his
      bidding,
      and hearken to the voice of his word.
21 Bless the Lord, all you his hosts,
      you ministers of his who do his will.
22 Bless the Lord, all you works of his, in all places of his dominion;
      bless the Lord, O my soul.

READING   **Revelation 12.7–12**

[7] And war broke out in heaven; Michael and his angels fought against the dragon. The dragon and his angels fought back, [8] but they were defeated, and there was no longer any place for them in heaven. [9] The great dragon was thrown down, that ancient serpent, who is called the Devil and Satan, the deceiver of the whole world—he was thrown down to the earth, and his angels were thrown down with him.

¹⁰ Then I heard a loud voice in heaven, proclaiming,
　'Now have come the salvation and the power
　　and the kingdom of our God
　　and the authority of his Messiah,
　for the accuser of our comrades has been thrown down,
　　who accuses them day and night before our God.
¹¹　But they have conquered him by the blood of the Lamb
　　and by the word of their testimony,
　for they did not cling to life even in the face of death.
¹²　Rejoice then, you heavens
　　and those who dwell in them!
　But woe to the earth and the sea,
　　for the devil has come down to you
　with great wrath,
　　because he knows that his time is short!'

GOSPEL   John 1.47–51

⁴⁷ When Jesus saw Nathanael coming towards him, he said of him, 'Here is truly an Israelite in whom there is no deceit!' ⁴⁸ Nathanael asked him, 'Where did you come to know me?' Jesus answered, 'I saw you under the fig tree before Philip called you.' ⁴⁹ Nathanael replied, 'Rabbi, you are the Son of God! You are the King of Israel!' ⁵⁰ Jesus answered, 'Do you believe because I told you that I saw you under the fig tree? You will see greater things than these.' ⁵¹ And he said to him, 'Very truly, I tell you, you will see heaven opened and the angels of God ascending and descending upon the Son of Man.'

OR

READING   Revelation 12.7–12

⁷ And war broke out in heaven; Michael and his angels fought against the dragon. The dragon and his angels fought back, ⁸ but they were defeated, and there was no longer any place for them in heaven. ⁹ The great dragon was thrown down, that ancient serpent, who is called the Devil and Satan, the deceiver of the whole world—he was thrown down to the earth, and his angels were thrown down with him.

¹⁰ Then I heard a loud voice in heaven, proclaiming,
　'Now have come the salvation and the power
　　and the kingdom of our God
　　and the authority of his Messiah,
　for the accuser of our comrades has been thrown down,
　　who accuses them day and night before our God.
¹¹ But they have conquered him by the blood of the Lamb
　　and by the word of their testimony,
　for they did not cling to life even in the face of death.
¹² Rejoice then, you heavens
　　and those who dwell in them!
　But woe to the earth and the sea,
　　for the devil has come down to you
　with great wrath,
　　because he knows that his time is short!'

PSALM   Psalm 103.19–22

¹⁹ The Lord has set his throne in heaven,
　　and his kingship has dominion over all.
²⁰ Bless the Lord, you angels of his, you mighty ones who do his
　　bidding,
　and hearken to the voice of his word.
²¹ Bless the Lord, all you his hosts,
　　you ministers of his who do his will.
²² Bless the Lord, all you works of his, in all places of his dominion;
　bless the Lord, O my soul.

READING   Hebrews 1.5–14

⁵ For to which of the angels did God ever say,
　'You are my Son;
　　today I have begotten you'?
Or again,
　'I will be his Father,
　　and he will be my Son'?
⁶ And again, when he brings the firstborn into the world, he says,
　'Let all God's angels worship him.'
⁷ Of the angels he says,
　'He makes his angels winds,
　　and his servants flames of fire.'

⁸ But of the Son he says,

    'Your throne, O God, is for ever and ever,
        and the righteous sceptre is the sceptre of your kingdom.
⁹   You have loved righteousness and hated wickedness;
    therefore God, your God, has anointed you
        with the oil of gladness beyond your companions.'
¹⁰ And,

    'In the beginning, Lord, you founded the earth,
        and the heavens are the work of your hands;
¹¹   they will perish, but you remain;
    they will all wear out like clothing;
¹²   like a cloak you will roll them up,
    and like clothing they will be changed.
    But you are the same,
        and your years will never end.'
¹³ But to which of the angels has he ever said,

    'Sit at my right hand
        until I make your enemies a footstool for your feet'?
¹⁴ Are not all angels spirits in the divine service, sent to serve for the sake of those who are to inherit salvation?

GOSPEL   John 1.47–51

⁴⁷ When Jesus saw Nathanael coming towards him, he said of him, 'Here is truly an Israelite in whom there is no deceit!' ⁴⁸ Nathanael asked him, 'Where did you come to know me?' Jesus answered, 'I saw you under the fig tree before Philip called you.' ⁴⁹ Nathanael replied, 'Rabbi, you are the Son of God! You are the King of Israel!' ⁵⁰ Jesus answered, 'Do you believe because I told you that I saw you under the fig tree? You will see greater things than these.' ⁵¹ And he said to him, 'Very truly, I tell you, you will see heaven opened and the angels of God ascending and descending upon the Son of Man.'

POST COMMUNION

Lord of heaven,
in this eucharist you have brought us near
   to an innumerable company of angels
   and to the spirits of the saints made perfect:
as in this food of our earthly pilgrimage
   we have shared their fellowship,
so may we come to share their joy in heaven;
through Jesus Christ our Lord.

LUKE
EVANGELIST

COLLECT

Almighty God,
you called Luke the physician,
whose praise is in the gospel,
to be an evangelist and physician of the soul:
by the grace of the Spirit
and through the wholesome medicine of the gospel,
give your Church the same love and power to heal;
through Jesus Christ your Son our Lord,
who is alive and reigns with you,
in the unity of the Holy Spirit,
one God, now and for ever.

READING

EITHER   **Isaiah 35.3–6**

³ Strengthen the weak hands,
     and make firm the feeble knees.
⁴ Say to those who are of a fearful heart,
     'Be strong, do not fear!
   Here is your God.
     He will come with vengeance,
   with terrible recompense.
     He will come and save you.'
⁵ Then the eyes of the blind shall be opened,
     and the ears of the deaf unstopped;
⁶ then the lame shall leap like a deer,
     and the tongue of the speechless sing for joy.
   For waters shall break forth in the wilderness,
     and streams in the desert.

OR   **Acts 16.6–12a**

⁶ They went through the region of Phrygia and Galatia, having been
forbidden by the Holy Spirit to speak the word in Asia. ⁷ When they had
come opposite Mysia, they attempted to go into Bithynia, but the Spirit of
Jesus did not allow them; ⁸ so, passing by Mysia, they went down to Troas.

⁹ During the night Paul had a vision: there stood a man of Macedonia pleading with him and saying, 'Come over to Macedonia and help us.' ¹⁰ When he had seen the vision, we immediately tried to cross over to Macedonia, being convinced that God had called us to proclaim the good news to them.

¹¹ We set sail from Troas and took a straight course to Samothrace, the following day to Neapolis, ¹² and from there to Philippi, which is a leading city of the district of Macedonia and a Roman colony.

PSALM   Psalm 147.1-7

1   Alleluia! How good it is to sing praises to our God!
    how pleasant it is to honour him with praise!
2   The Lord rebuilds Jerusalem;
    he gathers the exiles of Israel.
3   He heals the brokenhearted
    and binds up their wounds.
4   He counts the number of the stars
    and calls them all by their names.
5   Great is our Lord and mighty in power;
    there is no limit to his wisdom.
6   The Lord lifts up the lowly,
    but casts the wicked to the ground.
7   Sing to the Lord with thanksgiving;
    make music to our God upon the harp.

READING   2 Timothy 4.5-17

⁵ As for you, always be sober, endure suffering, do the work of an evangelist, carry out your ministry fully.

⁶ As for me, I am already being poured out as a libation, and the time of my departure has come. ⁷ I have fought the good fight, I have finished the race, I have kept the faith. ⁸ From now on there is reserved for me the crown of righteousness, which the Lord, the righteous judge, will give to me on that day, and not only to me but also to all who have longed for his appearing.

⁹ Do your best to come to me soon, ¹⁰ for Demas, in love with this present world, has deserted me and gone to Thessalonica; Crescens has gone to Galatia, Titus to Dalmatia. ¹¹ Only Luke is with me. Get Mark and bring him with you, for he is useful in my ministry. ¹² I have sent Tychicus to Ephesus. ¹³ When you come, bring the cloak that I left with Carpus at Troas, also the

books, and above all the parchments. [14] Alexander the coppersmith did me great harm; the Lord will pay him back for his deeds. [15] You also must beware of him, for he strongly opposed our message.

[16] At my first defence no one came to my support, but all deserted me. May it not be counted against them! [17] But the Lord stood by me and gave me strength, so that through me the message might be fully proclaimed and all the Gentiles might hear it. So I was rescued from the lion's mouth.

GOSPEL   Luke 10.1–9

[1] After this the Lord appointed seventy others and sent them on ahead of him in pairs to every town and place where he himself intended to go. [2] He said to them, 'The harvest is plentiful, but the labourers are few; therefore ask the Lord of the harvest to send out labourers into his harvest. [3] Go on your way. See, I am sending you out like lambs into the midst of wolves. [4] Carry no purse, no bag, no sandals; and greet no one on the road. [5] Whatever house you enter, first say, "Peace to this house!" [6] And if anyone is there who shares in peace, your peace will rest on that person; but if not, it will return to you. [7] Remain in the same house, eating and drinking whatever they provide, for the labourer deserves to be paid. Do not move about from house to house. [8] Whenever you enter a town and its people welcome you, eat what is set before you; [9] cure the sick who are there, and say to them, "The kingdom of God has come near to you." '

POST COMMUNION

EITHER

Almighty God,
who on the day of Pentecost
sent your Holy Spirit to the apostles
with the wind from heaven and in tongues of flame,
filling them with joy and boldness to preach the gospel:
by the power of the same Spirit
strengthen us to witness to your truth
and to draw everyone to the fire of your love;
through Jesus Christ our Lord.

OR

Lord God, the source of truth and love,
keep us faithful to the apostles' teaching and fellowship,
united in prayer and the breaking of bread,
and one in joy and simplicity of heart,
in Jesus Christ our Lord.

SIMON AND JUDE
APOSTLES

COLLECT

Almighty God,
who built your Church upon the foundation
   of the apostles and prophets,
with Jesus Christ himself as the chief corner-stone:
so join us together in unity of spirit by their doctrine,
that we may be made a holy temple acceptable to you;
through Jesus Christ your Son our Lord,
who is alive and reigns with you,
in the unity of the Holy Spirit,
one God, now and for ever.

READING   Isaiah 28.14–16

¹⁴ Therefore hear the word of the LORD, you scoffers
    who rule this people in Jerusalem.
¹⁵ Because you have said, 'We have made a covenant with death,
    and with Sheol we have an agreement;
  when the overwhelming scourge passes through
    it will not come to us;
  for we have made lies our refuge,
    and in falsehood we have taken shelter';
¹⁶ therefore thus says the Lord GOD,
  See, I am laying in Zion a foundation stone,
    a tested stone,
  a precious cornerstone, a sure foundation:
    'One who trusts will not panic.'

PSALM   Psalm 119.89–96

⁸⁹ O Lord, your word is everlasting;
    it stands firm in the heavens.
⁹⁰ Your faithfulness remains from one generation to another;
    you established the earth and it abides.
⁹¹ By your decree these continue to this day,
    for all things are your servants.

92 If my delight had not been in your law,
    I should have perished in my affliction.
93 I will never forget your commandments,
    because by them you give me life.
94 I am yours; O that you would save me!
    for I study your commandments.
95 Though the wicked lie in wait for me to destroy me,
    I will apply my mind to your decrees.
96 I see that all things come to an end,
    but your commandment has no bounds.

READING   Ephesians 2.19–22

19 So then you are no longer strangers and aliens, but you are citizens with the saints and also members of the household of God, 20 built upon the foundation of the apostles and prophets, with Christ Jesus himself as the cornerstone. 21 In him the whole structure is joined together and grows into a holy temple in the Lord; 22 in whom you also are built together spiritually into a dwelling-place for God.

GOSPEL   John 15.17–27

17 'I am giving you these commands so that you may love one another.

18 'If the world hates you, be aware that it hated me before it hated you. 19 If you belonged to the world, the world would love you as its own. Because you do not belong to the world, but I have chosen you out of the world—therefore the world hates you. 20 Remember the word that I said to you, "Servants are not greater than their master." If they persecuted me, they will persecute you; if they kept my word, they will keep yours also. 21 But they will do all these things to you on account of my name, because they do not know him who sent me. 22 If I had not come and spoken to them, they would not have sin; but now they have no excuse for their sin. 23 Whoever hates me hates my Father also. 24 If I had not done among them the works that no one else did, they would not have sin. But now they have seen and hated both me and my Father. 25 It was to fulfil the word that is written in their law, "They hated me without a cause."

26 'When the Advocate comes, whom I will send to you from the Father, the Spirit of truth who comes from the Father, he will testify on my behalf. 27 You also are to testify because you have been with me from the beginning.'

POST COMMUNION

EITHER

Almighty God,
who on the day of Pentecost
sent your Holy Spirit to the apostles
with the wind from heaven and in tongues of flame,
filling them with joy and boldness to preach the gospel:
by the power of the same Spirit
strengthen us to witness to your truth
and to draw everyone to the fire of your love;
through Jesus Christ our Lord.

OR

Lord God, the source of truth and love,
keep us faithful to the apostles' teaching and fellowship,
united in prayer and the breaking of bread,
and one in joy and simplicity of heart,
in Jesus Christ our Lord.

COMMEMORATION OF THE FAITHFUL DEPARTED (ALL SOULS' DAY)   2 NOVEMBER

LESSER FESTIVAL

COLLECT

Eternal God, our maker and redeemer,
grant us, with all the faithful departed,
the sure benefits of your Son's saving passion
   and glorious resurrection
that, in the last day,
when you gather up all things in Christ,
we may with them enjoy the fullness of your promises;
through Jesus Christ your Son our Lord,
who is alive and reigns with you,
in the unity of the Holy Spirit,
one God, now and for ever.

READING

EITHER   ### Lamentations 3.17–26, 31–33

¹⁷ My soul is bereft of peace;
   I have forgotten what happiness is;
¹⁸ so I say, 'Gone is my glory,
   and all that I had hoped for from the LORD.'
¹⁹ The thought of my affliction and my homelessness
   is wormwood and gall!
²⁰ My soul continually thinks of it
   and is bowed down within me.
²¹ But this I call to mind,
   and therefore I have hope:
²² The steadfast love of the LORD never ceases,
   his mercies never come to an end;
²³ they are new every morning;
   great is your faithfulness.
²⁴ 'The LORD is my portion,' says my soul,
   'therefore I will hope in him.'
²⁵ The LORD is good to those who wait for him,
   to the soul that seeks him.
²⁶ It is good that one should wait quietly
   for the salvation of the LORD.

³¹ For the Lord will not
   reject for ever.
³² Although he causes grief, he will have compassion
   according to the abundance of his steadfast love;
³³ for he does not willingly afflict
   or grieve anyone.

OR   ### Wisdom 3.1–9

¹ But the souls of the righteous are in the hand of God,
   and no torment will ever touch them.
² In the eyes of the foolish they seemed to have died,
   and their departure was thought to be a disaster,
³ and their going from us to be their destruction;
   but they are at peace.
⁴ For though in the sight of others they were punished,
   their hope is full of immortality.
⁵ Having been disciplined a little, they will receive great good,
   because God tested them and found them worthy of himself;

⁶ like gold in the furnace he tried them,
and like a sacrificial burnt-offering he accepted them.
⁷ In the time of their visitation they will shine forth,
and will run like sparks through the stubble.
⁸ They will govern nations and rule over peoples,
and the Lord will reign over them for ever.
⁹ Those who trust in him will understand truth,
and the faithful will abide with him in love,
because grace and mercy are upon his holy ones,
and he watches over his elect.

PSALM

EITHER   **Psalm 23**

¹ The Lord is my shepherd;
I shall not be in want.
² He makes me lie down in green pastures
and leads me beside still waters.
³ He revives my soul
and guides me along right pathways for his name's sake.
⁴ Though I walk through the valley of the shadow of death, I shall
fear no evil;
for you are with me; your rod and your staff, they comfort me.
⁵ You spread a table before me in the presence of those who trouble
me;
you have anointed my head with oil, and my cup is running over.
⁶ Surely your goodness and mercy shall follow me all the days of my
life,
and I will dwell in the house of the Lord for ever.

OR   **Psalm 27.1–7, 17–18**

¹ The Lord is my light and my salvation; whom then shall I fear?
the Lord is the strength of my life; of whom then shall I be afraid?
² When evildoers came upon me to eat up my flesh,
it was they, my foes and my adversaries, who stumbled and fell.
³ Though an army should encamp against me,
yet my heart shall not be afraid;
⁴ And though war should rise up against me,
yet will I put my trust in him.
⁵ One thing have I asked of the Lord; one thing I seek;
that I may dwell in the house of the Lord all the days of my life;

⁶ To behold the fair beauty of the Lord
and to seek him in his temple.

⁷ For in the day of trouble he shall keep me safe in his shelter;
he shall hide me in the secrecy of his dwelling and set me high
upon a rock.

¹⁷ What if I had not believed that I should see the goodness of the
Lord
in the land of the living!

¹⁸ O tarry and await the Lord's pleasure; be strong and he shall
comfort your heart;
wait patiently for the Lord.

READING

EITHER   **Romans 5.5–11**

⁵ And hope does not disappoint us, because God's love has been poured
into our hearts through the Holy Spirit that has been given to us.

⁶ For while we were still weak, at the right time Christ died for the
ungodly. ⁷ Indeed, rarely will anyone die for a righteous person—though
perhaps for a good person someone might actually dare to die. ⁸ But God
proves his love for us in that while we still were sinners Christ died for us.
⁹ Much more surely then, now that we have been justified by his blood, will
we be saved through him from the wrath of God. ¹⁰ For if while we were
enemies, we were reconciled to God through the death of his Son, much
more surely, having been reconciled, will we be saved by his life. ¹¹ But
more than that, we even boast in God through our Lord Jesus Christ,
through whom we have now received reconciliation.

OR   **1 Peter 1.3–9**

³ Blessed be the God and Father of our Lord Jesus Christ! By his great mercy
he has given us a new birth into a living hope through the resurrection of
Jesus Christ from the dead, ⁴ and into an inheritance that is imperishable,
undefiled, and unfading, kept in heaven for you, ⁵ who are being protected
by the power of God through faith for a salvation ready to be revealed in
the last time. ⁶ In this you rejoice, even if now for a little while you have
had to suffer various trials, ⁷ so that the genuineness of your faith—being
more precious than gold that, though perishable, is tested by fire—may be
found to result in praise and glory and honour when Jesus Christ is revealed.
⁸ Although you have not seen him, you love him; and even though you do

not see him now, you believe in him and rejoice with an indescribable and glorious joy, [9] for you are receiving the outcome of your faith, the salvation of your souls.

GOSPEL

EITHER   John 5.19–25

[19] Jesus said to them, 'Very truly, I tell you, the Son can do nothing on his own, but only what he sees the Father doing; for whatever the Father does, the Son does likewise. [20] The Father loves the Son and shows him all that he himself is doing; and he will show him greater works than these, so that you will be astonished. [21] Indeed, just as the Father raises the dead and gives them life, so also the Son gives life to whomsoever he wishes. [22] The Father judges no one but has given all judgement to the Son, [23] so that all may honour the Son just as they honour the Father. Anyone who does not honour the Son does not honour the Father who sent him. [24] Very truly, I tell you, anyone who hears my word and believes him who sent me has eternal life, and does not come under judgement, but has passed from death to life.

[25] 'Very truly, I tell you, the hour is coming, and is now here, when the dead will hear the voice of the Son of God, and those who hear will live.'

OR   John 6.37–40

[37] 'Everything that the Father gives me will come to me, and anyone who comes to me I will never drive away; [38] for I have come down from heaven, not to do my own will, but the will of him who sent me. [39] And this is the will of him who sent me, that I should lose nothing of all that he has given me, but raise it up on the last day. [40] This is indeed the will of my Father, that all who see the Son and believe in him may have eternal life; and I will raise them up on the last day.'

POST COMMUNION

God of love,
may the death and resurrection of Christ
which we have celebrated in this eucharist
bring us, with all the faithful departed,
into the peace of your eternal home.
We ask this in the name of Jesus Christ,
our rock and our salvation,
to whom be glory for time and for eternity.

THE SAINTS AND MARTYRS OF ENGLAND 8 NOVEMBER

LESSER FESTIVAL

COLLECT

God, whom the glorious company of the redeemed adore,
assembled from all times and places of your dominion:
we praise you for the saints of our own land
and for the many lamps their holiness has lit;
and we pray that we also may be numbered at last
with those who have done your will
   and declared your righteousness;
through Jesus Christ your Son our Lord,
who is alive and reigns with you,
in the unity of the Holy Spirit,
one God, now and for ever.

READING

EITHER   Isaiah 61.4–9

⁴ They shall build up the ancient ruins,
   they shall raise up the former devastations;
 they shall repair the ruined cities,
   the devastations of many generations.
⁵ Strangers shall stand and feed your flocks,
   foreigners shall till your land and dress your vines;
⁶ but you shall be called priests of the LORD,
   you shall be named ministers of our God;
 you shall enjoy the wealth of the nations,
   and in their riches you shall glory.
⁷ Because their shame was double,
   and dishonour was proclaimed as their lot,
 therefore they shall possess a double portion;
   everlasting joy shall be theirs.
⁸ For I the LORD love justice,
   I hate robbery and wrongdoing;
 I will faithfully give them their recompense,
   and I will make an everlasting covenant with them.
⁹ Their descendants shall be known among the nations,
   and their offspring among the peoples;
 all who see them shall acknowledge
   that they are a people whom the LORD has blessed.

OR   **Ecclesiasticus 44.1–15**

1 Let us now sing the praises of famous men,
     our ancestors in their generations.
2 The Lord apportioned to them great glory,
     his majesty from the beginning.
3 There were those who ruled in their kingdoms,
     and made a name for themselves by their valour;
     those who gave counsel because they were intelligent;
     those who spoke in prophetic oracles;
4 those who led the people by their counsels
     and by their knowledge of the people's lore;
     they were wise in their words of instruction;
5 those who composed musical tunes,
     or put verses in writing;
6 rich men endowed with resources,
     living peacefully in their homes—
7 all these were honoured in their generations,
     and were the pride of their times.
8 Some of them have left behind a name,
     so that others declare their praise.
9 But of others there is no memory;
     they have perished as though they had never existed;
     they have become as though they had never been born,
     they and their children after them.
10 But these also were godly men,
     whose righteous deeds have not been forgotten;
11 their wealth will remain with their descendants,
     and their inheritance with their children's children.
12 Their descendants stand by the covenants;
     their children also, for their sake.
13 Their offspring will continue for ever,
     and their glory will never be blotted out.
14 Their bodies are buried in peace,
     but their name lives on generation after generation.
15 The assembly declares their wisdom,
     and the congregation proclaims their praise.

PSALM   Psalm 15

1 Lord, who may dwell in your tabernacle?
     who may abide upon your holy hill?
2 Whoever leads a blameless life and does what is right,
     who speaks the truth from his heart.

3 There is no guile upon his tongue; he does no evil to his friend;
   he does not heap contempt upon his neighbour.
4 In his sight the wicked is rejected,
   but he honours those who fear the Lord.
5 He has sworn to do no wrong
   and does not take back his word.
6 He does not give his money in hope of gain,
   nor does he take a bribe against the innocent.
7 Whoever does these things
   shall never be overthrown.

READING   Revelation 19.5–10

5 And from the throne came a voice saying,
   'Praise our God,
      all you his servants,
   and all who fear him,
      small and great.'
6 Then I heard what seemed to be the voice of a great multitude, like the
sound of many waters and like the sound of mighty thunder-peals, crying
out,
   'Hallelujah!
   For the Lord our God
      the Almighty reigns.
7 Let us rejoice and exult
      and give him the glory,
   for the marriage of the Lamb has come,
      and his bride has made herself ready;
8 to her it has been granted to be clothed
      with fine linen, bright and pure'—
for the fine linen is the righteous deeds of the saints.

9 And the angel said to me, 'Write this: Blessed are those who are invited
to the marriage supper of the Lamb.' And he said to me, 'These are true
words of God.' 10 Then I fell down at his feet to worship him, but he said to
me, 'You must not do that! I am a fellow-servant with you and your comrades
who hold the testimony of Jesus. Worship God! For the testimony of Jesus
is the spirit of prophecy.'

GOSPEL   John 17.18–23

18 'As you have sent me into the world, so I have sent them into the world.
19 And for their sakes I sanctify myself, so that they also may be sanctified
in truth.

[20] 'I ask not only on behalf of these, but also on behalf of those who will believe in me through their word, [21] that they may all be one. As you, Father, are in me and I am in you, may they also be in us, so that the world may believe that you have sent me. [22] The glory that you have given me I have given them, so that they may be one, as we are one, [23] I in them and you in me, that they may become completely one, so that the world may know that you have sent me and have loved them even as you have loved me.'

POST COMMUNION

God, the source of all holiness
   and giver of all good things:
may we who have shared at this table
   as strangers and pilgrims here on earth
be welcomed with all your saints
   to the heavenly feast on the day of your kingdom;
through Jesus Christ our Lord.

ANDREW
APOSTLE   30 NOVEMBER

FESTIVAL

COLLECT

Almighty God,
who gave such grace to your apostle Saint Andrew
that he readily obeyed the call of your Son Jesus Christ
   and brought his brother with him:
call us by your holy word,
and give us grace to follow without delay
   and to tell the good news of your kingdom;
through Jesus Christ your Son our Lord,
who is alive and reigns with you,
in the unity of the Holy Spirit,
one God, now and for ever.

READING   Isaiah 52.7-10

7   How beautiful upon the mountains
        are the feet of the messenger who announces peace,
    who brings good news,
        who announces salvation,
        who says to Zion, 'Your God reigns.'
8   Listen! Your sentinels lift up their voices,
        together they sing for joy;
    for in plain sight they see
        the return of the Lord to Zion.
9   Break forth together into singing,
        you ruins of Jerusalem;
    for the Lord has comforted his people,
        he has redeemed Jerusalem.
10 The Lord has bared his holy arm
        before the eyes of all the nations;
    and all the ends of the earth shall see
        the salvation of our God.

PSALM   Psalm 19.1-6

1   The heavens declare the glory of God,
        and the firmament shows his handiwork.
2   One day tells its tale to another,
        and one night imparts knowledge to another.
3   Although they have no words or language,
        and their voices are not heard,
4   Their sound has gone out into all lands,
        and their message to the ends of the world.
5   In the deep has he set a pavilion for the sun;
        it comes forth like a bridegroom out of his chamber; it rejoices
        like a champion to run its course.
6   It goes forth from the uttermost edge of the heavens and runs
        about to the end of it again;
    nothing is hidden from its burning heat.

READING   Romans 10.12-18

12 For there is no distinction between Jew and Greek; the same Lord is Lord of all and is generous to all who call on him. 13 For, 'Everyone who calls on the name of the Lord shall be saved.'

14 But how are they to call on one in whom they have not believed? And how are they to believe in one of whom they have never heard? And how

are they to hear without someone to proclaim him? [15] And how are they to proclaim him unless they are sent? As it is written, 'How beautiful are the feet of those who bring good news!' [16] But not all have obeyed the good news; for Isaiah says, 'Lord, who has believed our message?' [17] So faith comes from what is heard, and what is heard comes through the word of Christ.

[18] But I ask, have they not heard? Indeed they have; for
  'Their voice has gone out to all the earth,
    and their words to the ends of the world.'

GOSPEL   Matthew 4.18–22

[18] As he walked by the Sea of Galilee, he saw two brothers, Simon, who is called Peter, and Andrew his brother, casting a net into the lake—for they were fishermen. [19] And he said to them, 'Follow me, and I will make you fish for people.' [20] Immediately they left their nets and followed him. [21] As he went from there, he saw two other brothers, James son of Zebedee and his brother John, in the boat with their father Zebedee, mending their nets, and he called them. [22] Immediately they left the boat and their father, and followed him.

POST COMMUNION

EITHER

Almighty God,
who on the day of Pentecost
sent your Holy Spirit to the apostles
with the wind from heaven and in tongues of flame,
filling them with joy and boldness to preach the gospel:
by the power of the same Spirit
strengthen us to witness to your truth
and to draw everyone to the fire of your love;
through Jesus Christ our Lord.

OR

Lord God, the source of truth and love,
keep us faithful to the apostles' teaching and fellowship,
united in prayer and the breaking of bread,
and one in joy and simplicity of heart,
in Jesus Christ our Lord.

STEPHEN
DEACON, FIRST MARTYR   26 DECEMBER

COLLECT

Gracious Father,
who gave the first martyr Stephen
grace to pray for those who took up stones against him:
grant that in all our sufferings for the truth
we may learn to love even our enemies
and to seek forgiveness for those who desire our hurt,
looking up to heaven to him who was crucified for us,
Jesus Christ, our mediator and advocate,
who is alive and reigns with you,
in the unity of the Holy Spirit,
one God, now and for ever.

EITHER

READING   2 Chronicles 24.20–22

²⁰ Then the spirit of God took possession of Zechariah son of the priest Jehoiada; he stood above the people and said to them, 'Thus says God: Why do you transgress the commandments of the LORD, so that you cannot prosper? Because you have forsaken the LORD, he has also forsaken you.' ²¹ But they conspired against him, and by command of the king they stoned him to death in the court of the house of the LORD. ²² King Joash did not remember the kindness that Jehoiada, Zechariah's father, had shown him, but killed his son. As he was dying, he said, 'May the LORD see and avenge!'

PSALM   Psalm 119.161–168

161 Rulers have persecuted me without a cause,
       but my heart stands in awe of your word.
162 I am as glad because of your promise
       as one who finds great spoils.
163 As for lies, I hate and abhor them,
       but your law is my love.
164 Seven times a day do I praise you,
       because of your righteous judgements.
165 Great peace have they who love your law;
       for them there is no stumbling block.
166 I have hoped for your salvation, O Lord,
       and I have fulfilled your commandments.

167 I have kept your decrees
and I have loved them deeply.
168 I have kept your commandments and decrees,
for all my ways are before you.

READING   Acts 7.51–60

51 'You stiff-necked people, uncircumcised in heart and ears, you are for ever opposing the Holy Spirit, just as your ancestors used to do. 52 Which of the prophets did your ancestors not persecute? They killed those who foretold the coming of the Righteous One, and now you have become his betrayers and murderers. 53 You are the ones that received the law as ordained by angels, and yet you have not kept it.'

54 When they heard these things, they became enraged and ground their teeth at Stephen. 55 But filled with the Holy Spirit, he gazed into heaven and saw the glory of God and Jesus standing at the right hand of God. 56 'Look,' he said, 'I see the heavens opened and the Son of Man standing at the right hand of God!' 57 But they covered their ears, and with a loud shout all rushed together against him. 58 Then they dragged him out of the city and began to stone him; and the witnesses laid their coats at the feet of a young man named Saul. 59 While they were stoning Stephen, he prayed, 'Lord Jesus, receive my spirit.' 60 Then he knelt down and cried out in a loud voice, 'Lord, do not hold this sin against them.' When he had said this, he died.

GOSPEL   Matthew 23.34–39

34 'Therefore I send you prophets, sages, and scribes, some of whom you will kill and crucify, and some you will flog in your synagogues and pursue from town to town, 35 so that upon you may come all the righteous blood shed on earth, from the blood of righteous Abel to the blood of Zechariah son of Barachiah, whom you murdered between the sanctuary and the altar. 36 Truly I tell you, all this will come upon this generation.

37 'Jerusalem, Jerusalem, the city that kills the prophets and stones those who are sent to it! How often have I desired to gather your children together as a hen gathers her brood under her wings, and you were not willing! 38 See, your house is left to you, desolate. 39 For I tell you, you will not see me again until you say, "Blessed is the one who comes in the name of the Lord." '

OR

READING   Acts 7.51-60

[51] 'You stiff-necked people, uncircumcised in heart and ears, you are for ever opposing the Holy Spirit, just as your ancestors used to do. [52] Which of the prophets did your ancestors not persecute? They killed those who foretold the coming of the Righteous One, and now you have become his betrayers and murderers. [53] You are the ones that received the law as ordained by angels, and yet you have not kept it.'

[54] When they heard these things, they became enraged and ground their teeth at Stephen. [55] But filled with the Holy Spirit, he gazed into heaven and saw the glory of God and Jesus standing at the right hand of God. [56] 'Look,' he said, 'I see the heavens opened and the Son of Man standing at the right hand of God!' [57] But they covered their ears, and with a loud shout all rushed together against him. [58] Then they dragged him out of the city and began to stone him; and the witnesses laid their coats at the feet of a young man named Saul. [59] While they were stoning Stephen, he prayed, 'Lord Jesus, receive my spirit.' [60] Then he knelt down and cried out in a loud voice, 'Lord, do not hold this sin against them.' When he had said this, he died.

PSALM   Psalm 119.161-168

[161] Rulers have persecuted me without a cause,
    but my heart stands in awe of your word.
[162] I am as glad because of your promise
    as one who finds great spoils.
[163] As for lies, I hate and abhor them,
    but your law is my love.
[164] Seven times a day do I praise you,
    because of your righteous judgements.
[165] Great peace have they who love your law;
    for them there is no stumbling block.
[166] I have hoped for your salvation, O Lord,
    and I have fulfilled your commandments.
[167] I have kept your decrees
    and I have loved them deeply.
[168] I have kept your commandments and decrees,
    for all my ways are before you.

READING   Galatians 2.16b–20

¹⁶ And we have come to believe in Christ Jesus, so that we might be justified by faith in Christ, and not by doing the works of the law, because no one will be justified by the works of the law. ¹⁷ But if, in our effort to be justified in Christ, we ourselves have been found to be sinners, is Christ then a servant of sin? Certainly not! ¹⁸ But if I build up again the very things that I once tore down, then I demonstrate that I am a transgressor. ¹⁹ For through the law I died to the law, so that I might live to God. I have been crucified with Christ; ²⁰ and it is no longer I who live, but it is Christ who lives in me. And the life I now live in the flesh I live by faith in the Son of God, who loved me and gave himself for me.

GOSPEL   Matthew 23.34–39

³⁴ 'Therefore I send you prophets, sages, and scribes, some of whom you will kill and crucify, and some you will flog in your synagogues and pursue from town to town, ³⁵ so that upon you may come all the righteous blood shed on earth, from the blood of righteous Abel to the blood of Zechariah son of Barachiah, whom you murdered between the sanctuary and the altar. ³⁶ Truly I tell you, all this will come upon this generation.

³⁷ 'Jerusalem, Jerusalem, the city that kills the prophets and stones those who are sent to it! How often have I desired to gather your children together as a hen gathers her brood under her wings, and you were not willing! ³⁸ See, your house is left to you, desolate. ³⁹ For I tell you, you will not see me again until you say, "Blessed is the one who comes in the name of the Lord." '

POST COMMUNION

Merciful Lord,
we thank you for the signs of your mercy
revealed in birth and death:
save us by the coming of your Son,
and give us joy in honouring Stephen,
first martyr of the new Israel;
through Jesus Christ our Lord.

JOHN
APOSTLE AND EVANGELIST 27 DECEMBER

COLLECT

Merciful Lord,
cast your bright beams of light upon the Church:
that, being enlightened by the teaching
    of your blessed apostle and evangelist Saint John,
we may so walk in the light of your truth
that we may at last attain to the light of everlasting life;
through Jesus Christ your incarnate Son our Lord,
who is alive and reigns with you,
in the unity of the Holy Spirit,
one God, now and for ever.

READING Exodus 33.7–11a

[7] Now Moses used to take the tent and pitch it outside the camp, far off from the camp; he called it the tent of meeting. And everyone who sought the LORD would go out to the tent of meeting, which was outside the camp. [8] Whenever Moses went out to the tent, all the people would rise and stand, each of them, at the entrance of their tents and watch Moses until he had gone into the tent. [9] When Moses entered the tent, the pillar of cloud would descend and stand at the entrance of the tent, and the LORD would speak with Moses. [10] When all the people saw the pillar of cloud standing at the entrance of the tent, all the people would rise and bow down, all of them, at the entrance of their tents. [11] Thus the LORD used to speak to Moses face to face, as one speaks to a friend.

PSALM Psalm 117

1   Praise the Lord, all you nations;
    laud him, all you peoples.
2   For his loving-kindness towards us is great,
    and the faithfulness of the Lord endures for ever. Alleluia!

READING 1 John 1.1–10

[1] We declare to you what was from the beginning, what we have heard, what we have seen with our eyes, what we have looked at and touched with our hands, concerning the word of life— [2] this life was revealed, and we have seen it and testify to it, and declare to you the eternal life that was

with the Father and was revealed to us— ³ we declare to you what we have seen and heard so that you also may have fellowship with us; and truly our fellowship is with the Father and with his Son Jesus Christ. ⁴ We are writing these things so that our joy may be complete.

⁵ This is the message we have heard from him and proclaim to you, that God is light and in him there is no darkness at all. ⁶ If we say that we have fellowship with him while we are walking in darkness, we lie and do not do what is true; ⁷ but if we walk in the light as he himself is in the light, we have fellowship with one another, and the blood of Jesus his Son cleanses us from all sin. ⁸ If we say that we have no sin, we deceive ourselves, and the truth is not in us. ⁹ If we confess our sins, he who is faithful and just will forgive us our sins and cleanse us from all unrighteousness. ¹⁰ If we say that we have not sinned, we make him a liar, and his word is not in us.

GOSPEL   John 21.19b–25

¹⁹ After this he said to him, 'Follow me.'

²⁰ Peter turned and saw the disciple whom Jesus loved following them; he was the one who had reclined next to Jesus at the supper and had said, 'Lord, who is it that is going to betray you?' ²¹ When Peter saw him, he said to Jesus, 'Lord, what about him?' ²² Jesus said to him, 'If it is my will that he remain until I come, what is that to you? Follow me!' ²³ So the rumour spread in the community that this disciple would not die. Yet Jesus did not say to him that he would not die, but, 'If it is my will that he remain until I come, what is that to you?'

²⁴ This is the disciple who is testifying to these things and has written them, and we know that his testimony is true. ²⁵ But there are also many other things that Jesus did; if every one of them were written down, I suppose that the world itself could not contain the books that would be written.

POST COMMUNION

Grant, O Lord, we pray,
that the Word made flesh
proclaimed by your apostle John
may, by the celebration of these holy mysteries,
ever abide and live within us;
through Jesus Christ our Lord.

THE HOLY INNOCENTS 28 DECEMBER

COLLECT

Heavenly Father,
whose children suffered at the hands of Herod,
though they had done no wrong:
by the suffering of your Son
and by the innocence of our lives
frustrate all evil designs
and establish your reign of justice and peace;
through Jesus Christ your Son our Lord,
who is alive and reigns with you,
in the unity of the Holy Spirit,
one God, now and for ever.

READING Jeremiah 31.15–17

15 Thus says the LORD:
    A voice is heard in Ramah,
        lamentation and bitter weeping.
    Rachel is weeping for her children;
        she refuses to be comforted for her children,
        because they are no more.
16 Thus says the LORD:
    Keep your voice from weeping,
        and your eyes from tears;
    for there is a reward for your work,
            says the LORD:
    they shall come back from the land of the enemy;
17 there is hope for your future,
            says the LORD:
    your children shall come back to their own country.

PSALM Psalm 124

1 If the Lord had not been on our side,
    let Israel now say;
2 If the Lord had not been on our side,
    when enemies rose up against us;
3 Then would they have swallowed us up alive
    in their fierce anger towards us;

4 Then would the waters have overwhelmed us
 and the torrent gone over us;
5 Then would the raging waters
 have gone right over us.
6 Blessèd be the Lord!
 he has not given us over to be a prey for their teeth.
7 We have escaped like a bird from the snare of the fowler;
 the snare is broken and we have escaped.
8 Our help is in the name of the Lord,
 the maker of heaven and earth.

READING   1 Corinthians 1.26–29

26 Consider your own call, brothers and sisters: not many of you were wise
by human standards, not many were powerful, not many were of noble
birth. 27 But God chose what is foolish in the world to shame the wise; God
chose what is weak in the world to shame the strong; 28 God chose what is
low and despised in the world, things that are not, to reduce to nothing
things that are, 29 so that no one might boast in the presence of God.

GOSPEL   Matthew 2.13–18

13 Now after they had left, an angel of the Lord appeared to Joseph in a
dream and said, 'Get up, take the child and his mother, and flee to Egypt,
and remain there until I tell you; for Herod is about to search for the child,
to destroy him.' 14 Then Joseph got up, took the child and his mother by
night, and went to Egypt, 15 and remained there until the death of Herod.
This was to fulfil what had been spoken by the Lord through the prophet,
'Out of Egypt I have called my son.'

16 When Herod saw that he had been tricked by the wise men, he was
infuriated, and he sent and killed all the children in and around Bethlehem
who were two years old or under, according to the time that he had learned
from the wise men. 17 Then was fulfilled what had been spoken through
the prophet Jeremiah:
18 'A voice was heard in Ramah,
  wailing and loud lamentation,
 Rachel weeping for her children;
  she refused to be consoled, because they are no more.'

POST COMMUNION

Lord Jesus Christ,
in your humility you have stooped to share our human life
with the most defenceless of your children:
may we who have received these gifts of your passion
rejoice in celebrating the witness of the holy innocents
    to the purity of your sacrifice
    made once for all upon the cross;
for you are alive and reign, now and for ever.

POST COMMUNION

COMMON OF THE SAINTS AND
SPECIAL OCCASIONS

COMMON OF THE SAINTS

SPECIAL OCCASIONS

FESTIVALS OF THE BLESSED VIRGIN MARY

THE BIRTH OF THE
BLESSED VIRGIN MARY
8 SEPTEMBER

THE CONCEPTION OF THE
BLESSED VIRGIN MARY
8 DECEMBER

The following prayers and readings are used on all these occasions

COLLECT

Almighty and everlasting God,
who stooped to raise fallen humanity
through the child-bearing of blessed Mary:
grant that we, who have seen your glory
    revealed in our human nature
and your love made perfect in our weakness,
may daily be renewed in your image
and conformed to the pattern of your Son,
Jesus Christ our Lord,
who is alive and reigns with you,
in the unity of the Holy Spirit,
one God, now and for ever.

Genesis 3.8–15, 20; Isaiah 7.10–14; Micah 5.1–4
Acts 1.12–14; Romans 8.18–30; Galatians 4.4–7
Psalms 45.11–18; 113; 131
Luke 1.26–38; Luke 1.39–47; John 19.25–27

POST COMMUNION

God most high,
whose handmaid bore the Word made flesh:
we thank you that in this sacrament of our redemption
you visit us with your Holy Spirit

and overshadow us by your power;
strengthen us to walk with Mary the joyful path of obedience
and so to bring forth the fruits of holiness;
through Jesus Christ our Lord.

MARTYRS

COLLECT

Almighty God,
by whose grace and power your holy martyr N
triumphed over suffering and was faithful unto death:
strengthen us with your grace,
that we may endure reproach and persecution
and faithfully bear witness to the name
   of Jesus Christ your Son our Lord,
who is alive and reigns with you,
in the unity of the Holy Spirit,
one God, now and for ever.

2 Chronicles 24.17–21; Isaiah 43.1–7; Jeremiah 11.18–20; Wisdom 4.10–15
Romans 8.35–39; 2 Corinthians 4.7–15; 2 Timothy 2.3–7, [8–13];
Hebrews 11.32–40; 1 Peter 4.12–19; Revelation 12.10–12a
Psalms 3; 11; 31.1–5; 44.18–23; 126
Matthew 10.16–22; Matthew 10.28–39; Matthew 16.24–26; John 12.24–26;
John 15.18–21

POST COMMUNION

EITHER

Eternal God,
who gave us this holy meal
in which we have celebrated the glory of the cross
and the victory of your martyr N:
by our communion with Christ
in his saving death and resurrection,
give us with all your saints the courage to conquer evil
and so to share the fruit of the tree of life;
through Jesus Christ our Lord.

OR

God our redeemer,
whose Church was strengthened by the blood of your martyr *N*:
so bind us, in life and death, to Christ's sacrifice
that our lives, broken and offered with his,
may carry his death and proclaim his resurrection in the world;
through Jesus Christ our Lord.

This general Post Communion is used for the following

AGNES
CHILD-MARTYR AT ROME, 304   21 JANUARY

COLLECT

Eternal God, shepherd of your sheep,
whose child Agnes was strengthened to bear witness
   in her living and her dying
to the true love of her redeemer:
grant us the power to understand, with all your saints,
what is the breadth and length and height and depth
and to know the love that surpasses knowledge,
even Jesus Christ your Son our Lord,
who is alive and reigns with you,
in the unity of the Holy Spirit,
one God, now and for ever.

also Revelation 7.13–17

CHARLES
KING AND MARTYR, 1649   30 JANUARY

COLLECT

King of kings and Lord of lords,
whose faithful servant Charles
prayed for those who persecuted him
and died in the living hope of your eternal kingdom:
grant us by your grace so to follow his example

that we may love and bless our enemies,
through the intercession of your Son, our Lord Jesus Christ,
who is alive and reigns with you,
in the unity of the Holy Spirit,
one God, now and for ever.

also Ecclesiasticus 2.12–17; 1 Timothy 6.12–16

JANANI LUWUM
ARCHBISHOP OF UGANDA, MARTYR, 1977   17 FEBRUARY

COLLECT

God of truth,
whose servant Janani Luwum walked in the light
and in his death defied the powers of darkness:
free us from fear of those who kill the body,
that we too may walk as children of light,
through him who overcame darkness
   by the power of the cross,
Jesus Christ your Son our Lord,
who is alive and reigns with you,
in the unity of the Holy Spirit,
one God, now and for ever.

also Ecclesiasticus 4.20–28; John 12.24–32

POLYCARP
BISHOP OF SMYRNA, MARTYR, c.155   23 FEBRUARY

COLLECT

Almighty God,
who gave to your servant Polycarp
boldness to confess the name of our Saviour Jesus Christ
   before the rulers of this world
and courage to die for his faith:
grant that we also may be ready
to give an answer for the faith that is in us
and to suffer gladly for the sake of our Lord Jesus Christ,

who is alive and reigns with you,
in the unity of the Holy Spirit,
one God, now and for ever.

also Revelation 2.8–11

PERPETUA, FELICITY, AND THEIR COMPANIONS
MARTYRS AT CARTHAGE, 203   7 MARCH

COLLECT

Holy God,
who gave great courage to Perpetua, Felicity,
    and their companions:
grant that we may be worthy to climb the ladder of sacrifice
and be received into the garden of peace;
through Jesus Christ your Son our Lord,
who is alive and reigns with you,
in the unity of the Holy Spirit,
one God, now and for ever.

especially Revelation 12.10–12a; *also* Wisdom 3.1–7

THOMAS CRANMER
ARCHBISHOP OF CANTERBURY,
REFORMATION MARTYR, 1556   21 MARCH

COLLECT

Father of all mercies,
who through the work of your servant Thomas Cranmer
    renewed the worship of your Church
and through his death
    revealed your strength in human weakness:
by your grace strengthen us to worship you
in spirit and in truth
and so to come to the joys of your everlasting kingdom;

through Jesus Christ our Mediator and Advocate,
who is alive and reigns with you,
in the unity of the Holy Spirit,
one God, now and for ever.

ALPHEGE
ARCHBISHOP OF CANTERBURY, MARTYR, 1012   19 APRIL

COLLECT

Merciful God,
who raised up your servant Alphege
to be a pastor of your people
and gave him grace to suffer for justice and true religion:
grant that we who celebrate his martyrdom
may know the power of the risen Christ in our hearts
and share his peace in lives offered to your service;
through Jesus Christ your Son our Lord,
who is alive and reigns with you,
in the unity of the Holy Spirit,
one God, now and for ever.

also Hebrews 5.1–4

JUSTIN
MARTYR AT ROME, *c.*165   1 JUNE

COLLECT

God our redeemer,
who through the folly of the cross taught your martyr Justin
the surpassing knowledge of Jesus Christ:
remove from us every kind of error
that we, like him, may be firmly grounded in the faith,
and make your name known to all peoples;

through Jesus Christ your Son our Lord,
who is alive and reigns with you,
in the unity of the Holy Spirit,
one God, now and for ever.

especially John 15.18–21; *also* 1 Maccabees 2.15–22; 1 Corinthians 1.18–25

BONIFACE (WYNFRITH) OF CREDITON
BISHOP, APOSTLE OF GERMANY, MARTYR, 754   5 JUNE

COLLECT

God our redeemer,
who called your servant Boniface
to preach the gospel among the German people
and to build up your Church in holiness:
grant that we may preserve in our hearts
that faith which he taught with his words
   and sealed with his blood,
and profess it in lives dedicated to your Son
Jesus Christ our Lord,
who is alive and reigns with you,
in the unity of the Holy Spirit,
one God, now and for ever.

also Acts 20.24–28

ALBAN
FIRST MARTYR OF BRITAIN, c.250   22 JUNE

COLLECT

Eternal Father,
when the gospel of Christ first came to our land
you gloriously confirmed the faith of Alban
by making him the first to win a martyr's crown:
grant that, following his example,
in the fellowship of the saints
we may worship you, the living God,
and give true witness to Jesus Christ your Son our Lord,

who is alive and reigns with you,
in the unity of the Holy Spirit,
one God, now and for ever.

especially 2 Timothy 2.3–13; John 12.24–26

OSWALD
KING OF NORTHUMBRIA, MARTYR, 642   5 AUGUST

COLLECT

Lord God almighty,
who so kindled the faith of King Oswald with your Spirit
that he set up the sign of the cross in his kingdom
and turned his people to the light of Christ:
grant that we, being fired by the same Spirit,
may always bear our cross before the world
and be found faithful servants of the gospel;
through Jesus Christ your Son our Lord,
who is alive and reigns with you,
in the unity of the Holy Spirit,
one God, now and for ever.

especially 1 Peter 4.12–19; John 16.29–33

LAURENCE
DEACON AT ROME, MARTYR, 258   10 AUGUST

COLLECT

Almighty God,
who made Laurence a loving servant of your people
and a wise steward of the treasures of your Church:
fire us with his example to love as he loved
    and to walk in the way that leads to eternal life;
through Jesus Christ your Son our Lord,
who is alive and reigns with you,
in the unity of the Holy Spirit,
one God, now and for ever.

also 2 Corinthians 9.6–10

CYPRIAN
BISHOP OF CARTHAGE, MARTYR, 258   15 SEPTEMBER

COLLECT

Holy God,
who brought Cyprian to faith in Christ,
made him a bishop in the Church
and crowned his witness with a martyr's death:
grant that, after his example,
we may love the Church and her teachings,
find your forgiveness within her fellowship
and so come to share the heavenly banquet
     you have prepared for us;
through Jesus Christ your Son our Lord,
who is alive and reigns with you,
in the unity of the Holy Spirit,
one God, now and for ever.

especially 1 Peter 4.12–19; *also* Matthew 18.18–22

JOHN COLERIDGE PATTESON
FIRST BISHOP OF MELANESIA, AND HIS
COMPANIONS, MARTYRS, 1871   20 SEPTEMBER

COLLECT

God of all tribes and peoples and tongues,
who called your servant John Coleridge Patteson
to witness in life and death to the gospel of Christ
amongst the peoples of Melanesia:
grant us to hear your call to service
and to respond trustfully and joyfully
to Jesus Christ our redeemer,
who is alive and reigns with you,
in the unity of the Holy Spirit,
one God, now and for ever.

especially 2 Chronicles 24.17–21; *also* Acts 7.55–60

WILLIAM TYNDALE
TRANSLATOR OF THE SCRIPTURES, REFORMATION MARTYR, 1536   6 OCTOBER

COLLECT

Lord, give to your people grace to hear and keep your word
that, after the example of your servant William Tyndale,
we may not only profess your gospel
but also be ready to suffer and die for it,
to the honour of your name;
through Jesus Christ your Son our Lord,
who is alive and reigns with you,
in the unity of the Holy Spirit,
one God, now and for ever.

also Proverbs 8.4–11; 2 Timothy 3.12–17

IGNATIUS
BISHOP OF ANTIOCH, MARTYR, c.107   17 OCTOBER

COLLECT

Feed us, O Lord, with the living bread
and make us drink deep of the cup of salvation
that, following the teaching of your bishop Ignatius
and rejoicing in the faith
   with which he embraced a martyr's death,
we may be nourished for that eternal life
   for which he longed;
through Jesus Christ your Son our Lord,
who is alive and reigns with you,
in the unity of the Holy Spirit,
one God, now and for ever.

also Philippians 3.7–12; John 6.52–58

JAMES HANNINGTON
BISHOP OF EASTERN EQUATORIAL AFRICA, MARTYR IN UGANDA, 1885

29 OCTOBER

COLLECT

Most merciful God,
who strengthened your Church by the steadfast courage
    of your martyr James Hannington:
grant that we also,
thankfully remembering his victory of faith,
may overcome what is evil
and glorify your holy name;
through Jesus Christ your Son our Lord,
who is alive and reigns with you,
in the unity of the Holy Spirit,
one God, now and for ever.

especially Matthew 10.28–39

EDMUND
KING OF THE EAST ANGLES, MARTYR, 870

20 NOVEMBER

COLLECT

Eternal God,
whose servant Edmund kept faith to the end,
both with you and with his people,
and glorified you by his death:
grant us such steadfastness of faith
that, with the noble army of martyrs,
we may come to enjoy the fullness of the resurrection life;
through Jesus Christ your Son our Lord,
who is alive and reigns with you,
in the unity of the Holy Spirit,
one God, now and for ever.

also Proverbs 20.28; 21.1–4, 7

CLEMENT
BISHOP OF ROME, MARTYR, c.100   23 NOVEMBER

COLLECT

Creator and Father of eternity,
whose martyr Clement bore witness with his blood
to the love he proclaimed and the gospel that he preached:
give us thankful hearts as we celebrate your faithfulness
    revealed to us in the lives of your saints
and strengthen us in our pilgrimage as we follow your Son,
Jesus Christ our Lord,
who is alive and reigns with you,
in the unity of the Holy Spirit,
one God, now and for ever.

also Philippians 3.17–4.3; Matthew 16.13–19

LUCY
MARTYR AT SYRACUSE, 304   13 DECEMBER

COLLECT

God our redeemer,
who gave light to the world that was in darkness
by the healing power of the Saviour's cross:
shed that light on us, we pray,
that with your martyr Lucy
we may, by the purity of our lives,
    reflect the light of Christ
and, by the merits of his passion,
    come to the light of everlasting life;
through Jesus Christ your Son our Lord,
who is alive and reigns with you,
in the unity of the Holy Spirit,
one God, now and for ever.

also Wisdom 3.1–7; 2 Corinthians 4.6–15

THOMAS BECKET
ARCHBISHOP OF CANTERBURY, MARTYR, 1170   29 DECEMBER

COLLECT

Lord God,
who gave grace to your servant Thomas Becket
to put aside all earthly fear
    and be faithful even to death:
grant that we, disregarding worldly esteem,
may fight all wrong,
uphold your rule,
and serve you to our life's end;
through Jesus Christ your Son our Lord,
who is alive and reigns with you,
in the unity of the Holy Spirit,
one God, now and for ever.

especially Matthew 10.28–33; *also* Ecclesiasticus 51.1–8

TEACHERS OF THE FAITH AND SPIRITUAL WRITERS

COLLECT

Almighty God,
who enlightened your Church
    by the teaching of your servant *N*:
enrich it evermore with your heavenly grace
and raise up faithful witnesses
who, by their life and teaching,
may proclaim the truth of your salvation;
through Jesus Christ your Son our Lord,
who is alive and reigns with you,
in the unity of the Holy Spirit,
one God, now and for ever.

1 Kings 3.[6–10,] 11–14; Proverbs 4.1–9; Wisdom 7.7–10, 15–16;
Ecclesiasticus 39.1–10
1 Corinthians 1.18–25; 1 Corinthians 2.1–10; 1 Corinthians 2.9–16;
Ephesians 3.8–12; 2 Timothy 4.1–8; Titus 2.1–8

Psalms 19.7–10; 34.11–17; 37.32–36; 119.85–96; 119.97–104
Matthew 5.13–19; Matthew 13.52–58; Matthew 23.8–12; Mark 4.1–9;
John 16.12–15

POST COMMUNION

God of truth,
whose Wisdom set her table
and invited us to eat the bread and drink the wine
    of the kingdom:
help us to lay aside all foolishness
and to live and walk in the way of insight,
that we may come with N
    to the eternal feast of heaven;
through Jesus Christ our Lord.

This general Post Communion is used for the following

BASIL THE GREAT AND GREGORY OF NAZIANZUS
BISHOPS, TEACHERS OF THE FAITH, 379 AND 389   2 JANUARY

COLLECT

Lord God,
whose servants Basil and Gregory
proclaimed the mystery of your Word made flesh,
to build up your Church in wisdom and strength:
grant that we may rejoice in his presence among us,
and so be brought with them to know
the power of your unending love;
through Jesus Christ your Son our Lord,
who is alive and reigns with you,
in the unity of the Holy Spirit,
one God, now and for ever.

especially 2 Timothy 4.1–8; Matthew 5.13–19

HILARY
BISHOP OF POITIERS, TEACHER OF THE FAITH, 367   13 JANUARY

COLLECT

Everlasting God,
whose servant Hilary
steadfastly confessed your Son Jesus Christ
   to be both human and divine:
grant us his gentle courtesy
to bring to all the message of redemption
   in the incarnate Christ,
who is alive and reigns with you,
in the unity of the Holy Spirit,
one God, now and for ever.

also 1 John 2.18–25; John 8.25–32

FRANCIS DE SALES
BISHOP OF GENEVA, TEACHER OF THE FAITH, 1622   24 JANUARY

COLLECT

Holy God,
who called your bishop Francis de Sales
to bring many to Christ through his devout life
and to renew your Church with patience and understanding:
grant that we may, by word and example,
reflect your gentleness and love to all we meet;
through Jesus Christ our Saviour,
who is alive and reigns with you,
in the unity of the Holy Spirit,
one God, now and for ever.

also Proverbs 3.13–18; John 3.17–21

THOMAS AQUINAS
PRIEST, PHILOSOPHER, TEACHER OF
THE FAITH, 1274   28 JANUARY

COLLECT

Eternal God,
who enriched your Church with the learning and holiness
    of your servant Thomas Aquinas:
give to all who seek you
a humble mind and a pure heart
that they may know your Son Jesus Christ
as the way, the truth and the life;
who is alive and reigns with you,
in the unity of the Holy Spirit,
one God, now and for ever.

especially Wisdom 7.7–10, 15–16; 1 Corinthians 2.9–16; John 16.12–15

WILLIAM LAW
PRIEST, SPIRITUAL WRITER, 1761   10 APRIL

COLLECT

Almighty God,
who called your servant William Law
to a devout and holy life:
grant that by your spirit of love
and through faithfulness in prayer
we may find the way to divine knowledge
and so come to see the hidden things of God;
through Jesus Christ your Son our Lord,
who is alive and reigns with you,
in the unity of the Holy Spirit,
one God, now and for ever.

especially 1 Corinthians 2.9–16; *also* Matthew 17.1–9

ANSELM
ABBOT OF LE BEC, ARCHBISHOP OF CANTERBURY, TEACHER OF THE FAITH, 1109
21 APRIL

COLLECT

Eternal God,
who gave great gifts to your servant Anselm
as a pastor and teacher:
grant that we, like him, may desire you with our whole heart
and, so desiring, may seek you
and, seeking, may find you;
through Jesus Christ your Son our Lord,
who is alive and reigns with you,
in the unity of the Holy Spirit,
one God, now and for ever.

also Wisdom 9.13–18; Romans 5.8–11

CATHERINE OF SIENA
TEACHER OF THE FAITH, 1380
29 APRIL

COLLECT

God of compassion,
who gave your servant Catherine of Siena
a wondrous love of the passion of Christ:
grant that your people
    may be united to him in his majesty
and rejoice for ever in the revelation of his glory;
who is alive and reigns with you,
in the unity of the Holy Spirit,
one God, now and for ever.

also Proverbs 8.1, 6–11; John 17.12–26

ATHANASIUS
BISHOP OF ALEXANDRIA, TEACHER OF THE FAITH, 373   2 MAY

COLLECT

Ever-living God,
whose servant Athanasius testified
   to the mystery of the Word made flesh for our salvation:
help us, with all your saints,
to contend for the truth
and to grow into the likeness of your Son,
Jesus Christ our Lord,
who is alive and reigns with you,
in the unity of the Holy Spirit,
one God, now and for ever.

also Ecclesiasticus 4.20–28; *also* Matthew 10.24–27

IRENAEUS
BISHOP OF LYONS, TEACHER OF THE FAITH, c.200   28 JUNE

COLLECT

God of peace,
who through the ministry of your servant Irenaeus
strengthened the true faith
and brought harmony to your Church:
keep us steadfast in your true religion,
and renew us in faith and love,
that we may always walk in the way that leads to eternal life;
through Jesus Christ your Son our Lord,
who is alive and reigns with you,
in the unity of the Holy Spirit,
one God, now and for ever.

also 2 Peter 1.16–21

GREGORY AND MACRINA

GREGORY, BISHOP OF NYSSA, AND HIS SISTER MACRINA, DEACONESS, TEACHERS OF THE FAITH, *c.*394 AND *c.*379   19 JULY

COLLECT

Lord of eternity, creator of all things,
in your Son Jesus Christ
    you open for us the way to resurrection
that we may enjoy your bountiful goodness:
may we who celebrate your servants Gregory and Macrina
press onwards in faith to your boundless love
and ever wonder at the miracle of your presence among us;
through Jesus Christ your Son our Lord,
who is alive and reigns with you,
in the unity of the Holy Spirit,
one God, now and for ever.

especially 1 Corinthians 2.9–13; *also* Wisdom 9.13–17

JEREMY TAYLOR

BISHOP OF DOWN AND CONNOR, TEACHER OF THE FAITH, 1667   13 AUGUST

COLLECT

Holy and loving God,
you dwell in the human heart
and make us partakers of the divine nature
in Christ our great high priest:
help us who remember your servant Jeremy Taylor
to put our trust in your heavenly promises
and follow a holy life in virtue and true godliness;
through Jesus Christ your Son our Lord,
who is alive and reigns with you,
in the unity of the Holy Spirit,
one God, now and for ever.

also Titus 2.7–8, 11–14

YEARS A, B, AND C

BERNARD
ABBOT OF CLAIRVAUX, TEACHER OF THE FAITH, 1153 20 AUGUST

COLLECT

Merciful redeemer,
who, by the life and preaching of your servant Bernard,
rekindled the radiant light of your Church:
grant us, in our generation,
to be inflamed with the same spirit of discipline and love,
and ever to walk before you as children of light;
through Jesus Christ your Son our Lord,
who is alive and reigns with you,
in the unity of the Holy Spirit,
one God, now and for ever.

especially Revelation 19.5–9

AUGUSTINE OF HIPPO
BISHOP OF HIPPO, TEACHER OF THE FAITH, 430   28 AUGUST

COLLECT

Merciful Lord,
who turned Augustine from his sins
    to be a faithful bishop and teacher:
grant that we may follow him in penitence and discipline
till our restless hearts find their rest in you;
through Jesus Christ your Son our Lord,
who is alive and reigns with you,
in the unity of the Holy Spirit,
one God, now and for ever.

especially Ecclesiasticus 39.1–10; *also* Romans 13.11–13

JOHN BUNYAN
SPIRITUAL WRITER, 1688   30 AUGUST

COLLECT

God of peace,
who called your servant John Bunyan
to be valiant for truth:
grant that as strangers and pilgrims
we may at the last
  rejoice with all Christian people in your heavenly city;
through Jesus Christ your Son our Lord,
who is alive and reigns with you,
in the unity of the Holy Spirit,
one God, now and for ever.

also Hebrews 12.1–2; Luke 21.21, 34–36

GREGORY THE GREAT
BISHOP OF ROME, TEACHER OF THE FAITH, 604   3 SEPTEMBER

COLLECT

Merciful Father,
who chose your bishop Gregory
to be a servant of the servants of God:
grant that, like him, we may ever long to serve you
by proclaiming your gospel to the nations,
and may ever rejoice to sing your praises;
through Jesus Christ your Son our Lord,
who is alive and reigns with you,
in the unity of the Holy Spirit,
one God, now and for ever.

also 1 Thessalonians 2.3–8

JOHN CHRYSOSTOM
BISHOP OF CONSTANTINOPLE, TEACHER OF THE FAITH, 407
13 SEPTEMBER

COLLECT

God of truth and love,
who gave to your servant John Chrysostom
eloquence to declare your righteousness
   in the great congregation
and courage to bear reproach for the honour of your name:
mercifully grant to those who minister your word
such excellence in preaching,
that all people may share with them
in the glory that shall be revealed;
through Jesus Christ your Son our Lord,
who is alive and reigns with you,
in the unity of the Holy Spirit,
one God, now and for ever.

especially Matthew 5.13–19; *also* Jeremiah 1.4–10

TERESA OF AVILA
TEACHER OF THE FAITH, 1582
15 OCTOBER

COLLECT

Merciful God,
who by your Spirit raised up your servant Teresa of Avila
to reveal to your Church the way of perfection:
grant that her teaching
may awaken in us a longing for holiness,
until we attain to the perfect union of love
in Jesus Christ your Son our Lord,
who is alive and reigns with you,
in the unity of the Holy Spirit,
one God, now and for ever.

also Romans 8.22–27

RICHARD HOOKER
PRIEST, ANGLICAN APOLOGIST, TEACHER OF THE FAITH, 1600   3 NOVEMBER

COLLECT

God of peace, the bond of all love,
who in your Son Jesus Christ have made the human race
   your inseparable dwelling place:
after the example of your servant Richard Hooker,
give grace to us your servants ever to rejoice
   in the true inheritance of your adopted children
and to show forth your praises now and ever;
through Jesus Christ your Son our Lord,
who is alive and reigns with you,
in the unity of the Holy Spirit,
one God, now and for ever.

especially John 16.12–15; *also* Ecclesiasticus 44.10–15

LEO THE GREAT
BISHOP OF ROME, TEACHER OF THE FAITH, 461   10 NOVEMBER

COLLECT

God our Father,
who made your servant Leo strong in the defence of the faith:
fill your Church with the spirit of truth
that, guided by humility and governed by love,
she may prevail against the powers of evil;
through Jesus Christ your Son our Lord,
who is alive and reigns with you,
in the unity of the Holy Spirit,
one God, now and for ever.

also 1 Peter 5.1–11

AMBROSE
BISHOP OF MILAN, TEACHER OF THE FAITH, 397   7 DECEMBER

COLLECT

God of hosts,
who called Ambrose from the governor's throne
to be a bishop in your Church
and an intrepid champion of your faithful people:
mercifully grant that, as he did not fear to rebuke rulers,
so we, with like courage,
    may contend for the faith we have received;
through Jesus Christ your Son our Lord,
who is alive and reigns with you,
in the unity of the Holy Spirit,
one God, now and for ever.

also Isaiah 41.9b–13; Luke 22.24–30

JOHN OF THE CROSS
POET, TEACHER OF THE FAITH, 1591   14 DECEMBER

COLLECT

O God, the judge of all,
who gave your servant John of the Cross
a warmth of nature, a strength of purpose
    and a mystical faith
that sustained him even in the darkness:
shed your light on all who love you
and grant them union of body and soul
in your Son Jesus Christ our Lord,
who is alive and reigns with you,
in the unity of the Holy Spirit,
one God, now and for ever.

especially 1 Corinthians 2.1–10; *also* John 14.18–23

BISHOPS AND OTHER PASTORS

COLLECT

EITHER

Eternal God,
you called N to proclaim your glory
   in a life of prayer and pastoral zeal:
keep the leaders of your Church faithful
and bless your people through their ministry,
that the Church may grow into the full stature
   of your Son Jesus Christ our Lord,
who is alive and reigns with you,
in the unity of the Holy Spirit,
one God, now and for ever.

OR, FOR A BISHOP

Almighty God,
the light of the faithful and shepherd of souls,
who set your servant N to be a bishop in the Church,
to feed your sheep by the word of Christ
and to guide them by good example:
give us grace to keep the faith of the Church
and to follow in the footsteps
   of Jesus Christ our Lord,
who is alive and reigns with you,
in the unity of the Holy Spirit,
one God, now and for ever.

1 Samuel 16.1, 6–13; Isaiah 6.1–8; Jeremiah 1.4–10; Ezekiel 3.16–21;
Malachi 2.5–7
Acts 20.28–35; 1 Corinthians 4.1–5; 2 Corinthians 4.1–2, [3–4,] 5–7, [8–10];
2 Corinthians 5.14–20; 1 Peter 5.1–4
Psalms 1; 15; 16.5–11; 96; 110
Matthew 11.25–30; Matthew 24.42–46; John 10.11–16; John 15.9–17;
John 21.15–17

POST COMMUNION

God, shepherd of your people,
whose servant N revealed the loving service of Christ
    in his/her ministry as a pastor of your people:
by this eucharist in which we share
awaken within us the love of Christ
and keep us faithful to our Christian calling;
through him who laid down his life for us,
but is alive and reigns with you, now and for ever.

This general Post Communion is used for the following

WULFSTAN
BISHOP OF WORCESTER, 1095   19 JANUARY

COLLECT

Lord God,
who raised up Wulfstan to be a bishop among your people
    and a leader of your Church:
help us, after his example,
    to live simply,
    to work diligently
    and to make your kingdom known;
through Jesus Christ your Son our Lord,
who is alive and reigns with you,
in the unity of the Holy Spirit,
one God, now and for ever.

especially Matthew 24.42–46

GEORGE HERBERT
PRIEST, POET, 1633   27 FEBRUARY

COLLECT

King of glory, king of peace,
who called your servant George Herbert
from the pursuit of worldly honours
to be a priest in the temple of his God and king:
grant us also the grace to offer ourselves with singleness of heart in
humble obedience to your service;
through Jesus Christ your Son our Lord,
who is alive and reigns with you,
in the unity of the Holy Spirit,
one God, now and for ever.

especially Malachi 2.5–7; Matthew 11.25–30; *also* Revelation 19.5–9

DAVID
BISHOP OF MENEVIA, PATRON OF WALES, *c.*601   1 MARCH

COLLECT

Almighty God,
who called your servant David
   to be a faithful and wise steward of your mysteries
   for the people of Wales:
in your mercy grant that,
   following his purity of life and zeal for the gospel of Christ,
we may with him receive the crown of everlasting life;
through Jesus Christ your Son our Lord,
who is alive and reigns with you,
in the unity of the Holy Spirit,
one God, now and for ever.

also 2 Samuel 23.1–4; Psalm 89.19–23, 25

EDWARD KING
BISHOP OF LINCOLN, 1910   8 MARCH

COLLECT

God of peace,
who gave such grace to your servant Edward King
that whomever he met he drew to Christ:
fill us, we pray, with tender sympathy and joyful faith,
that we also may win others
    to know the love that passes knowledge;
through him who is the shepherd and guardian of our souls,
Jesus Christ your Son our Lord,
who is alive and reigns with you,
in the unity of the Holy Spirit,
one God, now and for ever.

also Hebrews 13.1–8

DUNSTAN
ARCHBISHOP OF CANTERBURY, RESTORER OF
MONASTIC LIFE, 988   19 MAY

COLLECT

Almighty God,
who raised up Dunstan to be a true shepherd of the flock,
a restorer of monastic life
and a faithful counsellor to those in authority:
give to all pastors the same gifts of your Holy Spirit
that they may be true servants of Christ
    and of all his people;
through Jesus Christ your Son our Lord,
who is alive and reigns with you,
in the unity of the Holy Spirit,
one God, now and for ever.

especially Matthew 24.42–46; *also* Exodus 31.1–5

JOHN AND CHARLES WESLEY
EVANGELISTS, HYMN WRITERS, 1791 AND 1788   24 MAY

COLLECT

God of mercy,
who inspired John and Charles Wesley
   with zeal for your gospel:
grant to all people boldness to proclaim your word
and a heart ever to rejoice in singing your praises;
through Jesus Christ your Son our Lord,
who is alive and reigns with you,
in the unity of the Holy Spirit,
one God, now and for ever.

also Ephesians 5.15–20

AUGUSTINE OF CANTERBURY
FIRST ARCHBISHOP OF CANTERBURY, 605   26 MAY

COLLECT

Almighty God,
whose servant Augustine was sent as the apostle
   of the English people:
grant that as he laboured in the Spirit
to preach Christ's gospel in this land,
so all who hear the good news
may strive to make your truth known in all the world;
through Jesus Christ your Son our Lord,
who is alive and reigns with you,
in the unity of the Holy Spirit,
one God, now and for ever.

also 1 Thessalonians 2.2b-8; Matthew 13.31–33

THOMAS KEN

BISHOP OF BATH AND WELLS, NON-JUROR, HYMN WRITER, 1711   8 JUNE

COLLECT

O God, from whom all blessings flow,
by whose providence we are kept
and by whose grace we are directed:
help us, through the example of your servant Thomas Ken,
faithfully to keep your word,
humbly to accept adversity
and steadfastly to worship you;
through Jesus Christ your Son our Lord,
who is alive and reigns with you,
in the unity of the Holy Spirit,
one God, now and for ever.

especially 2 Corinthians 4.1–10; Matthew 24.42–46

RICHARD

BISHOP OF CHICHESTER, 1253   16 JUNE

COLLECT

Most merciful redeemer,
who gave to your bishop Richard a love of learning,
a zeal for souls and a devotion to the poor:
grant that, encouraged by his example,
we may know you more clearly,
    love you more dearly,
    and follow you more nearly,
day by day,
who with the Father and the Holy Spirit are alive and reign,
one God, now and for ever.

also John 21.15–19

JOHN KEBLE
PRIEST, TRACTARIAN, POET, 1866   14 JULY

COLLECT

Father of the eternal Word,
in whose encompassing love
all things in peace and order move:
grant that, as your servant John Keble
   adored you in all creation,
so we may have a humble heart of love
for the mysteries of your Church
and know your love to be new every morning,
in Jesus Christ your Son our Lord,
who is alive and reigns with you,
in the unity of the Holy Spirit,
one God, now and for ever.

also Lamentations 3.19–26; Matthew 5.1–8

SWITHUN
BISHOP OF WINCHESTER, *c*.862   15 JULY

COLLECT

Almighty God,
by whose grace we celebrate again
the feast of your servant Swithun:
grant that, as he governed with gentleness
   the people committed to his care,
so we, rejoicing in our Christian inheritance,
may always seek to build up your Church in unity and love;
through Jesus Christ your Son our Lord,
who is alive and reigns with you,
in the unity of the Holy Spirit,
one God, now and for ever.

also James 5.7–11, 13–18

LANCELOT ANDREWES
BISHOP OF WINCHESTER, SPIRITUAL
WRITER, 1626   25 SEPTEMBER

COLLECT

Lord God,
who gave to Lancelot Andrewes
   many gifts of your Holy Spirit,
making him a man of prayer and a pastor of your people:
perfect in us that which is lacking in your gifts,
   of faith, to increase it,
   of hope, to establish it,
   of love, to kindle it,
that we may live in the light of your grace and glory;
through Jesus Christ your Son our Lord,
who is alive and reigns with you,
in the unity of the Holy Spirit,
one God, now and for ever.

especially Isaiah 6.1–8

MARTIN OF TOURS
BISHOP OF TOURS, *c.*397   11 NOVEMBER

COLLECT

God all powerful,
who called Martin from the armies of this world
to be a faithful soldier of Christ:
give us grace to follow him
in his love and compassion for the needy,
and enable your Church to claim for all people
their inheritance as children of God;
through Jesus Christ your Son our Lord,
who is alive and reigns with you,
in the unity of the Holy Spirit,
one God, now and for ever.

also 1 Thessalonians 5.1–11; Matthew 25.34–40

CHARLES SIMEON
PRIEST, EVANGELICAL DIVINE, 1836   13 NOVEMBER

COLLECT

Eternal God,
who raised up Charles Simeon
    to preach the good news of Jesus Christ
and inspire your people in service and mission:
grant that we with all your Church may worship the Saviour,
turn in sorrow from our sins and walk in the way of holiness;
through Jesus Christ your Son our Lord,
who is alive and reigns with you,
in the unity of the Holy Spirit,
one God, now and for ever.

especially Malachi 2.5–7; *also* Colossians 1.3–8; Luke 8.4–8

HUGH
BISHOP OF LINCOLN, 1200   17 NOVEMBER

COLLECT

O God,
who endowed your servant Hugh
with a wise and cheerful boldness
and taught him to commend to earthly rulers
    the discipline of a holy life:
give us grace like him to be bold in the service of the gospel,
putting our confidence in Christ alone,
who is alive and reigns with you,
in the unity of the Holy Spirit,
one God, now and for ever.

also 1 Timothy 6.11–16

NICHOLAS
BISHOP OF MYRA, *c.*326   6 DECEMBER

COLLECT

Almighty Father, lover of souls,
who chose your servant Nicholas
   to be a bishop in the Church,
that he might give freely out of the treasures of your grace:
make us mindful of the needs of others
and, as we have received,
   so teach us also to give;
through Jesus Christ your Son our Lord,
who is alive and reigns with you,
in the unity of the Holy Spirit,
one God, now and for ever.

also Isaiah 61.1–3; 1 Timothy 6.6–11; Mark 10.13–16

MEMBERS OF RELIGIOUS COMMUNITIES

COLLECT

Almighty God,
by whose grace N, kindled with the fire of your love,
became a burning and a shining light in the Church:
inflame us with the same spirit of discipline and love,
that we may ever walk before you as children of light;
through Jesus Christ your Son our Lord,
who is alive and reigns with you,
in the unity of the Holy Spirit,
one God, now and for ever.

1 Kings 19.9–18; Proverbs 10.27–32; Song of Solomon 8.6–7;
Isaiah 61.10–62.5; Hosea 2.14–15, 19–20

Acts 4.32–35; 2 Corinthians 10.17–11.2; Philippians 3.7–14; 1 John 2.15–17;
Revelation 19.1, 5–9

Psalms 34.1–8; 112.1–9; 119.57–64; 123; 131

Matthew 11.25–30; Matthew 19.3–12; Matthew 19.23–30; Luke 9.57–62;
Luke 12.32–37

POST COMMUNION

Merciful God,
who gave such grace to your servant N
that he/she served you with singleness of heart
and loved you above all things:
help us, whose communion with you
    has been renewed in this sacrament,
to forsake all that holds us back from following Christ
and to grow into his likeness from glory to glory;
through Jesus Christ our Lord.

This general Post Communion is used for the following

AELRED OF HEXHAM
ABBOT OF RIEVAULX, 1167   12 JANUARY

COLLECT

Almighty God,
who endowed Aelred the abbot
with the gift of Christian friendship
and the wisdom to lead others in the way of holiness:
grant to your people that same spirit of mutual affection,
so that, in loving one another,
we may know the love of Christ
and rejoice in the eternal possession
    of your supreme goodness;
through Jesus Christ your Son our Lord,
who is alive and reigns with you,
in the unity of the Holy Spirit,
one God, now and for ever.

also Ecclesiasticus 15.1–6

ANTONY OF EGYPT
HERMIT, ABBOT, 356 17 JANUARY

COLLECT

Most gracious God,
who called your servant Antony to sell all that he had
and to serve you in the solitude of the desert:
by his example may we learn to deny ourselves
and to love you before all things;
through Jesus Christ your Son our Lord,
who is alive and reigns with you,
in the unity of the Holy Spirit,
one God, now and for ever.

especially Philippians 3.7–14, *also* Matthew 19.16–26

JULIAN OF NORWICH
SPIRITUAL WRITER, c.1417 8 MAY

COLLECT

Most holy God, the ground of our beseeching,
who through your servant Julian
revealed the wonders of your love:
grant that as we are created in your nature
   and restored by your grace,
our wills may be so made one with yours
that we may come to see you face to face
and gaze on you for ever;
through Jesus Christ your Son our Lord,
who is alive and reigns with you,
in the unity of the Holy Spirit,
one God, now and for ever.

also 1 Corinthians 13.8–13; Matthew 5.13–16

ALCUIN OF YORK
DEACON, ABBOT OF TOURS, 804 20 MAY

COLLECT

God of wisdom, eternal light,
who shone in the heart of your servant Alcuin,
revealing to him your power and pity:
scatter the darkness of our ignorance
that, with all our heart and mind and strength,
we may seek your face
and be brought with all your saints
to your holy presence;
through Jesus Christ your Son our Lord,
who is alive and reigns with you,
in the unity of the Holy Spirit,
one God, now and for ever.

also Colossians 3.12–16; John 4.19–24

THE VENERABLE BEDE
MONK AT JARROW, SCHOLAR, HISTORIAN, 735 25 MAY

COLLECT

God our maker,
whose Son Jesus Christ gave to your servant Bede
grace to drink in with joy
    the word that leads us to know you and to love you:
in your goodness
grant that we also may come at length to you,
the source of all wisdom,
and stand before your face;
through Jesus Christ your Son our Lord,
who is alive and reigns with you,
in the unity of the Holy Spirit,
one God, now and for ever.

also Ecclesiasticus 39.1–10

ETHELDREDA
ABBESS OF ELY, *c.*678   23 JUNE

COLLECT

Eternal God,
who bestowed such grace upon your servant Etheldreda
that she gave herself wholly to the life of prayer
    and to the service of your true religion:
grant that we, like her,
may so live our lives on earth seeking your kingdom
that by your guiding
we may be joined to the glorious fellowship of your saints;
through Jesus Christ your Son our Lord,
who is alive and reigns with you,
in the unity of the Holy Spirit,
one God, now and for ever.

also Matthew 25.1–13

BENEDICT OF NURSIA
ABBOT OF MONTE CASSINO, FATHER OF WESTERN
MONASTICISM, *c.*550   11 JULY

COLLECT

Eternal God,
who made Benedict a wise master
in the school of your service
and a guide to many called into community
    to follow the rule of Christ:
grant that we may put your love before all else
and seek with joy the way of your commandments;
through Jesus Christ your Son our Lord,
who is alive and reigns with you,
in the unity of the Holy Spirit,
one God, now and for ever.

also 1 Corinthians 3.10–11; Luke 18.18–22

DOMINIC
PRIEST, FOUNDER OF THE ORDER OF
PREACHERS, 1221   8 AUGUST

COLLECT

Almighty God,
whose servant Dominic grew in the knowledge of your truth
and formed an order of preachers
    to proclaim the faith of Christ:
by your grace give to all your people a love for your word
and a longing to share the gospel,
so that the whole world may come to know you
and your Son Jesus Christ our Lord,
who is alive and reigns with you,
in the unity of the Holy Spirit,
one God, now and for ever.

also Ecclesiasticus 39.1–10

CLARE OF ASSISI
FOUNDER OF THE MINORESSES
(POOR CLARES), 1253   11 AUGUST

COLLECT

God of peace,
who in the poverty of the blessed Clare
gave us a clear light to shine in the darkness of this world:
give us grace so to follow in her footsteps
that we may, at the last, rejoice with her
    in your eternal glory;
through Jesus Christ your Son our Lord,
who is alive and reigns with you,
in the unity of the Holy Spirit,
one God, now and for ever.

especially Song of Solomon 8.6–7

HILDEGARD
ABBESS OF BINGEN, VISIONARY, 1179   17 SEPTEMBER

COLLECT

Most glorious and holy God,
whose servant Hildegard, strong in the faith,
was caught up in the vision of your heavenly courts:
by the breath of your Spirit
open our eyes to glimpse your glory
and our lips to sing your praises with all the angels;
through Jesus Christ your Son our Lord,
who is alive and reigns with you,
in the unity of the Holy Spirit,
one God, now and for ever.

also 1 Corinthians 2.9–13; Luke 10.21–24

VINCENT DE PAUL
FOUNDER OF THE CONGREGATION OF THE
MISSION (LAZARISTS), 1660   27 SEPTEMBER

COLLECT

Merciful God,
whose servant Vincent de Paul,
by his ministry of preaching and pastoral care,
brought your love to the sick and the poor:
give to all your people a heart of compassion
that by word and action they may serve you
    in serving others in their need;
through Jesus Christ your Son our Lord,
who is alive and reigns with you,
in the unity of the Holy Spirit,
one God, now and for ever.

also 1 Corinthians 1.25–31; Matthew 25.34–40

FRANCIS OF ASSISI
FRIAR, DEACON, FOUNDER OF THE
FRIARS MINOR, 1226   4 OCTOBER

COLLECT

O God, you ever delight to reveal yourself
to the child-like and lowly of heart:
grant that, following the example of the blessed Francis,
we may count the wisdom of this world as foolishness
and know only Jesus Christ and him crucified,
who is alive and reigns with you,
in the unity of the Holy Spirit,
one God, now and for ever.

also Galatians 6.14–18; Luke 12.22–34

HILDA
ABBESS OF WHITBY, 680   19 NOVEMBER

COLLECT

Eternal God,
who made the abbess Hilda to shine like a jewel in our land
and through her holiness and leadership
    blessed your Church with new life and unity:
help us, like her, to yearn for the gospel of Christ
and to reconcile those who are divided;
through him who is alive and reigns with you,
in the unity of the Holy Spirit,
one God, now and for ever.

especially Isaiah 61.10–62.5

MISSIONARIES

COLLECT

Everlasting God,
whose servant N carried the good news of your Son
to the people of ...:
grant that we who commemorate his/her service
may know the hope of the gospel in our hearts
and manifest its light in all our ways;
through Jesus Christ your Son our Lord,
who is alive and reigns with you,
in the unity of the Holy Spirit,
one God, now and for ever.

Isaiah 52.7–10; Isaiah 61.1–3a; Ezekiel 34.11–16; Jonah 3.1–5

Acts 2.14, 22–36; Acts 13.46–49; Acts 16.6–10; Acts 26.19–23;
Romans 15.17–21; 2 Corinthians 5.11–6.2

Psalms 67; 87; 97; 100; 117

Matthew 9.35–38; Matthew 28.16–20; Mark 16.15–20; Luke 5.1–11;
Luke 10.1–9

POST COMMUNION

Holy Father,
who gathered us here around the table of your Son
to share this meal with the whole household of God:
in that new world where you reveal
    the fullness of your peace,
gather people of every race and language
to share with N and all your saints
in the eternal banquet of Jesus Christ our Lord.

This general Post Communion is used for the following

ANSKAR
ARCHBISHOP OF HAMBURG, MISSIONARY IN
DENMARK AND SWEDEN   3 FEBRUARY

COLLECT

God of grace and might,
who sent your servant Anskar
to spread the gospel to the Nordic peoples:
raise up, we pray, in our generation
   messengers of your good news
   and heralds of your kingdom
that the world may come to know
   the immeasurable riches of our Saviour Jesus Christ,
who is alive and reigns with you,
in the unity of the Holy Spirit,
one God, now and for ever.

especially Isaiah 52.7–10; *also* Romans 10.11–15

CYRIL AND METHODIUS
MISSIONARIES TO THE SLAVS, 869 AND 885   14 FEBRUARY

COLLECT

Lord of all,
who gave to your servants Cyril and Methodius
the gift of tongues to proclaim the gospel to the Slavs:
make your whole Church one as you are one
that all Christians may honour one another,
and east and west acknowledge
   one Lord, one faith, one baptism,
and you, the God and Father of all;
through Jesus Christ your Son our Lord,
who is alive and reigns with you,
in the unity of the Holy Spirit,
one God, now and for ever.

especially Isaiah 52.7–10; *also* Romans 10.11–15

CHAD
BISHOP OF LICHFIELD, MISSIONARY, 672   2 MARCH

COLLECT

Almighty God,
from the first fruits of the English nation
   who turned to Christ,
you called your servant Chad
to be an evangelist and bishop of his own people:
give us grace so to follow his peaceable nature,
   humble spirit and prayerful life,
that we may truly commend to others
the faith which we ourselves profess;
through Jesus Christ your Son our Lord,
who is alive and reigns with you,
in the unity of the Holy Spirit,
one God, now and for ever.

also 1 Timothy 6.11b–16

PATRICK
BISHOP, MISSIONARY, PATRON OF IRELAND, *c.*460   17 MARCH

COLLECT

Almighty God,
who in your providence chose your servant Patrick
to be the apostle of the Irish people:
keep alive in us the fire of the faith he kindled
and strengthen us in our pilgrimage
   towards the light of everlasting life;
through Jesus Christ your Son our Lord,
who is alive and reigns with you,
in the unity of the Holy Spirit,
one God, now and for ever.

also Psalm 91.1–4, 13–16; Luke 10.1–12, 17–20

CUTHBERT
BISHOP OF LINDISFARNE, MISSIONARY, 687   20 MARCH

COLLECT

Almighty God,
who called your servant Cuthbert from following the flock
to follow your Son and to be a shepherd of your people:
in your mercy, grant that we, following his example,
may bring those who are lost home to your fold;
through Jesus Christ your Son our Lord,
who is alive and reigns with you,
in the unity of the Holy Spirit,
one God, now and for ever.

especially Ezekiel 34.11–16; *also* Matthew 18.12–14

COLUMBA
ABBOT OF IONA, MISSIONARY, 597   9 JUNE

COLLECT

Almighty God,
who filled the heart of Columba
with the joy of the Holy Spirit
and with deep love for those in his care:
may your pilgrim people follow him,
strong in faith, sustained by hope,
and one in the love that binds us to you;
through Jesus Christ your Son our Lord,
who is alive and reigns with you,
in the unity of the Holy Spirit,
one God, now and for ever.

also Titus 2.11–15

AIDAN
BISHOP OF LINDISFARNE, MISSIONARY, 651   31 AUGUST

COLLECT

Everlasting God,
you sent the gentle bishop Aidan
to proclaim the gospel in this land:
grant us to live as he taught
in simplicity, humility, and love for the poor;
through Jesus Christ your Son our Lord,
who is alive and reigns with you,
in the unity of the Holy Spirit,
one God, now and for ever.

also 1 Corinthians 9.16–19

NINIAN
BISHOP OF GALLOWAY, APOSTLE OF THE
PICTS, *c.*432   16 SEPTEMBER

COLLECT

Almighty and everlasting God,
who called your servant Ninian to preach the gospel
    to the people of northern Britain:
raise up in this and every land
heralds and evangelists of your kingdom,
that your Church may make known the immeasurable riches
    of your Son our Saviour Jesus Christ,
who is alive and reigns with you,
in the unity of the Holy Spirit,
one God, now and for ever.

especially Acts 13.46–49; Mark 16.15–20

PAULINUS
BISHOP OF YORK, MISSIONARY, 644 — 10 OCTOBER

COLLECT

God our saviour,
who sent Paulinus to preach and to baptize,
and so to build up your Church in this land:
grant that, inspired by his example,
we may tell all the world of your truth,
that with him we may receive
   the reward you prepare for all your faithful servants;
through Jesus Christ your Son our Lord,
who is alive and reigns with you,
in the unity of the Holy Spirit,
one God, now and for ever.

especially Matthew 28.16–20

WILFRID OF RIPON
BISHOP, MISSIONARY, 709 — 12 OCTOBER

COLLECT

Almighty God,
who called our forebears to the light of the gospel
   by the preaching of your servant Wilfrid:
help us, who keep his life and labour in remembrance,
to glorify your name by following the example
   of his zeal and perseverance;
through Jesus Christ your Son our Lord,
who is alive and reigns with you,
in the unity of the Holy Spirit,
one God, now and for ever.

especially Luke 5.1–11; *also* 1 Corinthians 1.18–25

HENRY MARTYN

TRANSLATOR OF THE SCRIPTURES, MISSIONARY
IN INDIA AND PERSIA, 1812
19 OCTOBER

COLLECT

Almighty God,
who by your Holy Spirit gave Henry Martyn
a longing to tell the good news of Christ
and skill to translate the Scriptures:
by the same Spirit give us grace to offer you our gifts,
wherever you may lead, at whatever the cost;
through Jesus Christ your Son our Lord,
who is alive and reigns with you,
in the unity of the Holy Spirit,
one God, now and for ever.

especially Mark 16.15–20; *also* Isaiah 55.6–11

WILLIBRORD OF YORK

BISHOP, APOSTLE OF FRISIA, 739
7 NOVEMBER

COLLECT

God, the saviour of all,
you sent your bishop Willibrord from this land
to proclaim the good news to many peoples
and confirm them in their faith:
help us also to witness to your steadfast love
    by word and deed
so that your Church may increase
    and grow strong in holiness;
through Jesus Christ your Son our Lord,
who is alive and reigns with you, in the unity of the Holy Spirit,
one God, now and for ever.

especially Isaiah 52.7–10; Matthew 28.16–20

ANY SAINT

GENERAL

COLLECT

Almighty Father,
you have built up your Church
through the love and devotion of your saints:
inspire us to follow the example of N,
whom we commemorate today,
that we in our generation may rejoice with him/her
in the vision of your glory;
through Jesus Christ your Son our Lord,
who is alive and reigns with you,
in the unity of the Holy Spirit,
one God, now and for ever.

Genesis 12.1–4; Proverbs 8.1–11; Micah 6.6–8; Ecclesiasticus 2.7–13, [14–17]
Ephesians 3.14–19; Ephesians 6.11–18; Hebrews 13.7–8, 15–16;
James 2.14–17; 1 John 4.7–16; Revelation 21.[1–4,] 5–7
Psalms 32; 33.1–5; 119.1–8; 139.1–5, [6–12]; 145.8–13
Matthew 19.16–21; Matthew 25.1–13; Matthew 25.14–30; John 15.1–8;
John 17.20–26

POST COMMUNION

Any one of the following may be used

Faithful God,
who called N to serve you
and gave him/her joy in walking the path of holiness:
by this eucharist
   in which you renew within us the vision of your glory,
strengthen us all to follow the way of perfection
until we come to see you face to face;
through Jesus Christ our Lord.

God our redeemer,
who inspired N to witness to your love
and to work for the coming of your kingdom:

may we, who in this sacrament share the bread of heaven,
be fired by your Spirit to proclaim the gospel in our daily living
and never to rest content until your kingdom come,
on earth as it is in heaven;
through Jesus Christ our Lord.

Father,
from whom every family in heaven and on earth takes its name,
your servant N revealed your goodness
    in a life of tranquillity and service:
grant that we who have gathered in faith around this table
may like him/her know the love of Christ
    that surpasses knowledge
and be filled with all your fullness;
through Jesus Christ our Lord.

God, the source of all holiness
    and giver of all good things:
may we who have shared at this table
    as strangers and pilgrims here on earth
be welcomed with all your saints
    to the heavenly feast on the day of your kingdom;
through Jesus Christ our Lord.

CHRISTIAN RULERS

COLLECT

Sovereign God,
who called N to be a ruler among his/her people
and gave him/her grace to be their servant:
help us, following our Saviour Christ
in the path of humble service,
to see his kingdom set forward on earth
and to enjoy its fullness in heaven;
who is alive and reigns with you,
in the unity of the Holy Spirit,
one God, now and for ever.

1 Samuel 16.1–13a; 1 Kings 3.3–14
1 Timothy 2.1–6
Psalms 72.1–7; 99
Mark 10.42–45; Luke 14.27–33

POST COMMUNION

Any of the prayers given under 'Any Saint' (see page 1267) may be used

EDWARD THE CONFESSOR
KING OF ENGLAND, 1066   13 OCTOBER

COLLECT

Sovereign God,
who set your servant Edward
    upon the throne of an earthly kingdom
and inspired him with zeal for the kingdom of heaven:
grant that we may so confess the faith of Christ
    by word and deed,
that we may, with all your saints, inherit your eternal glory;
through Jesus Christ your Son our Lord,
who is alive and reigns with you,
in the unity of the Holy Spirit,
one God, now and for ever.

also 2 Samuel 23.1–5; 1 John 4.13–16

POST COMMUNION

God our redeemer,
who inspired Edward to witness to your love
and to work for the coming of your kingdom:
may we, who in this sacrament share the bread of heaven,
be fired by your Spirit to proclaim the gospel in our daily living
and never to rest content until your kingdom come,
on earth as it is in heaven;
through Jesus Christ our Lord.

or any of the prayers given under 'Any Saint' (see page 1267)

ALFRED THE GREAT

KING OF THE WEST SAXONS, SCHOLAR, 899   26 OCTOBER

COLLECT

God, our maker and redeemer,
we pray you of your great mercy
and by the power of your holy cross
to guide us by your will and to shield us from our foes:
that, after the example of your servant Alfred,
we may inwardly love you above all things;
through Jesus Christ your Son our Lord,
who is alive and reigns with you,
in the unity of the Holy Spirit,
one God, now and for ever.

also 2 Samuel 23.1–5; John 18.33–37

POST COMMUNION

God our redeemer,
who inspired Alfred to witness to your love
and to work for the coming of your kingdom:
may we, who in this sacrament share the bread of heaven,
be fired by your Spirit to proclaim the gospel in our daily living
and never to rest content until your kingdom come,
on earth as it is in heaven;
through Jesus Christ our Lord.

or any of the prayers given under 'Any Saint' (see page 1267)

MARGARET OF SCOTLAND
QUEEN OF SCOTLAND, PHILANTHROPIST,
REFORMER OF THE CHURCH, 1093   16 NOVEMBER

COLLECT

God, the ruler of all,
who called your servant Margaret to an earthly throne
and gave her zeal for your Church and love for your people
that she might advance your heavenly kingdom:
mercifully grant that we who commemorate her example
may be fruitful in good works
and attain to the glorious crown of your saints;
through Jesus Christ your Son our Lord,
who is alive and reigns with you,
in the unity of the Holy Spirit,
one God, now and for ever.

also Proverbs 31.10–12, 20, 26–31; 1 Corinthians 12.13–13.3; Matthew 25.34–46

POST COMMUNION

God our redeemer,
who inspired Margaret to witness to your love
and to work for the coming of your kingdom:
may we, who in this sacrament share the bread of heaven,
be fired by your Spirit to proclaim the gospel in our daily living
and never to rest content until your kingdom come,
on earth as it is in heaven;
through Jesus Christ our Lord.

or any of the prayers given under 'Any Saint' (see page 1267)

THOSE WORKING WITH THE POOR AND UNDERPRIVILEGED

COLLECT

Merciful God,
you have compassion on all that you have made
and your whole creation is enfolded in your love:
help us to stand firm for your truth,
to struggle against poverty,
and to share your love with our neighbour,
that with your servant N
we may be instruments of your peace;
through Jesus Christ your Son our Lord,
who is alive and reigns with you,
in the unity of the Holy Spirit,
one God, now and for ever.

Isaiah 58.6–11
Hebrews 13.1–3; 1 John 3.14–18
Psalms 82; 146.5–9
Matthew 5.1–12; Matthew 25.31–46

POST COMMUNION

Any of the prayers given under 'Any Saint' (see page 1267) may be used

JOSEPHINE BUTLER
SOCIAL REFORMER, 1906   30 MAY

COLLECT

God of compassion and love,
by whose grace your servant Josephine Butler
followed in the way of your Son
in caring for those in need:
help us like her to work with strength
for the restoration of all
to the dignity and freedom of those created in your image;
through Jesus Christ our Saviour,

who is alive and reigns with you,
in the unity of the Holy Spirit,
one God, now and for ever.

especially Isaiah 58.6–11; *also* 1 John 3.18–23; Matthew 9.10–13

POST COMMUNION

God our redeemer,
who inspired Josephine Butler to witness to your love
and to work for the coming of your kingdom:
may we, who in this sacrament share the bread of heaven,
be fired by your Spirit to proclaim the gospel in our daily living
and never to rest content until your kingdom come,
on earth as it is in heaven;
through Jesus Christ our Lord.

or any of the prayers given under 'Any Saint' (see page 1267)

WILLIAM WILBERFORCE
SOCIAL REFORMER, 1833   30 JULY

COLLECT

God our deliverer,
who sent your Son Jesus Christ
to set your people free from the slavery of sin:
grant that, as your servant William Wilberforce
    toiled against the sin of slavery,
so we may bring compassion to all
and work for the freedom of all the children of God;
through Jesus Christ your Son our Lord,
who is alive and reigns with you,
in the unity of the Holy Spirit,
one God, now and for ever.

also Job 31.16–23; Galatians 3.26–29; 4.6–7; Luke 4.16–21

POST COMMUNION

God our redeemer,
who inspired William Wilberforce to witness to your love
and to work for the coming of your kingdom:
may we, who in this sacrament share the bread of heaven,
be fired by your Spirit to proclaim the gospel in our daily living
and never to rest content until your kingdom come,
on earth as it is in heaven;
through Jesus Christ our Lord.

or any of the prayers given under 'Any Saint' (see page 1267)

ELIZABETH OF HUNGARY
PRINCESS OF THURINGIA, PHILANTHROPIST, 1231   18 NOVEMBER

COLLECT

Lord God,
who taught Elizabeth of Hungary
   to recognize and reverence Christ in the poor of this world:
by her example
strengthen us to love and serve the afflicted and the needy
and so to honour your Son, the servant king,
who is alive and reigns with you,
in the unity of the Holy Spirit,
one God, now and for ever.

especially Matthew 25.31–46; *also* Proverbs 31.10–31

POST COMMUNION

Faithful God,
who called Elizabeth of Hungary to serve you
and gave her joy in walking the path of holiness:
by this eucharist
   in which you renew within us the vision of your glory,

strengthen us all to follow the way of perfection
until we come to see you face to face;
through Jesus Christ our Lord.

or any of the prayers given under 'Any Saint' (see page 1267)

MEN AND WOMEN OF LEARNING

COLLECT

God our Father,
who gave wisdom and insight to your servant N
to fathom the depths of your love
and to understand your design for the world you have made:
grant us the help of your Holy Spirit
that we also may come to a full knowledge of your purposes
revealed in your Son Jesus Christ, our wisdom and our life;
who is alive and reigns with you,
in the unity of the Holy Spirit,
one God, now and for ever.

Proverbs 8.22–31; Ecclesiasticus 44.1–15
Philippians 4.7–8
Psalms 36.5–10; 49.1–4
Matthew 13.44–46, 52; John 7.14–18

POST COMMUNION

Any of the prayers given under 'Any Saint' (see page 1267) may be used

THOSE WHOSE HOLINESS WAS REVEALED IN MARRIAGE AND FAMILY LIFE

COLLECT

Eternal God,
whose love is revealed in the mystery of the Trinity:
help us, like your servant N,
to find in our human loving a mirror of your divine love

and to see in all your children our brothers and sisters in Christ,
who is alive and reigns with you,
in the unity of the Holy Spirit,
one God, now and for ever.

Proverbs 31.10–13, [14–18,] 19–20, [21–29,] 30–31; Tobit 8.4–7
1 Peter 3.1–9
Psalms 127; 128
Mark 3.31–35; Luke 10.38–42

POST COMMUNION

Any of the prayers given under 'Any Saint' (see page 1267) may be used

MARY SUMNER
FOUNDER OF THE MOTHERS' UNION, 1921   9 AUGUST

COLLECT

Faithful and loving God,
who called Mary Sumner to strive
    for the renewal of family life:
give us the gift of your Holy Spirit,
that through word, prayer and deed
    your family may be strengthened and your people served;
through Jesus Christ your Son our Lord,
who is alive and reigns with you,
in the unity of the Holy Spirit,
one God, now and for ever.

also Hebrews 13.1–5

POST COMMUNION

Father,
from whom every family in heaven and on earth takes its name,
your servant Mary Sumner revealed your goodness
    in a life of tranquillity and service:
grant that we who have gathered in faith around this table

may like her know the love of Christ
   that surpasses knowledge
and be filled with all your fullness;
through Jesus Christ our Lord.

or any of the prayers given under 'Any Saint' (see page 1267)

MONICA
MOTHER OF AUGUSTINE OF HIPPO, 387   27 AUGUST

COLLECT

Faithful God,
who strengthened Monica, the mother of Augustine,
   with wisdom,
and through her patient endurance encouraged him
   to seek after you:
give us the will to persist in prayer
that those who stray from you may be brought to faith
in your Son Jesus Christ our Lord,
who is alive and reigns with you,
in the unity of the Holy Spirit,
one God, now and for ever.

also Ecclesiasticus 26.1–3, 13–16

POST COMMUNION

Father,
from whom every family in heaven and on earth takes its name,
your servant Monica revealed your goodness
   in a life of tranquillity and service:
grant that we who have gathered in faith around this table
may like her know the love of Christ
   that surpasses knowledge
and be filled with all your fullness;
through Jesus Christ our Lord.

or any of the prayers given under 'Any Saint' (see page 1267)

THE GUIDANCE OF THE HOLY SPIRIT

COLLECT

EITHER

God, who from of old
taught the hearts of your faithful people
by sending to them the light of your Holy Spirit:
grant us by the same Spirit
to have a right judgement in all things
and evermore to rejoice in his holy comfort;
through the merits of Christ Jesus our Saviour,
who is alive and reigns with you,
in the unity of the Holy Spirit,
one God, now and for ever.

OR

Almighty God,
you have given your Holy Spirit to the Church
to lead us into all truth:
bless with the Spirit's grace and presence
    the members of this ... (*synod/PCC/etc.*);
keep us/them steadfast in faith and united in love,
that we/they may manifest your glory
and prepare the way of your kingdom;
through Jesus Christ your Son our Lord,
who is alive and reigns with you,
in the unity of the Holy Spirit,
one God, now and for ever.

Proverbs 24.3–7; Isaiah 30.15–21; Wisdom 9.13–17
Acts 15.23–29; Romans 8.22–27; 1 Corinthians 12.4–13
Psalms 25.1–9; 104.25–34; 143.8–10
Luke 14.27–33; John 14.23–26; John 16.13–15

POST COMMUNION

God of power,
whose Holy Spirit renews your people
in the bread and wine we bless and share:
may the boldness of the Spirit transform us,

the gentleness of the Spirit lead us,
and the gifts of the Spirit equip us
   to serve and worship you;
through Jesus Christ our Lord.

ROGATION DAYS

COLLECT

Any one of the following Collects may be used

Almighty God,
whose will it is that the earth and the sea
should bear fruit in due season:
bless the labours of those who work on land and sea,
grant us a good harvest
and the grace always to rejoice in your fatherly care;
through Jesus Christ your Son our Lord,
who is alive and reigns with you,
in the unity of the Holy Spirit,
one God, now and for ever.

Almighty God and Father,
you have so ordered our life
   that we are dependent on one another:
prosper those engaged in commerce and industry
and direct their minds and hands
that they may rightly use your gifts in the service of others;
through Jesus Christ your Son our Lord,
who is alive and reigns with you,
in the unity of the Holy Spirit,
one God, now and for ever.

God our Father,
you never cease the work you have begun
and prosper with your blessing all human labour:
make us wise and faithful stewards of your gifts
that we may serve the common good,
maintain the fabric of our world
and seek that justice where all may share
   the good things you pour upon us;
through Jesus Christ your Son our Lord,

who is alive and reigns with you,
in the unity of the Holy Spirit,
one God, now and for ever.

Deuteronomy 8.1–10; 1 Kings 8.35–40; Job 28.1–11
Philippians 4.4–7; 2 Thessalonians 3.6–13; 1 John 5.12–15
Psalms 104.22–31; 107.1–9; 121
Matthew 6.1–15; Mark 11.22–24; Luke 11.5–13

POST COMMUNION

God our creator,
you give seed for us to sow and bread for us to eat:
as you have blessed the fruit of our labour in this eucharist,
so we ask you to give all your children their daily bread,
that the world may praise you for your goodness;
through Jesus Christ our Lord.

MISSION AND EVANGELISM

COLLECT

Almighty God,
who called your Church to witness
that you were in Christ reconciling the world to yourself:
help us to proclaim the good news of your love,
that all who hear it may be drawn to you;
through him who was lifted up on the cross,
and reigns with you
in the unity of the Holy Spirit,
one God, now and for ever.

Isaiah 49.1–6; Isaiah 52.7–10; Micah 4.1–5
Acts 17.12–34; 2 Corinthians 5.14–6.2; Ephesians 2.13–22
Psalms 2; 46; 67
Matthew 5.13–16; Matthew 28.16–20; John 17.20–26

POST COMMUNION

Eternal God, giver of love and power,
your Son Jesus Christ has sent us into all the world
to preach the gospel of his kingdom:
confirm us in this mission,
and help us to live the good news we proclaim;
through Jesus Christ our Lord.

THE UNITY OF THE CHURCH

COLLECT

EITHER

Heavenly Father,
you have called us in the Body of your Son Jesus Christ
to continue his work of reconciliation
and reveal you to the world:
forgive us the sins which tear us apart;
give us the courage to overcome our fears
and to seek that unity which is your gift and your will;
through Jesus Christ your Son our Lord,
who is alive and reigns with you,
in the unity of the Holy Spirit,
one God, now and for ever.

OR

Lord Jesus Christ,
who said to your apostles,
'Peace I leave with you, my peace I give to you':
look not on our sins but on the faith of your Church
and grant it the peace and unity of your kingdom;
where you are alive and reign with the Father
in the unity of the Holy Spirit,
one God, now and for ever.

Jeremiah 33.6–9a; Ezekiel 36.23–28; Zephaniah 3.16–20
Ephesians 4.1–6; Colossians 3.9–17; 1 John 4.9–15
Psalms 100; 122; 133
Matthew 18.19–22; John 11.45–52; John 17.11b–23

POST COMMUNION

Eternal God and Father,
whose Son at supper prayed that his disciples might be one,
as he is one with you:
draw us closer to him,
that in common love and obedience to you
we may be united to one another
in the fellowship of the one Spirit,
that the world may believe that he is Lord, to your eternal glory;
through Jesus Christ our Lord.

THE PEACE OF THE WORLD

COLLECT

Almighty God,
from whom all thoughts of truth and peace proceed:
kindle, we pray, in the hearts of all, the true love of peace
and guide with your pure and peaceable wisdom
those who take counsel for the nations of the earth
that in tranquillity your kingdom may go forward,
till the earth is filled with the knowledge of your love;
through Jesus Christ your Son our Lord,
who is alive and reigns with you,
in the unity of the Holy Spirit,
one God, now and for ever.

Isaiah 9.1–6; Isaiah 57.15–19; Micah 4.1–5
Philippians 4.6–9; 1 Timothy 2.1–6; James 3.13–18
Psalms 40.14–17; 72.1–7; 85.8–13
Matthew 5.43–48; John 14.23–29; John 15.9–17

POST COMMUNION

God our Father,
your Son is our peace
and his cross the sign of reconciliation:
help us, who share the broken bread,
to bring together what is scattered
and to bind up what is wounded,
that Christ may bring in the everlasting kingdom of his peace;
who is alive and reigns, now and for ever.

SOCIAL JUSTICE AND RESPONSIBILITY

COLLECT

EITHER

Eternal God,
in whose perfect realm
no sword is drawn but the sword of righteousness,
and no strength known but the strength of love:
so guide and inspire the work of those who seek your kingdom
that all your people may find their security
in that love which casts out fear
and in the fellowship revealed to us
in Jesus Christ our Saviour,
who is alive and reigns with you,
in the unity of the Holy Spirit,
one God, now and for ever.

OR

Almighty and eternal God,
to whom we must all give account:
guide with your Spirit the ... of this (*city, society, etc.*),
that we/they may be faithful to the mind of Christ
and seek in all our/their purposes to enrich our common life;
through Jesus Christ your Son our Lord,
who is alive and reigns with you,
in the unity of the Holy Spirit,
one God, now and for ever.

Isaiah 32.15–20; Amos 5.21–24; Amos 8.4–7; Acts 5.1–11
Colossians 3.12–15; James 2.1–4
Psalms 31.21–24; 85.1–7; 146.4–9
Matthew 5.1–12; Matthew 25.31–46; Luke 16.19–31

POST COMMUNION

Blessed God,
help us, whom you have fed and satisfied in this eucharist,
to hunger and thirst for what is right;
help us, who here have rejoiced and been glad,
to stand with those who are persecuted and reviled;

help us, who here have glimpsed the life of heaven,
to strive for the cause of right
   and for the coming of the kingdom of Jesus Christ,
who is alive and reigns, now and for ever.

MINISTRY (INCLUDING EMBER DAYS)

COLLECT

FOR THE MINISTRY OF ALL CHRISTIAN PEOPLE

Almighty and everlasting God,
by whose Spirit the whole body of the Church
   is governed and sanctified:
hear our prayer which we offer for all your faithful people,
that in their vocation and ministry
they may serve you in holiness and truth
to the glory of your name;
through our Lord and Saviour Jesus Christ,
who is alive and reigns with you,
in the unity of the Holy Spirit,
one God, now and for ever.

FOR THOSE TO BE ORDAINED

Almighty God, the giver of all good gifts,
by your Holy Spirit you have appointed
   various orders of ministry in the Church:
look with mercy on your servants
   now called to be deacons and priests;
maintain them in truth and renew them in holiness,
that by word and good example they may faithfully serve you
to the glory of your name and the benefit of your Church;
through the merits of our Saviour Jesus Christ,
who is alive and reigns with you,
in the unity of the Holy Spirit,
one God, now and for ever.

FOR VOCATIONS

Almighty God,
you have entrusted to your Church
a share in the ministry of your Son our great high priest:

inspire by your Holy Spirit the hearts of many
to offer themselves for the ministry of your Church,
that strengthened by his power,
they may work for the increase of your kingdom
and set forward the eternal praise of your name;
through Jesus Christ your Son our Lord,
who is alive and reigns with you,
in the unity of the Holy Spirit,
one God, now and for ever.

FOR THE INAUGURATION OF A NEW MINISTRY

God our Father, Lord of all the world,
through your Son you have called us into the fellowship
    of your universal Church:
hear our prayer for your faithful people
that in their vocation and ministry
each may be an instrument of your love,
and give to your servant N now to be ... *(installed, inducted, etc.)*
the needful gifts of grace;
through our Lord and Saviour Jesus Christ,
who is alive and reigns with you,
in the unity of the Holy Spirit,
one God, now and for ever.

Numbers 11.16–17, 24–29; Numbers 27.15–23; 1 Samuel 16.1–13a;
Isaiah 6.1–8; Isaiah 61.1–3; Jeremiah 1.4–10
Acts 20.28–35; 1 Corinthians 3.3–11; Ephesians 4.4–16; Philippians 3.7–14
Psalms 40.8–13; 84.7–12; 89.19–25; 101.1–5, 7; 122
Luke 4.16–21; Luke 12.35–43; Luke 22.24–27; John 4.31–38; John 15.5–17

POST COMMUNION

EITHER

Heavenly Father,
whose ascended Son gave gifts of leadership and service
    to the Church:
strengthen us who have received this holy food
to be good stewards of your manifold grace,
through him who came not to be served but to serve,
    and give his life as a ransom for many,
Jesus Christ our Lord.

OR

Lord of the harvest,
you have fed your people in this sacrament
with the fruits of creation made holy by your Spirit:
by your grace raise up among us faithful labourers
to sow your word and reap the harvest of souls;
through Jesus Christ our Lord.

IN TIME OF TROUBLE

COLLECT

Sovereign God,
the defence of those who trust in you
and the strength of those who suffer:
look with mercy on our affliction
and deliver us through our mighty Saviour Jesus Christ,
who is alive and reigns with you,
in the unity of the Holy Spirit,
one God, now and for ever.

Genesis 9.8–17; Job 1.13–22; Isaiah 38.6–11
Romans 3.21–26; Romans 8.18–25; 2 Corinthians 8.1–5, 9
Psalms 86.1–7; 107.4–15; 142.1–7
Mark 4.35–41; Luke 12.1–7; John 16.31–33

POST COMMUNION

Almighty God,
whose Son gave us in this meal a pledge of your saving love
and a foretaste of your kingdom of justice and peace:
strengthen your people in their faith
that they may endure the sufferings of this present time
in expectation of the glory to be revealed;
through Jesus Christ our Lord.

FOR THE SOVEREIGN

COLLECT

Almighty God,
the fountain of all goodness,
bless our Sovereign Lady, Queen Elizabeth,
and all who are in authority under her;
that they may order all things
    in wisdom and equity, righteousness and peace,
to the honour and glory of your name
and the good of your Church and people;
through Jesus Christ your Son our Lord,
who is alive and reigns with you,
in the unity of the Holy Spirit,
one God, now and for ever.

Joshua 1.1–9; Proverbs 8.1–16
Romans 13.1–10; Revelation 21.22–22.4
Psalms 20; 101; 121
Matthew 22.16–22; Luke 22.24–30

POST COMMUNION

O God, the Father of our Lord Jesus Christ,
our only Saviour, the prince of peace:
give us grace seriously to lay to heart
the great dangers we are in by our unhappy divisions;
take away our hatred and prejudice
and whatever else may hinder us from godly union and concord,
that, as there is but one body, one Spirit
    and one hope of our calling,
one Lord, one faith, one baptism,
one God and Father of us all,
so may we henceforth be all of one heart and of one soul,
united in one holy bond of truth and peace, of faith and charity,
and may with one mind and one mouth glorify you;
through Jesus Christ our Lord.

INDEX OF READINGS

The index lists all the references for the readings from the Bible that are printed out in full in the Principal services. The index is arranged in order of the books of the Bible (with the Apocrypha after the New Testament), showing the Bible reference, abbreviated Name of day and Year. For details of any shorter variant readings that may be used, see the actual reference and reading at the day noted.

ABBREVIATIONS

The following abbreviations are used for the books of the Bible:

OLD TESTAMENT		NEW TESTAMENT		APOCRYPHAL/ DEUTEROCANONICAL BOOKS	
Gen	Genesis	Mt	Matthew		
Ex	Exodus	Mk	Mark	Tob	Tobit
Lev	Leviticus	Lk	Luke	Jdt	Judith
Num	Numbers	Jn	John	Add Esth	The Additions to
Deut	Deuteronomy	Acts	Acts of the		the Book of
Josh	Joshua		Apostles		Esther
Judg	Judges	Rom	Romans	Wis	Wisdom of
Ruth	Ruth	1 Cor	1 Corinthians		Solomon
1 Sam	1 Samuel	2 Cor	2 Corinthians	Sir	Ecclesiasticus, or
2 Sam	2 Samuel	Gal	Galatians		the Wisdom of
1 Kings	1 Kings	Eph	Ephesians		Jesus Son of
2 Kings	2 Kings	Phil	Philippians		Sirach
1 Chr	1 Chronicles	Col	Colossians	Bar	Baruch
2 Chr	2 Chronicles	1 Thess	1 Thessalonians	Let Jer	The Letter of
Ezra	Ezra	2 Thess	2 Thessalonians		Jeremiah
Neh	Nehemiah	1 Tim	1 Timothy	Song of	The Prayer of
Esth	Esther	2 Tim	2 Timothy	Thr	Azariah and the
Job	Job	Titus	Titus		Song of the Three
Ps	Psalms	Philem	Philemon		Jews
Prov	Proverbs	Heb	Hebrews	Sus	Susanna
Eccl	Ecclesiastes	Jas	James	Bel	Bel and the
Song	Song of Solomon	1 Pet	1 Peter		Dragon
Isa	Isaiah	2 Pet	2 Peter	1 Macc	1 Maccabees
Jer	Jeremiah	1 Jn	1 John	2 Macc	2 Maccabees
Lam	Lamentations	2 Jn	2 John	1 Esd	1 Esdras
Ezek	Ezekiel	3 Jn	3 John	Pr Man	Prayer of
Dan	Daniel	Jude	Jude		Manasseh
Hos	Hosea	Rev	Revelation	Ps 151	Psalm 151
Joel	Joel			3 Macc	3 Maccabees
Am	Amos			2 Esd	2 Esdras
Ob	Obadiah			4 Macc	4 Maccabees
Jon	Jonah				
Mic	Micah				
Nah	Nahum				
Hab	Habakkuk				
Zeph	Zephaniah				
Hag	Haggai				
Zech	Zechariah				
Mal	Malachi				

Ex	34.29–35	1 Before Lent	C
Lev	19.1–2, 9–18	Proper 3	A
Lev	19.1–2, 15–18	Proper 25	A
Num	6.22–27	Circumcision	A, B, C
Num	11.4–6, 10–16, 24–29	Proper 21	B
Num	11.24–30	Pentecost	A
Num	21.4–9	Lent 4	B
Num	21.4–9	Holy Cross	A, B, C
Deut	4.1–2, 6–9	Proper 17	B
Deut	5.12–15	Proper 4	B
Deut	6.1–9	4 Before Advent	B
Deut	8.7–18	Harvest Thanksgiving	A
Deut	11.18–21, 26–28	Proper 4	A
Deut	18.15–20	Epiphany 4	B
Deut	26.1–11	Lent 1	C
Deut	26.1–11	Harvest Thanksgiving	C
Deut	28.1–14	Harvest Thanksgiving	A
Deut	30.9–14	Proper 10	C
Deut	30.15–20	Proper 2	A
Deut	30.15–20	Proper 18	C
Deut	34.1–12	Proper 25	A
Josh	5.9–12	Lent 4	C
Josh	24.1–2, 14–18	Proper 16	B
1 Sam	1.20–28	Mothering Sunday	A, B, C
1 Sam	2.18–20, 26	Christmas 1	C
1 Sam	3.1–20	Epiphany 2	B
1 Sam	3.1–20	Proper 4	B
1 Sam	8.4–20; 11.14–15	Proper 5	B
1 Sam	15.34–16.13	Proper 6	B
1 Sam	16.1–13	Lent 4	A
1 Sam	17.1, 4–11, 19–23, 32–49	Proper 7	B
1 Sam	17.57–18.5, 10–16	Proper 7	B
2 Sam	1.1, 17–27	Proper 8	B
2 Sam	5.1–5, 9–10	Proper 9	B
2 Sam	6.1–5, 12–19	Proper 10	B
2 Sam	7.1–5, 8–11, 16	Christmas Eve	A, B, C
2 Sam	7.1–11, 16	Advent 4	B
2 Sam	7.1–14	Proper 11	B
2 Sam	7.4–16	Joseph	A, B, C
2 Sam	11.1–15	Proper 12	B
2 Sam	11.26–12.10, 13–15	Proper 6	C
2 Sam	11.26–12.13	Proper 13	B
2 Sam	18.5–9, 15, 31–33	Proper 14	B
1 Kings	2.10–12; 3.3–14	Proper 15	B
1 Kings	3.5–12	Proper 12	A
1 Kings	8.1, 6, 10–11, 22–30, 41–43	Proper 16	B
1 Kings	8.22–23, 41–43	Proper 4	C
1 Kings	8.22–30	Dedication Festival	A
1 Kings	17.8–16	Epiphany 4	A
1 Kings	17.8–24	Proper 5	C
1 Kings	17.17–24	Proper 5	C
1 Kings	18.20–39	Proper 4	C
1 Kings	19.1–15	Proper 7	C
1 Kings	19.4–8	Proper 14	B
1 Kings	19.9–18	Proper 14	A
1 Kings	19.15–16, 19–21	Proper 8	C
1 Kings	21.1–21	Proper 6	C

Ps	22.22–27	Holy Cross	A, B, C
Ps	22.22–30	Lent 2	B
Ps	22.24–30	Easter 5	B
Ps	23	Lent 4	A
Ps	23	Easter 4	A, B, C
Ps	23	Proper 11	B
Ps	23	Proper 23	A
Ps	23	All Souls' Day	A, B, C
Ps	24	Proper 10	B
Ps	24.1–6	All Saints' Day	B
Ps	24.1–10	Presentation	A, B, C
Ps	25.1–8	Proper 21	A
Ps	25.1–9	Advent 1	C
Ps	25.1–9	Lent 1	B
Ps	25.1–9	Proper 10	C
Ps	26	Proper 22	B
Ps	26.1–8	Proper 17	A
Ps	27	Lent 2	C
Ps	27.1, 5–13	Epiphany 3	A
Ps	27.1–7, 17–18	All Souls' Day	A, B, C
Ps	29	Baptism of Christ	A, B, C
Ps	29	Trinity Sunday	B
Ps	30	Proper 2	B
Ps	30	Easter 3	C
Ps	30	Proper 5	C
Ps	30	Proper 8	B
Ps	30	Proper 9	C
Ps	31.1–4, 15–16	Easter Eve	A, B, C
Ps	31.1–5, 15–16	Easter 5	A
Ps	31.1–5, 19–24	Proper 4	A
Ps	31.1–6	Thomas	A, B, C
Ps	31.9–16	Palm Sunday	A, B, C
Ps	32	Lent 1	A
Ps	32	Lent 4	C
Ps	32	Proper 6	C
Ps	32.1–8	4 Before Advent	C
Ps	33.1–5	All Saints' Day	A, B, C
Ps	33.1–12	Proper 5	A
Ps	33.12–22	Proper 14	C
Ps	34.1–8	Proper 14	B
Ps	34.1–8, 19–22	Proper 25	B
Ps	34.1–10	All Saints' Day	A
Ps	34.9–14	Proper 15	B
Ps	34.11–20	Mothering Sunday	A, B, C
Ps	34.15–22	Proper 16	B
Ps	36.5–10	Epiphany 2	C
Ps	36.5–10	Epiphany 4	A
Ps	36.5–11	Monday of Holy Week	A, B, C
Ps	37.1–10	Proper 22	C
Ps	37.1–12, 41–42	Proper 3	C
Ps	40.1–12	Epiphany 2	A
Ps	40.5–11	Annunciation	A, B, C
Ps	41	Proper 3	B
Ps	42.1–9	Mary Magdalene	A, B, C
Ps	42; 43	Easter Vigil	A, B, C
Ps	42; 43	Proper 7	C
Ps	43	4 Before Advent	A

INDEX OF READINGS